Poetry
Criticism

Guide to Gale Literary Criticism Series

For criticism on	Consult these Gale series
Authors now living or who died after December 31, 1999	*CONTEMPORARY LITERARY CRITICISM (CLC)*
Authors who died between 1900 and 1999	*TWENTIETH-CENTURY LITERARY CRITICISM (TCLC)*
Authors who died between 1800 and 1899	*NINETEENTH-CENTURY LITERATURE CRITICISM (NCLC)*
Authors who died between 1400 and 1799	*LITERATURE CRITICISM FROM 1400 TO 1800 (LC)* *SHAKESPEAREAN CRITICISM (SC)*
Authors who died before 1400	*CLASSICAL AND MEDIEVAL LITERATURE CRITICISM (CMLC)*
Authors of books for children and young adults	*CHILDREN'S LITERATURE REVIEW (CLR)*
Dramatists	*DRAMA CRITICISM (DC)*
Poets	*POETRY CRITICISM (PC)*
Short story writers	*SHORT STORY CRITICISM (SSC)*
Literary topics and movements	*HARLEM RENAISSANCE: A GALE CRITICAL COMPANION (HR)* *THE BEAT GENERATION: A GALE CRITICAL COMPANION (BG)* *FEMINISM IN LITERATURE: A GALE CRITICAL COMPANION (FL)* *GOTHIC LITERATURE: A GALE CRITICAL COMPANION (GL)*
Asian American writers of the last two hundred years	*ASIAN AMERICAN LITERATURE (AAL)*
Black writers of the past two hundred years	*BLACK LITERATURE CRITICISM (BLC-1)* *BLACK LITERATURE CRITICISM SUPPLEMENT (BLCS)* *BLACK LITERATURE CRITICISM: CLASSIC AND EMERGING AUTHORS SINCE 1950 (BLC-2)*
Hispanic writers of the late nineteenth and twentieth centuries	*HISPANIC LITERATURE CRITICISM (HLC)* *HISPANIC LITERATURE CRITICISM SUPPLEMENT (HLCS)*
Native North American writers and orators of the eighteenth, nineteenth, and twentieth centuries	*NATIVE NORTH AMERICAN LITERATURE (NNAL)*
Major authors from the Renaissance to the present	*WORLD LITERATURE CRITICISM, 1500 TO THE PRESENT (WLC)* *WORLD LITERATURE CRITICISM SUPPLEMENT (WLCS)*

ISSN 1052-4851

Poetry Criticism

Excerpts from Criticism of the Works of the Most Significant and Widely Studied Poets of World Literature

Volume 105

Michelle Lee
Project Editor

GALE
CENGAGE Learning

Detroit • New York • San Francisco • New Haven, Conn • Waterville, Maine • London

GALE
CENGAGE Learning·

Poetry Criticism, Vol. 105

Project Editor: Michelle Lee

Editorial: Dana Barnes, Sara Constantakis, Kathy D. Darrow, Kristen Dorsch, Dana Ferguson, Jeffrey W. Hunter, Michelle Kazensky, Jelena O. Krstović, Marie Toft, Lawrence J. Trudeau

Content Conversion: Katrina D. Coach, Gwen Tucker

Indexing Services: Factiva, Inc.

Rights and Acquisitions: Beth Beaufore, Barb McNeil, and Sara Teller

Composition and Electronic Capture: Gary Leach

Manufacturing: Rhonda Dover

Product Manager: Janet Witalec

For product information and technology assistance, contact us at
Gale Customer Support, 1-800-877-4253.
For permission to use material from this text or product,
submit all requests online at **www.cengage.com/permissions.**
Further permissions questions can be emailed to
permissionrequest@cengage.com

Gale
27500 Drake Rd.
Farmington Hills, MI, 48331-3535

LIBRARY OF CONGRESS CATALOG CARD NUMBER 81-640179

ISBN-13: 978-1-4144-4760-5
ISBN-10: 1-4144-4760-4

ISSN 1052-4851

Printed in the United States of America
1 2 3 4 5 6 7 14 13 12 11 10

Contents

Preface

*P*oetry Criticism (*PC*) presents significant criticism of the world's greatest poets and provides supplementary biographical and bibliographical material to guide the interested reader to a greater understanding of the genre and its creators. Although major poets and literary movements are covered in such Gale Literary Criticism series as *Contemporary Literary Criticism (CLC)*, *Twentieth-Century Literary Criticism (TCLC)*, *Nineteenth-Century Literature Criticism (NCLC)*, *Literature Criticism from 1400 to 1800 (LC)*, and *Classical and Medieval Literature Criticism (CMLC)*, *PC* offers more focused attention on poetry than is possible in the broader, survey-oriented entries on writers in these Gale series. Students, teachers, librarians, and researchers will find that the generous excerpts and supplementary material provided by *PC* supply them with the vital information needed to write a term paper on poetic technique, to examine a poet's most prominent themes, or to lead a poetry discussion group.

Scope of the Series

PC is designed to serve as an introduction to major poets of all eras and nationalities. Since these authors have inspired a great deal of relevant critical material, *PC* is necessarily selective, and the editors have chosen the most important published criticism to aid readers and students in their research. Each author entry presents a historical survey of the critical response to that author's work. The length of an entry is intended to reflect the amount of critical attention the author has received from critics writing in English and from foreign critics in translation. Every attempt has been made to identify and include the most significant essays on each author's work. In order to provide these important critical pieces, the editors sometimes reprint essays that have appeared elsewhere in Gale's Literary Criticism Series. Such duplication, however, never exceeds twenty percent of a *PC* volume.

Organization of the Book

Each *PC* entry consists of the following elements:

- The **Author Heading** cites the name under which the author most commonly wrote, followed by birth and death dates. Also located here are any name variations under which an author wrote, including transliterated forms for authors whose native languages use nonroman alphabets. If the author wrote consistently under a pseudonym, the pseudonym will be listed in the author heading and the author's actual name given in parenthesis on the first line of the biographical and critical introduction. Uncertain birth or death dates are indicated by question marks. Single-work entries are preceded by the title of the work and its date of publication.

- The **Introduction** contains background information that introduces the reader to the author and the critical debates surrounding his or her work.

- The list of **Principal Works** is ordered chronologically by date of first publication and lists the most important works by the author. The first section comprises poetry collections and book-length poems. The second section gives information on other major works by the author. For foreign authors, the editors have provided original foreign-language publication information and have selected what are considered the best and most complete English-language editions of their works.

- Reprinted **Criticism** is arranged chronologically in each entry to provide a useful perspective on changes in critical evaluation over time. All individual titles of poems and poetry collections by the author featured in the entry are printed in boldface type. The critic's name and the date of composition or publication of the critical work are given at the beginning of each piece of criticism. Unsigned criticism is preceded by the title of the source in which it appeared. Footnotes are reprinted at the end of each essay or excerpt. In the case of excerpted criticism, only those footnotes that pertain to the excerpted texts are included.

- Critical essays are prefaced by brief **Annotations** explicating each piece.

- A complete **Bibliographical Citation** of the original essay or book precedes each piece of criticism.

- An annotated bibliography of **Further Reading** appears at the end of each entry and suggests resources for additional study. In some cases, significant essays for which the editors could not obtain reprint rights are included here. Boxed material following the further reading list provides references to other biographical and critical sources on the author in series published by Gale.

Cumulative Indexes

A **Cumulative Author Index** lists all of the authors that appear in a wide variety of reference sources published by Gale, including *PC*. A complete list of these sources is found facing the first page of the Author Index. The index also includes birth and death dates and cross references between pseudonyms and actual names.

A **Cumulative Nationality Index** lists all authors featured in *PC* by nationality, followed by the number of the *PC* volume in which their entry appears.

A **Cumulative Title Index** lists in alphabetical order all individual poems, book-length poems, and collection titles contained in the *PC* series. Titles of poetry collections and separately published poems are printed in italics, while titles of individual poems are printed in roman type with quotation marks. Each title is followed by the author's last name and corresponding volume and page numbers where commentary on the work is located. English-language translations of original foreign-language titles are cross-referenced to the foreign titles so that all references to discussion of a work are combined in one listing.

Citing *Poetry Criticism*

When citing criticism reprinted in the Literary Criticism Series, students should provide complete bibliographic information so that the cited essay can be located in the original print or electronic source. Students who quote directly from reprinted criticism may use any accepted bibliographic format, such as University of Chicago Press style or Modern Language Association (MLA) style. Both the MLA and the University of Chicago formats are acceptable and recognized as being the current standards for citations. It is important, however, to choose one format for all citations; do not mix the two formats within a list of citations.

The examples below follow recommendations for preparing a bibliography set forth in *The Chicago Manual of Style*, 14th ed. (Chicago: The University of Chicago Press, 1993); the first example pertains to material drawn from periodicals, the second to material reprinted from books:

Linkin, Harriet Kramer. "The Language of Speakers in *Songs of Innocence and of Experience*." *Romanticism Past and Present* 10, no. 2 (summer 1986): 5-24. Reprinted in *Poetry Criticism*. Vol. 63, edited by Michelle Lee, 79-88. Detroit: Thomson Gale, 2005.

Glen, Heather. "Blake's Criticism of Moral Thinking in *Songs of Innocence and of Experience*." In *Interpreting Blake*, edited by Michael Phillips, 32-69. Cambridge: Cambridge University Press, 1978. Reprinted in *Poetry Criticism*. Vol. 63, edited by Michelle Lee, 34-51. Detroit: Thomson Gale, 2005.

Suggestions are Welcome

Readers who wish to suggest new features, topics, or authors to appear in future volumes, or who have other suggestions or comments are cordially invited to call, write, or fax the Associate Product Manager:

Product Manager, Literary Criticism Series
Gale
27500 Drake Road
Farmington Hills, MI 48331-3535
1-800-347-4253 (GALE)
Fax: 248-699-8054

Acknowledgments

The editors wish to thank the copyright holders of the criticism included in this volume and the permissions managers of many book and magazine publishing companies for assisting us in securing reproduction rights. Following is a list of the copyright holders who have granted us permission to reproduce material in this volume of *PC*. Every effort has been made to trace copyright, but if omissions have been made, please let us know.

COPYRIGHTED MATERIAL IN *PC*, VOLUME 105, WAS REPRODUCED FROM THE FOLLOWING PERIODICALS:

Colby Quarterly, v. XXXI, December, 1995. Reproduced by permission.—*English,* v. XVIII, autumn, 1969. Copyright © by the English Association, 1969. Reproduced by permission.—*French Forum,* v. 24, September, 1999; v. 30, fall, 2005; v. 32, winter, 2007. Copyright © 1999, 2005, 2007 by French Forum, Inc. All rights reserved. All reproduced by permission of the University of Nebraska Press.—*Irish University Review,* v. 13, spring, 1983. Copyright © 1983 by *Irish University Review.* Reproduced by permission.—*Journal of Medieval and Early Modern Studies,* v. 32, spring, 2002. Copyright, 2002, Duke University Press. All rights reserved. Used by permission of the publisher.—*Mississippi Quarterly,* v. 53, summer, 2000. Copyright © 2000 by Mississippi State University. Reproduced by permission.—*MLN,* v. 119 Supplement, January, 2004. Copyright © 2004 by the Johns Hopkins University Press. Reproduced by permission.—*Neophilologus,* v. 86, 2002 for "'Adieu vieille forest': Myth, Melancholia, and Ronsard's Family Trees" by Susan K. Silver; v. 91, 2007 for "Ronsard's *Folies Bergères*: The *Livret des Folastries* and Petrarch" by Lance K. Donaldson-Evans. Copyright © 2002, 2007 by Springer. Both reproduced with kind permission from Springer Science + Business Media and the respective authors.—*New Centennial Review,* v. 2, spring, 2002. Reproduced by permission.—*New Hibernia Review,* v. 8, spring, 2004 for "'All the Answers': The Influence of Auden on Kavanagh's Poetic Development" by John Redmond. Copyright © 2004 by the University of St. Thomas. All rights reserved. Reproduced by permission of the publisher and the author.—*Notes and Queries,* v. 55, March, 2008 for "Patrick Kavanagh and Horizon: A Source for R.S. Thomas's Use of 'Peasant'" by Samuel Perry. Copyright © 2008 by Oxford University Press. Reproduced by permission of the publisher and the author.—*Renaissance Studies,* v. 22, September, 2008. Copyright © 2008 by Basil Blackwell Ltd. Reproduced by permission of Blackwell Publishers.—*Romantic Review,* v. 84, March, 1993. Copyright © 1993 by the Trustees of Columbia University in the City of New York. Reproduced by permission.—*Sixteenth Century Journal,* v. XXVIII, winter, 1997. Republished with permission of Sixteenth Century Journal Publishers, Inc., conveyed through Copyright Clearance Center, Inc.—*Southern Literary Journal,* v. 31, spring, 1999. Copyright © 1999 by the University of North Carolina Press. Used by permission.—*Southern Review,* v. 31, summer, 1995 for "Underdeveloped Comedy: Patrick Kavanagh" by Declan Kiberd. Copyright © by Louisiana State University, 1995. Reproduced by permission of the author.—*Southern Review,* n.s. v. XXVII, 1991 for "Spiritual Matter in Fred Chappell's Poetry: A Prologue" by Dabney Stuart. Reproduced by permission of the author.—*Studies: An Irish Quarterly Review,* v. XLIX, autumn, 1960. Copyright © by Roland Burke Savage, S.J., editor. Reproduced by permission. / v. 93, winter, 2004. Reproduced by permission.—*Virginia Quarterly Review,* v. 68, spring, 1992. Copyright © 1992 by *Virginia Quarterly Review,* The University of Virginia. Reproduced by permission of the publisher.

COPYRIGHTED MATERIAL IN *PC*, VOLUME 105, WAS REPRODUCED FROM THE FOLLOWING BOOKS:

Agnew, Una. From *The Mystical Imagination of Patrick Kavanagh.* Columba Press, 1998. Copyright © 1998, Una Agnew. Reproduced by permission.—Allen, Michael. From "Provincialism and Recent Irish Poetry: The Importance of Patrick Kavanagh," in *Two Decades of Irish Writing: A Critical Survey.* Edited by Douglas Dunn. Dufour Editions, 1975. Copyright © by Michael Allen. Permission granted by Dufour Editions, Inc.—Bizzaro, Patrick. From "'Growth of a Poet's Mind' and the Problem of Autobiography: Distance and Point of View in the Writings of Fred Chappell," in *More Lights Than One: On the Fiction of Fred Chappell.* Edited by Patrick Bizzaro. Louisiana State University Press, 2004. Copyright © 2004 by Louisiana State University Press. All rights reserved. Reproduced by permission.—Conley, Tom. From "Ronsard on Speed: 'Ciel, air, & vens,'" in *In Memory of Elaine Marks: Life Writing, Writing Death.* Edited by Richard E. Goodkin. University of Wisconsin Press, 2007. Copyright © 2007 by the Board of Regents of the University of Wisconsin System. Reproduced by permission of the University of Wisconsin Press.—Cooper, Kate M. From "Reading Between the

Gale Literature Product Advisory Board

The members of the Gale Literature Product Advisory Board—reference librarians from public and academic library systems—represent a cross-section of our customer base and offer a variety of informed perspectives on both the presentation and content of our literature products. Advisory board members assess and define such quality issues as the relevance, currency, and usefulness of the author coverage, critical content, and literary topics included in our series; evaluate the layout, presentation, and general quality of our printed volumes; provide feedback on the criteria used for selecting authors and topics covered in our series; provide suggestions for potential enhancements to our series; identify any gaps in our coverage of authors or literary topics, recommending authors or topics for inclusion; analyze the appropriateness of our content and presentation for various user audiences, such as high school students, undergraduates, graduate students, librarians, and educators; and offer feedback on any proposed changes/enhancements to our series. We wish to thank the following advisors for their advice throughout the year.

Fred Chappell
1936-

(Full name Fred Davis Chappell) American poet, novelist, short story writer, and essayist.

INTRODUCTION

A prolific and highly accomplished poet and storyteller, Chappell is known for dark psychological novels in the Southern Gothic style and most especially for his poetry, which features vivid descriptions of his native Appalachia, an extensive knowledge of the classics, and a gently humorous approach to his subject matter.

BIOGRAPHICAL INFORMATION

Chappell was born on May 28, 1936, in the small mill town of Canton, in western North Carolina, to James Taylor and Anne Davis Chappell. Both his parents were teachers; however, his father left teaching to tend the family farm, supplementing his income with a job as a furniture retailer. From 1957 through 1964, Chappell worked at various jobs—as the general manager of a supply company, as the credit manager of a furniture company, and as a proofreader for Duke University Press—until he completed his education, earning a B.A. in 1961 and an M.A. in 1964, both from Duke University. Chappell then accepted a teaching position at Duke, where he served as professor of English for forty years until his retirement in 2004. In 1959, he married Susan Nichols, with whom he had a son, Heath. Chappell has earned a number of fellowships and awards, among them the Woodrow Wilson fellowship, a Rockefeller Foundation grant (1966), the National Institute and American Academy award in literature (1968), the Roanoke-Chowan Poetry Cup (1972, 1978, and 1979), the Bollingen Prize in Poetry (1985), the T. S. Eliot Prize (1993), and the Aiken Taylor Award in Poetry (1996). He served as Poet Laureate of North Carolina from 1997-2002. He continues to write and publish poetry and short stories.

MAJOR WORKS

In the 1960s, early in his literary career, Chappell produced novels that were dark, even grotesque, and filled with madness and violence—in keeping with the conventions of the Southern Gothic genre. In 1971, he issued his first volume of poetry, *The World between the Eyes,* characterized by lengthy descriptions of the way of life he enjoyed as a child in a small mountain town. He then produced a series of books that would later be collected in the highly-acclaimed 1981 volume *Midquest,* which was structured around the essential elements of earth, wind, fire, and water. Individually, the volumes are *River* (1975), *Bloodfire* (1978), *Wind Mountain* (1979), and *Earthsleep* (1980). The collected version features multiple poetic voices and perspectives as well as a variety of verse forms. In 1984, Chappell departed from his usual poetic technique and produced *Castle Tzingal,* a verse narrative set in medieval times. The work combines elements of suspense, grotesquerie, and humor in the form of a revenge tragedy. *First and Last Words* was published in 1989 and features the poet/narrator's appraisals of various literary figures and their works down through the ages. In 1993, Chappell published *C: Poems,* a satirical collection of one hundred poems and riddles, many based on the classics. Chappell's most recent collections of poetry are *Spring Garden: New and Selected Poems* (1995), centering on a day in a garden; *Family Gathering: Poems* (2000), inspired by a family reunion; the aptly named *Backsass* (2004), containing sarcastic and witty poems on various aspects of modern life; and *Shadow Box* (2009), featuring the poem-within-a-poem, hailed by reviewers as a new poetic form.

In addition to his poetry, Chappell has produced nine novels, two collections of essays, and three collections of short stories; the most recent, *Ancestors and Others: New and Selected Stories,* was published in 2009.

CRITICAL RECEPTION

Critical discussion of Chappell's work typically involves an assumed dichotomy between his early life in a rural mountain town and his later career at a top university—both of which inform his poetry as well as his prose. Michael McFee refers to Chappell's "split literary personality," characterized by 'Ole Fred,' the drinking, joking, and cussing narrator of *Midquest* versus Professor Chappell, "deeply and widely read, profoundly learned: a genuine scholar." Dabney Stuart has also studied the ways that Chappell "suggests the disparity of the two environments" and the manner in which structure "involves the paradigmatic polarization of rural and urban" in his work. Stuart cautions, however, against oversimplification, acknowledging that Chappell's work "is not as sharply bifurcated between the rural and the intellectual" as Stuart's introduction to *The Fred Chappell Reader* seems to imply. George Hovis contends that the "preoccupation with the farming life Chappell chose to leave," informs the poet's entire oeuvre, but it is *Midquest* that most clearly displays "the themes of exile from his Appalachian past and the struggle to reforge, through poetry, a unity with that past." John Lang believes that Chappell has achieved that unity, as the poet's "enormous range of allusions ties his individual Appalachian voices to many of the most significant features of the Western literary, philosophical, and religious traditions."

Kate M. Cooper employs French critical theory in her analysis of *Castle Tzingal,* an unusual poem for Chappell as it is set in neither of the poet's two worlds, but rather in the court of a mad king determined to assert total control over the subjects of his mythical kingdom. Other familiar dichotomies appear in the poem, however, between harmony and discord, "nature and culture, language and desire, poetry and power" which the critic contends "point not only to the problematic of its own writing, but also to the questions of production inherent to every literary undertaking." Cooper suggests that the work "may be read as a clue to the understanding of southern culture and literature" at the same time that it "also speaks with uncanny explicitness to the issues of contemporary French theory." Peter Makuck points out that despite the impressive range of diction, forms, voice, and subject matter within Chappell's body of work, there are a number of continuities that exist over the course of his career as a poet. Henry Taylor also finds "a consistency of style and approach" in Chappell's poetry. As an example, Taylor points to the speaker in "The World between the Eyes" from Chappell's poetry collection of the same name, "who, in various guises and at various ages, continues to be the means of perception throughout much of Chappell's poetry." The primary speaker in *Midquest,* "Ole Fred," has received a great deal of critical attention as a stand-in for Chappell himself, particularly since the poet and his poetic persona share the same birthday—their thirty-fifth—which Chappell considers the midpoint of life. Lang refers to the volume as a "semiautobiographical epic," and Patrick Bizzaro, noting that the narrators most often used in *Midquest* are either Ole Fred or 'I,' questions Chappell's insistence that neither of them "is identical to the author." Bizzaro claims that in studying Chappell's poetry, "readers might rightly feel that their educations have betrayed them," since their training in point of view is "inadequate to the task" of separating author from narrator. According to Bizzaro, "in all of Chappell's works the line separating Chappell as author from the narrators of his essays,

poems, and stories is so thin—at times nearly invisible"—that regardless of the genre, critics as well as readers have considered Chappell's work autobiographical.

PRINCIPAL WORKS

Poetry

The World between the Eyes 1971
River 1975
The Man Twice Married to Fire 1977
Bloodfire 1978
Awakening to Music 1979
Wind Mountain 1979
Earthsleep 1980
Driftlake: A Lieder Cycle 1981
*Midquest 1981
Castle Tzingal 1984
Source 1986
First and Last Words 1989
C: Poems 1993
Spring Garden: New and Selected Poems 1995
Family Gathering: Poems 2000
Backsass: Poems 2004
Shadow Box 2009

Other Major Works

It Is Time, Lord (novel) 1963
The Inkling (novel) 1965
Dagon (novel) 1968
The Gaudy Place (novel) 1972
Moments of Light (short stories) 1980
I Am One of You Forever (novel) 1985
The Fred Chappell Reader (poetry, novels, and short stories) 1987
Brighten the Corner Where You Are (novel) 1989
More Shapes than One (short stories) 1991
Plow Naked: Selected Writings on Poetry (essays) 1993
Farewell, I'm Bound to Leave You (short stories) 1996
A Way of Happening: Observations of Contemporary Poetry (essays) 1998
Look Back All the Green Valley (novel) 1999
Ancestors and Others: New and Selected Stories (short stories) 2009

*Includes *River, Bloodfire. Wind Mountain, and Earthsleep.*

CRITICISM

Dabney Stuart (essay date 1987)

SOURCE: Stuart, Dabney. "'What's Artichokes?': An Introduction to the Work of Fred Chappell." In *The Fred Chappell Reader,* pp. xi-xx. New York: St. Martin's Press, 1987.

[*In the following essay—written as an introduction to a collection of excerpts from Chappell's major works—Stuart discusses the place of Chappell's rural upbringing and of his Eastern education on his poetry and prose.*]

> *The child is father to the man, we say. Let me then praise my father, even salute him: for he stood there without any ulterior motive, furtively gazing into heaven: he didn't make a song about it, didn't dream of writing it up as a poem to be praised and admired—just stood there and gaped!*
>
>　　　　　　　　　　　　　—*John Stewart Collis*

In *Poison Pen,* his recent compendium of cultural and literary satire, novelist and poet George Garrett, faintly disguised, calls Fred Chappell the John-Boy Walton of American poetry. It's a facetious remark, of course, but there's enough truth in it to afford an unexpected entrance to Fred Chappell's work. Chappell was born May 28, 1936, and grew up on a farm in Canton, near Asheville, North Carolina, but his family poems in *Midquest* give a tougher, less whimsical access to the kind of hardscrabble farm life popularized in Earl Hamner's television series.

Midquest's narrator, "Ole Fred"—composed of Chappell's attitudes, memories, and experiences, but not identical with the author—celebrates his thirty-fifth birthday in four groups of poems, one series each for the elements once believed to have been the components of all matter—earth, air, fire, and water. He begins the second poem of the volume by quoting Dante—"Midway in this life I came to a darksome wood"—establishing another classical basis for what follows. I will come back to this, but the focus for now is Ole Fred's family, which populates the volume via monologue and dialogue (with Fred as a boy), centering its down-home humor, grit, and independence.

His grandparents and parents are the principals, sharply individualized, economically rendered, living at harmonious odds with each other in hard times, honoring each other's idiosyncrasies, complementing strength with weakness, weakness with strength. The mother's account of her unique courtship—J. T., who taught at the same schoolhouse, borrowed her slip to use in his class experiments with electricity, flying it past her

window like Ben Franklin's kite—acts as a screen memory that helps her not dwell too closely on how difficult life actually was. Her real code word is "hard." Fred's father, for whom money is scarce and a burden simultaneously ("Thinking of nothing but money makes me sick") burns a dollar bill to assert his freedom, and in another instance makes up for his son a beguiling tale in which he itemizes the contents of the layers of a hurricane. For the grandmother it's the disintegration of the family that is worrisome. Noting Fred's "bookishness," she fears he'll grow up to be a lawyer, becoming "second-generation-respectable." She also believes he can never cut loose from his roots altogether; she says to him,

> "Not all the money in this world can wash true-poor
> True rich. Fatback just won't change to artichokes."
>
> "What's artichokes?"
>
> 　　　　　　"Pray Jesus you'll never know.
> For if you do it'll be a sign you've grown
> Away from what you are. . . ."

Another central character, though not family, is Virgil Campbell, who runs a general store and generally keeps the community from hunkering too morosely on its problems. His first name echoes his literary predecessor, but one of the pitfalls Chappell successfully skirts is solemnity, and his guide through the difficulties of daily life navigates by means of humor. "Campbell," he writes in the introduction to *Midquest,* "is supposed to give to the whole its specifically regional, its Appalachian, context." In **"Dead Soldiers,"** instead of recalling disaster and loss, the focus is on Campbell's shooting his emptied jars of whiskey as they float from the basement of his store on floodwater. Eventually the bridge just upriver starts to sway and groan, so he takes a shot at it as it falls, becoming known as the man who killed the bridge.

There is, of course, more to such procedures than fun. Humor's relationship to survival and sanity is a matter for celebration on any account. To this Chappell adds, as a premise on which his "character" poems rest, the understanding of the psyche's way of turning its attention aside from events of disaster and grief to scenes and activities obliquely attached to them. Too direct a memory numbs; the indirect route makes us able to continue the trip. It's a compromise struck between facing reality head on and trying to evade it altogether, and is one reason this aspect of Chappell's work, though affectionate and open, is bracingly unsentimental (which helps, incidentally, to distinguish him further as a storyteller from John-Boy Walton).

The focus on rural character and situation I have approached through *Midquest* extends, unsurprisingly, into Chappell's prose as well. A cluster of four stories in *Moments of Light* could be considered as stages in the declension of the life of Mark Vance from the coherencies of rural experience to the debilitation of the city. Though he is not uniformly happy as a boy on the farm—indeed, one observes in his inattention and lack of will the seeds of later problems—he is nonetheless in an environment that requires certain contributions from him necessary to survival. If he doesn't get water to his father at work in the long sun, for instance, the man's labor will be more tortuous; if he's not responsible with his ignorance about items such as blasting caps, his life is at risk. He is also surrounded by people who care about him, and who seek to help him grow into a productive place among the family and its traditions.

In the university town where we later see him, however, he is cut off from such people and the land with which they share a covenant of nurture and increase. The result is a harrowing rootlessness. To feel how sharply Chappell suggests the disparity of the two environments one could compare the good-humored, brightly surprising introduction to sex Rosemary gives Mark (in "The Weather") with the dissolute, hollow visit he has with Norma in "The Thousand Ways."

One of the few black characters in Chappell's fiction, Stovebolt Johnson in "Blue Dive," acts as a central instance of civility, decorum, and balanced regard for both himself and other people. The dramatic structure again involves the paradigmatic polarization of rural and urban. This time, however, Chappell puts the big city dude—Locklear Hawkins, who runs the dive where Johnson seeks a job as a guitarist—in farm country, an inversion that enables him to have Johnson play with the homefield advantage. His ability to restrain his anger under considerable pressure is in part due to his being surrounded by people whose pace and habits he is familiar with and can therefore draw succor and support from. Chappell's phrase for a central quality of farmers is "inspired patience," an attribute that Johnson, though not a farmer, embodies.

Although over half of *Moments of Light* deals with other subjects, Chappell sets all of *I Am One of You Forever* on a farm. It is a series of stories, too, but they are loosely connected through form and characters to approximate a novel. Chappell's use of humorous exaggeration in many of the chapters is an obvious indication of the book's genial tone. *I Am One of You Forever* is also his most extensive dramatization of the values of a farm family's cohesion and support, which foster the mutual independence and growth of its members.

The various eccentric uncles who visit young Jess and his parents become involved in situations whose familiar American hyperbole (à la Paul Bunyan, Epaminondas, and Mark Twain) is, first of all, entertaining. It is also, I think, suggestive of one of the necessities in a

kind of life whose intimacy and death-defying routine are always simmering tensions that might eventually erupt in strife and disharmony. That necessity is the acceptance of idiosyncrasy and outright craziness. A farm family has to make room for its loonies, much as certain tribes of native Americans once did. Again, the issue is survival, and comic inventiveness plays a basic role.

One of the uncles out-Don Juans his namesake until his life is bogusly threatened; another's beard grows to incredible lengths; another, when he comes to visit, brings his coffin and sleeps in it. The pleasure of observing young Jess watch these men includes seeing him become alternately curious about and afraid of them, and, eventually, with his father's help, learning to incorporate them into his sense of life and its possibilities. Chappell complicates those possibilities by interpolating other considerations through occasional non-uncle chapters. The audience he desires, whatever else it may be, is not naive. Humor isn't escape, but accommodation; Chappell romanticizes neither it nor country life. Jess must confront, among other things, the loss of a close friend, the challenge of competition with other men, and the eternal need on a farm to rebuild what nature destroys and will destroy again. The following paragraph concludes "Overspill," a story about just such a destruction. Jess's mother has come home to find that the bridge built for her has been brought to nothing by a flood.

> *The tear on my mother's cheek got larger and larger. It detached from her face and became a shiny globe, widening outward like an inflating balloon. At first the tear floated in air between them, but as it expanded it took my mother and father into itself. I saw them suspended, separate but beginning to drift slowly toward one another. Then my mother looked past my father's shoulder, looked through the bright skin of the tear, at me. The tear enlarged until at last it took me in too. It was warm and salt. As soon as I got used to the strange light inside the tear, I began to swim clumsily toward my parents.*

Jess's vision here reveals better than any commentary the complex centrality of family life as I have been discussing it in Fred Chappell's work. But if he was born and raised in rural western North Carolina, he went east to a fancy college, "deserting," he says, "manual for intellectual labor," and has made his living as a teacher of literature and writing for twenty-two years. It would be a shock similar to encountering a black hole in space if his fiction and poetry didn't reflect the part humane letters has played in his life, too.

Chappell has been around long enough, in fact, for apocryphal rumors to have sprouted. He is alleged to have started writing before he could talk, and in his early teens to have printed reams of science fiction stories under an undivulged pseudonym. Fortunately, more dependable information is available about him as a poet in high school, and later during his checkered undergraduate career at Duke University. His **"Rimbaud Fire Letter to Jim Applewhite"** (in the *Bloodfire* section of *Midquest*) reveals, from an affectionately amused adult perspective, something of the intensity with which he immersed himself in his image of the feverish young *auteur.*

> Four things I knew: Rimbaud was genius pure;
> The colors of the vowels and verb tenses;
> That civilization was going up in fire;
> And how to derange every last one of my senses:
> Kind of a handbook on how to be weird and silly.

I don't want to veer toward biography here so much as to point at the fierce allegiance, however adolescent, to literature the poem recounts. It is one of three such letters in *Midquest,* written to other authors, that focus this allegiance, as well as a few of its particular objects: Rimbaud, Dante, and science fiction authors, especially Poe, H. P. Lovecraft, and H. G. Wells.

A cursory skimming of *Midquest* will show how pervasive Dante is, for instance. The conception of the book, as well as much of its overall structure, derives from *The Divine Comedy.* I've already mentioned the "darksome wood" beginnings of both poems, and Virgil Campbell's kinship to the Roman epic poet who guides Dante through hell to heaven. That *Midquest* lacks the inclusive theological system of Dante's trilogy is part of its meaning. It is, after all, written three-quarters of the way through an exhaustingly secular century, determined, it sometimes appears, to exceed past human horrors without the hope the church afforded in previous times. Chappell's poem, however, is no less serious in its scope and intention than *The Divine Comedy*; God and the Bible suffuse it. There are descents into hell (**"Cleaning the Well"**), rebirths (**"Bloodfire," "Fire Now Wakening on the River"**), frequent ponderings on flesh and spirit (**"Firewood"**), and no embarrassment accompanies the evocation of the spirits of the dead.

From this perspective even the discussion of literature in the playlet **"Hallowind"** (whose title, too, has religious implications) assumes an added spiritual dimension. Note this exchange between Ole Fred, Reynolds Price, and the personified rain:

FRED:

> The most symbolic line there is,
> And fullest of hard realities,
> Is Shakespearean: "Exeunt omnes."

REYNOLDS:

> Your poet's a foe to love and laughter.
> Here's the line one gives one's life for:

> "They all lived happily ever after."

THE RAIN:

> What say we work us up some brio
> And drown this silly wayward trio?
> *My* favorite line is "Ex Nihilo."

From "Ex Nihilo," with its suggestion of the creation, to "exeunt omnes" covers much of the ground human beings travel. When the narrator prays at the close of the opening poem in *Earthsleep,* "Hello Destiny, I'm harmless Fred, / Treat me sweet Please," he isn't asking for a favorable literary reputation.

The Divine Comedy is to *Midquest* as Vergil to Dante, I think. This is the most important antecedent evident in the poem, though Chaucer's *Canterbury Tales,* Byron's two comic epics, Browning's monologists, and Chekhov's tender, clear-eyed stories exert their acknowledged influences as well. Chappell cites others in his preface, adding that "some of the grand idols of my admiration—Baudelaire, Rimbaud, Rilke, Pound—did not show up, or appeared only in order to be made fun of."

It is in Chappell's early novels that those grand idols exert their power without the filter of distance and humor, more by their example of intoxicated, romantic sacrifice of everything for literature ("Be drunk with something," Baudelaire urged) than by any specific borrowing Chappell does. Thomas Mann and William Faulkner are among the more accessible pantries he raids for particular goodies, using shifting time perspectives and narration within narration in *It Is Time, Lord,* and, in *The Inkling* and *Dagon,* a sweaty determinism reminiscent of *The Sound and the Fury. The Gaudy Place,* a sprightlier, less hermetic book, has the multiple narrators of *As I Lay Dying,* as well as something of its mordant humor.

Still, taken together, Chappell's first four novels are very much his own; they receive a fine extended discussion by R. H. W. Dillard in *The Hollins Critic* (Volume X, Number 2). From the wider perspective of his later work, the first three of them constitute a little package of experiment and exorcism, a descent into the maelstrom it appears now to have been necessary to hazard and survive. They honor, as does all Chappell's output, the darker, inarticulate regions of human nature, the ineffable dreamwork done in those depths and the actual dreams that issue from them. They embody, however, as the work that follows them does not, the horrible possibility that the animal in us might indeed be severed from the articulation of mind and soul, and that human life might be reduced again to the mute, destructive servitude of the will. In these books the vision is unremittingly demonic, lacking the modest openness and broad curiosity, and the resulting humor, of the poetry and fiction that have followed them.

I began this focus on education and influence by using the phrase "humane letters" instead of "literature" because Chappell's reading includes an abundance of stuff from a variety of areas. Beyond Vergil, whose *Georgics* are relevant to a farm boy turned author, his classical interests include Lucretius, Horace, Pliny, and Ovid. His historical fiction, much of it uncollected, reveals more than a nodding acquaintance with an astronomer, Sir William Herschel, a botanist, Carl Linnaeus, a vain geographer, Maupertuis, and composers such as Haydn, Offenbach, and Mozart. Apparently minor figures from American cultural and theological history turn up, too, as witness Thomas Morton, whose experiences with his Merrymounters underpin the Puritan explorations (kin also to Hawthorne) in *Dagon*.

This is a partial list, indicative of the breadth of Chappell's interests, but not of ease with which he carries his erudition. It is not paraded, but subsumed into appropriate situation, event, and character, alluded to quietly enough to alert an informed reader without putting off a less informed one. *Castle Tzingal* and *Source,* his two most recent collections of poems, are further cases in point.

In the former, a verse novel in voices—almost, indeed, a play without stage directions—Chappell plies together, amidst a diversity of forms similar to *Midquest,* a number of allusive threads. The context and plot are medieval, as is enough of the vocabulary ("grutch," "frore") to suggest the period: a deranged king murders and decapitates a traveling minstrel whose isolated head continues to sing, haunting the surviving members of the court. The consequent societal- and self-destruction is Biblical in its visitation of sin upon the sinner, and assumes that humankind has an operative conscience despite the modern overlays of this or that theoretical utopian salve. A background twine is the legend of Orpheus, to which Chappell gives a science-fiction twist. Instead of being borne down the river Hebrus, the singer's "comely head," hidden in "a grotesque undercellar," is "suspended in fluids beside a gurgling retort."

Source shows Chappell moving through various image clusters in the book's earlier sections to a culminating vision that is atomic, explicitly based in Lucretius' depiction of the universe in *De Rerum Natura*. Chappell's use of Lucretius' atomism ranges from the minute—frost seen as "emery," a fog dissolving solid objects "into spirit"—to the intergalactic: the stars, in a representative instance, are a "bright fishnet lifting from darkness those broken / many heroes we read the mind with." Between these extremes the volume's individual poems show the illusorily solid human species carrying out its daily heroism, its sweet music, its longing for rest, as well as its potentially sudden joining up with the eternal smithereens.

Though from the outset of his career Chappell has published poems in which he observes particular details in nature, he has not, to my mind, ever been a "Nature" poet. The poems in *Source* offer a fresh illustration of this point. They refer consistently to such items as Queen Anne's lace, the milking of cows, the slow spread of evening, and much else we associate with the term *nature*. All these details, however, are perceived as parts of an inclusive vision of human experience, current and historical. Of all theories of matter, atomism by definition dwells most insistently on the discrete, but it also views its particulars from a unifying perspective.

Which brings me to the basic oversimplification of this introduction. Fred Chappell's work is not as sharply bifurcated between the rural and the intellectual as the convenient shape of my remarks has so far implied. It is also significantly more varied in its subject matter than I've had space to suggest. The second of these deficiencies will be easily remedied by dipping into the deliciously thick right-hand side of the volume you are holding. As for the misleading division itself let me conclude with a couple of observations.

John Stewart Collis' words at the head of this essay suggest the first one. Fred Chappell the author who thinks is Fred Chappell the farm boy grown up, and what he thinks about is partly unified by that process. His grandmother's warning that he might grow away from himself wasn't an old woman's ignorant fear, but it appears equally true that Ole Fred has grown toward himself as well, as any plant grows away from its necessary root to flower. The fifty years this has taken (so far) is misleading if one conceives of it spatially—a "long" time. It is more helpful to say it is *one* time. Fred Chappell is one person, though unfinished; in *Midquest* Ole Fred refers to himself as "halfway halved and halfway blent." Similarly, his thought is rooted in that gaping child, who, as we all do, took everything in without thought. Chappell's tireless, wide-ranging intellectual curiosity, and the poetry and fiction that issue from it, are the attempt to understand wholly that "ulterior motive," however complex, that comes with consciousness. Intellect is vapid if it doesn't proceed from feeling; the feeling intellect in search of ecstasy keeps the twin hopes of recovery and synthesis alive, the future positive.

Finally, Fred Chappell concludes a recent essay about Vergil's idealized vision of the farmer in his bucolic poetry with a paragraph that could as well be, and I suspect is, about himself.

> Most poets would make better lutenists than farmers.
> But even the most inept of us still feel close kinship
> with the man in the fields, with his life of ordered
> observation and inspired patience. That is the one life
> besides poetry and natural philosophy that still touches

an essential harmony of things, and when a civilization discards that way of life, it breaks the most fundamental covenant mankind can remember.

Kate M. Cooper (essay date 1990)

SOURCE: Cooper, Kate M. "Reading Between the Lines: Fred Chappell's *Castle Tzingal*." In *Southern Literature and Literary Theory,* edited by Jefferson Humphries, pp. 88-108. Athens, Ga.: University of Georgia Press, 1990.

[*In the following essay, Cooper provides a detailed analysis of Chappell's* Castle Tzingal *through the lens of French critical theory.*]

The remarks accompanying Fred Chappell's photograph in Mark Morrow's *Images of the Southern Writer* (University of Georgia Press, 1985) include a wry admission from the prize-winning poet/novelist: "There's something about a disembodied voice that gets me every time. I don't even dare answer the phone unless I know who it is. Salesmen call me up asking me to come look at condominiums or mountain chalets and I always agree to go. Of course, I never show up." Chappell's fetching confession countersigns the attitudes of several other writers depicted in Morrow's volume. When first approached about having a photographic portrait made, Walker Percy pithily but gently demurred: "Thanks, Mark, but I finally had to swear off getting my picture took. To feel foreign for several hours!" Eudora Welty's comment during her own photographic session is more resonant with Chappell's. After objecting to Morrow's choice of her home's hallway for the sitting, Welty finally conceded and settled herself in a chair that she used only when talking on the phone. She explained her opposition to the chair as a portrait site, saying that she associated it "with nothing but resignation and impatience." Reynolds Price's somewhat resolute stare at the camera shows a face half obscured by the shadows of lamplight; the same light that both clarifies and darkens his facial features illuminates the metallic sheen of a small statue near the border of the photograph, a statue that Price salvaged from a going-out-of-business sale in New York. After glossing over topics as diverse as the formation of a writer's sensibility, his experiences as a teacher, the comparatively recent southern literary renaissance, and the role of religion in southern fiction, the acclaimed novelist set aside his worry beads and answered Morrow's question about his own personal religious involvement with a curious reflection: "I'm eastern North Carolina, but that's all."[1]

Remarks such as these are anecdotally reassuring. A Columbia-trained physician and National Book Award winner who anticipates a sense of personal disorienta-tion strong enough to make him beg off from a photo session, a venerable stateswoman of southern letters who prefers a straight-drive Oldsmobile and a crisp relation to the phone, a widely traveled Oxonian scholar who would choose to live no further than sixty-five miles from his home town in North Carolina—all of these descriptions breed the impressions of genteel xenophobia, Arcadian nostalgia, and "rootedness" so often associated with the personalities of the American South and its literature in the twentieth century. Without a doubt, the richly evocative, almost tangible linguistic forms that convey such memorable figures of fiction as Price's Rosacoke Mustian, Percy's Binx Bolling, or Chappell's Virgil Campbell seem to require a reading of homogeneous signification, the assimilation of a language and its purveyors with a comfortable, histori-cally determined notion of place. The familiar content of southern literary production in the twentieth cen-tury—this textuality's persistent reflection upon the im-ages of nature and upon the structures of family, race, and church—perhaps encourages the unquestioned mi-metism and fulsome sense of community so often ap-parent in the criticism of southern literature. Just as an Italian reader may risk loss of critical distance when dealing with Dante, the southern reader may be especially vulnerable to the referential lure of much southern writing. But is it not even more absurd to seek dialectical possibilities between this seemingly referen-tial literature and the rarefied sophistication of contem-porary language theory?

When speaking of contemporary language theory, I am referring specifically to the conceptual influence that America has acknowledged in the writings of such French theorists as Jacques Derrida, Roland Barthes, Maurice Blanchot, and Jacques Lacan. Since the critical developments of these thinkers are so radically different in orientation, and since their thoughts affect such traditionally disparate disciplines as philosophy, semiot-ics, linguistics, literature, and psychoanalysis, it is impossible to establish strict homology or analogy between them. I allude to them here as a group only because of their shared focus upon language as a field of inquiry and because of their insistence upon the autonomy of language as both force and form. In ap-proximate terms, all of these theorists emphasize the intransitive character of the linguistic medium, the power of words as signs to defer indefinitely or even to deny the representation of reality in a text. The critical practice of each of these thinkers thus posits textuality (literary or other) as its own object, and shows how linguistic representation invariably asserts its own impure agency, its simultaneous status as vehicle of and obstacle to meaning.

Though the questions provoked by these theoretical stances admit no certain answers, the implications for contemporary critical thought are innumerable. Derridean inquiry, for example, is generally directed toward the historical and cultural significance of writing as that significance is inscribed within various texts. In brilliant readings of Plato and Freud, Nietzsche and Heidegger, Rousseau, Mallarmé and others, Derrida concentrates upon textual examples of the written sign and shows how these representations are both determined and determinative—how they respond to and define the western conceptual tradition.[2] Lacanian thought, on the other hand, is more distinctly concerned with the analytic experience and with linguistic phenomena in relation to the unconscious. Since Lacan's theory reformulates the structures of the unconscious elaborated by Freud, it accords less primacy to the status of the written sign than does Derridean thought. For Lacan, language plays a crucial role not only in the constitution of the human subject, but also in the larger set of human relations in which that subject exists.[3] Yet, of the theorists mentioned, Blanchot is the one who most consistently points to the fundamental ambivalence of language as a dilemma of literature, writing, and reading. His fiction and theoretical writings relentlessly invoke the destructive force of language, the power of words to falsify or annihilate the truth that they attempt to name. His theory repeatedly exposes the fallacies of literary mimesis and obsessively questions the writer's control over whatever it is he is trying to say. According to Blanchot, the act of writing opens an empty space between the world and what is written, a void that always exceeds the writing which creates it. What he calls "l'espace littéraire," the literary space, is paradoxically the place of literature's impossibility: the space emerging yet always retreating from the writer's efforts to appropriate it with words.[4]

These synopses are extremely rough, at the same time partial and overly general. However, they are necessary within this study for two reasons. First, by juxtaposing them to the personal confidences of the writers cited at the beginning of this essay, I hope to stress the superficial eccentricity of a critical reading that proposes discursive coherences between a southern literary text and the questions of French modernism. To call any form of literature "southern" is to ascribe it to a certifiable American tradition and, on some level, to assume a teleological relation between that literature and the locus of its production. As suggested, the often familiar idiom and repeated thematic reflections of southern narrative and poetry perhaps hasten identification between this literature and the area where it was written. Even from a purely demographic perspective, the density of literary production in the southeastern United States during the past forty years argues favorably for generic labeling of the sort that the term "southern" connotes.[5] But if the literature produced in this region is so clearly an evocation of place, is it not then highly questionable to

read it through a body of thought that radically problematizes literature's place? Here is where the surface eccentricity of the proposed reading lies.

My second motive for invoking contemporary French theory results from a more careful scrutiny of this eccentricity and a reordering of the questions it implies. Ultimately, to read a literary text merely as the mimetic expression of a geographical region is to consign each to the other and to ignore the specificity of both. Though such a critical practice may have a certain documentary utility, it fails to interrogate adequately the determinations of both literature and place, and thus encloses both in a static conceptual system. To immortalize William Faulkner as the apotheosis of southern literature is to say no more than that Faulkner wrote about the South and that the South of his period furnished him with the material of his opus. This kind of reading can account neither for the fact that Europe recognized him with greater enthusiasm and foresight than did America, nor for the fact that the South has been the site of America's most prolific (though erratic) literary production since the First World War.[6] Since it takes stock neither of the "whys" of a writer's project nor of the conditions subtending a culture's specificity, critical homologizing of this sort can only impair the strength of its own assumptions.

My intention, then, is not to reject a priori the possibility of causal relations between the literary text and the region of its production. Instead, through a reading informed by contemporary French theory, I shall relocate the question of literature's place within the terms of the literary text itself. Another look at the comments cited at the beginning of this discussion confirms the validity of my approach. Ultimately, all the authors quoted are conveying an awareness of the dynamically complex tension between the sign (verbal, written, photographic) and the determinants of an individual's being and place, the tension between linguistic or photographic images and the larger systems of difference (historical, political, ritual, and so on) used to specify a region and the individual's role within it. Walker Percy's statement is illustrative: for the novelist, having his picture "took" is tantamount to being humanly alienated, made "to feel foreign," uprooted from the appurtenances and rights of a culture. Given the fact that his photographic session finally took place on the front porch of his home in Covington, Louisiana, it is safe to say that Percy's understanding of human alienation in this case has more to do with the violent effect of the camera image than with any sort of physical displacement.[7] The "resignation and impatience" that Welty professes when at the mercy of the telephone betray a similar wary consciousness of the temporal and spatial differences arbitrarily imposed upon human existence by a cultural medium.

What these writers' comments seem to enjoin is a critical view of the literary text that treats the ontological implications of origin, history, and social order as problems of linguistic representation. Rarely have these issues been so forcibly addressed in contemporary American letters as in Fred Chappell's allegorical poem *Castle Tzingal*.[8] Similar to his acclaimed *Midquest* tetralogy and his more recent poetic collection *Source*,[9] *Castle Tzingal* is a formally structured verse work in which the four classical elements—earth, water, wind, and fire—play highly symbolic roles. But instead of the southern rural landscapes that serve as backdrop in so much of Chappell's poetry, the setting of *Castle Tzingal* is the mythical court of a deranged king, a mad monarch whose obsessive attempts to insure total control over his subjects lead to the dissolution of his own kingdom.

Chappell's achievement in *Castle Tzingal* consists in part of his customary mastery of innumerable verse forms and traditions, combined with the ever-startling novelty of his own style. The overriding singularity of *Castle Tzingal,* however, resides in the insights it lends to a range of crucial issues. The intricate series of articulations that this text establishes between nature and culture, language and desire, poetry and power, point not only to the problematics of its own writing but also to the questions of production inherent to every literary undertaking. And if *Castle Tzingal* may be read as a clue to the understanding of southern culture and literature, it also speaks with uncanny explicitness to the issues of contemporary French theory.

The poem is a series of monologues, ballades, dramatic dialogues, and epistles that tell a devastating story of political decay, moral corruption, and loss. The tale relates the search for a poet/harpist named Marco whose prolonged absence has disturbed King Tzingal's court (especially the King's wife, Queen Frynna) and the neighboring realm of the mad King's half brother, King Reynal. Knowledge of Marco's whereabouts and of the circumstances of his disappearance is the goal of a quest that King Reynal has delegated to his emissary and first cousin, Petrus. Petrus's mission leads him within the walls of Castle Tzingal to various encounters with the depraved King's grotesque subjects, encounters which he then resumes in report form for King Reynal. Inside the dank walls of the castle, however, Marco's absence is the disturbing evocation of a melodic, disembodied voice (see Chappell's comment at the beginning of this discussion) that haunts the sleep of King Tzingal's subjects and troubles the depths of their memory. The perturbing lyrics of the disembodied voice conjure madness in those who hear them, and finally impel Queen Frynna and Tzingal's old, pensioned Admiral to their deaths.

Causally, then, Marco's mysterious disappearance and his spectral reemergence in song are the pretext of all speech and activity in the textual world of *Castle Tzingal.* Though the mad King's castle is the site of the entire poem, the effects of Marco's absence upon the respective kingdoms of Reynal and Tzingal give rise to two separate understandings of political rule, social order, and genealogical filiation in the text.

The Courts of Harmony and Discord

In Reynal's realm, effective political rule and genealogical linking are coterminous. Petrus's relation to the king signals this overlay of royal and familial orders since the emissary is at the same time a titled member of the court and the monarch's first cousin. In this "other" kingdom, Marco's protracted absence represents not only dismemberment of the body politic but also an excision from the royal family tree. Petrus's first letter from Castle Tzingal to his regent comments on this genealogical relation between King Reynal and the poet:

> Of your nephew Marco, whose silent disappearance
> I've come here to trace,—not much.
> I have unveiled some puzzling hints
> And know that he stopped here indeed
> Last year, received the gracious encouragements
> Of Queen Frynna.
>
> (*Castle Tzingal*, p. 13)[10]

Further, under Reynal the solid bonds of polity and kinship are only enhanced by the affective ties that the kingdom's members profess for each other and for their lost poet. In his first report to Reynal, Petrus comments on the infected atmosphere of Castle Tzingal and its unsuitability for a youth of Marco's constitution:

> A lad devoted to sport in open fields, to song
> And skillful love-converse, as Marco was,
> Would have but villeyn company in this place
> And much dour argument.
>   . . . . .
> Marco's affections would not be for this place
> Or for these folk. And I do admit
> Neither is the liking of your close and faithful envoy.
>
> (pp. 13-14)

The concurrence of filial, affective, and political ties linking King Reynal and his subjects suggests that his reign has been one approaching holism, one in which the structures of kinship, authority, and desire have achieved a viable balance. If there is an equilibrium implied by the cohesiveness of these public and private structures, it is only reinforced by the solidity of the genealogical relations between the kingdom's members. As first cousins, Reynal and Petrus share a linear tie to the same ancestors; as uncle and nephew, Reynal and Marco are descended in different degrees from the same parents. All three genealogical links (between the King and his emissary, between Petrus and the poet Marco, between Marco and the King) imply marital or sibling alliances—lateral bonds—that remain absent in the language of the text. Bound in relations of both affinity and consanguinity, the members of this poem's "other" kingdom are allied in multidimensional terms.

But such is not the case inside the walls of Castle Tzingal. The mad king's rule is one of strict linearity, a governance that seeks to control even the erratic supervention of desire. In order to maintain his preeminent authority, Tzingal threatens his subjects with knowledge of their innermost fears and dreams, with the awareness of their own perverse humanity. In repeated attempts to assert his own supereminence, the obsessive King invokes either the illicit sexual conduct of his court members or their static purposelessness as mere functionaries in his realm. After one particularly brutal evening meal, the court's Astrologer reports the vitriolic tirade launched by Tzingal against the old Admiral:

> "Tell us," he told the Admiral, "how you took
> Zomara, and what you said when they struck
> Their colors. What joy
> That victory must have been! Or were you—
> As I have heard—below, buggering the pretty cabin
>   boy?"
> The Admiral stared unseeing into his plate.
> "I know," the King continued, "of field commissions
>   in battle.
> But to raise a lad from lackey to First Mate?
> I fear you take no prize for being subtle."
>
> (p. 27)

But neither is the Astrologer himself immune to King Tzingal's invective:

> "For you, Astrologer,"
> He said, "all energies of life have lost their savor.
> You are sick and cowardly and have betrayed
> Some best part of yourself. Do you recall
> The earnest scholar once you were and have since
>   unmade?"
>
> (p. 28)

Thus, desire and its vagaries constitute the target of Tzingal's barbarous threats. In the case of the old Admiral, the alleged secret of desire and ensuing act of sodomy make for a faulty and humiliating infraction under Tzingal's law. Perhaps most interesting is the fact that the wretched King views that infraction in terms of a hierarchical displacement ("But to raise a lad from lackey to First Mate?"). On the other hand, the Astrologer is accused by his regent of a lack of desire itself, a stagnation of the vital forces which had formerly infused his work. In either case, in the furtive expression of sexual desire or in the demonstration of its loss, King Tzingal's subjects are called wanton because they want.

The King takes pains to exempt himself from the circuits of desire that he mentions to recriminate his court members. Tzingal's marriage to Queen Frynna, though a plausible locus for the licit expression of sexual desire, is a purely formal and barren relation overridden by the harsh imposition of the monarch's order. The Queen views her own plight as the grotesque inversion of her childhood:

> In Castle Tzingal I sigh long sighs
> And wish I were a silly child again,
> Nestled beneath my father's stout roof
> And never stolen away to be the wife
> Of an iron and fruitless man.
>   . . . . .
> I am not suited for the intricate gloom
> And thorny intrigue of a blackguard time.
> There is a child, a sunny child
> Who dances within my breast and combs
> Her sunny hair and coddles a painted mammet.
> In these bleak years I am defiled
> By the drunken ambitions, the nightmare designs
> Of a petty Mahomet.
>
> (pp. 4-5)

The painted mammet of Queen Frynna's youth, the doll she embraced during childhood play, is now transformed into a false deity who alienates and repugns her with his possessive schemes. The royal couple's alliance is perhaps this poem's clearest expression of the sterilizing effects of an absolute, imposed order, a rule that alienates desire by seeking to appropriate it.

It is of course clear in the poem that Tzingal's consuming ardor in the poem is tantamount to poetic desire itself: the desire for total knowledge, truth, and the union of these two in an absolute expression. The fulminating regent seeks to fulfill this desire through the creation of the Homunculus, a miniature man made to order by the court Astrologer. Properly named Flyting but called Tweak throughout the poem, the Homunculus is the monarch's eyes and ears, a creature small enough to inhabit the undetected recesses of the castle walls and to accumulate the secrets of its denizens. Moreover, the tiny spy's loyalty to King Tzingal is unswerving:

> —Ah no, I can't be bribed to speak. Whatever
> Could you bribe me with?
> The things I dream of are forever
> Beyond my reach, sunk deep in earth
> Or at a human height.
>
> (p. 2)

PAPER, SCISSORS, ROCK: THE GO-BETWEENS

King Tzingal thus maintains control of his gloomy kingdom through the invasive scrutiny of his subjects' desires. To this end, Tweak is his most perfectly accomplished agent: in accordance with the King's command, the Homunculus spies upon the castle inhabitants, then reports the politics and gossip gleaned through his undetected surveillance. In the text, Tweak is a pure sign of the economy of knowledge—knowledge construed here in terms of plans for political rupture or as the secrets of personal desire. As the poem suggests, Tweak is tightly bound to the King in a relation of profound specularity: this "minim" man (and it is noteworthy that the adjective reads the same forward and backward) owes the debt of his existence to the King and thus reports the findings of his wily espionage only to the mad monarch:

> I'm silent in a dusty nook
> But in the Council Chamber I speak
> My mind straight out and am respected.
> No one can trust me but the King
> Who caused me to be made.
> That's my safety from the murderous boot
> And poison marmalade.
>
>   (p. 2)

The Homunculus serves all the deranged King's possessive designs: the order, agent, and reflection of political scheming and secret desire, Tweak stands within the poem as the perfectly efficient instrument of King Tzingal's complete dominion. By transmitting information to the King, he furnishes his sovereign's desire for absolute rule with the substance of knowledge.

But perhaps Tweak's most startling feature is his avowed immunity to the seduction of being loved:

> I have no love of being loved; a minim man
> Prefers to flourish by means of fear,
> To cast beyond his stature giant shade.
>
>   (p. 2)

What insures the miniature man's perfect efficacity in this role is his *lack* of affective need, and consequently, his insouciance regarding recognition for his services. Much as his name suggests, Tweak inhabits the elusive wrinkles of the text, and within them, gathers, withholds, and betrays all secrets. His omniscience is implied not only in the economy of his function in the poem but also in the circumstances of his creation. "Conceived with purpose" and "drawn up to plan" (p. 3), this minuscule model of a man represents the final achievement of the magic arts, the result of an elaborate alchemical rite:

> My father was a mage, my mother a pour
> Of mystery chemicals. I was born
> On a table bright with flame and glassware,
> And had no childhood except an ignorance
> Of politics and gossip.
>
>   (p. 1)

Tweak's omniscience in the poem may be allied to his fleeting omnipresence. Unlike the other figures in the realm who have distinctly ascribed private chambers in the castle, the little spy's only abode is a bottle through which he has perceptual access to all of the castle's hidden places—its nooks and crannies, cracks and crevices:

> I'm hardly the first man to live in a bottle
> And see the world through a different size.
> I'm the King's most privy counselor,
> And know the secrets lisped at midnight
> By love-performing ministers
> And cunning courtesans. I spy the spies
> Who never seek beneath their beds
> Or in the arras-folds hard by the banisters
> Of the shadowed gallery.
>
>   (p. 1)

Omniscient and omnipresent, exempt from the desire for personal recognition and betraying no human or tangible need, Tweak symbolizes the infallible alliance of knowledge and power. He stands in the text as the King's agent of authority, secure in his allegiance because of his unconcern for otherness or material gratification.

Yet there is something in the poem that ultimately overturns this rigid economy in which all knowledge is submitted to King Tzingal's glowering, intransigent rule. In the introductory stanzas of the poem, Tweak explains his own origins and privileged status in the castle to a strangely silent interlocutor. Much in the same way that he stirs anxiety and suspicion among the other figures in the text, the dwarf "tweaks" us as readers with a curious innuendo at the end of the first monologue:

> I was conceived with purpose, drawn up to plan
> And have a surer measure than a man.
> It's s [*sic*] rarefied temptation
> Could smudge my honesty,
> And as for what *you* offer . . .
>   Well, we'll see.
>
>   (p. 3)

Who is this "you" in the passage? Is the miniature man suggesting that his unwavering loyalty to the King might be swayed? If so, what possibly could decide this "minim man"—along with all the absolute inferences of his poetic form and function—to switch allegiance? And to what place or political group would his newfound allegiance be directed?

As the poem progresses, we are gradually led to assimilate this mysterious "you" in Tweak's introductory monologue with Petrus, King Reynal's Master Envoy. Paradoxically, Petrus's mission is similar to Tweak's because he has been engaged to discover the whereabouts of the poem's emblem of desire, the poet/harpist Marco. But unlike Tweak, for whom the royal command to gather information (especially the knowledge of hidden desire) has no purpose or compensatory value beyond the fulfillment of the task, Petrus is both personally and politically implicated in his fictional quest. What Petrus seeks is knowledge with a view toward restitution of desire's lost object; what the Homunculus seeks is knowledge of desire with a view toward its submission to Tzingal's absolute control. Marco's absence represents in both courts the pretext of all speech and activity; knowledge of his whereabouts is thus the subject and object of all quests in the poem.

Petrus's inquiry leads him into dialogue with several of the poem's characters, one of which is the Astrologer's Page, Pollio. Prior to Petrus's interview with the Astrologer, the Page introduces himself to the emissary and seizes the opportunity to engage in private conversation. He questions Petrus about the outside world, and finally recommends that the emissary purchase his debenture. To embellish the proposal Pollio enumerates some of the qualities that make him worthy as a servant:

> —Oh no, sir, I'm not unhappy here,
> But adventurous to roam the wider world:
> It's the youth blood in me, and curiosity.
> But I'm no featherwit, as soon you'd see,
> Were you my master. For I have a clever
> Way with secrets, how to weasel them out
> And noise them all abroad,
> Or how to keep them quiet as a shroud
>
>   . . . . .
>
> You'd find me, Master-Envoy, quicksilver-deft
> At any use or task, in bedchamber or in foyer.
>
> For there are matters, both of word and deed,
> That here have taken shape and would have value,
> If ever they be known outside these walls
> To rival principates; and all you
> Could ever desire to know is in my head.
>
>   (p. 10)

Like Tzingal's "minim man," the Page claims to withhold the quiet power of knowledge as well as the awareness of how and when to use that knowledge. Again like Tweak, Pollio's secrets and abilities are not limited to any one particular cognitive area: his services useful "in bedchamber or in foyer," the Page hints that his knowledge spans the official arena of politics as well as the private sphere of desire. But unlike the Homunculus, Pollio announces that his competence and loyalty may be had for the mere price of his debenture.

The successive interviews between Petrus, Tweak, and the Page not only lead to the eclipse of King Tzingal's mad designs, but also imply the dilemmas inherent to any attempt at poetic writing. If the poetic enterprise is the search for a totalizing linguistic form, for the perfect expression of man's experience and condition, then the three figures named above play major roles in demonstrating the seduction and pitfalls of that undertaking.

As go-betweens or intermediaries, these three figures occupy a privileged status in the poetic circuits of knowledge and desire; because of their access to both inner and outer worlds, they enjoy a certain immunity to the authorities whom they encounter or serve. Tweak, for example, operates in a circuit between King Tzingal and the deranged monarch's underlings or foes; through him, secrets and knowledge of the other are transformed into an armament of absolute control. Yet, the miniature man has no titular role or defined place in the oppressive government that he so effectively reinforces. Omnipresent, evanescent, and omniscient, combining in his poetic presence the inferences of authority, the fundamental elements of nature, and the highest achievement of the magic arts, Tweak informs and supersedes the hierarchy that he serves. As the mirror of the mad King's realm, he dwells in the fissures of the castle walls, ferreting out the frenzied desires of Tzingal's subjects. His rigorous economy and function within the text remain secure because of his imperviousness to the desires he detects and because of his professed resistance to the lure of recompense.

Pollio, too, is a liminal figure in the poem since he serves both the official and erotic interests of the court's Astrologer. Unlike Tweak, however, the Page is initially subservient to the bloodless lust and dead erudition of his master. The young servant claims to withhold a "nether history / Of Castle Tzingal" (p. 10) but will divulge his information to Petrus if the emissary assumes his debenture. Knowing how to dislodge and retain the secrets of their poetic world, Tweak and the Page suggest similar cognitive acuities. But their knowledge can be had only at a price, a price which for each reflects the specificity of his function and desire in the poem. Pollio's desire, openly claimed in the text, is for the experience of otherness or difference, for change from the withering stagnation and servitude that he lives with the Astrologer. Upon taking leave from his master, the Page decries the Astrologer's interpretive practices, strategies that wholly submit the signs of nature to the transient political ploys of men:

> How often have the stars said right
> As you interpret them?
> I have no fear to grapple whatever fate
> You foretell mine. I go to seek a saner home,
> Petrus my mentor and I no catamite.
> I hear no stars speak politics at night.
>
>   (p. 10)

Despite Tweak's claim that his services cannot be bought, Petrus finally comes up with the offer that causes the tiny spy to reveal the circumstances of Marco's disappearance. But what sort of leverage can be used with this minim man who symbolically combines the forces of nature, culture, knowledge, and art and who seems to lack nothing? What sort of promise could be made to Tweak that would cause him to divulge the required information and switch allegiance? Though the dilemma permits no facile solutions, King Reynal's Master-Envoy strikes an imaginative bargain that buys the information he's seeking:

Do you bear a more imaginative bribe
Than that you offered me when
You first approached me? I hope
You've racked your brain for—. . .
　　　　　　　　　　　　　　You say
That under King Reynal I'd have a duchy?
There's a thought might cause my fealty to slip.

　　　　　　　　　　　　　　　　　(p. 25)

Thus, this miniature man, this inscription of omniscience and omnipotence, will reveal his secrets in exchange for property—for the legitimacy implicit to the status of landowner in King Reynal's realm. Unlike the Page, who seeks a way out of the conditions of his servitude, Tweak is swayed by the prospect of having a place within a hierarchical structure.

Though accurate, the knowledge that Petrus's offer procures from Tweak comprises no glad tidings. The Homunculus tells Reynal's emissary that:

King Tzingal conceived a jealousy of the poet;
Gave orders for his murder
And then with his own hand chopped off his head.
He ordered my father Astrologer to do it
With a burning poison, but reserved the harder
Pleasure for his own royal sword.
He fancied you see that Marco and the Queen . . .
Well, you need no pictures drawn.
And there was no truth in it, not the least,
But King Tzingal never inquires for proof.

　　　　　　　　　　　　　　　　　(p. 25)

Nevertheless, the mission that King Reynal delegated to Petrus has been carried out, since the emissary was instructed to discover either Marco's whereabouts or the circumstances of his absence. With the news of the poet/harpist's decapitation at the hands of King Reynal, Petrus hastens to recommend retaliatory measures to his own regent.

Before scrutinizing the consequences of Petrus's retaliatory decision, let us examine a bit further this remarkable interlude between the Master-Envoy and King Tzingal's tiny spy. This scene between two of the poem's middle men is a pivotal interval in the text because it assembles the poem's major themes; moreover, this passage speaks with outstanding clarity to the wider-ranging questions of poetic production outlined in the beginning pages of this essay. Of the numerous clues to reading contained in this scene, three features are especially noteworthy.

The first of these concerns Petrus's formal status in the poem. Like Tweak and the Page, Petrus is a go-between, a messenger whose quest leads him to cross the boundary between distinct but neighboring orders. Unlike these two figures, however, Petrus maintains a balanced or harmonious relation to the titular authority he serves. Tweak ultimately controls and overrules King Tzingal

through a canny manipulation of the mad monarch's desires. Though Tzingal may use the secrets that Tweak confides to enforce obedience and terror among his subjects, the King himself is not humanly immune to the effects of the miniature man's information. Apprised of the Queen's fancy for Marco, Tzingal conceives a jealousy so overwhelming that he breaks his own rule by murdering the poet. The King's secret infraction then places him in an ambiguous relation to Tweak, because Tweak's knowledge of the murder carries a potential threat to the royal order. On the other hand, Pollio's persona suggests the subjugation of vital desire to a statically imposed order. Conformable with Tzingal's allegations, the master Astrologer has lost desire's creative impulse, and has reduced his magic art to a sterile formula of signs. The knowledge he imposes upon Pollio, along with the domestic and erotic services he exacts from the Page, betrays a disregard for the vitality apparent in the servant's competence and desire for knowledge.

By now it is evident that the order of authority examined here and represented in *Castle Tzingal* by various monarchs, magicians, and middle men is in a more extended sense a synonym for poetic language in its quest for universal signification. Considering that the poetic project is an attempt to express the pure note of meaning, the articulation of ultimate truth, we must recognize the profound ambivalence of that enterprise. How can one express that which is eternal, universal, and absolute through writing—a form of representation that has its own force, form, laws, and hierarchy? How can the poet express universal oneness through a medium that establishes and enforces difference? If Tweak and Pollio's verse performances in relation to their own masters remind us of the unstable and ultimately failed relation between language (hierarchy, order) and the expression of human desire, then Petrus's presence in the text ingeniously hypothesizes the possibility of that relation.

As the representative of this text's "other" kingdom, a realm in which political organization, family structure, and the forces of desire have apparently achieved a functional balance, Petrus stands forth in the poem as the missing link between Tzingal's dark, fractured regency and a nearly idyllic peace. Implied in his figure is the equilibrium of social hierarchy, kinship, and desire that is so sorely wanting inside Tzingal's court. But this balance, this strength that Petrus symbolizes is strangely conveyed in the language of the poem by his absence from all direct modes of speech. Petrus exists in the poem only as the silent interlocutor of a dialogue or as the origin of the various letters addressed to King Reynal. Always implied but never explicit, Petrus's agency in Tzingal's land is a silent one. This is the first significant feature of the dialogue between Petrus and Tweak.

Second, this passage is of foremost importance because of its place in the overall organization of the poem. Like most of Chappell's poetry, **Castle Tzingal** has a classically precise organization; a careful look at the dialogue between Petrus and Tweak shows us that it is the twelfth of twenty-three poetic segments. This versified conversation between two middle men thus constitutes, in the most literal and graphic sense, the absolute middle of the poem.

Finally, this dialogue is notable for the multiple ways that it alludes to absence as a vehicle of meaning. Through this dialogue, we will remember, Petrus learns of Marco's death at the hands of King Tzingal. Much like an attempt to enforce and control desire itself, the deranged monarch's act in killing the poet is similar to one of the aspects of poetic writing. By decapitating Marco, the monarch imposes the absence of ruptured loss and death upon his kingdom, thereby stirring the very frenzy of desire that he had hoped to deflect or quell. The song that then haunts the castle and points to Marco's absence mirrors the King's murderous act because it rends the continuity of sleep and evokes the schismatic pain of memory. The tale that Tweak tells is one of a tearing and murderous difference, a void signifying exclusion, dismemberment, loss, separation, and death. But Petrus's absence from all forms of direct speech in this passage (and throughout the poem) is an absence of a completely different nature. Petrus's exclusion from all direct forms of speech in the poem is a silence that unifies instead of one that divides and destroys. The knowledge he acquires from Tweak represents fulfillment and loss at the same time: fulfillment because in gathering the news of Marco's death, Petrus accomplishes the mission delegated to him, and loss because the news of Marco's death signifies a dolorous blow for all of King Reynal's realm. This dual signification of life and death implicit to Petrus's silence is repeated in the strategies he employs to gain Tweak's allegiance. By promising Tweak a place and property in Reynal's kingdom, Petrus manages to break the spy's ties of loyalty to Tzingal and to establish a new bond to Reynal. Though the nearly idyllic unity of Reynal's kingdom has been destroyed by the news of Marco's death, a reformulated, though slightly less pure, unity is hinted in the triple alliance of Petrus, Tweak, and the Page.

SOME OTHER PLACE, THE RIGHT PLACE

If I have dwelled at length on the roles of Petrus, Tweak, and the Page, it is because these are the only three figures of the poem to escape the murderous touch of Tzingal and the destruction of his kingdom by any means other than death. Tzingal's Admiral seeks the peace of death by hanging himself in his bedchamber, whereas Queen Frynna, more and more haunted by the ghostly melody that she hears during sleep, drinks a po-

tion that induces death's slumber. Finally, at Petrus's behest, Tweak serves the King a blood-searing elixir that brings on the monarch's own demise. Before he draws his final breath, Tzingal sees Tweak put a torch to his chamber's tapestries:

> I take the flambeau here
> And flame the curtain, and now the tapestry
> That celebrates your coronation we see flare
> Like the glory of holy martyrs.

(p. 45)

Thus, in a highly symbolic gesture, Tweak burns the tapestry depicting Tzingal's coronation before the dying King's eyes. In much the same way that Tzingal's murder of Marco placed the monarch at the mercy of the dwarf's whim, the image of Tzingal's coronation is here submitted to the consuming flames. The only remaining words of the poem are those of the Song for a Disembodied Voice.

The image of a burning edifice is a prominent motif in some of Chappell's other poetry,[11] and is often accompanied by a chaotic dispersion of voices. But if fire is a dominant motif in Chappell's writing, it is still only one of many elements that he uses to dramatize his largest concern: the ontological implications of poetry. In his poem **"A Prayer for Truth,"**[12] Chappell's hope is that his verse "find the solid places," that it not be abandoned to the more savage and unstable regions of earth. Is this not the foremost allusion of **Castle Tzingal** as well?

I have pointed out that Tweak, Petrus, and the Page are the only ones to escape unscathed from Tzingal's murderous rule and the ultimate devastation of his castle. But what remains to be emphasized is the very inviting relation between these three figures' names or titles and the components—material and cognitive—of poetic writing. As his name suggests, Tweak is that pinch of consciousness representative of the omniscience, skill, and perceptual infallibility necessary for the supreme articulation. The Page, on the other hand, is the one begging exposure to otherness and desire, similar to the blank page of writing that beckons to the poet's inscription. And finally, Petrus as a figure in the poem comes to signify the balance and solidity implied by the phonic and etymological resonances of his name. The name "Petrus" is phonically and graphically similar to the term "petrous," which as an adjective means "stony, hard, solid." As a noun, however, the petrous is a bone behind the temple that supports the inner ear, which is the physiological site of hearing and equilibrium. Both as an adjective and as a noun, the term derives from the Greek *petra*, "a rock." So with a little onomastic liberty, we may see in the threesome who are freed from Castle Tzingal's walls allegories of poetic creation: Tweak and Pollio, symbolizing omniscience, skill, desire, and the locus of writing, find a place with Petrus, the solid figure who assures their solidarity in another land. The scheme seems nearly perfect.

I say "nearly perfect" because, after the gloomy sojourn through Castle Tzingal, the prospect of renewed solidarity suggested by the silent withdrawal of Petrus, Tweak, and the Page must remain conjectural and slightly impure. As the Song for a Disembodied Voice so poignantly reminds us, "The happy season of the world has left no mark" (p. 31). In fact, if the possibility of restored unity obtains in the survivors' departure to the "other" place, that possibility is transmitted to the reader only by or as an absence. The text of *Castle Tzingal* emerges from an instance of originary loss or fractured perfection; throughout the text, the poem's writing consistently echoes that loss and postpones all possible restitution. The spectre of ruptured perfection revealed in Marco's disappearance and death will always taint the possibility of paradise regained. The decapitation of the poet/harpist is thus a nearly paradigmatic illustration of writing's ambivalence as invoked by Blanchot: in the language of *Castle Tzingal,* the perfection of truth is implied only by the graphic figures of its destruction or deferral.

Paradoxically, it is perhaps through these figures of loss or absence that we may best consider *Castle Tzingal* (or any of Chappell's poetry) exemplary of a southern literary tradition. In what may be termed a bifurcated concept of community, many writers of the American South since Faulkner have posited that the region's identity is rooted in a loss of faith in the redemptive potential of history and in a profoundly isolated view of the individual in society. Robert Penn Warren's novel *Flood,* for example, shows us a protagonist, Brad Tolliver, returning to his native town in Tennessee in an attempt to discover the connections between his adulthood and a more general, locatable notion of culture. Accompanied by a friend who will direct the movie of his script in the making, Brad visits a cemetery where he hopes to find the grave of a figure alive in his childhood memories. Recalling the impressive individuality of the deceased character, Brad turns his own memory into a larger reflection upon the South: "Hell, no Southerner believes that there is any South. He just believes that if he keeps on saying the word he will lose some of the angry lonesomeness." Further along, Brad remarks that southerners do not believe in God, but pray because they believe in "the black hole in the sky God left when He went away." Lewis Simpson's discussion of this and other works of southern literature after the First World War suggests that the sense of place so clearly discernible in much contemporary southern writing is a place of mourning and dream instead of a strictly mimetic representation.[13]

On both internal and external levels, *Castle Tzingal* stands as a sparkling demonstration of this premise:

forever seeking restoration of its own lost wholeness, the writing of the text constitutes that differential interval between the moment of solidarity's failure and the fervent, but silent intimation of its renewed possibility.

Notes

1. For the specific passages alluded to here, see Mark Morrow, *Images of the Southern Writer* (Athens: University of Georgia Press, 1985). The comments of Chappell, Percy, Welty, and Price appear respectively on pp. 8, 60, 86, and 62.

2. See in particular *L'Écriture et la différence* (Paris: Editions du Seuil, 1967) and for Plato, *La dissémination* (Paris: Editions du Seuil, 1972). Derrida's most notable discussion of Rousseau may be found in *De la grammatologie* (Paris: Editions de Minuit, 1967).

3. See in particular pp. 237-322, 401-36, 493-530, 685-96 in *Les Écrits* (Paris: Editions du Seuil, 1966).

4. See *L'espace littéraire* (Paris: Editions Gallimard, 1955).

5. In the introduction to his volume, Morrow mentions that nearly 450 southern writers published novels between 1940 and 1983. See *Images of the Southern Writer,* x.

6. Lewis Simpson, *The Dispossessed Garden: Pastoral and History in Southern Literature* (Baton Rouge: Louisiana State University Press, 1983). See especially chap. 3, "The Southern Recovery of Memory and History," pp. 65-100.

7. Percy has, of course, given us a provocative view on the impact of the camera image in his novel *The Movie Goer* (New York: Avon Books, 1960).

8. Fred Chappell, *Castle Tzingal* (Baton Rouge: Louisiana State University Press, 1984).

9. *Midquest: A Poem* (Baton Rouge: Louisiana State University Press, 1981) and *Source* (Baton Rouge: Louisiana State University Press, 1985).

10. This and all subsequent quotations of the poem are taken from the edition cited in note 8 above.

11. See his lyric rendition of a burning church, "My Grandfather's Church Goes Up," in *Midquest: A Poem,* pp. 74-77.

12. *Source,* p. 7.

13. Robert Penn Warren, *Flood: A Romance of Our Time* (New York: New American Library, 1965), pp. 143-44. I am indebted to Lewis Simpson for alluding to this work; see his discussion in *The Dispossessed Garden,* pp. 91-94.

Peter Makuck (essay date spring 1992)

SOURCE: Makuck, Peter. "Chappell's Continuities: First and Last Words." *Virginia Quarterly Review* 68, no. 2 (spring 1992): 315-36.

[*In the following essay, Makuck traces certain congruent elements of theme and style in Chappell's major works of poetry from* Midquest *to* First and Last Words.]

> I had learned, maybe without really knowing, that not even the steadfast mountains themselves were safe and unmoving, that the foundations of the earth were shaken and the connections between the stars become frail as a cobweb
>
> —Fred Chappell, *I Am One of You Forever.*

Since his tetralogy on the elements appeared under one cover as *Midquest* in 1981, Fred Chappell has published *Castle Tzingal* (1984), *Source* (1985), and *First and Last Words* (1989), all of which are linked, if not by voice, by an abiding concern with Ultimates, with faith and art, love and war. *Midquest* is an impressive compendium of forms and voices—poems that sing and laugh, paint and ponder, rhetorically expansive poems that tell stories and have a keen interest in the character and language of vivid mountain folk. Chappell's diction in the tetralogy ranges from pure lyricism to scatology, sometimes even within the same verse sentence, whereas the range in subsequent books is narrower, the difference, say, between symphonic and chamber music. Nonetheless, from *Midquest* to *First and Last Words* continuities exist.

Midquest, bookish but funny too, like the novels of Saul Bellow, is seriously concerned with the question of meaning. In one poem, Old Fred says, "Everything means something / Even if it's Nothing . . ." (171). In another, he wonders about death: "Not death, no, there is no / Death, only a deeper dreaming" (147). Elsewhere he describes passion or "bloodfire" as "the disease / necessary to know God" (91). In yet another poem, he asks, "but where / shall I sit when once this flesh is spirit?" (73). In one of the love poems to Susan, the prospect of loss threatens the speaker's faith in reunion beyond death, but at first his faith seems strong: *"We shall meet again on that other shore,"* he thinks, then plays with the phrase, "We shall meet again, we shall meet / When now touchless my hand on your breast is swimming . . ." (51). The operative word is "now," the eternal now, which is an important dimension in Chappell's work, but one which need not preclude the possibility of postmortem survival ("I'd like to believe anything is possible" [6]), or the necessity of further quest.

Though Chappell has written prayer poems, and the vocabulary of Christian belief proliferates in both his early and later work ("resurrection," "grace," "chri-

som," "baptism," "Christ," "Lord," "Eden," "Genesis," "temptation," "Paradise," "annunciation," "absolution," "faith," "mortal sin," "angels," "redeem," and so on), the poet's belief is not narrow or orthodox. In **"Birthday 35: Diary Entry,"** he writes:

> I'd sleep in the eiderdown of the True Believer
> And never nightmare about Either/Or
>
> If I had a different person in my head
> But this gnawing worm shows that I'm not dead.
>
> Therefore: either I live with doubt
> Or get out.
>
> (5)

Other poems in *Midquest* also make us realize that Old Fred will not rest complacently in the fundamental comfort of a Personal Savior, for a realistic look at the human predicament (at "photos of Hitler and the cordwood dead" [65] at "snail-white corpses / bloating the Mekong and Hudson" [48]) shortcircuits belief in a personal loving God. Further, Chappell's imagination is haunted by emptiness and nothingness, the latter word recurring frequently in his work. In **"Hallowind,"** a rich and wonderful dialogue poem about writing which features Old Fred, Reynolds Price, and Susan, the personified and annihilating elements have the last words:

> The Rain (to The Wind)
>
> What say we work us up some brio
> And drown this silly wayward trio?
> *My* favorite line is "Ex Nihilo."
>
> The Wind
>
> Leave them in peace, if peace there is
> For their clamorous little species;
> Let them relish their flimsy wishes.
> Tomorrow and tomorrow we
> Advance against them frightfully.
> This night at least they have their say
> Together; the force of Time
> Upon their arts, upon slant rhyme
> And paragraph delays for them.
> It's soon enough we dissolve
> Their names to dust, unmoving move
> Against their animal powers to love
> And weep and fear
>
> (138-139).

Love is a central value in Chappell's poetry, but whether love is eternal remains to be seen. In *Midquest,* perhaps the poet often ponders the question of immortality because he so intently watches the heavens with a chilly knowledge of late 20th-century astronomy, with a knowledge of *"vacant interlunar spaces"* (69). Chappell's skymaps do not necessarily indicate the direction of transcendence; they point to purity, wonder, mystery, as well as nothingness; they sometimes act as psychological mirrors of human projections, register positive and negative valences in the observer. At the end of Faulkner's *Sanctuary,* Horace Benbow, emotionally battered from having witnessed so much human savagery, looks on the beautiful April delta coming back to blossom and says: "You'd almost think there was some purpose to it." In the work of Fred Chappell, the night sky is a constant, a given, as is the alternately mocking and consoling delta landscape in Faulkner, the moody sea in Conrad, the eye-like sun in Flannery O'Connor, the enigmatic heath in Hardy. In *Midquest,* we have numerous references to stars, comets, constellations, planets, pulsars: "the stars / Splash down in the filth of morning newspapers" (4), "Pleiades / Streaked in my head like silver fleas" (16), "wrinkling stars in rings" (46), "mole-runs of starlight" (46), "our savage reverent assault upon the stars" (102), "the stark beginning where the first stars burned" (77), "the lancet / glance of the star" (69), "firepoint / constellations" (183), "the black stars whirling / collapsed to a nervous cinder" (185), "stillness like a star of ice" (137), "love that moves the sun and other stars" (187). A typical way Chappell uses stars can be seen in the following:

> The pure spirits stand among monsters and heroes,
> Orion, Hercules, Cassiopeia,
> And Draco and the Big and Little Bear.
> And we this hour, 28 May 1971,
> Are Gemini:
>   the Twins, each and the other
> Like the two-colored candleflame.
>
> *Torn sheet of light sizzles in the mirror.*
>
> The seeds, ignis semina, of fire
> Put forth in me their rootlets, the tree of fire
> Begins to shape itself
>
>   (56).

The method involves correspondences and analogies—ways of exploring and mapping relationships, both galactic and personal.

Chappell also pursues this method in *Source* where again we have a profusion of starlit poems, a "powder of stars," "a granary of stars," "savage stars," "star-tangled trees," "discolored stars," "a nebula of accident," and other celestial imagery. The negative element of dread that results from contemplating the black emptiness of outer space appears in **"Windows"** where Chappell identifies "the gray light" that "steals across the unforgiving vacancy, / the tired source of death is that impervious space / between galaxies" (50). In the face of death and those terrible spaces between the stars, "We huddle into ourselves. Beaten by / obscure longings. . . . And the prayed-for transformation / remains stone" (50).

The most positive and the loveliest stellar metaphor in *Source,* however, comes in the first lines of **"Latencies"**:

> First point of light and then another and another: the
>   stars
> come out, bright fishnet lifting from darkness those
>   broken
> many heroes we read the mind with
>
>   (25).

In this poem the starry configurations of myth point to latent possibilities of Time, both positive and negative. A trout troubling the river's surface "reinstates the dawn" and is "a latent prayer." A woman standing by a window reminds the speaker of a "decade of obliterate dreams," of regretted waste which causes him to say: "The window is a latent religion." But there is also a negative latency:

> Or consider the young man fishing the river. Now he
> has gone to be a soldier, he has become
> a latent garden of terrible American beauty roses
> which only the enemy bullets can make manifest
>
>   (25).

Chappell's meditations on the heavens, his *"vacant interlunar spaces"* and "impervious spaces between the galaxies" also suggest vacant and impervious spaces in the soul and recall both Pascal's God-bringing meditations on *"les espaces infinis"* and the God-less universe of Stephen Hawking (*A Brief History of Time*) or Joseph Wood Krutch (*The Modern Temper*). What is important to Chappell, however, is that we create our own god, with either capital or lower case. "I been sentenced doncha know to create reality / by the sweat of my brow, Bible sez so" (*Midquest* 73). Here and elsewhere in Chappell we have a sense of the poet as Job and are reminded of Santayana's famous statement that poetry is "religion which is no longer believed."

Castle Tzingal is in one sense an anomaly among Chappell's books in that it lacks a celestial backdrop. Indeed, *Tzingal* is an indoor, low-ceilinged narrative, the castle and most of its inhabitants locked in a godless winter of discontent, with no bucolic memory except perhaps a brief one that lives in the voice of the murdered poet:

> I'd make my song like the wind-tossed willow tree,
> Promiseful-green and all a-lilt . . .
> With sun-spangle from a pleachy sky. . . .
>   . . . . .
> But Arcady is fled and gone
> Until I rend the guilty sleep
> Of Castle Tzingal and, like the sun,
> Wither this black scheming up.
> I am no more alive,
> And all my murderers thrive
>
>   (16).

In this volume, appearing between **Source** and **First and Last Words** (both books in which he shows himself highly successful as well at short poems, poems of less than a page), Chappell once again interests himself in character and voice to tell, in dramatic monologue and soliloquy, the grim story of Castle Tzingal, a tale of paranoia, jealousy, murder, and the persistence of poetry. Though very different, **Castle Tzingal** puts one in mind of W. D. Snodgrass's *The Fuhrer Bunker* (as well an indoor if not underground narrative) where Hitler's minions "explain themselves," have their final say—cynical, pathetic, political, recriminating—before the last act and their final exits. It is ironic that Chappell's only book without starlight features an astronomer who is a diabolical opportunist, denizen of a cold and starless world haunted by a murdered poet's voice, the voice of lost light and redeeming love.

Of considerable importance in Chappell's work is the notion that love, religion, and art are ways to deny our nothingness. In fact, even in **Midquest**'s **"Hallowind,"** where oblivion seems triumphant, the assertion of emptiness is paradoxically a denial of it. No matter how often it is brought home to us that our lives are founded on and speeding toward nothingness, we must live them, Chappell seems to suggest, as if such were not the case. We must, with our imaginations, press back, or believe as Tertullian believed—*because* belief is absurd. With great difficulty, our fictions praise creation and become a form of prayer, an act of faith. In **Midquest**'s **"My Grandfather's Church Goes Up,"** a disembodied voice says:

> *Pilgrim, the past   becomes prayer*
> *becomes remembrance rock-real   of Resurrection*
> *when the Willer so willeth   works his wild wonders*
>
>   (77).

The poet, Old Fred often implies, is someone responsible for always being on duty, is someone haunted into song by the black yawn of Time. In **"Susan Bathing"** (**Midquest**), the link between poetry, religion, love, and time is deeply felt:

> that beauty too is Jesus . . . that
> unattending beauty is danger and mortal sin . . .
> I
> must cleave to speech, speech being my single
>   knowledge,
>   speech praise,
> though this speech clings only a soiled atomic
> instant about your bare feet before pouring fast to the
>   black
> mouth of the pipe to smother. . . .
>
>   (19).

Through Art, Chappell implies, we are able to know solace or experience The Scared. Art notices, art reminds. We have a responsibility to complete the world

by noticing—an act of perception that re-creates. "We've got to tune and turn the music ever. . . . / You wouldn't let the music of this world die. / Would you?" (115).

In Chappell's world, small natural sounds potentially aspire to the condition of music and are themselves the sources of music and poetry. In **Source, "Music as a Woman Imperfectly Perceived"** and **"Awakening to Music"** celebrate those soft daily sounds

> in air existing and just now coming to exist,
>
> as in a fog-quiet autumn dawn the three low
>   dew-cool notes of the mourning dove
>   across mist-washed grass and fence wire
> suffuse themselves to hearing
>
>   (20).

Sounds awaken other senses, and we smell "wilted perfume and stiff linen" as well as the lovely woman of the title. The world, of course, comes to us through the sound of words as well and becomes more intensely itself for the sounding. At the end of **"Awakening to Music,"** which recalls the speaker's waking in the predawn dark and stumbling to chores in the milking barn, we are presented a number of important questions:

> How would I get it back? Go to blood
> again, sleep the light green sleep?
> How can I wake, not waking to music?
>
>   (11).

The answer is he can't, and we can't. As Wallace Stevens tells us in *Noble Rider*, it helps us live our lives, it's connected with our survival. Stevens here is talking about the music of poetry and, quite often, so is Chappell, but, from **Midquest** on, he often celebrates classical music, and jazz, too. In **"The Highest Wind that Ever Blew,"** a poem of homage to Louis Armstrong, Old Fred says, "I couldn't count how many times / You saved my life" (99). Interesting, too, how the notion of art saving and renewing the world is underscored in the epigraph by Schopenhauer which Chappell chose for the poem: *"Music is the world over again."*

If music is a source of beauty and solace, if war is a source of ugliness and suffering, **Source** ponders the painful and intimate coexistence of these elements. Here and elsewhere in Chappell's poetry, the relationship between pain and beauty, peace and war is a major problem, but a problem not to be solved. And therein lies the meaning. There is no bottom line. The two elements constitute a mystery to be lived and not a problem to be solved. Further, the element of evil can be tracked to the individual self, the finger of accusation not smugly or easily pointed at others or the external world.

In **"The Virtues,"** Chappell says, "The vices are always hungry for my hands / But the virtues stay inside their houses like shy brown thrushes" (35). Then, interestingly, he personifies the virtues and makes them feminine, indicting the war-making side of man's nature:

> The virtues are widowed sisters.
> No man has been with them for many years.
>
> I believe they are waiting for cataclysm.
> They will open their doors
>
> When perfect ruin has taken down this city,
> Will wander forth and sift thoughtfully in the hot
>   rubble
>
> (35).

In *Source,* which often balances war and images of horror with those of bucolic peace, we come upon another poem about virtue, **"Humility,"** which offers the possibility of innocence recaptured. We have a country setting bathed in "vesper light" where "the martins slide / Above the cows at the warped pasture gate" (9). Humility is a virtue one cultivates, a virtue that one can freely choose to perfect. Chappell emphasizes the element of choice in the two final stanzas of the poem:

> This is the country we return to when
> For a moment we forget ourselves,
> When we watch the sleeping kitten quiver
> After long play, or rain comes down warm.
>
> Here we might choose to live always, here where
> Ugly rumors of ourselves do not reach,
> Where in the whisper-light of the kerosene lamp
> The deep Bible lies open like a turned-down bed
>
> (9).

All of the images tell us this is not the Bible that readily supplies appropriate quotation for various crimes needing justification. The Bible here supplies the daily bread of poetry, the possibility of grace, virtue, and peace. Like a book of poems, this is the Bible that few read or care to believe in.

If the dread of nothingness (the dark side of peace and quiet) weren't enough to endure, our hunger for the power that leads to war is also a theme that makes itself felt in *Midquest* and Chappell's subsequent volumes. The imagery of warfare is frequent and *homo homini lupus* a constant theme. There is a sense in which aggression is a form of deliverance or distraction from the painful perception of "unforgiving vacancy" between the stars, an unbearable vacancy, too, within the self. In this context one thinks of thematic parallels in Théophile Gauthier (*"plutôt la barbarie que l'ennui"*) or Walker Percy's *The Second Coming*: "Are we afraid that ordinary afternoons will be interrupted by gunfire, or do we hope they will?" Chappell, in **"Urlied"** (*Source*), has a fictional Lucretius say:

> "The comfort is, there's nothing personal in it.
> The seeds of things put forth foreordained fruit,
> Nothing's wasted, nothing crazy, nothing
> Out of nowhere to attack a man for nothing"
>
> (53).

Nothing five times repeated. It is this perception of nothingness, Chappell intimates, that either prompts song—is the primitive source of all song—or violence, for in the title poem **"Source,"** Chappell says that "An ancient wound troubles the river" where a "perfumed barge drifts by, bearing / The final viceroy to oblivion" (36). Faced with "oblivion," one will turn either to creation or to the destructive pursuit of power as a form of relief, deliverance from awareness.

II

In the beginning was the Word, and at the end, too, there will be words or, as Faulkner put it, man's "puny inexhaustible voice, still talking," still refusing to accept the end. Chappell's *First and Last Words* is about silence and talking, about words sacred and profane, about music and silence. More perhaps than his other volumes, this is a book about language and makers, about Chappell's pantheon of favorite musicians, artists, and literary forebears to whom he responds; it celebrates the continuity of genius throughout history while simultaneously transcending linear time by enacting dialogue with the work of great artists in an eternal now. The volume is full of homages and references (mostly classical): Homer, Aeschylus, Virgil, Livy, Catullus, The Bible, Schiller, Goethe, Livy, Tolstoy, Valéry, Hardy, Einstein, Auden, Vermeer, Fragonard, Watteau, Baudelaire and others. Though *First and Last Words* gives evidence of wide and deep reading, one would be hard put to describe it as exhibitionistic in motive. In fact, the reader's reaction to a wealth of presented ideas is like Chappell's own to the way, in "Subject Matter," Auden deals with "irrefrangible Newton at the close / of his bookish poem / that seemed somehow not bookish at all. / Seemed instead a colloquy." Early in *Midquest,* Old Fred's grandmother accuses him of being "bookish," but in that work the references (direct or indirect) to Rimbaud, Kierkegaard, Dante, and many other writers, painters, or musicians are often passed over quickly, well digested by the characters, the action, or the large canvas of the narrative. But in *First and Last Words* what was backstage most often comes to the fore, stands alone, and delivers clear statements of mixed feeling. The imagistic, glittering particulars reappear now and again, but less frequently than in previous volumes.

For Chappell, the notion of the quest has always been important, and here that quest for the highest things is associated again with the heavens, with the charting and mapping which we find, for example, in **"Voyagers,"** a poem based on Vermeer's painting "The Astronomer." Though Chappell does not mention the painting ("The Finding of Moses") within the painting, it is nonetheless clear that studying the heavens is metaphorically our proper spiritual destiny, is intimately connected with our need for guidance. Chappell's astronomer stands in a "room that silence studies like a science" with "his globe celestial, / His book that names the fixed and ambling stars, / Their ascensions, declinations, appointed seasons" (22). The illusion of order and control that naming brings to the learned astronomer is ironically treated in the poem's closure:

> . . . The oceans after all agree
> With what the astronomer tells the stars to do
> From his room at Delft with his little silver book
>
> (22).

We find the same sense of ourselves as vulnerable, searching creatures in **"Word"** where we have, in effect, a picture of the Writer as Sisyphus. Though we long for the order and seeming fixity that naming promises, we are never allowed rest or certainty, for:

> With the word I set down after
> the next word I set down,
> all is obliterate.
>
>   It becomes
> a blind white plain as far as anyone can see,
> a clean snowfield into which we march like children,
> printing our fine new names
>
> (27).

Frustration, vulnerability, uncertainty, and a sense of loneliness notwithstanding, it is more important in Chappell's scheme of things to keep the faith, to be a questor, a watcher of skies than not to be. That the unexamined life is not worth living appears as more of a religious than a philosophical idea in Tolstoy's "The Death of Ivan Ilych," a story which prompts Chappell to write, in **"Meanwhile,"** these beautifully balanced lines:

> At midnight in the panelled library he pours
> a brandy and tries to think about his life.
> He ponders instead his career which gleams
> like a samovar . . .
>
> (13).

The "meanwhile" of one's life, Chappell and Tolstoy imply, ought to be filled with more than "career" and society's guiding idea that "A man must get ahead in the world." If one goes for the con and buys into such intellectual junk bonds, one then lives in a "world that breaks its first and only promise."

Chappell's *First and Last Words* is so finely structured that his poems play against each other like wind chimes, and a contrasting sense of "meanwhile" is found in the poem **"Dipperful"** where the speaker is out wandering in the mountains on a hot day. An old country man offers him a drink which he gladly accepts. No career is at stake. Simply one man attuned to another and to the surrounding hills. Old Fred "drank the hill. Scatter of sand-motes sparkled / When I launched the gourd's blind belly back in the bucket, / And on my tongue the green hill sprouted ferns" (35). Unlike Ivan Ilych who lived to get ahead in the world, the old country man tells an attentive Fred:

> "I never got married, you see, never had
> To grub for other people. I worked enough
> To keep myself sufficient peace and quiet. . . ."
>
> He spat again and a swoon of flies unsettled,
> Then settled back. The early afternoon
> Began to climb the fields. "I've talked too much,"
> He said. "I wish I didn't talk so much."
> When he said that, the silence had its say
>
> (36).

Silence always takes the last word, and the quality of silence varies from poem to poem. In some cases, silence emphasizes vacancy, nothingness, loneliness, and is an aggressive, annihilating force; in others, silence isn't so much an absence of sound as a positive sensation, the barely audible music of small sounds that accompanies the night sky and, say, bats "tacking from star / to early star as if putting in to ports of call" (30). Related to silence, of course, is peace and the fleeting consolation provided by music itself.

First and Last Words has fewer poems about music than previous volumes, in fact only two (**"The Gift To Be Simple"** and **"Webern's Mountain"**), which is perhaps an ominous sign of the poet's darkening vision. The book is structured in such a way that harmony brought by music is threatened by our time. First we come to **"The Gift To Be Simple"** in which Chappell, with aphoristic force, speaks about the curative dimension of music: "For Order is a Music of such health and delight / That in hearing it newly we come round right" (15). If music measures the health of a human soul, then we live in plaguey times, for in **"Webern's Mountain"** German Fascism prepares "the clinical bonfire" for "Jews and poets." The poem closes with this potent image:

> Then it came apart, the stave-line filaments
> Of gleam snapped by a mortar shell, viola
> And cello strings dying under the tank treads
>
> (37-38).

In **"Observers,"** troubled and still pondering the unthinkable consequences of life without music, Chappell characterizes the late 20th century as a time of arbitrary starlight

Which is drifting toward the place where Mozart
goes unheard forever, which is punctuated by
the blackened matchstem that was Nagasaki

(44).

With fewer references to music, and poems about music, music itself seems under siege, the implications for civilization grave. But the closest to topicality that Chappell comes is a powerful short poem about the national scourge of drugs which ends, "A whole Manhattan of indifference, / A whole Miami of despair" (33). Despair indeed. What does one do when the music of civilization becomes moribund? Chappell does not provide an answer, but in key poems he has sentinel figures who remain faithful to heroic ideals in the most grinding of conditions, who embody virtues like humility, fidelity, patience, and courage.

"The Watchman" is a poem about the Trojan war and the faithful watch of a sentinel who sees, as he waits for the signal, "stars flitter stupidly overhead / Like an irritated squad of flies above a corpse" (7). Chappell nicely describes how war and endless waiting for the end enervate and make the watcher numb, and he skillfully accomplishes this indirectly by reference once again to the stars:

So many nights of silent skies
Have darkened his capacities
To comprehend. The arrow showers
Of meteors no longer startle; he no longer numbers
The familiar constellation stars.
The Great Bear lumbers
Over his spirit, leaving a shadow like a mortal bruise

(7).

In another war poem, **"Patience,"** which Chappell calls a "prologue to *The Georgics*," we find a traditional tension between country and city, peace and war. The irresistible rural setting is beautifully painted with a "hive of stars" that "immerses the dark porches where / The farmers muse" (9). The farm animals have a "patience almost mineral" and settle in sleep "to the ground like velvet boulders." But men, alas, do not have this kind of patience and abhor the vacuum of peace because it has nothing to do with the power they seem to crave. Chappell tells us that poets—wrongly perceived as unrealistic woolgatherers—have known this all along and provides a bloody and balancing imagery of war with "cottager mothers flung on the corpses of their children" (10). The poem concludes directly and with the implication that peace-war cycles (closely related to the book's country-city dialectic) are a mystery to be endured with something close to animal-like patience:

But nothing changes. The war grinds over the world
and all

Its politics, the soldiers marry the farmers' daughters
And tell their plowman sons about the fight at the
   Scaean Gate,
And the other sanguine braveries the dust has eaten.
Sundown still draws the chickens to their purring
   roost,
The cow to the milking stall, the farmer to his porch
   to watch
Whether the soaring constellations promise rain

(10).

Faced with various kinds of madness, ignorance, and absurdity, one must adopt an attitude, perhaps an attitude like the one in **"Stoic Poet"** (a prologue to Hardy's *The Dynasts*). The attitude is presented in this way: "He gains a knowledge would cause an easy man / to embitter and grow lean. / Terrors assail him, he holds steady, / absorbing the wounds of the world's every crime" (14). But perhaps the best, most intricate poem about learning such stoic balance is Chappell's fond recollection of his teacher / mentor Allen Tate in the extraordinary **"Afternoons with Allen"** where we are presented with a number of sharp contrasts: the active and the meditative, the quiet and the loud. Time has made its inevitable inroads on the speaker's old friend, Allen Tate, a veteran of literary wars, a man who has taken his stand more than once, and held ground. Frail now, he and the speaker reminisce while watching Vince Lombardi's Washington Redskins on TV. Chappell humorously creates a Paleface/ Redskin contrast by emphasizing Allen's "pale pale eyes" and by associating him with Valéry's intellectual Monsieur Teste. The Redskins lose, but Tate doesn't seem to care and smiles at the "unimportant score." He says, "It's their precision I like, like a machine . . . / like well made poetry." Perhaps Tate is indifferent to the final outcome because he realizes that victory is at best a fleeting illusion. In any event, historical hindsight gives added poignance and drama to this scene, for the famous coach perhaps already knew he was losing to cancer, his winning single season with the Redskins a triumph of absurd courage. And in the transitional light of a late October afternoon, we see Tate losing gracefully, sipping bourbon, smoking, and appraising the writers of his generation, Hemingway, Stein, and Pound, whose "talent crumbled into rant."

In a wonderful closure, Chappell associates Allen, Lombardi, and heroic Priam in one bold stroke:

For Lombardi
He fetched out of that high magniloquent head
A telling line of the Second Aeneid.

Forsitan et, Priami fuerint quae fata, requiras?

(16).

By having Allen conclude the poem with this untranslated, uninterpreted line from Virgil's second book of *The Aeneid*, Chappell links the fate of all three men (himself as well) and suggests something of the heroic. Chappell's stroke is bold, for the context of the line, compressing so much, means everything. It is especially important, and moving, to know that the line comes from the scene in which Pyrrhus, hot with freshly spilled blood, pursues Polites and kills him before Priam's and Hecuba's eyes. It is the genius of the quoted line that it is one of Virgil's great transitionals: "Perhaps now you will ask the doom of Priam?" What Priam does—an old man at this juncture—is strap on his armor to avenge the murder of his son. Hecuba, weeping and pleading with him, recognizes the gesture for what it is—futile, for Pyrrhus is much younger and virtually invincible. But Allen Tate (Chappell, too) seems to find a beautiful grace and nobility in the act, an exquisite example of dramatic refusal, an act of great courage and dignity in a situation of certain loss. And Lombardi and Tate in their different ways had also heard those heavy quick steps behind them, felt the advent of final defeat in their bones. Intransigence in the face of the inevitable. But to return to the poem's last line for a moment, it is worth noting that the music of this Latin line creates another kind of transition, the transition between sound and silence—the after-silence that announces annihilation, a theme that Chappell has been sounding through the book.

The first poem in *First and Last Words* is **"An Old Mountain Woman Reading the Book of Job"** and in a volume that largely interests itself in reading and writing and the sister arts of painting and music, Chappell could not have begun with a better poem in terms of structure. Beyond being a signature poem with mica-like glories that harks back to the great bucolic strengths of *Midquest,* **"An Old Mountain Woman Reading the Book of Job"** first sounds the themes of light against dark, sound against silence which, among other strategies, help *First and Last Words* to achieve its impressive unity. Surrounding this lonely widow on a stormy, "starless night," is a devouring silence, an aggressive menacing darkness. Chappell sets the scene in a painterly but realistic way, in a way that reminds one of those canvases of Georges de la Tour which often feature a solitary vigil-keeper in dramatic lamplight. It is a world

> . . . delivered to ungodly shadow.
> The darkness of her hand darkens the page.
> She straightens her bifocals in which the words,
> Reflected, jitter, then come to rest like moths.
> It is November. The woodstove shifts its log
> And grumbles. The night is longer than the fire
>
> (5).

Young poets could learn much from Chappell's example of how to establish a setting dramatically related to character with such speed and economy. This is a poem about strength of character—an old woman's refusal to cry out or be intimidated by the hostile emptiness about her; nor will she succumb to the Biblical consolation of Jesus or St. Paul. Not tonight. She tends her fire which, like her faith in God's goodness, is on the wane. We see a pitiful hunger for immortality, her own and that of her dead husband, but the poet's metaphor says it all: "The night is longer than the fire."

Alone after the death of her husband, she goes (almost perversely) to the Book of Job for sustenance, but instead of help or hope she experiences the painful absence, remembers her husband's Job-like silence through long suffering and herself feels "Job's bewilderment." There is no help. "St. Paul does not escape, / Not even Jesus shines clear tonight." Tonight is the operative word, for we know she will face another day, however bleak Chappell's closure seems, however final.

Pursuing again a similar kind of "balancing act" structure he described in the preface to *Midquest,* Chappell in *First and Last Words* gives us a tight book, a well proportioned, intricate structure. Beyond the sectional symmetry of nine prologues, nine epilogues, and entr'acte, there are certain kinds of thematic and imagistic mirrorings throughout. In some way, almost all the nine poems of the epilogue echo the nine earlier soundings of the prologue. Most obviously, the echoing companion of **"An Old Woman Reading the Book of Job"** is **"Scarecrow Colloquy."** The book thus opens and closes with sentinels of the night, watchers who wait with an acute sense of absence for some loving transcendent sign, memory both consolation and torment, heaven and hell. But language, too, is consolation, and the last words of the book are those of that puny, inexhaustible voice still talking to its self-made Other, whistling in the dark, making the nothingness point to a somethingness, something to keep away the dark crows of death.

Chappell in this last word, **"Scarecrow Colloquy,"** or "epilogue to the Gospels," again dramatizes silence and suffering without God. Though he is concerned with eschatology, nowhere does he attempt to justify the ways of God to man. The last poem, in fact, endorses a Hardyesque world, stark and beautifully frightening, presided over by a *deus absconditus.* Typically, the two voices of the poem are confronted with darkness and interstellar space. The speaker humorously greets the scarecrow in the first line as "Ragwisp" and "my Sentinel of the Stars," and tells him that he looks "entranced as St. Jerome." Chappell's use of the possessive adjective *my* seems to establish the scarecrow as an alter ego, a kind of externalized Watcher Within, and the poem can easily be seen as dialogue between Faith and Skepticism. The Scarecrow asks of the speaker some news of the *"man who nailed me up, left me to challenge / the courage of the crow . . ."* (56). But the unitalicized, world-weary voice of the speaker tells old

"Hayhead" that he is forgotten by his maker, there is no point in trying to "unfold the motive of your construction." The Scarecrow feels sure that the farmer, an absent and forgetful creator, must occasionally think about that cobbled up figure he placed in the field. Light in the farmhouse window on winter nights gives some hope to the lonely scarecrow who imagines his maker by a warm fireplace, smoking a meerschaum and dreaming of "his friend in God, the Scarecrow." No such luck. Throughout the poem, the skeptical speaker answers "Chaffstaff" in various ways that he is forgotten and better face up to it. Godot won't arrive, and, if he does, it doesn't matter anyway. But, after the speaker sarcastically tells him to keep the faith, Chappell significantly gives the poignant closure to the Scarecrow:

> I have spoken in the field until my voice became an
>   owl.
> I have surveyed the horizon until I lost my buttons.
> The fieldmouse heard my silence and gnawed my flesh
>   of grass.
> And still I stand here guarding the bones of Adam
>
>   (57).

I don't mean to treat the poem too seriously because Chappell obviously intends humor and wouldn't want us losing our buttons like the old Scarecrow. But this slapstick figure of suffering harks back and mirrors to some extent the old woman we met in the first poem. Though they refuse to submit to different fates, they are presented nonetheless as refusing to submit, keeping an absurd faith, and we are somehow ennobled by their suffering, by their dramatic no. Indirectly, Chappell suggests an image of the writer as watcher and Job-like recorder who must keep the faith—something not terribly far from a definition found in one of D. H. Lawrence's letters: "A work of art is an act of faith and one goes on writing, to the unseen witnesses."

In the best sense of the word, Fred Chappell is an old fashioned poet, one for whom writing is a spiritual project, not merely a game with words. Chappell's poems implicitly argue against the current literary/philosophical notion that words are problematically referential, or don't mean, or mean much. Chappell knows they mean plenty and, skillfully used, are capable of providing sustenance and solace. They are the fragile vessels that bear our lives and hopes, to which Chappell bears glowing witness. What Virgil—one of Old Fred's favorite poets—wrote in another context is equally true of Chappell's own creation: *Fervet opus.* The work is all aglow.

Dabney Stuart (essay date 1997)

SOURCE: Stuart, Dabney. "Spiritual Matter in Fred Chappell's Poetry: A Prologue." In *Dream Garden: The Poetic Vision of Fred Chappell,* edited by Patrick Bizzaro, pp. 48-70. Baton Rouge, La.: Louisiana State University Press, 1997.

[*In the following essay, Stuart discusses the spiritual content of Chappell's* Midquest.]

> Tanto giú cadde, che tutti argomenti
>   à la salute sua eran giá corti
> fuor che mostrarli le perdute genté.
>
>   —Dante, *Purgatorio,* XXX, 136-38

> Our faith must be earned from terror.
>
>   —Fred Chappell, **Bloodfire,** IX

FLESH AND SPIRIT

The first two words of the title of this essay are a subdued version of Fred Chappell's more spritely rhymed phrase "attar of matter" (in **"Firewood"**). I intend, however, the same complementary attachment of terms. Chappell's phrase suggests, in sound as well as substance, that there is an essence embedded in matter and releasable from it—a sweet, intangible spirit inexplicably meshed in the molecular arrangement of the elemental stuff of which all things, including human and other creatures, are composed. One direction in which Chappell aims the atomistic possibilities inherent in this perspective is Lucretian. The other primary direction is not, however, subject to the contained reshuffling of atoms. Chappell is more essentially preoccupied with and hopeful of images of release and transformation, which are Christian in their orientation. The two modes of understanding are, needless to say, not always cleanly separable.

Perhaps a finer distinction is in order. The Lucretian perspective doesn't employ the complementary duality of flesh and spirit but rather transposes it into the fluid, imperceptible molecular composition of apparently solid material bodies. This, of course, was Lucretius' understanding of how the transience of individual instances of forms could be reconciled with the equally obvious recurrence, apparently eternal, of the forms themselves. Individual people die, but the human race does not; we eat this carrot today, but another grows for us to eat tomorrow; we may pulverize this stone, but stones are everywhere. Mutation and recurrence are complementary motions, rearranging the atoms out of whose coalescence particular things are made, and because of whose dispersal they disappear. But the atoms are irreducible and everlasting, as is the process of rearrangement—carried out by the forces he called Love and Strife—by which perceptible forms occur, pass away, and recur.

The interpenetration of earth, air, fire, and water is one expression of the Lucretian dispensation in **Midquest** and seems to me in no need of elaborate elucidation.

The titles of the frame poems of Volumes II, III, and IV serve as sufficient indicators, as do the abundance of phrases in those same poems in which two or more of the elements cohere: "dewfired," for instance, and "Earthsmoke," "earth / with its mouths of wind," "water in stone," and "blind windcurrent of the soil." It shows more explicitly, however, in passages where Chappell uses Lucretius' terms and images. In **"Bloodfire Garden,"** it is in the fire of love that "we are / whole again, / our atoms driven and / interlocked as heat in air" (91-92). When the "untenable trombone tones" Chappell imagines riding "out upon the blue-bleached air" pops, it lets him "slide the effervescent atoms" alone (**"The Autumn Bleat of the Weathervane Trombone,"** 114-15). In the same poem, he refers to "the hail of impulse Nature keeps tossing over / Her shoulder" (115). The recurrent "coming apart to" constructions (as in "fire coming apart now to wind") extend this explicit evocation across some of the frame poems. In the world beyond the "four-square crucis of elements" in **"Earth Emergent Drifts the Fire River"** (a cold world of nothingness, which I will comment on in more detail later), "the single atoms stray / Lost and touchless" (146-47). This poem is, in fact, dotted with Lucretian infusions, perceptions more accessible because of the atomistic backdrop. As Fred wakes in the first poem of **Bloodfire,** "the seeds, ignis semina, of fire / Put forth in me their rootlets" (56).[1] *Ignis semina* is, in fact, a phrase from Lucretius, which Chappell identifies later in **"Firewood."**

"Susan Bathing" and **"Firewood"** comprise the two most probing, subtle, and thorough embodiments of the Lucretian vision in *Midquest.* They are rather miraculous poems in many ways, not least in their personal and local dimensions and in the careful psychological progression their disguised narrative lines reveal. But my space and context limit me to some brief comments on the process of atomistic transmutations that occur in **"Firewood."**

It is "Flame, flame" that Fred's ax strikes first; he imagines the fire in the hearth that the log he is splitting will eventually afford. The dimensions the language implies become more complex immediately, as he speaks of the "heart / red in the oak where sun / climbed vein by vein" (67). It's not until he tangles with the walnut log some seventy-five lines later that these implications begin to receive their fullest development. This time he sees "the life" of the blazing log, "yellow / red and orange and blue & hasting your dark gasses / starward, on the silverblue night splaying a new tree / shape, tree of spirit spread on the night wind" (69). This new tree lifted from the burning of the old one sifts "upward to the needle pricks of fire" of the constellations. The roots of the tree of fire

> sizzle in our fireplace, the
> ghostly arms of it embrace the moon, the lancet

glance of the star pierces its leafage, this tree
in our fireplace is the sun risen at midnight,
capillaries of heat light lift out the chimney,
the rose trellis of stars is afire, sun reaches
homeward again to the *vacant interlunar spaces,*
chimney is its shrunk trunk & pins our dwelling
to the earth and to the stars equally, this spirit
trunk in the chimney is the spine of the world.

(69)

Chappell suggests at least a double cycle here: the sun's energy enters the tree, causes it to grow, and then, in the burning of the logs, is released again into the vastness of space where it originated; the physical form of the tree rooted in the earth is released as a tree of spirit rooted in the hearth fire and foliated among the stars. That the stars themselves are fire spreads further the impress of transformation focused in this passage. The fire, however, remains mysterious, no matter the language invented to image it, because it gives us light in which to "read" everything but itself. It is also mortal. As the fire in the hearth dwindles so does the tree of spirit rising from it: "Lucretius' / seed of fire ignis semina is seed semina mortuis / . . . of death in that same split second" (70).

Three other sorts of transformations parallel this central one. In the brief parenthetical phrase that echoes the burden of **"My Grandmother Washes Her Feet"**— *"dirt we rose from, dirt we'll never forget"* (70)— human beings rise from the ground and are rooted there, no matter the changes that transpire in any individual life. Human will, similarly, may cast "forward / into the flesh of light itself / . . . angry against the stream of time" (70-71). Perhaps the poet, too, "*can* transform all / germens with an incantatory perception of what's / what or what's supposed" (71). These palimpsest possibilities layered against the basic image of the tree of spirit follow one another in the poem pell-mell, each growing from the other, the form enacting transformation while articulating its stages. The energy of language and prophetic will, twined together, leads Fred to a credo: it can make

> every tree that stands a *Christmas tree,* Christmas
> on Earth, though even as I recall the beautiful
> manifesto my faith flickers & dwindles, we are not
> born for the rarer destinies only for the rarest,
> we are born to enter the tree of smoke, backbone of
> the world of substance, born to smear our life stuff
> against the zodiac, & as I take down in matter
> the spine of the world & will send it up again in
> spirit a feeling that these things are so indelibly
> correct overtakes me.

(71)

Part of the primary drama of this extraordinary poem consists of its entertainment. It is interesting, first of all, various and full of surprising turns, holding together voice and attention (poet's and reader's), as well as holding out alternative ways of speaking about the relationship of matter to spirit. The Lucretian focus, a naturalistic philosophy both ancient and contemporary, balances, as it were, in the middle of a spectrum.

At one end is nothingness, the terrifying possibility that a "roaming / puddle of gravitons, a winter's night the black / hole, comes this way striding & yanks the tree / of light elongate like a sunny licorice down / the drain" (70).

Fred explicitly rejects the terror of nothingness, along with the will-less condition of Nirvana (which he has earlier called "a sterile and joyless blasphemy"), in the opening poem of *Earthsleep,* indicating by their juxtaposition that the latter is a version of the former. "What there is in emptiness," he says,

> . . . let it consume itself,
> Let it mass and flounder yonder from the skin
> Of things, let it not come nigh this hearth, this hold,
> This house, let the cloud of unbeing never touch
> Our garish boxes of fervor.
>
>   (146)

In the same series of refusals he seems also to include Lucretius' eternal atomistic dispersal and configuration; he mentions "another" world, "where no water sings with / Its breath of fire, where sunlight the cloud never / Ripens to peach, where the single atoms stray / Lost and touchless" (146-47). Lucretius' vision, I think, slides to the negative end of the spectrum here.[2] The double nadir of **"Susan Bathing,"** which produces abject fear in Fred, is first, that he will not be able to praise her adequately (in *River*'s **"Birthday 35,"** to have his mouth stopped is "despair") and second, that Susan will vaporize and disappear. After confronting such motions toward vacuum, Fred pushes his face "more fiercely" to Susan's breast and begins a series of allusive reprises of earlier poems that have centered on experiences of healing contact with people he loves.

It is not surprising given Fred's heritage that atomistic philosophy is insufficient, since Lucretius includes the soul among material things. A central thrust of his arguments in *De Rerum Natura* is to remove from his auditors their fear of punishment after life by arguing that the soul, like everything else, disperses into autonomous, anonymous atoms. There *was,* therefore, no hereafter to fear. This is not only too neat and reductive for a mind as probing, doubtful, and inventive as Fred Chappell's, it also dismisses too cerebrally what he has absorbed into the veins of his imagination from birth. If Lucretius had grown up with Fred's grandparents and parents, he would have rejected atomism, too. Chappell's profound disinclination also proceeds from his sensuality and, perhaps above all, from his unstaunchable love

of life. In his splendid essay on Lucretius in *Three Philosophical Poets,* George Santayana observed that at the bottom of Lucretius' insistent opposition to immortality was a fear of life.[3] Santayana called this an "untenable ideal." He asserted that "What is dreaded is the defeat of a present will directed upon life and its various undertakings. . . . To introduce ascetic discipline, to bring out the irony of experience, to expose the self-contradictions of the will, would be the true means of mitigating the love of life; and if the love of life were extinguished, the fear of death, like smoke rising from that fire, would have vanished also" (53).

Fred clearly is no ascetic. He seeks everywhere to embrace life, to fire the world with his will, in the local and temporal frame of *Midquest* to celebrate his birthday, and to continue his fundamentally hopeful, Dantesque journey toward light.

At the other extreme is the Christmas tree and its extension at the end of **"Firewood"** into images of marriage, procreation, and finally, salvation. The sexual and marital similes salted into the opening page of the poem (*e.g., "marriage / vow* joints," "nice girls back in high school") receive more serious resolution in such phrases as "the wedge goes in like semen" and "the river-clean smell of opened / flesh comes at me as the annunciation to Mary" (73). The latter reference also echoes the more extended annunciation passage in **"Susan Bathing."** Immediately following these focuses is Fred's assertion "I'm washed in the blood / of the sun," a variation of "blood of the Lamb" in a context suggesting, with **"Christmas on Earth,"** a Christian salvation, an implicit answer to the parenthetical question "but where / shall I sit when once this flesh is spirit?" (73) The "flesh! more flesh" at the heart of the riven log is analogous to the Christian incarnation and helps one understand the source of Fred's love of the earth and life on it that pervades *Midquest.* ("The flesh the earth is suits me fine" is a representative instance.) The poem following **"Firewood"** deals with a real fire, the conflagration that destroyed Fred's grandfather's church. Its concluding passage reinforces the sacramental, transforming vision of **"Firewood."** In form and language imitating Old English alliterative verse, the poem presents Fred and Susan coming to the site of the fire years later to find it altogether revivified, a "victory of spirit":

>   Time took it anew
> and changed that church-plot   to an enchanted chrisom
> of leaf and flower   of lithe light and shade.
>
> *Pilgrim, the past   becomes prayer*
> *becomes remembrance rock-real   of Resurrection*
> *when the Willer so willeth   works his wild wonders.*
>
>   (77)

This is stated as unequivocally as "the spine of the world" passage quoted above.

Other less extended instances of the Christian mode of transformation abound. The world was formed as "the purer spirits surged ever upward, / Shucking the gross pig-matter their bodies" (**"Fire Now Wakening on the River,"** 56). Sexual union in **"Bloodfire Garden"** burns the lovers "down again to the ghost of us, . . . Burnt-off, we are being prepared" (94). For the grandmother in **"Second Wind,"** the stirring of a slight breeze becomes "the breath of life. . . . / Renewal of spirit such as I could never / Deny" (106). In a richly evocative scene on Wind Mountain, "the resplendent house of spirit bursts around the body" (**"Earth Emergent Drifts the Fire River,"** 149). The four elements carried by the winds are "suffering of spirit, suffering of elements, / In one mass," in **"Dawn Wind Unlocks the River Sky"** (98). Both the poems celebrating jazz in *Wind Mountain* embody the idea from Schopenhauer that serves as epigraph in Chappell's homage to Louis Armstrong—*"Music is the world over again,"* but in impalpable sound, in another form altogether (99). At the close of that poem, man becomes "half funky animal, half pure music, / Meat and spirit drunk together" (102).

The spiritual choice I am suggesting *Midquest* reticulately and dramatically enacts is more sharply underlined by three poems at the close of *Source,* published in 1985, four years after *Midquest*'s serially printed volumes (1975, 1978, 1979, 1980) were collected into one. In **"Urlied,"** Chappell puts words (some anachronistic) into Lucretius' mouth, having him reject immortality via Rilke and the familiar anthropomorphism of Olympus. Conversely, Lucretius reiterates his "trust" in the forces of dissolution and coalescence (love / strife, Venus / Mars) and draws this comfort from his system: "There's nothing personal in it" (*Source,* 53). The evaluation is heavily ironic, however, being true as a description of the movement of matter but devastatingly false when applied to the emotional effect of losing one's identity. Chappell articulates this dreadful rift in the last section of the poem, where he evaluates Lucretius' endeavor as fundamentally courageous and integral but finally without solace. He leaves Lucretius in the "white fountain of delirium / Burning but not purified" (54), recalling both the close of T. S. Eliot's "The Fire Sermon" and the final stanza of his own **"Feverscape: The Silver Planet"** in *Midquest.* Once again, the Lucretian vision, for all its radically compelling perception into the material nature of things, is bleak and isolate, not transforming in a way Chappell finds desirable.

The other two poems set against **"Urlied"** involve ascent. **"Message"** employs Lucretian terminology, but Chappell's context involves three dimensions basically apostate to the Roman poet's system: the controlling metaphor of ascension; an increased understanding by the grief-stricken sufferer; and a concern with expressing that understanding in language. In choosing among his sorrows, the "he" of the poem becomes the measure of his own grief. In the opening lines' use of an angel as messenger "purely clothed in terror," there is also an implicit acceptance of this aspect of Rilke, contrasted to his dismissal by Lucretius in the preceding poem.

More telling still is **"Forever Mountain,"** the final poem in *Source.* Chappell presents his father ascending, after death, Mt. Pisgah, about fifteen miles southeast of Canton, North Carolina—Chappell's hometown but also the mountain from which God showed Moses the promised land. Words from the hymn "Sweet Hour of Prayer" are relevant to the vision the poem renders: "Til from Mt. Pisgah's lofty height / I view my home and take my flight." J. T. Chappell doesn't fly, but he does leisurely ascend the mountain, "taking the time / He's got a world of" (57). He observes "the quality of light come over him," spends a dreamful night, "rises glad and early and goes his way, / Taking by plateaus the mountain that possesses him." He has come a far piece from the Pilate-like figure he cut when we last saw him in *Midquest.* At the poem's close, Chappell's "vision blurs . . . with distance," Pisgah becomes Forever Mountain, "a cloud / That light turns gold, that wind dislimns." The shift from the figure of his father to Chappell's blurred vision has much the same effect as would an unmitigated focus on the father's assumption into a new form. We witness an ascension of body to light and transformation, the context and perspective explicitly biblical, implicitly Christian. Between **"Message"** and **"Forever Mountain,"** in fact, Chappell places a terse and rending avatar of another hymn, "O Sacred Head Now Wounded," concerned with the mocking of Jesus' suffering during his trial and crucifixion.

PRAYER; ORTHODOXIES

I called **"Forever Mountain"** a vision, but in an italicized line appended to the poem, Chappell calls it a prayer. It is noteworthy that it's not a vision or a wish or a hope, but specifically *a prayer. Source,* in fact, contains three other poems so labeled, each of them depicting a merging of the one who prays with the particular conditions he prays about ("about" in the sense of concerning, and circling). In the first, **"A Prayer for the Mountains,"** it is a peaceable kingdom he both accepts as existing and desires to exist, wanting to "share the sleep / Of the cool ground's mildest children" (5). In **"A Prayer for Slowness,"** he seeks to be not content but filled with giving, as the cow in the poem has "her rich welcome / . . . taken from her" (6). **"A Prayer for Truthfulness"** concerns the poet's release of his poem from his control into its own illumination, able to say finally "its last abandonment" (7). The three prayers are, in short, not self-focused or escapist or acquisitive; in fact, insofar as they ask for anything, it is a place among the portions of other creatures into which Chappell may meld his being and talent.

Prayer is, of course, as complex an area as the other spiritual matters in Fred Chappell's work. I'm no expert on it by any stretch of the imagination, but a few thoughts may at least serve to disperse its associations beyond mere petition.

The extraordinary act of paying conscious attention may be considered a form of prayer. Prayer may be a tonality, an indication in declarative statements or questions that the speaker is tuned somewhere to spiritual dimensions he may not be addressing directly. "Where've you been?" asked in a certain way, for instance, can be a prayer, as Kathy Mattea's recent song by that name shows. A lived life can be a prayer, though that is difficult to specify, except perhaps in the cases of some saints. Prayer is not necessarily even supplication but may be homage, or gratitude, or acceptance, or lament, or bewilderment spoken or enacted or felt toward the immanent presence of a power greater than oneself. It may be a habit or an attitude. In *Hamlet,* Claudius' prayer, though his thoughts "remain below," is still a prayer. That which impels our attention away from the self or turns the will toward imagination may, speaking as broadly as possible, be considered prayer. Chappell refers to *Midquest* in his Preface as "in its largest design a love poem" (xi); from a number of these perspectives, the book could also be thought of as a prayer.

Individual poems, too, embody this possibility. **"Susan Bathing"** is a prayer of worship, praise, and adoration, **"My Grandmother's Dream of Plowing,"** a prayer for release and forgiveness, **"My Father Allergic to Fire,"** for acknowledgement and continuance. And so on.

The prayers per se dispersed throughout *Midquest,* though not explicitly indicated as the ones in *Source,* are not so much disguised as diverse. Chappell composes and aims them variously.

"Birthday 35: Diary Entry" concludes with a prayer in the more traditional mode of petition: "Please, Lord. I want to go to some forever / Where water is, and live there" (7). Until the final three lines, the poem is a plea for an anthropomorphic afterlife (part of the pattern **"How to Build the Earthly Paradise"** and **"At the Grave of Virgil Campbell"** later extend) where current pleasures pertain, an "Elysium . . . plentifully planted / With trout streams and waterfalls and suburban / Swimming pools, and sufficient chaser for bourbon" (8). Its tone is wise-ass jaunty, its diction hip, its beat and vary-

ing line lengths accumulating a pseudo music-hall effect that seeks to minimize the prayerful imploring, much as a sophisticated dude cultivates a cool exterior to cover his sensitivity. But in the last three lines, the more serious underlying concern breaks through: he wants the water of heaven to wash away sin.

The going up in flames of Fred's grandfather's church (*Bloodfire,* VI) and the site's transformation seventeen years later "to the stark beginning where the first stars burned" (77) becomes the ground for the definition of prayer that ends the poem. What has been a catastrophe is subsequently seen as part of a reenactment of the resurrection of Jesus.

> Pilgrim, the past   becomes prayer
> becomes remembrance rock-real   of Resurrection
> when the Willer so willeth   works his wild won-
>   ders.
>
> (77)

"The Willer," presumably not a human being, is involved in the process of prayer defined here. The experience itself is prayer, in which the divine will is inextricably woven, suggesting that God's involvement in history is not limited to the incarnation of Jesus.

I'm not sure if the more dire self-immolation of the Buddhist monks in **"Bloodfire"** should be included in this context, but it seems possible. What miraculous renewal may be hidden in the most awful destruction is part of the dread mystery of God's will.

Chappell uses fire as an agent of transformation again in connection with prayer in **"Bloodfire Garden."** In a remarkable merging of garden and bed, brushfire and loinfire ("the disease / necessary to know God"), Fred remembers praying as he watched the blackberry vines, scythed and "raked up in barbarous heaps," put to the torch (92). It was, he says, a moment in which

> I went stark sane, feeling under my feet
> the hands of blackberry fire
> rummaging
> unfurrowed earth.
>
> (93)

What, if anything, he prays for is unspecified, but his act is imbedded in images that suggest not only fire as incipient plow ("rummaging": the area is being cleared for planting) but also the burning of human bodies ("frying lattice / of dry bones") and the incarnation of spirits ("ghosts began again to take flesh") (93). In the other half of the poem's context of burning—the bedroom—after the lovers' climax "a cool invisible smoke goes up / from our bodies, it is grateful / prayer, sigil / of warm silence between us" (94).

> In this garden our bed we have burned
> down again to the ghost of us . . .
>
> (94)

In both contexts, the burning down has resulted in renewal or the readying for it. "Burnt-off," the lovers "are being prepared"; the burning off of the wild blackberry vines is a preparation as well for new growth. The image of dry bones suggests the vulnerability of the apparently solid human body and has driven young Fred to sanity and prayer; the aftermath of the fire of sexual union is prayer as well, associated with gratitude. In this context, the fresh rain blowing up "out of the green isles / of Eden," with its implication of renewed creative harmony with the Creator, seems entirely appropriate (94).

Fred's first prayer, the one in **"Birthday 35"** to which I've referred above, follows a vision of Time in which he sees "nothing human,"

> No man, no woman,
>
> No animals or plants; only moon
> Upon moon, sterile stone
>
> Climbing the steep hill of void.
>
>   (7)

This waste land (part of a longer passage that I think consciously echoes T. S. Eliot's poem) leads to Fred's admission, "I was afraid." This process of a fearful vision of bleakness leading to prayer occurs again in at least two noteworthy places. In *Earthsleep* I, Fred talks to himself or, more accurately, to his "Mind," which he calls "Old Crusoe." In the context of wondering if they are both lost on "this bright and lonely spark" (149), he asks three questions about their eventual fate. The questions are directed at "Earth" but involve the other three elements central to *Midquest*. All of the alternatives are terrifying: "black waters streaming / Deathward," "In wind to suffer shorn of flesh," and "fire . . . the raging ecstasy / . . . of burning foreknowledge" (149). After such imagined vistas, the next utterance is a prayer.

>   Do not us Earth
> Remember.
>   Leave us, mud jumble of mirk
> And humus, tucked in the rock heart
> Of the mountain, in these stones are seeds of fire,
> Dream-seeds which taking root shall renew the world,
> Tree of Spirit lifting from the mountain of earth.
>
>   (149)

I take this prayer to be a refusal to identify the human creature as simply a concatenation of elemental substances. We are no more fully accounted for as such a composite than we are as Lucretian molecular aggregates or energy diminishing toward the cold willlessness of Nirvana. Human creatures are elemental, yes, but also infused with spirit. Fred's prayer here is childlike in its desire that Earth simply forget him and Susan and tend to some other business. They'll take a

spiritual form (the tree of spirit from **"Firewood"**) analogous to the earthly tree—an appeasing gesture?—and grow on transmuted, as spirit mysteriously grows. This eases into two afterprayers, asking "Earth" for gentleness and "Destiny" for sweet treatment. The tone and focus here is relief after the exhausting effort of imagination that precedes it.

The same process occurs finally in starker, more condensed form in the closing poem of the volume (and the book):

>   Here where I find
> I am I founder.
>   Lord Lord
> Let this lost dark not.
>
>   (186)

Not what? is the inevitable question. Swallow us up, as the sea overwhelms a foundering ship? That seems the most immediate likelihood. The prayer itself is so close to the terror that impels it that it cannot be completely uttered. The pattern of zeroes that occupy the volume (the "darkest vowel" of the well opening, for instance, the drains in the grandmother's and Susan's tub, the black hole in space in **"Firewood"**) has been perhaps the best preparation for what is most feared here from the dark.

These various spiritual radiations are rarely orthodox in any sense. But institutional Christian orthodoxies, too, occupy a substantial place in the spiritual experience of *Midquest*. The most accessibly presented are made part of the lives of Fred's forebears. Concerned for his salvation, his grandfather changes denominations (*River,* VII) and is baptized in the West Fork of the Pigeon River. Later, speaking from the grave (*Earthsleep,* IX), "Here where it's / Still not Absolute" (181-82), he awaits "Judgment Day / When we can see once more in the Judgment Book / All that we've seen already, each nook / And cranny of us forever on display" (182). The tone of the latter poem is nettled and testy, a strong modulation of the comic surface of the former one; in both poems, the man is of two minds about the perspectives the church has saddled him with, but there's no doubt he accepts its terms and forms, and takes them seriously.

These two poems deal with sacraments: baptism and burial. Fred's grandmother confronts another—marriage (*River,* VII), seeing this commitment as analogous to Caesar's Rubicon: *"If I cross this river I won't turn back."* When her husband dies (*Wind Mountain,* III) and she is faced with the public anonymity of everything, as well as the distracting hodge-podge of the funeral gathering, she wants to join him. Immediately, however, she aborts the idea on orthodox grounds: "It's a sin to want yourself to die" (103). She utters this fundamental belief before the poem is well begun, then suffers the family and their best intentions until, unable to take any more, she walks outdoors, away from the house, to a place "where the rose / Vine climbed the cowlot fence and looked away / Toward Chambers Cove" (105). It is also a place in her spiritual life "where everything is hard as flint: breathing, / Walking, crying even. It's a heathen / Sorrow over us" (105). In such a condition, she is unable to help herself, but in the immobilizing heat of the day, she feels a breeze stir, coming cornstalk leaf by cornstalk leaf across the field toward her. She understands this to be "the breath of life . . . / Renewal of spirit such as I could never / Deny and still name myself a believer" (106). This utterly convincing account ends with the freshening wind touching her face "so strong it poured on me the weight of grace" (106).

At the other extreme from this visitation of saving grace, Chappell places Fred's father's guilt over the manner in which he's buried Honey, an old mule dead after generations of labor on the farm (*Earthsleep,* III). Because the clayey ground makes the digging of a grave nearly impossible, J. T. breaks the animal's legs so he won't need so deep a hole. What he does and is witnessed doing is ineradicable, however, from his memory, in his "head for good and all and ever" (155). It's no wonder, given his account of it:

> I busted her legs.
> I busted her legs with the mattock, her eyes all open
> And watching me crack her bones and bulging out
> Farther slightly with every blow. These fields
> Were in her eyes, and a picture of me against
> The sky blood-raw savage with my mattock.
>
> (154)

"Heavy is how / I felt," he says, "empty-heavy and blue as poison" (154). The context of the poem is J. T.'s washing at the pump two weeks later. He scrubs his hands for "maybe seven minutes," dries them, and when he gives Fred the towel back, "there was his handprint, / Earth-colored, indelible, on the linen" (155). The figures of Pontius Pilate and Lady MacBeth lurk in the shadowy background here, and for the moment anyhow, no grace pours down on anything.

The mule is already dead when J. T. breaks her legs, and his sense of guilt is mostly a projection of his sensitivity and compassion. The experience revealed in the grandmother's dream of plowing (*Earthsleep,* VIII), however, is a fundamental sin, the bearing of a child either prior to her marriage to Frank or through adultery during it. The skillfully dovetailed phases of her dream show her progressively unsuccessful attempts to disguise her act, its issue, and their consequences. Frank's plowing, itself an unprecedented vision for her, provides an apt contextual metaphor: something hidden

is uncovered. Frank both unearths the object and asks the question that pitches the dream toward its identification: "*Is that your baby that was never mine?*" (179). Anne—the grandmother, too, is named for the first time in the book, becoming a person not wholly identified through a role—"expects" at the start of her dream a church bell to be turned up by the plow, an object associated with Frank's past misfortune (the burning of his church) rather than with her own sin. This is the first of the dream's series of displacements. The object turns out to be in its first incarnation a lump of gold, which she cradles "to [her] breast." Following Frank's question, Anne denies (to herself) it's a baby, but then suddenly "I knew it *was* a baby in my arm, / The strangest baby" (179). The displacements continue: the infant is compared to Jesus as he is depicted in the *Upper Room*—a daily devotional publication—and then becomes a "golden child" who will "bring us luck." The creature she holds, however, continues to metamorphose toward the truth the dream is unlayering, finally becoming "'an ugly little man,'" "an evil little goblin / With an evil smile" (179). This truth is, of course, how Anne feels about the child, a slow revelation of her shame and awful self-condemnation projected outward into the form the dream work has presented as separate from her. She wishes it dead, and—"the awfullest part" (180)—it dies. It's only after this that she is able to say, "It was my fault," but her admission of responsibility is focused only on her desire for the figure's death. Her guilt, insofar as she articulates it to Fred, to whom she's recounting the dream, seems focused on this, too; she also considers the child as separate from herself in its innocence at this point: "Whatever harm had the little goblin done?" (180). There seems no conscious owning up to her responsibility for its birth. Whether we are to take the death in the dream as indicating what happened to the actual baby is inconclusive, but the guilt is real enough: she has never waked from this dream. Incidentally, the revelation of this buried secret from her past casts a sharp light on her preoccupation in previous poems with the "Shadow Cousins," the profound hesitation she experienced before committing herself to marrying Frank, and our seeing her in two situations where she is washing something (her feet, her milk cans).[4]

These poems compose behavior and attitudes derived from sectarian Christian assumptions undergirding central aspects of what one might call primary theology. Suicide, adultery, and the wish to murder are sins; guilt is inevitably consequent upon sin; grace is God-given and mysterious, coming in unpredictable forms and at unpredictable times; the sacraments are inviolable, no matter how one might seek to hedge one's bets through them, their seriousness ingrained in the soul.

One of the assumptions inherent in *Midquest* appears to be that human beings, as Fred's grandmother fears, do grow away from their sources (this occurs both to individuals and to generations), but they appear to do so as a tree grows away from its roots, remaining one organism. Human beings are mobile, of course. I mean this analogy more to suggest temporal than spatial wholeness: as a tree grows in space, so a person grows in time. Human beings can make disorienting and potentially destructive choices, but there is as well a genetic and behavioral determinism woven into their development. *Midquest* embodies Fred Chappell's fulfillment of the grandmother's vision by becoming a professor and author, leaving the farm behind, deserting, as he says, "manual labor for intellectual labor." But the restless, doubt-ridden entertainments of his imaginative mind are largely informed by and directed at the physical, religious, and moral dimensions of the farm environment in which he was raised. I think this is the source, finally, of the spiritual and psychic healing and regeneration that *Midquest* seeks in its widest intention. In my context here, the central orthodox beliefs that define the family members seep into Fred's ways of probing his own diverse options.

This is clearest in the preoccupation with the relationship between matter and spirit—how to view incarnation—that pervades *Midquest* and informs much of Chappell's poetry subsequent to it. His terror in the face of nothingness and the anonymous dispersal of atoms is bearable because the Christian mode of understanding affords him a richer, more hopeful alternative. He is, of course, predisposed toward it, but too given to the mind's uncertainties to accept it without first testing the abysmal ontological possibilities that contradict it. His use of Dante's *Divine Comedy* as model and guide further underscores the influence orthodox configurations have on his work. (Below I comment on Dante more specifically.)[5]

Other more local instances arise frequently throughout the book. I have mentioned both the transformation Fred witnesses in *Bloodfire* VI and the serious note ("Washing away sin") toward which his prayer at the close of **"Birthday 35"** tends (8), and I will discuss his use of Jonah, Lazarus, and Joseph. Not surprisingly, in the pattern of praise for Susan in **"Susan Bathing,"** phrases from the Christian vocabulary of belief appear: *"plenia gratia"* (from the Catholic "Hail Mary" and Luke 1:28) in the Madonna passage; *"let there be,"* from the creation story in Genesis. As a whole, the poem and the narrator's role in it are informed by the conception of God as Word (John 1:1ff.). In **"Firewood,"** he alludes to man "in his fallen state." In *Earthsleep* VI, he tells the dead Virgil Campbell, "All the world is lit for your delight, / old Buddy, hook it to your hulk both hands, / It's a worship of God, though kinda primitive / I admit."

These last two examples are drops in the larger welter of Fred's ruminations about the afterlife. They range from the pleasant, relaxed, anthropomorphic excursions in such poems as **"The Peaceable Kingdom of Emerald Windows," "At the Grave of Virgil Campbell,"** and *Wind Mountain* V, to the bleak visions of nothingness in **"Firewood"** and *Earthsleep* I. What can be envisioned in familiar terms we can project ourselves into, evaluate and decide about, but a Christian vision of the soul's form after death is more troublesome. A genuine transformation—the Pauline idea of the "body imperishable" of I Corinthians, 35-57, for instance—is, like grace, a mystery and therefore by definition cannot be imaged (though the conditions of its mystery may be). Consequently, the alternative, desirable vision is only vaguely implied in *Midquest,* a spindrift of thought and faith. This quandary is sharply presented in **"Birthday 35"**:

> But, Lord, You stand on one side
>
> Of the infinite black ditch
> And I on the other. *And that's a bitch.*
>
> (7-8)

Fred is as fascinated, however, with how life may have begun as with what may follow it. From the touching desire to uncover with his grandfather "the final source of West Fork Pigeon River," through the brief hints in the opening poem of each volume about "how the world was formed," to the more complexly developed myths of creation in *Wind Mountain* V ("a slightly different Big Bang theory") and *River* IX ("The Novel"), he reveals an inventive, fervent desire to be present at beginnings (which in the myths at least, he is). The title section ("Two") of *Source* elaborates this impulse, being composed of scattered, disparate myths, many dealing with first causes, each apparently seeking to embody an "explanation," but finally explaining nothing.

In this preoccupation with the unknowns that border human life at either verge, he keeps in uneasy balance his inventive, informed intellectual curiosity and his spiritual tendency to accept the unknowable, or at least his place outside it. Here, as at so many other junctures of *Midquest,* a passage from **"Birthday 35,"** the true prelude to the volume, is pertinent:

> I'd sleep in the eiderdown of the True Believer
> And never nightmare about Either / Or
>
> If I had a different person in my head.
> But this gnawing worm shows that I'm not dead.
>
> Therefore: either I live with doubt
> Or get out.
>
> (5)

STRUCTURES

One may enter Chappell's *Midquest* at any point and find, as with all coherent visions emanating from a center, the basic terms and images that shadow the whole. The poems radiate from and revolve around a hub—though within most of them there is a nicely composed narrative linearity sometimes (*e.g.,* **"Susan Bathing," "Second Wind"**) reinforced by a psychological progression—so that one poem or a sequence of poems may enact the volume.

"Cleaning the Well" offers an instance of this, embodying in a single piece the general construction of *Midquest* as a Dantesque descent into hell and a rising toward light and redemption. Fred assists his grandfather in cleaning the well, the literal experience graphically presented from the double perspective of a young (eight-to ten-year-old) boy doing the work and an adult creating a shape for his memory. Chappell gives various indications of the figurative perspective from which he sees the experience and by which he wishes it evaluated. Dante's descent is, of course, the fundamental metaphoric enclosure, the "soundless dreaming / O" (14) of the well's mouth functioning effectively as a fearsome gate to the netherworld, prefiguring *Inferno*'s circles and the further possibility that nothingness may be at the bottom of things. The grandfather lowers Fred on pulley rope and harness, thus supporting him and becoming a "guide" (like Virgil) in a way appropriate to the context. The well itself is a version of the well at the center of the declining valleys of Malebolge through which Dante enters Cocytus, the frozen wasteland of the final circle of *Inferno*. Two of the boy's phrases particularize the broad connection. As he hits the water, he cries, "Whoo! It's *God / Damn* cold!" (14) and later, in response to his grandfather's asking how it's going, thinks, "It goes like Hell" (15). Two italicized phrases express more formally the implications of these colloquial ones: at the terrifying point where the boy has been reduced to the condition of a non-creature (nerveless, sexless, breathless, mindless, and bodiless) occur the words *"I shall arise never"* (15); similarly, at the other extreme of readjustment to the ground above, we read, *"I had not found death good"* (17).

Within the Dantesque frame, Chappell has Fred compare himself to Jonah, Joseph, and Lazarus, adding a biblical lens through which the homey, local experience is considered. A particularly telling merging of psychological insight and literary allusion takes place in this stanza (14). Fred's return to upper earth has disoriented him as much as had the earlier descent into the gelid water. He recalls the foreboding dark as "holy" and tries, in his new disorientation, "to fetch [it] / Back" (16). He then wonders if the three biblical figures had also been "ript untimely / From black wellspring of death" (16). There is the understanding of the human psyche's conservative nature, to want to remain in the condition to which it's become accustomed, so that the usual view of the miracles of the restoring of Jonah, Joseph, and Lazarus to the world is given an unexpected twist. In terms of the other allusive dimension here, Fred's resistance to

his return recalls the resistance to waking with which each of the four volumes of *Midquest* begins, itself derived partly from Dante's tendency to sleep or swoon when faced with the pressure of attention and discovery (e.g., *Inferno,* I, ll, III, 136, and V, 142; *Purgatorio,* XVIII, 145). Finally, "wellspring of death" encapsulates the paradoxical understanding the *Divine Comedy* assumes, eventually tracing back to the *felix culpa* of Christianity.

Poems VI, VII, and VIII of *Wind Mountain* accomplish as a series what **"Cleaning the Well"** does as a single poem. A comic inversion of the poem it precedes, **"My Father's Hurricane"** is a tall tale with which J. T. regales eleven-year-old Fred over "the ruins / Of an April supper" (116). The hurricane is immortalized as "Bad Egg," which suggests it is the destructive opposite of "Egg," the source of all life that Fred refers to hyperbolically in **"Birthday 35."** It is a five-layer conglomeration of all the stuff its power has uprooted and carried who knows where. J. T. travels upward through each layer, fending off young Fred's common-sense questions, until he reaches layer five, composed of "'Lovebirds, honeypies, sweethearts—whatever / You want to call them'" (119). The mother stops the story at the point where it tends toward raunchiness, the lovers "'Rolling and sporting in the wind like face cards / From a stag poker deck'" (120). The simile indicates the more serious substance the poem makes light of— lust and the gamble one takes with one's soul when one gives in to it. Paulo and Francesca are among those J. T. sees in layer five, and the potential cost of lust becomes even more sharply focused by Fred's question, "'But how did you get down without / Getting killed?'" (120). The answer to the question never comes, for the poem ends with J. T.'s voice cut off. Getting out is another story.

These last three details—the reference to Paulo and Francesca, the figurative implication that lust is a high-stakes gamble, and the allusion to death—would be sufficient to key the spiritual implications of this inverted hell. It is humorously presented, of course, and a dazzlingly inventive entertainment, but it is also from the outset suspiciously unsettling, beginning as it does with the comparison of J. T.'s cigarette smoke to a "dust cloud over a bombed-out city" (116).

The corrective to this odd *ascent* into a layer of "honeypies," begins with the title of the next poem. **"In Parte Ove Non E Che Luca"** is most of the final line of Canto IV of Dante's *Inferno,* and the poem it labels is a pretty fair country translation of Canto V. The chaotic uprooting of the previous poem becomes the "storm infernal" (Dante's *"bufera"* could be translated "hurricane") of the second circle of Hell. Here the winds also conflict, unceasingly driving the damned Spirits "onward with brute force":

Up they go to the very edge of the Course
  Of Ruin, complaining, lamenting, aghast.
  For them the Word Divine is sheer remorse.

Into this pain the lovers of flesh are thrust,
  All those who gave their human reason over
  To the delicious fever of carnal lust.

                       (122)

In short, J. T.'s "lovebirds" are here, hovering "in the torn air," and this time no humor relieves their predicament. Chappell, however, updates the population by adding Casanova, a couple of poets, and from his own book, Virgil Campbell.

Campbell, in response to Fred's request that his Master and guide, the *other* Virgil, stop and bring him over to them, becomes the subject and speaker (à la Francesca) of the third poem in this group, **"Three Sheets in the Wind: Virgil Campbell Confesses."** He tells his own tale, balancing formally J. T.'s hurricane story. It concerns his getting caught by his wife and the preacher *in flagrante delicto* with a willing country "gal you always hear about / And generally never meet" (124). It's another funny experience, well stitched together, but for all Campbell's ingratiating humor, cajolery, and wit, it is finally quite serious because of the context in which Chappell sets it. Ironies proceed from that context, too. The poem, a confession, begins with Campbell calling himself "a solid by God citizen," but his country is the second circle of the Inferno.⁶ He understands his youthful penchant for moonshine and women as "a kind of crazy" in his blood that "nothing but / The worst that can happen will ever get . . . out" (124). He then says, "The worst that can happen never happened to me," which is a lie, given his condition of damnation; it is also a sign of the rationalization and evasion of the truth that is traditionally characteristic of the damned. Virgil Campbell could have sold cider to Eve. His story leads him to make the familiar promise of those caught in a terrifying trap—he believes, sewed up in one of his wife's sheets, that he's died and gone to hell, and so he thinks

        how I'd do it all different if
I could only live my earthly life again:
I'd be a sweet and silent religious man.

                       (126)

He gets out of the story's *contretemps*, of course, and the final line of the poem, in which he decides to have a drink, indicates how ineptly he's kept that rash promise. "'Well, where's the harm?'" (127) he asks rhetorically, ready to bend his elbow, repeating the same question he's asked earlier in the poem in justifying with wonderful sophistic logic his adultery. The harm is perdition, no matter the charm of the lothario; Campbell is a convincing embodiment of the giving over of human reason "to the delicious fever of carnal lust." In

the larger series of poems centering on Virgil Campbell in *Midquest,* it's clear that Fred is affectionately and generously disposed toward him; Fred feels great kinship with Virgil in the last of these, **"At the Grave of Virgil Campbell."** But a lovable reprobate is still a reprobate, and in a book that takes seriously the fallen nature of humankind and traditional modes of dealing with that condition, the implications of this trio of poems are inescapable.

This group, then, repeats in extended form and with more widely varying tonalities the descent motif of **"Cleaning the Well,"** using Dante's model more pervasively, making explicit the dimension of Hell's eternal enclosure. These four poems focus also *Midquest*'s recurrent entertainment from different perspectives of the possibility of an afterlife and what spiritual alternatives face its central figure, the pilgrim Fred Chappell on his thirty-fifth birthday, pressing toward "the love that moves itself in light to loving."

Notes

1. Because both the author and the narrator of *Midquest* share the same name but are not identical to each other, I have used "Fred Chappell" or "Chappell" to refer to the former and "Fred" for the latter. Chappell comments on this matter in his Preface to *Midquest.*

2. A complementary comic rejection occurs in *Earthsleep,* IV, where "the Ideal World," Platonic in its evocative details, "sounds like a Grand Hotel / Emptied out because of chicken pox."

3. George Santayana, *Three Philosophical Poets* (Cambridge, Mass., 1910), 53.

4. Fred's guilt at turning his back on the voices of the poor (*Wind Mountain,* IX) may be considered part of this pattern.

5. The musical aspect of this part of Chappell's quest may be as crucial as the philosophical. The absence of jazz in Nirvana is another telling argument against its appeal.

6. I have taken Virgil Campbell's placement in the second circle of Dante's Hell so literally because of the sequence of these poems, particularly the segue between the second and third. The presence of J. T. Chappell as listener in the dramatic monologue of the confession complicates this choice, however. Is J. T. damned, too? Perhaps he is a *nonce* extension of Fred, a "listener" of context, no more trapped in hell than Dante was. Or perhaps we are gradually to ease back into the familiar general-store setting of "Firewater."

Henry Taylor (essay date 1997)

SOURCE: Taylor, Henry. "The World Was Plenty: The Poems of Fred Chappell." In *Dream Garden: The Poetic*

Vision of Fred Chappell, edited by Patrick Bizzaro, pp. 71-87. Baton Rouge, La.: Louisiana State University Press, 1997.

[*In the following essay, Taylor presents an overview of the subjects, styles, and continuities of Chappell's body of poetic writing.*]

When **The World between the Eyes,** Fred Chappell's first book of poems, appeared in 1971, he had published three novels and completed a fourth. The first three (*It Is Time, Lord,* 1963; *The Inkling,* 1965; *Dagon,* 1968) revealed not only a thorough command of the ingredients and conventions of southern gothic fiction but also a view of the world shaped by wide-ranging and tireless reading. They are brilliant, brief, allusive, densely textured, and difficult. They found skilled translators and came to be widely respected in France—a fact that Chappell acknowledged gratefully when Bob Edwards brought it up on National Public Radio's *Morning Edition* a few years ago. Chappell added, "But it should be remembered that this is a people with admiration also for Jerry Lewis and snails." In an afterword to *The Fred Chappell Reader* (1987), Chappell points out the shortcomings of his early fiction (though without disavowing it) and says that his ambition has shifted away from excessively intellectual experiments with form: "I have got to where I should like for my work to be humane, and I do not much care if it even becomes sentimental. Perhaps it would be nice if a few artists in our time decided to rejoin the human race, and I think that I would be glad to do so, however much I disagree with its politics" (486).

The humanity, clarity, and apparent directness of Chappell's more recent novels, *I Am One of You Forever* (1987) and *Brighten the Corner Where You Are* (1989) would seem to bear out this statement, though one begins with a narrator swimming through a teardrop, and the second begins with the protagonist's theft of the moon. If Chappell's fiction has undergone a noticeable transformation, his poetry has maintained a consistency of style and approach, even as its scope has extended to the book-length *Midquest* (1981). The title poem of **The World between the Eyes** presents a speaker who, in various guises and at various ages, continues to be the means of perception throughout much of Chappell's poetry. In this poem, he is a boy caught between the world his body inhabits and the world he finds in books. More precisely, he lives in a larger world that includes both:

> The house is chill, he wanders room and room,
> October is seething at the windows.
>
> Hands lax in his pockets. He sees
> Through it all. Man of the boring world,
> He dangles his cigarette and his dangerous charm.
>   "Ah, Comtesse, it's all too apparent,

> you know little of the ways of the Hindoo";
> Insouciant in jade cufflinks,
> While the skyline flickers with the Big Guns.
>
>   (12-13)

Here he shifts between the "real" world and his imagination, a little like Stephen Dedalus wishing he were the Count of Monte Cristo. As the poem proceeds, however, October works its magic not only on the house but also on the landscapes drawn in the books. Time is "charged past endurance with the future"(14), but the poem ends with the boy "blest in his skins, an old stone / House, and a sky eaten up with stars" (15).

"February" and **"Weird Tales"** emerge more purely from the two realms of rural childhood and literary fantasy, respectively. The first recounts a hog butchering from the boy's point of view; he is "dismayed / With delight"(3), "elated-drunk / With the horror"(4), as the hog is killed, scalded, gutted, cloven. For a while, the poem looks like something vegetarians might use to gain converts, but it takes in the brisk air, the joy of community ritual, and ends with a nostalgic tableau:

> And his bladder and his stomach sack! puffed
> Up and tied off and flung to the kids,
> Game balls, they bat them about,
> Running full tilt head down across the scattered yard.
> And then on a startled breeze
> The bladder's hoist, vaults high and gleams in the
>   sunlight
> And reflects on its shiny globe
> The sky a white square
> And the figures beneath, earnest figures
> Gazing straight up.
>
>   (5)

Imagination and recollection combine here into something more durable than the experience itself; and in **"Weird Tales,"** it is finally friendship that is the theme rather than the fascination with the obscure writers of horror and fantasy who supplied that magazine with material. The poem begins with an evocation of Lovecraft and proceeds to a kind of honor roll of

> . . . those who witnessed, away
> From the rant of commerce, the shriek of lying
>   newsprint,
> The innocent intimate truths that gnaw the marrow.
>
>   (40)

But the poem ends with love and gratitude expressed to Richard Dillard, author of *News of the Nile* (1971), the title poem of which makes beautiful and elaborate connections among sites along the Nile, flowing north as a train runs north to Wisconsin:

> Where August Derleth prints the books
> Of Lovecraft. . . .

And east of this train, south of Virginia,
In western North Carolina, Fred Chappell
Has written a novel, *Dagon,* and all these things
Come together, turn together, and will pass on
To come again. The Nile flows sluggish
And is thick with mud. It bears the news.[1]

Chappell's poem, in turn, becomes a letter, signed "Fred," and makes more connections; to add to them, I acknowledge here that Richard Dillard provided me with the information that Farnsworth Wright (1888-1940) was the editor of *Weird Tales.*

This news too the Nile bears, Richard Dillard,
Flowing past "Dongola, Kerma and Wawa";
Past Karloff double features, Lugosi revivals,
The spiderwebbed offices of Farnsworth Wright:
That rather than injustices and generals,
We choose to live with vampires, demons, ghouls.

(40-41)

Even the slighter poems in *The World between the Eyes* are fine examples of the delight to be taken in finding the right words, in the power of words and literature to transform the everyday. Near the end of the book there are five poems about baseball; their true subject is wit and the similes available to a person who has done some reading. The first of the five, **"Third Base Coach,"** begins and ends with literary comparisons:

He commands as mysteriously as
the ghost of Hamlet's father.
. . . . .
Like an Aeschylean tragedy he's static; baffling;
Boring; but.
Urgent with import.

(48)

Farther into the sequence, as a quotation from Ty Cobb describes a fast ball, and invented similes and jokes combine with those that appear to have originated on the field ("Trying to hit Wednesday with a bb gun"— **"Junk Ball,"** 51), the poems begin to revel in their slightness, reminding us that "it's just a game" is about the most ignorant statement that can be made to someone who takes a game seriously. In other words: people who think it's just a game had better play among themselves.

II

In 1963, a few months before Chappell published his first novel, Duke University Press published *Under Twenty-five,* an anthology of "Duke narrative and verse" edited by the distinguished creative-writing teacher William Blackburn.[2] Chappell is represented by two prose pieces and ten poems, only two of which were later collected in *The World between the Eyes.* Others are interesting primarily as evidence that Chappell was committed at an early age to using traditional forms, sometimes combining them with free verse or very loosely cadenced lines. **"Familiar Poem"** is in many ways the most ambitious of these poems; it is the meditation of a man lying awake beside his sleeping wife. The first of the four sections sets the scene, in a dark bedroom where "rain is sound"; the lines, moderately regular iambic pentameter, drift among rhyme schemes based on the quatrain, on five lines, and on seven. In mid-sentence, the section ends, and the form becomes looser iambic pentameter, unrhymed. The speaker's thoughts wander more noticeably, from his love for his wife, through poetic ambition as alchemy, to the knowledge of the writer's struggle to find, against "the onyx mirror of history past and future," the "bitter poison of salvation."

The third section is a sonnet. The octave addresses the sleeping wife and tries to characterize her dreams; the sestet addresses God and prays "that I may / Not be insane":

Let my love's dreams as spies
Into that trackless wild. When I trace back
My life, thought seems the suffering, slack
Thread preserving my self from the gray, gay
Narcotic mazes and hysteric skies.

(200)

In the fourth section, dawn arrives, and "reality" overcomes "imagination." As objects become discernible, "light is sound," and free verse embodies random observations of the waking world:

The sunlight shapes all objects, destroying images to
being.
I rise and turn and unravel
The ghost of myself from among the sheets.

(201)

"Familiar Poem" is sometimes self-consciously ambitious and contains more nearly "confessional" passages than Chappell has since allowed himself. He may have admitted some youthful follies and drawn upon autobiographical material, but he has done so without the self-importance that sometimes reveals itself in this poem. Most of the time, inhabiting the worlds of imagination and of dailiness is a source of joy in Chappell's work.

The poem's chief interest now, aside from its demonstration of a twenty-five-year-old poet's enormous promise, is that it is a clear forerunner of *Midquest* (1981), the superb long poem that first appeared as four separate volumes: *River* (1975), *Bloodfire* (1978), *Wind Mountain* (1979), and *Earthsleep* (1980).

Like **"Familiar Poem,"** each part of *Midquest* begins with a speaker awakening beside his sleeping wife; the phrase "light is sound" also appears at the beginning of

Earthsleep, in **"Earth Emergent Drifts the Fire River."** Furthermore, each of the waking poems rings some variation on the idea that in waking, the speaker must lose or abandon some essential part of himself. But the speaker of *Midquest* is ten years older than the author of **"Familiar Poem,"** and the author, most of the time, is older than that. At the Dantean midpoint of his life, the speaker takes stock and meditates—on his love for his wife, Susan; on the selves he has been and is becoming; and on the significance of place and family, of friendship, music, and literature.

As Chappell points out in a preface to the one-volume edition, each of the four parts of the poem consists of "eleven longish poems . . . covering four times the same twenty-four hours of the speaker's life" (ix). The date is May 28, 1971, his thirty-fifth birthday. Chappell goes on to declare that the speaker, named "Fred," is no more or less Fred Chappell than any of his other fictional characters and to explain a few of the principles according to which the poems are arranged. The organization allows the gradual unfolding of a life, a loose narrative, yet it also retains most of the advantages of a collection of shorter poems. There is little here that is not enriched by its context, but there is no single poem that could not stand outside the context. For this reason, the order imposed on the poems, though satisfying and persuasive, is not inevitable. Chappell's remarks set the reader up to notice certain large rhythms:

> And each of the volumes (except **Wind Mountain**) is organized as a balancing act. The first poem is mirrored by the last; the second by the next to last, and so on inward. But the sixth poem in each volume is companionless in that volume, and concerned with a garrulous old gentleman named Virgil Campbell, who is supposed to give to the whole its specifically regional, its Appalachian, context. The fifth poem in each is given to stream of consciousness and these interior monologues become discernibly more formal as the speaker begins to order his life. Each volume is dominated by a different element of the family, *River* by the grandparents, *Bloodfire* by the father, and there is a family reunion in *Earthsleep,* the part most shadowed by death. (In order to suggest the fluid and disordered nature of air, *Wind Mountain* was exempt from some of these requirements.)
>
> (ix-x)

It turns out that in *Bloodfire* (the second part), Virgil Campbell holds forth in the seventh poem, **"Firewater."** In the more loosely arranged *Wind Mountain,* he gets the eighth poem, as it happens; he does not settle back to the middle of a part until *Earthsleep.* My point is not to suggest that there is a mistake in the order of the poems or even in Chappell's description of it but rather to note that giving Virgil poems VI, VII, VIII, and VI, is just as effective as giving him VI every time. Only Chappell's prefatory remark brings attention to this matter. Other "mirrorings" and the consistently stream-of-consciousness fifth poems are perhaps regular enough in their recurrence to evoke recognition, but several of Chappell's self-imposed rules were more useful to him than to his readers, in something like the way in which syllabic meter can be useful: it is in itself inaudible but gives the poet something to work with and against.

Many of the poems are in loose blank verse or free verse. Various traditional forms are also used, from the Anglo-Saxon strong-stress meter of **"My Grandfather's Church Goes Up"** to the elaborate chant royal of **"My Mother's Hard Row to Hoe."** The several voices in the poems and the fully realized characters behind them help to keep the formal variety from becoming obtrusive; so, too, does Chappell's command of meters that range from the stately to the rollicking and his ability to work in many tones and genres.

The central "balancing act" in *Midquest* is the speaker's steady exploration of the tensions between his rural Appalachian childhood and his urban professional adulthood. His grandmother is perhaps the richest source of the earlier values and attitudes. She speaks most of four poems given to her, and Fred listens, occasionally asking questions or commenting; at times, she seems conscious of her role as informant but often she drifts from there into a spoken re-creation of a moment in the distant past. Her strength and independence, and the ways in which she accommodates these to marriage and widowhood, provide some of the most moving passages in *Midquest.*

The anecdotes and recollections of Fred's parents are either wildly funny or a sweet blend of nostalgia and a wish to be true to the difficult times. When his mother recalls their first meeting, she vacillates between the warmth of a funny story and insistence that their early life was "hard, hard, hard, hard, / Hard" (109). In **"My Father's Hurricane,"** his father indulges himself in a tall tale of being blown around in a wind that had everything on earth airborne, whereas in **"My Father Allergic to Fire,"** he tries to assume a heavy weight of guilt for a childish and ignorant initiation into the Ku Klux Klan.

Against the background of these poems and the rowdier episodes involving Virgil Campbell, Fred addresses love poems to Susan, beholds the changing landscapes of his past and present, recalls his attempts to play the trombone, and with graceful freedom from self-indulgence, explores the sources and nature of his literary ambitions. **"Science Fiction Water Letter to Guy Lillian"** begins as a thoughtful discussion of the genre's limitations and ends with a précis of Fred's own unwritten sci-fi novel; **"Rimbaud Fire Letter to Jim Applewhite"** is a painfully humorous evocation of youthful pretensions arising from misapprehensions of Rimbaud's life and work. If these poems were required reading in creative writing workshops, student writers would have less trouble understanding what it really means to take one's work seriously.

Throughout the book, there are echoes, sometimes respectful and sometimes parodic, of other writers: Wordsworth, Cummings, Eliot, Frost, and others come in for brief and witty allusions, and Dante, who stands behind the whole poem, is both translated and transformed in **Wind Mountain.** **"In Parte Ove Non E Che Luca"** begins as a somewhat colloquial but perfectly honorable rendering of Canto V of the *Inferno* and holds its own against other translations for fifty-one lines. When Dante begins to introduce individual victims of lust, however, building toward Francesca da Rimini, Chappell loosens his diction gradually as he introduces Casanova, Lord Byron, and James Dickey before turning back inward to his own poem:

> "Master, wait!" I said. "I recognize
> From childhood the round form, the red face
> Of Virgil Campbell, one of my father's cronies.

> "May I not hear what brought him such disgrace?"
> "Of course," he said, "I'll bid him to this place."

(123)

Among the best of the literary poems is **"Hallowind,"** the tenth poem in **Wind Mountain.** It is a "playlet," reminiscent of Yeats in length and metric but set in Durham in 1961; the characters are Reynolds Price, Susan, Fred, the rain, and the wind. In an argument about the nature of fiction, Fred pushes for the paradigms and myths discoverable in stories and Reynolds argues for each story's particularity until Susan enters with tea and cakes. She shifts the conversation toward conclusion, but the rain and the wind interrupt them. The wind's closing speech is a surprising and moving argument for what might be called the humanities:

> It's soon enough that we dissolve
> Their names to dust, unmoving move
> Against their animal powers to love
> And weep and fear. It's all too soon
> They grow as silent as the moon
> And lie in earth as naked bone.
> We'll let them sit and sip their tea
> Till midnight; then I'll shake the tree
> Outside their window, and drive the sea
> Upon the land, the mountain toward the Pole,
> The desert upon the glacier. And all
> They ever knew or hoped will fall
> To ash . . . Till then, though, let them speak
> And lighten the long dim heartache,
> And trifle, for sweet trifling's sake

(139)

This inclusive and loving recognition of the world we inhabit is the foundation on which **Midquest** stands. What this world is to us is touched on in a brief pas-

sage in *Brighten the Corner Where You Are.* The protagonist, Joe Robert Kirkman, is loosely based on Chappell's father; his son is the narrator. One full and fateful morning at the school where Joe Robert teaches science, he is visited by the parents of Lewis Dorson, a former student who returned from the Second World War unable to pick up his life and at last committed suicide. Joe Robert has just learned this from Lewis' mother:

> It was over between them forever now, but my father felt the need to say something, knowing there was nothing to say, yet knowing, too, that she would listen. It came out lame and hoarse: "I thought the world of him. More than that."

> "More than the world." She looked into his face. "I count on more."

> But that wasn't what he meant, whatever he meant. The world was what my father knew, nothing more or less, better or worse. The world was plenty. "We all do," he said.

(65-66)

III

In the ninth poem of **Bloodfire, "Burning the Frankenstein Monster: Elegiac Letter to Richard Dillard,"** Fred acknowledges a perception of Dillard's and adds, "But *The Inkling* is long out of print, bemuses not even my mother. / Let it smolder to ash on whatever forgotten shelf" (85). As luck would have it, my copy of *The Inkling* is holding up very well. Between the front cover and the flyleaf, there is a paper napkin on which in April, 1966, at the Pickwick in Greensboro, Fred Chappell scribbled these lines:

> When it's
> Ginsberg on the Ganges,
> Him with His hairy phalange,
> I'll be back
> Again, sweetheart,
> In the following stanges.

None of the other writers there assembled could rise to that challenge, which is quoted here for the fun of it, as an indication of Chappell's restless interest in saying the world and as an epigraph to the question of how a poet still in mid-career might follow a book as strong and deep as **Midquest.**

Writers tend to be more interested in their recent work than in work that has receded somewhat into the past. On the one hand, a young writer can be daunted to realize that a recent work is a vast improvement on earlier efforts; one wonders whether one can rise to that level again and what the writing life will be like if one cannot. On the other hand, a writer in middle age can sometimes face with relative equanimity the thought of having written already that work which he or she may not surpass. Gratitude for having achieved that work can even be liberating: now it will be easier to take greater risks or pursue more idiosyncratic impulses. By this time, the writer knows that one must first of all be interested in what one is doing. These notions arise from contemplation of the startling oddity and the surprising success of *Castle Tzingal* (1984), a poem consisting of twenty-three dramatic pieces, most of them monologues. The nine characters are occupants of a mythical principality under the rule of a mad king, remote in time and place. The imprecision of time, especially, is that of dream or of vaguely researched costume drama; the speakers use such words as *arras, florin, villeyn, catamite, scranny,* and *grutch,* but they also use words of more recent origin, as if to remind us that they are detached from real history.

As they certainly are. The first monologue is spoken by "the Homunculus," an eighteen-inch creature named Flyting but called Tweak. His account of his origins is a fine, humorous example of alchemical fantasy:

> I was born
> On a table bright with flame and glassware,
> And had no childhood except an ignorance
> Of politics and gossip. And what a boring year
> My childhood was. No company
> But the pottering alchemist, his cat
> Who wanted to gobble me up, and three
> Disgusting nodules of melting flesh
> That were earlier attempts at being me.
>
> (1)

Tweak is a gleefully wicked spy for the king, who suspects everybody of plotting against him. His queen pines for one Marco, a troubadour from a neighboring province, who has disappeared. Petrus, an envoy from Marco's father, gradually comes close to discovering that young man's grisly fate and in three poems sends reports back home. The Astrologer, the Admiral, and a Page all take their turns exposing their fears and treacheries, and they are all disturbed at times by the disembodied voice of Marco, who still manages to sing from his place not far this side of the grave.

The poem is another balancing act, and the reader teeters on the line between standing well back in arm's-length apprehension of the self-consciously literary language and allegory and being drawn into the melodramatic story. Among the forces that draw the reader in is the skill with which Chappell sometimes echoes the sound of anonymous balladry:

> *As the lone long wind unwinds*
> *Her bobbin of white thread*
> *She sings a song rejoicing*
> *That she never wed.*
>
> (5)

But if this were a bedtime story, it would be saved for the nights when the children had been very wicked, indeed. That is another of the forces that draw us into these seeming improbabilities. The disloyalty, self-interest, madness, and grief of Castle Tzingal are common enough in realms with which most of us are better acquainted. Marco's disembodied voice is that of poetry or even truth, and he wonders at the enormity of his punishment:

> No crime against humanity or God has yet deserved
> Such unimagined punishment, no black sin
> Received such frozen penalty.
>
> Until a mad king dabbled in chemistry.
> So I live on, if live I do,
> To wrinkle and pull tense the minds of those
> Who have created me what I am now
> Until a thorough justice arise.
>
> (31)

In our time, such words cause a chill of recognition. Our alchemy is farther-fetched even than that of Tzingal, and it has rendered us more vulnerable to madness. Many a poet in such a world has reason to feel like a disembodied voice, but Chappell tells his story with too much skill and too much pleasure in the resources of poetic form to be accused of losing hope.

IV

Source (1985) was Chappell's first full-length collection of short poems since his first book, though the publication history of individual poems shows that many of them were composed by the way while he was working on *Midquest* and *Castle Tzingal.* Furthermore, in 1979 he published *Awakening to Music,* a chapbook of fifteen poems, and in 1981, *Driftlake: A Lieder Cycle,* an elegant limited edition. *Source* contains five poems from *Awakening to Music*; *Driftlake* is left uncollected in favor of **"The Transformed Twilight,"** a second "lieder cycle" similar in form and length to the first. Between the two small books and the larger one, there are some important differences of tone and apparent intention. These are particularly evident in the revisions of the five poems from *Awakening to Music* and one, **"Seated Figure,"** reprinted from *The World between the Eyes.*

Awakening to Music is characterized by imaginative play carried toward extremes of verbal ingenuity, startling similes, and weird situations. A few, like **"Delayed by Mongol Forces at National Airport,"** posit wonderful premises but trail off into unsatisfying endings. Nonetheless, the title poem, a recollection of the pleasures and trials of caring for cattle, and **"Music as a Woman Imperfectly Perceived"** handsomely sustain their ambitious figures.

In one view, *Source* is concerned with such literary gains as may be extracted from various other kinds of losses. The first section of the book, "Child in the Fog," evokes scenes from a mountain childhood in poems simultaneously regretting their disappearance and rejoicing in the power of words to recall their shadows. Here, **"Awakening to Music"** has been enriched and simplified. Between the following two versions of the same passage, a strained simile has been taken out and the syntax eased:

> Or:
>> with hands frost-grained
>> from the bucket bail I'd clutch the brood-warm
>> teats and mother of God how
>> a cow would kick.
>>> The leg
>> like a diving board snapping off on second
>>> bounce.
>> As sudden as a door blown shut.
>> (In August they'd lash out
>> when thistle-thorns hid in the udders.)
>
> *(**Awakening**, 9)*

> Sometimes:
>> with hands frost-grained
>> from the bucket bail I'd clutch the brood-warm
>> teats and God help us how she'd kick a shapely
>> leg as sudden as a door blown shut.
>> Or just as quick in August when
>> thistle-thorns embedded in the udders
>
> *(**Source**, 10)*

It is at the end of the poem that the most thematically significant changes have been made. The first version's ending is explicit in stating the loss attendant on living past those days of herding and milking:

> And all those years I went clothed in this sleep,
> odor and heat of cows
> blanketed about my head,
> blear low fever I breathed passionately.
> How would I get it back? Go to blood
> again, sleep the light green sleep?
> How can anyone live truly, waking without cows?
>
> Then
> no more music.
>
> *(**Awakening**, 10)*

> And all those years I went clothed in this sleep,
> odor and warmth
> of cows blanketed about my head.
>
> How would I get it back?
> Go to blood again, sleep the light green sleep?
> How can I wake, not waking to music?
>
> *(**Source**, 11)*

The new last line allows for a paraphrase like "How can I help waking to music?" The emphasis shifts from what has gone forever to what has been retained.

In the second and third sections of the book, "Source" and "The Transformed Twilight," Chappell moves

beyond instances of personal loss to portrayals of the kind of destruction our age has taught us to consider. **"The Evening of the Second Day"** reports the vague movements of a band of people who have reverted to tribalism among the ruins of a city blasted almost beyond recognition. The lieder cycle is a love poem, but the speaker "can imagine no brutal history that will not be born" (43) and describes a few that already have been. Yet even the darkness of these poems is mitigated by the pleasure of **"Recovery of Sexual Desire After a Bad Cold"** or the wit of **"The Story."** The story thrives among such people as a farmer's wife and children and a jolly merchant but falls drunkenly among poets; when it is thoroughly derelict, the novelists find it.

The poems in the final section, "Forever Mountain," find various kinds of consolation in the knowledge that death is an eternal separation. The poem from which the section takes its title ends with the words *"This is a prayer"*; it is an affecting farewell to the poet's father, who is visualized moving in a leisurely way through a day and night on the mountainside until he is out of sight. **"Urleid"** revives Lucretius and his ideas of basic atoms free of supernatural will. The poem revels in anachronism, as Lucretius dismisses Olympus as a "drawing-room farce" and takes Rilke to task for his angels.

Lucretius is treated with more affection in *First and Last Words* (1989). In **"How the Job Gets Done,"** subtitled "an epilogue to Lucretius," a real battlefield becomes a literary battlefield, and the soil of a garden becomes a page. After the corpses and bones and weapons are dust, there is still

> in his garden the poet who labors to line-end,
> turns back like a sweating plowman to fold
> another loamy furrow over the crumbled palaces.
>
> (52)

The title of the collection arises from what Chappell is about in the first and third sections, which are devoted, respectively, to prologues and epilogues for various works of literature—*The Georgics* and *The Dynasts*, Livy and Lucretius, Goethe and Tolstoy, *The Wind in the Willows*. Chappell makes us at ease with what he is talking about, however familiar or unfamiliar the works he addresses. These poems are, for the most part, refreshingly accessible without being simple or simple-minded. Like most of the poems I have been looking at, they hover between the world of literature and the world we live in, as if it were sometimes hard to tell the difference.

The middle section of *First and Last Words*, "Entr'acte," contains a few miscellaneous poems—not closely related to the book's central concern but too good to have been left out—and a few poems that come at the life/literature dichotomy from the other direction. **"Word," "Literature," "The Reader,"** and **"The Garden"** are witty texts in which the world itself becomes a text. It would be tempting to say that the poems and the world become one, but Chappell seems to like that shimmering margin between them. The two propositions of **"The Garden"** are, first, that "The garden is a book about the gardener," and, second, that "The gardener is a book about her garden":

> She walks among these leaves as easy as morning
> Come to scatter its robins and tender noises.
> As the plants inhale the morning and its green light,
> The book is open once again that was never shut.
> What now we do not know we shall never know.
>
> (30)

The apparent directness of that passage, the casual paradox of the next-to-last line, indicate some of the qualities that keep these poems, with all their colloquy with other books, from being too literary to be believed. Chappell's intelligence has always been among the gifts he puts to most powerful use, because he knows how to keep it from being too showy. He learned this, as *Midquest* makes clear, from hanging around very bright but nonliterary people who speak their complicated minds in memorable country words. **"Dipperful"** gives us an encounter with an old man on a porch, under which his hounds are "warm spotted lumps of doze and quiver" (35). He speaks of walking for pleasure and walking to work. Then, echoing the wind at the end of **"Hallowind,"** remarks "'But if we didn't have the triflingness / To think back on, nobody would come this far'" (35).

"Remodeling the Hermit's Cabin" presents words of a builder named Reade who has accepted a contract to desecrate an old cabin for the new owner, who likes certain modern amenities. This is the poem's conclusion:

> "It looks kind of sad and busted, what we've done,"
> I said.
>   "That Florida feller will tack up plastic,"
> He said, "and put him in an ice machine,
> And have him a radar carport and a poodle
> He's trained to count his money. These modern days
> We're all a bunch of cowbirds, you know that?"
>
> (51)

This wonderful poem is presented as an epilogue to the Constitution of the United States. As with many of the other poems in *First and Last Words,* the connection is not forced or required for understanding. But the connections—even when we do need to make them before the poem is clear—are rich with amazing possibilities. A certain occupational hazard troubles some poets. As Tony Connor once put it, they "find poems in everything" and fear the failure "to feed silence to death."

But Fred Chappell has long since learned that durable poems, whatever perception or occasion gets them started, occupy a mysterious realm somewhere between where we are and what we speak. The difference between the trees among which he grew up and the trees in the sacred wood diminishes with each of his strong advances upon the wilderness.

Notes

1. R. H. W. Dillard, *News of the Nile: A Book of Poems by R. H. W. Dillard* (Chapel Hill, 1971), 27.

2. William Blackburn, ed., *Under Twenty-five: Duke Narrative and Verse, 1945-1962* (Durham, 1963).

Randolph Paul Runyon (essay date 1997)

SOURCE: Runyon, Randolph Paul. "Fred Chappell: Midquestions." In *Southern Writers at Century's End,* edited by Jeffrey J. Folks and James A. Perkins, pp. 185-200. Lexington, Ky.: University Press of Kentucky, 1997.

[*In the following essay, Runyon details the complex structural symmetries of Chappell's* Midquest.]

Born in western North Carolina, in 1936, Fred Chappell has drawn increasingly on his Appalachian heritage in recent years. His best works—the epic poem *Midquest* (1981) and the novel *I Am One of You Forever* (1985)—are rooted in a quasi-autobiographical network of recurring hill-country characters, including his parents and grandparents, various eccentric uncles, and general-store proprietor Virgil Campbell, whose prankish independence harks back to Sut Lovingood but whose first name has a deserved Old World resonance.

This is particularly true in *Midquest,* which takes place in the Dantean middle of the protagonist's life, his thirty-fifth birthday (as well as Fred Chappell's), and where Virgil is, if not guide, at least a constant presence. The poem is actually four books of eleven poems each in which "the first poem is mirrored by the last," according to Chappell in the Preface, "the second by the next to last, and so on inward. But the sixth poem in each volume is companionless in that volume, and concerned with a garrulous old gentleman named Virgil Campbell, who is supposed to give to the whole its specifically regional, its Appalachian, context" (ix-x). As David Paul Ragan has pointed out, however, this is somewhat "misleading" in its implication "that the regional context is conveyed primarily through [the Campbell poems] alone" (22). For plenty of the other poems in *Midquest* provide that regional context, too.

More troubling is Chappell's misleading the reader in the matter of the placement of the Virgil poems. Of the four volumes in the poem—***River, Bloodfire, Wind***

Mountain, and *Earthsleep*—of only the first and last is it true that "the sixth poem is . . . concerned with . . . Virgil Campbell." The Virgil poem in *Bloodfire,* "**Firewater,**" is the seventh poem; in *Wind Mountain* it is the eighth, "**Three Sheets in the Wind**"—a circumstance that is not immediately apparent in the table of contents, which does not display subtitles. If it had, such a misstatement could hardly have escaped notice, for the poem's full title is "**Three Sheets in the Wind: Virgil Campbell Confesses.**"[1] If the Preface is wrong in this particular, can we believe what else it says?

It is unusual for a poet to go to such trouble to detail the hidden architecture of his text. In the case of Fred Chappell it may even be a little suspicious. For in an essay first published in 1989, eight years after *Midquest,* he wrote in not entirely approving tones of the "modern epic poet" who "shall tell us" that his poem "'has a secret structure that is hidden by its bewildering surface.' Then he proceeds to point out to us"—as did Chappell himself—

> arcane principles of structure, unnoticed axioms of organization, subterranean networks of relationships, correspondences, and associations. And so it turns out that this object which has appeared to be so haphazard and patchwork can actually be clarified with a diagram. Aren't we all now reassured of the poet's sanity?
>
> Perhaps we are. Perhaps not. For it is a wild connect-the-dots scheme, this construction of the contemporary epic.
>
> [*Plow Naked* 89]

What kind of modern epic poem is he talking about? He goes on to allude to Pound's *Cantos,* Williams's *Paterson,* Olson's *Maximus Poems,* Zukovsky's *A,* and Crane's *The Bridge.* But is he also talking about *Midquest*? Perhaps not. Instead of "patchwork," the model his Preface claims is the "sampler," a display of fancy stitches: terza rima, tetrameter, rhymed couplets, chant royal, among others. Yet that refers not to the possible symmetrical relation of the poems to each other on the grounds of theme and language but to their various forms.

A more fitting description may be the "crazy-quilt" of the flesh of Dr. Frankenstein's creation in *Bloodfire*'s ninth poem, "**Burning the Frankenstein Monster**" (85). Particularly because this "innocent wistful crazy-quilt of dead flesh" in the Frankenstein poem seems to participate in the "balancing act" Chappell claims is going on in *Midquest,* an element in the mirroring that poem does of its symmetrical companion, "**My Father Allergic to Fire,**" the third poem in *Bloodfire.* The Frankenstein monster was unnaturally afraid of fire: "Why must poor Karloff . . . die, fire-fearing, / In the fire?" (85). Fred's father, despite the title, is allergic to only "One kind of fire." The Klan's burning crosses

make him vomit. When he was nine, he spied on a Klan meeting, was caught, and forced to join. They took matches and heated a pocket knife to burn a cross onto his shoulder. In recounting this episode, he "Peeled back" his clothes to show the cross to his son, who found he couldn't see it. "I stared into my father's skin. / A little pimple in a square of gray-pink flesh. / . . . no cross at all. / 'Can't you see it?' He pleaded like a child. // My father's innocent shoulder I almost kissed" (64). Fred subsequently yields to his father's desire and lies, saying that he can see the cross, though it's "awfully small." His father is relieved, for it loomed so large in his memory that it had to be there. If the reader of *Midquest,* mindful of the Preface's promise, stares at these two poems long enough, something will indeed appear: the father's "innocent" "flesh" will reappear, as if in a mirror, in the "innocent . . . flesh" of the "crazy-quilt" of which the monster was made.

In "**Burning the Frankenstein Monster,**" Chappell increases the mirroring effect by drawing out the father-son relationship between creator and monster, thus recalling the father-son situation grounding "**My Father Allergic to Fire**": Dr. Frankenstein "has fathered / A son" (86). Creator and created are "Father and son, with one instant of recognition between them." Fred's not being able to see the cross but saying he could might be termed a sort of false recognition. In another echo, in "**My Father Allergic to Fire,**" the father "*Peeled back* two layers / Of undershirt" (64) to bare his shoulder, while Fred's "vividest memory" of the Frankenstein film is the scene where the monster first sees sunlight, "pouring / Through the roof *peeled back* little by little, at last" (85).

This echoing effect is self-referential, and in an unsettling way. Fred fibbed when he told his father he could see the cross. Chappell, similarly, is not quite truthful when he tells us that the sixth poem will always be about Virgil Campbell. Is he telling the truth when he speaks of the mirroring effect of the poems? They certainly mirror in this instance, but we find ourselves in the very act of looking for evidence of it curiously foreshadowed by the poet's persona in "**My Father Allergic to Fire.**" Is Chappell drawing us into such a situation only to then suggest that we would be as untruthful as the son if we said we could see it?

To answer that question it might help to determine if the mirror effect is at work elsewhere, even though to do that might still be to play Chappell's game, even to fall victim to what may be a "rusty" on his part. But let's see where it takes us anyway. Consider "**Firewood**" and "**Firewater,**" the fifth and seventh poems in *Bloodfire.* In "**Firewood,**" Fred is chopping at a particularly difficult piece of oak, "blow on blow not yielding at all until / 28 strokes tear a jag / of shadow-lightning across the grooved / round top." Coincidence or not, this is the sixteenth of the forty-four poems in *Midquest* (which is divided into four books of eleven poems each), which means there are as many left as the number of strokes it will take to make a tear in the log. "Numbers," Chappell writes in the Preface, "are obviously important in the poem" (ix).[2] Are they important enough for there to be an allegorical parallel between the reader's hacking at *Midquest* to open up its secret (by rereading it over and over to find the promised mirror echoes, for instance) and the poet's chopping away at the oak?

Fred wields his ax to find what secret the wood will disclose, but discovers that its secret was already laid bare. The wood "at last torn open shows that all the secret / was merely the hardness itself" (68). A log is text, or at least texture: "there is I tell you in the texture of this log that / which taunts the mind." But in the end "nothing happens except that matter retains its smirking / hardness & just sits there" (72).

This smirking and sitting is mirrored in the tale Virgil Campbell tells in **"Firewater."** Big Mama, a notorious but never apprehended moonshiner, is invited to parade a model still down Main Street for the Hayesville centennial. "Sitting on a rocking chair on a wagon" and "Grinning grinning grinning," she waves to the deputy sheriff. For this is no pretend still, but a real one, "smoke just boiling out / Pretty as you please" and disabling the mule in the wagon behind, who passes out dead drunk from the fumes (79). Like the log displaying its secret that is no secret at all and that "smirking . . . just sits there," Big Mama sits in her chair "Rocking and grinning and rocking." For ten years the authorities had been trying to catch her at her trade, but they had not expected that she would respond to their invitation so literally. Yet she was breaking the law. The deputy stepped forward to announce that she was under arrest. Her sons then "stood up . . . / And threw down on the deputy three shotguns" (79). **"Firewood"** appropriately supplies the right term for such an impasse: "Mexican stand off is the closest you'll get," matter in the form of a near-impenetrable walnut log tells Fred (72).

Verbal echoes reveal that numerous elements of one poem have their counterparts in the other. "A cat would've by God laughed" in **"Firewater"** to see Big Mama still in action under the deputy's nose (79). Feline reaction to the main event is foreshadowed in the first line of **"Firewood,"** where "the cat is scared" by the fury with which Fred attacks the log (67). Near the end, Fred rests from his near-futile labor: "it could go / on like this forever since it forever has, better take / a moment's cigarette" (73). Similarly, at the end of **"Firewater"** Big Mama forsakes the moonshine business ("Ain't no profit in it" any more) for cigarettes: "Growing these Merry Widow cigarettes, / That's where they

make their money" (80). "I will sit on this log & breathe bluegray smoke," Fred says in **"Firewood,"** anticipating this time the mule that followed Big Mama's wagon: "Drunk as an owl, / Just from breathing the smoke that was pouring out / From Big Mama's *model* still" (79; italics in original).

Fred muses about finding "our unguessable double" in the heart of the log, not realizing that Chappell leads his readers, along the trail running from the Preface's remarks about mirror effects to such examples of it as these, to guess that his double may be an inebriated mule.

In the mirror effect **"Susan Bathing"** and **"My Grandfather Gets Doused"** (poems V and VII in *River,* to adopt Chappell's roman numeral numbering system) enact, one finds Fred's wife's double in the water that baptized his grandfather, and the doubling effect finds another self-referential description in the form of recycled Lucretian atoms. Fred imagines Susan's body "remaining yet sailed / away on streams on streams of atoms into the winds . . . sweetening now zephyrs / by Bermuda & Mykonos" (22), while the grandfather, repenting of having undergone a Baptist immersion in the waters of West Fork Pigeon River, is consoled by the thought that "The water that saved him was some place / Else now, washing away the sins / Of trout down past McKinnon Trace. // . . . 'What damn difference / Will it make?'" (33). Like the streams of atoms that make up Susan and the stream itself, atoms from one poem are "some place / Else now" (in fact, *now* itself is just such an atom, having first appeared in "sweetening now zephyrs" but now turning up here), drawn into another poem.

Likewise "a single tear reflecting my chest & face" (21) on the bathing Susan becomes a "double tear" in his grandfather's eye that is also a sign of Fred's presence: "He frowned // When he saw me gaping. A double tear / Bloomed at the rim of his eye" (31). Animals in **"Susan Bathing"** "go robed churchly in / white" (24) while the baptismal candidate had likewise been "togged . . . out in white" (31). In more general (and thus perhaps less interesting) terms, Susan's immersion in her bath anticipates the grandfather's in the river.

Similarly, the well-scrubbing in **"Cleaning the Well"** is reflected by the milk can-cleansing in **"My Grandmother Washes Her Vessels"** in *River* poems IV and VIII, though it is hardly surprising that two paired poems should be about such similar subjects in an eleven-poem sequence devoted to water. More intriguing is the fact that both the well into which the boy is let down by his grandfather and the channel into which his grandmother plunges her vessels reek of mortality. The *"spring*-run" is "a concrete grave" (34), while the deep and chilly hole into which the fearful boy descends is the "well*spring* of death" (16). Coming out at last, his task completed, he feels like "Jonah, Joseph, Lazarus," risen from the dead. With a taste for symmetry, Chappell has the formerly "white sun" of noon (14) turn "Yellow" (17) when the boy emerges an hour after he went in (yellow, and "Thin," it is too cold to warm him up that December day after his brush with chilly death), while just the opposite will happen in the other poem: The **"Yellow light"** of the August six-o'clock sun "entering / The bone-white milkhouse recharged itself white" (34).

If we went by titles alone, we might have been tempted to say **"My Grandmother Washes Her Vessels"** would have made a better match with **"My Grandmother Washes Her Feet,"** the third poem in *River*. But, going by the numbers, as Chappell implies we should, that poem is paired with the ninth, **"Science Fiction Water Letter to Guy Lillian."** The connection arises from what Fred's grandmother tells him about how "We sprouted from dirt" and that he should never forget it. "No Mam," he says, assuring her he won't. "Don't you say me No Mam yet. / Wait till you get your chance to deny it" (12-13). In the letter to Lillian, Fred outlines a projected science fiction novel in which "once upon this earth / Words had not the shape that now they shine in" (41). They lay upon the ground like objects; men had no ears to hear them with, no understanding of their possibility of signification. "The notion / Of *word* had not yet squiggled into being. / But there they were, twitchy to be discovered, / All words that in the world ever were or will." An extraterrestrial woman from Nirvan, "who'd been awarded / Mother of the Year" on that planet, lands on earth, and instructs the first man who comes along in the art of words (42). She takes him to a mountain, tells him this is what *"Water"* is, and the mountain, "Finally collapsing, like jello in an oven, to liquid" (43), becomes it. The man sprouts ears, and words now take on meaning at last, words like "Pomegranate. Baseball. Mouse. / Cadillac. Poem. Paradise. Cinnamon Doughnut." That first man called himself Adam, and Chappell calls his teacher "Our Lovely Mother" (43), as if, despite her origins, she were Eve, mother of us all.

This ultimate grandmother, mother of the human species, recalls Fred's grandmother in the other poem. Not just because she instructs her grandson concerning dirt, but because she does so concerning words. And in particular concerning words whose meaning and appropriate use will only become clear at some later time: she won't let him say "No Mam" to her yet. Later, she lets fall a word Fred doesn't know, and for that word too—like the words in the science fiction novel—its existence as an incomprehensible and unusable entity must long precede its use and comprehension: "'Fatback just won't change to artichokes.' // 'What's artichokes?' // 'Pray Jesus you'll never know. / For if

you do it'll be a sign you've grown / Away from what you are'" (12).

The jello that the mountain turns into as it liquefies recalls the "ancestral jelly" (13) into which Fred imagined himself "forcing warm rude fingers," which then sends us back to the other poem to meditate on the role of fingers there: "S-f [science fiction] is / . . . less pleasurable to / the fingers; a deliberate squeamishness obtains" (38). Though he has respect for some practitioners of the genre, and outlines a science fiction novel himself, Fred finds it too sterile. At this point we can start to see the real connection to the other poem. Fred here and his grandmother there are saying, at bottom, the same thing. We are born from dirt and we shouldn't pretend otherwise. "It's not the skeleton" in science fiction and ghost stories "that rattles me, but the flesh—/ or want of it." It has the color of blood "but not its taste." Science fiction "has no feel for pastness" (39). The grandmother does, though, and knows that "Just about the time you'll think your blood / Is clean, here will come dirt in a natural shape / You never dreamed" (12). Science fiction is guilty of the willful forgetting of the necessary connection between dirt and life the grandmother warned Fred against.

Elsewhere in *River,* the narrator's ascent to "this hill at midnight" (45) in **"On Stillpoint Hill at Midnight"** (X) was anticipated by the moon's "Climbing the steep hill of void" (7) "on a midnight full / of stars" (6) in **"Birthday 35: Diary Entry"** (II). Looking up from the riverbank to the hill the moon illumined, Fred in the latter poem "saw nothing human, / . . . No animals . . . only moon / Upon moon, sterile stone" (7), while in the other poem the opposite takes place as he considers "how stones will burgeon / into animals" (45), given enough geological time. The animals evolving from stone will eventually be "gnawing the ruled streets and lot corners / of suburbs" (45), thus demonstrating that life will emerge despite the present appearance of death, a situation in which the poet includes himself: "(I glow amidst the dead)." In **"Birthday 35"** gnawing is likewise the sign of life: "this gnawing worm shows that I'm not dead" (5).

Verbal echoes between the first and last (eleventh) in each book are for some reason sparser, though these poems always recount the same situation, the poet in bed with his wife at dawn (though this is less clear in **"Wind Subsides on the Earth River,"** the last poem in *Wind Mountain,* where it is night but not necessarily the end of night). As Chappell points out in the Preface, each of the four books together cover "the same twenty-four hours of the speaker's life" (ix). Only the first and last poems tend to evoke the same hour. As Karen Cherry points out, trees figure in the opening lines of each of the four first poems (117):

Deep morning. Before the trees take silhouettes

> ["The River Awakening in the Sea" (1)]

Morning. / First light shapes the trees

> ["Fire Now Wakening on the River" (55)]

Early half-light, dawnwind driving / The trees

> ["Dawn Wind Unlocks the River Sky" (97)]

The cool deep morning / Begins to fashion the trees

> ["Earth Emergent Drifts the Fire River" (145)]

The first line of the last poem in *River*:

> Again. Deep morning.
>
> > ["The River Seeks Again the Sea" (50)]

recalls the first line of the first:

> Deep morning.
>
> > ["The River Awakening in the Sea" (1)]

And what Fred's forehead does in one his mind does in the other:

> My forehead suckles your shoulder
>
> [1]
>
> my mind suckles your shoreless lonesomeness.
>
> [50]

The first poem of *Bloodfire* continues this theme, recalling the first poem of *River*: "My forehead enters your shoulder" (**"Fire Now Wakening on the River"** [55]).

Bloodfire's first anticipates its last through poison and sizzle:

> Boiled juices of poison oak
>
> [56]
>
> the poison / wild cherry
>
> [93]
>
> *Torn sheet of light sizzles in the mirror*
>
> [56]
>
> sizzle on the hard / vine ribs
>
> [93]

And Orion makes an appearance in both (56, 92).

More worthy of note, or at least more easily interpretable, is the way Baudelaire and Rimbaud, featured players in **"Rimbaud Fire Letter to Jim Applewhite"** (II), return in **"Bloodfire"** (X): "Here I turned / Back to the books that nurtured me / When I met evil first, learned / An implacable philosophy" (89). It is a literal turning back that is evoked here, inviting the reader to turn back to what the Preface said would be the companion poem to **"Bloodfire," "Rimbaud Fire Letter,"** where Fred makes it pretty clear that the books that had nurtured him were Rimbaud and Baudelaire. "That decade with Rimbaud I don't regret. / . . . Rimbaud was genius pure; / . . . Kind of a handbook on how to be weird and silly" (58). Baudelaire, in whose *Flowers of Evil* Fred apparently "met evil first," played an important role, too, in those formative years: His high school teachers "stood up for health and truth and light, / I stood up for Baudelaire and me" (59)—Baudelaire, in that formulation, representing a glorification of *le mal* that ran counter to all that health and truth and light.

"Let's don't wind up brilliant, young, and dead" (61), Fred says to Applewhite in the **"Rimbaud Fire Letter."** Which is exactly what happens to the young man whose fate is recounted in **"Bloodfire,"** who immolates himself in protest against the war in Vietnam. He "never could belong / To another army" (88) than that of the war protesters, while Fred in the other poem tried to enlist in the military, in pre-Vietnam days, but "They turned me down for the army" (60).

In the remaining pair in *Bloodfire* not yet mentioned, the "sickness" and "silver fire" of **"Feverscape: The Silver Planet"** (IV) find echoes in the episode Fred recounts in **"My Father Burns Washington"** (VIII) of how his father, "sick" of having to think "of nothing but money" (82) in the depths of the Depression, took out a dollar bill and set it on fire. "Money," the father complains. "It's the death / *Of the world*" (82; emphasis added), recalling the feverish boy's statement in the other poem: "I know well what sickness comes trembling over / the edge *of the world*" (66; emphasis added). Listening at night to his parents, downstairs lamenting their penury, the boy in **"My Father Burns Washington"** feared that "Money would climb / The stair . . . and, growling, try / The doorknob, enter upon us furiously" (81). Likewise, in the fever of various childhood illness, in **"Feverscape"** he finds his bedroom invaded by the silver planet whose "vast leaping / coronas fingered the medicine space I suffered in" and whose "White tentacles of camphor-smelling flame . . . lashed me" (65, 66).

His father breaks into open revolt against money's oppression. Likewise, Fred in the other poem declares that "Too long we have bared our backs, we / have bent our heads beneath the cruel silver fire" (66). In the context of **"Feverscape"** alone, it is not clear (at least to this reader) what Fred is talking about here, for the silver planet seems now (at the conclusion of the poem) to mean something significantly broader than the fever-induced hallucination it had been in his childhood. In the context it shares with **"My Father Burns Washington,"** however, a context Chappell's Preface makes licit, it seems that it may have something to do with money. Silver, after all, is money—though not the paper variety that lends itself so well to combustion. "It might have helped if I had known some French," as Fred says in **"Rimbaud Fire Letter"** (58), a language that makes that equation self-evident.

In elegant self-referential symmetry, a mirror that becomes a window ("The mirror like a burning window" [97]) in the first poem of *Wind Mountain* (**"Dawn Wind Unlocks the River Sky"**) finds its mirror reflection in windows that become mirrors ("reflections of Buicks in supermarket windows" [141]) in the last (**"Wind Subsides on the Earth River"**). In the next pair, "The weepy *eaves* peep down into the *rooms*" as "Wind and water drive against the windows" (emphasis added) in **"The Highest Wind That Ever Blew: Homage to Louis"** (II), while the wind and rain in **"Hallowind"** (X) "tear the ragged *eaves* as if / The world outside weren't *room* enough" (135; emphasis added). In **"Second Wind"** (III), Fred's grandmother is renewed by a welcome "cooling wind" after the death of her husband, though before it showed itself the day was so "hot and still" that there had been "Not the least little *breath* of air" (103; emphasis added), while in **"Remembering Wind Mountain at Sunset"** (IX), there is no wind but an ill one, whether it be the one that blows down from Freeze Land in winter or the coal stove wind of summer that hasn't "a *breath* of soothe in it" (132; emphasis added). The wind in **"Second Wind"** "was the breath of life to me," exclaimed the grandmother (106), while in **"Remembering Wind Mountain at Sunset"** we find "the wind robbing / them [the poor] of breath" (129). The opposition between the life-restoring wind in one poem and the death-dealing one in the other is internalized in **"Remembering Wind Mountain at Sunset"** by the realization that "the funny part is, come summer / same wind out of the same place" has the opposite effect from what it had in winter. Then, it went "over you / ice water," but now it "feels like it's pouring out of a coalstove" (131, 132). It is, in other words, another moment of self-reference, the same-yet-opposite quality of the wind in poem IX duplicating, and thus alluding to, the opposite-yet-same quality of the wind that blows through both poems.

Why then should Chappell declare in the Preface that *Wind Mountain* does *not* include such mirror effects as these: "each of the volumes (except *Wind Mountain*) is organized as a balancing act"? "In order to suggest the fluid and disordered nature of air," he says later in the same paragraph, "*Wind Mountain* was exempt from some of these requirements," the requirements just then mentioned being (1) that the poems be symmetrically paired, (2) that the sixth poem be "companionless" and

devoted to Virgil Campbell, (3) that the fifth be "given to stream of consciousness," and (4) that each volume be "dominated by a different element of the family"— *River* by the grandparents, *Bloodfire* by the father, and *Earthsleep,* "the part most shadowed by death," constituting a "family reunion." It is just after this sentence that he grants the third volume its exemption "from some of these requirements." But from which ones exactly? From the second to be sure, for Virgil appears there in the eighth poem, not the sixth. But this prompts the question why his is the *seventh* poem in *Bloodfire,* when no such exemption was granted that volume. *Wind Mountain* fulfills the third requirement, its fifth poem, **"The Autumn Blast of the Weathervane Trombone,"** being as much in the stream-of-consciousness genre as **"Susan's Morning Dream of Her Garden,"** the fifth in *Earthsleep,*[3] though not perhaps as Joycean as **"Susan Bathing"** (in *River*) and **"Firewood"** (in *Bloodfire*). Evidently he was thinking of the fourth requirement (the one he had most recently mentioned) in alluding to the freedom granted his third volume, for grandparents, mother and father appear with about equal frequency there.

But this does not exempt Chappell from the contradiction between the Preface's description and the reality of his poem with regard to the "balancing act." The Preface's account of the poem gives rise to more questions than answers, for *Wind Mountain* is in no way exempt from that requirement, as the two remaining pairs (and the three preceding) show. It obliges the reader who follows Chappell's implied advice to seek out the mirror echoes to risk discovering that Chappell not only fibbed about what would be found in the middle of each volume (not more than half the time is it Virgil Campbell) but did so as well about the structure of *Wind Mountain.*[4]

"My Mother Shoots the Breeze," the fourth poem in that volume, finds some remarkable reflections in the eighth, **"Three Sheets in the Wind: Virgil Campbell Confesses."** Fred's mother tells her son how she first met his father, who taught science in the high school where she taught languages. He asked for the loan of her slip so that he could make a kite to demonstrate Ben Franklin's lightning experiment. For her it was sexually arousing: "my slip, / Scented the way that I alone could know, / Flying past the windows made me warm" (108). J. T. went too far, however, flying the kite every day for two weeks. "It's time to show that man that I mean business." So she borrowed her father's shotgun and "blew the fool out of it, both barrels. / It floated up and down in a silk snow / Till there was nothing left. I can still remember / Your Pa's mouth open." They were married within a month. Sexuality is rampant, too, in **"Three Sheets in the Wind,"** in which Virgil Campbell confesses how his youthful indiscretions came to an end when his wife caught him in bed with another woman. "I leapt out / The window . . . praying that the shooting wouldn't hit me." But "The wind lifted a sheet" on the backyard clothesline and Virgil fell, knocked out cold with the sheet wound about him (126). When he came to, all he could see was whiteness. "It came to me that I was dead—/ She'd shot my vitals out—and here's the shroud / They buried me in." He tried to claw his way out, but she had sewn him in and was flailing away with a curtain rod. "*pow!* Pow pow pow*." He thought it was the beginning of the tortures of hell, prelude to burning oil and pitchforks. The parallels between these poems are as striking as any in *Midquest*: the slip and the sheet, both lifted up by the wind; the windows; the shooting; the sexual, and conjugal, context.

In the remaining pair, **"The Autumn Bleat of the Weathervane Trombone"** (V) anticipates the Dantean vision of **"In Parte Ove Non E Che Luca"** (VII), which begins as a translation of *Inferno*'s fifth canto, by imagining the afterlife of poets. The "fancy" that comes to Fred as he plays his trombone is that "poets after the loud labor of their lives / Are gathered to the sun," where they "speak in flame" and "lie a lot" (112). George Garrett will be there, and Applewhite and Tate and at least eight others. Fred, too, though the thought gives him pause. "Trapped in a burning eternity with a herd / Of poets, what kind of fate is that for a handsome / Lad" like him? There are poets too—Byron and James Dickey—in the "inferno" (121) the other poem describes. While the solar afterlife in **"The Autumn Bleat"** is a kind of heaven and this one hell, the poet's paradise is nevertheless "a burning eternity." In the mirror reversal these poems enact, what's positive in one is negative in the other. Fred's trombone-induced fancy leads him to see himself in a falling leaf of tulip poplar as a poet "cast from heaven," the heaven of all those poets in the sun. "It's too much *love of earth* that draws him thither, / . . . *The flesh* the earth it suits me fine" (113; emphasis added). This is precisely reversed (as in a mirror) in the other poem when "Into this pain the *lovers of flesh* are thrust" (122; emphasis added), lovers like Casanova, Byron, and Dickey. The parallel—and the reversal—could hardly be more clearly drawn.

A brief look at the final volume will round out this tour of *Midquest*'s mirrors. While *Earthsleep*'s first and last poems, like those in the preceding three volumes, appear less tightly linked than other pairs in the same volume, a **"Tree of Fire"** appears in each (150, 186). Both **"My Mother's Hard Row to Hoe"** (II) and **"Stillpoint Hill That Other Shore"** (X) speak of fatigue. When the mother was a child her day was filled with such unending farm chores that "It was a numbing torture to carry on." She always obeyed her mother's commands, "no never-mind how tired / I was" (151). In the tenth poem, "our limbs quiver, / exhaustion of stale guilt" (184), and the narrator "is avid for . . . sleep" (185).

In **"My Father Washes His Hands"** (III), Fred's father would like to wash his hands of farming and of the guilt of having had to break the dead mule's legs to get her to fit in the grave that blue clay made undiggable. "Two feet down we hit pipe clay as blue / And sticky as Buick paint." Nothing but "Blue glue" (153). Blueness becomes an echo internal to the poem when, sad at having broken Honey's legs as her dead eyes stared up at him, "The harder down I dug the bluer I got" (154). In **"My Grandfather Dishes the Dirt"** (IX), another grave poem, the grandfather speaks from his tomb and gives blueness a connotation the precise opposite of what it had in the other poem when the father got bluer the deeper he dug: "blue May days / Leap out in my grave sleep / Like sun-drunk butterflies" (181). Both Honey's grave and the grandfather's are full of blueness.

The ninth poem's title is somewhat misleading, as the grandfather has no dirt to dish, nothing much to say, except that he's content to remain ("I *like* it here" [italics in original]), awaiting Judgment Day. "Death disinherits / Us of wanting," though it is "kind of lonely" (181, 182) down there. "The dead I'm here to say have nothing to say. / . . . Let's let each other alone, for Jesus' sake" (182). The father in the other poem would have welcomed that sentiment, for, to his dismay, the dead mule has plenty to say and will not leave him alone. "Honey's not gone, / She's in my head for good and all and ever" (155). In her sleep he can "see her pawing up on her broken legs / Out of the blue mud . . . in her eyes the picture / Of me coming toward her with my mattock; / And talking in a woman's pitiful voice: / *Don't do it, J. T., you're breaking promises*" (italics in original).

The talking mule in **"My Father Washes His Hands"** is succeeded in the following poem, **"The Peaceable Kingdom of Emerald Windows"** (IV), by talking horses. "Bay Maude says to Jackson: 'Don't let's stop / At windrow-end, good fellow, I feel the edge / Of the world just barely beyond my hooftip'" (161). Indeed, *Midquest* is probably as rich in sequential echoes as it is in symmetrical ones. Donald Secreast points out, for example, that **"Cleaning the Well"** is preceded by Bubba Martin managing to fall into the well after shooting himself in **"My Grandmother Washes Her Feet,"** and that "the reflection of the lightbulb on the grandmother's glasses mirrors the two suns which the boy sees as he enters the well" (41).

The horses' conversation is part of a symmetrical echo as well, however, for in **"My Grandmother's Dream of Plowing"** (VIII) we again encounter "Jackson and

Maude whose heads went up and down / Like they agreed on what they were talking over" (178). In the grandmother's dream the horses' plow uncovers what appears to be "a big and shining lump of gold." They'd never have to worry about money again. Then she hears her husband's voice behind her: *"Is that your baby that was never mine?"* (italics in original). She looks again and it *is* a baby, "And this gold child was / Speaking to me. . . . / Except I couldn't hear" (179). And then it turns into a goblin. She found herself wishing it would die, and it does. It "sighed a sigh, and lay in my arms stone dead. / / . . . It turned into a stone, / And it was all my fault, wishing that way" (180). She wept. "And then you woke up," her grandson tells her. "'And now I know,' she said, 'I never woke.'" It's quite a nightmare, suggesting a whole other side to Fred's grandmother. As Dabney Stuart writes, "the revelation of this buried secret from her past casts a sharp light on her preoccupation in the previous poems about her with the 'Shadow Cousins'"—in **"My Grandmother Washes Her Feet"** (12)—"the profound hesitation she experienced before committing herself to marrying Frank, and our seeing her in two situations where she is washing something (her feet, her milk cans)" (214). And as Chappell says in the Preface, *Midquest* is "something like a verse novel" (ix).

Midquest should be read as a novel, and in connection with *I Am One of You Forever* and *Brighten the Corner Where You Are,* novels in which these characters recur, but it should also be read within the context it creates for itself, and in that respect it is intriguing that **"The Peaceable Kingdom of Emerald Windows"** should begin with talk of dreams and hidden babies: "Tree-dream, weed-dream, the man within the tree, / woman within the weed, babies inhabit / Tea roses" (156). This is a stream-of-consciousness poem, more so really than **"Susan's Morning Dream of Her Garden,"** which, as the fifth poem in *Earthsleep,* should, according to the Preface, have been the volume's example of that genre—yet another of the Preface's strange misstatements. In its stream may be found the essential elements of the grandmother's dream: babies to be found, as noted already; but also a "dream of stone" (156) to match the grandmother's dream of a stone dead baby turned to stone; hidden there too (like the babies in tea roses) may be found "the grandmother's tear of parting" (157), anticipating the grandmother's bitter tears at the baby's demise ("I . . . cried so hard I felt my eyes dissolve" [180]). Even the sex behind the grandmother's guilt is present here, with an echo involving sacks: the baby when it was just a lump of gold was "About as big as a twenty-five-pound sack / Of flour" (178), while in **"The Peaceable Kingdom"** "we can get it on / On the sacks of cottonseed meal . . . / No one not even the rain has such big tits, / Lend me your lip a minute, willya, lovechile?" (157). Not to mention the "Rains of semen."[5]

Finally, the last remaining pair: **"Susan's Morning Dream of Her Garden"** (V) and **"How to Build the Earthly Paradise: Letter to George Garrett"** (VII). Susan dreams of a garden where "the sweet rose invites her oriental suitors all // iridescent in green and *oil*" (164; emphasis added), while Fred dreams up an earthly paradise where with "Green / plants for / the heart's delectation, the rough-red / singing vine glows with fire-*oils*" (175; emphasis added). In her garden "into ground lean the lonely / and elaborate dead . . . / burbling one to another always"; in his, "the dead / are troublous in their cool sleep, they stir / and grumble." She reflects on "the way my hand goes into the dirt"; he imagines "a dirt so rich our warm rude fingers / tingle inside it." But their dreams diverge as well: Susan would improve upon the garden the natural world provides, importing elements from another world and time: "I am not replete or reconciled. // Garden, garden, will you not grow for me / a salon full of billets-doux and turtledoves? / . . . I long to belong to / the chipper elegance, those centuries where / the hand of man has never said an ugly word" (165). Fred, on the other hand, is happy with the way things are: "That's / how I'd / build it, the Earthly Paradise: no / different, how could it be?, from what / it was ever dreamed. . . . Is / it true / already, what if it's true already? and / we have but to touch out to see it" (176-77).

Thus it is that Susan wishes to retreat from the real world into her garden, and does not want to wake: "I'd be a fool, a woman's a fool, to be drawn back / into the waking world. . . . I'm snugging / deeper in the larder of dream" (165-66); while Fred "never no more will turn my back / upon" (177) the real world which is "no / different . . . from what . . . was ever dreamed." Fred wakes willingly from his dream, emerging from the door of his lair: "I'm coming belchlike out of / the cave, make way my friends make way, / here gleaming with unspotted dream"; Susan, however, has found another door, not the way out but a way deeper inside: "I'm diving to a door I sense below, / . . . that opens truly into the garden // . . . and can draw / my waking body in and there no one / can draw me out again."

And thus *Midquest* ends—that is, its trail of mirrors ends—the same way *I Am One of You Forever* concludes, with the uncanny phenomenon of shared dreams. In the last chapter of the novel, Jess discovers that Johnson Gibbs, Uncle Luden, and his father all appear to be dreaming the same dream, each saying the name "Helen" in their sleep. Then the three sleepers sit bolt up-right in their beds and stare at the same vision, which the boy thinks he can maybe see, too, but he's not sure: "If something had actually appeared . . . if I had seen something . . ." (182). Fred is less uncertain concerning what his father thinks he should be able to see, the cross on his shoulder in **"My Father Allergic to Fire."** Yet these are surely parallel moments in Chappell, the moment of instant recognition ("Father and son, with one instant of recognition between them" [**"Burning the Frankenstein Monster"** (87)], "all in a single instant—I saw something. I thought that I saw" [*I Am One of You Forever* (182)]) in which one seems to catch a glimpse of something one has seen before: "the features blurred . . . and yet familiar. . . . I was disturbed most of all by the unplaceable familiarity of the vision" (182-83). The poems in pairs, not just the last pair but all of them, seem to dream the same dream. The reader, given the conundrums the Preface poses, may never be quite sure that what he or she sees is what the poet sees. But Chappell seems to have written that quandary into his text.

Notes

1. It did not escape the notice of Henry Taylor, though he denies it any significance. "It turns out that in *Bloodfire* . . . Virgil Campbell holds forth in the seventh poem. . . . In the more loosely arranged *Wind Mountain,* he gets the eighth poem, as it happens; he does not settle back to the middle of a part until *Earthsleep*. My point is not to show that there is a mistake in the order of the poems, or even in Chappell's description of it; it is rather to notice that it is just as effective to give Virgil poems VI, VII, VIII, and VI, as it is to give him VI every time. It is only the prefatory remark that brings attention to this matter" (75). The Preface, in Taylor's view, doesn't count as part of the text.

2. Four, he goes on to say, "is the Pythagorean number representing World, and 4 × 11 = 44, the world twice, interior and exterior. Etc., etc." (ix).

3. Though, as I will later suggest, "Susan's Morning Dream of Her Garden" is not in fact *Earthsleep*'s stream-of-consciousness poem. That honor belongs to the fourth poem, "The Peaceable Kingdom of Emerald Windows."

4. David Paul Ragan, who pointed out that the declaration about Virgil Campbell giving *Midquest* its Appalachian context is a gross oversimplification, suggests what I have made explicit here, that the Preface is full of other misstatements as well: "like many of the statements in that Preface," the one about Virgil "is perhaps misleading" (22).

5. Or these lines: "We'll look up the dresses of tan-legged women oh boy / See the mouth in the moss. See Spot run. / World-wound, come and get me, I'm dying for blood" (158).

Works Cited

Chappell, Fred. *I Am One of You Forever.* Baton Rouge: Louisiana State UP, 1985.

———. *Midquest: A Poem.* Baton Rouge: Louisiana State UP, 1981.

———. *Plow Naked: Selected Writings on Poetry.* Ann Arbor: U of Michigan P, 1993.

Ragan, David Paul. "At the Grave of Sut Lovingood: Virgil Campbell in the Work of Fred Chappell." *Mississippi Quarterly* 37.1 (winter 1983-84): 21-30.

Taylor, Henry. *Compulsory Figures: Essays on Recent American Poets.* Baton Rouge: Louisiana State UP, 1992.

Michael McFee (essay date spring 1999)

SOURCE: McFee, Michael. "The Epigrammatical Fred Chappell." *Southern Literary Journal* 31, no. 2 (spring 1999): 95-108.

[*In the following essay, McFee argues that* C: Poems—*Chappell's volume of one hundred epigrams—while seemingly a stylistic anomaly in Chappell's overall body of work, may have been written in the form most suited to Chappell's poetic personality.*]

I

In a long poetic career distinguished by often-long poems of character and landscape and memory and flamboyant imagination, Fred Chappell's volume *C:*—his tenth, published in 1993, a collection of one hundred epigrams—may seem something of an anomaly, a surprising departure in style and tone and scope from earlier work. With the possible exception of *The World between the Eyes* (1973) and *Source* (1985), each poem in each of Chappell's collections is part of some preconceived larger design to the volume, not just another in a series of autonomous lyric verses. The forty-four extended poems in the Bollingen Prize-winning *Midquest* (1981)—a tetralogy composed of the individual books *River, Bloodfire, Wind Mountain,* and *Earthsleep*—mirror and echo each other, comprising an intricate multilayered verse novel modeled on Dante but set in Chappell's native western North Carolina mountains. *Castle Tzingal* (1984) is a haunting medieval moral tale, presented as a series of twenty-three dramatic monologues, and *First and Last Words* (1989) opens with nine prologues and concludes with nine epilogues to various literary classics.

The poems in *C*—unlike the substantial narratives in *Midquest* and other books—are short and pithy, true to the epigram tradition. Chappell does not group or pattern them for the reader in any deliberate way, by whole volume (as with *Castle Tzingal*) or in sections (as with *First and Last Words*): they are simply presented as numbers I through C. On first glance, then, and even after a reading or two, *C* may seem strangely out of place in Chappell's poetic oeuvre, a diverting but uncharacteristic detour. But is it, really? Or is it—as I would argue—his quintessential book, the one that discovers the ideal form for him to work in, the one best-suited to his split literary personality?

II

On the one side, we have "Ole Fred," the kind of persona readers rend to remember, a character of extreme Romantic temperament and habits. Ole Fred is feisty; he cusses, he jokes, he drinks, he misbehaves; he is cheerfully politically incorrect; he overstates and exaggerates. *Odi et amo!* is his Catullan motto. On the other side, though—overshadowed by his more boisterous and attention-grabbing half—is Professor Chappell, a Neo-classical polymath of the first order, deeply and widely read, profoundly learned: a genuine scholar. Professor Chappell speaks quietly but precisely; he alludes frequently but never shows off; his perspective is historical, across centuries and cultures. *Ars celare artem* is his Horatian motto.

Which is why the epigram, above all a feat of wit, is the ideal from or forum for this battle of the personae, for the literary psychomachia that has always given Fred Chappell's work such fascinating tension and tremendous strength. In spirit, the epigram is lively, often satirical the utterance of a decisive and opinionated character—say, an Ole Fred who wants to pronounce on politics or religion or love; in form, however the epigram is emphatically controlled, conservative, incisive, chiseled lines from a character who (like Professor Chappell) has looked hard and thought long and reduced the subject to its pithiest essence. Which is why, ultimately, *C* is Fred Chappell's *least* surprising book, his most inevitable volume, the one he (and his several sides) had to write someday.

III

C is also not too surprising given Chappell's academic past. Like the Latin poet Martial, who migrated from a remote Spanish province of the Roman Empire to its capital, young Fred went from the mountain isolation of Canton to the literary capital of Duke University, where—with other small-town undergrads like Reynolds Price and James Applewhite—he took William Blackburn's celebrated writing class. But Chappell also went back to Duke for a Master's degree in English literature, which was not (as would have been unthinkable at the time) a so-called "creative thesis," a slim apprentice novel or book of poetry, but a massive "Concordance to the English Poems of Samuel Johnson," four inches thick and 1,110 pages long, representing years of index cards and tedious typing, listing every word Dr. Johnson used in its line context. Why would Ole Fred (already a legendary figure) undertake such a project? At least in part, because he

needed to: to quote a stanza of the **"Rimbaud Fire Letter to James Applewhite"** in *Midquest,* about returning to his native mountains after Duke kicked him out,

> The only good thing was that I got married.
> And I watched the mountains until the mountains touched
> My mind and partly tore away my fire-red
> Vision of a universe besmirched.
> I started my Concordance to Samuel Johnson,
> And learned to list a proper footnote, got down
> To reading folks like Pope and Bertrand Bronson,
> And turned my back on the ashes of Paree-town.

(M [Midquest] 60-61)

His Rimbaud-inspired and -impaired "vision of a universe besmirched" was healed by a convergence of things: by his marriage to Susan, a constant steadying presence thereafter in his life and poems; by nature, the mountains around him; and by settling down in the world of the English Neo-classical poets and leaving the dissipated Romantic hell of Paris behind.

And in so doing, Chappell received a thorough immersion in and inclination toward the epigrammatic tradition. This includes eighteenth-century English poets like Alexander Pope, of course, with his famous "Epigram. Engraved on the Collar of a Dog Which I Gave to His Royal Highness": "I am his Highness' dog at Kew; / Pray tell me Sir, whose dog are you?", as well as Matthew Prior and Jonathan Swift and Dr. Johnson himself, who wrote epigrams "On Colley Cibber" and "On Hearing Mrs. Thrale Deliberate about Her Hat," among others. But it also includes epigrams in other languages and from other times: Dr. Johnson wrote some of his epigrams in Latin and in Greek, and he also translated epigrams from the French, including the haunting "Á Son Lit": "In bed we laugh, in bed we cry, / And born in bed, in bed we die; / The near approach a bed may show / Of human bliss to human woe." Johnson also did some translations from *The Greek Anthology,* the epigrammatic headwaters of Western literature, that vast Palatine gathering of over 4000 epigrams, ranging back to 700 B.C. and forward almost two millenia and across pretty much every imaginable subject, love and life and death and all the rest. True, Dr. Johnson did translate these Greek poems into Latin; but in *C,* Chappell gives us several helpfully rendered into modern English.

IV

In fact, to a degree, *C* itself is an anthology. Of the one hundred epigrams included, twenty-eight of them—over a quarter of the total poems—are translations or versions of epigrams written by other poets at other times. Besides the several Greeks, there are six epigrams by the prolific and most vigorous Roman master of the form, Martial, as well as one from Ausonius; there are several from Petrarch in the fourteenth century, one each from Rabelais and Buchanan in the sixteenth century, and many others from German, French, and especially Italian poets of the eighteenth, nineteenth, and twentieth centuries. One might well ask: Why are so many epigrams by so many other poets woven into the fabric of this volume, presented as part of a century of poems by Fred Chappell?

I think the answer has to do with the nature of the epigram and of epigrammatists. The epigram itself is a paradoxical form: it is topical, often provoked by a specific person or event, yet timeless, transcending the particulars of whatever triggered it and staying fresh for millenia. It is personal, dealing directly with the poet's experiences, and yet anonymous: it almost doesn't matter who the author of an epigram is—if it's a good one, it could apply to pretty much anyone, anywhere, at any time. For that reason, epigrammatists form a unique literary community, one that crosses the boundaries of schools and movements and centuries. They are keen-eyed, sharp-tongued observers of human comedy and folly; they tend to be conservative (or, more accurately, traditional) and cynical (though often romantic at heart); they take the long view of things; and, because they write what Lewis Turco called "terse verse with a cutting edge," with a limited range of technical options, their epigrams often sound somewhat alike, even if written centuries apart.

And so it actually makes perfect sense that Chappell would include so many epigrammatic brethren in his own book, or that he would rewrite a well-known epigram of the seventeenth century which was itself a version of a Martial poem, and call it **"The Truth at Last"**: "I do not love thee, Dr. Fell; / The reason why I'm going to tell / Although your lawyers threaten suit. / For I'm too sick to give a hoot" (*C* 17). An epigram is part of an ongoing literary conversation, an exchange of quick minds and pens, where the point is not the individual who wrote the poem as is often the case in late twentieth-century critical studies) but rather the truth and pithy eloquence of what's said. In that case, why not include poems by others that say something you admire, something you wish you'd said (and did say, somewhat, as translator), something that fits well with the original epigrams you have written?

V

Besides the Greek and Roman poets, and English masters of the form like Ben Jonson, Robert Herrick, and Walter Savage Landor, there is a less familiar epigrammatic tradition in this century, one that the well-read Professor Chappell is surely familiar with. Many modern and contemporary poets have tried their hand at epigrams, but the single name most associated with that

form in recent times is J. V. Cunningham, who lived from 1911 to 1985. He published six slim volumes featuring "short poems terminating in a point," as Dr. Johnson defined the form, experimenting with different ways of presenting those verses, finally settling—in the penultimate section of his 1971 *Collected Poems and Epigrams*—on a grouping called "A Century of Epigrams." Like Fred Chappell (F. C.), here is another C-poet (J. V. C.) collecting one hundred (C) poems.

But the similarities pretty much end there. Cunningham, for example, did do translations of some of the Roman epigrammatists, but he gathered them separately, in the final section of his *Collected Poems,* called "Latin Lines." And his own epigrams are very different from *C.* They tend to be shorter, averaging just over four lines each, the shortest a couplet, the longest only fifteen lines; Chappell's are fifty percent longer, averaging over six lines apiece, with the shortest a single line and the longest twenty-eight. And though they do treat some of the same subjects, like love—as in one of Cunningham's most famous poems, "Naked I came, naked I leave the scene, / And naked was my pastime in between" (*CPE* [*Collected Poems and Epigrams*] 48), which could have been written by Martial or Chappell—the tone of the two centuries of epigrams is quite different. Cunningham's are more Latinate, abstract, aloof, and chilly, if not downright dour and sour and sad, like distilled Philip Larkin. And their speaker is much more haunted by mortality, time's passage, darkness, death: he may declare, in an Ole Fred-like credo, "I like the trivial, vulgar, and exalted" (120), but in the end he is an isolated and somewhat desperate figure, saying, "Drink is my only medication / And loneliness my defence" (126). Cunningham's epigrams may be more classically classical than Chappell's more intensely chiseled, but they also seem less human somehow, less accessible and fun to read.

VI

Not that *C* is not classical! Far from it. Its title is, obviously, Roman, and four of its first five poems invoke or translate Latin and Greek masters. The opening epigram is called **"Proem"**:

> In such a book as this,
> The poet Martial says,
> Some of the epigrams
> Shall have seen better days,
> And some are hit-or-miss;
> But some—like telegrams—
> Deliver intelligence
> With such a sudden blaze
> The shine can make us wince.
>
> (*C* 1)

The epigram has always been a reflexive form, defining itself as it's being written: here, the author offers—if not definition—images for his epigrams. They are "like telegrams," terse messages delivered suddenly; they are like a flashlight or blinding flame, "a sudden blaze [whose] shine can make us wince" at their illuminations; and they deliver not wisecracks, not editorials, not passionate effusions, but "intelligence," both in the sense of knowledge and of secret information brought to light.

Having aligned himself with Martial and others in this opening fanfare of five epigrams, the distinctive voice of Ole Fred emerges in number six, a **"Rejoinder"** to the preceding poem, in which Martial listed "the things [fertile farm, good meals, faithful wife, etc.] that make life blest." "Now let's even up the score," Fred begins,

> And tell what things make life a bore:
> Sappy girls who kiss and tell;
> Televangelists's threats of hell;
> Whining chain saws, mating cats;
> Republicans; and Democrats;
> Expertly tearful on their knees,
> Plushlined senators copping pleas,
> Swearing by the Rocks of Ages
> That they did not molest their pages;
> Insurance forms and tax reports;
> Flabby jokes and lame retorts;
> Do-gooders, jocks, and feminists;
> Poems that are merely lists.
>
> (3)

In a way, this is the book's true overture, introducing many of the subjects treated in the subsequent epigrams—sex, religion, politics, and so on—as well as the gently self-deprecatory tone underlying the book. But it may also be somewhat misleading. *C* is not a book that relentlessly proceeds from topic to topic, deflating all the "things that make life a bore." One of its very human strengths, I think, is not just a range of topics but a range of tone, which is immediately evident in the following poem, the seventh, called **"Aubade,"** a tender morning love song addressed to Susan, two pentameter sestets with a much softer rhyme scheme than the preceding clipped tetrameter couplets. The speaker is gentle, inviting his wife to wake up and walk with him around the lake enjoying nature—which is exactly what he does in the following three epigrams, taking on the voices of flora and fauna. The imagistic daisy says, "Men build Parises and Zions; / I, wide meadows of Orions. / Rome took two thousand years, but in one day / I built a Milky Way" (5); the chipmunk says, with haiku-like quickness, "Don't blink, or / I'm gone, / Slow thinker" (5). These poems do introduce patterns or motifs—there is a **"Serenade"** toward the end of the book, to match the early **"Aubade,"** and there are three other substantial groupings of quietly amazing nature epigrams—but they also serve to make clear, early on, that *C* will not just be a book of "marble verses," satirical and incisive, but will display a more sympathetic imagination toward "the things that make life blest."

Not that there won't be plenty of satire in these epigrams, as demonstrated in the following two poems, **"Epitaph: The Poet"** ("I never truckled. / I never pandered. / I was born / To be remaindered.") and **"Epitaph: The Reprobate"** (6). The presence of these and several later epitaphs in *C* reminds us of one of the origins of the epigram, which at root means "inscription": literally, words carved into artifacts or votive offerings or headstones. It should also remind Chappell scholars of his earlier forays into the epitaph mode, which may have served as a warmup for this book. In chapter seven of the novel *I Am One of You Forever* (1985), "The Maker of One Coffin," young Jess goes out with his sepulchral Uncle Runkin to a local graveyard, where they discover and critique the epitaphs while looking for one good enough to go on his uncle's coffin lid. And in **"At the Grave of Virgil Campbell,"** late in *Midquest,* "half-smashed" Ole Fred invents some epitaphs for his late friend (like "HERE'S THE FIRST TIME IT WAS SAID / THAT VIRGIL CAMPBELL WAS GRAVELY LAID" or "EARTH, RECEIVE / YOUR PLAYFUL LOVER / TO HIS ONE SLEEP / WITH NO HANGOVER") and even a few for himself, including "HERE LIES FRED / IN HIS MOSS-GROWN MANSE. / IF HE'S NOT DEAD, / HE'S MISSING A DAMN GOOD CHANCE" (*M* 168).

Every epitaph may not be an epigram, but—in a way—every epigram is an epitaph, especially the satirical ones that sum up and dispatch a character: they are the last word, figuratively if not literally. With a few exceptions, the next twenty epigrams in *C*—numbers 13 through 32—are just such poems, skewering intellectuals, novelists, poets (including the author himself), literary critics, editors, and televangelists. One of the tests of a good epigram is its memorability, and these are among the most memorable poems in the book:

Upon a Confessional Poet

You've shown us all in stark undress
The sins you needed to confess.
If my peccadilloes were so small
I never would undress at all.

(*C* 7)

Literary Critic

Blandword died, and now his ghost
Drifts gray through lobby, office, hall.
Some mourn diminished presence; most
Can find no difference at all.

(10)

Televangelist

He claims that he'll reign equally
With Jesus in eternity.
But it's not like him to be willing
To give a partner equal billing.

(13)

What do all these little satires have in common? A hatred of pretentiousness, self-importance, self-indulgence, self-righteousness: the same things that have provoked poets into stinging epigrams for millenia.

VII

One thing you can say for Fred Chappell: he is not predictable. Every new book of poetry is a surprise, a conceptual departure from preceding books, a challenge to himself and his readers. In *C*, he incorporates that poetic variety into a single volume. Just when it seems he has settled into an entertaining satirical mode, lasering all the human folly around him, he goes in another direction altogether. Epigrams 33 through 35 are, in fact, prayers, blessings, **"Grace before Meat"**: "As this noon our meat we carve, / Bless us better than we deserve" (14). The last one is a bit Ogden-Nash-esque ("Bless our cone pones, Lord. But let us dream / They might be black currant muffins with strawberry jam and clotted double Devon cream" [14]), but the shift of tone from satire to blessing is genuine and swift and deliberate.

Though there's no need to be pedantic and map every subsequent shift in the book, this is in fact how its geography unfolds: satirical peaks, lyrical valleys (often nature poems), and a quietly articulated middle ground (often love poems) that can be remarkably powerful, like this one:

I Love You

Yet you were gone six days before
I took from the bedroom closet the dress,
The blue and white one that you wore
To that dinner party that was such a mess,
And fearfully hung it on the door
And sat before it in a chair,
Remembering what and when and where,
And touched it with a ghost's caress.

(27)

This picture of loss and regret and fear couldn't be farther from the swift caricature of a biting epitaph: it is in fact a subtle and complex portrait, the most hauntingly delicate of elegies.

VIII

I mentioned political epigrams in *C*, but will quote only one—an unexpectedly timely poem, about Jesse Helms, called

El Perfecto

Senator No sets out as referee
Of everything we read and think and see.
His justification for such stiff decreeing
Is being born a perfect human being

Without a jot of blemish, taint, or flaw,
The Dixie embodiment of Moral Law,
Quite fit and eager to pursue the quarrel
With God Whose handiwork he finds immoral.

(23)

Given recent arts-council funding controversies, how ironic that these lines should appear in a volume with this sentence at the front: "Publication of this book has been supported by a grant from the National Endowment for the Arts in Washington, D.C., a federal agency."

IX

At the heart of *C* is a series of poems about women and love, numbers 49 through 64—some bawdy, some delicate, some playful, like **"A Glorious Twilight,"** where "Susan is painting her nails / such a brilliant shade of bright / she seems to have sprouted 22 fingers . . . Be careful, I said, waving your phalanges about! / You're gonna burn the house down" (29). This deliberately central placement of such poems recalls *Midquest,* which Chappell called "in its largest designs a love poem" (*M* xi), a book where the opening, closing, and (usually) central poem of each section was centered on Susan. She is his Beatrice, his Eve, his muse, no less in *C* than in *Midquest* (or other books). Though "love" is not a word often associated with epigrams, at least in a non-ironic way, that's one thing that distinguishes *C* from other such collections: I think it may very well be, in its largest designs, a love poem. The epigrams at the end of the book move toward winter, toward darkness, toward night; but they also move toward home, the locus of love, where (in **"Serenade"**) the poet cozily invites, "Let's stay at home tonight and build a fire" (*C* 46).

X

Whenever someone asks me why today's poetry doesn't rhyme and isn't funny anymore, I reach for a book by Fred Chappell. Any book, really; because from the beginning, he has been a formal and a comic virtuoso, writing poems that are technically dazzling and often hilarious. That's also what a good epigrammatist must do, and that's just what he does in *C*.

Chappell has always been a subversive formalist, though, and he continues that mischievousness in this volume. He certainly writes plenty of epigrams in traditional couplets or quatrains, but he also enjoys tweaking the formal conventions, experimenting with free-verse epigrams; linked epigrams (often paired, though sometimes in larger groupings, as with **"Literary Critic"** and the six poems following it titled **"Another"**); and even one-line epigrams, like numbers 66 and 67, his abbreviated version of Pope's "Essay on Man":

Definition

The only animal that dares to play the bagpipes.

Corollary

Or wants to.

(32)

And in a nice combination of two ancient poetic forms, he writes three riddle-epigrams, including this one:

> However still and dark the night
> For the soldier it is light;
> When the silent stars abound
> For the guiltless it is sound;
> While days and nights their vigils keep
> In the graveyard it is deep.
>
> *(sleep)*

(43)

Chappell is always pushing the formal envelope, even as he honors it

And though he can certainly write powerful serious poems, Chappell's impulse has always been comic, toward verse that is genuinely funny if rarely "light." Epigrams suit his nature perfectly: they make a point but also make us laugh, like well-told and well-timed jokes. But their humor shouldn't be mistaken for superficiality, or their brevity for lack of effort on the poet's part; as Fred himself once said, "Comedy is much more serious than tragedy. . . . It says more about the conditions of people, the way people live day to day. Tragedy is wonderful, but the tragic view is sometimes too easy" (*PM* ["Interview with Fred Chappell," *Pembroke Magazine* 17] 133). Or as he writes in **"Stand-up Comic,"**

> Grimacing, sweating, he shrieks obscenities,
>   Bellows his punch lines again and again,
> Until we ask ourselves what kind of mirth
>   Could cause a man such tearing pain.
>
> (*C* 38)

This may be a portrait of Lenny Bruce or Eddie Murphy; but is it not also an exaggerated picture of the epigrammatist himself, the anger and painful effort beneath his mirth, Ole Fred's wild punch behind Professor Chappell's polished lines?

XI

C ends quietly. After the homey **"Serenade,"** there are three straightforward reverential **"Bedtime Prayers,"** balancing the three graces-before-meat said earlier. Poems 94 through 97 reprise the nature epigrams, with the natural world now entering winter darkness. The last three poems are valedictions: 98 is a generous farewell **"To Old Age,"** 99 is a feisty **"Apology"** or defense for *C* itself—

> If any line I've scribbled here
> Has caused a politician shame
> Or brought a quack a troubled night
> Or given a critic a twinge of fear
> Or made a poet's fame appear
> Transitory as candleflame,
> Why then, I gladly sign my name:
> Maybe I did something right.

(51)

—and, finally, number 100 finishes off book, poet, and tradition in only two lines, titled **"The Epigrammatist"**: "Mankind perishes. The world goes dark. / He racks his brain for a tart remark" (52). How appropriate, that the book should end where it began, with an epigram about epigrams, those "tart remarks" that can (as the first poem said) "deliver intelligence / With such a sudden blaze / The shine can make us wince."

Chappell called **Midquest,** in his preface to that book, "to some degree a reactionary work" (*M* x). It reacted against the prevailing poetic mode of "the brilliant autobiographical lyric" not only in its epic length, but also by developing "qualities sometimes lacking in the larger body of contemporary poetry: detachment, social scope, humor, portrayal of character and background, discursiveness, wide range of subject matter." I would like to suggest that *C* does exactly the same thing, in exactly the opposite direction: instead of developing these unfashionable qualities at length, in a "verse novel," he develops them (with the obvious exception of "discursiveness") in brief, in epigrams that—no less than **Midquest**—cultivate detachment, social scope, humor, portrayal of character and background, and a wide range of subject matter. And there's a beautiful irony to this reactionary decision: though *C* could not be more different from the typical book of contemporary poetry, it probably has a much better chance of being read and understood and enjoyed by the general public, whose appetite for poetry may have been dulled by generations of sober uninviting autobiographical lyrics, but who can still remember and quote light-verse epigrams by Dorothy Parker or Ogden Nash. I would like to think, quoting Chappell himself—current Poet Laureate of North Carolina, the state's most public poetic figure—and simply substituting the title *C* for **Midquest,** "that a reader may find *C* accessible and amusing even in its imperfections, and that some solace may be taken from it" (xi).

XII

One last point about the epigrammatical Fred Chappell. Yes, *C* was his magnum opus in this mode, but it wasn't his last word on epigrams. The book that followed two years later—**Spring Garden: New and Selected Poems** (1995)—reconfigured his poetic output in an intricate botanical and thematic manner, with sections on "The Good Life" and "The Garden of Love," or "Poems of

Character" and "Poems of Fantasy." The one section defined by its form, though, was "Epigrams," fifteen poems from two to twenty lines long, a dozen of them from *C* (*SG* [*Spring Garden*] 117-125). A dozen others from *C* were scattered throughout the other sections of **Spring Garden,** and five epigrams were brand-new.

This suggests several things to me. One is the centrality of epigrams to Chappell's vision of his entire poetic output; the other is that he's not done with epigrams yet. Way back at the beginning of **Midquest**—in the volume **River,** in 1975—he wrote,

> On paper I scribble mottoes and epigrams,
> Blessings and epithets, O-Holy's and Damn's—
>
> Not matter sufficient to guard a week by.
> The wisdom I hoard you could stuff in your eye.
>
> But *everything* means *something,* that's my faith;
> Despair begins when they stop my mouth.

> (*M* 4)

Those couplets were originally written about a quarter of a century ago. In them you can hear Ole Fred, with his epithets and throw-aways; in them you can hear Professor Chappell, who believes "*everything* means *something*"; and in them you definitely hear Fred Chappell the writer, who embodies both, who knows that he must keep scribbling because—as any writer would agree—"Despair begins when they stop my mouth." Obviously, no one can predict where Chappell's words will take him in future books of poetry, but I think the epigrammatical urge is a powerful one in him, and has been for many decades, and will continue to manifest itself well into MM, the next millenium.

Works Cited

Chappell, Fred. *C.* Baton Rouge: Louisiana State UP, 1993.

———. *Midquest.* Baton Rouge: Louisiana State UP, 1981.

———. *Spring Garden: New and Selected Poems.* Baton Rouge: Louisiana State UP, 1995.

Cunningham, J. V. *Collected Poems and Epigrams.* London: Faber and Faber, 1971.

Ruffin, Paul. "Interview with Fred Chappell." *Pembrok Magazine* 17 (1985): 131-135.

George Hovis (essay date summer 2000)

SOURCE: Hovis, George. "'When You Got True Dirt You Got Everything You Need': Forging an Appalachian Arcadia in Fred Chappell's *Midquest.*" *Mississippi Quarterly* 53, no. 3 (summer 2000): 389-414.

[*In the following essay, Hovis characterizes the purpose of Chappell's literary output—taking the body of work in its entirety, but most especially in* Midquest—*as an attempt to reconnect in an authentic way with his family's agrarian Appalachian past.*]

In his essay "The Poet and the Plowman," Fred Chappell ponders what he considers to be one of the fundamental issues facing poets ever since the classical age: the fact that it is impractical, if not impossible, to pursue both a life of poetry and a life of farming. As the essay begins, Chappell recalls long Sunday afternoons in the mid 1960s when he and his guest Allen Tate (who was then guest lecturing at the University of North Carolina at Greensboro) would watch TV football and bemoan the disappearance of their Latin skills, along with the diminishing allure of the "traditional attractions of farm life." [1] Chappell recalls Tate's conclusion that poets should be only "spectator farmers": "Then he would smile and say in his breathy ironic genteel Kentucky accent: 'But we would make dreadful farmers, Fred, you and I'" (p. 73). In Chappell's portrait of the aging Agrarian, Tate comes off unmistakably more comfortable in his resignation than does Chappell himself, who goes on restlessly to ponder the age-old kinship between the poet—or, more generally, the writer—and the plowman.

In much of Chappell's diverse oeuvre—which includes more than twenty books of poetry, fiction, and criticism—one finds a preoccupation with the farming life Chappell chose to leave. The themes of exile from his Appalachian past and the struggle to reforge, through poetry, a unity with that past are perhaps most clearly presented in what many consider the pinnacle of Chappell's career, the Bollingen Prize-winning long poem **Midquest** (1981). Though originally published separately as **River** (1975), **Bloodfire** (1978), **Wind Mountain** (1979), and **Earthsleep** (1980), the four volumes of **Midquest** were conceived as integral parts of a whole. Their achievement is made even more momentous by the fact that they compose half of an octave, completed by the four acclaimed novels in the Kirkman Quartet. [2] Both quartets involve the reminiscences of a middle-aged poet about his childhood on an Appalachian farm, a past he idealizes—in typical pastoral fashion—as a long-lost golden age, accessible now only through the imagination.

In the Preface to **Midquest,** Chappell describes the poem's semi-autobiographical "protagonist," Ole Fred, as a "demographic sample" of the twentieth century: "He was reared on a farm but has moved to the city; he has deserted manual for intellectual labor, is 'upwardly mobile'; he is cut off from his disappearing cultural traditions but finds them, in remembering, his real values."[3] This contrast between an ideal agrarian childhood and a corrupted urban age is one of the principal hallmarks of pastoral, which, as Frank Kermode notes, is always "an urban product."[4] Kermode observes that the "first condition of pastoral . . . is that there should be a sharp difference between two ways of life, the rustic and the urban. The city is an artificial product, and the pastoral poet invariably lives in it, or is the product of its schools and universities" (p. 14). Kermode's description fits Chappell, as well as "Ole Fred," whose idiom alternates between that of a learned poet and Appalachian vernacular.

Born in 1936 and reared on a farm near the mill town of Canton, North Carolina, Chappell grew up observing the remnants of a traditional culture. The "loud, smoky, noisome" Champion Paper and Fiber Company[5] is a ubiquitous presence in Chappell's pastorals, as is the figure of the farmer father tenaciously scratching out a living from the soil, and the dreamy adolescent boy destined to leave the farm for the Piedmont cities of Durham and Greensboro. The world Chappell describes is one very much in flux, which makes his recollections of childhood appear all the more valued. Kermode has noted that pastoral "flourishes at a particular moment in the urban development, the phase in which the relationship of metropolis and country is still evident, and there are no children (as there are now) who have never seen a cow" (p. 15). This precondition for pastoral sounds very like the necessity of the "backward glance" to the Southern literary renascence, or, more generally, to the experience of modernism. In each case, the artist has witnessed the disappearance of the old verities, an experience that leaves him dislocated, alienated, full of epistemological uncertainty, and longing for some touchstone of truth by which to reorient himself.

Chappell's geographical exile from Appalachia to the Piedmont cities of Durham and Greensboro has been further exacerbated by the fact that he is an extremely cultivated scholar who has pursued more than a casual interest in a variety of national literatures, translating writings from a variety of languages, writing a substantial body of criticism on poetry from outside his native region, and inevitably coming to see his native land through such an ecumenical vision. He has named Faulkner, Eliot, Pound, and Joyce among the important models especially of his earlier writing, and, like these and other great writers of the high modernist period, Chappell has responded to his loss of a traditional culture by reconstructing the raw materials in forms borrowed from both within and without the culture. *Midquest* is full of folk tales, jokes, and convincing accounts of farm life, and at the same time it abounds in literary allusions. It is a poem that consistently seeks subtly to situate local dramas in relation to the artistic, philosophical, and scientific touchstones of western

discourse, relying on sources as diverse as Plato, subatomic theory, and Louis Armstrong. The verse forms are as varied as terza rima, blank verse, Old English ode, syllabics, classical hexameter, Yeatsian tetrameter, rhymed couplets, and chant royal. Chappell humbly compares *Midquest* to "that elder American art form, the sampler [or quilt], each form standing for a different fancy stitch" (p. ix). Chappell's style conflates examples of high and low cultures and derives a high lyricism from a rural Appalachian vernacular, a strategy that both ennobles the rural subject matter and concretely locates the lyrical expression.

Many readers have noted what Michael McFee calls Chappell's "split literary personality." "On the one side," McFee explains,

> we have "Ole Fred," the kind of persona readers tend to remember, a character of extreme Romantic temperament and habits. Ole Fred is feisty; he cusses, he jokes, he drinks, he misbehaves; he is cheerfully politically incorrect; he overstates and exaggerates. . . . On the other side . . . is Professor Chappell, a neo-classical polymath of the first order, deeply and widely read, profoundly learned: a genuine scholar.[6]

This split literary persona arguably reflects an actual "split" within the writer, who understands himself and his world by means of two divided cultures, one belonging to his present life in the academy, and the other to his childhood on the Appalachian farm of his ancestors. In its largest design, *Midquest* attempts to heal this schism and restore a sense of wholeness by employing the breadth of the poet's learning to recreate the world of his childhood.

Following the model of Dante's *Divine Comedy*, each of the four volumes begins with Ole Fred awakening on his thirty-fifth birthday in a state of spiritual longing. Of the eleven poems that compose each volume, most take the form of dialogues with family members remembered from the poet's childhood. These recollections serve as a source of inspiration and direction for Ole Fred, who at mid-life finds himself disenchanted with his suburban existence. In **"Birthday 35: Diary Entry,"** the second poem in the first volume, Ole Fred pessimistically considers—from the comfort of his living room—the results of his life's work:

> On paper I scribble mottoes and epigrams,
> Blessings and epithets, O-Holy's and Damn's—
>
> Not matter sufficient to guard a week by.
> The wisdom I hoard you could stuff in your eye.
>
> (p. 4)

The heroic couplets enhance the comic deflation of his vocational crisis. Throughout the poem Ole Fred employs humor to shield himself from raw feelings of despair and loss, as well as from the fear that the spiritual restoration for which he yearns is no longer available.

Like the Wordsworth of the "Intimations" ode, Ole Fred is a poet who romantically longs for the transcendental inspiration of his boyhood but, doubting its availability, is willing to confront the reality of his present alienation:

> I'd like to believe anything is possible.
> That I could walk out on a midnight full
>
> Of stars and hear an omniscient Voice say,
> "Well, Fred, for a change you had a good day.
>
> You didn't do anything so terribly awful.
> Even your thoughts were mostly lawful.
>
> I'm pleased."—Or that by accident I'd find
> A tablet headed, *Carry this message to mankind.*
>
> But nothing like that is in the cards.
> Bit by scroungy bit knowledge affords
> Itself; . . .
>
> (p. 6)

Ole Fred pokes fun at his juvenile hopes that he would be *chosen* like Moses as a prophet. Inspiration comes to the now more mature poet not through flashes of "genius" or from the voice of a divine muse, but through hard work and careful observation, "bit by scroungy bit," by subjugating the self to an empirical world stingy with its revelations. For Chappell, however, the empirical world is, indeed, available to the patient, attentive observer. Furthermore, it can be described or captured in language. In a recent interview, he stated his unequivocal objection to the skepticism of poststructuralists, who insist that there is an immitigable rift between language and the empirical world:

> That's too easy, and . . . it refutes itself. If language cannot make a statement about the nature of reality that has any genuineness, then that defeats itself, because that's a statement and it's made of language, and it's just another statement. So, a blind dead end. Also it's just clearly demonstrable that this is not the case. We communicate with language. Mathematics is language. There is no communication we have without language. We don't know if we can even think without language. And it's obvious that we have changed the world in a thousand trillion different ways because we had ideas about it, because we formulated our ideas in language, set these down on paper at the time when we had paper or otherwise remembered and used this memory embedded in language to build pyramids, to fashion spears, to make rocket ships, vaccines. . . . So I just think that it's a crock. If one tried to imagine a universe in which this poststructuralist notion really applied, it's very strange, what Leibnitz might call a "monadic," existence, where one is self-enclosed entirely and impinged upon by objects, by reality, rather than engaging with it. There's something predictably defeatist in that kind of thinking. But we have a superstition that the gloomiest philosophy, the most violent actions, are the more genuine. And that's sophomoric.[7]

In this same interview, Chappell distances himself from his own early fiction, in which the mind is depicted as

what might, in fact, be called "monadic." For example, in his first novel, *It Is Time, Lord* (1963), the protagonist James Christopher describes the mind as "an isolated citadel standing in a desert . . . peopled only with thin ghosts."[8] This Eliotic novel presents a montage of fragmented childhood memories interspersed with scenes from James Christopher's current troubled life. Chappell's first novel is easily his most postmodern: it is impossible to recover from these fragments an underlying narrative of the past that would help to explain the present. Memory is corrupted by the present moment, just as the present is corrupted by memory. James Christopher describes the past as "an eternally current danger, in effect, a suicide. We desire the past, we call to it just as men who have fallen overboard an ocean liner call. . . . [I]t sours and rots like old meat in the mind" (pp. 34-35). An Appalachian Quentin Compson, James Christopher feels trapped by his familial and cultural past. In order to avoid Quentin's fate, he finds that he must repress childhood memories and live in the present.

Though James Christopher's family (especially his father) resembles that of Ole Fred and of Jess Kirkman of the Kirkman quartet, the attitudes of the later protagonists toward a familial past vary considerably from James Christopher's. The past is no longer a "suicide," but, rather, an antidote for the aridity of modern existence, a touchstone by which the poet finds meaning to live in the present. Furthermore, this changed relation to the past creates a more hopeful attitude about the relation of the individual mind to the empirical world. In contrast to James Christopher's description of the mind as "an isolated citadel standing in a desert" (p. 35), wasteland imagery appears in **"Birthday 35,"** not as an immitigable fate but, rather, as a spiritual condition to be avoided through a consistent effort to escape the prison of the isolated self:

> A wilderness of wind and ash.
>
> When I went to the river . . .
>
> I saw, darkened, my own face.
>
> On the bank of Time I saw nothing human,
>
> . . . only moon
> Upon moon, sterile stone
>
> Climbing the steep hill of void.
> And I was afraid.
>
> (p. 7)

This sterile landscape is characterized by dryness and uniformity; except for the reflection of Ole Fred's own face, the scene is drearily monotonous. He obviously fears his own tendency toward solipsism and the possibility that, as in the case of James Christopher, the world he observes or remembers is merely a projection of his own subconscious.

These lines clearly echo the language from the final section of *The Waste Land*: "Here is no water but only rock / Rock and no water and the sandy road."[9] Chappell's reaction to the dilemma is a parody of Eliot's climactic prayer, with Ole Fred praying for transcendence in the form of "Elysium . . . plentifully planted / With trout streams and waterfalls and suburban / Swimming pools, and sufficient chaser for bourbon" (p. 8). In characteristic fashion, he switches back and forth between adolescent cheekiness and heartfelt sincerity; these lines are immediately followed by a shift in tone from cynicism to reverential pleading. Note also that the suburban references are absent from the concluding lines:

> Lead me then, Lord, to the thundering valleys where
> Cool silver droplets feather the air;
>
> Where rain like thimbles smacks roofs of tin,
> Washing away sin;
>
> Where daily a vast and wholesome cloud
> Announces itself aloud.
>
>   Amen.
>
>   (p. 8)

The wasteland imagery in **"Birthday 35"** evokes Ole Fred's spiritual estrangement and draws a distinction, in typical pastoral fashion, between the emptiness of his present urban/suburban condition and the spiritual sustenance to be found in a long-past rural Golden Age.

The prayer for cleansing and quenching that ends **"Birthday 35"** is provisionally answered in the following poem, **"My Grandmother Washes Her Feet,"** a dramatic dialogue in which, while washing her feet, the grandmother lectures the boy Fred about the dangers of pretension and the unrecognized history of his family's less respectable side, which she accepts as family despite what mainstream society might see as undesirable idiosyncrasies. Again, intellectual pursuits occupy an antagonistic position to the farming life, as indicated in the grandmother's warning to the boy:

> You're bookish. I can see you easy a lawyer
> Or a county clerk in a big white suit and tie,
> Feeding the preacher and bribing the sheriff and the
>   judge.
> Second-generation-respectable
> Don't come to any better destiny.
> But it's dirt you rose from, dirt you'll bury in.
> Just about the time you'll think your blood
> Is clean, here will come dirt in a natural shape
> You never dreamed. . . .

> . . . When you got true dirt, you got
> Everything you need . . .
>
>   (p. 12)

The shift in consciousness that occurs from **"Birthday 35"** to the following **"My Grandmother Washes her Feet"**—from a jaded scholar, listening to himself pontificate in the prison of his suburban living room, to the mostly passive and humble boy auditor, receptive to the wisdom of another—reveals the strategy Chappell will employ in many of the following poems. He will consistently seek to escape self-absorption and alienation, which he identifies as the problem of his age, and make contact with a concrete and authentic world, evoked by the refrain of "dirt" throughout this poem.

Dirt here has multiple connotations: the basis of agriculture and the source of all life; a symbol for the cycle of life and death; and a representation of the eternal and substantial versus the ephemeral and superficial. *Dirt* also contains the Biblical allusions to the creation of Adam, as well as Original Sin. The latter ironically is changed by the pious grandmother into a positive attribute of the human condition, reminding us of our common proclivities to error, and thereby requiring one to assume a humility that acknowledges one's common humanity, a basic component of the ancient pastoral myths, which, as Kermode notes, portray the people of a Golden Age in their natural states as "hedonistic and sinless, though wanton" (p. 43). The grandmother's list of cousins in their "natural" states includes drunks, womanizers, a "Jackleg" preacher, and a great aunt named Paregoric Annie who would beg for drug-money by removing her glass eye and asking for assistance in replacing it. Fred idealizes these cousins as still vitally connected to the earth through farming, and thereby exempt from the fallen state and subsequent need for salvation attributed to civilized humanity. Fred longs to forge a lost connection to this extended family that the grandmother and her generation took for granted. In an effort to better visualize these shadow cousins he has never met, the boy Fred shapes their earthen effigies from the mud that soaks up his grandmother's footbath water. The adult Fred concludes the poem dejectedly, contemplating the economic necessity that forced his father to give up farming, then comparing himself unfavorably to his imagined cousins: "I never had the grit to stir those guts. / I never had the guts to stir that earth" (p. 13). The reciprocal substitution of the terms "grit," or its synonym "earth," with "guts" in these lines equates the terms syntactically and thereby conflates their meanings, an effect enhanced by the consonance in "grit" and "guts."

This same tendency to ennoble mountain folk by equating them physically with the land itself is found in *Brighten the Corner Where You Are* when Joe Robert is visited by Pruitt and Ginny Dorson, an extremely rural couple whom he characterizes as "silent farm folk from the genuine old-time mountain stock. . . . Salt of the earth: That was the common phrase for families like the Dorsons, but my father considered that it was all too common. Soul of the earth, he thought, earth's own earth" (p. 56). The purest expression of Chappell's longing for a complete reunification with his Appalachian heritage is found in his desire to be one with the earth itself, which Jess Kirkman symbolically achieves at the end of *Look Back All the Green Valley* (also the culmination of the entire octave), when he finds himself on a rainy night covered in the mud of his father's grave.

The Dorsons, Fred's "shadow cousins," the "dirt poor" as Fred's grandmother calls them (p. 12), and all the other "genuine old-time mountain" folk in Chappell's narratives figure the same way that shepherds figure in traditional pastoral poetry, as a liaison between the pure and simple world of Nature and the complicated and impure urban world of the pastoral poet. As J. E. Congleton explains, "The shepherd, actually, is half man and half Nature; he has enough in common with man to be his universal representative and has enough in common with Nature to be at one with it. Because the shepherd is so close to Nature, man, through him, can become united with Nature and consequently feel that he is a harmonious part of the whole and that his ideas are reconciled with the fundamental truths."[10] Through a study of his Appalachian "shepherds," Chappell similarly hopes to overcome his geographic and spiritual estrangement and get in touch with the simple, the concrete, what he feels to be his own essential nature.

The error of leaving the farm and forgetting one's birthright of "dirt" involves perhaps the dominant theme of *Midquest*: the loss of the concrete world through a process of abstraction. *Dirt* represents here the empirical world, unornamented by the imagination; this is Stevens's "things as they are," that most elusive of quantities, because the imagination, as Stevens and other modernists discovered, is hardly capable of registering sensory experience without resorting to metaphor and comparisons or even prefabricated formulae. The epistemological anxiety associated with language's inevitable process of abstracting concrete existence is, of course, not a problem new to the twentieth-century modernists. Kermode argues that the "great seventeenth-century war of Ancients and Moderns was really fought on divergent interpretations of Imitation, in the widest sense of the term" (p. 24), considering "Imitation" as the relation of art to its tradition and the extent to which working within such a tradition facilitates or hinders the writer's ability to describe faithfully the natural world. Kermode notes that in pastoral the ubiquitous opposition between town and

country always serves to suggest the more general opposition between Art and Nature, and that though this opposition is integral to all literary genres, nowhere is it "so evident and acute as in Pastoral" (p. 12). Pastoral promises a reunification with Nature by means of considering human culture at its most basic level, and yet, as Kermode observes, the challenge to the pastoral poet is to avoid merely an inauthentic imitation of established conventions. This challenge is one familiar to any reader of Southern literature. Just as the earlier pastorals often tended toward derivative accounts of shepherds and nymphs, Southern writers have felt the temptation toward predictable representations of pastoral types: the pure and virtuous belle, the noble colonel-father, the faithful Negro retainer, the hillbilly farmer.

In *Midquest* Chappell frequently calls attention to this problem, as in the poem **"Firewater,"** in which the boy Fred listens to his father and his father's drinking buddy Virgil Campbell as they lament the passing of the old ways and of the genuine Appalachian farmers. What their dialogue makes obvious to the reader is the difficulty of representing a "genuine" Appalachian farmer—as well as how the label itself implies a level of self-consciousness in which the organic and traditional have been extracted from their living medium to be displayed for their picturesque value. Virgil begins the poem by describing his recent visit to rural Clay County—where some of his backwater cousins live—for the purpose of watching their centennial celebration. The festival's main attraction was the "Grand Parade, / Celebrating their most famous products" (p. 78), with moonshine topping the list. In an effort to celebrate their culture, the local officials have traveled up Standing Indian Mountain to invite Big Mama and her family (whom they have been trying to prosecute for ten years) to "build a model still" and "waltz it down Main Street in broad daylight" (p. 79). The plan backfires during the middle of the parade when a mule following behind Big Mama's float staggers and then collapses, "Drunk as an owl, / Just from breathing the smoke that was pouring out / From Big Mama's *model* still" (p. 79). A deputy attempts to make an arrest, but "smiling so the crowd would think / It was part of the act" (p. 80), at which point

> Big Mama's boys stood up—
> Wearing phony beards, barefoot with beat-up hats,
> Just like the hillbillies in the funny papers—
> And threw down on the deputy three shotguns.
> Whether they were loaded I don't know.
> He didn't know. Except Big Mama's bunch
> *Nobody* knew.
>
> (p. 80)

The use of disguises here serves as a metafictional device, calling our attention to the stereotype and thus forcing us to guess at the authentic identity we are incapable of witnessing. These are the pastoral's real shepherds wearing shepherd masks. As Houston Baker notes of the minstrel mask and its adoption by black speakers during the Jim Crow era,[11] Big Mama's boys assume their hillbilly disguises as a means of protecting their genuine identities. That they alone know whether their guns are loaded further suggests their control over their own identity and culture and thereby invalidates Virgil and J. T.'s nostalgic lament of cultural erosion.

Throughout *Midquest,* Chappell faces the challenge of accurately describing Appalachian culture without self-consciously doing so. Of *I Am One of You Forever* Fred Hobson has noted a longing toward what Donald Davidson called "the autochthonous ideal," or the artist's total immersion in his culture, which results in a vision that is not aesthetically or critically separate from its subject matter. Hobson notes that despite the common appearance of this aspiration in Southern literature, it is nearly always doomed to failure, since the writer requires a certain critical distance from his culture to make sense of it.[12] *Midquest* thoroughly exploits this tension between critical distance and a longing for immersion, a tension Chappell has inherited from the two primary models of classical pastoral, Theocritus and Vergil; Chappell possesses the former's close familiarity with the language and folkways of his rural subjects, along with the latter's gifts of philosophy and penetrating analysis of the ways in which simple, rural characters represent fundamental aspects of the human experience. *Midquest* triumphs in its combination of these two pastoral modes, in its ability to locate the universal in the concrete and thus avoid the two pitfalls dreaded by Southern writers: local color and abstraction.

The difficulty of creating narrative that reveals the essential truths of his experience is a problem Chappell remembers tentatively facing as a teenage farm boy, when churning out dozens of formulaic science-fiction stories seemed infinitely simpler than writing realistically about the natural world around him:

> It was not that I had no realistic experience to write about; there was God's grand plenty of realism on a farm. But I found it impossible to organize experience into any kind of shape; reality may have had the advantage of authenticity but it had the disadvantage of stubbornness, of sheer perversity. It didn't want to be whittled, rearranged, or even comprehended; it just wanted to sit laconic in an ungainly lump and refuse to differentiate into parts.

> *(Plow, pp. 13-14)*

By choosing in *Midquest* to differentiate experience into four rubrics associated with the four pre-Socratic elements, Chappell examines experience at its most fundamental level. The effect of the repeated images of water, fire, air, and earth relentlessly locates human experience in a natural, primitive context. The speakers in these poems are constantly in contact with the natural elements and interpret their lives by means of metaphors derived from the natural world. In **"Second Wind,"** for example, the grandmother tells the boy Fred the story of his grandfather's funeral and embodies the despair she felt in the hot, still August weather; similarly, the freshening of a breeze breaks her emotional stasis and leads to hope.

Time in *Midquest* is cyclical, a concept reinforced by the poem's fourpart structure. In each volume the poet's birthday begins with first light and progresses toward evening. The farming community depicted in *Midquest* measures time in a pre-modern way, planting crops by the phases of the moon, paying attention to the progress of the seasons, locating memory by references not to calendar dates so much as to significant events, often natural disasters, such as the storm described in **"My Father's Hurricane."** Images of destruction and rebirth, almost always associated with one of the four elements, recur throughout *Midquest*. In *River,* for example, **"Dead Soldiers"** describes the flood of 1946, a natural disaster that affects all the farmers in the region and invites comparisons to the flood from *Genesis*. The following poem, **"My Grandfather Gets Doused,"** describes a church baptism that takes place in the same Pigeon River, and the subsequent poem, **"My Grandmother Washes Her Vessels,"** also develops the purification/baptism theme.

In the poems from *Bloodfire,* the themes of destruction and purification often occur together, as in **"My Grandfather's Church Goes Up."** Remembering the fire that destroyed his grandfather's church, Ole Fred represents the inferno as a transfiguration in which the material of the church is purified into its fundamental elements, which leads him to a recognition of how these same essences remain a continuing presence in his own life, even though their material manifestations may have changed. Chappell borrows the structure and alliterative pattern of an Old English Ode and employs an abundance of archaic and Anglo-Saxon-derived vocabulary to suggest the ancient quality of the culture; like the language of Old English (still retained in some Appalachian idioms), his grandfather's world is available to him in changed forms that are ubiquitous if not readily apparent. Fred's longing for that lost culture combines with the congregation's past hymns of longing for God, as well as with his sexual longings for Susan when the poet and his wife return to the abandoned church site for a picnic. Their amorous picnic gives way to a transcendental moment in which Fred experiences the return of his grandfather's spirit: "In happy half-sleep I heard or half heard / in the bliss of breeze breath of my grandfather" (p. 76). The poem's catalogue of images of transfiguration, mirrored by its fascination with lexical transformation, puts forth a faith in eternal presence and unity of life, a reality he believes to be overlooked because of the tendency to accept momentary states of being as separate from their pre-existing and subsequent states. As in Faulkner, for Chappell here the past is not dead—it is not even past:

> Pilgrim, the past   *becomes prayer*
> *becomes remembrance rock-real* *of Resurrection*
> *when the Willer so willeth* *works his wild won-*
> *ders.*

(p. 77)

Like Wordsworth's "spots in time," for Ole Fred significant moments from his personal and cultural past have a continued existence that must be accessed in order to achieve an awareness of life as an organic whole. Though these recollections are infrequent and ephemeral, and though the poet can do little more than wait patiently and passively for them, they are accompanied by such a profound dissolution of the normal distinctions between subject and object, past and present, that he affirms them as "rock-real."

The momentary perfect unity that Ole Fred experiences in **"My Grandfather's Church Goes Up"** is not often matched in *Midquest,* though it is consistently invoked and often approximated. Inherent even in the language we use to describe existence, Chappell points out, is the theme of estrangement from unity, how we rely upon familiar dialectics to make the world comprehensible, artificially dividing existence into body and spirit, subject and object, the spiritual and the secular, and other categories *ad infinitum.* Chappell views this tendency to dissect as a limitation of the human mind, a metaphysical state for which his cultural dislocation from his Appalachian past serves as an apt metaphor. Within this broader context, his longing for unity with the community of his childhood takes on a much greater significance. John Lang points out how throughout *Midquest* the central metaphor of marriage "testifies to the union—often a difficult one—of distinct personalities or qualities" and serves as an expression of the universal desire for "love," "order," and "harmony."[13] Both Lang and Dabney Stuart have addressed the poem's recurrent tension between body and spirit.[14] Lang notes Chappell's constant "impatience with the loss of the Creation, whether in Platonic idealism, Cartesian idealism, Emersonian Transcendentalism, or Protestant fundamentalism, with their tendency to denigrate the physical world" (p. 108). One finds the occasional overt rejection of such idealistic abstraction in poems such as **"The Autumn Bleat of the Weather-vane Trombone"** and **"Birthday 35: Diary Entry,"** but more frequently Chappell chooses to dramatize the ineffectualness and comic absurdity of such positions, as in **"My Grandfather Gets Doused,"** the account of his grandfather's abortive conversion to the Baptists' belief in instantaneous salvation, which Chappell writes

in a bawdy terza rima as a mock version of Dante's *Divine Comedy.* Also, in the several poems focusing on the sensualist Virgil Campbell, Chappell creates a character who consistently opposes the shams of local religionists who oppose his fun.

Despite this delight in the sensual world for its own sake, Chappell's strong metaphysical bent finds ample expression throughout *Midquest,* as in **"Firewood,"** **"The Peaceable Kingdom of Emerald Windows,"** and **"Susan Bathing,"** poems in which he takes pains to deify the material world, to oppose cold scientific rationality with a tentative transcendentalism. In the Preface, Chappell calls *Midquest* "in its largest design a love poem" (p. xi), which is obvious in the numerous poems Ole Fred addresses to his wife, Susan, especially the morning bedroom scenes. However, *Midquest* is concerned with multiple forms of love: erotic, platonic, divine, filial, and love of nature. Love, of course, has always been a main theme of pastoral poetry from classical times onward, and, with the influence of Neo-Platonism, the relation of physical and spiritual love became further developed and systematized (Kermode, p. 35). Though Lang is correct in stressing that Chappell is uncomfortable with Neo-Platonism's subjugation of the body to spirit, the essential desire for unity found in Neo-Platonism (as well as Emersonian Transcendentalism and backwoods Christianity) is an essential component of *Midquest*—and of Chappell's pastoral Kirkman novels. Throughout, love serves to draw the individual out of isolation and to make connection with another person, with God, with the earth itself.

The awakening address to Susan that begins each of the four volumes establishes the basic structure of address that most of the other poems follow, including the four poems in the form of letters, the many dramatic dialogues, and the prayers. In each, Chappell places an intended audience within the poem, emphasizing the use of language to make a connection, rather than—as in the first two parts of **"Birthday 35: Diary Entry"**—as cloistered, confessional expression. In **"Bloodfire Garden,"** he easily conflates "the disease / necessary to know God" with "the heat / in the animal calling to animals" and longs to return to a primal unity, to forget distinctions between the physical and the spiritual:

> *Take* me *into your world of blade and rock*
> *help me return* to when the sun
> first struck off in fury
> the boiling planets.

(p. 91)

"Bloodfire Garden" is a meditation on creation and procreation, relating scenes of sexual intercourse with his wife to boyhood episodes in early spring when he watched his father burning down the weeds and vines to prepare the garden for the growing season. He recalls witnessing in the garden the miracle of incarnation as "the ghosts began again to take flesh" (p. 93). The poem ends with a tight four-line stanza in which the four classical elements are envisioned in harmony, an image that periodically recurs throughout *Midquest,* each time evoking awe at the miraculous unity of creation, how the "jarring elements" (**"Earthsleep,"** p. 186) of fire, water, earth, and air, are held together in an apparently seamless whole, just as spirit and body in their natural states are unified and whole.

In such an optimistic poem abounding in transcendental images of unity, one of the most memorable stanzas depicts Fred as a boy of twelve in the woods at night, longing for the "gleam" of a "hunters' campfire / blinking" at him through the darkness, only to find himself separated from their warmth by the barrier of a dark river, in which he sees reflected "Orion / sliding the water calmly" (p. 92). As a mere reflection or counterfeit of the actual stars, the boy is doubly alienated from the celestial fires of Orion the Hunter, just as he is separated by the river from the terrestrial warmth of the hunters' fire, suggesting the pubescent boy's alienation from both man and God. The image is followed by an address to the adult poet's wife, "Now you warm me," indicating that the adolescent's recognition of desire has led to adult consummation. An alternate reading of the image of the reflected constellation would involve its antithetical relation to the image of the hunters' fire. Rather than duplicating the feeling of alienation, the vision of the stars in the water serves as a compensation. The tone of the stanza begins with a feverish desire to reach the hunters' fire and then shifts to a feeling of resignation and sublimity upon the boy's witnessing the divine order of the stars, their already cold fires made yet colder by their reflection in water. Inner, spiritual warmth comes in compensation for, or as a sublimation of, physical warmth, just as the poet's desire for the imagined childhood unity with family leads instead to a beatific image of an ordered cosmos, one in which the human longing for love and connection plays an integral part. *Midquest* and the subsequent Jess Kirkman novels abound with images of the alienated adolescent, but, unlike the alienation depicted in Chappell's early novels, in the later work alienation promises the possibility of reconciliation.

Lang observes that "For Chappell, genuine selfhood exists only in and through relationships to something outside the self" (p. 99). If this assessment is accurate, it can help us to understand the reasons for the deterioration of selfhood we find in the protagonists of his earlier gothic novels *It Is Time, Lord* and *Dagon.* These characters' schizophrenia and dementia are products of their alienation from any social context that would organize their psyches in a recognizable or meaningful pattern. In *Midquest,* Chappell reminds us of the need to avoid this trap when he frequently employs a dialectic between the alienated, self-absorbed imagination, and an imagination that is constituted by its contact with other family members, with farm labor, and with exposure to the elements themselves. **"Cleaning the Well"** begins "Two worlds there are. One you think / You know; the Other is the Well" (p. 14). He goes on to describe being lowered into the well by his grandfather with instructions to "Clean it out good" (p. 15), and imagines on the way down what he will find at the bottom: a "monster trove / Of blinding treasure . . . Ribcage of drowned warlock" (p. 14). Instead, he finds "Twelve plastic pearls, monopoly / Money, a greenish rotten cat, / Rubber knife, toy gun" (p. 15), detritus from his childhood. He also discovers physical and psychological anguish, "Precise accord / Of pain, disgust, and fear" (p. 15), and comes back up believing that he has died and returned from the dead, "Recalling something beyond recall" (p. 16). Like Poe's alienated narrators, the boy has discovered in this altered perspective a painful reality, from which he is normally protected by his daily life that is contextualized and defined by his relationships with other family members. At the end of the poem, when the cold and frightened child returns from the well exclaiming, "Down there I kept thinking I was dead," the grandfather retorts, "Aw, you're all right" (p. 17), reestablishing the boys sense of security and connectedness, but also dismissing the validity of his vision, attributing it simply to childish fancy and frailty. The reader is left in the same quandary as the boy, disoriented, plunged into the well, unsure which vision is the more valid.

"Feverscape: The Silver Planet" is another study of adolescent alienation. A tendency toward sickliness and an insatiable interest in science fiction coalesce in this depiction of the feverish nightmares that come to the bedridden boy. In **"Feverscape"** the isolated ego is purged through suffering, as it is throughout the *Bloodfire* poems. In **"Rimbaud Fireletter to Jim Applewhite,"** Fred looks back on his late teens and twenties with a mixture of nostalgia, condescension, and gratitude for having survived. He remembers the Durham beer joints where he and his poet friend nursed "the artificial fevers, wet [behind the ears] / With Falstaff beer" (p. 58), deeply under the influence of Rimbaud and Baudelaire. Chappell depicts this friendship in the same terms he uses to describe his friendship with his high school buddy Fuzz in **"A Pact With Faustus"**: two outsiders joined by their artistic interests and especially by a mutual interest in a Romantic literary hero whom they both emulate. The adolescent Fred is aware of the differences that separate him from others in his community but chooses to see his lack of social success as the artist's inevitable sacrifice:

> So passed my high school years. The senior prom
> I missed, and the girls, and all the thrilling sports.

My teachers asked me, "Boy, where you *from*?"
"From deep in a savage forest of unknown words."
The dialogue went downhill after that,
But our positions were clear respectively:
They stood up for health and truth and light,
I stood up for Baudelaire and me.

(pp. 58-59)

The boy's grandiose vision of himself becomes a source of comedy for the more mature poet, who is capable of valuing the adolescent's vision of artistic success while vicariously suffering for his naiveté: "Those were the days! . . .—But they went on and on and on. / The failure I saw myself grew darker and darker" (p. 60). This failure derives from an intuition of his own inauthenticity; the process of discovering his identity and his voice bears all the awkwardness of adolescence, a time in which he struggles to distinguish himself from his parents and community but also to determine the commonalties that bind them together.

Painfully, he recalls leaving the university: "They kicked me out and back to the hills I went / But not before they'd taught me how to see / Myself as halfway halved and halfway blent" (p. 60). In suffering this fragmentation of identity and values, Fred becomes what he calls in the preface a "demographic sample" of the twentieth century. His experience as an artist likewise resembles that of the early- to mid-twentieth-century artist. Like the high modernists, his oeuvre shows an interest in social fragmentation resulting from commercialization, urbanization, and technology (especially the world-shattering technologies unleashed during the World Wars), an obsession with the alienation that results from such fragmentation, a neo-Romantic privileging of the imagination rather than a strict adherence to verisimilitude, a self-reflexiveness that often tends toward metafiction, and a reliance upon multiple subjectivities to reveal an underlying unified reality.

Perhaps most significantly, Chappell shares with the modernists a growing distrust of Romanticism's emphasis on the individual and the solipsism such an aesthetic implies. With maturity, Chappell came to distance himself from the French Symbolists who had inspired his youth, and, like T. S. Eliot, he embraced the classical and neo-classical poets. Just as the later Eliot turned away from the incipient nihilism of *The Waste Land* to write the optimistic *Four Quartets,* Chappell "turned [his] back on the ashes of Paree-town" and began studying "folks like Pope and Bertrand Bronson," and the complete works of Samuel Johnson, for which he wrote a massive, 1,110-page Concordance as his Master's thesis (McFee, p. 97). This shift from a romantic to a classical sensibility is readily apparent when one compares the studies in alienation we find in Chappell's early four novels (1963-1973) with *Midquest* (1981) and the four Kirkman novels (1985-1999), in which Chappell depicts an ordered, harmonious society and, by extension, a harmonious universe. A structural comparison of these works yields similar findings. Unlike the montage of *It Is Time, Lord* (1963), a brilliant novel, which, nevertheless, resists not only closure but the production of any sort of stable meaning, *Midquest* presents an ordered repetition of image and event, which reflects a psychic balance and harmony rather than discord. The multiple subjectivities represented in *Midquest*'s dramatic monologues and dialogues create the sense of a community of interdependent speakers. Consider, for example, how the speakers in poems VI, VII, and VIII in *Wind Mountain* are linked by their relation to the Second Circle of Dante's Inferno, with VI introducing the allusion, VII developing it more fully and then explicitly introducing the windy confession of Virgil Campbell in VIII. The connections among poems are usually more subtle, though no less important. Often, adjacent poems in one of the four volumes are paired, as in VI, VII and VIII of *River,* poems dealing with themes of fallenness and redemption. Also, there are multiple connections among volumes, poems in the same position of each volume that present the same character, theme, and/or verse structure.

Lucinda Hardwick MacKethan argues that Southern pastorals have always been motivated by the "need of people in a rapidly changing world to have a vision of an understandable order."[15] According to MacKethan, a

> particular social structure becomes a dramatic mechanism . . . for examining systems of values for any one of a great variety of purposes, emotional and political as well as artistic. Southern literature in its own clear tradition is associated with strong judgments and a positive system of values—not always the same judgments or even the same system, to be sure, yet a literature that seems to insist on shared standards highly visible and widely articulated.

(pp. 5-6)

Throughout *Midquest* and the Kirkman Quartet, Chappell demonstrates just such an eager interest in the network of relationships that define the farming family, the basic political unit of yeoman society. Like Thomas Jefferson's yeoman utopia and Vergil's Golden Age, Chappell promotes yeomanry as the ideal society, one that makes possible the difficult balance between individual freedom and social integrity. This tension between the claim of the individual and the claims of society is at the heart of *Midquest* and is a tension Chappell seeks to resolve in part by demonstrating how the values of personal autonomy and responsibility are central to the frontier community's vision of itself (drawing attention to the often fine line between autonomy and alienation). In fact, it is the loss of autonomy on the part of the individual and the family that most demonstrates the decline of the community. Fred's father, J. T., is constantly lamenting that farming no longer remains economically viable, as in the poems

"My Father Burns Washington" and **"My Father Washes His Hands."** Both poems present the Appalachian farmer's transition from subsistence farming to the production of cash crops as a fall from grace, after which the farmer is dependent upon market prices and bank loans. Throughout *Midquest* Chappell simultaneously participates in and undercuts this sort of nostalgia. For example, in **"Firewater"** (discussed earlier) we are invited to take only half seriously J. T. and Virgil Campbell's lament of cultural erosion represented by the case of Big Mama and her rural family. Virgil explains that out of economic necessity Big Mama has "stopped running corn [whiskey]" and begun "Growing these Merry Widow cigarettes," a fact that leaves both Virgil and J. T. dejected and longing for the old times, mourning the disappearance of what they see as Appalachia's "eternal verities" of "poverty and whiskey and scratch-ankle farming" (p. 80). This comic elegy parodies the more serious longing for a stable order that appears throughout *Midquest.* Fred's father models the appropriate response to a universe in perpetual flux by proposing a toast "here at the end of the world" (p. 80). The tale of Big Mama itself reveals how, in the midst of change, Appalachian values of defiant independence hold their own—though, perhaps, in an ever more degraded form—exemplified by the moonshiners who merely change crops but remain outlaws, and by the name of the mountain where they live, "Standing Indian," which has lost any etymological connection to the indigenous Cherokee driven out on the Trail of Tears, but whose English name conjures the image of durability and defiance. Furthermore, the mountain now nourishes a race who, like the legendary Cherokee, value self-sufficiency and challenge centralized authority.

Midquest elegizes not simply personal and cultural loss but cosmic entropy. Like most of the poems that serve as frames for the four volumes, **"On Stillpoint Hill at Midnight"** is a meditation on the relation of the individual to the cosmic order. This poem, addressed to Susan, finds solace in the stability of their relationship while "creation dribbles / out the bottleneck of diminishment" (p. 46). He finds abundant evidence of universal social collapse: "murdered soldiers" in 1971 Vietnam, animals indifferently and wastefully slaughtered by humans, "rivers rotting to lye where the mill-drains vomit inky venom," and "babies thrust into sewer pipes" (p. 48). Nevertheless, like Whitman and Thoreau, whom he elsewhere looks to as optimistic visionaries (see **"Earth Emergent Drifts the Fire River,"** p. 147), Chappell finds in nature and human sexuality hope for the endless renewal of life and order, a theme explored from the very first poem of *Midquest,* **"The River Awakening in the Sea."** Here, in long lines and slightly hyperbolic images, both characteristic of Whitman, Chappell ennobles the human form by having Ole Fred describe his wife's body in terms of the natural

landscape: "My forehead suckles your shoulder, straining to hear / In you the headlong ocean, your blood, island-saying sea now. / Wild stretches, bound to every water, of seas in you" (p. 1). This passage expresses a transcendental faith in the connectedness of the individual to the vast physical universe, and even in the title one finds Emerson's primary metaphor for the Over-Soul, in which the material contiguity of sea and river represents the "influx of the Divine mind into our mind."[16] It should be acknowledged here that, as with most modernists, Chappell's repudiation of the Romantics is only a partial one, which he concedes in **"Fire-letter"** when Fred recalls his father's words: "Fire's in the bloodstream" (p. 61). Wordsworth and the American Romantics, in particular, resonate throughout *Midquest.* In contrast to the decadence of the late Romantics, their democratic optimism provides an image of the individual immersed in nature and connected with a cosmic order, which provides a source of inspiration for Chappell, even if his own optimism is often qualified by doubt.

"On Stillpoint Hill" mirrors the meditative quality of **"The River Awakening."** In both, the speaker attempts to merge with the mind of God and consider the present decline of civilization from the perspective of eternity, which allows him to witness the cyclic and eternally renewing processes of nature:

> consider how the giants went
> into earth
> patiently to wait themselves
> into stone;
> considering again how stones will burgeon
> into animals, erupting to four feet
> on glossy lawns,
> and gnawing the ruled streets and lot corners
> of suburbs
>
> (p. 45)

If, as several critics have pointed out, Susan serves as Fred's Beatrice in the poem's overarching journey toward redemption, in **"On Stillpoint Hill"** Fred takes the lead in imagining wholeness. In the tradition of the pastoral love lyric (and of Whitman's *Song of Myself*) Fred invites Susan to join him in immersing themselves in nature:

> We will rest simple,
> we will taste with our pores
> the powerful probabilities massing about
> indivisible infinite motes of water
> as the earth sweats itself
> in this springhead.
> Or come with me at 6 a.m.
> in the woods by the lake
>
> . . . . .
>
> We must lie careless as
> these forces foment,

we also must reflect every
fire of the heavens
and the cool effortless moon
trawling our faces.
Must read too the waters clouding us, . . .

(pp. 47-48)

Like Emerson's transparent eyeball, the poet must purge himself of ego and, passive and permeable to the forces of nature, record their impression upon his soul. At the same time, one finds the transcendentalists' egotistical optimism in the Whitmanian imperative that they "must reflect every fire of the heavens," ultimately placing the burden of perfect conservation of universal energy and order upon the poet. Elsewhere in the poem, Ole Fred boasts that "each upheaval that order is, / my stillness takes in" (p. 45). If we read the poem's protagonist as an Everyman, or "widely representative" (Preface, p. x), then, as with Whitman's persona in *Song of Myself,* we the readers are invited to identify closely with this persona and to follow his example of transcendental faith, so that what appears boasting is actually a democratic celebration of every person's promise of fulfillment through a connection to nature and the Divine.

One of the most readily apparent tensions throughout *Midquest* appears between the dramatic monologues and dialogues in Appalachian vernacular and the meditative, often free-verse poems such as **"On Stillpoint Hill"** and **"The River Awakening."** Other than the obvious differences in idiom and verse structure, there occurs a fundamental difference in scope, with the dramatic poems typically limited to the concrete world of Appalachia and the meditations often tending toward universal abstractions, as noted above. Considering that Chappell's aim throughout—even in the meditations—is to avoid abstraction, while, nevertheless, attaining the universal, the balance of the two poetic forms helps to accomplish this goal. In effect, his dramatic poems locate the meditations upon universal order in a concrete world, just as Whitman's abundant use of catalogues serves to embody Emerson's Transcendentalism. By associating the specific instance of Appalachian yeomanry with a cosmic order in which that culture's values are sustained, Chappell expresses faith in a Golden Age, accessible, if not in actuality, then at least through poetry.

The faith in sustainability—in a Divine order that manifests itself in the social order of an farming community—is essentially Jefferson's yeoman utopia or, earlier still, Vergil's Golden Age. In "The Poet and the Plowman," his essay on the *Georgics,* Chappell examines Vergil's dictum, "*Nudas ara, sere nudus,* Plow naked, naked sow," and declares, "The words are there to remind us of the ceremonial, and ultimately religious nature of farming; they remind us of the selfless rituals

we must undergo in order to keep faith" (*Plow,* p. 76). Further on, he continues this theme:

> The largest purpose of the *Georgics* is not to dignify, but to sanctify, honest farm labor. A reader who has not looked at it in a long time finds he has forgotten that the poem is full of stars. Even the smallest task must be undertaken in due season under the proper constellations. These prescriptions are not mere meteorology; they connect the order of the earth to the order of the stars. The farmer moves by the motion of the stars, and his labors determine the concerns of the government. The Roman State is not founded upon the soil, it is founded in the universe. And so were all the other civilizations which managed to endure for any length of time. If poets do not wish to study these matters and treat of them, they shirk their responsibilities and fail their society.

(p. 77)

Just as the hunter-farmers and Orion the Hunter are conflated in **"Bloodfire Garden,"** in this passage Chappell makes explicit his belief in the spiritual harmony that exists between yeomen and the cosmos. The language here is as confrontational as anything found in the Agrarians' manifesto, *I'll Take My Stand.* Chappell's conviction that the artist bears a responsibility to his public—that he should show that public a vision of its better self—is a distinctly pre-modern notion, and one of Chappell's most notable frustrations with contemporary poetry derives from his observation that the vast majority of it, good and bad, takes the shape of the "autobiographical lyric" with little in the way of "social scope" (*Midquest,* p. x). Private alienation is a topic Chappell himself thoroughly explored in his first four novels, one that he felt fortunate to escape in his poetry.

In *Midquest,* he turns away from a fascination with private reality to a consideration of cultural values, which, true to the agrarian culture he describes, are presented in a reverential tone that might be described as oftentimes prescriptive. Indeed, *Midquest* comes as close to the epic as anything we are likely to find in contemporary poetry. As with Vergil, for Chappell poetry's greatest value lies in its ability to capture not only a life but a world. Poetry has the ability to compensate for a life estranged from farming because poetry shares with farming so many spiritual values: "fatalism, renunciation, awe of nature, reverence for the earth" (*Plow,* p. 74), and "a life of ordered observation and inspired patience" (p. 79). Even in an age when social fragmentation is accepted as normative, when the world of the Appalachian farmer must seem to most readers as remote as Vergil's Golden Age, with *Midquest* Chappell convincingly portrays a life that "touches an essential harmony of things" (*Plow,* p. 79).

Notes

1. Fred Chappell, *Plow Naked: Selected Writings on Poetry* (Ann Arbor: University of Michigan Press, 1993), p. 73.

2. The Kirkman Quartet includes: *I Am One of You Forever* (Baton Rouge: Louisiana State University Press, 1985); *Brighten the Corner Where You Are* (New York: St. Martin's, 1989); *Farewell, I'm Bound to Leave You* (New York: Picador, 1996); and *Look Back All the Green Valley* (New York: Picador, 1999).

3. Fred Chappell, Preface, *Midquest: A Poem* (Baton Rouge: Louisiana State University Press, 1981), p. x.

4. Frank Kermode, *English Pastoral Poetry: From the Beginnings to Marvell* (New York: Barnes & Noble, 1952), p. 15.

5. Fred Chappell, "A Pact with Faustus," *Mississippi Quarterly,* 37 (1984); rpt. in *The Fred Chappell Reader,* ed. Dabney Stuart (New York: St. Martin's, 1987), p. 489.

6. Michael McFee, "The Epigrammatical Fred Chappell," *Southern Literary Journal,* 31 (Spring 1999), 96.

7. George Hovis, "An Interview with Fred Chappell," *Carolina Quarterly,* 52 (Fall/Winter 1999), 72-73.

8. Fred Chappell, *It Is Time, Lord* (1963; rpt., Baton Rouge: Louisiana State University Press, 1996), p. 35.

9. T. S. Eliot, *The Wasteland and Other Poems* (New York: Harvest, 1934), p. 42.

10. J. E. Congleton, *Theories of Pastoral Poetry in England, 1684-1798* (Gainesville: University of Florida Press, 1952), p. 4.

11. Houston A. Baker, *Modernism and the Harlem Renaissance* (Chicago: University of Chicago Press, 1987).

12. Fred Hobson, "Contemporary Southern Fiction and the Autochthonous Ideal," in *The Southern Writer in the Postmodern World* (Athens: University of Georgia Press, 1991), pp. 73-101.

13. John Lang, "Points of Kinship: Community and Allusion in Fred Chappell's *Midquest*," in *Dream Garden,* ed. Patrick Bizzaro (Baton Rouge: Louisiana State University Press, 1997), p. 98.

14. See Dabney Stuart, "Spiritual Matter in Fred Chappell's Poetry: A Prologue" (*Dream Garden,* pp. 48-70).

15. Lucinda Hardwick MacKethan, *The Dream of Arcady: Place and Time in Southern Literature* (Baton Rouge: Louisiana State University Press, 1980), p. 6.

16. Ralph Waldo Emerson, "The Over-Soul," in *Selected Writings of Emerson,* ed. Donald McQuade (New York: Modern Library College Edition, 1981), p. 253.

John Lang (essay date 2000)

SOURCE: Lang, John. "Shaping the Self in Poetry: *The World between the Eyes* and *Midquest*." In *Understanding Fred Chappell,* pp. 58-94. Columbia, S.C.: University of South Carolina Press, 2000.

[*In the following essay, Lang analyzes* The World between the Eyes *and* Midquest, *arguing that the latter—in part for its skillful blending of regional and universal concerns—is "one of the finest long poems in twentieth-century American literature."*]

By the time Chappell's first book of poems, **The World between the Eyes,** appeared in 1971, the author had already published three novels and had completed a draft of his fourth. Yet despite the variety of fictional forms in which he has worked, Chappell's first allegiance has always been to poetry, which he calls a "nobler sort of art" than fiction.[1] "It's enormously more fun writing poetry than fiction and nonfiction," he told an interviewer, "because of the concentration on themes and on language, particularly language. . . . It's also more difficult."[2] That challenge is one he has successfully embraced in ten book-length collections of poems as well as three chapbooks.[3]

Chappell's poetics derives from the organicism first espoused in American literature by Ralph Waldo Emerson, for whom the poem originates in "a thought so passionate and alive that, like the spirit of a plant or an animal, it has an architecture of its own, and adorns nature with a new thing."[4] As Chappell puts it, "Every work of art . . . creates its own separate aesthetic laws, the way in which it's to be understood. I think that really means that it must have created its own special way to be written if it's a genuine work of art."[5] Chappell has repeatedly avowed his commitment to the Horatian aims of literature, to entertain and to instruct, and has said that "the only important considerations" in assessing a poem or a book of poems "[are] that it be beautiful, honest, and interesting—that is, that it intrigue the mind or affect the feelings."[6] These aesthetic principles help to account for the range of forms that readers encounter in Chappell's poetry as well as the varied styles he uses. Chappell has often written in free verse, not just in traditional forms, while the range of such forms, especially in **Midquest,** demonstrates his mastery of poetic craft and technique. As for the absence of a distinctive poetic style in his work, Chappell has commented: "I'm not interested in creating a fixed poetic style for myself, but [in] matching each separate poem to the subject matter. I deliberately try to be as fluid as possible."[7]

Yet another important aesthetic principle governing Chappell's collections of poetry is his assumption that a book of poems should form a whole and not be simply a gathering of discrete individual poems. The four books that compose *Midquest,* each of them organized around one of the four classical elements, exhibit such unity, as does the text as a whole, which is subtitled *A Poem.* *Castle Tzingal* (1984) certainly has such unity, as do, in varying degrees, each of his subsequent volumes, whether the book's impression of wholeness results from similarity of themes and motifs, as in *Source* (1985); similarity of subject matter and approach, as in *First and Last Words* (1989); or similarity of poetic form, as in the epigrams of *C* (1993). Chappell's most important precursor in this regard is Charles Baudelaire's *Fleurs du mal.* "Baudelaire said," Chappell told an interviewer, "if you have twenty-four poems, the order of the poems makes up the twenty-fifth poem; that is, the design of the whole book is a poem itself."[8]

THE WORLD BETWEEN THE EYES

It is for the absence of such design, among other flaws, that Chappell has criticized *The World between the Eyes,* calling it "weak in conception and execution."[9] Yet while it is true that the thirty-seven poems collected in this initial volume lack the structural unity and the refinement of Chappell's later poetic compositions, the book contains a number of poems, as Kathryn Stripling Byer has noted, "which are [among] the most intense in contemporary poetry, almost overwhelming in their obsessive imagery and unrelenting rhythms."[10] These qualities are especially notable in the eight longer narrative poems that fill nearly half of the book's pages. In fact those eight poems—**"February," "The World between the Eyes," "The Farm," "The Father," "The Mother," "Tin Roof Blues," "Sunday,"** and **"The Dying"**—though often separated from one another by shorter lyric poems, can usefully be read as a sequence. Taken together, they provide an insightful portrait of the artist as child and young man, and they thus anticipate both the narrative structure of many of *Midquest*'s poems and some of that later volume's major subjects, themes, images, and stances.

The World between the Eyes opens with **"February,"** a poem that vividly describes, in a syntax often disjointed and a free verse that frequently employs an iambic base, a hog killing. This subject matter situates poet and reader squarely in the rural environment so typical of Chappell's work. The poem's events are presented from the perspective of "the boy," a semiautobiographical point of view to which Chappell returns not only in much of *Midquest* but also in *I Am One of You Forever*

and the other Kirkman novels. The child's ambivalence toward the hog killing is captured in such phrases as "dismayed / With delight" and "elated-drunk / With the horror."[11] The communal dimension of this activity is one of its most important features, for Chappell seeks to locate the reader not only in proximity to the natural world but also in relationships with others. Nature, through this "most unlikely prodigious pig" (5), affords the family both food and an occasion for affirming friendship and interdependence.

One of Chappell's pervasive poetic concerns has been his resistance to the self-absorption that characterizes so much contemporary poetry, the retreat into the individual psyche that marked the confessional poetry of the late 1950s and 1960s. Despite this concern, the longer narrative poems of *The World between the Eyes* do indeed record the efforts of "the child" to achieve individuation, self-identity. The title poem emphasizes the issue of subjectivity and the child's struggle for selfhood by opening with the boy imagining a scene of troops preparing for battle. Casting himself in the role of "the Swarthy Spy" who "hones a talent for precision" in his reports (12), the child becomes an emblem of the adult poet.

The title of this collection highlights the role that mind and imagination play in shaping the world. But the title also recalls the phrase "a bullet between the eyes," thereby reinforcing the child's sense of being menaced by the world, of being embattled. It is significant that these narrative poems begin with a hog killing and end, in **"The Dying,"** with the death of the boy's sister, while including in **"The Father"** the child's contemplation of suicide. Death haunts many of these poems, as it haunted Chappell's first three novels. The book's title is open to a third interpretation as well. The world between the eyes is also a world shared among various I's—that is, shared among different people (families, communities) and shared among the different selves (or different voices) that contribute to a single individual's identity. The child shares his world with his ancestors, with the past, as he wanders "the house of his fathers," "rooms of his fathers" (12). He shares it with his father and mother, with the inhabitants of Canton (in **"Tin Roof Blues"**), with the religious community in which his parents immerse him (in **"Sunday"**), with his dying sister, and with the natural phenomena portrayed in **"The Farm."** That poem too, as it moves from the work required by summer haying to the paralysis of winter, is shadowed by death: "Stupor of cold wide stars" (20), "The world, locked bone" (21).

To make a place for himself in such a world, the developing poet must master his memories, must overcome the stasis they often induce, and must come to recognize, like James Christopher of *It Is Time, Lord,* the resources they offer. Even more importantly, he must achieve a vision of the future, grounding that future in an accurate understanding of his past. Over against "things that bloom and burn," the child sets "words [that] bloom / and burn" (13) and embraces "his duty to read aright, / To know" (14). Surrounded by "signs" and filled with a sense of time "charged past endurance with the future" (14), the child of the title poem nevertheless realizes that "he's blest in his skins, an old stone / House, and a sky eaten up with stars" (15). Time and eternity are yoked in the images of house and star, and brooding on both is the figure of the developing poet.

Though Chappell grounds these narrative poems in the rural and in family, he does not idealize either of those subjects. The seasonal progression from summer to winter in **"The Farm"** makes this attitude clear, as does the difficulty of the work portrayed. The child's relationships with his father and mother, presented in two consecutive poems, the latter at the virtual midpoint of the book, reveal a similar ambivalence. The father's judgmental stance mirrors that of James Christopher's father in the "January" episodes of *It Is Time, Lord.* Yet the boy's success in fulfilling the task his father assigns—to discover a new spring to replenish the family's water supply—leads the child to a renewed sense of life's possibilities. Having rejected the temptation to commit suicide, he feels like "someone who's lived through his death, come out grinning, / Mind surcharged with the future" (27). While this easy confidence is treated ironically, the child does acquire a new sense of equanimity.

Although the boy's mother promptly shatters that equanimity, he is able to restore it, and what makes his resilience possible is humor—humor and a hard-won capacity for detachment. Significantly, it is precisely such a discovery of the usefulness of humor that helped effect the transition in Chappell's fiction from the gloom of *Dagon* to the lighter tone of *The Gaudy Place,* not to mention the broad comedy of many of the poems in **Midquest** and of many of the characters and events in the Kirkman tetralogy. What Chappell says of humor in Carolyn Kizer's poetry seems applicable to his own increasing reliance on humor after the publication of *Dagon*: "Kizer seems to look upon humor as one of the most welcome parts of her personal, as well as her human, heritage. It is for her not only necessary for balance and tolerance, it is a necessity for survival."[12]

For the child in **"The Mother,"** it is humor that enables him to triumph over hatred and rage. Storming out of the house, he longs to "squash it from sight with his palm" (29). Rejecting that option, he retreats to the woods to consider others. Yet the very shapes of his fantasies subvert their appeal: "Could live in the woods and eat bugs! / Or, handily build Snug Cabin, chink it with mud / . . . // Could murder his mother, conquer

the world! / Or, rob banks and live rich on the loot" (30). By acknowledging the absurdity of his fantasies, the child manages to return home.

In this poem at the midpoint of Chappell's first book of poetry, the child-poet comes to recognize that the function of the imagination is not to evade reality but to confront it and to illuminate it. The world between the eyes emerges from and engages with the world those eyes observe, not a world they invent. Chappell's later short stories and novels and poems reveal his penchant for fantasy, but it is fantasy in the service of a deeper understanding of life, not fantasy as an alternative to lived social experience. The child in **"The Mother"** returns home, "his pace . . . deliberately fashioned." Unlike the figure in this volume's **"Face to Face,"** who, standing at his door, decides that "he'll sleep the ditch tonight" (22), the child-poet "stops to take the measure of the family door. / And then he enters" (31). As Byer says of **"The Father"** and **"The Mother,"** "Each poem concludes with a real, earned breakthrough into a life-sustaining vision."[13] The return home that the latter poem records becomes the pivotal event in the poet's psychological and artistic development.

The eight longer narrative poems in **The World between the Eyes** are linked by repeated images and phrases; by their narrative structure; by the themes of time, mortality, family ties, and the function of the imagination; and, most importantly, by the figure of the boy or young man who appears in each of them. Although the poems are not presented as a sequence, they can profitably be read as one. Yet as the striking contrast between the endings of **"Face to Face"** and **"The Mother"** shows, Chappell has also established connections between several of the shorter poems in this volume and the longer narrative poems as well as connections among some of the shorter poems. Three poems on the poet's son, Heath, for example, serve as a bridge between the title poem and **"The Farm,"** depicting Heath's wrestling with the world of objects and his efforts to acquire a language expressive of his needs and feelings. Five witty poems on baseball are grouped together, illustrating Chappell's skill with figurative language and apt allusions as well as his sense of humor, but those poems fail to contribute to a sense of underlying unity in the book as a whole. Nevertheless, as Byer remarks, "What continues to fascinate any reader of **The World between the Eyes** is the range of voice, tone, and style the book displays."[14]

Such range has become one of the hallmarks of Chappell's achievement, not only in poetry but also in fiction. In other ways too **The World between the Eyes** adumbrates his later poetic forms, themes, and techniques. The ease with which he moves, for instance, from free verse to a variety of rhyme schemes, meters, and stanza structures is amply evident. His extensive use of narratives that focus on childhood memories and experiences provides another example of the continuity between this initial book of poems and his later work. Even the place names in some of these early narrative poems—Smathers Hill, Wind River—either reappear in *Midquest* or anticipate that book's dominant images. The allusiveness of Chappell's poetry, along with its philosophical concerns, is also evident at many points, starting with the volume's second poem, **"A Transcendental Idealist Dreams in Springtime,"** a poem dedicated to James Applewhite. That allusiveness marks even the opening and closing lines of **"Third Base Coach,"** with its references to the ghost of Hamlet's father and to Aeschylean tragedy. Chappell's willingness to address such seemingly unpoetic material and to dignify the products of popular culture is also apparent in a poem like **"Weird Tales,"** with its celebration of the practitioners of horror stories and science fiction. In form, moreover, **"Weird Tales"** is an epistolary poem, addressed to R. H. W. Dillard, and it thus looks forward to the four letter-poems that play a crucial role in *Midquest.*

Chappell chose to reprint only four poems from *The World between the Eyes* in *The Fred Chappell Reader,* but he selected ten of them (at times greatly revised) for inclusion in *Spring Garden.* While some of the poems—**"Erasures," "Guess Who," "The Survivors,"** and **"Northwest Airlines,"** among others—are indeed slight, a number of the poems remain of interest both for their insights into the poet's later development and for their own artistic merit.

MIDQUEST

In the title poem of *The World between the Eyes,* the narrator remarks of the child-poet, "Of the elements his is water" (14). It was, in fact, to water that Chappell turned in composing his next book of poems, *River* (1975), the first volume of what was to become *Midquest* (1981), his semiautobiographical epic, "something like a verse novel," as he notes in the preface to that book.[15] Chappell has traced the genesis of *Midquest* to **"Familiar Poem,"** first published in *The Archive* while he was a student at Duke.[16] But he didn't begin working on this material consciously, he says, until May 28, 1971, his thirty-fifth birthday, when he was preparing *The World between the Eyes* for publication. Early on Chappell realized the potential scope of this new body of material: "By the time I'd written the second poem [in *River*] . . . I saw the shape of the whole thing. Not the exact structure but the shape of it."[17] Asked by an interviewer, "How old were you when you found the grain [of your poetic sensibility] and kept going with it?" Chappell responded, "I was thirty-five. . . . I started writing *Midquest.* It became important to me. And that became the theme of the book—to take stock and change directions."[18] To another

interviewer Chappell remarked, "The whole poem, *Midquest,* is about rebirth."[19]

Now widely recognized as what Patrick Bizzaro calls "the structural and thematic centerpiece of Chappell's poetic achievement thus far,"[20] *Midquest* is an extraordinarily ambitious, complexly structured, deeply humane book. Some five thousand lines in length, it gathers together the four previously published volumes *River, Bloodfire* (1978), *Wind Mountain* (1979), and *Earthsleep* (1980). Each of those volumes consists of eleven poems, with each volume organized around one of the four elements—water, fire, air, and earth—that Pythagoras and other ancient philosophers viewed as fundamental to all life. Chappell allows each of these elements to assume a variety of meanings and also has them interact with and upon one another, as when he describes "the burning river of this morning / That earth and wind overtake" (187) or speaks of "the morning flush of loosed wind-spirit, exhalation / Of fire-seed and gusty waters and of every dirt" (98). In *Bloodfire* alone, the image of fire is linked to dawn, to a Rimbaudian derangement of the senses, to the Ku Klux Klan's cross burnings, to sexual desire, to spiritual longing, to Pentecost and the Christian symbolism associated with the Holy Spirit, to hellfire, to the violence of war, to martyrdom (political as well as religious), to hearth and home, to the fevers of physical illness, to natural disasters, to Lucretius's *ignis semina* as building blocks of the physical world, to illumination or revelation, to alcohol ("firewater"), to "fire / As symbolic of tortured, transcendent-striving will" (85), and to many other objects and significations. A similar multiplicity of meanings attaches to the other elements, allowing the poet enormous latitude for the exercise of his ingenuity while at the same time insuring a comprehensive and comprehensible focus for the book.

In addition to using the four elements as a unifying device within and between volumes, Chappell conjoins the four books that comprise *Midquest* in a number of other ways. Each volume opens, for instance, with the poet-narrator (Ole Fred) in bed with his wife, Susan, on the morning of his thirty-fifth birthday, and each volume closes with the couple back in bed. Susan likewise appears in at least one other poem in each volume. Ole Fred's grandparents and parents speak at length in various narrative poems throughout the four volumes. Yet another unifying character is Virgil Campbell, the country storekeeper first introduced in *It Is Time, Lord.* One poem in each of *Midquest*'s four volumes is devoted to Virgil, "who is supposed to give to the whole," Chappell states in the preface, "its specifically regional, its Appalachian, context" (x). Each volume also contains a lengthy stream-of-consciousness poem that meditates on such philosophical issues as the relationship between body and mind, flesh and spirit, time and eternity; and each volume contains a poem that portrays a natural disaster appropriate to the element around which that book is organized: a flood, a fire, a hurricane, and in *Earthsleep* death itself. Similarly helping to unify all four volumes are Chappell's varied allusions to and echoes of Dante's *Divine Comedy,* with its quest for moral and spiritual rebirth at the midpoint of one's life. The motif of pilgrimage is implicit throughout *Midquest,* as is Thoreau's idea that "morning is moral reform" (101). Chappell subtitles *Midquest* "A Poem," thus indicating the unity of impression to which the work aspires, and which, I believe, it achieves—a unity amidst astonishing and engaging variety. The careful design of the book infuses in the reader a sense both of order and of the richness of life's possibilities; yet *Midquest* never slights the struggles that are required to attain and sustain such a vision.

Chappell's preface to *Midquest* indicates a great deal about the author's intentions and about the book's design. The preface has generated some controversy, however, because of several inconsistencies between Chappell's statements there and the book's actual structure. Chappell notes, for example, that the sixth poem in each volume is devoted to Virgil Campbell, when in fact Virgil appears in the seventh poem of *Bloodfire* and the eighth poem of *Wind Mountain.* Likewise, Chappell claims that "the fifth poem in each [volume] is given to stream of consciousness" (x), though it seems clear that it is the fourth poem in *Earthsleep,* "The Peaceable Kingdom of Emerald Windows,"* that parallels the narrator's stream-of-consciousness meditations in *Midquest*'s first three volumes. Chappell also explains in the preface that "each of the volumes (except *Wind Mountain*) is organized as a balancing act. The first poem is mirrored by the last; the second by the next to last, and so on inward" (ix). Although Randolph Paul Runyon has traced many of these parallels, they ultimately seem far less significant than the narrative and thematic momentum of the book as it moves forward through the poems in a given volume and through the entire text. As Runyon himself concedes, "*Midquest* is probably as rich in sequential echoes as it is in symmetrical ones."[21]

Chappell's preface is more useful, it seems to me, in its comments on the poet's general intentions than on the book's details of design. Chappell characterizes *Midquest,* for instance, as "a reactionary work," one that aimed "to restore . . . qualities sometimes lacking in the larger body of contemporary poetry: detachment, social scope, humor, portrayal of character and background, discursiveness, wide range of subject matter" (x). The longer version of the preface that appeared in *The Small Farm,* a year prior to *Midquest*'s publication, helps to clarify to what and to whom the poet was reacting. There he indicates his dissatisfaction both with the autobiographical lyric and with the long poem as represented by Ezra Pound's *Cantos,* William Carlos Williams's *Paterson,* Charles Olson's *Maximus Poems,* Louis Zukovsky's *A,* and Hart Crane's *The Bridge.* These long poems he faults for their "structural failures" as they "limn down to lyric moments stuck together with the bland glue of raw data."[22] It is within the tradition of the long poem that Chappell places *Midquest,* and his achievement within that tradition is truly extraordinary. *Midquest* combines lyric, narrative, and meditative poems to create a larger structure that derives from the epic, most obviously Dante's *Divine Comedy.*

The title of one of Chappell's book reviews, reprinted in *A Way of Happening,* indicates his assessment of the contemporary long poem—"Piecework: The Longer Poem Returns." In that review he speaks of the "mosaic structures" rather than "extended wholes" that the majority of American long poems offer.[23] One of the consequences of such structures, as he points out in *Plow Naked,* is that "whatever the subject matter of the modern epic, and whatever the ostensible and announced themes, three secondary themes will inevitably be articulated[:] . . . disintegration, disconnection, and loneliness."[24] According to Chappell, "It is a wild connect-the-dots scheme, this construction of the contemporary epic," and he contrasts the fragmentation of perception and structure in such works with Homer's "faith that in fashioning a plot from all the random matter [of his world], he would find meaning, and a truth that would have value."[25] In *Midquest* the poet has striven for a sense of design, an architecture, in which "each part supports every other and a homogeneity of interest results."[26] While the resulting poem clearly lacks the narrative flow of *The Odyssey* or *The Aeneid,* it tries to recover the "sense of community with the people of the past" so often absent from the contemporary epic.[27] Instead of portraying Ole Fred in terms of disconnection and loneliness, Chappell presents him as rooted in family and place and as representative of both the folk culture of the Appalachian South and the formal literary culture of the university. The social dimension of Chappell's poetic vision cannot be overemphasized. As Robert Morgan has remarked: "There is an assumption of community in all [Chappell's] work, a sense of belonging not just to a family and a place . . . but also to the terrain of history. It is a community in time that is implied and evoked, a world of parents and ancestors both literal and literary."[28]

Chappell's reservations about the contemporary autobiographical lyric, like his reservations about the modern epic, stem from its loss of community, its creation of intensely private, fragmentary modes of consciousness. He also criticizes such lyrics for their "attenuation of subject matter" and their "phony mysticism, the substitution of excited language for hard-won perception."[29] Shaped by "the Symbolist prescription that the poet should be a seer, a prophet," the autobiographical lyric, in Chappell's opinion, has reinforced the Romantic notion of the poet as social outsider, as social outcast. Too often, then, he adds, "The subject matter to be perceived lay on or beyond the outer borders of common experience."[30]

Chappell's rejection of this last assumption pervades *Midquest.* As Henry Taylor has written, "*Midquest* is a poem celebrating the world most of us live in and the play of mind and language over it."[31] It is to human beings' ordinary yet remarkable relationships and experiences that Ole Fred turns in his portraits of his grandparents, parents, spouse, and friends. The sense of community is fundamental to the book, and that community extends well beyond the mountain setting of Ole Fred's childhood. Similarly, the self the poet portrays is not simply—or even primarily—an autobiographical self. While the figure of Ole Fred borrows heavily from the author's personal experiences, he is meant to be, like Dante the pilgrim or Walt Whitman's persona, "widely representative" (x). Chappell seeks not the novelties of private moments of illumination but the revelations that result from engagement with tradition and with other people. He resists entrapment in the isolated ego and rejects elitist conceptions of art; instead he situates the reader in a vivid social milieu and draws upon the oral tradition and folk materials to underscore his imagination's democratic inclusiveness. As the poet told an interviewer while the book was still in progress, "Although [*Midquest*] is autobiographical, in many ways, the last thing I want it to be about is the self. . . . And a sense of history, a sense of tradition, is one way to get away from the extremely *personal* tone of so much present-day poetry."[32]

While dissociating himself from the intensely subjective autobiographical lyric, Chappell does not—despite his disclaimer in the preface—sacrifice "intensity, urgency, metaphysical trial, emotional revelation" (x). Such qualities are regularly present in *Midquest,* particularly in the opening and closing poems of each volume and in Ole Fred's stream-of-consciousness meditations, but they occur within the larger context of the relationships, the extended sense of community and tradition, that the poem explores. Nor does Chappell abandon the idea of the poet as a seer, though he employs other conceptions of the poet's identity as well in order to recover for poetry the breadth of subject matter it enjoyed in pre-Symbolist eras. Spiritual vision is crucial to *Midquest,* a text in which Chappell affirms what he has called the traditional role of the poet "as celebrator of divinity and of the created objects of the universe."[33] As seer, Ole Fred embraces both body and spirit, sings the physical world without neglecting "the Mountains Outside Time" (169), and wonders whether the "Earthly Paradise" isn't already "among our amidst" (177). The meditative

poems in each volume are especially imbued with visionary insights, which manifest themselves at many other points in *Midquest* too.

Part of what distinguishes this book from Chappell's earlier work is its attitude toward the past. For James Christopher of *It Is Time, Lord,* the past was filled with memories of his father's misjudgment of him and memories of burning down his grandparents' house. For Peter Leland of *Dagon,* the weight of the past meant bondage to Mina and ensnarement in a degrading religious cult. Even for "the child" of the narrative poems in *The World between the Eyes,* the past is often tormenting as he struggles to come to terms with his father and mother, with his sense of alienation from community and church in **"Tin Roof Blues"** and **"Sunday,"** and with the death of his sister. For Ole Fred, however, as well as for his author, the past is a valuable resource, a strong foundation upon which to build. As Chappell says of his persona in the preface to *Midquest,* "He is cut off from his disappearing cultural traditions but finds them, in remembering, his real values" (x). Yet Chappell does not idealize or romanticize that past. The "Georgic center" of Chappell's poetry, in Don Johnson's phrase,[34] may be the farm, but like the Roman poet Virgil, Chappell is keenly aware of the hardships of agrarian living, especially on hardscrabble mountain farms, as a poem like **"My Father Washes His Hands"** demonstrates. Chappell is not a neo-Agrarian, but he does find in farming a meaningful—though not financially rewarding—lifestyle, one that heightens recognition of humanity's dependence on nature and that encourages both humility and a sense of stewardship. As he declares in his essay, "Poet and Plowman," "[Farming] is the one life besides poetry and natural philosophy that still touches an essential harmony of things, and when a civilization discards that way of life, it breaks the most fundamental covenant mankind can remember."[35] In *Midquest* farming also becomes a metaphor for the cultivation of the physical world that eventuates in spiritual vision. For Chappell, immersion in the physical world, not flight from it, leads to religious insight.

The agrarian tradition is only one dimension of the past that the poet celebrates in *Midquest.* Memories of his grandparents and parents as well as of Virgil Campbell elicit some of the book's most humorous and affectionate poems. Often those poems are monologues spoken by the characters themselves, though a younger Fred may serve as interlocutor. It is in such narrative poems as **"My Grandmother Washes Her Feet," "My Father Allergic to Fire," "Firewater," "My Mother Shoots the Breeze," "My Father's Hurricane,"** and **"Three Sheets in the Wind: Virgil Campbell Confesses"** that Chappell utilizes most effectively the oral tradition of his native Appalachia. At the same time, these narrative poems, with their vivid characters and incidents and their use of traditional folk materials, were inspired, Chappell says, by his admiration for Chaucer's achievement in *The Canterbury Tales.*[36]

The humor of the oral tradition—especially that distinctively American art form, the tall tale—had a major impact on the development of nineteenth-century literature in the United States, most notably in the writing of George Washington Harris and Mark Twain. Chappell's reading of both authors is apparent on more than one occasion in *Midquest* (and throughout the Kirkman tetralogy). Ole Fred's father's account of the multilayered windstorm in **"My Father's Hurricane,"** for instance, originates in the Washoe Zephyr that Twain describes in chapter 21 of *Roughing It.* And Harris's Sut Lovingood puts words in Virgil Campbell's mouth— *"Feet don't fail me now"*—in **"Three Sheets in the Wind."**[37]

Such borrowings and the frequent literary, musical, philosophical, and religious allusions in *Midquest* attest to the poet's celebration of the past and to the inclusiveness of his sense of community. His use of Dante's pilgrimage motif and other Dantean materials further affirms the continuity between past and present, as do the epigraphs he chooses for each of the book's four volumes, epigraphs taken from Melville, René Char, Dante, and Hawthorne, respectively. Of this group, only Char represents the twentieth century. The challenges faced by Chappell's "widely representative" persona are perennial human concerns.

Even while evoking the immense resources of the past, Chappell also emphasizes the importance of community in the present. This emphasis results not only from his attachment to place and to family but also from the poem's sociopolitical dimension and from the relationships Ole Fred cultivates with fellow writers. Sociopolitical issues are raised in each volume of *Midquest,* and the responsibilities of citizenship are never far from the poet's mind because the text's present, May 1971, finds the United States still fighting a war in Vietnam. **"Bloodfire"** deals most directly with that war, referring to its "fire-martyrs," "the immolated and self-immolated" (88). But the penultimate poem in *River* also speaks of "slow rain twitching wounds and eyelids / of murdered soldiers, / daily snail-white corpses / bloating the Mekong" (48). The opening poem of *Earthsleep* likewise notes how "fire colors the military maps, each village a red coal" (145). In addition to the bloodshed in Vietnam, Chappell protests economic injustice, from the paper mill's role in augmenting the flood's destruction in **"Dead Soldiers"** to the indifference of the rich toward the poor in **"Remembering Wind Mountain at Sunset."** By making such issues, including the racism alluded to in **"My Father Allergic to Fire,"** a significant part of the book, Chappell indicates that, for him, poetry is a means of confronting sociopolitical realities, not retreating from them into aestheticism.

Yet aesthetics, as distinct from aestheticism, is certainly another of the issues that *Midquest* addresses. The nature and function of the literary imagination have become one of the dominant themes in twentieth-century poetry, as is evident in the poetry of Wallace Stevens, for example. Unlike Stevens, however, for whom this theme is ubiquitous, Chappell assigns it a carefully delimited role in *Midquest,* as if to suggest that, for all its importance to the poet, it is only one of several ways of approaching the work of the mind. The poems in which aesthetic issues receive the most extended treatment are the playlet in which Reynolds Price appears and the four epistolary poems Ole Fred writes to friends and fellow writers Guy Lillian, James Applewhite, Richard Dillard, and George Garrett. Through their epistolary format, the latter poems reinforce the theme of community and help to dispel the image of the writer as *isolato.* These poems also reveal several of the major literary influences that shaped Chappell's imagination, influences he had learned to question. In **"Science Fiction Water Letter to Guy Lillian,"** for instance, the poet recalls his youthful fascination with this genre. Despite his continuing use of science fiction in a story like "The Somewhere Doors" (*More Shapes Than One*), this poem expresses Chappell's dissatisfaction with the genre, primarily because of its inattention to the physical world, its failure to develop a "feel for pastness," and its disregard for suffering (38-39). After this critique of science fiction, however, the poet proceeds to comment on the plight of contemporary poetry, especially among confessional poets, "still whining, like flawed Dylan records, about their poor / lost innocence" (40). Rejecting such an egocentric stance and its obsession with the personal past, Chappell proclaims, "Fresh wonders clamor for language," and he recommends (as T. S. Eliot's essays do) a return to Andrew Marvell and John Donne and Henry Vaughan, for "they had senses / alive apart from their egos, and took delight in / every new page of Natural Theology" (40).

This poem's emphasis on utilizing the senses to experience creation's abundance is echoed by the critique of the Symbolist sensibility set forth in **"Rimbaud Fire Letter to Jim Applewhite."** There Ole Fred renounces the derangement of the senses he had practiced so assiduously under Rimbaud's tutelage. What altered his poetic vision, he explains, following his suspension from Duke, was his return to the mountain landscape and then, following his re-enrollment at Duke, his immersion in the writings of Samuel Johnson, Alexander Pope, and other representatives of neoclassical rationalism. Yet Ole Fred signs this letter, only partly ironically, "Yours for terror and symbolism" (61), for symbolism—though not the Symbolist sensibility—informs all of *Midquest.* As for terror, that term, reminiscent perhaps of the emotion prompted by Rimbaud's "Drunken Boat," assumes for Chappell the added meaning of gazing into the abyss of suffering and meaninglessness. As he writes Richard Dillard in another of these epistolary poems, "Our faith must be earned from terror" (87) to be credible.

The aesthetic issues raised in the preceding epistolary poems are recapitulated in **"Hallowind"** and in the letter Chappell addresses to George Garrett titled **"How to Build the Earthly Paradise."** The playlet posits a contrast between Fred as poet and Reynolds Price as fiction writer, the former committed to generalizing symbols or archetypes, to a poetry of paradigms, the latter espousing "local clarities" (136) and declaring, "I regard the 'symbol' as a thief" (137). For Price, as Chappell presents him, "Poems are maimed by their timelessness, / . . . / The *symbol* is at last inhuman" (137; Chappell's italics). In actuality, of course, Chappell and Price write both fiction and poetry, and both authors use symbolism extensively. The conflict this poem articulates is intentionally oversimplified. In *Midquest* Chappell creates a text that reconciles the opposing principles the playlet depicts, combining the "local clarities" of the mountain community in which he was raised with the paradigm of spiritual quest limned in Dante's *Divine Comedy,* itself a poem steeped in symbolism and allegory. Chappell's use of the four elements as unifying images also contributes to the symbolic thrust of the poem, its archetypal and mythic dimensions. But at the same time, the images derived from those four elements anchor the text in the material world, in the realm of time and mortality, even as the pilgrim strives to soar toward eternity, toward a vision of the divine. It is precisely the substantiality of the Earthly Paradise—its composition from stone, sand, earth, water, air, plants and animals, men and women and children—that Ole Fred's epistle to Garrett insists upon. And the last word of that letter, before its valediction, is "yes," a word that voices both persona's and poet's affirmation of "the seething / homebrew of creation creating" (177). For Chappell both spiritual rebirth and authentic poetic insight depend upon this recognition of the wonder and mystery of nature and of human existence itself. As he writes in **"Susan Bathing,"** "Unattending beauty is danger & mortal sin," whereas "speech-praise" is the "instrument of unclosing and rising toward light" (19).

To enter the presence of such light is the ultimate goal of the pilgrim-poet in *Midquest,* as it is of Dante the pilgrim, and Chappell establishes many parallels between the two works. Both pilgrims commence their journeys in their thirty-fifth years; both have guides named Virgil; and both also experience divine love mediated by a woman (Beatrice, Susan). Though Virgil Campbell speaks for far earthier values than the author of the *Aeneid,* both Virgils are storytellers who, in different ways, represent the power of the vernacular. As in Dante's epic, the disappearance of *Midquest*'s Virgil from the text (Ole Fred visits his grave in the sixth poem of *Earthsleep*) is followed by a vision of the Earthly Paradise. Some of Chappell's parallels to Dante's poem occur in humorous contexts, as when Chappell, by adding Casanova, Lord Byron, and James Dickey, updates the Italian poet's Second Circle, where the carnal are punished. Chappell achieves similar humorous effects by using Dante's *terza rima* in Ole Fred's account of his grandfather's decision to hedge "his final bet" by converting from Methodism to "hard-believer / Baptist" (30), a conversion that necessitates baptism by total immersion, in the irreverently titled **"My Grandfather Gets Doused."** Such humorous adaptations of Dantean materials and poetic techniques are clearly meant to counterbalance the visionary flights of *Midquest*'s persona. Ole Fred lacks the certitude of his Dantean counterpart, and Chappell thus makes his pilgrim's affirmations more credible by detailing the "wilderness of doubt" (56) from which Fred's faith ultimately arises. The poet's skillful use of humor and irony, his perfectly timed moments of self-deprecation and self-mockery, strengthen the book.

"Birthday 35: Diary Entry," the second poem in *Midquest,* marks the point of departure for Ole Fred's spiritual quest and provides an effective example of the poet's self-directed humor and irony.

> Multiplying my age by 2 in my head,
> I'm a grandfather. Or dead.
>
> "Midway in this life I came to a darksome wood."
> But Dante, however befuddled, was Good.
>
> I'm still in flight, still unsteadily in pursuit,
> Always becoming more sordid, pale, and acute . . .
>
> (3)

In the book's opening poem Ole Fred is portrayed as "wishing never to wake" (2). His diary entry helps explain this impulse by describing the spiritual wasteland he wanders. Yet Ole Fred's response to this emptiness is not to despair but to pray. **"Birthday 35"** concludes with a prayer that runs for twenty-two lines. A striking admixture of the humorous, the grotesque, the self-ironic, and the sincere, that prayer distances readers from Ole Fred's longing for rebirth without undercutting the sincerity and significance of his yearning.

That yearning is powerfully conveyed in *Midquest*'s fourth poem too, **"Cleaning the Well,"** with its archetypal descent into the underworld, its confrontation with death. Hauled up into the light, the "most willing fish that was ever caught" (16), young Fred wonders, "Jonah, Joseph, Lazarus, / Were you delivered so?" (16) and remarks, *"I had not found death good"* (17; Chappell's italics). The prospect of death and the possibility of resurrection preoccupy Fred in many of the book's poems, especially in *Earthsleep,* for as his grandmother tells him as early as *Midquest*'s third poem, "It's dirt you rose from, dirt you'll bury in" (12). For her, this thought is more fact than threat, a fact of nature that does not negate her hope of resurrection. Indeed the natural and the supernatural cohabit throughout *Midquest,* as they frequently do in the Judeo-Christian tradition. Each of the four elements around which Chappell organizes *Midquest* assumes religious significance. Water, often a symbol of materiality, becomes an emblem of the intersection of time and eternity in **"The River Awakening in the Sea,"** as in Anne Bradstreet's "Contemplations." Water is also, in baptism, a means of grace, an instrument of spiritual regeneration. Fire is both instrument of divine wrath and means of purification. It witnesses to God's presence in the burning bush from which God spoke to Moses and in the tongues of flame associated with the Holy Spirit. Wind—bodiless, invisible, yet observable in its effects—is similarly linked to the Holy Spirit, and in **"Second Wind"** it touches Fred's grandmother with "the weight of grace" (106). Chappell regularly associates wind with music as well and has noted that "music probably stands in my poems most of the time for exaltation, exalted spirits, ecstatic visionary knowledge."[38] As for earth, with its gaping graves, it is the foundation of the Earthly Paradise and the soil from which the "Tree of Spirit lift[s] from the mountain of earth" (149) to "the Mountains Outside Time" (169).

Midquest is a poem that evokes the mythos of Eden and "a final shore" (141) beyond the fevered river of time. Implicit in the sleep of *Earthsleep* is the prospect of awakening, and the epigraph from Hawthorne that opens the book's final volume depicts the peaceful transition from waking to the "temporary death" of sleep, comparing that transition to the experience of dying itself. "So calm, perhaps, will be the final change; so undisturbed, as if among familiar things the entrance of the soul to its Eternal home" (143). Hawthorne's "perhaps" in this passage registers the ineluctable mystery of the human encounter with death, and the sketch from which Chappell excerpts this epigraph is titled "The Haunted Mind." Yet while the questions death poses are irresolvable for the mind situated on this side of the grave—as the varied definitions of the term "earthsleep" in *Midquest*'s closing poem indicate—Chappell concludes that poem by invoking Dante's vision of God: "The love that moves the sun and other stars / The love that moves itself in light to loving" (187). The first of these lines translates the final line of the *Paradiso,* while the second is Chappell's attempt to capture the tone and spirit of Dante's poem. In

the final line of **"Earthsleep"** Fred and Susan lie side by side "here in the earliest morning of the world" (187), an image suggestive not of death but of new life. Dabney Stuart is thus correct when he argues that Chappell is "preoccupied with and hopeful of images of release and transformation, which are Christian in their orientation."[39] The Fred who resists waking in *Midquest*'s opening poem learns to "invite the mornings" (185).[40]

In addition to tracing this explicitly religious quest, Chappell fills *Midquest* with metaphysical speculations of various sorts. For Chappell, the experience of wonder prompts not only spiritual meditation but also the reflections of poet and philosopher alike. Chappell's repeated probing of philosophical issues, what one critic has called Chappell's "abiding concern with Ultimates,"[41] contributes significantly to both the breadth of *Midquest*'s subject matter and the substantiality of its themes. Yet the book does not simply juxtapose humorous narrative poems with more somber meditative poems. Instead, Chappell's narrative poems address philosophical and religious themes while his meditative poems are leavened by a buoyant humor that prevents reader and poet alike from taking themselves too seriously. The book's more lyric poems—those, for example, that open and close each of the four volumes—are similarly infused with philosophical inquiry. In fact cosmogony is a recurring motif in the initial poems of *River, Bloodfire,* and *Wind Mountain,* introduced in each case by references to "how the world was formed" (2, 56, 98). Myths of origin are also evident in Ole Fred's "slightly different Big Bang theory" in **"The Autumn Bleat of the Weathervane Trombone"** ("In the beginning was the Trombone" [115]) and in the excerpt from his novel-in-progress in **"Science Fiction Water Letter"** (41-43). Obviously, a concern for cosmogony also underpins Chappell's use of the four elements to structure *Midquest.* Renouncing the abstraction of Plato's realm of Ideal Forms (as he had done in his early poem **"A Transcendental Idealist Dreams in Springtime"**), Chappell recurs to the pre-Socratic naturalistic era in Greek philosophy. What he offers, finally, is a profoundly incarnational view of the relationship between matter and spirit, time and eternity, a view shaped by Christian thought.

This incarnational perspective is most fully developed in *Midquest*'s four long meditative poems: **"Susan Bathing," "Firewood," "The Autumn Bleat of the Weathervane Trombone,"** and **"The Peaceable Kingdom of Emerald Windows."** The first two are single-sentence stream-of-consciousness poems, each seven pages in length, and they thus contrast in structure with the greater formal and syntactical clarity of the latter two poems, differences intended to mirror, Chappell says, his pilgrim's progress "as the speaker begins to order his life" (x). To term these poems "interior monologues," however, as Chappell does in the preface, is somewhat misleading, for each includes features of direct address that again reinforce the network of relationships in which the poet embeds Ole Fred.

"Susan Bathing" incorporates both philosophical and explicitly religious themes while also confirming Chappell's claim that *Midquest* is "in its largest design a love poem" (xi). The epigraph to **"Susan Bathing,"** taken from Pope's "Windsor Forest," asserts that harmonious confusion, not chaos, governs the world, and thus underscores the fundamental outlook of *Midquest* as a whole and the artistic impression of order that the book conveys. The Susan of this poem takes on a variety of identities. On the literal level she is simply Fred's wife, the object of his love, but marriage in *Midquest* assumes a metaphoric significance that extends well beyond its social function. Marriage illustrates the union of apparent opposites: not only women and men but also humankind and nature, as well as in Christian theology, the human and the divine. Susan herself functions allegorically in this poem both as Beatrice and as the Virgin Mary. In **"Susan Bathing"** body and spirit are conjoined, and Chappell's wide-ranging diction reflects this yoking of the earthy and the ethereal. In addition to her roles as Beatrice and Mary, Susan becomes the poet's muse, her "clean / flesh the synonym of love," eliciting his "speech praise" (23), reminding the poet of his "responsibilities to whatever is genuine" (19). In traditional Christian terms, the poet describes his will as "stricken and contort" and declares that "only intercession from / without can restore it" (21). Through Susan and the outpouring of praise she provokes, he gains access to self-transformation, "for once the mind prepares to praise & garbs / in worshipful robe it enlarges to plenitude" (19), a plenitude, as in the annunciation to Mary, "plena gratia" (20), full of grace. Significantly, it is the sight of Susan's body that prompts this epiphany, just as her physical act of bathing promises the poet spiritual regeneration.

In contrast to **"Susan Bathing,"** **"Firewood"** is less explicitly religious and more overtly philosophical in its exploration of the relationship between flesh and spirit, matter and mind. It too employs the metaphor of marriage, however, and discusses the role of art in bonding humanity and nature. Much more than **"Susan Bathing,"** **"Firewood"** confronts the fact of death and attempts to reconcile that fact with the longing for immortality. The wood Ole Fred splits in this poem is destined for his fireplace, where the sun (imaged as stored in the wood) will be released as heat and light, "the sun risen at midnight" to ascend "the rose trellis of stars . . . afire" (69). Burning, this wood will become "tree of spirit," with the poet's chimney linking the corporeal and the immaterial and suggesting humanity's dual identity as flesh and spirit—the world of spirit

symbolized, here as elsewhere in Chappell's work, by the stars. The chimney "pins our dwelling / to the earth and to the stars equally" (69), the poet observes. Yet despite the beauty and the rhetorical effect of an image like "the rose trellis of stars," Ole Fred remains skeptical, fearful that "the cold dark will tear our tree of fire / away complete" (69) and conscious that Lucretius's "seed of fire ignis semina is seed semina mortuis," that is, seed of death (70). Unable to endorse, as he once did, Rimbaud's conception of "the vatic will" (71) capable of utterly transforming reality through the powers of the poetic imagination, Ole Fred yields to thoughts of death. For a moment he even longs to jettison human consciousness in exchange for the apparent contentment of the animal world. But, finally, he can neither surrender the uniqueness of human selfhood nor evade its often anguished doubts. As he continues to wonder, "but where / shall I sit when once this flesh is spirit?" (73), the reader notices that Ole Fred has undercut the Lucretian view of a purely physical universe in the very formulation of that question. **"Firewood"** concludes by comparing the ultimately successful splitting of the wood to the annunciation to Mary and by depicting that experience as a kind of baptism: "I'm washed in the blood / of the sun, the ghostly holy of the deep deep log" (73). The punning religious diction here is meant to resolve, to some extent at least, the tensions between secular and sacred, flesh and spirit, time and eternity, that this poem examines. Yet, as Ole Fred states in the poem's final lines, "It doesn't come easy, I'm / here to tell you that."

What the other two long meditative poems in *Midquest* make clear is that, for Chappell, this "ghostly holy" is not to be sought at the expense of the physical world. To both **"The Autumn Bleat of the Weathervane Trombone"** and **"The Peaceable Kingdom of Emerald Windows,"** the poet introduces a new character, someone whom Ole Fred refers to as Uncle Body. This figure is intended to subvert the philosophical idealism espoused by Plato, Plotinus, Descartes, and Emerson as well as the otherworldliness of a Protestant Christianity too often misled by Gnostic and Neo-Platonic thought. For the Emerson of *Nature,* personal identity was purely a mental or spiritual phenomenon; even one's body belonged to the category of the "NOT ME."[42] The playfulness and linguistic exuberance of both these poems reflect the expansiveness of the poet's sense of self-hood. In **"The Autumn Bleat"** fall is less a time of decay than of rebirth. Yellow, gold, and blue are the dominant colors, the last recalling Wallace Stevens's use of blue as the color of the imagination in "The Man with the Blue Guitar." That connection is evident here in Fred's music, a "bluesy A" (115) emerging to drift "the bluebleached air" (114). As the title's term "bleat" implies, that music is scarcely elegant, but the poem provides a cornucopia of sound effects, of levels of diction and allusion too. "There's something in air in love with rounded notes, / The goldenrod's a-groan at the globèd beauty," Chappell writes, in lines of consciously exaggerated alliteration (110). "Bring me my trombone of burning gold, bring me / My harrowing desire," he adds, paraphrasing Blake's *Milton.* Obviously, Chappell takes risks in such passages, as he attempts to communicate Fred's vision of life's fullness; occasionally those fanciful flights collapse under the weight of their distended diction. In general, however, readers are likely to be borne along by the sweeping sense of elation Ole Fred expresses, by the sheer energy and inventiveness of his words.

Like **"Firewood,"** both **"Autumn Bleat"** and **"The Peaceable Kingdom of Emerald Windows"** address the fact of death. In contrast to **"Firewood"** the latter two poems actually contain portraits of the afterlife (as does *Earthsleep*'s **"At the Grave of Virgil Campbell"**). At times, these visions of the afterlife are wildly comic, verging on the blasphemous, as when Fred states his certainty that there is "Whiskey-after-Death" and refers to God as "the Holy Bartender" (173). But the different versions of the afterlife Ole Fred offers all have in common their being grounded upon human relationships and the physical world. In **"Autumn Bleat,"** for example, he anticipates—with some apprehension—the prospect of spending eternity in the company of his fellow poets. In **"Peaceable Kingdom"** it is naturalists like Gilbert White and William Bartram, a novelist like Colette, and "rare Ben Franklin" whom he envisions joining, all of them people firmly attached in their earthly lives to the physical world. Moreover, since the phrase "Emerald Windows" refers to raindrops, nature becomes precious in itself, associated through the color green with seasonal rebirth and providing a source of spiritual vision, a window on eternity. At odds with the philosophical idealism of Emerson, Chappell nevertheless seems to concur with the Transcendentalist precept, "Nature is the symbol of Spirit."

Yet while Ole Fred celebrates nature and renounces Nirvana as "a sterile and joyless blasphemy" (113), he is decidedly unwilling to resign himself to physicality alone. He refuses to surrender to matter his powers of mind and spirit. Thus in **"Autumn Bleat"** he attempts to induce Uncle Body to voyage with him through the realms of philosophical speculation: "To swim from Singapore / To Hermeneutics and through the Dardanelles / To Transcendentalism, back through the Straits / of Hegel" (113). Here, as in many other poems in *Midquest,* Chappell attempts to naturalize metaphysical thought and thus to create for poetry—and for its readers—a commitment to philosophical reflection, to the Socratic ideal of examined lives. Just as the Virgil of the *Georgics* identifies the natural philosopher (along with the farmer and the poet) as one of the three kinds of people most attuned to the harmonies of the universe, so Chappell makes philosophical thought one of

Midquest's central activities, along with farming and artistic creation and the religious quest itself.

Perhaps the most persistent philosophical and religious problem Chappell's book addresses, especially in **Earthsleep,** is human mortality, the inescapable reality that Martin Heidegger terms *Sein zum Tod* (being toward death). **"The Peaceable Kingdom,"** the meditative poem in that final volume, includes the statement, "Goodbye I perceive to be a human creature" (156). Yet the tone of that poem is not one of fear or anxiety but serenity. Chappell achieves this effect in part by invoking the utopian vision of the Edward Hicks painting mentioned in the title, in part by making green one of the poem's dominant colors (as that color predominates in **Earthsleep**), and in part by organizing the latter portions of the poem around the activity of harvesting hay. That activity, successfully completed despite the threat of rain, lends to the poem an aura of fruition and reaffirms the bonds of family and community which the entire book cultivates. Rejecting again idealism's "sleepy flea market of Forms" (158), Ole Fred emphasizes the goodness of the creation, informing Uncle Body, "All the world is lit for your delight" (159). Integral to this vision of oneness with nature are those passages in which the poet personifies Maude and Jackson, the horses pulling the hay wagon, endowing them with speech. Through this device Chappell bridges the accustomed gap between humanity and nature and suspends the reader's commitment to the purely factual. His appeal to a wider conception of truth encourages the reader to assent as well to his image of the sun nestling "in the form / In the hay in the world in the green green hand" (157).

Clearly the resolution **"The Peaceable Kingdom"** offers is more emotional than logical. Like the repeated sound of the church bell calling *home, home, home* at key points throughout the last two volumes of *Midquest* (100, 133, 161, 185), it appeals more to the heart than to the head. But Chappell has already conceded as much in **"Firewood"** in his account of the postlapsarian intellect as "all alert and doubtful" (72). What Chappell manages to accomplish in *Midquest*—and it is no small achievement in what is commonly considered a postmodern, post-Christian age—is to awaken readers to the presence of Spirit, both in nature and in themselves. The *Book of Earth,* as Ole Fred discovers, is "brimming over with matter, / Matter aye and spirit, too, each / And every page is chock to stupefying" (160). Or, as Fred puts it after visiting the site of a burned church in **"My Grandfather's Church Goes Up"**:

> Pilgrim, the past   becomes prayer
> becomes remembrance rock-real   of Resurrection
> when the Willer so willeth   works his wild wonders.

> (77; Chappell's italics)

Among the types of resurrection to which *Midquest* testifies is that of traditional poetic forms. **"My Grandfather's Church"** employs Anglo-Saxon alliterative verse; the epistolary poem to Richard Dillard is in elegiacs; the letter to Guy Lillian in syllabics; **"My Grandmother's Hard Row to Hoe"** uses chant royal. While blank verse and free verse predominate, other traditional forms abound: rhymed couplets in lines of varying lengths, heroic couplets, *terza rima,* Yeatsian tetrameter, even a variation on classical hexameter in **"Susan Bathing."** The rhyme scheme in the playlet **"Hallowind"** consists of three successively rhymed tetrameter lines, with the rhymes carrying over from one speaker to the next. In the grandmother's monologue in **"Second Wind"** the poet uses iambic pentameter octets based on an abba abba rhyme scheme, yet maintains the impression of a vernacular voice. Few poets since Robert Frost have captured the natural speaking voice as effectively as Chappell does in both rhymed forms and blank verse. The book's varied stanza structures—couplets, tercets, quatrains, sestets, octets, verse paragraphs of differing lengths, seven-page single-sentence stream-of-consciousness meditations—help keep the poems continually fresh as the reader accompanies Ole Fred on his quest. As one critic has remarked, "The poems fairly exult in their technical invention. . . . The range is extraordinary."[43] Chappell's skill with such structural matters is especially evident in the epistolary poem to George Garrett titled **"How to Build the Earthly Paradise."** There the poet creates a nine-line stanza, each end stopped, to represent the blocks of material used to construct this utopia. Each stanza opens and closes, moreover, with a single-syllable line, as if to evince the solidity of the workmanship, and the second and eighth lines contain just two syllables per line. The ponderous rhythms these four lines establish at each stanza's beginning and end suggest the thought and care that underlie the poet's making. Chappell's mastery of his craft is readily, though unostentatiously, apparent throughout *Midquest,* reminding readers of the poetic resources many contemporary poets have neglected in their commitment to free verse.

The revival of the narrative impulse in poetry is another of the aesthetic resurrections that this book attains. As one interviewer has noted, there are at least three kinds of narrative in *Midquest*: "the movement of images," "the repetition of narratives within a poem, the story lines themselves, the plots," and "the whole poetic narrative of the self, a biography of sorts."[44] It is in the second of these categories that the poet allows his gifts for storytelling their freest rein, particularly when his grandparents and parents and Virgil Campbell speak; and it is often in these poems (for example, **"My Father's Hurricane"** and **"Three Sheets in the Wind"**) that Chappell's comic vision reaches its greatest heights. Because of the accessibility and humor of these poems,

general readers as well as critics have sometimes seen them as the most distinctive or original aspect of the book. Yet for all their vividness and directness of appeal, these poems are subsumed within *Midquest*'s larger narrative and thematic structure, which is centered upon Ole Fred's search for moral and spiritual renewal and for a deeper understanding of his place both in the human community and in the cosmos.

Midquest is ultimately most original in its elaborate interweaving of the regional and the universal and in its intricacy of design, a design in which lyric, narrative, epistolary, and meditative poems echo and enrich one another. Chappell's enormous range of allusions ties his individual Appalachian voices to many of the most significant features of the Western literary, philosophical, and religious traditions. To declare, as one reviewer of *Earthsleep* did, that Chappell's "real subject" is "the hard but satisfyingly essential dirt-farming life as it used to be in the South," a subject from which the reviewer felt the poems in *Earthsleep* had strayed, is to badly misread both the poet's intentions and his accomplishment.[45] *Midquest* is a book that requires and rewards rereading. It is, to quote Kelly Cherry, "a terrifically . . . powerful poem, full of the pleasures of surfaces and the deep gratification of complex structure."[46] As the book receives the kind of searching critical analysis its achievement merits, it will increasingly be seen for what, in fact, it is—one of the finest long poems in twentieth-century American literature.

Notes

1. Broughton, "Fred Chappell," 118.

2. Palmer, "Fred Chappell," 407.

3. Chappell's three chapbooks—*The Man Twice Married to Fire* (Greensboro: Unicorn, 1977), *Awakening to Music* (Davidson, N.C.: Briarpatch, 1979), and *Driftlake: A Lieder Cycle* (Emory, Va.: Iron Mountain Press, 1981)—have often been erroneously listed among his book-length publications in standard reference works. "How I Lost It"—another title so listed—though planned, never appeared in print.

4. Ralph Waldo Emerson, *Selected Prose and Poetry,* 2d ed., ed. Reginald L. Cook (San Francisco: Rinehart, 1969), 124.

5. Stephenson, "'The Way It Is,'" 8.

6. Chappell, *A Way of Happening: Observations of Contemporary Poetry* (New York: Picador, 1998), 9.

7. Walsh, "Fred Chappell," 71.

8. Ibid., 75.

9. Chappell, "Fred Chappell," 122.

10. Kathryn Stripling Byer, "Turning the Windlass at the Well: Fred Chappell's Early Poetry," in *Dream Garden,* 88.

11. Chappell, *The World between the Eyes* (Baton Rouge: Louisiana State University Press, 1971), 3, 4. Further references noted parenthetically are to this edition.

12. Chappell, *Plow Naked: Selected Writings on Poetry* (Ann Arbor: University of Michigan Press, 1993), 112.

13. Byer, "Turning the Windlass at the Well," 93-94.

14. Ibid., 95.

15. Chappell, *Midquest* (Baton Rouge: Louisiana State University Press, 1981), ix. Further references noted parenthetically are to this edition.

16. Broughton, "Fred Chappell," 108. "Familiar Poem" is reprinted in *Under Twenty-five: Duke Narrative and Verse, 1945-1962,* ed. William Blackburn (Durham, N.C.: Duke University Press, 1963), 198-201.

17. Crane and Kirkland, "First and Last Words," 16.

18. Dannye Romine Powell, "Fred Chappell," in *Parting the Curtains: Interviews with Southern Writers* (Winston-Salem: Blair, 1994), 36.

19. Jackson, "On the Margins of Dreams," 156.

20. Bizzaro, "Introduction: Fred Chappell's Community of Readers," in *Dream Garden,* 4.

21. Randolph Paul Runyon, "Fred Chappell: Midquestions," in *Southern Writers at Century's End,* ed. Jeffrey J. Folks and James A. Perkins (Lexington: University of Kentucky Press, 1997), 197.

22. Chappell, "Midquest," *The Small Farm* 11-12 (Spring-Fall 1980): 13.

23. Chappell, *A Way of Happening,* 215.

24. Chappell, *Plow Naked,* 90.

25. Ibid., 89, 92.

26. Chappell, *A Way of Happening,* 235.

27. Chappell, *Plow Naked,* 91.

28. Morgan, "*Midquest* and the Gift of Narrative," in *Dream Garden,* 139.

29. Chappell, "Midquest," 13.

30. Ibid.

31. Taylor, "Fred Chappell," in *Contemporary Poets,* 6th ed., ed. Thomas Riggs (New York: St. James Press, 1996), 154.

32. Philip Pierson, "Interview with Fred Chappell," *New River Review* 2 (Spring 1977): 13. As Rodney Jones also notes, "We never have the sense that *Midquest* is inventing itself apart from other consciousness." See Jones's essay "The Large Vision: Fred Chappell's *Midquest,*" *Appalachian Journal* 9, no. 1 (1981): 63.

33. Chappell, "Towards a Beginning," *The Small Farm* 4-5 (Oct. 1976-Mar. 1977): 98.

34. Don Johnson, "The Cultivated Mind: The Georgic Center of Fred Chappell's Poetry," in *Dream Garden,* 170-79.

35. Chappell, *Plow Naked,* 79.

36. Pierson, "Interview with Fred Chappell," 11. See also Crane and Kirkland, "First and Last Words," 20.

37. For an extensive analysis of the sources of many of Chappell's allusions in *Midquest,* see John Lang, "Points of Kinship: Community and Allusion in Fred Chappell's *Midquest,*" in *Dream Garden,* 97-117.

38. Broughton, "Fred Chappell," 109.

39. Dabney Stuart, "Spiritual Matter in Fred Chappell's Poetry," in *Dream Garden,* 48.

40. Alan Nadel mistakenly assumes that Chappell's aim in *Midquest* is to "attempt to freeze the day of his 35th birthday," an attempt that Nadel calls "the governing futility of the whole tetralogy." See his essay "Quest and Midquest: Fred Chappell and the First-Person Personal Epic," *New England Review and Bread Loaf Quarterly* 6 (Winter 1983): 324.

41. Peter Makuck, "Chappell's Continuities: *First and Last Words,*" in *Dream Garden,* 180.

42. Emerson, *Selected Prose and Poetry,* 4.

43. Cherry, "The Idea of Odyssey in *Midquest,*" in *Dream Garden,* 122.

44. Jackson, "On the Margins of Dreams," 155.

45. Richard Tillinghast, "Scattered Nebulae," *Sewanee Review* 90, no. 2 (1982): 300.

46. Cherry, "The Idea of Odyssey in *Midquest,*" 132.

Bibliography

Works by Fred Chappell

Listed in order of publication.

Collections of Poetry

The World between the Eyes. Baton Rouge: Louisiana State University Press, 1971.

River. Baton Rouge: Louisiana State University Press, 1975.

Bloodfire. Baton Rouge: Louisiana State University Press, 1978.

Wind Mountain. Baton Rouge: Louisiana State University Press, 1979.

Earthsleep. Baton Rouge: Louisiana State University Press, 1980.

Midquest. Baton Rouge: Louisiana State University Press, 1981.

Castle Tzingal. Baton Rouge: Louisiana State University Press, 1984.

Source. Baton Rouge: Louisiana State University Press, 1985.

First and Last Words. Baton Rouge: Louisiana State University Press, 1989.

C. Baton Rouge: Louisiana State University Press, 1993.

Spring Garden: New and Selected Poems. Baton Rouge: Louisiana State University Press, 1995.

COLLECTIONS OF ESSAYS

Plow Naked: Selected Writings on Poetry. Ann Arbor: University of Michigan Press, 1993.

A Way of Happening: Observations of Contemporary Poetry. New York: Picador, 1998.

SELECTED UNCOLLECTED ESSAYS AND OTHER NONFICTION

"Fred Chappell." Vol. 4 of *Contemporary Authors Autobiography Series,* edited by Adele Sarkissian, 113-26. Detroit: Gale, 1986.

INTERVIEWS

Pierson, Philip. "Interview with Fred Chappell." *New River Review* 2 (Spring 1977): 5-16, 61-73.

Jackson, Richard. "On the Margins of Dreams." In *Acts of Mind: Conversations with Contemporary Poets,* edited by Richard Jackson. Tuscaloosa: University of Alabama Press, 1983.

Stephenson, Shelby. "'The Way It Is': An Interview with Fred Chappell." *Iron Mountain Review* 2 (Spring 1985): 7-11.

Broughton, Irv. "Fred Chappell." Vol. 3 of *The Writer's Mind: Interviews with American Authors.* Fayetteville: University of Arkansas Press, 1990.

Walsh, William J. "Fred Chappell." In *Speak So I Shall Know Thee: Interviews with Southern Writers.* Asheboro, N.C.: Down Home Press, 1990.

Palmer, Tersh. "Fred Chappell." *Appalachian Journal* 19, no. 4 (1992): 402-10.

Powell, Dannye Romine. "Fred Chappell." In *Parting the Curtains: Interviews with Southern Writers.* Winston-Salem, N.C.: John F. Blair, 1994.

Crane, Resa, and James Kirkland. "First and Last Words: A Conversation with Fred Chappell." In *Dream Garden: The Poetic Vision of Fred Chappell,* edited by Patrick Bizzaro. Baton Rouge: Louisiana State University Press, 1997.

SELECTED WORKS ABOUT CHAPPELL

Listed in alphabetical order by author.

BIBLIOGRAPHIES

Kibler, James Everett, Jr. "A Fred Chappell Bibliography, 1963-1983." *Mississippi Quarterly* 37 (Winter 1983-84): 63-88. Detailed record of Chappell's primary works.

BOOKS

Bizzaro, Patrick, ed. *Dream Garden: The Poetic Vision of Fred Chappell.* Baton Rouge: Louisiana State University Press, 1997. Extremely valuable collection of essays on Chappell's poetry through *Spring Garden.*

SELECTED CRITICAL AND BIOGRAPHICAL ESSAYS

Byer, Kathryn Stripling. "Turning the Windlass at the Well: Fred Chappell's Early Poetry." In *Dream Garden: The Poetic Vision of Fred Chappell,* edited by Patrick Bizzaro, 88-96. Baton Rouge: Louisiana State University Press, 1997. Excellent assessment of *The World between the Eyes,* especially its longer narrative poems.

Cherry, Kelly. "A Writer's Harmonious World." *Parnassus* 9 (Fall-Winter 1981): 115-29. Reprinted as "The Idea of Odyssey in *Midquest*" in *Dream Garden: The Poetic Vision of Fred Chappell,* edited by Patrick Bizzaro, 118-32. Baton Rouge: Louisiana State University Press, 1997. Detailed analysis of the motif of the spiritual journey in *Midquest.*

Johnson, Don. "The Cultivated Mind: The Georgic Center of Fred Chappell's Poetry." In *Dream Garden: The Poetic Vision of Fred Chappell,* edited by Patrick Bizzaro, 170-79. Baton Rouge: Louisiana State University Press, 1997. Informative discussion of Chappell's debt to Virgil and the agrarian vision of the *Georgics.*

Jones, Rodney. "The Large Vision: Fred Chappell's *Midquest.*" *Appalachian Journal* 9, no. 1 (1981): 59-65. Enthusiastic assessment of *Midquest* that emphasizes the volume's meditative poems.

Lang, John. "Points of Kinship: Community and Allusion in Fred Chappell's *Midquest.*" In *Dream Garden: The Poetic Vision of Fred Chappell,* edited by Patrick Bizzaro, 97-117. Baton Rouge: Louisiana State University Press, 1997. Includes a useful appendix that lists

Chappell's many references and allusions in this poem and that demonstrates the varied sources that have influenced his work.

Makuck, Peter. "Chappell's Continuities: *First and Last Words.*" *Virginia Quarterly Review* 68, no. 2 (1992): 315-36. Reprinted in *Dream Garden: The Poetic Vision of Fred Chappell,* edited by Patrick Bizzaro, 180-97. Baton Rouge: Louisiana State University Press, 1997. Perceptive placement of this volume in the context of Chappell's abiding philosophical and religious concerns.

Morgan, Robert. *"Midquest." American Poetry Review* 11 (July-Aug. 1982): 45-47. Reprinted as *"Midquest* and the Gift of Narrative" in *Dream Garden: The Poetic Vision of Fred Chappell,* edited by Patrick Bizzaro, 133-44. Baton Rouge: Louisiana State University Press, 1997. Also reprinted in Morgan's *Good Measure* (Baton Rouge: Louisiana State University Press, 1993). Superb analysis of *Midquest* as "lyric narrative."

Nadel, Alan. "Quest and Midquest: Fred Chappell and the First-Person Personal Epic." *New England Review and Bread Loaf Quarterly* 6 (Winter 1983): 323-31. Argues that Chappell's quest is doomed because it tries to freeze the day of his thirty-fifth birthday to stop the passage of time.

Runyon, Randolph Paul. "Fred Chappell: Midquestions." *Southern Writers at Century's Turn.* Ed. Jeffrey J. Folks and James A. Perkins, 185-200. Lexington: University Press of Kentucky, 1997. Detailed analysis of the "symmetrical" structure of *Midquest* and some of the inconsistencies between Chappell's preface and the poem's practice.

Stuart, Dabney. "Spiritual Matter in Fred Chappell's Poetry: A Prologue." *Southern Review* 27, no. 1 (1991): 200-220. Reprinted in *Dream Garden: The Poetic Vision of Fred Chappell,* edited by Patrick Bizzaro, 48-70. Baton Rouge: Louisiana State University Press, 1997. Brilliant discussion of the Lucretian and Christian influences on Chappell's poetry.

Patrick Bizzaro (essay date 2004)

SOURCE: Bizzaro, Patrick. "'Growth of a Poet's Mind' and the Problem of Autobiography: Distance and Point of View in the Writings of Fred Chappell." In *More Lights Than One: On the Fiction of Fred Chappell,* edited by Patrick Bizzaro, pp. 72-91. Baton Rouge, La.: Louisiana State University Press, 2004.

[*In the following essay, Bizzaro addresses the narrative aspects of Chappell's poetry and fiction, focusing in part on the various narrative voices—many of them autobiographical—employed in* Midquest *and the Kirkman Tetralogy.*]

Handling point of view is much more than a matter of picking a person or a narrative technique and sticking with it; rather, it involves carefully manipulating the distance between narrator and character, moving closer one minute, then farther away the next, so as to achieve the desired response from the reader.

—David Jauss, "From Long Shots to X-Rays"

Fred Chappell has been rightly praised for his ability to work in several genres effectively. Robert Morgan, for one, writes, "Among the poets of our time there are many with great ability for concentration of phrase and figure. . . . And there are many fine story writers and novelists among us. Since Frost, however, there has been virtually no one who can do both at once. . . . We should value all the more, therefore, a writer such as Fred Chappell, who can combine the two arts" (133). Morgan refers here to Chappell's use of narrative in both his poetry and fiction. For my purposes in this essay, I want to add to this praise of Chappell praise for his ability to write effectively in essay form, as both critic and creative essayist. So it should not surprise us that two of the matters brought to our attention in the Kirkman tetralogy—that the novels are concerned largely with Jess's education, with what Wordsworth calls the "growth of a poet's mind," and that, as a result, they invite us to pay particular attention to the relationship established between the narrator and the author— are perfectly comfortable in their relation to other of Chappell's works in other genres. No doubt one of Chappell's contributions to contemporary literature, indeed to postmodern thinking, is the way we view genre and voice since his central themes and his complex use of point of view are evident in his poems and essays as well as in his novels. This is particularly true of his major fictive accomplishment to date, the Kirkman tetralogy, novels structurally parallel to his four-volume poem *Midquest.*[1]

Both the Kirkman tetralogy and *Midquest* are in some ways concerned with the "growth of a poet's mind" and with the education of its narrators, Jess Kirkman and the "Ole Fred" or "I" of Chappell's poetry. In spite of his statements to the contrary, Chappell seems to self-consciously identify not only Jess and Ole Fred but his other narrators as well (including essayist Chappell and critic Chappell) with Fred Chappell the author. And he seems especially interested, in all three genres, in discussing the education of his narrators. That these narratives often overlap neither surprises the reader nor lessens the impact of the individual narratives. But the narratives do bring to mind other writers who, like Chappell, placed so much emphasis on themselves.

But Chappell seems to have already thought his way through this predicament. While readers still take quite seriously D. H. Lawrence's dictum to "never trust the teller, trust the tale," most will honor the author's denial that he has intentionally identified his narrators with himself. But in Chappell's case his various personae report similar narratives of the growth of the poet, if not narratives typically associated in all respects with *bildungsromane*.[2] No doubt the experiences given in these multi-genred, multi-volumed efforts are not identical with Chappell's life experiences any more than Wordsworth's "growth of a poet's mind," *The Prelude,* is an accurate depiction in every detail of Wordsworth's life. At most, these works are "partial autobiographies"—which, of course, in some ways erases them as autobiographies. We might look farther for comparisons. But more partial, and less autobiographical, indeed, are the other romantic works that come to mind, including Keats's *Endymion,* Byron's *Don Juan,* Pater's *Marius the Epicurean*—works in the subgenre "growth of a poet's mind" most often cited as prototypes of *bildungsromane* (see Buckley).

Still, in reading Chappell's writings, readers might rightly feel that their educations have betrayed them— or, if not betrayed them, been revealed as inadequate to the task. It is fairly standard these days to locate point of view in terms of "person." Though this is often a useful mechanism for discussing literature, since it enables us to determine "who" tells the story, it does not provide the tools necessary if our goal is to understand and appreciate narration, as we must in reading Chappell, in terms of what Wayne Booth calls "distance." As Booth notes in *The Rhetoric of Fiction,* distance may mean "distance in time and space, differences of social class or [in] conventions of speech or dress" (156). These elements of narrative distance—to use Booth's language, the distance between narrator (the one who tells the story) and implied author (the author's presence in the story as a second self)—give us a way to discuss point of view in Chappell's writings. Though I am opposed to reading Chappell's essays, poems, and stories as rhetorical in any reductive way, if we hope to understand Chappell's method of narration we must accept the notion that Chappell as author has intended to manipulate his subject and his audience to achieve particular ends and thus works rhetorically himself.[3]

The term *distance,* then, is the one that best describes the rhetorical manipulation Chappell has in mind. As Booth writes: "The *narrator* may be more or less distant from the *implied author*" (156, my emphasis). This essay will read Chappell for the skill he employs in distancing his narrator from the implied author and test in Chappell's writings the viability of Booth's longstanding and widely accepted position on the use of the implied author—that is, that the narrator and the implied author may exist simultaneously in a text and that they may be (are apt to be) identified in that text by a single name. More specifically, in personal essays such as "First Attempts" and "Welcome to High Culture" from

Plow Naked, Chappell, the implied author, speaks through a mature if judgmental voice and thus seems distant in time, place, and moral values from his youngish narrator, who describes the events that constitute growth as writer and poet. These events often bewilder the narrator, though they are understandable to the older, more experienced implied author. In poems from *Midquest,* Chappell uses a variety of strategies to manage point of view and manipulate his readers; **"Rimbaud Fire Letter to Jim Applewhite"** makes the most impressive use of distance through which Chappell the writer seems best able to demonstrate the point he wants to make about the poet's growth toward maturity. When read as we read *Midquest,* as a single work that comprises four parts, the novels likewise use a variety of means of distancing. And where Jess the narrator and the implied author agree, the implied author disappears entirely; the job of educating the poet is then complete. Since in all of Chappell's works the line separating Chappell as author from the narrators of his essays, poems, and stories (i.e., Chappell the critic, Ole Fred, "I," and Jess Kirkman) is so thin—at times nearly invisible—that accusations of having written autobiographically have been and continue to be leveled against Chappell. This essay concludes with some observations about Chappell as an autobiographical writer.

The Implied Author in Action: Harpooning the "Irascible Critic"

Narrators of Chappell's essays work together, often to achieve comic effect. As a result, Chappell's implied author provides various reminders of his presence, usually by offering inside views about or interpretations of the narrator's experiences, much as the critic Chappell offers judgments and interpretations about the works he discusses. Bakhtin provides an interesting description of this literary event in his assertion that multiple voices exist simultaneously in a text (what he calls *dialogism* or *polyphony*). Readers are directed to these changing voices in Chappell's essays when changes occur in tone.

The existence of these voices (and the distances between them) is quite apparent in Chappell's criticism, where judgments made by Chappell the critic are juxtaposed with judgments made by Chappell the implied author. Both voices may be heard: the critic Chappell who discusses the literary works in question, and the implied author who discusses Chappell the critic and criticism in general. These judgments are sometimes at odds. The implied author often doubts or makes light of the wisdom of Chappell the critic and, in Chappell's collections of critical and personal essays, *Plow Naked* and *A Way of Happening,* this encounter—Chappell as implied author with Chappell as critic—gives the works their distinctive character. Through the conflict these two voices create, Chappell is best able to teach and delight. In fact, Chappell seems aware of the different voices that sometimes wrestle for dominance in his critical essays: the critic speaks while the implied author justifies, ameliorates, extends, or simply undermines the critic's efforts.

For purposes of demonstrating how these two voices work together, let's look at "Maiden Voyages and Their Pilots" from *A Way of Happening.* This essay addresses the first books of six young writers. The cantankerous critic Chappell reaches several logical conclusions that come from the single critical judgment: "One trait that generally betrays a book as being a first effort is the usage of the first-person pronoun" (79). Later Chappell the critic makes more specific use of this judgment (and might even be commenting on the use of first-person in his own poetry): "The I of a poem is one of its methods of control, and when the poet forgets that the speaking I is not and should not be the same figure as the live person writing the poem, the result can be shymaking" (81). And yet another: "In most contemporary poems the I is simply a reporter of feelings and observations about incidents enjoyed or endured; rarely is the I physically involved in any significant action the poem might record" (82). But the voice of the critic in these examples is balanced by the more urbane, almost self-effacing implied author who confides in a voice distant in time, place, and moral value from the above: "I am only trying to understand the dramatic function of the I in our contemporary lyric poems and finding it to be a more complex chore than I had reckoned on" (83). The most distinctive characteristic of Chappell's criticism—the juxtaposition of a judgment with the repudiation or harpooning of the judge—arises from Chappell's use of voices in his essays. These often conflicting voices render an interesting juxtaposition in terms of temporality: the critic, focused on the here and now, alongside the implied author, who seems outside the time constraints of the essay. By considering one of Chappell's personal essays, we are able to see how this technique of narration works when Chappell writes about the "growth of a poet's mind" where the time and place of the bewildered "I" of the events (the narrator) is by necessity distant from that of the judgment-making "I," who often by his comments reinforces moral distance as well (the implied author).

In "First Attempts," from *Plow Naked,* the implied author does not reveal his presence except through occasional intrusions. In this essay and the one that follows it ("Welcome to High Culture"), we assume the implied author/poet Chappell has already grown into maturity since he recalls his stages of development, creating a distance in time and place between the implied author and the young narrator. While the narrator of the essay has a story to tell, the implied author moralizes—often humorously—on that story and more often than not does so by speaking cordially and directly to the reader. The first sentence of "First Attempts"

introduces the essay's warring voices: "The real beginning of a writer's compulsion to compose is difficult to discover and he must be a foolhardy author who will attempt to sound these strange, moiling storm-lit depths in search of an origin" (4). This is the voice of the implied author who recognizes in the narrator's willingness to tell the story of his origins as a writer a certain foolhardiness, separating himself, then, from the narrator, who seems not to know any better than to write such an essay. The narrator has a story to tell, as the implied author understands quite well: "He [the writer] has been forced to be objective about something, to try to see it in a light that permits description, however fumbling and inaccurate" (4). Because the implied author is a presence in the essay, a judge of the narrator's foolishness not only for writing on this particular subject but also for believing much that he believes, we tend to trust the voice of the implied author when we hear it, finding it, in Booth's term, "reliable," while we do not always trust or find reliable the voice of the one who narrates. That voice, after all, is often undermined and ridiculed in the essay by the implied author. A reader finds it difficult to trust them both.

Consistent with this view, the narrator goes on to portray the fantasies he held to as a beginning writer: "I knew what I would look like as a writer," he says, and "I knew too what I was supposed to look like while writing" (5). The author who is all along an implied presence soon intrudes, however, in the tone of the judgmental veteran: "I suspect that most writers are urged to their purpose by adolescent fantasies such as these, and that these day-dreams do not entirely evaporate with adolescence" (6). And what's more, "The steely frost of publication soon lays this pastel hope a-withering but never kills it entirely." The distance between implied author and narrator here is great, a distance in time, place, and moral value.

In "First Attempts," the large pronouncements, the less cautious statements of value and thus the more eloquent generalizations, are offered by the implied author, which may be why we tend to find him more knowledgeable and reliable than the narrator: "For me it is in the work that the final perfection of a life is lodged; the work is the life." And, "I have known any number of writers who were drunks, buffoons, knaves, clods, blowhards, sycophants, trimmers, charlatans, and egomaniacs; indeed, I can find episodes of my own life in which I have matched each of these descriptions and sometimes all of them together" (8). And, "Not that writers as a group are scurvier than other groups. Maybe it is a holdover from my adolescent glamourizing that I expect them to be better . . ." (8). The narrator then returns us to the story he wants to tell, and he does so without making the judgments that seem reserved for the implied author: "When I was a teenager the only contemporary writer whose personal life I knew anything about was Hemingway." As in his critical essays, Chappell the author employs two voices, one telling a story we may justifiably call "growth of a poet's mind"—this the tale told by the narrator—and the other commenting on the person telling the story, what that person says, and how it is told—this told by the implied author.

POINT OF VIEW IN *MIDQUEST*: SOME OBSERVATIONS

The narrators of poems in **Midquest,** as Chappell notes in his preface, are most often either "Ole Fred" or "I," neither of whom, the author says, is identical to the author. They are simply representative characters, "to some extent a demographic sample" (x). As in essays such as "First Attempts," poems in *Midquest* that take up the subject of Ole Fred's education (and he seems to be an active learner in nearly all of the poems) use techniques of narration that are more typically used in fiction. Poems in *Midquest* that address the education of the poet are explorations. As such, they most often depend for success (and even in some poems, for development) upon the presence of an "other." Distance between implied author, narrator, and this other (characters) is a major consideration insofar as the inevitable expression of values is concerned. How are narrators of these poems and the characters themselves used to manipulate the reader?

Chappell's narrators in these poems employ a wide range of vantage points from which to see the world Chappell has created. Rare, indeed, are poems that employ narrators other than Ole Fred or "I," but they do exist (including the narrators of **"Second Wind," "My Mother Shoots the Breeze," "Three Sheets in the Wind," "Susan's Morning Dream of Her Garden,"** and **"My Grandmother's Dream of Plowing"**). But these poems are dramatic monologues; as such, they imply the presence of a listener. The listener of these poems is the presence identified elsewhere as "I" or Ole Fred. The titles of these poems suggest the strategy used in *Farewell, I'm Bound to Leave You*: a poem titled **"*My* Mother Shoots the Breeze"** (emphasis mine) suggests that what follows in the poem is filtered and selected by someone other than the mother—the mother speaks through her child's recollection. In this particular poem, then, the implied author decides which details of the known experiences of "mother" will be given and how. The distance in this poem between implied author and narrator (the mother) is slim indeed. It is thus the implied author who decides to recall the "Old Times," for instance, as "cruelty and misery" or to recount the mother's post-secondary education and to make her "schoolbook proud." This strategy looks forward to *Farewell* and solves for Chappell some of the problems male authors confront when they narrate a story from a woman's point of view. By creating such

close, almost shared, perspectives for the implied author and the narrator, the implied author's "mother," Chappell manipulates his reader into thinking that the stated values are those of the mother. In fact, the values are those of Ole Fred or "I" who speaks through the narrator and serves as the implied author.

Chappell employs a similar strategy in **"Hollowind,"** in which the distance between implied author and the poem's characters is likewise manipulated. In his interview with Resa Crane and James Kirkland, Chappell says the conversation presented in **"Hollowind"** is a "[v]ery accurate reflection of a kind of continuing dialogue, or debate, that Reynolds [Price] and Jim Applewhite and I had in those days" (14). This is a trickier strategy for the reader to break through than the one used in **"My Mother Shoots the Breeze"** since one of the speakers here is identified as "Fred." But we cannot read this voice as that of the author Fred Chappell (or, in any case, if we do we cannot assume this person and the author of *Midquest* are one and the same). The Fred of this poem is a construction. If we assume he speaks for the author of **Midquest,** we are more apt to believe that Reynolds Price in the poem is, in fact, author Reynolds Price. But Reynolds of the poem is, likewise, a construction, perhaps sharing some qualities with the writer Reynolds Price; and the speaker who gives Reynolds his words and ideas is the implied author, so nearly identified with the multiple voices in this poem that a reader finds it difficult to tell them apart.

A third method of narration in the poems comprised in **Midquest** is the interview. This strategy seems to be a combination of the first two discussed, insofar as one speaker speaks to assumed listeners, as in **"My Mother Shoots the Breeze,"** but often in response to questions asked by a curious listener, Ole Fred, who serves as an interviewer. This strategy helps Chappell complete two tasks. For one, it gives the reader the sense that the "I" is distant from the speaker, called "father" in the poem, and at the same time it provides a mechanism in the poem for elaborating the events father wants to tell. The reader is thus given the sense that a distance exists between the implied author and the characters. But the implied author directs the exchange between the boy and his father; the boy serves as the doubting listener, pointing out inconsistencies and impossibilities in the father's story, and the father reacts to these intrusions with the refrain, "Don't interrupt me, boy. *I am coming to that*" (116). The values that insist that father adhere to reality, or at least argue logically, suggest the presence in the poem of yet another character entirely, the implied author.

"At the Grave of Virgil Campbell" provides a complex strategy for narration and looks forward to a similar strategy in the framework of *Look Back All the*

Green Valley. This poem is spoken by the "I" who addresses a now-deceased Virgil who, even in his silence, is a curious interviewer. These two begin in agreement: "I visit you half-smashed, you'll understand . . . Let's you and me / . . . tell some lies / To the worms and minerals" (167). What choice does Virgil have here? But since Virgil is linked to the values of another, the poem's implied author, he soon disagrees and challenges even in his silence. The point of departure where the deceased Virgil disagrees with the poem's narrator is over "some epitaphs." The narrator credits Virgil with finding the first epitaph "A little naked maybe." After three more epitaphs are offered, the narrator sees that the deceased cannot object after all: "I've got no business scribbling epitaphs / For wiser sounder ones who can't hit back" (168). This, of course, is an ironic statement since it implies that the deceased do have some control—that, in fact, they do hit back. But this strategy serves the author well since, like the interview strategy, one result is that it enables the author, through his implied presence in the poem, to continue, this time with epitaphs he's written for himself. Virgil is able to "hit back" nonetheless: "Howzat, / Old Mole, you think it's junky—portentous" (168). The drunken narrator gives Virgil just enough animation to make possible certain judgments that, like the first-person narrator of Chappell's critical essays, echo in the voice of the implied author.

Since it focuses exclusively on the growth of the poet's mind, **"Rimbaud Fire Letter to Jim Applewhite"** offers an interesting comparison with the essays "First Attempts" and "Welcome to High Culture," which address the same subject. This poem not only addresses the topic "growth of a poet's mind" but also employs a strategy of narration similar to the strategy employed in those essays. Both the essays and this poem rely upon two voices to narrate. One, the poem's narrator, has a story to tell. The other, the implied author, serves to comment on the story, how the story is told, and the person who tells it. And, finally, as in "First Attempts" and "Welcome to High Culture," the implied author is the mature poet reflecting upon his youth, and the narrator speaks in the voice of the young poet himself, who learns by his misdeeds. To use Booth's subtle distinctions concerning distance, these two voices are separated by their places in time if not always by moral value. The implied author seems to be interested in the young narrator's behavior but too tired to live it again.

The poem's title aptly prepares us for the "hard" learning the narrator must do in its reference to Rimbaud, whose debauchery is legendary, and by its position in *Midquest* as a "fire poem." The story told by the narrator recounts "the artificial fevers, wet / With Falstaff beer":

> I walked the railyard,
> Stumbling the moon-streaked tracks, reciting line
> After burning line I couldn't understand.

(58)

The narrator tells of problems with his parents ("My folks thought I was crazy"), the youthful certainty of how much he knew ("Four things I knew"), and his disposition during high school ("The senior prom / I missed, and the girls, and all the thrilling sports").

The implied author has something to say about this story and makes mature, if damning, judgments—as the implied author of the essays does—about the youthful narrator and the hard work that must be done to educate *this* poet. The poem begins in the voice of the implied author: "That decade with Rimbaud I don't regret. / But could not live again. Man, that was *hard*." During that foolhardy decade, says the implied author, "I formulated esoteric laws / That nothing ever obeyed, or ever will." Even lines from Rimbaud were, then, elusive: ". . . what they meant, or even what they *were*, / I never knew." The mature poet/implied author concludes that the youthful narrator was

> Kind of a handbook on how to be weird and silly.
> It might have helped if I had known some French,
> But like any other Haywood County hillbilly
> The simple thought of the language made me flinch.

(58)

As for his teachers, the implied author reflects, "They stood up for health and truth and light, / I stood up for Baudelaire and me" (59). And we are led to the next portion of this growth of a poet's mind with this, again, in the voice of the implied author: "The subject gets more and more embarrassing" until after naming the places where his "growth" took place—"Mayola's Chili House, / Annamaria's Pizza, Maitland's Top Hat, / the Pickwick, and that truly squalid place, / The Duchess"—the narrator confides, "Finally / They kicked me out, and back to the hills I went." Eventually, perhaps acknowledging a general lack of common sense, the narrator and implied author seem to become one, at least in values: "I watched the mountains until the mountains touched / My mind and partly tore away my fire-red / Vision of a universe besmirched" (60-1). Then he returned to book-learning and started his "Concordance to Samuel Johnson, / And learned to list a proper footnote, got down / To reading folks like Pope and Bertrand Bronson, / And turned my back on the ashes of Paree-town" (61).

No doubt, this tale only in part sides with the sensibly voiced implied author. In spite of his judgments, he merely "could not live again" the life the narrator describes. The very behavior the implied author seems unhappy to note seems just as necessary in the end as the bookish behavior he seems to favor. The growth of the poet's mind in **"Rimbaud Fire Letter to Jim Applewhite,"** recorded "for terror and symbolism," suggests by its strategy of story-telling that "growth" is a process that requires all the false steps that, when recorded and analyzed, show the distance not only in time, but in moral conviction, between the narrator and the implied author. As the poem ends, these two voices seem to speak in unison, narrowing dramatically the distance between the two in this poem. Narrative distance in the poem underscores the very symbolic process of maturing as a poet.

DISTANCE AS CHARACTER IN THE KIRKMAN TETRALOGY

Jess is the first-person narrator of each of the Kirkman novels. But Jess, like the narrators of the essays and poems by Chappell that deal with the growth of a poet's mind, is not always one person.[4] Often Jess is the young man narrating the novels' events. But on specific occasions and for specific reasons, Jess is also the mature poet looking back on his life. These two characters are not always in agreement, nor do they always live in the same place and time. Chappell skillfully uses distance to manipulate not only his readers, but his characters as well.

Clearly, when the implied author appears in the novel, Chappell intends to signal something. If we read the Kirkman novels as the story of Jess's education, we see that the distance between the narrator Jess and the implied author diminishes, as we've seen in **"Rimbaud Fire Letter,"** when the narrator Jess and the implied author share moral conviction and, thus, experience the world similarly. Not surprisingly, this convergence occurs more often at the end of a novel than at the beginning, as though the process of the novel is the process of closing that gap. As Jess learns more and develops into the poet the implied author *is* all along, fewer and fewer intrusions by the implied author are necessary. This convergence is clearly shown in *I Am One of You Forever,* in which the process of Jess's education as a poet is begun, and culminates in the very last utterance of the novel: "'Well, Jess, are you one of us or not?'" (184). The answer "yes" is implied by the title and entitles Jess to narrate the remaining novels in an effort to understand his teachers.

The opening sections of the quartet of novels provide excellent opportunities to demonstrate how these two voices, Jess the narrator's and the implied author's, contend under the identity of the first-person narrator. This interaction works in two directions, across individual novels to suggest, specifically in *Forever* and *Brighten,* young Jess's growth, and across the entire tetralogy to suggest that the implied author's comments on actions in these stories is intended to guide the reader's judgments about Jess; it is as if Chappell is educating not only Jess, but the readers who read the books in the order in which they were written. As a result, we might expect the implied author to do more work, provide greater amounts of guidance in the early novels (*Forever* and *Brighten*) than in the later novels (*Farewell* and *Look Back*). This pattern suggests that toward the end of the first two novels, young Jess has learned enough to receive the approval of the implied author and in the later books the implied-author-as-poet and Jess (and in judgments at least we might extend this to the reader) are most often in agreement, seeing this particular world similarly and accepting its boundaries. While Jess the poet learns in the last two books, distance in time and place lessens and most of the learning to be done is moral education.

Distance from the event in *Forever* is evident in the very first sentence: "Then there was one brief time when we didn't live in the big brick house with my grand-mother" (1). The novel begins *in medias res,* with the implied author in the midst, it seems, of telling other stories about his family and his upbringing, intruding in that implied sequence to tell *this* particular story. Likewise, *Brighten* is a recollection in which the distance is quickly established. The second sentence of the novel's opening section, "Moon," begins: "Those winter mornings were so cold that I felt I would ring like an anvil if my father touched me" (3). We see here the implied author recollecting the particular winter morning when the event occurs from among all winter mornings he might recall. He recalls these mornings from a time and place distant from the event itself.

In *Farewell,* Chappell uses a variation on this strategy. In this novel, a frame device is employed to distance the immediate event, Annie Barbara's imminent death, from Jess's recollection of stories told to him by his women-teachers. In this novel, Joe Robert and Jess are near enough in time, place, and moral value (we must keep in mind that the boy Jess is more like the boyish Joe Robert than the older, more mature Jess is) that fewer intrusions are necessary. It is Joe Robert who voices the purpose of the novel: "We will listen to the wind whisper and tell again the stories of women that your mother and grandmother need for you to hear" (5). Chappell may well have used this strategy to create the balance he needed in telling the growth of a poet's mind, asserting in this way that women's ways of knowing are as important to the poet's education as men's ways, the subject of *Brighten.*

Look Back chronicles Jess's final effort in obtaining his education as poet. Joe Robert is dead but, like Virgil Campbell of **"At the Grave of Virgil Campbell,"** he continues to challenge Jess's inventiveness. The novel, employing a frame device, opens and closes in the here and now: the grown Jess and two comrades (Ned and Tod) are in the graveyard at night, as a storm is threatening, to exhume Joe Robert's bones. The implied author is not a presence here. In fact, the judgment-maker at the end of the novel is Jess, the poet: "my father was the fox" (278). Though this novel goes on to play more rhetorical games with Jess—and thus with the reader—than the other three novels, Chappell has closed the distance between Jess and the implied author. Finally, they are the same moral person, in the same place and time, and the story told within that frame tests the accuracy of Jess's moral judgments about the Fox's secret life. From the perspective that this novel continues to tell the growth of a poet's mind, Joe Robert, even after his death, contributes to Jess's moral development.

When Chappell distances the implied author from the narrator, as he does to greatest effect at the beginning of *Forever* and *Brighten,* he allows the implied author to speak with authority and to guide our judgments as readers. In these first two books of the series, for instance, the location where events take place is different from the place the implied author (the mature Jess, the poet) inhabits and, as the following passage from the text shows, time is distant too: "*At this time* my mother was visiting her brother in California" (*Forever* 1, my emphasis). In order to manipulate his characters as well as his readers, Chappell lessens the distance between implied author and narrator so that time and place converge until the narrator places himself alongside his father: "So my father and I had to fumble along as best we could." Chappell closes the distance between Jess and Joe Robert to influence the reader's reaction: on the one hand, we feel with Jess his desire to be close to his father and, on the other, we sense that it might be easier for the young boy to get close to his father at this time and in this place than it may be later, for instance in *Look Back,* where Jess seems to barely understand Joe Robert.

Clearly, the voice of the implied author looking back to this place and time from another place and time is different from the voice of the narrator who exists in the same place and time as Joe Robert. But Chappell wants to close the gap between the moral Jess and the moral Joe Robert, and the novel's ending suggests that that job has been accomplished. By moral judgment as well as by the implied author's continuous reminders, Jess the twelve-year-old boy, and Joe Robert the boyish father eventually experience the world similarly. Only initiation into the world, including introduction to its various outlandish characters and to Joe Robert's way of perceiving them, needs to be done before the boy and the boyish adult will come to see things similarly. We find out in *Look Back,* however, that the mature Jess does not in every way understand Joe Robert. But this is a moral distance rather than a distance in time and place, indicating that Chappell would have us read that book as the book in which the last efforts to educate Jess must take place. Certainly, this view of Chappell's

use of distance requires that readers accept many of the fantastic elements in the book, elements that "The Overspill" introduces in microcosm (and that other chapters in *Forever* and *Brighten,* including well-known chapters titled "The Beard" in *Forever* and "Moon" in *Brighten,* take to their logical consequences). The convergence of time, place, and moral value between Jess and Joe Robert signals the divergence of these same elements of narrative distance between Jess the narrator and Jess the implied author until they, too, merge in recognition of the fantastic, that Joe Robert has all along been the Fox, at the end of *Look Back.*

Once connected in time and place and by the necessity that they "fumble along" in Jess's mother's absence, the implied narrator makes certain that we see why they get along, son and father: "We meet now on freshly neutral ground somewhere between my boyhood and his boyishness" (2). This is spoken by the grown Jess who, from the distance of time and in the voice of the wise authority, leads the reader into a greater understanding of the relationship between young Jess and his father. Jess is initiated into the world of boyish men, where wild imaginings are possible and pranks inevitable. The adult in the group, Jess's mom, needn't know or censor this way of acting and, we find out before chapter 1, this way of thinking: "We were clumsy housekeepers, there were lots of minor mishaps, and the tagline we formulated soonest was 'Let's just not tell Mama about this one.' I adored that thought."

Any number of intrusions by the implied author might be cited as guidelines used by Chappell to direct his readers' opinions. "The Overspill" details Joe Robert's effort to give his wife a welcome-home gift, "a small but elaborate bridge across the little creek that divided the yard and the garden" (3). From the distance of the grown Jess recalling the event, we are told the gift must be "something guaranteed to please a lady," even though young Jess wasn't told "what we were building." Judgments of value are made: "He must have been a handy carpenter," "the completed bridge appeared marvelous." These are the recollections of mature Jess, the implied author, and stand out as such because they are juxtaposed with judgments made in the voice of young Jess, who is closer in time and place (and eventually in moral values, at least at the end of this novel) to Joe Robert: "When I walked back and forth across the bridge I heard and felt a satisfactory drumming." Young Jess is so close to the event that his observations are greeted with the reservations we usually employ in hearing the judgments of a young boy. Only the more mature and distant and, therefore, the more reliable observations of the implied author guide us truly. Clearly, young Jess is correct in assessing the symbolic nature of the bridge, but we must implicitly know so because the speaker of the section's first sentence has *selected* this tale as the one to tell us, and we trust that speaker as mature and reliable. We see the young boy's unwitting insight that it will take the distance of time and place for him to truly understand that "in crossing the bridge I was entering a different world, not simply going into the garden." We recognize this as the voice of young Jess and understand that the implied author, mature Jess, Jess reflecting on this experience across time and space, now recognizes the significance of this bridge to his growth. The boundaries of this world, and Jess's experience in it, are far from restricting.

In fact, the effects of such distancing in the Kirkman tetralogy are multiple. First, Chappell is thus able to separate the voice of Jess from the voice of the implied author, creating a distance in time, place, and moral values between the two that serves as an aid to Chappell as he renders Jess's growth. By creating this distance, Chappell helps his readers make correct judgments—or, in any event, the same judgments as those made by the mature Jess, Jess the poet—about the process of that growth. Second, such distancing enables us to envision two times: the time when Jess is young and the time when Jess is a mature poet telling these tales. Third, it provides Chappell with two rhetorical strategies, which enable him to manipulate time and place. For one, we are continually reminded, by how they are told and arranged, that these stories are selections only, chosen from many that might have been told and, as selections, promise only to belong to the time between childhood and adulthood. And, for another, this distancing makes it possible for Chappell to effectively posit a thesis, which the remainder of the novel supports.

CONCLUSION: CHAPPELL AND AUTOBIOGRAPHY

Chappell is well aware that writers of autobiographical pieces are often accused of self-interest and conceit. He is also aware of the technical dilemma this places him in: if these are not autobiographical works, yet if they are intended to portray the education and growth of the central character and thus are written in first person, Chappell must devise a means of narrating these tales that permits him to at once deny that the "I" and Chappell himself are identical beings and yet permit Chappell the author and his audience to share knowledge that the characters, including the narrator, do not possess. Thus he finds it necessary to address this problem in defense of the accusation of autobiographical, even confessional, writing. He employs three different tactics in doing so, two of which are simple denials. The third, however, the subject of this essay, requires an analysis of Chappell's use of point of view in several of his essays, poems, and novels that deal with the growth of a poet's mind.

Chappell's recent interview with George Hovis gives us the opportunity to reflect upon one of these denials. In

it, Chappell explains why in *Look Back All the Green Valley* Jess Kirkman is given the pen name Fred Chappell:

> That confusion [between Chappell and his narrators] was beginning to become a real issue with me, because I don't like to be autobiographical. . . . There's no hard and fast dividing line between what you imagine and what you observe. What you observe, as in the Wordsworth line, you "half perceive and half create." . . . I thought that by reversing the ordinary expectations, where the real writer has a pen name— let's do it where the pen name has a real writer. That way we would establish a primacy of the imagination in the way this little universe is set up in these volumes. . . . And it would help answer that pesky question that I always get asked when I give public readings, "How much of this is real? Is that a real poem, or did you just make it up?"
>
> (69)

Chappell explains here his effort in *Look Back* to rid himself of accusations of writing autobiographically by establishing that the world of the novel is an imagined place, mostly separate from the real-life world Fred Chappell lives in. All observations, he argues, are a mixture of perception and imagining. This effort at explaining the link Chappell makes between Jess and himself would account for the events in the Kirkman novels if they existed apart from other of Chappell's work, but of course they don't. In a sense, as they elaborate the growth of the poet's mind, the poems and personal essays seem connected to the Kirkman novels, not to mention to *It Is Time, Lord.*

Chappell argues more convincingly and less defensively about the autobiographical elements of **Midquest** in the second of his denials when he places himself, as he does other writers whose works he criticizes, in historical context (see Bizzaro, "Teacher"). Chappell took the opportunity to dispense with any possible complaint of "self-conceit" in his poems when he was asked, long after writing some of the poems in **Midquest,** to write a preface to it, a kind of explanation of what he set out to accomplish. In that preface, Chappell seems to have had the accusation of self-concern in mind:

> Though he is called "Fred," the "I" of the poem is no more myself than any character in any novel I might choose to write. (And no less myself, either, I suppose.) He was constructed, as was Dante's persona, Dante, in order to be widely representative. He was reared on a farm but has moved to the city; he has deserted manual for intellectual labor, is "upwardly mobile"; he is cut off from his disappearing cultural tradition but finds them, in remembering, his real values. He is to some extent a demographic sample.
>
> (x)

But he is also to some extent Jess Kirkman.

The third tactic, the one this essay addresses, is Chappell's skillful and complex use of first-person narrative in his essays, poems, and stories when he addresses the growth of a poet's mind. Chappell insists upon separating his narrator from himself as author—especially when he addresses his education in *Plow Naked* and *A Way of Happening,* Ole Fred's education in a number of poems from **Midquest,** and Jess's education in the Kirkman novels—and thus introduces complexity to the narrator's descriptions and judgments. On the one hand, we know, because many of the events described portray the "mouthpiece" as immature (e.g., the childlike fantasies of what it would be like to be a successful writer, the sophomoric debauchery) that the narrator is sometimes unreliable. But on the other hand, judgments made (e.g., that childlike fantasies are correctable, that debauchery is not something a poet must or even can get "good" at) portray yet another voice entirely, somewhat cranky but certainly more reliable than the other voice we hear. Chappell claims to be neither of these voices or, in any event, they are no more Chappell, to paraphrase his denial in the preface to **Midquest,** than any other character he might create in any novel or poem or, we might add, any essay he might write. We learn much about Chappell the writer by how he deals with the dilemma these contradictory voices create for him, especially his insistence that he does not intend to identify either/any of these voices with himself.

The problem Chappell chooses to address by employing these three tactics, since he does not "like to be autobiographical," is what Keats labeled "the wordsworthian or egotistical sublime," which, in his oftcited letter to Woodhouse, Keats says "is a thing per se and stands alone" (I, 387).[5] Chappell understands in the preface to **Midquest** that the only way around the "egotistical sublime" is for the author to make his work *representative* and not *idiosyncratic.* For Chappell seems to be aware of what Wordsworth acknowledged in his famous letter to Sir George Beaumont about *The Prelude,* then unpublished, that it is "a thing unprecedented in literary history that a man should talk so much about himself" (Wayne 72). For whatever reason, Chappell prefers not to be accused of having talked "so much about himself." With Chappell, however, we find the accusation (I hesitate to call it a *problem*) of having written autobiographically made all the more complex by his efforts, arguably unprecedented, to write about the "growth of a poet's mind" in three genres: poetry, essay, and novel. No doubt readers who assume Chappell's writings to be autobiographical do so because they do not read for distance, as described in this essay, and thus attribute to autobiography what should be seen as artistry.

Notes

1. Unfortunately, a quartet of nonfiction works parallel to *Midquest* and the Kirkman tetralogy has not yet been written by Chappell.

2. In *Season of Youth,* Jerome Buckley lists "the principle characteristics" of the *bildungsroman* (p. 17), not all of which apply to the life of Jess Kirkman.

3. Admittedly, I will keep in mind the interrelationships long agreed upon concerning genres. For instance, Bakhtin writes in "Discourse on the Novel" that "The novel, and artistic prose in general, has the closest genetic family relationship to rhetorical forms." Chappell presents an interesting dilemma for the contemporary critic because his nonfiction and his poems often appropriate tactics usually associated with novels, connecting them in a familial relationship as well. This essay is interested, then, in what Chappell can teach us about genre as well as about narration.

4. A more conventional reading of these novels might argue that we all have voices in our heads that speak to each other, what Lev Vygotsky calls "inner voice." Saying so, however, does not adequately explain strategic uses of these voices, such as Chappell's.

5. Keats could not have referred to *The Prelude* in his letter to Woodhouse cited above. *The Prelude* was published nearly thirty years after Keats's death. But Keats acknowledges elsewhere *Tintern Abbey,* Wordsworth's other autobiographical poem concerned with the "growth of a poet's mind," and no doubt considers that poem an example of the egotistical sublime.

Works Cited

Bakhtin, Mikhail. "Discourse on the Novel." In *Critical Theory since 1965,* ed. Hazard Adams and Leroy Searle. Tallahassee: Florida State University Press, 1990.

Bizzaro, Patrick. "The Critic As Teacher: A Review of Fred Chappell's *A Way of Happening.*" *Asheville Poetry Review* 6, no. 1 (1999): 101-3.

Booth, Wayne. *The Rhetoric of Fiction.* 2nd ed. Chicago: University of Chicago Press, 1983.

Buckley, Jerome Hamilton. *Season of Youth: The Bildungsroman from Dickens to Golding.* Cambridge: Harvard University Press, 1974.

Crane, Resa, and James Kirkland. "First and Last Words: A Conversation with Fred Chappell." In *Dream Garden: The Poetic Vision of Fred Chappell,* ed. Patrick Bizzaro. Baton Rouge: Louisiana State University Press, 1997.

Jauss, David. "From Long Shots to X-Rays: Distance and Point of View in Fiction Writing." *Writer's Chronicle* 33, no. 1 (2000): 5-14, 17.

Keats, John. "Letter of May 3, 1818, to Woodhouse." In *The Letters of John Keats.* 2 vols. Cambridge: Harvard University Press, 1958, I.

Morgan, Robert. "*Midquest* and the Gift of Narrative." In *Dream Garden: The Poetic Vision of Fred Chappell,* ed. Patrick Bizzaro. Baton Rouge: Louisiana State University Press, 1997.

Wordsworth, William. "Letter of May 1, 1805, to Sir George Beaumont." In *Letters of William Wordsworth,* ed. Philip Wayne. London: Oxford University Press, 1933.

FURTHER READING

Criticism

Campbell, Hilbert. "Fred Chappell's Urn of Memory: *I Am One of You Forever.*" In *American Vein: Critical Readings in Appalachian Literature,* edited by Danny L. Miller, pp. 252-60. Athens, Ohio: Ohio University Press, 2005.

    Explores similarities in tone, theme, and structure between Chappell's novel *I Am One of You Forever* and the poetry collection *Midquest.*

Additional coverage of Chappell's life and career is contained in the following sources published by Gale: *Contemporary Authors,* **Vols. 5-8R, 198;** *Contemporary Authors Autobiographical Essay,* **Vol. 198;** *Contemporary Authors Autobiography Series,* **Vol. 4;** *Contemporary Authors New Revision Series,* **Vols. 8, 33, 67, 110;** *Contemporary Literary Criticism,* **Vols. 40, 78, 162;** *Contemporary Novelists,* **Ed. 6;** *Contemporary Poets,* **Eds. 6, 7;** *Contemporary Southern Writers;* *Dictionary of Literary Biography,* **Vols. 6, 105;** *Literature Resource Center;* **and** *St. James Guide to Horror, Ghost & Gothic Writers.*

Patrick Kavanagh
1904-1967

Irish poet, novelist, and critic.

For additional information on Kavanagh's life and career, see *PC,* Volume 33.

INTRODUCTION

Known for his realistic representations of the brutal conditions of life in rural Ireland, Kavanagh produced poetry at odds with the work of many of his contemporaries. He was critical of idyllic portraits of rural life and his work reveals an ambiguous view of his homeland. His most famous, and most controversial, work is the lengthy narrative poem *The Great Hunger* (1942).

BIOGRAPHICAL INFORMATION

The fourth of ten children, Kavanagh was born on a farm in Inniskeen, County Monaghan on October 21, 1904. His parents were Bridget Kavanagh and James Kavanagh, who worked as a shoemaker as well as a farmer. Kavanagh was also trained in that craft and after leaving school at an early age, he worked at both shoemaking and farming throughout his youth. At the same time, he read and wrote poetry, submitting his work to various publications, both local and national. In 1929 Kavanagh sent some of his poetry to the *Irish Statesman* whose editor, George Russell, offered encouragement, sent him books to further his education, and arranged introductions to various Dublin poets. Russell also published the poem "The Intangible"— Kavanagh's first publication in a literary magazine. His first volume of poetry appeared in 1936; two years later, Kavanagh went to London, where he lived for a brief period. In 1939 he moved to Dublin, earning a living writing newspaper articles and reviews while continuing to produce his own poetry and prose. Much of Kavanagh's writing was highly critical of the work of other poets, particularly regarding what he considered their idealized representations of rural Irish life.

In 1955, Kavanagh developed lung cancer, had one lung surgically removed, and spent his lengthy recovery period reflecting on his life and writing career. With a newly acquired appreciation of his environment and, according to some scholars, a newly acquired spiritual-ity, he began writing poetry again. He also embarked on a series of lectures in Ireland and America and served as a judge for the Guinness Poetry Awards. By 1960, his health began to fail and he wrote very little during his final years. Kavanagh died on November 30, 1967, after a brief stay in a Dublin nursing home; he is buried in his native village of Inniskeen.

MAJOR WORKS

Kavanagh's early work was published in a number of periodicals, among them the *Weekly Irish Independent,* the *Irish Statesman,* and *Dublin Magazine.* His first collection of poetry, *Ploughman and Other Poems,* was published in 1936; the volume contains thirty-one poems, among them the well-regarded "Ploughman," "Beech Tree," and "Inniskeen Road, July Evening." In 1942, Kavanagh produced *The Great Hunger,* a long narrative anti-pastoral poem filled with social criticism, disparaged by a number of critics, and later disavowed by Kavanagh himself. An abridged version of *The Great Hunger* was included in the 1947 collection, *A Soul for Sale,* along with eighteen other poems, among them "Stony Grey Soil," "Temptation in Harvest," and "A Wreath for Tom Moore's Statue." Most of the early poetry realistically described the landscape and life of rural Ireland, with the poet insisting on an accurate representation of the brutal mental and physical conditions under which the average farmer labored. Kavanagh also produced a number of verse satires ridiculing the idealized versions of country living that appeared in most pastoral poetry. With few exceptions, Kavanagh concentrated on prose during the next several years, and returned to poetry only after his long convalescence from surgery.

In his later work, Kavanagh attempted to put the self-described "whining" quality of his earlier work aside, along with the biting satirical tone directed at the work of other Irish poets. He took a different direction, towards the "business of love," in *Come Dance with Kitty Stobling, and Other Poems* (1960), a volume that was well received in both England and Ireland. In 1964, Kavanagh published *Collected Poems* and in 1972, five years after the poet's death, *The Complete Poems of Patrick Kavanagh* appeared.

In addition to his poetry, Kavanagh wrote *The Green Fool* (1938), considered a fictionalized autobiography or an autobiographical novel, and *Tarry Flynn* (1948), a novel that was banned in Ireland. Later adapted for the stage, *Tarry Flynn* was performed in 1966, at Dublin's Abbey Theatre. Kavanagh also produced a number of critical essays and published, along with his brother Peter, thirteen editions of *Kavanagh's Weekly: A Journal of Literature and Politics* (1952).

CRITICAL RECEPTION

Often categorized as a "peasant poet," a label he despised, Kavanagh was a controversial figure during his lifetime, and the reception of his poetry was uneven. Kavanagh's work as a reviewer and journalist—as well as his verse satires—made him an unpopular figure among his contemporaries, particularly those writers, artists, and institutions that were the targets of his merciless attacks. "Well-known for his cantankerousness in person, the poet proved equally contentious in his critical writings," neither of which won him many friends, maintains Thomas B. O'Grady. Kavanagh also attracted negative attention from the Catholic censors. All copies of the magazine *Horizon,* which published the first part of *The Great Hunger,* were confiscated by the Irish police because of a reference to masturbation. It was published in full later that year, but the "objectionable" material was excised from the version that appeared in *A Soul for Sale.* Kavanagh's novel *Tarry Flynn* was also banned in Ireland when it first appeared in 1948. Antoinette Quinn suggests that *The Great Hunger* "was not immediately successful" for other reasons as well—particularly in its apparent attempt to dispel pastoral views of rural Ireland. Quinn maintains, however, that the work was visionary with "its antenna-like sensitivity" to the fact that the public consciousness was beginning to shift away from idealized notions about country living, despite the desire of Irish politicians to cling to them. She, like a number of other recent critics, praises the work for its "documentary authenticity" and for Kavanagh's "fictional technique" that has more in common with cinema than with the stage, as the poet maintained. In general, Kavanagh's literary reputation has been growing in the years since his death. Alan Warner reports that "in Ireland he has been widely acclaimed as the greatest Irish poet since Yeats." Basil Payne too believes that Kavanagh's critical reputation will eventually rival that of Yeats. In his reassessment of Kavanagh's body of work, Payne acknowledges that Kavanagh's first book of poems "was a slight work of honest, unpretentious competence," but he praises the later volumes which demonstrate Kavanagh's development as a poet. In the later work, according to Payne, there is "no indignation that does not include forgiveness; nothing but pity for what the poet occasionally finds it necessary to satirise." Also noting the different tone of Kavanagh's poetry after his illness, Warner reports that "the sourness of satire fell away and he returned to praise of the commonplace, the discovery of wonder in the ordinary."

Kavanagh's feelings for his native land, as expressed in his poetry, were ambiguous and a number of scholars have commented on his "love/hate" relationship to his early environment. Seamus Heaney (see Further Reading), praising *The Great Hunger,* believes that the work was informed "by a desperate sense that life in that secluded spot is no book of pastoral hours but an enervating round of labour and lethargy." But Warner claims that "it was only in certain moods that he cried out against his birthplace as a 'savage area' where he lived 'the usual barbaric life of the Irish country poor.'" At the same time, Warner insists, Kavanagh had a lifelong "passionate attachment" to County Monaghan, described by the critic as "one of the humblest of the Irish counties." Darcy O'Brien also contends that Kavanagh's apparent ill will towards his homeland is misleading. She notes that, although he escaped to Dublin to further his literary career, "Inniskeen, ignorant, backward, slow, he understood and loved too well ever to reject, drawing on it all his life in verse." If Kavanagh's feelings for Inniskeen were conflicted, his feelings for Dublin—where he lived for thirty years—were apparently no less ambivalent; Heaney reports that Kavanagh himself called the move to Dublin "the worst mistake of my life." Adele Dalsimer, too, finds that in his poetry, Dublin is "either a hell or a Parnassus," as his feelings for it encompass simultaneously "the despair and the pain, the relief and the joy." Dalsimer sums up the poet's relationship to his surroundings this way: "[w]herever he was, he wanted to be somewhere else."

PRINCIPAL WORKS

Poetry

Ploughman and Other Poems 1936
The Great Hunger 1942
A Soul for Sale 1947
Recent Poems 1958
Come Dance with Kitty Stobling, and Other Poems 1960
Collected Poems 1964
The Complete Poems of Patrick Kavanagh 1972
Lough Derg 1978

Other Major Works

The Green Fool (fictionalized autobiography) 1938
Tarry Flynn: A Novel (novel) 1948
Self Portrait (autobiographical television script) 1964
Collected Prose (prose) 1967

Lapped Furrows: Correspondence, 1933-1967, Between Patrick and Peter Kavanagh, with Other Documents (letters) 1969

November Haggard: Uncollected Prose and Verse (prose and poetry) 1971

Love's Tortured Headland: A Sequel to Lapped Furrows (letters) 1974

By Night Unstarred: An Autobiographical Novel (novel) 1978

Kavanagh's Weekly: A Journal of Literature and Politics (anthology) 1981

CRITICISM

Basil Payne (essay date autumn 1960)

SOURCE: Payne, Basil. "The Poetry of Patrick Kavanagh." *Studies: An Irish Quarterly Review* 49, no. 195 (autumn 1960): 277-94.

[*In the following essay, written upon the publication of* Come Dance with Kitty Stobling, *Payne presents an overview of Kavanagh's work and argues that he should be seen as a poet of major stature on the order of Yeats.*]

The appearance—thirteen years after his last collection—of a new book of poems by Patrick Kavanagh[1] has, as the publishers' announcement mentions, given many readers in Britain their first opportunity to buy Kavanagh's work in collected form. The new collection has been well received by reviewers in Britain, and was the Summer choice of the Poetry Book Society. In Ireland, **Come Dance with Kitty Stobling** has also received favourable notices. This, one hopes, will encourage the relatively small number of persons here who actually read poetry, not only to buy the new volume, but also to re-read Kavanagh's earlier work. A re-assessment of Kavanagh's achievement seems overdue. This essay is an attempt at such a re-assessment.

When Patrick Kavanagh's first important collection of poems, **A Soul for Sale,** was published by Macmillan in 1947, it was enthusiastically received. It was not, of course, Kavanagh's first book of verse: **Ploughman and Other Poems,** a collection of early lyrics, had already appeared in 1936, but this was a slight work of honest, unpretentious competence. Despite, however, the assessment of one reviewer of **A Soul for Sale** that no comparable collection of importance had come from Ireland since the death of Yeats, the attitude of many of our present Irish critics and poets towards Kavanagh's poems has been apathetic or even frankly hostile, e.g.—

'There is one very fine poet in this country who can survive comparison with such writers as Edwin Muir and John Crowe Ransom. He is not, I regret, Patrick Kavanagh'.[2] Other Irish critics have, however, been more impressed. Mr James Plunkett contributed a very fine appraisal of **'The Great Hunger'** to *The Bell,* March 1952, which, however, concerned itself more with the sociological importance than the poetic merits of the poem; Mr Anthony Cronin provided a sensitive and excellent article on Kavanagh's work in the issue of *Nimbus*[3] in which almost half of the poems in the most recent collection were first published. (A further study by Mr John Montague was published in *Poetry Chicago* a few years ago, but unfortunately, I have not been able to procure a copy.) Too often, however, Kavanagh's stature as a poet has tended to be denigrated by Irish readers and aspirant poets—possibly perhaps because his colourful personality and his controversial journalism have deflected attention from its fulcrum, the poet, to the swingboats he stubbornly pushes under our noses.

The collection, **A Soul for Sale,** is a slim volume of some fifty odd pages, roughly half of which is taken up by Kavanagh's longest and most ambitious poem, **'The Great Hunger'.** The others, eighteen in number, are all poems of clarity, and even austerity, of style, but palpitating with the vigour and freshness of 'illuminated innocence'—even when they are concerned with the most adult experience. Their outstanding qualities are candour and intensity—qualities not sufficient of themselves to make great poetry, but which, allied to an exceptional technical accomplishment, can generate universal significance from the most everyday experience—the stuff of all real poetry.

'The Great Hunger' is Kavanagh's longest and most ambitious poem. Asked what it is *about,* one might answer that it is a relentless and unequivocal picture of Patrick Maguire, an Irish 'peasant ploughman, who is half a vegetable'; a slave to his bitter acres which possess him body and soul; subjected to the domination of an aged matriarch, of his sparse lands and of the externals of his religion; cheated, too, in turn by each of his three captors; an old, lonely and hard-working bachelor, for whom our hearts cry out with Kavanagh's

> Watch him, watch him, that man on a hill whose spirit
> Is a wet sack flapping about the knees of time.
> He lives that his little fields may stay fertile when his own body
> Is spread in the bottom of a ditch under two coulters in Christ's name.

'The Great Hunger' is about this; but it is also about much more. It is about the loneliness and frustration that has a niche in all our hearts and engulfs some of us; it is, at the same time, about the mysterious powers of love and humility; the tendril beauty and the raw savagery of nature; the self-deception of the heart of man; the whip of faith to the flagging spirit; the *holiness* of the Imagination. It is told in a taut, realistic and distinctly personal style, which gives it the excitement of an epic and the intensity of a pure lyric.

For the reader's convenience the poem is divided into fourteen sections, but the divisions are of little importance. The presentation is in many ways cinemascopic—the general background and landscape projected on a wide screen, and against this background numerous close shots taken of the principal protagonists at the daily, monthly and yearly round of toil, idle diversion, or 'quiet desperation'. The flash-back from our first introduction to Maguire at the age of sixty-five gathering potatoes with his men on a hillside on an October afternoon, to his youth, thirties and middle-age, is a well-tried device, but one which is eminently successful here, where the poet's sharp projection of the beauty in the endless procession of the seasons is so skilfully interwoven with the sad procession of Maguire's disappointment and loneliness to his imminent defeat. And yet, despite the despondent moralistic tone in the last few lines of the poem

> No hope, no lust.
> The hungry field
> Screams the apocalypse of clay
> In every corner of this land.

our ultimate feeling is not that we have witnessed a study of failure; the society responsible for the tragedy of Maguire is censured by the poet, but the heart of the poem is *a presentation of the situation* in full dispassion of intellect and compassion of feeling, rather than *the posing of a solution*. One is reminded of Emily Dickenson, or perhaps Tchehov. The enduring power of love, in spite of whatever mere peripheral experience of it is superimposed by sinister, extraneous forces, is implicit in the poem. For, as Tchehov says, 'One would need to be God to decide which are the failures and which are the successes in life'.

The most remarkable technical achievement in **'The Great Hunger'** is, perhaps, its unity—the conclusion is itself contained in the opening line of the poem:

> Clay is the word and clay is the flesh.

In such realistic writing where the movement is from the particular to the universal, there is no room for the roses, eagles, fur or faeces of the symbolists. The image is valid in its own right; its power is in its startling matter-of-factness:

> A dog lying on a torn jacket under a heeled-up cart,
> A horse nosing along the posied headland, trailing
> A rusty plough. Three heads hanging between wide-
>   apart legs.

Already, on the first page of the poem, a *tension* is generated, which maintained with remarkable skill and consistency throughout, and relieved only by occasional deliberate alterations in rhythm which Kavanagh cleverly interposes—as he occasionally lets our imaginations sidle with Maguire's from the main predicament:

> The goldfinches on the railway paling were worth
>   looking at—
> A man might imagine then
> Himself in Brazil and these the birds of paradise
> And the Amazon and the romance traced on the school
>   map lived again.

Then we are jerked back violently to the treadmill again, as a crumpled leaf from the whitethorn bushes

> Darts like a frightened robin

or Maguire's mother, 'Tall hard as a Protestant spire', comes

> down the stairs barefoot at the kettle-call
> And talked to her son sharply: "Did you let
> The hens out, you?"

And so, back again to the peasant's routine; to the growing crops and 'the ridges he never loved'. Nobody, we are told,

> will ever know how much tortured poetry
>   the pulled weeds on the ridge wrote
> Before they withered in the July sun.
> Nobody will ever read the wild, sprawling, scrawling
>   mad woman's signature.
> The hysteria and the boredom of the enclosed nun of
>   his thought.
> Like the afterbirth of a cow stretched on a branch in
>   the wind
> Life dried in the veins of these women and men.

The image of the animal's afterbirth may seem an obvious one for a poet who has himself worked as a farmer to choose. Its impact, however, is well judged. The tragedy of Maguire, and of all the lonely or frustrated whose prototype he is, is that superficially it seems a mere backwash of tragedy, going unnoticed because it is repeated thousands of times everywhere:

> No mad hooves galloping in the sky
> But the weak, washy way of true tragedy—
> A sick horse nosing around the meadow for a clean
>   place to die.

One is reminded of Auden's *Musée des Beaux Arts*

> even the dreadful martyrdom must run its
>   course
> Anyhow in a corner, some untidy spot
> Where the dogs go on with their doggy life and the
>   torturer's horse
> Scratches its innocent behind on a tree.

Kavanagh, being a poet-artist, must, of course, do more than merely show us Maguire's predicament; he must present his peasant tragic-hero to us in all the complexities of our fallen human nature. Our compassion for Maguire must embrace sympathy and understanding for his sins and failings; but the sins and failings must be identified for what they are; no more and no less. Kavanagh, wisely I think, does not shirk this fact: Maguire

> Suspicious in his youth as a rat near strange bread
> When girls laughed

cannot walk the easy road to destiny. His sin of lonely lechery is committed, admitted, and committed again. But (again rightly), Kavanagh does not become hysterical about sex; the temptations of middle-age are different from those of youth, but man is equally vulnerable to them; and one falls:

> The priest from the altar called Patrick Maguire's
>   name
> To hold the collecting box in the chapel door
> During all the Sundays in May.
> His neighbours envied him his holy rise,
> But he walked down from the church with affected
>   indifference
> And took the measure of heaven angel-wise.

But if Kavanagh is a realist, he is also a Catholic to whom the words faith, hope and charity have real meaning: religion is not Maguire's bugbear. It is the matriarchal-circumscribed insistence on its externals which deludes. Kavanagh is, in fact, that (nowadays) rare thing, a good *religious* poet; religious in the sense that Shakespeare and Keats and Blake are all in their different ways religious poets, no less than Vaughan, and St John of the Cross and Gerard Manley Hopkins; religious, even perhaps in the sense that Thomas Merton found Joyce religious, despite Joyce's apostasy; religious, again, despite some of the neo-existentialist futilities in **'The Great Hunger'**:

> Sitting on a wooden gate
> Sitting on a wooden gate
> Sitting on a wooden gate
> He didn't give a damn.
> Said whatever came into his head
> Said whatever came into his head
> Said whatever came into his head
> And inconsequently sang.

And again,

> Evening at the cross-roads—
> Heavy heads nodding out words as wise
> As the rumination of cows after milking.
> From the ragged surface a boy picks up
> A piece of gravel and stares at it—and then
> He flings it across the elm tree on to the railway.
> It means nothing,
> Not a damn thing.

In suggesting that Kavanagh is a fine religious poet, I do not, of course, imply that his *themes* are specifically religious, although most of the poems in *A Soul for Sale* are most recognizably Catholic in atmosphere—as in Langland and Chaucer. **'The Great Hunger'**, especially, has some fine and courageous religious imagery, e.g.

> These men know God the Father in a tree
> The Holy Spirit is the rising sap
> And Christ will be the green leaves that will come
> At Easter from the sealed and guarded tomb.

Such sharp spiritual realism not only enriches the fabric of the poem, but following on the image of the 'dead sparrow' and 'old waistcoat' among the blackthorn shadows in the ditch, tightens the texture as effectively as Eliot's sudden image of the children 'hidden excitedly containing laughter' in *Four Quartets*. Kavanagh has, in a way, something in common with the later Eliot, not only in his choice of the right words and the right tone when his language is most direct and simple, but in his insistence on prayer and humility and forgiveness in the business of living:

> O let us kneel where the blind ploughman kneels
> And learn to live without despairing
> In a mud-walled space—
> Illiterate, unknown and unknowing.

But something more is required. There is the injunction to positive love and positive virtue (like Eliot's 'We must be still and still moving / into another intensity / For a further union, a deeper communion . . .'):

> He helped a poor woman whose cow
> Had died on her:
> He dragged home a drunken man on a winter's night
> And one rare moment he heard the young people play-
>   ing on the railway stile
> And he wished them happiness and whatever they
>   most desired from life.

It would be wrong, however, for anyone (as yet, perhaps, unfamiliar with **'The Great Hunger'**) to imagine from this that Kavanagh is a mere Catholic or sociological apologist masquerading in verse. The poetry, as all good poetry should, exists for its own sake. The fact that the poet's personal poetic vision also embodies an orthodox spiritual point of view does not at all lessen the quality of the poetry.

Occasionally, however, Kavanagh does comment specifically on the Catholic scene and the Church, as in **'Father Mat'**, or a much later poem, **'House Party to Celebrate the Destruction of the Roman Catholic Church in Ireland'**. In the latter he whimsically satirizes a woman novelist and her fulminating pretensions—

Her book was out, and did she devastate
the Roman Catholic Church on every page
And in Seamus's house they met to celebrate
With giggles high the dying monster's rage.

Meantime, Kavanagh notes laconically, in far-off
parishes of Cork and Kerry

Old priests walked homeless in the winter air
As Seamus poured another pale dry sherry.

It is, of course, a minor poem of Kavanagh's, but
interesting in that it shows forcibly his insistence on
truth in things minor as well as major; an insistence
which, however, now recognizes truth as 'the most
entertaining type of communication', rather than the
bludgeon of the poet-sitting-in judgement (as in **'A
Wreath for Tom Moore's Statue'**). **'Father Mat',** an
early poem of about a hundred lines, is, however, of
considerable significance in that it is one of the few
poems in the collection *A Soul for Sale* which gives a
hint of Kavanagh's later development. Here, instead of
the spancelled peasant, Maguire, we are given a picture
of an old country priest hearing Confessions on a sunny
evening in May, hemmed in not by the fields, this time;
nor by the tedious litanies of sins; nor yet by the
spiritual pride of the consciously-aspiring saint;
hemmed in, however, by the dancer of temptation 'that
dances in the hearts of men', to which all of us are
exposed, whether the temptation is that of the poet to
tear himself loose from fields that nurtured him, yet
'burgled his bank of youth'; or of the man who is not a
poet to abandon the truth which he knows lingers
vaguely but persistently in his heart. In this poem, Kavanagh is, in fact, asserting the identity of the real world
and the imagination, as Keats in the famous letter to
Bailey said he was sure of nothing but the holiness of
the Heart's affections and the truth of Imagination. This
is the kernal of Kavanagh's importance. The poet must
not only aspire to truth; he must *dedicate* himself to
truth, and even—without blasphemy—*be* truth. For the
ordinary man any deflection from truth is regrettable or
sinful; for the poet it is, poetically speaking, sacrilegious. This righteous conviction and dedication cannot,
of itself, *make* a poet; but without it no poet will ever
achieve universality. How about Kavanagh? In a
hundred years' time—if there be a hundred years'
time—I think Kavanagh, despite his slim output, is as
likely to be read as Yeats. 'Yeats,' says Kavanagh, 'was
a poet, and he invented many writers. He invented
Synge, and Lady Gregory, and he was largely responsible for F. R. Higgins'. Many will quarrel with this
dismissal of Synge; personally I find the prevalent near-
idolatry of his *kitsch* dramaturgy very puzzling. Might
one venture further and say that Yeats himself was the
makings of a very great poet—and then he invented
Yeats? Perhaps.

Apart from **'The Great Hunger'**, the poems in *A Soul
for Sale* which project the earlier Kavanagh ethos most

sharply are, I think, **'Stony Grey Soil'**; **'A Wreath for
Tom Moore's Statue'** and **'Temptation in Harvest'**.
In them, we find the poet arrogantly striding in gaunt
grandeur into the market-place, and overturning the
traders' tables where 'fake love, fake thoughts, fake
ideal' are wantonly and vicariously purveyed, e.g. **'A
Wreath for Tom Moore's Statue'**:

The cowardice of Ireland is in his statue
No poet's honoured when they wreath this stone,
An old shopkeeper who has dealt in the marrow-bone
Of his neighbours looks at you,
Dim-eyed, degenerate, he is admiring his god.
The bank manager who pays his monthly confession
The tedious narrative of a mediocrity's passion
The shallow, safe sins that never become a flood
To sweep themselves away . . .

It is very intense, and savagely certain of the poet's
own integrity. But for all its power of directness it is, I
think, less effective than the oblique, satirical approach
to the subject by, say, Mervyn Wall in *The Unfortunate
Fursey,* or the hilarious incisiveness of Myles na Gopaleen in *Faustus Kelly.* Kavanagh's later poetry has, as
Mr Anthony Cronin points out, great gains of subtlety,
irony and humour, without sacrificing any of its earlier
imaginative intensity. The difference can perhaps be
explained by saying that in his later work Kavanagh
transcends his suffering. Certainly, earlier poems such
as **'Stony Grey Soil'** would, but for the sheer brilliance
of the technical accomplishment, be destroyed by their
own larvae of self-pity;

O stony grey soil of Monaghan
The laugh from my love you thieved;
You took the gay child of my passion
And gave me your clod-conceived.
You flung a ditch on my vision
Of beauty, love and truth.
O stony grey soil of Monaghan
You burgled my bank of youth!

Yet, the tone is removed from the *saeva indignatio* of
Swift. Kavanagh, even in the early poems, is, behind
the fury, capable of much love, much vitality and much
fresh innocent intensity, as in **'A Christmas
Childhood'**:

My father payed the melodion;
My mother milked the cows.
And I had a prayer like a white rose pinned
On the virgin Mary's blouse.

'Temptation in Harvest', a poem of just less than a
hundred lines is concerned with a predicament which
has been a recurrent motif in much of Kavanagh's later
work both in verse and prose: the poet, troubled and
self-reproachful for his decision to uproot himself from
the environment in which he has been nurtured and set
off for his Utopia of Art and Letters, e.g.

And yet, having sown a couple of acres of barley in
May I walked off. I felt that I shouldn't have done it,
that I was acting by some untruthful principle that had
been created.[4]

The dilemma is posed forcibly by the image in the opening lines:

A poplar leaf was spiked upon a thorn
Above the hedge like a flag of surrender
That the year held out. I was afraid to wonder
At capitulation in a field of corn.

It is a poem which illustrates exceptionally well Kavanagh's *power* over words—a near-perfect equivalence
of thought and expression.[5] It is, in a way, a poem in
the romantic tradition. The sudden appearance of the
old woman who whispers from a bush to the poet to

stand in
The shadow of the ricks until she passes;
You cannot eat what grows upon Parnassus—
And she is going there as sure as sin.

shatters both the seeming security of the real world of
the blackberry lane-way which the poet knows, and
also the seeming glory of the City of the Kings to which
he is being drawn. As in the German *Novelle,* she
becomes (imaginatively anyway) an emissary from the
supernatural who has crossed the border to reality; the
frontier separating the real and the imagined becomes
more and more tenuous, and the spirit is left trapped in
a no-man's-land of confusion and imminent disaster. In
the German *Novelle* the supernatural element is capable
of two contrasting interpretations. It can be a power
external to, and independent of, man, or it may be taken
as a product of the irrational activity of man's mind. A
similar duality of tension is generated in Kavanagh's
poem:

Earth, earth! I dragged my feet off the ground.
Labourers, animals armed with farm tools,
Ringed me. The one open gap had larch poles
Across it now by memory secured and bound
The flaggers in the swamp were the reserves
Waiting to lift their dim nostalgic arms
The moment I would move.

Even the atmosphere in the closing passage of the poem
has, behind its realism, a romantic strain reminiscent of
Keats's Nightingale Ode, as Kavanagh going 'to follow
her who winked at me', turns on a September evening

Away from the ricks, the sheds, the cabbage-garden.
The stones in the street, the thrush song in the tree,
The potato-pits, the flaggers in the swamp.

'Temptation in Harvest' is possibly the most completely satisfying in *A Soul for Sale.* It is not surprising
that the experience which poem engendered it should
continue to preoccupy Kavanagh so persistently.

* * *

'All we learn from experience', says Kavanagh, writing
in *Nonplus,* 'is the way from simplicity back to
simplicity'. It is not a new or startling statement. The
path of the greatest poets, saints and mystics has always
been from the trust and acceptance of childhood,
through doubt and 'dark night of the soul' back again to
the serenity and acceptance of childhood. Back,
however, to a different serenity; different, in that it is
not an accidental endowment, but a state of grace
struggled for and realized. 'The agonizing pincer-jaws
of heaven'—as Kavanagh put it in an early poem—are
as yet not quite breached, but they are no longer agonizing; the intuition of ultimate reality, of which the pilgrim
was before but vaguely aware, is now sure and
confident, and can be proclaimed confidently by the
poet through symbols from the world of common
experience. The poetry is more direct, subtle, humorous
and generous. Such poetry seldom has a wide audience;
ostensibly it is often too ebullient to be considered really important by many serious critics. Yet who could
quarrel with Kavanagh's statement that

Laughter is the most poetic thing in life, that is the
right kind of loving laughter. When, after a lifetime of
struggle we produce the quintessence of ourselves, it
will be something gay and young.[6]

Certainly not Shakespeare. Not Blake. Not Dylan
Thomas. Patrick Kavanagh's poetry since *A Soul for
Sale* is a progression from experience to innocence;
from gaunt grandeur to rectitude; from the grip of the
earlier grim, land-locked myth to the liberation of the
passively recognized, and gladly embraced, state of
holiness of the Imagination.

A provocative and important essay of Kavanagh's, From
Monaghan to the Grand Canal published in *Studies* in
Spring 1959, is in many ways his poetic statement of
faith. In it, amongst other things, he comments somewhat severely on his earlier work, especially **'Pegasus',**
the opening poem in *A Soul for Sale.* 'One can see,' he
says, 'the embarrassing impertinence and weakness of it
all, the dissolute character whining'. Continuing, he
comments that 'there has always been a big market in
England for the synthetic Irish thing', and declaims the
poetic merits of having 'roots in the soil'.

What are our roots?   What is our material?
Real roots lie in our capacity for love and its abandon.
The material itself has no special value; it is what our
    imagination
and love does to it.

It is easy to fall into the temptation of being impatient
with a writer who disowns earlier work so insistently,
and even facetiously. O'Casey, for instance, with *The
Plough and the Stars* and *Juno and the Paycock* behind,

cuts an arrogant, and at times ludicrous figure, as he proudly hollers out the dawn of the new O'Casey of *Cock-a-Doodle-Dandy,* or bids us gather in an admiring circle around *The Bishop's Bonfire.* But there is a difference, and Kavanagh's phrase 'the dissolute character whining' touches upon it. Kavanagh has rightly put the 'whine' behind him and the new man is, I believe, a better poet. Moreover, this capacity for love and its abandon is undoubtedly one of the most striking qualities of Kavanagh's later poetry. The appearance of **Come Dance with Kitty Stobling** enables us to assess more adequately Kavanagh's real accomplishment as a poet. Until its publication, the poems had to be hunted for in back numbers of literary periodicals, e.g. *Nimbus, Encounter, Horizon, Time and Tide,* and—in Ireland—*Studies, The Irish Times* and *Nonplus.* Dispersed so widely, the poems were easily missed or ill-absorbed; the high quality of the sonnets which re-appear in the new book was too easily diffused in the opacity of some—but not all—of the longer satirical pieces, e.g. **'The Paddiad',** a satire on Irish men-of-letters which, despite some incisive irony, is, I think, largely banal. The banality, however, is not in the *fact* of the satire, but in the fact that it seems merely to bawdlerize in long-winded—but extremely funny—verse, the still-centre of wounded love which Kavanagh presents with such concentrated precision in the sonnets.

The banal has, however, an important place in life and in art; in the poet's crucible it can be refined till the granulated residue is 'violently beautiful', e.g. the sonnet **'Canal Bank Walk',** a poem which must be read many times before its astonishing fusion of thought and rhythm can be fully absorbed:

> Leafy-with-love banks and the green waters of the
>   canal
> Pouring redemption for me, that I do
> The will of God, wallow in the habitual, the banal,
> Grow with nature again as before I grew.

Suffering and joy are indistinguishable from each other as they leap together into fusion in the shout of the poet—a shout which is however as artistically controlled in its language as Schiller's 'Ode of Joy' or Beethoven's great echo of it in the Choral Symphony. Here, Kavanagh tells us, as it were in parenthesis, is

> the Word
> Eloquently new and abandoned to its delirious beat.

How different it all is from the whine of the Romantics, as in Shelly's 'Ode to the West Wind':

> Make me they lyre even as the forest is:
> What if my leaves are falling like its own!

Kavanagh's equivalent evocation?

> O Unworn world enrapture me, encapture me in a
>   web

Of fabulous grass and eternal voices by a beach,
Feed the gaping need of my senses, give me ad lib
To pray unselfconsciously with overflowing speech
For this sould needs to be honoured with a new dress
   woven
From green and blue things and arguments that cannot
   be proven.

'Canal Bank Walk' is the first poem in Kavanagh's new collection, and effectively sounds the pitch of the poet's development since **A Soul for Sale.** Whilst the basic impact of Kavanagh's earlier poetry in **A Soul for Sale** is tragic, whereas the impact of his later verse is comic—in the sense that Shakespeare's *The Tempest* is a comedy *vis-à-vis,* say, *King Lear* or *Hamlet*—it would be a mistake to imagine that there is a cleavage between the two, either in content or technique. Each has fundamentally the same *inner* vision; there is merely a shift in form and in emphasis, and a noticeable shedding of naivety. Throughout, Kavanagh is concerned fundamentally with seeing

> the newness that was in every stale thing
> When we looked at it as children; the spirit-shocking
> Wonder in a black slanting Ulster hill.

That is, the ordinary and the humdrum transmuted and given universal significance by the alchemy of Imagination. The real tragedy for anyone is not to be astonished at a stick carried down a stream,

> Or at the undying difference in the corner of a field.

Yet it has taken thirteen years for these poems to appear in book form. Why? Partly at least because:

> In Ireland one is up against the fact that very few care for or understand the creative spirit. You can come across by being Irish in manner and spirit, but when you attempt to offer them the real thing it's no go. When I started to write what is the real thing three years ago, there was not much response, except possibly from Stephen Spender who described it as 'violently beautiful'.[7]

But, as I have said before, there is no *whine* in these later poems, no indignation that does not include forgiveness; nothing but pity for what the poet occasionally finds it necessary to satirise, as in these lines from **'Is'**:

> The important thing is not
> To imagine one ought
> Have something to say,
> A *raison d'être,* a plot for the play.
> The only true teaching
> Subsists in watching
> Things moving or just colour
> Without comment from the scholar.
> To look on is enough
> In the business of love.

The 'business of love' is Kavanagh's fundamental concern as a poet. 'Lovers alone lovers protect' he says in *Prelude,* one of the more successful of his longer quasi-satirical poems; quasi, because satire itself is confronted and surmounted in the poet's grim self-analysis:

> But satire is unfruitful prayer,
> Only wild shoots of pity there,
> And you must go inland and be
> Lost in compassion's ecstasy

In **'Yellow Vestment'**—another sonnet—he repeats the injunction to love and recognizes its implications

> For love's sake we must only consider whatever
>   widens
> The field of the faithful's activity.

Again, in **'The One',** love is shown as a pale but true reflection of God's Love, yet at the same time contained within the latter:

> Green, blue, yellow and red—
> God is down in the swamps and marshes
> Sensational as April and almost incredible the flower-
>   ing of our catharsis.

In another fine sonnet, **'October',** the timelessness of love's mystery and pain is the only truth of which the poet is still certain in middle age as he was at nineteen:

> O leafy yellowness you create for me
> A world that was and now is poised above time,
> I do not need to puzzle out Eternity
> As I walk this aboreal street on the edge of a town.
> The breeze too, even the temperature
> And pattern of movement is precisely the same
> As broke my heart for youth passing. Now I am sure
> Of something. Something will be mine wherever I am.

Kavanagh's great advance in technique is best seen in such poems as **'Auditors In'**; **'Intimate Parnassus'**; **'The Hero'**; **'The Hospital'**; **'Dear Folks'** and the title-poem **'Come Dance with Kitty Stobling'**. In these poems, his judicious handling of the conversational and the cliché-emotion, as well as the cliché-phrase, is superior by far to Auden's, though Auden is generally accepted as a master of this type of technical excellence. Auden, however, in striving to avoid taking himself seriously, swings the pendulum too far towards the jocular; the poem frequently, therefore, misfires (e.g. 'Heavy Date'); one suspects the poet is not really *involved* as he should be. Kavanagh, however, effectively takes a stand of inner peace in the midst of outer confusion

>   somewhere to stay
> Doesn't matter. What is distressing
> Is waking eagerly to go nowhere in particular.

The sonnet **'Come Dance with Kitty Stobling'** is, in my opinion, not entirely successful despite its brilliantly arresting opening:

> No, no, no, I know I was not important as I moved
> Through the colourful country, I was but a single
> Item in the picture, the namer not the beloved.

It is, however, an extremely fine poem with an elasticity of rhythm and phrase which compels attention.

> O dance with Kitty Stobling I outrageously
> Cried out-of-sense to them, while their timorous paces
> Stumbled behind Jove's page boy paging me.
> I had a very pleasant journey, thank you sincerely
> For giving me my madness back, or nearly.

The poem, **'Intimate Parnassus',** though less arresting on first reading, seems to me to resolve the poet's predicament with more mature assurance:

> Men are what they are, and what they do
> Is their own business. If they praise
> The gods or jeer at them, the gods can not
> Be moved, involved or hurt.

And again, the injunction to love, but to be controlled in one's art:

> Poet, you have reason to be sympathetic—
> Count them the beautiful unbroken
> And then forget them
> As things aside from the main purpose
> Which is to be
> Passive, observing with a steady eye.

Yeats, in 'Under Ben Bulben', is scarcely more indomitable.

In **'The Hero'** the poet is shown as

> an ordinary man, a man full of honour

refusing to be corrupted by those who would make him their false idol:

> They had the wrong ideas of a god
> Who once all know becomes ridiculous.
> —I am as obvious as an auctioneer
> Dreaming of twenty thousand pounds a year.
> At this they roared in the streets and became quite
>   hysterical
> And he knew he was the cause of this noise—
> Yet he had acted reasonably, had performed no
>   miracle,
> Had spoken in a conventional voice,
> And he said: surely you can
> See that I am an ordinary man?

But in the end his contempt for the mean and the petty and the insincere, with their ludicrous cheer and sick applause, dissolves; even satire seems irrelevant. 'Humility', as Eliot tells us, 'is endless'. And Kavanagh echoes the sentiment:

> And for the insincere city
> He felt a profound pity.

Humility, then, and innocence and compassion are the beginning, the middle, and the end of the long road of experience. A simple formula? An easy solution? No.

Kavanagh's depth of psychological insight never falters, and the mystery pulses all the time behind the casual phrase, the everyday effort; as the closing couplet of the excellent sonnet, **'The Hospital'**, has it:

> For we must record love's mystery without claptrap,
> Snatch out of time the passionate transitory.[8]

Kavanagh, it may be protested, is too self-consciously the artist in these later poems to be valid or stimulating as a poet. The poems themselves are the best answer to this criticism. The work of the best artists and the best poets, as their art matures, strives towards a quality, which, for the want of a more satisfactory description, I shall call 'absoluteness'. Ultimately, they are humble before the discovery that all poetry and all art, however near-perfect it may strive to be, is a compromise. There is much in common between the incarcerated artist fumbling towards expression and the sin-weighted soul stumbling towards God. The attempt itself is an integral part of the artist's achievement and the sinner's redemption; as such, it also must be included in the artist's work. Such *self-awareness* is an outstanding quality of much of the best modern poetry. Jacques Maritain (writing on Baudelaire) says that the 'self-awareness and sense of its own freedom that poetry has gained in modern times, place him from the very start at the centre of the citadel'. Likewise, Kavanagh's ultimate appeal—and importance—as a poet is the appeal to the experience of poetry itself. Even his astonishing development of technique must be identified, as Kavanagh himself claims, as 'a spiritual quality, a condition of mind, or an ability to invoke a condition of mind'.

It is this latter quality which gives Kavanagh's poetry its merits of *freedom* and *uniqueness*. Or, to quote Maritain again (in *Creative Intuition in Art and Poetry*), poetry, as such, is served by the intellect, but has its own mode of knowledge. Neither is it subject to religion, since it is in its essence free. Faith and the intellect, however, affect poetry *indirectly* via the whole life of any man that poetry inhabits. Pursued to its extreme, we can see, as Kavanagh admits, that Plato may not be far wrong in suggesting that the poet is a menace. But, to quote Kavanagh again, there is little danger of his menacing Dublin or Ireland generally! Nevertheless, as he says in **'Dear Folks'**:

> The main thing is to continue,
> To walk Parnassus right into the sunset
> Detached in love where pygmies cannot pin you
> To the ground like Gulliver. So good luck and cheers.

Notes

1. *Come Dance with Kitty Stobling and Other Poems* by Patrick Kavanagh. London: Longmans. 1960. Pp. 44. 10s. 6d.

2. Dr Denis Donoghue in *The Month,* March 1957.

3. 'Innocence and Experience, the Poetry of Patrick Kavanagh' (*Nimbus,* Winter 1956).

4. 'Patrick Kavanagh: From Monaghan to the Grand Canal' (*Studies,* Spring 1959).

5. In this, I differ from the view of Dr Denis Donoghue (writing in *The Month,* March 1957) that 'the main defect in Mr Kavanagh's writing' is 'an inadequate grasp of the potentialities of language as a penetrative instrument'.

6. 'Patrick Kavanagh: From Monaghan to the Grand Canal' (*Studies,* Spring 1959).

7. 'Patrick Kavanagh: From Monaghan to the Grand Canal' (*Studies,* Spring 1959).

8. When this sonnet first appeared in *Nimbus* the final couplet read 'For we must set in words the mystery without claptrap / Experience so light-hearted appears transitory'. The new version is, I think, much stronger.

Alan Warner (essay date autumn 1969)

SOURCE: Warner, Alan. "The Poetry of Patrick Kavanagh (1904-1967)." *English* 18, no. 102 (autumn 1969): 98-103.

[*In the following essay, Warner speculates on Kavanagh's literary legacy and posits that Kavanagh will still be favorably regarded "in a hundred years or so."*]

'In a hundred years from now the only thing that will be remembered about this savage area is that I lived here awhile among the pigs.' This angry and dangerous boast comes from Tarry Flynn, alias Patrick Kavanagh; it may well prove prophetic.

In 1967, the year of his death, Kavanagh's name appeared for the first time in *Who's Who.* In the same year he was awarded a handsome poetry bursary by the Arts Council in London. In Ireland he has been widely acclaimed as the greatest Irish poet since Yeats. Even outside Ireland he has received high praise. A. Alvarez, reviewing his **Collected Poems** in 1964, referred to him as 'the best poet Ireland now has'. In a hundred years from now will he take his place beside Clare and Burns, or will he be half-forgotten like Stephen Duck and Robert Bloomfield?

Kavanagh hated being classed as a peasant poet, but it is not unfair to include him in their ranks. For the first thirty years of his life he belonged to the world of *Tarry Flynn,* to the little fields of Monaghan. It was only in certain moods that he cried out against his birthplace as a 'savage area' where he lived 'the usual barbaric life of the Irish country poor'. To the end of his days he had a passionate attachment to 'the stony grey soil of Monaghan', and most of his best work is rooted in the world of his youth.

He was born on 21 October 1904, in the townland of Mucker in the parish of Inniskeen, Co. Monaghan. Monaghan is in the northern half of Ireland and it formed part of the old province of Ulster, but it was included in the Republic of Ireland when the country was partitioned in 1921. It is one of the humblest of the Irish counties, possessing neither mountains nor sea-coast. It is separated by Louth from the sea and it is squeezed against the borders of modern Ulster between Fermanagh and Armagh. It has been called the county of the little hills. Passing through it one notices the hills characteristically divided into triangular fields, because this proved to be the most suitable way of dealing with the drainage. The land is not rich and it is mostly farmed by small peasant farmers. The towns—Monaghan, Castleblayney, Carrickmacross—are small market-towns. But although the landscape is unremarkable it possesses ample peace and beauty for those who look with the eyes of familiarity and affection. The hills may be small but there are fine views from them away to the sea in the east and to the mountains in the north-west. Many a time Kavanagh lifted his eyes from his 'hungry hills' at Shancoduff to see Slieve Gullion, or the sea shining in the distance beyond the plain of Louth.

> My hills hoard the bright shillings of March
> While the sun searches in every pocket.
> They are my Alps and I have climbed the Matterhorn
> With a sheaf of hay for three perishing calves.

Kavanagh's father was a country shoemaker who managed to save a little money and buy some land. His mother was a simple peasant woman without any schooling, but she was a shrewd judge of men and animals and her conversation had a racy edge that Kavanagh recalls in the pages of *Tarry Flynn*. As a boy he attended the local National School until the age of thirteen. Then he left to work on the land. He also learnt something of his father's trade of shoemaking but he never became a master of it.

Meantime he had begun to make verses. His first efforts were ballads about local events such as football matches and weddings. Later he contributed to the verse corner of a Dublin Sunday newspaper. Years afterwards he recalled as one of the great moments of his life the day his brother came up to the threshing machine where he was working and handed him a letter from the newspaper editor accepting some of his verses.

These early poems were published in 1928 and 1929. At this time he had never heard of W. B. Yeats. His only models were the other poems in the verse corner

and his school anthologies, where Tennyson and Longfellow were strongly represented. It is not surprising that he later on described his own early verses as 'atrocious'. It was the *Irish Statesman,* a chance copy of which fell into his hands at a local fair, that first opened wider literary horizons to him. The *Irish Statesman* was a Dublin literary journal edited by A. E., which ceased publication in 1930.

In 1936 Kavanagh's first volume of poetry, ***Ploughman and Other Poems,*** was published by Macmillan. It revealed a distinct lyric gift but had little originality. In 1939 he finally left the land and went to Dublin to embark on a life of poetry, poverty, and journalism. He eked out a precarious living by reviewing books for the *Irish Times* and by writing a gossip column for the *Irish Press* under the pseudonym of Piers Plowman. For a time he accepted the role of the Irish peasant poet, but he soon grew tired of self-conscious Irishness and became disillusioned with the Dublin literary world:

> 'When I came to Dublin in 1939 the Irish literary affair was still booming. It was the notion that Dublin was a literary metropolis and Ireland, as invented and patented by Yeats, Lady Gregory and Synge, a spiritual entity. It was full of writers and poets and I am afraid I thought their work had the Irish quality. The conversation in Poet's Pub had the richness and copiosity that H. W. Nevinson said all Dublin conversation had. To me, even then, it was tiresome drivel between journalists and civil servants. No humour at all. And, of course, they thought so much of poetry they didn't believe in the poet eating.'

In 1942 Kavanagh published a remarkable poem, **'The Great Hunger'.** On the strength of this poem alone he is entitled to serious consideration as a significant and original twentieth-century poet. For a long time it was little known and not easy to come by. It is now available in his ***Collected Poems,*** in a separate edition published in paperback by MacGibbon & Kee, and is included in the *Penguin Book of Longer Contemporary Poems* (1966).

There is no pastoral sentimentality about this poem. Indeed it is strongly anti-pastoral and it depicts the restricted and frustrated life of 'the peasant ploughman who is half a vegetable'. The central figure in the poem is Patrick Maguire, whose 'great hunger' for life and love is frustrated by a narrow prudence. At the age of sixty-five he remains unmarried, tied to his old mother and his little fields, 'a man who made a field his bride'. The poem opens with a sombre picture of the monotonous toil of the potato-gatherers:

> Clay is the word and clay is the flesh
> Where the potato-gatherers like mechanized scare-crows move
> Along the side-fall of the hill—Maguire and his men.
> If we watch them an hour is there anything we can prove

Of life as it is broken-backed over the Book
Of Death?

The poem is not simply a drab documentary of the potato fields. Although Maguire is firmly pinned to earth, his feet in the clay and the dung, yet there are times when he laughs and sees the sunlight and has glimpses of joy and eternity. He also has more ordinary comforts and compensations: gossip and cards, and a bob each way on the Derby. He goes to Mass on Sundays and attains the dignity of holding the collecting box at the chapel door. Yet he remains a pathetic figure. The worst thing about his life is not the fourteen-hour day that he works for years, but the mixture of narrow morality and caution that keeps him away from the girls until it is too late:

Who bent the coin of my destiny
That it stuck in the slot?

There is nothing for him to look forward to but death, when he 'will hardly remember that life happened to him'.

Patrick Maguire, the old peasant, can neither be
    damned nor glorified:
The grave yard where he will lie will just be a deep-
    drilled potato field
Where the seed gets no chance to come through
To the fun of the sun.
The tongue in his mouth is the root of a yew.
Silence, silence, the story is done.

Kavanagh came to dislike **'The Great Hunger'**. In introducing a broadcast of it on the B. B. C. Third Programme in 1960, he said that it was far too strong for honesty. 'In places, the poem here is a cry, a howl . . . there's no laughter in it . . . the poem remains tragedy because it is not completely born.' In *Self-Portrait* he remarked that it lacked the 'nobility and repose of poetry'. His own criticism is penetrating, but he carries it too far. It is true that there is a note of stridency in the poem, a raw edge:

O Christ! I am locked in a stable with pigs and cows
    for ever.

But the situation described in the poem demands a cry. Kavanagh is really admitting this at the end of his own introduction:

'Of course, I ought to mention that I was born and bred and reared in such a society and amid such a landscape as *The Great Hunger* describes. Many features of that country of small farms have disappeared. The horse has gone from the agricultural scene, and the heeled-up cart of the potato fields has now been replaced by tractor and trailer, but for all that, the life that is lived there remains practically the same—sad, grey, twisted, blind—and just awful.'

Although the main impact of the poem is tragic it is not entirely without laughter or repose. There are some vivid evocations of rural life that move with relaxed colloquial ease. The card game, for example:

Kate, throw another sod on that fire.
One of the card-players laughs and spits
Into the flame across a shoulder.
Outside, a noise like a rat
Among the hen-roosts. The cock crows over
The frosted townland of the night.
Eleven o'clock and still the game
Goes on and the players seem to be
Drunk in an Orient opium den.
Midnight, one o'clock, two.
Somebody's leg has fallen asleep.
What about home? Maguire, are you
Using your double-tree this week?
Why? do you want it? Play the ace.
There's it, and that's the last card for me.
A wonderful night, we had. Duffy's place
Is very convenient. Is that a ghost or a tree?
And so they go home with dragging feet
And their voices rumble like laden carts.
And they are happy as the dead or sleeping . . .
I should have led that ace of hearts.

Even before **'The Great Hunger'** Kavanagh was beginning to find a voice and style of his own. There are a number of poems, most of them later published in *A Soul for Sale* (1947) but many of them written much earlier, that make an original contribution to English pastoral poetry. They include **'Shancoduff'**, **'Peace'**, **'A Christmas Childhood'**, **'The Long Garden'**, **'Art McCooey'**, and **'Spraying the Potatoes.'** To these could be added some later poems that express similar moods and feelings—**'Innocence'**, **'Kerr's Ass'**, **'Epic'**, and **'In Memory of My Mother'**. These are mostly poems of reminiscence. Kavanagh, now committed to the streets and pubs of Dublin and London, looks back to the world of Mucker and his youth. The following extract from one of his *Envoy* diaries suggests the mood in which he wrote:

'On this breezy October day sitting looking out of a window in London, I am vividly back in a small potato field, turning out the drills of potatoes. Unconscious. Didn't know my age. And the yellow briar leaves with holes in them and the pock-marked poplar leaves and the dry clay and the wonderful appetite it gives. O love.'

He writes from inside this world, as a man who once took part in country tasks, who loved and praised the commonplace:

The tracks of cattle to a drinking-place
A green stone lying sideways in a ditch
Or any common sight.

Kavanagh shares with Wordsworth a sense of wonder at the common face of earth, an awareness of 'joy in widest commonalty spread'. But he is quite unlike Wordsworth in his perception and expression of it. He sees first, not the large appearances of cloud and lake, the tall rock, the mountain, and the deep and gloomy wood, but the detail of humble rural life, the potato pits, the nettles, the old bucket flung in a ditch:

> One side of the potato pits was white with frost—
> How wonderful that was, how wonderful! . . .
>
> A water-hen screeched in the bog,
> Mass-going feet
> Crunched the water-ice on the pot-holes,
> Somebody wistfully twisted the bellows wheel.

Kavanagh had his feet more firmly planted in the dung and the clay than Wordsworth. He recalls the common country tasks he once performed, such as spraying the potatoes:

> The barrels of blue potato-spray
> Stood on a headland of July . . .
>
> And over that potato field
> A lazy veil of woven sun.
> Dandelions growing on headlands
> Showing their unloved hearts to everyone.

In the midst of the commonplace he perceives, in Vaughan's phrase, 'bright shoots of everlastingness'. Beauty and wonder grow alongside the trivial and the sordid:

> In the sow's rootings where the hen scratches
> We dipped our fingers in the pockets of God.

After *A Soul for Sale* Kavanagh's poetry went through a lean period until 1955. He wrote some satires on the literary and cultural scene in Dublin, but with one or two exceptions (for example, **'House Party to Celebrate the Destruction of the Roman Catholic Church in Ireland'** and **'Who Killed James Joyce?'**) they are poor. He wrote a good deal of prose in this period. *Tarry Flynn,* an autobiographical novel, appeared in 1948, and he contributed a series of vivid and vigorous diaries to the magazine *Envoy*. He also produced the lively and provocative *Kavanagh's Weekly* in 1952.

In 1955 Kavanagh was in the Rialto Hospital in Dublin with cancer of the lung. He had one lung removed, and surviving this drastic operation he walked out into a warm summer and lay on the banks of the Grand Canal. Only then, he maintains in his *Self-Portrait,* did he become a poet. Certainly he had a remarkable burst of poetic energy. The sourness of satire fell away and he returned to praise of the commonplace, the discovery of wonder in the ordinary. This time he celebrates Dublin, particularly the Grand Canal, but there are also references back to Monaghan:

> Leafy-with-love banks and the green waters of the
>   canal

> Pouring redemption for me, that I do
> The will of God, wallow in the habitual, the banal,
> Grow with nature again as before I grew,
> The bright stick trapped, the breeze adding a third
> Party to the couple kissing on an old seat,
> And a bird gathering materials for the nest for the
>   Word
> Eloquently new and abandoned to its delirious beat.

He experienced a mood of acceptance, abandon, and love that embraced even the ward of the hospital. It finds expression in **'October'**:

> I want to throw myself on the public street without
>   caring
> For anything but the prayering that the earth offers.

These poems, together with some gay and jaunty personal pieces, such as **'Song at Fifty'** and **'If ever you go to Dublin Town'**, were published along with a mixed bag of earlier verse in *Come Dance with Kitty Stobling* (1960). After this Kavanagh produced little poetry. His occasional later pieces suggest a drying up of poetic springs, an exhaustion of spiritual energy. In **'Personal Problem'** he complains that he lacks a subject:

> If I could rewrite a famous tale
> Or perhaps return to a midnight calving,
> This cow sacred on a Hindu scale—
> So there it is my friends. What am I to do
> With the void growing more awful every hour?
> I lacked a classical discipline. I grew
> Uncultivated and now the soil turns sour . . .

The soil was perhaps turning sour in his last few years and it is to his credit that he did not flog it feverishly to produce a few poor blooms of poetry. Although his total output was modest he had already produced enough poetry and prose to entitle him to a place in the history of literature.

In a review of *The Green Fool* (1938), a semi-fictional autobiography, Harold Nicolson remarked: 'Patrick Kavanagh for all he knows may become the Robert Burns of Eire. He is a poet and a peasant.' But Kavanagh did not become the Irish Burns, though he has some things in common with Burns, especially in his comic moods. If Burns had ever written a novel it might well have included some of the scenes found in *Tarry Flynn.* But more than a century of Irish poverty and puritanism (Catholic puritanism of a special Irish brand) separates Kavanagh from Burns. *The Midnight Court,* written in Irish in the late eighteenth century by Brian Merriman, has more of Burns in it than **'The Great Hunger'** has.

Burns had behind him a great Scottish folk tradition, a tradition based on song and speech. He was a folk poet in a way that Kavanagh could not be. In the world into which Kavanagh was born only faint traces of an oral tradition still lingered. *Tit-Bits,* the *Irish Weekly Independent,* the verse pages of *Old Moore's Almanac,* and *Ireland's Own* had largely replaced folk-tale and folk-song. The situation grew worse as the years passed. Kavanagh commented on it in an article in the *Irish Farmers' Journal* entitled 'Land Without Song':

> 'The great defect in rural Ireland in recent years has been the absence of an integrated culture. The old songs and the old stories that held a society together are gone.
>
> 'I remember remarking on this to a priest, who agreed with me, when we were crossing the Atlantic. There were a couple of hundred Irish emigrants on the ship and sometimes I would go down to the bar to join them. Not a song of their own they had. What they had was imitations of film stars. They tried to do Al Jolson complete with actions, and surely it would take a tear from a stone. I couldn't endure it and one evening I started to sing "The Rising of the Moon", but they wouldn't have it.
>
> 'When I was growing up the songs of Burns were common currency. Today these would be considered highbrow and are only to be heard in sophisticated society.'

Certainly Kavanagh was unable to latch on to a popular tradition in the way that Burns could; he had to pull himself up by his own boot-straps and find a poetic mode of his own.

Born into the century of the common man and growing up in an Ireland that had achieved national independence, he had none of the humble deference to social superiors that is evident in earlier peasant poets. He recognized no social superiors and he was often bitter and contemptuous about the public patronage of the arts. He preserved his independence and his poverty. The result was not altogether fortunate; it led to a certain souring of the spirit. Although he was treated generously by individuals and by some authorities, he retained a rancour towards those at the top. It appears in a late poem addressed to Yeats:

> Yes Yeats it was damn easy for you protected
> By the middle classes and the Big Houses
> To talk about the sixty year old public protected
> Man sheltered by the dim Victorian Muses.

Kavanagh may well be the last of the peasant poets. Even if peasants and small farmers survive the technological changes of this century their children will increasingly share in the benefits of the welfare state. It is less likely now that a boy will be lost, even in a remote country place, in a fog of unknowing. Seamus Heaney and John Montague, for example, were both bred on small Irish farms, but neither could really be considered a peasant poet. Although both of them write about the countryside, neither of them belongs to a rural community in the way that Kavanagh did. Both

had a secondary school and university education; both, at the age of thirty, were inside the world of literature in a way that Kavanagh was not.

Kavanagh never became reconciled to the world of literature. In this respect he has some affinity with the peasant poets of the late eighteenth and early nineteenth centuries. W. Kenneth Richmond, in his book on *Poetry and the People,* writes of 'The Peasant's Revolt', which he defines as 'an attempt to emancipate poetry from literature'. The attempt failed because the poets were not strong enough to resist the influence of the literary world. Hogg and Clare adopted the modes and language of polite literature, and even Burns imitated the effete and genteel poetic diction of his day.

Polite literature presented a much more solid front in Clare's day than in Kavanagh's. There is no longer a need for a 'peasant's revolt' against the closed ranks of literature. Many of the most respected literary figures of our time are rebels or outcasts. Indeed we find Kavanagh complaining at one time that a writer who hasn't done a spell in prison is almost out of the swim. But in spite of the freedom of attitude and language in the modern world of letters, Kavanagh steadily declined to become a man of letters. He retained to the end a mistrust and dislike, part peasant perhaps, part personal, of the world of culture, especially the academic world.

It would be wrong to think of Kavanagh simply as a countryman. He belongs to the streets of Dublin as much as the fields of Monaghan:

> If ever you go to Dublin town
> In a hundred years or so
> Inquire for me in Baggot Street
> And what I was like to know.
> O he was a queer one,
> Fol dol the di do,
> He was a queer one
> I tell you.

He was certainly a queer one, awkward but alive, refusing any of the roles that the literary world or the academic world would have liked him to adopt, remaining to the end, in Thomas Kinsella's words, 'an outcast Corvine figure embittered by disillusion, hugging the cold comfort of his honesty and craft'. His angular personality was both strength and weakness. He is describing his own creative processes at the end of **'Art McCooey'**:

> Unlearnedly and unreasonably poetry is shaped
> Awkwardly but alive in the unmeasured womb.

In his slender and uneven output there are enough of those 'lines that speak the passionate heart' to ensure that his work will still be read in a hundred years or so.

Darcy O'Brien (essay date 1975)

SOURCE: O'Brien, Darcy. "Stony Grey Soil." In *Patrick Kavanagh*, pp. 27-41. Lewisburg, Penn.: Bucknell University Press, 1975.

[*In the following excerpt, O'Brien characterizes Kavanagh's poetic challenge following the publication of* The Great Hunger—*which Kavanagh himself later disavowed—as the attempt to sincerely convey his ambiguous relationship with the land of his native County Monaghan.*]

In later years Kavanagh took to disparaging *The Great Hunger.* There were "some queer and terrible things" in it "but it lacks the nobility and repose of great poetry." It began to seem overdone, overstated. He wondered whether the Vice Squad had been right after all: "There is something wrong with a work of art, some kinetic vulgarity in it when it is visible to policemen. . . . *The Great Hunger* is tragedy and Tragedy is underdeveloped Comedy, not fully born. Had I stuck to the tragic thing in *The Great Hunger* I would have found many powerful friends."

Such remarks are partly the poet's predictable disowning of early work and partly the preference of an older man for grays over the blacks and whites of his youth. But for all its power the poem never did represent with any degree of fullness or completeness Kavanagh's attitudes and feelings about the land. Here is a tired aesthetic problem: "sincerity." Ought we to care a whit whether a poet believes in what he says as long as he says it well? Probably not. But if "sincerity" ought to be no issue for the reader, it can become one for the writer. Kavanagh never mastered Yeats's trick of changing masks comfortably from poem to poem.

I believe that *The Great Hunger* was written as a polemic not so much against the land as against sentimental literary lies about the land. Kavanagh was cynical about the reputations that had been gained by these lies; yet he had still more to be cynical about when his own lie, "the tragic thing in *The Great Hunger,*" proved profitable too. He began to notice that his dishonest poems, or poems reflecting one rather than two or seven sides of a subject, attracted the most attention. They helped to sound a steady note of either lamentation or exultation, for the benefit of one-track ears. One of his least favorite poems, **"Memory of Brother Michael"** (1944), became the most frequently anthologized. ("A nettle-wild grave . . . Ireland's stage. . . .") It has just the right clap-trap, the perfect cliché-touch. The Irish thing.

Kavanagh's poetic problem after *The Great Hunger* was to find a way of getting in some of the things he had excluded without sacrificing all the queer and ter-

rible aspects. His earlier work (1930-39) consisted mainly of pious encomiums: "I find a star-lovely art / In a dark sod. / Joy that it timeless! O heart / That knows God! / (**"Ploughman,"** 1930)" But this was as much a distortion as the apocalypse of clay. We can gather from his two autobiographical novels, *The Green Fool* (1938) and *Tarry Flynn* (1947), and from his letters and fugitive journalism, how varied and complicated Kavanagh's relation to the land actually was.

Benedict Kiely has described *The Green Fool,* accurately, as being "as honest and unaffected and happy and humorous a book as any young poet ever wrote about himself." Yet its publishing history was a disaster. After his first book of verse, **Ploughman and Other Poems,** had come out in 1936, Kavanagh went to London to try to get involved in the literary scene. He quickly ran out of money, tried selling coronation medals in the company of an amputee, and passed himself off to a newspaper as the man who had blown up the statue of George II in Dublin, earning a guinea for his lie. But Helen Waddell, the novelist, was kind to him and suggested that he write an autobiographical novel. Kavanagh returned to Ireland and completed the book in a year.

Shortly after publication *The Green Fool* was withdrawn, and Kavanagh earned neither fame nor a penny from it, though a little notoriety. Oliver St. John Gogarty (Joyce's model for Buck Mulligan in *Ulysses*) took offense, or said he did, at a certain passage, in which Kavanagh tells of arriving in Dublin after a pilgrimage on foot from his home in Inniskeen, County Monaghan. Knocking, uninvited, on Gogarty's door, "I mistook Gogarty's white-robed maid for his wife—or his mistress. I expected every poet to have a spare wife." This is hardly malicious: if it cuts at anything it is at the country boy's gaucherie. But Gogarty sued successfully for £100 damages and killed the book. Later he joked that he had been offended by the implication that he had but one mistress. Later, too, Kavanagh claimed to have invented the entire incident.

It is one of the few instances known in which Gogarty, who had a vicious tongue but was capable of kindness, lived up to the meanness of character Joyce ascribed to him. Obviously the withdrawal of the book seriously affected Kavanagh's career. *The Green Fool* might well have been a success, for it has a mature, easy tone that Kavanagh was not to recapture for many years, and the savagery of *The Great Hunger* must have been born in part out of his literary frustrations. In the course of describing the blossoming of a poetic soul *The Green Fool* touches on countless details of country life that are of anthropological as well as literary interest.

Kavanagh's father, James, a shoemaker by trade, married Bridget Quinn of Tullerain, County Louth, in 1897. They had ten children, Annie, Mary, Bridget, Patrick (born October 21, 1904), Lucy, Theresa, Josie, James (who died in infancy), Cecelia, and Peter (born March 19, 1916). The original family house in Inniskeen, near the Armagh border of County Monaghan was a traditional Irish cabin, wedge-shaped "to trick the western winds," with two rooms and a kitchen, built and first thatched in 1791. But in 1909, when Patrick was about five, it was torn down and a new house, two-storied and slate-roofed, was built on its foundations. Patrick remembered his father's supplying the two masons who built the house with two dozen bottles of porter a day; they built a healthy structure, light, dry, and roomy. Neighbors were of the opinion that the Kavanaghs must have got a legacy to be able to afford it, but the shoemaker Kavanagh worked hard, from six in the morning till near midnight each day. (His workshop was the kitchen, alive with the talk of customers and journeyman cobblers, telling of their travels.) In addition Kavanagh's mother did a small bit of farming with her children's help. There were about four acres of land and two acres of bog attached to the house, and an acre or two more could be rented from a nearby estate. The Kavanaghs kept about six dozen hens, three cows, and four pigs fattening. Whenever they attempted to add a fifth pig, one would die, so they stuck to the four.

Such were the rudiments of the life portrayed in **The Great Hunger** but Kavanagh's attitude toward them had more of tolerance and affection than bitter resentment in it, and he returned to Inniskeen regularly throughout his life, in thought, verse, and person, oftener as he grew older. The stunted hills with their outcroppings of rock, hills neither grand nor fertile, held his attention. **The Great Hunger** by itself can mislead one into thinking that Kavanagh's was the case of the Irish writer who finds home conditions so intolerable that he must, so he says, like Shaw or Joyce, flee to save himself. He had literary ambitions and he went, eventually, to Dublin to further them, but Inniskeen, ignorant, backward, slow, he understood and loved too well ever to reject, drawing on it all his life in verse. At times, to be sure, he railed against it:

> O stony grey soil of Monaghan
> The laugh from my love you thieved;
> You took the gay child of my passion
>
> And gave me your clod-conceived. . . .
> You sang on steaming dunghills
> A song of cowards' brood,
> You perfumed my clothes with weasel itch,
> You fed me on swinish food.
>
> (**"Stony Grey Soil,"** 1940)

Hate can make a poem strong. Kavanagh had been living in Dublin for over a year when he wrote **"Stony Grey Soil,"** and the city makes every countryman hate himself for awhile. But he knew and eventually expressed that Inniskeen was a way of life, like any other, and that only his unsureness about himself had made him hate it: "Ashamed of what I loved / I flung her from me and called her a ditch / Although she was smiling at me with violets . . ." (**"Innocence,"** 1950)

In *The Green Fool*, as later in *Tarry Flynn*, the character and the characters of Inniskeen come across as so varied and so intense that one looks on in fascination and with little enough of either approval or disgust. Had Gogarty not got there first, certain people who appear in the book are said to have been threatening libel suits, but then the Irish are a litigious folk. Certainly Kavanagh does not spare himself from humorous treatment, as when he describes how he taunted the son of the Protestant sexton and then ran for his life from the wrath of the boy's father. Everyone seems to get his due, and no more.

There is nothing stage-Irish here, the observations are too precise for that. We get a sharply focused picture of a specific region and proof that there are not one or two but hundreds of Irelands tucked away among low hills or high mountains, black-soiled valleys or white-stoned coasts; a country as yet unhomogenized by the mass media; a place where crossing a stream can bring a change of accent and custom.

Historically County Monaghan is part of the province of Ulster, a name lately debased into a synonymn for Northern Ireland, whereas Ulster embraces the nine northernmost of Ireland's 32 counties, Northern Ireland but six of these. One detects many of the characteristics of the Ulsterman among the Kavanaghs and their neighbors. These are people with razor edges round their personalities. Extravagant speech is rare. Conversations are apt to be blunt though ironical and often witty, with little of the baroque evasiveness characteristic of the south and west. A cow has died and it is buried at night to avoid the public disgrace of the loss of property. But one neighbor-woman sniffs things out:

> "Who was that ye had out there?"
>
> "Biddy Magee."
>
> "A bad-minded article."
>
> "She heard the cow died."
>
> "Well, let her hear away. The cow's gone now and all our bad luck be with her!"
>
> "Amen."

Or take this exchange over the death of a generally despised policeman, known for his strict enforcement of the law against herding animals in the road. Constable Kinsella had joined the British Army at the outbreak of the First World War and was killed the first week:

> "Kinsella was a bad article," one of our neighbors said.
>
> "A bad pill surely," was the reply.

"It was the price of him," people said, "he couldn't have better luck."

This sort of acid banter embodies the psychology and general outlook of Kavanagh country. Inniskeen lies in a townland (or district) called Mucker, meaning in corrupted Irish-Gaelic a place where pigs breed in abundance, and you had to begin with irony, born in a place with such a name as that. Life was pepper and salt and nothing too marvelous might be expected from it. Kavanagh, however, had dreams. "I was in my mother's arms clinging with my small hands to the security of her shoulder. I saw into a far mysterious place that I had long associated with Wordsworth's Ode on Immortality. I believed for many years that I had looked back into a world from whence I came. And perhaps I had." As a dreamer he was regarded as something of a fool (hence the title of the book), the butt of jokes at wake, fair, or dance. But, he writes, "being made a fool of is good for the soul. It produces a sensitivity of one kind or another; it makes a man into something unusual, a saint or a poet or an imbecile." He did not blame the people who needed a fool about. There were others who cared for him deeply. An old story: the poet very much of the people, yet set apart from most; nothing, however, of the poet set entirely apart, no Zarathustra nonsense.

"In our house," Kavanagh writes, "the most important subjects were the saying of the Rosary each evening and the making of money. Ours was a united house, there was only one purse let it be full or empty. In other houses the man held to what he could make from cattle or corn, the wife would have to supply the kitchen from the proceeds of butter and eggs. Everybody was poor and proud. My parents didn't know anything to be proud of, so they just carried on." Religion was taken seriously but the priests were judged on their merits as human beings, one regarded as a saint, another as an idiot, with reverence due not them but the function they fulfilled. Throughout his life Kavanagh was neither anti-nor pro-clerical, and he was always Ulster-practical about his relations with the Church. Later, during hard times in Dublin, he would accept quietly small sums of money from the Reverend John McQuaid, the ultra-conservative Archbishop of Dublin.

When Kavanagh was about six years old he went to confession for the first time, not sure why, since his sins were not bothering him much and no one had told him to go. Old Father MacElroy, white-haired and deaf, asked him what sins he remembered, and the child confessed he had committed adultery and stolen from the press.

"Well now, you mustn't steal from the press any more," he advised me tenderly. "And for your penance," he hurriedly summoned up, "for your penance you'll say . . . No, you'll come in and serve my Mass on Sunday."

I take it that young Patrick had no idea what adultery was and that the deaf priest convinced himself he wasn't hearing properly. What comes across, apart from the humor, is matter-of-fact kindliness. Other priests, particularly those who preach hysterically against sex, Kavanagh merely laughs at. They are of no great importance, simply part of the landscape. The nightly Rosary is often a bore, but also a family ritual, like tea or the daily chores. Reading *The Green Fool* one can understand why, if we are to believe certain surveys, most Irish Catholics cease practicing their religion when they emigrate to Birmingham, Manchester, Liverpool, or London. At home Catholicism is worn comfortably and thoughtlessly, but in a different society the faith loses its integral function. The religion is not renounced, only left behind and on lonely evenings remembered regretfully, like family faces.

Except for his dreaming and a fascination with poetry from the age of eight or nine, Kavanagh passed his youth like the rest of the lads, thinning turnips, spraying the potatoes, hauling dung in a cart, and, sporadically, attending the Kednaminsha grade school. He often played truant and quit school forever at the age of twelve. The long summer evenings, when the light would not fail till after ten, were good for mischief. There was the occasional salmon poaching in the River Fane, penny pitching, cards, and more exotic pastimes, catching and killing bees and giving them a wake with pipes and tobacco and whiskey: the deceased were buried like Pharaohs in matchbox coffins under pyramids of dust. To the boy

> It was the garden of the golden apples
> A long garden between a railway and a road. . . .
>
> In the thistly hedge old boots were flying sandals
> By which we travelled through the childhood skies,
> Old buckets rusty-holed with half-hung handles
> Were drums to play when old men married wives.
>
> **("The Long Garden,"** 1946)

Kavanagh would visit the Carrick Fair, perhaps driving a heifer for sale, and watch bargains being struck in the old manner, a third party bringing the hands of the hagglers together when a fair price had been reached. Once when he was in his early twenties, he sold himself out to hire as a laborer for a Cavan farmer.

"Were ye ever hired afore?" my man said.

"No," I answered.

"Well, before I bid anything, can ye milk?"

"I can milk anything but a hen," I said.

"Ha, ha, ha," they laughed, but only like men to whom laughter caused pain.

The arrangement did not last long. The farmer kept getting him up earlier and earlier, the food got worse and worse, and to his relief Kavanagh managed to get himself fired, after breaking a plough.

In 1921 Kavanagh involved himself with the I. R. A., never formally joining but helping out with the pulling down of telegraph wires. His sympathies were Republican (this was the Civil War period) but he thought of his activities more as pranks than as serious military maneuvers. Three of his crowd, however, were caught, lined up against the Dundalk jail wall and shot by the Free Staters. Kavanagh was purged of any simple-minded sort of patriotism or anti-British feeling by the spectacle of Irishmen slaughtering each other, and he came to regard his own limited participation with an amused contempt.

After his failure as a hired hand, his father apprenticed him to the shoemaker's trade, but he was bored by it, so the family managed to purchase an extra three acres of land, his watery hills, he would later call them. He farmed them, but it was only at poetry that he worked hard, from early on: "Around twelve or so I took to the poeming, as it is called. Quite a lot of terror filled the hearts of my parents when they heard the news. 'Was he going to be another Bard?'" There was a local bard, a cripple with an ass and cart and a crockery business, who called himself the Bard of Callenberg. Kavanagh gives the right comic touch to his description of this vestige of the *fili,* druidic poets of pre-Christian Ireland, known especially for their satire, which had the power to kill. Once, after Kavanagh had begun to publish verses in the Poet's Corner of the *Weekly Independent* and in the *Dundalk Democrat,* an agitated man called on him: "Ye can do a great deal for me . . . I'm an unfortunate man livin' among the worst of bad neighbors; night, noon and mornin' they have me persecuted. I want ye to make a ballad on them, a good, strong, poisonous ballad. . . . I'll give ye the facts, and you'll make the ballad." He gave the names of his neighbors and their nicknames, which of them had bastard blood and which had been accused of theft, a crime more disgraceful than murder in Ireland. It looked to be "the bones of a good ballad." But Kavanagh asked three pounds for it, and the man had only the price of a couple of bottles of porter. He left, saying he could get a solicitor cheaper. Aside from its comicality the incident illustrates Kavanagh's Ulster hard-headedness and foreshadows his later devotion to satirical verse, which if it had not the power to kill, could wound.

The earliest influences on Kavanagh's poetry were romantic, the lyrics of Thomas Moore and James Clarence Mangan, which he found in school texts. They spoke to his imagination of what was fantastic and unreal and they fed his dreams. Over the years his technique advanced and his perceptions widened and sharpened. It was his imaginative sense or longing and not any active disgust with Inniskeen that caused him to walk like a pilgrim to Dublin in 1930. He had been reading William Carleton, the author of *Traits and Stories of the Irish Peasantry* (1830-33), who, as he tells in his *Life,* made a similar journey on foot as a poor scholar, and one can be sure that Kavanagh had Carleton as a hero in his head as he made his way south through Slane, begging successfully in some places and getting doors slammed in his face at others, inquiring at last at the National Library of Gogarty's address and supposedly having his misfortunate encounter with Gogarty's maid. George Russell (AE), who had played an important role in the Literary Renaissance both as a writer and as an encourager of young talent, had already printed three of Kavanagh's poems in the *Irish Statesman,* and when Kavanagh called on him, luck changed. Russell loaded Kavanagh up with books—Emerson, Melville, Dostoevsky, Whitman, James Stephens, Liam O'Flaherty, Frank O'Connor and others—and with kindness. From that point on Kavanagh's sights were set on Dublin, though he did not move there permanently until 1939.

His mixed emotions about finally departing Inniskeen are crystallized in *Tarry Flynn,* completed in 1947, published the next year, and reprinted twice since. The novel was adapted for the stage by P. J. O'Connor and Pat Layde; it had a successful run at the Abbey in 1966 and has been revived frequently since at various theaters around the country. The stage version confines itself mainly to the humorous episodes of the book, the feuds between families, the sharp speech of the mother ("What in the name of the devil's father are you looking for at such an hour of the morning? Are you going to go to Mass at all or do you mean to be at home with them atself? . . . Looking on top of the dresser! Mind you don't put the big awkward hooves on one of them chickens that's under you."), the elaborate attempts to marry-off daughters, the comical intensities of country religion. A girl is knocked off her bicycle at a crossroads by local louts. This causes the parish priest to work himself into a fit over the plague of lust that he sees devastating the townland: "Rapscallions of hell," he preaches, "curmudgeons of the devil that are less civilised than the natives of the Congo. Like a lot of pigs that you were after throwing cayenne pepper among. . . ." He brings in the Redemptorist fathers, famous for their puritanical strictures, for a mission against sex. Of course there is hardly any sex at all going on in the place, but the Redemptorists have the effect of firing everyone up.

A wonderful episode, and typical of *Tarry Flynn.* It covers much of the same ground as *The Green Fool,* but Kavanagh's experience with the law of libel induced him to protect himself with fiction, so the names are changed to protect the innocent author, and the setting is nominally County Cavan. Aesthetically it is superior to the earlier work, more humorous, tighter, and more coherent by virtue of its controlling theme, the inevitable departure from the countryside of its young poet-hero Tarry.

The time span of the book is confined to Kavanagh's (or Tarry's) late twenties, that prolonged adolescence that is the burden and the pleasure of Irish youth. Kavanagh's father, with whom he had been very close, had died in 1929, and so in the novel the mother is head of the household, immensely strong, with a curl to her tongue, but as for Tarry, "she loved that son more than any mother ever loved a son. She hardly knew why. There was something so natural about him, so real and so innocent and which yet looked like badness." He does his work about the place, but he dreams and reads in the fields, and at night he scribbles away at verse. He loves a girl but is too shy to declare it. He loves his district but in his fantasy-ridden mind he dwells elsewhere, somewhere, nowhere. Finally an uncle visits and urges Tarry to leave with him. There'll be a job and money to spend. "It's not what you make but what you spend that makes you rich." Abruptly, Tarry decides to go. He appears for breakfast in his good suit, and the mother knows. Her lips move, but there are no words. "Then a storm of sobs swept over her and words came in a deluge. 'Your nice wee place; your strong farm; your wee room for your writing, your room for your writing.'"

Kavanagh leaves us at last with the pain of uprooting and the beauty of what Tarry loves. No bitterness, no resentment at the stony grey soil, only sadness and confusion at the power of home and the urge to leave it. Kavanagh had gone away with a book already published, another published though aborted, and literary prospects and contacts established in Dublin. Tarry has none of these, but his regret is Kavanagh's own. He had to leave to try himself in the world, but lest we be in any doubt of the price, he ends the novel with a poem and these lines: "And then I came to the haggard gate, / And I knew as I entered that I had come / Through fields that were part of no earthly estate."

Michael Allen (essay date 1975)

SOURCE: Allen, Michael. "Provincialism and Recent Irish Poetry: The Importance of Patrick Kavanagh." In *Two Decades of Irish Writing: A Critical Survey,* edited by Douglas Dunn, pp. 23-36. Chester Springs, Penn.: Dufour Editions, 1975.

[*In the following essay, Allen argues that the preoccupation with provincialism in Irish poetry—embarked upon by Seamus Deane—can, in Kavanagh's case, be seen as productive. Allen goes on to discuss Kavanagh's influence on later Irish poetry with respect to the issue of provincialism.*]

Provincialism was a major European social and literary preoccupation in the nineteenth century; but why does it still remain such a central concern in Ireland? Seamus

Deane's suggestion (in the preceding essay [Irish Poetry and Irish Nationalism: A Survey]) that Ireland was a provincial backwater between 1930 and 1955 is a variation on Daniel Corkery's general notion that Ireland is most provincial when most peaceful. One explanation of the continued Irish concern with this issue must obviously have to do with her relationship with England: the custom that lies upon her '"heavy as frost and deep almost as life"', Corkery says, is not her 'own custom, it is England's'. Louis MacNeice, in his book on Yeats, offers another explanation: that Ireland may sometimes be united against England, but is always divided against herself, characterized above all by an intensity of local feeling. 'A man from the next parish is a foreigner.' The example of Patrick Kavanagh, the most influential poet to have lived with Deane's twenty-five years of provincialism, shows that the preoccupation can be fruitful as well as debilitating; it lends support to both the above explanations which may thus be taken as complementary rather than contradictory.

As a nineteenth-century idea, the pejorative notion of provincialism, 'pertaining to a narrow and limited environment', appealed to that sense of superiority on grounds of mobility and wide acquaintance with the best people on which upper class people thrived socially. Their own presumably broad and expansive environment they could see as 'cosmopolitan' or 'metropolitan'; their way of life as 'urbane'. For intellectuals and artists these socially accepted, opposed or overlapping 'catchwords' (A. O. Lovejoy) offered the idea of the whole world as a structured hierarchical system of places. One's art, one's style, one's flow of thought, it was assumed, would profit from location in, or free access to, places high up in the hierarchy like Paris or London. Those doomed to places lower down could be pitied or patronized. Matthew Arnold snobbishly introduced this idea of provincialism to the English literary journals in the course of popularizing the critical terminology of Sainte-Beuve in 1864. The provincial note, he said, occurred in the writer 'left too much to himself' with 'ignorance and platitude all round him' too far from a 'supposed centre of correct information, correct judgement, correct taste'. Writing produced in such circumstances would, he said, exaggerate 'the value of its ideas' or rather 'give one idea too much prominence at the expense of others'. This sense of 'provincial' was immediately taken up in the critical essays in Victorian periodicals, the literary talk in London *salons.* But Arnold's very high standards, his castigation of the whole of English culture as provincial in comparison with that of France, tended to get lost when the distinction was used by, say, Thackeray and his circle: they would use it to dignify their own ethos and patronize a Charlotte Brontë or a Thomas Hardy. It probably seemed no more than common sense to assume that such provincial writers were inferior in cultural advantage and could only profit by gaining mobility and access to superior circles. George Eliot accepted her assimilation into the metropolitan melting pot gratefully; Charlotte Brontë half accepted the benefits of her London links. Even the young Hardy accepted the assumption initially, deciding that, as a writer, he must have his headquarters in or near London.

It seems clear to us now that for a writer whose art is uniquely dependent on a native love of a particular terrain, an authentic sense of a local society, such considerations might seem irrelevant (Faulkner is the most obvious modern example). While Hardy conceded the value of the metropolitan visits which continued after he had settled in Dorchester, his confidence in his own gifts led him to repudiate the basic premisses of urbane patronage. 'Arnold is wrong about provincialism', he wrote, 'if he means anything more than a provincialism of style and manner . . . A certain provincialism of feeling is invaluable. It is of the essence of individuality and is largely made up of that crude enthusiasm without which no great thoughts are thought, no great deeds done.' We can speculate that like Clym Yeobright he had originally renounced the provinces for a metropolis where he thought customs and values would be infinitely superior; but that he too found that he was putting off 'one sort of life' for another that was 'not better than the one he had known before. It was simply different.' He still recognized the limitations of provincial society in terms which partially reflect Arnold's: the scene of *The Woodlanders* for instance is 'a place where may usually be found more meditation than action and more listlessness than meditation; where reasoning proceeds on narrow premisses . . .' But it is important that he added 'and results in inferences wildly imaginative'. The relationship between these inferences and his own 'provincialism of feeling', 'individuality', 'enthusiasm' was to be established and objectified through the creation of a self-contained fictional world. Genteel and cosmopolitan characters and scenes could be subordinated or excluded since 'there was quite enough human nature in Wessex for one man's literary purpose'. This conception of art rooted in the re-creation of an authentic self-contained regional world reached its height when Faulkner, an even more intransigent provincial, discovered what could be achieved by writing about his own little postage stamp of native soil, sublimating the actual into the apocryphal. These formulations are suggestive of the mode of Patrick Kavanagh's best work. What is more, the nineteenth-century 'debate' in which they germinated remains relevant in Ireland, where Yeats played Arnold's role and Kavanagh (I shall maintain) played Hardy's. In his book on the Southern writer, Cleanth Brooks argues that Hardy and Faulkner both gained great artistic strength from their identification with provincial cultures in a period when the intellectual and social values of the metropolitan commercial and cultural centres were defective. He is wrong, however,

to place Yeats alongside these authors. Certainly Yeats was not a thoroughgoing cosmopolitan; he earned Joyce's rebuke ('a treacherous instinct of adaptability') in as much as he was not prepared to reject Irish literary circles for their 'temporising and poltroonery, their attitude of timid covert revolt on all issues not purely national' as Joyce did. But this was precisely because Dublin was as important to him as Sligo: he differs from the other writers referred to by Brooks in that he had no intimate and exclusive relationship with a rural traditional culture. In fact, in *Autobiographies* he described Irish culture in Arnoldian terms. He said that the incessant attempt to communicate with 'ignorant or still worse half-ignorant men' produced a 'sense of strain' for the writer; and because Ireland offered 'no ideas and ideals . . . no aesthetic culture or taste' wide reading frequently became mere pedantry. He resembled Arnold in his application of these strictures to a national culture he was finally, himself, committed to; Arnold's remedy for provincialism in England, an Academy on the French model, was one of Yeats's own most cherished Dublin projects; his only advice on the individual level was that talented young men should leave Ireland entirely between the ages of eighteen and twenty-five (the implication being that they should then return to Dublin to assist in the construction of a national metropolis). And though Yeats continued to regard the town as 'unmannerly' he did, as the century progressed, superintend the growth there of a recognizable literary establishment which accepted as credentials either a measure of genteel cosmopolitanism like his own or a 'genuine' peasant-pastoral *naïveté* which would be patronized.

Patrick Kavanagh was more like Hardy than like Yeats, though lacking in either's artistic stature. As the young Hardy thought it essential to migrate to London to be a writer so the young Kavanagh set out for Dublin, believing it, he said later, to have been transformed into 'a literary metropolis' by Yeats, Lady Gregory and Synge. What he brought with him was an exact and authentic sense of his own region, a fresh and subversive verbal gift, a capacity to integrate these talents in original ways. And he too was to find that he was putting off 'one sort of life' for another that was 'not better than the one he had known before. It was simply different.' He was aware that his own genius was akin to Hardy's, that their similar cases could be summed up in such a phrase as 'roots in the soil'. What he tried to record as a difference between them ('Could any man be more remote from the simple elemental folk of Wessex than Hardy?') is not really a difference. Admittedly, Kavanagh was a small farmer while Hardy trained as an architect; but what made both men different from their 'folk' was their literary vocation, and their overwhelming need to justify themselves in the face of genteel metropolitan literary establishments to which they were outsiders.

Kavanagh's initial reception in Dublin literary circles was kindly enough; but in his view it was essentially patronizing, requiring that he should play the role of the unlettered peasant poet among the literati. He also discovered that the 'famed Dublin literary conversation' seemed to him 'tiresome drivel between journalists and civil servants'. In fact, what Kavanagh was offered by the genteel establishment when he came to Dublin was exactly what Hardy had been offered by the English establishment—a patronized role as a naïve peasant-pastoral writer. And like Hardy he refused to accept it. By what he said and what he wrote (The *Collected Pruse* with its anti-genteel title provides ample illustration as does Section IV of the **Collected Poems**) he alienated himself from the Dublin literary establishment; and in his alienation he wildly and erratically assumed either that he should have stayed at home or that Dublin lacked the advantages of London (an opinion which could only alienate him further). On the one hand, he repeatedly and mournfully doubted the distinction upon which his migration had been based, wondering if he had missed 'the big emotional gesture', wasted in malignant Dublin what could have been his four glorious years in Monaghan. On the other hand, he would suggest that what he was missing in Dublin were the intellectual life, inquiring minds, adventurous publishers, aristocratic belief in the importance of poets, which were available in London. In the latter mood, while he was exaggerating the cultural advantages of London, he did put his finger on the attraction which a major publishing centre is bound to have for writers, and the way this conditioned an envious hostility in Dublin: there was hardly a book published in Ireland, he said, that hadn't been rejected by every London publisher; and 'the provincial mentality' was 'to attack what it secretly worships'.

One can see that two overlapping social situations (one involving the relationship between London and Dublin, the other that between Dublin and Monaghan) prompted that obsessive preoccupation with provincialism which dominates the *Collected Pruse*. (The occasional interest in Joycean cosmopolitanism there and in Section IV of the **Poems** is more theoretical since it never corresponded to a real possibility for Kavanagh.) His contradictory feelings on the subject were only fully resolved in the poetry (as we shall see); he resolved them polemically however by concluding that there were only two mentalities informing poetry: that of the provincial, who has 'no mind of his own', and who 'does not trust what his eyes see until he has heard what the metropolis . . . has to say on any subject'; and the 'parochial' mentality, that of the writer who 'is never in any doubt about the social and artistic validity of his parish'. This position is based on antagonism to urbane gentility as patently as Hardy's was when he praised provincialism as 'the essence of individuality', characterized by the 'crude enthusiasm without which

no great thoughts are thought, no great deeds done'. Kavanagh too wished to applaud a tendency outside metropolitan or cosmopolitan circles towards 'individuality' ('no mind of his own') and 'enthusiasm' ('never in any doubt'). But he assumes that the word 'provincial' is beyond reclamation from its pejorative implications; and so he concentrates his attention on the paradoxical purification of the word 'parochial' from derogatory nuances. The 'parochial' writer for Kavanagh (and Hardy and Faulkner obviously qualify) works with the intimately known rural society and landscape and is successful if these come alive and work in the realized artistic creation: the writer's 'parish' provides authenticity, and a self-dependent myth upon which the writer can build. He must, however, guard against the 'bravado which takes pleasure in the notion that the potato patch is the ultimate' with 'the right kind of sensitive courage and the right kind of sensitive humility'. We must ask a little later, in the light of Kavanagh's own achievement, what he meant by this.

Yeats, writing about his own early novel, shows that he had learned from Irish regional fiction the aesthetic principle of 'parochial' writing. He saw that it should focus on those who love their native places without perhaps, loving Ireland, exploiting the way that they make their native town into their whole world. While *John Sherman* does not as a novel add distinction to this formula, *Tarry Flynn,* Kavanagh's most sustained major achievement certainly does. But Yeats also acknowledged the strange double-bind of which the Irish writer's preoccupation with provincialism is symptomatic when he said of such novels that their characters 'do not travel and are shut off from England by the whole breadth of Ireland'. He could not help being aware of the further dimension with which the Arnoldian 'frame' could trouble 'parochial' writing.

'Shancoduff' (1934) shows how early these considerations were affecting Kavanagh. It is a celebration of his own locale as a complete and self-contained world; but by virtue of this fact it has to recognize the alternative view:

> My black hills have never seen the sun rising,
> Eternally they look north toward Armagh.
> Lot's wife would not be salt if she had been
> Incurious as my black hills that are happy
> When dawn whitens Glassdrummond chapel.

Words like 'black' and 'north', the depressive sound of the mundane place-names, Shancoduff, Glassdrummond, the inveterately rural and provincial ring of 'Armagh' almost allow us to take up the vernacular pejorative implication of 'Eternally'. The stanza hinges on that word, which finally retains its traditional (religious and artistic) force in association with the perpetually arrested vision of whiteness artistically heightened by a 'north light', the chapel backed up by the ancient religious capital of Ireland. Somewhere behind the poem, the knowledge that Armagh was once the 'metropolis', the bishop's seat, is balanced against the fascination with the wicked city which had ruined Lot's wife. And the concern with provincialism conditions the impeded development, the openendedness of the poem. Against the mainly euphoric literary clichés of the speaker in the second stanza ('They are my Alps and I have climbed the Matterhorn') is set the dour realism of the (mobile) cattle-drovers:

> 'Who owns them hungry hills
> That the water-hen and snipe must have forsaken?'

The ambiguity of 'poor' in the penultimate line does not (and is not intended to) resolve the issue entirely:

> 'A poet? Then by heavens he must be poor'
> I hear and is my heart not badly shaken?

With his migration to Dublin five years later this central conflict was to become more urgent and painful for Kavanagh. He always resisted the simple assumption that the 'centre' was a better place to be. But it is only rarely that the 'parochial' writer in Kavanagh's sense, having achieved through his own mobility a new perspective, a point-of-vantage from which to view his own parish, can afford to exclude some formal or dramatic equivalent from his art. Examples would be the figure of the 'returned native' who often acts as the ironic focus of disillusionment and regret in Hardy's novels; or Faulkner's carefully staged re-enactment of his provincial drama at an ostensible cultural centre with the 'sophisticate' Shreve as ringmaster. *Tarry Flynn* works successfully without such devices because of its triumphantly concrete style, its assured address to the reader (who is persuaded by its very openendedness to agree that Tarry is 'not a country man, but merely a man living. And life was the same everywhere'). But despite the 'parochial' virtues of *The Great Hunger,* freshness, clarity, authenticity and compassion, it lacks a formal centre of control and judgement: and falls back too readily upon overbearing sententiousness or the deliberate use of bathetic rhythms to define its attitude to central figure (Maguire) and central theme (rural provincial deprivation).

The important thing about the formal and dramatic points-of-vantage in Hardy and Faulkner referred to above is that they function ironically. In mid-nineteenth-century writing (for example, *Middlemarch, Shirley, Villette*) comparable devices at least partially implied the validity of a more expansive mode of life beyond the provincial milieu: but in Hardy and Faulkner they tend to suggest the moral bankruptcy of bourgeois-genteel 'central' culture, and formally reinforce the reverberations of the 'parochial' drama. How could Kavanagh, in lyric poetry with no obviously experimental tendencies, achieve a similar ironic perspective?

One strategy, after moving to Dublin in 1939, was to write about the Second World War from a national viewpoint rather as Hardy and Edward Thomas wrote about the First. The speaker in 'Peace' wonders whether he should be 'here' in neutral Ireland rather than in war-torn Europe ('Ireland is most provincial when most peaceful'?); 'here' becomes precise, however, only in a characteristic local landscape ('leaf-lapped furrow', 'old plough', 'weedy ridge', 'saddle-harrow') which breaks through the immediate pretext of the poem (England/Ireland) to reveal the tensions arising from Kavanagh's departure from his childhood landscape for Dublin:

> Out of that childhood country what fools climb
> To fight with tyrants Love and Life and Time?

The attempt to equate Monaghan with Ireland (in the phase of his verse which he later condemned for its exploitation of a pseudo-Irish poetic identity) is not successful. In fact, he is thrown back on a vocabulary of rhetorical abstractions (as in that final line of **'Peace'**) by the out-dated poetic strategy he has chosen.

Another over-literary frame of reference in the poetry of this period is the ninetyish idea of Parnassus. **'Temptation in Harvest',** explores the personal implications for the poet of the life objectively realized in *The Great Hunger.* The poem depicts a 'returned native' reliving the desire to be an uncomplicated countryman 'on an ash-tree's limb / Sawing a stick for a post', to love the local landscape and care for his ricks without intellectual ambition; he tries to ignore the inevitable fate of such men, left 'on their backs in muddiness'. But the opposite alternative, the journey, is imaged (rather emptily) in the inviting glance of a passing girl (the muse). The speaker remembers asking himself

> Could I go
> Over the fields to the City of the Kings
> Where art, music, letters are the real things?

In the memory, labourers, animals, landscape and an old country woman (the poet's mother?) urge him to stay at home ('You cannot eat what grows upon Parnassus / And she is going there sure as sin.'); but he turns

> Away from the ricks, the sheds, the cabbage garden,
> The stones of the street, the thrush song in the tree
> The potato pits, the flaggers in the swamp;
> From the country heart that hardly learned to harden

to 'follow her who winked at me'. The poem's strength resides in its 'parochial' vividness. But it is sabotaged by the clichéd attempt to fuse Kavanagh's real-life migratory experience with a symbolic Parnassian journey.

The poet was soon experiencing and expressing the traumatic conflicts arising from his failure to adjust to the Dublin literary situation: but the best poems of the period find subtle new uses for his familiar Monaghan materials. **'Innocence',** for instance, is an attempt to counter the pejorative view of the poet's provincial background, the urbane conviction that he is limited by his origins:

> They laughed at one I loved—
> The triangular hill that hung
> Under the Big Forth. They said
> That I was bounded by the whitethorn hedges
> Of the little farm and did not know the world.
> But I knew that love's doorway to life
> Is the same doorway everywhere.

As the poem proceeds an initial repudiation of his roots ('Ashamed of what I loved') is succeeded by a mystical or magical state ('back in her briary arms') in which

> I know nothing of women,
> Nothing of cities,
> I cannot die
> Unless I walk outside these whitethorn hedges.

The poem is an advance upon **'Temptation in Harvest'** in the way that the feminine figure (both muse and mother) is now imperceptibly present in the local imagery giving concrete particularity to the central assertion that 'love's doorway to life / Is the same doorway everywhere'. The symbolism functions delicately to persuade us that the local scene is a 'universal stage' as it does in *Tarry Flynn*. But Kavanagh is still excluding rather than ironically encompassing the patronizingly urbane stand-point which was perturbing him, looking backwards rather than towards the resolution of his present conflicts. One sees this evasion in **'Auditors In',** which turns away from 'the sour soil of a town where all roots canker', claiming to have arrived at 'The placeless Heaven that's under all our noses'. Kavanagh could not write well about a 'placeless Heaven'. His strength was his capacity for a deep and intense engagement with place, and he was still coming to terms with a new location.

He achieved this in two stages: the first was necessary for his emotional and intellectual development but produced bad poetry; in the second, however, he seems to me to have achieved at times the kind of ironic perspective which gives formal completeness to 'parochial' writing. The low point of his poetic career (and a temporary betrayal of what it represents) came with the writing of drab satiric poems about the provincial mediocrity of Dublin which invoke the superior cosmopolitan alternatives (London and Paris) recognized by 'Stephen Dedalus', Yeats and the O'Casey of *Inishfallen, Fare Thee Well* (**'The Paddiad'**). In these poems there is no doubt that Kavanagh becomes a provincial in the sense of his own later definition. He has ceased to trust what his eyes see and directs his aspirations towards a superior

'metropolis'. In so doing he gives temporary assent to the nineteenth-century genteel 'frame' and all its superior assumptions. Ironically, he takes this position in order to attack a literary establishment which is urging the celebration of Irish culture as 'the last preserve / Of Eden' where genius walks 'with feet rooted in the native soil' (**'The Defeated'**) as well as arranging cosmopolitan opportunities for its politically influential members (**'Irish Stew'**). He seems later to have regarded this phase of his poetry as one of spiritual death from which the next phase emerged as a kind of spiritual rebirth.

This painfully devastated period ended with his libel suit against *The Leader*: an occasion which can be seen as a ritual punishment of the hubristic outsider who was refusing (Kavanagh said this) to play the inferior role allotted to him. In some ways it was like the drubbing Hardy received after the publication of *Jude the Obscure*, though in Kavanagh's case the wounds were self-invited. The crucial recognition wrung from him during the traumatic trial proceedings was his commitment to Dublin as locale: 'I love the place. Why should I come and stay in it if I didn't?' It seems to be with this acceptance of his love for the place he had journeyed to (in full recognition that it was as 'provincial' as the place he had left) that the final fruits of his genius emerged. (Though we are in a position, as he was not, to recognize the characteristically Irish overlap of two social situations which made this resolution possible.)

A number of late lyrics which many people (including the poet) have considered to be the height of Kavanagh's poetic achievement hinge upon the fully dramatized and minutely realized motif of a completed journey. When he found himself experiencing in 1955 'the same emotion' on the Grand Canal Bank as back in Monaghan his poetry reached some kind of parallel resolution: **'Canal Bank Walk'** and its companion poems celebrate his new ability to 'grow with nature again as before I grew'. Earlier he had said (still drawing on his vapid ninetyish idea of poetry) 'In the presence of the Parnassian authority we are provincials nowhere'. But now the minute particulars of Dublin as locale (canal seats and bridges and water, city streets and trees and hospitals) allowed the affectionate superimposition of one provincial milieu upon another, the discovery in concrete terms that we are provincials everywhere.

The late poetry is still very uneven. Its anti-genteel centre is Kavanagh's self-presentation as one of the Dublin dispossessed: sometimes with the makings of a folk-hero (**'If Ever You Go to Dublin Town'**); more often as a down-and-out migrant 'enduring' the spare deprivation of streets, hospitals, bridges, benches, garages. The 'I' of this poetry is as recognizably a scapegoat figure as is Hardy's Jude in his latter days in Christminster. ('Poetry made me a sort of outcast . . .', wrote Kavanagh, introducing his **Collected Poems,** 'I do not believe in sacrifice yet it seems that I was sacrificed'.) But he is consciously a scapegoat—recognizing in **'Come Dance with Kitty Stobling'** how Dublin society had recalled him to his familiar rural social role:

> I had a very pleasant journey, thank you sincerely
> For giving me my madness back, or nearly.

He is the scapegoat as comic poet: he brings with him from his rural past spells and exorcisms for the urban present; and the subtle gaieties of his late rhythms play with transformative power over his deep sense of his double role as provincial victim. As he walks 'this arboreal street on the edge of a town':

> The breeze too, even the temperature
> And pattern of movement is precisely the same
> As broke my heart for youth passing. Now I am sure
> Of something. Something will be mine wherever I am.
> I want to throw myself on the public street without
>   caring
> For anything but the prayering that the earth offers.
> It is October over all my life and the light is staring
> As it caught me once in a plantation by the fox
>   coverts.
> A man is ploughing ground for winter wheat
> And my nineteen years weigh heavily on my feet.

(**'October'**)

The sharp ambiguities, indicative of unresolved tensions, of poems like **'Shancoduff'** have relaxed into a new rich solving movement consistent with 'the prayering that the earth offers': this movement, however, plays against the unease of the half-rhymes; and unearned securities are excluded by the placing of 'I am sure' at the end of the line, the hint of misgiving in the repeated 'something'; and also the ominous associations of 'staring', 'caught', 'ground for winter wheat', 'weigh heavily'. As in the best writing of this kind (compare some of Emily Dickinson's poems as well as Hardy's) the isolation and curtailment of life's possibilities induced by the provincial milieu (past and present) is subtly universalized by the seasonal landscape (so concrete in the past, so consciously abstract in the present). The ritual permanence discovered in this double perspective *is* the poem. And the successful formula which reveals a rural provincial spareness, a traditional ritual stance, in a shabby urban landscape works with other juxtapositions, other recognizable journeys:

> Only thus can I attune
> To despair an illness like winter alone in Leeds.

(**'Winter in Leeds'**)

> The winkers that had no choke-band
> The collar and the reins . . .

> In Ealing Broadway, London Town
> I name their several names . . .

(**'Kerr's Ass'**)

Seamus Deane points out that Kavanagh has had more influence than Yeats over recent Irish poetry. I am suggesting that Kavanagh may be having the same kind of effect on the development of Irish writing ('because he was there') as Hardy has had on the development of English writing: the arrest and reversal of a whole nineteenth-century way of thinking about literary location. (Since my emphasis has been on the power of social roles and ideas as well as on the influence of poetry, it is only fair to point out that Hardy's influence in England was reinforced by social changes which have established less genteel assumptions about literary location; and which are less advanced in Ireland.) The poetic careers of John Montague and Seamus Heaney offer two interesting test-cases for this hypothesis.

Montague began writing earlier than Heaney, assimilating as Heaney did, London modes like that of *New Lines,* but looking towards Dublin as his nation's literary capital. The two dominant models for an Irish poetic career in the late fifties were still the naïve nationalistic peasant-poet and the cosmopolitan (who should now look to Rome, Paris or the U.S.A. rather than London). In the latter category, a poet like Thomas MacGreevy had been (according to his dust-jacket) identifying himself 'with the European intelligences in Irish poetry—Montgomery, Coffey and Devlin'; a poet like Desmond O'Grady was just then moving from Paris to Rome and the patronage of Ezra Pound. It is not surprising that Montague should have adopted the explicit notion of a tradition of fruitful cosmopolitanism which he later traces in his essay 'The Impact of International Modern Poetry on Irish Writing' from Yeats and Joyce through Denis Devlin to himself. The poems in his first book are not unlike some of Kavanagh's in their delicate and authentic use of the rural childhood landscape and society. But the search for a point-of-vantage seizes on cosmopolitan possibilities, Rome visited, Auschwitz remembered or an abstracted aesthetic tradition:

> One stood until the bucket brimmed
> Inhaling the musty smell of unpicked berries,
> That heavy greenness fostered by water.

> Recovering the scene, I had hoped to stylize it,
> Like the portrait of an Egyptian water-carrier . . .

('The Water Carrier')

In a brief satiric poem 'Regionalism or Portrait of the Artist as a Model Farmer' he impersonates an Irish rural poet who shields the 'tuber' he has planted from

> Foreign beetles and exotic weeds,
> Complicated continental breeds

in the incoherent belief that the purity of his gift will comfort him in his 'fierce anonymity'. The sheer vigour of the impersonation suggests that Montague has some instinctive sympathy for the position he is satirizing. But his over-all aesthetic commitment at this point in his career is clear enough.

His second book, *A Chosen Light* (1967) assumes in the title sequence that an appropriate point-of-vantage has been achieved in a cosmopolitan setting; that a symbolic journey has been accomplished, 'from Tyrone to the rue Daguerre'. Such a journey is assimilated into the make-up of the volume: the Paris locale is used to encapsulate (always sensitively) the remembered Irish past. But this principle of development is not sustained. A fragile retractive sequence in the next book *Tides* (called, significantly, 'The Pale Light') moves away from the cosmopolitan perspective achieved in *A Chosen Light*: it begins by contemplating 'the shelf of Europe', 'the dome of the casino' ('North Sea'), 'the Stadz-muzeum at Bruges' ('Coming Events') but goes on to register (in terms of human relationship and poetic development) the need for a diminuendo, for

>   the slow
> 　 climb
> 　　 down.

After this, the cosmopolitan point-of-vantage as such disappears from Montague's poetry. And his next book, *The Rough Field* (1972) returns to rural Tyrone for its subject matter, reprinting several earlier poems in the search for some kind of new locally-rooted perspective.

How are we to explain this reversal? Kavanagh's **Come Dance with Kitty Stobling** was published in 1960, his **Collected Poems** in 1964. And in 1966 Heaney was widely praised for his first book, *Death of a Naturalist* about which he said: 'I have no need to write a poem to Patrick Kavanagh; I wrote *Death of a Naturalist*'. But the possibility of being a 'parochial' poet in Kavanagh's sense was clearly there in Montague's early poetry too. A selection of his poems appeared in an anthology *Six Irish Poets* in 1962; and the editor, Robin Skelton, praised in his introduction, the way Irish poetry could still base itself firmly on 'natural resources . . . the sense of belonging' and thereby gain a 'real vitality'. It was about this time, Montague says, that he began to plan *The Rough Field*.

Despite the affectionate re-creation of the locale, there is, throughout Montague's book, a careful, ruefully hesitant poetic voice to be heard conceding, movingly, an alienation, a lack of ultimate direction, summed up in the refrain-line: 'for all my circling, a failure to return'. One is reminded of the central preoccupation of Kavanagh's later poetry, 'return in departure'. But Montague is unable to achieve that kind of vitally ironic point-of-vantage, formally vindicated, which distinguishes Kavanagh's best last poems. And the self-

conscious attempt to construct an over-all viewpoint for the book, using historical quotations, woodcuts, and verse-reportage to universalize the poet's local materials by reference to the 'Ulster Crisis' is no substitute.

That it is intended to be a substitute, and to remind us in an underhand way of the poet's cosmopolitanism is clear from the back cover: '. . . the New Road I describe runs through Normandy as well as Tyrone. And experience of agitations in Paris and Berkeley taught me that the violence of disputing factions is more than a local phenomenon.' One is reminded of Kavanagh's primary stipulation for the 'parochial' writer: that he should never show 'any doubt about the social and artistic validity of his parish'. The importance of this stipulation, his definition implies, is that any concession to genteel cosmopolitanism in the context of such writing would devitalize the poetry. This would be my complaint about *The Rough Field*. Whether from the nature of his gifts or because of an accident of timing, Montague has not shown himself so far to be capable of following and profiting from Kavanagh's achievement. Heaney, on the other hand, has never shown any doubt about the social and artistic validity of his parish.

In Heaney's earlier poems the imaginative implications of the local society and terrain, viewed often with a childhood intensity, are presented with subtlety and vigour, and with no hint of self-conscious humility. It is probably this essential confidence in the utility of the re-created internally consistent region of his poems that he was admitting to having inherited from Kavanagh. But this is possibly not the whole of his debt. In his second and third books he too begins to embody in key poems a crucial relationship between poetic development and the motif of the journey away from roots. In 'Bogland', 'The Wool Trade', 'Westering' and 'The Tollund Man' he shows himself to have learned how to work with specific ironic vantage-points which may seem to illuminate, but are in fact illuminated by the 'parochial' materials.

We are probably now in a position to see what Kavanagh meant by his injunction that the parochial writer should guard against the bravado that takes the potato patch for the ultimate with 'the right kind of sensitive courage and the right kind of sensitive humility'. He did not mean that the writer should avoid technical influence from literary mainstreams; Auden is as important to the making of Kavanagh's own later rhythms as Roethke and Hughes have been to the growth of Heaney's poetic idiom. What he was advocating (for a particular *kind* of writer) was the delicate adjustment of social and poetic strategies to the changing pressures of the poet's own most authentic experience. The aim was to remain free of the sapping and enervating currents of establishmentarian uniformity (which in Ireland still tended to keep alive the nineteenth-century tradition of genteel cosmopolitanism and its subordinate convention of naïve peasant pastoralism). Kavanagh was an innovator in Ireland as much by what he stood for as by what he wrote: the wastefulness, the false directions, the personal over-assertiveness which sometimes characterize his poetic career, also provide pointers to directions in which his successors need not move because he did. Heaney's writing to some extent emerges from the same ambiguous concern with provincialism that we find in Kavanagh and Montague. But because of Kavanagh he could begin from a position of strength. In his work the personal and intellectual underpinnings are entirely hidden, leaving us to respond to the way the local materials emerge into the constantly developing, fluid yet certain poetic point of view.

Robert Welch (essay date spring 1983)

SOURCE: Welch, Robert. "Language as Pilgrimage: Lough Derg Poems of Patrick Kavanagh and Denis Devlin." *Irish University Review* 13, no. 1 (spring 1983): 54-66.

[*In the following essay, Welch compares Kavanagh's* Lough Derg *with Denis Devlin's poem of the same name.*]

To go on pilgrimage is to take stock, to stop the ordinary passage of time and look for another kind of time, another way of reckoning. If writing is involved with using language as a kind of judging, in making words open up to scrutiny of themselves and what they may be thought to mean, then it is no surprise that the pilgrimage should have become a literary genre. To be a pilgrim is to try to direct life to a new attentiveness, sharpened by consideration of ending; to write is to embark into language, in the full clear knowledge that a conclusion must be reached, and that the strength or otherwise of that conclusion will depend on the conduct of the language, on how well the writer has tried to bring his language into focus, into clarity. The writer's rhythm is his reckoning. The movements of his voices as he tries to limn out his thoughts let us know whether he is trying to pull a fast one, and get to the end before his time, or whether he is a real pilgrim in his language, opening to the form of reckoning he has chosen.

Lough Derg, in the South of Donegal, has become a place of pilgrimage for centuries: by the time Dante wrote the bleak shores and islands of the lake had been visited by many Europeans. Donnchadh Mór O Dhálaigh, who died in 1244 tells of his journey there, but is baffled that he could not weep for pity of Christ's bruises and wounds:

> Truagh mo thuras ar Loch Dearg
> a rígh na gceall a's na gclog,
> do chaoineadh do chneadh 's do chréacht
> 's nach dtig dear thar mo rosg.

> (Alas, my journey to Lough Derg
> for weeping your wounds and cuts,
> king of Church and bell,
> when no tear came over my eye.)

The two poems that are the subject of this essay, Denis Devlin's "Lough Derg" and Patrick Kavanagh's poem of the same title share the mood of baffled questioning, the fear of sterility, the need for strong emotion that the medieval poem effortlessly states, in all the clarity of its spiritual directness. Lough Derg is not a place to generate an easy idea of transformation of life redeemed by miracle: it is a place that pushes the pilgrim back into himself, into his own dreariness, lack of spontaneity, and coldness, and then he must make of that what he can. That is the journey that these two poems of the nineteen-forties undertake: what is to be said in neutral Ireland ("that froze for want of Europe" in Kavanagh's phrase)?; what use is faith?; what kind of language can open up to a dialogue of the mortal self and the soul?

Both poems are deeply experimental in that they are poems of risk; they are deep spiritual reckonings that attempt to find authentic speech. Despite Devlin's apparent tightness of form (his stanzas bristle with a sense of containment) both poems are very open in their inner forms: the way the thinking in each moves is reckless and exploratory, visceral in its nervous transitions. Both poems are also hidden: Devlin's meaning and emotion are difficult of access, demanding patience and quiet attentiveness of the reader; Kavanagh's remained unpublished until 1978 (when it appeared in two different editions), and it too is elusive in its meaning and significance, its deceptively casual technique easily reassuring the unwary that it is some form of spiritual amble through the oddities of wartime Irish society. Both are poems marked by temperament but the temperaments are widely different: Devlin's arcane and obtuse, working with an intensity of concentration; Kavanagh's expansive and fiery, trying to find a way of expressing the spirituality of ordinary people and their lives. The poems exemplify two aspects of Irish religious tradition: the realisation of spirit seen as a matter of hermetic enclosure, in Devlin; in Kavanagh it is seen as a matter of extension through sympathy. But in both these ambitious poems there is a freedom from the spectre of Yeats. Each handles his material in his own way and each apprehends his world directly and clearly.

I mention Yeats because he too came to write a poem on Lough Derg:

> Round Lough Derg's holy island I went upon the
>   stones,

> I prayed at all the Stations upon my marrow-bones,
> And there I found an old man, and though I prayed all
>   day
> And that old man beside me, nothing would he say
> *But fol de rol de rolly O*

("The Pilgrim")

This late Yeatsian gaiety is frantic and awesome: the ludicrous refrain lurches up to not knowing, to not being able to say anything with any certainty with a fierce insouciance that might be called Nietzschean. In moments like these (and they are to be found throughout the later Yeats) he has got into the inner feeling of bleak nothingness, when nothing matters, when it may seem to make no odds who or how you kill, or how many, that is one of the facts of our modern spiritual condition. If nothing matters, then, as Saul Bellow has pointed out, it is perfectly right and logical that we butcher each other in as cruel a way as possible. This, let me stress, is *one* of the facts of our modern spiritual condition: Kavanagh and Devlin, both Catholic, explore other possibilities.

Kavanagh's *Lough Derg* was written in 1942 (he tells us in the poem) and is a kind of diastole to the systole of *The Great Hunger* published in the same year. Where the landscape and mood of *The Great Hunger* revolve around the consciousness of one man, Maguire, the stance being narrative, the guiding voice in *Lough Derg* does not locate itself in so easily identifiable a way: it is much more fluid, in keeping with what the poem sets out to do. It, like other pilgrimage poems before it, wants to "take all shapes of souls as a living theme . . . No truth oppresses." It is an opening out to experience, a comic opening after the withdrawal of *The Great Hunger.* It wants to say and to celebrate the religious experience of ordinary people, the

> Mothers whose daughters are Final Medicals,
> Too heavy-hipped for thinking,
> Wives whose husbands have angina pectoris,
> Wives whose husbands have taken to drinking.

Kavanagh in this poem has the Romantic desire to be "a man speaking to men", as classically defined by Wordsworth in the preface to the second edition of *Lyrical Ballads,* a phrase which now, through over-familiarity, has become something of a cliché, but that should not blind us to its revolutionary import. For poets like Wordsworth and Kavanagh the poet *is* speaking the real language of men by getting them to read their own nature through a language which comprehends it. Thus the poetry becomes an invocation of "the spirit of life" (another, lesser known phrase, from the preface) that is in the poet, in the reader and in the Universe itself ("volitions and passions as manifested in the goings-on of the Universe"—Wordsworth again). This may seem like Romantic claptrap but it must be pointed out that this idealism need in no way estrange the poet

from the material world: in fact, properly understood and sustained by an unremitting energy of attention, it drives the poet into deeper and deeper relation with the common, the ordinary, the everyday. The material world may be seen to be charged with spiritual potential. This is the vision not just of Wordsworth, but of Blake before him, and of Kavanagh. It also fires the thought of Teilhard de Chardin and bearing this in mind one is brought to ask: are we only now beginning to understand the full spiritual implications of the Romantic vision? The human sympathy, the extensive imaginative charity of Kavanagh's vision in *Lough Derg* is, along with Yeats's reaction to meaninglessness, a fact of our modern spiritual condition.

The opening section of *Lough Derg* sets out Kavanagh's objective: to take this pilgrimage and show its inner aspect, how the "Castleblaney grocer trapped in the moment's need / puts out a hand and writes what he cannot read." But he also shows that this involves no easy transubstantiation of the familiar: it is difficult to pick out "the silver strands / Of the individual . . . through the fabric of prison anonymity", all the more so because in Ireland so much of the sense of self (so evident in Wordsworth's self-delight) and of history is ruined that often it is difficult to know where to start. So much demands speech:

>   . . . a heap
> Of stones anywhere is consecrated
> by love's terrible need.

but that way madness lies. It is not possible to sing everything, so in a vastly convincing technical stroke, beautifully worked because issuing out of artistic and psychological need, alarming because of the artless way it gets out of the risk of generalising about the individual and history, a kind of plot starts to emerge. Three people detached themselves from the general category of pilgrim: Robert Fitzsimmons; Aggie Meegan; and an ex-monk from Dublin. Gradually something of their stories unfold: Fitzsimmons, a half-hearted pilgrim is a country pedant who talks beyond his feelings, a false philosopher; Aggie, to whom he is drawn, a girl who has been in trouble. The way their brief exchanges are presented, tentatively, obliquely, gives a sense of the difficulty of telling the truth about anyone. The complicated way people react to each other is held and celebrated in these lines:

> Aggie Meegan passed by
> To vigil. Robert was puzzled, where
> Grew the germ of this crooked prayer?
> The girl thrilling as joy's despair.

The rhyme emphasises the thrill of the realisation where the old Sidneian paradox, "joy's despair", speaks again: the poetry is true to life, speaking the "real language of men".

Aggie Meegan tells Fitzsimmons her story of "Birth, bastardy, and murder"; the ex-monk tells him that he has learned patience:

> That laws for the mown hay
> Will not serve for that which is growing.

Then they fade out of the story, "almost"; becoming again "part of the flood of humanity / Anonymous, never to write or be written." After this engagement with the particular, difficult and troubled as it is, the poem returns to the general scene, fuelled by the realisation of individual trouble. And now, for the first time, the "poet" appears on the scene, asking questions, involved. He is now seen as a pilgrim as well, trying to understand, without attitude, preconception, superiority. The writing that follows, moving towards the poem's end, is an impressive exercise in Wordsworthian "wise passiveness", poetry not as judging, categorising, sneering, but poetry as pure extension of understanding, poetry trying to find the words to activate or reactivate love—love of others; love of Ireland, its smallness, hopelessness, generosity; and love of self, (not egoism) without which all the rest darkens into rancour. It would be easy to underestimate the sense of poetic absence which allows the sorry condition of the man from Leitrim to stand clear in the following. This is Shakespearian self-abnegation, not the impersonality of Eliot:

> 'And who are you?', said the poet speaking to
> the old Leitrim man.
> He said, 'I can tell you
> What I am.
> Servant girls bred my servility:
> When I stoop,
> It is my mother's mother mother's mother
> Each one in turn being called in to spread—
> "Wider with your legs" the master of the house said.
> Domestic servants taken, back and front.
> That's why I'm servile.

The poem moves on to give us, in Shakespearian sonnet form, the prayers of different people on the pilgrimage. It seems appropriate that for a poetry like this, that seeks to limn out and to bring to stand the lives and secrecies of others in a language steadfastly simple and attentive, such as might be really used by man, Kavanagh makes use of the Shakespearian sonnet, that great vehicle for the registering of pain and the expense of selflessness. Here is one of these gaunt, scrupulous sonnets, fiery with realisation:

> O Sacred Heart of Jesus I ask of you
> A job so I can settle down and marry;
> I want to live a decent life. And through
> The flames of St. Patrick's Purgatory
> I go offering every stone-bruise, all my hunger;
> In the back-room of my penance I am wearing
> An inside-shirt for charity. How longer
> Must a fifty-shilling a week job be day-dreaming?
> The dole and empty minds and empty pockets,

> Old films that break the eye-balls in their sockets.
> A toss-pit. This is the life for such as me.
> And I know a girl and I know a room to be let
> And a job in a builder's yard to be given yet.

This tells us a great deal about wartime Ireland, but it tells us just as much about ourselves. It makes us ask questions, because of what we have been brought to see in the poem. How good is our human sympathy? The reader becomes a pilgrim to a form of language that may be shared.

At the end of the poem Kavanagh acknowledges that in it he only gets hold of half the truth:

> The half untrue:
> Of this story is his pride's rhythm.

But now more than ever is the exemplary attentiveness of Kavanagh required, his readiness to try again to bring about that free community of speech of which the Romantics dreamed, where the reader will be "really" touched by what he is brought to see.

Against Kavanagh's gentleness, his informing idea that language can be effective in creating a community of understanding and sympathy we might place Denis Devlin's harsh, uncompromising and Jansenist statement that:

> Not all
> The men of God nor the priests of mankind
> Can mend or explain the good and broke, not one
> Generous with love prove communion.

Devlin's God is the hidden God of the Jansenists and of Pascal: to presume a communion with Him by any human means is to presume too much. He is only caught in the unexpected harmonies that break into the bleak ardour of discipline. And discipline is all. The pilgrimage that the poet enters into when he opens into his poem is not an open affair driven by expectancies of innocence. From the start rigour is emphasised; patience predominates; the mood is bleak. Speech, by means of which it is possible to betray everything by lurching into the loutishness of emotion (or learning, as Beckett would have it), is to be watched. Metre and stanza are not modes of realisation of sympathy: they are icons of watchfulness and caution, checks, reminders of imperfection, mortification. Verse is penance, a numbering of time while awaiting the grace to which there is no entitlement.

God's inscrutability is emphasised in the two opening stanzas. The pilgrims are seen, as rude, intrusive, as if they would cajole Him into benign simplicity:

> The poor in spirit on their rosary rounds
> The jobbers with their whiskey-angered eyes,
> The pink bank clerks, the tip-hat papal counts,

And drab, kind women their tonsured mockery tries,
Glad invalids on penitential feet
Walk the Lord's majesty like their village street.

With mullioned Europe shattered, this Northwest,
Rude-sainted isle would pray it whole again:
(Peasant Apollo! Troy is worn to rest.)
Europe that humanised the sacred bane
Of God's chance who yet laughed in his mind
And balanced thief and saint: were they this kind?

Were the Europeans who humanised the terrifying puzzle of God's judgement on the thief and the saint like these jobbers, these "tip-hat papal counts" who, even on Lough Derg "try" the women to see if they can score with their "tonsured mockery"? By "tonsured mockery" Devlin means, I think, a certain kind of pious wheedling indecency that the polite papal count goes in for, and we see from this that Devlin's stance is, at least in part, satiric. But he acknowledges himself a part of this motley resumption; he too is a pilgrim:

Ours, passive, for man's gradual wisdom take
Firefly instinct dreamed out into law.

The Irish have, for all sorts of reasons, been out of the gradual accumulation of wisdom that is a part of European tradition: instead the "firefly instinct", unstable and unreliable as it is, has been solidified into law, and Devlin here, in his typically complex manner, seems to be suggesting that a sensuality fires Irish rigidity, thereby making emotional life a tangle of unknowing, fear and lust and devotion all implicated. With such confusion in the interior the outward forms are clung to:

All is simple and symbol in their world,
The incomprehended rendered fabulous.
Sin teases life whose natural fruits witheld
Sour the deprived nor bloom for timely loss:

the next phrase strikes home with a rhythmic jump:

Clan Jansen!

but Devlin's qualifying mind is in action even here. This is not a label; he is not calling the Irish Jansenists, aware, as he is, of the profound force of Jansenist belief. These are *Clan* Jansen, Irish Jansenists, lessened, because of history, and so caught in crudity and lack of consciousness

less what magnanimity leavens,
Man's wept out, fitful, magniloquent heavens

Where prayer was praise, O Lord! The Temple trumpets
Cascaded down Thy sunny pavilions of air . . .

The "sunny pavilions of air" is the lightsome joy that relieves the watchful mind, fortified against sentiment by discipline; the air of grace that breaks into Pascal's dark and rigorous mind without expectation or deserving.

Devlin's thought, so far having pondered how good or how bad the human mind is at becoming aware of itself, now goes out into a consideration of what happened when Man arrived at consciousness, and how these pilgrims of Lough Derg stand with reference to that. He comes to this theme by an extraordinary series of associative and exploratory jumps. From Jansen he moves to the "sunny pavilion" of the Jansenist conscience when it is illuminated by grace; from this he moves to a bravura evocation of Judaic colour and celebration, a way of voicing the inner tones of the watchful mind as it releases itself in joy; then to the Greeks and their light because he is beginning to think of geometry as an emblem of the brain emerging into consciousness of itself as an ordering principle. The push of the brain, then, trying to clear the confusion in its cells is bold in its striving for great consciousness. Against this push into intelligence, how may these pilgrims, and Devlin himself, be measured? All of this seems like a terrible jumble, and my bald summary cannot give a sense of the swift passages of Devlin's thinking in a language that crackles like electricity, but this kind of thinking shows his relationship with the "firefly instinct" he has spoken of earlier as being characteristic of the Irish. It is also the kind of thinking, exploratory, troubled, humane, that one finds in Devlin's master, Montaigne.

Let us go back to Devlin's description of the strivings of consciousness:

It was said stone dreams and animal sleeps and man
Is awake; but sleep with its drama on us bred
Animal articulate, only somnambulist can
Conscience like Cawdor give the blood its head
For the dim moors to reign through druids again.
O first Geometer! tangent-feelered brain

Clearing by inches the encircled eyes,
Bolder than the peasant tiger whose autumn beauty
Sags in the expletive kill, or the sacrifice
Of dearth puffed positive in the stance of duty
With which these pilgrims would propitiate
Their fears . . .

We are, he is saying, articulate animals, speech being bred in us through the drama of sleep. This sleep is the sleep of potential consciousness as it evolves, through struggle, in matter. (Devlin's evolutionism here is very close to Teilhard de Chardin's in *Activation of Energy* and elsewhere.) Once the phenomenon of speech occurs then there is no going back to a quasi-animal state, except through a kind of somnambulism: conscience is like Cawdor, it can "sleep no more". The "first geometer" is the brain, and it is also, ambiguously, God in us, as it moves into clarity in boldness, a boldness greater than the heroic violence of the half-animal, half-human, "peasant-tiger" and greater also than the "sacrifice" of the pilgrims, which Devlin's restless mind now anatomises. Theirs is the sacrifice of a spiritual and material poverty resigned to and even made positive ("puffed positive") by assuming appropriate attitudes of humiliation, obedience and willingness. This is arrogant, though, "puffed", in that there is an expectation that this will make everything all right, will "propitiate / *Their* fears". Such an attitude, Devlin is implying in the glancing argument of the poem, is a form of somnambulism, a denial of the brain's drive into more complete awareness, a "spirit bureaucracy", a turning away from responsibility.

But then, in another turn of thought, another *essai,* he acknowledges that this piety is built, "in part", upon the old monks of the "Merovingian Centuries" in their "convents of coracles" who went out, into Europe, "to give without demand". Our missionaries are "doughed in dogma, who never have dared". But (and again Devlin changes his thought) they are:

No better or worse than I who, in my books,
Have angered at the stake with Bruno and, by the
  rope
Watt Tyler swung from, leagued with shifty looks
To fuse the next rebellion with the desperate
Serfs in the sane need to eat and get;

Have praised, on its thunderous canvas, the Florentine
  smile
As man took to wearing his death, his own . . .
In soul, reborn as body's appetite:
Now languisht back in body's amber light,

Now is consumed.

Devlin's pilgrimages into history have meant that he has sympathised, has understood, has praised. He has grasped the inner meanings (as he sees them) of the Florentine canvasses, where consciousness has reached such a peak that men begin to take their own deaths upon themselves (this is the revelation of the Botticelli smile), to accept it into their souls, where it is reborn as the immense sensual paean of Renaissance erotic love, where the orgasm was a death from which the lovers, Phoenix-like, would revive. But that intense glorification of the body has "languisht" into an amber light, which the Botticelli canvasses would seem to foretell, and which was consumed. Leaving what? What is the result of Devlin's inquiry into the past? He doesn't know. The poem again sceptically turns aside from the gathering pressure to conclude by issuing another challenge to our comprehension:

Hell is to know our natural empire used
Wrong, by mind's moulting, brute divinities.
The vanishing tiger's saved, his blood transfused.

So much for the evolution of consciousness. The tiger of animality, over which the brain attempted to gain

precedence, is back. The old gods, "brute divinities" once more "give the blood its head" and Devlin's native city

        Glasgow town
Burns high enough to screen the stars and moon.

We seem to be coming full circle. There seems no way out, nothing to be said, and the poem moves very close to a gloomier version of Yeats's *Fol de rol de rolly O*":

        All indiscriminate, man, stone, animal
Are woken up in nightmare. What John the Blind
From Patmos saw works and we speak it . . .

What use pilgrimage?; what use speech?; what use poetry? We are close to what Montaigne (in Florio's translation of "An Apologie of Raymond Sebond") called the "absolute surceasing and suspense of judgement". Nothing to be said, nothing to be done. There is only tiredness, exhaustion, futile and ludicrous attempts at friendship:

Behind the eyes the winged ascension flags,
For want of spirit by the market blurbed,
And if hands touch, such fraternity sags
Frightened this side the dikes of death disturbed
Like Aran Islands' bibulous, unclean seas:
Pieta: but the limbs ache; it is not peace.

There is a kind of poet (and Devlin is one of these) to whom the will is vital. The intelligence and emotional honesty of Devlin's pilgrim poem has brought him to this impasse, but the imagination refuses to luxuriate in this dejection. Another stanza opens with resolution, renewed caution, vigilance, acknowledging the "hearts' hunger" for something beyond the impasse of twentieth century nihilism. The writing becomes a form of exertion:

Then to see less, look little, let hearts' hunger
Feed on water and berries. The pilgrims sing:
Life will fare well from elder to younger . . .

That last line seems to me to be profound and moving in its directness and simplicity. The intellectual poet, full of irony, has put it all away and refuses to argue himself out of the dilemma; he is released from it by the pilgrims singing. There is no assertion, by Devlin, that all will be well; but there is no denial either of what it is that the pilgrims sing. It may be that "we pray to ourself", but (again the exploration, as in Montaigne, of the other possibility);

        The metal moon, unspent
Virgin eternity sleeping in the mind,
Excites the form of prayer without content;
Whitethorn lightens, delicate and blind,
The negro mountain, and so, knelt on her sod,
This woman beside me murmuring *My God! My God!*

As in all good poetry, there is no message; the mountain is lightened by the moonlight and "so" the woman beside the I moves into speech, into prayer, and the poem records this transformation. It does not explain it or rationalise it as a way out of any dilemma of faith (the moment is too simple for that); but it does not underrate it either.

As in Kavanagh's poem there is a movement into the words of prayer spoken by a pilgrim, but whereas in Kavanagh, verse is used to sharpen our realisation of the conditions out of which the pilgrims come, here only four bare syllables are recorded. Devlin's language is not trying to establish a community of realisation (as Kavanagh's is). There is "no one generous with love" who can prove communion. But there is the moment of grace, of lightening, the unexpected; and that moment must be given its value, even if only in four syllables.

Kavanagh's poem is written out of the conviction that some kind of sharing of experience and of feeling is possible, and his language tries to activate that sharing. It would be this kind of language that men would really use if they could see. He wants the neglected lives of Ireland, the servile, the falsely devout, the unhappy, to stand clear in his verse and this means that he thinks of verse as something sanctioned by community. Poetry is communion. In this he looks back to Wordsworth, with whose thoughts on these matters he has strong affinities. In modern Irish literature the person he seems closest to among his predecessors is Lady Gregory, who also always thought of art in terms of community; to whom literature was not just words on the page, but a means of drawing life and language together in communion. For both of them poetry should seek the Platonic ideal of mending the broken circuits of language and community.

Devlin, it seems, has not an ounce of Platonism in his make-up. In "Jansenist Journey" there is an extraordinarily moving passage about the "black-faced scapegoat, Guilt" the pilgrim brothers take with them:

> He bucked the wild flowers with flashing horns,
>
>> These freshets garlic to his taste,
>> But I put no trust in him no trust.

"No trust". Versing is not spelling out the patterns always there, always to be seen if we only allow ourselves to open our eyes. Versing is caution not trusting, watching the language. Whatever meaning may be arrived at is always perilous, not to be trusted, under siege from within and without. All is ambiguous; there are no conclusions. All conditions are altering, and it is not possible, even, to hold a coherent argument for very long without immense effort and strain. Montaigne is the dominating presence here, but as in Montaigne,

Devlin's sense of the difficulty of knowing anything for sure does not degenerate into a lethargy of Pyrrhonist sloth, or a Belacqua-like somnambulism (as mocked at in Beckett's *More Pricks than Kicks*). The writing remains alert and he keeps the language open for possibility, without cajoling it. His verse is a numbered time as he waits, not for Godot, but for God's grace. And sometimes it is there: "delicate and blind".

And so we have Kavanagh's amplitude and expansiveness; Devlin's uncertainty and caution. The danger for Kavanagh (and we see him in this trouble later on in his career) is that he will try to sacramentalise the trivial and thereby expend his energy; for Devlin the danger is that he will retire into a language too remote from ordinary concerns through scruple of conscience.

My own concluding thought would be that Irish poetry has still not learned enough of the serious artistry of either poet: Kavanagh's visionary openness has often degenerated into emotive rant; Devlin's profound not-knowing has become the indifference that comes from knowing nothing.

Adele Dalsimer (essay date 1984)

SOURCE: Dalsimer, Adele. "Hell and Parnassus by the Canal Bank: Patrick Kavanagh's Dublin." In *The Irish Writer and the City,* edited by Maurice Harmon, pp. 136-43. Gerrards Cross, England: Colin Smythe, 1984.

[*In the following essay, Dalsimer discusses Kavanagh's changing feeling for, and poetic treatment of, the city of Dublin.*]

Surely no nation of writers has been more migratory than the Irish. An alienated sense of place seems, in fact, a prerequisite for the Irish imagination. Even Patrick Kavanagh, thought to be the poet most firmly rooted in Irish soil, was rarely content with his surroundings. Wherever he was, he wanted to be somewhere else. Whether in Inniskeen or Dublin, London or New York, he wanted to go elsewhere or simply back where he had been. Writing about Tarry Flynn, Darcy O'Brien remarked, 'He loves his district but in his fantasy-ridden mind he dwells elsewhere, somewhere, nowhere.'[1] O'Brien might have been describing Kavanagh himself.

Kavanagh's sense of dislocation vascillated primarily between Dublin and Inniskeen. Having left his home in Monaghan for the city, he railed at Dublin, wishing he had 'stood in bed. Or in Monaghan.'[2] In Inniskeen, he insisted he belonged to Dublin: 'I go false in Mucker poems . . . I never belonged there. Terrible, ignorant, vulgar place Inniskeen . . . I shall hardly ever go there again except for a day or so.'[3]

In the poetic expression of this conflict, Kavanagh's Dublin is characterized by two dichotomous metaphors. The city appears in his poetry as either a hell or a Parnassus, and although, as some of his critics have suggested,[4] Kavanagh overworks his metaphoric arrangements in predictable and, at times, even conventional ways, these motifs do suggest effectively the range of feelings the city aroused in him—the despair and the pain, the relief and the joy.

The search for Parnassus was central and lifelong. Kavanagh desired the 'true abandon and gaiety of heart' which 'spring from the sense of authority, confidence, and courage of the man who is on the sacred mountain.'[5] The greatest authors, Melville for example, possessed that 'gay abandon':[6] they 'had "the true Parnassian note. Godlike. Both passionate and uncaring at the same time".'[7] Kavanagh believed that atop his personal Parnassus, he, too, would be liberated to create. Above earthly distractions and free of human entanglements, he would write with a joy and authority uncontaminated by mundane concerns. At rare moments Kavanagh realized that such freedom could arise only internally—from a state of inner quietude—but more often he sought his peace and his Parnassus externally, believing that, in the right place, he would produce the right poetry.

From the start the quest for Parnassus was implicit in his poetry. The old white goat nibbling at the herbs of wisdom—the 'herbs of the Secret of Life'[8]—on the slopes of Slieve Donard, the black hills of Shancoduff, the dusty attic room, all point to the early hold the Parnassian myth had on Kavanagh.

In *Tarry Flynn*, Kavanagh describes his Parnassian ideal and indicates that, for a time, he believed he had found it in Monaghan: 'Tarry went upstairs . . . This corner was his Parnassus, the constant point above time . . . He carried out his ritual, for the Muse is attracted and held by the little gestures just as women are . . . He crossed his legs, got out the puce pencil and the blue notepaper and let his mind become passive . . . The net of earthly intrigue could not catch him here. He was on a level with the horizon—and it was a level on which there was laughter. Looking down at his own misfortunes he thought them funny now. From this height he could see himself losing his temper with the Finnegans and the Carlins and hating his neighbours and he moved the figures on the landscape, made them speak, and was filled with the joy in his own power.'[9]

But Inniskeen was not high enough to liberate Kavanagh, and by the time he was thirty-three, his rural existence had become stultifying. Frustrated by the idea of staying in one place all his life and detesting the more boring chores of the farm, he worried about associating only with people who were unaware of, or insensitive to, his aesthetic perceptions. He feared that life on the farm would blunt his talent; his little Parnassus began to seem too small and too limiting.[10] The earth that had stifled Patrick Maguire seemed about to suffocate him. He had been deluded when he believed that he could create in Monaghan. In fact, its 'stony grey soil' had 'clogged the feet of [his] boyhood;' it had deceived him into believing that his stumble 'Had the poise and stride of Apollo. / And his voice my thick-tongued mumble.' Rather than creating an artist, Inniskeen had 'flung a ditch' on his 'vision / Of beauty, love and truth.'[11] As he later commented, 'My childhood experience was the usual barbaric life of the Irish country poor . . . Poverty is a mental condition . . . The real poverty was the lack of enlightenment to go out and get under the moon. I am afraid this fog of unknowing affected me dreadfully.'[12] Thus Kavanagh set out for the city.

The sonnet sequence **'Temptation in Harvest'** is the poetic expression of Kavanagh's conflicted decision to leave the farm for Dublin,[13] and, in these poems, Dublin, not Inniskeen, becomes the Parnassus that beckons him from the clay, 'from the stones of the street, the sheds, the hedges' with the promise of creativity and real art. It is his 'City of Kings / Where art, music, letters are the real things.' Kavanagh presents the temptations of the city as a feminine seduction by his muse, but more important, as a seduction from the farm to Parnassus:

> An old woman whispered from behind the bush:
> 'Stand in
> The shadows of the ricks until she passes;
> You cannot eat what grows upon Parnassus—
> And she is going there as sure as sin.'

But the poet does not heed this warning; the heights of Parnassus are his goal, and he turns

> Away from the ricks, the sheds, the cabbage garden,
> The stones of the street, the thrush song in the tree,
> The potato-pits, the flaggers in the swamp;—
> From the country heart that hardly learned to harden,
> From the spotlight of an old kitchen lamp

and follows 'her who winked at [him]'.[14]

But if Parnassus had been improbable in Monaghan, it was impossible in Dublin. Unable to eke out a living, alienated from the city's literary society, hungry, and lonely, Kavanagh soon viewed Dublin as an enemy and himself as an empty, wasted failure. Even more than he had decried his corroding country existence, he bemoaned his decision to leave the farm and come to Dublin. 'With no background, no job or prospects of one, I came to Dublin and since then I have never stopped regretting it'.[15] 'I came to Dublin in 1939. That was the first act of the tragedy, the folly . . . I cannot out of my experience look upon my so coming as anything but insanity.'[16] His life in Dublin seemed an endless struggle with the 'very city of hate.'[17] 'What,' he asked himself, 'possessed me to think that in coming to Dublin I was coming to a place that was an improvement on my native fields? Here was I casting myself into the den of beasts. There was nothing of inspiration here. There were no poets here. There was absolutely nothing here for me.'[18]

In **'Intimate Parnassus,'** Kavanagh depicts his creative failure in Dublin and his wish—seemingly impossible—to remain aloof and detached from his unsatisfying environment:

> It is not cold on the mountain, human women
> Fall like ripe fruit while mere men
> Are climbing out on dangerous branches
> Of banking, insurance, and shops; going
> To the theatre; becoming
> Acquainted with actors; unhappily
> Pretending to a knowledge of art.
> Poet . . . forget them
> As things aside from the main purpose
> Which is to be
> Passive, observing with a steady eye.[19]

Kavanagh had come to Dublin for a 'peep into the Temple of the Muses,'[20] but instead had heard the 'demon's terrifying yell: / There is no place as perfect as our hell.'[21] Dreams of Appollonian creativity had become nightmares of inauthentic art, and in the frustration of disappointed expectations, Kavanagh transformed his Parnassus into his Inferno. He wrote to his brother Peter in March, 1951, 'I am writing away. I have got a good deal out of Dublin which I have established as Hell.'[22]

The idiosyncratic hell that Kavanagh constructs in such poems as **'The Paddiad,' 'The Defeated,'** and **'Adventures in the Bohemian Jungle'** is based on the poet's failed artistic dreams. Its torments are aesthetic. *By Night Unstarred* portrays the Dublin scene that by now held for Kavanagh all the tortures of the damned: 'He called into the Pub where the poets who do not write met on Monday and Thursday evenings. There they were all of them sitting praising each other, and talking literature all the time . . . The conversation at the tables was the usual drivel. There were no standards of criticism. That destructive element of inarticulate Dublin society . . . was here represented. A poisonous element, bitter, clever, good at making hurtful witticisms about their neighbours. But they had nothing creative to their name. Some of them achieved a reputation for scintillating wit but the final effect was injury to the soul.'[23] What makes Dublin a hell for Kavanagh is its seeming animadversion of art. There are no aesthetic standards in his Dublin—just cronyism and mutual back-scratching. Financial reward is the only goal.

Inhabited by would-be artists and writers who delight in the accoutrements of art, but lack the vision and integrity to look at themselves and their world honestly, the city is an artistic sham. Its writers are frauds, exploiting their Irishness while ignoring the authentic Irish spirit.

In his poems, Kavanagh recreates this scene so that 'the whole social and cultural world of Irish art becomes a living hell for the intelligent and sensitive,'[24] and it is a hell that disquiets us with its tepid qualities:

> . . . here in this nondescript land
> Everything is second hand:
> Nothing ardently growing,
> Nothing, coming, nothing going,
> Tepid fevers, nothing hot,
> None alive enough to rot;
> Nothing clearly defined . . .
> Every head is challenged. Friend,
> This is hell you've brought me to.
> Where's the gate that we came through?[25]

The devil in this Inferno is Dublin's lack of artistic integrity and creative energy. He is Mediocrity, 'most generous-tempered of the gods' who

> listens to the vilest odes,
> Aye, and not just idle praise!
> For these the devil highly pays.
>
> Far and near he screws his eyes
> In search of what will never rise,
> Souls that are fusty, safe, and dim,
> These are the geniuses of the land to him.[26]

As Brendan Kennelly has suggested, Kavanagh began to sound 'like a rural Faustus brought face to face with the hell of hypocritical mediocrity.'[27]

But like the exiled Dante with whom he identified, Kavanagh eventually left Hell for Paradise—and he did not have to journey far. In 1955, on the banks of the Grand Canal, Dublin became a true Parnassus. Operated on in March of that year for cancer of the lung, Kavanagh recovered completely, shocking a Dublin that had already planned his funeral (he was to be waked in the City Hall). Kavanagh viewed his recovery as a miracle. Like Yeats, he now believed, 'We are blest by everything, Everything we look upon is blest.' Having lost his lung, Kavanagh also lost his bitterness, and, no longer tormented by feelings of futility or the pain of dislocation, he discovered a new bond between himself and his surroundings. Kavanagh felt reborn, and with his rebirth, Dublin shed its infernal characteristics and assumed the longed for Parnassian attributes. The City's transformation is explicit in **'Lines Written on a Seat on the Grand Canal, Dublin, Erected to the Memory of Mrs. Dermot O'Brien'**:

> No one will speak in prose,
> Who finds his way to these Parnassian islands.[28]

and in **'Dear Folks'**:

> Just a line to remind my friends that after much trouble
>
> Of one kind and another I am back in circulation.
>
>   . . . The main thing is to continue,
>   To walk Parnassus right into the sunset
>   Detached in love where pygmies cannot pin you
>   To the ground like Gulliver.[29]

Kavanagh had finally found the freedom of 'Mount Olympus laughter-roaring unsolemn / Where no one is angry and satirical,'[30] and he could maintain the detachment simply to watch

>   Thing moving or just colour
>   Without comment from the scholar.
>   To look on is enough
>   In the business of love.[31]

In the joy of his rebirth, Kavanagh was able to look with equanimity not only on the Dublin of his present, but also on the Inniskeen of his past. For the next several years, before his final illness overtook him— wakening a bitterness greater than before—he viewed with contentment his rural youth and his urban maturity, and acknowledged that both Inniskeen and Dublin had contributed to his growth as a poet. Briefly, but lovingly, he accepted the city's pavements and the 'passion of primrose banks in May.' As he poignantly wrote in **'Question to Life'**:

>   When all is said and done a considerable
>   Portion of loving is found in inanimate
>   Nature, and a man need not feel miserable
>   . . . . .
>   . . . there is always the passing gift of affection
>   Tossed from the window of high charity
>   In the office girl and the civil servant section
>   And these are no despicable commodity.
>   So be reposed and praise, praise, praise
>   The way it happened and the way it is.[32]

By the banks of the Grand Canal, Kavanagh's Hell had, for a short while, become his Parnassus.

Notes

1. *Patrick Kavanagh* (Lewisburg: Bucknell University Press), p. 40.

2. *November Haggard*, Peter Kavanagh, Ed. (New York; Peter Kavanagh Hand Press, 1971), p. 75.

3. Peter Kavanagh, *Sacred Keeper* (The Curragh, Ireland: Goldsmith Press, 1979). p. 337.

4. In 'Provincialism and Recent Irish Poetry: The Importance of Patrick Kavanagh,' Michael Allen has written 'Another over-literary frame of reference is the ninetyish idea of Parnassus;' Allen sees Kavanagh's attempt to fuse his 'real-life migra-

tory experience with a symbolic Parnassian journey' as 'clichéd.' (*Two Decades of Irish Writing*, Douglas Dunn, Ed. [Chester Springs: Dufour Editions, 1975], pp. 29-30). John Jordan comments, 'Mr Kavanagh's defects are grave. A catalogue of them would include over-reliance on portentous abstractions, the mandarin platitude . . . an uneasy acquaintance with Greek mythology (he must never again mention Parnassus, in any form).' Jordan adds, however, 'But for me the defects are often in themselves contributory to the success of individual poems, breaking up the light and refracting it.' ('Mr. Kavanagh's Progress,' *Studies*, XLIX [Autumn, 1960], p. 303.)

5. 'Patrick Kavanagh on Poetry,' *Journal of Irish Literature*, VI (January, 1977), p. 69.

6. Ibid.

7. Anthony Cronin, *Dead as Doornails* (Swords, Ireland: Poolbeg Press, 1980), p. 76.

8. *Collected Poems* (New York: W. W. Norton, 1964), p. 5.

9. (New York: Penguin Books, 1978), pp. 177-178.

10. John Nemo, *Patrick Kavanagh* (Boston: Twayne Publishers, 1979), p. 20.

11. *Collected Poems*, p. 82.

12. *Self-Portrait* (Dublin: Dolmen Press, 1975), p. 9.

13. Seamus Heaney, 'The Poetry of Patrick Kavanagh: From Monaghan to the Grand Canal,' *Two Decades of Irish Writing*, Douglas Dunn, Ed. (Chester Springs: Dufour Editions, 1975), p. 110.

14. *Collected Poems*, pp. 67-68.

15. *Sacred Keeper*, p. 60.

16. *November Haggard*, p. 74.

17. *Collected Poems*, p. 89.

18. *November Haggard*, p. 74.

19. *Collected Poems*, p. 164.

20. p. 100.

21. p. 99.

22. *Lapped Furrows*, Peter Kavanagh, Ed. (New York: Peter Kavanagh Hand Press, 1969), p. 163.

23. (The Curragh, Ireland: Goldsmith Press, 1977), pp. 162-163.

24. John Nemo, 'A Joust with the Philistines: Patrick Kavanagh's Cultural Criticism,' *Journal of Irish Literature*, IV (May, 1975), p. 73.

25. *Collected Poems*, p. 108.

26. p. 91.

27. 'Patrick Kavanagh,' *Ariel*, I (July, 1970), p. 19.

28. *Collected Poems*, p. 150.

29. p. 151.

30. p. 155.

31. p. 154.

32. p. 164.

Antoinette Quinn (essay date 1991)

SOURCE: Quinn, Antoinette. "Voice of the People: *The Great Hunger*." In *Patrick Kavanagh: Born-Again Romantic*, pp. 123-58. New York : Gill and Macmillan, 1991.

[*In the following essay, Quinn provides a detailed analysis of* The Great Hunger, *focusing in part on the work's varied style and emotional range.*]

In *The Great Hunger* Kavanagh returns to a terrain he had already lightheartedly traversed in *The Green Fool*. Once again his narrator is a native informant taking the reader on a conducted tour of his own neighbourhood. On this occasion his parish is named Donaghmoyne rather than Inniskeen but, since these two parishes were once, in fact, united, both autobiography and poem present the same people and the same land. Only four years separate the two works. Yet all has changed utterly; a terrible hideousness, inconceivable to the genial narrator of *The Green Fool*, has been born, a terrifying vision of a way of life that had once seemed full of blessings. *The Great Hunger* subverts the benign narrative of *The Green Fool*. To turn from its concluding pages to the opening lines of *The Great Hunger* is not simply to encounter an alternative version of the same text; it is to change imaginative worlds. It is to move from this:

> As we picked up the tubers the smells rising from the dry brown clay were a tonic to revive the weariest body, the loneliest spirit. Turning over the soil, our fingers were turning the pages in the Book of Life . . .

to this:

> Clay is the word and clay is the flesh
> Where the potato-gatherers like mechanised scare-
>   crows move
> Along the side-fall of the hill—Maguire and his men.
> If we watch them an hour is there anything we can
>   prove
> Of life as it is broken-backed over the Book
>   Of Death?

The rhetoric here is biblical, the voice that of the angry prophet, crying out in an Irish wilderness, railing against the desecration of sacred human life. His opening words shock the complacent Irish reader out of his *laissez-faire* lethargy with their powerful perversion of a fundamental tenet of Christian faith:

> And the Word was made flesh . . .

Twice daily the Angelus bell reminded country Catholics of the reality of Christ's incarnation, yet the ethos of the small farm daily denied the evangelical truth in which all professed to believe. What they worshipped was a false God made of clay, sacrificing body and soul in his service. The land of Ireland is deconsecrated in this deeply religious poem, where clay connotes the negation of body and soul and of all human and divine intercourse, the victory of death over life; and the Irish farmer is reduced to a corpse ('a bag of wet clay'), his fields to a cemetery.

The Great Hunger may seem to be a reading from the Book of Death, yet its prophetic condemnation of rural Ireland as a wasteland is inspired by an intensely Christian interpretation of the holiness of human life. Christ's incarnation is here envisioned not as some far off divine event but as a present metaphysicality, a quickening spirit that sanctifies the flesh. The poem's vision is Johannine in its identification of God as light and life and *Logos*. Its God is, above all, a creative God, rejoicing in human sensuality, sexuality, fertility; not a repressively puritanical deity, approving the closed lips, closed legs and closed minds of the Irish poor. In a parish where 'five hundred hearts' are 'hungry for life' and women proffer unwanted wombs, the tabernacle is 'pregnant', for 'God's truth is life'. The cautious, thrifty, prudish gospel emanating from a rural 'Respectability that knows the price of all things' (and, presumably, the value of nothing) and 'marks God's truth in pounds and pence and farthings' is apocryphal. According to Kavanagh's evangel what God abhors is sexual inhibition, not sexual licence:

> For the strangled impulse there is no redemption.

Kavanagh's God is not some remote, unattainable, abstract absolute; he is immanent in life's ordinary quotidian round, in 'the bits and pieces of Everyday'. The farm folk, 'hurrying' to Sunday mass, ignore the sacramentality of their weekday lives. They dissociate the eucharist from their daily bread, failing to recognise that

> In a crumb of bread the whole mystery is.

Their God has been distorted into the custodian of a post-Famine peasant ethos, wanting his people to endure rather than enjoy, rewarding the respectable with a church collecting-box, or lighting the farmer's way to the grave with a blessed candle when he finally reaches the end of his long day's dying. A peasant priesthood colludes with this peasant version of Catholicism in which economic prudence and material self-interest masquerade as morality. The country chapel has been converted into a coffin, grimly clamping down on human desires, 'pressing its low ceiling over them'. The fierce anger that empowers *The Great Hunger* is the wrath of the biblical seer, lifting 'a moment to Prophecy / Out of the clayey hours'. He concludes with oracular authority, warning of the terrible 'apocalypse' in store for a land that has blasphemed against the incarnate Christ by raising up a false clay god in his stead.

The Great Hunger is as visionary in its critique of a historical epoch as Blake's 'America: A Prophecy', though it substitutes figurative fiction for mythic abstraction. The living death of small-farm Ireland is represented through the biography of the elderly bachelor farmer, Patrick Maguire. His name, ironically combining that of the national apostle and the parish priest of Inniskeen,[1] marks him out as a typical Irish country Catholic. Patrick Maguire is an overworked slave, brutalised, vegetised even, by a life of unremitting drudgery, culturally deprived, compelled to be chaste, and forbidden to marry until impotent from age. He is the victim of a religiously enforced rural economy which values property and propriety at the expense of love and self-fulfilment. Maguire's human energies are gradually absorbed by devotion to his fields, while his psycho-sexual yearnings are simultaneously suppressed to the point of extinction. Human fertility is sacrificed to agricultural productivity:

> He lives that his little fields may stay fertile when his
>   own body
> Is spread in the bottom of a ditch under two coulters
>   crossed in Christ's Name.

As a tale of wasted human potential *The Great Hunger* centres on Maguire's celibacy, focusing with grim relentlessness on a lifetime of sexual evasions pathetically interwoven with aspirations towards marriage (or, in his later years, even some groping of unsuspecting schoolgirls), and eventually culminating in a lonely, hopeless, sterile old age. His failure to achieve the normal expression of his manhood is attributed to the reinforcement of sexual timidity and inexperience by economic and ecclesiastical precept:

> Religion, the fields and the fear of the Lord
> And Ignorance giving him the coward's blow . . .

Maguire's predicament is exacerbated by a combination of filial obligation and maternal manipulation. He is trapped in a pernicious Irish rural system of belated male marriage which he himself, if he were not doomed to perish childless, would be condemned to perpetuate. His widowed mother is only twenty six years his senior; the farmhouse is her home. It is in her interest to blackmail her son into celibacy, exploiting the dictates of economic expediency and Catholic morality to maintain her dominant position as head of the household, fearful that if her son's sexual curiosity is encouraged she will be unable to deter him from marriage. Mrs Maguire trusts that 'the push of nature' will thwart her efforts in the long term but, instead, her son is slowly emasculated by matriarchy. He procrastinates, masturbates, sublimates. Patrick Maguire has fallen victim to the stereotypical Irish mother / son relationship that precludes all other relationships, a grotesque Oedipal parody in which she is 'wife and mother in one' and he upholds their marriage contract. By the verbal sleight of substituting 'to' for 'until' Kavanagh makes such fidelity tantamount to being 'faithful to death'. When Mrs Maguire dies, aged ninety-one, 'the knuckle-bones' are 'cutting the skin of her son's backside' and he is sixty-five. The Maguires' case is extreme, but not untypical. Such a sustained, sterile, mutual dependency violates the natural order all around them:

> The cows and horses breed,
> And the potato-seed
> Gives a bud and a root and rots
> In the good mother's way with her sons;
> The fledged bird is thrown
> From the nest—on its own.
> But the peasant in his little acres is tied
> To a mother's womb by the wind-toughened navel-
>   cord . . .

Patrick Maguire's biography is presented, for the most part, in an extended flashback. He is already an old mechanised scarecrow when first encountered in his potato field and because his role is that of representative subsistence farmer, his childhood and adolescence are disregarded. What the poem sets out to evoke is the texture of his adult life, not only his doings and sayings but his most private fantasies, fears and frustrations. Kavanagh could get under the skin of the tillage farmer because, to some extent, it was his own skin too, yet Maguire is an autonomous dramatic creation and not a disguised self-portrait. Poet and character differ not only in the matter of age in that Maguire's biography begins at approximately the age where Kavanagh's rural autobiography left off. They differ fundamentally in that Maguire is emphatically neither a poet nor an intellectual, merely an 'illiterate, unknown and unknowing'. Though 'not born blind' and 'not always blind' ('sometimes . . . these men know God the Father in a tree'), the peasant, with very rare exceptions, is deprived of that visionary imagination which transfigured the Inniskeen landscape for Kavanagh and enabled him to transcend the horror and the boredom of country life. Peasantry in *The Great Hunger* is defined, as the poet would much later define it in *Self-Portrait,* less as a station in life than as a state of semi-consciousness, remote from imaginative awareness. The peasant is a 'half-vegetable', little better than the potatoes he picks,

> Who can react to sun and rain and sometimes even
> Regret that the Maker of Light had not touched him
>   more intensely.
> Brought him up from the sub-soil to an existence
> Of conscious joy . . .

Nevertheless, a shared Christian name indicates Kavanagh's recognition that poet and character have something in common. The aged, resigned slave who will never escape from the tyranny of his little tillage fields embodies a fate which, but for the grace of imagination, might have been the poet's own. Possibly the dire alternative over which, as elder son and mainstay of a female household, he brooded as he struggled to free himself from the bonds of home. Certainly, the narrator of *The Great Hunger* renders the deprivations and limited consolations of Maguire's life from young manhood to old age with the familiarity of one who has foreknown and foresuffered all.

Whereas the narrator of *The Green Fool* was also the book's hero, in *The Great Hunger* Kavanagh takes advantage of his own recent professional distance from subsistence farming to sever the relationship between poet and farmer. The poet figure now serves as an interpreter of country life, mediating between an uninitiated urban or non-Irish readership and an illiterate peasantry. Maguire's biography is filtered through a controlling narrative consciousness; it is a realist but also an exemplary fiction. Maguire is an Irish rural Everyman and the omniscient narrator's prophetic role is to witness to his story's representativeness and to warn of its consequence. He is both angry on his character's behalf and ironic at his expense.

Though Maguire is a pathetic or derisory spectacle displayed for the reader's empathy or enlightenment, the structural metaphor of tragic theatre, invoked in the poem's opening lines to separate commentator and character, is misleading. It does signal an important change of literary direction from the lyrical and comic genres Kavanagh had formerly deployed. To invest small-farm misery with the dignity and gravity of tragedy was a way of elevating a humble situation by assigning it to an aggrandising literary category, just as, ten years later, he would defiantly entitle a sonnet about a 'local row', **'Epic'**. Here he draws attention to his own subversiveness by declaring that Maguire's case history demands a redefinition or a revision of the tragic category. What *The Great Hunger* presents is a realist or 'true tragedy', neither heroic nor spectacular. It is a drama of non-event, telling a 'weak' and 'washy' tale; its hero is an anti-hero, lacking in vision, energy, courage or resolve. It treats of an obscure life passed in an ugly world, brutal, lonely, wretched, downcast; a life that is really a protracted death; not 'mad hooves galloping in the sky', but 'A sick horse nosing around the meadow for a clean place to die'. The heavens do not blaze forth the death of Irish farmers.

While *The Great Hunger* sometimes calls for an empathetic response to Maguire's plight, it does not do so with any consistency. 'Let us salute him without irony', the narrator demands in part XIII, before he reintroduces his tragic metaphor. A change of tone is called for because here, as throughout much of the poem, sympathy is blocked by narrative irony. At thirty-five Maguire 'could take the sparrow's bow'; at sixty-five his whistling saddens his terrier dog; and the applause that greets the conclusion of his biography is less cathartic than ironic, more a boo than a boo hoo, a zany whoop of relief that 'The story is done'. If the poem must be assigned a genre, then it comes closer to tragicomedy than to tragedy and, probably, closer to black comedy than to either.

Kavanagh refers to his narrative enterprise in theatrical metaphors, yet fictional technique in *The Great Hunger* is really cinematic,[2] rather than dramatic, short on dialogue, highly visual and scenically mobile. The narrator substitutes for both camera and sound recording and also serves as a voice-over. Its cinematic technique prevents this poem from settling into either tragedy or comedy, for gravity is often displaced by irony, a pathetic image spliced with a comic. It is a destabilising technique, even threatening the prophetic voice-over through undignified realist juxtaposition. The poem, organised as a montage, is extraordinarily flexible, continually altering angle and direction, zooming from a long shot of farm workers on the side-fall of a hill to a close up of a dog lying on a torn jacket under a heeled-up cart, cutting from breakfast time in the Maguire kitchen to a headland at dawn, from Maguire at mass to his occasion of sin in the Yellow Meadow, from a night's card-playing in a firelit kitchen to a frosty February morning in bleached white fields. Maguire's life is framed with rapid changes of focus and from a deliberately diverting play of angles. The camera tracks him as he ducks and weaves, his 'dream' fluctuating 'like the cloud-swung wind'.

It is to a large extent its innovatory technique that liberates the poem from the conventions of Abbey 'peasant quality' (the notorious 'pq'), enabling Kavanagh to achieve a more documentary presentation of small-farm life. Moving out from the confines of the proscenium arch he covers new ground. He shoots a good deal of outdoor footage, accompanying the farmer into the fields as he collects 'the scattered harness and baskets' after a day's potato picking, gathers 'the loose stones off the ridge', walks 'among his cattle' or loads 'the day-scoured implements on the cart / As the shadows of evening poplars crookened the furrows'. His presentation is selective, avoiding the tedium of a full scale presentation, panning from the hills, where neighbours watch 'with all the sharpened interest of rivalry' as Maguire ploughs in a black March wind, to a close up of the headland:

Primroses and the unearthly start of ferns
Among the blackthorn shadows in the ditch,
A dead sparrow and an old waistcoat . . .

The camera eye does not distinguish between pretty and ugly images and here neither is edited out. *The Great Hunger* abounds in authentic shots of country life: savants swapping knowledge in the pub; heavy-headed ruminants nodding at the crossroads; Maguire on the railway slope watching children picking flowers; girls 'sitting on the grass banks of lanes / Stretch-legged and lingering staring'; a dying mother reaching 'five bony crooks under the tick' to find five pounds for masses; Agnes picking her steps through wet grass, holding her skirts 'sensationally up' for Maguire's benefit. Selectivity is exercised with such unobtrusiveness that there is no sense of an imposed order or a measured comprehensiveness. The delightful redundance of Kavanagh's approach is evident, for instance, in the February morning sequence in part XII, which pans from the frozen white hills to a candid camera shot of Maguire clapping his arms, prancing on crisp roots, shouting to warm himself, buckleaping about the potato pit. Such quirkiness takes the didacticism out of documentary.

By clever cutting, occasional brief flashbacks, and dispensing with linking narrative, Kavanagh solved the problem of organisation he had already confronted in *The Green Fool,* the difficulty of combining the linearity of biography with the repetitiveness of agricultural cycles and rural routines. Whereas in *The Green Fool* he felt compelled to treat of a farming chore in some detail in one chapter and never revert to it, his new technique permitted him to return to the same locations, chapel, tillage field or potato pit, and the same actions, ploughing or potato harvesting, varying the camera angle and distance or the length, pace and detail of a sequence. Again and again Maguire is filmed with his dog and there are brief late allusions to such earlier sequences as the card playing or his masturbation over the kitchen hearth. So *The Green Fool*'s artificial division of labour is avoided, a better sense of the repetitive texture of the farmer's life is conveyed, recurrence is exploited to indicate monotony or the repeated evasion of opportunity, and the turning of the rural calendar marks 'the slow and speedier' passage of time. *The Great Hunger,* despite its deliberate discontinuities, is a unified coherent whole, in which each sequence is inspired by the same religious vision, designed to show an aspect of the same rural catastrophe.

The skilfully edited chapel episode in part IV reveals Kavanagh's narrative technique at work. A self-contained sequence it, nevertheless, refers backwards and forwards into the poem and contributes both playfully and seriously to its central theme of the meaning and misunderstanding of Christ's incarnation:

Maguire knelt beside a pillar where he could spit
Without being seen. He turned an old prayer round:

'Jesus, Mary and Joseph pray for us
Now and at the Hour.' Heaven dazzled death.
'Wonder should I cross-plough that turnip-ground.'
The tension broke. The congregation lifted its head
As one man and coughed in unison.
Five hundred hearts were hungry for life—
Who lives in Christ shall never die the death.
And the candle-lit Altar and the flowers
And the pregnant Tabernacle lifted a moment to
   Prophecy
Out of the clayey hours.
Maguire sprinkled his face with holy water
As the congregation stood up for the Last Gospel.
He rubbed the dust off his knees with his palm, and
   then
Coughed the prayer phlegm up from his throat and
   sighed: Amen.

The sequence opens with a comic, realist close-up of Maguire at mass, obliquely noting his omission of the allusion to death in his routine prayer and taking amused cognisance of the fact that the colourful religious spectacle may distract him from the fear of death, but not from his agricultural preoccupations. The subject of death, a central symbolic obsession in this poem, is introduced by the narrator but evaded by the character's ellipsis. He overlooks death and concentrates on a heavenly afterlife, or displaces the grave with his 'turnip-ground'. Yet his prayer is one that ironically conjoins the immediate present and the hour of death.

The narrative then cuts to the moment after the Elevation and the camera is turned on the rest of the congregation, comically clearing their throats after the obligatory ritual silence. What is emphasised about this humorous rustic chorus is its 'unison'. Maguire is here both 'one man' and everyman. The narrator now shifts into his vatic mode to provide a visionary interpretation of the eucharist, seeing the consecrated bread and wine as the divine satisfaction of the parishioners' appetite, presenting transubstantiation as an image of divine incarnation. The title metaphor is defined as a people's hunger for life and love. Life in Christ is opposed to death but the Christian triumph of life is acknowledged to be as momentary as the elevation itself for this rural congregation. Christ has not impregnated their world; before and after the elevation stretches a horizontal plane of 'clayey hours'. Significantly, the chapel sequence is preceded by the fields' message that 'only Time can bless' and succeeded by Maguire's failure to avail of the sexual blessing he is offered in the Yellow Meadow which he, puritanically, mistranslates as sexual temptation. The spirit quickens but the letter kills and sexual sin is writ large in Maguire's Catholic consciousness. As the narrator interprets the prophetic meaning of the divine incarnation the camera focuses on the aesthetically beautiful altar, candle lit and flower adorned.

Abruptly the screenplay cuts to the Last Gospel and to the chapel porch where Maguire, as was customary among less devout males, is making an early escape. He is caught in slow motion, gesturing towards blessing himself, cleaning the dust off his good Sunday trousers (he has probably been kneeling on the floor at the back of the chapel so that he can slip out easily) and indulging the smoker's cough he was restraining during mass. His actions are both comic, realist and, also, ironic because he is shaking off and expectorating whatever religious experience he has just undergone. 'Amen', the last word in the passage, is an apt word to fade out on. It signals the conclusion of Maguire's devotions, the separation of mass from the world outside the chapel, and his passive, fatalistic, 'So be it' attitude to life. The sequence reveals the narrator's religious vision and his character's blindness to it. Maguire emerges completely unaffected from a potentially transcendental occasion. This passage illustrates Kavanagh's mastery of a narrative technique that combines comic realism with a visionary critique that embraces humour, irony, compassion and prophetic faith. His narrator mediates between the *Logos* and the clay words of everyday. By virtue of its cinematic art *The Great Hunger* presents an almost unbearably bleak biography in an entertainingly varied manner, with subtle modulations or outrageous transitions between shots and numerous changes of pace and mood.

To praise *The Great Hunger* for its 'breathtaking honesty' has become something of a critical commonplace, but its documentary authenticity never stops short at realism. Kavanagh's is a visionary and fiercely moral imagination, obsessed with meaning, finding God or the 'hungry fiend' 'in the bits and pieces of Everyday'. His God is not 'all / In one place, complete and labelled like a case in a railway store',[3] a piece of baggage to be deposited in the 'Left Luggage' office, when inconvenient. He is not pre-packaged for Sunday consumption. From the outset *The Great Hunger* is concerned not just with daily 'life as it is' realistically, but with what scene and action signify religiously. 'Is there anything we can prove . . . ?' is the poem's first question. The potato gatherers of the opening lines move between metaphors. Cinematic technique enabled Kavanagh to apply what he called a 'carnal method' to his visionary critique of Irish rural society.[4] Where previously he, like Maguire, often 'read the symbol too sharply', so that objects tended to fade and disappear in the light of his religious or aesthetic vision, the camera which converts everything into image, gives a metonymic dimension to his metaphoric readings.

There is often so little disjunction between realist detail and figurative interpretation in *The Great Hunger* that metaphor is unobtrusive and even contributes to the documentary process: the farmer's spirit is 'a wet sack flapping about the knees of time' or 'the mark of a hoof in a guttery gap'; a deep-drilled potato field or two coulters lying crossed in a ditch suggest a grave and headstone; morality is like 'a bush' in a gap 'weighted with boulders'; 'the green of after-grass' symbolises life's aftermath; the bachelor is an unbroken colt trembling his head and running free of the halter. Maguire sighs 'like the brown breeze in the thistles' and the mumble of rural speech is compared to 'the rumination of cows after milking' or to the rumbling of 'laden carts'. Metonymy often contributes an ironic edge to the poem's symbolism as when a biblical 'strait way' is achieved for the peasant's passage to the afterlife 'by the angles / Where the plough missed or a spade stands, straitening the way'. The reader is frequently 'diverted' by such angles. Its splicing of metonymy and metaphor creates a continuity and coherence between *The Great Hunger*'s documentary and visionary dimensions. Only when the voice-over is too predominant, the freeze-frame too prolonged, does the poem's palpable design become too obtrusive.

The primary contraries in *The Great Hunger* are life and death; its symbolic drama is the defeat of spirituality and sexuality by inertia, cowardice, enslavement to matter and a perverted morality. In Kavanagh's christened world psychosexual energies are sacred; sexual intercourse is as sacramental as matrimony; to refuse the claims of the flesh is sacrilegious. It is a Blakean universe where 'everything that lives is holy / Life delights in life'. Before this late arousal of his sexual imagination Kavanagh's poetry had inhabited a land where 'flesh was a thought more spiritual than music'. He had side-stepped the sexual by adopting a childhood perspective or projecting himself as poet rather than man. Although girlish presences hover in **'Spraying the Potatoes'** and **'Art McCooey'**, they are never brought to 'lust nearness'. The poet is merely playing with 'the frilly edges of reality'; he is 'lost in the mists where "genesis" begins'. *The Great Hunger*, however, is explicitly and insistently sexual in thought, word, deed and omission. Now ordinary farm images are invested with phallic significance:

> A dog lying on a torn jacket under a heeled-up cart,
> A horse nosing along the posied headland, trailing
> A rusty plough. Three heads hanging between wide-apart
> Legs. October playing a symphony on a slack wire paling . . .

Or less droopily, Maguire raping the earth that an earlier Kavanagh ploughman had painted brown:

> The twisting sod rolls over on her back—
> The virgin screams before the irresistible sock . . .

Planting seed takes on connotations of 'sensuous groping'; picking potatoes becomes an occasion for sexual innuendo:

What is he looking for there?
He thinks it is a potato, but we know better
Than his mud-gloved fingers probe in this insensitive
   hair . . .

Harrowing is a phallic activity; a horse eating clover lips 'late passion'; cows and foal mare are surrogate wives; Maguire's devotion to his farm is uxorious, making 'a field his bride'. The repressed Irish country Catholic displaces his sexual energies on to his crops and his stock. He ekes out his sterile days in a fecund, burgeoning, teeming world where cows and horses breed, grass and corn flourish, potatoes and weeds proliferate.

To refuse the 'fruited Tree of life' in *The Great Hunger* is to indulge a perverse appetite for death. Necrophilia and a prostrate worship of a life-denying scripture are fused in the image of the potato gatherers bent 'broken-backed over the Book of Death'. Kavanagh exploits the metonymic connections of clay with agriculture, inhumation and the decomposed corpse to establish a metaphoric association between farming and the funereal, devotion to the land and death wish. His peasant is ground down and buried alive: the 'mud-walled space' allocated to him in part XI is a coffin; the potato pit he pats smooth in part XIV is 'a new-piled grave'. The poem's black comedy is at its most macabre in its ironic fantasia on Maguire's 'afterlife': his comfortable familiarity with a subterranean existence or his compensatory posthumous paradise, full of exhilarating alternatives to his present deprivations. The story concludes with the grim acknowledgment that there may be no 'unearthly law'; that Maguire has not sufficient spirit to be either damned or glorified; that he is not alive enough to warrant reincarnation. So the poem circles back to the image with which it had begun, that of the potato field as a graveyard, the bitter truth being that in the Irish farmer's case there is little to choose between being over it or under it.

There is now no 'ditch' on Kavanagh's 'vision'. No scene or event is too mean or trivial or ugly to be included in his verse. Nothing human is foreign to him, no place or action so unsanctified as to be off-limits. Maguire spits, grunts, coughs, cleans his arse, masturbates. In 1941 such realism in Irish poetry was revolutionary. Kavanagh's flouting of literary decorum was too extreme even for Macmillan who had already published Yeats's late, physically explicit verse. Unaccountably, they permitted the masturbation sequences but drew the line at allowing Maguire to clean his arse with grass, and all but the first eight lines of part II were bowdlerised when the poem was collected in *A Soul for Sale* (1947). In Ireland, surprisingly, *The Great Hunger* escaped the censor, probably because it was originally published in a limited edition of 250 copies, or because Mrs O'Grundy rarely read poetry.[5]

The passage of time is frequently marked throughout *The Great Hunger*: the time of day, the month or season, the flight of years, hallooed away like greedy crows. April and October are key months in Maguire's calendar. April, the time for sowing seed, is a cruel month, reminding him and the reader that, through an obsession with ensuring the fertility of his fields, he himself is failing to propagate. He has sacrificed parenthood to protect 'the seed of an acre'. October is the symbolic month in which *The Great Hunger* begins and ends. Not only does it herald the approach of winter, even more significantly, it is a time when potatoes are picked and, therefore, a crucial month in Irish folk mythology. Through title, timing, location and the use of the potato as a recurrent motif Kavanagh establishes a consistent analogy between the psychic and sexual deprivation that is depopulating and destroying rural Ireland in the twentieth century and the Famine that ravaged the country in the mid-nineteenth century. *The Great Hunger* is almost a Famine centenary poem.

Famine is a potent, anti-heroic national myth, stirring atavistic fears, rousing racial memories of extreme indignity and humiliation as well as of impoverishment, suffering and death. The victims of the Famine, were, as in *The Great Hunger,* the ordinary Irish poor, people who lived in degradation and died ignominiously. Like T. S. Eliot's *Waste Land* myths this Irish historical disaster myth embraces both place and people, the physical and the psychic, connecting natural and human disease and decay; but Kavanagh's method, unlike Eliot's, is not allusive. The title of *The Great Hunger* provides the only direct clue to the poem's central historical symbol and contemporary parallels are subtly suggested, not explicitly adverted to, throughout the text. Knowledge of the poem's prior myth is taken for granted and readers are invited to discover implicit historical comparisons and ironies. The supreme historical irony, which Kavanagh appears to have intuited and which social historians have since largely substantiated, is that the infrequency or belatedness of marriages in twentieth-century rural Ireland was a consequence of the Famine.[6] Previously, so the historical argument runs, an agreeable carelessness had prevailed in matters of land and marriage; afterwards, the economics of survival took precedence over all other considerations, and agricultural prosperity was achieved at the cost of self-expression and self-fulfilment. That cult and culture of the potato so savagely mocked in *The Great Hunger* had set in. The potato crop flourished but human lives were blighted.

In *The Great Hunger* a civilisation and its discontents are revealed rhetorically, fictionally and symbolically. Kavanagh had read Joyce for the first time in 1937, and *The Great Hunger* may be read as a rural sequel to *Dubliners*, a poetic version of the *Provincials* that Joyce probably recognised he lacked the necessary experience to write. Joyce, whom O'Faoláin and O'Connor opposed to Yeats as the contemporary Irish writer's exemplary author, would have disapproved of Kavanagh's narrative technique with its all too visible narrator. Nevertheless, Maguire is the Dubliner's country cousin, psychologically paralysed, immobilised by an inertia endemic in his rural acculturation.

His entrapment is enacted in the poem's structure and reiterated through image and metaphor. The technique of extended flashback predestines him to a lifetime of sexual failure. His ambitions and aspirations to escape misery through marriage are foredoomed. The reader watches him writhe on a death-baited hook, with that almost unbearably unrelieved pessimism which only dramatic irony can induce. He is caught in the noose of the poem's circular narrative and also circumscribed by the narrator's insistence on applying circular metaphors to his routine existence. He is compared to an athlete running round and round a grass track where there is no finishing line, a goat mooching about the tree stump to which it is tethered, a sick horse nosing around a meadow looking for a clean place to die. So accustomed is he to a treadmill existence that he hopes for nothing better in the future than a different circle, one 'curved to his own will'. Maguire's immobility is further emphasised through such narrative metaphors as being gripped, 'tied', 'tethered', 'stuck in the slot'. The narrator is cruelly ironic about his failure to recognise that he is a farmer under field-arrest and a prisoner of conscience to boot when he is prevented from acting out his sexual fantasies by a fear of jail, scathingly rendered as a reluctance to 'serve . . . time'. Even the ordinary farmyard chore of locking and unlocking the henhouse acquires disturbing metaphoric overtones when Maguire finally reaches the claustrophobic awareness that he himself is both brutalised and incarcerated:

> Oh Christ! I am locked in a stable with pigs and cows
>   forever.

The desperate narrative question, 'Is there no escape?' elicits the doubly emphatic negative response, 'No escape. No escape.'

Monotony is suggested through the metaphor of unvarying melody. 'A new rhythm is a new life' and Maguire cannot change his tune. Seasonal recurrence is exploited to symbolise repetitiveness, not renewal, with the adjective 'another' ironically connoting sameness as well as transience:

> A year passed and another hurried after it . . .

and

> Another field whitened in the April air . . .

Time cannot bless. It is experienced as a continuum because there is nothing to look forward to:

> There is no tomorrow
> No future but only time stretched for the mowing of
>   the hay
> Or putting an axle in a turf-barrow . . .

For all its morbid inevitability, its structural trajectory from cemetery to cemetery, *The Great Hunger* is not an unmitigatedly grave poem. Though it writes the obituary of a man and a culture, its tone is not elegiac. Its narrative modes are too versatile, its moods too changeable, its cinematic technique too flexible, to induce a continuously mournful response. In fact, there is a good deal of comedy interspersed throughout the *saeva indignatio* of this poem. Maguire's mother may be the wicked witch of the north, an ugly domineering harpy, but, pictured in the kitchen and even in her last illness, she is a comic grotesque. The deathbed scene is blackly humorous. No keening voices exhort the 'men from the fields' to 'tread softly, softly'. Kavanagh later complained that Colum's rendering of peasant death was charming but superficial, based on 'cliché-phrase and -emotion'.[7] Here he disperses 'old sentimentality' by the realist detail of sending Mary Anne 'to boil the calves their gruel', and by his reductive, un-Lycidas-like play with water imagery:

> The holy water was sprinkled on the bed-clothes
> And her children stood around the bed and cried
>   because it was too late for crying.
> A mother dead! The tired sentiment:
> 'Mother mother' was a shallow pool
> Where sorrow hardly could wash its feet . . .

Crowd scenes in the pub, at the crossroads and the card playing, the rival farmers perched on neighbouring hills as Maguire ploughs, may reveal the intellectual limitations, boredom and intrusiveness of village life, but they are also very funny. The poem includes several such amusing sequences: rosary time in Barney Meegan's; Maguire's promotion to the position of church collector; the whist playing in Duffy's and the elderly bachelor's autobiographical reflection, 'I should have led that ace of hearts.'

Structurally, *The Great Hunger* is divided into fourteen parts, perhaps to suggest the epic dimensions of the subject, though as befits a poem, whose theme is the death wish of a culture, it begins well past the *in medias res* phase of its anti-hero's life. The first and last parts, both of which have an outdoor October setting, provide a structural frame, establishing the narrator in his role of commentator, inappropriately applying the metaphor of theatre to the intervening action, introducing Maguire at the beginning, and at the end projecting his posthumous fate and proclaiming the doom of the rural culture he represents. Formally, *The Great Hunger* is even more versatile and varied than its fourteen-part structure might suggest, most parts consisting of a montage of different sequences, with successive sequences separated by paragraphing as well as by variations in line length, rhyming and rhythmic patterns.

Kavanagh also exploits the abrupt transitions of montage to effect unexpected juxtapositions and disconcerting connections between the poem's successive parts. So the mercenary religious arithmetic with which part III concludes:

> O to be wise
> As Respectability that knows the price of all things
> And marks God's truth in pounds and pence and
>   farthings.

is reversed at the beginning of part IV:

> April, and no one able to calculate
> How far is it to harvest . . .

Maguire's lewd nocturnal indoor dreams at the end of part V are immediately contrasted with his more conventional and, even religious, outdoor, daytime dreams in part VI. Here his three wishes also echo the half religious/half fairytale aspirations of Barney Meegan's daughter in part V, an echo which serves to show that, though Maguire is no bisexual Tiresias figure, his fantasies and frustrations are shared by country parishioners of both sexes. The narrator's prophetic observation, 'In a crumb of bread the whole mystery is', almost chokes on its irreverent recollection of the chunk of loaf Maguire consumed with his cocoa before masturbating. A striking image of sexual and creative frustration at the end of part VI, the 'speechless muse', is instantly displaced by the scheming, manipulative accents of Mrs Maguire, conning her son into sexual abstinence at the beginning of part VII. The 'intellectual life' of the pub in part X reflects sardonically on the transmission of oral culture at the conclusion of part IX. Such structural interplay, which is a feature of Kavanagh's narrative throughout *The Great Hunger,* introduces a subtle quirkiness into his formal presentation. Despite his retention of a central protagonist and a controlling narrator, his technique is modernist, discontinuous and multifaceted.

Rhyme, almost always unobtrusively present, is only occasionally foregrounded, usually for comic or satiric effect, as in those lines which Macmillan expurgated from part II:

> O he loved his mother
> Above all others.
> O he loved his ploughs
> And he loved his cows
> And his happiest dream
> Was to clean his arse
> With perennial grass
> On the bank of some summer stream;
> To smoke his pipe

> In a sheltered gripe
> In the middle of July—
> His face in a mist
> And two stones in his fist
> And an impotent worm on his thigh.

The rhythmic beat is mockingly accentuated here and in part VIII where the use of an improvisational jazz technique points up Maguire's psychological paralysis:

> Sitting on a wooden gate,
> Sitting on a wooden gate,
> Sitting on a wooden gate
> He didn't care a damn.
> Said whatever came into his head,
> Said whatever came into his head,
> Said whatever came into his head
> And inconsequently sang.
> Inconsequently sang
> While his world withered away . . .

Here the repetitive monotony of Maguire's life is playfully transposed into a series of lilting refrains, yet the narrator is also ironic about his character's insouciant mood. The frivolity of popular song, with its privileging of rhythm over meaning, captures the sense of frittered time and opportunity as Maguire masturbates in a land where love is freely available and 'young women' run 'wild' and dream 'of a child'. Maguire here uses religion to rationalise his inhibitions, so his effort to secure his sexual position on the gate is highly ironic:

> He locked his body with his knees . . .

Kavanagh deploys a technique of free indirect narration interspersed with direct narrative commentary to catch his character's mood and to condemn it, yet since both are played to the same tune, not only are the transitions less obvious but the effect is more chilling. One of the unfortunate Maguire's few interludes of well-being is uncomfortably counterpointed. The sequence concludes by replaying its introductory refrain, this time accompanying it with a still musical, yet sardonic, sexual thrust:

> But while he caught high ecstasies
> Life slipped between the bars.

The Great Hunger's ludic 'wooden gate' melody is a far cry from **'Address to an Old Wooden Gate'**, twelve years previously. Eliot's 'Shakes-pe-her-ian rag' may echo behind Kavanagh's satiric refrains but, if so, the influence has been so well absorbed as to be inaudible. The modernisation of Kavanagh's muse seems to have been hastened by his admiration for the 'fresh young attitude and vocabulary' of Stephen Spender, Dylan Thomas and W. H. Auden, whose poetry was transfused with 'the blood of life-as-it-is-lived'.[8] Kavanagh learned from Auden how to zoom in on the precise images that evoke a way of life and to reproduce the speech rhythms that catch the texture of a particular culture. He knew how to adapt from the English middle-class ambience and tone of well-bred disdain in

> Pardon the studied taste that could refuse
> The golf-house quick one and the rector's tea[9]

to register with comic neutrality the shriller refusals and niggardly kindliness of Irish Catholic farmers. In an understatedly ironic sequence Maguire and his sister, childless, unmarried, sexually frustrated by their prudent Catholicism, confront the children whom the church sends fund raising to their door:

> His sister Mary Anne spat poison at the children
> Who sometimes came to the door selling raffle tickets
> For holy funds.
> 'Get out you little tramps!' she would scream
> As she shook to the hens an apronful of crumbs,[10]
> But Patrick often put his hand deep down
> In his trouser-pocket and fingered out a penny
> Or maybe a tobacco-stained caramel.
> 'You're soft' said the sister 'with other people's money
> It's not a bit funny' . . .

While the brief lyric, **'War and Peace'**, is embarrassingly derivative of Auden's 'O What is that Sound?', in *The Great Hunger* this new literary influence is unrecognisable.[11]

What is remarkable about the changing rhythms of this long poem is their adaptability to a wide diversity of narrative situations, moods and voices. Most impressive of all, perhaps, is Kavanagh's ability to create a conversational rhythm that not only mimics the Monaghan accent but is attuned to his characters' unvoiced moods. In the crossroads sequence in part V, for instance, the narrative captures the men's vacuous apathy through simile and documentary realism, the slight stir of uneventful events; and through a sluggish pacing that imitates the almost stationary inertia it evokes:

> Evening at the cross-roads—
> Heavy heads nodding out words as wise
> As the rumination of cows after milking.
> From the ragged road surface a boy picks up
> A piece of gravel and stares at it—and then
> He flings it across the elm tree on to the railway.
> It means nothing,
> Not a damn thing.
> Somebody is coming over the metal railway bridge
> And his hob-nailed boots on the arches sound like a gong
> Calling men awake. But the bridge is too narrow—
> The men lift their heads a moment. That was only John,
> So they dream on.

A double interruption of drowsiness by insignificant action, accompanied by a double interruption of long lines by lines of four syllables, four monosyllables on two

occasions, mimes the occasional jerking into wakefulness of these somnolent revellers. The boy's sense of futility is particularly well enacted through falling rhythms and a minimally negative colloquial speech. Such subtle adaptation of narrative commentary to country speech patterns and moods shows that in addition to a sharp eye for the authentic images that summon up a country scene and an ear alert to the nuances of local speech, Kavanagh was also sensitive to the inner psychic rhythms of the country farmer. Without any intrusive narrative moralising he succeeds in conjuring up a drab and dreary ambience, evoking the dispiritedness that is his central theme. Meaninglessness and damnation are unobtrusively allied in the boy's action, which repeats one of the elderly Maguire's futile actions in part I. Dream in *The Great Hunger* has not the Romantic connotations it had in Kavanagh's early lyrics; it now refers to fantasy, particularly sexual fantasy, or, more often, to 'things half-born to mind', the submerged, subconscious psycho-sexual longings of an oppressed people:

> And sensual sleep dreams subtly underground . . .

By replacing the stage Irishman with a cinematic Irishman, Kavanagh not merely freed himself from comic convention, static, indoor presentation, and theatrical propriety; more importantly, for his purposes, he shifted the emphasis from dramatic dialogue to dumb show, found a way of portraying muteness and repression. Unlike the stage-Irishman, the cinematic Irishman does not have to talk entertainingly to earn his literary keep. He need hardly speak aloud at all. Exhausted and oppressed by fourteen-hour days of drudgery, he need only mutter a few clichés from the betting shop, pub or card game, by way of social intercourse:

> 'A treble, full multiple odds . . . That's flat porter
>   . . .'

or

> 'Cut for trump'.

Maguire is silent throughout most of *The Great Hunger*. The only subject on which he waxes even a little eloquent, is work. On this topic he sometimes manages two or three consecutive lines and once even rises to eleven:

> 'Move forward the basket and balance it steady
> In this hollow. Pull down the shafts of that cart, Joe,
> And straddle the horse' Maguire calls.
> 'The wind's over Brannagan's, now that means rain.
> Graip up some withered stalks and see that no potato falls
> Over the tail-board going down the ruckety pass—
> And *that's* a job we'll have to do in December,
> Gravel it and build a kerb on the bog-side. Is that
>   Cassidy's ass

Out in my clover? Curse o' God—
Where is that dog?
Never where he's wanted' . . .

After this Maguire 'grunts and spits' and lapses into his customary incommunicativeness. This is the realist speech of rural Ireland as Kavanagh heard it, neither imaginatively lyrical nor rumbustiously wordy, the terse practical language of a culture obsessed by a work ethic and by economy, control and constraint. Maguire's is the voice of a man 'bounded by the hedges of [his] little farm', the peasant proprietor, preoccupied by the job in hand or the job to follow, vigilant about his crops, angered by wastefulness or neighbourly exploitation, moved to utterance by the necessity to issue orders and protect what he owns.

Speech is never, where Maguire is concerned, a vehicle for communicating private hopes, disappointments, fears and anxieties. These remain repressed, unvoiced. It is the narrator who makes us privy to the frustrations and fantasies that trouble his consciousness. In public Maguire conceals his worries and his lusts, masks the desires he cannot master, learns to adopt a guise of 'respectability and righteousness'. With supreme narrative irony he is portrayed in 'an old judge's pose' immediately after he has decided to substitute masturbation for the groping of schoolgirls, a secret 'crime'

The law's long arm could not serve with 'time'.

The Great Hunger's rural community is scarce with words because what matters most cannot be spoken. Taciturnity is inseparable from repression. To venture beyond the limits of local cliché, of communal passwords, would be an act of self-identification or self-discovery, and self-denial is their established code: 'No' is 'in every sentence of their story'. For all its devotion to 'pq' the Abbey could not enact what Kavanagh envisaged as the tragedy of rural Ireland, because dialogue was essentially false to the close-mouthed, suppressed suffering he wished to see articulated. Silence was for him the Irish countryman's most personal speech.

Ireland's language crisis was not, for Kavanagh, as for so many of his contemporaries, the seemingly inexorable disappearance of Gaelic; it was the absence of any real verbal communication. So great was the divergence between the official, imprimatured version of Irish conduct and the impermissible, instinctual impulse towards extra-marital sexuality or maternity in a land of late marriages that a whole countryside was quietly dying. Rural Ireland had become a place of full bellies and empty wombs. In *The Great Hunger* even the female body-language of loosed buttons and 'skirts lifted sensationally up' is a one-sided dialogue that elicits no answering male sign. The capitalised, religiously inhibiting word, 'Sin', intervenes between

sexual invitation and response. Kavanagh's Ireland is silent as a graveyard; its people are censored into vegetal muteness; their deepest instincts lie buried:

The tongue in [their] mouth is the root of a yew.

His potato-picking epic sets out to unearth a different hidden Ireland than nationalist cultural historians like Daniel Corkery wished to reveal. The hugely disproportionate ratio of commentary to speech in *The Great Hunger* may sometimes make the narrative appear overdetermined, yet it is also its most powerful medium of condemnation. These people require a narrator; they are incapable of even beginning to tell their own story. They need an interpreter who understands the sign-language of the deaf and dumb.

The narrator of *The Great Hunger* is acutely aware of the undone vast, all the unscripted lives whose misery will never be chronicled. The life-in-death of Patrick Maguire to which he witnesses is only one among the numerous unwritten biographies of countrymen and women; his uneventful drama is representative of a tragedy being mutely re-enacted in 'every corner of this land'. Not even the full story of Maguire's silent suffering can be told; there is much that is irretrievable, illegible:

Nobody will ever know how much tortured poetry the
  pulled weeds on the ridge wrote
Before they withered in the July sun,
Nobody will ever read the wild, sprawling, scrawling
  mad woman's signature,
The hysteria and the boredom of the enclosed nun of
  his thought.
Like the afterbirth of a cow stretched on a branch in
  the wind
Life dried in the veins of these women and men . . .

Here 'the pulled weeds on the ridge' suggest marginalisation, unwanted fertility, the destruction of what is alive but unloved. Self-identification and loss of sexual control both signify lunacy. The mad-woman-in-the-attic image modulates into the religious image of the enclosed nun, with its connotations of a secret life hidden behind defensive walls, vowed to silence and to celibacy, frustrated yet self-prevented from participation in human intercourse, an entombment exalted by country Catholicism:

Religion's walls expand to the push of nature.
  Morality yields
To sense—but not in little tillage fields . . .

Repressed within the subconsciousness of the Irish rural male is the image of his female counterpart (mad woman, nun) whose human fulfilment he denies, a secret knowledge of the torments he is inflicting on her in the process of torturing himself. *The Great Hunger* is populated with neglected, uncourted women: Eileen

Farrelly, the girl in the Yellow Meadow, Agnes, Kitty and Molly, Barney Meegan's daughter, Kate, who minds the kitchen fire while the men play cards; girls laughing like 'fillies in season', sitting 'stretch-legged and lingering staring', praying for 'health and wealth and love', or running 'wild' dreaming 'of a child'. Their fate is embodied in Maguire's own sister, Mary Anne, who endures the 'purgatory of middle-aged virginity', turns into an embittered spinster, spitting 'poison at . . . children' and ends her days, tight-legged, tight-lipped and frizzled up 'like the wick of an oil-less lamp', an unwise biblical virgin relocated in Donaghmoyne. Behind these women stands the Catholic icon of the Blessed Virgin, 'Queen of Heaven, the ocean's star', symbolising the Church's ideal of chastity, an ideal that has contributed to Maguire's sexual inhibition:

> Which of these men
> Loved the light and the queen
> Too long virgin?

The cult of the virgin queen may well be indistinguishable from worship of the 'hungry fiend'. Today, the Irish Constitution champions the rights of the unborn. In Kavanagh's terrible prophetic vision the born in rural Ireland are reduced from persons to animal 'afterbirths', their lives stretched out in the fields, disregarded, until they dry up and wither silently away.

'A man is what is written on the label', but what if he cannot communicate, or what if the 'passing world' refuses to 'look closer' and decipher his illiterate scrawl? In *The Great Hunger* Kavanagh takes on the literary responsibility he had envisaged in **'Peasant'**, to articulate the 'hoarse cry' of his people, to represent those who

> Have never scratched in any kind of hand
> On any wall . . .

In this poem we hear the muffled language of a submerged, suppressed race:

> Their voices through the darkness sound like voices
>   from a cave,
> A dull thudding far away, futile, feeble, far away . . .

We read the 'left-handed' message they wish to write on the page, a more sinister text than the received version of pastoral.

The Great Hunger exposes a nationwide conspiracy of lies, secrecy and silence: a false paradisal perception of Irish country life sponsored by post-colonial chauvinism and national economic expediency, and enforced by a combination of religious precept and a cautious, thrifty, small-farm ethos. What this angry poem demonstrates is that the cover-up connived at by state, church, literary convention and peasant morality is

tantamount, not just to the burial of a problem, but to the burial of a race. The solution to Maguire's puzzlement over his distorted, misshapen, paralysed existence:

> Who bent the coin of my destiny
> That it stuck in the slot?

is written into the title and central symbolism of the poem. Kavanagh's rural Ireland is caught in a timewarp, still traumatised by the economic shock of the Famine. As he wrote, neutral Ireland was isolated from world history, psychologically stagnant, frozen 'for want of Europe', undergoing a self-inflicted genocide. Kavanagh had a lifelong dislike of journalistic notions of the important, so it is not surprising that he bypassed the 'headlines of war' to focus on life in a backward Irish village. He could not have known about the concentration camps yet if he had, on the evidence of his later 'Epic', he would still have written as he did, recognising that a people can be suffocated to death in other ways than in the gas chamber.

The Great Hunger bypasses official Irish national history, even more blatantly than European war, which at least gets a mention in the pub sequence. The rise and fall of Parnell, the 1916 Rising, the Treaty, the Civil War, all would have occurred in the lifetime of a character who was sixty-five some time before 1941. However, Maguire's life goes onward the same though dynasties pass. Ageing is presented as a prolongation of personal misery, a repetition of personal despair, not as a device for chronicling nationally important events. In the Ireland of 1941 social history still tended to be marginalised by political history and heroic biography. What Kavanagh is inventing is an Irish social history in the guise of a social critique, recording the way common country people lived in the 'unwritten spaces between the lines' of orthodox history books, bringing to his documentation the persuasiveness of the prophetic historian.

At the conclusion of *The Great Hunger* the camera pans from the lone figure of the aged Maguire to the horizons of Ireland:

> He stands in the doorway of his house
> A ragged sculpture of the wind
> October creaks the rotted mattress
> The bedposts fall. No hope. No. No lust.
> The hungry fiend
> Screams the apocalypse of clay
> In every corner of this land.

Here Maguire stands freeze-framed, more image than man, a silent icon shaped by adverse weather. His raggedness recalls his scarecrow attitude at the beginning of the poem, though this soul will not clap its hands and louder sing for every tatter in its mortal dress. Instead part VIII's inconsequential song has ceased;

part I's October symphony plays a different, though equally ironic, sexual tune. Lust's disappearance is equated, through apposition, with hopelessness. The hunger of the title is now personified as an anti-Christ; the farmer's field has been metamorphosed into a fiend. A poem that began with a perverse parody of divine revelation concludes with the annunciation of an anti-Logos. Word disintegrates into a wordless scream. This final scream echoes the scream of Maguire's unborn children and of the excited girls 'in season' in part I, the 'hysteria' of the unmated woman of Maguire's fantasy in part IX, but it is also the cry of the victims of Ireland's twentieth-century famine. It is the voice of the oppressed and repressed from every country parish, clamouring to be heard and heeded, and resonating beyond the poem into *après-texte* Ireland: the terrible primal protest of a whole people being buried alive, before the clay finally smothers them.

In *The Great Hunger* the people's need has created a voice. Its narrative gives utterance to inarticulate peasant Ireland, as if the very stones were crying out, speaking the unspoken and unspeakable, defying the taboo that keeps desperation quiet, unsaying the pastoral platitudes, gainsaying the literary myths of the noble savage and the prelapsarian peasant. The 'speechless muse' has found a language.

If *The Great Hunger* aimed at changing the fanciful establishment view of rural Ireland as a primitivist Eden, it was not immediately successful. Almost a year after its publication de Valera made his notorious St Patrick's Day broadcast to the Irish people in which he communicated his political fantasy of small-farm Ireland:

> That Ireland which we dreamed of would be the home of a people who valued material wealth only as a basis of right living, of a people who were satisfied with frugal comfort and devoted their leisure to the things of the spirit; a land whose countryside would be bright with cosy homesteads, whose fields and villages would be joyous with sounds of industry, the romping of sturdy children, the contests of athletic youths, the laughter of comely maidens; whose firesides would be the forums of the wisdom of serene old age.[12]

De Valera's vision of small-farm Ireland is indeed such stuff as politicians' and poets' dreams were made on before the advent of *The Great Hunger.* How anachronistically hollow his oratory sounds by contrast with the bleak honesty of Kavanagh's poem. One of *The Great Hunger*'s claims to the status of major poem, as the cultural historian, Terence Brown, has pointed out, is its antenna-like sensitivity to 'the shifts of consciousness that determine a people's future'.[13]

Had Kavanagh intended to broadcast to the nation would he have been content to publish his poem in a semi-private edition and not reprint it until 1947?

However, it was its social concern that led him to repudiate *The Great Hunger* in his last years. He condemned it for its preoccupation with 'the woes of the poor' which prevented it from achieving 'the nobility and repose of poetry'. It was, he declared, a 'tragedy' and 'Tragedy is underdeveloped Comedy, not fully born.' Such a definition of the tragic aesthetic is undoubtedly debatable. What is certain is that his dismissal of *The Great Hunger* as tragedy has some validity within the context of his own poetics where comedy represents a detached, disengaged art, and tragedy, as its aesthetic contrary, represents an engaged, committed art. That *The Great Hunger* was 'visible to policemen', the older poet considered, betrayed its 'kinetic vulgarity'. It had the obviousness of a poem addressed to a mass audience; whereas 'a true poet', as opposed to a rhetorician, 'is selfish and implacable', content to state 'the position' and 'not care whether his words change anything or not'.[14]

This is not merely a sensational recantation of an early masterpiece; it is a criticism that focuses unerringly on the poem's central weakness, its over-determined narrative. It is, indeed, the case that *The Great Hunger* is at its least persuasive when it is at its most audience-conscious, when its designs on the reader are too palpable; specifically, when the role of the narrator upstages that of the chief protagonist. A conflict between rhetoric and drama is, however, inherent in the nature of the poem.

The Great Hunger is formally problematic when the control exercised by its ubiquitous and dictatorial narrator is too obtrusive. Sometimes this failure is one of tone as in the overly pedagogic approach in the first paragraph, 'is there anything we can prove' or the patronising, 'He thinks . . . but we know better', later in part I. Sometimes the narrator is unduly reflexive as when, conscious that he is taking poetry into a new terrain, he invites Imagination to accompany him in the opening and closing parts of the poem. Sometimes he abandons exemplary fiction for a more direct rhetorical engagement with his reader as in his appeal for empathy in part XI or his ironic attack on primitivism in part XIII. His hortatory stance in part XI:

> Let us kneel where he kneels
> And feel what he feels . . .

might be attributed to a lack of confidence in his own fictional powers of evocation, a failure to see that the pity is in the poetry already. One might argue that *The Great Hunger* is weakened by Kavanagh's failure to contain his new anti-Romantic and anti-Revivalist polemic within the confines of his fiction. When Maguire 'grunts and spits / Through a clay-wattled moustache' the reader detects a mischievous gibe at idyllic life on Innisfree. However, the satiric representation of primitivism in such lines as

> *There* is the source from which all cultures rise,
> And all religions,
> *There* is the pool in which the poet dips
> And the musician.
> Without the peasant base civilisation must die,
> Unless the clay is in the mouth the singer's singing is
>   useless.
> The travellers touch the roots of the grass and feel
>   renewed
> When they grasp the steering wheels again . . .

does not stop short at sneering at tourists and trippers and debunking a Revivalist ideology, triumphally proclaimed by Yeats:

> John Synge, I and Augusta Gregory, thought
> All that we did, all that we said or sang
> Must come from contact with the soil, from that
> Contact everything Antaeus-like grew strong . . .

More fundamentally, it disposes of a literary myth of the importance of peasantry which had flourished in English poetry since Wordsworth published the preface to the *Lyrical Ballads*. Nevertheless, such a frontal rhetorical assault was unnecessary because Kavanagh had by then almost completed the alternative fiction that demythologises peasantry, had demonstrated that having 'roots in the soil' is uncomfortably close to vegetable status.

Unfortunately, the rhetorical defects of *The Great Hunger* are almost inseparable from its virtues. It is primarily a dogmatic poem; its fiction is not autotelic and is only a means to its didactic end. By dehyphenating his customary role of poet-farmer and distributing it between two characters Kavanagh created a non-autobiographical poet figure, a lay narrator with no function other than that of commentator. The authoritativeness of this narrative voice is due, in large measure, to the fact that it is disembodied, rhetorical rather than dramatic. It does not provide a partial or limited view such as that of the cattle drovers in **'Shancoduff'**; it presents a reliable, responsible overview. One of the principal functions assigned to the narrator is to compensate for the myopia or partial sightedness of the poem's fictional characters by the clarity and comprehensiveness of his own religious vision. He supplies a dimension absent from, or usually concealed from view, in the poem's fictional world, a visionary criterion by which this world can be judged and found wanting. Maguire is perturbed by his inability to arrive at a mathematical religious certitude, a 'certain standard, measured and known'. The narrator enjoys just such certitude since he is a religious prophet, representing God's viewpoint: registering divine anger and amusement, pronouncing divine judgment, promising divine retribution. The poet who had loitered palely around the altar in his early verse has become a theologian and mounted the pulpit. To take away the 'messianic compulsion'[15] that Kavanagh later complained of is to

diminish the poem. Message and medium, vision and rhetoric, are inseparable in *The Great Hunger*.

The emotional instability of the narrator's response, which varies between anger, irony, amusement and compassion, may be identified with the complexity of Kavanagh's own emotional attitude to life in Inniskeen, or, to give him greater credit, with his dramatisation of such an attitude. It is an attitude aphoristically summed up in a phrase he quotes from Chesterton, to 'love the city enough to set fire to it'.[16]

Kavanagh did love the country enough to burn it. A love almost indistinguishable from hatred and a destructiveness bred of love: this is the complex of passions to which Maguire's drama is essential, yet subsidiary. Donaghmoyne is but a combustible to Kavanagh's fiery prophetic vision. *The Great Hunger* is a marriage of heaven and hell.

Notes

1. Canon Bernard Maguire, ('Salamanca Barney'), Rector of the Irish College, Salamanca, 1898-1907; Parish Priest of Inniskeen; 1915-48.

2. Kavanagh's cinematic technique was first noticed by James Plunkett in a pioneering article on *The Great Hunger*, 'The Pulled Weeds on the Ridge', *The Bell*, March 1952. Kavanagh became film critic for *The Standard* in 1946.

3. This image, which appears in the Cuala Press edition only, explains the part played by the personified Hope in later versions of the poem.

4. 'A Strange Irish Poet', *The Irish Times*, 30 and 31 March 1945.

5. Kavanagh was visited by two Gardaí Siochana in connection with the January 1942 number of *Horizon*, though the interview appears to have been conducted in a friendly manner. Some copies of this number of the journal were seized but, while there appears to be no consensus as to why the Irish authorities took exception to it, it is generally agreed that 'The Old Peasant', as the excerpt from *The Great Hunger* was entitled, was not the reason.

6. See Terence Brown, *Ireland, A Social and Cultural History, 1922-1985*, Fontana, London 1986, 21.

7. 'From Monaghan to the Grand Canal', *Studies*, spring 1959.

8. 'Liberators', *The Irish Times*, 15 August 1942.

9. Kavanagh later quoted these lines from Auden's 1935 poem, 'To a Writer on his Birthday' in 'Auden and the Creative Mind', *Envoy*, June 1951.

10. 'Apronful' in the Cuala Press and *A Soul for Sale* versions. 'Armful', introduced in *Collected Poems* and *Complete Poems,* does not make sense and would seem to be a misprint.

11. *The Irish Press,* 18 March 1943.

12. ibid.

13. Brown, op cit, 187.

14. 'Author's Note', *Collected Poems.*

15. ibid.

16. *November Haggard,* Peter Kavanagh ed, New York 1977, 59.

Primary Sources

The Green Fool, Michael Joseph, London 1938.

The Great Hunger, Cuala Press, Dublin 1942.

A Soul for Sale, Macmillan, London 1947.

Tarry Flynn, Pilot Press, London 1948.

Self-Portrait, Dolmen Press, Dublin 1964.

November Haggard, Uncollected Prose and Verse of Patrick Kavanagh, selected, arranged and edited by Peter Kavanagh, Peter Kavanagh Hand Press, New York 1971.

Patrick Kavanagh, The Complete Poems, collected, arranged and edited by Peter Kavanagh, Peter Kavanagh Hand Press, New York 1972.

By Night Unstarred, An Autobiographical Novel, edited by Peter Kavanagh, Goldsmith Press, The Curragh, Ireland 1977.

Declan Kiberd (essay date summer 1995)

SOURCE: Kiberd, Declan. "Underdeveloped Comedy: Patrick Kavanagh." *Southern Review* 31, no. 3 (summer 1995): 714-25.

[*In the following essay, Kiberd draws parallels between Kavanagh and Samuel Beckett as practitioners of "minor literature" as the term is defined by French critical theorists Gilles Deleuze and Felix Guattari.*]

The writer of a minor literature. according to Gilles Deleuze and Felix Guattari, "feeds himself on abstinence" and tears out of language "all the qualities of underdevelopment that it has tried to hide." He tries to "make it cry with an extremely sober and rigorous cry." What these critics are defining is a place made sumptuous by destitution, in which writers "oppose the op-pressed quality of a language to its oppressive quality" in the attempt to locate those points of underdevelopment at which a new kind of art becomes possible.

In these terms Samuel Beckett must stand as the pre-eminent resistance writer, as one who has always hated the languages of masters and who has tried to remain a stranger within his own language. First he sought impoverishment by writing in learner's French as an escape from the baroque excesses of the Anglo-Irish tradition, in which wit and wordplay were ritually expected by English readers of Irish users of their language. In French, Beckett could write with the myopic literalism of a careful student of a second language. For an Irish author to embrace French in this way was an act of linguistic self-denial.

Decades later, having achieved fame as a brilliant writer of that language, Beckett again rejected mastery, returning in works like *Company to English,* lest his "stain upon the silence" seem made too easily. In that late period his works grew shorter, as if their maker was a kind of literary anorexic, straining for "the blessedness of absence," for the point at which underdevelopment shades into silence. "This is becoming really insignificant," laments a character in *Waiting for Godot,* only to be told, "Not enough." The less Beckett had to say, the better he said it; the slimmer his texts became, the weightier the analyses they seemed to generate.

For most of his life Beckett knew failure as others know the air they breathe, so when recognition and success came, they could not deflect him from his mission: he had breathed "vivifying" defeat too long to want to abandon it now. To be an artist was to fail, but to give that failure a form; and so Beckett, more than any other, deserved the description of one who gave a voice to the voiceless. Whereas Joyce had chosen enrichment, Beckett stripped everything down and took everything out. In a rare interview he offered Israel Shenker a piercingly lucid self-estimate:

> The kind of work I do is one in which I'm not master of my material. The more Joyce knew the more he could. I'm working with impotence, ignorance. I don't think ignorance has been exploited in the past. There seems to be a kind of aesthetic axiom that expression is achievement—must be an achievement. My little exploration is that whole zone of being that has always been set aside by artists as something unusable—as something by definition incompatible with art.

The helplessness of one who lives where there is nothing to express, nothing with which to express, along with the obligation to express, seems a feasible description of the post-colonial artist. Reared in a cultural vacuum, fatigued by the representational naivete of realist artists of the colonial power, and twitching with the urge to leave some trace behind, he can feed only on abstinence.

Patrick Kavanagh, though Beckett's contemporary, is seldom seen in relation to him, perhaps because their backgrounds, talents, and destinies were so very different; and yet they had a great deal in common, not least an obsession with the notion of expressive underdevelopment. Kavanagh embarked on a very Beckettian study of the mind of God, without the assistance of Christian mythology. This mythology had sustained him in youth, until he decided it was just a beautiful fairy-story:

> No System, no Plan,
> Yeatsian invention
> No all-over
> Organisational prover.
> Let words laugh
> And people be stimulated by our stuff.
> . . . . .
> Beckett's garbage-can
> Contains all our man
> Who without fright on his face
> Dominates the place
> And makes all feel
> That all is well.
>
> **("Mermaid Tavern")**

The Plan is a Yeatsian invention, parodied by System with a capital S; but against this false literary project Kavanagh pits the author of *Endgame*. The reason there is no fright, despite the extreme situation, is that Beckett has found the release of laughter. He has taken failure, made it his subject, and laughed at it, just as Kavanagh could mock his own in the caustic **"If Ever You Go to Dublin Town"**:

> I saw his name with a hundred others
> In a book in the library,
> It said he had never fully achieved
> His potentiality.
> O he was slothful,
> Fol dol the di do,
> He was slothful
> I tell you.

That might be Belacqua, or Murphy, or Malone, agreeing with Beckett and ram van Velde that to be an artist is to fail as nobody else has failed—a point made even more poignantly in Kavanagh's self-mockingly titled **"Portrait of the Artist"**: "A man of talent who lacked the little more / That makes the difference / Between success and failure." To one who saw Irish society as mere "pastiche" with no "overall purpose," Beckett's remedy, to "put despair and futility on the stage for us to laugh at them," was the only option. This strategy Kavanagh contrasted with that of "academic writers ready to offer a large illuminating symbol . . . as if society were a solid, unified Victorian lie." He thereby endorsed Beckett's 1934 essay on Irish poetry, which praised modernists and denigrated well-upholstered antiquarians. Kavanagh also followed Beckett in asserting that the old-world certainties of Gaelic heroes had

interest for "none but the academic." The answer to the sense of doom was not to avoid tears, but to revert to laughter after they had dried. Otherwise a people would know only emotional and spiritual underdevelopment: for, as Kavanagh put it in his Author's Note in the ***Collected Poems,*** "Tragedy is underdeveloped Comedy, not fully born."

It was just such an underdevelopment that Kavanagh explored in ***The Great Hunger.*** The world of subsistence farming he evokes in this long poem of 1942 shows us lowercase tragedy, according to Kavanagh, not the uppercase kind that "is underdeveloped Comedy." It is a place of dire underdevelopment—economic, religious, and intellectual; and the poem is a fierce anti-pastoral, which won the admiration of Cyril Connolly, Stephen Spender, and I. W. Auden for its cultivated, banal repetitions and its slack line-endings. The title seems to promise a study of heroic nineteenth-century peasants, but the text delivers a nihilistic account of unheroic farmers in the twentieth. All this is framed sarcastically in the cinematic techniques of a curious First World anatomizing the Third.

The camera pans in on the potato-gatherers at the start, creating a sort of anti-travelogue: "If we watch them an hour is there anything we can prove / Of life as it is broken-backed over the Book / Of Death?"—but the voice grows increasingly impatient and caustic in its parody of pastoralism, for this is a voice of one who has read not only the rural landscape but William Empson too:

> The world looks on
> And talks of the peasant:
> The peasant has no worries;
> In his little lyrical fields
> He ploughs and sows;
> He eats fresh food,
> He loves fresh women,
> He is his own master
> As it was in the Beginning
> The simpleness of peasant life.
> The birds that sing for him are eternal choirs,
> Everywhere he walks there are flowers.
> His heart is pure,
> His mind is clear,
> He can talk to God as Moses and Isaiah talked—
> The peasant who is only one remove from the beasts
>   he drives.
> The travellers stop their cars to gape over the green
>   bank into his fields:—
> There is the source from which all cultures rise,
> And all religions,
> There is the pool in which the poet dips
> And the musician.
> Without the peasant base civilisation must die,
> Unless the clay is in the mouth the singer's singing is
>   useless.
> The travellers touch the roots of the grass and feel
>   renewed
> When they grasp the steering wheels again.

The subject, as in Beckett, is how one dies a little every day; and the attempt in each section is to find a tense adequate to the plight of one whose life has ended but is not yet over. The world of nature blooms and reproduces while Paddy Maguire looks impotently on, denied even the dubious pleasure of a climactic ending:

> No crash,
> No drama.
> That was how his life happened.
> No mad hooves galloping in the sky.
> But the weak, washy way of true tragedy—
> A sick horse nosing around the meadow for a clean
>   place to die.

That final line is expanded to a slack endlessness, and the passage asserts what Beckett adumbrated: the impossibility of old-fashioned tragedy, with its moment of clarification, and its redefinition as a matter of everyday numbness. The plight of Paddy Maguire is at once absurd and Christian, absurd because it reflects the unexamined Christianity of a rural Ireland whose mothers tell their sons, "Now go to Mass and pray and confess your sins / And you'll have all the luck."

The result is a man who never achieves even a rudimentary consciousness, a peasant in Kavanagh's anti-revivalist definition of the species: "Although the literal idea of the peasant is of a farm-labouring person, in fact a peasant is all that mass of mankind which lives below a certain level of consciousness. They live in the dark cave of the unconscious and they scream when they see the light." That is a description of a Joycean rather than a Yeatsian peasant, and a knowing throwback to the bare-breasted woman who beckoned across a half-door to the passing youth in *A Portrait of the Artist as a Young Man,* and who seemed to Stephen "a type of her race and of his own, a batlike soul waking to the consciousness of itself in darkness and secrecy and loneliness." Like those revivalist poets denounced by Beckett, Maguire never awakes to self-perception.

The Great Hunger is a reworking of Beckett's 1934 thesis: that the failure of the revivalists to explore self was the inevitable consequence of their resort for subject-matter to an uncritical celebration of peasant life. Kavanagh eventually concluded that his involvement with the theme was so deep that he too had fallen into the trap of excessive care. "Not caring is really a sense of values and feeling of confidence," he concluded. "A man who cares is not the master." Instead, he is the victim of the tragedy that is underdevelopment and of the underdevelopment that is Tragedy.

The birth-pangs of a developed comedy became, after ***The Great Hunger,*** Kavanagh's abiding theme. In Joyce's equation of the artist with the omnipotent God, high above his creation, paring his fingernails, Kavanagh found his desired wisdom. Kavanagh remained confident that the existence of a benevolent deity permitted man to take himself less seriously: once God existed, if only as a cosmic force, the idea of man became comical. Thus was born the philosophy of "not caring." Excessive solemnity became, within this new code, a form of blasphemy, or at least a vulgar sentimentality (since it was sentimental to invest things with more significance than God gave them).

The remoteness that is the necessary condition for such laughter allows the poet to question his own ridiculous pretensions to power or majesty. In the poems Kavanagh seldom emulates Beckett in making direct statements that mock the act of writing, but such declarations come frequently in the prose: "Stupid poets think that by taking subjects of public importance it will help their work to survive. There is nothing as dead and damned as an important thing." Within the poetry these assaults are evident in a rejection of the portentous or the significant. Accepting that his duty is not to theorize but to record, Kavanagh rejects the temptation to allegory, endorsing Beckett's aphorism "No symbols where none intended."

Above all, Kavanagh deflected solemnity by his delight in deliberate technical risk, by his attempt to write a looser and more prosaic type of line that steadfastly resisted the seductions of Irish rhetoric. Beckett called this the attempt to write without style; Kavanagh explained the aspiration more colourfully, as the urge "to play a true note on a dead slack string." Where Joyce had tried to make prose more poetic, Kavanagh would attempt to render poetry more prosaic. He believed that the delight of Irish talk lay not in exotic Synge-song, but in ordinariness. So in his later poems he ran the risk of banality, even cliche: absurdism and not caring became both his subject and his technique:

"Lines Written on a Seat on the Grand Canal, Dublin, Erected to the Memory of Mrs Dermot O'Brien"

> O commemorate me where there is water,
> Canal water preferably, so stilly
> Greeny at the heart of summer. Brother
> Commemorate me thus beautifully.
> Where by a lock Niagariously roars
> The falls for those who sit in the tremendous silence
> Of mid-July. No one will speak in prose
> Who finds his way to these Parnassian islands.
> A swan goes by head low with many apologies,
> Fantastic light looks through the eyes of bridges—
> And look! a barge comes bringing from Athy
> And other far-flung towns mythologies.
> O commemorate me with no hero-courageous
> Tomb—just a canal-bank seat for the passer-by.

One could point to a dozen risks knowingly taken here, the most obvious being that a veteran of the "Baggot Street Gallop" should ask for commemoration where there is water. Technically, one notes the use of repetition, as of a man forming and reforming in leisurely fashion the elements of a sentence—"water . . . canal water, preferably"—until he gets it right. (This is the characteristic mannerism of Beckett's prose in the trilogy.) The use of the Dublinese -y conveys a sense that the adjective found is an approximation, not a true hit. The effect of one line reeling into the next, without end-stopping, is compounded in the last couplet by the use of a hyphenated word at the moment of transition, as if the poem were the work of a slightly tipsy man. "Hero-courageous" is a relaxed, childlike composite, yet it topples into "tomb"; and the off-key ending clinches the effect of poetic indifference to audience response: "just" reduces the claims made for a poet's immortality, and the sentence collapses into silence on its last, awkward word, "passer-by."

Darcy O'Brien has pointed to Kavanagh's eschewing of conventional rhyme (water/brother, roars/prose, bridges/courageous, silence/islands) in a poem that wreaks havoc with the sonnet, the strictest and most austere of forms. The deflation of Yeatsian intensities is completed with that swan, shy instead of superb, and the use of Athy to mock that titular abstraction "mythologies."

"Lines Written on a Seat on the Grand Canal" was, literally and metaphorically, a watershed in Kavanagh's life, a moment when he discovered that "my purpose was to have no purpose." So the later Kavanagh could follow Beckett in admitting the futility of all knowledge: "Making the statement is enough-there are no answers / To any real question. . . ." Beckett's Molloy had concluded that the desire to know is a pernicious habit that can be redeemed only by concrete experience of physical objects. This is also Kavanagh's conclusion: sometime in the 1950s he decided that great poetry is simply an inventory of objects known and loved. So he follows Beckett's example and places his persona in a hospital's terminal ward, then sets out on his inventory of kitsch:

> A year ago I fell in love with the functional ward
> Of a chest hospital: square cubicles in a row
> Plain concrete, wash basins—an art lover's woe,
> Not counting how the fellow in the next bed snored.
> . . . . .
> This is what love does to things: the Rialto Bridge,
> The main gate that was bent by a heavy lorry,
> The seat at the back of a shed that was a suntrap.
> Naming these things is the love-act and its pledge;
> For we must record love's mystery without claptrap,
> Snatch out of time the passionate transitory.
>
> **("The Hospital")**

In this situation, the poet is namer rather than beloved, and his devotion to objects gives him back a sense of his reality.

The great difference between Kavanagh and Beckett—apart from the obvious one between a talent and a genius—lies in their attitudes to God. Both assert the limits of human knowledge, reject pat symbolic systems, and warn of the dangers of logic and the vital necessity of mystery. "If we go on in a logical way we come to cage bars," says Kavanagh: "We must not ask the ultimate question. 'Why?' is God." This is rather like the absurdist's conviction that events simply happen and that only a fool seeks causes. A secular absurdist like Beckett is by no means sure God is there, but he continues to study and to curse Him anyway. For Kavanagh the value of God as an idea arises from the fact that arguments about Him cannot be proven. Beckett is suspicious about the "leap of faith," but he too yearns for an inscrutable to adore, and so his Molloy seeks and finds mystery in the beautiful, incomprehensible patterns traced by dancing bees. Moran says with rapture: "Here is something I can study all my life and never understand." That is precisely what Kavanagh concludes about the mind of God:

> We have tested and tasted too much, lover—
> Through a chink too wide there comes in no wonder.
> . . . . .
> Won't we be rich, my love and I, and please
> God we shall not ask for reason's payment,
> The why of heart-breaking strangeness in dreeping
>   hedges
> Nor analyse God's breath in common statement.

Such analysis would anyway have proved impossible to a poet who sought to ravish the ineffable without the assistance of the available mythologies. For the Christian myth, Yeats had substituted A Vision, preferring to create his own system rather than be enslaved by another's. Kavanagh rejected even this option as a questionable luxury. He. chose to define himself without the props afforded by system, and he often paid an artistic price for that loneliness, in bad poems and half-realised themes. It was of him that Brendan Kennelly said: "[A] man without a mythology is a man confronting famine." But Kavanagh had the courage to make that attempt.

As a critic, Kavanagh has been underestimated and misunderstood. He had only contempt for the wilful cultivation of Irishness in writing: "Irishness is a form of anti-art," he wrote, "a way of posing as a poet without actually being one." He dubbed such pseudo-poets "buckleppers" and defined the bucklep as follows: ". . . an act performed by a man eager to display his merit and exuberance as a true Gael. He gallivants along some street in Dublin and suddenly he will leap into the air with a shout, causing his heels to strike hard against his buttock cheeks. This is buckleppin'." All of this was explained in a voice close to that of his friend, the Gaelic satirist Brian O'Nolan, but it was also the voice of Kavanagh's exemplar, Samuel Beckett, who in the 1934 essay had dismissed those poets who tried to reproduce Gaelic prosody in English as antiquarians in flight from self-awareness.

This was Kavanagh's view as well, detailed in his devastating essay on F. R. Higgins:

> Writing about F. R. Higgins is a problem—the problem of exploring a labyrinth that leads nowhere. There is also the problem of keeping oneself from accepting the fraudulent premises and invalid symbols established by the subject. The work of F. R. Higgins is based on an illusion—on a myth which he pretended to believe.
>
> The myth and illusion was "Ireland."
>
> One must try to get some things straight about the man: He was a Protestant.
>
> He most desperately wanted to be what mystically or poetically does not exist, an "Irishman."
>
> Nearly everything about Higgins would need to be put in inverted commas. All this was the essence of insincerity, for sincerity means giving all of oneself to one's work, being absolutely real. For all his pleasant verse Higgins was a dabbler.

Part of Higgins's factitiousness lay in his attempt to build up Dublin as a theme, a stratagem Kavanagh called "a gerrymandering of the constituencies of the soul." Higgins failed to realize that Dublin derived its literary glamour from Joyce, not Joyce from Dublin.

It is hard, of course, to separate anti-Protestantism from anti-pastoralism in Kavanagh's criticism, but it should be emphasised that he was never theologically anti-Protestant. He was merely opposed to the use of pastoral formulae by Protestant writers who were foolishly trying to compensate for a self-diagnosed lack of Irishness. When the editor who published the Higgins essay told Kavanagh it gave the impression that he thought a Protestant could not be an Irish writer and asked him to make it clear in a footnote that this was not the case, what Kavanagh produced in response was far more interesting than a mere correction of the misunderstanding:

> My immediate reaction would be: Who wants to be an Irish writer?
>
> A man is what he is, and if there is some mystical quality in the Nation or the race it will ooze through the skin. Many Protestants, doubting that their Irishism would ooze, have painted it on from the outside.
>
> National characteristics are superficial qualities and are not the stuff with which the poet deals.

Deep down, of course, Kavanagh did not believe in a national essence. On one famous occasion, he announced that while Daniel Corkery, Frank O'Connor, and company were cranking out their "Ireland" stuff, the real writers of contemporary Ireland were W. H. Auden and George Barker.

These analyses make complete sense only if removed from the constricting Irish context of the mid-century. Kavanagh was a genuinely post-colonial thinker and poet, one who had emptied his mind of the categories devised by colonialist and anti-colonialist alike. He was the first to expose the ways Irish revivalism was complicit with its putative enemy, sanitising slurs and reworking jaded categories—hence his charge that it was "a thoroughgoing English-bred lie." Given his rural origins, Kavanagh saw that what appeared to be essential traits of the Irish peasantry were to be found in most societies with little economic development and saw too that the notion of Irish essence was an ideological veil cast by a ruling class over its own self-interests. Why fetishise such a thing?

This analysis of revivalism was consistent with Fanon's account of the second phase of decolonisation, when intellectuals behave like foreign tourists in their own country, "going native" in patently excessive ways. Because he refused that role, Kavanagh remained as incomprehensible to most English critics as Fanon did to most French intellectuals. It was almost a point of pride to the man who was "never much considered by the English critics" that Joyce's *Portrait,* when it appeared in 1916, got no review in England. Neither Joyce nor Kavanagh had any truck with Irishness.

Kavanagh was alert to the danger that certain "radicals," in denouncing revivalist nationalism, might breathe new life into it by furthering the illusion that, three decades after "independence," it still counted for something. Of such people he savagely wrote: "They are not Lilliputian cranks as some outsiders scream; / They are the official liberal opposition and part of the regime." The problem such "liberals" could never face was the one Kavanagh confronted and solved: the fact that anti-nationalism is neither a political ideology nor a literary philosophy, but a neurotic reaction.

Kavanagh cited Sean O'Casey as a tell-tale instance of such neurosis and lamented his failure to transcend this fixation on Ireland: "O'Casey is loved in Ireland because, however he attacks, he always accepts the theme of Ireland. To deny Ireland as a spiritual entity leaves so many people floundering—without art." Kavanagh mischievously noted that the anticlericalism of many Irish Stalinists was much admired by the clerics themselves because it helped to persuade them that they were still important. Attacks on the Catholic Church had become almost de rigueur in a certain kind of play, a kind that posed a challenge to audiences keen to demonstrate how far they had travelled in terms of liberal sophistication in those early decades of independence. What Kavanagh wrote in 1914 of the contemporary Abbey Theatre (in The Bell) could have been repeated, without inaccuracy, for the next forty years:

> You have plays in which barbarous characters are set up so that audiences can feel superior. The audiences which only yesterday were humble folk in the small fields have taken over the function of the idiotic Ascendancy, and authors have turned up to invent a lower order that one can be superior about.
>
> Great liberality is permitted towards these mythical characters in the case of murder, infanticide, drunken-

ness and outrageous brawling. The new middle class audience of theatre and books is falling backwards in its effort to prove itself broad-minded. . . .

That new class was stuck fast, repudiating its earlier nationalism but refusing, lest it be construed as an admission that the native elites had some of the same weaknesses to be found elsewhere in the post-colonial world, to adopt the analysis that could have given meaning to that repudiation. Kavanagh was remorseless in his judgement of those weaknesses: but he was also one of the first artists in the English language to take up the theme of underdevelopment.

Thomas B. O'Grady (essay date December 1995)

SOURCE: O'Grady, Thomas B. "Poetics and Polemics: The Politics of Patrick Kavanagh's 'Spraying the Potatoes.'" *Colby Quarterly* 31, no. 4 (December 1995): 242-52.

[*In the following essay, O'Grady discusses Kavanagh's poem "Spraying the Potatoes" as a poetic response to the controversy engendered by his acerbic review of Maurice Walsh's novel* The Hill Is Mine.]

In many respects, **"Spraying the Potatoes,"** a relatively early lyric first collected in *A Soul for Sale* (1947), epitomizes both the thematic vision and the poetic technique of Patrick Kavanagh. Thematically, the poem obviously reflects Kavanagh's preoccupation with rural subject matter throughout his career. Focusing on a crucial (if rarely recorded) aspect of farm husbandry, the poem has a clear affinity with those other verses of Kavanagh's—early and late—which discover an essentially transcendent potential in the familiar seasonal labors of ploughing, harrowing, sowing, and harvesting which the poet had engaged in during his boyhood and young manhood in County Monaghan. Technically, **"Spraying the Potatoes"** reflects Kavanagh's generally casual attitude toward both prosodic and stylistic concerns which afflicts much of his poetry. Composed in quatrains of loose iambic tetrameter lines occasionally, and arbitrarily, extended to pentameter, the poem is characterized both by memorably vivid imagery— "The axle-roll of a rut-locked cart / Broke the burnt stick of noon in two"—and by artless and irrelevant diction: "We talked and our talk was a theme of kings, / A theme for strings." With similar inconsistency, it is distinguished both by Kavanagh's trademark attention to local detail in his identifying the potatoes as Kerr's Pinks and Arran Banners and by a distractingly abrupt shift in point of view, from the immediacy of the first-person perspective of the first seven stanzas to the detached omniscience of the third-person in the final stanza (*Complete Poems* 72-73).

Yet, while unto themselves those intrinsic qualities— thematic and technical—of **"Spraying the Potatoes"** help to locate the poem centrally in Kavanagh's *oeuvre,* their significance is even more resonant in light of the poem's provenance in the midst of one of the many controversies provoked by Kavanagh during his career as commentator and reviewer for various Dublin journals and magazines. Well-known for his cantankerousness in person, the poet proved equally contentious in his critical writings, subjecting to ruthless scrutiny both individuals and institutions in his frequently insightful—but sometimes merely inciting—articles and columns published over several decades in *The Irish Times, The Standard, The Bell, Envoy,* and many other publications (including, of course, *Kavanagh's Weekly,* a short-lived tabloid of cultural commentary and criticism founded and written almost exclusively by the poet and his brother Peter). From F. R. Higgins to Frank O'Connor, from *The Capuchin Annual* to the New Critics, from local Art Councils to continental painters, the targets of Kavanagh's more merciless offensives were themselves usually inoffensive by most reasonable standards, as reflected in several cases in dissenting responses printed in letters to the editor—or indeed as reflected in at least one instance in an editorial disclaimer accompanying Kavanagh's patently questionable diatribe.

Of all of the controversies associated with Kavanagh, however, that initiated by his review of Maurice Walsh's novel *The Hill is Mine* in July of 1940 may reveal most acutely the extent to which the poet, while never truly the "green fool" of his purported autobiography published in 1938, nonetheless continued to find in the rustic simplicity of his life "Ere Dublin taught him to be wise" (*Complete Poems* 20) a consolation—if not quite an antidote—for the pseudo-urbanity of the Irish metropolis that he had adopted as his home in the late 1930s. As Antoinette Quinn has observed of Kavanagh's relocation from Inniskeen to Dublin, "once he was at a physical remove from his home place he experienced a Romantic 'return in Departure' and 1939 to 1942 were four glorious years for his poetry. Now that he had abandoned his few paternal acres he was at last content to breathe his native air and to farm the land imaginatively in poem after poem" (88). In the case of **"Spraying the Potatoes"**—written, as the poet's brother annotates it, in "response to the controversy" created by Kavanagh's review of Walsh's novel (*Complete Poems* 393), and first published in *The Irish Times* one week after that review, on July 27, 1940—not only the immediacy of the evocation of rural experience but equally the very form and substance of the poem *qua* poem represent a major statement of Kavanagh's true "aesthetic." Subsequently compromising this aesthetic during the latter half of the 1940s and the first half of the '50s to indulge that antithetical impulse toward inelegant and vitriolic expression in his vindictive exposés of and harangues against the Dublin literary establishment, Kavanagh would muse in 1964: "Curious this, how I had started off with the right simplicity, indifferent to crude reason and then ploughed my way through complexities of anger, hatred and ill-will towards the faults of man, and came back to where I started" (*Self-Portrait* 26).

I

Curious, too, that Kavanagh's review of *The Hill is Mine* should have precipitated—or at least anticipated—those twisted furrows (as it were) of his middle years as poet. Not yet the literary and cinematic footnote that he would eventually become after the silver-screen adaptation in 1952 of his 1935 short story "The Quiet Man," Maurice Walsh was nonetheless an innocuously popular writer during his lifetime, and his tenth book is neither more nor less enduring than the twenty-odd other works of fiction that he published between 1926 and 1964. Set in the highlands of Scotland (a native of North Kerry, Walsh worked for several years as a Scottish customs and excise officer before settling in Stillorgan, Co. Dublin, and maintained a life-long affection for Scottish settings, for Scottish women—he married one—and for Scotch whiskey), *The Hill is Mine* actually bears a coincidental resemblance to "The Quiet Man" which, as a romantic corrective to the dogmatic—or dogged—realism of George Moore's "Home Sickness" (1903), represents an important variation on the theme of the "returned Yank." Recounting in colorful detail the initiation of a young American rancher into the ways and the wiles of the lords and the ladies—and even more the laddies—who inhabit the countryside around the small "croft" he has inherited from his grandmother, the novel pretends to little more than wholesome entertainment. Perhaps not surprisingly, the book was a best-seller in Dublin throughout July of 1940, and contemporary reviews were almost unanimously complimentary.

Indeed, Kavanagh's own review of *The Hill is Mine*, concluding with the judgment that the novel "may not appeal to literary readers, but it will delight all who enjoy a romantic story, told with great skill, and sometimes illuminated by a poet's vision," is ultimately—if not quite unequivocally—favorable.[1] Appreciating Walsh's ability to ground the "fantasy" of his narrative "upon the crags of reality" and admiring his charming "sense of humour," Kavanagh complains only that the novel suffers from an excess of "bonnie, boring Scotland" and from a lack of engaging moral ambiguity—"a slight flavour of real sin," as he puts it (*Irish Times*, July 20, 1940). As generous as it is judicious, this reading of *The Hill is Mine* should have proved exceptionable to none but the most ardent of Maurice Walsh's loyal readers—had Kavanagh for once refrained from using the occasion of a review to offer critical commentary not only on the book at hand but also on

other matters of less immediate relevance. But, as John Nemo has observed, Kavanagh displayed even in his earliest published criticism the inclination toward wide-ranging proclamations that was to characterize his critical writing throughout his career:

> Impulsive, egotistical and perpetually romantic, when he examined either life or literature he tended to communicate his creative intensity rather than detail his intellectual response. As a result, when he turned his energies to criticism he often over-reacted, declaring absolutes and making generalizations which satisfied his artistic passion but confused his critical position.
>
> ("The Green Knight" 283)

Typically enough, then, his review of Walsh's novel includes if not devastating broadsides then at least agitating asides directed at more or less innocent bystanders in what would escalate over the years into the poet's personal war against the forces of literary and cultural philistinism in Ireland.

Plausibly, Kavanagh may have intended to provoke more than mere thought in his readers by his casual dismissal of the "empty virtuosity" of Hopkins and Eliot and the later Yeats and Joyce and his unrestrained discrediting of "stupid, boring books, like *Gone With the Wind*." Probably, however, he could not have expected his irrelevant declaration that "The boy scout may be said to represent civilisation at its lowest"—an offhanded follow-up to his observation that Walsh's characters incline toward "the open-air boy scout type"—to act as the primary catalyst to an unusually prolonged and singularly profuse disputation among readers of *The Irish Times*. Responding to a letter to the editor signed "F. L. J." published on July 22nd which took exception to Kavanagh's "remarkable, and quite unnecessary opinions," one Oscar Love initiated on July 23rd an epistolary exchange which would continue, under the heading "Literary Criticism," for more than a fortnight, involving a full fifty letters composed by—ostensibly—almost forty different correspondents (*Irish Times*, July 22-August 7, 1940).[2] Seemingly perturbed by the arbitrariness of critical pronouncements, Love asserted that Kavanagh "made a slight error" in demeaning the boy scout:

> It would have been wiser to omit the word "scout." The boy represents civilisation at its lowest, and long may he remain so. Only the grown man develops and rejoices in the art of destruction.

Failing to detect the obviously intended irony of Love's statement in its chastening allusion to literary critics like Kavanagh, not only F. L. J. but also Harold C. Brown and Frank E. Prenton Jones responded on July 24th in righteous defense of the Boy Scout movement. Their letters in turn prompted a rebuttal by Love, followed the next day by counter-rebuttals by both F. L. J.

and Jones. "I prithee let this bedlamite orchestra play on," reader M. C. Ahern exhorted *The Irish Times* on July 26th, as if any circulation-conscious editor would even consider interrupting a debate of such apparently spontaneous combustibility.[3]

For the next week-and-a-half, in fact, the controversy generated by Kavanagh's review of *The Hill is Mine* produced a true polyphony of Dublin opinion: from Ewart Milne's apologia for his fellow poet in the face of "the gnats' nest" he had disturbed by his review to anonymous and pseudonymous comparisons of the Boy Scout movement and the Hitler-Jugend; from Dublin wit Niall Montgomery's expression of incredulity that the traditionally West Briton *Irish Times* should publish a comment even glancingly critical of Yeats to various correspondents' musings on the aptness of the sewer as a metaphor for belletristic ambition and accomplishment in Ireland. The remarkably disparate chorus of accents and attitudes notwithstanding, the cumulative effect of missives ranging in tone from the presumably earnest—a recommendation by R. H. S. on July 30th of Spinoza as "the greatest literary critic of all time"—to the certifiably inane—Judy Clifford's account on July 27th of her disappointing meeting with some Boy Scouts in Co. Wicklow—was, perhaps inevitably, a decided facetiousness. For in another literary footnote associated with Maurice Walsh, many of the more blusterous (or preposterous) responses to Kavanagh's review—including letters written backwards (to reflect the direction the discussion seemed to be moving) or in imitation of Joyce's recently published *Finnegans Wake*—evidently originated with just one writer: the already pseudonymous litterateur Flann O'Brien. Resurrecting the spirit of two lesser controversies that he had enlivened with his friend Niall Montgomery in *The Irish Times* in 1939 and earlier in 1940, O'Brien—or Brian O'Nolan as he was properly known—would shortly parlay the public interest in these mock debates into the regular column "Cruiskeen Lawn" published under the byline Myles na Gopaleen; on this occasion, however, the adoption by the prodigiously polynomial O'Nolan of monikers as diverse as Oscar Love, Lir O'Connor, Miss (alas) Luna O'Connor, W. R. Lambkin, and Whit Cassidy appears to have had no purpose other than to annoy the burgeoning rustic man of letters Patrick Kavanagh.

Indeed, although Kavanagh's review had obviously invited reaction, the pedal point in the ensuing correspondence shifted gradually but unmistakably from Kavanagh the critic to Kavanagh the artist as more and more voices entered the contrapuntal imbroglio. The first of two especially captious motifs appeared four days after the review when Frank E. Prenton Jones recollected with disgust a "short story" written by Kavanagh "some months ago, which dealt with the lower order of potato-diggers and their vulgar remarks about the serving maids of the village." Impressively, given that the piece alluded to seems to be neither the anecdote "Planting the Potatoes" which was printed in *The Irish Times* on May 4, 1940 nor even the pastoral reminiscence published on October 25, 1939 as "A Rural Irish Contrast" to the war in Europe but rather a sketch entitled "Sentimental Ploughman" which appeared on May 30, 1939—almost fourteen months before the Walsh review—Oscar Love confidently patronized it the next day as "a delightful article," observing that "Mr. Jones should recognise that the lowest orders are more original than university graduates, for they are not moulded in the college sausage machine." Just as impressively, N. S. Harvey of Co. Tipperary and F. L. J. of Glasnevin confidently corroborated Jones's very specific recollection of a very minor bit of hack writing on Kavanagh's part, and other contributors to the debate referred to it with rather unlikely familiarity as well.

With possibly even less provocation, a number of readers—led by "F. O'Brien" on July 29th—responded with similar picayune faultfinding to the publication of Kavanagh's poem **"Spraying the Potatoes"** one week into the Walsh controversy. Inspired by the poem's being printed inside a border that made it look like a five-pound note, O'Brien wrote:

> I had naturally enough inferred that our bank notes were being treated periodically with a suitable germicide, a practice which has long been a commonplace of enlightened monetary science in Australia. When I realised that the heading had reference to some verses by Mr. Patrick Kavanagh dealing with the part played by chemistry in modern farming, my chargrin [sic] may be imagined. . . . Perhaps the *Irish Times*, tireless champion of our peasantry, will oblige us with a series in this strain covering such rural complexities as inflamed goat-udders, warble-pocked shorthorn, contagious abortion, non-ovoid oviducts and nervous disorders among the gentlemen who pay the rent.

The following day, Lir O'Connor, apostrophizing to Kavanagh, declared that the poem would not suffice as "convincing literary proof of your existence," and Oscar Love feigned sympathy for the poet, wondering: "Is Mr. Kavanagh crazy? He now puts another weapon in his critics' hands. In **'Spraying the Potatoes'**—which my ten-year-old niece enjoyed reading—Mr. Kavanagh writes of 'young girls swinging from the sky.' It is really indecent to write thus of a parachutist in slacks." More pettily (and less wittily) a reader employing as a pseudonym the chemical formula "$Cu SO_4$"—for the compound sprayed on potatoes—refused to acknowledge a typesetting error in the fourth stanza of the poem: "In one line a wasp is poised on the edge of a barrel; in the next he is afloat on the surface of the liquor. A brimful barrel would explain it, but it is hardly worth explaining." Several days later, an apparent competitor—"$Na_2 Co_3$"—complained:

Another appreciative reader of poetry is perturbed by the thought that the blossoms of Arran Banners, described as blue, are in reality white. It is doubtful if poetic licence permits such an inaccuracy as this, and I think Mr. Kavanagh should severely reprimand his Muse for not having consulted the Department of Agriculture's leaflet on potatoes (sent free on application) before inspiring him.

II

Understandably, in light of the many abrasive remarks directed toward Kavanagh personally during this two-week riot of epistolography, a commentator writing in *The Honest Ulsterman* three decades after the fact might imagine Kavanagh's being utterly bemused by both the extent and the nature of the response elicited by his review of *The Hill is Mine*:

> Poor Kavanagh. God knows he had plenty of real problems to contend with. He must have been bewildered at this sudden eruption of quite causeless, meaningless schoolboy agression [sic] conducted by such a frighteningly united bunch of juvenile delinquents. The message must have been clear to him— 'You are not one of us. You are not of our class. You have not had our education. You are not a Dubliner. Shut up or get out.'

(Jude the Obscure 29)

Contesting this supposition, Flann O'Brien's biographer Anthony Cronin claims that "Kavanagh does not seem to have interpreted the correspondence this way; and in later years anyway he had certainly no animus against Brian O'Nolan on the head of it" (121). The poet's brother Peter actually recalls that "Patrick and I enjoyed it immensely" (*Sacred Keeper* 97); and, indeed, Kavanagh's own letter to the editor which finally closed the controversy on August 7th acknowledges that, while "all very adolescent," the exchange of letters was also "at times faintly amusing." He took particular satisfaction in reading the letters in the afterglow of his original review:

> In my review of Maurice Walsh's "The Hill is Mine" I referred to the empty virtuosity of artists who were expert in the art of saying nothing. Ploughmen without land. One of my critics said it was a wistful remark, and, maybe, it was; but if ever a critic was proved right, all round, by his critics it happened this time.

Concluding with uncharacteristic equanimity that "On the serious letters I do not intend to comment here," Kavanagh seemingly decided in his conventional response to the controversy to defer direct confrontation with the philistine faction he perceived as enjoying majority rule in Dublin's literary and cultural politics.

As an unconventional "response to the controversy," however, Kavanagh's poem **"Spraying the Potatoes,"** published on *The Irish Times* book page about halfway

through the Walsh debate, represents a subtle—even a subversive—expression of the delicate but desirable equipoise among polemics, poetics and literary politics that would subsequently elude the poet for almost two decades. For as the stone (as it were) in the midst of all, the poem does truly trouble, in terms Kavanagh suggested in 1958 in a lecture series entitled "Studies in the Technique of Poetry,"[4] that stream of condescension—hurtful or playful—which finally engulfed the essential integrity of his review of *The Hill is Mine*. His mind, the poet asserted in his fourth lecture delivered at University College Dublin, "keeps saying that it is only by realising the full folly and nature of society and the things it will accept in the way of culture that you can understand the necessity for your own polemic, the need to state your own point of view" ("Extracts" 61); of course, beginning with **"A Wreath for Tom Moore's Statue"** in 1944 and continuing well into the 1950s with such poems as **"The Wake of the Books," "The Paddiad," "The Defeated,"** and **"The Christmas Mummers,"** Kavanagh had elected against his own better judgment to follow **"The Road to Hate"** (*Complete Poems* 211) as his response to the hostility he experienced on the streets, in the pubs, and in the literary parlors of Dublin. But in **"Spraying the Potatoes"** he seems clearly to transform the sense of absolute displacement which would determine so much of that later verse into a statement of absolute transcendence of the sort he described in his seventh lecture:

> A poet is interested in his own private world; he luxuriates in telling the truth; he never argues or holds a symposium to find out what to think on any given subject. Neither does a poet preach; he makes statements about what is. The statement floats free of common didacticism in a realm of pure logic; you can walk around it and examine it but you can do nothing about it. You can only attack the person of the man who released the statement, and that is the thing generally done. Only a few brave virtuous people are willing to recognize and honour the Logos when they experience it.

("Extracts" 68)

For Kavanagh, then, as for fellow Ulster poet-in-exile (and preeminent Kavanagh apologist) Seamus Heaney, who muses thirty years later on the response of some poets of contemporary Northern Ireland to a literary politics of at least equal volatility, "The only reliable release for the poet was the appeasement of the achieved poem":

> In that liberated moment, when the lyric discovers its buoyant completion, when the timeless formal pleasure comes to its fullness and exhaustion, in that moment of self-justification and self-obliteration the poet makes contact with the plane of consciousness where he is at once intensified in his being and detached from his predicaments.

("Place and Displacement" 163)

Thus, to the extent that they reflect what Heaney emphasizes as "the profound relation . . . between poetic technique and historical situation" (164), even the stylistic and prosodic imperfections of **"Spraying the Potatoes"** reinforce the subtle and subversive "polemic" of Kavanagh's poem. For as Heaney observes in his essay "Feeling into Words," poetic technique must be distinguished from the learned "skill of making," from mere poetic craft:

> Technique . . . involves not only a poet's way with words, his management of metre, rhythm and verbal texture; it involves also a definition of his stance towards life, a definition of his own reality. It involves the discovery of ways to go out of his normal cognitive bounds and raid the inarticulate: a dynamic alertness that mediates between the origins of feeling in memory and experience and the formal ploys that express these in a work of art.
>
> (47)

Or as Kavanagh asserts more succinctly in the first of his 1958 lectures, "The question of technique is not simply a matter of grammar and syntax or anything as easy as that. It has to do with the mystical" ("Extracts" 57).

Obviously, the "mystical" dimension of **"Spraying the Potatoes"** involves the process by which the poet's lyrical recollection of the life he had abandoned to pursue his muse can sustain him in the face of the inhospitable reception given him by Dublin's literary establishment. "So does a poem bring a world alive in my mind," he would write more than a quarter-century later in the second of his **"Shancoduff"** poems, an impressionistic but unsentimental evocation of that same Inniskeen townland he had first extolled in verse in 1934: immersing himself once more in a world of rushy fields, of scythes and flails, of knapsack sprayers—"Put on four barrels / Filled with a porringer tin"—Kavanagh acknowledges in 1966 his completion of clearly the same sort of "long day's journey into night and day the same day" (**Complete Poems** 346-47) that he had undertaken during the Walsh controversy in 1940. The affectionately reproduced details of the first seven stanzas of **"Spraying the Potatoes"** thus affording him a literary transportation truly beyond the Pale, the unfelicitously transplanted countryman Kavanagh achieves in the third-person perspective of the final stanza of the poem—

> And poet lost to potato-fields,
> Remembering the lime and copper smell
> Of the spraying barrels he is not lost
> Or till blossomed stalks cannot weave a spell—

a literal transcendence of the kind hinted at in the ninth of his UCD lectures: "The purpose of technique is to enable us to detach our experience from ourselves and see it as a thing apart" ("Extracts" 73).

III

Subtly, then, but surely, **"Spraying the Potatoes"** substantiates Heaney's insistence that "The idea of poetry as a symbolic resolution of opposing truths, the idea of the poem as having its existence in a realm separate from the discourse of politics, does not absolve it or the poet from political status" ("Place and Displacement" 164). Just as subtly, however, the poem reveals the transience of its own transcendence in validating Heaney's corollary that the poet can be "stretched between politics and transcendence, and is often displaced from a confidence in a single position by his disposition to be affected by all positions, negatively rather than positively capable" (164). For in acknowledging the intrinsic fickleness of nature at the same time that it presents the possibility for romantic engagement with nature, **"Spraying the Potatoes"** serves as a poetic milestone—a referential point of both departure and return—not only with regard to Kavanagh's **"Adventures in the Bohemian Jungle"** (as he entitled one of his more caustic satires directed against literary and cultural Dublin), but also with regard to his verses of the early 1940s which manifest such seemingly deep-rooted antipathy toward the same world and life that he had celebrated during the first dozen years of his career as poet.

Of course, **"Spraying the Potatoes"** does not approach the fullest articulation of that antipathy, found in the jaundiced perspective of **The Great Hunger,** first published in 1942 and subsequently reprinted with **"Spraying the Potatoes"** in **A Soul for Sale** five years later. Yet, introducing in the fourth stanza of the poem, through his dispassionate description of the lethal potency of the lime and copper compound used to combat potato blight—"A wasp was floating / Dead on a sunken briar leaf / Over a copper-poisoned ocean"—a counter to his more typically whimsical personification of the wild roses, the potato-stalks and the dandelions as "young girls" with "unloved hearts" which had constituted the first three stanzas, Kavanagh seems truly to anticipate the spirit of dis-ease with rural living which would occasionally find expression in his verse in the next decade-and-a-half. Indeed, by employing the conventionally romantic mode of the lyric to depict and reflect upon a farming chore of a decidedly unromantic and truly consequential sort,[5] Kavanagh ultimately (albeit without apparent conscious design) locates the poem in conspicuous apposition to **"Stony Grey Soil,"** the poem printed immediately after it in the chronologically arranged **Complete Poems** and the earliest expression of his temperamental—if temporary—rejection of the hills and the fields of Inniskeen and environs which had so inspired him from his earliest poetic efforts:

> O stony grey soil of Monaghan
> The laugh from my love you thieved;

You took the gay child of my passion
And gave me your clod-conceived.

(Complete Poems 73)

First printed in *The Bell* in October of 1940, this poem, seemingly presenting through its emphasis on the dark underside of Irish country life a pronounced contrast to the prevailing transcendence of **"Spraying the Potatoes,"** actually brings into high relief the equivocation which quietly but insistently infiltrates the earlier poem. Even Kavanagh's redirecting his attention in the penultimate stanza to the plants and the flowers to dismiss the old man who interrupts his reverie—"O roses / The old man dies in the young girl's frown"—may be read as a willful (as opposed to a more characteristically wistful) repression of the sobering threat of blight inevitably suggested by the preventive measure of spraying and vaguely yet ominously mused upon by the old man's echoing "an ancient farming prayer."

As Antoinette Quinn has remarked, Kavanagh had allowed "worldly doubt to trouble poetic faith" (45) as early as the mid-1930s, taking literally to heart the negative evaluation of his black-hilled holding by insensitive cattle-drovers: "I hear and is my heart not badly shaken?" (**Complete Poems** 13). In 1951, beginning to disentangle himself from the "complexities of anger, hatred and ill-will towards the faults of man" which so possessed him during the 1940s, he recalled the aftereffect of that first **"Shancoduff"** poem in verses appropriately entitled **"Innocence"**: "Ashamed of what I loved," he admits, "I flung her from me and called her a ditch / Although she was smiling at me with violets." Briefly revisiting those familiar fields, however, he realizes that "I cannot die / Unless I walk outside these white-thorn hedges" (**Complete Poems** 241-42). In this respect, while straddling the boundary (as it were) between affection for and disaffection with the life of the Irish countryman—presumably the hedges in **"Innocence"** are the same ones that "the gulls like old newspapers are blown clear of . . . luckily" in **The Great Hunger** (**Complete Poems** 80)—**"Spraying the Potatoes"** may ultimately affirm its transcendent and transporting lyricism and function as a poetic landmark warranting Patrick Kavanagh's eventual willing and willful return, in the last half-dozen years of his life and career, to a Monaghan both actual and imaginary: to that "right simplicity" he had so abruptly abandoned in the aftermath of the Walsh controversy in the summer of 1940.

Notes

1. Nine years later, however, Kavanagh would show considerably less generosity toward Walsh in casting him—according to the poet's brother Peter (*Complete Poems* 400)—as "the Devil Mediocrity" in his poem "The Paddiad":

He has written many Catholic novels,
None of which mention devils:
Daring men, beautiful women,
Nothing about muck or midden,
Wholesome atmosphere—Why must
So-called artists deal with lust?

(Complete Poems 213)

2. A representative selection of these letters has been reprinted in John Wyse Jackson, ed., *Myles Before Myles* (203-26).

3. Indeed, according to Peter Kavanagh (*Sacred Keeper* 92), the editor himself of *The Irish Times*, R. M. Smyllie, contributed a letter on July 31st over the pseudonym (The) O'Madan.

4. As Peter Kavanagh mentions in a note in *The Complete Poems* (401-02), these lectures were misdated 1956 in *November Haggard*.

5. In a note to "Spraying the Potatoes" Peter Kavanagh explains: "To prevent 'the blight' potatoes had to be sprayed at least twice—in June and July, using a mixture of copper-sulphate and washing soda melted in a forty-gallon barrel of water. The barrel was placed conveniently on the headland. A two-gallon capacity back-carried sprayer was rented in the Village. Patrick sprayed the potatoes by walking up and down each furrow, the sprayer on his back. Around forty pounds weight or more. You came home tired after that day's work" (*The Complete Poems* 392).

Works Cited

CRONIN, ANTHONY. *No Laughing Matter: The Life and Times of Flann O'Brien*. London: Paladin, 1990.

HEANEY, SEAMUS. "Feeling into Words." *Preoccupations: Selected Prose, 1968-1978*. New York: Farrar, Straus, Giroux, 41-60.

———. "Place and Displacement: Reflections on Some Recent Poetry from Northern Ireland." *The Agni Review* 22 (1985): 158-77.

JACKSON, JOHN WYSE, ed. *Myles Before Myles: A Selection of the Earlier Writing of Brian O'Nolan*. London: Grafton, 1988.

JUDE THE OBSCURE. "The H. U. Business Section." *The Honest Ulsterman* 32 (Jan./Feb. 1972): 28-33.

KAVANAGH, PATRICK. *The Complete Poems*. New York: The Peter Kavanagh Hand Press, 1972.

———. "Extracts from Ten Lectures Delivered at University College Dublin in 1956 [sic 1958] Entitled 'Studies in the Technique of Poetry.'" *November Haggard: Uncollected Prose and Verse of Patrick Kavanagh*. Ed. Peter Kavanagh. New York: The Peter Kavanagh Hand Press, 1971, 55-76.

———. "Maurice Walsh's New Novel," *The Irish Times* 20 July 1940.

———. *Self-Portrait.* 2nd ed. Dublin: Dolmen, 1975.

KAVANAGH, PETER. *Sacred Keeper: A Biography of Patrick Kavanagh.* Orono, Me.: The National Poetry Foundation, 1984.

"Literary Criticism." *The Irish Times* 22 July-7 August 1940.

NEMO, JOHN. "The Green Knight: Patrick Kavanagh's Venture into Criticism." *Studies* LXIII, 251 (Autumn 1974): 282-94.

QUINN, ANTOINETTE. *Patrick Kavanagh: A Critical Study.* Syracuse: Syracuse Univ. Press, 1991.

Una Agnew (essay date 1998)

SOURCE: Agnew, Una. "Patrick Kavanagh: A Mystical Writer?" In *The Mystical Imagination of Patrick Kavanagh,* pp. 17-44. Dublin: Columba Press, 1998.

[*In the following essay, Agnew examines the nature of mysticism and argues that Kavanagh's work offers many examples of the convergence of mysticism and poetry.*]

There is, of course, a poetic movement which sees poetry materialistically. The writers of this school see no transcendent nature in the poet; they are practical chaps, excellent technicians. But somehow or other I have a belief in poetry as a mystical thing, and a dangerous thing.

(*Collected Poems,* Martin, Brian and O'Keeffe, 1964, p. xiii.)

PART ONE

KAVANAGH: A MYSTICAL POET?

When Patrick Kavanagh announced his belief in poetry as 'a mystical thing and a dangerous thing', no one seemed to pay attention. This unusual declaration, which appeared in the introduction to his first major poetry collection (1964), went largely unnoticed by scholars and critics alike. Indeed, Kavanagh's strong roots in the Catholic religion and his life-long pre-occupation with eternal questionings, give credence to his claim. But how serious is his assertion that poetry, of its essence, is mystical? And does his work demonstrate this? To test the validity of his statement, it is necessary to bear with me while I examine with some care what mysticism is, and if it can fittingly describe Kavanagh's work.

WHAT IS MYSTICISM?

Evelyn Underhill (1875-1941) outlines the principal characteristics of the mystic in her classic work, *Mysticism*.[1] She is helpful in that she is herself a poet as well as a spiritual writer. The mystic, she holds, is firstly a seeker who passionately follows the pursuit of beauty, goodness or truth. The lifelong quest for the Holy Grail is the object of mystical love. St John of the Cross's quest for his 'Beloved' is immortalised in his famous 'Spiritual Canticle', a poem of delectable but painful longing:

Where have you hidden,
Beloved, and left me moaning?
You fled like the stag
After wounding me . . .[2]

Mystical knowledge belongs in a category of its own. The mystic stands in sharp contrast to the empirical scientist who generally regards mystical knowledge as unreliable and unworthy of consideration. The mystic, on the other hand, holds to have seen, or at least glimpsed, a vision of beauty beyond the veil of custom or calculation. This revelation is authentic knowledge, but can be grasped only in images and symbols.

Once the vision of beauty, truth, or goodness has been glimpsed, the mystic is smitten with desire for this cherished goal. In St John's case, he has been 'wounded' at the deepest centre of his soul. He relentlessly seeks a 'way out' or a 'way back', restlessly yearning to be at home in the heart of Essential Being.[3]

Restless and uneasy with platitudes, the mystic seeks to know things in their essence. This desire for knowledge is part of the quest for perfection. And, for the mystic, knowing goes beyond mere rational knowledge. It is coupled with a desire for union with reality, and often consists in a direct intuition of truth. The mystic frequently knows, without being able to explain why.

The mystic above all seeks to love. The lover, the poet and the mystic experience the joy of 'seeing into the heart of things'. With the writer St Exupéry they affirm that it is with the heart that one sees. To love with one's whole being, intellect, emotions and volition, is intrinsically mystical. Through love, doors fly open which logic has battered on in vain.[4] Reason can speak, but it is only love that sings.[5] The mystic is well aware that there exists a life beyond reach of the senses.

More and more, the mystic experiences a level of consciousness beyond the ordinary. The awakening of the hidden faculty of the soul opens up a level of awareness which produces experiences of great joy, alternating with profound desolation. The mystic encounters life with greater intensity and sensitivity than most. As is the case with poet and mystic William Blake (1757-1827), one becomes periodically 'drunk with . . . vision' or, as in the Christian tradition, 'inebriated' with Christ.[6]

Single-mindedly the mystic follows the hidden Paradise of Love. Once the glory of transcendent beauty has been glimpsed, he remains dissatisfied with anything less. Those who become 'drunk with God' through visions or ecstasy, find it more difficult to return to mundane realities. The mystic gone astray is in danger of seeking compensatory substances such as drugs or alcohol as substitutes for the exquisite 'Bread of Angels'. At best, the mystical life is one lived in a kind of limbo, always seeking paradise yet attaining little but its merest glimpse.

At certain points along the way, there occur periods of darkness and disillusionment. This experience may seem to overwhelm the subject with deprivation of light and solace. Darkness, however, can be interpreted as a time of gestation or purgation, during which the soul is drawn even closer to its beloved object:

> Oh night that was my guide!
> Oh darkness dearer than the morning's pride,
> Oh night that joined the lover
> To the beloved bride
> Transfiguring them each into the other.[7]

This purgation is aptly described by T. S. Eliot, who resonates deeply with the mystical darkness of St John of the Cross. Darkness, for Eliot, is a time of waiting:

> I said to my soul, be still, and let the dark come upon
>   you
> Which shall be the darkness of God . . .[8]

Emerging from a period of purification, the mystic is prepared for further awakenings of spirit.

The mystic's secret knowledge[9] cuts him or her adrift from ordinary people, and imposes a kind of involuntary exile. The pursuit of vision requires complete dedication. One becomes impatient with all that is false in oneself and in one's world. The mystic is not simply a dreamer, but one who is engaged energetically with life, tirelessly discerning what is true from what is false. Periodically the mystic skirts a mental state akin to madness, a state of psychic openness which brings blessing and torture in its wake. Thus, the mystical state can be dangerous in that it can unhinge the mind, drive it to the edge of sanity or carry it to unbidden heights only to sink it once more into troughs of darkness.

The poet's claim to be a mystic lies in the fact that he or she 'has achieved a passionate communion with deeper levels of life than those with which we usually deal'.[10] Such a poet is Walt Whitman, admired greatly by Patrick Kavanagh. Above all, the poet-mystic is a visionary. The mystical soul sees beyond the surface of the ordinary and penetrates the mystery at the heart of all things. This was particularly obvious in the Celtic mystical tradition, where the veil between earth and heaven is thin. Joseph Mary Plunkett (1887-1916) was possessed of a mystical awareness of God's presence in the created world around him. He saw Christ traced on elements of the natural world:

> I see his blood upon the rose
> And in the stars the glory of his eyes,
> His body gleams amid eternal snows,
> His tears fall from the skies.[11]

In summary, Underhill states that the emergence of the mystic in society is a recurring phenomenon. Life for the mystic becomes a mysterious search, guided and inspired by an innate 'spiritual spark' or transcendent faculty. Such powers remain dormant in many, and yet are available to all. Speaking of this 'divine spark' she sees it emerge from 'the still point' or 'apex of the soul' and gradually become dominant in the mystic's life. Possessed of a secret knowledge, the mystic wends a solitary path through life, sometimes elated by vision, oftentimes living in a dark, abandoned contemplation. The 'inner eye of love' is a Zen Buddhist expression for this mystical faculty, which gradually leads to enlightenment.[12] Mystical vision is little understood in our modern world. It can evoke admiration, but also irritation and ridicule, when others fail to understand it.[13] In this the poet and mystic have much in common.

THE POET AND THE MYSTIC

Henri Bremond points out that the poet and mystic share a common ground.[14] Both have an instinct for the transcendent and enjoy fleeting glimpses of the mystery that surrounds everyday life. This is made clear in the poetry of Francis Thompson:

> O world invisible, we view thee,
> O world intangible, we touch thee,
> O world unknowable, we know thee,
> Inapprehensible, we clutch thee!

Experiences of poetry and mysticism belong to the same order of knowledge, a knowledge of the heart.[15] The mystic, Bremond says, is 'graced with an immediate intuition of God'. Poet and mystic alike rely on intuition, that immediate grasp of the truth, beyond reason or analysis. The essential difference between them is principally one of communication. The poet trades in the magic of words as a vehicle for expression, while the mystic takes refuge in contemplative silence. While both may have a profound experience, one is greater in communication, the other in interior communion. In terms of communication, the mystic is 'less' than the poet. One is greater by experience, the other by expression. Though they share the same terrain, their goals differ. The 'mystical state' of the poet cannot be said to be identical with the 'state of grace' experienced by the mystic. Yet they are not mutually exclusive. Both share parallel moments which spill over onto the terrain of the other, making it sometimes impossible to tell them apart.

For the religious mystic, a glimpse of the glory of God demands a rigorous *ascesis* of bringing one's life into conformity with the graces gratuitously received. The poet-mystic, on the other hand, assumes the discipline of bringing experience to birth in poetry, and is often consumed with a prophetic mission to restore for mankind the integrity of the universe. A margin of incommunicability, nevertheless, generally lingers in the experience of both.

The mystic who is *also* an artist will attempt to describe in images and symbols what is seen and heard. 'Painting, poetry and music,' argues Blake, are 'the three powers in man of conversing with Paradise.'[16] The poet longs to capture the elusive beauty of Eden. Martin Heidegger sees the poet as the one who senses the banishment of 'the gods' from the earth. Poets, he believes, detect 'the trace of the fugitive gods' and 'stay on (their) tracks'. Their mission is seen to be that of leading fellow mortals back to the path of 'the holy'. The artist acts, then, as prophet for the people, seeking to grasp their dreams and echo their aspirations. Yeats, echoing Blake, clearly envisions a spiritual role for the artist when he exhorts his fellow Irish poets to 'learn their trade':

> Poet and sculptor do the work
> Nor let the modish painter shirk
> What his great forefathers did,
> Bring the soul of man to God . . .[17]

Poet and mystic together experience intermittent states of light and darkness, sunshine and shadow, agony and ecstasy: all of which, from Blake's standpoint, are 'eternal'.[18] The poet and mystic are close to one another in their mutual quest for beauty, which 'tends of itself to unite us to God'.[19] Poetry and mysticism, then, have similar sources and can, in certain cases, be synonymous. Although they may express themselves differently, they reflect and illumine one another.

THE MYSTICAL PATH

Strangely, it is the mystic who teaches us to better understand the poet.[20] Mystical development can help us comprehend the development of the poet's mystical imagination. It provides us with a 'rough sketch' of the poetic mind. Among all those writing about mysticism, Underhill best outlines the process.[21] Mystical development involves *three* main stages: Awakening, Purification, and Illumination. This schema originated with the Neo-Platonists and is valid for all metaphysical systems.

Awakening constitutes the first opening of the eyes of the mystical sense. This can occur gradually from childhood, as in the case of the French mystic Madame Guyon, or suddenly on the roadside, as in the case of St Paul. An experience of acute pain or pleasure can be instrumental in the awakening process. Nature mystics are possessed of a high degree of perceptive vision. Like Blake and the Celtic mystics, they can 'see a world in a grain of sand / And heaven in a wild flower'. The mystic has a sense of awakening from sleep to a world that is new.

Purification can accompany or follow upon awakening. Each new level of insight and self-understanding causes the mystic to shed superficial ways of being. Illness and suffering can be instrumental in the purification process, as was the case with Julian of Norwich and St Ignatius of Loyola. Poverty and destitution, loneliness and rejection can frequently be sources of purification. Inner cleansing takes place through letting go of the ego. This is often called the *via negativa* or the negative experience of God. These dark passages of the mystic's formation are ascetical in nature. Self-denial, penance and exile were frequently chosen by Celtic monks of the early Irish church who embraced the search for God. The interior suffering of Gerard Manley Hopkins and T. S. Eliot was the refining fire of their souls. Hurt, ridicule and disparagement were instrumental in the soul-formation of mystical poets and artists, not least among them Patrick Kavanagh, for whom poverty and rejection were part of a life-long purification.

Illumination occurs when mystical consciousness, no longer clouded by custom, becomes lucid and awake. Wordsworth best evokes this stage in his 'Tintern Abbey', when he experiences the quieting of bodily sense and awakening of spiritual vision: 'we are laid asleep in body and become a living soul'. The soul, alive and fully awake at last, is illumined, so that 'we see into the life of things'. This mystical seeing occurs in a specifically religious context for Hopkins when he becomes dazzled by a transformed vision of the world. 'God's Grandeur', he sees, is an energy that 'charges' the universe with splendour:

> The world is charged with the grandeur of God
> It will flame out, like shook foil;
> It gathers to a greatness, like the ooze of oil
> Crushed.[22]

Here illumination takes on a sacramental character which is of interest when we come to consider the poet Patrick Kavanagh. The radiance of God's presence is the fruit of an expanded consciousness. This radiance is all-pervasive; it becomes 'resplendent in the meanest things'.[23]

A similar view of sacramentality is described by Eliade when he speaks about primitive man's capacity to converse with the sacredness of the cosmos. 'Tilling . . . the clay put(s) primitive man into a universe steeped in the sacred'.[24] The mountain or the tree are not simply items on the horizon but sacred places linking earth and heaven. Primitive man was unconsciously a symbolic thinker. He preserved a sense of the sacred amid daily life. Modern technology has, for the most part, robbed humankind of a sense of the sacredness of matter. Thus the cosmos has become de-sanctified. In the words of Heidegger, 'the gods have fled' . . . and 'the divine radiance has become extinguished in the world's history'.[25] The poet and mystic can recover, in moments of illumination, a sense of the cosmos as hierophanic. Poetry can reconstitute the earth as sacred. This radiant vision, or sacramental presence of God, is experienced as illumination in the Christian mystical tradition.

Ecstasy is a degree of illumination where the mystic is seized by an awareness so total, so absorbing that he experiences himself outside time and space. In this state, one remains momentarily freed from the constraints of time and space. Experience of this kind usually leads to further purification. In some cases, there is a total dying to self in what St John calls the 'Dark Night' of the soul. Some mystics reach a state of surrender so complete that there ensues 'a mystical marriage'; an intense union with God.

Transformation is the natural outcome of mystical life. A person becomes changed inwardly because of the intensity of this personal inner journey. There is a gradual 'rebirthing', sometimes dramatic, sometimes barely perceptible in the personality. What is most obvious is that the person achieves inner peace; is at one within the self, radiating a deep, imperturbable inner joy. The equanimity that ensues is not the end, but the beginning of new levels of enlightenment.

SUMMARY

This brief examination of mysticism, along with the distinctions between the poet and the mystic, help clarify what is meant by the mystical dimension of poetry. Underhill's description of mystical states and stages is particularly helpful. She especially, among all those writing on mysticism, presents the clearest pattern of mystical development: Awakening, Purification, Illumination and Transformation.[26] Bremond has drawn useful parallels between mysticism and poetry, showing that sublime mystical states shed light on what happens in the poetic process.[27] Together these experts present us with a useful set of guidelines to apply to Patrick Kavanagh's work as a poet and writer.

In view of Kavanagh's claim for poetry as mystical and John Jordan's assessment of him as 'an instinctive theologian', it is necessary to attempt to evaluate these statements and settle the question once for all.[28] Is there a mystical dimension to Kavanagh's work? The mystic regularly undergoes scrutiny from both theology and psychology, to test every 'spirit' against self-delusion.[29] Poetic states must likewise surrender to investigation. Mystical science sheds light on the workings of the mystical imagination. It is reasonable to suggest that a poet such as Kavanagh be tested, with advantage to poetry and mysticism alike.

PART TWO

MYSTICAL ELEMENTS IN KAVANAGH'S WORK

The questions now to be asked are: Does the poet Patrick Kavanagh fulfil any or all of the characteristics typical of the mystic? Was he gifted with a level of consciousness above the ordinary? Was he a seeker of Beauty and of God? Was he gifted with intuitive knowledge and did this knowledge stretch beyond the confines of rational knowledge and common sense? Did he, in the course of his life, achieve illumination or, in Underhill's words, 'sacramental expansion'?[30] Did he succeed in piercing the veil and disclosing the eternal? Did he follow the traditional mystical path of Awakening, Purification, Illumination and Transformation?

MYSTICAL AWARENESS

The Green Fool portrays Kavanagh as a young man, emerging self-consciously as a dreamer and seer. He seems to be possessed of certain visionary tendencies at least. He is often perplexed by what he sees; for example 'the strange beautiful light' on 'the Drumgonnelly Hills':

> 'Do you see anything very beautiful and strange on those hills?' I asked my brother as we cycled together to a football match in Dundalk. 'This free-wheel is missing,' and he gave it a vigorous crack with the heel of his shoe. 'Is it on Drumgonnelly Hills?'
>
> 'Yes?'
>
> 'Do you mean the general beauty of the landscape?'
>
> 'Something beyond that, beyond that,' I said.
>
> 'Them hills are fine no doubt.'
>
> 'And is that all you see?'
>
> 'This free-wheel is missing again,' he said. 'I'll have to get down and put a drop of oil on it.'
>
> We got moving again. 'What were we talking about?'
>
> 'Beauty', I said.[31]

In this short passage, the awakening of an early mystical consciousness can be discerned. Mystical imagination is juxtaposed with the rather bald realism of 'This free-wheel is missing' or the even more vision-damping analysis: 'Do you mean the general beauty of the landscape?' Patrick Kavanagh is gradually becoming aware of the lonely world of the poet, whose experience is not understood, not even by his brother. No earth-bound eye can reach this place which, in biblical terms, 'no eye has seen nor ear has heard' (1 Cor 2:9). The 'strange light' mentioned in his early autobiography is converted later into religious coinage as 'the Holy Spirit on the hills'.[32]

At home in Inniskeen, it dawns slowly on Kavanagh that the world he inhabits is different. At moments of heightened awareness he receives meanings and messages that come from the 'hills of the imagination, far beyond the flat fields of common sense'.[33] He finds within himself the 'half-god' who can 'see the immortal in things mortal'; a kind of mythological god-man brooding over the ancient territory of Farney and the Fews. During his High Court proceedings of February, 1954, when he sued *The Leader* for allegedly libellous remarks and defamation of character, he stated unambiguously that his reference to going 'over the fields to the City of Kings' was mystical by implication. Emphatically he proclaimed: 'I am speaking mystically of God, of the City without Walls' and not of any 'mortal city'.[34]

His early period of development he called an 'angelhood' or 'the angel while . . .' when, with typical Kavanagh originality, he experienced God as 'unstirred mud in a shallow pool'. His vision was clear and open to possibilities. He guarded this gift jealously, refusing to expose 'moments innocent with revelation' to the vulgarity of 'the market-place'. The market-place was ignorant of his 'transfigured hills' his 'Edenic landscape'. To speak of them was to risk losing them forever. Kavanagh's Eden is where, like Blake, he sings his 'Songs of Innocence' in a mood of rapt 'starriness'.

The penalty for sharing his treasure was severe. His spirit was shocked by those who neither saw nor understood what he saw. He was both angered and hurt at being misunderstood, feelings which contributed to a life of on-going purification:

> . . . I told of that beatific wonder to clods and disillusioned lovers. I asked if they didn't see something beyond the hills of Glassdrummond. They laughed and said I was mad.[35]

His Eden, or 'garden of the golden apples', becomes occasionally sullied by twisted thinking of people who distrust what he considered to be 'innocent and lovely'. Sadly, these people 'twist awry' the original blessedness of life, and perceive only guilt and sinfulness in 'the dark places of soul':

> We are a dark people,
> Our eyes are ever turned
> Inward
> Watching the liar who twists
> The hill-paths awry.
> O false fondler with what
> Was made lovely
> In a garden!
>
> ('**Dark Ireland**')

Even though he moved away from his 'childhood country', he retains his 'Eden-flowering mind' which, though prone to disenchantment by falsehood and hypocrisy, is still allowed blossom. Kavanagh is one of Bremond's 'elite' among the poets and mystics who 'penetrate the lost paradise'.[36] He recaptures once more his sense of 'fields that are part of no earthly estate'. At such times his world, as in '**A Christmas Childhood**', becomes 'wonderful', 'magical' and capable of being distilled into a symbol of mystical prayer: white, wordless, iridescent, transcendent . . . 'a white rose pinned / on the Virgin Mary's blouse'.

His 'garden of the golden apples',[37] a strip of garden 'between a railway and a road' is transformed into a paradise where miracles are commonplace and time eternal. Here mystical knowledge is bestowed on the poet by the strange light of the new moon. The structure of the lines yields happily to 'the expanded voltage' of the experience. Kavanagh is rapt as he remembers:

> And when the sun went down into Drumcatton
> And the New Moon by its little finger swung
> From the telegraph wires, we knew how God had happened
> And what the blackbird in the whitethorn sang.
>
> ('**The Long Garden**')

He feels he had, at this moment, an insight into God and God's earthly revelation. This world was neither worn nor pedestrian but magical and mystical. Nothing is soiled or sordid or out of tune with the harmony experienced. Here paganism and Christianity intermingle, united in primeval innocence. In Kavanagh's imaginative landscape, Slieve Gullion is a 'sacred mountain' and 'place of mystery', exuding pagan splendour, yet blending harmoniously with the simple radiance of the newly built Catholic church in its foothills. This is 'Glassdrummond chapel', a place of brightness, contrasting favourably with the dark north-facing beauty of Shancoduff.

Little wonder that he envisioned his life as being on a different plane from others, his rhyme in '**Come Dance with Kitty Stobling**', 'cavorting on mile-high stilts'. Bewildered, 'the unnerved crowds' looked up 'with terror in their rational faces'. The poet in this instance may appear contemptuous towards the non-poetic. Is he arrogant, a victim of spiritual pride? Or is he rather like Yeat's 'Malachi Stilt-Jack', metaphorically stalking 'the terrible novelty of the night' 'like a barnacle goose / Far up in the stretches of night'. Kitty Stobling and Malachi Stilt-Jack are both outrageous characters, which present a comic view of the awkward, vulnerable position of the poet vis-à-vis society. The essential loneliness and exile of the poet is made abundantly clear.

Ironically, Kavanagh longed for the ordinary sense of belonging to mundane activities of town and country:

> And sometimes I am sorry when the grass
> Is growing over the stones in quiet hollows
> And the cocksfoot leans across the rutted cart-pass
> That I am not the voice of country fellows

Who now are standing by some headland talking
Of turnips and potatoes or young corn . . .

('Peace')

He wished to live on the plane of farming, football,
horse-racing and everyday commonalities, but he could
not survive without the vision that transported him 'on
mile-high stilts' above 'the timorous paces' and the
tediousness of the crowd who lacked imagination. Often
he portrays the arrogance and impatience of one who
sees a different vision and hears 'a different drummer'.
Occasionally he begs compassion for his own eccentricity and vulnerability from those whom he loved and
trusted and asks a prayer for one 'who walked apart on
the hills'. Too well he knew the price of 'loving life's
miracles of stone and grass . . .' That price was loneliness and isolation.

MYSTICAL SEEING

Kavanagh sees beyond the surface of everyday life. He
senses, like William Blake and Elizabeth Barrett-
Browning (1806-1861), a radiance in life around him.
His earth too is 'crammed with heaven'. Herein lies,
perhaps, the greatest proof of his mystical imagination.
In his early work he is almost intoxicated by vision. He
celebrates this early clear-sightedness in words that
point to veritable glimpses of heaven. He is the darling
of whatever God he worships:

> The gods of poetry are generous: they give every young
> poet a year's salary which he hasn't worked for; they
> let him take one peep into every tabernacle; they give
> him transcendent power. While he is learning the craft
> of verse and getting ready his tools, they present him
> with wonderful lines which he thinks are his own. In
> those days I had vision. I saw upon the little hills and
> in the eyes of small flowers beauty too delicately rare
> for carnal words.[38]

From the common experience of ploughing and harrowing in spring he sees into the mystery of quickening
life. At this early stage of his career, he also analogously
envisions the first seeds of his poetry. He foresees the
mystical fruitfulness of clay when he leaves 'the check
rein slack' and surrenders to 'the harrow('s) play'.
Already he has become wise to the role of 'the worm's
opinion' and the 'pointed harrow-pins' of life. His vision has become capable of penetrating the potency of
'seed' scattered 'on the dark eternity of April's clay':

> This seed is potent as the seed
> Of knowledge in the Hebrew Book.
> So drive your horses in the creed
> Of God the Father as a stook.

('To the Man After the Harrow')

Mystical vision reaches farther than the human eye, and
acquires a dark knowledge, a wisdom learned only in
the mystical 'cloud of unknowing'.[39] For Kavanagh, a
spiritual journey as well as a poetic one has been initiated. He is entering 'the mist where Genesis begins'.
The symbols of sower and seed propel him deeply into
Biblical territory: 'unless the grain of wheat falls to the
ground and dies it remains only a single grain' (Jn
12:24). Does he foresee the harrowing of his own soul
as a prerequisite for a harvest of poetry? Symbolically
and mystically he is being transformed by the land that
bore him, by the landscape that enshrines his spirit. He
is being made into 'a carbon copy' of his surrounding
hills:

> O Monaghan hills when is writ your story
> A carbon copy will unfold my being.

('Monaghan Hills')

Ploughing for Kavanagh becomes real contemplation as
well as a symbol of his poetic art. His instrument, the
swing-plough, though crude and clumsy by modern
standards, provides an ideal opportunity for the two
activities he so often pursues in tandem: 'poetry and
prayer'. As a young poet, he has unabashed confidence
in his ability to do both:

> I find a star-lovely art
> In a dark sod.
> Joy that is timeless! O heart
> That knows God!

('Ploughman')

With considerable assurance of his visionary powers, he
sets about learning his poetic art, with only the most
rudimentary education at his disposal. He asserts
unambiguously in an early poem, **'Plough Horses'**
(1938), that he owes his clarity of vision to the unseal-
ing of his eyes by the power of the Holy Spirit. Yet, he
surprises his reader by asserting that the visionary form
he contemplates has been shaped at the hand of Phidias,
the celebrated fifth-century BC Greek sculptor. This
knowledge, undoubtedly gleaned from schoolbook
sources, serves to strengthen Kavanagh's natural mystical ability.[40] He masters the classical allusion with
remarkable ease. Meanwhile, his 'third eye', or 'inner
eye',[41] sees beyond the animal shape. In Eliade's terms,
he had easy access to the sacred dimension of the
cosmos,[42] the prerogative of primitive man:

> The cosmos being a hierophany and human existence
> sacred, work possessed a liturgical value which still
> survives, albeit obscurely, among rural populations of
> contemporary Europe. What is especially important to
> emphasise is the possibility given to primitive man to
> immerse himself in the sacred by his own work as a
> *homo faber* and as creator and manipulator of tools.[43]

As a simple ploughman, and not a very skillful one by
all accounts, Kavanagh's poetic genius sees two
ordinary farmyard 'nags' transformed under his gaze.
He has experienced something of the power of the Holy
Spirit in this early epiphany:

Seeing with eyes the Spirit unsealed
Plough-horses in a quiet field.

                                        (**'Plough Horses'**)

Not only does Kavanagh see beneath the surface of life
but he shows himself to be Celtic in mind-set, by attributing life to the fields and trees themselves. He not
only finds 'the immortal in things mortal' but knows
that the fields in turn have witnessed 'the immortal'
within him. They speak to his spirit in a wordless
conversation—a mystical communion:

> There was I, me face black, sitting on the sate-board,
> me legs crossed, letting the fields look at me. Ah, the
> fields looked at me more than I at them, at this moment
> they are still staring at me.[44]

In an even more compelling way, his hawthorn ditches
'smile at (him) with violets', and the bluebells 'under
the big trees' think of him with lovers' delight. The
items in Kavanagh's landscape are as alive as those of
the ninth century Celtic monk:

> A wall of woodland overlooks me.
> A blackbird sings me a song (no lie!)
> Above my book, with its lines laid out,
> The birds in their music sing to me.[45]

By the time he writes **'Primrose'** (1939), he has
established himself as a poet with visionary powers.
This 'one small primrose', bearing the signature of the
Holy Spirit at its centre, speaks eloquently to him of the
transfigured Christ. Vision has become interiorised for
the poet and reaches towards a Being who is God:

> I look at Christ transfigured without fear
> The light was very beautiful and kind,
> And where the Holy Ghost in flame had signed
> I read it through the lenses of a tear.

Kavanagh as a poet is by now advancing on the road of
mystical knowledge.

Secret Knowledge

As a boy, Patrick Kavanagh loved to rummage in the
'thalidge', a sort of semi-loft over the kitchen of his
maternal grandfather, Oul' Quinn's, thatched cottage.
Here he glimpsed hints of a world of mystery and
romance. He delighted in his 'museum that never had
known a curator'—a place 'rich with ancient smells'
where one might expect to find an old pike or a Fenian
gun . . .'[46] This descriptive passage from his autobiography presents a boy innocently in love with secret
knowledge, and showing a predilection for the hidden,
the obscure, the unsophisticated. He learned to relish
'dark truths' which generally went unnoticed. He was
extraordinarily precocious in realising that in remote
rural places there existed 'the secret archives of peasant
minds of which no official document has ever been

made'. The travelling workmen, 'journeymen cobblers',
who brought these 'dark truths' into view were the
delight of his boyhood.[47]

In his early teens Kavanagh listened intently to the
conversation of neighbours around his father's work-
bench. He read and learned by heart chosen texts from
old schoolbooks and from the newspaper bought daily
by his father. Following the trend of the current
educational system, there was an undue emphasis in the
Kavanagh home on the accumulation of facts: local history, mythology, politics and folklore. His father, Peter
said, wished to fill Patrick's head with lore which he
had collected from *Titbits* and *Answers*.[48]

Patrick, however, soon learned to trust his own 'animal-
remembering mind' which he discovered is superior to
much of the knowledge which is more academic or
merely informational. He may have compensated a little,
at first, for his secretly felt lack of educational opportunity. So-called intellectual knowledge, he says,
taught him 'far too many things', endangering thereby
his mystical song and vision. He complains in his address 'To Knowledge' that he is angry at his loss of 'the
speech of mountains', and at falling victim to the false
promise of erudition. He who could once steer 'by night
unstarred' and 'pray with stone and water' has placed
his 'lamp of contemplation' in jeopardy by aspiring to
worship knowledge. It was a long road ahead to come
to accept his mystical gifts or to own his poetic
predispositions:

> It wasn't considered manly to feel any poetic emotion.
> If a scene was beautiful you didn't say so. A man in
> love with anything was daft.[49]

True to his mystical instinct, he knew that analysis,
explanation or reason were inadequate tools for the
spirit. His poem **'Advent'** expresses the need to be
purged of cerebral excesses and of the temptation to be
over-analytical:

> . . . and please
> God we shall not ask for reason's payment,
> The why of heart-breaking strangeness in dreeping
>   hedges
> Nor analyse God's breath in common statement.

                                                  (**'Advent'**)

For Kavanagh, the rational, the superficial and the
sophisticated belonged to 'secular wisdom' and to the
'secular city'. They belonged also to every 'tedious
man' who lacks imagination, deprived of consort with
the gods. Illumination, enlightenment, vision, are given
only to those prepared to surrender forever the glamour
of ego-titillating knowledge:

> We have thrown into the dustbin the clay-minted
>   wages

Of pleasure, knowledge and the conscious hour—
And Christ comes with a January flower.

'Revelation', Kavanagh admits, 'comes as an aside.' It comes unbidden in an essentially non-academic way but, nevertheless, as compelling as is the appearance of an early spring flower. Kavanagh boldly claims that mystical knowledge, though difficult of access, soars higher than reason and attains its goal with precision:

And I have a feeling
Through a hole in reason's ceiling;
We can fly to knowledge
Without ever going to college.

(**'To Hell with Commonsense'**)

The chink in reason becomes the sacred threshold of a knowledge that 'passeth understanding'. St John of the Cross's description of a moment of high contemplation has certain marked likenesses to that experienced by the poet:

He who truly arrives there
Cuts free from himself;
All that he knew before
Now seems worthless,
And his knowledge so soars
That he is left unknowing
Transcending all knowledge.[50]

The mystic, in the language of St John, soars to an unknowing transcendent knowledge. True enlightenment, or that 'flash of Divine Intelligence',[51] is the moment of genuine insight and illumination. Waiting in a state of unknowing is often a preliminary to mystical insight. Given to occasional outward rapt behaviour, neighbours presumed Kavanagh to be unsound of mind. Nevertheless, lost in reverie, he continued to plough his mystical furrow. He remained faithful to hidden knowledge, paying ultimate homage as an accomplished poet in **'Canal Bank Walk'** to 'arguments that cannot be proven'.

'Remote places', 'ancient smells', 'secret archives of peasant-minds'; these attracted the poet towards the contemplation of mysterious things. He felt at home in this strange, unchartered territory.

MYSTICAL LOVING

Revelation, though normally gratuitously bestowed on the poet-mystic, can sometimes be facilitated by contemplation:

To look on is enough
In the business of love

'Is')

Ultimately Kavanagh sees loving contemplation as the supreme activity of the poet. Kavanagh loves secretly, passionately, constantly and universally. 'For,' he says

'nothing whatever is by love debarred.' (**'The Hospital'**) He loves 'girls in red blouses', 'dandelions growing on headlands', buckets 'with half-hung handles', weeds, a gate 'bent by a lorry', bits of road and upturned carts.[52] Everything he loves becomes transformed. The intensity of love reaches mystical proportions when he contemplates a scene from the Rialto Hospital in March 1955:

This is what love does to things: the Rialto Bridge,
The main gate that was bent by a heavy lorry,
The seat at the back of a shed that was a suntrap.
Naming these things is the love-act and its pledge;
For we must record love's mystery without claptrap,
Snatch out of time the passionate transitory.

(**'The Hospital'**)

It must be remembered that this was the Kavanagh who had undergone surgery for lung cancer and had survived!

Some years previously (1950), while 'in exile' in London, memory of details from his past re-awaken his slumbering 'god of imagination'. The names of almost-forgotten farmyard harness, names hidden 'in the unrecorded archives of rural minds' become transformed through the poet's naming ritual:

The winkers that had no choke-band,
The collar and the reins . . .
In Ealing Broadway, London Town
I name their several names
Until a world comes to life—
Morning, the silent bog,

And the God of imagination waking
In a Mucker fog.

(**'Kerr's Ass'**)

Naming in this case belongs to the creative act of God described in the Book of Genesis. To be named, biblically speaking, is a pledge of immortality. It is a supremely mystical and creative event, since naming can invoke the hidden power of the named. Recalling and reciting the names of beloved objects and place-names can resemble the repetition of the mystic's mantra which gradually induces a heightened state of consciousness akin to inspired poetic activity.[53] For Kavanagh in particular, naming evokes a realisation of divine presence. Thus, memory plays an important role in the creative process. 'On the stem of memory' he insists, 'imaginations blossom'. (**'Why Sorrow?'**) The mystic ritually re-members the object of love and recreates a new state of being-in-love:

And remembering you
O Sion, whom I loved,
In that sweet memory
I wept even more.[54]

In summary, Kavanagh was undoubtedly a self-styled lover. Love, requited and unrequited, rendered him vulnerable. The 'lovers that (he) could not have', inflicted on him a purification designed by the 'agonising pincer-jaws of heaven'. (**'Sanctity'**) Kavanagh knew only the language of Christian sanctification to describe his painful condition. But for this very reason, his love became mystical, capable of transforming the banalities and failures of life into shining radiances.

MYSTICAL TIME

One of the striking gifts of the mystic is his sense of the timeless. He can see the past in the present, and be simultaneously transported by a sudden flash of intuition into a timeless synthesis. For Kavanagh, local history and folklore provided foundational data which awakened his imagination and allowed him to see beyond recorded facts. He developed this habit in youth, as is seen in a fragment of juvenilia written about the Land Agent, Stuart Trench, who was alleged to have treated his tenants, and Kavanagh's ancestors in particular, with cruelty and disdain. Unable to pay their rent, the Callans, his grandmother's people, had had their land confiscated and succeeded only with difficulty in retaining a roof over their heads. The Agent's residence at Essex Castle, Carrickmacross, had, since 1888, become a convent-school where Kavanagh's contemporaries, including his sister Lucy, went to school:

> Today I see in my mind's eye
> A shadow of the Trenche's (*sic*) great
> Pass slowly through the convent gate,
> Those haters of the Celtic race
> Who lived to see their own disgrace
> And lived to see a convent grand
> Beneath the roof where oft they planned
> Destruction for the weak and small
> Who dared to break the landlord's thrall.[55]

> (**'Juvenilia'**)

This was one of Kavanagh's earliest attempts at poetry. Whatever its technical defects, it is clear that his intuitive faculty is already active. Time barriers crumble, nearness and distance intermingle as, in a mood of contemplation, he peers through the corridors of history and finds the 'mills of God' which grind slowly but 'grind exceedingly fine'. The rent-offices of the great Stuart Trench are slowly replaced by 'a convent grand', signalling a new era for this locality. A once-detested landlord's den, which repeatedly 'planned destruction' for the small farmers of the Bath Estate, is transformed. Kavanagh may intuitively have sensed something of Trench's harsh decisions that touched his ancestors, not merely when their land was taken from them, but more poignantly still, when his grandfather Patrick Kevany, the local schoolteacher, was banished from the area.[56]

Kavanagh's sense of mystical time becomes more explicit in his contemplation of the poplar trees which grow on Mucker lane. He recalled helping to plant these, selecting the straightest saplings with his father who imagined their future possibilities:

> My father dreamt forests, he is dead—
> And there are poplar forests in the waste places
> And on the banks of drains.

> (**'Poplars'**)

The trees, now fully grown, appear to the poet to link heaven and earth, past and present. The evocations of sun and earth link these trees with the Celtic underground gods, the mythological Tuatha Dé Danann who share the earth with mortals. Mention of his dead father evokes the world of the mortal and immortal Kavanaghs. 'These straightest spears of sky.' Are they trees? Or are they Kavanaghs? Throughout the poem our gaze is focused on his dead father, even now 'peering through the branched sky'. These trees will endure. They have, like other trees, 'caught him in their mysteries', since it is here 'among the poplars' that the spirit of his mother also walks:

> I do not think of you lying in the wet clay
> Of a Monaghan graveyard; I see
> You walking down a lane among the poplars
> On your way to the station . . .

> (**'In Memory of My Mother'**)

Father, mother and offspring are symbolically metamorphosed in a row of poplar trees. Once again, the poet transcends the barriers of chronological time.

An incident recounted by Kavanagh's nephew, Kieran Markey, recalls how in the 1950s, when his uncle Patrick took him, then a young boy, out of doors to play football in the garden, he became easily tired of the youngster. He would say, 'Leave me alone now, I want to do a bit of dramin' to myself,' whereupon he would lean against a tree and look off into the distance towards 'Cassidy's hanging hill', or towards Woods' fields, the setting of **'The Great Hunger'**, or Rocksavage and the 'triangular field' he loved. Kieran Markey had no idea that his uncle was even then caught in the grip of his 'fantasy soaring mind' or mystically communing with his hidden paradise.[57]

Kavanagh was frustrated, in youth, by the ceaseless round of farming chores which violated the rhythms of his poetic soul. As a farm-hand, working for a neighbour, he found the incessant pace of life irksome; the constant 'nag of jobs waiting to be done', a vicious circle, 'a wheel without a spoke of time missing'.[58] The much-needed 'spoke of time' was essential to the contemplation he needed as a poet. 'To get to know one small field or the corner of one is a life-time's experience'.[59] This is the language of the contemplative, as well as that of the poet. 'It's what the imagination does to things that makes them big.' At another time he speaks of 'moments as big as years', making one aware that time and space expand immeasurably in the mind of the poet and mystic.[60]

Kavanagh can occasionally appear to be outside time, contemplating his life from the standpoint of history. To his friend Tarry Lennon[61] (Eusebius Cassidy) he would say, as they worked together digging or sowing potatoes, 'Some day, people will say that you dug this ground with me.' Later in Dublin, he is even more confident that his name will survive:

> On Pembroke Road look out for my ghost,
> Dishevelled with shoes untied,
> Playing through the railings with little children
> Whose children have long since died.

> **('If ever you go to Dublin Town')**

Time past, present and future mingle uncannily, producing a deliberately eerie effect. A sense of ghostliness is achieved by blending the more permanent elements of life with the transitory ones: railings, children, a well-known Dublin street (Pembroke Road), and his own ghost wandering there 'dishevelled with shoes untied'. Prophetically he was correct. His loneliness, his humour, his eccentric cantankerousness, his spirituality and unfulfilled ambition still haunt Pembroke Road and vindicate the poet's 'trick of time' that makes the past present and sees the future now!

Dark Knowledge

As well as experiencing moments of mystical radiance, Kavanagh also underwent periods of spiritual darkness and painful emptiness. Vague murmurings of inner anguish can be detected in early lines which hint at some hellish experience:

> Child do not go
> Into the dark places of soul
> For there the lean wolves whine,
> The lean grey wolves.

> **('To A Child')**

It is difficult to interpret the sadness and rejection which surrounds some of the poet's earliest attempts at verse. In his **'Address to an Old Wooden Gate'** he depicts himself as 'the scorn of women,' rejected, laughed at, abused, like the 'old wooden gate'. He and the gate are kindred spirits:

> But you and I are kindred, Ruined Gate,
> For both of us have met the self-same fate.

> **('Juvenilia')**

He fluctuates between seeing himself as the darling child of the gods and as their persecuted servant. He often sounds the most sorrowful and rejected of mortals. He knows personal hurt from his native surroundings where 'the worm's opinion' and 'pointed harrow pins' cut deeply into his poetic sensibilities. His religious scruples, his 'monsters of despair', threaten him in a dark church while waiting for confession. Sexual confu-

sions tortured the delicacy of his conscience. These were, no doubt, the 'uncouth monsters', 'the nightmare of the soul and the fathers of remorse'[62] inflicted by a harsh religious teaching. He refers scathingly to 'a childhood perverted by Christian moralists'. But is there not something more that weighs on the poet's mind? The story of his lost genealogy will be discussed fully in Chapter Five.

The greatest exorcism of despair in Kavanagh, and perhaps the most complete expression of his 'dark night', was undoubtedly **'The Great Hunger'**. Spectre-like, the inhabitants of **'The Great Hunger'** groan with the anguish of unlived life. Physical, mental, emotional and spiritual famine stalk the land, bringing not death but half-life to these rural people. Kavanagh's personal nightmares are perhaps best expressed in such lines as:

> Life dried in the veins of these women and men:
> The grey and grief and unlove,
> The bones in the backs of their hands,
> And the chapel pressing its low ceiling over them.

Kavanagh is as powerful in his dark imagery as he is radiant in his spiritual seeing. His apocalypse of clay screams not only throughout 'every corner of this land' but also into the soul of every sympathetic reader. Its hysterical laugh is that of the defeated. One suspects that this dark dream emanated from the depths of his own psyche, where life was experienced at times as 'sad, grey, twisted, blind, just awful'.[63] Clay, often experienced as fruitful, is also experienced as dead and infertile as 'putty spread on stones' (***Lough Derg***). The poet's cry to 'the stony grey soil of Monaghan' is that of one robbed, forsaken, abandoned—even raped. His sharp Jansenistic upbringing frequently pruned life that is budding, green and full of promise. There remains for him only, on occasion, the sterile life of current pieties and religious hypocrisy which degenerated into a claustrophobia of popular devotion.

In religious terms Kavanagh's purification is endless. Though vigorously expressed in **'The Great Hunger'**, his despair, disillusionment and felt absence of God, is often suppressed and only given expression through the less worthy medium of angry, satirical verse.

Conclusion

At the beginning of this chapter we noted the general characteristics of the mystical path. It is seen to follow a spiral or maze-like movement, moving forward towards an unknown goal, yet frequently returning back on itself toward the point of departure. Kavanagh began with a springtime of poems written out of a vision of ordinary life in his Monaghan landscape. He returned, towards the end of his life, in **'Canal Bank Walk',** to the belief that, all along, this had been God's will for him. His pursuit of poetry may not exactly match the classical mystical pattern, but he did seem to be possessed of a desire to pursue a spiritual goal. The object of his desire, he knew, would be costly in personal terms. It would cost him 'something not sold for a penny / In the slums of the Mind'. For the desired prize he would be tireless in his efforts to 'climb the unending stair'. **'Ascetic'**

Though this poem **'Ascetic'** was written as early as 1930, its idealistic and self-conscious sentiments alert us to the truth that Kavanagh is a seeker in a mysterious territory—'in the other lands'. He is not interested in poetry as a technician; it is the hidden spark of the Divine that he seeks. He is prepared to work in difficult and lonely circumstances to pursue his goal. In the 1940s he renews his resolution and, though momentarily tempted to renege on his dream, as suggested in **'Temptation in Harvest'** (1945-46), he follows unflinchingly the beckoning 'wink' of his vocation. Though struggling with a series of failures in the early 50s, he is resolved to start again: 'I at the bottom will start.' This is the resolute promise he makes to himself in **'Auditors In'** (1951). It is not surprising that towards the end of his life, in spite of the many vicissitudes endured, Kavanagh can claim his inheritance before the final day of reckoning—'the opening of that holy door'. By then he knows that he will endure only because he has scorned interest in 'anything but the soul'.

Scant attention has, until now, been paid to Kavanagh's mystical propensities, yet there is abundant evidence of their existence. His visionary seeing, loving, knowing and his genuine insight into God's presence in everyday life is evident throughout his work. The sacramentality of ordinary life becomes the special focus of his attention, though he does not discount 'the dark places of the soul' as sources of purifying knowledge. Mystically, he crosses barriers of time and space as he embarks on his spiritual quest. On arrival in the dangerous territory of the mystic, he has, on his own admission, both taken fright and flight. Poetically speaking he 'became airborne', a flight that culminated in his 'hegira' on the banks of the Grand Canal in 1955.[64] The frightful element in his development involved an on-going purification, almost to the point of despair.

Kavanagh was undoubtedly a dreamer and a visionary, despite his outer cantankerous behaviour both in Inniskeen and Dublin. He told of his 'beatific wonder' to people whom he thought would understand but they laughed and thought he was mad.[65] Nevertheless, in his own intensely idiosyncratic way, I believe that he underwent the classic mystical pathway, outlined by Underhill, of Awakening, Purification and Illumination. Only a chosen few could see that his life was transformed towards the end. The nature of his personal encounter with God was hidden from most. This intensely personal aspect of his life he reserved for intimate friends, but above all for expression in poetry.

Notes

1. Evelyn Underhill, (Mrs Steward Moore), *Mysticism,* New York: E. P. Dutton and Co, Inc, Dutton Paperback ed., 1961, pp. 70-94.

2. St John of the Cross, 'The Spiritual Canticle' in *The Collected Works of St John of the Cross,* trans. Kieran Kavanaugh, O. C. D. and Otilio Rodriguez, O. C. D., Washington, DC: Institute of Carmelite Studies, 1973, p. 712. All further references to the writings of St John are taken from this edition unless otherwise stated.

3. Underhill, pp. 1-2.

4. Underhill, p. 48.

5. Joseph de Maistre quoted by Henri Bremond, *Prayer and Poetry,* London: Burns Oates and Washbourne Ltd, 1927, introductory quotations, n.p.

6. From the prayer *Anima Christi,* 'Blood of Christ, inebriate me'. See Underhill (1911), p. 235.

7. Roy Campbell trans., 'Upon a Gloomy Night', *Collected Poems,* III London: The Bodley Head Ltd, 1960, p. 47.

8. 'East Coker,' *Four Quartets,* New York: Harcourt, Brace and World, Inc., 1943, pp. 27-8.

9. William Johnston, *The Inner Eye of Love,* London: William Collins and Sons Ltd, 1978, p. 16.

10. Underhill, *Practical Mysticism,* New York: E. P. Dutton and Co, Inc, 1915, p. 9.

11. Brendan Kennelly ed., Joseph Mary Plunkett, 'I See His Blood Upon the Rose', *The Penguin Book of Irish Verse,* London: Penguin Books, 1970. p. 301.

12. William Johnston, p. 39.

13. Underhill (1911), p. 94.

14. Bremond, pp. 187-200.

15. Bremond, p. 187.

16. Underhill, p. 74. Blake's words are also quoted by W. B. Yeats, *Essays and Introductions,* London: Macmillan and Co Ltd, 1961, p. 117.

17. W. B. Yeats, 'Under Ben Bulben,' *Collected Poems,* ed. Augustine Martin, London: Arrow Books Ltd. An Arena Book, 1990 p. 342.

18. William Blake, 'Jerusalem,' in *Poetry and Prose of William Blake,* ed. Geoffrey Keynes, Bloomsbury, The Nonesuch Press, 1927, iii, pp. 649-702.

19. Quoted by Bremond, p. 199.

20. Bremond, p. 84 and p. 90.

21. Harvey D. Egan, *What are they saying about Mysticism?* New York: Paulist Press, 1982, pp. 42-50.

22. Gerard Manley Hopkins, *Poems and Prose,* H. Gardner ed., Middlesex, England: Penguin Books, 1953, p. 27.

23. Underhill, pp. 169-70. See also S. Foster Damon, *William Blake: His Philosophy and Symbols,* Gloucester, Mass., Peter Smith, 1958, p. 2. Here the five states of mystical development are successfully applied to the poetry of William Blake.

24. Mircea Eliade, *The Forge and the Crucible,* tr. Stephen Corrin, New York: Harper and Row, 1962, p. 142-4.

25. Martin Heidegger, 'What are Poets For?' in *Poetry, Language, Thought,* New York: Harper and Row Publishers Inc., 1971, p. 91.

26. Harvey Egan, *What are they saying about Mysticism?* New York: Paulist Press, 1982, p. 42.

27. Bremond, p. 187.

28. John Jordan, 'Mr Kavanagh's Progress,' *Studies,* 49 (Fall, 1960), p. 297.

29. The science of spiritual guidance practised in religious traditions east and west, had as its aim the discernment of true and false spirits.

30. Egan, p. 43.

31. Patrick Kavanagh, *The Green Fool,* London: Penguin Book, 1975, p. 201. All quotations are from this edition.

32. Patrick Kavanagh, *Tarry Flynn,* London: Penguin Books, 1978, p. 29. All quotations are from this edition.

33. *The Green Fool,* p. 194.

34. *Collected Pruse,* London: Martin, Brian and O'Keeffe, 1964, p. 198.

35. *The Green Fool,* p. 123.

36. Bremond, p. 88.

37. The edition of this poem entitled 'The Long Garden' published in *Collected Poems* by Brian and O'Keeffe in 1972 is preferable, to the edition as it appears in the long poem 'Why Sorrow?' as edited by Peter Kavanagh in *The Complete Poems,* New York: The Peter Kavanagh Hand Press, 1972.

38. *The Green Fool,* pp. 200-201.

39. William Johnston, ed. *The Cloud of Unknowing and the Book of Privy Counseling,* New York: Image Books, 1973.

40. *Sixth Reading Book,* Dublin: Alex Thom and Co, Ltd, 1889, Notes, p. 421, often referred to as the 'Sixth Book'.

41. Kavanagh refers to his 'third eye' in a poem entitled 'Remembered Country', p. 49. The notion of 'the third eye' is Indian in origin and denotes enlightenment. It is represented in Indian culture by the round spot painted on the forehead, the eye of true vision, contrasted with the illusory world of the flesh. See Johnston, pp. 143-151.

42. Kavanagh may have borrowed the reference to the Greek sculptor from 'Under Ben Bulben' by W. B. Yeats. It is more likely that he learned of Phidias from the 'Sixth Book', one of the Royal Readers, Dublin: Alex Thom and Co, Ltd, 1889, which he read after he had left primary school. The first lesson in this reader is a piece by Addison entitled 'Education compared to Sculpture', pp. 1-2. Aristotle's doctrine of substantial forms is referred to. He tells us that 'a statue lies hid (sic) in a block of marble', . . . 'The figure is in stone, the sculptor only finds it.' Phidias (432 BC) and Praxiteles (324 BC) are named as master-sculptors gifted with 'nice touches and finishings'. Explanatory notes in these readers provided comprehensive information.

43. Mircea Eliade, p. 144.

44. *Collected Pruse,* p. 33.

45. *The New Oxford Book of Irish Verse,* ed. Thomas Kinsella, Oxford: OUP, 1986, No. 19, p. 30.

46. *The Green Fool,* p. 74.

47. ibid., p. 180.

48. English magazines filled with snippets of information. *Titbits* is still being published at Stamford Street, London, SE1 9LS. The contents of these publications were the subject of conversation around the shoemaker's bench in the Kavanagh home.

49. *The Green Fool,* p. 154.

50. St John of the Cross, 'Stanzas Concerning an Ecstasy experienced in High Contemplation.' p. 719.

51. *Collected Pruse,* p. 195.

52. 'Is', 'Spraying the Potatoes' and 'The Long Garden' are among the poems to which I refer here.

53. For a further example of ritual naming see Brian Friel, 'Faith Healer', *Selected Plays,* London: Faber and Faber, 1984, pp. 327-376 at 332. Here the repetition of 'Kinlochbervie, Inverbervie, / Inverdruie, Invergordon, / . . . ,' acts as a kind of incantation whose very mention can effect healing.

54. St John of the Cross, 'A Romance on the Psalm "By the Waters of Babylon"', p. 733.

55. For the historical background to this poem see Peadar Livingstone, *The Monaghan Story,* Enniskillen: Clogher Historical Society, Watergate Press, 1980, p. 179. Kavanagh's information is accurate.

56. See Chapter Five for a full account of this incident.

57. Interview with Kieran Markey, nephew of the poet, January, 1991.

58. *The Green Fool,* p. 125.

59. *Irish Farmers Journal,* Sept 1, 1962.

60. 'Moments As Big As Years', *Creation,* July, 1957.

61. From an interview with Mr Terence Lennon, Hackballscross. August, 1990.

62. *The Green Fool,* p. 150.

63. *November Haggard,* Peter Kavanagh ed., New York, 1971, p. 16.

64. *Self Portrait,* p. 28.

65. *The Green Fool,* p. 123.

Alan A. Gillis (essay date 2001)

SOURCE: Gillis, Alan A. "Patrick Kavanagh's Poetics of the Peasant." In *Critical Ireland: New Essays in Literature and Culture,* edited by Alan A. Gillis and Aaron Kelly, pp. 87-95. Dublin: Four Courts Press, 2001.

[*In the following essay, Gillis analyzes the largely negative, but nuanced, view of the country and of peasant life presented in Kavanagh's long poem* The Great Hunger.]

As is well known, *The Great Hunger* attempted to vandalize Ireland's self-image. What might be called the ideology of ruralism provided a circuitry of images and ideas through which the collective Irish imagination conceived itself to be essentially Romantic. Roy Foster writes that de Valera's 'vision of Ireland . . . was of small agricultural units, each self-sufficiently supporting a frugal family; industrious, Gaelicist and anti-materialist. His ideal, like the popular literary versions, was built on the basis of a fundamentally dignified and ancient peasant way of life'.[1] Yet by the late 1930s, what Sean O'Faolain called a 'wholesale flight from the fields' was underway.[2] A Commission on Emigration later acknowledged a 'psychological and economic malaise' borne from the 'relative loneliness, dullness and generally unattractive nature of life in many parts of rural Ireland'.[3] And in this emerging context, ruralism was seen to be shrouding Ireland's modernization and poverty. Writers like O'Faolain and Kavanagh thus viewed it with increasing contempt. In *The Great Hunger,* the deteriorating effects of economic change in the country are manifest with the palpability of disease.

The poem parodies ruralism's amorphous structure of ideals:

> The peasant has no worries;
> In his little lyrical fields
> He ploughs and sows;
> He eats fresh food,
> He loves fresh women,
> He is his own master
> As it was in the Beginning
> The simpleness of peasant life.
> The birds that sing for him are eternal choirs,
> Everywhere he walks there are flowers.
> His heart is pure,
> His mind is clear,
> He can talk to God as Moses and Isaiah talked—
> The peasant who is only one remove from the beasts
>   he drives.[4]

If we disregard Kavanagh's irony for a moment, it is clear that ruralism provides a utopian alternative to modernity. By exploding these lyrical fields, Kavanagh fragments the ideal of an organic society integrated with nature, upon which Irish Ireland was founded.

At the core of this ideal is ruralism's great chain of being, in which each entity obtains autonomy within a broader, naturalized amalgamation. Kavanagh's scene is synecdochically structured: the lyrical fields stand for the world; the birds, beasts and flowers stand for the entirety of nature; and the peasant stands for humanity, deriving meaning through an intrinsic relationship with the totality. At the same time, the birds, beasts, flowers and fields stand for aspects of each other and of man and God (and vice versa).[5] Taking offence at this, Kavanagh represents the peasant as an alienated and overworked wreck. His poem insists that Maguire, the man-of-the-earth bereft of the complexities of modernity, is at root no closer to nature than an office clerk. And yet, the poem's power is partially derived through its relationship with pastoral utopianism. It is highly conscious of its own fragmentation, a fallen world in thrall to the promise of synecdochic integration. For example, the first line, 'Clay is the word and clay is the flesh', by the very nature of its mimicry, denotes a secular world conscious of Christ's absence.[6] The line initiates a momentum of desire. The homology of each hemistich, 'Clay is the word' / 'clay is the flesh', draws them together; the caesural 'and' is almost like a pivot upon which they could be folded into one another, yet it simultaneously divides them in parallel isolation. And this gesture of intimated but withheld union is paradigmatic, not just of Christianity, but of many Romantic poetic modes, such as Yeats' early apocalyptic symbolism.

If we disregard the line's poetic structure, however, the message is that word and flesh *do* combine in clay, just as they do in Christ. In other words, the apocalypse has already happened. The opening nihilism of the poem suggests that clay denotes a vacuum of meaning, that this is an apocalypse of non-significance. But clay is more equivocal than this. Elsewhere we are told that 'Unless the clay is in the mouth the singer's singing is useless'.[7] When hardened, clay normally connotes stasis and death. But when wet it is malleable, and clay is inextricably bound up with the imagery of creation. The substitution of clay for Christ, then, is only superficially negative. But it does get rid of immaterialism. The poem's rejection of Christ signifies that the confrontation between word and flesh, or consciousness and the world, is to be mediated directly. The church is said, in a clumsy phrase, to lift 'Prophecy out of the clayey hours', and makes Maguire rush 'beyond the thing / To the unreal'.[8] This is part of his tragedy and why the church must be condemned. Against such abstraction, language, if it became clay-like, would retain body, substance, and relevance to the brute materiality of nature. Concomitantly, if clay became language-like, it would be anthropomorphized and malleable to human subjects. Thus clay-language would be a mid-point between consciousness and nature, and a culture bound by such language would be the antithesis of

> . . . that metaphysical land
> Where flesh was a thought more spiritual than music
> Among the stars—out of the reach of the peasant's
> hand.[9]

This frisson between senses, in the opening line, engenders a dialectic that runs throughout the poem. Maguire is alienated primarily because of his consuming labour, his need to impose order on an otherwise unproductive nature, so that he and his family can eat. It is this predicament which shatters any vestige of pastoral idealism. Yet one image in the poem tells us

> These men know God the father in a tree:
> The Holy Spirit is the rising sap,
> And Christ will be the green leaves that will come
> At Easter from the sealed and guarded tomb.[10]

Here, the feminine earth is a locus of death, a tomb, transfigured into a womb through propagation with the phallic tree. Both feminine matter and masculine energy are necessary for life. This image stands as a kind of master-image, a magnet pulling Maguire's desire. Conventionally, within Romanticism, the task of impregnating fallen nature with divinity is passed over to man. And in this sense, Maguire's plight is that of

the failed Romantic artist. The poem sends him on a quest for synecdochic integration, and his perpetually thwarted desire for this is mostly figured through his interminable sexual yearning.

The other side of the dialectic, though, works against this Romantic propulsion. In one passage, we are told

> . . . Maguire learns
> As the horses turn slowly round the which is which
> Of love and fear and things half born to mind.
> He stands between the plough-handles and he sees
> At the end of a long furrow his name signed
> Among the poets, prostitute's. With all miseries
> He is one. Here with the unfortunate
> Who for half moments of paradise
> Pay out good days and wait and wait
> For sunlight-woven cloaks.[11]

Maguire's signature, his identity, is bound up with that of the poet and prostitute, word and flesh. The 'sunlight-woven cloaks' echo Yeats' embroidered cloths of heaven, linking the passage to his symbolist poetics.[12] But the prolonged wait for these cloaks proves that the symbolist world is entirely proleptic. The satiation of desire is always expected in this world, but, like Godot, never quite turns up. Maguire senses that his name (word) will be inscribed in the soil (flesh), yet this is posited as a telos, something that will happen at 'the end of a long furrow' (when he is dead). In the meantime, something half-sensed or barely intuited is to recompense. Kavanagh thus implicitly critiques such symbolism as an opiate for the masses, a blockade against knowledge and agency, a poetic attuned to masturbation rather than consummation.

Against this, the poem claims that 'God is in the bits and pieces of Everyday'.[13] A poetic based on the positive connotations of clay seems is offered as an alternative to synecdochic Romanticism. Within this alternative, to focus on clay or corporeal matter is to focus on the here and now. And much of *The Great Hunger* is, accordingly, metonymic. More than this, the world of clay, as opposed to the world of Christ, enables things to stand for, within bounds, whatever the perceiver makes of them. Therefore, metonymic apprehension is spliced with metaphor to allow a verisimilar depiction of contiguous reality illuminated by the depth created by imaginative association. In this mode, Maguire is sometimes released from pining for total meaning, and is allowed to get on with simply being in the world. And yet the absence of a sense of total order, the destabilization of meaning, always shadows this aspect of the poem with doubt, with an intimation of its own limitations.

Thus the poem spins recurrent loops of non-resolution. Apocalyptic tropes are dismissed in places, but the synecdochic urge towards integration remains constant.

Likewise, a metonymic-metaphorical apprehension is sometimes embraced, but then is dismissed elsewhere. Every articulation and gesture is made within the wider context of alternative perspectives. The poem is therefore panoptic and ironic. It is put together by a process of juxtaposition that is surprisingly reminiscent of Pound, or at least of other long poems that develop the tenets of Imagism. *The Great Hunger* is built of perpetual shifts in focus and tone. At the same time, however, the poem utilises a narrator who supposedly guides the images. Vivid imagery is often accompanied with a rhetorical heavy-handedness which comes from over-zealous prompts for readers to connect image and narrative. This develops a gap between narrative message (one of monotony, waste and tragedy), and aesthetic experience (one of variety, energy and polysemy). And this tension between the poem's ironic sophistication and its overbearing fatalism is tangible throughout.

The narrative voice plays off the deeper, ironic structures of the poem. For example, after a passage that condemns the church for stemming instinct, we are told: 'For the strangled impulse there is no redemption'.[14] The assurance and attractiveness of the thought suggests this is the poem's, or Kavanagh's, true point of view. But this sentiment is surely questioned when consideration turns to 'Schoolgirls of thirteen', who 'Would see no political intrigue in an old man's friendship'—an idea that is only discarded because

> . . . there was danger of talk
> And jails are narrower than the five-sod ridge
> And colder than the black hills facing Armagh in February.[15]

In ways such as this, the narration swamps the reader in a tide of irresolution, reducing us to the level of Maguire. As Kavanagh castigates his society's image of the peasant, he replaces it with a kaleidoscope of perspectives upon an enigma.

Like Maguire, the reader is trapped by an irony that is ultimately negative: avenues of possibility almost inevitably turn out to be cul de sacs, forcing a return to the one-way passage towards futility. The ironic gamesmanship and play with modes of representation, the vivid creation of a metonymic-metaphorical verisimilitude, the polysemic experience encountered in much of the imagery: all of this works dialectically against, but cannot stem the tide of, the poem's superimposition of a tragic narrative.

But ironically, as the poem progresses towards its apocalypse, it articulates with evermore clarity an argument against apocalypticism. Just before the final section, we are explicitly told there were 'No mad hooves galloping in the sky'.[16] And even at the poem's powerful climax, the apocalypse is reached in the context of yet more unanswered questions:

> Maybe he will be born again, a bird of an angel's conceit
> To sing the gospel of life . . .
> Will that be? will that be?
> Or is the earth right that laughs: haw haw
> And does not believe
> In an unearthly law.

Interestingly, this last question lacks a question mark, most likely to deflect attention away from the indecision, in order to garner momentum for the conclusion:

> . . . No hope. No. No lust.
> The hungry fiend
> Screams the apocalypse of clay
> In every corner of this land.[17]

But the apocalypse can only be read in the context of the two unanswerable questions: Is there a God? Is there a natural order?

The ending has powerful connotations. One could read into it the revelation of a God who is angry at the absence of faith, or the revelation of a nature that has not been understood and thus appears vengeful. But such connotations are predicated upon a teleological dynamic that is contrary to the poem's assertion that Maguire's life entails 'No crash, / No drama'.[18] The apocalyptic ending in fact works against the poem's dominant sense of irresolution, providing an emotive punch to counteract it with.

We began, however, with ruralism, whose great chain of being perpetuates the illusion that Ireland is a self-enclosed entity cut off from modernist change and international forces. The synecdochic propensity to relate the lyrical fields with the whole of Ireland engenders a sense of the nation effused with idealism. It should now be clear that, underneath its surface attack, *The Great Hunger* remains dialectically structured by the trope that forms the basis of such ruralism. Arguably, it is of continuing aesthetic importance because of its immersion in the thought structures that it condemns. Indeed, Kavanagh's paradoxical complex of poetic modes, the tensions within the poem's tropic structure, provide an interesting point of intersection with the cultural-historical perspectives through which it might be contextualized.

By maintaining an apocalyptic structure, the poem recognizes the emotional pull of romantic nationalism, the apparent symbolic abyss of any alternative. The alternative that *is* postulated, a kind of metonymic apprehension of the world, content to forgo the stability of static integration with a fixed cosmic order, might be compared to the mode of historical thought articulated by Sean O'Faolain. O'Faolain is posited, in *The Field Day Anthology of Irish Writing,* as one of Ireland's first historical 'revisionists', whose rejection of Romantic-historical thought came in tandem with a view of Ireland as modern and European. Undoubtedly, O'Faolain's (and others') categorical rejection of Romanticism provided Kavanagh with a positive aesthetic alternative: pragmatic Realism. The distinction between O'Faolain's pragmatic realism and Irish Ireland's Romanticism provide a backdrop to the contradictions of Kavanagh's poem.[19] Yet *The Great Hunger* also indicates how the two shadow each other.

Terence Brown argues how prototypical revisionists such as O'Faolain predicated their vision, like de Valera, on a conception of Ireland's autonomy:

> There was a sense . . . in which the writers and the politicians were not in fundamental disagreement. They may have differed on the historical basis of contemporary Irish society and disagreed profoundly in their conscious assessment of the quality of Irish life, but they shared a faith that the Irish future would depend on . . . a commitment to the essential worth of Irish experience.[20]

Kavanagh's poem likewise shows a commitment to the country in the midst of its assault. In a sense, his rural scene is as enclosed as the lyrical fields he would explode. In the 1930s (as before and after), the Irish countryside was incontrovertibly politicized: rightwing Fine Gael activists and leftwing Republican initiatives both found root support amongst farmers. But Kavanagh's poem is utterly bereft of such politics and recent history. The one reference to WWII emphasises the community's isolation from it.

One of the dominant motifs in the poem involves boundaries and their transgression. Images of hedges and walls proliferate, symbolizing boundaries between the self and alterity. It is implied that Maguire must break through them if he is to transform his alienated mode of existence. And his failure to do so reflects the poem's own imprisonment within an apocalyptic narrative structure, the debilitating retention of the desire for synecdochic enclosure.

Kavanagh's use of a predetermined tragic narrative or enclosed form, which his poem energetically reacts against, is a means of critique using the emotive force of negation. He inverts idealistic Romanticism to such an extent that its retention becomes quite obscene. Nevertheless, although *The Great Hunger* critiques the non-transgression of boundaries of the self, Kavanagh would later base his poetic on the necessity of a perpetual and fraught dialectic between self and alterity.[21] Without some form of boundaries or sense of self, there can be nothing: the utopia of hybridity is as empty as the utopia of self-sufficient homogeneity.

In many ways, Kavanagh's hedges are a thorn in the side of Irish historical thought, because questions of autonomy and openness continually prove to be a site

of incessant contradiction for modes of historical interpretation. For example, Terry Eagleton writes of the Famine as a kind of abyss in historical thought that scatters the sense of the nation and history throughout space and time.[22] Yet the Famine simultaneously becomes a symbol of unity: the experience of disaster strengthening the communal sense of self. In a similar manner, O'Faolain's historiography opens the door to Europe and international forces, yet this ultimately serves to strengthen the sense of nation by altering its foundations so that it can survive the epistemic shift to Modernity.

To an extent, then, *The Great Hunger* reveals the limitations of the historiographical models available to Irish studies. We have noted that Ireland was experiencing deep-structural economic change during the time of the poem. And whilst the 'base' is in transition, Marxists say, any paradigmatic form through which civilization chooses to conceive of itself will be unstable and founded on contradiction. Maguire's poverty remains constant, but the poem deflects attention away from this towards explorations of aesthetic and interpretative models, all of which are futile. Seamus Deane has conceived of Irish historiography as dualistic: the only possible alternatives for historical thought lie with either apocalypse or boredom.[23] Kavanagh, describing Maguire, points out 'The hysteria and the boredom of the enclosed nun of his thought', which makes plain, contra Deane, the felt need for a prescription against these emotions.[24] A formulation such as Deane's is synecdochically closed off, occluding the possibility of a historical perspective predicated on the analysis of global economic transformation, or on a consideration of class inequality within Ireland.

Then again, Marxism's internationalism is predicated on a conception of the ineluctable interrelationship of historical objects and forces. If one node along an interconnected chain is altered, the qualitative nature of the whole is transformed. As a mode of historical thought, therefore, Marxism is based on the trope of synecdoche as much as nationalism is. Just as revisionism attacks Romanticism but retains the boundaries of nationhood, so internationalist perspectives lead to yet another synecdochic formulation, to the extent that most are predicated on explanatory models that explain diachronic change within synchronic contexts.

This perpetual movement away from synecdoche that somehow leads back to it again reflects the dynamics that structure *The Great Hunger.* It might be that the insistent recurrence of synecdoche points to the fallacy of criticising it, or, by extension, the concept of organicism. The trope or concept is of relative value, dependent on its particular usage. Although Kavanagh attacks the hypocrisy of Romanticism in relation to contemporary destitution, it is the synecdochic propensity to understand things as interconnected within a provisional whole that brings contradiction to light in the first place. Perhaps more importantly, it is the idea of patterned interconnectivity that provides the impetus to resolve those contradictions. Organicism, whilst exponentially unfashionable at the moment, is one half of most formulations of dialectical change. Kavanagh could not critique rural destitution without an awareness of something better. The challenge that **The Great Hunger** lays down for Irish critics is to decide what their 'something better' might be.

Notes

1. Roy Foster, *Modern Ireland 1600-1972* (London: Penguin, 1989) 538.

2. Sean O'Faoláin, 'Silent Ireland', *The Bell,* 6:5 (August 1943) 464.

3. Terence Brown, *Ireland: A Social and Cultural History 1922-1985* (London: Fontana, 1985) 184-5.

4. Patrick Kavanagh, *Selected Poems,* ed. Antoinette Quinn (London: Penguin, 1996) 40.

5. Hayden White describes synecdoche as a trope that posits 'an *intrinsic* relationship of shared *qualities*'. Thus, a synecdoche combines elements 'in the manner of an *integration* within a whole that is *qualitatively* different from the sum of the parts'. Synecdoche 'suggests a relationship among the parts . . . which is qualitative in nature and in which all of the parts participate'. *Metahistory: The Historical Imagination in Nineteenth-Century Europe* (London: Johns Hopkins UP) 35-6.

6. *Selected Poems* 18.

7. Ibid. 41.

8. Ibid. 25.

9. Ibid. 29.

10. Ibid. 23.

11. Ibid. 24.

12. 'Had I the heaven's embroidered cloths / Enwrought with golden and silver light', W. B. Yeats, *Collected Poems* (London: Picador, 1990) 81.

13. Kavanagh, *Selected Poems* 28.

14. Ibid. 25.

15. Ibid. 35.

16. Ibid. 42.

17. Ibid. 44.

18. Ibid. 41.

19. O'Faolain, along with Frank O'Connor and Liam O'Flaherty, had a direct influence on Kavanagh's writing in the period leading up to and throughout the writing of 'The Great Hunger'. See Antoinette Quinn's *Patrick Kavanagh: Born Again Romantic* (Dublin: Gill and Macmillan, 1991).

20. Brown, *Ireland: A Social and Cultural History* 159.

21. Kavanagh's poem 'Innocence' contains the lines 'They said / That I was bounded by the whitethorn hedges / Of the little farm and did not know the world'. But it ends 'I cannot die / Unless I walk outside these whitethorn hedges'. *Selected Poems* 101.

22. 'Part of the horror of the Famine is its atavistic nature—the mind-shaking fact that an event with all the premodern character of a medieval pestilence happened in Ireland with frightening recentness. This deathly origin then shatters space as well as time, unmaking the nation and scattering Irish history across the globe'. *Heathcliff and the Great Hunger: Studies in Irish Culture* (London: Verso, 1995) 14.

23. *Strange Country: Modernity and Nationhood in Irish Writing since 1790* (Oxford: Clarendon, 1987).

24. Kavanagh, *Selected Poems* 31.

John McAuliffe (essay date 2001)

SOURCE: McAuliffe, John. "Urban Hymns: The City, Desire and Theology in Austin Clarke and Patrick Kavanagh." In *Critical Ireland: New Essays in Literature and Culture,* edited by Alan A. Gillis and Aaron Kelly, pp. 166-73. Dublin: Four Courts Press, 2001.

[*In the following essay, McAuliffe discusses the place of the city, and of Dublin in particular, in the poetry of Kavanagh and Austin Clarke.*]

The city has rarely been central to poetry in the Irish republic. Patrick Kavanagh, the laureate of the Free State, is primarily read for his early lyrics, the canal bank poems and **'The Great Hunger',** poems that are at the heart of a still-thriving pastoral tradition in Irish poetry. Austin Clarke's poetic character is more difficult to establish; he is usually read as either the Anglo-Gaelic poet of 'The Lost Heifer' and 'The Blackbird of Derrycairn', or as one of the State's most effective but erratic satirists. While neither man has been much considered as an urban poet, I will argue that reading both in an urban context clarifies critical ideas about their central pre-occupations. I will focus on their work in the mid-1950s when, for the first time, they both lived and published poetry in the same city.[1]

Although both men wrote about London and New York, Dublin is the central metropolis in their work. This is the Dublin of Archbishop John Charles McQuaid, a man with whom both poets had connections. Clarke's mother famously disinherited her anti-clerical son by willing the family home to the Dublin diocese; on the other hand, McQuaid intervened to find Kavanagh a job first in the 1940s as a film reviewer and later as a UCD lecturer, in addition to granting him irregular financial assistance, probably McQuaid's greatest contribution to Irish intellectual life at this time.[2] Otherwise, an exacting, abstract city of god loomed over Dublin, shadowing every corner of the city, as is most evident in the Marian year 1954. This was a starting point for an intensive church-building programme and also led to the institution of the Angelus bells on RTE radio. In a recent essay, the poet Thomas McCarthy points out that, although it was originally a one-year honour to the virgin which RTE took off the air at the end of 1954, the angelus broadcast was reinstituted due to public demand in 1955 and is still with us.[3] So, during Clarke and Kavanagh's lifetime, the city of Dublin is primarily defined by the increasingly powerful presence of Catholicism. The church dominates Ireland's cultural discourse as well as its political life and physical landscape. There is not much sign of a counterculture—with the passing of Yeats' generation, both poets describe the city's literary culture as impoverished and in constant retreat.

However, they respond very differently to this social situation. In effect, though hardly in intention, Kavanagh's poetry after **'The Great Hunger'** is receptive to if not supportive of Ireland's and Dublin's Catholicization. This will be clearer after an examination of those poems that take an urban theme. The city is present even in Kavanagh's earliest lyric poems, written in Monaghan. In **'Gay Cities'**, Kavanagh imagines himself in the city, 'crushed and shoved in the rude / unknowing throng'; in **'Ascetic',** he sees the poet searching the 'slums of Mind' for the invaluable, elusive material for poetry (11, 5). In **'At Noon',** the city is identified with self-destructive desire:

> Now at the passionate noon
> The no-good dames
> Tatoo my flesh with the indelible
> Ink of lust.
>
> What are these dim rooms
> And red ghost-lamps?
> Tell me this city's name,
> New York or Paris?
>
> Heaven was somewhere about
> A child ideal.
> Ah! The disillusioned one cried,
> You have come too far
>
>   (22).

In the well-known **'Memory of my Father',** this sense of displacement in an anonymous, amoral, brutal urban world is also present: 'Every old man I see / Reminds me of my father', he begins, as he walks down London's Gardiner Street, and the poem concludes

> Every old man I see
> In October-coloured weather
> Seems to say to me:
> 'I was once your father'
>
>   (69).

Again the city is a place where man wanders, lost and orphaned, without community or family. For Kavanagh, this is no liberation, and there is a constant desire to return to the more secure identities of rural life, however harsh that life may be.

For Kavanagh, the city is never a subject in itself; the poems are grounded in a formulaic opposition where the city is always present as the flipside of a child's rural life. The poems are **'The Lake Isle of Inisfree',** rewritten time after time, setting up a simple opposition: the world of pavements, roadways and adulthood against the field, the lane and childhood. The poems ignore current political usages of that rural vision, images that culminate in de Valera's famous 1941 St Patrick's Day speech. They also ignore Yeats' own complication of that rural scene, they ignore Clarke's epic revisions of that Irish landscape which see it as an arduous stage for the humbling of man, and later, they ignore his own **'The Great Hunger',** the great poem that he spent much of his career repudiating.

At this point, it is worth noting that, and this may be already clear, much of Kavanagh's least interesting poetry is on an urban theme. When he does attempt to transform the city, to see it as a viable place for writing, he writes an utterly odd poem like **'Phoenix'** that attaches his characteristic redemptive conclusion to the grim and clichéd image of the urban scrap-yard,

> A Leeds furnace
> Is the Phoenix
> From whose death-wings on this scrap-heap
> Will rise
> Mechanic vigour.
> We believe.
> Now is the Faith-dawn
>
>   (6).

This oddity apart, an anti-modern posture continues to predicate all of Kavanagh's poetry, although other, more concrete urban spaces are introduced and consistently examined in the 1950s. The city at mid-century is characterized by two settings, the pub and the street—the former is the court where Kavanagh judges his contemporaries and bewails the unParnassian nature of city life and the problem of 'literary gloom'. (In poems like **'If you ever go to Dublin Town / Look for me on Pembroke Road'**, Kavanagh is dying to be remembered, and dying to be gone too). Many of these poems take the form of ballads and verse drama and have been clearly discussed by Antoinette Quinn in her account of Kavanagh's self-representation as a heroic figure.[4]

The other kind of city poem is set on the street, usually the site of the opportunistic male gaze. In **'The Rowley Mile'**, a poem that imitates the disconcertingly uncomfortable trajectory of **'On Raglan Road'** (187), **'Grafton Street Admiration'** (130), **'Good By Ladies'** (209), and **'Along the Grand Canal'** (297), the poet approaches a woman after an exchange of glances, only to be rebuffed:

> The street was full of eyes that stared
> At something very odd.
> I tried to imagine how little means
> Such a contretemps to God.
> I followed her a few slow yards
> 'Please just one minute stop'
> And then I dashed with urgent tread
> Into a corner shop.
>
> As I walked down that sunny street
> I was a broken man
> Thanks to an Irish girl
> But is true to the plan
> Taught her by old Gummy Granny—
> You must try out your power with a smile,
> But come to the test hard reality must
> Make the pace on the Rowley Mile

(260).

The city street, as in his earliest poems, is the occasion of desire but only ever provides frustrating glimpses of another lifestyle that can never be realized. But even when successful, the city can get in the lover's way, intruding as the despoiler of innocent nostalgia: in **'Love in a Meadow'**,

> She waved her body in the circle sign
> Of love purely born without side;
> The earth's contour, she orbited to my pride,
> Sin and unsin.
> But the critic asking questions ran
> From the fright of the dawn
> To weep later on an urban lawn
> For the undone,
> God-gifted man

(289).

Love and art can only be contained and sustained in the unthinking, stable setting of rural life and Kavanagh's vision of love and the good life is always the backward, northwestern look. In poems like **'Miss Universe'** where the body is actually graphically *mentioned*, it is never in an urban context and religious prescriptions are never more than a couple of lines away:

> O the sensual throb
> Of the explosive body and tumultuous thighs!

> Adown a summer lane comes Miss Universe
> She whom no lecher's art can rob
> Though she is not the virgin who was wise

(291).

When he writes positively of the city, in the canal bank poems, it is a domesticated city, connected to the rural world—'the barge comes bringing from Athy / And other far-flung towns mythologies.'[5] Or, it is a city whose sense of community is comically rural and familial in its intimacy: 'And be excited to meet old acquaintances such as / A branch in the water and a cocksfoot of this year's growth / And be able to say I knew your father and your mother both.'[6]. In a fine early poem like **'The 6:40 from Amiens Street'**, reader and protagonist are soon transported into the pastoral scene where Kavanagh's lyrical intensity safely retreats from the problematic conservatism of contemporary Catholicism. That poem begins:

> O is it 1940
> Or a thousand years ago
> We are not going home by train
> We are riding through the snow

(75).

Where Kavanagh retreats from the ruins and rubble, the transformations and the multiplicity of city life, Austin Clarke celebrates the unsettling power of the urban to produce disorder and change. Clarke was born in Dublin's North inner city and he received his primary and secondary education there and in Limerick—he completed a BA and an MA at UCD, where he taught for a short time; he then spent 15 years working as book-reviewer in London. The city, however, does not appear as a subject in Clarke's work until late in his career, with the publication of the short book of satires *Ancient Lights*. In 1955, at the age of 59, Clarke approaches the city of Dublin and its governance. Gone is the harsh, wet and windy natural landscape of the early work, gone too is the recourse to Gaelic myth and symbol; in its stead is an urgency that insists on the modern city as the battleground of civilization. Clarke, to paraphrase Eavan Boland, passes on myth and moves into history. It is telling that the first poem in the collection, 'Celebrations', takes its form from the ballad 'Who fears to speak of '98?': Clarke's poem begins 'Who dare complain or be ashamed / Of liberties our arms have taken?' (195). The ballad form and Clarke's role as satirist, both ashamed and complaining about the state, clearly announce the new turn his poetry has taken. After 1955, Clarke consistently refers to urban life and contemporary political and religious intrigue—his satires will be a reliable map to the changing state. As Thomas McCarthy puts it: 'in the 1950s faith had a vibrant street-life. Clarke follows this life around the Free State like a well-rehearsed heckler.'[7]

In the title poem of *Ancient Lights,* he meditates at length upon his radical decision to write poetry that is specifically grounded in an urban environment. It is a central poem for any understanding of Clarke's later work, as a close reading illustrates.[8] The poem's title is typical of Clarke's rich contextual subtlety—it refers to the building law that allows tenants to object to any new building that obstructs daylight naturally entering their windows. Until recently, objectors had only to chalk the words 'Ancient Light' on the house wall to protect their right. Clarke's poem is an equivalent writing on the wall, defending the natural light of the protagonist from the construction that the church places on his words and his place. Crudely expressed, the poem's theme is the Church's domination of the young poet's mental and physical landscape. Clarke begins:

> When all of us wore smaller shoes
> And knew the next world better than
> The knots we broke, I used to hurry
> On missions of my own to Capel
> Street, Bolton Street and Granby Row
> To see what man has made.[9]

The stanza immediately concerns itself with spatial definition: Clarke contrasts the well-known 'next world' (of heaven and hell) with the actual living reality of which the terrified child is hardly aware. Line 5 ironically contrasts the shopping streets of Capel et al ('what man has made') with the divinely authorized church. The boy's obsessive concern with other worldly knowledge is evident in the pun of the third line where he 'breaks the knots' of shoelaces and also, unknowingly, the 'thou shalt nots' of the ten commandments. A further pun on 'missions' contrasts the errands on which children are sent with the religious Missions to the non-Catholic world.

The stanza continues

> But darkness
> Was roomed with fears. Sleep, stripped by woes
> I had been taught, beat door, leaped landing,
> Lied down the banisters of naught.

The darkness of the night (and later the Church and its confessional) is imbued with fear, due to the taught 'woes' that populate his imagination. Then, Clarke puns on 'landing', denoting the top of a staircase but also the groundedness of human life that eludes him since he has entered the fantastic world of superstition and fear. The 'lying' on the banister sends him on a rollercoaster ride out of the physical world and describes the child's utter rootlessness in the arcane unreality of dogma: the 'naught' from which he cannot escape into reality.

The next two stanzas describe the reason for the child's terror, the false confession where he unwittingly confessed to sins of the flesh, 'immodest look . . . un-

necessary touch.' The fourth and fifth stanzas recount a liberating incident outside the church, when the child witnesses a cage bird devoured by sparrows, an event that he is unable to prevent. Confronted by mortality, the child despairs, but moments later a 'bronze bird' attacking the sparrows is distracted by the child's shouts. The 'lesson' is this: 'Pity / Could raise some littleness from dust,' a striking thought that grants agency and a sacrilegiously godlike power of resurrection to the young child. The next stanza relates this notion to the adult world that Clarke now inhabits, 'among the hatreds of rent Europe', and praises freethinkers, Martin Luther and Clarke's namesake, St Augustine.

The final stanzas again return to the moment of liberation that freed his childhood from oppressive religious strictures, and the scene is again the city street, where the child takes shelter from a downpour in the doorway of the heretic protestant church, (the Black Church where, superstition has it, if you walk twice round, after dark, you will meet the devil himself).[10] The city, undogmatic, open still to accident and dialogue offers Clarke salvation:

> Still, still I remember awful downpour
> Cabbing Mountjoy Street, spun loneliness
> Veiling almost the Protestant church,
> Two backyards from my very home,
> I dared to shelter at locked door.
> There, walled by heresy, my fears
> Were solved. I had absolved myself:
> Feast-day effulgence, as though I gained
> For life a plenary indulgence.

Clarke sets out his beliefs and writes that he can and has absolved himself—the location is symbolic, on a busy, rainy street, at the door of the Protestant church, like Martin Luther before him. His use of sacramental language grants the church an almost bridal appearance, the rain baptizes his new fearlessness. By judicious punning the last stanza also recovers for secular use the language of confession (by the poet's apt choice of verb and image for the concluding downpour: he hears 'half our heavens' pass through the street sewer's confessional grille), mass (the pun on 'services') and papal election ('New smoke flew up'). The Catholic Church's dominance of language and the urban scene is fiercely contested and the last stanza also diminishes religion's abstract spirituality, concentrating instead on the physical and human landscapes that underpin and here undermine such Catholic structures.

The stanza finally forces our attention on mortality, the body, and the excremental street:

> The sun came out, new smoke flew up,
> The gutters of the Black Church rang
> With services. Waste water mocked
> The ballcocks: down-pipes sparrowing,
> And all around the spires of Dublin

Such swallowing in the air, such cowling
To keep high offices pure: I heard
From shore to shore, the iron gratings
Take half our heavens with a roar.

In 'Ancient Lights', Clarke describes the terrain which his imagination habitually inhabits thereafter, an area familiar to residents of Dublin and readers of Clarke's work. With a typically allusive wit, Clarke illuminates a moment of crisis when powerful forces test the identity of the individual. There is no over-reaching search for closure: rather, Clarke is content to represent characters living in doubt, uncertainty and confusion, a state that is imagined as the babbling city street. The poem's difficulty, the reticence of its style, is itself a rebuke to the kind of preaching and oversimplification that defined the political and religious morality of Roman Catholic Ireland.

To conclude, and to finally refer to this paper's title, neither poet is able to write the kind of conformist urban hymn that the age demanded—Kavanagh's conservative religious sensibility conceives of the city as irretrievably a place of fear, desire and sin. On the other hand, Clarke squares up to his urban situation, but he produces poems that deliberately evade the simplicity that characterizes popular song. Clarke's city is the place where he sings from his own dissonant hymn sheet, where he discovers a way out of the mass devotions that characterized Irish religious practice during his lifetime.

Notes

1. All quotations from poems are taken from Austin Clarke, *Collected Poems* (Dublin: Dolmen, 1974) and Patrick Kavanagh, *The Complete Poems* (Newbridge: Goldsmith, 1991). Further references are to these editions and are cited in the text.

2. John Cooney *Archbishop John Charles McQuaid: Ruler of Catholic Ireland* (Dublin: O'Brien, 1999) 142, 459.

3. Thomas McCarthy, *Gardens of Remembrance* (Dublin: New Island, 1998) 196.

4. Antoinette Quinn, *Patrick Kavanagh: Born Again Romantic* (Dublin: Gill and Macmillan, 1991)

5. 'Lines Written on a Seat . . .' (295).

6. 'Cool Water Under Bridges' (296).

7. McCarthy 196.

8. This close reading is indebted to other readers of the poem, including Maurice Harmon, *Austin Clarke: A Critical Introduction* (Dublin: Wolfhound, 1989) 154-9; and W. J. McCormack *Austin Clarke: Selected Poems* Dublin: Lilliput, 1991) 234-5.

9. 'Ancient Lights' 199-201. All further quotations are from this text.

10. Austin Clarke, *Twice round the Black Church: Early Memories of Ireland and England* (Dublin: Moytura, 1990 [1962]) 22.

Una Agnew (essay date winter 2004)

SOURCE: Agnew, Una. "The God of Patrick Kavanagh." *Studies: An Irish Quarterly Review* 93, no. 372 (winter 2004): 437-47.

[*In the following essay, Agnew discusses Kavanagh's career-long exploration into the nature of God and the Absolute, focusing on the organic and feminine characteristics of Kavanagh's God.*]

Writers, poets, philosophers and theologians alike, have grappled to find suitable language to describe the overarching Mystery that surrounds our lives. God has been severally named as: "Creator", "Ground of Being", "Uncaused Cause", "Ineffable Mystery" "Nurturing Mother" "Eternal Father" . . . the list is endless. Gerard Manley Hopkins bravely attempts to encapsulate the physical energy and grace of Christ in the dynamic flight of "The Windhover";[1] Patrick Kavanagh contemplates Christ transfigured at the heart of a primrose[2]. There is a strong mystical tradition that sees the darkness at the edges of human experience as God's mysterious presence and contemplation as the key to encountering that dark un-knowing[3].

KAVANAGH PERSISTENTLY TRIES TO FIGURE OUT GOD!

No one has more repeatedly or more persistently grappled with attempts to figure God out, in his writing, than Patrick Kavanagh. Many of his critics are almost embarrassed that God, and the mysteries of religion are so prevalent in his work. It is perhaps, not "cool" to speak of Kavanagh's God. More popular, without doubt, are his smart-alecky statements, raucous outbursts, dubious hygiene and general contempt for convention. Most anecdotal material relating to the poet's life tends to portray him in his outrageous persona, a garb deliberately adopted to protect and even conceal his inner self, his mystical imagination and delicate lyricism. None of these anecdotal moments, however brutally recounted, render him impervious to divine illumination. This, I believe, is the triumph of Patrick Kavanagh. Indeed, his attempts at concealment have never fooled his real admirers.

From the beginning, Kavanagh's understanding of God is soundly based on a God who cannot be manipulated, not even by dutiful religiosity. Although he feels empty and unproductive, he lays rightful claim to the gratuitous and compassionate nature of God's bounty: *I who have not sown / I too / By God's grace may come to harvest / And proud, As the bowed / Reaper at the Assumption / Murmur thanksgiving*[4]. Here he deliberately counters an over-reliance on human effort and slavish effort at meriting grace, with a hint of liberating perspective. His imagination reaches out and brings a breath of fresh air—a breath of infinity to the boxed Pelagian atmosphere of early twentieth century spirituality in Ireland. Kavanagh's God consistently seeks to break the current moulds of stagnant religious practice. God for him is One who is neither solemn nor boring, who, delightfully, is allowed *"to surprise us"*. Surprise comes in the nature of unexpected joy, leniency, gentleness and understanding, especially toward those who are down in their luck. This God is merciful; One who blinks at human failure, and looks instead at the desire of the heart to be open to life. The poet dares to look into the mind of God and even put words in God's mouth when he pleads for a less flawed personality for himself: *"One day I asked God to give me perfection"* . . . He then delineates in some detail, how he wants to be *"smooth and courteous"*, *"the world's virtuous prize"*. Kavanagh's God is quick to respond and nimble of tongue! *"And God spoke out of Heaven / The only gift in my giving is yours, Life!"* Belief in life was, for the poet, the foundation of virtue. His tribute to his mother, after her death, was that she was *"so rich with life"* *"so full of repose"*: Kavanagh's personal cry of despair in sensing that life might be passing him by, is not unlike that of Hopkins who, at the end, pleaded in anguish with his Lord: *Mine O thou Lord of life, send my roots rain.*[5] In a similar state of barrenness, Kavanagh cries out: *"Can a man grow from the dead clod of failure some consoling flower?"* and ends the prayer with: *O God! can a man find You when he lies with his face downwards / And his nose in the rubble that was his achievement?*[6]. He concludes with a cry from the heart: *"O God give us purpose"*. It seems clear, throughout the course of the years, that purpose in life for the poet was identical with belief in God.

Early Scepticism

Early in his writing life, he is skeptical of the "numerical God" of novenas, Missions and highly institutionalised religious practices. Lough Derg's *"three days too goodness"* was destined, he felt, to induce an artificial temporary conversion rather than true attrition. On the contrary, it is the touching human stories of Lough Derg's pilgrims; "the penance of the poor" that provide him with real evidence of faith, wrapped simultaneously in semi-heretical packaging. On the one hand, he witnessed the extortionist cry of middle-class respectability for further prosperity and worldly success, and, on the other, the heartfelt cry of broken people who craved some basic human needs. He pokes respectful

fun at the heresy that *"nine"* repetitions of any devotion could automatically secure eternal salvation, once for all. Likewise, the euphoria of a parish Mission that ended "in a blaze of candles", with mass renunciation of "the world, the flesh and the devil" he estimated, was unrealistic in "clayey hours" for the subsistence-farming community of South Monaghan[7]. It was, nevertheless, in the ordinary moments, and in unexpected places where *"the sow roots and the hen scratches"* that pockets of God numinously appear[8]. Kavanagh fully subscribed to a God of little things, a God who inhabits the *"bits and pieces of everyday"*. Thus he articulated a spirituality, soundly Incarnational, yet lacking official sanction and promotion at this time.

Creating His Own Images of God Out of Personal Experience

Kavanagh undoubtedly probed religion further than the average churchgoer of his time. He experienced prayer differently from current Church practice, as he walked alone in his fields and on the hills. Addressing the spirit of the dead Joan Russell, a young girl with whom he was once in love, he petitions her earnestly: *And pray / For him who walked apart / On the hills / Loving life's miracles . . .*[9] From his youth, he acknowledges a mixture of puzzlement and delight in his acutely-felt visionary sense. He recalls an incident when, cycling to Dundalk with his brother, he stops to remark on a strange mystical light on the Drumgonnelly hills. He soon realises that he is alone in his vision. He believed, nevertheless, that "on the hills and in the eyes of small flowers" was a "beauty too delicately rare for carnal words"[10]. He also depicts *Tarry Flynn* as "rapt to the silly heavens" in the wake of having seen "the Holy Spirit on the hills"[11]. It was this mixed blessing of being a visionary among people who considered him mentally unhinged, which propelled him towards poetry as a means of self-expression. Despite his unpretentious background and simple education, he saw miracles of God's artistry in stones, streams, weeds and hedges, throughout the little fields of Mucker and Shancoduff. Each season brought its own marvels: *"the wafer-ice on the potholes"* at Christmas, the dancing whitethorn hedges of *"April's ecstasy"* in spring. *"Dandelions growing on headlands"*, hazy veils of *"woven sun"*, the *"frivelled blossoms"* of green potato-stalks: all brought an enchantment characteristic of *"no earthly estate"*[12]. Many of these early, and still unguarded statements of innocent vision, are found in his autobiography *The Green Fool* (1938).

Still, at the launch of his poetic career, he could be lured by the attraction of *"beauty the world did not touch"*. With nose pressed to the earth, he marvelled at a *"God"* who was *"unstirred mud in a shallow pool"*[13]. There was something virginal and perhaps a little unreal in this early vision. He had not reached the spiritual maturity of finding the tracks of God in *"guttery gaps"*.

He is similarly rapt while gazing at spirit-filled spaces in an empty stubble field, or at *"moonlight that stays forever in a tree"*.[14] *Spirit-shocking* is a word chosen by the poet for the mystical vision he has come to experience. A sense of the sacred everywhere indicates that Kavanagh was gifted with intuitive knowledge, more akin to mystical awareness than to conventional theology. The presence of mystery all around, he believed, was the Holy Spirit, the breath of God, *ruah* that hovered over the earth. It often puzzled him why people were intent on pushing *"closed, the doors that God holds open"* as if in their anxiety, they failed to see God in the beauty around them[15]. As a young man, he marvelled at being given "access into every tabernacle" and gratuitously gifted with lyrical words to match (*The Green Fool*). As an apprentice farmer, he pondered over seed growing invisibly in the dark earth; a reflection of God's creativity at work. He knew that this vision aptly paralleled his own genesis as a poet. While the harrowing of his poetic life was painful, it seemed to be the inevitable preparation for the eventual garnering of a literary harvest. Planting crops or writing poems were parallel Genesis moments when Kavanagh's *"God of imagination"* was *"waking in a Mucker fog"*[16].

His Unique Dedication to the Holy Ghost

The origin and source of his gift of poetry, Kavanagh concluded, must be derived from a "breath of Divine Intelligence", a "celestial fire" which was always young and elemental[17]. It is the Holy Spirit who seems to endow him with the power to write. At such moments of poetic creativity he feels *"baptised by fire and by the Holy Spirit"*. It is difficult to interpret this level of experience which seems to have manifested itself as a kind of aura that emanated from the poet even when seated alone in a pub[18]. Suffice it to say that he often felt inspired from a place deep within himself as words poured untrammelled from his pen. Though settling at times for the use of conventional religious language when he recognises the signature of "The Holy Ghost" at the heart of a primrose or sees "God the Father" in a tree, he generally avoided conventional religious clichés and catechism definitions when dealing with God. Despite wanting to side-step convention, it is noticeable that his grasp of the doctrine of the Holy Spirit and his understanding of the sacrament of Confirmation are soundly rooted in the Reilly catechism where a special section was reserved for those to be confirmed[19]. But Kavanagh could always surpass the language of orthodoxy. His *Holy Spirit* can turn *"the Bedlam of the little fields"* into a song, can *"brood"* over harrowed fields, incubate new life and, yes, even "renew the face of the earth"!

A Life-long Progression of Images in Tune with Personal Growth

There is an interesting progression in the variety of Kavanagh's allusions to God, as he moves from youth to later life. He may have over- idealised his notion of God in a illuminating moment, *"when the sun comes through a gap"* in **The Great Hunger,** yet, at parallel moments he was equally aware of God as a stern, forbidding parent, who frowns disapprovingly on a pleasurable stroll with his girl-friend, in the bluebell woods of Dunshaughlin. More chilling still is the God who, in church, calls forth *"monsters of despair / to terrify deep into the soul"* in the sombre atmosphere created by *"two guttering candles"*. It was when Kavanagh had nothing to lose after his cancer operation, that his eyes were opened eventually to a God as passionate and all-caressing as any earthly lover. The vagaries of his star-crossed life are readily available throughout his writings. This biographical movement makes it easier to follow his pilgrim journey, intent on finding the transcendent meaning of life, despite its cruel circumstances. His efforts at containing despair, underline his personal struggle with survival. Counselling himself to equanimity, he strains to achieve the perspective necessary to remain in the role of being a celebrant of life. *"And do not lose love's resolution / though face to face with destitution"* is his salutary advice to himself. His brother Peter's abiding memory of him all through the Dublin years was that he laughed and made others laugh, despite almost unmitigated poverty[20]. Patrick's was a spirituality that sought, to embrace the earthy, the commonplace, the self-styled "humorosity" of life, as well as its profoundly mystical dimension. A modest hermeneutical study of his God-images, such as is attempted in this article, reveals his considerable theological exploration of God-images, as well as a definite progression in his spiritual development. A sense of the overwhelming spiritual health and mental wholeness of the man, despite physical ill-health and outward eccentricities, was the picture of Kavanagh that remained with John Jordan in his "Tribute to Patrick Kavanagh" in the January edition of *Hibernia*, 1968.

It is not surprising to find that Kavanagh's God is organic, One who lives in a *"dark sod"* of earth as well as in the delicate beauty of weeds and flowers. God speaks, progressively manifesting Himself or Herself in the multi-faceted aspects of earth. God is immanently present in the resilience of incubating seeds, in the real but hidden mystery of *"the rising sap"*, the surprise January flower, the luxuriant growth of a turnip-field, a cut-away bog in full bloom and in the aura of a tree-lined street in autumn. These are but a few of the images that begin to carry the import of Kavanagh's God-talk. The landmarks of his own life-story also profoundly influence the God-images he produces. Flushed with new levels of creative energy; and endowed with a new eloquence, Kavanagh rejoices in the promise of a newly furnished *"nest for the Word"* to celebrate his recovery from lung cancer in 1955. Here, from his perch on the Grand Canal, he is reinstated in his God-given identity as one inspired to do

God's will through poetry. This God fortuitously *"pours redemption"* and re-baptises the poet in his mission to the ordinary. Back in his native bogland, he further acknowledges the presence of this *"sensational"* God, who crowns the *"backward"* places of life in glory. Unforgettably, Kavanagh's *"beautiful, beautiful, beautiful God / was breathing His love by a cut-away bog"*.[21]

It is easy to see that Kavanagh's earlier idyllic image of God *"as unstirred mud"*, was One who did not mix with dirt! Now, as the poet grows apace with The-God-who-grows, *"pockets of God"* are everywhere. This God is profligate, spilling beauty with abandon. If, in an earlier stage of life he feels that *heaven* must be stolen *"while God is in the town"* now heaven is *"under all our noses"*[22]. The image of God in **"Lough Derg"**, who *"lies down beside him like a woman"* is consistent with a new mystical perception of One *"who caresses the daily and nightly earth"* a God, not judging at all but One who *"refuses to take failure for an answer"* and is surprisingly unlike those to whom world gives importance. Flagrantly he declares: *"I met God the Father on the street. . . . he was not a man who would be appointed to a board / or impress a bishop / or gathering of art lovers."* Kavanagh was subversive in his ideas of God; he was indeed the first Irish theologian who lays claim to the possibility of a feminine God, generous in praise, understanding of the poet, and affirming of creativity. He may not have been a true feminist, yet his declaration that *"surely my God is feminine"* is well ahead of his time and might have carried more theological clout, had Kavanagh achieved the literary status that was his due. Only now, one hundred years after his birth, do people see in Kavanagh, the glimmer of a more all-embracing God.

This so-called "uneducated" poet explores a whole gamut of God-images, persistently chipping away at all that is not God until a firm intuition of God remains. Indeed, for all his created images and analogies, Kavanagh knows that God is ultimately beyond what is imaginable. God is the Absolute, the Beyond in the midst of life and in the poet's own words is *"the Mind that has baulked the profoundest of mortals"*.[23] The rest is silence.

KAVANAGH'S CONTRIBUTION TO IRISH THEOLOGY

This poet's significant contribution to Irish theology, then, is to have been tenacious in his search for God in whom he had unshakeable faith. He deploys the full scope of his mystical imagination to lend new freshness to timeworn religious doctrines and showed how the Irish landscape and indeed *"the unconscious streets of Dublin"* were redolent with unacknowledged God-life. Courageously he put to rout all that was not God in an effort to serve the truth. He returned again and again to the dignity of the human condition, the indestructibility of the soul's pact with its Creator. He treated serious subjects such as God, failure and religion with the lightest of touches and lent his imagination and lyricism to the mysteriously compelling agenda of *"being true to God"*. His constant chipping away at all that is not God opens up a window on a Mystery that begs contemplation. Gifted with what John Montague has recently called, a "seismic energy" that emanated from him as it were a radar[24] he was possessed also of a seismic faith that could, not only move mountains, but could also mystically transform the smallest piece of earth into *"a placeless heaven"*. For him, *"the whole mystery"* was in *"a crumb"*. Like any good farmer he was watchful too, lest "the clean springs of his religion" be polluted with false teachings and for this reason he castigated the anti-life mentality of Church and State alike; a society that preached fear of sex and suspicion of human love[25]. He knew very well that the worst excesses of his contemporary Church had distorted the real face of God who had come to be preached as a stern, authoritative, killjoy, who spoiled the fun of life and cruelly *"cut all the green branches."* Breaking traditional moulds he proclaims outrageously that God is in *"a kiss"*, in *"a laugh"* and is the adornment not the disfigurement of the human condition; a genuine *pearl necklace*! What an extraordinary spiritual liberation for himself and for anyone who takes him at his word!

Kavanagh's work is crammed with theological statement. He is in constant dialogue within himself, arguing back and forth, vehemently refuting doctrines that are false, while stoutly affirming *"God's truth in common statement"*. His God was *"not all in one place complete and labeled like a suitcase in a railway station"*.[26] This is a strong indictment of what was then a current trend in theology: a highly apologetic faith that relied on proofs for the existence of God, sustained with penny catechism answers. The Incarnate God was kept under lock and key in the tabernacle; the Holy of Holies was apart in the church sanctuary. Little wonder that Kavanagh pleaded for a God present in the *"bits and pieces"* of life, and a heaven that peeped delightfully *"between the ricks of hay and straw"*. A packed and labeled suitcase, Kavanagh pleaded, was a far-from-adequate metaphor for God. His Incarnate God, on the contrary, was conceived by the Holy Spirit in the pristine "green meadows" of spring, grew and flowered in sunlight, and was susceptible to withering *"(into) the Futile One"* through willful lack of worship[27]. No one who reads Kavanagh carefully can accuse him of pantheistic worship; he is too steeped in Catholic teaching for that. He sees God in nature but knows, in unerring rectitude, that nature is not God!

KAVANAGH'S FINAL GOD-ENCOUNTER

When Kavanagh was breathing his last breaths of life in the Merrion Nursing Home on the night of November

29th, 1967 he was murmuring audibly a simple prayer of faith: "O God I believe". Which of Kavanagh's Gods, one wonders, was with him at the end? I suspect that, in this hour of physical diminishment, he was once again experiencing the final harrowing of his soul-territory. Yet, here he was also inwardly confident that his crop was saved and his harvest home! Moments later, as the night edged towards morning, he would, no doubt, *"swagger celestially home"*[28] in the caressing embrace of a Beatific Presence, whose face would, for a final time, surprise him with a familiarity born of a lifetime's relationship[29].

Notes

1. W. H. Gardner (ed.) *Gerard Manley Hopkins: Poems and Prose,* (Harmondsworth: Penguin Books, 1953/63) p. 30.

2. "Primrose", p. 70. See Patrick Kavanagh, *The Complete Poems,* ed. Peter Kavanagh (New York and Newbridge, Co Kildare, 1984). Unless otherwise stated all quotations from Kavanagh's poems will be from this edition. The title of the poem will be given in a footnote, unless this is already obvious from the context.

3. Denys Turner, *The Darkness of God: Negativity in Christian Mysticism,* Cambridge University Press, 1995, pp 1-4.

4. "I may Reap" p. 8.

5. *Thou art indeed just, Lord* Gardner p. 67

6. The poems referred to here are: "Having Confessed" p. 256 and "From Failure Up" p. 161.

7. See *Tarry Flynn,* Penguin Classics edition, Chapter One.

8. *Collected Poems, ed. Antoinette Quinn,* "The Long Garden", pp. 17-18

9. "Joan Russell" p. 207-8. Member of a well-known Dublin family. Lines from this poem were chosen by Kavanagh's brother Peter for the inscription on his grave in Inniskeen.

10. *The Green Fool* p.?

11. *Tarry Flynn* p. 29-30

12. "A Christmas Childhood", p. 143-145,"April" p. 20, "Spraying the Potatoes" p. 72 and "Tarry Flynn" p. 141. See also Tom Stack, *No Earthly Estate,* The Columba Press, 2002.

13. "A Christmas Childhood, Part I, p. 144, "Remembered Country" p. 49.

14. "On Looking into E. V. Rieu's Homer" p. 238.

15. "Lough Derg" p. 104 with oblique reference also to "Auditor's In" p. 242-245.

16. "Kerr's Ass" p. 254.

17. Collected Pruse, p. 225

18. The poet Paul Durcan referred to one such moment which he witnessed himself in Baggot Street during the 1960s.

19. The Reilly Catechism was compiled by Bishop O'Reilly (1690-1758) and used mostly in the Ulster counties. It was renowned for the brevity of its answers, which would have suited Kavanagh. e.g. Q. Who created you and placed you in the world? A. God. [Reilly Catechism, p. 16].

20. Peter Kavanagh in dialogue with John Waters of the *Irish Times,* at Trinity College Dublin, July 22nd, 2004. This point was made during the question and answer session.

21. "The One" p. 291

22. "The Long Garden", part of long poem "Why Sorrow" pp. 170-171, "Bluebells for Love" p. 159.

23. "The One" p. 291

24. "Memories of Patrick Kavanagh": a talk given by John Montague at "The Raglan Road Festival," Inniskeen Rural and Literary Centre, July 2004

25. *Kavanagh's Weekly,* "Sex and Christianity" (May 24th, 1952), p. 7

26. I am indebted to Antoinette Quinn's *Collected Poems* (1999) for her helpful and first time inclusion of these lines, which for many years had been excluded from editions of the "Great Hunger".

27. "Auditors In" p. 241

28. From "The Great Hunger" p. 104.

29. See Agnew on Kavanagh's death in *The Mystical Imagination of Patrick Kavanagh* 1998, PP 224-227, where two sources of information are acknowledged: Peter Kavanagh's *Love's Tortured Headlands,* New York: 1978 and Mrs Flo Connaughton who nursed him at the end.

John Redmond (essay date spring 2004)

SOURCE: Redmond, John. "'All the Answers': The Influence of Auden on Kavanagh's Poetic Development." *New Hibernia Review* 8, no. 1 (spring 2004): 21-34.

[*In the following essay, Redmond explores the influence of W. H. Auden on Kavanagh's poetry, focusing in particular on the shift in Kavanagh's style marked by the publication of* The Great Hunger *in 1941.*]

We are used to reading Patrick Kavanagh's poetry with reference to literary standpoints for which Kavanagh himself had little time. We see him as an exemplary corrective to the pieties of the Irish Literary Revival, as instructively hostile to the politics of literary Dublin. Our approval of him often takes a negative form because we have such a sharp idea, thanks to his poems and essays, of what he stood against. When our approval takes the positive form of endorsing what he stood for, it is articulated hazily. We think of him—vaguely, sweepingly—as a literary innocent wiping the slate of Irish poetry clean, ushering in a poetic Year Zero to the new state. Seamus Deane's description of the typical poem we encounter in Kavanagh's first book **Ploughman and Other Poems** illustrates this point well. "The poem is translucent. Kavanagh emerges as he entered, still persistently himself. He is a bare-faced poet. No masks. In this he is revolutionary."[1]

The picture of Kavanagh as unaffected and, by extension, uninfluenced tends to be ahistorical and has led to some awkward critical emphases. To take one example, the collection of essays *Modernism and Ireland: The Poetry of the 1930s* explicitly excludes Kavanagh despite the obvious modernist procedures of **The Great Hunger**.[2] Admittedly, Kavanagh's most important long poem was composed in 1941, but the editors do not cite this date as a reason to exclude him. The tendency to perceive Kavanagh as having been "naive" and "uninfluenced" while, at the same time, characterizing such others of the period as Brian Coffey, Denis Devlin, and Thomas McGreevey as positively influenced and smartly up-to-date distorts a fair picture of the period.

Kavanagh's work, especially **The Great Hunger,** relates to the second wave of English modernism associated with—indeed instigated by—W. H. Auden. This version of modernism, highly influential in the 1930s, was notably anxious to connect with a general audience. Therefore, Kavanagh is partly unoriginal. He is a poet sharply aware of, and anxious about, his influences. Kavanagh's undisguised admiration for the work of W. H. Auden crops up many times in his prose. In his essay "Pietism and Poetry," for example, he places Auden in the company of Yeats and Eliot.[3] Not so daring a move, but in "Literature and the Universities" he goes still further and puts Auden in the company of Milton and Shakespeare (*Pruse* 236-40). In his most considered treatment of the English poet, the essay "Auden and the Creative Mind," comparisons with Shakespeare are repeatedly made: "Shakespeare and Auden in common give the impression that they have found a formula and that they could employ ghosts to turn out their particular line till there would be no need for another poet for a long time" (*Pruse* 250-51). Not only does the essay strikingly affirm the value of Auden's work, it also holds his poetry out as a corrective to the influence of Yeats. A further piece emphasizing the instructive cosmopoli-

tanism of the English poet coopts Auden into the pantheon of Irish writers:

> Those 'Ireland' writers, who are still writing . . . could not see that the writers of Ireland were no longer Corkery and O'Connor and the others but Auden and George Barker—anyone anywhere who at least appreciated, if he could not cure, their misfortune.

> (*Pruse* 266)

Despite Kavanagh's loud acknowledgement of his admiration for Auden, Auden's influence on Kavanagh's work has been little remarked on and less analyzed. There have been few incentives for politically minded Irish criticism, either revisionist or nationalist, to read Kavanagh's career in the light of Auden's influence. Typically, critical acknowledgements of Auden's influence are made in passing and are relatively unfocused. The major critical biography by Antoinette Quinn acknowledges Auden's influence a few times, but does not treat the subject in detail. While she recognizes that by 1941 Auden was a general influence on Kavanagh's poetry, she observes that with respect to ". . .*The Great Hunger* this new literary influence is unrecognisable."[4] Quinn, in turn, has difficulty explaining Kavanagh's enormous leap in style from the poems of the 1930s to **The Great Hunger.** One strategy she adopts is to cite the influence of a number of prose writers on Kavanagh—Sean O'Faolain, Frank O'Connor, and Peadar O'Donnell—and to explain Kavanagh's change of style as a digestion of their socially concerned writings. Quinn also proposes that we see **The Great Hunger** as "a rural sequel" to Joyce's *Dubliners*.[5] Yet the styles of *Dubliners* and **The Great Hunger** are fundamentally different. Joyce's "nicely polished looking-glass" is a coolly narrated study in subtlety and understatement. Rather than coolness and subtlety the narrator of **The Great Hunger** offers us by turns agitation, crudity, lyricism, and finger-wagging. It is precisely such narrative excesses that Auden's influence goes far to explain.

One of the few extended efforts to address the question of Auden's influence was made by Douglas Houston, who observed that "To focus on relations between the poetries of Patrick Kavanagh and W. H. Auden is less to trade in stylistic influence than to discern imaginative and spiritual affinities."[6] Like other commentators, Houston hesitates to credit Auden with a direct influence on Kavanagh. However, Auden's influence on Kavanagh, which is especially noticeable in the long poem **The Great Hunger,** is both direct and considerable, to such a degree that it is possible to read Kavanagh's entire career in a new way.

Kavanagh's poetic career may be considered in four stages, each roughly associated with a decade and defined by three elements: anxiety (or the lack of it); complexity (or the lack of it); and, in the person of the speaker, plurality (or the lack of it). The first stage, associated with the 1930s and his first book *Ploughman and Other Poems,* may be broadly characterized by a simple, serene, "I am." The second stage, associated with the long poems of the 1940s, is characterized by a complex, anxious, collective voice: a "we are" in *The Great Hunger* and a mixture of second person and third person in **"Loch Derg"** and **"Why Sorrow?"** The third stage, associated with the **"Canal Bank"** poems of the 1950s, is characterized by a complex, serene "I am." The fourth stage, associated with the technical collapse of the 1960s, is characterized by a simple, anxious "I am." Kavanagh's anxieties (or their relief) in all these periods revolve around his relationship to an audience—a typical problem for the Auden generation, which sought to avoid the ivory tower aloofness of high modernism. His complexities, or the lack of them, in these periods revolve around the strategic process of managing these anxieties, seen after his social-prophet phase in the self-conscious "not-caring" of the **"Canal Bank"** poems.

The use of a voice speaking on behalf of a collective is characteristic of one phase only, but that is the crucial transitional phase of *The Great Hunger.* Auden's influence causes the shift from stage one to stage two. Through his encounter with Auden's poems, a question is asked of the "I-persona" of stage one: what is his relationship to other people, to an audience? The huge leap in terms of style from *Ploughman* to *The Great Hunger* can be explained only by an intense encounter between Kavanagh and Auden's poetry of the 1930s. In *The Great Hunger,* the I-persona usefully described by Deane is replaced, except for a few instances of reported speech, by a "we-persona." It is this replacement which truly earns Deane's adjective "revolutionary." Instead of a subject whose concerns are, for the most part, private and internal, we find a subject that is deeply concerned with the public and external. As Houston points out: "By the time of **'The Great Hunger'**, Kavanagh's diagnostic attitude to rural Ireland's social ills is perhaps indicative that he had been nudged in such a direction by Auden's example."[7] From the very first section of this poem, which draws us into the spiritual predicament of the farmer Patrick Maguire, we are aware that we are about to be offered a kind of guided tour around this man's life by an indeterminate third party. The we-persona is introduced in the fourth line: "If we watch them an hour is there anything we can prove / Of life. . . ."[8] The speaker immediately marks out his emotional distance from the subject, which is also a way of marking his distance from emotion. This mode of chilly appraisal is one closely associated with Auden's early style:

> Consider if you will how lovers stand
> In brief adherence, straining to preserve
> Too long the suction of goodbye. . . .[9]

Auden's speaker offers us information in an extravagantly disinterested way through the language of the professor turning to the slidescreen. By comparison, in *The Great Hunger* we find a remarkable air of finality in the comments that Kavanagh's speaker makes. The tense which he uses is baldly unconditional—"We will wait and watch the tragedy to the last curtain" (*CP* [*The Complete Poems*] 80). The speaker's tone is assured and decided, superior to both audience and subject. The reference to a theater curtain is significant. It reminds us that a brisk and irritable tone of instruction—widespread in Auden's work—is especially noticeable in his verse drama of the 1930s. Often, in those plays which Auden cowrote with Christopher Isherwood, we encounter the presenter who knows exactly what is going to happen in such lines as: "We show you man caught in the trap of his terror, destroying himself" (*EA* [*The English Auden: Poems, Essays and Dramatic Writings 1927-1939*] 280); "We would show you at first an English village: you shall choose its location" (*EA* 282); and: "We will show you what he has done."[10]

This sort of self-consciously superior presentation is frequently found in *The Great Hunger.* Time and again, Kavanagh's we-persona lurches into a sudden intensity for his subject: "Watch him, watch him, that man on a hill whose spirit / Is a wet sack flapping about the knees of time." (*CP* 81). While not abandoning his knowingness, the speaker's imperative repetition betrays another tone, this time of the warder watching the dangerous prisoner. Again, it is a tone powerfully present in Auden's work, as in this dramatic chorus from *The Dog Beneath the Skin* (1935): "Watch him asleep and waking / Dreaming of continuous sexual enjoyment or perpetual applause" (*EA* 231). This language figuratively accords power to the speaker over his audience. This dominating voice is far removed from the uncomplicated "I am" of *Ploughman.* The speaker of *The Dog Beneath the Skin* is adopting an authoritative tone, that of the prophet, superior to the audience and in mature possession of his voice. This shift of the speaker's stance is borne out of crisis, however, rather than out of conviction. *The Great Hunger* soon undermines this voice's air of superior detachment, for example in section 6:

> Men build their heavens as they build their circles
> Of friends. God is in the bits and pieces of Everyday—
> A kiss here and a laugh again, and sometimes tears,
> A pearl necklace round the neck of poverty.

> (*CP* 88)

This tone is closer to Kavanagh's original voice—colloquial and casual. It is as though the instructor has got off his podium to join his audience in a sudden show of fraternity and solidarity. The breaking off from a focus on scientific detachment to a focus on entertaining personal anxieties is reminiscent of a stanza in Auden's "Spain 1937":

And the investigator peers through his instruments
At the inhuman provinces, the virile bacillus
  Or enormous Jupiter finished:
But the lives of my friends. I inquire, I inquire.

                                        (*EA* 211)

In these lines, however, the sentiments are expressed by a character, not by the controlling voice of the poem.

In section 13 of *The Great Hunger,* the speaker again puts his detachment aside in order to direct a tirade against some patronizing tourists who are observing Maguire from their cars. Then, as suddenly as the knowing tone vanishes, it returns:

That was how his life happened.
No mad hooves galloping in the sky,
But the weak, washy way of true tragedy—
A sick horse nosing around the meadow for a clean
  place to die.

                                        (*CP* 101)

As Basil Payne has indicated, these lines recall of the idea of tragedy in Auden's "'Musée Des Beaux Arts,'" especially when Auden points out where the "dreadful martyrdom" occurs: "Where the dogs go on with their doggy life and the torturer's horse / scratches its innocent behind on a tree" (*EA* 237).[11] In both poems, the long line imitates the casual motions of a horse and the place, "some untidy spot," is of no particular importance. Here, as in so many other parts of *The Great Hunger,* the we-persona appears to be an amalgam of the unresolved relations between Kavanagh, his audience, and Auden. In these moments, we might usefully see the poem as an example of what Harold Bloom calls "covenant-love." Kavanagh, the ephebe, attempts to accommodate the voice of the strong precursor, Auden, to his own voice. This adaptation would explain many of the poem's deep inconsistencies of tone.

Kavanagh may have been attracted to the voice of Auden's verse plays because of their roots in English ritual drama. The simplified, expressionist use of character in these works may throw light on the use of character in *The Great Hunger.* Consider, for example, the use of figures. There is a sinister undercurrent in *The Great Hunger* associated with the occasional appearance of dolls and idols. At the end of Section 6, for instance, Maguire's three wishes, "Health and wealth and love," have become inanimate things with an eerily human likeness: "And his three wishes were three stones too sharp to sit on, / Too hard to carve. Three frozen idols of a speechless muse" (*CP* 88). In section 12, the opposite process is demonstrated. The mother and children become like dead things: "she held the strings of her children's Punch and Judy" (*CP* 99). Like many of the rigid, ossified forms in the poem, the puppet figures seem to be embodied neuroses. It is striking that Kavanagh uses devices that were also an integral part of

Auden's early poetry. In Auden's *The Orators* (1932), for example, dolls are used to denote perverted lovers: ". . . voice toneless, they stoop, their gait wooden like a galvanised doll so that one involuntarily exclaims on meeting, 'You really oughtn't to be out in weather like this'" (*EA* 63).

One link between Kavanagh and Auden, in this respect, is provided by the mumming tradition. Auden employed a form of the mummer's play in his early, highly innovative charade *Paid on Both Sides* (1928). In that play, as Katherine Worth remarks, ". . . one is reminded of 'Sweeney Agonistes' in the violence of its break with realism, its feelings for spontaneous, popular forms of English drama, especially pantomime and the most primitive form of all, the Mummer's Play."[12] Two characters from the mumming tradition appear in the charade: the "Man-Woman" and the "Doctor." Auden liked to use such characters because, as he put it, ". . . drama is not suited to the analysis of character, which is the province of the novel. Dramatic characters are simplified, easily recognised and over life-size." Dramatic speech, as Auden conceived of it, should have ". . . the same compressed, significant and undocumentary character as dramatic movement" (*EA* 273). The drama therefore is led by the audience. But, however familiar the actions of such characters may be to the audience, they must also have an undeniable strangeness. The performance, ritual in nature, forgets the origins of the ritual elements. It is both familiar and strange.

We are reminded that throughout his career—but especially in his social-prophet phase—Kavanagh wrote mini-verse-dramas, including **"Bardic Dust," "The Paddiad,"** and **"Adventures in the Bohemian Jungle."** These featured a tour guide and a variety of voices representing various contemporary types. **"The Wake of the Books"** and **"The Christmas Mummers"** would also be included, both of which explicitly draw on the mumming tradition. To the latter poem, Kavanagh appended an "explanation" beginning: "The custom of Mummers or rhymers going around before Christmas performing in rural kitchens still lives on in some parts of Ireland. Each Mummer re-presents some historical or nonsensical character" (*CP* 270). Elements of this tradition converge in very suggestive ways in *The Great Hunger.* England has had many types of this drama. In Ireland, however, where the plays, according to A. Gailey, ". . . may be described as Hero-Combat plays," there were fewer types.[13] This type of play was popular along the eastern seaboard and in Ulster.[14] Another pattern was that of the Wooing (or Bridal, or Plough) play. Herbert Halpert writes that, in some of these plays, ". . . the act of ploughing or of making a plough is connected with mimicry of the sexual act . . ."—a description obviously relevant to *The Great Hunger.*[15] Often, a man dressed as a "female" was wooed by a

Ploughboy whom she would reject in favor of a fool. Gailey thinks that Ireland may have had versions of this play.[16] The use of the plough and the use of the Man-Woman certainly chime with *The Great Hunger*. The latter, for instance, may be seen in the absence of a father or in a line like ". . . it cut him up in the middle, till he became more woman than man" (*CP* 94).

Plainly, *The Great Hunger* uses two of the central devices of the mumming tradition: the reduction of characters to caricatures, combined with the ritual scapegoating of such characters in order to achieve dramatic ends. If one needs to be reminded of the poem's dramatic nature—which puts us in mind of Tom McIntyre's later expressionist treatment of the work—one need only look to its final section where we are told in an ironic tone: "The curtain falls—/ Applause applause" (*CP* 103). The real irony is that no audience exists except for Kavanagh himself. He is the only one who can render the final applause. Maguire is Kavanagh's scapegoat, his Fool.

The problem of audience is crucial to *The Great Hunger*. By using tones derived from Auden, Kavanagh's speaker gained a certain figurative power, as well as an audience, imagined and actual, over which to wield it. These tones were, of course, contrived, but their contrivance meant an incipient strategic reversal of Auden's influence. This reversal is not fully accomplished in *The Great Hunger*. We must wait until the 1950s to see Kavanagh overcome Auden's power entirely. Nevertheless, some powerful deflection of Auden's influence does take place, which is illustrated with Kavanagh's use of the crucial trope of panorama.

There is no more powerful trope in early Auden than that of panorama. It is particularly evident in the choruses of his verse drama, which seem to have struck Kavanagh so strongly, as in the following from *The Dog Beneath the Skin*:

> The Summer holds: upon its glittering lake
> Lie Europe and the islands; many rivers
> Wrinkling its surface like a ploughman's palm.
> Under the bellies of the grazing horses
> On the far side of posts and bridges
> The vigorous shadows dwindle; nothing wavers.
>
> (*EA* 281)

A further example from the same play:

> . . . From the square surrounded by Georgian houses,
>   taking the lurching tram eastward
> South of the ship-cranes, of the Slythe canal: Stopping
>   at Fruby and Drulger Street,
> Past boys ball-using: shrill in alleys.
> Passing the cinemas blazing with bulbs: bowers of
>   bliss
> Where thousands are holding hands: they gape at the
>   tropical vegetation, at the Ionic pillars and the organ
>   solo.
>
> (*EA* 279)

These panoramas allow the speaker to aggregate extreme power unto himself. They confer on him the strength and grandiose status of an omniscient eye. After the power of the light, such panoramas are often clinched by a closing sound, like the organ solo above. The sound's meaning may be entirely obscure, as in poem "XII" from Auden's *Poems* (1930):

> From scars where kestrels hover,
> The leader looking over
> Into the happy valley,
> Orchard and curving river,
> May turn away to see
> The slow fastidious line
> That disciplines the fell,
> Hear curlew's creaking call
>
> (*EA* 28)

The omniscient being is also an omnivorous being. The light that illuminates all things is also a consuming fire. Kavanagh recognized such energy as a defining quality in Auden's poetry: "A great poet is a monster who eats up everything. Shakespeare left nothing for those who came after him and it looks as if Auden is doing the same" (*Pruse* 248-49). The clear anxiety in this passage is that Kavanagh, thanks to Auden, will be poetically redundant. How significant then, that the most lyrical and moving passage of *The Great Hunger* should be a great high panorama which closes with a most human sound:

> The fields were bleached white,
> The wooden tubs full of water
> Were white in the winds
> That blew through Brannagan's Gap on their way from
>   Siberia;
> The cows on the grassless heights
> Followed the hay that had wings—
> The February fodder that hung itself on the black
>   branches
> Of the hill-top hedge.
> A man stood beside a potato-pit
> And clapped his arms
> And pranced on the crisp roots
> And shouted to warm himself.
>
> (*CP* 98)

Here is a man shouting to warm himself, yet remaining cold. Here, the narrator of *The Great Hunger* sheds his "we-persona" and reaches back through this representative man to his first simple "I am." A passage in Harold Bloom's *The Breaking of the Vessels* may be useful here:

> The problem of restoring to the world original and eternal beauty is solved by the redemption of the soul. The ruin or the blank that we see when we look at nature is in our own eye. The axis of vision is not coincident with the axis of things so they appear not transparent but opaque. . . .[17]

What is the nature of the ruin or blank which Kavanagh's speaker sees in *The Great Hunger*? Is its origin inside or outside him? The speaker does not know. He is in a state of literary and existential uncertainty, hence his wild ambivalence.

Kavanagh is trying to restore his original way of seeing things, so he must move from Auden's trope of panorama to change the axis of his vision. The eye of Kavanagh's passage is still omniscient; but, rather than seeing everything, it begins to see through everything. That is why the things in this panorama are seen without color, in terms of presence or absence of light. Kavanagh's axis of vision, which would shift entirely by the 1950s, has already been slightly altered. Rather than looking at what the eye's visionary fire illuminates, his eye is beginning to look at the fire.

Before Kavanagh could successfully overcome the strains of Auden's voice in his poetry, he had to work through the difficulty of leaving that voice behind. How was a poet so conscious of poetic worthiness to deal with an influential precursor whom he acknowledged to be far worthier than himself? Kavanagh's conception of "the great poet" is evidently Darwinian: "I scarcely believe in the theory of the 'mute inglorious Milton'. There might well be mute Bowens or Priestleys or Blundens, but hardly a Milton, a Shakespeare, an Auden" (*Pruse* 266). The strong poet will out. But was *he* a Blunden or an Auden? On what scale was *he* built? In the poetry after *The Great Hunger*—in a poem like **"Winter in Leeds,"** for example—one can still see the clinical tones of the early Auden:

> To take something as a subject, indifferent
> To personal affection I have been considering
> An ancient saga for my instrument

> (*CP* 335)

The abstract, distant tone is created through diction: "subject," "indifferent," "considering," "instrument." It is the voice of the professor back on his podium. The air of authority derives from the absence of words with emotional resonance—everything is to appear measured and controlled. The problem with Kavanagh using this tone is that his handling of it is not subtle enough to make it come alive. We see this voice again in Kavanagh's **"October"**:

> As I walk this arboreal street on the edge of town,
> The breeze too, even the temperature
> And pattern of movement is precisely the same. . . .

> (*CP* 292)

These lines are straightforward enough, and that is exactly the problem. Kavanagh treats the scene like a detached scientific observer. By contrast, when Auden sharply separates a speaker from the object of his vision, it is only to show that the detachment is a neurotic illusion. The fractured personality of the Airman in "The Orators," for instance, uses the same diction of measurement, but the effect is troublingly ironic:

> Mean temperature 34F
> Fair. Some cumulus cloud at 10,000 feet. Wind
>   easterly and moderate.
> Hands in perfect order.

> (*EA* 94)

Here, the measuring voice returns to its site of production and exposes its deficiency, since the phrase, "Hands in perfect order" refers to the Airman's onanistic tendencies. These lines emphasize how the efforts of Kavanagh to gain authority for his speakers lacks an essential subtlety.

While Kavanagh often adopted an air of knowingness, he knew that it was another's air. Thus he turned from public writing about subjects to the private subject of writing. Influence becomes a topic—sometimes concealed, more often explicit—in his poems and with it, inevitably, Auden:

> Having read Spenser who could stop the Thames
> To hear his Prothalamion—and no wonder!
> I fell back defeated from the miracle.
> The Freudean [*sic*] river clinical
> Is grey with silt
> To high romance inimical—
> Grey Liffey run less sadly with my guilt.
>
> Auden knows all the answers, and the question
> Is where we can find a question to ask
> We ring all the changes on the emotions
> Re-weave and re-weave the shoddy
> Vary the tilt
> Of the dead body—
> Grey Liffey run less drearily with my guilt.

> (*CP* 271)

There can hardly be a poem more explicitly anxious about influence than this one, **"Grey Liffey."** Spenser, like Auden, is seen as a prophet whose poetry is so dramatically potent that it can change the world. As Spenser is the acknowledged poetic master of the old romance world, so Auden is the acknowledged poetic master of the modern Freudian one. Kavanagh wonders how he can exist as a poet with such strong precursors so powerfully present. As he writes about influence, the metaphor of water becomes increasingly useful to him. Water can be used to speak about sources as well as about qualities of essence. Kavanagh is not Spenser—he cannot command the waters to stop—but he can at least demand that they "run less drearily." In other words, he can do nothing about the flow of the water, but he can change its quality. Like the panorama in section 12 of *The Great Hunger,* this focus on water is evidence of a shift in Kavanagh's vision—a shift less concerned with the message than the medium. This is why the poem is a tense mixture of single and plural pronouns.

The final thing to note about the poem is the question of finding a question. Because Auden has, as Kavanagh would have it, exhausted the worthwhile things to say, what is there left to say but this? The only true subject is the position of the latecomer. **"Grey Liffey"** is, therefore, a highly significant prelude to Kavanagh's most successful poems which all take influence as their subject and which include the Canal Bank sonnets.

As soon as Kavanagh realized that, in philosophical, psychological, and social terms, he had nothing profound to say, he was in a position to "give back" the measured, knowing terms that he had borrowed from Auden. He could then write, casually, about nothing. The poem **"Is"** provides a good example:

> The important thing is not
> To imagine one ought
> Have something to say
> A raison d'être, a plot for the play.
>
> (*CP* 287)

As in section 12 of *The Great Hunger*, Kavanagh's eye begins again to look through living nature. We are reminded of what Seamus Heaney wrote in his essay "The Placeless Heaven: Another Look at Kavanagh": "In the poetry of Kavanagh's later period, embodied first in 'Epic' and then, in the late 1950s, in the Canal Bank Sonnets, a definite change is perceptible. We might say that now the world is more pervious to his vision than he is pervious to the world."[18] With nothing as his subject and with water as his image and metaphor, providing examples of purification, reduction, and emptiness, Kavanagh loses his anxiety about his audience and about Auden. We see this clearly in **"Is"**:

> Mention water again
> Always virginal,
> Always original,
> It washes out Original Sin.
>
> (*CP* 287)

These lines bring us back to **"Grey Liffey,"** in which he spoke about "guilt." Kavanagh felt guilty because he knew much of his poetry was tainted by a fatal falseness of tone and subject matter. Because subject matter is effectively absent in **"Is,"** the speaker is correspondingly free of anxiety.

In Kavanagh's various Canal Bank poems, passivity becomes part of the process of emptying out the poetic self, of concentrating on the poet's own original voice, of returning to "I am." The trope of panorama is now completely inverted. Auden, as previously seen, uses the trope to give his speakers the apparent power of omniscience—they project light onto the world and see it anew. Kavanagh's speaker, however, does not project light. He instead remains passive and the light is brought to him. **"Lines Written on a Seat on the Grand Canal"** provides an example:

> A swan goes by head low with many apologies,
> Fantastic light looks through the eyes of bridges—

> And look! A barge comes bringing from Athy
> And other far-flung towns mythologies.
>
> (*CP* 295)

Another example comes from **"Cool Water Under Bridges"**: "The thrilling immortal grass and those sunsets / That look at me from Crumlin . . . (*CP* 297) The difference between these examples and an early poem like **"Stony Grey Soil"** is to be found in the quality of the light. In **"Stony Grey Soil,"** the speaker is not so passive and the light is correspondingly duller:

> Mullahinsha, Drummeril, Black Shanco—
> Wherever I turn I see
> In the stony grey soil of Monaghan
> Dead loves that were born for me[.]
>
> (*CP* 74)

"Whatever is grey," Ludwig Wittgenstein once noted, "does not look grey. Everything grey looks as though it is being illuminated."[19] Just as Kavanagh always thought that he was trying to illuminate a dull audience, most of his early poetry made strenuous efforts to illuminate dull objects. The speaker in **"Stony Grey Soil"** must turn and see only disappointing gray. But in the Canal Bank poems, Kavanagh is no longer the illuminator—he is the illuminated.

Only in a poem about influence could this shift be so dramatically accomplished. In his later poems, Kavanagh is forced to recognize his own position in relation to Auden's. Kavanagh is both downstream of Auden's poetic source and lit up by Auden's illuminating eye. He uses the force of Auden's panoramic trope in the only way possible—by being the vision rather than the visionary. Kavanagh empties himself out so much that he becomes a poetic object: "just a canal-bank seat for the passer-by." These poems create their essential frisson in the intimation of the moment before change, of the moment before the light comes through "the eyes of bridges," of the moment before a child is conceived by the couple sitting on "an old seat," of the moment before the pure poet must eventually submit to influence, of the moment of "I am." This is why these poems return to their beginnings as Kavanagh returns to his.

It is not surprising that Kavanagh is unable to maintain this high level of poetic performance. It is logical and perhaps fitting that this poetic phase, his highest point of achievement, should be momentary. After the "Canal Bank" poems, Kavanagh returns to the position of the subject and, therefore, to the straight-forward influence of Auden. Introducing the simple, anxious "I am" of his final phase, he returns to his audience and begins once more to make social statements of an unconvincing sort, realizing bitterly that his poetry is in decline. The short poem **"No Poetic Authorisation"** distills these feelings:

I come to advise you on the moral position
For nobody is more cognizant of the awful fate
Of him who is a nobody in his own mind
With no poetic authorization.

(CP 339)

Kavanagh's Darwinian conception of "the great poet" meant that he always faced the danger of becoming "a nobody in his own mind." Paradoxically, he was most successful when he wrote as a nobody, because when he wrote about "nothing" he was writing about that which most preoccupied him. **"Winter in Leeds"** ends with the despair of someone who believes they are nothing:

There it is my friends. What am I to do
And the void growing more awful every hour.
I lacked a classic discipline. I grew
Uncultivated and now the soil turns sour,
Needs to be revived with a great story not my own
Of heroes enormous who do astounding deeds
Out of this world. Only thus can I attune
To despair an illness like winter alone in Leeds.

(CP 335)

Here, Kavanagh has returned to the problems that he solved in the "Canal Bank" poems. Grayness returns in the image of the "soil," and the return of the problem of audience is signalled by the phrase "my friends." The latter causes a renewed and fatal uncertainty of tone. In the poem **"Thank You, Thank You,"** for instance, he is unable to decide whether he should preach or flatter his audience:

Come I'm beginning to get pretentious
Beginning to message for instead
Of expressing how glad
I am to have lived to feel the radiance
Of a holy living audience.

(CP 350)

Kavanagh's sensitivity to what made a poet weak or strong was so acute that influence and power became the most important themes in his writing. When he discarded the influence of Auden from his poems, he became successful. By coming in contact with Auden's poetry, Kavanagh faced troubling questions about audience, causing a shift in stance and tone decisively registered in **The Great Hunger.** Auden's influence was subsequently deflected—and questions of audience deferred—in the later Canal Bank poems. However, in his last poems, the twin problems of Auden and audience return and Kavanagh's poetic voice collapses, thus reinforcing the enabling and disabling power of poetic influence.

Notes

1. Seamus Deane, "Irish Poetry and Nationalism" in *Two Decades of Irish Writing* ed. Douglas Dunn (Cheadle: Carcanet, 1975), p. 10.

2. See *Modernism and Ireland: The Poetry of the 1930s,* ed. Alex Davis and Patricia Coughlan (Cork: Cork University Press, 1995).

3. Patrick Kavanagh, "Pietism and Poetry" in *Collected Pruse* (London: Martin Brian and O'Keefe, 1973), p. 244; hereafter cited parenthetically, thus: (*Pruse* 244).

4. Antoinette Quinn, *Patrick Kavanagh: Born-again Romantic* (Dublin: Gill and Macmillan, 1991), p. 146.

5. Quinn, p. 139.

6. Douglas Houston, "Landscapes of the Heart: Parallels in the Poetries of Kavanagh and Auden" in *Studies,* 77 (Winter, 1988), 445.

7. Houston, 446.

8. Patrick Kavanagh, *The Complete Poems,* ed. Peter Kavanagh (New York: The Peter Kavanagh Hand Press, 1972), p. 80; hereafter cited parenthetically, thus: (*CP* 80).

9. W. H. Auden, *The English Auden: Poems, Essays and Dramatic Writings 1927-1939,* ed. Edward Mendelson (London: Faber and Faber, 1977), p. 438; hereafter cited parenthetically, thus: (*EA* 438).

10. W. H. Auden and Christopher Isherwood, *Plays and Other Dramatic Writings by W. H. Auden, 1928-1938,* ed. Edward Mendelson (Princeton: Princeton University Press, 1988), p. 241.

11. Basil Payne, "The Poetry of Patrick Kavanagh," *Studies,* 49 (1960), 282.

12. Katherine Worth, *Revolutions in Modern English Drama* (London: Bell, 1972), pp. 106-07.

13. A. Gailey, *Irish Folk Drama* (Cork: Mercier Press, 1969), p. 69.

14. E. C. Cawte, A. Helm, N. Peacock, *English Ritual Drama* (London: Folklore Society, 1967), p. 35.

15. Herbert Halpert, "A Typology of Mumming" in *Christmas Mumming in Newfoundland: Essays in Anthropology, Folklore and History,* ed. H. Halpert, G. M. Story (Toronto: University of Toronto Press, 1969), p. 57.

16. Gailey, p. 69.

17. Harold Bloom, *The Breaking of the Vessels* (Chicago: University of Chicago Press, 1982), p. 76.

18. Seamus Heaney, "The Placeless Heaven: Another Look at Kavanagh" in *The Government of the Tongue: The T. S. Eliot Memorial Lectures and Other Critical Writings* (London: Faber, 1988), p. 5.

19. Ludwig Wittgenstein, *Remarks on Colour,* ed. G.
     E. M. Anscombe (Oxford: Blackwell, 1977), p. 7.

Samuel Perry (essay date March 2008)

SOURCE: Perry, Samuel. "Patrick Kavanagh and *Horizon*: A Source for R. S. Thomas's Use of 'Peasant.'" *Notes and Queries* 55, no. 1 (March 2008): 80-2.

[*In the following essay, Perry addresses the influence of Kavanagh's* The Great Hunger *on the work of Welsh poet R. S. Thomas.*]

The poetry of R. S. Thomas began appearing in literary periodicals in 1939, seven years before the publication of his first volume *The Stones of the Field* (1946). A significant amount of Thomas's poetry remains uncollected and Sandra Anstey has pointed out that many of his earliest poems exhibit a pronouncedly Georgian style of writing.[1] This was something which Thomas was to lament, attributing the tendency to a highly conservative poetic education:

> In the late twenties, at a time when I should have been
> in touch with what Eliot, Joyce and Pound were doing,
> I was receiving my ideas of poetry via Palgrave's
> *Golden Treasury,* and through such Georgian verse as
> was compulsory reading for my examinations in
> English. I was also a confirmed open-air nature lover
> so that such verses as I then achieved myself were
> almost bound to be about trees and fields and skies and
> seas. No bad thing if I had been familiar with the poets
> who knew how to deal maturely with such material,
> Wordsworth and Hardy for instance. But my efforts
> were based on the weaker poems of Shelley and the
> more sugary ones of the Georgians.[2]

When he moved to Manafon in 1942, Thomas was faced with the question of how to write about a community which was dominated by the day-to-day struggle to make a living from the land, a materialistic culture which simply could not be reconciled with the young priest's Wordsworthian ideals. As Tony Brown has recently observed, it is here, within the context of Thomas's dilemma about how he could attempt to write about the Welsh hill-farming culture in a much more direct way than his Georgian techniques and tones would allow, that we can appreciate the vital role that Patrick Kavanagh's *The Great Hunger* played in the development of Thomas's poetic methodology and register, Kavanagh himself having broken free from an early attachment to the Georgian style.[3]

There are signs that Thomas drew inspiration from the way in which the narrator of *The Great Hunger* records the mannerisms of Patrick Maguire and invites the reader to 'wait and watch' the farmer as he goes about his daily tasks: 'collecting the scattered harness and baskets' after a day's potato picking; gathering 'the loose stones off the ridges'; walking among his cattle or 'load[ing] the day-scoured implements on the cart'.[4] At the beginning of Thomas's 'Out of the Hills' (1946) we are met with the image of the hill farmer 'ambling with his cattle from the starved pastures' before being encouraged to 'follow him down' to the village below.[5] Similarly, in 'A Peasant' (1946) the reader is invited to picture Iago Prytherch 'Docking mangels . . . churning the crude earth / To a stiff sea of clods that glint in the wind' and later to 'see' the labourer 'fixed in his chair / Motionless except when he leans to gob in the fire'.[6] As Anstey suggests, the attention to detail that we get in these early poems is of considerable significance, because it provides clear evidence of Thomas's awakening to the richness of his surroundings at Manafon as a subject matter for poetry, and marks the beginning of his movement away from a nature poetry written in the style of the Georgians to one which engages with the full experience of rural life.[7] In short, we are witnessing the emergence of an authentic poetic voice from the shadows of 1940s neo-Georgian pastoral, a development which was later recognized by Thomas himself:

> My awakening to the possibility of a more robust poetry
> came with my removal to my first incumbency in the
> Montgomeryshire foothills in 1942. I came in contact
> for the first time with the rough farm folk of the upland
> valleys. These were pre-tractor days. Their life was a
> hard slog in wind and mire on hill slopes with the oc-
> casional brief idyllic interludes. Their life and their at-
> titudes administered an inward shock to my Georgian
> sensibility. I responded with the first of my poems about
> Iago Prytherch, a sort of prototype of this kind of
> farmer. It was called 'A Peasant'.[8]

A measure of the speed with which R. S. Thomas took to his new poetic terrain can be gained from the fact that 'A Peasant' was first published in *Life and Letters Today* in 1943, less than a year after Thomas made the move to Montgomeryshire and not long after he had written his neo-Georgian poems of the late 1930s.[9] The question lies in how we can account for such a rapid development of methodology and register, and the answer must include the likelihood that Thomas began to read *The Great Hunger* shortly after arriving in Manafon. This seems even more plausible when we consider Thomas's use of the word 'peasant', for as M. Wynn Thomas has noted,[10] when reading the comments passed by certain critics on the early poems it is worth bearing in mind Raymond Williams's words regarding the terms appropriate for a mature discussion of Hardy:

> First, we had better drop 'peasant' alto-
> gether. Where Hardy lived and worked, as in
> most other parts of England, there were
> virtually no peasants, although 'peasantry'
> as a generic word for country people was
> still used by writers. The actual country
> people were landowners, tenant farmers,
> dealers, craftsmen, and labourers.[11]

One might add that the 'peasantry' of mid-Wales (a term ultimately derived from feudal social structures) were, like Hardy's rural workers decades before, part of a capitalist economy, a fact of which R. S. Thomas, as their priest, was all too aware. It is by no means implausible, then, that the only reason Thomas uses the term 'peasant' in his early poetry is because, like those poetic mannerisms that he seems to have absorbed from Kavanagh, he had encountered it whilst reading **The Great Hunger.** In fact, though Thomas did buy the full-length Cuala Press edition of Kavanagh's poem, he may first have read parts I, II, III, and 26 lines of Part IV, which were published in the London-based journal *Horizon* in January 1942, under the title '**The Old Peasant**'.[12] It is a link which has not previously been made, and its credibility is strengthened by the fact that Thomas himself contributed to *Horizon*: his poem 'Homo Sapiens 1941' appeared there in October 1941.[13] It seems certain, therefore, given that not only did they share friends and literary acquaintances but were also publishing in the same journals and often within only a few months of each other, that Thomas was very much alive to the work of Kavanagh, and would have read **The Great Hunger** shortly after its publication in April 1942.[14]

Notes

1. Sandra Anstey, 'Some Uncollected Poems and Variant Readings from the Early Work of R. S. Thomas', *The Page's Drift: R. S. Thomas at Eighty,* ed. M. Wynn Thomas (Bridgend, 1993) 22-35, 23 (hereafter *PD*). A volume of R. S. Thomas's uncollected poems is currently being compiled by Tony Brown and Jason Walford Davies, co-directors of the R. S. Thomas Study Centre at the University of Wales, Bangor.

2. The Critical Forum: 'R. S. Thomas and Ted Hughes read and discuss their own poems' (Sussex, 1978). Quoted by Anstey, *PD* 23.

3. Tony Brown, *R. S. Thomas* (Cardiff, 2006) 18-19. Kavanagh's first collection, *Ploughman and Other Poems* (1936), encouraged by his friend and mentor 'A. E.' (George Russell 1867-1935), contains a number of mystical, neo-Georgian lyrics. In 'To a Blackbird', for example, the sweet sound of the bird's song is set against a picturesque background of lakes and hills.

4. Patrick Kavanagh, *Selected Poems* (London, 1996) 19-34.

5. R. S. Thomas, *Collected Poems 1945-1990* (London, 1993) 1 (hereafter *CP*).

6. *CP*, 4.

7. *PD*, 27-8.

8. Quoted by Anstey, *PD* 28.

9. *Life and Letters Today,* xxxvi/67 (1943), 154.

10. M. Wynn Thomas, *Internal Difference: Twentieth-Century Writing in Wales* (Cardiff, 1992) 110.

11. Raymond Williams, *The English Novel from Dickens to Lawrence* (St Albans, 1974), 82.

12. *Horizon,* v/25 (1942), 12-17. That R. S. Thomas did own the Cuala Press edition has been confirmed by the poet's son, Gwydion Thomas. Email to Tony Brown, October 2005.

13. *Horizon,* iv/22 (1941), 232.

14. We know that in 1939 Kavanagh published three poems—'Primrose', 'Memory of my Father', and 'Anna Quinn'—in the Autumn edition of Seamus O'Sullivan's *The Dublin Magazine,* and that R. S. Thomas contributed two poems—'The Bat' and 'Cyclamen'—to the following July-September issue. The first complete edition of *The Great Hunger* was published by Cuala Press in April 1942. It was later printed as the concluding poem in *A Soul for Sale.* However, lines 9-32 of section II were omitted on grounds of obscenity.

FURTHER READING

Criticism

Alexander, Alan. "The Laughter of Paddy Kavanagh." *Poetry Australia,* no. 73 (February 1980): 20-6.
> Provides a brief survey of the comic elements in Kavanagh's work.

Bradley, Anthony G. "Pastoral in Modern Irish Poetry." *Concerning Poetry* 14, no. 2 (fall 1981): 79-96.
> Examines the post-Yeatsian pastoral poetry of Kavanagh and John Montague, finding it "both earthy and intellectual."

Faherty, Michael. "Lost, Unhappy and at Home: The Robinson Crusoe Complex in Contemporary Irish Poetry." In *The Classical World and the Mediterranean,* edited by Giuseppe Serpillo and Donatella Badin, pp. 371-78. Cagliari, Italy: Universitá di Sassari / Tema, 1996.
> Discusses Kavanagh's love/hate relationship with the rural area of his native Inniskeen in County Monaghan, particularly evident in the poem "Inniskeen Road: July Evening."

Heaney, Seamus. "The Poetry of Patrick Kavanagh: From Monaghan to the Grand Canal." In *Two Decades of Irish Writing: A Critical Survey,* edited by Douglas Dunn, pp. 105-117. Chester Springs, Penn.: Dufour Editions, 1975.
> Discusses Kavanagh's complicated and conflicted relationship with his native Monaghan county.

Kavanagh, Patrick. "Patrick Kavanagh on Poetry." *Journal of Irish Literature* 6, no. 1 (January 1977): 69-70.

Kavanagh's brief discussion of the role of the poet in relation to his audience.

Warner, Alan. "A Poet in the Fields." In *Clay Is the Word: Patrick Kavanagh 1904-1967,* pp. 46-65. Dublin: Dolmen Press, 1973.

Argues that despite Kavanagh's own negative assessment of the poem, *The Great Hunger* has much to recommend it.

Pierre de Ronsard
1524-1585

French poet and critic.

For additional information on Ronsard's life and career, see *PC,* Volume 11.

INTRODUCTION

A prominent figure in the French Renaissance, Ronsard was a talented and imaginative writer who produced an impressive volume of work in a number of different poetic forms, including sonnets, odes, elegies, and hymns. He also embraced a wide range of themes and metrical styles and became known for his precise use of language. During his lifetime, Ronsard's work was enormously popular, and although his reputation declined from the mid-seventeenth century until the mid-nineteenth century, it has since been reevaluated and his position as an important lyric poet restored.

BIOGRAPHICAL INFORMATION

Much of the biographical information about Ronsard is considered less than reliable, but it is believed that he was born on September 11, 1524, at the Château de la Possonière in Couture-sur-Loir in the Vendôme. Ronsard was the youngest of four surviving children born to Jeanne Chaudrier and Louis de Ronsard, a minor nobleman. Ronsard was primarily educated at home where he acquired a thorough knowledge and deep appreciation of nature, particularly that of his immediate surroundings. He developed a lifelong love of his native province, an affection which informed his poetry throughout his career. When he was nine years old, Ronsard left his home region to begin his formal education in Paris at the Collège de Navarre. He stayed only one semester before returning to his parents' home. At the age of twelve, he began serving as a page at the French court, then served briefly in Scotland. In 1538, he returned to France, hoping to start a career in the military and the diplomatic corps; however, his poor health forced him to give up those plans. He again returned to his childhood home, where he embarked on a career in literature, intent on producing poetry in French at a time when the prevailing aesthetic climate demanded composition in Latin. The success he enjoyed from his early work encouraged him to continue writing and to branch out into other styles and poetic forms. In

1559, Ronsard assumed the position of official court poet, and in keeping with his duties, began writing verses in honor of various dignitaries and occasional pieces commemorating important events. Ronsard's final years were spent at Saint-Cosme Priory near Tours and at Croixval Priory. He devoted much of his time to the revision of his earlier works—a task that consumed him throughout his long career as a poet. He died at Saint-Cosme on December 28, 1585.

MAJOR WORKS

Ronsard produced a large body of work during almost fifty years as a poet from his first effort in 1538, "Ode de Pierre de Ronsard a Jacques Peletier," to *Les derniers vers de Pierre de Ronsard,* published posthumously in 1586. In the intervening years, he produced a great many volumes of poetry as well as numerous revisions and republications of many of them. He embraced a variety of styles from the primarily Horatian and Pindaric *Les quatre premiers livres des odes* (1550) to the Petrarchan *Les amours* (1552), *Continuation des amours* (1555), and *Nouvelle continuation des amours* (1556). He also produced two books of Homeric verse, *Les hymnes* (1555) and *Le second livre des hymnes* (1556). With the publication of *Les œvres* in 1560, Ronsard turned to poetry based on more public themes, promoting his religious and political beliefs which included devotion to Catholicism and the emerging French nation. His most overtly political works include *Discours des miseres de ce temps, a la Royne mere du Roy* (1562) and *Remonstrance au people de France* (1563). Both were revised and reissued twice, while *Les œvres* went through no less than six revisions from 1560 to a posthumous edition in 1587. *Le livret de folastries* (1553) has been considered by some critics to be Ronsard's most innovative—even subversive—volume since it was decidedly anti-Petrarchan and seemed to violate most of the poetic conventions of its day. In addition to his poetry, Ronsard produced a volume of criticism, *Abrege de l'art poëtique François,* in 1565.

CRITICAL RECEPTION

According to Cathy Yandell, Ronsard was obsessed with youth, expressed within his poetry by his use of the *carpe diem* motif. Acknowledging that there was an established tradition of *carpe diem* poetry in early modern France (and elsewhere) dating back to classical times, she believes that Ronsard was not only an important figure in the revival of the tradition but that he transformed its conventions in significant ways. Ronsard's poems, unlike his classical models, separate the poet/speaker from the object of his seduction, suggesting that *she* will grow old, whereas *he* will conquer time along with her inhibitions.

Ronsard's constant efforts to identify himself with various mythical and literary precursors (Apollo, Homer, Achilles) has been studied by Sara Sturm-Maddox, who reports in particular on Ronsard's desire to be known as the French Petrarch. Although he modeled some of his poetry on the work of Petrarch, Sturm-Maddox notes that he began to compose in the Petrarchan style rather late compared to some of his competitors, such as Joachim Du Bellay and Maurice Scève. Lance K. Donaldson-Evans reports that Ronsard initially tried to resist the neo-Petrarchan style that was all the rage in France, but "was forced to capitulate to the prevailing mode in his *Amours,* since his *Odes* had not brought him the fame and glory he hoped." Ronsard's work was considered more explicitly physical than that of the "chaste" Italian poet and he was criticized for altering Petrarch's meaning and tone with the addition of erotic elements. Matthew Gumpert examines *Les Amours Diverses* 45, contending that it is "certainly Ronsard's most obscene poem," and notes that it was disparaged by contemporary critics. According to Gumpert, "while it appears to have lost much of its shock value today, it continues to be neglected." Gerard DeFaux also discusses the differences between Petrarch and Ronsard: "For Petrarch, there was only Laura . . . for Ronsard, we have an impressive list of idols: Cassandre, Marie, Sinope, Astrée, Genèvre, Hélène." According to Donaldson-Evans, *Livret des Folastries* (1553) was actually an anti-Petrarchan text and "may well be Ronsard's most subversive collection, calling into question the prevailing poetic practice of his contemporaries."

Cynthia Skenazi notes that Ronsard, who was named *poëte du roi* in 1554, kept himself informed regarding the political atmosphere of France, attending to every shift in royal politics—often with the composition of an appropriate poem to meet the requirements of the moment. As an example, Skenazi cites his publication of *Exhortation au Camp du Roy pour bien combattre le jour de la bataille* written to inspire the French troops preparing for battle with the Spanish; however, when the parties entered into negotiations before the initial hostilities ensued, Ronsard quickly issued *Exhortation pour la paix* in support of Henry II's peace efforts, followed by *La paix, Au Roy* intended to encourage acceptance of the peace treaty being considered. However, opposing this evidence of Ronsard's service to the king and to the emerging French nation, is the large amount of poetry displaying his obvious pride and devotion concerning his native region—the Vendôme. Louisa Mackenzie explains the competing loyalties Ronsard and other sixteenth-century French poets felt as, on the one hand, they were participating—through their poetry—in the formation of a new national identity at the same time they were celebrating, and mourning the loss of, the glory days of their respective regions. According to Mackenzie, "the Vendômois region is constructed, in Ronsard's lyrics, as a metaphor for a prelapsarian world of poetry that excludes the tensions of contemporary France, a world ordered first and foremost by poetry and poets, a world of aristocratic virtue and value, immune from sectarian strife and historical disruptions." Both Mackenzie and Susan K. Silver have studied Ronsard's *Elegie XXIIII,* one of Ronsard's final poems, in which he protests the logging of the forest surrounding his family's estate. Silver reports that in the poem Ronsard "weaves together personal and legendary tales of loss and disempowerment," since he was being overshadowed at court by a younger poet at the same time the woodcutters were destroying the Gâtine Forest.

PRINCIPAL WORKS

Poetry

Avantentrée du Roy trescrestien à Paris 1549

L'hymne de France 1549

Ode de la paix 1550

Les quatre premiers livres des odes de Pierre de Ronsard, ensemble son bocage 1550; revised edition, 1555

Les amours de P. de Ronsard vandomois, ensemble le cinquiesme de ses odes 1552; revised editions, 1553, 1557, 1560, 1578

Les cinquieme des odes, augmente; ensemble la harangue que fit Monseigneur le duc de Guise aus soudars de Mez le iour qu'il pensoit avoir l'assaut 1553

Le livret de folastries à Janot Parisien 1553; revised edition, 1584

Les odes 1553

Le bocage 1554

Continuation des amours 1555; revised edition, 1557

Hymne de Bacus, avec la version latine de Iean Dorat 1555

Les hymnes de P. de Ronsard a tresillustre et reverendissime Odet, cardinal de Chastillon [Hercule Chrestien; partial translation] 1555

Les meslanges 1555; revised edition, 1555

Nouvelle continuation des amours 1556

Le second livre des hymnes 1556

Exhortation au camp du Roy pour bien combatre le iour de la bataille 1558

Exhortation pour la paix 1558

Chant de liesse, au Roy 1559

Chant pastoral sur les nopces de Monseigneur Charles duc de Lorraine & Madame Claude fille II du Roy 1559

Discours a treshault et trespuissant prince, Monseigneur le duc de Savoye; chant pastoral a Madame Marguerite duchesse de Savoye; plus, XXIII inscriptions en faveur de quelques grands seigneurs 1559

L'hymne de tresillustre prince Charles cardinal de Lorraine 1559

La paix, au Roy 1559

Le second livre des meslanges 1559

Suyte de l'hymne de tresillustre prince Charles cardinal de Lorraine 1559

Les œvres de P. de Ronsard, gentilhomme vandomois [*Songs and Sonnets of Pierre de Ronsard, Gentleman of Vendomois*; partial translation] 1560; revised editions, 1567, 1571, 1572-73, 1578, 1584, 1587

Elegie sur le despart de la Royne Marie retournant à son royaume d'Escosse 1561

Continuation du discourse des miseres de ce temps, a la Royne 1562; revised edition, 1564

Discours des miseres de ce temps, a la Royne mere du Roy [*A Discours of the Present Troobles in Fraune, and Miseries of This Tyme, Compyled by Peter Ronsard Gentilman of Vandome, and Dedicated unto the Quene Mother*] 1562; revised editions, 1563, 1568

Elegie sur les troubles d'Amboise, 1560 1562; revised edition, 1563

Institution pour l'adolescence du Roy tres-chrestien Charles neufiesme de ce nom 1562

Remonstrance au people de France 1563; revised editions, 1564, 1572

Response de P. de Ronsard aux injuret et calomnies 1563

Les trois livres du recueil des nouvelles poesies 1563

Elegies, mascarades et bergerie 1565

Les nues, ou nouvelles 1565

Le septiesme livre des poemes 1569

Le sixiesme livre des poemes 1569

Les quatre premiers livres de la Franciade 1572; revised editions, 1573, 1574

Le tombeau du feu Roy tres-chrestien Charles IX, prince tres-debonnaire, tres-vertueux & tres-eloquent 1574

Les estoilles a Monsieur de Pibrac, et deux responses a deux elegies envoyées par le feu Roy Charles à Ronsard 1575

Le tombeau de tresillustre princesse Marguerite de France, duchesse de Savoye 1575

Panegyrique de la renommee, a Henry Troisiesme, Roy de France & de Poloigne 1579

Les derniers vers de Pierre de Ronsard 1586

Œvres inédites de Pierre de Ronsard 1855

Pierre de Ronsard: Œvres complètes. 20 vols. (poetry and criticism) 1914-75

Other Major Works

Abrege de l'art poëtique François (criticism) 1565

CRITICISM

Jerry C. Nash (essay date March 1993)

SOURCE: Nash, Jerry C. "'Fantastiquant mille monstres bossus': Poetic Incongruities, Poetic Epiphanies, and the Writerly Semiosis of Pierre De Ronsard." *Romanic Review* 84, no. 2 (March 1993): 143-62.

[*In the following essay, Nash examines Ronsard's use of "imaginary ekphrasis"—visual images portrayed verbally rather than through the use of real-world referents—in his poetry. Ronsard's poems "L'Ombre du cheval" and "Je veux chanter en ces vers ma tristesse" serve as examples of this practice.*]

In his latest study on an intriguing subject that was for him both "exhilarating" and "exasperating," Murray Krieger defines ekphrasis in these terms: "the literary representation of visual art, real or imaginary." The kind of ekphrasis that deals with the "real" is of course the art of mimesis, what Krieger calls "enargeia I," that is, the "sensible" or sense-oriented perception and portrayal of the mimetic real. Ekphrasis which strives to capture the "imaginary," a writer's art of semiosis, Krieger discusses as "enargeia II," that is, the "intelligible" or mind-oriented perception and portrayal of the semiotic imaginary.[1] My discussion of Pierre de Ronsard will consider only one side of his captivating poetic of ekphrasis, namely, his verbally semiotic presentations of the visual imaginary, his intelligible perceptions and creations of enargeia II. Other studies have already explored Ronsard's debt to the ekphrastic principle of imitation as it relates to and attempts to portray the mimetic real.[2] What remains is to examine this other discourse and level of meaning in Ronsard, his writerly semiosis of seeing and of showing which truly became a poetic obsession for him just as it did for Joachim Du Bellay and Maurice Sceve, as I have written on elsewhere.[3]

Exhilarating and exasperating are indeed perfect ways to describe the writerly as well as readerly activity involved in the literary phenomenology of ekphrasis. This is especially the case when a poet is concerned with coming to terms with the imaginary real, with what another contemporary critic of Poetics, Michael Riffaterre, calls the "fictional truth" and triumph of semiosis over mimesis.[4] The exasperating side of Ronsard's poetic project can be seen in the many failure-poems one encounters in his *Amours,* such as the "eye-defeating" and thus art-defeating impasse which the poet acknowledges and describes early on in **"Cassandre XIX."**[5] In addition to failure in love, the familiar thematics of unrequited love, this poem is also a statement about poetic sterility and poetic failure, and it is the beloved Cassandre herself in her Trojan role as prophetess who conveys this to the poet. His rewards and legacy, she tells him in the first two stanzas, can only be an early death and unaccomplished life, lackluster writings, and scorn and ridicule by his readers in the future. In sum, as Cassandre sees it: "Tu bastiras sur l'incertain du sable, / Et vainement tu peindras dans les cieulx." Worse still, Cassandre's dire and defeating predictions on the poet's failure and future seem to be confirmed by the ultimate sign of divine authority, as the poem's closural image "seals" the matter once and for all (i.e., the image of a lightning flash as an ill-fated omen which the poet "sees" on his "right" hand):

> Ainsi disoit la Nymphe qui m'afolle,
> Lors que le ciel pour seeller sa parolle
> D'un dextre esclair fut presage a mes yeulx.

Two other early poems are also about artistic failure: **"Cassandre XXVIII"** and **"XXIX."** The reader does not have to wait until the Marie-cycle of love poems to find confirmation of such a failure in poetic seeing and feeling and showing, contrary to what most critics, and especially Olivier Pot most recently, have argued.[6] **"Cassandre XXVIII"** is very revealing to show the poet showing the writing of mimesis as failure, or, to be more precise, to show the poet recognizing a failure in the sensible, sense-satisfying purpose of the mimetic vision and its writing. At first, the poet seems to be telling us that this ineffable beauty of Cassandre that has so enslaved him and caused his "senses" to "trouble" his reason is to be found in the many objects or entities of nature itself. This beauty the poet does see and feel through the perceiving senses of the body "painted in them":

> Je ne voy pre, fleur, antre, ny rivage,
> Champ, roc, ny boys, ny flotz dedans le Loyr,
> Que, peite en eulx, il ne me semble voyr
> Ceste beaulte qui me tient en servage.

Up to this point, the mimetic vision and the writing of it are both working well for the poet. But, as the poet informs us in the poem's last tercet, when it comes to pursuing this beauty in them, he is left with the realization that Love has sent him forms that really have no substance, for they all seem to disappear ("s'enfuir"), leaving the poet with only an "empty real." Alongside deception in love, the poet is also pointing out to the reader another deception, that of mimetic perception and its portrayal. The sensible illusion and reality af-

forded by ekphrasis as mimesis are indeed deceptive and parallel the despair and deception and failure in love which the poet is also describing. As the poet poignantly puts it in the last line: "Et pour le vray je ne pren que le vuide."

This failure in the realist project, in mimetic art, that is, the inability of the poet to accept sensible perceptions or visions as real and meaningful and to turn them into adequate and self-satisfying words and images that succeed in bridging the gap between feeling and world, is also the subject of **"Cassandre XXIX."** The first two quatrains of this sonnet also show the poet indulging an exceptionally sensible, highly sensual, even erotic fantasy, with the poet's arms imitating the intimate embrace of the vine-plant. Again, up to this point in the poem, things appear to be working well for the poet and for the reader. However, by the time we reach the end of this poem too, the poet's mimetic vision has been deconstructed and disintegrates completely, leaving him once again abandoned and dismayed:

> Mais ce portraict qui nage dans mes yeulx,
> Fraude tousjours ma joye entrerompue.
> Et tu me fuis au meillieu de mon bien,
> Comme l'esclair qui se finist en rien,
> Ou comme au vent s'esvanouit la nue.

In his "songe divin" of the mimetic real, which is the real subject and problem in this poem, the poet's vision of self as vine-plant enjoying physical intimacy with the beloved becomes ultimately a failed vision. The poet is literally left with "nothing" ("rien"), with the "self-consuming" ("s'evanouir") and unsatisfying vision and feeling and art of non-meaning and non-presence. This failure-poem, like the ones above, does not at all confirm the much discussed and much admired Pleiade realist project and its principle of ekphrasis as mimesis, an aesthetic and writerly principle which Henri Weber (in La Creation poetique . . .) was one of the first to praise and to explore in Ronsard's poetic texts: Ronsard's "desir fondamental de cueillir dans la realite les sensations les plus intenses pour en tirer une delectation exaltante"; or, as Weber continues to paint the picture of Ronsard as the successful poet in harmony verbally with depicting the mimetic real: ". . . aux mots memes qui peignent le monde reel, Ronsard sait en general associer par le seul effet du rythme la joie de l'artiste qui decouvre ce monde, alors la description devient poesie" (125). As we have already seen, and there are other failure-poems in Cassandre one could turn to, such notions as "la joie de l'artiste" and indeed of poetry itself as ekphrasis are totally antithetical to the message being conveyed in **"XIX,"** **"XXVIII,"** and **"XXIX,"** truly poems of despair and defeat in matters of love and of art.[7]

Fortunately however, **"Cassandre XIX"** does offer a clue as how to reverse artistic sterility and failure, and how to change despair and defeat into joy and poetry.

Such a reversal begins, necessarily, with poems and statements such as those considered above which acknowledge failure, ones highlighting the very impossibility or at least the tenuousness and unacceptability of the mimetic project and process, with its sense-oriented aesthetic, in coming to terms with the ineffability of the love experience. Moreover, the best textual indication that mimetic failure is not Ronsard's final position on poetic seeing and showing lies in the ambiguity afforded in the closure of **"Cassandre XIX"**: the seemingly ill-fated omen of a lightning flash ("dextre esclair") on the poet's right hand. Can this image and sign, contrary to the view of Ronsard's various editors who have commented on it, not be interpreted differently, even in the exact opposite way as a favorable sign intended to lead the poet, and the reader, out of exasperation and failure to exhilaration and triumph? Elsewhere (**"LVII"**), the poet clearly signals that his torment and misfortune, like those of Sisyphus and Tantalus, are associated with a left hand. And in another place (**"CLX"**), perhaps even more revealing, we are told that his true potential as poet is to be found in "rightly" interpreting "intelligibly" ("dextrement") the prophecy of his fate. Only through a more intelligible perception and presentation, Ronsard reassures himself and his reader, can he as poet envision Cassandre/the Vendemois countryside (Gastine Forest, Loire River) raised to the poetic power of the Muse Thalia/Mount Parnassus (Apollo's Laurel, Castalia Spring):

> Si dextrement l'augure j'ay receu,
> Et si mon oeil ne fut hyer deceu
> Des doulx regardz de ma doulce Thalie,
> Dorenavant poete me ferez,
> Et par la France appellez vous serez,
> L'un mon laurier, l'aultre ma Castalie.

The "dextre esclair" in **"Cassandre XIX,"** as with the "dextrement" in the line above from **"CLX,"** may be a sign of melancholy, as Ronsard's various editors have presented it, but it also points to something the opposite. As pure metanoia, a change in direction of the mind and thus in poetic direction and definition, it stands as a sign of a different potential and way of writing and of showing, and of the potential success and miracle of the poet-pen-paper relationship in this different mode and aesthetic resisting and rejecting the realist aesthetic, opting instead to control its/their own destiny. This image announces the poet's receptivity to an alternative semiotic kind of writing, an other mode of discourse which the poet acknowledges might be more apt and more satisfying epistemologically and literarily. To verbalize "Intelligibly" visions of the ineffable, to capture in words through pen and paper the "flashing" significance and the realities not of this world but of mind and art, these are the poetic possibilities of a semiotic consciousness being suggested in **"Cassandre XIX"** and **"CLX."** We have actually already begun to see this semiotic of the word at work in **"Cassandre CLX"** just quoted, in the magical visionary itinery and transformation of Cassandre/Vendome becoming Thalia/Mount Parnassus. Thanks to the symbolic images of myth and allegory that increase the distance between signifier and signified, thanks to a reduced mimetic ambition whose increased unconcern with the things of the real world can better provide the poet and the reader with visionary access to the sacred and the ineffable, Ronsard's fabulous inventions or semiotic constructs will house not real people and real things and real spaces but will give life to and find another space and place for the verbal-visual ineffable in its infinite remove from such realities. Only then can the poet claim, as he does in **"CLX,"** that thanks to such marvelous non-mimetic creations: "Dorenavant poete me ferez."

There is no finer poem in all of Ronsard's works to help us see and understand and appreciate this poet's belief in and performance of a writerly semiosis and the brand of ekphrasis he was truly obsessed with than the chanson **"Je veux chanter en ces vers ma tristesse,"** found in the *Amours de Marie.*[8] A song of melancholy and sadness turned into joyful vision and verbal presentation of this vision is precisely this poem's triumph. Ronsard's semiotic mode of presentation is what is being highlighted when the poet avows in lines 22-24 that his purpose in this poem is to "fantastiqu[er] mille monstres bossus, / Hommes, oiseaux, et Chimeres cornues." He is telling us that his art of semiosis, and his understanding now of ekphrasis, will necessarily be involved with poetic incongruities and aberrations ("mille monstres bossus"), from where poetic epiphanies will be derived, that is, will be created. However, before discussing these incongruous yet epiphanic creations, we do need to consider a great poem in the Italian Renaissance that served as an intertext, or rather a countertext, for Ronsard. The French poet's conscious rewriting of his Italian model will be of help in understanding the semiotic constructs of **"Je veux chanter."**

Ronsard's chanson is supposedly, and has been identified by all editors of Ronsard as being, an imitation of Petrarch's *Rime sparse* 127.[9] Petrarch's poem is about love's ecstasy and the clear mimetic analogies between the beauties of nature and Laura, the poet's beloved. In this poem, conventional ekphrasis as enargeia I is certainly at work where language functions on the level of imitation (imitatio) itself. Petrarch's poetic images, encapsulating the art of the mimetic real, vividly and credibly portray their natural-sign objects as if in a painting. The Italian poet is creating with his verbal "images" analogues to the visual images of the painter, thereby affirming the transferability of 'things' between verbal and visual systems of representation. Like Ronsard, who tells us he must sing his song of grief if only in order to alleviate it or lessen it, Petrarch had similarly acknowledged in his own sorrowful song a therapeutic function of art:

> But still, however much of the story of my suffering I
> find written
> by his [Love's] very own hand, in the midst of my
> heart where I
> so often return, I shall speak out, because sighs take a
> truce and
> there is help for sorrow when one speaks. I say that
> although I
> gaze intent and fixed on a thousand different things, I
> see only
> one lady and her lovely face.
>
>   (7-14)

But with the last idea just quoted from Petrarch, there is something new and very different from what Ronsard will write. Petrarch is already affirming for him the inseparability and the intense satisfaction of vision, focused on nature, on external reality, and the beloved object. His song will be concerned with the mimetic union and unity of "a thousand different things" on which the poet "gaze[s] intent and fixed" and where he "see[s] only one lady and her lovely face." The remainder of the poem is a description of these sensibly-felt "things" of the mimetic real that is Laura/Nature, that is, Laura as natural-sign objects. Her presence and absence parallel the luminous rising and dark setting of the sun:

> If I see the sun rise, I sense the approach of the light
> that enamors
> me; if setting at evening, I seem to see her when she
> departs, leaving
> all in darkness behind her,
>
>   (66-70)

The sense-illuminating art of mimesis is, as Petrarch tells us, his principal poetic purpose in this poem, as it appears to be in the whole of the Rime sparse:

> . . . when the strange idea came to me to tell in so
> few pages in how
> many places the flower of all beauties, remaining in
> herself, has scattered her light.
>
>   (87-90)

This is why the poet can believe that Laura as "light," as "the flower of all beauties," can bring him to see in and through her the perfected excellence of nature itself. Whether he is "gazing at leaves on a branch or violets on the ground" (29-30), or viewing "from afar new snow on the hills" (43-44), or seeing "white with crimson roses in a vase of gold" (71-72), it is always the mimetic vision that permits him to see "the face of her who excels all other wonders with the three excellences gathered in her" (74-76), that is, the floral white, crimson, and gold above. This Italian poet has been

conveying supernal beauty through the sensibly-signifying art of mimesis. He has been relying on a conventional sign system, one operating exclusively through the senses to the imperative "voy" being used five times to reinforce our understanding of this vision, finding a home, rest, and delight "en ce monde si ample," in the same worldly divine illumination that Petrarch took refuge in: Helene as the morning sun, her eyes as stars shining like a bright lantern in a temple, or the warm beam of her eyes bringing forth an eternal springtime, in a word, and controlling image, her "love radiance" ("ses flames amoureuses") embellishing the earth and enchanting the heavens. Helene in this picture is, in the ultimate mimetic analysis, "des beautez le portrait & l'exemple" of the here-and-now "en ce monde si ample." She is mimesis personified.[10]

However, there is another, a totally different side to Ronsard, as I have been suggesting, one which can best be seen and appreciated by juxtaposing it with the poet's, and Petrarch's, mimetic side discussed above. This other side to Ronsard is, I believe, the artistic consequence of his doubts and questionings of mimetic portrayal, which we analyzed at some length at the beginning of this study. In his "different" creations, Ronsard will no longer be concerned with the mimetic art of representation, but with the semiotic art of presentation. Both poetic perspective and literary ontology are now radically different from what we have just observed in Ronsard and in Petrarch. This new verbal-visual writerly semiosis as ekphrasis is obsessed not with poetic similarities and unity but with poetic dissimilarities and incongruities, even with monsters and monstrosities and other aberrations of reality. This can all be seen in his poem-song, **"Je veux chanter en ces vers ma tristesse,"** one of his finest portrayals of poetic incongruities, and poetic epiphanies. As indicated earlier, this marvelous song is supposedly an imitation of Petrarch's Song 127. However, in Ronsard's version, the poet is deliberately subverting the mimetic value of Petrarch's pre-text to highlight and emphasize another, perhaps more captivating process of signifying. As we shall see, he is clearly opting in **"Je veux chanter"** for a semiotic mode of writing as both a resistance and a response to reality, and to mimetic representations of reality.[11]

The genesis of **"Je veux chanter"** is identical to that of *Rime sparse* 127. In the "absence" of Marie the beloved object (3: "Veu que je suis absent de ma maistresse"; 6: "Pour le depart de ma maistresse absente"), the only thing left for the poet to do is to sing his song of sorrow (5: "Tour ne mourir il faut donc que je chante"). Here there are obviously two meanings contained in the notion of absence. As with Petrarch, Ronsard's poet is separated from the beloved, thus, a physical absence. Unlike in Petrarch, for Ronsard's poet the beloved is also absent around him: she is an object "absented."

Thus, the poet can only construct, through mental and poetic images, the presentation of an absent reality. This reality is certainly not to be, and cannot be, found around him, for he cannot "see" it with the "body's eye" anywhere he looks. The sensible world, and the sensory instrument par excellence of perceiving this world—the poet's very eyes—will not lead the poet this time to transcendent seeing and showing, to ekphrasis and to epiphany. As the poet acknowledges once again his all-too-familiar impasse in sensible perception: "Tant par les yeux nos esprits sont deceus" (24).

Since the poet cannot see in anything real the beauty he looks for, he is forced to turn away from ordinary vision of the external world and to turn inward—to the inner eye, the "unreal" eye ("oelliade trompee") of the "mind-soul," as he calls it—for another source of vision. Mental imaging is clearly being made the prerequisite to poetic imaging, the mind's ability to conceive and produce pictures:

> Ainsi je vois d'une oeillade trompee
> Cette beaute dont je suis deprave,
> Qui par les yeux dedans l'ame frappee,
> M'a vivement son portrait engrave.
>
> (29-32)

It is no longer the bodily, mimetic eye of "raison" connecting sight to actual presence, but the inner eye of "une fausse et vaine illusion" bestowing the creative insight of a presence-in-absence that the poet must now rely on for revelation and portrayal and meaning. Semiotic negation replaces logocentric affirmation as a poetic principle. Here is another of Ronsard's recognitions of this intriguing kind of semiotic seeing, which will lead the poet to showing in words the illusions of mind and art:

> Mais ma raison est si bien corrompue
> Par une fausse et vaine illusion,
> Que nuit et jour je la porte en la vue,
> Et sans la voir j'en ai la vision.
>
> (17-20)

His newly-acquired "deviant" kind of vision, as with its ineffable object, in frustrating and negating "reason" and normal or conventional sight is therefore called "une fausse et vaine illusion" ("une faulce imagination" as it is called in earlier editions), which permits the poet day and night to have "imaginings," that is, to visualize and verbalize both her and itself. Of course, the imaginings or creations of the poet's "fausse et vaine illusion" have nothing to do with the real world, hence the incongruous yet very apt wording Ronsard uses in designating his faculty of the imagination. They, and it, actually function to re-think and re-create this world. The contemplative and creative activity of the poet now is like the sailors who row with the "percep-tion" of a broken oar (26-27: "En haute mer, a puissance de bras / Tirent la rame, ils l'imaginent torte") or, as the reader is also encouraged to see this impossible activity, like the sky-gazer "qui contemple les nues, / Fantastiquant mille monstres bossus, / Hommes, oiseaux et Chimeres cornues" (21-23). Needless to say, the reader is a very long way now from Petrarch's "flower of all beauties" in Song 127 and the "jardin" in *Helene III*.

This highly incongruous, even monstrous, ineffable beauty to be perceived and portrayed so vividly by the "eye of the mind-soul" (29-32) is what the poet focuses on and pursues in the last two-thirds of this remarkable poem. Whether climbing in the mountains or walking in the woods alongside a stream, he avows how "tousjours a l'oeil ce beau portrait me suit" (36), that is, the "image" of this beauty of Marie as "beaute amere" which the poet's "unreal eye" has made in its moments of sublime derangement (29-32).[12] The verbal constructions "j'appergoy" and "je pense voir," used eleven times to reinforce and give credibility to the workings of the poet's other, inner eye, introduce or dominate virtually every stanza that follows. "To perceive" is the same for Ronsard as "to think in order to see." Seeing as thinking precedes words as mental image precedes poetic image. Imagination is what turns mental image into poetic image. The creations of the poet's imagination are pure constructs of mind and art, of a writerly semiosis, which are now strangely yet credibly non-mimetic. This is why Ronsard refers to his faculty of imagination as "illusion," and as "fausse." This faculty is not at all real, but incredible, to the world, yet very real, credible, to the poet, for it satisfies and makes possible his own different and unique view of things. The poet's deviant imagination in the process of conceiving mental-verbal-visual monstrosities just may, in its unexpected and mimetically meaning-negating inventions, offer a better means of signifying the beauty of the ineffable. And it is not as much in Ronsard to visualize the verbal as it is to verbalize the visual (to turn thought and words into images). Which is to say that he is a poet intent on creating an other world more than he is a painter interested in depicting this world. To borrow the insightful words of John Berger which this writer-critic uses to indicate "another" (intelligible, mind-oriented) way of seeing, for Ronsard too "seeing [thought as imaging] comes before words." Ronsard now writes, not what he can see, but what he is capable of thinking and imagining.[13] This is really why Ronsard tells us so repeatedly in his chanson: "Je pense voir. . . ." Simply put, he turns to the mind, not to nature or external reality, for vision and creation.

Poetic incongruities of enargeia II are the products of this mental and linguistic operation and aberration, of Ronsard's other way of seeing and of writing. The reader's ability to participate in the poet's thoughts, even the most incongruous and outrageous and seemingly impossible, is crucial to Ronsard's writerly semiosis. This reader must share with the poet the challenge of the semiotic relationship between signs and referents, words, and things. One of Ronsard's favorite images and metaphors which the reader encounters in so many of his poems is of course the rose in its resplendent and ephemeral beauty, to which the poet mimetically equates the beauty of the beloved, usually with an ulterior motive in mind. In **"Je veux chanter"** however, the natural-sign status of the rose is not one of similarity but of difference. The kind of rose that Ronsard sees this time in Marie does not conform to the real-life cycle of the rose in nature, with its fragile beauty and brief life span justifying the poet's plea of carpe diem. She/it never dies in the poet's mind, or imagination:

> Quand j'apercois la rose sur l'epine,
> Je pense voir de ses levres le teint;
> La rose au soir de sa couleur decline,
> L'autre couleur jamais ne se deteint.

> (49-52)

Marie is indeed portrayed not through the transparently clear, sense-satisfying representation of mimesis but through the intensely empathy-provoking, intelligible presentation of the poet's semiotic consciousness. As an object existing in and being portrayed by mind, she is presented to the reader's mind not in an all resplendent and reassuring light but in the uneasy identification of her with intelligible, phantastic entities, such as the curved side of the Moon, that is, a bow and arrow ready to strike:

> Si le Croissant au premier mois j'avise,
> Je pense voir son sourcil ressemblant
> A l'arc d'un Turc qui la sagette a mise
> Dedans la coche et menace le blanc.

> (41-44)

In order to come to terms with and to depict the chanson's overriding theme of presence-in-absence, the poet will also turn to the allegorical figure of "Ceres la bletiere, / Ayant le front orne de son present" to sustain him in the real absence around him of Marie (9-10). Or, he sees and portrays the beauty of Marie in the fantastic form and image of this ripening wheat whose frizzled blades as the result of plowing become the beloved's silk hair full of curls blowing in the wind:

> Si j'apercois quelque champ qui blondoie
> D'epis frises au travers des sillons,
> Je pense voir ses beaux cheveaux de soie
> Epars au vent en mille crepillons.

> (37-40)

Ronsard too, like William Blake later, was able to see a "Heaven" in, of all things, a wild flower, in Marie as one of these "fleurs en quelque pree":

> Quand j'apercois les fleurs en quelque pree
> Ouvrir leur robe au lever du Soleil,
> Je pense voir de sa face pourpree
> S'epanouir le beau lustre vermeil.

> (53-56)

And the wording "en quelled free" is quite significant. It is just as meaningfully and intentionally indefinite as similar wording is later in another marvelous writer of semiosis, in Stephen Marlene: "Je is: tune fleer!" For Marlene as for Ronsard, this imaginary or intelligible kind of flower as "libelants de tours bouquets" is "la notion pure," that is, "idle mere ate suave."[14] In both poets, words are being used to call forth an intelligible reality of the imaginary as opposed to the sensible specific of the real: wild flowers in some meadow, those contained in a "meadow" within the mind of the poet, as opposed to actual flowers in one of the real world. Like Maharanees "absented" flower in all bouquets (i.e., in no real bouquet), which is this writer's mental-verbal image of "idea itself and sweet," Ronsard's own "images" of the verbally ineffable are also pure constructs of mind and art created to convey their own special world of a writerly semiosis. They do this by reducing mimetic fidelity and precision in order to capture the more indirect semiotic power of the aesthetic sign.

As such, Ronsard was also able to see, and to translate, his vision of the ineffable Marie in a wild oak tree:

> Si j'apercois quelque chene sauvage,
> Qui jusqu'au ciel eleve ses rameaux
> Je pense voir sa taille et son corsage,
> Ses pieds, sa greve et ses jumeaux.

> (57-60)

Another semiotic re-creation of vision and of world can be seen in the "splashing noise" which the poet describes next as coming from a "clear" stream:

> Si j'entends bruire une fontaine claire,
> Je pense ouir sa voix dessus le bord,
> Qui se plaignant de ma triste misere,
> M'appelle a soi pour me donner confort.

> (61-64)

In the very next stanza, the poet explains the real reason for all of these strange poetic and mental incongruities, his phantasms, his fantastic forms. They are the products of joyful melancholy:

> Voila comment, pour etre fantastique,
> En cent facons ses beautes j'apercoi,
> Et m'ejouis d'etre melancolique,
> Pour recevoir tant de formes en moi.

> (65-68)

The recovery of semiotic vision from the melancholy associated with a perceived failure in mimetic perception and creation, of insight from sight, and the joyful portrayal of that new-found vision and order are Ronsard's ultimate triumph in **"Je veux chanter."** The poet is creating his own self-standing and self-satisfying universe in which he is now able to take utmost delight. Love for him is indeed the fury of a deranged and dissonant fantasy: "Nommant ce mal fureur de fantaisie" (71). There is no real cure for this melancholic disease of the poet's amorous pains, or at least no conventional cure for this "maladie" which "les medecins . . . savent bien juger" but "qui ne se peut par herbes soulager" (69-70, 72). His fate, like that of a few other committed love poets, is to suffer the happiness he can create from it, the happiness of his amorous pains in their state of unhappiness, these "amoureuses peines, / Dont le bonheur n'est sinon que malheur" (75-76).

But, as we have already seen, it is through this very sickness that health can be restored, through this unhappiness that happiness is possible, in the passage from an old (poetic) order and its failed expectations to creatively-renewed life, one in which the poet can loudly and defiantly proclaim: "Et m'ejouis d'etre melancolique"! The poet's melancholy is ultimately a positive, not negative, sign and a necessary and redeeming condition for semiotic production, for seeing and showing "dextrement" (**"Cassandre CLX"**: "intelligibly," "differently"). With this understanding, the poet's incongruities and aberrations, his chanson, are not really for him, as he hopes for his reader, so illusory or outlandish or unreal as they might appear at first. As the poet takes pains to reassure Marie on this crucial point, we read in the poem's last stanza: "ce n'est tromperie / Des visions que je raconte ici" (78-79). She and they—the poet's "amorous care"—are very real for him, and are even his epiphanies, for the poet carries them night and day in his mind (80). Giving new life and new meaning and new forms to the "black ink of melancholy" is truly Ronsard's triumph in this chanson, just as it was for Shakespeare in his own melancholic love lyrics, as Jean Starobinski has shown in his analysis of Sonnet 114. Ronsard too was able to transform the black ink of despair (Starobinski: "les desordres de l'esprit") into something of great human worth and value in the redemptive and liberating reality of art:

> Le fond tenebreux comporte la chance del'eclat, si on
> lui superpose
> une matiere lisse. Shakespeare le devine, en evoquant
> le miracle
> d'un amour qui resplendit, sauve des ravages univer-
> sels du Temps,
> dans l'encre noire du poeme [. . .] La melancolie de-
> venue encre
> devient enfin le tain grace auquel l'image rayonne.[15]

And here is how Krieger describes the same triumph in Shakespeare, which, as I have been arguing, I also believe to have been Ronsard's. He too is concerned

with, and quotes from, Shakespeare's Sonnet 114, a poem very close in semiotic perspective and mode to Ronsard's intriguing chanson: "To make of monsters and things indigest / Such cherubins as your sweet self resemble." He then will explain how, in Shakespeare as in other writers who share and develop the same deviant kind of perspective, such "strangely incongruous, dreamlike—if sometimes nightmarish—equivalences [can] abound in the redemption produced by monstrosity" and how "all readings [can] end in an identity—despite the great discrepancy—between sign and referent" (137). Sonnet 114's illusory metamorphosis of "monsters" and "things indigest" into "cherubins," in a word, its "magic semiotic," is achieved through the semiotic possibilities of the verbally intelligible image: "Through the alembic of his words the poet achieves his function as alchemist." [. . .] What the poet's eye sees has been transformed by the mind's power to superimpose its own seeing upon it, under the power of love that teaches the eye "this alchemy" (140).

What we have been discussing is of course the self-sufficiency and autonomy of the poetic text, the poem as ultimate intelligible image and universe, and its hermeneutic independence from everything but itself, and especially from the "real" world. This is exactly what Ronsard intends us to understand in his chanson when he acknowledges his own obsession with "fantastiquant mille monstres bossus, / Hommes, oiseaux, et Chimeres cornues," that is, when he equates the beloved ineffable Marie with an ominous configuration of "le Croissant," with "Ceres la bletiere," with "quelque champ qui blondoie / D'epis frises au travers des sillons," with one of these "fleurs en quelque pree," with "quelque chene sauvage," and so forth. These are the products of the mind's eye, of the poet's intelligible imagination (his "fausse et vaine illusion" or "faulce imagination" or "fureur de fantaisie"). Ronsard pushes poetic language and imagery and vision up to and at times beyond their usual referential intelligibility for meaning and value. This semiotic consciousness is what gives him vision of the absented Marie: "Et sans la voir [with [sans l'avoir' also surely intended by Ronsard] j'en ai la vision." It is also what provides him with the forms in which to present his vision: "Pour recevoir tant de formes en moi."[16]

These forms of fantasy truly abound in Ronsard's oeuvre, his semiotic constructs which affirm their own charm of being and of not being. They are not limited to his love lyrics, though the latter are especially suited to his writerly semiosis. In **"La Lyre,"** for example, mind alone as creative intelligence is viewed as responsible for translating vision and constructing text:

> Quant a Pallas qui sort de la cervelle,
> C'est de l'esprit l'oeuvre toute nouvelle
> Que le penser luy [Jupiter] a fait concevoir.[17]

Ronsard is aligning himself here on the subject of poetic conception and creation with the most intelligible of all mythic figures and their accomplishments, with Jupiter and Minerva. Ronsard will also indicate what kind of lyric writing he is really intrigued by. The poet will affirm once again the necessity of his "fureur de fantaisie" so crucial, as we saw, to **"Je veux chanter,"** that is, his melancholic condition and inspiration for lyric writing:

> Quand la fureur me laisse, tout soudain
> Plume et papier me tombent de la main.
>
> (323)

He will specifically ask himself what kind of writing will best serve his purpose, will best translate the melancholic disposition of both Jean Belot, to whom **"La Lyre"** is dedicated, and himself:

> Par quel escrit faut-il que je commence
> Pour envoyer des Muses la semence,
> J'enten mes vers, par toute Europe, i fin
> Que ton renom survive apres ta fin?
>
> (325)

Ronsard will give us the answer. Poetry aspiring to excellence and to permanence begins and ends in the mind of its author-reader, and above all else must speak to and captivate this mind with strange and novel creations. Invoking the inward-outward dichotomy and duality of Socrates as an apt image of Belot, and of himself, to convey this idea ("Lors de ta voix distile l'eloquence / Un vray Socrate," 326), Ronsard is obviously fascinated, as he hopes Belot and his reader will be, by this Socrates-image. For, as Ronsard sees it, its grotesque and highly incongruous exterior ("En front severe, en oeil melancolique," 325) does conceal an inner linguistic and creative charm capable of conceiving "dix mille odeurs estranges et nouvelles / . . . / Par la vertu de ta langue qui pousse / Un hamecon aux coeurs, tant elle est douce" (327). As is obvious by now, the poet is addressing himself as much as he is his friend and benefactor Belot in this poem, for the real subject of **"La Lyre"** has to do with the aesthetics of a writerly semiosis, with Ronsard's own semiotically enticing "odeurs estranges et nouvelles."

Monstrously strange and novel images are also the subject of **"Folastrie VIII,"** which offers the reader another application or "writing" by Ronsard of enargeia II, of the intelligible operation of mind and art. This poem, like important sections of **"Je veux chanter,"** has to do with clouds, and a state of verbal-visual drunkenness and blindness:

> Je voy deca, je voy dela,
> Je voy mille bestes cornues,
> Mille marmotz dedans les nues.
>
> (761)

. . . . .

> Voyci deux nuages tous plains
> De Mores, qui n'ont point de mains,
> Ny de corps, et ont les visages
> Semblables a des chatz sauvages.
>
> (762)

Once again, the poet is on the semiotic path toward the epiphanic recreation and redemption found in, created through, verbal-visual monstrosity. Through his intentionally "strange" images, the poet is also presenting a view of "drunkenness" as a textual reflection upon the creation of signs. Seen from a semiotic perspective, this view translates his awareness of the arbitrariness of signs and language, with one fictional, self-referential process of imaging (the seeing and showing here in clouds of "mille bestes cornues," of "mille marmot") at work within another (the seeing and showing there in clouds of "Mores," of "chatz sauvages"). It is not too unreal to see here that Ronsard has constructed a semiotic mise en abyme. As self-referential fiction, this text is, I believe, calling into question the representational function of writing by emphasizing the ability of the poetic imagination to turn in upon itself and away from the real world. What the poet "sees" and shows in **"Folastrie VIII"** is, once again, the unique signifying creations of the poem, not conventional earthly objects.

Nowhere in Ronsard, finally, is his writerly semiosis, his intelligible art of mind over (mimetic) sense, so captivatingly shown and seen than in his painting-poem, **"L'Ombre du cheval"** (373), which I have saved for discussion last. This poem is a superb and magical embodiment of ekphrasis as enargeia II and the writing of the two principal features that define this kind of ekphrasis: "the literary depiction of a painting and also the figurative use of such a depiction" (Riffaterre 127), a definition we have been applying to Ronsard's texts throughout this study. It is written again to his friend Belot, ostensibly to thank him for a painting of a horse, but which Ronsard the poet prefers to read as a verbal emblem:

> Amy Belot, que l'honneur accompagne,
> Tu m'as donne non un cheval d'Espagne,
> Mais l'ombre vain d'un cheval par escrit,
> Que je comprens seulement en esprit.
> Je ne le puis ny par les yeux comprendre
> Ny par la main; il ne se laisse prendre,
> Chose invisible, et fantome me suit,
> Ainsi qu'on voit en nos songes de nuit
> Se presenter je ne scay quels images
> Sans corps, sans mains, sans bras et sans visages.

We have already seen this "horse," this mental monster, depicted above in the many verbal-visual constructs of Ronsard's ekphrasis as enargeia II. This time, the writerly ineffable is not a horse at all but "l'ombre vain d'un cheval par escrit," which can only be understood in the place where it was created, and where it must be read and interpreted—in the poet's and the reader's mind ("Que je comprens seulement en esprit"). As a "chose invisible, et fantome," the horse in question cannot be comprehended by the eyes of the body ("Je ne le puis ny par les yeux comprendre"), nor through the sense of touch ("Ny par la main.") It is totally resistant to sensible perception. This horse must be visualized by the mind's eye just as one encounters "images" in a dream, that is, through intelligible perceptions totally lacking in sensible features i.e., through images "sans corps, sans mains, sans bras et sans visages"). Of course, it is not a question in this poem of picturing a real horse at all, but of verbally conceiving "the imaging of the horse," the very title of the poem. This must take place at moments totally removed from reality, moments when mind and art are liberated from sensible reality, such as those of "drunkenness" or "blindness" (as we saw above in other poems), or those of sleep or the dream state, as the picture is being presented to us now:

> Ton cheval. . . .
> Que seulement en dormant j'appercoy;
> Car autrement ton cheval je ne voy.
> Plus en songeant ton cheval je me donne.
>
> (373)

The horse in the poem, and to be correct one needs to say "as the poem," is distanced in every conceivable way from a real horse. This one does not gallop: "Mais ton cheval, fantome, ne chemine" (374). But it does do other marvelous things, which a real horse cannot do:

> Il vole en l'air, boit en l'air, d'air se paist;
> C'est un corps d'air, l'air seulement luy plaist
> Et la fumee et le vent et le songe,
> Et dedans l'air seulement il s'allonge.
>
> (374)

As with **"Je veux chanter," "L'Ombre du cheval"** is a captivating and convincing demonstration that the realist project is inherently incompatible with a view of the poetic text as a self-conscious and self-contained artifice. The ineffable existence or "world" of the "horse" portrayed so exquisitely in the above lines serves no other purpose than to affirm the ontological status of this "world" in the text, and the power of language to create the illusion that this "world" is "real." For in the final analysis, all that can really be said about this horse is that it is like these

> . . . jumens qui en tournant l'entree
> De leur nature au vent Zephyrien,
> Sur le Printemps, vont concevant de rein.
>
> (375)

"To go about conceiving nothing" as a principle and preoccupation of literary perception and discourse has been the real subject of this study of Ronsard's ek-

phrastic art. At the end of **"L'Ombre du cheval,"** Ronsards specifically calls this art of "nothing" his "vers raillards" (375). His is an art that is monstrously and incongruously "playful" or "witty" ("raillard"), an art which at its best is a playful statement on and performance of the autonomy of language itself. But this art of "nothing" should not be construed as trivial. Ronsard's writing of "rien" in "vers raillards" is always being related by the poet and owes its very existence to the poet's coming to terms with the Renaissance theoretical issue of literary re/presentation, with what today we view to be the tension between critical emphases on mimesis and metafictionality, on referentiality and self-referentiality. As we have seen in so many ways and forms, Ronsard's verbal-visual ineffable as "nothing," his writing of the "fantastic," requires a highly intelligible, incongruous, non-mimetic mode of presentation that replaces, as Todorov argues throughout his book on this subject, the mimetic credible as real with the semiotic fantastic as real.[18] This art of the fantastic is, to quote Krieger on this same point, one "that shifts the burden of the poem from its dependence on external objects of imitation and places it on the verbal inventions that respond to the visions produced by the poet's 'wit'" (127). For a poet like Ronsard, as in the case of a poet like Mallarme and his visions and constructs of "Rien" (Mondor/Jean-Aubry 27), this creative wit that is the ekphrastic mode of semiosis—the writerly brilliance of Ronsard's "vers raillards," or of his "dextre esclair" as we saw it presented at the beginning of this study—this wit is quite possibly the ultimate source of epiphany, of revelatory meaning.

In the end, however, it is up to the reader to assess the meaning and value of ekphrasis in Ronsard's texts. This reader will need to figure out in particular what Ronsard meant when he wrote, in qualifying his poetic creations and fictions: "ce n'est que Poesie" (Weber 318). The statement can best be understood, I believe, as poetry as pure invention of the mind and as reflector of its own self-contained system. Ronsard's fictitious mimesis thrives on the symbolic, visual malleability of the verbal image, on all these "ombre[s] vain [s] . . . par escrit" that are the writerly constructs of his opaque semiosis: Marie as the curved side of the Moon, the aesthetics of **"La Lyre"** ushering forth "dix mille odeurs estranges et nouvelles, "the imaging of "mille monstres bossus" or of "mille bestes cornues," a pictured horse intelligibly depicted verbally, and so forth. Ronsard has only one word for all these strange but epiphanic creations. He calls them "Poesie."[19]

Notes

1. *Ekphrasis: The Illusion of the Natural Sign* (Baltimore: The Johns Hopkins University Press, 1992) 67ff., 93ff. Krieger's Ekphrasis is nothing less than seminal and has been very helpful in my

own work on this subject in Renaissance poetry and poetics. We will be returning to him later in this essay. All italics in this study are mine, unless otherwise indicated, as are all translations into English.

2. See, among many others one could cite, the following representative studies: Henri Weber, *La Creation poetique au [XVI.sup.e] siecle en France* (Paris: Nizet, 1955), especially 235-396 (wherein Ronsard figures prominently in the discussion of the love themes and imagery in the Pleiade production); Roberto E. Campo, "A Poem to A Painter: The Elegie of Janet and Ronsard's Dilemma of Ambivalence," *French Forum* 12 (1987): 273-87; Margaret M. McGowan, *Ideal Forms in the Age of Ronsard* (Berkeley: University of California Press, 1985); Donald Stone, Jr., *Ronsard's Sonnet Cycles: A Study in Tone and Vision* (New Haven: Yale University Press, 1966); Elaine Limbrick, "L'Oeil du poete: vision et perspective dans la poesie francaise de la Renaissance," *Etudes litteraires* 20 (1987): 13-26. The essay by Limbrick comes the closest to the aesthetic views on Ronsard which the present essay will develop. This critic is not, however, interested in the theoretical implications of ekphrasis, which I believe can be of great help in understanding a heretofore neglected side (critical and poetic: semiotic) of this Renaissance prince of poets.

3. The interest in and performance of a writerly semiosis, as opposed to a writerly mimesis, by Sceve and Du Bellay are subjects explored in my book, *The Love Aesthetics of Maurice Sceve: Poetry and Struggle* (Cambridge: Cambridge University Press, 1991), and my essay, "The Poetics of Seeing and Showing: Du Bellay's Love Lyrics," in Barbara C. Bowen and Jerry C. Nash, editors, *Lapidary Inscriptions: Renaissance Essays for Donald Stone, Jr.* (Lexington: French Forum, 1991) 45-59.

4. This is the very title of Riffaterre's book, as well as the subject he treats therein: *Fictional Truth* (Baltimore: The Johns Hopkins University Press, 1990). More later from Riffaterre.

5. *Les Amours,* Henri and Catherine Weber, editors (Paris: Garnier, 1985).

6. This critical notion of Ronsard's constructive epistemology of inspiration (the idealism of Neo-Platonism) located in Cassandre, yielding to skeptical epistemology and artistic failure in Marie (mannerism), is a major structuring principle in Pot's discussion of Ronsard's love lyrics. See his inspiration et melancolie: l'epistemologie poetique dans les *Amours de Ronsard* (Geneva: Droz, 1990). I do not believe that evolution and sequen-

tiality fully explain Ronsard's failure-poems. These surface throughout his love cycles and are connected to a perceived, and demonstrated, artistic failure in the realist project, to mimesis itself failing the poet, as much as they are to any notion of cyclical-epistemological evolution. This point will become more apparent as the present essay unfolds.

7. For other approaches to writerly impasse in other poems of Ronsard, see Terence Cave, "Enargeia: Erasmus and the Rhetoric of Presence in the Sixteenth Century," *L'Esprit Createur* 16 (1976): 5-19; and also Claude-Gilbert Dubois, "Itineraire et impasses de la 'Vive Representation" au [XVI.sup.e] siecle," in *La Litterature de la Renaissance: Melanges d'histoire et de critique litteraires offerts a Henri Weber,* Marguerite Soulie and Robert Aulotte, editors (Geneva: Slatkine, 1984) 405-425.

8. I will be using here the edition by Albert-Marie Schmidt for quoting this chanson (80 lines, 20 quatrains) since it, unlike the Weber edition, gives the latest, and very important, emendations of this poem made by Ronsard himself in 1578-87. *Les Amours* (Paris: Gallimard, 1964). Since I quote from this poem so extensively, and since line numbers are not given by Schmidt, I am providing them to facilitate referencing.

9. Robert M. Durling, editor and translator, *Petrarch's Lyric Poems* (Cambridge, Massachusetts: Harvard University Press, 1976) 248-55.

10. This is the kind of interpretation presented so well by Stone 207-10.

11. Ronsard's writerly semiosis as enargeia II will also lend support to the view of more involvement by him in Renaissance Neo-Platonism than has been generally allowed by critics. As Krieger has argued and shown, enargeia II is the literary essence in the Renaissance of an ekphrastic, verbally art-defining Neo-Platonism. Through it, the "extravagant metaphysical demands of Christian Neo-Platonism" were met, precisely in observing the fundamental distinction between the sensible reality of the profane, portrayed transparently as the mimetic real by the painter, or by a painterly-oriented poet, and the intelligible reality of the sacred and ineffable, presented opaquely as the verbal emblem by the writer: "For Renaissance Neo-Platonists, moved by a desire to save poetry and make it an instrument for our salvation, the potential object of imitation was, in the main, to vary with the art: a sensible object for the visual arts and an intelligible object for the verbal arts" (142).

12. Though he does not consider Ronsard, Jean-Michel Rabate examines the aesthetics of "beaute

amere" in his exciting book, *La Beaute amere: Fragments d'esthetiques* (Seyssel: Editions du Champ Vallon, 1986).

13. *Ways of Seeing* (London: British Broadcasting Corporation and Penguin Books, 1972) 7.

14. Crise de vers, Henri Mondor and G. Jean-Aubry, editors, *Stephane Mallarme, Oeuvres completes* (Paris: Gallimard, 1945) 368.

15. "L'Encre de la melancolie," *La Nouvelle Revue Francaise* 123 (1963): 423.

16. Ronsard's recognitions of his receptivity to the "forms" of the "mind's eye" clearly underscore his involvement in a writerly semiosis. As Riffaterre has shown (in *Fictional Truth*), this mode of seeing and of writing is always "opposed to referentiality, the assumed relationship between a sign and nonverbal objects taken to be reality" (130). This is why "form, being obviously contrived [thus Ronsard's recognition of his 'faulce imagination'], betrays the band of its maker and signals fictionality [the 'dextre esclair' of Ronsard's 'fausse et vaine illusion']" (63). It should also be clear by now that I have altered the representational itinerary that Pot in his book argues to be Ronsard's. He interprets Cassandre in Neo-Platonic accents as all light and mimesis, and Marie as darkness and failure, whose "manierisme . . . prend le parti inverse: l'enjeu, c'est simplement le jeu" (283, Pot's italics). He does however, at the end of his study, suggest that semiosis just may play a larger role in Ronsard's art than has been allowed (458). This notion is precisely what I have wished to explore in the present study, and to give to Marie, and to "Je veux chanter" in particular, a more positive assessment, as well as to other of Ronsard's less valued or less acclaimed texts, those that do not participate in the poet's project and triumph of mimesis.

17. Gustave Cohen, editor, *Ronsard, Oeuvres completes* (Paris: Gallimard, 1950) II 324. The lines within poems in the Cohen edition are not numbered. My references are to page numbers. This edition and volume will be used for the remainder of Ronsard's poems, unless otherwise indicated.

18. Tzvetan Todorov, *Introduction a la litterature fantastique* (Paris: Seuil, 1970). Though more interested in the social role and implications of the fantastic, Todorov does offer many useful observations on the purely literary implications of the fantastic, such as we have been studying them in Ronsard. One is that "le fantastique permet de franchir certaines limites [of the mind, of mental and verbal perception] inaccessibles tant qu'on n'a pas recours a lui" (166). It does this through

its compatibility with a writerly semiosis and its incompatibility with mimetic representation, through its "metaphysique du reel et de l'imaginaire" (176), through its "antithese entre le verbal et le transverbal, entre le reel et l'irreel" (183).

19. Ronsard's writerly semiosis is also the kind of writing Hans Robert Jauss has in mind when he speaks of this "other, more essential world [which] opens up to us in and through the lyric experience." *Aesthetic Experience and Literary Hermeneutics,* Michael Shaw, translator (Minneapolis: University of Minnesota Press, 1982) 259. For Jauss too, as for Krieger, giving life and meaning to this "world" of mind and art is the objective and the challenge of both writing and reading.

Cathy Yandell (essay date winter 1997)

SOURCE: Yandell, Cathy. "*Carpe Diem* Revisited: Ronsard's Temporal Ploys." *Sixteenth Century Journal* 28, no. 4 (winter 1997): 1281-298.

[*In the following essay, Yandell discusses the* carpe diem *motif in Ronsard's poetry, contending that the poet was preoccupied with youth and terrified of growing old.*]

Ronsard's lyric poetry reveals an adamant attachment to youth and a pronounced terror of aging, neither of which is convincingly assuaged even in the *Derniers vers.* These anxieties, embodied in various corporal images throughout Ronsard's poetic corpus, find their most powerful expression in the *carpe diem* motif, which represents the poet's ultimate attempt to triumph over time and the aging body. Neither explicitly succumbing to Chronos's devastation of his own body nor stoically accepting it, Ronsard's speaker in the *carpe diem* motif rhetorically masters the lady's time, ravishing her body by the ravaging of old age. Cassandre, Janne, and Hélène, all consigned at some point to a shriveled future within the poet's verses, function for Ronsard as his doubles, whose bodies enact the aging the poet so forcefully dreads for himself elsewhere in his work. An analysis of this phenomenon sheds light on the relationship between the human body and temporality in Ronsard's poetic corpus.

> *For women are as Roses, whose faire flowre Being once displaid, doth fall that verie howre.*

Orsino to Viola in Shakespeare's *Twelfth Night* (2:4:36-39)

The carpe diem ("pluck the day") motif, whose onomastic origins can be traced to Horace, permeates not only classical Greek and Latin poetry but also lyric poetry from fifteenth-century Italy to sixteenth-century Spain to seventeenth-century England.[1] Few students of English literature are unfamiliar with Robert Herrick's

"Corinna's Going a Maying," John Donne's "The Anagram," William Shakespeare's Sonnets 3 and 4, or Andrew Marvell's "To His Coy Mistress." Similarly, in the Spanish tradition, Garcilaso de la Vega's "En tanto que de rosa y azucena," Luis de Góngora's "Mientras por competir con tu cabello," Lupercio Leonardo de Argensola's "Ojalà suyo así llamar pudiera," and Francisco de Quevedo y Villegas's "A una mujer afeitada" form part of a large corpus of *carpe diem* poems. But it is perhaps in early modern France in general, and in the Pléiade in particular, that the *carpe diem* motif reaches its apogee. As Paul Laumonier humorously phrases it, "le vieux thème est dans l'air, et l'air en est saturé"[2] (the old theme is in the air, and the air is saturated with it). Pierre de Ronsard figures prominently in this tradition, which he both embraces and transforms.

Construed traditionally as "a compliment and an invitation" and more recently as "an instrument of seduction," *carpe diem* has received much critical mention but little sustained attention.[3] Perhaps this comparative dearth of scholarly scrutiny results from what appears to be a too obvious functioning of the literary motif. Even the most casual reader notes that the poet who invokes the *carpe diem* motif is attempting to convince the addressee, often through a comparison of the young girl to the ephemeral rose, that she should love him now while the time is ripe. But what is the nature of this tactic? How does it function, both rhetorically and psychologically? Is the poet's ultimate message an epicurean exhortation to "gather rosebuds while ye may," or do other rhetorical elements in the poems obfuscate that reading? Ronsard's *carpe diem* poems reveal not only multiple responses to these questions but also the poet's own assumptions about time, the topos that is explicitly problematized by the motif.

Ronsard's complex and original adaptation of the *carpe diem* motif can perhaps best be illustrated by juxtaposing his texts with the classical sources that he sets out to imitate. When Ronsard began to adopt the *carpe diem* motif in the mid-sixteenth century, a number of Latin, Greek, and more contemporary models were available to him. *The Greek Anthology* had been published in Florence in 1494 by Janus Lascaris and reprinted several times, including one printing in Paris by Josse Bade in 1531. Johannes Stobaeus's *Florilegium*, from which Ronsard borrowed many erotic-bacchic fragments, was published in Venice in 1535 by Bartholomeo Zanetti Casterzagense, in 1543 in Zurich by Froschoverus, and again in Basle in 1549 by Joannes Oporinus.[4] Horace's *Opera* and specifically the *Carmina* enjoyed a great popularity at the end of the fifteenth and the beginning of the sixteenth centuries, with numerous editions published in Venice, Florence, and then Paris (Simon de Colines, 1528). In addition to these classical sources, the *carpe diem* motif experienced a rebirth in the late-fifteenth-century Italian poetry

of the *Petrarchisti*, Lorenzo de' Medici and Poliziano.[5] Ronsard also read Johannes Secundus, which led him to other neo-Latins, notably Marullus, whose *Epigrammata & Hymni* had been published in Florence in 1497 and in Paris in 1529.

Many subtle differences exist among the various sorts of *carpe diem* poems, but the most prototypical form of the genre features the older male poet, with distinctly erotic designs, exhorting the younger female addressee to take advantage of the present moment. Propertius urges Cynthia to taste of life's pleasures now, for her kisses will fall like petals from a festive garland (*Elegies*, II, 15). Ovid reminds a young Roman woman that years flow like water; she will regret having pushed away her lover as she lies in her solitary bed in later years. She should gather the rose before it wilts and falls of its own accord (*Ars Amatoria*, II, vv. 59-80). In this representative form, three constitutive elements interact within the space of the poem, all conflicting with a diametric opposite and creating a tension that the poem proposes to resolve: the rose in its withered avatar clashes with its vigorous, youthful representation; the poet in most cases expresses an explicit or implicit contention with the addressee; and the menacing future (illustrated by the projected declining, aging body of the addressee) opposes the epicurean present (incarnated in the currently glowing, youthful body of the addressee).

I will argue here that Ronsard's poet exploits these tensions in his *carpe diem* poems more explicitly than do his classical models and that his staging of the tensions betrays certain of the poet's attitudes toward temporality, gender, and the body. Consider as a first example the paradigmatic sonnet **"Je vous envoye un bouquet que ma main"** (1572) with respect to its most frequently cited model, Rufinus's "To Rhodoklea."[6]

> Here Rhodoklea
> is a garland
> a braid of delicate
> flowers laced
> by my own hands
> there are lilies
> roses
> moist anemones
> soft narcissus
> dark-gleaming violets
> wear it
> cease to be haughty
> both flowers and you
> will cease one day[7]

Je vous envoye un bouquet que ma main
Vint de trier de ces fleurs épanies:
Qui ne les eust à ce vespre cuillies,
Cheutes à terre elles fussent demain.
Cela vous soit un exemple certain
Que vos beautés, bien qu'elles soient fleuries,
En peu de tems cherront toutes flétries,

Et comme fleurs periront tout soudain.
Le tems s'en va, le tems s'en va, ma Dame
Las! le tems non, mais nous nous en allons,
Et tost serons estendus sous la lame:
Et des amours desquelles nous parlons
Quand serons morts n'en sera plus nouvelle:
Pour-ce aimés moi, ce pendant qu'estes belle.

(*L.,* [*Oeuvres Complètes,* ed. Paul Laumonier] 7:152; *P.,*
[*Oeuvres Complètes,* ed. Jean Céard, Daniel Ménager, and
Michel Simonin] 1:270)[8]

(I am sending you a bouquet that my hand / Just picked
among these blossoming flowers / Tomorrow they
would have fallen / Had no one picked them today. /
Let this be an unmistakable lesson to you: / Your
beauty, although it is flourishing / In little time will be
gone / And like flowers, it will suddenly perish. / Time
is fleeting, time is fleeting, my Lady / Alas! Not time,
but we are fleeting, / and soon we will lie under stone.
And of the loves we now speak, / there will be no
more news when we are dead. / Thus love me now,
while you are still beautiful.)

The tensions cited above generate the movement of
both poems but much more obviously in the case of
Ronsard. Both poems insist on the flight of time and
both compare the young addressee to freshly picked
flowers. Both poets highlight their own authority. Rufinus's narrator emphasizes his role of weaving together
the garland, and Ronsard's speaker underscores that it
is his own hand that picked the flowers in order to take
advantage of their finest moment. In both cases, the
poet fully intends to reap benefits from the addressee's
beauty if she is so inclined. Rufinus's invitation, "wear
it / cease to be haughty," is the suggestive equivalent of
Ronsard's "Pour-ce aimés moy." In contrast to the
concise idea of Rufinus's poem, however, the elaboration and development of the motif in the French sonnet
create a quite different message.

The images of both poems lead to the conclusion that
the lovers must act before death sets in: "both flowers
and you / will cease one day," "cheutes à terre elles
fussent demain," "comme fleurs periront tout soudain,"
"tost serons estendus sous la lame."[9] Ronsard's speaker,
unlike Rufinus's, rhetorically identifies with the lady in
that both poet and addressee will someday die: "le tems
s'en va, ma Dame / Las! le tems non, mais nous nous
en allons." Yet the identification of the first-person-
plural pronoun extends only to death and not to the
problem of aging. Given the paradigm of the older male
poet/young girl, it is of course predictable that Ronsard
would not conclude the sonnet with a reference to his
own youth. The sonnet unfolds according to a principle
of commonality, however, with one exception: both
speaker and addressee will someday die, but within the
rhetoric of the poem, only one of them will grow old.
Five lines of the sestet proclaim the advent of death as
the preeminent reason to love now, but the last line
diverts the logical progression of the poem and

substitutes the implication of the lady's eclipsed beauty
("while you are [still] beautiful") for their mutual death.

In Ronsard's sonnet the poet is thus rhetorically connected to the addressee through the use of the unifying
first-person pronoun and then distanced from her
through the pronounced shift back to the second person
singular. The subjective dynamics within the poem mirror this tension. The poet establishes a connection with
the addressee both by the implicit suggestion of sexual
attraction and by his evocation of their mutual destiny.
A severance between the poet and the addressee takes
place, however, when Ronsard's speaker evokes her
youthful beauty that will soon vanish. The shift from
"nous" to "vous" and from "quand serons morts" to "ce
pendant qu'estes belle" is reminiscent of Tonto's
quintessential "what do you mean 'we,' Paleface?" By
rhetorically joining the lady in their mutual expectation
of death and then separating himself from her (from her
loss of youth), Ronsard's poet manifests a more
pronounced desire to gain mastery over both fleeting
time and the lady's aging than does his classical model.[10]
The 1567 elegy "J'ay ce matin amassé de ma main"
provides another clear example of the poet's insistence
on the flower's atrophy and loss of beauty rather than
its death, but this time the poet magnifies the fusion of
the flower and the addressee to illustrate the lady's
vanishing desirability. Thomas Greene notes in Ronsard
"the tendency of a woman's body to become a landscape
and conversely, of a landscape to become her body, a
tendency so subtle and pervasive as almost to merit the
term *Joycean.*"[11] This reciprocity develops particularly
in the beginning of the elegy where the earth's bosom
has produced a bouquet worthy of the lady's breast. It
is doubtless not coincidental that in this elegy Ronsard's speaker temporarily loses himself in a few
uncharacteristically repetitive verses: "Elle est vermeille, et vous estes vermeille. / Sa blancheur est à la
vostre pareille. / Elle est d'azur, vostre esprit et vos
yeux /Ont pour couleur le bel azur des cieux. / Elle a le
gris pour sa parure mise, / Et vous aimez la belle
couleur grise" (L., 14:148; P., 2:353), insisting upon the
collapse of modifiers and artfully coalescing the woman-
flower so that the human and herbaceous qualities
become interchangeable:

Plus il ne reste à vous dire, maistresse,
Que tout ainsi que ceste fleur se laisse
Passer soudain, perdant grace et vigueur,
Et tombe à terre atteinte de langueur,
Sans estre plus des Amans desirée
Comme une fleur toute desfigurée,
Vostre âge ainsi verdoyant s'en-ira
Et comme fleur sans grace perira.

(*L.,* 14:148; *P.,* 2:354-55)

(It remains to be said, my lady, / That just as a flower
fades suddenly, losing its grace and vigor, / And falls,
languishing, to the ground / No longer desired by any

lovers, / Like a disfigured flower, / [So] your flourishing age will flee / And like a flower will perish gracelessly.)

In this elegy it is the anthropomorphic flower, not the lady, replaced by the substantive "âge," who languishes, becomes disfigured, and fails to attract lovers. This referential indeterminacy that humanizes the flower also serves to dehumanize the addressee who "without grace will die." But once again, while death punctuates the poet's comparison, it is in no way the central problem posed by the elegy. There are six specific mentions of the loss of attractiveness to lovers and the deterioration of physical beauty in the elegy, whereas death (in the form of the verb "périr") figures only once.[12] Aging appears as a threat greater than death to the addressee in several of Ronsard's models as well,[13] but Ronsard's poet personalizes the temporal implications of the motif and accords them corporality, thus emphasizing the poet's authority in setting the clock forward. Ronsard's imitation of an epigram by Julianus from *The Greek Anthology* corroborates this claim:

> Maria is proud; but do thou, mighty Justice, take vengeance on the hauteur of that arrogant lass,—not by death, O Queen, but on the contrary may she reach the grey hairs of age, may her hard face come to wrinkles. May the grey hairs avenge my tears: may her beauty suffer for the error of her soul, as it was the cause of it.[14]

> Je ne veux point la mort de celle qui arreste
> Mon coeur en sa prison: mais, Amour, pour venger
> Mes larmes de six ans, fay ses cheveux changer,
> Et seme bien espais des neiges sur sa teste.
>   Si tu veux, la vengeance est desja toute preste:
> Tu accourcis les ans, tu les peux allonger:
> Ne souffres en ton camp ton soudard outrager.
> Que vieille elle devienne, ottroyant ma requeste.
>   Elle se glorifie en ses cheveux frisez,
> En sa verde jeunesse, en ses yeux aiguisez,
> Qui tirent dans les coeurs mille pointes encloses.
>   Pourquoy te braves-tu de cela qui n'est rien?
> La beauté n'est que vent, la beauté n'est pas bien,
> Les beautez en un jour s'en-vont comme les roses.

(*L.,* 17:245; *P.,* 1:373)

(I do not wish the death of the one who holds / My heart in her prison. But Amor, to avenge / My tears of six years, change the color of her hair, / And sow thick snow upon her head. / If you wish, vengeance is all ready. / You shorten the years, you can lengthen them as well: Do not let your soldier be injured in your camp. / Make her old—grant my plea. / She glorifies in her curly locks, / In her green youth, in her sharp eyes / That pierce my heart with a thousand arrows. / Why do you play the gallant with something worthless? / Beauty is only wind, beauty is not a possession, / Beauties vanish in a day like roses.)

Ronsard's speaker, even while imploring Eros's aid, establishes his own voice from the outset ("je," "mon coeur," "mes larmes," "ton soudard"), which highlights

his agency in the premature aging of the lady. The sixteenth-century poet insists more than does his Greek model upon the addressee's former beauty by furnishing concrete examples of the "before" as contrasted with the "after" ("cheveux frisez," "verde jeunesse," and "yeux aiguisez," which are all revealed to be ephemeral). Maintaining his authority in the physical realm, Ronsard omits the moral dimension introduced by Julianus ("May her beauty suffer for the error of her soul"). Ronsard's speaker (still the "je" introduced in the first quatrain) concludes his sonnet by evoking the transitory nature of beauty, as illustrated by two physical images: wind and roses. Thus once again Ronsard's poet rhetorically emphasizes his authority in the workings of time upon the lady and insists on her former beauty (and by extension the stakes involved in time's devastation of it) more than does the classical model.

Why, in these poems and elsewhere, is aging depicted as a fate worse than death? Why does the threat of the aging body prove to be such a prominent rhetorical strategy for Ronsard's poet, especially in comparison to his classical models? Female beauty in sixteenth-century France, as in fifteenth-century Italy, was a central preoccupation of artists and poets, to which the *Blasons poétiques du corps féminin* and many other works attest.[15] Judging from observations of male contemporaries, beauty and youth are not dissociable in the cultural sensibilities of early modern Europe. Vives's *Institution de la femme chrétienne,* first published in French translation in the 1540s, cites physical considerations as important factors in a man's choosing a wife, and first mentioned among those is age.[16] Erasmus incites girls to marry while they are still "in the bloom of youth," which he specifies as about seventeen years old.[17] Similarly, Estienne Pasquier warns that girls should not delay marriage lest their perfect ripeness pass, and he estimates the ideal nubile age to be twenty years.[18] Aging women figure prominently as the subject of derision in a number of sixteenth-century proverbs collected by Le Roux de Lincy, including "Temps pommelé, pomme ridée et femme fardée ne sont pas de longue durée" (Hazy weather, shriveled apple, and painted woman do not last long) and "Celuy qui prend la vieille femme, / Ayme l'argent plus que la dame" (He who takes an old wife loves money more than the lady).[19]

Thus it would appear that since youthful beauty is especially important to a woman in sixteenth-century France, at least from the perspectives cited, the threat of her losing that beauty by aging would be the most powerful of taunts. We could then agree with Henri Weber that in this poem Ronsard perhaps "a jugé que cet argument touchait plus directement l'orgueil féminin" (thought that this argument more directly touched feminine pride).[20] But that temptingly tidy conclusion fails to take into account the poet's terror about the future in general and about the effects of time on his own body in particular. As early as 1555 in "Quand je suis vingt ou trente mois / Sans retourner en Vando-mois" (*L.,* 7:98; *P.,* 1:806), the poet at age thirty, to the bemusement of many twentieth-century readers, already laments that his youth is fleeting: "Mais tousjours ma jeunesse fuit, / Et la vieillesse qui me suit, / De jeune en vieillard me transforme" (my youth is continually fleeting, and old age follows me, transforming me from a young to an old man).

Ronsard's perennial consternation at the problem of aging is corroborated in Creore's *Word Index,* which cites over six hundred references to forms of "vieux" and over eight hundred to forms of "jeune." The poet's anxiety about growing old translates first into his privileging the moment of youth, which finds one of its earliest expressions in **"Dedans des Prés je vis une Dryade"** in the first book of the *Amours*:

> Dedans des Prez je vis une Dryade,
> Qui comme fleur s'assisoyt par les fleurs,
> Et mignotoyt un chappeau de couleurs,
> Eschevelée, en simple verdugade.
>   De ce jour là ma raison fut malade,
> Mon cueur pensif, mes yeulx chargez de pleurs,
> Moy triste et lent: tel amas de douleurs
> En ma franchise imprima son oeillade.
>   Là je senty dedans mes yeulx voller
> Un doulx venin, qui se vint escouler
> Au fond de l'ame: et depuis cest oultrage,
>   Comme un beau lis, au moy de Juin blessé
> D'un ray trop chault, languist à chef baissée,
> Je me consume au plus verd de mon age.

> (*L.,* 4:53 [1552]; *P.,* 1:55)

(In the meadow I saw a dryad / Sitting as a flower among flowers, / Sweetly donning a colorful hat, / Tousled, in a simple dress. / From this day forward my judgment grew weak, / My heart pensive, my eyes filled with tears, / I became sorrowful and slow. / Her gaze engraved such a heavy mark upon my liberty. / I felt a sweet venom fly into my eyes, flowing into the depths of my soul. And since this shattering event, / Just as a beautiful lily wounded by scorching rays in June / Languishes with its head bowed, / [So] I am wasting away in the prime of my youth.)

This sonnet enumerates love's melancholic effects on the poet, with a conclusion highlighting the speaker's youth. Reflections on the budding beauty of the dryad in the form of a flower immediately give way to the poet's Petrarchan introspection regarding his own state, translated by the predominance of first-person referents: "*ma* raison," "*mon* cueur pensif, *mes* yeulx," "moy triste et lent." The first tercet, troped in an *innamoramento,* elaborates the poet's condition brought about by the young dryad-flower.[21] The second tercet predictably exploits the image of the flower with its head down (recalling Virgil's description of the death of Euryalus in the *Aeneid,* IX, 435-37); but, quite unpredictably, the flower in the last tercet represents no longer the dryad

but the poet himself, languishing as he is consumed by melancholy in his youth. This insistence on the poet's youth is certainly not a commonplace within the tradition of *innamoramento* poems.[22] What is even more striking in the sonnet and what distinguishes Ronsard from his classical models the most clearly is this substitution of the poet for the lady as the referent of the metaphorical flower.[23]

The woman-flower rhetorically metamorphosed into a man-flower within the space of the poem signals a blurring of genders as well as of identities. The substitution of one flower for the other once again stages a complex connection between poet and addressee; the Other both represents and does not represent himself, as evidenced in **"Je vous envoie un bouquet"** above. The Other is she who in amatory terms conquers him and whom he seeks to conquer, either by causing her aging within the poem (as in **"Je ne veux point la mort"**) or by seeking her affection and her favors (as in the poem under consideration here), a connection often severed within the register of his *carpe diem* poems. The last line of the sonnet, completely focused on the poet's inner state (underscored by the reflexive verb form), insists on his separateness and summarizes his regrets about his own premature aging; in contrast to the "flower seated among flowers" who remains stable throughout the sonnet, the poet sees the "greenness" of his youth destroyed.

The attraction of youth for Ronsard lies not only in the promise of the future for the young poet, thwarted in the preceding poem, but also in an erotic proclivity for budding female sensuality in the aging poet:

> J'aime un bouton vermeil entre-esclos au matin,
> Non la rose du soir, qui au Soleil se lâche:
>   J'aime un corps de jeunesse en son printemps
>   fleury:
> J'aime une jeune bouche, un baiser enfantin
> Encore non souillé d'une rude moustache,
> Et qui n'a point senty le poil blanc d'un mary.

> (*L.,* 17:326 [1569]; *P.,* 1:453)

(I like a ruby bud half-opened in the morning / Not the rose of evening, which is weary in the sun, / I like a youthful body in its blossoming spring / I like a young mouth, a child-like kiss / Not yet sullied by a rough mustache, / And which has never felt a husband's grey beard.)

This implicit fusion of the pure, pristine young woman and the unspoiled morning rosebud recalls *Les triumphes de la noble et amoureuse dame et l'art de honnestement aymer* (1535) by Jean Bouchet, who espouses the theory that, like flowers, a young girl's beauty fades if she is kissed or touched too much, "car le lys representant virginité pert incontinent sa beauté par attouchemens" (because the lily representing virginity quickly loses its beauty by being handled).[24] While on the one hand, the poet in this context relishes the inexperienced lover, on the other, Ronsard's name has never figured among the advocates of preservation of female purity. Indeed, he chides the resisting Marie for despising nature (*L.,* 7:254; *P.,* 1:194) and for imagining honor "dedans son esprit sot" (*L.,* 7:138; *P.,* 1:273) (in her foolish mind).

The second book of the **"Sonnets pour Helene"** offers other examples of the poet's shunning societal strictures on sexual expression when such principles interfere with his erotic designs, as in the following 1578 sonnet:

> Cest honneur, ceste loy sont noms pleins d'imposture
> Que vous alleguez tant, sottement inventez
> De nos peres réveurs, par lesquels vous ostez
> Et forcez les presents les meilleurs de Nature,
> Vous trompez votre sexe et lui faites injure. . . .

> (*L.,* 17:266; *P.,* 1:460)

(This honor and this law that you invoke so much are insidious, stupidly invented by our idle fathers. By [this honor], you abolish and constrain the best gifts of Nature, you deceive and abuse your sex. . . .)

Given Ronsard's unwavering adherence to orthodoxy in matters of state, as a fierce supporter of the kings he served, and religion, as a loyal Catholic, Ronsard's critique of contemporary sexual mores in this sonnet can be read as either exceptional or self-interested. I see evidence for both conclusions.

Challenging sexual mores in a more comprehensive way, Ronsard launches a *boutade* in the **Continuation des Amours,** musing that if Petrarch didn't gain Laura's favors, the poet from Arezzo should never have continued his devotion to her for thirty years:

> . . . car à voir son escrit,
> Il estoit esveillé d'un trop gentil esprit
> Pour estre sot trente ans, abusant sa jeunesse,
> Et sa Muse, au giron d'une seule maitresse:
> Ou bien il jouissoit de sa Laurette, ou bien
> Il estoit un grand fat d'aymer sans avoir rien. . . .

> (*L.,* 7:317; *P.,* 1:168-69)

(Judging from his work, [Petrarch] had too fine a mind to be such a fool / for thirty years, wasting his youth and his Muse, attached to the same / lady. Either he was finding physical pleasure with his little Laura, / or else he was an idiot to love without getting anything. . . .)

In this passage Ronsard's speaker not only challenges Petrarch's inability to secure Laura's physical affection, but he also specifically deplores the loss of Petrarch's youth because of it.

In addition to Ronsard's unmitigated passion for youth, the poet's aversion to aging and the aged is revealed in countless poems, from the more general psychological

reservations, "Pource je porte en l'ame une amere tristesse, / Dequoy mon pied s'avance aux faubourgs de vieillesse" (My soul carries a bitter sadness that I am headed for the realm of old age) (*L.,* 18:42; *P.,* 1:442),[25] to the specific fear of physical debility, "tant de malheurs / Que la vieillesse apporte, entre tant de douleurs . . ." (so many misfortunes that old age brings, amidst so much pain . . .) (*L.,* 18:265-6; *P.,* 2:612).

Several critics of Ronsard have concluded that the poet eventually rises above the questions of the flourishing or deteriorating physical body and accedes to a higher spiritual plane.[26] Indeed, Ronsard's speaker's sanguine tone when addressing the older "Sinope" in the first sonnet of a series devoted to her seems initially to mark the poet's acceptance of aging and its effects:[27]

> L'an se rajeunissoit en sa verde jouvence,
> Quand je m'épris de vous, ma Sinope cruelle;
> Seize ans estoyent la fleur de vostre âge nouvelle,
> Et vostre teint sentoit encore son enfance.

> . . . . .

> Vous aviez d'une infante encor la contenance,
> La parolle, et les pas; vostre bouche estoit belle,
> Vostre front, et voz mains dignes d'une immortelle
> Et vostre oeil, qui me fait trespasser quand j'y pense.

> Et si pour le jourd'huy voz beautez si parfaites
>   Ne sont comme autrefois, je n'en suis moins ravy,
> Car je n'ay pas égard à cela que vous estes,
> Mais au dous souvenir des beautez que je vy.

> (*L.,* 10:87; *P.,* 1:277)

(The year was renewed in its fresh youth when I was taken with you, my cruel Sinope. Sixteen years were the flower of your new age, and your countenance seemed still in its childhood. You still had the look, the speech and the step of a royal daughter. Your forehead, your hands (worthy of an immortal) and your eyes make me die just thinking about them. . . . And if today your perfect beauties are no longer as they were before, I am none the less thrilled, for I do not heed what you are, but rather the sweet memory of the beauties I saw.)

The poet disconcerts the reader by the *pointe* of the last line, however, rejecting any stoic acceptance of the effects of age. Diverting the question of Sinope's diminishing beauty, the speaker retains instead the *image* of her more alluring youth. Sinope's current, faded incarnation is emphatically supplanted by the memory of her younger avatar. The poet thus in no way transcends the loss of the young woman's beauty in favor of loftier considerations. On the contrary, he freezes in his mind the image of her former pulchritude by winding backward Mnemosyne's clock.

Here, as is so often the case in Ronsard's love lyrics, behind the problem of the Other looms the larger, more consuming question of the self. The fourth **"Sonnet à**

Sinope," which appears in the cycle shortly after **"L'an se rajeunissoit,"** sheds considerable light on the poet's regrets about his own aging and his jealousy of a younger suitor:

> Or de vostre inconstance accuser je me doy,
> Vous fournissant d'amy qui fut plus beau que moy,
> Plus jeune et plus dispos, mais non d'amour si forte.
>
> (**L.,** 10:89; **P.,** 1:278)

(Now I must blame myself for your inconstancy, / Furnishing you with a lover more handsome, / Younger and nimbler than I, but whose love is less strong.)

The poet consecrates the remaining sonnets to his loss of Sinope, culminating in the final poem where he renounces his quest: "C'est trop aymé, pauvre Ronsard, delaisse / D'estre plus sot, et le temps despendu / A prochasser l'amour d'une maistresse . . ." (**L.,** 10:100; **P.,** 1:278) (You have loved too much, poor Ronsard, cease / Being a fool and wasting time chasing after a mistress's love). Thus in light of the concluding sonnets of the cycle, the speaker's insistence on Sinope's declining beauty in the first sonnet can be glossed as a mask, a deflection, a substitute for the poet's discouragement about his own aging and his inveterate sense of loss.

What, then, is the relationship between Ronsard's apparent obsession with youth discernible throughout his work and the *carpe diem* poems? It seems clear from the preceding examples that the poet temporarily circumvents the question of his own aging (and of the alterity it represents) by projecting it onto the Other, incarnated textually in the female addressee.[28] The specific functioning of this projection is particularly apparent in Ronsard's 1550 **"A Janne impitoyable,"** which imitates Horace's ode "Ad Ligurinum" (IV, 10).[29] The odes of both Ronsard and his model are concerned with time's control over physical as well as psychological human destiny. They address, both rhetorically and psychologically, the dimension of aging that divides the self from itself, a phenomenon that Montaigne describes succinctly: "moy à cette heure et moy tantost sommes bien deux."[30] A commonplace in literary depictions of aging holds that the speaker does not recognize in the mirror his or her old face, which bears little resemblance to the "authentic" younger self. Horace's poet employs this image very convincingly when addressing the young Ligurinus:

> O crudelis adhuc et Veneris muneribus potens
> insperata tuae cum veniet pluma superbiae
> et, quae nunc umeris involitant, deciderint comae,
> nunc et qui color est puniceae flore prior rosae
> mutatus, Ligurine, in faciem verterit hispidam,
> dices "heu," *quotiens te speculo videris alterum,*
> "quae mens est hodie, cur eadem non puero fuit,
> vel cur his animis incolumes non redeunt genae?"

(Ah, how cruel you are while you are still master of Venus' Gifts! / When your cheek of disdain comes to be plumed with an unwelcome down, / When cascades of your hair, falling in full waves to your shoulders now, Start to thin and shed, when into rose-damask of fleshly tint / Harshness comes and a changed roughness of face, then, Ligurinus, then, / *As your mirror reflects someone unknown,* you will protest: "Alas!, / What I now understand, why did I not see as a lad? Or else, / May I not have again cheeks unimpaired, suiting what I know now?"[31]

Ronsard's ode threatens Janne with a similar fate:

> Jeune beauté, mais trop outrecuidée
>   Des presens de Venus,
> Quand tu voirras ta peau estre ridée
>   Et tes cheveux chenus,
> Contre le temps et contre toy rebelle
>   Diras en te tançant:
> "Que ne pensois-je alors que j'estois belle
>   Ce que je vais pensant?
> Ou bien pourquoi à mon desir pareille
>   Ne suis-je maintenant?
> La beauté semble à la rose vermeille
>   Qui meurt incontinent."
> —Voilà les vers tragiques et la plainte
>   Qu'au ciel tu envoyras,
> Incontinent que ta face dépainte
>   Par le temps tu voirras.
> Tu sçais combien ardemment je t'adore,
>   Indocile à pitié,
> Et tu me fuis, et tu ne veux encore
>   Te joindre à ta moitié.
> O de Paphos et de Cypre regente,
>   Deesse aux noirs sourcis!
> Plustost encor que le temps, sois vengente
>
>   . . . . .
>
> Et du brandon dont les coeurs tu enflames
>   Des jumens tout autour,
> Brusle-la moy, à fin que de ses flames
>   Je me rie à mon tour.
>
>   (**L.,** 2:33-35; **P.,** 1:761-62)

(Young beauty, too proud of Venus's gifts, when you see your wrinkled skin and grey hair rebellious against time and you, you'll chide yourself, saying "Why didn't I think what I do now when I was beautiful? Or why am I not as I wish now? Beauty, like the crimson rose, dies suddenly."—You'll exclaim these tragic jeremiads to the heavens, as you see your face quickly worn by time. You know how ardently I love you, [but] obstinate and unmerciful, you escape me, not wishing to join your other half. O queen of Paphos and Cyprus, goddess with black eyebrows! Even more than time, take revenge and with the torch you use to ignite young girls' hearts, fire her up for me, so that I can have my turn to laugh.)

On a first reading, the poems appear to be identical in the relationship between poet and addressee. Each poet desires the young addressee, who has not reciprocated his love, and both poets taunt the young object of desire, threatening old age and regret. But significant differences in the poems arise in the poets' rhetorical strategies, and some of these differences are attributable to the fact that Horace's addressee is male whereas Ronsard's is female. Voltaire, in his epistle to Horace, "n'a pas osé lui parler de son Ligurinus," and Laumonier, speaking of Horace in *Ronsard, poète lyrique,* expresses the same reservation.[32] Though the distinctions between the homoerotic lyric in Horace and the heterosexual lyric in Ronsard would be compelling to pursue, they extend beyond the scope of the present study. What is of particular interest to us in this context are the techniques by which Ronsard's poet once again establishes a semblance of connection with the addressee, only to replace it with a more detached stance, thus highlighting the sixteenth-century poet's mastery of the addressee and her time.[33]

The structure of the odes initially appears similar, in that both poems are predicated on an axis of when/then: *When* all these physical changes befall you, both poets stipulate, *then* you will see the light. Both addressees are made to speak of their moment of alienation followed by cognition. As the poems progress, however, a significant structural difference between the two poems emerges. In the Horatian ode, the paternal speaker willingly relinquishes the power of speech to his son/lover so that youth articulates his own belated discovery. Ligurinus thus has the last word. In contrast, Ronsard's speaker frames the lady's words (almost identical to Ligurinus's) within his own discourse, providing an exegesis and an elaboration such that the concluding message remains the poet's own. The poet's voice further enters the ode more explicitly in the form of a monologue to the addressee in line 17, "Tu sçais bien combien ardemment je t'adore," and the speaker's voice continues to dominate the remainder of the poem. The psychological underpinning of this form of *carpe diem,* the rhetorical aging of a lover who spurns the poet, functions similarly in the two poems in that both poets seek retribution for love refused. But Ronsard's ode far surpasses the Horatian ode in its depiction of difference and conflict. In the Horatian ode, the speaker details Ligurinus's present beauty in concrete terms, evoking his "cascades of . . . hair, falling in full waves" and his "rose-damask of fleshly tint," whereas Ronsard's speaker, apparently unwilling in this context to concede any semblance of complimentary language, describes the lady's beauty simply as "outrecuidée" (proud, haughty). In "Ad Ligurinum," the relationship between the speaker and the addressee remains implicit, since the speaker is nowhere present in the poem, and the only concrete indication of the speaker's position emerges in the first words of the ode: "O crudelis. . . ." The mirror image in line 6 of the Horatian ode evinces a relationship in which both identity and alterity are suggested and where, it could be argued, the *alter* ("different one") resembles the aged speaker more than he resembles the youthful Ligurinus.

Ronsard's speaker, unlike Horace's, enters fully into the poem beginning in line 17, proclaiming his ardor,

chastising Janne explicitly for fleeing his advances, and invoking Venus's vengeance upon her. Whereas in Horace, the conflict between narrator and narratee remains implicit, in Ronsard, the poem becomes a battlefield in which the speaker general triumphs, reserving for himself the last laugh. This last laugh adds a temporal dimension as well, since it transports the sonnet from the register of a future perspective of the present (the regrets of the young woman) back to the present ("Tu sçais combien ardemment je t'adore") and again the implied future of the imperative ("Brusle-la moy"), thus insisting even more on the tensions provoked by time's linear progression. Horace's ode, on the other hand, despite its insistence on fleeting time, remains rhetorically situated in the future. The Ronsardian ode thus stages the temporal tensions more dynamically both by its shift in time and by the intervention of the narrator. The sixteenth-century poet once again establishes his personal complicity with time and its powers more forcefully than does his classical model.

The tone Horace's poet adopts when directing a *carpe diem* poem to a male other than an elusive lover is, not surprisingly, even more complicitous than in his ode to Ligurinus. In the well-known "Aequam memento rebus in arduis," ("Remember, when life's path is steep," II, 3), addressed to Dellius, the tone of the ode suggests a vital connection between poet and addressee as the first counsels the second to partake of wines and perfumes "while Fortune and youth allow."

Several of Ronsard's poems on the subject of savoring the present moment, replete with wilting roses, are also addressed to men (as friends and colleagues, ostensibly, not as elusive lovers like Ligurinus), and in those odes and sonnets the poet establishes a tone of camaraderie, as in "Verson ces roses en ce vin," dedicated to Aubert:

> La belle Rose du printemps,
> Aubert, admoneste les hommes
> Passer joyeusement le temps,
> Et pendant que jeunes nous sommes,
> Esbattre la fleur de nos ans. . . .
>
> (*L.,* 7:190;*P.,* 1:841)

(The beautiful spring rose, Aubert, incites men to pass the time joyously, and while we are young, to relish the flower of our years. . . .)

The explicit identification of the poet with the addressee predicates a kind of shared history that nullifies the conflict present in the motif when the addressee is a spurning female lover. Predictably, in this context Ronsard's menacing depictions of old age vanish and his epicurean urgings become egalitarian and untainted by spite.

Does Ronsard's speaker ever identify with a female addressee when he writes of the ravages of time? To a limited degree, yes. In **"Comme une belle fleur assise** entre les fleurs," for example, the poet deplores "l'importune vieillesse [qui] nous suit," and the tone reveals the poet's indisputable complicity with the female addressee. Yet it is "le coup d'Amour" and not the human body that withers and grows old in this poem: **"Amour et les fleurs ne durent qu'un Print-emps"** (*L.*, 17: 224; *P.*, 1:364). In the 1550 ode **"Nimphe aus beaus yeus,"** also, Ronsard's poet allies himself with Cassandre by the first-person plural pronoun: "Incontinent nous mourrons . . . / Donc cependant que l'âge nous convie / De nous esbattre, es-gayon nostre vie. / Ne vois-tu le temps qui s'enfuit, / Et la vieillesse qui nous suit" (*L.*, 2:127-28; *P.*, 1:807-8) (Suddenly we will die . . . / So while our age still bids us / To dally, let's make our lives more mirthful. / Don't you see that time is fleeing, / And old age follows us). In both of these examples, however, time's devastation remains abstract; the reader will note the absence of references to the aging poet's own body in the context of his exhortation to pluck the day.

In his extensive study of time in Ronsard, Malcolm D. Quainton concludes that for Ronsard, "human happi-ness and wisdom are seen to reside in a submission to the rhythmic variety of time and in a stoical acceptance of man's inevitable transience in the name of cosmic harmony."[34] But the poet writes in a multiplicity of registers.[35] I have argued that Ronsard's lyric poetry reveals an adamant attachment to youth and a pro-nounced terror of aging, neither of which is convinc-ingly assuaged even in the **Derniers vers.** These attach-ments and fears, embodied in various corporal images throughout Ronsard's poetic corpus, find their most powerful expression in the *carpe diem* motif, which represents the poet's ultimate attempt to triumph over time and the aging body. Neither explicitly succumbing to Chronos's devastation of his own body nor stoically accepting it, as the above examples have illustrated, Ronsard's speaker in the *carpe diem* motif rhetorically masters the lady's time, ravishing her body by the ravaging of old age. Cassandre, Janne, and Hélène, all consigned at some point to a shriveled future within the poet's verses, function for Ronsard's speaker as his doubles whose bodies enact the aging the poet so force-fully dreads for himself elsewhere in his work.[36]

These physical projections into the future also reveal a paradoxical functioning of *carpe diem* in Ronsard's poetic corpus. While the motif's didactic message incites readers to relish the present moment, to round out, as it were, time's advancement, the repeated im-ages contrasting youthful and aging bodies unfold in a mercilessly linear time frame. In *Physics*, Aristotle as-serts that time is no more made up of instants than a line is made up of points. But as points can be established on a line, so Ronsard's employment of the *carpe diem* motif freezes in time fixed images of corporeal flower-ing and withering. Seizing textually not the moment but

the human body, Ronsard's poet, rhetorically if not epistemologically, takes time into his hands and makes it his own.

Notes

1. From the ode to Leuconoë: "Carpe diem, quam minimum credula postero" (Reap the harvest of today, putting as little trust as may be in the morrow!), *The Odes and Epodes*, trans. C. E. Ben-nett, Loeb Classical Library, 33 (Cambridge, Mass: Harvard UP, 1968), Ode I, 11, 32-33.

2. Paul Laumonier, *Ronsard, poète lyrique: Étude historique et littéraire* (Paris: Hachette, 1923; reprint, Geneva: Slatkine, 1972), 587.

3. Donald Stone, *Ronsard's Sonnet Cycles: A Study in Tone and Vision* (New Haven: Yale UP, 1966), 6; Elizabeth Berg, "Iconoclastic Moments: Read-ing the *Sonnets for Helene*, Writing the Portuguese Letters," in *The Poetics of Gender*, ed. Nancy K. Miller (New York: Columbia UP, 1986), 208. In their monumental studies of Ronsard and sixteenth-century poets, both Laumonier, *Ronsard, poète lyrique*, 560-634, esp. 581-91; and Henri Weber, *La création poétique au seizième siècle en France* (Paris: Nizet, 1955), 333-56, each devote a section to the *carpe diem* motif in the *Amours*. Stone, *Ronsard's Sonnet Cycles*, 6ff., treats the question briefly; and more recently Elizabeth Berg has given a feminist reading of the *Sonnets pour Helene* with some attention to the motif. Ricardo Quinones, *The Renaissance Discovery of Time* (Cambridge, Mass.: Harvard UP, 1972), is an excellent study that refers to *carpe diem* as an exhortation never to waste time, but there is no consideration of the motif as a rhetorical device. Richard Glasser, *Time in French Life and Thought*, trans. C. G. Pearson (Manchester: Manchester UP, 1972), 143, mentions *carpe diem* as an indication of the changing attitudes toward time and as the antidote to Ronsard's philosophy of the eternal: "Only that which resisted time was valuable and genuine," Glasser, *Time*, 168. See also Yvonne Bellenger, "Le vocabulaire de la journée et des moments dans la poésie du XVIe siècle," *Revue Belge de Philologie et d'Histoire* 5 (1977): 760-84; Tom Conley, *The Graphic Unconscious* (Cambridge: Cambridge UP, 1992), 106ff.; and Malcolm D. Quainton, *Ronsard's Ordered Chaos: Visions of Flux and Stability in the Poetry of Pierre de Ronsard* (Manchester: Manchester UP, 1980), 121-26.

4. For further development of these borrowings, see Laumonier, *Ronsard, poète lyrique*, 596-98; and Henri Chamard, *Histoire de la Pléiade* (Paris: Di-dier, 1939-1940), 70.

5. Lorenzo de Medici, *Poesie volgari* (Venice: Aldo Manuzio, 1554); Poliziano, Agnolo, and Lorenzo de Medici, *Canzone* (Florence: Giunti, 1568).

6. A number of other influences can be cited: Petrarch's "I'mi vivea" and more generally erotic epigrams from Asclepiades, Agathias, and Rufinus; see Laumonier, *Ronsard, poète lyrique*, 585-91; James Hutton, *The Greek Anthology in France and in the Latin Writers of the Netherlands to the Year 1800* (Ithaca: Cornell UP, 1946), 350-74; and Weber, *La création poétique*, 341-50. In most cases, Ronsard does not imitate a single, indisputable work but rather conflates several sources. In this study I have chosen to work with the most obvious models, which lend themselves best to close readings when juxtaposed with the Ronsardian texts. But other classical sources that I have consulted also support the theses I advance here. For a very interesting study of the phenomenon of multiple sources in Ronsard, see Edwin Duval, "Ronsard's Conflation of Classical Texts," *Classical and Modern Literature: A Quarterly* 4 (1981): 255-66.

7. *Anthologia Palatina*, 5.74, in *The Greek Anthology*, trans. Alan Marshfield, ed. Peter Jay (Oxford: Oxford UP, 1973), 306.

8. The first of these (*L.*) refers to *Oeuvres complètes*, ed. Paul Laumonier (Paris: Société des Textes Français Modernes, 1914-1975); and the second (*P.*) to *Oeuvres complètes*, ed. Jean Céard, Daniel Ménager, and Michel Simonin, Bibliotheque de la Pléiade, 45-46, 2 vols. (Paris: Gallimard, 1993-1994).

9. Quainton, *Ronsard's Ordered Chaos*, 122, shows the progression of rhyming words of the octet and its depiction of the destruction wrought by time and the movement from life to death: "epanie, demain, fleuries, flétries, soudain."

10. Compare also the 1569 "Dame au gros coeur, pourquoy t'espargnes-tu?" (*L.*, 15:121; *P.*, 2:885) which Hutton, *Greek Anthology*, 361, calls a "mere translation" of an epigram by Asclepiades (5.85). Indeed, the idea of the two poems is identical except that Ronsard adds a dimension of physical aging absent from the original ("cependant que tu es jeune et belle"). Compare also "Douce beauté, meurdriere de ma vie" (*L.*, 6:219; *P.*, 1:92).

11. Thomas M. Greene, *The Light in Troy: Imitation and Discovery in Renaissance Poetry* (New Haven: Yale UP, 1982), 205. See also François Rigolot, "Rhétorique de la métamorphose chez Ronsard," in *Textes et Intertextes: Études sur le seizième siècle pour Alfred Glauser*, ed. Floyd Grey and Marcel Tetel (Paris: Nizet, 1979), 152,

who notes in the ode "Mignonne, allons voir" the alternation between the woman as rose and the rose as woman. See also *Oeuvres complètes de Ronsard*, ed. Gustave Cohen, Bibliotheque de la Pléiade, 2 vols. (Paris: Gallimard, 1950), 1:1081; and Husserl, cited by M. Merleau-Ponty, *Le visible et l'invisible* (Paris: Gallimard, 1964), 203.

12. However, as Leonard Johnson deftly points out, "with death once is enough" (note on the manuscript).

13. See Horace, *Carmina*, IV, x; Propertius, *Elegies*, III, xxv; Meleager's "Garland"; Hutton, *Greek Anthology*, 155.

14. *Anthologia Palatina*, 5.298, Hutton, *Greek Anthology*, 372.

15. See Elizabeth Cropper, "The Beauty of Women: Problems in the Rhetoric of Renaissance Portraiture," in *Rewriting the Renaissance: The Discourses of Sexual Difference in Early Modern Europe*, ed. Margaret W. Ferguson, Maureen Quilligan, and Nancy J. Vickers (Chicago: U Chicago P, 1986), 175-90; Ruth Kelso, *Doctrine for the Lady of the Renaissance* (Urbana: U Illinois P, 1956 and 1978), 136-209; Nancy J. Vickers, "Diana Described: Scattered Woman and Scattered Rhyme," *Critical Inquiry* 8 (1976): 265-79; Alison Saunders, *The Sixteenth-Century Blason Poétique* (Berne: Peter Lang, 1981); Cathy Yandell, "A la recherche du corps perdu: A Capstone of the Renaissance *blasons anatomiques*," *Romance Notes* 26(1986): 135-42.

16. Juan Luis Vives, *Institution de la femme chrétienne*, trans. Pierre de Changy (Lyon: S. Sabon, n.d.), 225. This passage is also reproduced in Guillerm, *Le miroir des femmes* (Lille: Presses Universitaires de Lille, 1983), 86.

17. *The Colloquies of Erasmus*, trans. Craig R. Thompson (Chicago: U Chicago P, 1975), 104.

18. Letter 10 of book 22, in *Lettres familières*, ed. Dorothy Thickett (Geneva: Droz, 1974), 408. Compare also Francesco Barbaro, *Deux livres de l'estat du mariage*, trans. Claude Joly (Paris: Guillaume de Luyne, 1567), 29, who recommends choosing a young wife because a younger woman will more willingly accept instructions. For further treatment of the question of age and marriageability in sixteenth-century Paris, see Barbara Diefendorf, *Paris City Councillors in the Sixteenth Century: The Politics of Patrimony* (Princeton: Princeton UP, 1983), 179ff.

19. Le Roux de Lincy, *Le Livre des proverbes français et leur emploi dans la littérature du Moyen Age et de la Renaissance* (Paris: A. Delahays, 1859),

1:133, 220. For other examples of this phenom-enon, see Jacques Bailbé, "Le thème de la vieille femme dans la poésie satirique du 16e siècle et début du 17e siècle," *Bibliothèque d'Humanisme et Renaissance* 26 (1964): 98-119.

20. Laumonier, *La création poétique,* 347. Compare also his similar conclusion in Laumonier, *Ronsard poète lyrique,* 579.

21. Compare also Petrarch's *Rime Sparse,* CLIX, in *Petrarch's Lyric Poems,* ed. Robert Durling (Cambridge, Mass.: Harvard UP, 1976), 304.

22. Compare, for example, Petrarch, *Rime Sparse,* 1-3, pp. 36-39, 61, 138-39; Maurice Scève, *Delie,* I-XXX, in *Poètes du Seizième Siècle,* ed. Albert-Marie Schmidt (Paris: Gallimard, 1953), 75-85.

23. Weber, *La création poétique,* 248, notes simply that the lily referring to the poet joins and completes the evocation of spring flowers in the first quatrain. The sonnet "En vain pour vous ce bouquet je compose" (*L.,* 15:212; *P.,* 1:243-44) also includes a final image of the pining poet as wilting flower: "Comme je suis fany pour l'amour d'elle" (I am wilted out of love for her), whereas the epigram by Meleager on which it is based (5.143) limits the flower image to the addressee Heliodora. A comparison between the poet and the rose carries a different meaning in "Pren ceste rose aimable comme toy" (*L.,* 15:204; *P.,* 1:72-73), where the poet's life of suffering, unlike that of the rose, is seen to have no end.

24. Jean Bouchet, *Les Triumphes de la noble et amoureuse dame, et l'art de honnestement aymer* (Paris: Galliot du Pré, 1535), 21.

25. Other passages are far too numerous to develop here. See, for example, "Epitaphe de Feu Mon-seigneur d'Annebault" (*L.,* 13:182-83; *P.,* 2:917); "Celuy qui est mort aujourdhuy" (*L.,* 7:281; *P.,* 1:785); and "Voicy le temps, Hurault, qui joyeux nous convie" (*L.,* 17:380; *P.,* 2:340). Gilbert Gad-offre, *Les Quatre saisons de Ronsard,* 13, 15, notes Ronsard's early obsession with death, but he also concludes that "Ronsard est un grand anxieux," which he attributes in large part to the tumultuous political and cultural environment of the second half of Ronsard's life. Compare also "Joyeuse suy ton nom qui joyeux te convie," verse 61, "Car l'age le meilleur s'enfuit dés la jeunesse" (For the best age already begins to escape us beginning in childhood) (*L.,* 18:119; *P.,* 2:298).

26. See, for example, Isidore Silver, *Ronsard and the Grecian Lyre,* vol. 3 (Geneva: Droz, 1987), 164; Quainton, *Ronsard's Ordered Chaos,* 110-15; Yvonne Bellenger, "Temps mythique et mythes du temps dans les Hymnes de Ronsard (*Hymnes* de

1555-56 et de 1563)," in *Le Temps et la durée dans la littérature au Moyen Age et à la Renais-sance,* ed. Yvonne Bellenger (Paris: Nizet, 1986), 179-92.

27. Yvonne Bellenger, "Temps mythique," 178, in fact reads this poem as a confirmation of Ronsard's privileging love over beauty.

28. See Jean Laplanche and J.-B. Pontalis's definition of "projection," in *Dictionnaire de la psychanal-yse,* ed. Roland Chemama (Paris: Presses Univer-sitaires de France, 1981), 345: "the subject at-tributes to another the tendencies, desires, etc., that he repudiates in himself" (my translation).

29. Compare also Horace, *Carmina,* I, 25, vv. 9-19 and III, 26.

30. *Essais,* ed. Maurice Rat (Paris: Gallimard, 1962), 2:403 (III, 9). For a contemporary psychoanalytic reading of this question, see Kathleen Woodward, "The Mirror Stage of Old Age," in *Memory and Desire: Aging—Literature—Psychoanalysis,* ed. Kathleen Woodward and Murray M. Schwartz (Bloomington: Indiana UP, 1986).

31. Ode IV, 10, in *Odes and Epodes,* trans. Bennett, 324. The English translation is by Charles E. Pas-sage, *The Complete Works of Horace* (New York: Frederick Ungar, 1983), my emphasis.

32. Laumonier, *Ronsard, poète lyrique,* 581.

33. Compare also Horace's "Ode to Lyce" (*Carmina,* IV, 13), a post-*carpe diem* apostrophe addressed to the now aged former lover. Here the poet is distanced from the female addressee throughout the ode, and the speaker's presence in the text is limited to two first-person references: "Audiuere, Lyce, di mea uota" (The gods, O Lyce, have heard my imprecations) and "Quid habes illius, illius, / quae spirabat amores, / quae me surpuerat mihi" (What remains now of that beauty that our love breathed, that overtook me . . .). On the poet's distance from himself and his own youth, see Michael C. Putnam, *Artifices of Eternity: Hora-ce's Fourth Book of Odes* (Ithaca: Cornell UP, 1986), 227.

34. Quainton, *Ronsard's Ordered Chaos,* 127.

35. In the editors' introduction to the Pléiade reedition of Ronsard's works, they note Ronsard's ability to "se multiplier," in this case by his borrowing from other authors without engaging in servile imita-tion; *Oeuvres complètes,* ed. Céard, Ménager, and Simonin, 1:xxvi.

36. In a different context, Michel Simonin, "Hélène avant Surgères: pour une lecture humaniste des *Sonnets pour Hélène*," in *Sur des vers de Ron-*

sard, 1585-1985: Actes du colloque international, ed. Marcel Tetel (Paris: Aux amateurs de livres, 1990), 127-43, has ably demonstrated the importance of the notions of la gémellité ("twinship") and of the double in the Sonnets pour Hélenè.

JoAnn DellaNeva (essay date September 1999)

SOURCE: DellaNeva, JoAnn. "Teaching Du Bellay a Lesson: Ronsard's Rewriting of Ariosto's Sonnets." French Forum 24, no. 3 (September 1999): 285-301.

[In the following essay, DellaNeva examines the literary rivalry between Joachim Du Bellay and Ronsard, focusing on Ronsard's rewriting of Ariosto's sonnets—a task first undertaken by Du Bellay.]

In the preface to his first edition of the Olive, published in 1549, Joachim Du Bellay, the upstart French literary theorist and sonneteer, unabashedly offers this admission of his indebtedness to Italian sources: "Vrayment je confesse avoir imité Petrarque, et non luy seulement, mais aussi l'Arioste et d'autres modernes Italiens: pource qu'en l'argument que je traicte, je n'en ay point trouvé de meilleurs."[1] Indeed, numerous later critics and editors have agreed that Du Bellay borrows so extensively from Italian texts that his Olive appears to be at times a virtual tissue of citations, taken not only from the great Trecento master, Petrarch, but also from his followers.[2] Prominent among these other texts, is, of course, as Du Bellay himself indicated, Ariosto's masterpiece, the romance Orlando furioso. But a third set of important sources is the more nebulous category of "d'autres modernes Italiens" which consists primarily of a host of lesser-known Italian texts found in the so-called Giolito anthologies, a series of compilations of contemporary poetry of varying quality whose first volume was published in 1545, just four years prior to the Olive.[3]

While these anthologies contain a selection from many poets whose names are today largely unknown, they also incorporate a number of texts from more famous authors, such as Bembo and Ariosto, whose reputations are such that they can hardly be classified as "minor."[4] Nevertheless, neither Bembo nor Ariosto approaches the renown or status of the great lyric master Petrarch: for the Rime sparse had by this time acquired the rank of a genuine classic and were perceived as belonging to a more distant past, while the poems of Bembo and Ariosto were very nearly contemporary and thus more popular compositions. Moreover, the literary reputations of Bembo and Ariosto do not stem primarily (or at least not exclusively) from their lyric creations. Instead, Bembo's literary endeavors comprise primarily prose works, both in Italian and in his excruciatingly correct

Ciceronian Latin;[5] the case of Ariosto is even clearer, for his masterpiece was undoubtedly his romance, which was often favorably compared to the epics of Homer and Virgil.[6] When Du Bellay and his fellow Pléiade poets turn to the lyrics of Bembo and Ariosto for inspiration, they do so, then, in the knowledge that they were using the opere minore of eminent authors whose main claim to fame lay elsewhere.

Certainly, a significant number of poems in the Olive clearly are patent reworkings of passages from the Orlando furioso, a text whose lively and highly sensual descriptions provided models of erotic discourse lacking in the Rime sparse of Petrarch.[7] Yet Du Bellay appears to privilege Ariosto's minor lyrics even more so than his romance, especially in the first edition of the Olive. Of the 50 original poems of the 1549 Olive, at least 21 have Ariostean subtexts; of these, nine are drawn from the Furioso, while 12 are taken from his Rime, which were published separately in 1537, 1546, and 1547. Indeed, the very first poem of the Olive combines a reference to the major Petrarchan subtext with a reworking of one of Ariosto's poems.[8] The final verse of this poem ("Egal un jour au Laurier immortel") constitutes, no doubt, an allusion to Petrarch's Rime sparse, in which the Italian poet sang of his twin desires of winning the laurel, symbol of poetic glory, and the love of his mistress, Laura.[9] Thus, when Du Bellay prays to render the olive branch, his evergreen symbol of glory and the namesake of his own beloved, the equal of Petrarch's laurel, he clearly places this text within the Petrarchan tradition while at the same time engaging in open rivalry with it. But Petrarch's verses are not the only ones evoked in this all-important initial poem. For Du Bellay's rhetorical structure of refusal of more famous branches is reminiscent of a similar recusatio enacted in Ariosto's sonnet 7, in which another evergreen branch, the juniper, representing his beloved Ginevra, is destined to crown the Italian poet:[10] "Non voglio, e Febo e Bacco mi perdoni, / Che lor frondi mi mostrino poeta, / Ma ch'un genebro sia che mi coroni."[11] Like Olive 1, this sonnet explains the choice of the poet's preferred branch in terms of his lady's name: "il nome ha di colei che mi prescrive / termine e leggi a' travagliati spirti." The evocation of this intertext—a poem published in Ariosto's Opere minore and one of the four Ariostean sonnets found in the Giolito anthology—at such a strategic location, the very threshold of the Olive, is doubly significant: for it attests to the role that will be played by Ariosto's lyrics as well as by the Italian anthologies in the remainder of Du Bellay's canzoniere.

Just how clearly this signal of a significant intertextual presence was heard among Du Bellay's earliest readers can be judged by the case of Pierre de Ronsard, the foremost poet of the Pléiade school and Du Bellay's chief poetic rival. Admittedly, Ronsard was a privileged reader of the *Olive,* one of those *cognoscenti* for whom Du Bellay claims to be writing and to whom he apparently showed early versions of his poems in order to garner his advice, as he also admits in the preface to his expanded, second edition of the *Olive,* published in 1550.[12] That Ronsard read Du Bellay's poems attentively, and with an eye toward catching their Italian models, cannot be disputed, thanks to the physical evidence provided by his own personal copies of the first two volumes of the Giolito anthologies now housed in the Bibliothèque Nationale. For Ronsard heavily marked certain Italian verses, annotating those which were used as subtexts in the *Olive*—including the sonnet of Ariosto on which *Olive* 1 is based—with the name "Bellay" written in the margins.

There has been much speculation as to why Ronsard felt compelled to mark Du Bellay's sources in this manner; the general consensus among critics has been that he wished to avoid using these same sources in his own petrarchist poetry, the *Amours* dedicated to Cassandre, which he first published in 1552. Raymond Lebègue, for example, explains that Ronsard so annotated the anthologies "parce qu'il n'est pas le premier poète français qui compose un recueil de sonnets amoureux. Il a été précédé par Du Bellay. . . . Aussi prend-il soin de dépister les imitations de Du Bellay, afin de ne pas marcher sur ses brisées, et d'apporter à la poésie française des nouveautés" (278).[13] Earlier, Prosper Blanchemain had similarly stated that the markings signaled "des vers imités par Du Bellay, vers que Ronsard ne voulait pas imiter lui-même, et qu'il notait dans ce but" (59).[14] Likewise, Bodo L. O. Richter declared that "the Prince of Poets made no attempts to prove his superiority by elaborating the same Italian sonnets which Du Bellay had found attractive."[15] According to this scenario, then, in a courtly gesture of deference to textual priority, Ronsard avoided a direct confrontation with Du Bellay by choosing to use only texts not already imitated in the *Olive.*

But this ostensibly reasonable explanation warrants further investigation, particularly in light of the fact that, despite the obvious admiration each espoused for the other, these two men were adversaries whose poetic identities and lyric expressions were no doubt forged, at least in part, one in response to the other.[16] Indeed, it is a well-documented fact of literary history that Du Bellay engaged in open—and often bitter—contention with Ronsard in his later poetic collection, the *Regrets,* and that he did not hesitate to rewrite at least one of his countryman's most famous sonnets, "Je vouldroy bien richement jaunissant," in an effort to establish a poetic individuality distinct from that of his more celebrated compatriot.[17] From this perspective, it would be exceedingly naive to think that, in 1552, Ronsard would not have attempted to imitate the same texts already reworked by Du Bellay; to the contrary, one might

expect that the poet of the *Amours*—never one to be accused of humility—would view this as a golden opportunity to establish his superiority over the singer of Olive. In this way, Du Bellay's later displays of rivalry with Ronsard could be interpreted primarily as a reaction against Ronsard's earlier volley in his *Amours.* Only a careful comparative analysis—a micro-reading—of these poems can resolve the question of whether or not Ronsard used the same minor sources, specifically the lyrics of Ariosto, as had Du Bellay and, if so, what significance this might have in situating the beginnings of the Du Bellay-Ronsard conflict long before the publication of the *Regrets.*

Ariosto's works do indeed constitute a significant subtext for Ronsard's *Amours,* though not nearly to the same extent as they do for Du Bellay's *Olive.* While both poets make use of key passages—indeed, very often the same key passages—from the *Orlando furioso,* Ronsard's rewritings of Ariosto's lyrics are more modest. Instead, Ronsard appears to favor the other eminent "modern Italian poet," Bembo, basing the liminal poem of the *Amours,* known as the "Vœu," on the first poem of Bembo's *Rime.*[18] Nevertheless, the reader of the *Amours* cannot go for long without encountering the shadow of Ariosto, as well as of Du Bellay, for Sonnet 3, "Dans le serain de sa jumelle flamme," quickly attracts the reader's attention.[19] This sonnet maintains a three-part correspondence of imagery (yeux/ flammes; Amour/arc; cheveux/retz d'or) that is reminiscent of *Olive* 10, which, along with *Olive* 19, was considered to be the first example of a "sonnet rapporté" written in French.[20] Both *Olive* 10 and *Amours* 3 refer to the personified figure of Love, the flame of passion, and the net of the lady's hair, and a good deal of this imagery has been inspired by Ariosto's sonnet 9. The Italian source text is built around two series of extended metaphors: the Petrarchan clichés of the lady's hair as a net that entraps the lover and her eyes as arrows which penetrate his being.[21] These two series of images are developed throughout the quatrains, which contain a network of vocabulary related to bows and arrows, on the one hand, and entrapment, on the other hand. These metaphors are not pursued in the tercets, however; instead, the poet expresses his Lady's refusal to be moved to pity and his own perverse pleasure in suffering that so typifies the Petrarchan love tradition.

When Du Bellay reworks this sonnet in *Olive* 10, he elaborates on its repetitive structure and develops a three-part correspondence instead of repeating Ariosto's two-part series of metaphors. The French poet retains Ariosto's image of the beloved's hair as a net and of her eyes as arrows, but also adds a third conceit from the petrarchist repertoire: the image of Love as a flame that sets his heart on fire.[22] Unlike Ariosto, Du Bellay sustains these metaphors throughout the entire sonnet. Beginning with the second quatrain, Du Bellay provides a series of related words for each set of images: he enumerates the sources of suffering ("neudz, flamme, coup"), the antidotes to this pain ("fer, liqueur, mede-cine," which are related to the verbs "briser, eteindre, guerir") and fills the poem with other three-part enumerations such as "ayme, adore et prise." In this way, this poem must be read vertically as well as horizontally, with virtual columns of related images as its support. Throughout the poem, Du Bellay includes a number of lexical reminiscences from his Italian model, though they are sometimes employed in a new context (for example, "aspra/apre," "adorare/adorer," and the similarly sounding but differently signifying verb forms "prese/prise"). Finally, again like Ariosto, Du Bellay ends his poem with the peculiarly petrarchist claim of taking pleasure ("piacer/plaisir") in suffering, indeed dying, in this fashion.

While Du Bellay has certainly managed to write a *tour de force* that outdoes its Italian model in terms of complexity, Ronsard's third sonnet, by comparison, does not make use of quite so elaborate a structure. Ronsard employs a number of similar extended meta-phors, but also changes some of this imagery, for example, by assigning the element of fire not to the figure of Love but to the lady's eyes and reserving the bow and arrow imagery for Amour. But what is perhaps of greatest interest is that Ronsard would soon appear to rewrite his own poem, reprising the same imagery, in sonnet 17, "Par un destin dedans mon cuoeur demeure," a far more complete—and complex—*sonnet rapporté,* the only such poem to be indisputably assigned to Ron-sard.[23] The French poet here retains the eye and hair imagery present in the texts of Ariosto and Du Bellay, and maintains the changes he had already enacted in sonnet 3, making Cassandra's hair the source of the net and its related images of tying and knotting while her eyes are described as flames. But he substitutes a somewhat different third image for Du Bellay's innova-tive figure of Amour which he himself had evoked in sonnet 3: for, in sonnet 17, he conjures for the first time the image of the beloved's hand which tightly grasps the lover in a nearly suffocating grip, so that, in his new poem, all the figures are parts of his lady's body. In eliminating the extraneous figure of Amour and replac-ing it with his lady's hand, Ronsard succeeds in tighten-ing the structure of Du Bellay's poem by focusing on his beloved and her body, insisting more forcefully on human interaction and emphasizing the tangible—and violent—nature of his experience. In so doing, he ap-pears to be giving Du Bellay a lesson on the best way to develop poetic figures, a lesson the author of the *Quintil Horatian*—which severely criticized many of Du Bellay's imitative sonnets—thought necessary precisely for this poem: "Tout ce sonnet est de connex-ion mal jointe, et mal liez y sont les liens avec le feu et le trait. . . . Appren donq à bien figurer" (quoted in *Olive* 65).

Ronsard's final tercet is considerably different from those of his dual sources. There is here no final admis-sion of taking pleasure in this suffering, as in the poems of Du Bellay and Ariosto. Instead, Ronsard suggests that, were he an Ovid, he would merely metamorphose his lady's eye into a star, her hand into a lily, and her hair into a silken net, none of which poses any serious threat to the well-being of the lover. This final allusion, which has no counterpart in either of the source texts, could be read as a metatextual signal, one that suggests a playful literary awareness of the power of the author to transform the lady and her body parts—and by exten-sion, the poems of his sources—to suit his purposes. The implication seems to be that all great poets, like Ovid, engage in a kind of metamorphosis of body and text, one that is linked not to some kind of magical or divine force, but to the powers of poetic creation.

Given Ariosto's penchant for sensual description, it is not surprising that many of the sonnets reworked by Du Bellay, and later by Ronsard, deal with the beloved's beautiful body. Thus, another example of Ronsard's reworking of an Ariostean sonnet already imitated by Du Bellay is poem 183 of the **Amours de Cassandre,** a poem which responds to *Olive* 7 and is based on Arios-to's well-known sonnet 25, "Madonna sete bella."[24] Ari-osto's poem is structured by the rhetorical device of *ef-fictio,* the head-to-toe enumeration of the lady's admirable body parts.[25] Here, Ariosto displays great verbal virtuosity, repeating the adjective "bella" and the command "miri," or "behold," as well as its cognate "mirabile," implying that his lady is not only worthy of admiration but also (to use a word coming from the same root) truly a miracle of nature. Yet, in the manner of the witty Quattrocento petrarchists, Ariosto cannot resist ending his sonnet with this striking *pointe* or punch line: no matter how worthy of praise and wonder is the sight of his lady, it is his own fidelity that deserves even more admiration.

In his extremely close adaptation of the Italian sonnet, Du Bellay begins by virtually translating its first two verses, including the decidedly disappointing and imprecise Italian noun "cosa," uninspiringly rendered as "chose."[26] Du Bellay only slightly modifies Ariosto's opening lines by using the more pagan epithet "Déesse" instead of the religiously charged "Madonna." Likewise, he gives a similar rendition of Ariosto's last verse, turn-ing the admiration towards his own faithfulness. In between, he enumerates most of the same beautiful body parts as his source, in the same order, praising his lady's brow, eyes, mouth, hair, bosom, and hand, neglecting only her neck and arm. Nevertheless, many of these body parts are described somewhat differently in Du Bellay's poem. While Ariosto had explicitly referred to his lady's eyes as stars ("l'una e l'altra stella"), Du Bellay merely implies the metaphor when he speaks of their "clarté saincte" (a variation on Ariosto's "lume santo") as guiding and leading him, much as stars serve that purpose for sailors. Du Bellay also makes some substantial changes to Ariosto's descriptions in the second quatrain, where the beloved's breath is deemed superior to the sweet smells of the Orient, and where her golden hair is said to render the brightness of the sun dark and worthless. Ariosto had, of course, explicitly mentioned the sweetness emanating from his lady's mouth ("che dolce ha il riso e dolce ha la favella"), but Du Bellay's imagery is clearly more expansive, lending the lady an exotic air. While Ariosto's lady's locks were said to aid Amor in weaving a net to entrap the hapless lover, Olive's golden hair is obviously most noteworthy for its brilliance. Nevertheless, this notion of entrapment is evoked elsewhere in Du Bellay's poem, where Olive's hand is described as binding and holding his own heart.

Ronsard's variation on this sonnet offers some even more striking variations that can be read as direct responses to—if not vaguely hidden expressions of rivalry towards—both Ariosto and Du Bellay.[27] As if giving his compatriot a lesson on the inappropriateness of closely translating from the Italian source, particularly when that source is not especially striking in its imagery, Ronsard eliminates the first two verses of the Ariosto sonnet, which Du Bellay had rendered nearly word for word. As a result, Ronsard also avoided the quasi-religious appellations of "Déesse" or "Madonna" used by his predecessors, words which emphasized the heavenly qualities of their ladies, a fact that is further reinforced elsewhere thanks to their use of such adjectives as miraculous ("mirabile"), divine, and celestial. Ronsard, instead, seems to suggest that his lady is quite definitely not a goddess nor a particularly virtuous figure, but rather a mortal woman, albeit one with extraordinary charms. This is made explicit in the second quatrain, in which Ronsard adds references to two myths that did not appear in either the Ariosto or the Du Bellay sonnet: that of Jupiter's passion for the mortal women Leda and Europa, for whom he donned the disguise of a swan and a bull, respectively, in order to accomplish his surreptitious seduction. In these myths, it is significant that the powerful god Jupiter quite literally descends from the heavens to earth to attain his coveted prize, thus further emphasizing her mortal (and his immortal) nature. By analogy, then, it is the poet-lover Ronsard who assumes the role of the divine being, while the beloved Cassandre remains the mortal object of his desire. This situation is, of course, quite unusual in the petrarchist tradition, for there, as shown in the two source poems, it is the beloved who is most often divine and who might bestow a measure of immortality on her poet in thanks for his verses written in her favor.[28]

Still, despite her mortal nature, Cassandre possesses some remarkable features, which the poet clearly enumerates. Like his predecessors, Ronsard praises his lady's hair, brow, hand, mouth, and eyes, though—somewhat surprisingly, given his customary sensual inclination—he does not mention her bosom, which both earlier poets had likened to alabaster. Indeed, this detail had bestowed on both Olive and Ariosto's beloved a stony quality, making them appear to be virtual statues. Ronsard's mistress, on the other hand, is likened to another artistic medium, a painting, on which is portrayed the poet-lover's own suffering. Yet the quality of stoniness remains pertinent in Ronsard's poem, though here it is the beloved who, like Medusa, can turn others to stone, including Medusa herself. This comparison to Medusa endows the lady with a distinct power that was lacking in the previous mythological allusions to Leda and Europa, but its association with cruelty betrays a certain ambivalence regarding his assessment of her "sweet smile." Indeed, while both Ariosto and Du Bellay provide a straightforward encomium in their pieces, Ronsard's poem hardly flatters this lady who ages him before his time and whose brow depicts "le gaing de mon dommage." There is a disturbing edge to Ronsard's poem, conveyed especially by these classical allusions, which suggest, on the one hand, the latent threat of violation and exploitation of the lady's vulnerability (as in the myths of Leda and Europa) and, on the other hand, an assertion of her own aggressive nature (thanks to the image of Medusa).

Ronsard's description of his lady differs in one other significant respect from his sources. In those poems, the lady's eyes were described as stars, explicitly by Ariosto and implicitly by Du Bellay. Cassandre's eyes, however, are likened to twin suns, a far more brilliant source of light. Indeed, in case that fact of nature had not occurred to the reader familiar with his sources, Ronsard draws attention to this phenomenon by referring, in his last tercet, to the sun which "efface les moindres feux." Given his predecessors' descriptions of their lady's eyes to the lesser lights that are the stars, one could be justified in reading this tercet, which ostensibly refers only to the admirable quality of his own fidelity, as a clever but subtle expression of rivalry, one that proclaims the superiority of his Cassandre over the beloveds of Ariosto and Du Bellay, and by extension, of his poetry over that of his predecessors.

The next poem in Du Bellay's sequence, sonnet eight, also closely follows an Ariostean sonnet, number 10, where, once again, the lady's body parts, in this case, her blond hair, are the subject of an elaborate *blason*.[29] Both Du Bellay and Ariosto begin by questioning their own powers to sing adequately of their ladies' beauty when they can barely describe even one part of her body, her golden locks. In the second stanza, each poet declares that, indeed, even the ancient Greek and Latin poets, renowned for their eloquence, would scarcely be able to manage this task. In the first tercet, each poet goes on to describe his lady's tresses in similar terms. Both poets end their sonnet with a similar image of dying as a swan and in silence. Immediately before this image, each poet expresses a wish to receive inspiration from a higher source. For Ariosto, this would come from biting the laurel, like Ascreo, that is, Hesiod, whose home was the town Ascro on Mt. Helicon, the seat of the muses, where their sacred fountain, the Hippocrene, is located; for Du Bellay, this inspiration would come from drinking from this sacred fountain itself.

These poems clearly have a counterpart in Ronsard's **Amours de Cassandre,** sonnet 170, which follows a similar movement but acquires a somewhat different tone.[30] Ronsard begins by situating himself with respect to various sources of inspiration in a double gesture of refusal: despite what he had declared in the *Vœu* which had opened his *canzoniere*—a poem which likewise referred to the Hippocrene source—he has *not* witnessed the nightly dance of the Muses nor has he drunk from the Ascrean fountain, which sprung from the foot of the winged horse Pegasus. Ronsard's image of drinking from Ascrean waters is significant and may be taken as a signal of his combined reading of Ariosto's sonnet and Du Bellay's poem; for he seems to have borrowed the name "Ascrée" from the former, while taking the imbibing image from the latter.

In his second stanza, Ronsard reveals what really is his personal source of inspiration: namely the eye of his lady, not Parnassus ("Ton œil, . . . non Parnase"). Though his source text spoke of the beloved's hair, not eyes, this movement from one body part to another can be explained, at least in part, by the phonemic similarities between the word "beaulx raiz"—used here as a metonym for Cassandre's eyes—and the thoroughly Petrarchan expression "retz," which Ronsard himself had used in sonnets 3 and 17 to refer to the lady's hair as a net which entraps him. In naming his beloved's eye as the source responsible for his eloquence, Ronsard thus asserts that he does not depend on any external agent of inspiration—Muses, sacred fountains, and the like; rather, his inspiration is contained within the love experience itself. Despite the ostensible hypothetical situation suggested by the word "si," Ronsard does not, really, question his ability to sing of his mistress adequately, as had his predecessors. Instead, with typical self-confidence, he proclaims the self-sufficiency of his poetry, which is emphasized not only by the bold words "Je fu poete," found *en rejet* in verse 6, but also by this stanza's insistence on the first person singular possessive adjectives, "*ma* voix," "*ma* lyre," and "*ma* rime." It is only in the final tercet that Ronsard expresses some doubts about the ability of his lady's beauty to be appreciated and adequately praised. Yet at no time does Ronsard claim this inability for himself; rather it is his era, "nostre âge," that is not deemed

worthy to speak of such unfathomable beauty. This criticism of his contemporaries presumably extends to his rival Du Bellay, if indeed it is not entirely aimed at him.

While Ronsard's sonnet is thus far quite different in its message from the inexpressibility topos used by both Du Bellay and Ariosto, Ronsard's first tercet is, however, somewhat more reminiscent of his predecessors' texts, thanks to its allusions to previous examples of poetic eloquence. Here, however, the reference is not to the distant Greek and Roman traditions but to Petrarch, denoted by the epithet "le Thuscan," who sang not only of his beloved Laura but also of his native Florence and the river Sorgue which coursed through that region of France in which his love story took place. In this way, Ronsard's reference to the great literary tradition of the past is not only more specific than the vague allusion to the "greche e latine scole" or the "romain [et]atique sçavoir" found in the texts of Ariosto and Du Bellay: it is also more pertinent to the context of love poetry as it refers to the single most important model for the genre Ronsard is engaged in writing. Nevertheless, Ronsard has not entirely abandoned the notion of famous Greek and Roman texts mentioned in his sources. Instead, he cleverly incorporates allusions to the works of the most celebrated writers of each of these traditions—the Greek writer Hesiod and the Roman poets Horace and Ovid—by means of the images he selects and develops. In addition to referring to Hesiod by the figure of metonomy ("l'onde d'Ascrée"), as had Ariosto, Ronsard reprises the image of the dance of the Muses that is found at the beginning of the *Theogony*, thus rendering the reference to Hesiod himself all the more felicitous. In the same way, Ronsard's hypothetical articulation of the pleasure his verses might bring recalls one of the odes of Horace, while his assertion that experience, not Helicon, inspires his poetry is an Ovidian echo from the *Ars Amatoria*.[31]

This penchant for incorporating textual reminiscences or key imagery from previous texts instead of merely mentioning the master author's name can also be seen in the passage dealing with Petrarch. For it is significant that Ronsard does not refer to the beloved Laura by her name; rather, as Petrarch himself most often did, he evokes her presence through the device of paronomasia, using the French equivalent of the Italian word "alloro," or laurel, which Ariosto had employed in his sonnet. Though the epithet "le Thuscan" and the reference to Florence emphasize the foreignness of the great master, Ronsard's allusions to France as the home of Cassandre as well as of the legendary Laura suggest that his lady is the rightful inheritor of Laura's legacy, thereby establishing a patriotic connection between the two women who were separated not so much by space as by time. The implication is that, had Cassandre not been born too late, *she* would have become the subject of Petrarch's masterful verses instead of Laura. Indeed, the superiority of Cassandre over the mistresses so lovingly described in his source texts is evoked in a subtle but effective expression of one-upmanship: for, while Du Bellay's Olive enjoyed a merely terrestrial beauty, "qui decore *le monde*," and the loveliness of Ariosto's lady, was "angeliche e divine," Ronsard describes *his* lady's beauty as *"plus que* divine."

Lest it be assumed that Ronsard's rewriting of Ariosto and Du Bellay was always predicated upon the techniques of hyperbole, one should consider another poem, sonnet 105, which establishes the rivalry by means of litotes or understatement rather than exaggeration. This poem is a reworking of Ariosto's sonnet 13, which develops the image of the sweet prison of love.[32] Here, the Italian poet explains why he, unlike other prisoners, rejoices in his state. With an ever-mounting exuberance—evoked by the five-part repetition of the conjunction "ma"—Ariosto describes his love's highly sensual delights ("benigne accoglienze, complessi licenziosi, parole sciolte da ogni fren"). His poem reaches a crescendo in the last tercet, where he admits that these pleasures will culminate in the bestowal of thousands and thousands of sweet kisses, "dolci baci, dolcemente impressi, ben mille e mille e mille e mille volte."

In a similar vein, Du Bellay's prison of love, which is described in sonnet 33, is also sweet.[33] Using what by now appears to be his trademark technique of translating—or at least closely following—the first two verses of his model, Du Bellay does modify that source somewhat by assigning the role of jailor to his lady's eyes rather than to his own love for her. In a swift divergence from his Ariostean source, Du Bellay inserts, in his second quatrain, a recollection of a famous Petrarchan sonnet, R 61 ("Benedetto sia"), a poem remarkable for its extended use of anaphora. In the third stanza, however, Du Bellay no less abruptly returns to his Ariostean model, this time condensing the Italian's second quatrain into his tercet, with a considerable number of close lexical reminiscences in his description of how other prisoners are naturally saddened by their condition, fearing "la loy et le juge severe." In his last stanza, Du Bellay declares, in a manner reminiscent of his source, that the sweetness of his own experience stems from the fact that, though imprisoned, he enjoys "mile doux motz, doulcement exprimez, mil' doux baisers, doulcement imprimez." Du Bellay thus shows remarkable restraint by correcting his model's exuberance, rejecting the four-fold repetition of the "mille baci" and settling for a mere one thousand kisses.

Ronsard, however, takes this one step further and appears to give yet another lesson to his countryman.[34] Unlike Du Bellay's poem, Ronsard's text begins quite differently from the Ariostean model; the only textual reminiscence is a rather distant one, in the use of the word "law" which was found in both source texts. It is only in verse six, with the appearance of the delightful prison motif, that one can detect the influence of Ariosto and Du Bellay, though Ronsard, significantly, eliminates the *contaminatio* of Petrarch's sonnet that pervaded the second quatrain of his compatriot's poem. Ronsard's tercets reveal this influence even more strongly, with their lexical echoes of Du Bellay ("lié/ lien"), Ariosto ("martìr/martirer"), and both texts simultaneously ("dolce/dolcement/doulx/doulcement"). But it is also here that Ronsard's poem differs most from those of his predecessors. In a masterful example of understatement, Ronsard declares that the sweetness of his prison stems from a far more modest reward: the hope of a *single* kiss, "un *seul* baiser," which clearly is worth more than the thousands bestowed by previous literary ladies.

One can continue to add to the examples presented here of how Ronsard, far from avoiding the same sources as his compatriot Du Bellay, sometimes reworked the identical text. Indeed, despite the protestations of the Pléiade that the imitation of other French poets is to be avoided at all costs, it is clear that Ronsard's reworkings of Ariosto were often mediated by the recently published imitations of his chief petrarchist challenger, Du Bellay.[35] Yet, Ronsard by no means duplicated what his countryman had already produced. At the risk of falling prey to the intentional fallacy, one might say that Ronsard appears to give Du Bellay a number of lessons concerning what he perceives to be the proper method of literary imitation: avoiding close translation, improving upon the structure of the source, making the new poem distinctively his own by the addition of other images and rhetorical devices, and by suggesting that, in some cases, less is more. In this way, Ronsard appears to engage in a double act of intertextual contention, carefully reading both his petrarchist compatriot and his Italian model with great curiosity in a spirit of rivalry. And it is perhaps these "lessons" that so incensed Du Bellay, leading the exiled poet to feel compelled to bare his indignation in the sonnets of the *Regrets.*[36]

Notes

1. Joachim Du Bellay, *L'Olive,* ed. Ernesta Caldarini (Geneva: Droz, 1974) 169. All subsequent references to the *Olive* are to this edition and will be given in the body of the text.

2. See on this point Caldarini's edition as well as her article, "Nuove fonti dell'*Olive*," BHR [*Bibliothèque d'Humanisme et Renaissance*] 27 (1965): 395-434 and Joseph Vianey, "Les Sources italiennes de l'*Olive*," *Annales internationales de l'histoire. Congrès de Paris 1900* (Paris: Colin, 1901) 71-104.

3. For more on the Giolito anthologies, see Louise George Clubb and William G. Clubb, "Building a

Lyric Canon: Gabriel Giolito and the Rival Anthologists, 1545-1590," *Italica* 68 (1991): 332-344.

4. The first volume of the Giolito anthologies opens with 17 poems by Bembo and also contains three sonnets by Ariosto. The second volume contains an additional poem by Ariosto. See the *Rime diverse di molti eccellentissimi auttori nuovamente raccolte. Libro Primo* (Venice: Giolito, 1545) and the *Rime di diversi nobili huomini et eccellenti poeti nella lingua thoscana. Libro secondo* (Venice: Giolito, 1547).

5. In his *Deffence,* Du Bellay portrays Bembo as a "converted" Ciceronian who finally found the proper path to literary fame through his vernacular poems: ". . . maintz bons espris de notre tens, combien qu'ilz eussent ja acquis un bruyt non vulgaire entre les Latins, se sont neantmoins convertiz à leur Langue maternelle. . . . Je me contenteray de nommer ce docte cardinal Pierre Bembe, duquel je doute si onques homme immita plus curieusement Ciceron." In *La Deffence et illustration de la langue francoyse,* ed. Henri Chamard (1948; Paris: Didier, 1966) 189-90.

6. See Du Bellay, for example, who cites Ariosto as one who "j'oseray' (n'estoit la saincteté des vieulx poëmes) comparer à un Homere & Virgile." *Deffence* 128.

7. For more on the imitation of Ariosto, consult Vianey, "L'Arioste et la Pléiade," *Bulletin Italien* 1 (1901): 295-317; Alexander Cioranescu, *L'Arioste en France* (1939; rpt. Turin: Bottega d'Erasmo, 1970) and Alice Cameron, *The Influence of Ariosto's Epic and Lyric Poetry on Ronsard and His Group* (Baltimore: Johns Hopkins, 1930).

8. "Je ne quiers pas la fameuse couronne, / Sainct ornement du Dieu au chef doré, / Ou que du Dieu aux Indes adoré / Le gay chapeau la teste m'environne. / Encores moins veulx-je que l'on me donne / Le mol rameau en Cypre decoré: / Celuy qui est d'Athenes honoré, / Seul je le veulx, et le Ciel me l'ordonne. / O tige heureux, que la sage Déesse / En sa tutelle et garde a voulu prendre, / Pour faire honneur à son sacré autel! / Orne mon chef, donne moy hardiesse / De te chanter, qui espere te rendre / Egal un jour au Laurier immortel."

9. For more on the role of the beloved's name and its symbolic representation in the text, consult François Rigolot, *Poétique et onomastique* (Geneva: Droz, 1977).

10. See on this point Rigolot, "Du Bellay et la poésie de refus," *BHR* 26 (1974): 489-502.

11. Ludovico Ariosto, *Opere,* ed. Adriano Seroni (Milan: Mursia, n.d.).

12. "[J]e m'osay bien avanturer de mettre en lumiere mes petites poësies: après toutesfois les avoir communiquées à ceux que je pensoy' bien estre clervoyans en telles choses, singulierement à Pierre de Ronsard . . . pour la bonne opinion que j'ay toujours eue de son vif esprit, exacte sçavoir et solide jugement en nostre poësie françoise." *L'Olive* 45.

13. "Un volume de vers annotés par Ronsard," *Bulletin du Bibliophile et du Bibliothécaire* (1951): 272-80.

14. "La description d'un volume ayant appartenu à Ronsard," *Bulletin de la Société Archéologique, Scientifique et Littéraire du Vendômois* 14 (1875): 58-68.

15. "The Place of the Minor Italian Poets in the Works of Ronsard and Du Bellay," Dissertation, University of Pennsylvania, 1951, 224.

16. See, for example, Isamu Takata, "Poétique de l'*Olive* et des Amours: L'ombre de Du Bellay chez Ronsard," in *Du Bellay: Actes du colloque international d'Angers 26/29 mars 1989* (Angers: Presses de l'Université d'Angers, 1990) 509-21. Ronsard refers to his relationship with Du Bellay in the preface to his *Odes* of 1550: ". . . Joachim du Bellai, duquel le jugement, l'etude pareille, la longue frequentation, et l'ardant desir de reveiller la poësie Françoise avant nous foible et languissante . . . nous a rendus presque semblables d'esprit, d'inventions, et de labeur." See *Critical Prefaces of the French Renaissance,* ed. Bernard Weinberg (Evanston, IL: Northwestern UP, 1950) 146-47.

17. "Dans les *Regrets,* un dialogue se poursuit entre Du Bellay et Ronsard, qui contraste et situe deux poétiques." Floyd Gray, *La Poétique de Du Bellay* (Paris: Nizet, 1978) 79. See also on this point Rigolot, "Du Bellay et la poésie de refus," 493-97.

18. For more on Ronsard's use of Bembo, see Charles Dédéyan, "Ronsard et Bembo," in *Ronsard e l'Italia, Ronsard in Italia* (Fasano: Schena, 1988) 27-51 and Henri Weber, "Le Songe dans les *Amours* de Ronsard," *Op. Cit.: Revue de Littératures Française et Comparée* 9 (1997): 57-62. Weber's classic *La Création poétique au XVIe siècle en France* (Paris: Nizet, 1955) is also an excellent source for this subject.

19. "Dans le serain de sa jumelle flamme / Je vis Amour, qui son arc desbandoit, / Et sus mon cœur le brandon éspandoit, / Qui des plus froids les moëlles enflamme. / Puis çà puis là pres les yeux de ma dame / Entre cent fleurs un retz d'or me tendoit, / Qui tout crespu blondement descendoit /

A flotz ondez pour enlasser mon ame. / Qu'eussay-je faict? l'Archer estoit si doulx, / Si doulx son feu, si doulx l'or de ses noudz, / Qu'en leurs filetz encore je m'oublie: / Mais cest oubli ne me tourmente point, / Tant doulcement le doux Archer me poingt, / Le feu me brusle, & l'or crespe me lie." From *Les Amours*, ed. Henri Weber and Catherine Weber (Paris: Garnier, 1963).

20. *Olive* 10 reads: "Ces cheveux d'or sont les liens, Madame, / Dont fut premier ma liberté surprise, / Amour la flamme autour du cœur eprise, / Ces yeux le traict qui me transperse l'ame, / Fors sont les neudz, apre et vive la flamme, / Le coup, de main à tyrer bien apprise, / Et toutesfois j'ayme, j'adore et prise / Ce qui m'etraint, qui me brusle et entame. / Pour briser donq', pour eteindre et guerir / Ce dur lien, ceste ardeur, ceste playe, / Je ne quier fer, liqueur ny medicine: / L'heur et plaisir que ce m'est de perir / De telle main, ne permect que j'essaye / Glayve trenchant, ny froydeur, ny racine." For Du Bellay's use of the *sonnet rapporté*, see Estienne Pasquier, "Lettre à M. Tabourot," in *Lettres* (Lyon: Jean Veyrat, 1597) 329 r as well as Estienne Tabourot, *Les Bigarrures* (Paris: Richer, 1603) 106 v.

21. "La rete fu di queste fila d'oro / In che 'l mio pensier vago intricò l'ale, / E queste ciglia l'arco, i sguardi il strale, / Il feritor questi begli occhi fòro. / Io son ferito, io son prigion per loro, / La piaga in mezo 'l core aspra e mortale, / La prigion forte; e pur in tanto male, / E chi ferimmi e chi mi prese adoro. / Per la dolce cagion del languir mio / O del morir, se potrà tanto 'l duolo, / Languendo godo, e di morir disio; / Pur ch'ella, non sappiendo il piacer ch'io / Del languir m'abbia o del morir, d'un solo / Sospir mi degni o d'altro affetto pio."

22. Vianey claims that the French revision is less successful than the Italian original because "Du Bellay a éprouvé le besoin de compliquer les complications du modèle." See "L'Arioste et la Pléiade," 80. Cioranescu (274) suggests that the flame image is borrowed from Ariosto's *Furioso,* while Cameron (21) proposes that the presence of the flame image in both Du Bellay and Ronsard and its absence in Ariosto suggest that Du Bellay's sonnet was more influential on Ronsard than the original Italian poem.

23. "Par un destin dedans mon cuœur demeure, / L'œil, & la main, & le crin delié, / Qui m'ont si fort, bruslé, serré, lié / Qu'ars, prins, lassé, par eulx fault que je meure. / Le feu, la serre, & le ret à toute heure, / Ardant, pressant, nouant mon amitié, / Occise aux piedz de ma fiere moitié / Font par sa mort ma vie estre meilleure. / Oeil, main & crin, qui flammez & gennez, / Et r'enlassez mon cœur que vous tenez: / Au labyrint de vostre crespe voye. / Hé que ne suis je Ovide bien disant! / Oeil tu seroys un bel Astre luisant, / Main un beau lis, crin un beau ret de soye." For the unique nature of this *sonnet rapporté* within the œuvre of Ronsard, see Paul Laumonier's note to this poem in his edition of the *Amours, Œuvres complètes* 4 (1925; Paris: Nizet, 1982).

24. For more on this set of imitations, see Weber, *La Création poétique* 263-65 and Takata (512) who finds Du Bellay's description "statique et en quelque sorte objective," while Ronsard's is "dynamique, dramatique et mythologique."

25. "Madonna, sète bella e bella tanto, / Ch'io non veggio di voi cosa più bella; / Miri la fronte o l'una e l'altra stella / Che mi scorgon la via col lume santo; / Miri la bocca, a cui sola do vanto / Che dolce ha il riso e dolce ha la favella, / E l'aureo crine, ond'Amor fece quella / Rete che mi fu tesa d'ogni canto; / O di terso alabastro il collo e il seno, / O braccia o mano, e quanto finalmente / Di voi si mira, e quanto se ne crede, / Tutto è mirabil certo; non di meno / Non starò ch'io non dica arditamente / Che più mirabil molto è la mia fede."

26. "De grand' beauté ma Déesse est si pleine, / Que je ne voy' chose au monde plus belle. / Soit que le front je voye, ou les yeulx d'elle, / Dont la clarté saincte me guyde et meine: / Soit ceste bouche, où souspire une halaine / Qui les odeurs des Arabes excelle: / Soit ce chef d'or, qui rendroit l'estincelle / Du beau Soleil honteuse, obscure et vaine: / Soient ces coustaux d'albastre, et main polie, / Qui mon cœur serre, enferme, estreinct et lie, / Bref, ce que d'elle on peult ou voir ou croyre, / Tout est divin, celeste, incomparable: / Mais j'ose bien me donner ceste gloyre, / Que ma constance est trop plus admirable."

27. "Son chef est d'or, son front est un tableau / Où je voy peint le gaing de mon dommage, / Belle est sa main, qui me fait devant l'age / Changer de teint, de cheveulx, & de peau. / Belle est sa bouche, & son soleil jumeau, / De neige & feu s'embellit son visage, / Pour qui Juppin reprendroyt le plumage, / Ore d'un Cygne, or le poyl d'un toreau. / Doux est son ris, qui la Meduse mesme / Endurciroyt en quelque roche blesme, / Vangeant d'un coup cent mille crualtez. / Mais tout ainsi que le Soleil efface / Les moindres feux: ainsi ma foy surpasse / Le plus parfaict de toutes ses beaultez."

28. For more on these myths and the violation of the Petrarchan tradition, see JoAnn DellaNeva, "Ravishing Beauties in the *Amours* of Ronsard: Rape, Mythology and the Petrarchist Tradition," *Neophilologus* 73 (1989): 23-35.

29. "Auray'-je bien de louer le pouvoir / Ceste beauté, qui decore le monde, / Quand pour orner sa chevelure blonde / Je sens ma langue ineptement mouvoir? / Ny le romain ny l'atique sçavoir / Quoy que là fust l'ecolle de faconde, / Aux cheveulx mesme, où le fin or abonde, / Eussent bien faict à demy leur devoir. / Quand je les voy' si reluysans et blons, / Entrenouez, crespes, egaulx et longs, / Je m'esmerveille, et fay' telle complaincte: / Puis que pour vous (cheveulx) j'ay tel martyre, / Que n'ay-je beu à la fontaine saincte? / Je mourroy' cygne, où je meurs sans mot dire." The Ariostean source reads: "Com'esser può che dignamente io lodi / Vostre bellezze angeliche e divine / Se mi par ch'a dir sol del biondo crine / Volga la lingua inettamente e snodi? / Quelli alti stili e quelli dolci modi / Non basterian, che già greche e latine / Scole insegnaro, a dire il mezo e il fine / D'ogni lor loda alli aurei crespi nodi, / E 'l mirar quanto sian lucide e quanto / Lunghe ed ugual le ricche fila d'oro / Materia potrian dar d'eterno canto. / Deh, morso avess'io, come Ascreo, l'alloro! / Di queste, se non d'altro, direi tanto, / Che morrei cigno, ove tacendo io moro."

30. "Je ne suis point, Muses, acoustumé / De voir la nuict vostre dance sacrée: / Je n'ay point beu dedans l'onde d'Ascrée, / Fille du pied du cheval emplumé. / De tes beaulx raiz chastement allumé / Je fu poëte: & si ma voix recrée, / Et si ma lyre, ou si ma rime agrée, / Ton œil en soit, non Parnase estimé. / Certes le ciel te debvoit à la France, / Quand le Thuscan, & Sorgue, & sa Florence, / Et son Laurier engrava dans les cieux: / Ore trop tard beaulté plus que divine, / Tu vois nostre âge, helas, qui n'est plus digne / Tant seulement de parler de tes yeulx."

31. See Hesiod, *Theogony* 1-8, Horace, *Odes* 4: 3, 22-24 and Ovid, *Ars Amatoria* 1: 27-28. These allusions are mentioned in Weber's notes to this sonnet.

32. "Aventuroso carcere soave, / Dove né per furor né per dispetto, / Ma per amor e per pietà distretto / La bella e dolce mia nemica m'have; / Gli altri prigioni al volger de la chiave / S'attristano, io m'allegro: che diletto / E non martìr, vita e non morte aspetto, / Né giudice sever né legge grave, / Ma benigne accoglienze, ma complessi / Licenziosi, ma parole sciolte / Da ogni fren, ma risi, vezzi e giochi; / Ma dolci baci, dolcemente impressi / Ben mille e mille e mille e mille volte; / E, se potran contarsi, anche fien pochi."

33. "O prison doulce, où captif je demeure / Non par dedaing, force ou inimitié, / Mais par les yeulx de ma doulce moitié, / Qui m'y tiendra jusq'à tant que je meure. / O l'an heureux, le mois, le jour et l'heure, / Que mon cœur fut avecq' elle allié! / O l'heureux nœu, par qui j'y fu' lié, / Bien que souvent je plain', souspire et pleure! / Tous prisonniers, vous etes en soucy, / Craignant la loy et le juge severe: / Moy plus heureux, je ne suis pas ainsi. / Mile doulx motz, doulcement exprimez, / Mil' doulx baisers, doulcement imprimez, / Sont les tormens où ma foy persevere." For more on this sonnet and its models, consult Robert Griffin, *Coronation of the Poet: Joachim Du Bellay's Debt to the Trivium* (Berkeley: U of California P, 1969) 102-03.

34. "Si doulcement le souvenir me tente / De la mieleuse & fieleuse saison, / Où je perdi la loy de ma raison, / Qu'autre douleur ma peine ne contente. / Je ne veulx point en la playe de tente / Qu'Amour me fit, pour avoir guarison, / Et ne veulx point, qu'on m'ouvre la prison, / Pour affranchir autre part mon attente. / Plus que venin je fuy la liberté, / Tant j'ay grand peur de me voyr escarté / Du doulx lien qui doulcement offense: / Et m'est honneur de me voyr martirer, / Soubz un espoyr quelquefoys de tirer / Un seul baiser pour toute recompense."

35. In the preface to his *Odes* of 1550, Ronsard had written: ". . . l'imitation des nostres m'est tant odieuse . . . que pour cette raison je me suis éloigné d'eus, prenant stile apart, sens apart, euvre apart." See *Critical Prefaces of the French Renaissance* 146.

36. A version of this article was read at the Sixteenth Century Studies Conference in October, 1998. I should like to thank the participants of that session, especially Sara Sturm-Maddox, William J. Kennedy, and Deborah Lesko Baker, as well as the anonymous referees of this paper, for their most valuable comments.

Sara Sturm-Maddox (essay date 1999)

SOURCE: Sturm-Maddox, Sara. "Lyric Self-Fashioning: From 'le Gaulois Apollon' to 'le Pétrarque français.'" In *Ronsard, Petrarch, and the* Amours, pp. 6-35. Gainesville, Fla.: University Press of Florida, 1999.

[*In the following essay, Sturm-Maddox examines Ronsard's attempts at creating his own literary legacy as the French Apollo, the French Homer, and the French Petrarch through self-identification with his literary and mythical precursors in his poetry.*]

When Hélène de Surgères identified Pierre de Ronsard as "the Apollo of our age, the Homer of France," her double nomination was hardly original. In fact, it inscribes itself—appropriately enough, in a poem—as a move in the poet's own game.[1] The second element of the compliment, of course, responds to the onomastic play through which Ronsard often represented Hélène herself, celebrating the dedicatee of his last collection of love lyrics through her name, "so fatal a name" "sung by Homer so many times" (*SH* [*Sonets pour Helene*] I, 3; 16, 9).[2] The double title bestowed by Hélène upon her poet, however, reminds us also that Ronsard's game was fundamentally one, not only of representation, but of self-representation, a game in which, many years before the publication of the **Sonets pour Helene,** he had not hesitated to designate himself as the "Gaulois Apollon."[3]

It is easy to pass over such a gesture, to read it as merely typical of an age of hyperbolic eulogies.[4] In what was also an age of patronage, moreover, this particular variety of antonomasia was virtually ubiquitous, as poets vied for prestige and often for more substantial reward.[5] From a fortuitous convergence of humanist enthusiasm for the *gloire* of the classical age with the aspirations of the French nobility and their courtier-poets, there emerged what might well be characterized as a culture of impersonation, one rich in affinities with the Elizabethan court and destined to reach its apogee in the following century in the adulation of the Roi Soleil.[6] Not only were royal patrons or potential patrons compared in terms of their virtue and their heroism to the gods and heroes enthusiastically proclaimed by the humanists as the standards of glory. They might also be rendered, in a sort of ascribed impersonation, with all the attributes and even the costume of the classical personage in question; in a particularly remarkable example, François I is represented in a miniature with the combined attributes of Mars, Minerva, Mercury, and Diana, an iconography made explicit in the accompanying poem.[7] Or they might be cast as divinities in royal pageantry, as in Hugues Salel's *Chant poétique présenté au Roy le premier jour de l'an 1549* in which the gods of Olympus dance before Henri II, whose own role is that of Jupiter replacing Saturn.[8]

Ronsard was an enthusiastic participant in this culture, bestowing titles with a largesse equal to that which he hoped to inspire through his encomia. In **"La Lyre,"** the poem in which he identifies himself as the "Gaulois Apollon," his patron Belot, praised for his eloquence, is "a true Socrates"; the Cardinal de Lorraine, praised too for his eloquence as royal emissary, is the "Mercury of the French"; Montmorency and the Duc de Guise are celebrated as "two new Achilles."[9] Mythological figures, divinities, exemplary historical personages are all reborn under his pen in the powerful men and women of sixteenth-century France, a phenomenon appropriate to the poet's task as Ronsard defined it in the preface to his *Odes*: "C'est le vrai but d'un poëte Liriq de celebrer jusques à l'extremité celui qu'il entreprend de louer" [It

is the true objective of a Lyric poet to celebrate to the limit the one he undertakes to praise].[10] Read in this light, Ronsard's self-promotion may appear as no more than evidence that poets could undertake to praise themselves just as they undertook to praise patrons, could reward themselves even as they rewarded patrons; as Henri II was portrayed as now one god, now another, and as Catherine de Médicis was praised as the "Juno of France" and the Duchess of Savoie as "the new Pallas,"[11] so the "Gaulois Apollo" could be recognized in Pierre de Ronsard.

It should not be overlooked, however, that this latter self-titling, advanced during the years when Ronsard was the rising poet of a generation, was also a gesture of entitlement. Apollo was much invoked in the period as the presiding deity of poetic *fureur,* and many were the poets who declared themselves the beneficiaries of his inspiration.[12] So too Ronsard, as in the Apolline *fureur* that he associates with his poetic project in the **Hymne de l'Esté**:

> Nouveau Cygne emplumé je veux voller bien hault,
> Et veux comme l'Esté avoir l'estomaq chaut
> Des chaleurs d'Apollon, courant par la carriere
> Des Muses. . . .[13]
>
> A new feathered swan, I want to fly high, and, like Summer, feel my breast warmed with Apollo's heat, coursing along the path of the Muses. . . .

But while others sought variously to valorize their status as "enfanz des dieuz" and as recipients of "quelque divine afflation" such as that claimed for poets by Sébillet in his *Art poétique* of 1548,[14] Ronsard in his self-styling as the "Gaulois Apollon" laid a more direct, and unmediated, claim to lyric preeminence. Not only would he, as he repeatedly vaunted, conceive his works under the sway of the furies of both love and prophecy:[15] he would *be* a new Apollo, one in whom the Gallic muse was incarnate.[16]

France, it seems, had for some time been looking for a new Apollo, or so one might conclude from the public musings on the renewal of poetry that appeared close upon each other in a period beginning some thirty years before Hélène's compliment to Ronsard. And Ronsard, as early as 1550, was looking for a title. In that year, publishing the first book of his *Odes,* he announced his restoration of the lyre to its former glory, by which he was now honored in his turn: "C'est toy," he tells the instrument, "qui fais que Ronsard soit esleu / Harpeur François" [It is you who bring about Ronsard's selection as French Harpist] (**"A sa lyre,"** *L* [*Oeuvres complètes*, ed. Paul Laumonier] I, p. 162). The title doubles that which he unambiguously claimed for himself in the preface to that same work, where he declared to his reader: "quand tu m'appelleras le premier auteur Lirique François . . . lors tu me rendras ce que tu me dois" [when you call me the first French Lyric author . . . then you shall render me what is my due]—a declaration concerning which Marc-Antoine de Muret felt obliged to defend him against the accusation of excessive self-praise.[17] Muret's defense, that such claims were almost conventional, may appear somewhat disingenuous: "cette coutume de se loüer est commune aveques tous les excellans poëtes qui jamais furent" [this custom of self-praise is common among all the excellent poets of all time].[18] In fact, however, it was, like Ronsard's pronouncement, part of a project of cultural initiation directed toward the reader that would render the latter capable of awarding the title to its legitimate claimant.[19]

The title that Ronsard here presents for the reader to confer upon him signals not only his renewal in French of a poetic form highly esteemed in antiquity but also that the form in question is closely associated with music.[20] Its emphasis, quite obviously, was both a reflection of and an appeal to reigning fashion at court. Court poets as well as professional musicians in concert accompanied themselves in song, and numbers of courtiers both played and sang. So did ladies: the poet of the **Amours** will twice recall Cassandre's song on the occasion of his *innamoramento,* first her "chant marié gentiment / Avec mes vers animez de son poulce" [song gracefully married to my verses given life by her thumb] (*A* [*Amours*] 38), and again that song "lors qu'à son luth ses doits elle embesongne, / Et qu'elle dit le branle de Bourgogne, / Qu'elle disoit, le jour que je fus pris" [when she sets her fingers to her lute and sings the "branle de Bourgogne," that she was singing the day I was captured] (*A* 108).[21] In Lyon, Louise Labé penned memorable portraits of both herself and her beloved as skilled players of the instrument.[22] The fashion, like many others at the French court in the mid-sixteenth century, was set in Italy, and it was no doubt not for purely musical reasons that Ronsard called attention to "l'usage de la lire aujourd'hui resuscitée en Italie, laquelle lire seule peut et doit animer les vers, et leur donner le juste poi de leur gravité" [the use, revived today in Italy, of the lyre, which alone can and must give life to the verses, and give them the full weight of their solemnity] (*L* I, p. 48).

Against this background, Ronsard's self-styling as the "Gaulois Apollon" comes into better focus. Among the poets of the sixteenth century, as in other eras, lute and lyre take on a sense that is metaphoric, metapoetic, or metatextual.[23] Petrarch offered a precedent in a well-known poem, imitated by Du Bellay, in which he proclaims his inadequacy to speak of Laura:

> sì dirà ben: "Quello ove questi aspira
> è cosa da stancare Atene, Arpino,
> Mantova et Smirna, et l'una et l'altra lira."
>
> (*R* [*Petrarch's Lyric Poems: The Rime sparse and Other Lyrics*] 247, 9-11)

then he will say: "What this man aspires to would exhaust Athens, Arpinum, Mantua, and Smyrna, and both one and the other lyre."

Du Bellay expands this catalog in which the two lyres stand for the Greek and Latin lyric traditions by placing Petrarch himself at its head, a gesture that serves in turn as preparation for his reference to a Ronsard who would, along with other "modern"—French—poets, be unable to capture successfully the beauty of Olive:

> Ne cetuy là qui naguere a faict lire
> En lettres d'or gravé sur son rivage
> Le vieil honneur de l'une et l'autre lire.
>
> (*O* [Du Bellay's *Olive*] 62, 12-14)[24]

Nor that one there who once gave us to read, in letters of gold engraved upon his bank, the ancient honor of both one and the other lyre.

The lyre, along with the lute with which it was sometimes interchangeable, figured in common but considerably imprecise usage to designate a variety of poetic modes; it could also be invoked to distinguish between pagan and Christian poetry, as in Du Bellay's *La Lyre Chrestienne.*[25] The instrument, as Terence Cave notes, "occupies a privileged place in the Ronsardian corpus as a figure of poetry."[26] Striking in the case of Ronsard, however, is his recurrent representation not only of the instrument but of the poet in the act of playing it. He may well, in fact, have played the lyre, and possibly also the lute and the guitar.[27] But for our purpose the emphasis is important because it draws the attention of the reader, not to the imitative or competitive relation between the original text and the new text, but to the figure of the poet, who assumes the posture of the imitated master, be he ancient—as Pindar or Homer—or, like Apollo, divine.

Here the practice of imitation promulgated in the poetics of Ronsard and his contemporaries is deflected from the written to the performative act, to take on a new meaning as impersonation. Highly theatrical in this context, it is fully in keeping with a theatrical age in which, as Gilbert Gadoffre reminds us, the poet might claim for himself a privileged place in a world peopled by heroes as "the demiurge of this universe of mirrors," able to deify mortals as well as resuscitate the dead.[28] Ronsard, particularly insistent in this form of self-representation, was also particularly versatile in his self-casting as actor in this theater. Already in 1550, the year of his much-vaunted renewal of the lyric lyre in the first collection of the **Odes,** he imagined other uses for the instrument. Was France awaiting a new Homer, or perhaps a new Virgil? He would respond in epic vein, announcing the ambitious project of a dynastic epic to celebrate the House of Valois.[29] In his **Franciade,** named for the putative founder of the line, Ronsard would, he told the Muses, "chanter mon Francion sur vostre lyre" [sing of my Francus upon your lyre]; he would, he promised the king's sister Marguerite, write of her "plus haultement. . . . Lors que hardy je publiray le tige Troyen de [ta] race" [in a more exalted manner . . . when boldly I shall treat of the Trojan root of (your) race], reminding her that "mon luc premiere-ment / Aux François montra la voie / De sonner si pro-prement" [It was my lute that first showed the French the way to sound it so well].[30]

To show the way: such, of course, was the announced project of Du Bellay's *Deffence et illustration de la langue françoyse* whose publication preceded that of the *Odes* by a single year, the immediately acknowl-edged manifesto in which imitation of preeminent earlier poets such as Homer was advanced as the avenue of renewal for French poetry.[31] Ronsard's early enthusi-asm for the *Franciade* project, however, was not ef-fectively matched by that of its intended patrons; nor did the early *Odes* meet with the resounding and endur-ing success of which he confidently boasted in his preface. Did the circumstances result in a crisis of orientation, as Dassonville suggests?[32] In any case, it resulted in a change of orientation. Disposed once again to alter his course, Ronsard took his cue from two very recent works that had been rewarded with considerable success. Both were Petrarchan collections: Du Bellay's *Olive,* the sequence of love lyrics for which the *Def-fence et illustration* was intended to serve as preface, and Pontus de Tyard's *Erreurs amoureuses* of 1549.

Intent as ever to inscribe his own career into the poetic record of his time, Ronsard now explicitly locates his new orientation in the wake of Du Bellay and Tyard, at-tributing it, of course, not to poetic fashion but to love. In the poem **"A Jean de la Peruse, Poete,"** which passes in review the poetic endeavors of recent decades, he recalls first his own early efforts to "marier les Odes à la Lyre," then the amorous verses recording "les pas-sions" of an enamored Du Bellay and the "amoureux ennuy" of an enamored Tyard. Struck in his turn by Cupid's arrow, he affirms, he had turned, like them, to sing of love:

> Comme ces deux de mesme fleche attaint,
> (Tant peult amour) helas! je fu contraint
> Dessus le luth autres chansons apprendre,
> Pensant flechir l'orgueil de ma Cassandre.

> (*L* V, p. 259)

Struck like those two by the same arrow, (so much can love do) alas! I was constrained to learn other songs to the lute, thinking to bend the pride of my Cassandre.

Soon thereafter he composed a variant of this story, again placing his adoption of the Petrarchan mode under the sign of love but setting it off now against his preparation of the *Franciade*:

> N'agueres chanter je voulois
> Comme Francus au bord Gaulois
> Avecq' sa troupe vint descendre,
> Mais mon Luth pincé de mon doy,
> Ne vouloit en despit de moi
> Que chanter Amour & Cassandre.

> (*L* VI, p. 133)

In those days I wanted to sing of how Francus descended with his troops to the Gaulish border, but my Lute, strummed by my fingers, wanted despite myself only to sing of Love and Cassandre.

This version of his new poetic enterprise is given a more dramatic, indeed epic coloration in the *Amours* said to have been composed in response to that urging:

> Ja desja Mars ma trompe avoit choisie,
> Et, dans mes vers ja françoys, devisoyt:
> Sus ma fureur ja sa lance aiguizoit,
> Epoinçonnant ma brave poësie.
> Ja d'une horreur la Gaule estoit saisie,
> Et soubz le fer ja Sene treluisoit,
> Et ja Francus à son bord conduisoit
> L'ombre d'Hector, & l'honneur de l'Asie,
> Quand l'archerot emplumé par le dos
> D'un trait certain me playant jusqu'à l'os,
> De sa grandeur le sainct prestre m'ordonne:
> Armes adieu. Le Myrte Paphien
> Ne cede point au Laurien Delphien,
> Quand de sa main Amour mesme le donne.

> (*A* 71)

Already Mars had selected my trumpet, and in my verses now in French was composing: in my furor he was sharpening his lance, spurring on my brave poetry. Already Gaul was seized by horror and the Seine sparkled beneath the blade, and already Francus led to its bank the shade of Hector and the honor of Asia, when the winged archer, wounding me to the bone with an unerring shot, ordained me the sacred priest of his greatness. Arms farewell. The Paphian Myrtle does not yield to the Delphic Laurel, when Love himself awards it with his hand.

Here, with the evocation of his work on the *Franciade,* Ronsard effectively rewrites the Petrarchan scene of the innamoramento, blending the figures of a bellicose Mars and of Apolline fureur into that of Cupid as archer. The gesture asserts his uniqueness while proclaiming his filiation, creating a central component of his poetic autobiography in progress.

The change might not, of course, be definitive. In the **"Elegie à Cassandre,"** included in the *Pièces du Bocage* of 1554, he protested the necessity to abandon his newly successful love poetry in favor of more martial matters, at the king's behest: "& si faut que ma lyre / Pendüe au croc ne m'ose plus rien dire" [my lyre, stored upon its hook, no longer dares tell me anything] and the new collection of *Odes* published in 1555 defines itself as a farewell to the lyre, abandoned now in favor of the martial trumpet:[33]

Mais or,' par le commandement
Du Roi, ta Lyre j'abandonne
Pour entonner plus hautement
La grand' trompette de Bellonne. . . .

(*L* VII, pp. 66-67)

But now, by the King's command, I abandon your Lyre to sound more forcefully the great trumpet of Bellonne. . . .

Not only the lyre but the lute as well: both must be set aside, he tells Cassandre in an **"Elegie,"** as he takes up the trumpet to sing of the king's prowess:

Donques en vain je me paissois d'espoir
De faire un jour à la Thuscane voir
Que nôtre France, autant qu'elle, est heureuse
A soupirer une pleinte amoureuse . . .
Mon oeil, mon coeur, ma Cassandre, ma vie,
Hé! qu'à bon droit tu dois porter d'envie
A ce grant Roi, qui ne veut plus soufrir
Qu'à mes chansons ton nom se vienne ofrir.
C'est lui qui veut qu'en trompette j'échange
Mon Luc, afin d'entonner sa louange,
Non de lui seul, mais de tous ses aïeus
Qui sont issus de la race des Dieus.
Je le ferai puis qu'il me le commande . . .

(*L* VI, pp. 57-58)

Thus in vain I nourished the hope to one day make Tuscany see that our France, as much as she, is happy to sigh forth an amorous plaint . . . My eye, my heart, my Cassandre, my life, Oh! by rights you must envy this great King, who no longer wishes your name to inspire my songs. He it is who wills that I exchange my lute for the trumpet, to sound forth his praise; not his alone, but that of all his ancestors, issued from the race of the Gods. I shall do it since he commands me . . .

Yet Ronsard holds out hope for both his poetry and Cassandre, for the king, having himself some experience in love, will surely allow him to return to his more intimate theme:

S'il l'a senti, ma coulpe est effacée,
Et sa grandeur ne sera courroucée
Qu'à mon retour des horribles combas
Hors de son croc mon Luc j'aveigne à bas,
Le pincetant, & qu'en lieu des alarmes
Je chante Amour, tes beautés, & mes larmes . . .

(53-58)

If he has heard it, my fault is erased, and his grandeur will not be angered that on my return from the horrible battle I draw down my lute from its hook, strumming it, and that instead of alarms I sing Love, your beauties, and my tears . . .

Nor will this transposition signal a diminution of his own "heroic" status, for he goes on to claim a remarkable precursor. Ferocious Achilles, he tells Cassandre, upon returning to camp from battle, took advantage of just such an interlude to take up the lute:

Ainsi Achile apres avoir par terre
Tant fait mourir de soudars en la guerre
Son Luc doré prenoit entre ses mains
Teintes encor de meurdres inhumains,
Et vis à vis du fils de Menetie
Chantoit l'amour de Briseis s'amie . . ."

(61-66)

Thus Achilles, after casting so many soldiers dead to the earth in the melee, took his gilded Lute in those hands still tinged with inhuman carnage, and face to face with Menetie's son he sang the love of his beloved Briseis . . .

then suddenly took up arms again to return to combat "plus vaillant." In the same way, Ronsard assures his lady, as the king retires from combat and disarms himself in his tent, her poet will find the occasion to sing her praises: "De sur le Luc à l'heure ton Ronsard / te chantera" [your Ronsard will sing of you upon the lute in time] (72-73).

"Ainsi Achile . . . Ainsi ton Ronsard": the passage testifies eloquently to Ronsard's characteristic strategy of self-representation. The allusion, it has been noted, is inaccurate, and its deflection is significant: in the passage of *Iliad* IX to which he refers, the hero sings not of love but of the valiant deeds of the warriors.[34] In Ronsard's poem the fierce Achilles is rewritten as a lyric poet; he is pressed into service as model for a new poet, one who radically alters a canonized ancient text while at the same time he invents a contemporary fiction offered to the reader as the historical instance of his poem. In this extraordinarily flamboyant gesture, we find what we might be tempted once again to characterize, not as imitation, but as impersonation.

A final example confirms the striking pliability of these representations which Ronsard molded to the needs of his own poetic persona as he wove the new thread almost seamlessly into the old, into the literary representation of what he repeatedly termed the web of his life, the "trame de sa vie." For in fact, in abandoning the ode and the epic to devote himself to the love sonnet currently in favor, he abandoned neither the lyre nor his identification with Apollo. On the contrary, his stance as musician is central to his adaptation of the Petrarchan posture to his own measure in his first lyric collection. The adaptation is readily carried out: in the *Rime sparse* now to be imitated, had not Petrarch himself established an identity with Apollo through the Ovidian myth of the laurel? Now, in the first poem of the 1552 **Amours** to allude to his poetic celebration of the lady, Ronsard writes to a Cassandre cast here as Medusa:

Moy donc rocher, si dextrement je n'use
L'outil des Seurs pour ta gloire esbaucher,
Qu'un seul Tuscan est digne de toucher,
Non le changé, mais le changeur accuse.

(*A* 8, 5-8)

If I then, a stone, fail to use skillfully the instrument of the Sisters to set forth your glory, one that a single Tuscan is worthy to touch, accuse, not the transformed one, but the transformer.

But he is not to be deterred: "Bien mille fois & mille," he records, "j'ay tenté / De fredonner sus les nerfz de ma lyre . . . Le nom, qu'Amour dans le coeur m'a planté" [Thousands and thousands of times I have tried to hum to the strings of my lyre the name that Love implanted in my heart] (*A* 27, 1-4). The thematic thrust of the sonnet closely echoes Petrarch's declaration of his inability to record his lady's name, as Ronsard's editors routinely observe; like Petrarch's poet, Ronsard's lyric protagonist has been unable to inscribe the name on paper, and like him he remains without voice: "Più volte già per dir le labbra apersi, / poi rimase la voce in mezzo 'l petto" [many times already have I opened my lips to speak, but then my voice has remained within my breast] (*R* 20, 9-10); "la voix fraude ma bouche, / Et voulant dire en vain je suis béant" [the voice evades my mouth, and wishing to speak, in vain I am merely gaping] (*A* 27, 13-14). But Ronsard adds the instrumentality of the lyre, defining his desire to "dire" as an attempt at song.

For this song he claims as precursor a mythic Apollo presented in a later poem in the collection as "ce grand Dieu le pere de la lyre" [this great God the father of the lyre] (*A* 116). The god, we learn, also sang in vain:

Pour la douleur, qu'amour veult que je sente,
  Ainsi que moy, Phebus, tu lamentoys,
  Quand amoureux, loing du ciel tu chantoys
  Pres d'Ilion sus les rives de Xanthe.
Pinçant en vain ta lyre blandissante,
  Et fleurs, & flots, mal sain, tu enchantoys,
  Non la beauté qu'en l'ame tu sentoys
  Dans le plus doulx d'une playe esgrissante.

(*A* 36, 1-8)

On account of the pain that love wills me to feel, you, Phoebus, lamented just as I do, when, enamored, you sang far from the heavens on the banks of the Xanthe. Strumming your caressing lyre in vain, you enchanted flowers and waves in your distress, but not the beauty that you felt in your soul in the sweetest part of a keen painful wound.

Petrarch, drawing on Ovidian story for a configuration of mythological elements, had repeatedly presented an Apollo who laments his loss of the nymph Daphne. The Apollo who voices his amorous frustration to the accompaniment of his lyre, however, is not found in the *Rime sparse,* and that is highly suggestive. Here the lyre that distinguishes Ronsard's poet-persona of the early *Amours* from that of Petrarch in the *Rime* is placed in the hands of his mythological double as well, lending authority to the conversion of the poet's voice from the epic to the amorous mode, and status to the languishing figure playing a lyre that now is "blandissante."[35]

                    * * *

It was thus as part of a broader strategy of impersonation that Ronsard adopted his new Petrarchan posture, with an enthusiasm that hardly concealed his ambition. His French contemporaries, he declared in the **"Elegie a Cassandre,"** were inept as love poets, some crude and licentious, others unable to master the master's art to sing of "les amours":

L'on trop enflé les chante grossement,
L'un enervé les traine bassement,
L'un nous despaint une amie paillarde,
L'un plus aus vers qu'aus sentences regarde
Et ne peut onc, tant se sceut desguiser,
Aprendre l'art de bien Petrarquiser.

(*L* VI, p. 59)

One, too puffed up, sings of them inflatedly, another, irritated, drags them low, another paints for us a bawdy lover, yet another attends more to verse than to meaning and can never, however he covers it up, learn the art of Petrarchising well.

But Ronsard . . . Ronsard would be different. If only he could sing of Cassandre as he wished, he assured her and his reader in a poem to which we shall return, he would surpass poets both classical and modern:

Que n'ay-je, Dame, & la plume & la grace
  Divine autant que j'ay la volonté,
  Par mes escritz tu seroys surmonté,
  Vieil enchanteur des vieulx rochers de Thrace.
Plus hault encor que Pindare, ou qu'Horace,
  J'appenderoys à ta divinité
  Un livre enflé de telle gravité,
  Que Du Bellay luy quitteroyt la place.
Si vive encore Laure par l'Univers
  Ne fuit volant dessus les Thusques vers,
  Que nostre siecle heureusement estime,
Comme ton nom, honneur des vers françoys,
  Hault elevé par le vent de ma voix
  S'en voleroyt sus l'aisle de ma rime.

(*A* 73)

Lady, had I but pen and grace as sublime as my will, in my writings you, ancient enchanter of the ancient rocks of Thrace, would be surpassed. Higher still than Pindar or than Horace, I would append upon your divinity a book swelled with such solemnity that Du Bellay would abandon the field to it. As live as the name Laura flies through the Universe borne upon the Tuscan verses that our century happily esteems, so your name, honor of French verses, raised on high by the wind of my voice would take flight on the wing of my rhyme.

It is interesting that while the name of Homer is prominent elsewhere in the first collection of the *Amours,* introduced through the mythological associations of the name of Cassandre, Ronsard makes no mention here of the ancient poet. But it is sufficiently evident that the master against whom Ronsard measures himself is not only, not principally, Homer.[36] Instead we find not only Du Bellay, successful imitator of Petrarch, but Petrarch as well.

This latter suggestion of incipient rivalry, like the avowedly new orientation of Ronsard's poetic enterprise, was not wholly unprepared. For if Ronsard clearly aspired to the title of "Homère de la France," the title which Hélène in a playful key and others with far more solemnity were to award him, his poetic aspirations from a very early date had taken on an alternative cast. And that cast is suggested in his early self-designation as the "Gaulois Apollon," which began our exploration of his poetic self-fashioning. For it can hardly have escaped his notice, attentive as he was to gestures of poetic entitlement, that Maurice Scève, in a famous dizain, had identified Petrarch as the "Tuscan Apollo."[37] Adopting the stance of the "Gaulois Apollon," Ronsard created the formula for an equation through which he might hope one day to distinguish himself as "le Pétrarque français." It was a calculated ratio whose significance was not to be lost on his contemporaries, among them Etienne Jodelle, who succinctly defined its strategy as one of impersonation:

> Pétrarque Italien, pour un Phébus se faire,
> De l'immortel laurier alla choisir le nom;
> Notre Ronsard Français ne tâche aussi sinon
> Par l'amour de Cassandre un Phébus contrefaire.[38]

> The Italian Petrarch, to make himself a Phoebus, chose the name of the immortal laurel; our French Ronsard strives for nothing else than to impersonate a Phoebus through the love of Cassandre.

Thus Ronsard was to lay claim not only to the role of the mythical Apollo but also to parity with the most admired "modern" poet, the Petrarch who had for more than a century dictated the dominant poetic mode in Italy and who had, in the generation preceding Ronsard's, come to be acknowledged as the model of lyric poetry in France as well.[39]

To be the "French Petrarch": to some of Ronsard's contemporaries, and especially to his fellow aspirants to poetic glory, it may have seemed an odd ambition on his part, for he was a relative latecomer to the Petrarchan mode. Although the *Odes* contain much love poetry, that poetry is hardly Petrarchan, underlining instead the intensity of the lover's desire and postulating several ladies as its object; here, concludes Paul Laumonier, we are "at the Antipodes" of Petrarch.[40] Ronsard's earliest mentions of Petrarch in fact occur in comments not on his own poems but on those of others, and in them "Petrarch" is clearly a "text." Before 1545, to Peletier du Mans, who was attempting to translate Petrarch, Ronsard advanced as part of his portrait of his ideal *amie* "Qu'el'seust par cueur tout cela qu'a chanté / Petrarcque en Amours tant vanté / Ou la Rose par

Meun décritte" [that she know by heart all that Petrarch, so highly esteemed in Love, had sung, or the Rose depicted by Meun] (**"Ode a Jacques Peletier des beautez qu'il voudroit en s'amie"**; *L* I, p. 6). This "amie" herself is far from the Petrarchan mistress; most of Ronsard's poem is explicit physical description, a list of desiderata for a mistress not only young but "inconstant & volage, / Follatre, & digne de tel age" [inconstant and flighty, playful, and worthy of her age]. Does her knowledge of Petrarch's love lyrics and of Jean de Meun's *Roman de la Rose* attest to her literary culture, or instead to her amatory inclination, like that of the young female reader whose acquaintance with Petrarch Ronsard had indicted as serving only "fins de coquetterie"?

> La fille preste à marier, accorde
> Trop librement sa chanson à la corde
> D'un pouce curieus:
> Et veut encore Petrarque retenir
> Affin que mieus ell' puisse entretenir
> L'amant luxurieus.

> (*L* II, pp. 190-91)

The young girl ready to marry tunes her song too freely to the string with a curious thumb: and seeks too to remember her Petrarch in order better to entertain a lustful lover.

In any case, here the ladies—imaginary or real—are perhaps only responding in kind to the attentions of their lovers. Those attentions were denounced with varying proportions of ridicule or indignation, whether real or feigned, by observers of the courtly scene at mid-century, some of whom were at the same time ardent participants in its poetic rituals.[41] In a more serious vein, Théodore de Bèze, in the preface to his *Abraham sacrifiant* (1550), opposes the solemnity of Christian praise of God to the frivolity of poets who flattered their patrons or their ladies—their "idoles"—by attempting to "petrarquiser un sonnet,"[42] an enterprise whose dubious issue is acknowledged by the impatient poet in the **Amours** who pleads with his lady either to reward or to reject his suit outright because he is unable to conduct it according to fashion, to "petrarquiser" sufficiently:

> Dy l'un des deux, sans tant me desguiser
>   Le peu d'amour que ton semblant me porte:
>   Je ne scauroy, veu ma peine si forte,
>   Tant lamenter ne tant petrarquiser.
> Si tu le veulx, que sert de refuser
>   Ce doulx present dont l'espoir me conforte?
>   Si non, pourquoy, d'une esperance morte
>   Pais tu ma vie affin de l'abuser?

> (*A* 123, 1-8)[43]

Say one or the other, without so much disguising the scant love that your manner shows me: I could not, given the intensity of my pain, lament or Petrarchize so much. If you want it, what use is it to refuse that sweet gift whose hope comforts me? If not, why sustain my life with a dead hope in order to disappoint it?

To readers familiar with Ronsard's **Odes,** his professed ambition to rival Petrarch may have seemed odd for other reasons as well. Those accustomed to his emphatic pronouncements of poetic intent would surely have recalled that only two years before the publication of the **Amours** dedicated to Cassandre, in the preface to the **Odes** and at the same time that he vaunted his accomplishments in the lofty vein of a Pindar, Ronsard had taken the offensive in his own defense: "Je ne fai point de doute que ma Poësie tant varie ne semble facheuse aus oreilles de nos rimeurs, & principalement des courtizans, qui n'admirent qu'un petit sonnet petrarquizé, ou quelque mignardise d'amour qui continue tousjours en son propos" [I have no doubt whatever that my often-varied Poetry will seem unwelcome to the ears of our rhymers, and especially our courtiers, who admire only a little "petrarchized" sonnet or some affected bit of amorous flattery that is invariable in its intention] (**L** I, p. 47)—those unable to "aprendre l'art de bien Petrarquiser" of whom he was scornfully to complain.

But already Ronsard was writing verses inspired by and in imitation of Petrarch, verses that disclose a project far more ambitious than that of producing a "petit sonnet petrarquizé." Already he takes aim at an entitlement and at a title: that of the French Petrarch.[44] He was not unprepared to undertake such a venture, for his early, extensive, and direct acquaintance with a number of Italian poets has been amply chronicled.[45] And there is textual evidence of Ronsard's attentive reading of Petrarch during that formative period in which we find, in Laumonier's phrase, "the stammerings of his Muse" (**L** I, p. xxi)—evidence found in his earliest lyric practice, even before the first collection of the **Amours** in 1552.

As Laumonier discovered, the publication of the **Hymne de France** in 1550 included at its end two love lyrics, a **"Fantaisie à sa dame"** and a **"Sonnet à elle-même."**[46] The latter poem, Ronsard's first published sonnet, is a close imitation, for the most part a paraphrase, of Petrarch's sonnet 220, "Onde tolse Amor l'oro e di qual vena" [Where and from what mine did Love take the gold] praising the beauteous attributes of the beloved. It is something of a set piece and unremarkable of its type, differing little from the efforts of other French poets who were already engaged in translating and imitating the Italian master. The **"Fantaisie,"** however, more complex and more original, affords a pertinent test case for a reconsideration of Ronsard's early response to Petrarch's lyrics.

Ronsard's **"Fantaisie"** is cast in the form of a dream-vision for which a well-known Petrarchan source has been easily identified: canzone 323 of the *Rime sparse,*

"Standomi un giorno solo a la fenestra," already translated by Clément Marot as "Visions de Pétrarque." The speaker of *R* 323 represents the death of his beloved lady through six allegorical visions, in each of which an object of contemplation—a noble wild creature, a laden ship, a laurel plant, a fountain, a phoenix, a lady—is fatally transformed and destroyed before the eyes of the poet, who is present merely as spectator.[47] In Ronsard's **"Fantaisie"** it is the poet himself who is subjected to a series of transformations, which allow the dreamer to penetrate unobserved into the chamber of a lady who remains very much alive; at their conclusion, he boasts of having witnessed the unsuspecting object of his desire

> Montrer la jambe & la cuisse charnue,
> Ce corps, ce ventre & ce sein coloré,
> Ainçois ivoire en oeuvre elaboré,
> Où j'avisoy une & une autre pomme,
> Dans ceste neige aller & venir, comme
> Les ondes font se jouant à leur bord,
> Quand le vent est ne tranquille ne fort.

show a leg and a well-fleshed thigh, that body, that belly and that flushed breast like well-worked ivory, where I observed one and another apple rise and fall within that snowiness, like the waves do in playing on their shore when the wind is neither still nor strong.

Read against Petrarch's canzone 323, these verses are entirely unexpected, and their effect is not attenuated by the fact that Ronsard here closely imitates another Italian source to which he would frequently return, Ariosto's portrait of Alcina in the *Orlando Furioso.*[48] The contrast is the more startling because the representations of the lady throughout Petrarch's *R* 323 are among the most distanced of the entire Italian collection: she appears in human rather than allegorical guise only in the final stanza, and here too, "sì leggiadra et bella Donna" [a Lady so joyous and beautiful], she is not fully revealed to the observer's view, her "parti supreme," or highest parts, being "avolte d'una nebbia oscura" [wrapped in a dark mist]. Not surprisingly, the contrast between the two poems figures large in the debate that opposes an "erotic" Ronsard to a "chaste" Petrarch: this erotic pretext, Dassonville exclaims, alters the tone, the object, and the meaning of the model poem.[49]

The relation merits reexamination, however, for despite the affinities suggested by the casting of both *R* 323 and Ronsard's **"Fantaisie"** as visions, the primary Petrarchan inspiration of Ronsard's poem is not the allegorical "canzone delle visioni" but another canzone, *R* 23, "nel dolce tempo de la prima etade" [in the sweet time of my first age].[50] In this poem, as in Ronsard's, the successive metamorphoses are not those of allegorical images to which the poet is witness but those of the subject himself. All of these transformations have direct Ovidian models: as the poet becomes a laurel, a swan, a stone, a weeping fountain, a disembodied voice, and finally a stag, they recall the fates of Daphne, Cygnus, Battus, Biblis, Echo, and Acteon.[51] Ronsard's persona finds himself carried away through the skies to become first a cloud, then a shower of rain, a rock, a fountain, a swan, a flower, a disembodied shade. Each transformation preceding the sight of the lady, exactly as in Petrarch's canzone, prompts the expression of his subjugation to the will of the beloved, his impotent lament at her rejection of his suit, his attempt to pronounce her name and to praise her. Only the final transformation in Ronsard's poem, the single one that follows the vision of the lady's nakedness cited above, departs from this pattern, conforming instead to *Rime* 323: here, in an image derived from that of a ship's destruction that figures the lady herself in Petrarch's poem, the poet is finally transformed into a ship threatened with disaster.

Among these metamorphoses, it is the swan image that has attracted the particular attention of readers because, in this very early poem, it sets out a claim to poetic fame, indeed to poetic immortality:

> Et tout ainsi que j'avoy dans ce monde
> Fait éternel vostre nom par mon onde,
> Voulant remplir tout le ciel de son loz,
> La plume aux flans, l'aesle me creut au doz:
> Et nouveau cygne aloy par l'univers,
> Chantant de vous les louanges en vers. . . .

> (31-36)

And just as I had made your name eternal in this world by my wave, wishing to fill all heaven with its praise, feathers sprouted on my body, and wings on my back: and, new swan, I went through the universe singing your praises in verse. . . .

The image has also attracted critical attention as evidence of Ronsard's departure from the Petrarchan model: here he follows the example of classical precursors who had identified the poet with the swan as the creature able to exalt to the heavens the name of a person worthy of celebration and commemoration. The image was early adopted by others among the classicizing young poets of the Pléiade;[52] Du Bellay's *Olive* again affords numerous examples, as in his praise of Scève as "Cygne nouveau, qui voles en chantant / Du chault rivage au froid hiperborée" [new Swan, who flies in singing from the warm shore to the farthest northern cold] (*O* 105)[53] and in the apostrophe of the final poem: "Quel cigne encor' des cignes le plus beau / Te prêta l'aele?" [What swan again most beautiful of swans lent you his wing?] (*O* 115). The passage in Ronsard's **"Fantaisie"** clearly reflects this tradition, anticipating the claim to poetic immortality that he was shortly to advance in the ending of Book IV of his *Odes*: "J'ai fini mon ouvrage . . . Toujours toujours, sans que jamais je meure / Je volerai tout vif par l'univers" (*L* I, p. 152) [I have finished my work . . . Forever and ever,

without ever knowing death, I shall fly alive through the universe].[54]

Ronsard's triumphant soaring swan, whose transformation results from the success of his enterprise to praise the lady's name, stands in almost complete contrast with the swan transformation of Petrarch's metamorphosis canzone:

> Né meno ancor m'agghiaccia
> l'esser coverto poi di bianche piume
> allor che folminato et morto giacque
> il mio sperar che tropp'alto montava;
> che perch'io non sapea dove né quando
> me 'l ritrovasse, solo, lagrimando,
> là 've tolto mi fu, dì et notte andava
> ricercando dallato e dentro a l'acque;
> et giamai poi la mia lingua non tacque
> mentre poteo del suo cader maligno,
> ond'io presi col suon color d'un cigno.

> (*R* 23, 50-60)

Nor do I fear less for having been later covered with white feathers, when thunderstruck and dead lay my hope that was mounting too high; for, since I did not know where or when I would recover it, alone and weeping I went night and day where it had been taken from me, looking for it beside and within the waters; and from then on my tongue was never silent about its evil fall, as long as it had power; and I took on with the sound of a swan its color.

Petrarch here adapts another classical motif, that of the lamenting swan whose song is sweetest as it approaches death, which was also to be adopted by some of Ronsard's contemporaries, Du Bellay among them, as early as 1549.[55] Du Bellay's poet, protesting his inability to express his "martyre," may appear to present a contradictory opinion as he exclaims, "Je mourroy' cygne, où je meurs sans mot dire" [I shall die a swan, where I die without speaking a word] (*O* 8),[56] but he foretells in a later poem that "De cest oyseau prendray le blanc pennaige, / Qui en chantant plaingt la fin de son aage / Aux bordz herbus du recourbé Mëandre" [I shall take on the white plumage of that swan that, singing, lamented the end of its life on the grassy banks of the winding Meander] (*O* 59). The swan form in *R* 23, unlike Ronsard's and Du Bellay's, is the result of an unwitting and unwilling transformation, a figure of frustration whose movement is represented now, not as flight but as a fruitless search "beside and within the waters," and its song, not the praise of the beloved, but a wordless lament.

Are we then to conclude that Ronsard is here "unfaithful . . . to Petrarch's lesson" and that by this gesture he deliberately distances himself from the *Rime sparse*?[57] That ready conclusion would lead us to neglect a connection that has far-reaching implications for his later imitation of Petrarch. For once again closer examination is required, because the swan metamorphosis in Petrarch's canzone is doubled in that same poem by that of another bird, one that appears not in the series of the poet-lover's transformations but in the *commiato*, in the confident boast that he has been "l'uccel che più per l'aere poggia / alzando lei che ne' miei detti onoro" [the bird that rises highest in the air raising her that in my words I honor].

The presence of this source text is critical for our reading of Ronsard's claim of poetic triumph in the **"Fantaisie à sa dame,"** for in the commiato of *Rime* 23 the context is quite specific and quite unlike that of the series of metamorphoses of the frustrated poet-as-victim in the body of the poem. Here each transformation alludes to one of the metamorphoses through which an enamored Jupiter takes on a mortal form, bird or animal, so as to possess the human object of his desire; in the verses cited, the god assumes the form of an eagle to carry Ganymede off to Olympus. Of this image of triumphant flight Petrarch makes a figure of triumphant poetry, as the speaker of his poem raises to the skies the lady honored in his verse. And Ronsard's poem follows Petrarch's lead, with a highly suggestive innovation: while his description of avian metamorphosis follows that of the lover's swan transformation in the Italian poem, it is the bird of the commiato of *R* 23 that inspires his own claim of poetic achievement. This is the Petrarch to whose achievement Du Bellay had early aspired, as he recalls in his "Complainte du Desesperé":

> Alors que parmy la France
> Du beau Cygne de Florence
> J'alloys adorant les pas,
> Dont les plumes j'ay tirées,
> Qui des ailes mal cirées
> Le vol n'imiteront pas. . . .[58]

> while I went through France adoring the traces of the handsome swan of Florence, whose feathers I have plucked, whose flight my poorly waxed wings will not imitate. . . .

And it is the soaring Petrarch repeatedly evoked by Ronsard.[59] His assimilation of the bird images is confirmed in the **"Elegie ou Amour Oyseau,"** where he identifies Petrarch as "ce Florentin, / Que Cygne par ses vers surmonta le Destin" [this Florentine who as a Swan overcame Fate by his verses] (*L* XV, p. 210), taken up again in his **"Elegie Au Sieur Barthelemi Del-Bene"** (*L* XVIII, pp. 253ff.) to whom he accords the title of

> . . . second Cygne apres le Florentin
> Que l'art, & le sçavoir, l'Amour, & le Destin,
> Firent voler si haut sur Sorgue la riviere,
> Qu'il laissa de bien loing tous les autres derriere

> . . . second Swan after the Florentine, whom art, knowledge, Love, and Fate made to fly so high above the river Sorgue that he left all others far behind.[60]

* * *

Ample evidence exists, then, that in this early phase of his lyric production Ronsard was not a dilatory and servile imitator of the current poetic mode; on the contrary, he was an excellent reader of Petrarch. But what he found in the *Rime sparse* was more than the affectation of a poetic fashion implied in his declaration of an inability to "tant petrarquiser" to win his lady's favors. The definitions that proliferated in the period are in this regard suggestive: Théodore de Bèze, for example, had added to his deprecation of poets devoting themselves only to the attempt to "petrarquiser un sonnet" that of a posturing that was affective as well as poetic, to "faire l'amoureux transy" [play the transfixed lover]; a more sympathetic or at least ostensibly neutral Muret annotates Ronsard's verb "Petrarquiser" in a sonnet from the first collection of the *Amours* (*A* 123) with the identical phrase: "faire de l'amoureus transi, comme Petrarque" (*L* IV, p. 96), and J. Lemaire suggests something very similar, to imitate "'le bon Petrarque, en amours le vrai maistre.'"[61] While these *gloses* appear to emphasize the sense of affectation—"une hypocrisie ou une imposture," as Yvonne Bellenger comments, "l'idée d'un amour tout en tromperie, tout en feintes, en somme d'un mensonge"[62]—the suggestion of role-playing in these substitutions of "faire" for "écrire" may have particular implications, especially in the case of Ronsard, for the practice of writing as well.

The latter verb, of course, is implicit, for all of these author-commentators are attempting to define modes of lyric writing. A particularly suggestive example of the many possibilities of "writing like Petrarch" is a poem by Jodelle that takes as its point of departure this version of the innamoramento in the *Rime sparse*:

> Era il giorno ch'al sol si scoloraro
> per la pietà del suo fattore i rai
> quando i' fui preso, et non me ne guardai,
> ché i be' vostr'occhi, Donna, mi legaro.
> Tempo non mi parea da far riparo
> contr'a' colpi d'Amor; però m'andai
> secur, senza sospetto, onde i miei guai
> nel commune dolor s'incominciaro.
> Trovommi Amor del tutto disarmato,
> et aperta la via per gli occhi al core
> che di lagrime son fatti uscio et varco.
> Però al mio parer non li fu onore
> ferir me de saetta in quello stato,
> a voi armata non mostrar pur l'arco.

> (*R* 3)

> It was the day when the sun's rays turned pale with grief for his Maker when I was taken, and I did not defend myself against it, for your lovely eyes, Lady, bound me. It did not seem to me a time for being on guard against Love's blows; therefore I went confident and without fear, and so my misfortunes began in the midst of the universal woe. Love found me altogether

disarmed, and the way open through my eyes to my heart, my eyes which are now the portal and passageway of tears. Therefore, as it seems to me, it got him no honor to strike me with an arrow in that state, and not even to show his bow to you, who were armed.

Very early in the *Rime,* Petrarch's sonnet recontextualizes Love's assault on the unsuspecting poet within a collective Christian frame. The quatrains of Jodelle's sonnet, opening with the "communes douleurs" that make the reader's identification of the source poem inevitable and immediate, paraphrase the Italian poem in the third person while affording its explication in the insistence on the common experience, both of the universal grief appropriate to Good Friday—for "tous coeurs chrétiens"—and of vulnerability to Love's ruses, that "dépourvus nous surprennent."

> Aux communes douleurs qui poindre en ce jour viennent
> Tous coeurs chrétiens, Pétrarque alla chanter qu'il prit
> De ses douleurs la source, et par là nous apprit
> Que les ruses d'Amour dépourvus nous surprennent.
> En ces jours où les cieux, la mort, les pleurs retiennent
> Nos coeurs ardents, quel lieu reste au feu qui l'éprit?
> Il ne se gardait pas du lacs qui le surprit
> Non plus que moi des rets qui plus fort me reprennent.

In the communal sorrows that pierce all Christian hearts on that day, Petrarch was to sing that he took the source of his own sorrows, and by that he taught us that the ruses of Love take us by surprise. On such days when the heavens, death, and tears occupy our ardent hearts, what place is left for the fire that took him? He was not on guard against the snare that surprised him, no more than I was against the snares that hold me stronger still.

The last of these verses effectively identifies the poet's experience with that of Petrarch within this common vulnerability, but only to set up a contrast that will at last imply that Jodelle's suffering in love transcends even that of its famous exemplar:

> Bien qu'Amour sache assez qu'il est en moi trop fort,
> Pour croître du tourment, non du désir, l'effort,
> Il arme la peur froide, et l'aigre défiance.

Although Love knows full well that he is too strong within me, it is to heighten the force of the torment, not of desire, that he arms my cold fear and my sharp mistrust.

The concluding tercet then justifies the insertion of the Petrarchan episode in his own "story," in that it serves to render, in highly dramatic terms, not the innamoramento but the fear of losing a love already known:

> Pétrarque à l'heur eût pu perdre sans grand'douleur
> L'heur inconnu; ma perte aurait, las! ce malheur
> D'avoir de l'heur perdu si haute connaissance.[63]

Petrarch could have lost the happiness he had never known without great pain; my loss, alas! would have the misfortune of knowing the lost happiness so very well.

Jodelle's evocative retelling of a well-known Petrarchan scene reminds us that from its earliest circulation, and despite the fact that it was not always circulated or, eventually, published in the same form, Petrarch's collection of *rime sparse* was associated with a story. In fact, the history of the early reception of the collection is bound up with story-making. Biographical annotations proliferated in the editions circulating widely in Italy and Europe;[64] Petrarch's Italian commentators, well known to Ronsard, contributed substantially to a reading of the collection in which Petrarch as protagonist of an exemplary love story took priority over considerations of form and style.[65] Vellutello's extremely influential commentary in fact intervenes in the sequence as Petrarch determined it, reordering the poems to project a unified narrative corresponding to events in Petrarch's life.[66] The popular 1528 edition of the *Rime* contained not only the commentary by Vellutello and, like most other editions, a *vita* of Petrarch, but also a half dozen pages entitled "Origine di Madonna Laura con la descrittione di Valclusa e del luogo ove il poeta a principio di lei s'innamorò" [The origins of my lady Laura with the description of Vaucluse and of the place where the poet first fell in love with her], along with a map of the Vaucluse.[67]

The story, of course, is in one sense illusory, in the very form of the lyric collection: it is belied first by the designation of the poems as "scattered rhymes" in the first verse of the proemial sonnet, and then by the formally independent status of the lyrics themselves.[68] But the poems read in sequence nonetheless induce in the reader a presumption of story. Since the appearance of Pierre de Nolhac's 1886 edition based on the partially autograph manuscript containing the poet's last revisions, readers have probed the rich variety of ways in which the individual poems are organized into the sequence.[69] But during the intervening centuries too, Petrarch's poems "read together" provoked and teased his readers toward that presumption of story, one that received a justification from Bembo well over a century after Petrarch's death. Bembo's emphasis was critical in defining a mode of lyric *imitatio* that would be vastly influential throughout the sixteenth century: it insisted on the form of the vernacular *canzoniere* as testimony to the poet's *vicenda sentimentale,* which is in turn the text's fictional substratum, its structural justification.[70]

The result was readily exported to France. Petrarch's vernacular lyrics had been accessible to the cultivated public in manuscript form in the preceding century, but from the early years of the sixteenth century the large numbers of printed editions of the *Rime* contributed substantially to the dissemination of the canzoniere as lyric model.[71] In 1552-53, Luigi Alamanni published his own collection of love poems commemorating a "destin amoureux" enacted near Avignon and Vaucluse. With these *Opere Toscane* written in Tuscan and published in Lyon, observes Olivier Millet, Alamanni already effects a symbolic implanting of a poetic culture, based on the Petrarch of the *Rime,* that united Italy and France.[72] His dedication of the poems to the glory of a receptive François I both responded and contributed to a "royal culture" in which François I took an interest that was not only direct but active.[73] The presumed discovery of Laura's burial site by Scève in 1533 in a church in Avignon generated sufficient interest that the king, passing through the city, arranged a visit to the tomb, where he was reported to have immediately composed an epitaph for Laura.[74]

Some fifteen years later, Vasquin Philieul published a translation of Petrarch's poems "in vita di Madonna Laura" under the title of *Laure d'Avignon.*[75] The collection, the only integral French translation undertaken in the sixteenth century, was not only immensely influential in its experimentation with the sonnet form;[76] it also affords telling evidence of the particularized reception of the *Rime* as "story." Philieul based his translation on Vellutello's edition and ordering, and like Vellutello, he accompanied the poems with frequent and occasionally detailed commentary, appearing now as brief prose passages or "arguments" preceding the translated texts. And those passages, taken together, represent the Petrarchan collection as a story of which each poem is to be read as an episode. Philieul frequently offers a precise place and circumstance to account for the composition in question. The explanation that prefaces the translation of *Rime* 108, "Aventuroso più d'altro terreno" [Luckier than any other ground] is suggestive of the degree of his imaginative involvement: "Estant Petrarque ainsi solitaire à Vaucluse, fut visité d'une compagnie d'Avignon, qui estoit allée veoir la fontaine de la Sorgue, et en icelle compagnie estoit madame Laure. Or ne fault dire si l'on y fit grand chere. Icy Petrarque escript à son amy Senuce, benissans le lieu, qui avait eu la grace que sa dame y fust" [Thus Petrarch, when alone in Vaucluse, received the visit of a group from Avignon who had gone to see the fountain of the Sorgue, and among them was madame Laura. It hardly needs be said that there was a warm welcome. Here Petrarch wrote to his friend Sennuccio, blessing the place that had been graced with his lady's presence].[77]

Ronsard was not the first among Petrarch's French successors to demonstrate a keen awareness not only of the Italian poet's status as master of the individual lyric but of his status as protagonist in a "story" as well. Marot had published, in 1539, a translation of *Six sonnets de Pétrarque,* sonnets which, Jean Balsamo observes, were of seminal importance particularly in their attestation to

the structure of Petrarch's collection as a whole.[78] But Marot did not appear eager to exploit the potential of his innovative gesture,[79] and Scève, whose name was repeatedly associated with Petrarch's following the presumed discovery of Laura's tomb,[80] chose for his own lyric collection a form foreign to the Italian: the *dizain* whose very grammar and syntax, as Rigolot observes, appear to block the perception of a narrative continuity to which the *Rime* invites the reader.[81] But the *Délie* is a substantial collection, and it acquires its coherence as recueil in large part from what Doranne Fenoaltea terms the "narrative pre-text," a love story never narrated but accessible to the reader—indeed, formulated by the reader—through logical and pragmatic presupposition. And the reader familiar with the rhetoric of Petrarchan poetry will recognize in the first verse of the first poem of the *Délie,* in the evocation of the poet's "ieunes erreurs" corresponding to the "primo giovenile errore" of *Rime* 1, the particular type of love story to be expected.[82]

In fact, Scève's strategy of situating himself in relation to the poet's story in the *Rime sparse* is called explicitly to the reader's attention in several references in the *Délie* to Petrarch and his Laura/laurel. These may establish contrast: *D* 388 invokes both the impotence of reason to resist Love's assault in the staging of the innamoramento (*R* 2) and Petrarch's account of his frustrated pursuit leading only to "[il] lauro onde si coglie / acerbo frutto" [the laurel, whence one gathers bitter fruit] (*R* 6) to convey the contrast between Petrarch's recall of youthful vulnerability and his own more advanced age:

> Donc ce Thuscan pour vaine vtilité
> Trouue le goust de son Laurier amer:
> Car de ieunesse il aprint a l'aymer.
> Et en Automne Amour, ce Dieu volage,
> Quand me voulois de la raison armer,
> A preualu contre sens, & contre aage.[83]

> Thus it is in vain that this Tuscan finds the taste of his Laurel bitter: for he learned in his youth to love it. And in Autumn Love, that inconstant god, when I sought to arm myself with reason, prevailed against sense and against age.

Other poems too, alluding to Apollo's pursuit and ultimate celebration of an unyielding Daphne, evoke Petrarch's adaptation of the myth of the laurel to his own poet's story.[84] In the last of these, the well-known poem in which he entitles Petrarch the "Thuscan Apollo," he addresses the Rhone that flows through "mainte riue amoureuse,"

> Baingnant les piedz de celle terre heureuse,
> Ou ce Thuscan Apollo sa ieunesse
> Si bien forma, qu'a iamais sa vieillesse
> Verdoyera a toute eternité;

(*D* 417)

Bathing the feet of that happy land, where that Tuscan Apollo formed his youth so well that his old age will be verdant through all eternity;

and now, to the story of this poet who had won his own poetic immortality, is added that of Maurice Scève,

> . . . ou Amour ma premiere liesse
> A desrobée a immortalité.

> . . . there where Love stole away my first happiness from immortality.

Scève's dizain, as has been often noted, is a rewriting of *R* 208, playing, like the Italian original, on the name of the river Rhone: "rapido fiume . . . rodendo intorno (onde 'l tuo nome prendi)" [swift river . . . gnawing a way for yourself (whence you take your name)], "fle-uue rongeant pour t'attiltrer le nom / De la roideur . . ." [river gnawing away to gain yourself the name of rapidity].[85] But with the introduction of his own lyric persona, of course, we read as well the desire to replace Petrarch's love poetry with his own.[86]

For Du Bellay, the poetic lineage here suggested opened further possibilities for succession. His praise of Scève, as Jerry Nash points out, is frequently related, through the symbolism of the Rhone and its confluence with the Saône, to his praise of Petrarch and is central to his own claim to poetic immortality:

> L'Arne superbe adore sur sa rive
> Du sainct Laurier la branche tousjours vive,
> Et ta Delie enfle ta Saone lente.
> Mon Loire aussi, demydieu par mes vers,
> Bruslé d'amour etent les braz ouvers
> Au tige heureux, qu'à ses rives je plante.

(*O* 105, 9-14)[87]

The proud Arno adores on its bank the ever green branch of the sacred Laurel, and your slow-running Saone nurtures your Delie. My Loire too, demigod through my verses, scalded by love extends its open arms to the favored sapling that I plant on its banks.

Du Bellay, who assured his place in literary history with the doctrine of imitation published in the *Deffence* of 1549, avowed in that same year, in the first preface to the *Olive,* his own imitation of Italian poets, Petrarch first among them: "Vrayment je confesse avoir imité Petrarque" [In truth I confess having imitated Petrarch].[88] But Du Bellay in practice goes beyond his own ambitious theory, for with regard to the *Olive* the phrase "to imitate Petrarch" does not render adequately the relation between the new poet and the old. In a poem (*O* 84) otherwise inspired by another source (Sannazaro's *Arcadia*), the initial verse "Seul et pensif par la deserte plaine," translated from the opening of *R* 132, assumes the function of an exordium which, as Caldarini points out, proposes a type of assimilation of the poet to Petrarch.[89] Here the experience of the poet

of the *Rime sparse* is no longer evoked as that of another; instead, the third-person allusion and the first-person speaker's voice are collapsed into one.

Du Bellay's ambition is, of course, to *equal* Petrarch: Olive against Laura, olive against laurel, explicit in the opening sonnet as the poet addresses the garland of olive branches from which the collection draws its title: "Orne mon chef, donne moy hardiesse / De te chanter, qui espere te rendre / Egal un jour au Laurier immortel" [Bedeck my head, give me the boldness to sing of you, hoping to render you one day equal to the immortal Laurel].[90] Some years later, that ambition was to be mocked by Du Bellay himself, in a poem addressed to a lady with all the beauty of Laura:

> Pourquoy de moy a vous donc souhaitté
> D'estre sacree à l'immortalité,
> Si vostre nom d'un seul Petrarque est digne?
> Je ne sçay par d'où vient ce desir là,
> Fors qu'il vous plaist nous monstrer par cela
> Que d'un Corbeau vous pouvez faire un Cygne.[91]

Why have you then hoped to be consecrated to immortality by me, when your name is worthy of Petrarch alone? I know not what prompts that desire, unless it pleases you to show us thereby that you can make a Swan of a Crow.

But in the unbounded optimism of the poetic climate of 1549-50, Du Bellay's advertisement of his imitative strategy is suggestive, and so is Ronsard's recorded response, for it is in these terms that Ronsard promptly sends Du Bellay his encouragement:

> Si tu montres au jour tes vers
> Entés dans le tronc d'une olive,
> Qui hausse sa perruque vive
> Jusque à l'egal des lauriers vers.

(*L* II, p. 39)

If you one day show your verses grafted in the trunk of an olive tree, that raises its living leafy crown as high as the laurel verses.

It is not surprising, then, that it was by invoking not the style but the "story" of the *Rime sparse* that a supportive Ronsard had responded to his friend's professed ambition before the publication of the *Olive,* to predict for that recueil the glory of the canzoniere written for Laura:

> Une Laure plus heureuse
> Te soit un nouveau souci,
> Et que ta plume amoureuse
> Engrave à son tour aussi
> Des contens l'heur & le bien,
> A celle fin que nostre siecle encore
> Comme le vieil, en te lisant t'honore,
> Pour gaster l'encre si bien.

that a happier Laura be your new concern, and that your amorous pen engrave too in turn the happiness and good fortune of its contentment, to the end that our century again, like the former, honor you in reading you for having expended your ink so well.

And here Ronsard characterizes that relation in a way that foreshadows his own strategy of assimilation, as he praises the Du Bellay who shows him some verses as having "l'âme de Pétrarque":

> . . . son livre antiq' tu ne leus onques,
> Et tu écris ainsi comme lui, donques
> Le méme esprit est en toi.
>
> *(L* II, pp. 65-66)

> . . . you never read his ancient book, and you write thus like him, therefore the same spirit is in you.

It would be difficult to overestimate the importance of this declaration. This is not a rhetoric of imitation; it is the opposite, a denial of imitation, in that it is ostensibly prompted by Du Bellay's *not* having read Petrarch—although Du Bellay, as we have seen, belies that suggestion in his 1549 preface to the *Olive*. We might even call it instead a rhetoric of reincarnation, the same rhetoric that Du Bellay himself employs in the negative sense when he evokes the Homer who had immortalized the Greek heroes:

> Puis que les cieux m'avoient predestiné
> A vous aymer, digne object de celuy
> Par qui Achille est encor' aujourdjuy
> Contre les Grecz pour s'amye obstiné,
> Pourquoy aussi n'avoient-ilz ordonné
> Renaitre en moy l'ame et l'esprit de luy?
>
> *(O* 20, 1-6)

> Since the heavens had predestined me to love you, object worthy of him through whom Achilles is still relentless against the Greeks today for his beloved, why did they not also ordain his soul and his spirit reborn in me?

Here Du Bellay's theoretical meditation in the *Deffence* is suggestive in a rather unusual way. In a famous passage, the young poet explains the success of the revered Latin masters:

> Immitant les meilleurs aucteurs Grecz, se transformant en eux, les devorant, & apres les avoir bien digerez, les convertissant en sang & nouriture, se proposant, chacun selon son naturel & l'argument qu'il vouloit elire, le meilleur aucteur, dont ils observoint diligemment toutes les plus rares & exquises vertuz . . .

> Imitating the best Greek authors, transforming themselves into the Greeks, devouring them, and after having well digested them, converting them into blood and nourishment, they proposed the best author as a pattern, each according to his natural bent and the argument he wished to elect; they diligently observed all of the rarest and most exquisite virtues of the model author . . . [92]

Metaphors for the process of imitation abounded in the Renaissance; Petrarch himself had advanced one that, drawn from Seneca, was to have a long posterity, likening the poet to the bee that makes sweet new honey from many flowers.[93] Du Bellay's metaphor of innutrition in this passage is more carnal, more violent, than many others representing the process in similar ways: the devouring of the target author and that author's conversion through the digestive process into the very substance, the very blood and nourishment, to feed the hunger of the aspiring new author. But the essential paradox of his recommendation lies in its opening, not with the process of innutrition, but with its contrary: that of the new author transforming himself into the model author.[94] As Thomas Greene comments, this figurative account is something of an offense to logic: "The imitator simultaneously and paradoxically becomes his model and makes the model part of himself by innutrition"; in contrast, in Ronsard's own writing about poetry, the apian metaphor is present but reduces or suppresses the element of transformation, and the innutrition metaphor is absent.[95] But the transformation of the self into the other remains, and it is highly suggestive for a poet who aspired to be known as a "new"—a French—Petrarch.

The suggestion of reincarnation in Du Bellay's rhetorical posturing in *O* 20 goes beyond his source from the Giolito anthology readily identified through other elements of the poem.[96] It also goes well beyond the figuration of the poet—Scève, Du Bellay, Petrarch, or another—who self-consciously poses with lyre or lute or has himself portrayed as crowned with laurel, as Ronsard is portrayed in the frontispiece of the ***Amours.*** The conventional nature of their postures was fully apparent; they were adopting a common literary role. Etienne Pasquier wrote in 1555, in response to the question of the "sincerity" of the love experience apparently common to Petrarch and so many of his imitators: "Ainsi ne fault-il trouver trop estrange, si accommodans leurs escrits au subject qui semble estre du tout voüé à la jeunesse (en laquelle à present ils vivent) ils se sont proposez faire les passionez dans leurs oeuvres pour servir d'un bon miroüer à tout le monde?" [Thus must we find it terribly strange, if in adjusting their writing to the subject that seems wholly devoted to the time of youth (in which they are at present living) they have proposed to play the enamored in their works to serve as an accurate mirror of all around them?] Many years later, Ronsard would invoke this same commonsense principle in his own defense, going on to mock his accusers with the accusation of a naive reading:

> Je suis fol, Predicant, quand j'ay la plume en main,
> Mais quand je n'escri plus, j'a le cerveau bien sain
>
> . . .
>
> Tu sembles aux enfans qui contemplent es nues
> Des rochers, des Geans, des Chimeres cornues,
> Et ont de tel object le cerveau tant esmeu,

Qu'ils pensent estre vray l'ondoyant qu'ils ont veu,
Ainsi tu penses vrais les vers dont je me joüe.[97]

I am quite mad, Preacher, when I have my pen in hand,
but when I stop writing, my brain is quite healthy. . . .
You are like the children who see in the clouds rocks,
Giants, horned Chimera, and have their brains so
moved by such objects that they think the shifting shape
they have seen to be true; in the same way you think
true the verses with which I play.

But Ronsard had attracted the criticisms addressed to
him in part because of the manner of his own response
to Petrarch, a response that fully exploited the recognition that the poetic voice of the lyric collection, speaking in the first person to tell his own story, was a poetic
persona with a particular story to tell—a realization
with far-reaching consequences for his own lyric collections. Much recent reexploration of Renaissance writing
has demonstrated that, as the editor of a recent volume
concludes, "it is in and through fiction(s) that the most
adventurous (and sometimes precarious) conceptualiza-
tions of the self appear,"[98] and the fiction-making that
Ronsard found in the lyric collection of *Rime sparse*
took a characteristically idiosyncratic turn, with far-
reaching consequences, in the development of his own
poetic "self."

Notes

Petrarch's poems and their English versions are cited
from *Petrarch's Lyric Poems: The Rime sparse and
Other Lyrics* (= *R*), translated and edited by Robert M.
Durling (Cambridge: Harvard University Press, 1967).
Translations from Ronsard and other French and Italian
poets, unless attributed, are my own. Ronsard poems
from *Les Amours,* unless otherwise indicated, are cited
from Henri Weber and Catherine Weber, eds. (Paris:
Dunod, 1993): *A* = *Amours* 1552-53, *MM* = "Sur la
mort de Marie," *SH* = *Sonets pour Helene.* Other Ronsard citations are from *Pierre de Ronsard: Oeuvres
complètes,* ed. Paul Laumonier, continued by Raymond
Lebègue and Isidore Silver, 20 vols. (Paris: Société des
Textes Français Modernes, 1914-75), cited as *L* with
volume and page number. Unless otherwise indicated,
Du Bellay's *Olive* (= *O*) is cited from the edition by E.
Caldarini (Geneva: Droz, 1974).

1. Hélène's phrase, flattering for the poet, is less so
for the lover, for it was her game as well, she having welcomed his attentions "pour avoir (ses)
chansons." On the exchange between Hélène /
"Minerve" and Ronsard / "Bilhard" see Fernand
Desonay, *Ronsard poète de l'amour,* III (Brussels:
Duculot, 1959), pp. 205-6 and 18.

2. As Homer, so Ronsard: ". . . pour sujet fertil
Homere t'a choisie," he tells Hélène (*SH* [*Sonets
pour Helene*] II: 37, 5). For the importance of
onomastics in the collection see Nathalie Dauvois,
Mnémosyne: Ronsard, une poétique de la mémoire
(Paris: Champion, 1992), pp. 198-215.

3. "La Lyre," *L* [*Pierre de Ronsard: Oeuvres complètes,* ed. Paul Laumonier] XV, p. 28.

4. The phrase is that of Terence Cave, *The Cornucopian Text: Problems of Writing in the French
Renaissance* (Oxford: Clarendon, 1979), p. 262.

5. For detailed discussion see Guy Demerson, *La
Mythologie classique dans l'oeuvre lyrique de la
Pléiade* (Geneva: Droz, 1972), ch. 9, "Le Lyrisme
de la Pléiade et l'essor de la poésie de cour," and
Françoise Bardon, *Le Portrait mythologique à la
cour de France sous Henri IV et Louis XIII* (Paris:
Picard, 1974), esp. pp. 276-79.

6. The range of pageantry and personae through
which Elizabeth was celebrated has been the
object of considerable study; some telling examples are found in Stephen Greenblatt, *Renaissance Self-Fashioning: From More to Shakespeare*
(Chicago: University of Chicago Press, 1980), pp.
165-69. For the political importance of such
representations in the reign of Louis XIV see
Virginia Scott, "The Fall of Phaeton: The Son of
the Sun God in the Theatre of the Sun King,"
French Studies 48 (1994): pp. 141-54.

7. "François I en allégorie divine," c. 1545, Paris,
Bibliothèque Nationale, reproduced in *La cour de
François Ier: Gouverner autrement* (Centre Na-
tional de Documentation Pédagogique, 1996).

8. See Françoise Joukovsky, *La Gloire dans la poésie
française et néolatine du XVIe siècle* (Geneva:
Droz, 1969), who cites from *La chasse royalle*
Salel's description of Marie d'Autriche as a
mounted Diana fully armed for the hunt (pp. 179-
80). For Ronsard's role in the composition of
spectacles from 1564 to 1570, see Daniel Ménager,
Ronsard: Le Roi, le poète et les hommes (Geneva:
Droz, 1979), pp. 323-32, and Michel Dassonville,
Ronsard: Etude historique et littéraire, V (Geneva:
Droz, 1990), pp. 89-98.

9. For Charles as new Mercury see Hymne V, "De
Charles Cardinal de Lorraine" (*L* IX, p. 29); "les
forts Guisians" are celebrated in the first ode of
Le Quatriesme Livre des Odes (*L* VII, p. 90); in
another poem Ronsard becomes Ennius to the
Cardinal's brother's Scipio: "Je chante vos hon-
neurs, qui seuls me pourront faire / Aussi bon Ennius en chantant vostre frere, / Comme en guerre
il s'est fait Scipion des François" (*L* X, p. 82).

10. "A Monsieur de Belot," *L* VI, p. 27; *L* I, p. 48.
For the memorial function of such appellations
see Dauvois, *Mnémosyne,* esp. "le modèle et
l'exemple," pp. 21-37.

11. As Philippe Desan observes, "Apollo, Jupiter, Hercules and Henri II became interchangeable"; see
"The Tribulations of a Young Poet: Ronsard from

1547 to 1552" in *Renaissance Rereadings: Intertext and Context,* ed. Maryanne Cline Horowitz et al. (Urbana: University of Illinois Press, 1988), p. 195. For the "Ode à la Reine" and the inscription for Marguerite de Savoie see *L* VII, p. 36; *L* IX, p. 197.

12. On the adoption by sixteenth-century poets of the neoplatonist theory of inspiration see Françoise Joukovsky-Micha, *Poésie et mythologie au XVIe siècle* (Paris: Nizet, 1969), pp. 123-41.

13. *L* XII, p. 35. On Apollo as poet-god as well as sun-god in the *Hyme de l'Esté* see Cave, *Cornucopian Text,* pp. 248-49, and for the association of fire with poetry here see André Gendre, "Aspects du feu dans l'imaginaire de Ronsard amoureux," in *Ronsard et les éléments,* ed. André Gendre (Geneva: Droz, 1992), p. 179.

14. Thomas Sébillet, *Art poétique françoys,* cited in Joukovsky-Micha, *Poésie et mythologie,* p. 133.

15. On this "dual seizure" see the examples in Robert J. Clements, "Ronsard and Ficino on the Four Furies," *Romanic Review* 45 (1954): pp. 161-69.

16. On Ronsard's transposition of the neoplatonist *fureur* from poetry to love in the 1552 *Amours* see Terence Cave, "Ronsard as Apollo: Myth, Poetry and Experience in a Renaissance Sonnet-Cycle," in *Image and Symbol in the Renaissance, Yale French Studies* 47 (1972): pp. 76-78.

17. As Fernand Desonay observes, "Moins qu'à des poèmes qui auront à être 'mesurés à la lyre,' c'est à Pindare, c'est à la réputation de Pindare que songe notre jeune autant qu'audacieux gentilhomme vendômois"; see *Ronsard poète de l'amour. Livre premier. Cassandre* (Brussels: Palais des Académies, 1952), pp. 72-73, 116, n. 29.

18. *Préface de Marc-Antoine de Muret sur ses "Commentaires"* (cf. *L* V, xxiv), cited by Desonay, *Ronsard poète de l'amour,* p. 72.

19. See Claude Faisant, "L'Herméneutique du sens caché dans les discours prefaciels de Ronsard," *Versants* 15 (1989): this "interlocuteur privilégié du poète-préfacier, joue en fait le rôle d'un médiateur: il permet à Ronsard non seulement de pressentir les résistances du public réel, mais d'en infléchir surtout les attentes et de modeler aussi peu à peu une opinion à son écoute" (p. 101). On this explicit reader "associé quelquefois à la reconnaissance de cette gloire" see also André Gendre, "Lecteur 'esthétique' et lecteur 'éthique' dans les liminaires de la poésie française de 1549 à la fin du siècle" (p. 127).

20. In his *Art poétique* of 1548, Thomas Sébillet had noted that the verses of the ode were necessarily short because they were to be played to a lute or similar instrument, and in his own preface Ronsard restricts the designation of "lyrique" to short verses meant to be accompanied by "un instrument à cordes pincées"; see Gilbert Gadoffre, *Ronsard par lui-même* (2nd ed. Paris: Seuil, 1994), pp. 89-90.

21. As Weber notes, the theme of the lady singing the poet's verses to the accompaniment of her lute is frequent among the Petrarchist poets; cf. Pontus de Tyard, *Erreurs Amoureuses,* I, 42, and Du Bellay, *Olive,* 94.

22. Addressing the beloved: "Quand j'aperçoy ton blond chef couronné / D'un laurier verd, faire un Lut si bien pleindre . . ." (X, 1-2); and of herself, the famous "Lut, compagnon de ma calamité" (XII), and XIV: "Tant que ma main pourra les cordes tendre / Du mignart Lut, pour tes graces chanter" (5-6). *Louise Labé: Oeuvres complètes,* ed. François Rigolot (Paris: Flammarion, 1986).

23. Marcel Tetel, "Le luth et la lyre de l'école lyonnaise," in *Il Rinascimento a Lione,* ed. A. Possenti and G. Mastrangelo (Rome: Edizioni dell'Ateneo, 1988), p. 951.

24. See JoAnn DellaNeva, "Illustrating the *Deffence*: Imitation and Poetic Perfection in Du Bellay's *Olive,*" *French Review* 61 (1987): pp. 45-47. This lyre does not refer to the *Amours,* which were yet to appear, but to the *Odes*; the reference is of particular interest because, as Caldarini notes of this poem, the expression "en lettres d'or" is a Petrarchan echo from *R* [*Petrarch's Lyric Poems: The Rime sparse and Other Lyrics*] 93, 2 in which Amor tells the poet: "Scrivi quel che vedesti in lettre d'oro" (*Olive* ed., p. 116).

25. Du Bellay, *Oeuvres poétiques,* IV, ed. Henri Chamard (Paris: E. Cornely, 1908), vv. 17-20, 73-80; Du Bellay contrasts this lyre to the "luc vanteur" praising princes, "ces faulx dieux." Ronsard will later depict Orpheus breaking his "luc payen" to follow the "chanson chrestienne" in his ode *Aux Soeurs Seymours*; see Michel Dassonville, *Ronsard: Etude historique et littéraire, III: Prince des Poètes ou Poète des Princes* (Geneva: Droz, 1976), pp. 19-20.

26. Cave, *Cornucopian Text,* p. 267; on the poem as a whole see pp. 256-68.

27. For discussion of the varied critical opinion on the question, see Isidore Silver, *Ronsard and the Hellenistic Renaissance in France,* Part II: *Ronsard and the Grecian Lyre* (Geneva: Droz, 1981), pp. 83-112.

28. In his *Art poétique,* Gadoffre observes, Peletier du Mans characterizes the poet as a hero who presents himself as "la plus spectable personne du théâtre,

et ce théâtre est l'Univers'" (*Ronsard,* p. 20). Examples are abundant in Du Bellay's *Deffence,* in theatrical metaphors that drew the indignant objections of Barthélemy Aneau; see Margaret Ferguson, *Trials of Desire: Renaissance Defenses of Poetry* (New Haven: Yale University Press, 1983), p. 21. On the "motif héroïque" of the poet's enterprise see also Enea Balmas, *Littérature française: La Renaissance, II (1548-1570)* (Paris: Arthaud, 1974), pp. 74-75.

29. See Albert Py, *Imitation et Renaissance dans la poésie de Ronsard* (Geneva: Droz, 1984), who remarks that "la *Franciade* est présente dans des pièces bien antérieures à 1572" (p. 120).

30. "Ode à Michel de l'Hospital" (*L* III, pp. 148, 163); see Dassonville, *Prince des Poètes,* pp. 15-16. The text is dated by Laumonier as 1549.

31. Joachim Du Bellay, *Deffence et illustration de la langue françoyse,* ed. Henri Chamard (Paris: Didier, 1961).

32. Dassonville, *Prince des Poètes,* pp. 13-24. The crisis is reflected, he suggests, in the small number and the tenor of Ronsard's published pieces from fall 1550 until the publication of the early *Amours* in fall 1552.

33. See Dauvois, *Mnémosyne,* p. 103; these verses, she observes, are "déjà des 'avant-jeux' de l'oeuvre épique."

34. See Weber, ed., p. 605, note. The episode evidently caught Ronsard's imagination; he describes the Cardinal of Lorraine also playing the lute to evoke the heroic deeds of his family, "Comme Achille faisoit pour s'alleger un peu, / Bien qu'en l'ost des Gregeois Hector ruast le feu, / Et que l'horrible effroy de la trompe entonnée / Criast contre le bruit de la Lyre sonnée" (Hymne V of Book I, "De Charles Cardinal de Lorraine").

35. See the comments of Dauvois, *Mnémosyne,* pp. 194-96.

36. In fact, Ronsard's allegiance to the name of Homer is not matched by that to Homer's text; he finds much of his Cassandre instead in Virgil (*Aeneid* II and III) and in Lycophron. See Jacques Pineaux, "Ronsard et Homère dans les 'Amours' de Cassandre," *RHLF* [*Revue d'histoire Littéraire de la France*] 86 (1986): pp. 650-58.

37. *Délie* 417. On Scève's imitative strategy in this poem see Lori Walters, "Un mythe fondamental de la *Délie*—Maurice Scève—Prométhée," *Romanic Review* 80 (1989): p. 183.

38. Etienne Jodelle, *L'Amour obscur,* ed. Robert Melançon (Paris: La Différence, 1991), p. 63 (poem XLI, vv. 5-8).

39. For a useful reappraisal of the reception of Petrarch in France see Jean Balsamo, *Les Rencontres des Muses: Italianisme et anti-italianisme dans les Lettres françaises de la fin du XVIe siècle* (Geneva: Slatkine, 1992), pp. 217-54.

40. See Paul Laumonier, "Ronsard poète pétrarquiste avant 1550," in *Mélanges Gustave Lanson* (Paris: Hachette, 1922), p. 109. Laumonier points out that in these poems for Cassandre Ronsard takes as his models poets such as Catullus, Ovid, and the Latin poet Jean Second and that he celebrates other ladies in equally sensuous accents borrowed from yet other poets. On the "veine gauloise" of Ronsard's poetry in this period see also Desonay, *Ronsard poète de l'amour. Livre premier. Cassandre,* p. 58.

41. For examples see Yvonne Bellenger, "Pétrarquisme et contr'amours chez quelques poètes français du XVIe siècle," in *Der Petrarkistische Diskurs,* ed. Klaus W. Hempfer and Gerhard Regn (Stuttgart: Franz Steiner Verlag, 1993), pp. 353-73, esp. pp. 359-60.

42. See Balmas, *Littérature française,* p. 73.

43. See André Gendre, ed., *Les Amours et les Folastries (1552-1560)* (Paris: Le Livre de Poche, 1993), p. 484: in this "sonnet étonnant, Ronsard supplie sa belle de mettre fin à son manège pétrarquiste et de dire clairement oui ou non," but only to reestablish "le *dissidio* pétrarquiste" in what follows.

44. See Marc Bensimon, "Introduction" to Ronsard, *Les Amours* (Paris: GF-Flammarion, 1981), p. 16.

45. See, for example, Pierre de Nolhac, *Ronsard et l'Humanisme* (Paris: Champion, 1921), p. 224; Charles Dédéyan, "Ronsard et Bembo," in *Ronsard e l'Italia/Ronsard in Italia,* Atti del I° Convegno del Gruppo di Studio sul Cinquecento francese (Fasano di Puglia: Schena, 1988), p. 32.

46. Laumonier, "Ronsard poète pétrarquiste," pp. 112-14. The poems appear among the "premières pièces" in *L* I, pp. 35-39.

47. On this poem see Fredi Chiappelli, *Studi sul linguaggio del Petrarca: La canzone delle visioni* (Florence: Olschki, 1971).

48. *Orlando Furioso,* VII, xiv (see *L* I, p. 38, n. 1; Laumonier, "Ronsard poète pétrarquiste," p. 114).

49. Dassonville, *Prince des Poètes,* p. 25.

50. Laumonier suggests both the first and the third canzoni of the *Rime* as Ronsard's inspiration and observes correlations with other poems by Petrarch as well (*L* I, pp. 35-39); in "Ronsard poète pétrarquiste" he notes that vv. 21-38 are from stanzas 3 and 6 of "Nel dolce tempo" (p. 112).

51. For Petrarch's versions of these Ovidian episodes, see Dennis Dutschke, *Francesco Petrarca: Canzone XXIII from First to Final Version* (Ravenna: Longo, 1977).

52. See Joukovsky, *La Gloire,* esp. p. 335.

53. Du Bellay here imitates an Italian sonnet by Hercole Bentivoglio; see Ernesta Caldarini, "Nuove fonti italiane dell'*Olive,*" *BHR* [*Bibliothèque d'Humanisme et Renaissance*] 27 (1965): pp. 411-12.

54. This flight "par l'univers" is the same that Ronsard would wish to achieve for Cassandre's name to make its renown equal to that of Laura in the poem "Que n'ay-je, Dame, & la plume & la grace" cited above. For this "horizontal"—earthly—concept of the poet's flight see David Cowling, "Ronsard, Du Bellay et Ennius: L'Image du vol dans une ode de Ronsard," *Nouvelle Revue du seizième siècle* 9 (1991): pp. 45-53.

55. Joukovsky cites as example Du Bellay's ode "De l'immortalité des poëtes" (*La Gloire,* pp. 335-38).

56. Calderini points out the translation of the final verse of Ariosto's sonnet X, "che morrei cigno, ove tacendo io moro," and that Barthélemy Aneau clearly regarded the motif as affectation, objecting that "swans die without singing, whatever the fables say" (*L'Olive,* ed., p. 63).

57. Desonay, *Ronsard poète de l'amour. Livre premier. Cassandre,* p. 75: "chez Pétrarque, au contraire, le poète ne se compare à un cygne que parce que, devenu chenu à la suite des refus de Laura, il n'a plus d'autre consolation que de pleurer, aux rives du fleuve, ses espérances mortes."

58. Here as elsewhere, Du Bellay combines the swan image with the story of Icarus; see Mark Eigeldinger, "Le mythe d'Icare dans la poésie française du XVIe siècle," *Cahiers de l'Association Internationale des Etudes françaises* 25 (1973): esp. pp. 265-66.

59. For Ronsard's various mentions of Petrarch see Rosa Maria Frigo, "Pétrarque devant le Tribunal de Ronsard," *Ronsard e l'Italia/Ronsard in Italia* (Fasano di Puglia: Schena, 1988), and on this poem, p. 174.

60. This flattering attribution, a response to Delbene, was not unambiguous: "Rabaissé par son interlocuteur au rang, même illustre, d' 'imitateur' de Pétrarque, Ronsard, en retour, [lui] accordait bien volontiers ce title." See Jean Balsamo, "Note sur l'*Elégie à Bartolomeo Delbene Florentin,*" *Revue des Amis de Ronsard* 10 (1997): esp. pp. 154-55.

61. The latter examples are cited by Frigo, "Pétrarque devant le Tribunal de Ronsard," p. 168.

62. Yvonne Bellenger, "Ronsard imitateur infidèle de Pétrarque," in *Petrarca e la cultura europea,* ed. Luisa Rotondi Secchi Tarugi (Milan: Nuovi Orizzonti, 1997), p. 228.

63. Jodelle, *L'amour obscure,* pp. 65-66 (sonnet XLIV).

64. See Giovanni Parenti, "L'Infedeltà di Penelope e il Petrarchismo di Ronsard," *BHR* 49 (1987): pp. 558-60.

65. See L. Baldacci, *Il petrarchismo italiano nel Cinquecento* (Milan-Naples: Riccardo Ricciardi, 1957), ch. 1, "Il Petrarca specchio di vita"; Enrico Carrara, "La leggenda di Laura," in his *Studi Petrarcheschi e altri scritti* (Turin: Bottega d'Erasmo, 1959), pp. 79-111; François Lecercle, "La fabrique du texte: Les commentaires du *Canzoniere* de Pétrarque à la Renaissance," *Etudes de littérature ancienne* 3 (1987): pp. 167-80.

66. See William J. Kennedy, *Authorizing Petrarch* (Ithaca: Cornell University Press, 1994), pp. 45-52.

67. See Terence Cave, "Scève's *Délie*: Correcting Petrarch's Errors," in *Pre-Pléiade Poetry,* ed. Jerry C. Nash (Lexington, Ky.: French Forum, 1985), p. 113; for an astute discussion of the detail of these components see Kennedy, *Authorizing Petrarch,* pp. 45-52.

68. The fact distances the collection from its noted precursor, Dante's "libello" known as the *Vita Nuova,* in which the lyrics are inserted into a retrospective narrative that offers the reader both an account of personal experience and its "meaning." For Petrarch's response to the *Vita Nuova* see Sara Sturm-Maddox, *Petrarch's Metamorphoses: Text and Subtext in the Rime sparse* (Columbia: University of Missouri Press, 1985), ch. 3: "Dante and Beatrice: The Stilnovist Subtext."

69. See Marco Santagata, "Connessioni intertestuali nel *Canzoniere* del Petrarca," *Strumenti critici* 26 (1975): pp. 80-112, and Sturm-Maddox, *Petrarch's Metamorphoses.* See also Silvia Longhi, "Il tutto e le parti nel sistema di un canzoniere (Giovanni Della Casa)," *Strumenti critici* 13 (1979): pp. 265-300.

70. See Roberto Fedi, *La memoria della poesia: Canzonieri, lirici e libri di rime nel Rinascimento* (Rome: Salerno, 1990), pp. 74-75. Bembo, he suggests, marks the transition from a "weak" fifteenth-century Petrarchism to one that seeks to establish its own uncontested warrant of lyricism in part through the imposition of a *cornice,* or frame story.

71. In part through Bembo's attentions, both as editor (1501) and as author of the *Prose della volgar lingua* (1525), the vernacular Petrarch was "revitalized' and put into circulation as textual example"; some 167 editions of the *Rime* were published in Italy during the sixteenth century. See Fedi, *La memoria della poesia,* pp. 35, 43-48.

72. Olivier Millet, "Le tombeau de la morte et la voix du poète: la mémoire de Pétrarque en France autour de 1533," in *Regards sur le passé dans l'Europe des XVIe-XVIIe siècles* (Bern: Lang, 1997), p. 189.

73. See Jean Balsamo, "Marot et les origines du pétrarquisme français (1530-1540)," in *Clément Marot, "Prince des poëtes françois" 1496-1996,* ed. Gérard Defaux and Michel Simonin (Paris: Champion, 1997), pp. 325-31; and J. E. Kane, "L'italianisme dans l'oeuvre poétique de François Ier," *Studi francesi* 84 (1984): pp. 485-94.

74. On Scève's "discovery" see Verdun L. Saulnier, *Maurice Scève* (Paris: Klincksieck, 1948-49), 1: pp. 38-48; Enzo Giudici, "Bilancio di un 'annosa questione': Maurice Scève e la 'scoperta' della 'tomba' di Laura," *Quaderni di filologia e lingue romanze. Ricerche svolte nell'Università di Maserata* (Rome: Ed. dell'Ateneo, 1980), 2: 7-70; Millet, "Le tombeau de la morte"; and Balsamo, "Marot et les origines du pétrarquisme français," in whose view the "discovery" was probably organized by Alamanni and promoted a connection between the king and Petrarch, "deux François," for political ends (pp. 529-30). Gérard Defaux cites further indications of the king's decisive role in the diffusion of Petrarchism in France in 1533-34 in "Des poèmes oubliés de Clément Marot: Le 'prince des Poetes Françoys' et *Les fleurs de Poesie* de 1534," *Travaux de Littérature* 5 (1992): pp. 37-65; see esp. p. 54.

75. The poems were to appear, under the same title, as the first book of Philieul's translation of *Toutes les Euvres vulgaires de Francoys Petrarque* in 1555; see Giovanna Bellati, "Il primo traduttore del *Canzoniere* petrarchesco nel Rinascimento francese: Vasquin Philieul," *Aevum* 59 (1985): 371-73.

76. Balsamo characterizes the collection as a "laboratory of forms" that in fact created the French sonnet (*Les Rencontres des Muses,* p. 222).

77. *Laure d'Avignon de Vasquin Philieul* (Paris: Actes Sud-Papiers, 1987), p. 27. Bellati notes that, again like Vellutello, Philieul frequently stresses the connections between groups of poems read as moments of a single episode (p. 379).

78. The six sonnets chosen by Marot for translation demonstrate his understanding of the structure of the *recueil* and that he accepted it as a coherent ensemble of texts ("Marot et les origines du pétrarquisme," p. 333). Enea Balmas suggests that both Marot and Peletier attempt to achieve a "thematic" suggestion of the Italian collection as a whole, in presenting their translations of a few poems in the order of the original and respecting the traditional selection "in vita" and "in morte." See "Prime traduzioni del *Canzoniere* nel Cinquecento francese," in *Traduzione e tradizione europea del Petrarca* (Padua: Antenore, 1975), pp. 47-50.

79. Balsamo, for whom Marot was the inventor of French "Petrarchism," comments that he seems to have had "a strange reticence with regard to his invention" ("Marot et les origines du pétrarquisme français," p. 336).

80. An account of the "discovery" was included in the preface to an Italian edition of the *Rime* that Jean de Tournes dedicated to the Lyonnais poet in 1545, one year after the appearance of the *Délie*. See the observations of JoAnn DellaNeva, *Song and Counter-Song: Scève's "Délie" and Petrarch's "Rime"* (Lexington, Ky.: French Forum, 1983), p. 19.

81. See François Rigolot, *Le texte de la Renaissance, des Rhétoriqueurs à Montaigne* (Geneva: Droz, 1982), pp. 176-77.

82. Doranne Fenoaltea, *"Si haulte Architecture": The Design of Scève's "Délie"* (Lexington, Ky.: French Forum, 1982), pp. 23-24; Cave, "Scève's *Délie*," pp. 112-14. The reader might also recognize the impact of the *Trionfi*, Petrarch's own rewriting in a different key of the story of his love for Laura, particularly significant in the closing poem of the *Délie*; see Cave, "Scève's *Délie*," pp. 114-16. The *Délie* is cited from *Maurice Scève: Délie,* ed. I. D. McFarlane (Cambridge, England: Cambridge University Press, 1966) (= *D*).

83. For the importance of this poem in defining Scève's broad imitative strategy, his "rewriting" of Petrarch, see DellaNeva, *Song and Counter-Song,* pp. 25-32; see also Doranne Fenoaltea, "Establishing Contrasts: An Aspect of Scève's Use of Petrarch's Poetry in the *Délie*," *Studi francesi* 55 (1975): pp. 18-19. Nancy Frelick calls attention also to Scève's other allusion to the bitterness of the laurel (*D* 310); see *Délie as Other: Toward a Poetics of Desire in Scève's Délie* (Lexington, Ky.: French Forum, 1994), pp. 77-78.

84. See JoAnn DellaNeva, "Poetry, Metamorphosis, and the Laurel: Ovid, Petrarch, and Scève," *French Forum* 7 (1982): pp. 197-209. Simone Perrier points out that in these poems—dizains 102, 175, 388, 407, and 417—is sketched "une démarche

d'appropriation du laurier de Pétrarque-Apollon, ce laurier amoureux *et* poétique"; see "Inscription et écriture dans *Délie*," *Europe* nos. 691-92 (1986): 139-50; here p. 145.

85. See especially Hans Staub, "Rhodanus rodens: Métamorphoses d'un thème poétique de Pétrarque à Maurice Scève," *Studi di Letteratura Francese* 4 (1975): pp. 106-23; Fenoaltea, "Establishing Contrasts," pp. 19-20.

86. See DellaNeva, *Song and Counter-Song*, pp. 32-39; Walters, "Un mythe fondamental de la *Délie*," p. 183. For the *Rime* as the "negative intertext" of the *Délie* see Rigolot, *Le Texte de la Renaissance*, pp. 173-77.

87. Jerry C. Nash, "'Mont côtoyant le Fleuve et la Cité': Scève, Lyons, and Love," *French Review* 69 (1996): p. 944.

88. For the text of the 1559 preface "Au Lecteur" see Caldarini, ed., *L'Olive*, pp. 167-70.

89. Ibid., p. 13.

90. For Du Bellay's strategy in this poem see William J. Kennedy, "Ronsard's Petrarchan Textuality," *Romanic Review* 77 (1986): pp. 91-92; JoAnn DellaNeva, "Du Bellay: Reader of Scève, Reader of Petrarch," *Romanic Review* 79 (1988): pp. 402-03.

91. *Oeuvres poétiques, II: Recueils de Sonnets,* ed. Henri Chamard (rept. Paris: Marcel Didier, 1970), pp. 240-41.

92. Du Bellay, *Deffence*; text and translation cited from Margaret Ferguson, *Trials of Desire*, p. 42.

93. On this metaphor see Thomas M. Greene, "Petrarch and the Humanist Hermeneutic," in *Italian Literature, Roots and Branches: Essays in Honor of Thomas Goddard Bergin*, ed. G. Rimanelli and K. J. Atchity (New Haven: Yale University Press, 1976), pp. 215-17, and G. W. Pigman III, "Versions of Imitation in the Renaissance," *Renaissance Quarterly* 33 (1980): pp. 4-7.

94. Du Bellay does not insist on the model here, but it is repeated in the treatise: "Mais entende celuy qui voudra immiter, que ce n'est chose facile de bien suivre les vertuz d'un bon aucteur, & quasi comme se transformer en lui" [But he who wishes to imitate should understand that it is not an easy thing to follow well the virtues of a good author, and almost (as it were) transform oneself into him].

95. Thomas M. Greene, *The Light in Troy: Imitation and Discovery in Renaissance Lyric* (New Haven: Yale University Press, 1982), pp. 192, 194, 198-99.

96. Caldarini, *L'Olive,* notes the sonnet by G. Mozzarello published in Giolito I, p. 70.

97. Pasquier (*Le Monophile*, 1555) and Ronsard ("Response aux injures") are cited by Hermann Lindner, "Petrarkismus, Komödie, Stilistik: Normerfüllung und Normdekonstruktion in Ronsard's *Sonnets pour Hélène*," recalling the fundamental ontological difference between *Textproduzent* and *Textsprecher*, in *Der Petrarkistische Diskurs*, ed. Klaus W. Hempfer and Gerhard Regn (Stuttgart: Franz Steiner Verlag, 1993), pp. 392-93 (n. 24) and 398 (n. 50).

98. John O'Brien, "Foreword: Mercurian Exegesis," in *(Re)Interprétations: Etudes sur le seizième siècle*, ed. John O'Brien and Terence Cave (Ann Arbor: Department of Romance Languages, University of Michigan, 1995), p. 4.

Cynthia Skenazi (essay date 2000)

SOURCE: Skenazi, Cynthia. "*Dispositio* as an Art of Peace in Ronsard's Poetry." In *Peace and Negotiation: Strategies for Coexistence in the Middle Ages and the Renaissance*, edited by Diane Wolfthal, pp. 195-211. Turnhout, Belgium: Brepols, 2000.

[*In the following essay, Skenazi discusses the ordering of poetry within Ronsard's poetic* oeuvre, *which the poet revised throughout his lifetime as he considered the arrangement of poems to be as important as their composition.*]

Until his death, Pierre de Ronsard continually revised the order of his *Oeuvres*. In his *Oraison funèbre de Monsieur de Ronsard*, Jacques Davy Du Perron remarks that Ronsard organized his poems "comme il vouloit qu'ils feussent leuz et recitez a l'advenir" (the way he wanted [them] to be recited and read by future generations).[1] This preoccupation with order comes as no surprise, since Ronsard considered *dispositio* as closely related to *inventio*. In his *Abbregé de l'art poëtique françois* (1565), he wrote: ". . . & ne fault point douter, qu'apres avoir bien & hautement inventé, que la belle disposition de vers ne s'ensuyve, d'autant que la disposition suit l'invention mere de toutes choses, comme l'ombre faict le corps. . . . la disposition despend de la belle invention, laquelle consiste en une elegante et parfaicte collocation et ordre des choses inventées, et ne permet pas ce qui appartient à un lieu soit mis en l'autre . . ." (one should not doubt that after having well and highly invented, a good disposition of verses should follow, for disposition follows invention, which is the mother of all things, as the shadow follows the body . . . dispositio depends on *inventio*; it is an elegant and perfect arrangement and ordering of things invented, and it does not permit that which belongs to one place be put in another one).[2] Whereas, in rhetorical terms, *dispositio* is a matter of arrangement, *inventio* is a process of finding or conceiving the things to be ordered. In a well-known passage of the *Abbregé de l'art poëtique françois,* Ronsard wrote: "L'invention n'est autre chose que le bon naturel d'une imagination concevant les Idées & formes de toutes choses qui se peuvent imaginer tant celestes que terrestres, animées ou inanimes [*sic*], pour apres les representer, descrire & imiter . . ." (Invention is nothing else but the good nature of an imagination conceiving Ideas and forms of all things one can imagine, whether celestial or terrestrial, animated or inanimated, so as to represent them, describe them, and imitate them; XIV.12-13). The function of *dispositio* and *inventio* was a central question in contemporary rhetorical treatises. Ronsard did not go as far as Jacques Peletier du Mans who, in his *Art Poétique* (1544), considered *dispositio* as part of *inventio.*[3] Nevertheless, he saw them as closely interwoven.

Drawing upon such observations, critics have attempted to interpret the order of some of Ronsard's collections despite the fact that this kind of exegesis raises obvious methodological problems:[4] several centuries later, some implications of the order of a group of poems or the reasons for its transformation from one edition to another are forever lost. One can easily invent an order by making connections that Ronsard did not have in mind or by neglecting some relations intentionally made by the poet. In a broader sense, any interpretation of *dispositio* heavily depends on the critic's acquaintance with Ronsard's culture and with the historical context of the day. In spite of these limitations, it is nevertheless possible to detect some "patterns of intention" in the order of a group of texts. Although *dispositio* cannot be deciphered or translated like a coded message, I shall argue that it contributes to an objectification of a shared meaning between a writer and his targeted audience.

By analyzing the order of several poems on peace by Ronsard, I wish to explore some implications of *dispositio* as a spatial metalanguage. In these texts, order—which is at the heart of Ronsard's representation of peace—provides the poet with a strategy for making the practice of an "official" type of poetry (aiming at idealizing the French kingdom) fully compatible with the expression of Ronsard's own ambitions. In this respect, *dispositio* is essential for fashioning a composite identity of the nation and of Henri II as fierce warriors and as lovers of peace, but it also provides the poet an opportunity to convey his sincere desire to see his country at peace in an increasingly unstable political context.

War and Peace: Fashioning a French National Identity

A brief reminder of some historical events of the day might help us situate Ronsard's poems. From 1558 to 1559, Ronsard wrote several poems on the events leading to the signing of the treaty of Cateau-Cambrésis between France and Spain. Signed on April 1559, this treaty was of utmost importance for France since it put an end to centuries of wars in Italy. In 1557, the French had been defeated by the Duc de Savoie (the ally of the Spanish) at Saint-Quentin, during the siege of which the Connétable Anne de Montmorency was captured. In early 1558, François de Guise had retaliated by the capture of Calais from the English, and in June he had taken Thionville. However, the Maréchal de Termes suffered a major defeat at Gravelines. In late August, the French army led by François de Guise was facing the Spanish soldiers close to Amiens, and Henri II and Philip II of Spain had rejoined their troops. In September or October 1558, Ronsard published an *Exhortation au Camp du Roy pour bien combattre le jour de la bataille* to cheer up the French warriors. But rather than fight, the two kings began negotiating for peace. Both of them were increasingly concerned with internal political problems that required their immediate attention: an economic crisis, increasing social tensions, and alarming religious turmoils were threatening the stability of both countries.[5] The peace conference resumed at the Abbaye de Cercamp on 8 October 1558, and Ronsard quickly published an *Exhortation pour la Paix.* After 14 October 1558 (the date of Mellin de Saint-Gelais's death), the poet was named *conseiller et aumônier ordinaire du roi* and received a pension of 1,200 pounds and other favors. The promotion, which fully justified his 1554 title of *poëte du roi,* encouraged him to support Henri II's politics more zealously than ever. Obviously, the treaty of Cateau-Cambrésis was then being discussed, and Ronsard wrote a poem entitled *La Paix, Au Roy* claiming to convince Henri II to welcome peace.[6] A few weeks later, a *Chant de liesse* celebrated the settlement. Splendid feasts and royal weddings (among them, Marguerite, Henri II's sister, to Philibert-Emmanuel de Savoie) sealed the treaty, and a host of texts written by Du Bellay, Belleau, Aubert, and Des Autels welcomed the long-awaited peace.

Ronsard was clearly well informed about every political decision. The poet needed, however, to be aware of more than shifts in royal politics. The celebration of peace also required diplomatic skills, for the nobility, and especially the king, relied heavily on their military prowess to reaffirm their social identity.[7] A closer look at the sequence of *Exhortation au Camp du Roy, Exhortation pour la Paix,* and of *La Paix, Au Roy* reveals that Ronsard ordered them to portray his fellow citizens as fierce warriors *and* as lovers of peace.[8] In the first of these pieces, the *Exhortation au Camp du*

Roy, written in honor of the French warriors camping at Amiens in August 1558, Ronsard draws upon chivalrous ideals revived at the court of Henri II by fashionable books such as *Amadis de Gaule* and the *Roman de la Rose.* From the start, the poet praises Henri II, "nostre Roy, qui luymesme en personne, Veut les armes au poing deffendre sa couronne" (our King, who, in person, wants to defend his crown arms in fist; IX.4-5, lines 17-18). Following a hierarchical order, he then celebrates the nobles for giving their soldiers an example of courage and determination:

> Vous, les plus grands Seigneurs, montrez vous dili-
> 　gens
> A renger bien en ordre & vous & tous vos gens,
> Que la noble vertu de vostre race antique
> Ne soit point demantie en cest honneur bellique,
> Mais comme grans Seigneurs & les premiers du sang
> En defiant la mort, tenez le premier rang,
> Et par vostre vertu (qu'on ne sçauroit abattre)
> Montrez à vos soldas le chemin de combattre.
>
> 　　　　　　　　　　　　　　　(IX.5, lines 19-26)

(You, the highest Lords, show yourself diligent to put yourself and your people well in order, may the noble virtue of your ancient breed not be contradicted in this military honor, but like high Lords, and first of your breed, by challenging death, keep the first rank, and by your virtue [impossible to defeat] show your soldiers how to fight.)

In a very suggestive way, Ronsard imagines the noise of the cannons, the cries of the wounded soldiers; he describes the dead lying on the battlefield and ends the poem by predicting the forthcoming victory of the French army (IX.7-10, lines 1-112). The poet claims to be the voice of the nation and draws upon literary commonplaces of patriotic war poetry to go beyond the celebration of a factual event. Indeed, his poem elevates the warriors to a higher significance and validates their fight by immortalizing their memory (IX.10-11, lines 113-36).

Some critics have read the order of Ronsard's sequence as the sign of the poet's servility.[9] Yet, if the poet is willing to serve the king, he also proudly claims in other poems that he is not the other's servant.[10] Futhermore, this interpretation ignores Ronsard's preoccupation with ordering his texts. Rather than stress Ronsard's incoherences, the arrangement of the two poems emphasizes the protean intelligence of a court poet who gracefully accommodates to the changing moves of the prince. Contemporary treatises on courtly behavior (such as the famous *Cortegiano* by Baldassare Castiglione)[11] did indeed stress the need for the courtier to quickly adapt to the difficulties and contradictions of court life. In the sequence of the two *Exhortations,* this flexibility has poetic implications since it allows Ronsard to display fully his rhetorical skills by adopting the classical form of the debate (the *disputatio pro et contra*). The poet shows that he can be equally convincing either in a poem in favor of war or in a piece against it.

Furthermore, such an organization has obvious patriotic implications. By placing the **Exhortation pour la Paix** immediately after the **Exhortation au Camp du Roy pour bien combattre le jour de la bataille,** Ronsard exploits the sudden shift in royal politics and the chronological order of events. The repetition of the word *"Exhortation"* in the title of the two pieces contributes to their association in the reader's mind, creating a complex French identity, one which combines the strength of the perfect warrior with the spiritual virtues of the Christian deeply committed to peace. In an Erasmian spirit,[12] the **Exhortation pour la Paix** now encourages all Christians to cease their fratricide and to join together. The poet reminds his audience that war is for lions, wolves, and tigers, not for Christians; if Christians must fight, they should fight the Turks, usurpers of the Holy Land, and their natural enemies (IX.18-20, lines 57-79). Indeed this claim strikes an ironic note as Ronsard addresses the warriors of the *two* armies and, therefore, reminds the very Catholic Philip II of Spain of the essential law of brotherly love in the Gospels (Matt. 22.37-40; Mark 12.29-31; Luke 10.27). In this poem, concord is a process of civilization that Ronsard situates in a larger perspective by narrating the action of the cosmic peace to which I shall return shortly.

In the two **Exhortations,** the constant use of literary commonplaces on war and peace oversimplifies the portrait of the French elite and intensifies its persuasive effects. It comes as no surprise to notice that these poems were immediately translated into Latin (by Jean Dorat and François Thoor) so as to publicize to a broader audience in northern Europe a nationalistic representation of France as a paragon of chivalric *and* Christian humanist values.[13]

La Paix, Au Roy, which follows the two **Exhortations,** elaborates on their composite representation of French identity to emphasize the assumption that the end of war is peace. Ronsard now celebrates Henri II's spiritual journey from the perfect warrior to the guardian of peace. From the beginning of his reign (in 1547) to October 1558, Henri II had been almost continuously at war.[14] Significantly, the king, who was very fond of violent exercises, died in a tournament during the feasts celebrating the treaty of Cateau-Cambrésis. From the first lines of this poem, Ronsard therefore rightly observes

> Sire, quiconque soit qui fera votre histoire,
> Honorant vostre nom d'eternelle memoire,
> A fin qu'à tout jamais les peuples à venir
> De vos belles vertuz se puissent souvenir,

Dira, depuis le jour que nostre Roy vous fustes,
Et le sceptre François dans la main vous receustes,
Que vous n'avez cessé en guerre avoir vescu,
Meintenant le veinqueur, meintenant le veincu:
Dira, que vostre esprit (tresmagnanime Prince)
Ne s'est pas contenté de sa seulle province,
Mais par divers moyens, & par diverses fois
A tenté d'augmenter l'empire des François.

(IX.103-4, lines 1-11)

(Sire, whoever will write your history, honoring your name by eternal memory so that all the people to come would remember your beautiful virtues, will say that since the day you became king and received the French sceptre in your hand, you never stopped living in war; at times you were the victor, at times the vanquished party. This writer will say that your mind, very magnanimous Prince, was not satisfied with his only province, but through diverse means, and diverse occasions, attempted to expand the empire of the French people.)

The poet then proceeds by powerful contrasts, opposing the disadvantages of war, plunging mankind into sorrow, to the benefits of concord, bringing life's happiness. Once again, the argumentation heavily draws upon literary commonplaces, but, as in the two **Exhortations,** the use of rhetoric is a crucial part of Ronsard's strategy. After the celebration of the bravery and fortitude of the king, he stresses the powers to be derived from eloquence, moderation, and civility. Persuasion is more efficient and more fruitful than brutal strength (IX.113, lines 203-5). The poet therefore reminds his forty-year-old dedicatee that mature age has other pleasures than military prowess, pleasures that can flourish only when the country is at peace:

Il vaudroit beaucoup mieux, vous qui venez sur l'age
Ja grison, gouverner vostre Royal menage,
Vostre femme pudique, & voz nobles Enfans
Qu'aquerir par danger des lauriers triomphans:
Il vaudroit beaucoup mieux joyeusement bien vivre,
Ou bâtir vostre Louvre, ou lire dans un livre,
Ou chasser es forests, que tant vous travailler,
Et pour un peu de bien si long temps batailler.
Que souhaitez vous plus? la Fortune est muable,
Vous avez fait de vous meinte preuve honorable.
Il suffist, il suffist, il est temps desormais
Fouller la guerre aux pieds, & n'en parler jamais.

(IX.114, lines 221-32)

(It would be much more preferable, now that you are getting old, already with gray hair, to take care of your royal family, your chaste wife, and your noble children rather than to acquire through danger the laurels of triumph. It would be much more preferable to live joyfully well, or to build your Louvre, or to read a book, or to hunt in the forests, than to work so much, and to fight so much for such a little profit. What more do you wish? Fortune is changing; you have given many honorable proofs of your value. It is enough, it is enough; it is now time to trample war underfoot and never to speak of it again.)

Ronsard's concern for the king's cultural mission was significant since, according to contemporary sources, Henri II was not interested in literature.[15] But at the same time, the poet's description of his dedicatee's spiritual journey was also a way of flattering the king's imperialist ambitions. By welcoming peace and protecting the artists after a time of glorious conquests, the king would obviously follow the glorious example of the Roman emperor Augustus. The representation of Henri II as the French Augustus, a commonplace in the arts and letters of the time,[16] also serves Ronsard's self-propaganda; if Virgil and Horace helped secure Augustus's eternal fame, poets like Ronsard and architects like Pierre Lescot (who was renovating the Louvre) would bring the kingdom an everlasting fame. Henri II's love for peace will therefore be more fruitful than his youthful passion for war.[17] Ronsard's implicit association of Henri II with the emperor Augustus had several other diplomatic purposes as well. First, it allowed the poet to omit any specific allusion to the treaty of Cateau-Cambrésis, which was a total failure for France since, among other things, it meant the loss of the kingdom's possessions in nothern Italy. Second, by praising the king's prowess at war, Ronsard was putting the powerful Guises on his side, since members of this family played an important role in the French wars against Spain. Third, Ronsard advocated the views of Montmorency who, in contrast to the Guises, was an ardent proponent of peace and probably influenced the king's decision to sign the treaty of Cateau-Cambrésis.

In the two **Exhortations** and in **La Paix, Au Roy,** historical events mediate the construction of a complex French national and royal identity combining chivalric values with humanist and cultural interests. To create this composite image of fortitude and civility, the crucial strategy is *dispositio*. The sequence demonstrates the art of a court poet who ingeniously exploits the political situation so as to flatter the French elite. Yet this celebration is fully compatible with Ronsard's sincere patriotism; by their content and their order, the three poems emphasize the poet's will to serve his king well, under any circumstances, and to be a public personality by praising every major event in his country.

I wish now to investigate the implications of this perspective in the **Ode de la Paix** and in the *dispositio* of the Pindaric odes of Book I of Ronsard's **Odes** from 1560 to 1587. In these poems, as we shall see, peace is again a process of ordering.

THE "ODE DE LA PAIX" AND THE "DISPOSITIO"
OF THE PINDARIC ODES FROM BOOK I OF THE
"ODES" (1560-87)

The **Ode de la Paix** had initially been written for the 1550 peace between France and England. By adapting a prestigious Greek model—Pindar—in the vernacular,

Ronsard was actively contributing to the *translatio studii* in favor of France.[18] Furthermore, as a song of harmony with the cosmic order, the genre of the ode was an ideal way of situating the praise of the royal politics in a larger perspective. In order to celebrate the 1550 settlement, the poem first describes the fabulous origins of the universe as a process of organization. A mythic peace chases away chaos and combines the various parts of the cosmos (in the Greek sense of arrangement) in a coherent whole:

> C'est toy [la Paix] qui desus ton echine
> Soustiens ferme ceste machine,
> Medecinant chaque element
> Quand une humeur par trop abonde,
> Pour joindre les membres du monde
> D'un contrepois egallement.

> (III.24-25, lines 319-24)

(It is you who on your back solidly supports the world, curing each element when one humour abounds too much, joining the members of the world in a good balance.)

The same fable is repeated in the ***Exhortation pour la Paix,*** and in ***La Paix, Au Roy***:

> La Paix premierement composa ce grand monde,
> La paix mist l'air, le feu, toute la terre, & l'onde
> En paisible amitié, & la paix querella
> Au Chaos le discord, & le chassa delà
> Pour accorder ce Tout . . .

> (***Exhortation pour la Paix,*** IX.25, lines 195-99)

(Peace first composed this large world, Peace accorded the air, fire, all the earth, and the water in peaceful friendship, and Peace quarrelled with Discord in Chaos and chased it out so as to articulate this Whole.)

> Apres avoir par ordre arrangé la machine,
> Et lié ce grand Corps d'une amitié divine,
> Elle fist atacher à cent cheines de fer
> Le malheureux Discord aux abysmes d'Enfer

> (***La Paix, Au Roy,*** IX.108, lines 73-76)

(After having arranged the world through order and linked this large body with a divine friendship, Peace had poor Discord attached by a hundred iron chains to the abyss of Inferno.)

As critics have stressed, Ronsard's description of the organizing function of the mythic peace draws upon several classical sources that include Aristotle's *Metaphysics* and Ficino's *Commentary on Plato's Symposium.*[19] Furthermore, these lines also recall one of the widely known theses of St. Augustine on peace. In the *De Civitate Dei,* he remarks: "Pax itaque corporis est ordinata temperatura partium" (Peace of the body is the well organized balance of its parts; 19.13).[20] Ronsard's lines interpret St. Augustine's observation in pagan terms: the "body" now takes on a cosmological meaning.

In the ***Ode de la Paix,*** the universe and the kingdom of France are organized according to the same principles: the king reproduces in his country the ordering action of the cosmic peace. The representation of the king as a mediator between two "worlds" fully complies with Marsilio Ficino's philosophy. As André Chastel writes, "An original feature of Ficino's ontology is the theory of the *primum in aliquo genere* that puts at the top of each group of visible or invisible individuals a privileged being responsible for harmonizing this group with the immediate superior step."[21] In Ronsard's poem, the superiority of the king is not an understanding of things themselves but rather an intuition of the connections between the cosmos and human realms. In the ***Ode de la Paix,*** the history of French monarchy as a whole is oriented toward the restoration of that order. Francion, the legendary ancestor of the kings of France, is informed of this mission by prediction:

> C'est ce Henri qui batira
> Les Pergames de notre ville,
> Laquelle plus ne sentira
> Le fer meurtrier d'un autre Achille.

> (III.20, lines 257-60)

(It is this Henri who will build the Troy of our city that will no longer feel the murderous iron of another Achilles.)

This prediction (the foundation by Henri II of a new Troy where peace will flourish) would be accomplished through centuries of phases of peace and war that correspond to alternating periods of discord and concord at the cosmic level. After this epic section comes a hymn to political peace and the virtues of Henri II, of which generosity is not the least. After a brief digression about the practice of poetry, Ronsard offers the king poetic immortality and, in exchange for his gift, requests the king's protection and a financial reward.

In 1552, Ronsard inserted the ***Ode de la Paix*** into Book V of the ***Odes.*** Eight years later, the poem was placed at the opening of Book I of the ***Odes*** (in the first edition of the ***Oeuvres,*** in 1560), to celebrated the treaty of Cateau-Cambrésis. In contrast to the constant revision of the order of the poems of the ***Odes*** from one edition to the next, the *dispositio* of this first section (the Pindaric section) became definitive in 1560:[22]

(1) Ode au Roi (previously entitled ***Ode de la Paix***)

(2) A lui-mesme

(3) A la Roine sa femme

(4) A Madame Marguerite, soeur du Roi, Duchesse de Savoie

(5) Au reverendissime Prince Charles Cardinal de Lorraine

(6) La Victoire de François de Bourbon, Conte d'Anguien, à Cerizoles

(7) Au Seigneur de Carnavalet

(8) Usure à luimesme

(9) La Victoire de Gui de Chabot, seigneur de Jarnac

(10) A Michel de L'Hospital, chancelier de France

(11) A Jouachim Du Bellai Angevin

(12) A Bouju, Angevin

(13) A Jan d'Aurat

(14) A Anthoine de Baïf

(15) A Jan Martin[23]

By placing the *Ode de la Paix* at the beginning of the Pindaric section, Ronsard fully elaborated on its prediction and celebrated the ideal city founded by the king and inhabited by exemplary contemporary figures.[24] In a hierarchical manner, first comes Henri II who is the only dedicatee of two odes closely linked (odes 1 and 2),[25] then the royal family (the queen and Henri II's sister, odes 3 and 4), the noble warriors who are ranked according to their births and their responsibilities (odes 5-10 and 12), and finally the writers who bestow immortality on all these heroes (odes 11 and 13-15). The sequence combines the praise of nobility with the celebration of arms and of culture: by his or her exemplary virtues, everyone contributes to the well-functioning of the kingdom. Peace is the natural consequence of such a careful organization: the *dispositio* of the Pindaric odes offers a visual and spatial interpretation of St. Augustine's most famous thesis on peace. In chapter 19 of the *De Civitate Dei,* upon which Ronsard partly drew his representation of cosmic peace, St. Augustine wrote that "ordo est parium dispariumque rerum sua cuique loca tribuens dispositio" (order is the disposition of beings equal and inequal, by designating to each one the place that is suitable). St. Augustine then remarked: "Pax omnium rerum tranquillitas ordinis" (Peace is the tranquillity of the order of all things; 19.13). In the *dispositio* of Ronsard's Pindaric section, St. Augustine's Christian perspective on peace and order takes on a civic meaning. As in chapter 19 of the *De Civitate Dei,* but at a social level, the order of the poems visually associates hierarchy with the notion of joining together under the king's authority to form the perfect community epitomized by such a well-organized parade. The banquet described in ode 2 celebrates the conviviality of the idealized city founded by Henri II:

> Comme un qui prend une coupe,
> Seul honneur de son tresor,
> Et donne à boire à la troupe
> Du vin qui rit dedans l'or:
> Ainsi versant la rousée,
> Dont ma langue est arousée,
> Sus la race de VALOIS,
> En mon dous Nectar j'abreuve
> Le plus grand Roi qui se treuve,
> Soit en armes ou en lois.

(I.61, lines 1-10)

(Like one who takes a goblet, the only honor of his treasure, and gives the troop to drink wine which smiles within the gold, so pouring the dew with which my tongue is watered on the breed of Valois, with my sweet nectar, I water the greatest king that ever exists, either in arms or in law.)

After the *Ode de la Paix,* the guests at the banquet thank the king for making this reunion possible. The poet is the ambassador of the newly founded city; his voice expresses the joy of the community as a whole. The song and the wine circulate from one person to another, and the circle of guests keeps growing. The poet calls upon everyone to rejoice at the feast of words and food and extends his invitation to the reader.[26]

The constant reference in these odes to the Pindaric (and Horatian) *topos* of *ut architectura poesis* (poetry is like architecture) takes on its full meaning; Ronsard uses the musical origin of the ode (which is a song)[27] to build the "monument of a melody," in Paul Valéry's words.[28] In this section, *dispositio* is an art of textures. An observation on the transitions in Ovid's *Metamorphoses* made by Quintilian, which was later rephrased by Jacques Peletier du Mans, describes this process well: in these poems, Ronsard "il a invanté la maniere de lier tant de diverses Fables ansamble, e de donner a toutes leur place si propre, qu'il samble que ce soet une narracion perpetuele" (invented a way of linking so many different fables together, and giving to all of them the most appropriate place, so that it seems to be a perpetual narration).[29] As critics have stressed, a complex process of digressions and amplifications orchestrates the fifteen odes as well as each ode in particular—especially the longer ones such as the *Ode de la Paix* and the *Ode to Michel de L'Hospital.*[30]

A passage of transition between the epic episode and the hymn to political peace in the *Ode de la Paix* epitomizes this poetic practice:

> Celui qui en peu de vers
> Etraint un sujet divers,
> Se mét au chef la couronne:
> De cette fleur que voici,
> Et de celle, & celle aussi,
> La mouche son miel façonne.
>
> Diversement, ô Paix heureuse,
> Tu es la garde vigoureuse
> Des peuples, & de leurs cités:
> Des roiaumes les clefs tu portes
> Tu ouvres des villes les portes,
> Serenant leurs adversités.

(III.23-24, lines 295-306)

(He who in a few lines embraces a diverse subject puts a crown on his head; from this flower, and this one, and this one too the bee makes its honey. In various ways, O happy Peace, you are the vigorous guardian of the people and of their cities; you carry the keys of kingdoms, you open the doors of cities, calming their hostilities.)

The bee and the crown are royal attributes and announce the hymn to political peace, which is developed in the second stanza. However, the weaving of the crown and the gathering work of the bee also refer to the activity of the poet, who is able to create a unique piece of art by combining various borrowings and by coordinating heterogeneous motives in a homogeneous poem. The poet is to the ode what the king is to the city: both of them draw upon a cosmic model to maintain an organic relation between the elements constitutive of their respective "worlds."

By valuing hierarchy and cohesion, the *dispositio* of the fifteen odes spatializes the "official" story of the kingdom: such a flattering representation excludes any allusion to existing social tensions.[31] Yet when Ronsard published the first edition of his *Oeuvres* (1560), the very notions underlining the *dispositio* of the Pindaric odes became more and more critical of aspects of French politics. Questions of order, organic coherence, and, consequently, of peace were at stake. The main goal of the treaty of Cateau-Cambrésis (April 1559) was to focus on the inner turmoils threatening the kingdom's stability; for Henri II, the alliance with Spain meant reinforcing religious intolerance. The Protestants were immediately conscious of the danger. In a letter dated 17 August 1558 Macar wrote to Calvin: "If the king obtains peace, he will put all his soul and his good, as he claims, in a war against the Lutherans to destroy to the root their breed and their name." Two months after the signing of the treaty, the Edict of Ecouen (2 June 1559) stated Henri II's firm intention not to be "troubled by this damned enterprise by the heretical enemies of our faith and religion."[32] In 1560, when Ronsard published his first edition of the *Oeuvres,* the instability in France was even worse. Henri II was dead, and François II, his successor, soon passed away. Yet the poet kept the dedication of the *Odes* to Henri II as if he literally did not know to whom he could offer his work and decided that the best strategy was to put it under a dead king's protection. Right after the turmoils at Amboise (March 1559), and before the massacre of Vassy, which marked the beginning of the first civil war (March 1562), who could possibly believe in a peace-keeping monarch or a collective devotion to the king?[33] In this perspective, the *dispositio* of the Pindaric odes veils and unveils the weaknesses and the incompetency of royal authority. The only place left for order and peace is ultimately the space defined by the sequence of these poems: a non-space organized by the poet rather than by the king. This is a pre-baroque point of view as defined by Gilles Deleuze: "The specificity of the baroque is not to fall into illusion or to escape from it.

It is to realize something with the illusion itself, or to give it a spiritual presence by reassembling bits and pieces in a collective unity."[34]

The imaginary palace described in ode I in Book II of the *Odes* could epitomize the political implications of this endeavor. In this poem, Ronsard echoed Pindar to address Henri II:

> Je te veil bâtir une ode,
> La maçonnant à la mode
> De tes palais honnorés,
> Qui voulontiers ont l'entrée
> De grands marbres acoutrée
> Et de haus piliers dorés,
>
> Affin que le frond de l'euvre
> Tout le bâtiment dequeuvre
> Estant richement vétu:
> Ainsi (PRINCE) je veil mettre
> Au premier trait de mon mettre
> Ta louange & ta vertu.
>
> (I.167, lines 1-12)

(I want to build you an ode, rendering it according to the fashion of your honored palaces which used to have the entry decorated with large marbles and golden high pillars, so that the facade of the work reveals the building as a whole, as richly decorated. Likewise, Prince, I want to put at the beginning of my rhyme your praise and your virtue.)

When the king of France was losing his aura, Ronsard offered him a triumphal entrance. The palace did not exist and was located in a fictitious world and time. Only the creative power of the artist could decorate the entrance in the most luxurious way in order to inspire an attitude of respect to a beholder standing in front of this imaginary and empty building.

Several centuries later, in our current *ère du soupçon,* these verses may well appear as the work of an opportunistic flatterer. Yet such a perspective would blatantly misunderstand and even ignore the poet's sincere patriotism and his will to serve the king and to celebrate his country. Ronsard's position at the court was that of *conseiller du roi,* and the poet did indeed try to act as a royal counselor—a view inspired by a classical tradition. Through and by the staging of an illusion, the poet attempted to convince the reader that such a magnificent spectacle was indeed possible. In this perspective, the order of the Pindaric odes functions as a *rappel à l'ordre; dispositio* teaches the king and the court the art of textures, and it reminds the reader and the dedicatees of serving the king in the interest of peace. The poet's claim of the efficiency of his art draws upon a Neoplatonist faith in the moral effects of poetry and song. The genre of the ode reinforces this didactic message: in Ronsard's own words, the ode aims at celebrating "celebrer jusques à l'extremité" (to the very end; I.48). Through exaggeration, the song intends to act heavily on the audience's emotions and opinions. Yet the approval of the audience is already inscribed into the text since, by definition, the ode assimilates the poet to the spokesman and the leader of an idealized community.

Like the king, the poet of the Pindaric odes represents himself as a mediator between the divine and the human realms: both of them have an intuitive understanding of the supernatural meaning of history. The importance of poetry as an art of teaching peace is further elaborated on the **Ode à Michel de L'Hospital,** which was incorporated into the Pindaric section of Book I of the **Odes** at the same time as the **Ode de la Paix** in the first edition of the **Oeuvres** (1560). In many ways, the two poems carry on a dialogue. By their length, both are in striking contrast with the other poems of the Pindaric sequence. Just like the **Ode de la Paix,** the **Ode à Michel de L'Hospital** uses myth to narrate the genesis of the universe: the poem describes a gigantomachy inspired by Hesiod's verses (a major intertext of the description of the origins of the universe in the **Ode de la Paix**) to celebrate the institution of concord and order.[35] The praise of Henri II, the founder of civic peace in the **Ode de la Paix,** is further elaborated in the praise of his chancellor, the patron of poetry. This art is ultimately the only way of bringing peace back in France and of giving the nation immortal fame. The poet predicts that L'Hospital will defeat the armies of Ignorance;[36] the Muses will then reestablish the principles of cosmic harmony in the kingdom and in their people,[37] and an age of peace and culture will soon flourish. The birth of the chancellor is therefore part of a larger encomium of the divine gift of poetry to human beings.

Ronsard's claim that poetry can shape the basic values of a collectivity and will bring peace back in France raises broader questions. Can poetry influence the social order? What kind of reception (or reading) theory does such a perspective imply? In a more general sense, is art an efficient tool for political propaganda and how can one measure its persuasive effects? Some events contemporary to Ronsard's edition of the **Oeuvres** may provide a way to frame these complex issues. Interestingly, during this period of political instability, the court adopted strategies very similar to Ronsard's Pindaric odes. A growing number of royal entries and of feasts (Ronsard participated in some of them) repeatedly staged idyllic and peaceful societies, or well-organized and idealized cities.[38] Like Ronsard's poems, these allegorical representations aimed at clarifying social relations and warding off the fear of civil wars. However, by elevating contemporary events to the status of myth, such figural language reinterprets them. In a similar way, the massive display of erudition in the Pindaric odes (an aspect harshly criticized by Marot's disciples

at the publication of the first edition of the **Odes** in 1550) drastically limits the didactic impact of these poems: Ronsard's targeted audience is obviously a small circle of learned readers who are already convinced of the ontological and social value of poetry. Just like the royal entries and the feasts, Ronsard's attempt to fashion an imaginary national identity ultimately emphasized the inability of royal power to control the increasing internal turmoils that would culminate in the St. Bartholomew's Day Massacre of the Protestants (24 August 1572). Peace was as fragile and artificial as its artistic representations.

Notes

I thank Heather Campbell for her insightful comment on this essay and for her help with the translation. I also thank Nancy Virtue for her suggestions.

1. Jacques Davy du Perron, *Oraison funèbre sur la mort de Monsieur de Ronsard,* ed. Michel Simonin (Geneva, 1985), pp. 105-6. This and all subsequent translations are my own.

2. Ronsard, *Oeuvres complètes,* ed. Paul Laumonier (Paris, 1914-75), XIV.13-14. All subsequent quotations from Ronsard's works are taken from Laumonier's twenty-volume edition and are cited parenthetically by volume, page, and line number.

3. Jacques Peletier du Mans, *Art poétique françois,* ed. Jacques Boulanger (Paris, 1930), p. 89.

4. Among other essays focusing on the *dispositio* of some of Ronsard's collections, see Yvonne Bellenger, "L'organisation du *Bocage royal* de 1584," in *Ronsard en son IVe centenaire,* ed. Yvonne Bellenger, Jean Céard, Daniel Ménager, Michel Simonin (Geneva, 1988), 1:61-71; Philip Ford, *Ronsard's Hymnes: A Literary and Iconographical Study,* Medieval & Renaissance Texts & Studies 157 (Tempe, Ariz., 1997); Doranne Fenoaltea, *Du palais au jardin: L'architecture des Odes de Ronsard* (Geneva, 1990).

5. Henri II also had a personal reason for desiring the end to hostilities: the growing popularity of François de Guise, the hero of Calais and Thionville, was a danger to the king's authority.

6. Lucien Romier, *Les Origines politiques des guerres de religion* (Paris, 1914) 1:191-293, 297-390. Paul Laumonier (IX.103) suggested that Ronsard had written the poem before the signing of the treaty, whereas James Hutton, *Themes of Peace in Renaissance Poetry,* ed. Rita Guerlac (Ithaca, 1984), p. 107, situated the composition of this text after the official date of the settlement. The treaty was dated 2 and 3 April 1559.

7. On this question, see, for instance, Michael Wintroub, "Civilizing the Savage and Making a King:

The Royal Entry Festival of Henri II (Rouen, 1550)," *Sixteenth Century Journal* 29 (1998), 465-94.

8. Significantly, despite other arrangement changes in the pieces of the various editions of the *Oeuvres,* Ronsard deliberately maintained the sequence of the two *Exhortations* followed by *La Paix, Au Roy* untouched. In 1560, the three poems were incorporated in this order into the third Book of *Poemes* in Ronsard's first edition of the *Oeuvres.* In the following editions of the *Oeuvres* (from 1567 to 1573), all three pieces moved (again, in the same order) to the second Book of the *Poemes,* then to the first Book (in the 1578 edition of the *Oeuvres*), and finally to the second Book (in the 1584 and 1587 editions of the *Oeuvres*).

9. On these critics see Jean Céard, "Cosmologie et politique dans l'oeuvre et la pensée de Ronsard," in *Ronsard et Montaigne écrivains engagés?,* ed. Michel Dassonville (Lexington, Ky., 1985), p. 41. Céard also objects to their interpretation.

10. On this aspect, see Ullrich Langer, *Invention, Death, and Self-Definition in the Poetry of Pierre de Ronsard* (Stanford, 1986), p. 82.

11. Baldassare Castiglione, *The Book of the Courtier,* ed. and trans. George Bull (Baltimore, 1967), book 2, chap. 25.

12. On the Erasmian intertext of Ronsard's call for peace, see the Pléiade edition of Ronsard's *Oeuvres complètes,* ed. Jean Céard, Daniel Ménager, and Michel Simonin (Paris, 1994), 2:1526 nn. 4, 6.

13. The translations of the two *Exhortations* were published in separate plaquettes.

14. For a complete list of these wars, see Laumonier, IX.103 n. 2.

15. An Italian visitor had this suggestive comment on Henri II: "Non stimando sua Maesta le lettere molto, gli uomini letterati sono in poca considerazione" (quoted by Romier, *Origines politiques,* 1:27).

16. The four sculptures of Glory, Abundance, Peace, and Fame carved by Jean Goujon on one of the Louvre's façades provide an apt example of Henri II's imperialist ambitions: these four statues were the emblems of Augustus's reign. See Verner Hoffmann, "Le Louvre d'Henri II: un palais impérial," *Bulletin de la Société de l'histoire de l'art français* 34 (1982), 7-15.

17. Michael Wintroub, "Civilizing the Savage," p. 490, mentions an analogous strategy: at the 1549 entry of Henri II into Paris, the city fashioned a composite representation of Henri II as combining the strength of the Libyan Hercules and the prudence, eloquence, and justice of the Gallic Hercules.

18. Ronsard was also challenging the followers of Marot: Marot had set the biblical *Psalms* into verses, and Ronsard, in return, was reviving a collective song from pagan origin. In contrast to the medieval and biblical genres used by Marot and his disciples, Ronsard was committed to the ancients; in contrast to them also, his poetry valued erudition. On the first edition of the *Odes* and on the relations between Ronsard's collection and Du Bellay's *Deffence et Illustration de la langue françoyse,* see Doranne Fenoaltea, *Du Palais au jardin,* pp. 1-42.

19. See Jean Céard, "Cosmologie et politique dans l'oeuvre et la pensée de Ronsard," in *Ronsard et Montaigne écrivains engagés?,* pp. 41-55; and Malcolm Quainton, *Ronsard's Ordered Chaos: Visions of Flux and Stability in the Poetry of Ronsard* (Manchester, 1980), p. 15.

20. St. Augustine, *Oeuvres complètes,* ed. and trans. Péronne, Ecalle, Vincent, and Charpentier (Paris, 1873), 23:512. All further references to this text are taken from the same edition.

21. André Chastel, *Marsile Ficin et l'art* (Geneva, 1964), p. 81.

22. On the various changes of the order of the poems from one edition to another one, see the Pléiade edition of Ronsard's *Oeuvres complètes,* 1:1479-88.

23. For the spelling of these titles, I follow the 1560 edition of the *Oeuvres.*

24. See Daniel Ménager, *Ronsard: Le roi, le poète et les hommes* (Geneva, 1979), p. 135 f.

25. Carnavalet is also celebrated in two odes, but, as the title "Usure, à luy-mesme" makes clear, the second poem is but an addition to the first one. Ronsard is following Pindar's model.

26. See François Rouget, *Apothéose d'Orphée: L'esthétique de l'ode en France au XVIe siècle: De Sébillet à Scaliger* (Geneva, 1994), p. 58.

27. On Ronsard's interest in music, see Isidore Silver, *Ronsard and the Hellenic Renaissance in France: Ronsard and the Grecian Lyre,* vol. 2 (Geneva, 1985).

28. Paul Valéry, *Eupalinos et l'architecte* (Paris, 1945), p. 41.

29. Jacques Peletier du Mans, *Art poétique françois,* pp. 90-91. Peletier's treatise was published five

years after the *Ode de la Paix,* but this remark rephrases an observation made by Quintilian, *Institutio oratoria,* ed. Jean Cousin (Paris, 1977), 4:77.

30. See Quainton, *Ronsard's Ordered Chaos,* pp. 57-59; and Guy Demerson, *La mythologie classique dans l'oeuvre lyrique de la Pléiade* (Geneva, 1972), pp. 114-16.

31. See Daniel Ménager, *Ronsard,* p. 13f.

32. The two passages are quoted by Isidore Silver, *Ronsard and the Grecian Lyre,* vol. 2, part 2, *Ronsard and the Hellenic Renaissance in France* (Geneva, 1985), pp. 224-25.

33. This melancholic view is inscribed into the Pindaric form, which refers to a mythic Greece. See Ménager, *Ronsard,* p. 135.

34. Gilles Deleuze, *Le pli: Leibniz et le baroque* (Paris, 1988), p. 170.

35. In the *Ode à Michel de L'Hospital,* Jupiter could be seen as an allegorical representation of Henri II defeating the giants: this representation would then echo the description of the king ordering the country in the *Ode to Peace.* The *Ode à Michel de L'Hospital* opens with the song of the Muses and alludes to a quarrel between Minerva and Neptune on the sovereignty of Athens. Neptune epitomizes war, and Minerva peace (III.128-29).

36. This remark was inspired by Neoplatonism and was a commonplace in the arts and letters in Ronsard's time.

37. See Guy Demerson, *La mythologie classique,* p. 122f.

38. Ronsard participated in the artistic organization of Charles IX's entry into Paris in March 1571. He also wrote several *bergeries* and pastorals for the feasts Catherine de' Medici organized at Fontainebleau in 1564. See also Ménager, *Ronsard,* pp. 319-54.

Tom Conley (essay date spring 2002)

SOURCE: Conley, Tom. "Ronsard on Edge: 'Les Amours d'Eurymédon et Callirée' (1570)." *New Centennial Review* 2, no. 1 (spring 2002): 33-54.

[In the following essay, Conley explores the way Ronsard assumed the role of ethnographer in the landscape he created within the poem "Les Amours d'Eurymédon et Callirée."]

Work on travel in early modern Europe has grown at a Malthusian pace since the 1992 quincentenniel celebrating the discoveries of the New World. Recent research

has shown, contrary to public festivals in 1892 that ranked Thomas Edison on a par with Christopher Columbus, that *discovery* might well be replaced by *encounter,* and that indeed, if his *Libro de las profecias* is kept in mind, *conquest* might well be a more fitting substantive for what we know about "encounter." Shortly after Columbus's three voyages, flotillas of ships headed west, and conquest and colonization moved at full tilt.[1] Other studies have demonstrated that despite the ambition of Iberian programs an overall feeling of manifest destiny driving Europeans to the new shores may not have prevailed as it had in Seville and similar cities. French settlers soon established an adventitious network of trade as *coureurs de bois* living along the eastern coast of the realm they called "antarctic France." In the years of the wars of religion French motives and policies behind a modest colonial expedition at the Bay of "Guanabara" (Rio de Janeiro) ended in abysmal failure, as did another, with René de Laudonnière, on the eastern shores of Florida.

Impact of travel to the New World upon the Old has also been revised. It has been correct to think that the inventions of moveable type and artificial perspective were of a tenor equal to the Columbian discoveries. Yet historians who work closer to home, in their own national traditions, who seek to depict life as it had been lived from day to day in the murkier depths of reality as they had been sensed by anyone and everyone, have discovered that for most people the New World might have always been "over there." And, if it were really there, it meant little in the midst of the travails of daily life. Rabelais, whose intuition of the new space was acute, folded the idea of the New World into the mouth and upon the tongue of his eponymous hero of *Pantagruel* (1532). He transposed its exotic wonder into a familiar landscape of the Touraine. When he continued the narrations of the adventures of his prince, in drawing on Jacques Cartier's relation of his voyage to Canada among other models for the *Quart Livre* (1548 and 1551), he aims his ships in self-negating directions. They move at once to the east and the west.[2] The reader is left wondering if the expedition is based on a satirical or mental cartography that ultimately leads nowhere. And for Montaigne, an inner and perilous voyage into the crannies and the folds of the self, in an *"espineuse entreprinse, et plus qu'il ne semble, de suyvre une alleure si vagabonde que celle de nostre esprit; de penetrer les profondeurs opaques de ses replis internes; de choisir et arrester tant de menus airs de ses agitations"* [a thorny enterprise, and greater than it seems, to follow an allure so vagabond as that of our thoughts; to penetrate the opaque depths of its inner folds; to choose and arrest so many of the slightest stirrings of its agitations],[3] becomes the prevailing subject of the *Essais.* He devotes a short but telling chapter to the New World in "Of Cannibals," in which the material he culls is entirely third-hand, taken from the cosmographers whom he takes to task for being overblown and false where in their views topographers are veracious, exacting, and unremittingly balanced. The "topographers" he discovers are the Indians he invents from memory of an earlier trip he reports having taken to Rouen in about 1562.

If the New World was "over there," its impact was measured in shapes perceived and known and spaces cultivated "right here." It probably exercised, nonetheless, a productively alienating view of familiar places. Perhaps the idea of strange lands with exotic flora and fauna caused individuals to look closely at their own spaces with a sharpened historical focus. What had been a familiar and fairly unremarkable landscape at home suddenly turned into a picture whose worth was relative to others from adjacent or more remote places. That the art of print culture gave new and sudden value to views of the country and the city in cosmographies and local histories is a fact to which historians of the book have attested.[4] It suffices to page through any of the editions of Sebastian Münster to see that the wonder of a discovery and encounter with local worlds was running parallel with that of new ones.

The generalities of the three paragraphs above risk rehearsing many of the commonplaces that fill histories of early modern space and travel. They are set forward here to beg a question concerning voyage and consciousness in early modern poetry that suddenly embraces— and too, estranges—the areas of its own origins. Court poets write verse that situates them in autobiographical places in order, it seems, to inaugurate a spatial consciousness based on particularity, difference, and even local variation. The same consciousness emerges in the context of the growth of a commanding and unified "self" of national signature that allows these relations to be described and celebrated. Within the domain of print culture these poets become both divine cosmographers and wily topographers. They blend formulas taken from classical spaces, from the older worlds they rejuvenate and animate through translation of Greek and Latin into vernacular idioms, in fresh and arresting style, in discourses that remain inimitable because of the complexities of their mimicry in vernacular idioms as varied as the geographies of their usage.

In adapting classical sources to their own quasi-autobiographical enterprises the poets appear to be consubstantial with their poems. They explore sylvan and inhabited spaces as might an ethnographer who discovers alterity in a new world. The poet becomes an anthropologist when he describes familiar places in light of the novelty of oceanic discoveries. Dramatic alterations of local space in the work of French poets of the middle years of the sixteenth century might be of import comparable to the fruits of encounter in worlds far away.[5] It can be argued that the new sensibility to landscape and topography in lyric at the same time betrays a centralizing and a royalist consciousness through which the poet informs his Mycenas of what indeed can be known of their kingdom. That land is the subject of lyrical distortion indicates that the area, like the vernacular, is a playground as well as a heritage, a site where the most ostensibly sophisticated of all human activities, writing and hunting, sojourning and visiting, living and loving, are celebrated.

The aim of this short essay is to see how Pierre de Ronsard creates a self-image that blends into the landscape of his making, and how that image bears resemblance to one of an ethnographer who, in his own milieu, *passes through* both strange and familiar lands. He creates the latter by constructing topographies riddled with words, with images. He makes the space of his poems a function of movement that alters and heightens self-consciousness. Familiar land becomes a new world all the while it is of an avowedly classical aspect. In **"Les Amours d'Eurymédon et Callirée"** the site is somewhere out of the city, in the thick and bramble of woods that are probably, at the same time, close to the green forests around the chateau of Fontainebleau. The poem is set at the edge of the country and the court, in a liminal area between a sylvan space populated by nymphs, gods, goddesses, and dryads and a world of the noble court facing the violence and terror of religious conflict.

A somewhat later work in Ronsard's cycles of love, **"Les Amours d'Eurymédon et Callirée"** does not, upon cursory view, bear an immediate sign of the poet attached to a local or a national landscape. First published in 1578 under the same title, and changed into **"Les Vers d'Eurymédon et Callirée"** in the 1584 edition of the poet's *Oeuvres complètes,* the work is a composite allegory. By 1570 Ronsard had made clear his view as a Catholic and a Royalist in his new genre, the *Discours,* that had been launched to quash the Protestant "hydra" after the official beginnings of the Wars of Religion in 1562. Charles IX (born June 2, 1550), the second son of Henri II, the late king and husband of Catherine de Medici, had been in power since May 15, 1561, the date of his coronation in the cathedral of Reims. The leadership of France had been left to the Regent-Mother since Henri's death ten days after the spike of a lance had accidentally lodged in his left eye during a sportive tournament in Paris. Ronsard's relations with the new Mycenas grew appreciably over the greater part of a decade of turmoil. From 1568 to 1570 the poet retired to his properties in the Touraine, where he "dedicated himself to rustic life, especially to gardening."[6] In 1570 he returned to the court. Shortly after the Peace of Saint-Germain in early August, which ended the third of the Wars of Religion, Ronsard began composing the text of **"Eurymédon et**

Callirée." Although it would be published four years after the death of its royal dedicatee (Charles died on May 30, 1574), the work was probably circulated in the court with the aim not only to please and advise the young king but also to curry favor with Queen Catherine.

In 1570 Charles was twenty. An adolescent, he was in the "April of his age." Rumor had it that a passion for hunting, rendering him insensitive to the fondness of the female sex, was tempered by the interest of a "very pretty, wise, and honest young lady" whom he served "more to fashion and entertain his own graces than for any other purpose, there being nothing, he used to say, that would better fashion a young man than to have love struck in a handsome and noble subject."[7] In his compact allegory Ronsard dramatizes and celebrates the good auguries of the sudden turn of sentiment. He implicitly offers sage counsel to the young monarch from the standpoint of a 54-year-old bard who has seen and lived the passions of love and who, he adds, might offer the king some tips about balancing the drives of libido with the tasks of statecraft. The young woman in question is Anne d'Atri d'Acquaviva, a Neapolitan lady of honor in the entourage of the Queen mother. The circumstances of the publication of the allegory are complicated by the fact that Ronsard had not been ready to include it in his ***Oeuvres complètes.*** In wishing to keep the memory of the late king intact after his death in 1574, he also would be doing honor to the young lady, who had recently begun a literary career. By retarding the publication Ronsard would thus indicate to readers that the seeds of the fruits of her wisdom had been planted beforehand, in her amorous intrigue with the king, for which he serves as a privileged chronicler.[8] In all events, informed historians speculate that the composition had begun early in 1570 because, first, the work "happens to correspond with Ronsard's return from a retreat that kept the poet far from the court for over two years" and, second, it amounts to a "'total allegorization' of life in the court, indeed, to a "divination of its character by way of the living water and animated fire of a conquering moment in which contradictions get lost in metamorphosis."[9]

The poem is a strange creature. Counting 464 lines, it is composed of six units of different shape and style. Part I (96 lines) is written in sixteen *stances* in alexandrines, in embraced rhymes that follow an initial couplet inaugurating each *stance.* Spoken from the point of view of Eurymédon in the guise of Charles IX, the words tell Callirée, who is Anne d'Acquaviva, that his love is firm and that the world may go topsy-turvy before he would ever alter his affections for her. With jeweled concision he intones,

> *Et tout sera changé plustost qu'Eurymédon*
> *Oublie les amours qu'il porte à Callirée.*[10]

> [And all will be changed before Eurymédon
> Forgets the loves he brings to Callirée.]

Part II (114 alexandrines in eighteen *stances*) is of identical prosody, but it is spoken by a narrator telling of Eurymédon's love of venery, of Venus's metamorphosis into Diana, a stratagem she invents in order to transform the king's cynegetic passions into those of love. Venus-Diana wounds him with a shaft she fires from her bow. Smitten, confused, and perplexed, Eurymédon knows not what to do.

> *Il vouloit aux rochers et aux forests parler:*
> *Mais il ne peut jamais sa langue desmesler.*
>
> (ll. 109-10).

> [To the rocks and forests he wanted to talk.
> But in confusion his tongue would only balk.]

Part III, entitled "Le Baing de Callirée," is told from Eurymédon's crazed point of view. Composed of 80 alexandrines in rhymed couplets, it relates his dream of transforming himself into a woman in order to enter Callirée's private bath. He would be able to see and touch her, fondle her, and wash her shamelessly to his heart's delight:

> *Je pourrois sans vergogne à son baing me trouver,*
> *La voir, l'ouyr, sentir, la toucher & laver.. . . .*
>
> (ll. 23-24)

> [Without shame in her bath I'd be with her,
> See, hear, smell, and touch her, be her washer. . . .]

In his madness he avows that he is so impassioned that he would rather succumb to blindness than never behold her again.

Part IV, "Elegie du poète" (134 lines in alexandrines, in rhymed couplets, the *stances* in successive units of different groupings and successions of stanzas, conveys the old poet's advice to the young Eurymédon. It treats of love, passion, constancy, statecraft, and the beauty of amorous congress when imagined through the filter of the bard's written verse.[11] Part V, "Chanson par stances" (seven quatrains in decasyllabic measure, each in enclosing rhymes) does *not* indicate who is speaking. It seems to be Eurymédon, who develops a conceit comparing the effects of love to the flow of water in order to have him temper his passion and to beg the listener—Anne d'Acquaviva—to slake his thirst with her generous fluids, or even be transformed into a spring in order better "to follow the steps" (l. 8) of the princess. Part VI buckles the work with a sonnet entitled "Callirée parle contre la chasse" [Callirée speaks against hunting]. It affirms the lady's distaste for venery and her fear that her beloved Eurymédon might become another Adonis, a handsome lover killed, it is implied, like Meleager, by a wild boar unleashed by Diana (upon Mars's supplication in the frenzy of his jealousy over Venus's infidelity to him).[12]

The entire poem is faithful to Ronsard's innovation of interlacing masculine and feminine rhymes. It attests to formal virtue of the first order by uniting the different voices and styles of address (or even fantasy) in each section. And surely the biographical material that flickers in the circumstantial aspect of the poem lends to the whole a mosaic or even tessellated form: a dialogue is established between a young man who seems to be a variant of Hippolytus and a wizened poet who has known and written of love. The text allows the voices of the protagonists to speak cautiously about a future bond that would do honor to both of them. The thematic leitmotifs of fire and water, of warmth and cold, along with the background of the forest and the court, relate the aqueous name of the king's erotic object to the décor of the country and city.

In the reception and pedagogy of the text most critical interest has been drawn to the poet's avowal that, as his hair becomes grey and his face furrowed with wrinkles, love is more and more a passion of language; in turn, poetry is the site where he can confer with himself and temper his conflicting drives and desires. As if he were cribbing one of the early sonnets of Du Bellay's *Regrets* of 1558, he writes thus of poetry, a silent and secret interlocutor who accompanies him wherever he goes:

> *Je luy dis mes secrets: je la trouve fidelle*
> *Et soulage mon mal de si douce façon*
> *Que rien contre l'Amour n'est bon que la chanson.*
> *La Muse est mon confort, qui de sa voix excellente*
> *(Tant son charme est puissant) Amour, quand elle*
> * chante.*

> (ll. 124-28)

> *[I tell her my secrets, I find faith in her face,*
> *And calm my ills with such ease and grace*
> *That no remedy to love is better than song.*
> *The muse is my comfort, with her excellent voice*
> *(So powerful her charm), Love is my only choice.]*

The poet's all-encompassing vocation, his labor of love, is nonetheless greater than that of the young king. Yet it comes at the cost of experience, of living, seeing, and writing; its example now allows the prince to discern that for as long as he is yoked with passion he will be unable to esteem the worth of the land over which he reigns:

> *Ma fortune, un bon-heur passe la vostre, Prince.*
> *Que vous sert maintenant vostre riche province,*
> *Que vous sert vostre sceptre & vostre honneur royal?*
> *Cela ne peut guarir en amour vostre mal,*
> *Cela ne refroidit le feu qui vous allume:*

> *Où je suis soulagé par le bien de ma plume,*
> *Qui deschargent mon coeur de mille affections,*
> *Emporte dans le vent toutes mes passions*

> (ll. 115-23)

> *[My fortune, a happiness exceeds yours, Prince.*
> *What can be the use of your rich province,*
> *What sense of might and honor can you feel*
> *When in your veins you feel ills congeal?*
> *It does not dampen for us the fire and fume*
> *That warm me by the virtue of my plume,*
> *That calm my heart from a thousand affections*
> *And send to the winds all of my passions.]*

The poet's confession that he and his poem are one, indeed, that the consolation of lyric takes the form of the simulacrum of love, is framed by two couplets of similar design that set love in the context of statecraft. First:

> *Que vous sert maintenant vostre riche prince,*
> *Que vous sert vostre sceptre et vostre homneur royal?*

> (ll. 116-17)

And then:

> *Que le ciel soit ton pere, & la mer ta nourrice,*
> *Que tu sois citoyen d'Amathonte ou d'Eryce*

> (ll. 131-32)

> *[May the heavens be your father, the sea your midwife*
> *May you be from Amathonte or Eryce for your life]*

ends the confession and serves as a threshold to the final couplet beseeching Cupid to return to France with the intent of tempering the prince, who remains, nonetheless, a faithful subject of the god of love.

> *Vien demeurer en France, & soulage l'ardeur*
> *De mon prince, qui vit sujet de ta grandeur.*

> (ll. 133-34)

> *[Come to live in France, and calm the ardor*
> *Of my prince, living subject of your great order.]*

Crucial to the architecture of the imprecation is the allusion to the province and kingdom of France, a place known and esteemed more than Amathonte and Eryce, sites recognized in geographical dictionaries of mythology for being dedicated to Venus. France and its lands are as immediate and striking as the forests and the fauna described elsewhere in the poem. Amathonte and Eryce also refer to the recondite lexicon of the *Amours* of 1552, in which Ronsard built a sonnet around the alluring toponyms in order to celebrate a strangeness identical to the passion of love and to describe a temple for which he would offer himself as a sacrificial victim.[13] At this juncture the poet beckons the prince to look *through* the passion of venery-as-love in order to see his nation from a just perspective. At the same time the poet constructs a webbing of events past and present in his own oeuvre to show, albeit indirectly, that his former desire to immolate himself in honor of Cassandre [thus reducing his body to the ash contained in her own name (Cas-*cendre*)] was misplaced. But now, seen through the experience of other writings about love, the figure becomes an effective form of political counsel. It can modify and temper his noble interlocutor. Ronsard's overweaning narcissism of the 1550s has suddenly become stately and pragmatic.

The whole poem seems to turn on the double axis of these words. In the balance are the landscape of the nation and the life of the court, especially insofar as the future of the Valois genealogy is at stake. *Ardeur* carries back to the description of a forest sullied by the zeal of hunters. When Venus dresses in travesty of Diana she aims to turn Charles into the figure that had been central to the decorative schemes that Henry II, his late father, had enjoyed in the 1550s. Acteon is invoked to raise consciousness, on the one hand about an iconography that had dominated the court while, on the other, it draws attention to the state of the country in the passage of time from 1552 up to 1570.

> *Je porte, disoit elle, & l'arc & et le brandon*
> *Maintenant pour blesser le coeur d'Eurymedon,*
> *Qui, nouvel Acteon, de ses meutes tormente*
> *Le repos des forests, rend les buissons deserts*
> *Ensanglante les bois du meurtre de mes Cerfs . . .*

> (II, ll. 13-17)

> [*I now, she said, have found the bow and the fire*
> *To wound Eurymedon and to fuel his ire.*
> *Yes, a new Acteon with his packs of dogs*
> *He torments the calm and makes the forests clear,*
> *And bloodies the woods by murdering my Deer . . .*]

Potentiated energy is sapped when the forests are rid of their wildlife and when, in a remarkable figure of speech, the wilds are bloodied by senseless slaughter. When Venus-Diana finds her prey, after her Acteon has been shown to be a hunter without equal [through a tour-de-force that describes his passion with cynegetic virtuosity (ll. 49-53)], the landscape becomes a veinous form that mixes fantasy of rivers, antlers, blood vessels, possibly forest paths, and surely roots and branches that confuse the shapes of trees with the lines of genealogical schemes.[14] One twisted trait refers to others of similar vital order. A prevailing Petrarchan topos is that of the body figured as bark or dead wood that the poet leaves behind in the movement of his ascension toward immortalization. In sonnet 104 of the *Amours* he sighs, when seeing Cupid taking aim with a bow and an arrow that will strike the poet's own body, "Avant mes jours, j'ay grand'peur de laisser / Le verd fardeau de cette je-

une escorce" [Before my days I much fear leaving / The green burden of this young bark] (p. 66, ll. 3-4). The conventional *bois verd* that he wishes would be detonating powder (*pouldre d'amorce*, l. 8) opposes the forest and its innuendo of venery (*bois abois* or barking of dogs, and *verd* going toward, *vers, erres,* tracks of the beast) to the ardor and flame of the sonnet of 1552.

In another sonnet of similar vintage the poet cannot force destiny in view of his beloved prior "to being clothed in this new bark" (*Ains que vestir ceste escorce nouvelle*). Suddenly a sensation of heat runs through his body, ". . . adonq de moëlle en moëlle, / De nerfz en nerfz, de conduitz en conduitz, / Vient à mon cueur, dont j'ay vescu depuis, / Or en plaisir, or en peine cruelle" (108, p. 102, ll. 4-8) [and then from marrow to marrow, / From nerve to nerve, channel to channel, / It reaches my heart through a passage narrow, / Now in pleasure, then in pain, cutting path and furrow]. The lines of poetry trace the effect of a drug circulating in the poet's veins where things animal and vegetal are assimilated, from the skin or covering of dead epidermis to living liquids in continuous passage. The lines engrave the flow of vital fluids and the poisons infecting them. Now, in a poem added to the *Amours,* in the *Septiesme Livre des poèmes* (published in 1569, at the time he was crafting **"Eurymédon et Callirée"**) Ronsard describes how a friendly salutation from his lover flows into and through his body with narcotic force so strong that he is led to take pleasures in the vices that result:

> *De veine en veine, & d'artere en artere,*
> *De nerfz en nerfz le salut me passa*
> *Que l'autre jour Madame prononça,*
> *Me promenant tout triste & solitaire.*
> *Il fut si doux que je ne puis m'en taire. . . .*

> (20, p. 325, ll. 1-4)

> [*From artery to artery, from vein to vein,*
> *From nerve to nerve, her words cut a path*
> *Right where Madame said "hello" with a laugh.*
> *Alone and sad, my composure I tried to feign.*
> *It was so sweet my words I couldn't regain. . . .*]

The evolution of the figure from 1555 to 1567 indicates that the *experience* of the narcosis is heightened with emphasis on the passage of the "controlled substance" through the body. Ramification of sensation under the skin is so stressed that the image resembles the pattern of a cervine's antlers that branch outward and forward.

In **"Eurymédon"** the figure is reiterated three times, respectively, in parts II, III, and IV. It is in concord with the leitmotif of flowing liquid that animates the secret name, *Acquaviva,* that runs through the poem. It also lends a contour to the virtual landscape of the verse. When Venus/Diane beholds the hunter who is her quarry she cries out to warn him that she will jolt him with languor, and that as a result his only remedy will be found in the muses and in poetry.

> *D'une telle langueur mes ennemis je paye.*
> *En lieu de chiens, de trompe, & de bocages verds,*
> *Il te faudra chercher les Muses & les vers,*
> *Pour soulager le mal qui naistra de ta playe.*
>
> (II, ll. 81-84)

> *[With such languor my enemies do I ground.*
> *In place of hound, horn, forest of greenish sheen*
> *You'll need Muses and poetry, for bloody spleen*
> *To be soothed of the ills born of your wound.]*

The poison of the arrow that has struck the hunter, causing his blood to boil like water in which a red-hot poker is plunged, has a strangely depressive (and indeed mannered) effect of turning him into a zombie. The potion went to the bottom of his heart,

> *Passa de nerf en nerf, passa de veine en veine*
>
> (l. 88)

> *[Passed from nerve to nerve, passed from vein to vein]*

before it happened that he could no longer command the hunt in his own words or even speak at will "to the rocks and the forest" (l. 109). The man whose prey was crowned with antlers has become so anesthetized that the lines of his body acquire the moribund traits of an expiring cervine.

In the dream that ensues in part III, in which Eurymédon would like to be transformed into a woman in order to behold Callirée in the nude, the dumbfounded lover avows that by having "dipped her hand into my veins" (l. 54), she ought to purge her sin by plunging her entire body in the warm waters of a bath he has readied for her. He might behold her and even realize that as Acteon, were she to accord him her love, he would have no misgivings in sprouting antlers on his head (ll. 70-71). In part IV the wise poet (ll. 11-16) begins the second stanza of his elegy to Eurymédon in the fashion of an autopsy (Ronsard seeing himself in the landscape of his own body) that sums up and redirects the figures deployed up to this moment:

> *Les hommes ne sont faits de matieres contraires:*
> *Nous avons comme vous des nerfs & des arteres,*
> *Nous avons de nature un mesme corps que vous,*
> *Chair, muscles & tendons, cartilage & pouls,*
> *Mesme coeur, mesme sang, poumons & mesmes veines,*
> *Et souffrons comme vous les plaisirs et les peines.*
>
> (IV, ll. 11-16).

> *[Men are not made of things called contraries.*
> *Like you we have nerves and arteries,*

> *Like you we have a same body and nothing else:*
> *Flesh, muscle, tendons, cartilage and pulse,*
> *Same heart, same blood, same lungs and veins,*
> *And like you suffer the same pleasures and pains.]*

The human body is a living landscape animated by love. "[L]e propre sujet des hommes c'est aimer" (l. 18) [The very nature of man is to love]. The description of the heartfelt confusion of contrary forces by which we live in toss and stir is capped by the figure of a tree bearing bitter fruits "qu' Amour de son arbre nous donne" (l. 31) [that with its tree Love bears for us]. It is of a distasteful "leaf, flower, and root." All of a sudden the tree transmutes into a conceit that flows through an adventitious webbing of signifiers (*a-m-r*) ramifying from *Amour* to *amer* and from *amer* to *la mer,* following a lineage or stock that originates in the sea (with the birth of Venus) and that is suckled in "a savage forest":

> *Le tige en est amer, qui corrompt nostre corps,*
> *Amer par le dedans, amer par le dehors:*
> *Et bref amer par tout, comme ayant son lignage*
> *De la mer, & nourry dans un desert sauvage.*
>
> (ll. 33-36)

> *[Its stem is bitter, our body it corrodes, I confide,*
> *It is both bitter inside and bitter outside:*
> *In brief bitter everywhere, having as lineage*
> *The sea, and is nourished in lands ever savage.]*

The abstract figure under which are subsumed the veins and ganglia of nerves in the body includes the genealogy of love, the passage from sea to a primitive landscape, and memory of the horns of the cervine in the iconography of the myth of Diana and Acteon. Even the inner pattern of signifying graphemes constitutes a meristematic branching. An itinerary of perpetual splitting is visible. In the tale the poet tells to his patron about the bitter character of the persona of love, he reminds the youth that Cupid grows into his life as a thoughtless hunter, "luy mesme sans patron, allant par les forests" (IV, l. 49) [himself without order, going through the woods] who, willy-nilly, shoots bucks and does before leaving the wilds in search of human prey in urban places. "Des bois vint aux citez tirer droict aux humains" (IV, l. 53) [From the woods came to the cities to aim directly at humans].

The lesson afforded the young prince is that he must not forget the sylvan origins of his own passions all the while he is in the court. The discourse shows that love bears a military aspect that ought, it is suggested, to be harnessed for practical ends (l. 68), even when the "sulfer of love makes him suffer ("En voz veines le soulfre amoureux alluma") (l. 70). His passions are part of a landscape that needs to be defended. The bard's own reminiscences of his past are marshaled to inform and counsel about the present state of things. If, as it is likely, the backward glance is indeed a hinge on which the allegory turns, the last two parts of the poem (v and vi) move forward by virtue of the presence of the autobiographical past. The "Chanson par stances" sung by Eurymédon is in decasyllables that recall the conceits of passion that the younger Ronsard (at age twenty-eight) had crafted in the **Amours** of 1552. The young prince is transformed into an adolescent Ronsard when he pines for Callirée-Acquaviva in liquid figures drawn from the well of the sonnets that had wept over images of Cassandra. The leader who wanted to become a woman now wishes to be water that will mix and flow with his lady's liquids of love. The words of his song hark back to the **Amours**.

> Ah belle eau vive, ah fille d'un rocher,
> Qui fuis toujours pour ma peine fatale,
> Ne souffre plus que je sois un Tantale,
> Laisse ma soif en tes eaux estancher
>
> (v, ll. 1-4)

> [Ah daughter of stone, ah wafting lake,
> With water fleeing, for me fatal and callous,
> May I never suffer in becoming a Tantalus:
> Would my thirst your fluids ever slake]

is shaped from

> Je voudrois estre Ixion & Tantale,
> Dessus la roüe, & dans les eaux là bas:
> Et quelque fois presser entre mes bras
> Cette beauté qui les anges égale
>
> (45, p. 30, ll. 1-4)

> [Would I be a Tantalus or an Ixion,
> In the waters or chained to the wheel
> And sometime my in arms' grasp feel
> This beauty who is not an angelic fiction],

just as

> Fils de Venus, enfant ingenieux,
> Je te supply pour alleger ma peine
> Que tout mon corps ne soit qu'une fonteine,
> Et que mon sang je verse par les yeux
>
> (v, ll. 13-16)

> [Son of Venus, crafty infant who defies,
> To alleviate my pain, I beg to you and sing
> To turn my body into a watery spring,
> And to pour my blood through my eyes]

is drawn from

> Je vouldroy bien afin d'aiser ma peine
> Estre un Narcisse, & elle une fontaine
> Pour m'y plonger une nuict à sejour
>
> (20, p. 15, ll. 9-11)

> [I'd wish, in order to ease my pain
> To be a Narcissus, and she a spring
> In which, without end my body I'd fling]

indicating over and again that a double metamorphosis is being staged. In its economy Ronsard relives former passion through the imagination of the prince that he assimilates in his newer writing; likewise, the prince rehearses the youth of Ronsard by miming his poet's lines, thus tempering himself by internalizing the literal example given by the past master.

A new temper issues from the displacements of each into the other. The counsel that is given to Eurymédon comes through the binocular vision of the old poet looking both back to the wild province of his early writing and forward to slaking his amorous thirst when he considers the condition of the king's body in respect to that of the nation. In the coda to the poem, the sonnet spoken by Callirée in alexandrines, the young lady reminds the prince of the beauty of the "silence des bois" [silence of the woods] and of life therein,

> Et les Nymphes qui sont dans les arbres naissantes
>
> (l. 4)

> [And the Nymphs in the trees who are being born]

where otherwise violence is senselessly practiced. Callirée reveals her solicitude by fearing that Eurymédon will be killed by a wild boar ("quelque sangler," l. 11), a figure that seems to convey both political and mythological charge. The final line suggests that a death-like sign, a chiasm, remains in the visual inversion referring to Ronsard's own treatments of the love of Venus and Adonis in the last two lines, the cornerstone of the poem:

> Que le deuil ne me fasse une Venus nouvelle,
> Et la mort ne le face un nouvel Adonis.
>
> (ll. 13-14)

> [May grief not turn me into another Venus
> And may death not him into another Adonis.]

She alludes to the equivocal figure of the woods whence the poem began, where signs of the birth of civilization and nation were construed to be evident, but where human forces were running amok. It could be that the Wars of Religion are felt through an ambivalence about venery, and that the process of tempering coming with the liquid treatment of Anne d'Acquaviva's name conveys doubt, caution, and a sense of perspective about the state of France in 1570. Whatever the implied message may be, the poet draws the attention of the court back to a sylvan world, a world against which its mannered elegance is set in profile. It also participates in a greater project, one of a national topography, that mixes a renewed awareness of the landscape, the city, the country, and the ecology of the nation past and present. That it works at once through the multiple and modulated voices of the poet living different moments of his career and the voices of three other personages (Diana, Eurymédon, and Callirée) further animates the allegory.

The temporal shifts also signal a change in style. The text moves from self-consciousness to a new awareness about a world in peril. Taken in the context of discovery, encounter, and conquest, **"Les Amours d'Eurymédon et Callirée"** marks a poetics and a politics of conservation and circumspection. The poem turns *inward,* toward personal and national space, in order to move *outward* and ahead. Its stern view of venery is reflected to a degree in an earlier "poem" entitled **"La Chasse, à Jean Brinon"** [Hunting, for Jean Brinon], purporting to be an encomium of the sport but effectively turning away from a myth-history of illustrious hunters of ages past and toward a *blason* of the dedicatees's faithful dog in the here-and-now of his own life and times.[15] The poem, like the cynegetic rhapsody in the second part of **"Eurymédon et Callirée,"** is built from tessellations of myth and jargon. The description of the canine effectively wins over the title, and the pleasure of the hunt is not in the murder of the quarry. It resides, rather, in the delicate and mannered treatment of sylvan space. After the trophy of a "branched deer" (*cerf branchu*) is suspended from "some forked tree" (*quelque arbre fourchu,* ll. 105-6) to celebrate *Pan forestier,* joy is taken when the party sleeps near a "cerulean stream" on "soft grass" (*l'herbe mollette*) in order to see and hear in the distance of the landscape the staging of an eclogue, what might indeed be the poem itself. Therein, too, the pleasures, the hunter feels

> *Ô Dieux! De manger és bocages*
> *Du fromage et du lait et des fraises sauvages,*
> *Ou secouer le fruit d'un pommeux arbrisseau*
> *Ou de perdre la soif dans le prochain ruisseau*
>
> (ll. 115-18)

> *[O Gods! To eat within the groves*
> *Cheese, milk, and wild strawberries in droves,*
> *Or to shake the fruit of an appled treelet*
> *Or to slake our thirst in a nearby rivulet]*

before he returns to the lodge to see a faithful wife at rest, in bed, anxiously awaiting her husband for fear of danger or of succumbing to the charms of woodland nymphs.

"La Chasse" is an encomium of what Ronsard calls a "poem" through the comparison of a forest to a specific kind of tree. Where poetry is "a field of diverse appearance," a poem is now and again a flower or a single oak, an elm, a cypress (a homonym of "near here," *cy près*) that the artisan turns into an implement of human economy. Poetry is to the poem as a cosmographic image of the world is to a local or a topographical view, just as a portrait of a sitter is to a depiction of his or her ear or eye.[16] A poem is a tree in a forest that is turned toward a productive end. It is aware of its sylvan origins and remains in proximity to its birthplace in body and soul. Such is what is amplified in the allegorical tour-de-force in the inner voyage and the encounters that define much of the psychogeography of **"Eurymédon et Callirée."** The national landscape that the myths inhabit has become as important as the myths themselves. It is yoked to an allegorical design that ties French spaces to the royal lineage that is asked to nurture and protect them. On edge, at the edge of a picture of the court and its milieu, Ronsard frets over their future. The exploration of local times and spaces in the poet's milieu becomes a project of an order that complements greater movements east and west. With it comes an anthropology that mixes myth, analysis of the psyche, geography, and allegory. What is witnessed in the form of **"Eurymédon et Callirée"** may be a vital moment in the relation of poetry and nation to human science.

Notes

1. As shown, among others, by William A. and Carla Phillips, *The Worlds of Christopher Columbus* (New York: Cambridge University Press, 1992); and Bernard Vincent, *1492: L'Année admirable* (Paris: Aubier, 1991).

2. Mireille Huchon, "Notice" to her presentation of *Le Quart Livre,* in her critical edition of *Rabelais: Oeuvres complètes* (Paris: Gallimard/Pléiade, 1994), 1460.

3. Montaigne, *Essais,* ed. Albert Thibaudet and Maurice Rat (Paris: Gallimard/Pléiade, 1950), 415. All translations from the French are mine.

4. Jean-Marc Chatelain and Laurent Pinon, "L'Intervention de l'image et ses rapports avec le texte de la Renaissance," in *La Naissance du livre moderne: Mise en page et mise en texte du livre français (XIVe-XVIIe siècles)* edited by Henri-Jean Martin (Paris: Editions du Cercle de la Librairie, 2000), 36-71.

5. See Roland Greene, *Unrequited Conquests: Love and Empire in the Colonial Americas* (Chicago: University of Chicago Press, 1999).

6. Jean Céard, Daniel Ménager, and Michel Simonin, eds., introduction and chronology, *Ronsard: Oeuvres complètes,* vol. 1 (Paris: Gallimard/Pléiade, 1993), lxx.

7. The words are taken from the *Mémoires* of the Duc de Brantôme, cited by Henri and Catherine Weber in the introduction to their critical edition of *Ronsard: Les Amours* (Paris: Garnier, 1963/ 1998 reedition), xxvii.

8. Céard et al., *Ronsard: Oeuvres complètes,* 351.

9. Ibid., 1344 and 1346. The editors cite the observations of Marcel Raymond in "Sur les 'Amours d'Eurymédon et Callirée'" in *De Jean Lemaire de Belges à Jean Giraudoux: Mélanges Pierre Jourda* (Paris: Nizet, 1970), 13. They add that Ronsard's scribe, Amadis Jamyn, had composed a work of the same title in 1575, but probably in imitation of the master. Philippe Desportes, who changed the courtly style after his rise to power in 1573, wrote a poem entitled "A Callirée" in his first works of 1575. The topic was therefore of the style of the day. Its "mannered" temper showed that the poem, as we shall note, marked a turning point in composition, style, and vision of the nation.

10. Lines 95-95, Weber and Weber, *Ronsard: Les Amours,* 351. All reference to this poem and other texts of the *Amours* will be drawn from this edition.

11. It is difficult to discern a clear pattern, yet the recurrence and resemblance of given blocks of verse invite study of a hidden architecture. The numerical succession of *stances* is thus: 6-4-6-20-10-6-6-4-6-6-6-6-4-4-6-4-6-4-8-14-6.

12. The Weber and Weber edition (713 n2) elucidates the poet's blending of two myths of gods killed by wild pigs. Céard et al. note that at the end of the sonnet Callirée's feelings are revealed. She had concealed her fears for the young man in the first quatrains (in which she defends the gods), whereas in the tercets she defends wild beasts in lament over the abuse of nature (1349 n1).

13. Cf. *Amours* 125 (ed. Weber and Weber, 78):

> *Un coing vrayment, plus seur ne plus propice*
> *A deceler un tourment amoureux,*
> *N'est point dans Cypre, ou dans les plus heureux*
> *Vergers de Gnide, Amathonte, ou d'Eryce.*

> *[A little place, truly sure and propitious*
> *To reveal a torment amorous, and vicious,*
> *Is not in the jagged hills of Cyprus,*
> *Or the groves of Gnide, Amthonte or Eryce.]*

14. In *The Self-Made Map: Cartographic Writing in Early Modern France* (Minneapolis: University of Minnesota Press, 1996), it is shown that the legends to some maps blend potamographic lines with those of noble genealogy (242-43). Represen-

tations of rivers are shown bearing resemblance to family trees. A similar effect of confused filiation is felt here.

15. "La Chasse, à Jean Brinon," in Céard et al., *Ronsard: Oeuvres complètes,* 2:684-89. In alexandrines and counting 220 lines, the poem was first published in 1560 in the initial edition of Ronsard's *Oeuvres.* The editors note that "perhaps on the occasion of this new publication the poet begins to conceive the idea of the genre of the poem as he will define it in an important posthumous piece" (1486), in whose first twelve lines we read (also in Céard et al., 2:849):

> *Poëme et Poësie ont grande différence.*
> *Poësie est un pré de diverse aparence,*
> *Orgueilleux de ses biens, et riche de ses fleurs,*
> *Diapré, peinturé de cent mille couleurs,*
> *Qui fournist de boucquets les amantes Pucelles,*
> *Et de vivres les camps des Abeilles nouvelles.*
> *Poëme est une fleur, ou comme en des Forés*
> *Un seul Chesne, un seul Orme, un Sapin, un Cyprés,*
> *Qu'un nerveux charpentier tourne en courbes charrues,*
> *Ou en carreaux voutez des navires ventrues,*
> *Pour aller voir apres de Thetis les dangers*
> *Et les bords enrichis des biens des estrangers.*

> *[Poems and poetry are of great difference.*
> *Poetry is a field of diverse appearance,*
> *Boasting of its riches, furnished with flowers,*
> *Diapered, painted with a hundred thousand colors,*
> *That furnishes bouquets for many virgin damsels,*
> *And for fields of bees its many pollened petals.*
> *A poem is a flower, or as in the Forests*

> *A single Oak, a single Elm, a Pine, a Cypress*

> *A busy carpenter will turn into a curved plow*
> *Or in bent beams behind a squat galleon's prow*
> *In order to sail and see Thetis with its dangers,*
> *And shores enriched by the goods of strangers.]*

16. Illustrated in Pieter Apian, *Cosmographia* (Paris, 1524, and many other editions).

Louisa Mackenzie (essay date spring 2002)

SOURCE: Mackenzie, Louisa. "'Ce ne sont pas des bois': Poetry, Regionalism, and Loss in the Forest of Ronsard's Gâtine." *Journal of Medieval and Early Modern Studies* 32, no. 2 (spring 2002): 343-74.

[In the following essay, Mackenzie discusses Ronsard as a regional poet devoted to the idealized representations of his native Vendômois—particularly the forest of Gâtine—in his lyric poetry.]

Regionalism is a somewhat contested category of recent literary criticism. Often conceived of largely as a bulwark against the dangers of nationalism's violent exclusivity, regionalism has itself been problematized, as Roberto Dainotto writes in *Place in Literature*: "regionalism is merely taking the place and role that once was given to nationalism: they speak the same language, they foster the same desires, menacing and *unheimlich,* of purity and authenticity."[1] A region, for Dainotto, is a Lefebvrian *espace,* defined not by boundaries that are "natural" or geographic so much as by ideological boundaries, the exclusion of all that might tarnish the "beautiful discourse of what we ought to be." Regionalism, then, is a desire for an originary and pristine culture; regional literature, the imagining of that culture, a fantasy both poetic and communitarian in which literature is seen to be the ideal expression of a certain kind of community, and vice versa. Contiguous to Derridean *différance,* then, "because the region *is* not, it always defers itself to a hypothetical future that is the coming back of an original past—the realization, in other words, of what was always supposed to be."[2] Regional literature is a pastoral sensibility that operates through the exclusion of whatever is defined as the greater process of history and the nation.[3]

My starting point is this notion of region as a metaphor for yearning—yearning for the return, always differed, of an idealized past—and for the self-conscious exclusion of all perceived threats to the possible return of this past. For my purposes, "region" means a mental space, a *lieu de mémoire,* a place where lost wholeness is reconstructed, lamented, hoped for again.[4] It is a pastoral and literary version of what the Marxist geographer David Harvey has called a "space of hope."[5] There are certain associations between writers and such regions that have become almost antonomastic—that is, the name of a region suggests that of the artist, or vice versa (Thoreau and Walden being a prime example). That there are such associations, often very strong, between sixteenth-century French poets and their various regions of origin might surprise some readers looking for evidence of enthusiastic effacing of regional difference in the service of an emergent nationalism.[6] At a time when ideas of France as a nation were just starting to coalesce, and when Joachim Du Bellay had called French poets to unite and found a golden era of French literary nationhood, poets nevertheless continued to celebrate their regional loyalties often over and above their loyalties to France as a whole. The homesick Du Bellay wrote oft-cited eulogies to his native Anjou while in Rome—today the assiduous Du Bellay reader can visit the eponymous museum in his home province. The Lyonnais Maurice Scève and Louise Labé wrote into their poetry a sense of their geographical difference and distance from the north. And even a casual reader of Ronsard will quickly pick up that Ronsard is Vendômois.

This essay takes the case study of Pierre de Ronsard's presentation of his native Vendômois in his lyric landscapes, and in particular one landmark therein: the forest of Gâtine.[7] Landscape, in particular the garden, has been well studied with respect to sixteenth-century French writing,[8] and there is much recent interest on the intersection of early modern cartography and literature.[9] Also well studied are more general and philosophical notions of "nature" in Renaissance literature. Nature was of course as multivalenced a concept then as it is now: it was invoked by writers both as a transcendent source of order and also as a source of variety and flux.[10] This essay is a study of landscape in that it considers regional space in poetry as a vehicle for ideology, constructed as a "safe haven" or space of resistance against certain historical processes. It is a study of nature in that nature imitated from classical poets seems to stand for a lost poetic and moral order, the rhetorical counterpart to current events represented by an actual threat to the local trees. I trace Ronsard's early construction of the forest in his *Odes,* and offer a close reading and reconsideration of the later, spuriously titled **"Elégie contre les bûcherons de la forêt de Gâtine,"** in which Ronsard, prompted by the sale and logging of the forest in 1572, tells the woodsmen that they are murdering the goddesses who inhabit the trees. The Vendômois region is constructed, in Ronsard's lyrics, as a metaphor for a prelapsarian world of poetry that excludes the tensions of contemporary France, a world ordered first and foremost by poetry and poets, a world of aristocratic virtue and value, immune from sectarian strife and historical disruptions. At stake in this regionalism are questions of identity, both individual and collective: the status of the Catholic, of the aristocratic landowner, and of the poet and poetry themselves in a France whose future must have looked very uncertain in all these respects. In other words, local landscape is defined by an agonistic relationship to history; the forest, more than a poetic convention, more even than a bid for renown (although it is certainly that), allows the poet to contest some of the most powerful social changes of his time.

The forest of Gâtine is named directly ten times in Ronsard's *œuvre,* and many more times by implication.[11] By naming the forest several times throughout his work, Ronsard establishes it in his readers' minds as a poetically significant place. It is in the books of odes (1550) that Ronsard establishes the Gâtine as a place that enables and inspires creativity—his own, to be exact. The ode entitled *A sa lyre,* the final ode of the *Premier Livre des Odes,* is the first ode to name directly the Gâtine, at least in the ordering of the 1584 *Œuvres,* which we are following here.[12] It is significant that the first instance of naming the forest comes in a poem addressed to an object whose image is so directly associated with poetic inspiration, and—for Ronsard—with his own reputation.[13] It is also the final ode of its book, a position, following Horace's *Exegi monumentum,* often reserved in lyric tradition for meditations on the poet's own fame and fortune. Ronsard's entire poem is heavily derivative of both Horace and Pindar, whom he harnesses without any apparent embarrassment to further his reputation.[14]

Pindar's first Pythian Ode starts thus:

> O golden lyre, that art owned alike by Apollo and by the violet-tressed Muses! thou lyre, which the footstep heareth, as it beginneth the gladsome dance; lyre, whose notes the singers obey, whenever, with thy quivering strings, thou preparest to strike up the prelude of the choir-leading overture![15]

Ronsard begins his ode with a close transcription:

> Lyre dorée, où Phoebus seulement
> Et les neuf soeurs ont part egalement
> Le seul confort qui *mes* tristesses tue
> Que la danse oit, et toute s'esvertue
> De t'obeyr, et mesurer ses pas
> Sous tes fredons accordez par compas
> Lors qu'en sonnant tu marques la cadance
> De l'avant-jeu, le guide de la danse.
>
> 　　　　　　　　　　　(1-8, my emphasis)

> [Golden lyre, to whom only
> Phoebus and the nine Muses have a claim,
> The only comfort of my sorrows,
> Whom the dance hears, and entirely strives
> To follow you, and to measure its steps
> By your well-tuned strings,
> When with your playing you mark the cadence
> Of the overture, which leads the dance.][16]

This is, for the most part, a very close imitation of the source. However Ronsard does make one important innovation: while Pindar presents an encomium to lyres in general, with no particular poet associated with its creative power, Ronsard in the third line introduces himself, the "moi." Ronsard may start off like Pindar, attributing the lyre "only" to Apollo and the Muses; however, he immediately modifies this trope by adding himself to the list. Ronsard thus creates a much closer association between the lyre and his own poetry. And while the voice of the first-person starts off relatively weakly—not as predicate but simply as the possessor of sadness acted upon by the lyre—there is a transition in the third verse, where in the same sentence Ronsard moves from past to present through precisely the grammatical mediation of the lyre, which allows him to use the "je" self-referentially. After a verse based on the continuation of the Pindaric source, in which Ronsard expounds on the theme of the power of lyric song over the gods, the poem moves closer to home, in all senses:

> Celuy ne vit le cher-mignon des Dieux
> A qui deplaist ton chant melodieux,
> *Heureuse Lyre,* honneur de *mon* enfance,
> Je te sonnay devant tous *en la France.*
>
> 　　　　　　　　　　　(17-20, my emphasis)

> [He who dislikes your melodious song
> Never saw the beloved of the Gods,
> *Blessed Lyre,* honour of *my* youth,
> Above all others *in France* it was I who made you speak.]

The first two lines here are still Pindaric in inspiration,[17] but after the mention of the "blessed Lyre" Ronsard departs from his source and speaks on his own terms. The lyre, then, has a mediating function both syntactically, in the structure of the sentence, and poetically: it is Ronsard's "lyre," or his creative capacity, which allows him to thus transform past into present, or exemplars into himself. Such an act of transformation and creation works on the level of geography also, as it is appropriated initially for France as a whole. Greece and Italy are replaced by "la France."

Ronsard then proceeds to describe his imitative process in terms of the discovery and revival of an old rusty lyre. His reading and assimilation of classical poets is presented as a lengthy, loving curative act: he stumbles across an ancient lyre, out of tune and barely playable, coaxes it back into shape, and sings with it:

> 　　　　. . . quand premierement
> Je te trouvay, tu sonnois durement,
> 　　　　. . . . .
>
> Lors j'eu pitié de te voir mal-en-point,
> 　　　　. . . . .
>
> Je pillay Thebe, et saccageay la Pouille,
> T'enrichissant de leur belle despouille.
> Et lors en France avec toy je chantay,
> Et jeune d'ans sur le Loir. . . .
>
> 　　　　　　　　　　　(21-34)

> [. . . when first
> I found you, your sound was harsh
> 　　　. . . . .
>
> Then I took pity, seeing you in bad shape
> 　　　. . . . .
>
> I pillaged Thebes, and put Apulia to sack
> To adorn you with their sumptuous treasure.
> Then I sang with you in France,
> And in my youth on the Loir. . . .]

It is at the point of assimilation of the classics that regional land—as opposed to the space of France—is introduced into the poem, and that regionalist poetic ambition almost replaces the national. Pindar and Horace are named metonymically by their homelands, Thebes and Apulia, and these two Greek places are replaced, through Ronsard's efforts, not just by France, but by Ronsard's own home region in particular, the Vendômois (represented by the Loir river). There is an interesting variant maintained in editions up to 1578: in this section of the poem, Ronsard had proposed that both he and Du Bellay were due the credit of the renaissance of French lyric, Du Bellay also named metonymically by his homeland:

> Je t'envoiai sous le pousse Angevin
> Qui depuis moi t'a si bien fredonnée
> Qu'a nous deux seuls la gloire en soit donnée.
>
> (37-39)

> [I entrusted you then to Angevin hands
> Which strummed you so well, second to me,
> That to only the two of us is glory due.]

However, after the 1578 edition, Ronsard evidently became rather more jealous of his share of the credit, and dropped Du Bellay from the cursus. By the last edition of his lifetime, Ronsard presents himself alone as the vehicle by which the worthy ancients are brought into France; he figures himself almost as the reinventor of the French nation. If he presents France as a whole benefiting from his pillaging of Pindar and Horace, it is also quite clear whence in France this munificence emanates: his own Vendômois, superior this time to Du Bellay's Anjou, rather than collaborating with it. Geography is, as in Du Bellay, replaced by chorography, but in Ronsard chorography is affirmative; there is not the disillusionment that Du Bellay feels toward his homeland at the end of his *Regrets*.[18] Rather, the Vendômois is presented as the capital of poetic France, a place of pure poetry thanks to its association with Ronsard himself. It is at this point in **A sa lyre,** in the context of redemptive chorography, that the Gâtine enters the picture. Like the Loir, which appears again beside it, the naming of the Gâtine is inspired by a Horatian intertext. Horace's third ode of the fourth book contrasts sporting achievement with the superior glory of being known as a poet.[19] At the point of transition between athletics and poetry, Horace evokes the forest and the river as agents of poetic fame:

> But the waters that flow past the productive Tiber,
> And the thick leafy canopy of the glades
> Will make him famous by the song of Aeolius.[20]

Ronsard writes:

> Mais ma Gastine, et le haut crin des bois
> Qui vont bornant mon fleuve Vandomois,
> Le Dieu bouquin qui la Neufaune entourne,
> Et le saint choeur qui en Braye sejourne,
> Le feront tel, que par tout l'univers
> Se cognoistra renommé par ses vers.
>
> (45-50)

> [But my Gâtine, and the high canopy of the trees
> Which runs alongside my Vendomois river,
> The goatlike God who inhabits the Neufaune valley,
> And the blessed choir that resides in the valley of Braye,
> Will make him so famous that throughout the whole universe
> He will be recognized through his poetry.]

Where Horace names the river but not the wood, Ronsard names the wood but not the river (he has named the Loir already in this ode). This is another moment where the past and the present seem to coexist in suspension, in a landscape of pure poetry and of Ronsard's invention. The named forest brings the poem into the space of the French sixteenth-century lyric, but the Horatian intertext anchors it still in the domain of the ancient masters. The winner obviously is Ronsard himself, as he transforms the triumphant ending of Horace's ode into a triumph for himself. Horace writes:

> This is all your gift,
> That I am pointed out by the finger of passers-by
> As the poet of Roman lyric,
> It is your gift that I am inspired and that I please, if I do please.[21]

And Ronsard:

> C'est toy qui fais que Ronsard soit esleu
> Harpeur François, et quand on le rencontre
> Qu'avec le doigt par la rue on le monstre.
> Si je plais donc, si je sçay contenter
> Si mon renom la France veut chanter,
> Si de mon front les estoiles je passe,
> Certes mon Luth cela vient de ta grace.
>
> (62-68)

> [It is thanks to you that Ronsard is elected
> The lyricist of France, and that when he is seen
> In the street, people point him out.
> If then I please, if I give pleasure,
> If France sings my praises,
> If my head stands above the stars,
> Indeed, my Lute, this is by your grace.]

Note the expansion, or *dilatio,* of Horace by Ronsard. Ronsard is not only pointed out in the street, but his whole country sings his praises and he stands above the stars. The classical poets are there not to trouble his reputation but to bolster it: he has no compunction about trumping his exemplars.

This presentation, at the end of the first book of odes, of the Gâtine as a place closely associated with Ronsard's own poetic reputation gives rise to a cluster of odes about the forest in the second book. In the short ode entitled **A la forest de Gastine,** another piece of early composition, the forest is again presented as a refuge from strife and as a place where the poet may renew his connection with the Muses.[22] There is nothing particularly unusual about this presentation of the forest per se. What makes it notable, for our purposes, is that it is framed by a contrast between present and past. The first stanza reads:

> Couché sous tes ombrages vers
> Gastine, je te chante
> Autant que les Grecs par leurs vers
> La forest d'Erymanthe.[23]
>
>   (1-4)
>
> [Lying in your leafy shadows,
> Gastine, I sing of you
> As much as the Greeks in their verse
> Sang about the forest on Erymanthus.]

The first verse is dissected in the middle by a time line, signaled by the very Ronsardian transition "autant que": what is above it belongs to the present moment of composition, and what is below, to the past moment which inspired the present. So it is not clear what is being admired here: the forest itself, or the Greeks' admiration of theirs. The referent is obscured all the more by the fact that this is not simply an evocation of the Greeks, but of Horace's reference to this forest in his ode "Dianam tenerae dicite virgines."[24] It is a confusion with which Ronsard plays, simultaneously to name a contemporary French forest and to turn his admiration of it into admiration of the Greeks' admiration as suggested to him by a Latin poet.

Ronsard at once privileges the local and actual, and overwrites it with the past and foreign. What is at stake in this double movement becomes apparent if one reads the Horatian source to the end. Horace's address to young men and women to pray respectively to Apollo and Diana concludes by saying that doing so will protect them from plague and famine—an evocation of the grain shortage of 23 B.C.—and that these troubles will instead be visited upon the Britons and Persians. Horace moves from ritualized encomium, which is the context in which the woods on Erymanthus are mentioned, to mention of actual problems facing citizens of Augustan Rome:

> Young maidens, praise Diana
>   . . . . .
>
> Praise her who takes delight in rivers and the canopy
>   of the woods,
> That stand out on the cold Algidus mountains,
> Who delights in the black woods of Erymanthus
> Or the green woods of Cragus.
>   . . . . .
>
> He [Apollo] shall drive off bitter war and miserable
>   famine
> And plague from the Romans and the leader Caesar,
> And send them to the Persians and Britons,
> Moved by your prayer.[25]

The lyric geography of the ode is thus not only contrasted with real troubles, but presented as a refuge and protection from such troubles. The movement of Ronsard's ode is very similar. He, too, is constructing the Gâtine as a place of refuge from the reality of the present moment. He is not entirely presenting himself fleeing from the present; rather, he is rebuilding the present as he would wish it to be, a world ordered by his poetry. Ronsard is the mediator between the moment and place he inhabits, and the lost, idealized world of classical poetry, and his mediation, unlike Du Bellay's, has the potential to redeem the present through the past. While Horace's ode praises Apollo's power to ward off suffering, the main body of Ronsard's ode deals, not surprisingly, with his own poetic process, which replaces the classical divinities of his source. He is, indirectly, making quite a claim for the transformative power of his verse, but the reader can only understand this by supplying what is suppressed from his intertext—the power of Apollo himself. Ronsard replaces this power with images of himself communing with the Muses in the woods of Gâtine: he then wishes that the woods be always full of sylvan spirits, and that they remain untainted by present troubles. He presents the woods as a refuge from day to day cares, and his poetry as an activity which will somehow guarantee the survival of such places of refuge, since it is only, as he makes clear, through his mediation that the woods are thus transformed:

> Car malin, celer je ne puis
> A la race future
> De combien obligé je suis
> A ta belle verdure:
> Toy, qui sous l'abry de tes bois
> Ravy d'esprit m'amuses;
> Toy, qui fais qu'à toutes les fois
> Me respondent les Muses.
> Toy, par qui de *ce mechant soin*
> Tout franc je me delivre,
> Lors qu'en toy je me pers bien loin
> *Parlant avec un livre.*
> Tes bocages soient tousjours pleins
> D'amoureuses *brigades,*
> De Satyres et de Sylvains,
> La crainte des Naiades.
> En toy habite desormais
> Des Muses le college,
> Et ton bois ne sente jamais
> *La flame sacrilege.*
>
>   (5-24, my emphasis)
>
> [I cannot be so ungrateful as to hide
> From future generations
> How much I am obliged
> To your beautiful greenery:
> You, who in the shade of your woods
> Occupy my delighted spirit:
> You, thanks to whom always
> The Muses make reply to me:

You, through whom from *this heavy care*
I escape freely,
When I lose myself far in you,
Conversing with a book.
May your groves be forever full
Of amorous *troops,*
Of Satyres and of Silvans,
The dread of the Naiads.
Henceforth in you
May the College of the Muses live,
And may your woods never catch a hint
Of *the flame of sacrilege.*]

The first time mortal worries are mentioned (line 8) is as "mechant soin," which recalls in a general sense Horace's "atra cura" from his ode "Odi profanum," as well as more particularly Ronsard's own "soin meurtrier" from an ode in the same collection, called "Contre les avaricieux."[26] The Horatian ode deals primarily with the short-sighted and greedy accumulation of wealth for its own sake, a critique picked up and dealt with in great detail in Ronsard's own ode against the avaricious. So this first mention of the cares from which the poet is seeking shelter brings the specter of capitalism into the text: then, at the end of the ode, we see the poet hoping that the forest will never be burned up by the "flame of sacrilege"—a reference to the Protestant movement in France. Capitalism and Protestantism are thus both presented as evils from which the poet is trying to flee, an association which will come up again, as we shall see, in the elegy on the Gâtine. And the forest itself is not merely a shelter for the poet but is represented through poetry itself as a utopian answer to the problems he has just evoked, a place where past can redeem present. That the forest is more about poetry than about the Gâtine as a real space is made clear not only by Ronsard's depiction of his creative process (and the fact that he loses himself in the woods in order to "talk to a book"), but also by the play in line 18 on the word *brigade*—the former name of the Pléiade. The avatars of French poetry are transformed—through poetry itself—into typical denizens of the lyric forest, companions of naiads and satyrs.

Ronsard, then, has created a certain reader response; the reader of Ronsard's early collections has the Gâtine mapped out as the place that both creates and is created by Ronsard's particular genius. His lyric abounds with moments of prophesy in which he imagines future readers visiting the Vendômois region as an act of homage to him. In an early sonnet, "Cesse tes pleurs, mon livre," the poet imagines a future reader visiting his "pays"[27] and admiring not so much the countryside per se, but the poet—Ronsard—who was born there.

> Quelqu'un après mille ans, de mes vers étonné,
> Voudra dedans mon Loir comme en Permesse boire
> Et, voyant mon pays, à peine voudra croire
> Que d'un si petit champ tel poète soit né.
>
> (5-8)[28]

[In one thousand years, some admiring reader
Will want to drink from my Loir as from Parnassus,
And, on seeing my homeland, he will scarcely believe
That such a great poet was born of such a small land.]

Such prophetic moments are typical of Ronsard's lyric Vendômois: in a closed logical loop, the poet constructs landscape to send the reader back, through landscape, to the poet himself.[29] Ronsard, in a kind of performative statement, says he is famous, and makes himself so. The efficacy of such a gesture can be seen four hundred years later in the following moment of mimetic appreciation. Edmond Rocher, author of the tellingly titled *Pierre de Ronsard, Prince des Poètes,* cites these very lines by Ronsard and obediently transforms himself into exactly the reader Ronsard is prefiguring. His book is an account of his ecstatic "pilgrimage" to the Vendômois, where he walks reverentially, stopping to admire various landmarks celebrated by the poet.

> C'est en longeant les rives du Loir que j'évoque cette vigoureuse image du premier prince des poètes. Et je me plais à suivre sa grande ombre en ses promenades familières, au long de la rivière, autour de ses prieurés, de ses demeures de plaisance, et, relisant ses vers et retrouvant ses pas, durant l'accomplissement de ce pieux pélerinage, je sens que l'admiration et l'émotion prennent en moi une ferveur tout intime. Il aima cette gracieuse rivière comme en cette heure de solitude je me sens l'aimer.[30]

> [It is while walking along the banks of the Loir that I evoke this powerful image of the first Prince of Poets. And I take delight in following his long shadow on his familiar walks, along the river, around his priories, his favorite spots, and as I reread his poetry and trace his steps, during the realization of this worshipful pilgrimage, I feel personal, fervent admiration and emotion rising within me. He loved this graceful river as I feel I do in this moment of solitude.]

Rocher's experience of landscape is directly—and exclusively—mediated through Ronsard; the objects of his admiration have been preselected for him by Ronsard's poetry.[31] One wonders whether Rocher has a volume of Ronsard in hand while walking, or whether seeing the landmarks is itself a kind of "rereading," and in fact there is little difference. The acts of reading Ronsard and appreciating natural beauty are simultaneous.

Ronsard's Vendômois in his poetry, as he intends it to be read and as Rocher obligingly reads it, is practically synonymous with "pure" poetry, that is, a world symbolically ordered only by the processes of poetry and imagination, and not by other, modern (for Ronsard) processes of ordering—notably, the processes of capitalism and of Protestantism.[32] The forest in Ronsard's Vendômois is constructed as a refuge from both. The forest is a space sacred to poetry, a contrast to the real space of Ronsard's France, a place where the poet, Midas-like, turns everything he sees into pure poetry. This invocation of a poetically ordered space presents a harsh critique of present values. Central to this critique is the invocation of ancient authorities, whom he invokes as allies, belonging to the world whose passing he mourns and standing in contrast to the threats from the actual world he inhabits.[33] Any threat to the stability of the ideal world he constructs is countered by a return to the classics, by a reconstructing of his territory as the land of classical poetry and the dying values it stands for. Unlike Du Bellay, who as I show elsewhere never does work out the anxieties inherent in his relationship to his exemplars but rather lets them stand as his own particular "voice,"[34] Ronsard's relationship to classical poets is affirmative; he almost literally builds them into his poetic landscape as refuges from assaults by present corruption. Poetry and the past, Ronsard suggests in his Vendômois landscapes, have the potential to redeem the present.[35]

The uncomfortable reality of Protestant capitalist France is never far, though, and threatens to erase entirely this fragile lyric utopia. And its integrity and potential is challenged in the elegy on the clearcutting of the forest, where the trees—and by implication his own lyric world and the entire tradition—start falling down around him. In this poem, the *Elégie XXIIII*, the trees of the Gâtine are presented as sites of ideological contention where the stability of the ideal lyric world is radically challenged by intrusions from the modern world, and where the only protection comes from the invocation of the past symbolically ordered. The lyric traditions associated with trees, allied with the representation of a real forest, the Gâtine, allow Ronsard to foreground the struggle between past and present, a struggle which is ultimately a moral one, between a lost world of moral wholeness and an actual world of strife and degradation. Ronsard mourns a lost mimetic and poetic order represented by the past, and seeks to rebuild it in the present in his landscapes. His poetry stands precisely for this lost order—a pre-Protestant, precapitalist, aristocratic ethic that alone could turn the nation back from the brink of destruction.

The *Elégie XXIIII* is a combination of historical fact, reflection on the poetic process, and imitation of classical poets so bewildering that it merits consideration at length. The presentation of the forest is complicated from the outset by the fact that historical events render it impossible to continue idealizing the Gâtine. The forest belonged to the Bourbon-Vendôme family. For most of Ronsard's life, it had remained essentially untouched—perhaps the poet's sense of easy access through the forest to the world of classical poetry came in part from the pristine state in which it had been preserved. However, this was to change after 1572, the year in which Henri de Bourbon became king of Na-

varre and the debts of his family were estimated at one million *livres*. The council of the town of Vendôme recommended the sale of the Gâtine as the most propitious way to reestablish the family finances. Henry promptly accepted the recommendation, hired a surveyor, and in 1573 the trees started to fall.[36] This event lies behind the twenty-fourth elegy, though whether it provided the initial inspiration for the poem has been debated, as we shall see.

How does the poet react when the real-life emblem for his poetry is menaced? How is this threat transformed into poetry? Ronsard has presented the forest throughout his corpus as the place most intimately connected with his output, and it is not surprising that the deforestation stands for the threatened end of Ronsard's poetry. Since he allies his own output so closely with that of his exemplars, deforestation also represents the end of the ordering of classical poetry and the entire lyric tradition with all its redemptive potential. Since he has presented the forest standing for a certain moral order, as a refuge from modern ills, it is again not surprising that the deforestation stands for all that is wrong with the society he inhabits.

The twenty-fourth elegy is often anthologized under the title **"Elégie contre les bûcherons de la forêt de Gâtine"** [Elegy against the woodcutters of the Gâtine]. But this title appears for the first time in a posthumous edition of 1624, added by the editors; Ronsard simply called it *Elégie XXIIII*. The spurious editorial title, obviously determined by a certain kind of reading of the poem, has in turn determined most modern readings, which tend to read it primarily as a touching defense by Ronsard of the forest and trees he loved.[37] Indeed, in volumes that do not give the whole poem, the extract almost always starts on the line that is addressed directly to the woodcutters.[38] It is undeniable that Ronsard's poem is in part a reaction to the events of 1572. However, there is much more at stake; the poem is, and is not, about the particular events in the Gâtine. The forest is not even named in the poem; the association with the Gâtine, while it would have been obvious to any contemporary reader, is not as direct as the spurious title suggests. But it would be foolish to suggest the other extreme: that the poem has nothing to do with historical events in the Gâtine. The answer lies between the two: on the one hand, it is a meditation on poetry and what it could do, brimming with classical references to the point of not seeing the wood for the Ovids and Horaces. On the other, it is an obvious reaction to, and critique of, certain historical events and people. Ronsard takes as his point of departure a contemporary event, but transforms it into a literary event, without however completely overwriting the history that produced it. Throughout the poem, we see this tension between real and imagined space, past and present, literature and other discourses, especially economic. And it is precisely in the coincidence of history and poetry that meaning is constructed, as we shall see.

The false title, and the starting line of anthologized extracts of *Elégie XXIIII*, precondition the reader to see the addressee of the poem as the woodcutter. This unfortunately obscures another addressee, much more important for the historical context of the poem: Henri de Bourbon, king of Navarre, owner of the forest, the man who agreed to its sale, a Protestant, and the future king of France. The curse at the start of the poem is not, I believe, destined for the woodcutter, but for Henri, as Ute Margarete Saine has suggested,[39] and as lines 4-10 make clear:

> Quiconque aura premier la main embesongnée
> A te couper, forest, d'une dure congnée,
> Qu'il puisse s'enferrer de son propre baston,
> Et sente en l'estomac la faim d'Erisichthon,
> Qui coupa de Cerés le Chesne venerable,
> Et qui gourmand de tout, de tout insatiable,
> Les boeufs et les moutons de sa mere esgorgea,
> Puis pressé de la faim, soy-mesme se mangea:
> Ainsi puisse engloutir ses rentes et sa terre,
> Et se devore apres par les dents de la guerre.
>
> (1-10)

> [Whosoever first turns his hand
> To cut you, forest, with a hard axe,
> May he spike himself with his own stick,
> And feel in his stomach the hunger of Erisichthon,
> Who cut Ceres's sacred oak tree
> And who, greedy and insatiable for everything
> Ate his mother's sheep and cattle,
> Then, spurred by hunger, ate himself:
> Thus may he swallow up his money and land,
> And then devour himself with the teeth of war.]

Saine argues that the hand was not the body part instrumental to felling trees, and contrasts the hand with the arm in the later direct address to the woodcutter, concluding that the giving of the hand, in the first line, is the royal mandate for the sale, and thus Henri is implied from the beginning. While it is true that the root for *mandate* (*mandat* in French) is the Latin *manu dato*, I am not sure that the reference to Henri is apparent in this first line. Rather, we are not sure until the mention of Erisichthon to whom this curse applies; the comparison with a king, and the mention of money, land, and capital invested on war are clearly not applicable to a woodcutter, and focus the criticism on the royal agent of destruction, Henri. The criticism is made all the more direct by the fact that the apogée of the curse, lines 9-18, is the first part of the poem that is entirely original, that is, not imitated from classical sources.

The first eight lines are a conflation of Horace and Ovid that initially obscures the historical fact of deforestation and only gradually makes clear who is the object of Ronsard's fury. Even the initial direct address to the forest ("à te couper, forest") is mediated by Horace, who opens his ode "Ille et nefasto te posuit die" thus:

> He both planted you on an unlucky day, tree,
> Whoever did so in the first place, and also with a
>   sacrilegious hand
> Raised you for the danger of posterity
> And the shame of the village.[40]

Horace's ode is a humorously exaggerated account of a tree of the Sabine farm falling and nearly crushing him. His mock fury is directed against the person who planted the tree in the first place. Ronsard's tone is anything but light, and rather than cursing the planter of the trees, he focuses on the agents of the wood's falling. This transformation of Horace, the mention of the person responsible for the destruction, allows him to bring Ovid's Erisichthon into his poem, a figure who introduces the themes of sacrilege, punishment, and violence, all applied to a *king*.[41] In Ovid, Erisichthon is a powerful king who "scorned the gods"; the measure of his godlessness is shown when he "violated the sacred grove of Ceres with the axe." Initially, his slaves are wielding the axe. However, they hesitate when they come to a venerable oak tree, surrounded by wreaths and votive tablets, at which point the king snatches an axe and starts to chop. Blood streams from the tree; a slave who tries to hold back the king's arm is beheaded for his "pious thought." The voice of a nymph from inside the tree assures the king that he will be punished. At the behest of her nymphs, Ceres curses him with insatiable Famine, who leads him to eat his entire inheritance ("patrias") and property ("census"—a word also encompassing high social standing), to attempt to sell his daughter, and ultimately to consume himself.

The myth of Erisichthon focuses sharp criticism on the figure of the king, and much of Ovid's moral vocabulary—greed, sacrilege, consummation—is picked up by Ronsard. Central to Ovid's myth is the idea of appropriate and adequate punishment. Erisichthon is punished by Famine, the opposite ("contraria") to Ceres the goddess of natural abundance. If he has sinned by not respecting the vitality and inspiritedness embodied by Ceres, he will be visited by dearth and famine, and will be unable to find any satisfaction from the world. Ronsard similarly wishes an appropriate punishment upon his king, whose sin is to attribute economic value to a sacred place; pushing the sin to its extreme, he wishes an infinite accumulation of debts and interest, and ultimately financial ruination in a kind of bourgeois, capitalist speculative hell:

> Qu'il puisse, pour vanger le sang de nos forests,
> Toujours nouveaux emprunts sur nouveaux interests
> Devoir a l'usurier, et qu'en fin il consomme
> Tout son bien à payer la principale somme.
> Que tousjours sans repos ne face en son cerveau

Que tramer pour-neant quelque dessein nouveau,
Porté d'impatience et de fureur diverse
Et de mauvais conseil qui les hommes renverse.

(11-18)

[So that the blood of our forests may be avenged,
May the interest on his debts be forever accumulating,
And in order to pay back the principal,
May he end up spending his entire fortune.
May his mind always restlessly be hatching
Some useless new scheme or other,
Driven by impatience, by fits of anger,
And by bad advice which is the downfall of men.]

These lines are the first and only lines purely of Ronsard's invention, and as such they would stand out to a contemporary reader familiar with the sources. A new, threatening kind of vocabulary is introduced into the idealized space of lyric (the old forest) and into the domain of classical poetry, a vocabulary of capitalist accumulation, debt, compound interest (presumably), and restless speculation on new, ill-advised ventures. This is the world antithetical to poetry, or to the ordering of Ronsard's poetry, and the image of the falling trees allows him a powerful visual correlative to the idea of the destruction of a certain moral and poetic order by an emerging capitalist order.[42]

In this scheme, the woodcutter cannot count for much. He is the mere agent of forces beyond his control; in both Ronsard and Ovid, it is quite clear on whose shoulders blame should fall—those of powerful men in the position of making such decisions. Erisichthon's slaves, the real woodcutters, are the men who *refuse* to fell the sacred oak, and one man even loses his head for holding back the king's arm. In Ronsard, this moment of detention of the arm about to take a stroke is incorporated into a direct address, in the best-known line of the poem, "Escoute, buscheron, arreste un peu le bras." But, given the Ovidian intertext in which the king himself is the man with the axe, even this address is complicated. The "buscheron" is Henri himself, put in the position of Erisichthon by direct intertextual reference:

Escoute, Bucheron, arreste un peu le bras,
Ce ne sont pas des bois que tu jectes à bas,
Ne vois-tu pas le sang lequel desgoute à force
Des Nymphes qui vivoyent dessous la dure escorce?
Sacrilege meurdrier. . . .

(19-23)

[Listen, woodcutter, hold your arm right there,
This is not a wood which you cut down,
Don't you see the fast flow of the blood
Of the Nymphs who used to live under the thick bark?
Sacrilegious murderer. . . .]

Line 20 is to be taken quite seriously: these are not woods, or not only woods, or even only nymphs; they are also poetry itself, the vanishing poetry of the literary golden age, and of Ronsard himself.[43] The place of the crime is as much Ovid's sacred grove as it is the Gâtine: lines 21 and 23 are direct echoes of the Latin source.[44] The story of Erisichthon has much more than a comparative function in Ronsard's logic; he is not merely wishing a punishment on a woodcutter "like" the punishment of Erisichthon; rather, through the mythical king, he is making the agent of blame a king himself—Henri. The concluding epithet, "sacrilegious murderer," brings together Henri's greed and his religion. Ronsard seems to suggest that capitalist accumulation and Protestantism go hand in hand. At any rate, they both form the moral horizon against which Ronsard rails, and to which the Gâtine of his poetry stands in contrast.[45]

One might object that, since neither Henri nor the Gâtine are directly named, it is speculative to assume that they are the intended referents. Were the events of 1572 the inspiration for the poem? The *terminus ad quem* of the poem is 1584, the date of publication, but Ian McFarlane has suggested that "Ronsard composed at least part of his poem any time after 1553," the date of publication of a neo-Latin source by Gervais Sepin which McFarlane was the first to point out.[46] The similarities between Sepin and Ronsard are striking, but it does not follow that because a model poem was in circulation in the 1550s Ronsard must have begun composing his poem then. He certainly had Sepin in mind, perhaps even to hand, but it is clear nevertheless that the finished poem was intended as a response to the sale and clearing of the Gâtine. Ronsard wrote the bulk of his *Elégies* in the 1570s. He returned to his native Vendômois, disabused of life at court, in 1576, a date by which the forest had been surveyed, divided into parcels, and indeed clear-cut in certain parts. The resulting poem may draw on much more than biography or history, but there is no reason to doubt that the composition was prompted by Henri's decision and its visible results.

However it is also true that Henri is, in the poem, symptomatic of greater social trends. The elegy is not just about Henri's Protestantism, but about the effects of Protestantism—or more specifically the religious schism—on the nation; nor is it only about Henri's particular financial situation, but rather criticizes the general tendency in sixteenth-century French discourse to consider value in economic terms. A writer whom Ronsard may have had in mind is Bernard Palissy, who unites the figure of the Protestant with that of the socially mobile bourgeois. Palissy enjoyed protection from some of the most powerful families in France, and he and Ronsard flourished at the same time, so it is highly possible that Ronsard was familiar with his work at least by hearsay if not personally. In 1563 Palissy published his *Recepte Veritable*, which might attract more interest from Ronsard scholars if it were known under its more provocative full name, *Les Moyens de devenir riche ou Recepte Veritable par laquelle tous les hommes de la France pourront apprendre à multiplier et augmenter leurs trésors.*[47] From the title at least, there could hardly be a clearer representative of the "avaricieux" mentality Ronsard so lambastes in poems such as the "Hymne de l'Or," or the above-mentioned "Contre les avaricieux." Palissy was Protestant and working-class, he prided himself on not reading Greek or Latin and on his status as an artisan with practical knowledge who had pulled himself up through sheer hard work and skill. He represented all that Ronsard so despised about his world—social fluidity and promotion of the bourgeois, rejection of learning, Protestant and populist religion.

In his *Recepte Veritable,* Palissy discusses the cutting of trees, in a passage which could be an implied intertext for Ronsard's elegy, and if not, it at least makes for an interesting case study of the kinds of discourses around trees and wood to which Ronsard objects. Palissy talks of wood as the nation's most important economic resource, since every trade depends on it, and he insists on the need to manage carefully any clearcutting so as to ensure a future supply of timber. Palissy has no quibble with the idea of felling trees, but he insists on replanting, and on felling the right trees at the right time. This highly utilitarian discourse around the value of trees to the economic survival of the country is a direct contrast to Ronsard's notions of poetic value, and the contrast is also distinctly valenced along class lines. The reception of Palissy among the greater literary community in Renaissance France has not been researched at all; attention has focused on Palissy as a forerunner of certain scientific techniques and discourses. Until such work is done, all that can be said is that Palissy's work, and his status as a working-class Protestant, crystallizes many of the perceived threats to the trees of Ronsard's Gâtine.

The transition in the middle of **Elégie XXIIII** makes it clear that the forest in question is the Gâtine: Ronsard starts to bid farewell to lyric convention in general, and then to his own work in particular. As we have seen, the reader is trained by the early poems to associate the Gâtine with Ronsard's inspiration and genius, so, when Ronsard addresses the forest as the place where he heard Apollo's arrows, tuned his lyre, and other clichés of lyric creation, we ourselves supply the name. However, Ronsard takes a while to get there. First he takes leave of a panoply of lyric topoi, evocations mostly of Virgil:

> Forest, haute maison des oiseaux bocagers,[48]
> Plus le Cerf solitaire et les Chevreuls legers
> Ne paistront sous ton ombre, et ta verte criniere
> Plus du Soleil d'este ne rompra la lumiere.
> Plus l'amoureux Pasteur sur un tronq adossé,
> Enflant son flageolet à quatre trous persé,[49]

> Son mastin à ses pieds, à son flanc la houlette,
> Ne dira plus l'ardeur de sa belle Janette:
> Tout deviendra muet, Echo sera sans voix:
> Tu deviendras campagne, et en lieu de tes bois,
> Dont l'ombrage incertain lentement se remue,[50]
> Tu sentiras le soc, le coutre et la charrue:[51]
> Tu perdras ton silence, et haletans d'effroy
> Ny Satyres, ny Pans ne viendront plus chez toy.

(27-40)

> [Forest, high refuge of woodland birds,
> No longer will the solitary hart and the lightfooted roes
> Graze in your shadow, and your green canopy
> Will no longer filter summer sunbeams.
> The amorous shepherd, leaning against a tree trunk,
> Playing his four-holed wooden pipe,
> His hound at his feet, his crook by his side,
> Will no longer speak of his passion for the lovely Janette:
> All will become quiet, Echo will have no voice,
> You will become farmland, and instead of your woods
> Whose quivering shadow slowly changes,
> You will feel the ploughshare, the coulter and the plough:
> Your silence will be lost, and, gasping with fear,
> Satyrs and Pans will come to you no more.]

This is a sweeping adieu to the golden age, to the entire world of pastoral and lyric poetry whose integrity is destroyed by the greed of the king. The "amoureux pasteur" is, of course, Tityrus, the emblem of lyric ease and contentment in the face of dispossession, who has an affective and creative relationship with his land. By silencing this shepherd, Ronsard is effectively silencing himself, erasing the possibility of tranquil enjoyment and refuge from the world's cares. However, there is a play on the concept of silence, which shows the conflict of two different discourses, one of which is silenced and the other not. Line 35 is about the vanishing of lyric poetry; its voices will no longer be heard in the forest, and "all will become quiet." In line 39 however, we read, "you will lose your silence." The felled forest is simultaneously a place of silence and of cacophony, which is only possible if two different kinds of noise are at stake. The silence is the absence of the poetic order; the noise, the presence of exploitative capitalist activity.

This elegy is, in part, a gesture of capitulation of the former to the latter, a kind of epitaph of a certain kind of poetry. While it is neither "the last poem of the last volume of poetry published in Ronsard's lifetime," nor even "the last poem of his elegy cycle," as Saine rather oddly claims, it does still deserve to be read as a testament to lyric and the world it stands for in Ronsard.[52] If it was in fact written on the occasion of Ronsard's return to the Vendômois in 1576, it is one of the last poems he wrote, even if it does not conveniently occupy the final pages of the 1584 edition. The accumulation of adieus in the second half of the poem gives it the air of a funereal oration. Ronsard starts the formal farewells with his own poetic voice, a trope which he has built up throughout his earlier work:

> Adieu vieille forest, le jouet de Zephyre,
> Où premier j'accorday les langues de ma lyre,
> Où premier j'entendi les fleches resonner
> D'Apollon. . . .
>
> (41-44)

> [Goodbye, old forest, Zephyr's plaything,
> Where first I tuned the languages of my lyre,
> Where first I heard quiver the arrows
> Of Apollo. . . .]

Next to go is the commemorative and religious function of the trees, harking back to Erisichthon's sacrilege:

> Adieu vieille forest, adieu testes sacrées,
> De tableaux et de fleurs autrefois honorées.
>
> (49-50)

> [Goodbye, old forest, goodbye sacred heads,
> once honored with paintings and flowers.]

And finally, a farewell to the kind of society and individual that the trees stand for, a lost world of upstanding heroes:

> Adieu Chesnes, couronnes aux vaillans citoyens.
>
> (55)

> [Farewell, oak trees, the crowns of valiant citizens.]

The intertext here is Virgil, not the *Eclogues* or *Georgics,* but the *Aeneid,* the epic of the founding of Rome. The line is from the dead Anchises's eulogistic prediction about the future Roman state:

> What youths! See how much courage they display
> Their temples adorned with the civic oak![53]

The civic oak was awarded to one who had saved a fellow citizen in battle. This is one of the most optimistic and patriotic moments in the *Aeneid,* and through his imitation, Ronsard is evoking a now-lost world of civic virtue, of a nation of valiant soldiers and just wars, precisely the kind of nation sixteenth-century France, to Ronsard, is not.

Thus far in the poem, Ronsard has written a complex web of references to historical fact, to real space, to poetic space, to his own poetic project and his harnessing of his exemplars. It is in the interplay between them that meaning is constructed: for example, in the layering of the example of Erisichthon onto the curse against the agents of destruction of the Gâtine, the "woodcut-

ter" becomes Henri de Navarre. The image of the felled trees also evokes that of the truncated family tree—the Navarre line will soon replace the Valois dynasty, Henri being the one who "fells" the Valois tree. In the figure of Erisichthon, two principal characteristics are crystallized, avarice and sacrilege, which are transferred to Henri and become symptomatic of the corruption of the age. The Gâtine, constructed throughout Ronsard's work as a place of poetry untouched by mundane corruption, is destroyed; the capitalists and Protestants win. The forest, historically a space whose use was already strongly contested,[54] becomes in Ronsard a space contested between the poet and poetry on one side, and the king and economics on the other. Lyric poets are presented as the last bastion of a righteous, precapitalist, Virgilian kind of society where all are God-fearing and there is no economic demand made upon land; but as the trees fall, so does the world of lyric, and Ronsard and his chosen allies—Virgil, Horace, and Ovid—run from the scene of destruction like the woodland spirits of his poem.

The image of a lost ideal world is helpful for our understanding of the curious ending of the elegy, which leaves most readers stumped, so to speak, to the point that most choose simply to ignore it. Ian McFarlane is one of the few readers to have tackled the issue of the apparent lack of unity of the poem; however, he sees discontinuity between the Horatian and Ovidian beginning, almost half of the poem, and the rest, which is for him a "rich treatment" of "the themes of Nature and Time."[55] Unfortunately, McFarlane does not explain the last few lines for us. I see no problem with the first half, the overlap of Horace with the Erisichthon myth and the events surrounding the sale of the forest; all seems to coalesce around Henri, a symbol of the ills of the time. The last eight lines of the poem fit much less comfortably into this interpretive schema:

> Que l'homme est malheureux qui au monde se fie!
> O Dieux, que veritable est la Philosophie,
> Qui dit que toute chose à la fin perira,
> Et qu'en changeant de forme une autre vestira:
> De Tempé la vallée un jour sera montagne,
> Et la cyme d'Athos une large campagne,
> Neptune quelque fois de blé sera couvert,
> La matière demeure, et la forme se perd.
>
> (61-68)

> [How miserable is the man who trusts in the world!
> O gods, how true is that philosophy
> That says everything perishes in the end,
> And as it changes form, assumes a new one:
> The valley of Tempe will one day be a mountain,
> And the summit of Athos a wide plain,
> The ocean will at some time be covered in wheat.
> Matter remains, and form is lost.]

Michel Jeanneret, in his study of metamorphosis in sixteenth-century art and literature, *Perpetuum mobile,* uses the last line of Ronsard's *Elégie XXIIII,* "La matière demeure, et la forme se perd," as his epigraph.[56] Ronsard, for Jeanneret, seeks a "puissance de redressement" in the process of transformation, a recycling of death into life. Ronsard does indeed seem to be taking consolation from the fact that all landscapes shift and change—a classical commonplace since Ovid. But more is at stake, surely, than a *consolatio*. What Ronsard has just presented is not the force of Nature acting on the shape of the land, but the rapid and destructive effect of human activity. And there is a complex intertextual game being played with his sources in these last few lines that reveals a profound meditation on the transformative power not only of nature, but of poetry itself.

Ronsard's inspiration now is Lucretian and Ovidian. Once again, it is helpful to look beyond the immediate intertextual lines to the source texts surrounding them. The Lucretian lines paraphrased by Ronsard say "the earth is diminished and grows again," and "all things gradually decay and go to the reef of destruction, outworn by the ancient lapse of years."[57] These last lines, at the end of Lucretius's second book, come in the context of a mildly ironic commentary on the human tendency to idealize bygone times—precisely what Ronsard has been doing. The farmer in Lucretius "compares times present with times past and often praises the fortunes of his father," and "grumbles how the old world, full of piety, supported life with great ease on a narrow domain." It is this farmer who does not understand that "all things gradually decay." Ronsard seems to be taking a final jibe at himself, ironizing the very process by which he built up the Gâtine, the Vendômois, and his poetry as representative of a lost moral order.

However, he contrasts this with another intertext, Pythagoras's teachings in the last book of Ovid's *Metamorphoses*. This is a long discourse with several particular lines that Ronsard seems to have in mind: "all things change, but nothing dies. . . . Nothing is constant in the whole world. . . . nothing lasts long under the same form."[58] However Pythagoras starts his disquisition with a praise of the lost golden age which stands in contrast to the Lucretian irony. This juxtaposition of self-irony with apparently serious and wistful yearning of the lost age is Ronsard's message. While pointing out, through his reference to Lucretius, the very poetic process by which such an age is constructed by poets, he also seems to maintain, with Ovid's Pythagoras, the validity of such visions, and the fact that poets will always seek to construct such "spaces of hope" faced with the degradation of their time.

In *Spaces of Hope,* David Harvey takes Henri Lefebvre to task. In *The Production of Space,*[59] says Harvey, Lefebvre objects to the closing-off, the authoritarian act of definition and exclusion inherent in the act of imagining an alternative space to the capitalist space we inhabit. However, according to Harvey, Lefebvre provides us with no alternatives and leaves us hanging in "an agonistic romanticism of perpetually unfulfilled longing and desire."[60] Harvey addresses the question of how to fulfill this longing by insisting on the primacy of the imagination—"we cannot ignore the question of the imagination"—in a retort to the Thatcherite defense of globalized capitalist culture, "the Thatcherite doctrine that 'there is no alternative,'" and "the inability to find an 'optimism of the intellect' with which to work through alternatives."[61] In Harvey, we have perhaps a modern correlative to Ronsard's response to threats to the world of the imagination. The Harvey of the Pléiade imagines his utopia in regional space—the forest of Gâtine in the Vendômois.

Notes

Thanks to Tim Hampton, Paul Alpers, and Nick Paige for close reading and invaluable comments. Thanks also to Christian Biet of Paris X and to his students for friendly and constructive suggestions.

1. Roberto M. Dainotto, *Place in Literature: Regions, Cultures, Communities* (Ithaca: Cornell University Press, 2000), 173. Dainotto's introduction offers a comprehensive survey of the nationalist/regionalist debate, including ways in which these terms have been used, or not, by Marxist and postcolonial critics.

2. Ibid., 11.

3. For a powerful discussion applied to Renaissance literature of pastoral as a fragile protection against history, see David Quint's reading of Jacopo Sannazaro's *Arcadia* in the second chapter of his *Origin and Originality in Renaissance Literature: Versions of the Source* (New Haven: Yale University Press, 1983), 43-80.

4. The collection edited by Philippe Nys, *Le jardin, art et lieu de mémoire* (Besançon: Editions de l'Imprimeur, 1995), considers the Renaissance garden as spatialized, static, and solid incarnations of various verbal *mementi*: "le jardin est ainsi comme une écriture qui vient au secours de la parole qui s'envole" (25). See also, for a discussion of the classical rhetorical *ars memorativa* rooted in commonplaces, Frances Yates, *The Art of Memory* (Chicago: University of Chicago Press, 1966).

5. David Harvey, *Spaces of Hope* (Berkeley: University of California Press, 2000).

6. Nationalism itself is a problematic term, of course. Richard Helgerson's *Forms of Nationhood: The Elizabethan Writing of England* (Chicago: Univer-

sity of Chicago Press, 1992), shows that the Renaissance English imagining of nationhood was by no means monolithic. However, the case of France was different; I believe that there was in France, much earlier than in England, a more coherent sense of belonging to what we now recognize as a "nation." See Colette Beaune's *Naissance de la nation France* (Paris: Gallimard, 1985). For a study of the history of statehood on the European scale, see Hugh Seton-Watson's *Nations and States* (London: Methuen, 1977); and *Conquest and Coalescence: The Shaping of the State in Early Modern Europe,* ed. Mark Greengrass (London: Arnold, 1991). For the figurations of "literary nationhood" in early modern France, see Timothy Hampton, *Literature and Nation in the Sixteenth Century: Inventing Renaissance France* (Cornell: Cornell University Press, 2000). Benedict Anderson's nuanced study *Imagined Communities: Reflections on the Origin and Spread of Nationalism* (London: Verso, 1983) is still authoritative, and reminds us that "nationalism" is an Enlightenment concept while showing how prenationalist communities imagined themselves.

7. I use the word *landscape* in the sense understood by scholars of the visual arts, that is, a motivated selection and representation of a part of the raw material of nature. See Anne Cauquelin's *L'invention du paysage* (Paris: Plon, 1985). Guy Demerson has defined the written landscape, also, as a "fragment de nature, qui est dé-fini illusoirement et provisoirement," in his conclusion to the collection of essays *Le paysage à la Renaissance,* ed. Yves Giraud (Fribourg: Editions Universitaires Fribourg Suisse, 1988), 327. This is not to suggest, however, that the concept of nature is not itself culturally constructed. The history of the idea of nature has in fact been quite well studied, from R. G. Collingwood's *The Idea of Nature* (Oxford: Clarendon Press, 1945), to Neil Evernden's *The Social Creation of Nature* (Baltimore: Johns Hopkins University Press, 1992). My own reading is not of "nature" but of "landscape" in Pléiade poetry. See Françoise Joukovsky, *Paysages de la Renaissance* (Paris: P.U.F., 1974), for one of the first considerations of landscapes, as opposed to nature, in French Renaissance poetry.

8. Nowhere did literary and actual landscapes meet as closely as in the gardens of the sixteenth century. The incredibly detailed description of the fictional gardens, monuments, and statues in the *Hypnerotomachia Poliphili* (1499) was imitated in actual gardens throughout France and Italy for over a century afterwards. For the reception in France of the *Polyphilus,* see Gilles Polizzi's introduction to his edition of Martin's text, *Le songe de Poliphile* (Paris: Imprimerie nationale, 1994). For the importance of the Italian garden style in France—and the mass importing by French royalty of Italian landscape gardeners—see Terry Comito, *The Idea of the Garden in the Renaissance* (New Brunswick, N.J.: Rutgers University Press, 1978), chap. 1, and chap. 3 for Italian and French literary gardens. See Nys, *Le Jardin,* for a collection of essays dealing with both French and Italian case studies. There are many studies by landscape architects of the Renaissance garden, in particular the Italian model: a good overview of gardens in early modern Europe as a whole—with good photographs—is Torsten Olaf Enge's *Garden Architecture in Europe, 1450-1800: From the Villa Garden of the Italian Renaissance to the English Landscape Garden* (Koln: Taschen, 1990).

9. See, in particular, Frank Lestringant, *Ecrire le monde à la Renaissance: quinze études sur Rabelais, Postel, Bodin et la littérature géographique* (Caen: Paradigme, 1993). Tom Conley, in *The Self-Made Map: Cartographic Writing in Early Modern France* (Minneapolis: University of Minnesota Press, 1996), uses a more psychoanalytic approach to identify a cartographic "unconscious" in many Renaissance writers.

10. See, for example, Michel Jeanneret's important study of movement and metamorphosis in Renaissance writing and painting, *Perpetuum mobile: Métamorphoses des corps et des œuvres de Vinci à Montaigne* (Paris: Macula, 1997), which addresses the widespread humanist fascination with natural flux and variety over fixity and predictable order, and the rhetorical problems presented by a subject that resists the ordering of the text. His book is nicely complemented by Danièle Duport, *Les jardins qui sentent le sauvage: Ronsard et la poétique du paysage* (Geneva: Droz, 2000), who considers the philosophical notion that the ordering of nature is somehow reflected in poetic order, showing that Ronsard's nature is presented as a space in which the poet dialogues with his exemplars and into which he inscribes his own particular poetic manifesto.

11. See the following, all found in vol. 1 of Pierre de Ronsard, *Œuvres Complètes* (Paris: Gallimard, 1993): the odes *A sa lyre,* "Lyre dorée, ou Phoebus seulement" (676-78); *O terre fortunée,* "Des-Autels, qui redore" (699-700); *A la forest de Gastine,* "Couché sous tes ombrages vers" (703-4); ode to Gaspar d'Auvergne, "Gaspard, qui loing de Peguse" (a transposition of Horace I, xxxi, "Quid dedicatum poscit Apollinum"), (782-83); *A son lut,* "Si autre-fois sous l'ombre de Gastine" (962-65); the sonnets "Ciel, air et vents" (7-8); "Je te

hay peuple" (87-88); "Saincte Gastine, o douce secretaire" (111); "Que Gastine ait tout le chef jaunissant" (491); and the "Voyage de Tours" (204-11). Hereafter, Ronsard's works are cited parenthetically in the text by line numbers. For references to shorter poems, I give incipits—or titles when possible—as well as the page numbers for the Pléiade edition, rather than the number of a particular poem or even, in certain cases, the name of the collection in which it appears. Ronsard regularly reorganized his entire corpus, shifting poems from one collection to another, cutting them entirely from new editions, reorganizing the order within a collection, or adding new material. This makes the task of editing Ronsard an unenviable one. It also renders virtually redundant many designations of poems—especially the earlier works—by number and collection. For the sustained discussion of the twenty-fourth elegy, however, I will use the title *Elégie* XXIIII, since I shall argue the importance of there being no title in the first edition.

12. I follow the *recentiores superiores* policy of the editors of the Pléiade volumes, who give the ordering of the 1584 *Œuvres* since it was the last edition supervised by Ronsard himself.

13. For an extensive study of the image of the lyre in Ronsard, see Isidore Silver, *Ronsard and the Grecian Lyre* (Geneva: Droz, 1981). Françoise Joukovsky has written an impressive study of the theme of glory in French Renaissance poetry, *La gloire dans la poésie française et néolatine du 16e siècle: des rhétoriqueurs à Agrippa d'Aubigné* (Geneva: Droz, 1969); with respect to Ronsard, see in particular 204-14, and for the theme of glory inscribed in landscape, 323-64.

14. For exact borrowings from Pindar and Horace, see the notes to the Pléiade *Œuvres complètes*, ed. Jean Céard, Daniel Ménager, and Michael Simonin (Paris: Gallimard, 1994), 1515. Pindar's first Pythian, which Ronsard transcribes at the start of his ode, concludes with a reflection on fame particularly appropriate to Ronsard, though Ronsard does not use it here: "When men are dead and gone, it is only the loud acclaim of praise that surviveth mortals and revealeth their manner of life to chroniclers and to bards alike." Translation by Sir J. E. Sandys, Pindar's *Odes*, Loeb Classical Library (Cambridge: Harvard University Press, 1915).

15. Pindar, *Odes*, 1.

16. All translations are my own. I have tried simply to convey the literal sense of the French. Any translation, particularly of poetry, is an art in itself, and not one I claim to have mastered.

17. From Pindar, *Odes*, lines 13-14 of the first Pythia: "But all the beings that Zeus hath not loved, are astonished when they hear the voice of the Pierides."

18. The distinction between geography (mapping on a national scale) and chorography (mapping of a small region) is discussed by Lestringant, *Ecrire le monde*, chap. 1.

19. Interestingly, this ode comes right after a long encomiastic ode to Pindar, the "sports poet" of the Greeks.

20. Horace, *Odes and Epodes*, ed. Paul Shorey and Gordon J. Laing (Chicago: Sanborn, 1919), lines 10-12, my translation [Sed quae Tibur aquae fertile praefluunt, / Et spissae nemorum comae / Fingent Aeolio carmine nobilem]. All citations of *Odes and Epodes* in the essay refer to the odes.

21. Ibid., lines 21-24, my translation [Totum muneris hoc tuist, / Quod monstror digito praetereuntium / Romanae fidicen lyrae: / Quod spiro et placeo, si placeo, tuumst]. This itself seems to be a transformation of the image of the lyric poet being pointed out and laughed at in public places for his unrequited love for a woman. There is some interesting work to be done on such moments of public recognition in lyric.

22. This ode appeared in the first edition of the *Quatre Premiers Livres des Odes* (1550). The original text was substantially different from Ronsard's rewrite appearing in all editions after 1555. However, the contrast I discuss is operative in both versions of this particular ode, suggesting that it was structurally and thematically important enough for Ronsard to have kept it despite other significant changes.

23. Erymanthus: a mountain in Arcadia, a supposed haunt of Diana.

24. Horace, *Odes and Epodes*, I, xxi, line 7.

25. Ibid., lines 1-16: "Dianam tenerae dicite virgines / . . . / Vos laetam fluviis et nemorum coma / Quaecumque aut gelido prominet Algido, / Nigris aut Erymanthi / Silvis aut viridis Cragi. / . . . / Hic bellum lacrimosum, hic miseram famen / Pestemque a populo et principe Caesare in / Persas atque Britannos / Vestra motus aget prece."

26. Horace, *Odes and Epodes*, III, i, line 40; Ronsard, *Le Second Livre des Odes*, Ode IV, line 11 (*Œuvres*, 1:686).

27. The sense of *pays* in sixteenth-century French is much closer to the sense preserved in the modern Italian *paese*, that is, a local region rather than a nation.

28. This sonnet first appeared in the *Bocage* of 1554; in 1584, it concludes the first section of *Second livre des Amours de Marie* (*Œuvres*, 1:247).

29. Françoise Joukowsky, in "Qu'est-ce qu'un paysage?" in Giraud, *Le paysage à la Renaissance*, 55-66, has linked the constantly shifting landscapes to the construction of the poet's interior "moi esthétique"; they exist primarily to glorify the poet's own power of invention, constituting a Mallarmean "autonomous whole" which is about nothing more and nothing less than itself: "this reduced nature . . . is in fact an autonomous whole that creates its own space. . . . The landscape thus displays the self-sufficiency of the work of art, a world turned in on itself" (my trans.). This reading is helpful in that it highlights the importance of the Ronsardian poetic ego and his careful (some might say shameless) construction of his own reputation. However, what happens to this poetic self when it imitates its exemplar poets is a question Joukowsky does not raise. While no reader of Ronsard could ever dispute the self-serving dimension of much of his poetry, his relationship to his exemplars is a vital part of how he constructs his monument to himself.

30. Edmond Rocher, *Pierre de Ronsard, Prince des Poètes* (Paris: P.U.F., 1924), 29.

31. The field of "ecocriticism" has produced some good theoretical work on this relationship between text and landscape. See, for a starting point, the essays by Christopher Manes, "Nature and Silence," and Alison Byerly, "The Uses of Landscape," in *The Ecocriticism Reader*, ed. Cheryl Glotfelty and Harold Fromm (Athens: University of Georgia Press, 1996), 15-29, 52-68, as well as the editors' introduction. The practice of ecocritical reading, however, is almost exclusively applied to English and American literature, and within those, to the genre of nature writing. It is one of the aims of this project to show that ecocritical theory can inform readings of texts from other countries and of genres in which the post-Romantic human relationship to nature is not the primary concern.

32. Such a coupling might smack of Weberian causality; however, I am not arguing a causal relationship between Protestantism and capitalism, or any kind of relationship beyond the fact that they are objects of direct attack by Ronsard.

33. Thomas Greene, *The Light in Troy* (New Haven: Yale University Press, 1982), 201-213, addresses the issue of imitation in a particularly subtle reading of Ronsard's nature, in which he shows the fluid movement between the landscape and some other shape, for example, the female body. As Greene shows, such transformations are themselves acts of imitation, not of nature but of other writers, particularly Petrarch and Pindar. What Greene's reading does not do is consider moments in which Ronsard's nature is indubitably French and modern and cannot be anything else.

34. For an excellent reading of Du Bellay's hesitant poetic voice, see François Rigolot, "Du Bellay et la poésie du refus," *Bibliothèque d'Humanisme et de Renaissance* 36 (1974): 489-502. Rigolot points out, in a direct contrast with Ronsard, that much of what we perceive as Du Bellay's poetic individuality comes from his use of negations, his preference for formulae such as "je ne veulx point," "je ne suis point," etc.

35. The idea of a redemptive design in the natural order has been discussed with reference to Sidney and Shakespeare by Eric LaGuardia in *Nature Redeemed* (The Hague: Mouton, 1966). He argues that the "fallen" state of the natural world—located in sensuality and the body's desire—is perfected by poetry not through intervention from a separate divine order but through potential within nature itself. His focus is the literary idea of chaste love, which reconciles the natural and the divine orders.

36. The forest was sold in small parcels, and the sale took a long time. The details of the sale can be found in R. Caisso's article, "La vente de la forêt de Gâtine au temps de Ronsard," *Humanisme et Renaissance* 4 (1937): 274-85.

37. This is, for example, Caisso's reading. Since his is still an essential article on the details of the sale, many editors assume that his reading of the poem is also authoritative. It was not really challenged until Ian McFarlane's article "Neo-Latin Verse, Some New Discoveries: A Possible Source of Ronsard's *Elégie xxiv*," in *Modern Language Review* 54 (1959): 24-28. Donald Wilson, in *Ronsard, Poet of Nature* (Manchester: Manchester University Press, 1961), which is more useful as a compendium of Renaissance notions of nature than as an original reading of Ronsard, at least suggests that Ronsard's treatment of the logging is "anything but realistic in tone" (115), but does not expand his discussion.

38. In Raphaël Larrère and Olivier Nougarède, *Des hommes et des forêts* (Paris: Gallimard, 1993), 49, for example, this very extract is given in bold type at the beginning of a chapter, enlisting the poet's words rhetorically as a simple protest.

39. Ute Margarete Saine, "Dreaming the Forest of Gâtine: Ecology and Antiquity in Ronsard," *Cincinnati Romance Review* 9 (1990): 1-12. While there

are certain problems with this article, such as the fact that the concept of "ecology" is not put into question, this particular point of her argument is well taken.

40. Horace, *Odes and Epodes,* II, xiii, lines 1-4: "Ille et nefaste te posuit die, / Quicumque primum, et sacrilega manu / Produxit, arbos, in nepotum / Perniciem opprobiumque pagi."

41. Ovid, *Metamorphoses* VIII, lines 741-878. From Ovid, *Metamorphoses I, Books I-VIII,* trans. Frank Justus Miller, Loeb Classical Library (Cambridge: Harvard University Press, 1966).

42. One could invoke several scholars here: concepts I find particularly pertinent include Raymond Rogers's "residual and emergent forms" and "residual cultural records," in *Nature and the Crisis of Modernity* (New York: Black Rose Books, 1994). An emergent form is a new mentality or paradigm that is imposed upon an older one, the "residual form," and which eventually replaces it. The processes of capital are an emergent form, replacing precapitalist economies and determinants of value. These latter are thus "residual" forms which persist for a while in spaces such as literature, as a "residual cultural record," a strong sense of the loss of a vanishing way of life or of thought, a moment of protest against the new way. Ronsard's apparent protest against the logging of the Gâtine is just such a "residual cultural record," or protest against precisely the new processes of capitalistic evaluation of nature. I am not arguing a causal relationship between Protestantism and capitalism, so I am reluctant to engage Max Weber.

43. This is not, however, a study of Golden Age tropes in Ronsard. Elizabeth Armstrong, in *Ronsard and the Age of Gold* (Cambridge: Cambridge University Press, 1968), has traced Ronsard's use of the trope exhaustively enough for it not to be my concern here. Whereas Armstrong discusses Ronsard's landscapes as part of the repertoire of Golden Age clichés. I ask what it is about certain landscapes—the forest in particular—which allows the past/present confrontation to be staged, and what the stakes are.

44. Ovid, *Metamorphoses* VIII, line 762: "haud aliter fluxit discusso cortice sanguis"; and 771: "nympha sub hoc ego sum Cereri gratissima ligno."

45. I am reluctant to attribute any protoecological dimension to this poem, but cannot resist at least pointing to a relevant incident in modern environmental history. In 1971, the Sierra Club took Disney to court over the latter's plan to develop certain areas of the Sequoia National Park in California. Their defense was original: they defended the individual rights and "interests" of the trees as legal entities—essentially humanizing the trees as Ronsard does. French environmentalists have shown great interest in this case; see, for example, Luc Ferry's discussion in the first chapter of his *Le nouvel ordre écologique: L'arbre, l'animal et l'homme* (Paris: Grasset, 1992).

46. Ian McFarlane, "Neo-Latin Verse," 28.

47. There is a good modern critical edition by Keith Cameron (Geneva: Droz, 1988); however, the title is abbreviated to *Recepte Veritable.*

48. The image of the trees as houses for birds is in Virgil, Georgic ii, line 209; see Virgil, *Eclogues, Georgics, Aeneid I-VI,* trans. H. Rushton, Loeb Classical Library (Cambridge: Harvard University Press, 1994). For a consideration of Ronsard's sensibility to the animal world in his poetry, see Hélène Nais, *Les animaux dans la poésie française de la Renaissance: Science, Symbolique, Poésie* (Paris: Dider, 1961).

49. Virgil, *Eclogues, Georgics, Aeneid I-VI,* Eclogue i, lines 1-2.

50. Ibid., Eclogue v, line 5.

51. Ovid, *Metamorphoses* I, lines 101-2.

52. Saine, "Dreaming the Forest," 4-5. This is one of several factual errors in her paper. The *Elégie xxiiii* appeared for the first time in the *Œuvres* of 1584. It was not the last but the penultimate poem of the cycle, followed by (of course) *Elégie xxv,* an invective against a court "mignon" who had mocked Ronsard's *Franciade.* And the elegy cycle itself was far from being the last in the 1584 edition: it was followed by the hymns, the "Livres des poèmes," the epitaphs, and the "Discours des misères de ce temps."

53. Virgil, *Eclogues, Georgics, Aeneid I-VI,* Aeneid VI, lines 771-72: "Qui iuvenes! quantas ostentant, aspice, viris, / atque umbrata gerunt civili tempora quercu!"

54. The right to use the forest—wood, game, and land—for subsistence needs had been guaranteed to the people in most regions of France by local custom, although there were of course many conflicting interests and particularly royal restrictions imposed on common use. In the sixteenth century, however, many more of these local customs start to be eroded by the Crown than in the Middle Ages: scores of royal edicts were aimed at centralizing forest management and at excluding all but the Crown and landed nobility from the right to hunt. See, for an exhaustive history of the forest in Renaissance France, Michel Devèze, *La vie de la forêt française au XVIe siècle,* 2 vols. (Paris: S.E.V.P.E.N., 1961).

55. McFarlane, "Neo-Latin Verse," 28.

56. Jeanneret, *Perpetuum mobile,* 31-33. In his discussion of this one line, he puts Ronsard's sensibility to the inconstancy of form in the greater context or an Aristotelian displacement of the Platonic primacy of Form.

57. Lucretius, *De rerum natura* V, 260; II, 1173-74; trans. W. H. D. Rouse, Loeb Classical Library (Cambridge: Harvard University Press, 1997).

58. Ovid, *Metamorphoses* XV, 236 ff.

59. Henri Lefebvre, *The Production of Space* (Oxford: Clarendon Press, 1991).

60. Harvey, *Spaces of Hope,* 183.

61. Ibid., 7.

Susan K. Silver (essay date 2002)

SOURCE: Silver, Susan K. "'Adieu vieille forest . . .': Myth, Melancholia, and Ronsard's Family Trees." *Neophilologus* 86 (2002): 33-43.

[*In the following essay, Silver discusses Ronsard's poem of loss and disempowerment,* Elegie XXIIII, *prompted by the destruction of the Gâtine forest, but referring also to his own declining position at the court.*]

> *Escoute, Bucheron (arreste un peu le bras)*
>
> Ronsard, "**Elégie XXIIII**"

In 1573, the French Protestant king Henri de Navarre, faced with mounting debts inherited from his father and increased by the religious wars, decided to sell some royal forests, among them the *forêt de Gastine*. This forest contained the family estate of Loys de Ronsard, father of the Pléiade poet. Although the family property was granted to Pierre de Ronsard's father in recognition of royal service, the land all around was to come under the axe.[1] According to the local *Conseil de Vendôme*, the Gastine forest was home to "les plus haultz et beaulx chesnes propres à ouvrager." Three hundred and ten *arpents* (about 310 acres) were said to be covered exclusively with oak trees. Ironically, one of the units of royal measure employed in parcelling out the forest land was the *chesnée* (100 *chesnées* = 1 arpent),[2] thus making a tree the literal measure of its own destruction.

Self-destruction is the motivating theme behind Ronsard's elegy to his native forest, "**Elégie XXIIII**." The myth employed to transmit this theme is drawn from Ovid's *Metamorphoses*. It is the myth of Erysichthon, the monarch who felled the oak tree sacred to Ceres and whose punishment leads to his eventual self-devouring. In Ovid's account, Erysichthon first orders his men to cut down the great oak and, when they resist, grabs the axe himself. The tree trembles and groans as the king cuts into it; blood flows from its bark. When one of his men tries to stop the sacrilege, Erysichthon turns on him and slices off his head. The great oak falls and, as it collapses, crushes many other trees in the sacred grove.[3]

As punishment, Erysichthon is cursed by Ceres, grain goddess of plenty, to be racked by Famine, her emaciated counterpart. In his famished state, Erysichthon will devour everything around him, sell all his treasure and even his own daughter. When all else is consumed, he turns to the last thing he possesses. In Ovid's account, ". . . the wretched Erysichthon then began to rend his flesh, to bite his limbs, to feed on his own body."[4]

Ronsard's "**Elégie XXIIII**," written in his later years at the courts of Charles IX and Henri III, weaves together personal and legendary tales of loss and disempowerment. At court, Ronsard was being eclipsed by the younger, more fashionable poet, Philippe Desportes. At home, he was losing the forest of his lyric *jeunesse* to an enemy king, an outsider unable to see the significance of his act:

> Escoute, Bucheron (arreste un peu le bras)
> Ce ne sont pas des bois que tu jettes à bas,
> Ne vois-tu pas le sang lequel degoute à force
> Des Nymphes qui vivoyent dessous la dure escorce?[5]
>
> (19-22)

The poet's choice of the Erysichthon tale allows him to filter personal anxieties through the mythological figure of a shrinking self. Moreover, lurking in Erysichthon's shadow is another mythic figure—Cronos—the Golden Age god who castrated his father and swallowed his children. In the Renaissance imaginary, Cronos often appears as the allegorical *Temps Dévorateur,* figure of time's devastation.

In his "Abbregé de l'art poëtique françois" (1565), Ronsard had recommended that poets fortify their writing against the effects of time by matching beautiful subjects to vivid descriptions:

> . . . [C]ar tout ainsi qu'on ne peult veritablement dire un corps humain beau, plaisant & accomply s'il n'est composé de sang, venes, arteres & tendons, & surtout d'une plaisante couleur: ainsi la poësie ne peut estre plaisante ny parfaicte sans belles inventions, descriptions, comparaisons, qui sont les ners & la vie du livre qui veult forcer les siecles *pour demourer de toute memoire victorieux & maistre du temps.*[6]

For Ronsard, vanquishing Cronos means appropriating the latter's role as *le Temps Dévorateur* and usurping his power through writing. In "**Elégie XXIIII**," the poet embellishes Ovid's myth of Erysichthon, widely known in the Renaissance,[7] in order to highlight the woodcutter's greed for economic gain. Like Erysichthon, having consumed all of his goods, the woodcutter is left with only his own body for nourishment:

> Et qui gourmand de tout, de tout insatiable,
> Les boeufs & les moutons de sa mère esgorgea,
> Puis pressé de la faim, soy-mesme se mangea . . .[8]
>
> (6-8).

The brief one-line mention of physical self-cannibalism is, however, quickly returned to an economic register:

> Ainsi puisse engloutir ses rentes & sa terre,
> Et se devore apres par les dents de la guerre.
>   Qu'il puisse pour vanger le sang de nos forests,
> Tousjours nouveaux emprunts sur nouveaux interests
> Devoir à l'usurier, & qu'en fin il consomme
> Tout son bien à payer la principale somme.
>
> (9-14)

Whereas Ovid's Erysichthon is driven to *dévorer sa fortune* and deplete his economic resources to the point where he is left to feed on himself, Ronsard's woodcutter is identified with "ses rentes & sa terre" which, in the poet's curse, he is obliged to swallow up (*engloutir*) and which then leads to his self-devouring by "les dents de la guerre." The teeth of war are represented as a part of the woodcutter's own body, the part that allows him to *se dévorer.* They echo the imprecation of the third verse, "Qu'il puisse s'enferrer de son propre baston," which precedes the cannibal curse, "Et sente en l'estomac la faim d'Erysichthon," both common proverbial expressions. By making the proverbial figural, the poet fills empty words with new significance, revitalizing by historicizing them.

Positioned for revenge from the opening verse, the poet's verdict against the woodcutter is swift in **"Elégie XXIIII."** His malediction appears in verses three and four, while verses one and two have the resonance of a lover addressing the dead body of the beloved:

> Quiconque aura premier la main embesongnée
> A te couper, forest, d'une dure congnée. . . .
>
> (1-2)

An act of aggressive vengeance against a monarch is doubly veiled in this poem. The use of an anonymous subject in the opening verse transfers the blame away from the real seller, and therefore murderer, of the woods to a simple woodsman *quiconque* who may safely be attacked. The courtier poet cannot castigate/castrate a king without deposing him first. Cloaking his criticism of a monarch in the imitation of a tale from Ovid's *Metamorphoses* gives the poet free rein, reverses their respective power positions, and allows him to avenge the wrong done to his native forest, his first meeting-place with the muses of poetry. Beginning with

cutting/castrating and consuming/cannibalizing images, the poem moves toward a retrospective melancholy, a nostalgia for the lost Golden Age of gratification from mother muses and father oracles.

It is in the gap between the past state of fulfillment and the present state of lack that the poet inserts himself in an attempt at reparation and renewal. The pen which dismembers the woodcutter who has murdered the nymphs, reducing the former to isolated body parts— hand, stomach, teeth, and arm—tries then to "re-member" the lost forest and thereby to mitigate the poet's loss. The nostalgic poet as melancholy cannibal[9] ingests his mythological parents and mingles them with his personal history.[10]

Ullrich Langer has observed that the space between imitation and emulation, where Ronsard affirms his identity as a poet, is grounded in the melancholy contemplation of a dwindling self. "Sadness and death," he notes, "are subjects of those who come *afterwards.* Writing is thus a paradoxical enterprise: if one affirms oneself in adding something to that which has preceded, what one adds is one's own "degeneration.""[11] In **"Elégie XXIIII,"** the loss of the forest, of the nymphs, of the muses and the oracles allows for the "finding" or *inventio* of a poetic voice. Death and dearth in the natural world bring about new life in poetry, engender an abundance of words capable of replacing, by signifying, lost things.

The poet's continued quest for artistic achievement and glory is also a refusal of death, closure, and finality. For the poet as for Erysichthon, the outside cannot be consumed fast enough to fill the inside and to offset a rapidly changing world. *Le Temps Dévorateur,* Cronos, or Saturn, under whose sign the melancholy poet is born,[12] gradually feeds on his body just as the devouring woodcutter is feeding on the forest. The poet ages, the world changes, and younger poets are bound to take his place. As his world and his poetic sources are drained of life and disappear, so too will the voice of the poet vanish into silence.

In Ronsard's work, the threat of extinction is frequently offset by the creation of a foreign body with which the *moi du poète* can eventually, if only momentarily, be identified. Whereas in the elegy to the *forêt de Gastine* the foreign body is a forest, in **"Le Pin"** it is a single tree, part of the poet's own garden which he fears will be cut down by the Protestant Louis de Condé's approaching army.[13] The prospect of this future loss gives rise to a poem in honor of the poet's pine tree. His own tree is quickly conflated with the pine tree into which the mythological figure Attis was transformed by the goddess Cybele.

In this way, the cutting of the poet's own pine is turned into a tale of castration and madness. According to the legend of Attis, it was in a state of mad frenzy brought on him by the angered Cybele, of whose cult he was a member, that Attis castrated himself. The mother-goddess later forgave him, giving him new life by transforming him into a pine tree.

In Ronsard's poem, Attis's religious transformation and regeneration mirrors the *fureur poétique* which turns the poet into something other than himself and transforms him into a reflection of divine power.[14] Attis's loss is shown to be the poet's gain, as it is what leads him to tell a story of his own through appropriation of the ancient myth. To have voice is to have power, both over nature and over art, over foreign models and over literary rivals:[15]

> Jadis Catulle en sa langue Romaine,
> Nous la conta come venant des Grecs,
> Et moy François en me joüant apres
> Je la diray, afin que telle histoire,
> En tous endroitz fleurisse par memoire.[16]
>
> (30-34)

The prospect of personal property destruction at the hands of a Protestant leader of foreign mercenaries encourages a reading of this poem as a nationalistic defense against an attacking other. The need to affirm his own identity as both Frenchman and fabulist ("Et moi Françoys en me joüant après . . .") demonstrates the extent to which that identity appears threatened.[17]

Castration and impotence are conjured by literary creation and regeneration. This creation is itself engendered by cannibalistic imitation, the incorporation and assimilation of ancient mythographers and their myths. Ronsard, using the Renaissance euphemism *tesmoings* to signify genitals ("Et ses tesmoings d'un caillou moissonna"), links the castration to an elimination of voice or narrative as well as to a loss of virilty. Attis in castrating himself lost not only his *tesmoings*/testicles but also, and perhaps more importantly for the poet, he lost his story, his testimony, his *témoignage*.[18] This semantic condensation allows for the representation of multiple losses: loss of patrimony, loss of narrative authority,[19] and loss of the visible signifier or evidence of manhood.

The poet's attempts to restore Attis's losses will serve as a kind of self-defense, since, for Ronsard, poetic production is closely connected to the concept of fecundity.[20] Ronsard demonstrates his intolerance of the negative implications of castration, that is, the impossibility of regeneration, by interrupting the story he has set out to tell in order to reprove Attis directly for his self-mutilation:

> O bon Atys! aveuglé de malheur,
> Tu te coupas le membre le meilleur,
> Tes deux tesmoings, gros de glere foeconde,
> Sans qui seroit un desert ce grand Monde:

> Ce n'est ton doigt, ton oreille, ou ta main,
> Mais les autheurs de tout le genre humain.
>
> (47-52)

The finger, the ear, and the hand are all important parts of the authorial body, but the true generative power resides in *le membre le meilleur*, unquestionably functioning here as phallic signifier.

As in the elegy to the *forêt de Gastine*, the hand is a privileged figure in **"Le Pin."** Cursed by Attis as the agent of castration and death, the *main* metonymically signifies both the *manie* and the *manière* of his dreadful act:

> Meschantes mains, pourquoy coupastes vous
> De tout mon corps le membre le plus doux?
> Meschantes mains, bourrelles de ma vie,
> Que je vous porte & de haine & d'envie!
>
> (75-78)

The mannerism of the style, enlarging two members of the male body, the *tesmoings* and the *mains*, beyond natural proportion in order to inspire awe in the reader, supplements the cannibalistic method of text production through dismemberment and assimilation of emulated classical authors. The myth which Ronsard had borrowed from Catullus, Ovid, and other ancient sources, he then incorporates into his personal history and uses as a moral commentary on his own condition. He vows that the *furor poeticus* will never so deprive him of his reason that he cannot engender poems ("Ce n'est pas moy qui achepte si cher / Un repentir . . ." 128-129).

"Le Pin" might be seen as a figuration of the poet's relation to his own writing or, more aptly, his own rewriting. Like Montaigne, Ronsard was a lifelong revisor of his work, much to the chagrin of some of his contemporaries. One of them, Estienne Pasquier, unsuspectingly figures the poet as a literary Attis, when criticizing the 1584 edition of Ronsard's poetry:

> . . . [D]eux ou trois ans avant son decés estant affoibly d'un long aage, . . . [Ronsard] fit reimprimer toutes ses poësies en un grand, et gros volume, dont il reforma l'oeconomie generale, *chastra* son livre de plusieurs belles et gaillardes inventions qu'il condamna à une perpetuelle prison, changea des vers tous entiers, dans quelques uns y mit d'autres paroles, qui n'estoient de telle pointe, que les premieres. . . . Ne considerant que combien qu'il fut le pere . . . [il] n'appartient à une facheuse vieillesse de juger des coups d'une gaillarde jeunesse.[21]

Constantly taking away from and adding to his ever-changing *oeuvre*, Ronsard personifies two of the mythological figures of his poems, embodying them at the level of literary production and reproduction. Recent critics, describing Ronsard's writing process as one of inflation and deflation, supplementation and retraction,[22] also appear to cast the author in the Erysichthon/Attis role. This critical investment in Ronsard's own self-representation is in part due to the fact that, like Montaigne, Ronsard saw and reflected himself as both an imitator and a model for imitation, both a consumer and a product for consumption.

It is as model and exegete of his own work that Ronsard inserts himself at the end of his fable in **"Le Pin"** to unmask its allegory and reveal a hidden truth. Attis was never castrated, claims the poet. The story was simply an ancient cautionary tale, one he explains to Attis himself in the poem:

> Ainsi de toy les Grecs on devisé,
> Qui par ta fable ont le peuple avisé,
> O bon Atys! qu'un Philosophe sage
> Doibt come toy estre un home sauvage:
> Se faire un Pin, c'est fréquenter les bois,
> Fuir Citez, Bourgades & Bourgeois,
> Cybele aimer: elle ne signifie
> A mon advis que la Philosophie
>
> (131-138)
>
> . . . . .
>
> Tu n'as coupé (ce n'est que Poésie)
> Tes deux tesmoings: mais de ta fantaisie
> Tu arrachas folles affections,
> Mondains plaisirs, humaines passions,
> Qui te troublaient, pour heureusement vivre,
> Et contempler ta Cybele et la suivre.
>
> (145-150)

Denying the sterility implied by Attis's castration, Ronsard restores the wholeness and thus potency of his poetic double. However for Attis the sexual restoration comes at a price, one which will assure the poet's own future regeneration:

> A Dieu, Atys, si cette vieille fable
> que je te chante au coeur t'est agréable,
> Je ne requiers pour tout loyer sinon
> Qu'au vent ton Pin puisse siffler mon nom.
>
> (157-160)

"Le Pin" ends with the metamorphosis of the poet into his transformed subject. Attis, his pine, and the poet are fused into the sound of the author's name in the wind. The poet's body, sick and feverish as he reveals in the closing verses,[23] his loss of status to rival poets at court, his threatened property destruction, are all turned into a new body, the body of the poem.

Similarly, at the end of **"Elégie XXIIII,"** a Pythagorean view regarding the conservation of matter determines that ". . . toute chose à la fin perira / Et qu'en changeant de forme une autre vestira." Michel Jeanneret has affirmed that this idea is consonant with the history of *imitatio* itself, which could be viewed as a chain of metamorphosis.[24] In Ronsard's writing, *imitatio* could also be viewed as a chain of consumption and the elegy to the *forêt de Gastine* as one example of textual self-cannibalism. Pieces of **"Le Pin,"** first published in 1569, were borrowed and later transformed into **"Elégie XXIIII,"** published in 1584.[25] Enriching the later poem with select fragments of the earlier one, Ronsard's self-imitation echoes Erysichthon's auto-cannibalism.

The chain of *imitatio* thus links Ovid and Catullus to Ronsard in the 1569 poem, and Ronsard to Ronsard in the poem of 1584. Like Erysichthon, the poet, after having consumed the available outside material, turns to the inside, to his own literary body, for sustenance. Such auto-cannibalism perhaps sheds new light on the final image of form-changing in **"Elégie XXIIII."** By means of a Pythagorean flux, the poet would defer his complete self-consumption, could figure himself transformed rather than devoured, metamorphosed, rather than depleted. Just as Catullus's and Ovid's versions of ancient myths are appropriated and turned into a new textual *corpus,* so Ronsard's later appropriation of his earlier works allows him to succeed himself.

The poet as Erysichthon, a figure of auto-cannibalism who sustains himself by depleting himself, who loses his identity by gaining multiple identities, and whose appetite for success continually sends him back to his own body of writing and rewriting, remains one of Ronsard's most prominent mythological alter egos. Attis, also a metaphor of literary production, together with Erysichthon, may be fused into the master mythological signifier, Cronos, the Devourer/Castrator, Incorporator/Dismemberer at work in the writing process itself.

One of the last poems Ronsard wrote before his death, an elegy to Philippes Desportes, employs the figure of Saturn, or Cronos, to disempower and dispense with his rival and successor at Henry III's court.[26] Having worked all his life to achieve immortality as a poet, Ronsard, in the only poem he ever addressed to his young rival, paints a picture of artistic death and decay in which Cronos, as *le Temps Dévorateur,* wields the upper hand:

> Nous devons à la Mort & nous & nos ouvrages:
> Nous mourrons les premiers, le long reply des âges
> En roulant engloutist nos oeuvres à la fin:
> Ainsi le veut Nature & le puissant Destin.[27]
>
> (1-4)

In this elegy Ronsard incorporates both the mythical figure (Cronos) and the subject (Desportes), the latter figuring as a weaker, somewhat deteriorated version of Ronsard himself.[28] Desportes is advised not to aspire to a literary future, for *le Temps Dévorateur* spares no one: "Pour ce les Grecs ont dit, que glout de faim extreme / Saturne devoroit ses propres enfans mesme

. . ." (33-34). Ronsard was less pessimistic, however, when it came to projecting his own literary immortality. During the same period in which he was composing a devouring Saturn to dispense with Desportes's future renown, he was, in a sonnet to Hélène, assuring his own enduring reputation. Once again, a pine tree dedicated to the goddess Cybele will stand in place of the poet and bear his name:

> Je plante en ta faveur cest arbre de Cybelle,
> Ce Pin, où tes honneurs se liront tous les jours:
> J'ay gravé sur le tronc nos noms et nos amours,
> Qui croistront à l'envy de l'escorce nouvelle. . . .[29]

In this sonnet, the pine tree that was felled in **"Le Pin,"** is, like Attis, reborn and blessed with immortality. For the poet, inscribing his name in the sacred pine is a means of defeating *le Temps Dévorateur* and, more importantly, of achieving victory over a contemporary literary rival. For Ronsard's solid and venerable name will not only grow with the tree, but it will grow *à l'envy de l'escorce nouvelle.* In this perspective, rival poets such as Desportes are all surface and no substance. Ronsard's writing, on the other hand, is an elemental essence, the matter itself which time cannot devour nor younger poets replace. The final line of **"Elégie XXIIII,"** therefore, resonates in the poet's own literary history as a defensive strategy against a castrating/devouring Cronos: "La matière demeure, et la forme se perd."

Yet perhaps the most significant poetic transformation was yet to come, an ironic twist of Devouring Time. Ronsard's celebrated address to the Gastine woodcutter would eventually be incorporated by Philippe Desportes in one of his own elegies. The line of verse in Desportes's poem stands as both hommage and ironic response to the literary figure who inspired it, the one in whose shadow the younger poet would continue to create, and to imitate, in penning his own version of the master's verse, "Ne me fay point mourir, arreste un peu ton bras. . . ."[30]

Notes

1. See R. Caisso, "La Vente de la forêt de Gastine à l'époque de Ronsard," *Humanisme et Renaissance* 4 (1937): 274-285; and Ute Margarete Saine, "Dreaming the Forest of Gatine: Ecology and Antiquity in Ronsard," *Cincinnati Romance Review* (1990): 1-12.

2. Caisso 283, 276.

3. Ovid. *The Metamorphoses,* trans. Allen Mandelbaum (New York: Harcourt Brace, 1993), book VIII, 277-283.

4. Ovid 283.

5. Ronsard, *Oeuvres complètes,* ed. Paul Laumonier, vol. 18 (Paris: Librairie Marcel Didier, 1967), 144.

6. Ronsard, *Oeuvres complètes,* ed. Laumonier, vol. 14, p. 10, my emphasis.

7. Guy Demerson, *La Mythologie classique dans l'oeuvre de la Pléiade* (Genève: Librairie Droz, 1972), 196.

8. Ronsard, *Oeuvres complètes,* ed. Laumonier, vol. 18: 143-144.

9. On Ronsard and melancholy, see Oliver Pot, *Inspiration et mélancolie: L'Epistémologie poétique dans les "Amours" de Ronsard* (Genève: Droz, 1990). Regarding melancholy cannibalism, Julia Kristeva writes: "L'imaginaire cannibalique mélancolique est un désaveu de la réalité de la perte ainsi que de la mort. Il manifeste l'angoisse de perdre l'autre en faisant survivre le moi, certes abandonné, mais non séparé de ce qui le nourrit encore et toujours et se métamorphose en lui—qui ressuscite aussi—par cette dévoration." *Soleil noir: Dépression et mélancolie* (Paris: Gallimard, 1987), 21.

10. On the mixing of the autobiographical and the mythological registers and the connection to an abundance/deprivation motif in Ronsard's poetry, see Terence Cave, "Mythes de l'abondance et de la privation chez Ronsard," *Cahiers de l'Association Internationale des Etudes Françaises* 25 (1973): 247-260.

11. Langer, *Invention, Death, and Self-Definitions in the Poetry of Pierre de Ronsard* (Saratoga, CA: ANMA Libri & Co., 1986), 53.

12. See Raymond Klibansky, Erwin Panofsky, and Fritz Saxl, *Saturn and Melancholy: Studies in the History of Natural Philosophy, Religion, and Art* (New York: Basic Books, Inc.: 1964), 127-150.

13. Laumonier, vol. 15: 178, Note 2.

14. In *Totem and Taboo,* Freud traces the development of religions to "two inciting factors, the son's sense of guilt and his defiance," which cause him to strive to replace the father god. Attis and other young males who were loved by maternal goddesses, represent the coming of a new agricultural, patriarchal order, according to Freud, in which the son's "incestuous libido" could find "symbolic satisfaction in labouring over mother earth." The price of this satisfaction, however, as symbolized in the tales of Attis, Adonis and others, is castration or divine punishment by the father, *Totem and Taboo: Resemblances Between the Psychic Lives of Savages and Neurotics* (New York: New Republic, Inc., 1927), 265-266. In Ronsard's elegy to the *forest de Gastine,* it is indeed the desire to penetrate the earth with *le soc, le coutre,* and *la charrue* which constitutes man's transgression and brings about the cutting/castration of the forest/body.

15. See Albert Py, *Imitation et Renaissance dans la poésie de Ronsard* (Genève: Droz, 1984) Chapitre II, "Voix de Ronsard, *voix* chez Ronsard," 71-98, and Cave, "Mythes de l'abondance" for a treatment of "Le Pin" and poetic productivity.

16. Ed. Laumonier, vol. 15: 179-180.

17. François Rigolot has observed that Ronsard's erotic poetry and his national poetry are not nearly the separate and distinct genres that they have been claimed to be. See *Poétique et onomastique: L'Exemple de la Renaissance* (Genève: Droz, 1977), 208.

18. Edmond Huguet, *Dictionnaire de la langue française au seizième siècle* (Paris: Edouard Champion, 1925), vol. 7.

19. In his study of Renaissance literary imitation, Antoine Compagnon traces rhetorical *citatio,* or borrowing from authoritative models, to both *témoignage* (in Latin, *citatio* meant testifying before the tribunal) and *auctoritas,* or the authority of an outside *exemplum.* See *La Seconde Main ou le travail de la citation* (Paris: Editions du Seuil, 1979), 140-141.

20. Cave, "Mythes de l'abondance," 247-260.

21. Quoted in Louis Terreaux, *Ronsard, Correcteur de ses oeuvres: Les variantes des "Odes" et des deux premiers livres des "Amours"* (Genève: Droz, 1968), 14, my emphasis.

22. See Cave, Langer, Terreaux.

23. On illness, medicinal plants, and the writing process in this and other of Ronsard's poems, see S. Silver, "'La Salade' and Ronsard's Writing Cure," *Romanic Review,* 89:1 (1998): 21-36. On *imitatio* in Ronsard's poetics of nature, see Danièle Duport, *Les Jardins qui sentent le sauvage: Ronsard et la poétique du paysage* (Genève: Droz, 2000).

24. Michel Jeanneret, ". . . Et la forme se perd: Structures mobiles à la Renaissance," *Littérature* 85 (1992): 29. On Ronsard and metamorphosis, see also Jeanneret's *Perpetuum mobile: Métamorphoses des corps et des oeuvres da Vinci à Montaigne* (Paris: Editions Macula, 1997), Kathleen Ann Perry, *Another Reality: Metamorphosis and the Imagination in the Poetry of Ovid, Petrarch, and Ronsard* (New York: Lang, 1989), Leonard Barkan, *The Gods Made Flesh: Metamorphosis & the Pursuit of Paganism* (New Haven: Yale UP, 1986), 215-221, and Terence Cave, *The Cornucopian Text: Problems of Writing in the French Renaissance* (Oxford: Clarendon Press, 1979), 223-270. On metamorphosis in Renaissance poetics, see Guy Demerson, dir., *Poétiques de la méta-morphose* (Saint-Etienne: Publications de l'Université, 1981), Gisèle Mathieu-Castellani, dir., *La Métamorphose dans la poésie baroque française et anglaise* (Tubingen: Gunter Narr, et Paris: Jean-Michel Place, 1980), and François Rigolot, *Le Texte de la Renaissance: Des Rhétoriqueurs à Montaigne* (Genève: Droz, 1982), 187-198.

25. Caisso 281; Laumonier, vol. 15: 178, note 3.

26. For a fuller treatment of Ronsard's elegy to Desportes and its role as a palinode, or recantation, see Langer, *Invention, Death and Self-Definitions,* Chapter 6, 89-96.

27. Laumonier, vol. 18:1, 247, 249.

28. Langer 94.

29. Ronsard, ed. Bensimon and Martin, 292.

30. Philippe Desportes, *Oeuvres de Philippe Desportes.* ed. Alfred Michiels (Paris: Adolphe Delahays, 1858), 239. See Helmut Hatzfeld, "The Style of Philippe Desportes," *Symposium* 7.1 (1953): 266.

Stephen Murphy (essay date 2002)

SOURCE: Murphy, Stephen. "Catherine, Cybele, and Ronsard's Witnesses." In *High Anxiety: Masculinity in Crisis in Early Modern France,* edited by Kathleen P. Long, pp. 55-70. Kirksville, Mo.: Truman State University Press, 2002.

[*In the following essay, Murphy examines themes of self-emasculation and censorship in "Le Pin," a 1569 narrative poem based on the story of Attis and Cybele.*]

My point of departure and return is **"Le Pin,"** *a curious poem which first appears in* **Le Septiesme livre des Poëmes** *of 1569. Its narrative core is a retelling of the story of Attis and Cybele; in particular, the moment when the maddened Attis castrates himself, followed by his lament for his situation, and then his metamorphosis into a pine tree. The bloody catastrophe provides an occasion for the poet's commentary. As he first reports the self-emasculation, the disapproving poet exclaims:*

(45) Ta raison fut en fureur convertie,
(46) Qui te coupas ta meilleure partie:
(47) O bon Atys! aveuglé de malheur,
(48) Tu te coupas le membre le meilleur,
(49) Tes deux tesmoings, gros de glere foeconde,
(50) Sans qui seroit un desert ce grand Monde:
(51) Ce n'est ton doigt, ton oreille, ou ta main,
(52) Mais les autheurs de tout le genre humain.[1]

(45) [Your reason was turned into madness,
(46) Dear Attis, who cut off your best part!

(47) Blinded by misfortune,
(48) You cut off your best member,
(49) Your two *tesmoings,* Full of fertile glair,
(50) Without which this whole world
        Would be a desert;
(51) Not your finger, your ear, or your hand,
(52) But the authors of all the human race.]

This condemnation is expressed with the voice of a familiar Ronsard, the putative naturalist who reveres universal fecundity and is scandalized by its negation. However, the story's conclusion (the transformation of Attis into a pine tree by the goddess Cybele) introduces another interpretation of the central event. This is an allegorical interpretation, which takes Attis as the seeker of philosophical wisdom and Cybele as Philosophy (137-38)[2]:

(145) Tu n'as coupé (ce n'est que Poësie)
(146) Tes deux tesmoings: mais de ta fantaisie
(147) Tu arrachas folles affections,
(148) Mondains plaisirs, humaines passions,
(149) Qui te troubloient, pour heureusement vivre,
(150) Et contempler ta Cybele & la suyvre.

(145) [You did not cut off (that's only Poetry)
(146) Your two *tesmoings*; rather, you tore away
        from your
(147) Imagination those mad inclinations,
(148) Worldly pleasures and human passions
(149) Which troubled you, in order to live happily
(150) And contemplate your Cybele and follow her.]

How are we to take these contradictory apostrophes to Attis? True, the rhetorical turn of *correctio* or epanorthosis is common enough in Ronsard's poetry.[3] We could also say simply that the original condemnation concerns the immediate sense of the story, while the later commendation applies to the moral allegory Ronsard draws from it.[4] A long mythographic tradition attempts just such a revisionist reading of the Attis myth, including notably the emperor Julian's apologia for Cybele, Lucretius, and Saint Augustine.[5] But particular attention to one word may reveal in Ronsard's story of Attis and Cybele a wider-ranging importance and a more radical contradiction.

That word occurs in both the passages already cited (as well as v. 40), namely, *tesmoings.* Is it, as the editor, Paul Laumonier, declares, merely "un synonyme discret de testicules"?[6] Of course, such a gloss provides a starting point; what may appear obscure upon a first reading becomes clear when we realize that Ronsard is treating *tesmoings* as if it had the same ambiguity as Latin *testes.* The twin meanings of witness and testicles provided a pun to Latin writers at least since Plautus.[7] The pun persists in Romance languages, including compounds. We find *testimoni* with this double sense in sixteenth-century Italian texts: in at least one Roman pasquinade, and in *novelle* by Bandello and Firenzuola.[8] In French, Ronsard is not the first to use *tesmoings* in this way. It

shows up in Des Périer's *Nouvelles Recreations* (1558), and most instructively, in Baïf's comedy *Le Brave* (1567).[9] The latter was a version of Plautus's *Miles Gloriosus,* near the end of which the double meaning of *testes* lends itself to a legal pun: "si posthac prehendero ego te hic, carebis testibus" [If I ever catch you here again, you will be lacking your testicles/witnesses][10] Through the use of *témoins,* Baïf's version maintains Plautus's pun:

> Si jamais ceans te retreuve,
> J'auray les témoins pour la preuve"[11]
>
> [If I ever find you in here again,
> I'll have the *témoins* to prove it]

An awareness of the potential for double meaning in this word enables us to see an extra dimension in other, apparently innocent, passages. For example, in revision to his "Response aux injures" from 1567 on, Ronsard writes to his Protestant adversary: "Tes escris sont tesmoins que tu m'as desrobé"[12] [Your writings are *tesmoins* which you have stolen from me]. So that the question in interpreting **"Le Pin"** becomes: How can we understand both testicles and witness in the poem?

Tesmoings works in a way similar to what Michael Riffaterre calls "hypogram-generating dual signs. . . . Finding himself unable to understand the word as given in the text and as determined by grammatical function, the reader is forced to look elsewhere for a second, albeit simultaneous, interpretation, and to read a pun into the word."[13] The reader of **"Le Pin"** is likely to be brought up short by the inappropriateness to this context of *tesmoings* in its normal, ocular, or legal sense. "Ungrammaticality is . . . maximal, since the text has to extrapolate beyond a single language in order to find a homonym."[14] In earlier French uses of the pun, some indicator points towards Latin for the requisite ambiguity—whether that indicator be the Italian *novella* tradition, with its more Latinate vocabulary, or Plautus's text behind Baïf's play. In Ronsard's case, context encourages that extrapolation to Latin; namely, the setting of classical myth and, in particular, the intertext explicitly provided by Catullus's *carmen* 63.[15] The effect resembles that of a new coinage; or as Boileau puts it in his condemnation of Ronsard, "en français parlant grec et latin."[16]

Thus far, the pun possesses an intertextual status. But another contemporary occurrence complicates the matter by its dependence on the historical situation. In June 1575 the Parisian chronicler and collector of texts Pierre de l'Estoile noted that Queen Mother Catherine de Médicis had fallen ill, apparently after eating too many "crestes et rognons de coq" [cock's combs and testicles], of which she was quite fond.[17] L'Estoile dutifully recorded a series of four Latin epigrams which subsequently circulated in Paris. For the following month he offered a larger number of poems in French and Latin, several of which develop political metaphors from the Queen Mother's gluttony. Here are two from June and one from July which may serve as examples:

(1)

Foemina miraris, Salica cur lege refixa,
Audax imperio Gallica colla premat.
Evirat, heu! Gallos, cristas testesque revellens:
Imperium in Gallos inde virago tenet.

[You marvel how a woman,
      After annulling the Salic law,
Boldly presses Gallic necks to her authority.
Alas! she unmans cocks (*Galli*), tearing off their crests
   and testicles;
A virago holds sway over the French (*Galli*).]

(2)

Semper testiculos Gallorum prodiga coenat
Foemina, et hunc avide quum vorat illa cibum,
Compressis dicit labris: "Sic Gallica castro
Pector[a], sic Gallos eviro, sic subigo!"[18]

[An unbridled woman dines on the testicles of cocks
   (*Galli*)
And, as she devours this food,
She smacks her lips and says, "Thus I castrate Gallic
   courage,
Thus I unman the French (*Galli*), thus I subdue
   them!"]

(3)

Quid mirum Gallos instructos grandibus olim
Testibus, Eunuchos nunc evasisse vietos!
Foemina magna Deum Mater, peregrina, profusa,
Altera nunc Cybele, magnas invecta per urbes,
Sublimisque in equis, Gallos, gentem omnipotentem
Olim, castratos hodie atque virilibus orbos

Membris, esse sibi famulos, mollesque ministros
Atque Sacerdotes, sine mente et mentula inertes,
Cogit. Sic Galli, servato nomine, sed re

Amissâ, Cybelen Gallii, Eunuchique sequuntur.[19]

[What wonder if the French (*Galli*), formerly equipped
   with great *testes*,
Now turn out to be shrivelled eunuchs?
A mighty woman, Mother of the gods, an extravagant
   foreigner,
Another Cybele, borne loftily through mighty cities
   on horseback,
Compels the French (*Galli*), formerly an all-powerful
   people,
Now castrated and deprived of their virile member,
To be her servants and flabby priests, weak of mind
   and member.

Thus the French (*Galli*), maintaining the name but
   lacking the thing,
Follow Cybele as emasculated priests (*Gallii*) and
   eunuchs.]

As the first two texts show, the author or authors use *testes* interchangeably with *testiculi,* in the fairly straightforward sense of "testicles." There may be more here than meets the eye, however, as elsewhere L'Estoile shows awareness of the possibilities for punning on both *testes* and *témoins.*[20] Admittedly, the poet spends more metaphoric energy on the ambiguity of *Galli,* at once "cocks" and "Frenchmen." In this way Catherine's voracity provides a lesson concerning both nationalism and gender; she becomes a virago violating the Salic law and thereby unmanning good Frenchmen. But between June and July someone discovered a more interesting pun, based on the triple sense of Galli: not only cocks (that is, the gastronomic occasion) and Frenchmen (the political lesson), but also the emasculated priests of the goddess Cybele. By means of this pun on Galli, Catherine's sins take on gastronomical, political, and mythological dimensions. A satiric use of mythology becomes a vehicle for the political attack. The French males' shameful subjection is specified as the procession of Cybele and her priests, made famous by Lucretius and Virgil.[21]

Moreover, L'Estoile's texts are not only playing off classical pretexts; in numerous public festivities of these years, the identification of Catherine with a triumphant imperial Cybele was standard iconography. For example, in their "Tour de France" of 1564 through 1566, Catherine and Charles IX found the royal entry to Bayonne adorned with a tableau representing the Queen Mother surrounded by her children. The anonymous verses attached identify the latter as "les fruicts de Sibelle feconde."[22] Verses in both Latin and French by Jean Passerat for the entry to Troyes echo the same terms.[23] An even more precise precedent is supplied by the official gift bestowed by the city of Paris on Charles IX upon his official entry there in 1571. This gift was also a centerpiece of the public ceremony itself. It comprised, on a pedestal, a triumphal chariot drawn by the figures of two lions; in the chariot, "Cibelle mere des Dieux, representant la Roine mere du Roy," surrounded by her divine children Neptune, Pluto, and Juno (representing respectively the dukes of Anjou and Alençon, and Marguerite). Twin columns supported the figure of Jupiter, representing the king.[24] If there were any doubt that the 1571 spectacle staged a *mise-en-scène* of the Virgilian passage, it is laid to rest by the appropriate verses from the *Aeneid,* inscribed on the pedestal beneath the chariot.[25] The account of the 1571 royal entries, published by Simon Bouquet the following year, contains not only a detailed description of the divine chariot, but other reiterations of the central mythological identification.[26] In this light, we are bound to be interested by the fact that Ronsard himself collaborated on all aspects of the ceremony.[27]

In addition to those nearly contemporary, public portrayals of the Queen Mother as Cybele, there is a literary fact to consider. As any reader of Ronsard knows, he too liked to identify Catherine with Cybele. In the 1555 ode **"A la Royne Mere"** which became the second in the **Third Book of Odes,** he calls her "une autre Mere Cybelle."[28] Similarly, this identificatioon appears in the eclogue **"Daphnis et Thyrsis"** of 1564, and in the **"Bergerie"** and **"Les Nues, ou Nouvelles,"** both of 1565, all major poems which establish some of the standard pastoral/mythological identifications of the French court in the 1560s and later.[29] The motivation for equating Catherine with Cybele in these poems, as elsewhere, is evidently the regal fertility which belatedly bestowed upon France an abundant royal family. Baïf calls her the "Mère de la France," or Magna Mater.[30] "Plus que Rhea nostre Royne est feconde / De beaux enfans" [Our queen is more fertile in beautiful children than Rhea], declares Ronsard in 1559, making the common identification of Rhea with Cybele as mother of the gods.[31] In such passages the poet operates in the Virgilian tradition of a revered imperial Cybele, famously imitated by Du Bellay in the sixth sonnet of the *Antiquitez de Rome*.[32] Such a tradition also includes Cybele's role in the *Franciade* as a tutelary deity for the epic's hero Francus (as Athena is for Odysseus or Venus for Aeneas), actively promoting the foundation of the French royal dynasty.[33] At the center of Ronsardian mythology, as it harmonizes with official iconography, Magna Mater reigns. Her fertility bestows the races of gods and of kings, and so provides a foundation for Ronsard's poetry.

In contrast to that "high" Cybele, there also exists a tradition of a "low," satirical Cybele, which Ronsard also continues. This latter tradition emphasizes the goddess's age, which makes inappropriate her passion for young Attis, as well as the grotesque procession of her castrati/priests carrying on the custom established by Attis. This picture develops in the antipagan polemics of early Christian writers such as Arnobius, Firmicus Maternus, and Prudentius.[34] One of Ronsard's *Folastries* as well as his **"Palinodie à Denise"** his **"Dithyrambes,"** and a sonnet of the *Nouvelle continuation des Amours* all represent, in various combinations, the goddess as "une vieille ridée" and the grotesque procession of "les escouillés de Cybele."[35] When the poet himself enters the picture, he makes an explicit effort to dissociate himself from the worship of Cybele, emphasizing that "entre Atys et moy il y a difference."[36] On the one hand, the declaration of that difference belongs to the lover / poet's obligatory phallic swagger. But in addition, the distinction of poet and Attis as mutually exclusive, as well as the grotesqueness and sterility associated with the goddess, make Cybele a figure inimical to poetry.

It is not my intention to survey the figure of Cybele in the works of Ronsard,[37] but I would like to suggest that the existence of a "high" and a "low" Cybele does not mean we can simply separate some occurrences as one and some as the other form of the figure. Rather, both Cybeles are always present in varying doses. The imperial Mother, surrounded by the triumphant evidence of her fertility, is shadowed by the satirical hag leading her sterile crew. After all, a similar ambivalence characterizes ancient attitudes towards the goddess, an Earth mother wielding power over both life and death.[38] And Ronsard's version of that ambivalence is what makes the identification Catherine/Cybele a questionable homage. To put it in terms of intertexts: Ronsard cannot pretend that the queen, the Queen Mother, is only the Virgilian Cybele; she cannot hide the traces of the Catullan Cybele, provoker of superstition, madness, and self-mutilation.

Catherine's iconographical doubleness, matching the doubleness of Cybele, is reflected onomastically in the striking use of the name Catin. There are two Catins for Ronsard: one is the old slut of the third **Folastrie,** who resembles one of the wrinkled "escouillés de Cybele," and illustrates the more recent development of the name in French as a derogatory common noun.[39] The other Catin, as we find her named in a characteristically pastoral manner in the eclogue **"Daphnis et Thyrsis,"** represents Catherine de Médicis. That is, Daphnis and Thyrsis are transparently Charles IX and the future Henri III, singing the praises of their mother Catin: "Douce elle m'a nourry, comme autrefois Cybelle / Sur les mons Idéans nourrissoit ses enfans"[40] [Kindly she nursed me, just as Cybele used to nurse her children on the hills of Ida].

Of course, Catherine de Médicis as represented by contemporary testimony does strike us as an ambiguous figure, reducible to neither the panegyrics nor the invectives. She appears as a somewhat mannish widow insistently dressed in black, and so of uncertain gender; Etienne Jodelle declares, by way of praising her, "nous avons en une Royne un Roy" [in a queen we have a king].[41] During the long minority of Charles IX she was the closest thing to a monarch in France, and the well-known effeminacy of Henri III only put into higher relief Catherine's contrary image. She was also notorious for her doubleness in politics: it was uncertain, at any given moment, whether she was pursuing her middle course by favoring, or appearing to favor, the Catholic extremists or the Protestants.

But that last word returns to the question of witness in the central ideological conflict of the age. The Protestants owe their very name to the act of witnessing. We might tentatively distinguish three varieties of that act that characterize Calvinism. First, *témoin* and *témoignage* are theologically weighted terms running throughout Calvin's works. In the *Institutions,* for example, he crucially defines sacrament as a "tesmoignage de la grace de Dieu" [a manifestation of the grace of God].[42] The Reformers notoriously insist upon the sovereignty of that testament which is scripture. In the Bible and in sacraments, God is the one who testifies—that is, signifies his will.

Second, those who die for their faith act as witnesses. For Calvin, to suffer martyrdom is "rendre tesmoignage à la verité de Dieu au besoing" [to bear witness to God's truth when necessary].[43] In Crespin and Goulart's *Histoire des Martyrs,* Protestant martyrs are persistently called *témoings.*[44] Such nomenclature follows the tradition of biblical translation, of Greek *martus* and *marturia/marturion* into Latin *testis* and *testimonium* and from Latin into the vernaculars.[45] The testimony of such martyrs consists in the very fact of their public suffering, but they may also speak out to openly declare their belief; finally, the details of their suffering may become eloquent corporeal signs.[46] Hence the martyr's achievement, if I might appropriate Ronsard's words from another context: "Faisant son sang le tesmoing de sa Foy" [Making his blood the witness of his faith].[47] The suffering body is a witness.

And, perhaps most pertinently, a third sort of testimony lies at the heart of Protestant historiography and martyrology, which show a keen sense of duty to the memory of the victims. The historian's act of witnessing combats the attempts of orthodoxy to impose forgetfulness—and I am not referring to attempts in any vague sense. A formula that recurs in at least two of the peace treaties during the civil wars calls for the following: that the memory of past atrocities (for example, Saint Bartholomew's Day) "demeurera esteincte et assoupie, comme de choses non advenues" [will be annulled and suppressed, as if they had never happened].[48] Those texts are recorded in Agrippa d'Aubigné's *Histoire universelle*; and of course, his *Tragiques* is obviously and explicitly an epic of witness, particularly in the central books **"La Chambre dorée," "Les Feux,"** and **"Les Fers,"** with their catalogues of injustice and their visual appeal. In this last variety, literary witness, we find the text itself as *témoin.*

Hence, three subjects of witness: God, the martyr, and the writer. Hence also, two principal media of witness: the body and the text, whether that text be scriptural or historiographic/poetic. Protestant literary practice typically mingles these varieties, but the ultimate object of witness remains the same: Christian truth. Ronsard's myth also contains a divinity and a suffering and signifying body. On the other hand, his account obviously lacks the element of univocal signification; as I began by noting, contradictory interpretations open and close the narrative of **"Le Pin."** Semiotic similarities and hermeneutic differences connect Ronsard's Attis with the contemporary discourse of witnessing.

In the course of the 1560s it became clear that the Queen Mother was a persecutor of Protestant witnesses.

I would suggest that the widespread polemic image of Catherine as the castrating Mother (as in L'Estoile) is based on the pun, usually hidden, that confounds *testes* with *testes, témoin/testicle* with *témoin/witness.* On the other hand, Ronsard's own opposition to the Protestants, as voiced in his **Discours des misères** is based on a suspicion of the potency of witness unbridled by tradition or social norms. The poet's orthodoxy amounts to a politicization of the myth interpretation offered by the emperor Julian: Attis's castration represents "the checking of the unlimited" (*epoche tes apeirias*).[49] The common Catholic reproach, that Luther and Calvin opened the door to scriptural interpretation by everyone, voices a fear of excess, figurable both conceptually and corporeally.

That the integrity of *témoins* in the physical sense was an important political principle can be seen in an anecdote told by d'Aubigné. The gentleman Villandry was almost put to death for playfully grabbing Charles IX by "les parties honteuses." Such an action constituted a capital crime according to the laws, "qui ostent la vie à tous ceux qui prennent leur Souverain en tel endroit" [which condemn to death all those who take hold of their sovereign in such a place].[50] Villandry was saved from execution through the intervention of Admiral Coligny, who was himself later castrated as part of the ritual mutilation of his corpse on Saint Bartholomew's Day.[51] The perceived deviations of the body politic could be expiated on real bodies. Those real bodies, as martyrs bearing witness, could subsequently become textual bodies of peculiar power; a tendency exemplified strikingly by the hagiography of Coligny and his fellow victims of 1572.

The process can be summarized abstractly: the threat of a dangerous excess of witness, followed by the suppression of that witness, followed by its textual recuperation. Such a pattern hinges on what must be paradoxically called the productive role of castration.

Putting it that way may at first appear irrelevant to Ronsard. Attis is a figure of the poet.[52] As I earlier expressed it in Ronsard's words, "[les] escris sont tesmoins," and what Attis loses are explicitly called *autheurs* (v. 52). The Queen Mother deprived Ronsard of his *escris/tesmoins* by imposing silence. This she did by forbidding any more polemic pamphlets after the peace of Amboise in March 1563, and so, it might be claimed, putting an end to the series of **Discours des misères.** However, that gesture of negation does not mean simply silencing the poet. If we follow Daniel Ménager in reading the **Discours** as realizing the dead end of historical discourse, and their suspension as the return to "pure" poetry (that is, to an apparently nonpolemical poetry), we can see the Queen Mother's decree equally well in another light.[53] She is, in a sense, the one to thank for the mythological delirium of the four seasonal **Hymnes** as well as the other poems of the 1560s attesting to Ronsard's turn away from political poetry.

True, for some of Ronsard's contemporaries, as might be expected, castration constitutes an unambiguous image of censorship. Such is the case in the anecdote shared by Béroalde de Verville in *Le Moyen de parvenir* and d'Aubigné in *Les Avantures du Baron de Faeneste,* in which the artistic representation in a church of an excessively well endowed devil is subsequently deprived of his obscene feature by a censorious orthodoxy: painterly or sculptural castration.[54] In a similar vein, Montaigne recalls how Pope Paul IV "chastra" ancient sculptures in Rome "pour ne corrompre la veue" [in order not to corrupt sight].[55] For Ronsard, however, the gesture is more complex. He takes the Attis myth to mean "Un Philosophe sage / Doibt . . . estre un home sauvage: / Se faire un Pin, c'est frequenter les bois," and so forth [A wise philosopher (and thus a poet) must be a wild man; to become a pine tree is to haunt the woods] (133-35). What is constituted by the castration and metamorphosis of Attis is, so to speak, the forest of Gastine. The resemblance of **"Le Pin"** to the late elegy "Contre les bûcheronsy . . ." is based on similar phrasing early in both poems, their common perception of mythological figures beneath the *écorce* of nature, and their common positing of such a forest as the locus for poetic inspiration.[56] Ronsard recalls Ovid's allusion to the transformed Attis, where the Latin poet includes the pine in an enumeration of all the trees flocking to hear the poetry of Orpheus.[57] That Ovidian scene presents an enduring and much-imitated image of the supreme power of poetry.[58]

The pine tree becomes part of the locus of poetry through Attis's mutilation, but this is only part of a larger phenomenon. Poets may in fact be constituted by a radical lack. Ronsard's biographer Claude Binet calls the deafness which changed his poet's life "ce malheur bien-heureux," and makes an explicit parallel between that handicap and Homer's blindness.[59] Du Bellay takes the same tack in his "Hymne de la Surdité," addressed to Ronsard. Like Binet, he considers his friend's good fortune to consist in the necessary abandonment of a courtier's life. The place opposed to the court and, of course, far friendlier to poetic inspiration, is a woodland setting. This redirection from the court to poetry resembles the blessing that the Queen Mother's command of political silence bestowed on the poet of the *Discours des misères.*

Ronsard goes further in his "Responce aux injures," where he makes blindness a cause of the greatness of the primordial poets such as Homer, Thamyras, and Stesichorus. He takes his own example and Du Bellay's to show that what held true in archaic times for blindness holds true for deafness in the present day, in a sort of *translatio* of handicaps.[60] This homology between

deafness and blindness as sources of poetry is relevant for several reasons. First, in Ronsard's case the visual element of witness takes over from the lost sense of hearing. As Binet puts it: "il pensa de transferer l'office des oreilles aux yeux par la lecture des bons livres" [it occurred to him to transfer the ears' office to the eyes by reading good books].[61] The poet's deafness is the image of ocular maiming (Ronsard = Homer), and it finds compensation in the seeing that generates texts: literary practice as *témoignage* of an absence. Moreover, we might listen to Freud, whose anthropological speculation proposes blinding as a substitute for castration (Oedipus, for example).[62] Such a substitution provides a new dimension for the maiming that founds poetry.

Some form of self-emasculation and inspiration are associated in Ronsard's poetry as early as the declaration in the 1552 **Amours**: "Je suis semblable à la prestresse folle" [I am like the mad priestess].[63] It may be that Ronsard accentuates gender ambiguity most in his erotic poetry,[64] but a similar process turns up elsewhere. In his **"Dithyrambes"** for Jodelle's "Pompe du bouc" and in the **"Hymne de Bacus,"** Ronsard includes himself among the inspired followers of Dionysus/Bacchus. In the first case he establishes a parallel between the Bacchic triumph and the procession of Cybele and her followers, while in the second he repeatedly refers to the female gender of the Bacchantes, his companions.[65] What this amounts to in both poems is an assimilation of the poet to the castrated or female devotees of the god(s); he becomes a transvestite spying on mysteries like Pentheus, but sympathetic and undetected.

Ronsard concludes **"Le Pin"** with a reference to the fever from which he currently suffers, and a recognition that "La Muse peut alleger le soucy"[66] [The muse can lighten cares]. This bald commonplace takes on new meaning when we notice just how frequently the poet refers to his illness in the **Sixiesme** and **Septiesme livres des Poëmes,** and how intimate the link is between illness and poetic creation. Amadis Jamyn's liminary sonnet to the **Sixiesme livre** introduces Ronsard's sudden burst of composition as the direct result of a god-given quartan fever.[67] Many allusions in both books reaffirm an association between febrile illness and febrile creativity.[68] In the present poem and the collection that first contains it, with an explicit autobiographical note and in the cherished setting of Saint-Cosme, Ronsard plays variations on the theme of poetry as pathology or maiming.

What is more, although **"Le Pin"** narrates the story of a mortal and a goddess, which translates most obviously to an allegory of royalty and its dependent, the productivity of castration also exists in the intertextual realm. When Ronsard uses these terms in accusing his Protestant opponent, "Tes escris sont tesmoins que tu m'as desrobé," he is speaking metaphorically but not at all vaguely. The Protestants robbed him most clearly in the two **Palinodies** which appeared anonymously in 1563. These consist mostly of Ronsard's own verses, from his **"Elégie à Guillaume des Autels"** and the **"Discours à la Royne,"** so that he was certainly justified in accusing them of stealing his textual potency.[69] Ronsard also suffered in later years what might be considered hermeneutical theft. A Protestant pamphlet of 1574, *Le Réveille-matin des François,* cited and interpreted certain passages in the fourth book of the *Françiade* as using figures of the dreadful Merovingian dynasty to refer to members of the reigning Valois family.[70] The epic poet was thus interpreted as subverting the royal authority that his poem had aimed to legitimize. On the other hand, from the Protestant point of view, Ronsard's problem was that he had already lost the power of witness by betraying what had previously seemed promising to adherents of the Reformation.[71] Their mockery of him as "Grand Prestre de Cybele" condemns, first, a poet who wastes his time with pagan mythology and, second, one who has sought to advance his career through the unnatural occupation of cleric.[72] By both deeds, which both amount to self-mutilation, he has declined to testify.

So the gesture of mutilation, of oneself or another, stages an interplay among powers in the intertextual, ideological, and political realms. And that interplay is literarily fertile.[73] Likewise, a process takes place in Ronsard's imaginary. The castration of Attis leads to the erection of the pine tree, and provides the condition necessary for the pursuit of wisdom (which means being a poet); on the other hand, the cutting down of the forest of Gastine entails the death (or at least the dispersal) of poetic inspiration at the same time it inspires the poet to lament that fact. However violent the clash, it is not a matter of a simple opposition between cornucopian/genital fecundity on one side and sterility on the other.

Ronsard's second, positive interpretation of the Attis myth (cited above) continues with this quasi-Platonic distinction:

(151) L'home est Centaure: en bas il est
                cheval,
(152) Et home en haut, d'embas vient tout
                le mal,
(153) Si la raison, qui est l'home, ne guide
(154) Cet animal & ne luy tient la bride.[74]

(151) [Man is a centaur. Below he is a
                horse,
(152) Human above. All evil comes from
                below,
(153) If reason, which is human,
(154) Does not guide this animal and hold
                it reined in.]

The image of the rein of reason needed to control a double human nature, which comes from the *Phaedrus,*

should not obscure what is different and troubling in Ronsard's version. First, of course, there are not two horses in question as for Plato, but one creature simultaneously man and beast. This more intimate association of good and bad is joined to a neat corporeal distinction: "en bas . . . en haut." In these lines, as in a quite similar passage of the prose discourse, "Des vertus intellectuelles et morales," there is nothing surprising in finding the lower body condemned as the locus of base sensuality.[75] Nor is it incongruous that the interpretation represents as discipline (*guide, tient la bride*) what the myth represents as castration, or irreversible negation. But it turns out that both reason and madness perform the same function of purification. The effect of Attis's *fureur* ends up as the effect of reason—what makes humanity truly human.

What makes the poet a poet, what makes man human; finally, it is the same act that also creates human society. After all, Attis is a lawgiver. His cultic activity takes place in public, and his defining gesture has social circumstances and consequences. The social paradox of Ronsard's Attis myth is encapsulated in a formal element, as are the paradoxes of poetics and anthropology. The poetic cliché reads: madness at the inception of poetry; the anthropological cliché: a man becomes truly human by taming his irrational impulses. **"Le Pin"** serves as a reminder of the corporeal violence underlying those clichés. In particular, the striking rhyme near the end (133-34) sharpens the point: *sage/sauvage.* As for the social dimension, consider the startling parataxis of lines 39-40: "Premier, [Attis] & loix & statutz leur donna, / Et ses tesmoings d'un caillou moissonna" [Attis was the first to give them laws and statutes, and reaped his *tesmoings* with a flint]. That mysterious *et,* apparently so feeble as it connects the two clauses, provides the link between private and public, violence and construction, the intimate body and the body politic. It holds in balance the possible meanings of simultaneity (both . . . and) as well as temporal sequence (first . . . then). It suggests a connection between intimate violence and the foundation of civilization, but avoids being explicit. That minimal conjunction is a microcosm of the relationship between Ronsard's pun in **"Le Pin"** and the larger dialectic of witness contemporary with his text. There is no question of causality or precedence between the two realms, although they do share a common dynamic structure: excess (madness), suppression (castration), recuperation (text). Ronsard's poetic practice, placed in its context, reminds us of the physical destruction as well as the poetic fecundity that crisis may bring about. It is no longer possible to ignore the social dimension of textual maneuvers, or to ignore the force behind signification.[76]

The fate of Attis's—and Ronsard's—*tesmoings* poses a problem of excess meaning. The fate of *et* in line 40 possesses, in this connection, at least a symbolic importance. In the 1584 edition of Ronsard's *Œuvres,* the distich reads: "Loix et statuts ministre leur donna, / Puis ses tesmoins d'un caillou moissonna." The excision of *et* and its replacement by *puis* means a reduction of ambiguity and the promotion of a clearer narrative chronology: first, the productive religious/social activity, then the private violence. The aging poet, revising for the final collective edition before his death, cuts along with *et* some of the semantic excess from his poem. Nevertheless, much flourishes still beneath Attis's blow.

Notes

1. I cite the first edition: Pierre de Ronsard, *Œuvres complètes,* ed. Paul Laumonier et al., 20 vols. (Paris: Société de Textes Français Modernes, 1914-75), 15:178-85. All volumes of the Laumonier edition will be indicated as Lm. For the version in the 1584 *Œuvres,* see Pierre de Ronsard, *Œuvres complètes,* ed. Jean Céard, Daniel Ménager, and Michel Simonin, 2 vols. (Paris: Gallimard, 1993-94), 2:735-39. This edition will be indicated as Pl. The revisions are not numerous, especially after about v. 40.

2. For the equation Cybele = Nature, see the posthumous "Preface sur la Franciade"; Lm. 16:355; Pl. 1:1179.

3. As in such expressions as "Je faux"; for example, *Sonnets pour Helene* 2:30; 2:49 (1584) (Lm. 17:271; Pl. 1:404), or "Mais non," for example, in the poem that becomes the liminary sonnet for the 1584 *Œuvres* (Pl. 1:3; modified from the Lm. 4:85). See also Alex L. Gordon, *Ronsard et la rhétorique* (Geneva: Droz, 1970), 169-72; Marc-Antoine de Muret, *Commentaires au premier livre des* Amours *de Ronsard,* ed. Jacques Chomarat et al. (Geneva: Droz, 1985), 94ff.

4. See Terence Cave, "Ronsard's Mythological Universe," *Ronsard the Poet,* ed. Terence Cave (London: Methuen, 1973), 181-208, esp. 200-201 on "Le Pin"; Ann Moss, "New Myths for Old?" in *Ronsard in Cambridge,* ed. Philip Ford and Gillian Jondorf (Cambridge: Cambridge University Press, 1986), 55-66, esp. 61-64.

5. Julian, Oration 5, "To the Mother of the Gods"; for Ronsard's possible acquaintance with it, see Géralde Nakam, "Le mythe de Cybèle ou la terre et l'arbre dans l'oeuvre de Ronsard," *Ronsard et la Grèce 1585-1985,* ed. Kyriaki Christodoulou (Paris: Nizet, 1988), 89 n.; Lucretius *De rerum natura,* 2:600-660; Augustine *De civitate Dei* 7.24 (citing Varro). The first offers a metaphysical allegory, the latter two a naturalistic one.

6. Lm. 15:180. According to *A Dictionarie of the French and English Tongues,* ed. Randall Cotgrave (1632-), *tesmoings* "are (sometimes) a man's

testicles, or stones." He cites the proverb "Tesmoing passe lettre," as does Littré, who gives both nouns in the plural.

7. J. N. Adams, *The Latin Sexual Vocabulary* (London: Duckworth, 1982), 67.

8. *Pasquinate romane del Cinquecento,* ed. Valerio Marucci et al., 2 vols. (Rome: Salerno, 1983), 1:311-12; Matteo Bandello, *Tutte le opere,* ed. Francesco Flora, vol. 1 (Milan: Mondadori, 1934), 838, 843; Agnolo Firenzuola, *Le Novelle,* ed. Eugenio Ragni (Milan: Salerno, 1971), Giornata prima, novella quarta, secs. 35 and 44. The pun turns up again in Tassoni, *La Secchia rapita* 5.13.

9. Des Périers, *Nouvelles* 15 and 60. The use of the pun in the novella tradition concerns a stock situation (a trapped adulterer forced to castrate himself in order to escape) already imagined by Horace, *Serm* 1:2:45-46. For the stock situation, cf. no. 85 of *Les Cent nouvelles,* and nouvelle 26 of Nicolas de Troyes, *Grand parangon.*

10. Plautus, *Miles Gloriosus* 1426 in *Comoediae,* vol. 2, ed. W. M. Lindsay (Oxford: Oxford University Press, 1904). Cf. Curculio 31: "quod amas amato testibus presentibus."

11. Jean-Antoine de Baif, *Le Brave,* ed. Simone Maser (Geneva: Droz, 1979), vv. 3992-93. Ronsard participated in the premiere of this play, composing verses for one of its entr'actes (Lm. 14:201-2; Pl. 2:1122-23).

12. Lm. 11:117; Pl. 2:1044.

13. Michael Riffaterre, *Semiotics of Poetry* (Bloomington: Indiana University Press, 1978), 94. Riffaterre draws his main example from Francis Ponge's use of *artificier* (with the latent Latin *artifex*) in one of his *Douze petits ecrits.*

14. Riffaterre, *Semiotics of Poetry,* 95.

15. Catullus is named at v. 30. For the background of this intertext, see Mary Morrison, "Ronsard and Catullus: The Influence of the Teaching of Marc-Antoine Muret," *Bibliothèque d'Humanisme et Renaissance* 18 (1956): 240-74.

16. Boileau, *Art poétique,* 1:126.

17. Pierre de L'Estoile, *Registre-Journal du règne de Henri III,* ed. Madeleine Lazard and Gilbert Schrenck, vol. 1 (Geneva: Droz, 1992), 172. "Rognons de coq" were thought to be an aphrodisiac; see "La Bouquinade" attributed to Ronsard (Lm. 18:394; Pl. 2:1238).

18. L'Estoile, *Registre-Journal,* ed. Lazard and Schrenck, 172. I make what seems a necessary correction in the last line.

19. L'Estoile, *Registre-Journal,* ed. Lazard and Schrenck, 189. In 1586 the chronicler records another pasquinade which mentions Cybele and declares: "Vrai est qu'on ne vit onques Poule / Tant de braves Coqs commander," but he specifies in a note that Poule refers to Henri III; L'Estoile, *Journal pour le règne de Henri III,* ed. Louis-Raymond Lefèvre (Paris: Gallimard, 1943), 474, 477.

20. Cf. L'Estoile, *Journal pour le règne,* ed. Lefèvre, 174.

21. *De rerum natura* 2:600-643; Aeneid 6.784-87.

22. *The Royal Tour of France by Charles IX and Catherine de' Medici: Festivals and Entries 1564-66,* ed. Victor E. Graham and W. McAllister Johnson (Toronto: University of Toronto Press, 1979), 114.

23. *Royal Tour of France,* ed. Graham and Johnson, 177, 182, including this distich for a statue of Cybele (referring to the Trojan origin of the French monarchy): "Alma Phrygum Cybele, Phrygio de sanguine creto / Effundo Regi pleno mea munera cornu.'

24. *The Paris Entries of Charles IX and Elisabeth of Austria 1571,* ed. Victor E. Graham and W. McAllister Johnson (Toronto: University of Toronto Press, 1974), 188.

25. *Paris Entries,* ed. Graham and Johnson, 189: "Foelix prole parens, qualis Berecenthia mater / Invehitur curru Phrygias turrita per urbes, / Laeta deum partu, centum complexa nepotes." The Virgilian passage (*Aeneid* 6.784-86) begins "felix prole virum," but is otherwise identical.

26. *Paris Entries,* ed. Graham and Johnson, liminary sonnet by Bouquet to the Queen Mother, 101, and sonnet by Guy du Faur de Pibrac, 124.

27. See also Jean Doral's verses, cited in *Paris Entries,* ed. Graham and Johnson, 62.

28. Lm. 7:35; Pl. 1:726.

29. Lm. 12:157; Pl. 2:218. Lm. 13:97; Pl. 2:154. Lm. 13:277; Pl. 2:1121. During the reign of her husband, Henri II, Catherine was understandably more often represented as Juno; see Edouard Bourciez, *Les Moeurs polies et la littérature de cour sous Henri II* (Paris: Hachette, 1886), 177, 183-85.

30. Baif, *Euvres en rime,* ed. Ch. Marty-Laveaux, 5 vols. (Geneva: Slatkine, 1966), "dedication" of *Le Premier des Meteores,* 2:3, and *Troisieme livre des Passetems,* 4.365.

31. Lm. 9:195; Pl. 2:283.

32. Cf. Guy Demerson, *La Mythologie classique dans l'oeuvre lyrique de la Pléiade* (Geneva: Droz, 1972), 331-32.

33. As Nakam, "Le mythe de Cybèle," 90, comments, "La Franciade doit tout a Cybèle."

34. For the texts, see Hugo Hepding, *Attis: Seine Mythen und sein Kult* (Berlin: A. Topelmann, 1967), 37-45, 47-51, 64-67.

35. Lm. 5:24; Pl. 1:297. Lm. 1:252; Pl. 1:711. Lm. 5:61; Pl. 1:563. Lm. 7:275; Pl. 1:202. Not to mention Joachim Du Bellay, *Œuvres poétiques,* ed. Henri Chamard and Geneviève Demerson, 8 vols. (Paris: Société des Textes Français Modernes, 1908-85), 1:135, 5.10, 7.83. In the last of these poems ("Epigramma 2") Du Bellay, like L'Estoile's texts, plays on *Galli/Galli* and the opposition between French virility and oriental (whether Italian or Phrygian) "semivirility." There exists a Virgilian intertext for this Cybele and her procession as for the "high" version: *Aeneid* 9.614-20.

36. Lm. 7:275; Pl. 1:202. The less-than-tragic use of the myth is evident in Belleau's coy comment on this sonnet: "Il celle un autre point duquel il lui [= Attis] voudroit moins resembler," as he refers to Catullus's account; Remy Belleau, *Commentaire au second livre des Amours de Ronsard,* ed. Marie-Madeleine Fontaine and François Lecercle (Geneva: Droz, 1986), 47. Cf. Demerson, *La Mythologie classique,* 377.

37. This has already been done, albeit briefly, by Donald Stone, "Poetry and the Attis Legend," *Studi di letteratura francese* 12 (1986): 143-58; and by Nakam, "Le mythe de Cybèle."

38. See Maarten J. Vermaseren, *Cybele and Attis: The Myth and the Cult* (London: Thames and Hudson, 1977), 9-11.

39. Lm 5:21-29; Pl. 1:295-99. Cf. a violent poem in French against the Queen Mother, recorded by L'Estoile, *Registre-Journal,* ed. Lazard and Schrenck, 188, which apostrophizes her as "Catin." These verses and four subsequent Latin epigrams are glossed in the margin thus: "Katin" (187-90).

40. Lm. 12:157; Pl. 2:218. For other examples of Catin as a pastoral character, see Belleau, *Bergerie.*

41. Etienne Jodelle, *Œuvres complètes,* ed. Enea Balmas, 2 vols. (Paris: Gallimard, 1965), 1:205.

42. Jean Calvin, *Institution de la religion chrestienne,* ed. Abel Lefranc et al. (Paris: H. Champion, 1911), 565.

43. Calvin, *Three French Treatises,* ed. Francis M. Higman (London: Athlone Press, 1970), 143

44. See also Catharine Randall Coats, *Embodying the Word: Textual Resurrection in the Martyrological Narratives of Foxe, Crespin, de Bèze, and d'Aubigné* (New York: Peter Lang, 1992).

45. See for example the important uses in Rev. 1:4-5 and 1.9. One of the Protestants who engaged Ronsard in the polemic of the *Discours des misères* makes the identification *tesmoin = martire*; see *La Polémique protestante contre Ronsard*, ed. Jacques Pineaux, 2 vols. (Paris: Didier, 1973), 423.

46. Theodore Agrippa D'Aubigné, *Les Tragiques*, provides the clearest examples. In addition to the numerous uses of *tesmoin* as "martyr" and *tesmoignage* as "martyrdom" in the martyrological book, "Les Feux" (vv. 605, 625, 741, 746, 1097, 1130, 1155), see "La Chambre dorée," 651-52: "Que Dieu a ses tesmoins a donné maintesfois, / La langue estant couppée, une celeste voix"; see Theodore Agrippa D'Aubigné, *Œuvres*, ed. Henri Weber et al. (Paris: Gallimard, 1969).

47. Lm. 15:104; Pl. 2:393 (revised).

48. Theodore Agrippa D'Aubigné, *Histoire universelle*, ed. André Thierry, 10 vols. (Geneva: Droz, 1981-99), 4.143, 7.242.

49. Julian, *Oration 5*, "To the Mother of the Gods," 167C.

50. D'Aubigné, *Histoire universelle*, 3:301.

51. See Simon Goulart, *Mémoires de l'Estat de France sous Charles Neufiesme*, 3 vols. (Mendelbourg: H. Wolf, 1578-79), 1:209r.

52. See I. D. McFarlane, "Aspects of Ronsard's Poetic Vision," *Ronsard the Poet*, 56. Nakam, "Le mythe de Cybèle," 98, sees the three elements of the myth as symbolizing the moments of poetic creation: Cybele, "la fécondité de l'inspiration"; the Corybantes (with Attis), furor; the pine, "l'écriture créatrice."

53. See Daniel Ménager, *Ronsard: Le Roi, le Poète et les Hommes* (Geneva: Droz, 1979), 187-274, esp. 253, 266, 270.

54. D'Aubigné, *Œuvres*, 804; Béroalde de Verville, *Le Moyen de parvenir*, ed. Hélène Moreau and André Tournon, 2 vols. (Aix-en-Provence: Publications Université de Provence; Marseille: Diffusion Jean Laffitte, 1984), 2:118-24. Cf. Catharine Randall Coats, "The Devil's Phallus: Humanistic vs. Theological Notions of Writing in Béroalde de Verville and Agrippa d'Aubigné," *Stanford French Review* 13 (1989): 37-48; and Michael J. Giordano, "Transgression and Castration in *Le Moyen de parvenir*: A Reading of 'Chapitre General' (1.29)," *Studies on Béroalde de Verville*, ed. Giordano (Paris: Biblio 17-Papers on French Seventeenth-Century Literature, 1992), 109-38.

55. Michel de Montaigne, *Œuvres complètes*, ed. Albert Thibaudet and Maurice Rat (Paris: Gallimard, 1962), 837 (*Essais* 3:5).

56. "Elegie," 24 (Lm. 18.143-47; Pl. 2:408-9). Cf. "Le Pin," vv. 9-10, and "Elegie," 1-2 (similar structure and vocabulary already noted by Laumonier 15.178 n.); "Le Pin," 16-17, and "Elegie," 4 (the myth of Erysichthon); "Le Pin," 21, and "Elegie," 22 (nymphs beneath the bark); "Le Pin," 23-34, and "Elegie," 41-48 (poetry and tree[s]). For Ronsard's forest as a place of inspiration, cf. the ode "A la forest de Gastine" (Lm. 1:243-45; Pl. 1:703-4); the sonnet "Sainte Gastine . . ." (Lm. 4.128; Pl. 1:111); Elizabeth Armstrong, *Ronsard and the Age of Gold* (Cambridge: Cambridge University Press, 1968), 185-88.

57. Ovid *Metamorphoses* 10.86-105 (103-5 for the pine).

58. For example, "L'Orphee," vv. 347-49 (Lm. 12:142; Pl. 2:363); "Hymne de France," 9 (Lm. 1:24; Pl. 2:647); or "A son luc," 122-24 (Lm. 2:162; Pl. 1:965).

59. Claude Binet, *La Vie de P. de Ronsard (1586)*, ed. Paul Laumonier (Geneva: Slatkine, 1969), 7-8. Cf. the verses by Dorat cited by Pierre de Nolhac, *Ronsard et l'humanisme* (Paris: H. Champion, 1966), 82n.

60. Lm. 11:129-30; Pl. 2:1049. Is it only a coincidence that he adduces Du Bellay's example thus: "Tesmoing est du Bellay qui comme moy fut sourd"? His Protestant opponents also make the comparison between him and Thamyras, Homer, etc., albeit mockingly; see *La Polémique protestante*, 356-57.

61. Binet, *La Vie de P. de Ronsard*, 9.

62. Sigmund Freud, *Totem and Taboo*, trans. James Strachey (New York: Norton, 1950), 161.

63. Lm. 4.31; Pl. 1:38.

64. See Lawrence D. Kritzman, "Le corps de la fiction et la fiction du corps chez Ronsard," *Sur des vers de Ronsard 1585-1985*, ed. Marcel Tetel (Paris: Aux Amateurs de Livres, 1990), 71-83.

65. Lm. 5.53-76; Pl. 1:560-69, esp. vv. 103-7, 138; and Lm. 6.176-90; Pl. 2:594-601; esp. vv. 179-210, a graphic description of his own divine furor.

66. Lm. 15.179, v. 168.

67. Lm. 15.14.

68. In the *Sixiesme livre,* see: "Le Chat," vv. 91, 110; "Les Parolles que dit Calypson," 150, 263; "La Salade," 34; "L'Ombre du cheval," 85. In the *Septiesme livre,* see: "Elegie au seigneur Pierre du Lac," 17; "Le Soucy du jardin," 29, 85-90; "Le Pin," 165-70; "Le Rossignol," 79-81. See also sonnets 1, 2, 3, and 5: "Elegie, ou Amour oyseau," 1-26; "Elegie: Pour vous aymer," 1-4; "Elegie à A. Jamyn"; "Elegie: Seule apres Dieu," 43-52. As noted by D. B. Wilson, *Ronsard Poet of Nature* (Manchester: Manchester University Press, 1961), 108n, Ficino in his *De triplici vita* suggests that the "*fiebvre quarte* is a disease particularly appropriate to the *studieux.*"

69. Ronsard, cited in *La Polémique protestante,* 5-27. The second *Palinodie* is addressed—like Ronsard's "Discours"—to the Queen Mother. For the response to this accusation (Ronsard had already stolen the riches he accuses others of taking from him), see *La Polémique protestante,* 236, 369-72.

70. See Eusebe Philadelphe, *Le Reveille-matin des François et de leurs voisins* (Edinburgh: Jacques James, 1574), 109-16; Ménager, *Ronsard: Le Roi,* 289 and nn. 88-90. Cf. the extended comparison of Catherine to Brunehaut in the *Discours merveilleux de la vie, actions & deportemens de Catherine de Medicis Royne mere,* in Simon Goulart, *Mémoires de l'Estat de France,* 3:345r-349r (as in *Le Reveille-matin*).

71. See Ménager, *Ronsard: Le Roi,* 250-51.

72. For the "Grand Prestre de Cybele," see *La Polémique protestante,* 296, 507; cf. p. 517 to see what Ronsard has cut or will cut in order to advance himself in the church. The declaration in that polemic (336) that Ronsard knows the galliambic meter, of which Catullus's *carmen* 63 is the sole extant example, not to mention a reference to the ancient custom of castrating priests (342), also allude to the poet's involvement with the matter of Attis.

73. Note the vocabulary of both play and fertility in the lines that introduce Ronsard's retelling of the Attis myth, vv. 32-34: "Et moy François en me joüant apres / Je la diray, afin que telle histoire, / En tous endroitz fleurisse par memoire" [And I, a Frenchman, in playing hereafter / I will tell it, so that such a story, / May flourish everywhere in the memory].

74. The passage 151-54 is the only one in the poem, apart from 129-30, to be set apart by sententious quotation marks.

75. Lm. 18.456; Pl. 2:1191.

76. See Jacques Derrida, *L'écriture et la différence* (Paris: Seuil, 1967), 9-49.

Cathy Yandell (essay date 2003)

SOURCE: Yandell, Cathy. "Rhetoric and Virility in Ronsard's *Folastries*." In *Masculinities in Sixteenth-Century France,* edited by Philip Ford and Paul White, pp. 85-101. Cambridge: Cambridge French Colloquia, 2006.

[*In the following essay, originally presented in 2003, Yandell discusses Ronsard's challenge to masculinist ideals in the hybrid poems of* Le Livret de folastries *(1553).*]

In April of 1553, *Le Livret de folastries* was published anonymously by the same printer who had produced Ronsard's *Amours* the preceding year. These poems appeared four months after the resolution of Ronsard's famous quarrel with Saint-Gelais, itself a microcosm of the larger conflict between the lofty, classically inspired poets of Du Bellay's *Deffence* and Ronsard's *Odes,* on the one hand, and the Italianate court poets producing lighter fare, on the other.[1] Yet the larger stylistic conflict was far from resolved. Ronsard again sought public approval for his poetic experiments two years later in the first sonnet of the *Continuation des Amours,* 'Thiard, chacun disoit a mon commencement', in which the poet lamented the multi-headed monster, the fickle public, who found fault with both his high and his low styles.[2]

This literary conflict is significant in the context of the *Folastries* because it announces the hybridity that dominates the collection, a hybridity that is not only stylistic, but also sexual and generic. From the outset, the anonymous publication of the *Folastries* reveals the blurred relationship between the poet and his work. Acknowledging the complexity of the concept of 'masculinity', particularly within the context of sixteenth-century culture, one can nonetheless profitably pose the question: to what extent can the poetic identity that Ronsard establishes within the collection be said to be male or masculine? In these potentially most 'masculinist' of poems, both *gaillards* and *gaulois,* does what might be called 'masculine' rhetoric prevail? I will argue here that it does not, and that the virility embodied in the poems is frequently mollified or challenged. Ronsard both posits and subverts masculine ideals in the *Folastries.*

The present essay will not be the first to suggest sexual ambivalence in Ronsard's work. In 'Ronsard the Poet, Ronsard the Hermaphrodite', Ann Moss fruitfully studies the ambiguous sexuality in several of Ronsard's mythological poems of the 1560s. Lawrence Kritzman explores Ronsard's 'phallocentric masquerade' in the *Amours* of 1552, and Kirk Read calls attention to Ronsard's lactating mentor in 'A Jan Dorat'. Daniel Ménager treats the stylistic effects of Ronsard's use of the female voice, and I examine more specifically Ronsard's assumption of a lesbian voice in his elegy of 1567. In another study, I address Ronsard's substituting male for female referents, as when the poet himself becomes a flower in **'Dedans des Prez je vis une Dryade'**.[3] But the 'folastries', arguably the poems most fraught with sexual ambivalence, have heretofore been neglected in criticism focusing on the problems of gender.

From the outset, the **_Folastries_** situate themselves within an isotopy (to use Greimas's term) or a semantic field of sexuality.[4] Both the title and the epigraph of the collection signal a blurring of genders or sexual behaviours. 'Folastrerie', which replaced 'folastrie' during the course of the sixteenth century, is defined by Cotgrave as 'fond [meaning 'foolish' in the sixteenth century] trickes, lascivious prankes, wanton fashions, effeminate actions'. Since the collection was printed by Veuve Maurice de La Porte in five hundred copies, the anonymous collection was intended to be a commercial success, perhaps because of its licentious nature.[5] However, its author assures readers on the title page in a distich from Catullus 16 that the salacious verses should not be read as reflecting the author's own character:

> Nam castum esse decet pium poëtam
> Ipsum, versiculos nihil necesse est.[6]

(For the sacred poet ought to be chaste himself, though his poems need not be so.)

That an unidentified poet should seek to protect his reputation is curious if not paradoxical. Against what is the nameless poet seeking protection? Many literary historians agree that erotic literature was for the most part well accepted in the French Renaissance and that modern pornographic literature—both marginal and transgressive—is inconceivable before the Reformation and especially before Classicism. Indeed, Jean-Marie Goulemot has argued hyperbolically that 'foul language, scatological descriptions, and scenes of joyous fornication abound everywhere in the literature of the [pre-modern] time: from Rabelais to Sorel's *Francion*. They constitute an essential part of the literary production of the period'.[7] Yet if there were no norms to transgress, why did Ronsard publish anonymously? Could it be that his anonymity served as a subterfuge to test the critical waters for his lower, bolder style? If so, Ronsard's wager produced mixed results: the **_Folastries_** were well received by at least some of his contemporaries. Pierre des Mireurs, immediately guessing the author's identity, wrote laconically: 'Descendat quantum volet e sublimi sacrae poesis fastigio, semper Terpander erit' ('As much as he descends from the heights of sacred poetry, he will still be Terpander').[8] Olivier de Magny, in his own imitation of the **_Folastries_** published in 1554, praises the grace and perfection of 'ce livret de doctes folies'.[9] Charles Fontaine, a disciple of the Ma-

rotic school, also predictably assesses the collection in laudatory terms.[10] The ultimate measure of success for Ronsard's anonymous experiment can be ascertained by the poet's choice to republish almost all of the *folastries* under his own name in later collections.

The fact remains, however, that at the time of their publication, the **_Folastries_** were inextricably embroiled in literary quarrels. Five days after the *privilège du roi* had been issued, Henry's entourage complained of the poems, citing their libidinous turpitude and their affront to good morals.[11] To complicate matters further, Ronsard's epigraph is extracted from Catullus's response to another literary quarrel, this one about the sexual practices of its author:

> Pedicabo ego vos et irrumabo,
> Aureli pathice et cinaede Furi,
> qui me ex versiculis meis putastis,
> quod sunt molliculi, parum pudicum.

(1. I'll bugger you and stuff you, you catamite Aurelius and you pervert Furius, who have supposed me to be immodest, on account of my verses, because these are rather naughty.)

(Trans. Francis W. Cornish, 1913)

(2. I'll fuck the pair of you as you prefer it, oral Aurelius, anal Furius, who read my verses but misread their author: you think that *I'm* effeminate, since *they* are!)

(Trans. Charles Martin, 1992)[12]

The origins of this passage would have been well known to Ronsard's humanist readers. Because Catullus had written a so-called Sapphic ode, that is a *basium* poem in which the poet begs his lover for kisses, he is accused by Aurelius and Furius of being a sodomite. While this charge may initially appear illogical since Catullus's lover is female, the operative element is not the lover's gender, but rather his role. Both their accusations and Catullus's threat in these hendecasyllabic verses involve sexual passivity. It is interesting to note that the term 'molliculi' is translated in 1913 as 'naughty' and in 1992 as 'effeminate'. A number of classical scholars now agree that the term 'mollis' denotes in Roman times not homosexuality or woman-like behaviour per se, but passivity or penetrability in sexual relations with either gender.[13] Nonetheless, in other poems, notably those addressed to Juventius, Catullus's speaker describes in detail his homosexual desire. Ironically, then, Ronsard has chosen an extremely sexually charged passage to defend himself against charges of extremely sexualised poetry.

In addition to the sexual ambiguity present in Ronsard's model, his poet also uses imagery befitting a female in a preface to 'Janot Parisien', identified by Laumonier as Jean de Baïf. Ronsard describes himself (pp. 4-5) as ravished by the muses to conceive his verses:

Livre que les sœurs Thespiennes,
Dessus les rives Pympléennes,
Ravi, me firent concevoir,
Quand jeune garson j'allay voir
Le brisement de leur cadance
Et Apollon le guidedance.

While Catullus has been acknowledged as Ronsard's model for this preface, the Roman poet refers neither to ravishing nor to conceiving. Indeed, Catullus evokes the image of polishing his book with pumice stone, and, save a mention of his 'patrona virgo' (p. 3), sexual allusions are completely absent from his preface. Ronsard thus departs from his model not only by sexualising the metaphor for his book, but also by assuming in the process a feminised body capable of conception.

Ronsard enacts a further sexualising of the preface—albeit playfully—by addressing to 'Janot' the expression 'tu m'aymes mieux, / Ny que ton Cœur, ny que tes yeux' (p. 4). Readers of Catullus would recognise this expression as describing Lesbia's attachment to her pet sparrow, with whom (as we all know) Lesbia often played 'whilst she [held it] in her lap' (Catullus 2, p. 3). Once again the sexual implications in the text arise dialogically in relation to Catullus, the invisible but omnipresent model.

The poet of the *Folastries* thus establishes a problematic relationship with his publication in a number of ways—by his absent name, by his radically new style, and by his poet's sexuality, which through imitation is in constant dialogue with that of his model. Given that this collection situates itself under the aegis of sexuality, readers might well expect to find Ronsard, 'poète de la conquête amoureuse',[14] the most 'virile' or manly in his most lascivious collection of poems. Upon closer examination, however, it becomes clear that Ronsard's poet is strangely lacking in virility—'virile', that is, in its sixteenth-century reading, namely 'manlie' (as in *vir*), 'bold, courageous, valiant, strong, substantiall'.[15]

To what extent does the lyric narrator, Ronsard's 'je', fulfil masculine ideals as delineated in these sixteenth-century definitions? In both cultural and literary terms, the proving grounds for such a question remain constant: the bed (or verdant pasture) and the battlefield, that is, sexual conquest and military valour.[16]

To be sure, erotic episodes abound in the *Folastries,* as in the pastoral **'Jaquet et Robine'.** Of the eight poems bearing the title of *Folastries,* only this one recounts an unproblematic coupling. The staging of the amorous exploits of Jacquet and Robine includes the rhetoric of exchange and reciprocity from the rustic poem's opening:

Jaquet ayme autant sa Robine
Qu'une pucelle sa poupine,

Robine ayme autant son Jaquet
Qu'un amoureux fait son bouquet.
O amourettes doucelettes,
O doucelettes amourettes,
O couple d'amis bien heureux,
Ensemble aimez et amoureux.

(pp. 29-30)

These verses establish both linguistic symmetry and a blurring of genders. First, the names Jaquet and Robine recall the prototypical characters of French pastoral, Robin and Marion, except that the masculine 'Robin' figures here in its feminine form, Robine, and the diminutive that traditionally designates the young woman, Marie-on, now applies to the young man, Jacques-et. Symmetry is created not only by the lines 'Jaquet ayme autant / . . . / Robine ayme autant', but also by the *rejet* following the enjambment of each verse which logically should follow the other verse in question. In this arrangement, Jaquet loves as a girl (*une pucelle*) and Robine loves as a boy (*un amoureux*). As if further to reflect a perfect semantic symmetry, the anaphoric verses 5 and 6 are identical save the chiastic reversal of 'amourettes' and 'doucelettes'. While Catullus frequently uses the rhetorical figure chiasmus, the diagonal arrangement of terms as in the Greek letter X, never is it used to establish an equalising effect as it is throughout Ronsard's fourth *Folastrie.* Finally, the abundance of terms denoting togetherness and equality throughout the poem is striking, as evidenced in lines 7 and 8 above: *couple / amis / ensemble / aimez / amoureux.*

The erotic vision sketched in this pastoral proves to be unrealistic, symmetrically depicted in almost caricatural terms: just as Jaquet spies his mistress's 'grosse motte . . . et son petit cas barbelu', so Robine eyes his 'trib-art qui luy pendoit entre les jambes' (pp. 32-3). Their desires are united in the text with the repetition of the word 'rouge', once for Jaquet and once for Robine: his member is 'Plus rouge que les rouges flames / Qu'elle atisoit songneusement' (p. 33). When this mutual magnetism reaches its pinnacle ten lines later, the female Robine initiates the consummation: 'Si tu n'aymes mieux ta galette / Que ta mignarde Robinette, / Je te pry, Jaquet, jauche moy . . .' (p. 33). The shepherd and shepherdess's erotic antics are such that, upon observing them, even the goats mimetically begin to copulate. In rhetorical terms, also, copula are so readily understood as to be unnecessary: 'O couple d'amans bien heureux, / Ensemble aymez, et amoureux' (p. 34).

Both Catullus's and Ronsard's pastoral poems conclude with an elegiac description of reciprocal love, yet in quite different ways. While Ronsard's Jaquet and Robine are united in parallel rhetorical terms, Catullus's lovers Septimius and Acme (Catullus 45, 53), though blessed by Venus, are shown to have distinctly male and female ways of loving. Catullus's male Septimius prefers Acme to the military conquests of Syria and Britain, whereas Acme's desire is to take her fill of love and pleasure only in Septimius: 'unam Septimius misellus Acmen / mavolt quam Syrias Britanniasque: uno in Septimio fidelis Acme / facit delicias libidinesque' (Catullus 45, p. 54).

Not coincidentally, Ronsard's pastoral poem portraying a symmetrical coupling is also the only *Folastrie* in which no poetic *je* is present. Like Montaigne, who in painting himself 'tout nud' reveals only those weaknesses he imagines that the reader will find endearing (such as being too quick in sex and having a poor memory), so Ronsard's poet in the *Folastries* assumes the voice of the former or thwarted lover, the loser, the has-been. Failure, sometimes stigmatised as effeminate, takes on a humorous dimension in the *Folastries*.[17] This comic stance invites the reader both to side with the underdog and to bemoan the bumbling poet's fate.

A dog of a different sort plays the protagonist in *Folastrie 5* and successfully obstructs Ronsard's poet's amorous success. Poets from the Greek Anthology as well as Catullus and Ovid had written praises of various animals, especially dogs.[18] Here Ronsard takes the opposite position, chastising the dog for betraying him and his mistress in the midst of their secret lovemaking. The poem begins with the traditional image of the faithful dog, companion to historic heroes:

> Au viel temps que l'enfant de Rhée
> N'avoit la terre dedorée,
> Les Heroes ne dedaignoient
> Les chiens qui les accompagnoient,
> Fidelles gardes de leur trace . . .

> (p. 35)

The Golden Age sets the stage for Ronsard's tale, before the dethroning of Chronos by Zeus and before the poet's own fall from amorous grace. But the masculine image of heroes and their valiant dogs is undercut by a humorous interruption:

> Mais toy, chien de mechante race,
>
> . . . . .
>
> Desloyal et traistre mastin,
> Japant à la porte fermée
> De la chambre, où ma mieux aymée
> Me dorlotoyt entre ses bras,
> Counillant de jour dans les dras . . .

> (p. 36)

In this passage, the poet is depicted as doubly passive, identified in both cases by the objective pronoun: the dog discovers him as he is being fondled by his 'mieux aymée'. The verbs *combler, japer, dorloter,* and *couniller* are carried out not by the poet but by the dog and

the mistress. When the speaker finally takes action in the poem, 'Tout seul je faisoy la chosette / Avecque elle dans sa couchette' (p. 36), the mannerist diminutives serve to diminish any masculine power that the speaker might otherwise have claimed. The only other instances of the poet's assuming the subjective pronoun in the poem are followed by the pluperfect subjunctive, describing the poetry he would have written in honour of the dog, had circumstances been different: 'Je t'eusse fait chien immortel, / Et t'eusse mis parmy les signes, / Entre les astres plus insignes' (p. 37). Thus in all these examples, the poetic 'je' is in some sense emasculated, physically by the interruption of the sex act within the poem, and grammatically by its position as object, or as subject to a purely putative action.

A final foiling of Ronsard's erotic designs illustrates the extent to which Ronsard's poet depicts himself as equally priapic but more sexually thwarted than any of his models, Catullus, Martial, and Johannes Secundus. The image is identical in all of the poets, namely an erect penis futilely protruding into a tunic, but in Catullus, the first-person narrator is awaiting his lover's arrival and urging her to hurry. Martial employs the image to chide his prudish reader, and Johannes Secundus, after evoking the same image, returns to a vision of union through a kiss.[19] In contrast, Ronsard's poet in *Folastrie 3* remains perpetually frustrated with no hope of relief. Since his lubricious lover has changed her ways, now refusing her services, the poet's sufferings are visibly manifest:

> Ainsi depuis une semeine,
> La longue roydeur de ma veine,
> Pourneant rouge et bien enpoint,
> Bat ma chemise et mon proupoint.
> Qu' cent diables soit la prestresse
> Qui a bigotté ma maistresse.

> (p. 28)

In this poem, the shrivelled and repentant Catin serves as the antagonistic impediment to the poet's fulfilment. The poet's former lover has been converted by Catin, who in her youth serviced priests and monks, rich and poor alike, 'Pourveu qu'il servist bien en chambre / Et qu'il eust plus d'un pié de membre'. Now, because of the old woman's influence, the poet's mistress rejects his every move:

> Si qu'or, quand baiser je la veux,
> Elle me tire les cheveux:
> Si je veux tater sa cuissette,
> Ou fesser sa fesse grossete
> Ou si je mez la main dedans
> Ses tetins, elle à coups de dens
> Me dechire tout le visage,
> Comme un singe émeu contre un page.

> (p. 27)

Once again, despite the poet's former success, now he remains either the object of his mistress's ire ('elle me tire les cheveux' . . . 'me dechire tout le visage'), or the ineffectual, desiring subject ('quand baiser je la veux', 'si je veux tater'). The speaker's only action is preceded by the hypothetical 'si' and thwarted in the poem by the mistress—here depicted as a masculine ape—with her violent response.

So much for manly pursuits in the bedroom. Ronsard's poet also fails on the battlefield by subverting the masculine ideal of military prowess, particularly in *Folastrie 2*. In this heptasyllabic poem (again stylistically modelled on Catullus's hendecasyllables), the poet's comfortable access to his lover has been foiled by her brothers' return home from war. The poet's plan consists in sending them off again to fight as soon as possible, appealing to their patriotism: '. . . allez Soldars, / Allez bienheureux gendarmes, / Allez, et vestez les armes, / Secourez la fleur de lis' (p. 18). The poet first develops an incitement of the brothers to glory, followed by an attempt to induce guilt should they choose not to serve their country:

> A ce bel œuvre, guerriers,
> Ne serez vous des premiers?
> Ah, que vous aurez de honte
> Si un autre vous raconte
> Combien le Roy print de fors,
> Combien de gens seront mors . . .
>
>   (p. 20)

The mock heroic praise of military might humorously undercuts the power of this most masculine of institutions. Ronsard had established himself in the *Odes* of 1550 as a great promoter of Henri II's battles and victories. Here, however, the poet's triumph will consist in having his mistress to himself if her brothers return to war—but his success will be achieved by cunning rather than by conquest:

> Soldars, ne cagnardez point
> Suivez le train de voz Peres,
> Et raportez à voz Meres
> Double honneur, et double bien:
> Sans vous je garderay bien
> Vos sœurs: allez donc gendarmes . . .
>
>   (p. 21)

The principal refrain of the poem, 'Le bon Bacchus portelance / Soit tous-jours votre defence', underscores the sword's double edge as it figures metaphorically in both the world of war and the world of pleasure. Interestingly, in the midst of images of masculine warriors, Bacchus or Dionysus appears as a sexually ambivalent contrast. Often termed 'the effeminate god', under his soft, rounded appearance Bacchus is said to hide nerves of steel and Herculean strength, thus uniting woman's beauty and man's force.

The last two poems in the *Folastries,* two parallel sonnets blazoning male and female genitalia, provide a final example of Ronsard's blurring of genders through-out the collection. What is striking is not the difference between the sonnets, which would be expected given the clearly masculine point of view of the poet's voice, but rather the similarities between the two. First, both adopt a strongly religious and chivalric vocabulary. The verses 'Sans toi le Monde un Chaos se feroit' (l. 9) and '. . . combien à ton honneur / Doit on de vœux, combien de sacrifices' (ll. 13-14) of the first poem announce the laudatory lines 'Je te salue, ô vermeillette fante' of the second (*P.* [*Œuvres complètes,* Pléiade edition] I, p. 571). The prayer addressed to the genitals is of course reminiscent of the quintessential 'Je te salue Marie pleine de grâce' and especially the eleventh-century *Salve Regina*: 'Je te salue O Reine, Mère de miséricorde.' The repetition of 'ô' in Ronsard's blazon ('ô vermeillette fante . . . ô bienheuré pertuis . . . ô petit trou') further recalls the *Salve Regina,* 'O clémente, ô si bonne, ô douce, Vierge Marie'. Just as readers are called upon to offer sacrifices to the male organ in the first sonnet, so are all 'vers galans' invited to worship the female organ on bended knee in the second.

Rhetorical consonances between the two poems abound as well. Both Marotic sonnets are constructed as apostrophes to the genitals, calling them into being and thereby creating the speaker's subjectivity.[20] Further, both sonnets include active verbs describing the genitals' achievements: *poindre, choquer, rendre,* and *domter.* Paradoxically, while the term 'combat' figures in the sonnet to male genitalia, the only conquering that occurs in the two poems is accomplished by the female genitalia, 'Qui à ton gré domtes les plus rebelles'. A *contrepet* in line 13 of the first sonnet, proposed by the most recent editors of Ronsard, 'Par qui l'on vit' / 'Par lui con vit', produces an internal rime in lines 13 and 14 ('con' / 'doit-on'), and again creates a parallel: just as the male genitals figure in the sonnet for the female, so the female genitals are suggested in the sonnet for the male.

The use of images in the sonnets further obscures a clearly gendered reading. The initial image of the first sonnet, the lance, draws from chivalric imagery, and the terms 'combat', 'choquer', and 'poindre' in the quatrains continue the bellicose rhetoric. Yet in the final tercet of the sonnet, when the reader might well anticipate victory in the battles mentioned in lines 4 and 11, the rhetoric of manlihood is instead strangely sublimated or moralised. The 'lance au bout d'or' becomes the 'instrument de bon heur / Par qui lon vit',[21] and the sonnet ends with the male member not in conquest but in a position of reception, receiving sacrifices. Similarly, while the female genitalia are depicted in the first tercet as taming even the most rebellious, at the end of the poem, they too become a passive object of worship.

While Baldassari Olimpo degli Alessandri has been suggested as the inspiration both for these sonnets and for the collected blasons of the 1540s, no poem to a male body part can be found in Olimpo, nor is there any attempt in the *Blasons anatomiques* to construct parallel poems to male and female genitals.[22] Ronsard's original juxtaposing of these rhetorically parallel poems seemingly underscores the poet's desire to provide equal exposure, as it were, with the effect of complicating the preponderantly male discourse.

One might argue that in all lyric poetry, the indeterminate 'I' is in perpetual contingency, and thus that the male voice is never entirely stable. Yet while the semi-lyric genre of *ineptiae* or *nugae* inherited from Catullus is said to have a more supple rhythm in distinction to the ode, allowing the poet freer expression, it does not necessarily lend itself to a less masculine rhetoric. Olivier de Magny, for example, whose *Gayetez* published in 1554 were directly inspired by both Catullus and the *Folastries,* asserts a 'substantiall' masculine voice by employing terms of conquest and force, as in the lyric addressed to Denis Durant:

> Toutes les fois que j'aperçoi
> Ma nymfelette aupres de toi,
> Qui te tend à demy farouche
> Sa petite vermeille bouche,
> Lors que captive soubz ta main
> Je te vois, fierement humain,
> Forcer sa levre cramoisie
> A te donner de l'ambrosie . . .[23]

This use of terms denoting power echoes other passages in which Magny employs more imperatives than does Ronsard, indicating a tension between man and woman, as well as a desire for domination of the addressee.[24] In contrast to Magny, then, Ronsard invents in his collection a rhetoric that is patently lacking in masculine *virtus.*

Unlike Magny, Ronsard's poet undoes expectations for virile or 'manlie' behaviour in both amorous and military exploits in the *Folastries.* Ultimately, what would become of Ronsard's highly sexed and ambivalently gendered *style bas*?[25] The prefatory poem to the *Nouvelle Continuation des Amours* in 1556 responds in part to this question.[26] The preface is dedicated to the Parisian humanist Jean de Morel, who had apparently criticised the *Folastries* three years earlier. Through the use of mythological characters and hypotyposis, or vivid description, Ronsard initially sets a lofty tone for his new work. The poet might seem at first glance to be assuring his colleague that he has repented from the follies of the *Folastries,* as he offers verses more acceptable to Morel's easily offended sensibility:

> Et plus dignes de toy qui n'as l'oreille attainte
> Sinon de chastes vers d'une Muse tressainte,
> Qui parle sagement, et qui point ne rougit
> De honte, ny l'auteur ny celuy qui la lit.

(P. II, p. 823)

Yet these assurances form only part of the equation, and the rest of the poem systematically dismantles their claim. A note in the *princeps* edition exhorts the reader to consult Apollonius's fourth *Argonautica* for a better understanding of the elegy.[27] Like Apollonius, Ronsard recounts the gift of a clump of earth from the sea god Triton to Euphemus. Euphemus then dreams that the clump of earth is transformed into a young woman with whom he physically unites. When Euphemus awakens, Jason interprets the symbolic meaning of the dream: if Euphemus casts the clump of earth into the sea, it will become an island on which his descendants will flourish. Ronsard's recounting of the tale once again draws upon implicit sexual imagery:

> Or la nuict il songea qu'une douce rousée
> De laict avoit par tout cest motte arrousée,
> Qu'il tenoit cherement embrassé en son sein,
> Et qu'elle se changeoit en fille sous sa main,
> Et que luy tout ardant de la grand beauté d'elle
> Accolloit par amour ceste jeune pucelle,
> Qui sembloit dans le lict piteusement crier
> Comme une de quinze ans que lon va marier.

(Ronsard, P. II. 821)

. . . Euphemus bethought him of a dream of the night, reverencing the glorious son of Maia. For it seemed to him that the god-given clod of earth held in his palm close to his breast was being suckled by white streams of milk, and that from it, little though it was, grew a woman like a virgin; and he, overcome by strong desire, lay with her in love's embrace; and united with her he pitied her, as though she were a maiden whom he was feeding with his own milk.

(Apollonius, ll. 1731-1740)[28]

Whereas in Apollonius, the earth-woman drinks milk from the maternal Euphemus's breast, in Ronsard the more masculine 'milk' sprays the earth, the 'motte', which is not coincidentally the same term Ronsard had used to describe female genitals in the *Folastries.* Further, the sixteenth-century poet insists more on Euphemus's sexual power over the young virgin, who cries out in the marriage bed. These examples demonstrate Ronsard's rendering of Euphemus as more stereotypically masculine than that of Apollonius.

Yet once again the masculinity that Ronsard erects in the poem is followed by precious images undermining that stance. The poet asserts that his verses, unassuming and tiny like a stream, form a favourable contrast to oceanic and torrential works.

> Un petit ruisselet a tousjours l'onde nette:
> Aussi le papillon et la gentile avette
> Y vont puiser de l'eau, et non en ces torrens
> Qui tonnent d'un grand bruit par les roches courans.
> Petits Sonets bien-faits, belles Chansons petites,
> Petits Discours gentils, sont les fleurs des Charites
> . . .

(P. II. 822)

The word 'petit' appears four times within the six verses, and 'gentil' twice. The dainty diminutive 'ruisselet', along with references to flowers and butterflies, hardly describes a land of masculine conquest. But here the paradox emerges: in this poetic scene, smaller and sweeter are better. Comparing his work to Euphemus's bit of earth, which when thrown into the sea becomes a beautiful island, Ronsard notes that his 'petit labeur' is not as small as one might think, and indeed perhaps it is worth more than grandiose offerings:

> Peut estre qu'il vaut mieux que la grosse apparence
> De ces tomes enflez, de gloire convoiteux,
> Qui sont fardez de mots sourcilleux et vanteux,
> Empoullez et masquez, où rien ne se descœuvre
> Que l'arrogant jargon d'un ambicieux œuvre.

(P. II. 822)

Further asserting his ability to write as he chooses, Ronsard's poet renounces responsibility for the reception of his work by calling upon Morel, and by extension all his readers, to choose among verses, both 'graves' and 'fols', as a bee among flowers.[29]

Resisting a clearly masculine discourse and univocal poetic style, Ronsard reveals in the ***Folastries*** both his dialogic relationship to gender and his ultimate adherence to the principle of *varietas*. The subsequent ***Discours à Jean Morel,*** ostensibly a palliative to appease Ronsard's detractors, serves instead as a manifesto of the poet's commitment to literary experimentation. Just as the sex act between the nubile maiden and Euphemus in the ***Discours*** serves as a metaphor for poetic production, so the sexualised language of the ***Folastries*** announces Ronsard's hybrid style. In both cases, the place of gender in the poems remains unstable, as virile rhetoric is at once established and challenged. In the final argument of the ***Discours à Jean Morel,*** the poet asserts that like Nature itself, his poetry will be both high and low, 'ore mal, ore bien . . . une herbe venimeuse / Tout aupres d'une bonne' (*P.* II. 823). Perfection, the poet concludes, belongs only to God . . . and poetry, he implies, to humanity.

Notes

1. See Melin de Saint-Gelays, *Œuvres,* ed. Prosper Blanchemain (Paris: Paul Daffis, Bibliothèque Elzévirienne, 1873), I. 23-5. Du Bellay specifically recommended as a form the hendecasyllabic, following Catullus, Pontanus, and Johannes Secundus, in *Deffence et Illustration de la langue francoyse* (Geneva: Droz, 2001), p. 137.

2. Pierre de Ronsard, *Œuvres complètes,* Bibliothèque de la Pléiade, ed. Jean Céard, Daniel Ménager, and Michel Simonin (Paris: Gallimard, 1993-4), I. 172. The Pléiade edition will hereafter be designated by '*P*'.

3. Ann Moss, 'Ronsard the Poet, Ronsard the Hermaphrodite', *Ronsard, figure de la variété,* ed. Colette H. Winn (Geneva: Droz, 2002), pp. 115-23; Lawrence D. Kritzman, *The Rhetoric of Sexuality and the Literature of the French Renaissance* (Cambridge: Cambridge University Press, 1991), pp. 113-29; Kirk Read, *High Anxiety: Masculinity in Crisis in Early Modern France,* ed. Kathleen Perry Long, (Kirksville: Truman State University Press, 2002), pp. 71-87; Daniel Ménager, 'L'Amour au féminin', *Sur des vers de Ronsard, 1585-1985* (Paris: Aux amateurs de livres, 1990), pp. 105-16; Cathy Yandell, '*L'Amour au féminin?* Ronsard and Pontus de Tyard Speaking as Women', *Ronsard, figure de la variété,* op. cit, pp. 65-83; *Carpe Corpus: Time and Gender in Early Modern France* (Newark: University of Delaware Press; London: Associated University Presses, 2000), pp. 72-5.

4. 'Isotopy' is defined by A. J. Greimas as 'a complex of manifold semantic categories making possible the uniform reading' of a text. Greimas, *Du sens* (Paris: Seuil, 1979), p. 88; cited by Umberto Eco, *Interpretation and Overinterpretation,* ed. Stefan Collini (Cambridge: Cambridge University Press, 1992), p. 62.

5. Randle Cotgrave, *A Dictionarie of the French and English Tongues* (London, 1611; rpt Columbia: University of South Carolina Press, 1968). See also Michel Simonin, *Ronsard* (Paris: Fayard, 1990), pp. 144-5.

6. Pierre de Ronsard, *Œuvres complètes* (Paris: Société des Textes Français Modernes, 1914-75), V. 1. According to some classical scholars, Catullus was the first to claim that a poet's character cannot be inferred from his work. See *The Poems of Catullus,* ed. Guy Lee (Oxford: Clarendon, 1990), p. 154. Charles Fontaine had already used this same distich to exonerate his youthful follies in his *Fontaine d'amour* of 1546. See Ronsard, ed. Laumonier, V. vii. Unless otherwise indicated, all subsequent references to Ronsard will be from the fifth volume of the Laumonier edition.

7. Jean-Marie Goulemot, *Forbidden Texts,* trans. James Simpson (Philadelphia: University of Pennsylvania Press, 1994), p. 11. See also David Dorais, 'Les Païens de la Pléiade: L'Érotisme dans les *Folastries* de Ronsard et dans les *Gayetez* d'Olivier de Magny', *Renaissance and Reformation/Renaissance et Réforme* 23: 3 (1999), p. 66.

8. Pierre de Nolhac, 'Documents nouveaux sur la Pléiade: Ronsard, Du Bellay', *Revue d'Histoire littéraire* (1899), p. 358.

9. O. de Magny, *Les Gayetez,* ed. Allistair McKay (Geneva: Droz, 1968), p. 55.

10. 'Ne creins, ne creins, Ronsard, ce dous stile pour-suivre, / Stile qui te fera, non moins que l'autre, vivre: / Autre, obscur et scabreux, s'il ne fait à blamer, / Si se fait-il pourtant trop plus creindre qu'aymer.' Charles Fontaine, *Odes, enigmes, et épigrammes* (Lyon: J. Citoys, 1557), p. 67. See also Marcel Raymond, *L'Influence de Ronsard sur la poésie française, 1550-1585* (1927; Geneva: Slatkine Reprints, 1993), I. 32-3.

11. Simonin, op. cit., pp. 145-6.

12. *Catullus, Tibullus, Pervigilium Veneris,* trans. Francis Warre Cornish, Loeb Classical Library (Cambridge, MA: Harvard University Press; London: William Heinemann, 1937), pp. 22-3; Charles Martin, *Catullus* (New Haven: Yale University Press, 1992), p. 78. Subsequent references will be to the Loeb edition.

13. 'Mollis' comes from the verb *mollesco,* to become soft or gentle. Compare Iarbas's declaration in *Aeneid* IV. 215 that Aeneas is a 'Paris', again not necessarily homosexual but passive. On the anachronistic concepts of 'heterosexual' and 'homosexual' as applied to Roman society, see Craig Williams's *Roman Homosexuality: Ideologies of Masculinity in Classical Antiquity* (Oxford: Oxford University Press, 1999) and James L. Butrica's review of *The Priapus Poems,* ed. Richard W. Hooper (Urbana and Chicago: University of Illinois Press, 1999) in the *Bryn Mawr Classical Review* 23: 2 (2000), http://ccat.sas.upenn.edu/bmcr/2000/2000-02-23.html. Jonathan Walters notes 'the Roman sexual protocol that defined men [of high rank] as impenetrable penetrators', a status that symbolically protected the male body from invasion by a more powerful external force. See 'Invading the Roman Body: Manliness and Impenetrability in Roman Thought', *Roman Sexuality,* ed. Judith P. Hallett and Marilyn B. Skinner (Princeton: Princeton University Press, 1997), pp. 29-43.

14. André Gendre, *Ronsard, poète de la conquête amoureuse* (Neuchâtel: Éditions de La Baconnière, 1970).

15. Cotgrave, op. cit.

16. Compare François Billon's claim that Louise Labé was skilled in 'tout honneste exercice viril, et par especial aux Armes', *Le Fort inexpugnable de l'honneur du Sexe Femenin* (Paris: Ian d'Allyer, 1555), p. 15.

17. On the notion of failure as effeminate and 'psychic virility' in Catullus, see Marilyn B. Skinner, '*Ego Mulier*: The Construction of Male Sexuality in Catullus', *Roman Sexuality,* op. cit., p. 146.

18. Catullus 2. 3. In the Greek Anthology, birds sing love songs or interrupt erotic dreams: *The Greek Anthology,* ed. Peter Jay (Oxford: Oxford University Press, 1973), IX. 286 (p. 202), and IX. 87 (p. 203). See also Marot, *Œuvres poétiques,* ed. Gérard Defaux (Paris: Bordas, 1993), II. 210.

19. Catullus 32; Martial, *Epigrams,* XI. 16: 'If you are too grave, Reader, you can go from here where you will . . . How often will your stiffness push out your robe, although you be sterner than Curius and Fabricius!', trans. [Mitchell Starrett Buck] ([New York?]: Privately Printed for Subscribers Only, [1921]), p. 305. Compare Johannes Secundus, *Basium* XIV, *Le Livre des baisers,* ed. Thierry Sandre (Paris: Renaudot et Cie, 1989), p. 70:

> Tanti istas ego ut osculationes
> Imbelles faciam, superba, vestras,
> Ut, nervo toties rigens supino,
> Pertundam tunicas meas tuasque,
> Et, desiderio furens inani,
> Tabescam miser, aestuante vena?

> Quo fugis? Remane; nec hos ocellos,
> Nec nega mihi flammeum labellum.
> Te jam, te volo basiare, mollis,
> Molli mollior anseris medula.

(Do you think I'm so taken by these debilitating kisses, haughty one, that are yours, if, every time I stiffen like a pulled bow, I have to protrude through my clothing and yours, and afterwards, furious from my own unsuccessful desire, I am consumed, my pulse beating feverishly? Where are you going? Don't go. Stay. Don't refuse me those eyes, nor your lips that enflame me. Yes, I want to kiss you, my sweet, you who are softer than a gosling's down [my translation]).

20. See Jonathan Culler, 'Apostrophe', *Diacritics* 7: 4 (1977), pp. 59-69 and 'Reading Lyric', *Yale French Studies* 98 (1985), pp. 98-106.

21. This turn is reminiscent of Clément Marot's famous blazon in which the 'Beau tetin', an erotic enticer, is transformed into the bearer of an infant's milk. See Marot, *Œuvres complètes,* ed. cit., II. 241-2.

22. Baldassare de Olimpo degli Alessandri (Olympo de Sassoferrato), *Pegasea* (Venice: Bernardino di Bindoni, 1539). In the French collection of anatomical blazons, the 'Blason du con' and the 'Blason du con de la pucelle', have no male counterparts. *S'ensuivent les blasons anatomiques du corps femenin.* ([Paris]: Charles Langelier, 1543), f. D2^r-D3^r. The digital facsimile can be consulted online at http://iris.lib.virginia.edu/speccol/gordon/gordonimages/_B53/.

23. Olivier de Magny, *Les Gayetez,* ed. Allistair McKay (Geneva: Droz, 1968), p. 25.

24. See David Dorais, op. cit., pp. 67-8.

25. Concerning the stylistic function of eroticism in the *Folastries,* David Dorais argues that the erotic qualities serve to illustrate a different concept of love from that of the 1552 *Amours* and announce the carnal desire, rather than the Petrarchan adoration, that will dominate the *Continuation des Amours* (p. 66). Claude Faisant suggests that since the poet's ardour in the *Folastries* is neither sincere nor serious, the obscenity of the poems can be seen as an accessory to the burlesque, creating dissonance to produce a parodic effect; 'L'Érotisme dans les *Folastries* de Ronsard', *Europe* 247-62 (November-December 1986), p. 61. Michel Jeanneret concludes that Ronsard's opting for the *style bas* has the effect of including voices other than his own in the text; 'Les Amours de Marie: inscription de la deuxième personne et stratégies dialogiques', *Sur des vers de Ronsard* (1585-1985), op. cit., pp. 61-70. See also François Rigolot, *Poésie et Renaissance* (Paris: Seuil, 2002), p. 198.

26. I am grateful to Marc-André Wiesmann for having called my attention to this poem in relation to the *Folastries.*

27. P. II. 1531-2, n. 1. The note also refers readers to Pindar's fourth Pythian Ode. Pindar's ode recounts some of the story of Euphemus and the clump of earth, but with no mention of his dream.

28. Apollonius, *Argonautica,* The Online Medieval and Classical Library, http://omacl.org/Argonautica/book4.html.

29.   Ainsin en feuilletant ce mine petit ouvrage
       Tu sçauras bien tirer (comme prudent et sage)
       Les vers qui seront fols, amoureux, esvantez,
       D'avec ceux qui seront plus gravement chantez.

                                           (P. II. 823)

Gérard Defaux (essay date January 2004)

SOURCE: Defaux, Gérard. "Facing the Marot Generation: Ronsard's *giovenili errori.*" *MLN* 119, no. 1 (January 2004): S299-S326.

[*In the following essay, Defaux praises Ronsard as a poetic innovator, but contends that he was undone by his vanity and his inability to distinguish truth from myth.*]

> Tousjours l'humilité gaigne le cœur de tous:
> Au contraire l'orgueil attise le courrous.
>
>   —Ronsard

> Toutesfois tu doibz penser, que les Arz, et
> Sciences n'ont receu leur perfection tout à coup,
> et d'une mesme Main: ainçoys, par succession
> de longues Années, chacun y conferant quelque
> portion de son Industrie, sont parvenues au
> point de leur excellence.
>
>   —Du Bellay

For someone who, as I just did, spent some ten or twelve rewarding years of his life in Marotland, the rediscovery of the "new" or, rather—the correction is Du Bellay's—of the "ancient renewed poetry" (l'ancienne renouvelée poësie),[1] the shock is brutal, unavoidable. One is suddenly overwhelmed with a feeling of Gidian *estrangement.* Nothing looks the same anymore. The picture, its content and disposition, forms, colors, technique and point of perspective, everything has been all altered, deeply transformed. Contrary to what is currently said, it is not properly speaking a "revolution"—a term too strong, and inaccurate—but rather a transmutation or, to be even more precise, a profound and thorough *valorization* of the poetic process. Before 1549-1550, poetry was an "art," better, it was a trade, a "métier," a "rhétorique seconde" or "métrifiée" (a *second* or *versified* rhetoric) in the hands less of "poets" than of "facteurs," "acteurs" and "escrivains," that is people who made, spoke, acted and wrote, a collection of tricks, practices and recipes, of fixed and inherited forms, which were scrupulously transmitted from fathers to sons or masters to disciples; and it abruptly becomes *furor,* enthusiasm and divine inspiration, frenzy, magic and music, language of the Gods. It is not any longer learned and taught, but given, it descends from Heaven like grace, it becomes a sign of election, of ethical and social advancement. Not only God is no longer in all human beings, not only is He *in nobis,* exclusively *in nobis,* we the Chosen, we the Elect, the "Soothsayers" and the "Magi," we the "priests of the Muses," the "interpreters," "ministers" and "prophets" of the gods, *nous les hommes divins* (us "the god-like men," θεῖοι, διοι)[2]—but He is not the same God at all. The Christian God of Marguerite de Navarre and Marot has been properly displaced by the pagan gods of Ronsard. On Mount Parnassus, Virgil, Horace and Ovid, Homer, Pindar, Aratus and Anacreon replace David, they overtly challenge the very existence, the mystical and lyrical splendors of the Psalms. Generally speaking, with very rare exceptions—that, for example, of Nicolas Denisot and Lancelot Carle[3]—Eros prevails over Anteros, the "little Love" triumphs over the "great" one.[4] And this triumph is not of an ephemeral and Petrarchan nature, it sets, in our history, a point of no-return. From there on, *philautia (amor sui)* and idolatry, self-love and love of the creature, a new and lyrical religion of greed, lust and glory take precedence over "true" and "perfect Love," that is, *Caritas, Agapè,* the Johannic and Pauline Love of God and of God's creatures through Him.

Likewise, before 1549-1550, poetry was characterized by its "elegance," its "naturalness," "facility" and Ovidian "fluidity," its "transparence," its desire to please the "popular" and the "vulgar," to reach in fact the greatest possible number of readers through a deliberate use of "la commune maniere de parler"—the most "common manner of speaking." And it becomes suddenly lofty, impassioned, boastful and superb, deliberately obscure, not to say hermetic, inaccessible in its haughtiness and so studied, so elaborated, so affected, so full of "rare et antique érudition" (rare and Classical lore)[5] that, in order to be understood it requires the help of a "guide and interpreter."[6] It soars, it hovers and looks down from above like some Pindaric eagle, its patent and only ambition being to keep its distance, to stay aloof, to flee the common and ignorant herd, the *vulgum pecus,* to proclaim its difference, its grandeur, its crushing and glorious superiority. When, in 1533, Clément Marot, the "poete Gallique," could still say that his father Jehan had been "un illustre poete François" (an illustrious French Poet) "sans sçavoir aucunes Lettres ne Grecques ne Latines" (without knowing at all Greek and Latin letters),[7] on the contrary, in 1549-1550, Ronsard and Du Bellay wage war against what they both call "le vilain monstre Ignorance" (Ignorance, this vile and ugly monster),[8] they cannot imagine, to "illustrate" their vernacular, a better solution than the shameless "imitation," the systematic "looting" and "unearthing" of the Ancients. In more than one way, and in the span of no more than twenty years, all the signs take on opposite meanings. What was black becomes white, and vice versa. We are witnessing a perfect reversal, a Horatian movement from one extreme to the other: *Nil medium est: cum vitant stulti vitia, in contraria / currunt.* And, when one thinks about it, by its very nature this reversal was in fact not only predictable, but properly speaking necessary, unavoidable. Things could not have been different, since what we are dealing with here is essentially an *agonistic* phenomenon,[9] I mean a clash, a confrontation between two generations of poets: one, that of Marot, Saint-Gelais, Heroët, Sébillet, Salel, etc., which has the obvious advantage of being already there, of occupying all the terrain, of being solidly established at court and well received by ladies, princes and kings; the other, that of the young and ambitious disciples of Jean Dorat, whose obsessive dream and ambition is to dislodge those formidable opponents— they were indeed formidable—, to plunge them definitively, as fast as it can be done, into the pit of oblivion. In order to be heard and survive, they can do nothing but fight, make a lot of noise, generate turmoil, exaggeration and drama.

It is in this struggle, this brutal clash between the immediate past and the emerging present, that I personally locate the main reason, the most plausible explanation for those *giovenili errori* which are part of the title of this study. We all know that life is an endless *Comedy of errors.* But some of us are not as prone to err as others. Petrarch, for example—see the first sonnet of his Canzoniere—speaks of what he calls his first youthful error: *in sul mio primo giovenile errore.* This first (and fatal) error took place, as we all know, on "Mille trecento ventisette, a punto / su l'ora prima, il dí sesto d'Aprile,"[10] when his path crossed for the first time that of Laura. If we were to follow this line of argument, we could immediately see a huge difference between Ronsard and Petrarch. For Petrarch, there was only Laura. On the contrary, for Ronsard, we have an impressive list of idols: Cassandre, Marie, Sinope, Astrée, Genèvre, Hélène, plus a residue of what he himself calls *Amours diverses.* But I am not talking here about this type of wandering. What I have in mind is quite different. I am thinking not of what Pontus de Tyard calls *erreurs amoureuses,* erotic errors (or wanderings), but of poetic ones. And, in this domain, as we all know, Ronsard is the absolute champion, he has no match, he comes out first without even the beginning of a dispute. We all remember the legitimate reactions of the great majority of his contemporaries to the **Pindaric Odes** of 1550 and the **Amours** of 1552, their critiques and bewilderment: *obstupuerunt stupore magno.* The poetic beginnings of Ronsard were mainly *un succès de scandale.* They alienated almost everybody, but Dorat, Baïf, Muret and a few other *graeculi*—mainly those prone to believe that Τὰ χαλετὰ καλά, "what is difficult to comprehend is always beautiful."[11] Even Du Bellay, in spite of his friendship and desire to support and praise the "French Pindar," had great difficulties in following him all the way.[12] Let's forget here the "historical error" which, according to Paul Laumonier and Isidore Silver,[13] he made when he decided to transplant the Pindaric Ode into the French soil. Horace was right: to emulate Pindar, to resuscitate him, is an impossible task; and the poet who dares trying will fail and share Icarus's fate. Let's talk instead about his heavy pedantry, this irresistible urge which, like the young Pico della Mirandola, always pushed him, "full of pride and desirous of glory and men's praise," "to make a show of his cunning."[14] Ronsard was not only a great poet, he was also a reincarnation of Rabelais's *écolier limousin,* a somewhat ridiculous *pédant de collège* "qui parlait Grec en François" (who spoke Greek in French). Let's talk also about his boastful arrogance and devouring ambition— what, in his Preface to the **Odes** of 1550, he himself calls, only to deny it, his "ambitieuse presumption" (ambitious presumption);[15] his childish, not to say infantile lust for power and glory—indeed, he was a real *glutton-for-glory,* a "gourmand de gloire," a "glouton de louange" (*ibid.,* 993-94). Let's not forget his blatant ingratitude vis-à-vis his immediate predecessors, the fact, for example, that he dares say he saw in their poetry absolutely nothing that could satisfy him, that, in its very essence, this poetry was nothing but a "monstruous error" (*ibid.,* 995). In addition, let's mention his rather laughable desire to be the first—*le premier*—in everything, absolutely everything: "*le premier* auteur lirique François," (*the first* French lyrical author, *ibid.,* 994); *the first* to have brought to France not only the Ode, but its very name (*ibid.,* 995); *the first* to have "deterré" (unearthed) with his bare hands Callimachus, Simonides, Pindar, all the "vieux liriques," not to forget Horace—even Horace;[16] *the first* to have "invented" and "traced" new paths leading to "immortality," to have inspired others, shown them the light, the truth and the way, and convinced them to walk in his glorious (and ground-breaking) footsteps;[17] *the first* to have brought together music and poetry, the words and the lyre;[18] *the first* also to have given a new life and dignity to the French alexandrine and sung the praise of his own *patrie*.[19] As Binet, his first biographer, puts it, his main purpose was to let the world know, to proclaim *urbi et orbi, à son de trompe,* that "la Poësie est née avec luy en France"—that "Poetry (that is, great Poetry, true Poetry) was born with him in France."[20] Humble and modest Ronsard.[21] In the domain of this all too human activity which consists in singing one's own praise, blowing one's own horn or one's own trumpet, only Erasmus's *Moria* could, I think, be compared to him. It is certainly not by chance that Ronsard rhymes in French with "vantard" and "bragard." Ronsard knew it, and exploited shamelessly this poetic (and Cratylic) echo. In a poem dated 1569 and entitled **"Le Rossignol" (The Nightingale)**,[22] he writes the following, illustrating for us the well-known statement according to which *la rime*—indeed—*a souvent ses raisons*:

> Et je dirois, si j'estois un bragard
> Que Rossignol vient du nom de Ronsard.
> Mais ce n'est moy qui ma musique vante:
> Soit bien ou mal, Rossignolet, je chante . . .
>
> [And I would say, if I were a braggart
> That Nightingale comes from the name Ronsard.
> But I am not like those who praise their own Music:
> Either good or bad, little Nightingale, I sing . . .]

Let's not be dupes of this ostentatious modesty. These four lines contain at least two big lies. First, as we just said, Ronsard—Hic est ille—spent his time singing his own praise. Second, the conditional mode "If I were, I would say" is totally irrelevant in his case. He was a braggart, a pathological braggart, somebody who could not resist—and I quote him here—"Le plaisir qu'on reçoit d'apparoistre bien grand" (The pleasure one feels to appear really great).[23]

Some of us may still today admire this young conqueror, salute his boldness, his courage and pride, his genius—and I believe they have good reasons for doing so. But, whatever we think of him, we have no choice but to acknowledge that he was unable to keep and maintain his original pace. In fact, all scholars seem to agree on this, he started too strong and too fast. He did not walk, he ran, he precipitated himself, he was, as Silver once said, properly "carried away" by his enthusiasm.[24] He

wanted to be another Pindar, a new poetic eagle, and he fell—gloriously, but badly. And when I say he fell, I mean *he,* Ronsard, *he* much more than his poetry. If his poetry as such was criticized, it was, I think, because of him. The negative judgment passed by his contemporaries, Guillaume des Autels, Mellin, de Saint-Gelais, Barthelémy Aneau and many others, was above all the price he had to pay for his presumption, his aggressive stance, his insulting arrogance, the fact that he despised others, that he looked down at them, from above, *du haut de sa grandeur.* He had not yet understood—those are also his words, but they will not come out of his pen before 1579—that where "l'humilité gagne le cœur de tous: / Au contraire l'orgueil attize le courroux"—where "humility always wins over all hearts; on the contrary pride stirs up anger."[25]

But what made him so vain and so full of himself, so convinced of his own importance, was not only his temperament, the Jupiterian and Herculean image he possessed of himself,[26] but a belief, a myth he shared with all XVIth-century humanists. Allow me now to develop this point. Because I think it is quite a crucial one, one which, not only for Ronsard, but for us, had and still has—or might have—today rather devastating consequences in the domains of literary history and criticism.

Let's start with us, literary critics and historians. As I have indicated a number of times in the past—in particular about the reception afforded Clément Marot's work[27]—the entrenched prejudices that we have long maintained vis-à-vis the two to three poetic generations prior to that of 1550 are all the more unpardonable because they are not ours strictly speaking. Where we thought we were simply doing our job, that is thinking, trying to understand, giving free reign to our critical spirit, others, in truth, dictated to us without our knowledge not only what we were to believe and say, but also what we were to feel—even worse: what we had to see and how we had to see it. And, like Panurge's docile sheep, we have followed without the least qualm, without even being astonished by the evident similarity existing between the so-called "judgments" that we were making and that of the young ambitious members of the Pléiade, Du Bellay and Ronsard, authors of a poetic manifesto whose notorious celebrity nonetheless fails to mask their incoherencies, weaknesses, and bad faith. We also have not seen that the indisputable success of this intelligent, insolent, and brilliant bluff comes first and foremost from the fact that it magisterially exploits what we might call the founding myth of the Renaissance, a myth put in place in the XVth century and the beginning of the XVIth by such humanists as Valla, Erasmus, Budé, and Rabelais. And, in my opinion, all of Ronsard's *giovenili errori,* or at least most of them—let's not forget, in our analysis, the individual component, what I just called the Jupiterian temperament—derive from this fundamental assumption, this confusion between myth and truth, myth and history.

For it is, in fact, the existence of this myth which historically speaking explains everything from the success of the *Deffence et illustration* to the critical blindness from which we are barely recovering today. When, after many hesitations, in 1549, Ronsard and Du Bellay decide to make themselves known, they essentially do it by adopting as their own certainties then shared by the vast majority of their contemporaries. Long before the famous philosophers of the Age of Enlightenment, long also before the Marxist ideologues who followed them, and carried along by the real enthusiasm they feel for "la restitution des bonnes lettres" (the restoration of good letters) and the heroic struggle against "the ugly monster Ignorance," they turned themselves into staunch supporters of progress—Progress with a capital P. They loudly proclaim the superiority of their own era over preceding ones. The static and Manichean opposition they sketch between the past and the present is well-known; and yet, historically speaking, nothing is more illusory and more untenable, nothing could be more false. It is not because the things of this world—and the world itself, this "branloire perenne" (perennial movement), change, not because all these things obey what Michel Jeanneret calls the principle of *perpetuum mobile*,[28] that they always drag us along towards something better. All we can say is that they transform themselves, that they evolve, that they are unable to stay in place. And that's it. The movement that carries them "forward," as we perhaps say too naively is not necessarily positive. Strictly speaking, it might not even have a goal, and even less a significant or global structure. It might not lead toward anything, nor correspond to any "intention," and even less to a teleology or to some kind of transcendence, nor be anything other than that "perpetual multiplication and vicissitude of forms," that derisory trampling described by Montaigne in his chapter "Des coches," namely a way of not "going," but "prowling" and "swirling around," "walking in place, here and there," like drunkards or blind people. But this doubt never comes to the mind of Dorat's disciples; or, if they sense it, they feign to ignore it. They seem intimately persuaded that the movement which carries them and in which they participate with the greatest enthusiasm has a most positive meaning, that it is leading them somewhere, toward a greater light—totally unaware of the bloody denial that history will soon force upon them. The optimism which characterizes them dictates, about the past in general and the Middle Ages in particular, this polemical, caricatural, and deformed vision some of us have not yet totally forgotten today, that of an age of "ignorance," "Cimmerian darkness" and "barbarism"—the "obscure" and "calamitous" age of the Goths evoked by Gargantua in his famous exhortatory epistle of 1532.[29] The

mistake we habitually make in reading these lines is to fail to take into account their persuasiveness, the strength of the evidence and truth that, for the most enlightened minds, they possessed at that time. It is as though the irony and laughter with which Rabelais had purposefully endowed them had finally rendered them inoffensive, as if the grotesquely irresistible catalog of the "magnifique librairie de Saint-Victor," or the uncanny encounter of the curious, omniscient, and nomadic Panurge, had forever undermined the seriousness of the statement itself. However, thanks to Rabelais's creative genius, it is not only a fiction which takes form and materializes before our very eyes, but also a myth, and a highly successful myth at that. In fact, the good giant invents absolutely nothing; he expresses in his very essence the credo of the moment, he speaks exactly like Valla, Erasmus, Vives, and Budé—especially Budé—even going as far in his brand new optimism not only to adorn his gigantic "mythologies" with sentences taken from the *De studio litterarum,* Budé's work published in 1532, but also, and in an even more symbolic manner, to transform his giant's fictional letter into a kind of French commentary on one of the letters sent by the great Hellenist to his son Dreux Budé on May 8, 1519 and published the following year.[30] Let's recall here the most well-known passage of Gargantua's letter:[31]

> Mais encores que mon feu pere de bonne memoire Grand gousier eust adonné tout son estude, à ce que je proffitasse en toute perfection et sçavoir politique, et que mon labeur et estude correspondit tresbien, voire encore outrepassast son desir: toutesfoys comme tu peulx bien entendre, le temps n'estoit tant idoine ne commode es lettres comme est de present, et n'avoys copie de telz precepteurs comme tu as cu. Le temps estoit encores tenebreux et sentant l'infelicité et calamité des Gothz, qui avoient mis à destruction toute bonne literature. Mais, par la bonté divine, la lumiere et dignité a esté de mon eage rendue es lettres, et y voy tel amendement que, de present, à difficulté seroys receu en la premiere classe des petitz grimaulx, qui en mon eage virile, estoys (non à tord) reputé le plus sçavant du dict siecle. [. . .] Maintenant toutes disciplines sont restituées, les langues instaurées, Grecque, sans laquelle c'est honte que une personne se die sçavant, Hebraicque, Caldaicque, Latine. Les impressions tant elegantes et correctes en usance, qui ont esté inventées de mon eage par inspiration divine, comme à contrefil l'artillerie par suggestion diabolicque. Tout le monde est plein de gens savans, de precepteurs tresdoctes, de librairies tresamples, qu'il m'est advis que ny au temps de Platon, ny de Ciceron, ny de Papinian, n'estoit telle commodité d'estude qu'on y veoit maintenant. Et ne se fauldra plus doresnavant trouver en place ny en compaignie, qui ne sera bien expoly en l'officine de Minerve.

> [But although my deceased father of happy memory Grand gousier had bent his best endeavours to make me profit in all perfection and political knowledge, and that my labor and study was fully corresponding to, yea, went beyond his expectations: nevertheless, as

thou may well understand, the time then was not so proper and fit for learning as it is at present, neither had I plenty of good masters such as thou hast had. For the time was darksome, obscured with clouds of ignorance, and smacking of the infelicity and calamity of the Goths, who had brought to destruction all good literature. But, by God's goodness, in my day light and dignity have been restored to letters, and I see such improvement in these that at present I would hardly be accepted unto the first form of the little Grammar school-boys, I who, in my prime, was reputed (not wrongly) the most learned of my age [. . .] Now all branches of learning are reestablished, languages restored to their pristine purity: Greek, without which it is shameful for a man to call himself learned; Hebrew, Arabic, Chaldean and Latin. Printing likewise is now in use, so elegant, and so correct, that better cannot be imagined, an art, which was invented in my time by divine inspiration, as, conversely, was artillery through the Devil's suggestion. The whole world is full of educated people, of most learned teachers, of well-stocked libraries; and, in my judgment, neither in Plato's time, nor Cicero's, nor Papinian's, were there such facilities as we see now for intellectual and scholarly pursuits; and henceforth no one should appear in public or in company if he has not been pretty well polished in Minerva's workshop.]

Looking back toward that era which we still call for lack of a better term the Middle Ages, Budé affirms likewise in his *De studio* that those unfortunate and cursed centuries brought with them such misery that they destroyed every kind of literary life and intellectual enterprise on this earth. Without having apparently any sense of exaggerating in the least, he emphasizes that they were centuries during which letters and eloquence fell into silence and the darkness of oblivion, centuries during which mortals themselves, burdened by all kinds of disasters and calamities, lived or rather vegetated in the abyss of bestiality and the crassest ignorance, estranged from any life of the mind. In his blindness, Budé even talks about another "great flood"—*Literarum bonarum diluvium*.[32] And if the world today is reborn, if it finally returns to life and light, it is thanks to all these "Herculeses" and these "Heraclideses," these incomparable "heroes of the nation of Letters" (*heroes quidam nationis literariae*) whose exploits and hard work were responsible for the "restoration of learning." In fact, says Budé, a Budé who sees things just as Ronsard soon will see them, the intellectual and moral regeneration of Western civilization could not have taken place without these great men. They are the agents, the indispensable motors of the Renaissance which characterizes this new era, this most exalting and richest period of all which, because of printing, that "divine" invention, finally sees the complete resurgence of all the splendors of a world which disappeared all too quickly. Rarely has such a fragile conviction expressed itself in a stronger and nobler way by means of a lyricism which constantly tends towards the sublime. Having read the great legendary Pico della

Mirandola and in particular his *Oratio de hominis dignitate,* Budé the humanist is already a true existentialist—an existentialist long before existentialism existed. He believes, as Sartre will later, that existence precedes essence. Identical to that of Erasmus, his credo consists of these few words: one is not born a man, one becomes one—*Homines non nascuntur, sed finguntur.*[33] Or, to say the same thing differently, the humanist believes that man defines himself, makes himself, sculpts himself. Man is not the pure product of nature, but of his culture, of what Budé calls *cultus* or *cultura animi.*[34] And the only way to "make," to "forge a man" ("fingere hominem")[35] is, according to him, to "cultivate his soul," to "fertilize" it and give it life by means of "the semen of *bonae literae.*"[36] Learning does not only better those who engage in it, but also makes them men in the full and proper sense of the term, defining their "humanity." Without it, man would be nothing but an animal, a brute incapable of developing his reason and his language—his *ratio* and oratio—of attaining and perfecting in himself and by himself the ideal form inscribed since time immemorial by God in His creature. *Homo miraculum inter animantia*: Budé finally asks with pride, what is human reason if not nature brought to its ultimate point of perfection by the study of literature, that is, by humanist ideology and pedagogy? And where does this eminence, this "principality" that all our philosophers attribute to the soul, come from, if not from "learned eloquence," from "articulate and graceful language"?[37]

Now, with just a difference of registers, this is exactly the way Ronsard and his friends Du Bellay and Baïf expressed themselves twenty years later. Nothing could better justify their enterprise than the opposition they also discover between the past and the present. And if their vision is not as apocalyptic as that of their immediate predecessors, it is, nevertheless, nourished by the same fundamental certainty and, in addition, infused with urgency, arrogance, and even a condescension unknown and unprecedented until them. Where Budé maintained, in the name of cultural transcendence, a deep-seated conviction of fighting nobly for a better world, a world regenerated and embellished by the Mind, the Spirit, the Logos, Du Bellay and Ronsard have clearly a much more pragmatic aim. As I said earlier, what motivated them—and Ronsard above all others—was simply *fama,* ambition, power, and glory, what John calls in his first Epistle vv. 15-16, *ambitio sæculi,* that is the "love of the world and everything which is in it."[38] In the desire that animates them—the desire to believe in their own importance, to make a name for themselves, to be the only ones who matter—their goal was perhaps less one of "defending" and "illustrating" the French language than of obliterating the incontestable merits of their most direct rivals, indeed, erasing purely and simply the latter from the memories of their contemporaries. As we can easily see, the question is no longer for them what it was for Budé, Erasmus or Rabelais—that of an ideological confrontation: it has become a conflict between generations. If they affirm in a rhetorical way that they do not want to criticize "the simplicity" and "ignorance" of their "majeurs" (ancestors), the "truth," however, and a very convenient one at that, compels them to state that those ancestors were nothing but mediocre "farmers," very poor managers of the cultural treasure which had been entrusted to them. Much more concerned with "doing well than saying well," they have, in fact, more often than not, unfortunately "contented" themselves with "expressing their conceptions through unadorned words, without art or embellishment" ("avec paroles nues, sans art et ornement") of any kind, and have consequently handed down to us a language so poor that it needs today, if it wants to be heard, if it dares to appear and perform in public, to be adorned, enriched with "les plumes d'autruy"—others's feathers.[39] From a language that was "venerable by its antiquity,"[40] as venerable in fact as Greek, Latin or Italian could be, their guilty "negligence" made a gross and poorly polished instrument, as a matter of fact one totally unfit for expressing the great conceptions of the mind.

If the lack of ambition of these poor managers is regrettable and visible everywhere, it especially comes to light in the domain of poetry. With the sole exception of the "obscure," the "overly obscure" Maurice Scève, Ronsard and his friend argue at the outset that one cannot even speak of poetry since their only concern seems to have been to compose their works in a style which when all is said and done is indistinguishable from "la commune maniere de parler" (the ordinary manner of speaking). In fact, the illustrious Clément Marot, their "prince" and "standard bearer," spent his life, in his own words, "rhyming in prose,"[41] cultivating "facility," "simplicity," and "transparence"—"the natural." And what a strange choice of word, "natural." Not only did Marot ever manage to climb the heights of Mount Parnassus, but he also never seemed to have thought that such heights might exist.[42] He was too much a poet of the people, a poet who does not soar, but who crawls, a creator whose genius was too limited, who was unable to understand that poetry is "capable de quelque plus hault, et meilleur Style, que celuy, dont nous nous sommes si longuement contentez" (capable of some greater and better style than which satisfied us for so long); capable as well of "une forme de Poësie beaucoup plus exquise" (a far more exquisite form)[43] than the modest and lowly one in which he and his generation unfortunately enclosed and contented themselves. Du Bellay and Ronsard do not limit their criticism to Clément Marot. Considering themselves "the first (notice "the first") to have dared to introduce in France a quasi-new kind of poetry"[44]—I suppose that we should believe them, simply because they say so—they lump together, subject

to the same accusation, all of Marot's colleagues and disciples, Mellin de Saint-Gelais, Antoine Heroët, and the others, Jean Bouchet, Michel d'Amboise, Victor Brodeau and Bertrand de La Borderie, Charles de Sainte-Marthe and Charles Fontaine, Eustorg de Beaulieu, Claude Chappuys, Almanque Papillon, François Habert, Marguerite de Navarre and Hugues Salel, all those whom, in their insulting contempt, they do not even name. What these so-called poets lacked above all, they claim, was "knowledge," knowledge which as Horace says in his *Ars poetica* is "the beginning, the very source (*fons*) of good writing."[45] Except for Mellin de Saint-Gelais who had the good sense not to "publish anything under his name" (123-24), they all wrote too much, much too much. No glory could be less deserved than theirs. For even if it is true that they did not lack style and wit—and it is hard to think differently, indeed, especially when one is dealing with court poets as accomplished as Marot and Saint-Gelais. Even if it is also true that in their way they "illustrated our vernacular" and that in spite of everything one can say against them, France is forever in their "debt" (126), it remains, and that is the essential thing, that "we"—we, that is, the poets, writers, and thinkers of the generation of 1550, we the saviors, we the warriors, we the best ones—"can do much better," go beyond these "little things" (128) that in their carefreeness, their carelessness, they published too quickly and without thinking. Even if it is known, the severe verdict which Ronsard and Du Bellay handed down is worth being recalled here in its entirety. It has value for us as an example, as a paradigm. As we all remember, Ronsard, in the Preface of 1550 to his **Four Books of Odes,** shows no mercy whatsoever for his predecessors. Even if he feels obligated to hail Clément Marot as "la seulle lumiere en ses ans de la vulgaire poësie" [the only light in his years of vulgar poetry),[46] he nevertheless, in the very same paragraph, passes on his immediate predecessors—all of them—a judgment as insulting and rude as it is unfair. I have carefully looked around, he says, and my search has left me empty-handed. Believe me, Reader, I did not find in "our French poets anything really good enough to be imitated" (chose qui fust suffisante d'imiter). In fact, nothing they wrote is worth being remembered: the language they used is unfit, still "en son enfance" (in its infancy); they lacked audacity, curiosity and invention; and their production is so poor that the only reasonable solution is to *s'éloigner d'eux,* not only to get away from them as fast and as far as we can, to forget and to flee, but, to adopt, out of reaction, "stile apart, sens apart, euvre apart" [style aloof, meaning aloof, work aloof). The idea of having to "imitate" them, continues Ronsard, is "odious" to my mind and heart. I would loathe having "anything common with such a monstrous error" ["ne desirant avoir rien de commun avecq' une si monstrueuse erreur"). Compared to this aggressive and insulting posture, Du Bellay's *Deffence* looks almost innocuous and sweet. First concerning French language itself (80-81):

> Ainsi puys-je dire de nostre Langue, qui commence encores à fleurir, sans fructifier: ou plus tost, comme une Plante & Vergette, n'a point encores fleury, tant se fault qu'elle ait apporté tout le fruit, qu'elle pouroit bien produyre. Cela, certainement, non pour le default de la Nature d'elle, aussi apte à engendrer, que les autres; mais pour la couple de ceux qui l'ont euë en garde, et ne l'ont cultivée à suffisance: ains comme une plante sauvaige, en celuy mesme desert où elle avoit commencé à naitre, sans jamais l'arrouser, la tailler, ny defendre des Ronces & Epines qui lui faisoient umbre, l'ont laissé envieillir, & quasi mourir.

> I can speak primarily of our tongue, which now begins to flower without bearing fruit; or rather, like a plant and small shoot, has not yet flowered, still less borne all the fruit that it might well produce. That, certainly, does not derive from any defect in the nature thereof, which is as apt to engender as others; the fault lies rather in those who were to guard the plant, and did not cultivate it sufficiently, treating it instead like a wild plant in that same desert where it had begun to live; without even watering it, or pruning, or protecting it from brambles and thorns which shaded it, they have let it grow old and almost die.

Now concerning the poetic achievements, or rather the obvious shortcomings, of the preceding generation, Clément Marot showing the way, and receiving most of the direct and heavy blows. As we all know, if dead people cannot feel the bites, neither can they themselves bite—mordre—anymore. So Du Bellay has no reason to restrain himself (128):

> Qu'on ne m'allegue point icy, quelques uns des nostres, qui sans doctrine, à tout le moins non autre, que mediocre, ont acquis grand bruyt en nostre vulgaire. Ceux, qui admirent volontiers les petites choses, et desprisent ce qui excede leur jugement, en feront tel cas qu'ils voudront: mais je scay bien que les scavans ne les mettront en autre Ranc, que de ceux qui parlent bien François, et qui ont (comme disoit Ciceron des anciens Auteurs Romains) bon Esprit, mais bien peu d'Artifice.

> Please, do not use here as an argument the fact that some of our poets have acquired a great reputation in our vulgar tongue, being if not totally deprived of doctrine (erudition), at least endowed with no more than a mediocre one. Those who usually relish in little things and despise what exceeds the limits of their judgment, will do what they want with those poets. But I know quite well that real savants will not put them above the level of those who had a good command of the French language and who (as Cicero said of ancient Roman writers) had good spirit, but not enough art.

According to Ronsard and Du Bellay, nothing is easier to establish than the truth of these largely negative assessments. If the "poverty" which continues to plague our language constitutes in itself sufficient proof of the cultural incompetence of our "modern" poets, one must also simultaneously recognize and salute the progress accomplished since the beginning, that is from the *Romance of the Rose* by Guillaume de Lorris and Jean de Meung; and, once the problems have been outlined, propose radical and new solutions. What makes Ronsard and Du Bellay's texts irresistible and immediately seductive is that rather than being an indictment—an indictment as scathing as it is unjust—they constitute first and foremost a call to action, a general mobilization of the energies of the nation. Their entire persuasive force comes from the fact that the conquering reasoning which it contains convinces us and at the same time compels us, draws for us on the page, step by step, between the point of departure and the point of arrival, both the road already travelled and the one still ahead, generating in us freedom and confidence, heartening certainties, a space and a spirit in which everything suddenly becomes possible. All things considered, it is less a matter in this case of innovating, of creating *ab ovo, ex nihilo,* than of accelerating a movement which already exists and which took birth under Francis the First. In this specific area, this great king deserves, according to Du Bellay and, to a lesser extent, Ronsard, all the praise. He is, indeed, the protecting "father of letters and *lettrés,*" that "king *musagetes*" (leader of the Muses) unanimously praised by scholars, poets and humanists, the Marots, the Tusanuses and the Budés of the preceding generation. In truth, Du Bellay adds, France "owes him no less than Rome owed to Augustus"[47]—which says it all. His worth will have been to have conceived and inaugurated in France an authentic *politique culturelle,* a cultural policy. What History will remember him for is that he was the first to restore "in his noble kingdom [. . .] all the fine arts, letters, and sciences to their ancient dignity." It is due to his personal initiative that, setting aside Latin and Greek, philosophers, poets and historians, physicians, jurists and orators finally "learn[ed] to speak French"; through his leadership—and a most decisive leadership at that, a truly "royal" one—, that the French tongue, "encore rampante à terre" (still crawling on the ground), started timidly to "raise its head and get on its feet"; finally, it is under his reign that the French language regained its natural, inborn "elegance," thanks in particular to the systematic practice of translation, a practice that has made of it, if not the equal, at least "the faithful interpreter of all the other languages."[48] If this program has borne fruit, it must, nevertheless, be not only pursued, but also improved, built upon. One must aim even higher, go farther, intensify the movement, provide it with other means of action, and give it a new spirit. One must no longer be satisfied with existing practices but understand that the moment has finally come, after "elocution" and "disposition"—what Ronsard and Du Bellay call "elegance" or "spirit," "style"—to address the major problem of "invention," of *varietas* and *copia*. In short, to bring to its end, to its epiphany and triumph, the national "Renaissance" now underway.

It is at this point in their common demonstration—everything we know and see leads us to believe they worked together, at least in the beginning—that Du Bellay and Ronsard, Ronsard and Du Bellay, best reveal to the attentive reader the global historical vision which informs their passionate and powerful discourse. As I have already suggested with regard to humanists like Budé and Rabelais, this vision—their vision[49]—is entirely carried out and structured by the idea of progress. In the humanist myth, this idea is crucial, fundamental, it is not a key among others, but *the* key, it plays the role of first principle. Not content to define the perspectives to be adopted, it dictates to the eye what it must see and to the thought what it must comprehend, how it must react, the way in which it will interpret what has been perceived. Hence, it is anything but an innocent principle—there are no innocent principles. He who speaks of progress speaks in fact not only of movement, evolution, but also of progression toward something better, for example a hope, a light, an utopia. And this progression is as necessary as it is inevitable. It carries everything in its wake, explains and justifies everything, subjects everything to its law. The journey it describes is always the same; it is a required journey, which leads us of necessity from a minus to a plus—towards something greater. Beginning with the imperfection of origins, it always establishes levels toward a perfection which must come—and which, as a result, takes on the appearance of a vibrant and glorious epiphany. For example, in the case of the linguistic phenomenon which interested the young poets of the Pléiade, we are asked successively to look at:

1) a "poor" language, "gross and poorly polished" ("pauvre, scabreux et mal poly"), the result of the cultural "negligence" and abysmal "ignorance of our *majeurs.*"

2) a language which, even though it is "still crawling on the ground" ("rampant encore à terre"), is beginning, thanks to an intelligent and well-orchestrated policy, "to raise its head" and "get on its feet" ("hausser la tête et se lever sur pieds"), to give itself, not without *bravura,* an "elegance" and a "style"—an intermediary step whose spirit could be expressed in its entirety in the motto of the printer Etienne Dolet, *scabra dolo,* one of the pioneers along with Geofroy Tory, Clément Marot, and François Rabelais, of the "amplification," "defense and illustration" of the French language.[50]

3) finally, a language which thanks to the "richness of invention," the *copia* with which it will soon be endowed through imitation, will necessarily attain "the excellence and light of the other more famous ones" ("l'excellence et lumiere des autres plus fameux"), Greek, Latin, and Italian.

Just as logically, in the poetic domain, we experience and witness, in the very same way:

1) an era of stagnation, of non-intervention and non-culture, in short, the medieval era of "barbarism," "ignorance" and "Cimmerian darkness."

2) an era called "modern," that of Mellin de Saint-Gelais, Antoine Heroët, Maurice Scève and, of course, Clément Marot, whose presence endures, era in which the so-called "modern," while implying something better, a progress, nevertheless brings to mind an overall impression of incompleteness, dullness and regrettable mediocrity.

3) finally an era—should we already call it "post modern"?—characterized on the contrary by innovation, growth, and controlled fecundity, intervention, and planning at all levels. It goes without saying, in this scheme, that the first period just evoked—that of the "ancient French Poets"—is necessarily the least worthy of our attention. According to Du Bellay himself, Guillaume de Lorris, Jean de Meung, and the others only appear to remind us that our language is "venerable because of its antiquity." If they can still be read, there are but very few things in them "that may be imitated by the moderns." And those "Moderns" themselves, even in spite of the qualities attributed to them—*l'esprit,* wit, plus cultivation and mastery of the French language; even in spite of the fact that they were the first beneficiaries of Francis the First's cultural policy, suffer the same fate as their distant predecessors. The mediocrity of their knowledge, their lack of boldness, ambition, and intellectual curiosity, the strange preference they all had and always manifested for the "style bas" ("low style"), "la commune maniere de parler" (the ordinary manner of speaking), the obsolete genres that they stubbornly cultivated, those gothic and medieval "episseries"—rondeaux, ballads, chants royaux, virelais, chansons, etc.—that are performed at the Floral Games of Toulouse or at the Puy of Rouen, all of this turns them into models which are too poor and "monstruous" to be imitated. That is why Du Bellay and Ronsard strongly condemn this practice common among their immediate predecessors, the so-called "moderns," which, when one wants to become a poet, especially a French poet, and learn the trade, consists in finding one's inspiration in "domestic examples," "imitating at random (à pied levé) the most famous authors of our tongue"—a practice our young conquerors, our new prophets and "ministers of God," qualify as "pernicious and worthless for our vulgar tongue" ("vicieuse et de nul profit à nostre vulgaire"), since in sum it simply comes down to giving back to our language "what was already its own" ("ce qui estoit

déjà à lui").[51] The solution, as we all know—a rather paradoxical solution stemming from the pen of a champion, a "defender" of the French language—is found, on the contrary, in the "recourse to foreign examples" ("le recours aux exemples étrangers"), in the "imitation," not to mention the "looting," "pillaging," ("pillage") of the best Greek and Latin authors.[52] Since the Ancients were "more learned than the people of our time" ("plus sçavans que les hommes de nostre aege"), it is toward them that we must turn if we wish to "augment" ("accroistre") our language and at the same time give a more exquisite and richer form to our poetry. Here again, the anthem, while well-known, deserves to be quoted and thought about. The chapter from which it is taken is entitled "What Kinds of Poems Must the French Poet Elect" ("Quel genres de poëmes doit elire le poëte François").[53] We will have, after Etienne Pasquier and the great Jean-Baptiste de La Curne de Sainte-Palaye, to wait for Madame de Staël and the beginning of the XIXth century in order to understand, with the help of Goethe, Bürger, and Schiller, that the proper solution is to be found perhaps elsewhere than with the Ancients, that an imported culture exposes those who import it to the risk of no longer knowing exactly who they are, that a "poetic Renaissance"—a "literature," a "culture" truly worthy of this name—can only be "national," *Gallique,* that, in no case, as Rabelais will say in the Prologue to the alleged *Fifth Book,*[54] can it be the achievement of "rappetasseurs de vieilles ferrailles latines, revendeurs de vieux motz latins tout moisis et incertains" ("patchers of old Latin scrap iron, resellers of old moldy and uncertain Latin words"):

> Lis donc et relis premierement (ô Poète futur), fueillette de main nocturne & journelle les exemplaires Grecz & Latins: puis me laisse toutes ces vieilles poësies Françoyses aux jeux Floraux de Thoulouze & au Puy de Rouan: comme rondeaux, ballades, vyrelaiz, chantz royaulx, chansons & autres telles episseries, qui corrompent le goust de nostre langue & ne servent si non à porter tesmoingnage de nostre ignorance [. . .] jette toy à ces plaisans epigrammes [. . .] Distille ces pitoyables elegies, à l'exemple d'un Ovide, d'un Tibulle ou d'un Properce. Chante moy ces odes, incongneues encor' de la Muse Françoyse, d'un luc bien accordé au son de la lyre Grecque et Romaine [. . .] Sonne moy ces beaux sonnetz [. . .] Chante moy ces plaisantes ecclogues rustiques à l'exemple de Théocrit & de Virgile . . .

> Accordingly, first read and read again (o future Poet), turn over night and day Greek and Latins Exemplars; and then leave all those old French pieces of poetry—like rondeaux, ballads, virelais, chants royaux, songs—for the Floral games of Toulouse and the Puy of Rouen: all such "episseries" which corrupt, denature the taste of our language & serve no purpose but that of bringing our ignorance to light [. . .] Throw yourself into those pleasant epigrams [. . .] Distil those pitiable elegies, following an Ovid, a Tibullus or a Propertius [. . .] Sing me those odes, still unknown of the French Muse, with a lute well attuned to the sound of the Greek and Roman lyre [. . .] Strike me those beautiful sonnets [. . .] Sing me those pleasant and rustic eclogues, following Theocritus's and Virgil's exemple . . .

However, with regard to the humanist myth of progress and its consequences, Pierre de Ronsard will have the last word. After all, one of his first gestures—in fact, as early as 1550—was to appropriate for himself the title that Clément Marot's contemporaries and disciples had spontaneously attributed to him, that of "Prince of French Poets," and in one of his earliest Pindaric odes he has the knack of saying everything and of making us grasp it in the space of a few verses, in a simple and crude way. His youthful arrogance and his boldness are all the more visible because, goaded by a rather silly, yet understandable desire for emulation, a desire to rival and fight his illustrious model by confronting him on his own ground, he rewrites one of his very last compositions, the "Epistle of Spring 1544, sent [. . .] to Monsieur d'Anguyen, Lieutenant pour le Roy de là les Montz" ("King's Lieutenant for the territory beyond the Alps"), on the occasion of the brilliant victory that this young hero had just won at Cérisoles.[55] Ronsard says, in substance, that it would be useless to contest the talent of his predecessor.

Nevertheless, one must not forget that Marot could only be the poet of his own age; and, Ronsard adds, this age was mediocre, the language it possessed was still in its infancy, barely uncoarsened and "poorly polished," incapable, in the babblings of its beginnings of welcoming and even less of expressing great poetic invention. Hence, when one recognizes in Marot the "only poetic light in the vernacular of his age," "la seulle lumiere de vulgaire poësie de son âge," it must be immediately stated that this period, hardly out of Gothic darkness, had not sufficiently tasted learning and ancient knowledge to be able to properly honor the Muses. One can say about Marot all the good one wishes, but the "Hymn" that he addressed to the new Hero, the proud Count of Enghien, is certainly far from equaling "the merits of his glory." Therefore, affirms Ronsard, it is not he whose "luth premierement / Aux François monstra la voye / De sonner si proprement" (whose "lute firstly / To the French showed the way / To sing as one should sing");[56] it is not he, but I, I Ronsard—*Moi, Moi Moi, encore Moi,* and nobody else:[57]

> Je confesse bien qu'à l'heure
> Sa plume estoit la meilleure
> Pour ombrager simplement
> Les premiers traits seulement.
> Estant nay d'ung meilleur âge,
> Et plus que luy studieux,
> Je veux parfaire l'ouvrage
> D'un art plus laborieux . . .

> I willingly confess that at the time
> His pen was the very best

To simply adumbrate
Only the first strokes.
Being born in a better age
And more than him studious,
I want to bring to perfection that work
By means of a more laborious art.

If Ronsard was wrong to believe as naively as he apparently did in Progress,[58] we will not forget here that this fundamental error of perception went far beyond him and the shaping of his poetic career. It had in fact, and I am afraid it still has today, consequences of a wider and more far-reaching importance. For nearly five centuries, the logic engendered by this so-called "historical" vision of the phenomena and the type of reasoning to which it implicitly leads condemned the poets of the Marot generation and their predecessors, the "grands rhétoriqueurs," to indifference, condescension, and contempt. And what for Ronsard's *fama* can be looked at as a *felix culpa,* a real blessing—it gave him all the justifications he needed to act as he did and believe what he believed—, becomes for us, literary critics and historians, a shame, an unforgivable mistake, the very proof than we can easily be blinded by prejudice. For, if it already places Clément Marot and his "treschers freres" in poetry in an unenviable light and situation—no matter their qualities, they are evidently less good, coming as they do before the others—, it can only hurt Alain Chartier, André de La Vigne, Jean Molinet, Octovian de Saint-Gelais and Guillaume Cretin all the more, not to mention Jehan Marot himself. Faced with this "schéma progressiste" ("progressive scheme")[59] which has for us the stamp of authority, which is used without even noticing it, as if it went without saying, what kind of arguments could the poor *rhétoriqueurs* invoke in their defense? Although Clément Marot worked for the great king Francis the First and although he began to feel the beneficial effects of the "restoration of learning," even if only in a mediocre fashion, those who formed him belonged to the *end*, the *waning* of the Middle Ages, to the reign of Louis XII and *grande rhétorique,* that is to say to a period in history and in literature which, as Huizinga says in a work still being read today, can only be seen as a period of *decline.*[60]

By taking the full measure of the automatisms of thought which, especially since Michelet and the overly famous *Tableau* of Saint-Beuve,[61] the arbitrary designations of "Middle Ages" and "Renaissance" impose on us, one naturally comes to the conclusion that these terms should perhaps be reconsidered and rethought in a radical way, perhaps even abandoned, or at the very least used with the greatest circumspection. If it is true that for the historian periodization seems inevitable, it should never weigh on his thought like a straight jacket or a candle snuffer and become for him a source of error and dangerous blindness. The 20 pages that Sainte-Beuve devoted to Clément Marot in 1828 are nothing more than an unconscious rewriting of the discourse

that, in the years 1549-1550, Ronsard and Du Bellay put forth in their aggressive and arrogant manifestos. In them one recognizes all the ingredients of the myth of progress, a myth in which we believe today more than ever: yes Marot, the author of *L'Adolescence clementine,* "represents old French poetry in its greatest purity"; but he is constantly judged in the light of Ronsard, perceived according to a perspective and criteria put in place by Erasmus, Budé, Rabelais, and the Poets of the Pléiade themselves. When all is said and done, he exists only to prepare that which comes after him, those lyrical splendors which he was not even able to imagine. He had "une causcrie facile et sans ambition" (a "glib tongue and ambitionless way of speaking"), "un génie léger accomodé à la médiocrité du temps" (a "faint genius in tune with the mediocrity of the time"); "he invented nothing, but skillfully used everything at hand" ("il n'a rien inventé, mais s'est habilement servi de tout"); etc. All the prejudices of the Pléiade are there, all their convictions and beliefs, especially the movement, as natural as it is necessary, which seems to go on its own, toward a light, towards something better. As we have seen, critics have not stopped repeating this argument, imitating it in a way that is both mechanical and sterile. My suggestion here—and my hope—will be that the time has finally come to reject the myth and reclaim the paths of history.

Notes

1. See Bellenger/Du Bellay, 1982 (1908), Preface "Au Lecteur" (To the Reader) of *L'Olive,* second edition (1550), 12, lines 34-35.

2. Chamard/Du Bellay, 1982(1908), *L'Olive,* 123, sonnet CXIV, line 4: "l'humble prestre des Muses" (the humble priest of the Muses). Ronsard, 1993, ode "A Michel de l'Hospital, Chancelier de France," I, 637. lines 349-52 (Calliope speaking to Jupiter): "Donne nous encor d'avantage / La tourbe des chantres divins, / Les Poëtes et les Devins, / Et les Prophetes en partage" (Give moreover to us / A multitude of divine singers, / Poets, Soothsayers, / And Prophets as our share); 640, lines 477-80: "Ceux que je veux faire Poëtes / [. . .] / Seront nommez les interpretes / Des Dieux, et de leur volonté (Those I want to make Poets / [. . .] / Will be called the interpreters / Of the Gods and their Will); 642, line 548: "les Poëtes divins" (the divine Poets); 643, line 567: "Prestres sacrez" (sacred Priests); *ibid.,* line 569: "Poëtes saints" (holy Poets). Ode "A Du Bellay Angevin, poëte excellent", I, 668, lines 1-2: "Celuy qui ne nous honore / Comme Prophetes des Dieux," etc. (He who does not honor us / As Prophets of the Gods); lines 13-14: ". . . la fantaisie / De leurs Prestres agitez" (the fantasy / of their frenzied Priests); lines 24-25: "Les ministres plus parfaits / De la Deité profonde" (The most perfect ministers

/ Of the profound Deity). Ode "A Calliope," 683, line 31: "Dieu est en nous" (God is in us). Ode "Au Roy Henri II," 725, lines 142-43: "Les ministres des Dieux / Les Poëtes sacrez," (The sacred Poets / Ministers of God); Ode "A son Lut," 963, lines 53-54: "Ce sont les seuls interpretes / Des hauts Dieux que les Poëtes" (The Poets are high Gods's unique interpreters). Discours "A tresillustre Prince Charles Cardinal de Lorraine, II, 76, line 218: "les ministres de Dieu" (God's ministers), etc. On this poetic credo, this consecration and auto-sanctification of the Poet, see—*inter alia*—Vianey, 1946; Joukovsky, 1969; Rouget, 1994.

3. See Denisot, 1553; Carle, 1561 and 1562; Grente/Simonin, 2001, 226-27 (Carle) and 335-37 (Denisot).

4. On the couple Eros-Anteros and its history in the first part of the XVIth century, see Defaux, 1993 and 1994a; Langer/Miernowski, 1994. See also Lefranc/Marguerite, 1896, 301-12 ("La distinction du vray amour par Dixains").

5. Monferran/Du Bellay, 2001, 133 ("et qu'il n'y ait vers, où n'aparoisse quelque vestige de rare et antique erudition").

6. On this point, see Ménager, 1979, 25: "Objet difficile, l'ode du premier recueil [. . .] ressemble à la terre où débarque un étranger, à la recherche du guide et de l'interprète." (Of difficult access, the ode of 1550 [. . .] looks like a new-found land, a land which, to be explored, requires the help of a guide and interpreter.)

7. See Defaux/Mantovani, 1999, 3; and Defaux, forthcoming, "'Vivre je veulx pour l'honneur de la France' [. . .]," forthcoming Actes du Colloque *Lyon et l'illustration de la langue française à la Renaissance.*

8. Céard/Ronsard, 1993, ode "A Madame Marguerite, sœur du Roy, Duchesse de Savoye," I, 611, lines 54-56.

9. On this phenomenon—the cultural or literary *agôn*—, see Defaux, 1995 and 1997.

10. Blanc/Petrarch, 1988, Rime 211, 356, lines 12-14.

11. Illuminating commentary on this Greek proverb in Laumonier, 1909, 345.

12. On the *agôn* between the two poets-the new *Dioscuri,* the *Fratres Pindaridas,* see Defaux, 2003c.

13. Laumonier, 1909, 342: "Les odes pindariques furent donc une brillante erreur esthétique de Ronsard. Elles furent surtout une erreur historique . . ." (Ronsard's Pindaric odes are consequently a brilliant aesthetic error. They were above all an historical error); followed by Silver, 1937, 123.

14. See Pico della Mirandola, 1557, folio 3; Rigg/More, 1890, 9-10: "OF HIS MYNDE AND VAYNGLORI-OUSE DISPICIONS OF ROME. Now had he ben.vii. yere conversaunt in these studies whan full of pryde & desyrous of glory and mannes prayse (for yet was he not kendled in yᶜ love of God), he went to Rome, and there (covetyunge to make a show of his connynge [. . .] ix. C. questions he purposed . . ."

15. Céard/Ronsard, 1993, I, 994.

16. Céard/Ronsard, 1993, ode "A Madame Marguerite, sœur du Roy," I, 612, lines 85-96; ode "A Calliope," 683, lines 36-37; and Preface, 995.

17. *Ibid.,* I, 994-95; see also Ronsard's "Discours contre Fortune, à Odet de Coligny," II, 772, lines 84-85: out of fairness, the best poets of the time cannot but recognize that "Indompté du travail tout le premier je suis / Qui de Grece ay conduit les Muses en la France" (Through hard work, *I was the very first* / To bring Poetry from Greece to France). Same (amplified) statement in his "Response aux injures et calomnies," II, 1066, lines 943-66.

18. *Ibid.,* ode "A Antoine de Baïf," I, 661, lines 20-21; ode "A sa Lyre," I, 676-78, lines 19-32; "A Jean de la Peruse, Poete," II, 682, lines 14-15.

19. *Ibid.,* liminary epistle to the *Franciade,* I, 1184; "Hymne de France," II, 652, lines 209-210.

20. Laumonier/Binet, 1910 (1586), 13.

21. Believe it or not, his constant bragging does not prevent Ronsard from speaking of "his natural modesty" ("la modestic de [s]on naturel," II, 1086). My ennemies, says the poet, compare me with "ce glorieux escrimeur Amyqus" (Amycus, this glorious fighter) and criticize me for being "un magnifique vanteur" (a magnificent braggart). But they forget only one thing: I do not brag, I tell the truth ("si est-ce toutesfois que ma vanterie est veritable"). It is quite interesting to discover today that, following the great (and somehow naive) Emile Faguet, 1894, 205, Chamard, 1900, 94, and Laumonier, 1909, 19, accepted the idea of a "timide" (shy) Ronsard, "modeste comme il sied à un débutant" (modest as befits a beginner, *sic*), "ami du calme et du repos" (friend of calm and tranquillity), "peu fait pour la lutte, et en particulier pour la lutte littéraire" (not really cut out for struggling, especially in literary matters, re-*sic*). Are we speaking here of the same Ronsard?

22. Céard/Ronsard, 1993, II, 739, lines 15-18.

23. *Ibid.,* "Discours contre Fortune," II, 779, line 380.

24. Silver, 1937, 7.

25. Céard/Ronsard, 1993, "Panégyrique de la Renom-mée," II, 11, lines 167-68.

26. See for example Ronsard's "Elegie à Marie," I, 245, lines 45-46: "Et moy d'autre costé assis au mesme lieu [that is, "au sommet d'un pilier vener-able," "at the top of a venerable column"), / Je se-rois remarquable en la forme d'un Dieu . . ." (And on the other side, I, sitting in the same place, / In the guise of a God I would be noteworthy).

27. See for example Defaux, 1996, "Introduction," 15-30; Defaux/Mantovani, 1999, "Introduction." ix-xlvii. Etc.

28. Jeanneret, [1997].

29. See also, in Huchon/Rabelais, 1994, 979, the first sentence of the dedicatory epistle to André Ti-raqueau in J. Manardi's *Epistolarum medicinalium tomus secundus,* Lyons, Seb. Gryphius, June 1532, fol. 2: "Qui fit, Tiraquelle doctissime, ut in hac tanta seculi nostri luce, quo disciplinas omneis meliores singulari quodam deorum munere postliminio receptas videmus, passim inueniantur, quibus sic affectis esse contigit, ut e densa illa Gothici temporis caligine plusquam Cimmeria ad conspicuam solis facem oculos attollere aut nolint, aut nequeant?" (How does it happen, very learned Tiraqueau, that, in the very vivid light of our age, an age in which, thanks to a singular favor of the gods, all the highest disciplines have been brought back to life, we see here and there people of such affections that, coming out of the dense and more than Cimmerian obcurity of Gothic times, they either do not want or cannot look upwards at the dazzling torch of the Sun?)

30. See Delaruelle/Budé, 1907, letter 31, 57-58; Gad-offre, 1997, 50-51. What Gadoffre sees in Gargan-tua's famous letter is "un circuit de progrès." One cannot but agree. On the Budé-Rabelais relations, see also de La Garanderie, 1983, 151-167; De-faux, 1997, 53-55.

31. Huchon/Rabelais, 1994, 243-244.

32. La Garanderie/Budé, 1988, 50-51, lines 206-211 and 219; 82-83, lines 736-39: "cum ex tanta clade tantoque diluvio, quod tandíu mortales in caligine densa disciplinarum tenuit: literæ tum græcæ, tum earum æmulæ latinæ, emersa sint . . ." (it so hap-pens that Greek Letters and their emulators, Latin Letters, have just emerged from a disaster and flood of such a magnitude that it had for a long time kept mortals in the dense obscurity of ignorance). See also 52-53, lines 230-32; 92-93, lines 894-98, etc.

33. Margolin/Erasme, 1966, 69. Margolin also quotes the *De conscribendis epistolis* of 1521: "nativitas non facit hominem, sed humanaæ naturæ capacem.

Quod nascitur, ceu rudis quædam materia est, in-stitutio formam inducit." On this humanist credo, Chomarat, 1981, I, 66-71, is quite useful.

34. La Garanderie/Budé, 1988, 70-71, lines 541-42 and 547; 82-83, line 754.

35. *Ibid.,* 100-101, lines 1031-33: "Quod hominem est fingere, hoc est hominum ad rationem formalem sui generis absoluere, ut rerum humanarum pru-dentiam divinarumque teneat" (To 'make' a man is to realize in him the perfection of his kind, to enrich him with the knowledge of divine and hu-man things).

36. *Ibid.,* 78-79, lines 672-74: "progredi ad summum oportet disciplinæ orbícularís, indéque semína legere ad conceptus animorum."

37. *Ibid.,* 84-85, lines 784-85; 88-89, lines 826-28: ". . . quæ nihil est aliud in se perfecta, & ad sum-mam perducta natura"; 66-67, lines 488-490: "Ita qui rerum humanarum dívînarumque adeptus est prudentiam, cum orationis facultate, recte, apte, & eleganter compolitæ, is absolutionem sui generis censetur adeptus esse." (Consequently, he who has acquired knowledge of things divine and human, and at the same time mastery over the art of speak-ing, is commonly regarded as someone who has achieved within himself the absolute perfection of his own kind).

38. On the *ambitio sæculi* theme, see Joukovsky, 1969.

39. Monferran/Du Bellay, 2001, 79-82 (Part One, chap. III: "Pourquoy la langue Françoyse n'est si riche que la Grecque, et latine"—Why the French language is not as rich as Greek, and Latin) and 95-96.

40. *Ibid.,* 121 (Part Two, chap. II: "Des Poëtes Françoys"—Of French Poets).

41. Defaux/Marot, 1990, 145-46, *L'Adolescence clem-entine,* Rondeau XXIII, line 12: "Je rime en prose (& peult estre) en raison" (I rhyme in prose and perhaps with reason).

42. On this point, side by side with Du Bellay's *Def-fence,* see for example Céard/Ronsard, 1993, limi-nary epistle to the *Franciade,* I, 1166: "La plus grande partie de ceux qui escrivent de nostre temps, se trainent enervez à fleur de terre, comme foibles chenilles, qui n'ont encore la force de grimper aux festes des arbres, lesquelles se con-tentent sculement de paistre la basse humeur de la terre, sans affecter la nourriture des hautes cimes, ausquelles elles ne peuvent attaindre à cause de leur imbecillité." (The greatest part of those who write today crawl bloodless on the ground, like weak caterpillars. Since they do not have yet the strength to climb on top of the trees, they content

themselves with feeding on dirt without even desiring more heavenly nourishment—a nourishment which their own imbecility puts out of their reach.)

43. Monferran/Du Bellay, 2001, respectively 121 and 126.

44. Ibid., 120: "Je sçay bien que beaucoup me reprendront, qui ay osé le premier des Françoys introduyre quasi comme une nouvelle Poësie". In my opinion, if one thing proves that Ronsard and Du Bellay wrote the Deffence together, it is this very sentence.

45. *Ibid.,* 123: ". . . disant qu'en l'un [that is Clément Marot] default ce, qui est le commencement de bien escrire, c'est le Sçavoir." Cf. Horace, *De arte poetica liber,* line 309 ("Scribendi recte sapere principium est et fons").

46. Ronsard, 1993, 995.

47. Monferran/Du Bellay, 106: ". . . le Roy François, je dy celuy François, à qui la France ne doit moins qu'à Auguste Romme".

48. *Ibid.,* 83: "Mais à qui apres Dieu rendrons-nous grace d'un tel benefice, si non à nostre feu bon Roy, et Pere Françoys premier de ce nom, et de toutes vertuz? Je dy premier, d'autant qu'il a en son noble Royaume premierement restitué tous les bons Ars, et Sciences en leur ancienne dignité: et si a nostre Langaige au paravant scabreux, et mal poly, rendu elegant, et si non tant copieux, qu'il poura bien estre, pour le moins fidele Interprete de tous les autres."; 92: ". . . faire tant que nostre Langue, encores rampante à terre, puisse hausser la teste, et s'eslever sur piedz."

49. Everybody, in the sixteenth century, believe in this myth, even those who, ultimately, will be its victims. See, for example, Victor Brodeau's "Rondeau responsif", Defaux/Marot, 1990, 174: "Le temps depuis, qui tout or fine et affine . . ." (Since then, Time, which refines gold, makes it better . . .). Conviction shared by Marot himself, *ibid.,* 143: "Car tout ainsi que le feu l'or affine, / Le temps a faict nostre langue plus fine" (For, in the same way as fire refines gold, time has refined our tongue).

50. On this topic, see Longeon, 1989.

51. Monferran/Du Bellay, 2001, 94-95.

52. *Ibid.,* 93: Part One, chap. VIII, "D'amplifier la Langue Françoyse par l'immitation des anciens Aucteurs Grecz et Romains."

53. *Ibid.,* 131-38: Part Two, chap. IV.

54. Huchon/Rabelais, 1994, 727. Same biting satire in Monferran/Du Bellay, 2001, 110 ("ces Reblanchisseurs de murailles"). On this topic, see Defaux, 2003a and b.

55. Defaux/Marot, 1993, 707-709. On Ronsard's attitude and feelings towards Marot, see Laumonier, 1909, 18 ("Les lauriers de Marot l'empêchaient de dormir"—"Marot's laurels gave him sleepless nights"), followed by Rouget, 1994, 28-29. See also Cérard/Ronsard, 1993, ode "Au fleuve du Loir," I, 954, lines 9-12: "Si Calliope m'est prospere, / Fameux *comme le Lot,* j'espere / Te faire un jour nombrer / Aux rangs des caux qu'on prise" (If Calliope smiles to me, / I hope to make you as famous as the Lot / And put you on the map / Among the most renowned streams). Moreover Binet tells us (Laumouier, 1910, 10, lines 3-20) that, in his first years, before "le seigneur Paul" made him discover Virgil's poetic beauties, Ronsard had "tousjours en main quelque Poëte François [. . .], un Jean Lemaire de Belges, un Romant de la Rose, et les œuvres de Coquillart et de Clement Marot . . ." (he had always with him the works of some French Poet—among which those of Clément Marot). In Binet's last version of Ronsard's *Vie* (1597), Coquillart disappears from this short list.

56. Ronsard, 1993, Ode "A Madame Marguerite, sœur du Roy," 1, 6, lines 90-92.

57. *Ibid.,* "La victoire de François de Bourbon, comte d'Anguien, à Cerisoles," 614, lines 1-12. See also, for a sharp criticism of Marot's low style and desire to please the "vulgaire", in the same ode, first Epode, 615, lines 29-36. In Binet's passage quoted above, we read that Ronsard considered his French predecessors as Virgil considered Ennius, that is as "les immondices dont il tiroit de belles limures d'or" (the dirt out of which he extracted beautiful filings of gold). Ronsard's poetic arrogance is as insulting as it it shameless.

58. Another example (among many others) of this belief may be found in the ode "A sa Lyre" (Céard/Ronsard, 1993, I, 677, lines 19-24: "Heureuse Lyre, honneur de mon enfance, / Je te sonnay devant tous en le France / De peu à peu: car quand premierement / Je te trouvay, tu sonnois rudement, / Tu n'avois fust ny cordes qui valussent, / Ne qui respondre aux lois de mon doigt peussent" (Happy Lyre, the honor of my youth, / Before all others in France, I started playing you / Little by little: for when I first / Got hold of you, you sounded a harsh sound, / Your strings and body were not worth a penny, / Nor could they respond to the commands of my fingers).

59. Mantovani, forthcoming.

60. Huizinga, 1961. A correction worthy of our attention: Payot, Huizinga's publisher, finally decided in 1977 to change the French title and replace "Déclin" by "Automne," the exact translation of

the original Dutch title of 1919, *Hersttij der mid-delleeuwen.* On this, see Rigolot, 1992.

61. Sainte-Beuve, 1828, 19-39.

Bibliography

Blanc, Pierre, ed. 1988. *Pétrarque. Canzoniere. Le Chansonnier.* Paris.

Carle, Lancelot (de). 1561. *L'Ecclesiaste de Salomon, paraphrasé en vers françois / . . . /. Avec quelques sonnets chrestiens.* Paris.

———. 1562. *Le Cantique des cantiques de Salomon, paraphrasé en vers françois.* Paris.

Céard, Jean, Daniel Ménager and Michel Simonin, eds. 1993. *Ronsard. Œuvres complètes.* 2 vols. Paris.

Chamard, Henri, ed. (with Yvonne Bellenger for vol. I [1982] and Geneviève Demerson for vols. VII and VIII [1984 and 1985]) 1908-1985. *Joachim Du Bellay. Œuvres poétiques.* Paris.

———. 1900. *Joachim du Bellay 1522-1560.* Lille. Reprint Geneva, 1978.

Chomarat, Jacques. 1981. *Grammaire et rhétorique chez Erasme.* 2 vols. Paris.

de La Garanderie, Marie-Madelaine, ed. and transl. 1988. *Guillaume Budé. L'Etude des Lettres. Principes pour sa juste et commode institution. De studio literarum recte et commode instituendo.* Paris.

———. 1983. "Rabelais et Budé". In *Mélanges Franco Simone,* IV, 151-67.

Defaux, Gérard, ed. 1990 and 1993. *Clément Marot. Œuvres poétiques complètes.* 2 vols. Paris.

———. 1993. "Les deux Amours de Clément Marot," *Rivista di letterature moderne e comparate,* XLVI.1: 1-30.

———. 1994a. "Marot et 'Ferme Amour': essai de mise au point." In Langer/Miernowski, eds., 1994, 137-67.

———, ed. 1994b. *François Rabelais. Pantagruel.* Paris.

———. 1995. "Rabelais and the Monsters of Antiphysis," *MLN,* 110: 1017-42.

———. 1996. *Le Poète en son jardin. Etude sur Clément Marot et L'Adolescence clementine.* Paris.

———. 1997. *Rabelais agonistes: du rieur au prophète. Etudes sur 'Pantagruel,' 'Gargantua,' 'Le Quart Livre.'* Geneva, 13-66.

———and Thierry Mantovani. eds. 1999. *Jehan Marot. Les deux Recueils.* Geneva, TLF.

———, ed. 2003a. *Lyon et l'illustration de la langue française à la Renaissance.* Lyon.

———. 2003b. "'Vivre je veulx pour l'honneur de la France': Marot, Tory, Rabelais et le cas Etienne Dolet," in Defaux, 2003a.

———. 2003c. "'Moy ton Poëte, ayant premier osé . . .': Du Bellay, Ronsard et l'Envie." In Cité des hommes, Cité de Dieu. Travaux sur la littérature de la Renaissance en l'honneur de Daniel Ménager, Michel Magnien and Jean Céard eds, Geneva, 197-205.

Delaruelle, Louis. 1907. *Répertoire analytique de la Correspondance de Guillaume Budé.* Paris. Reprint, Geneva, 1974.

Denisot, Nicolas. 1553. *Cantiques du premier advenement de JesuChrist.* Paris.

Faguet, Emile. 1894. *Seizième siècle. Etudes littéraires.* Paris.

Gadoffre, Gilbert. 1997. *La révolution culturelle dans la France des humanistes.* Geneva.

Grente, Georges, and Michel Simonin. 2001. *Dictionnaire des Lettres Françaises. Le XVIᵉ siècle.* Paris.

Huchon, Mireille, and François Moureau. 1994. *Rabelais. Œuvres complètes,* Paris.

Huizinga, J. 1961. *Le Déclin du Moyen Age.* Paris.

Jeanneret, Michel. [1997]. *Perpetuum mobile. Métamorphoses des corps et des œuvres de Vinci à Montaigne.* Paris.

Joukovsky, Françoise. 1969. *La Gloire dans la poésie française et néo-latine du XVIᵉ siècle.* Geneva.

Langer, Ullrich and Jan Miernowski, eds. 1994. *Anteros.* Caen.

Laumonier, Paul. 1909. *Ronsard, poète lyrique. Etude historique et littéraire.* Paris.

Laumonier, Paul, ed. 1910. *Claude Binet. La Vie de P. de Ronsard (1586).* Paris.

Lefranc, Abel, ed. 1896. *Les dernières poésies de Marguerite de Navarre.* Paris,

Longeon, Claude, ed. 1989. *Premiers combats pour la langue française.* Paris.

Magnien, Michel, Jean Céard et al., eds. 2003. Cité des hommes, Cité de Dieu. Travaux sur la littérature de la Renaissance en l'honneur de *Daniel Ménager.* Geneva.

Mantovani, Thierry. Forthcoming. *Dans l'atelier du rythmeur. Contribution à l'étude des techniques de versification chez Jean et Clément Marot, Guillaume Cretin et André de La Vigne.* Paris.

Margolin, Jean-Claude, ed. 1966. *Erasme. De pueris statim et liberaliter instituendis.* Geneva, THR.

Ménager, Daniel. *Ronsard. Le Roi, le Poète et les Hommes.* Geneva, THR.

Monferran, Jean-Charles, ed. 2001. *Joachim Du Bellay. La Deffence, et illustration de la langue françoyse.* Geneva, TLF.

Pico della Mirandola. 1557. *Opera omnia.* Basel.

Rigg, J. M., Esqu. 1890. *Giovanni Pico della Mirandola: His Life by his Nephew Giovanni Francesco Pico. Also Three of his Letters; His Interpretation of Psalm XVI; His Twelve Rules of a Christian Life; His Twelve Points of a Perfect Lover; And his Deprecatory Hymn to God.* London.

Rigolot, François, 1992. "Rhétorique de l'automne: pour en finir avec le Moyen Age et la Renaissance," *Rhétoriques fin de siècle,* François Cornilliat & Mary Shaw eds, Paris, 27-41.

Rouget, François. 1994. *L'Apothéose d'Orphée. L'esthétique de l'ode en France au XVIᵉ siècle de Sébillet à Scaliger (1548-1561).* Geneva.

Sainte-Beuve, Charles A. 1828. *Tableau historique et critique de la poésie française et du théâtre français au XVIᵉ siècle.* Paris, 19-39.

Silver, Isidore. 1937. *The Pindaric Odes of Ronsard.* Paris.

Vianey, Joseph. 1946. *Les Odes de Ronsard.* Paris.

Matthew Gumpert (essay date fall 2005)

SOURCE: Gumpert, Matthew. "Supplementarity and the Sonnet: A Reading of Ronsard's *Les Amours Diverses* 45." *French Forum* 30, no. 3 (fall 2005): 17-42.

[*In the following essay, Gumpert discusses Ronsard's "most obscene poem," which was disparaged by contemporary critics and neglected by later ones.*]

[these imitations are mere nonsense]

Lysistrata l.159[1]

INTRODUCTION: EXAMPLES AND SUPPLEMENTS

Les Amours Diverses 45 is almost certainly Ronsard's most obscene poem. Critics in the past have not been kind to it. And while it appears to have lost much of its shock value today, it continues to be neglected. But there may be something to learn from this sonnet, and this neglect. One of the questions we might want to ask is whether it is the subject itself we find distasteful, or the fact that it is represented so explicitly. It is possible that what sets Ronsard's sonnet apart, and has made it something of an embarrassment to its readers, is simply the explicitness with which it tells the story most sonnets—and in particular Petrarchan sonnets—tell: that of desire as supplementarity, a matter of substitution and deferral. Looked at in this way, the scenario of substitu-

tion sketched out by Ronsard's sonnet appears, perversely enough, less perverse. Read against the background of early modern writings on sex as something scandalous, Ronsard's *Les Amours Diverses* 45 may remind us to what extent there is something scandalous about all writing, and something scandalous about the fact that we enjoy it.

I am suggesting, in effect, that *Les Amours Diverses* 45 is an exemplary piece of writing. But what does it mean, in fact, to be *exemplary*? To answer that question, let me begin with the *example* of Derrida, whose now famous—indeed, exemplary—discussion of the supplement in *Of Grammatology* (141-64) relies to a large extent, in turn, on the example of Rousseau. In both the *Confessions* and *Emile,* Derrida points out (150), Rousseau calls masturbation a "dangerous supplement," an addition to and substitute for "normal" sexuality. Of course Derrida does not begin his meditations on the supplement with *this* example. Supplements, Derrida points out, play key roles throughout Rousseau's writings, and indeed, in all writing: education is a supplement to nature, fantasy a supplement to physical contact, and writing a supplement to speech. In each pair something culturally privileged and normative is compensated for, and potentially replaced by, something ancillary and perverse:[2]

> The supplement adds itself, it is a surplus. . . . But the supplement supplements. It adds only to replace. It intervenes or insinuates itself *in-the-place-of*; if it fills, it is as if one fills a void. . . . This second signification of the supplement [i.e., replacement] cannot be separated from the first [completion].
>
> (144-45)

The fact, however, that the supplement can replace that which it was asked to complete suggests that the supplement is prior to and constitutive of that which it called upon to supplement. Writing may appear to be an adjunct to speech, but "[i]f 'writing' signifies inscription and especially the durable institution of a sign . . . then writing in general covers the entire field of linguistic signs" (*Grammatology* 44). Both "speech" and "writing" are thus, potentially, only variant forms of what Derrida sometimes calls *archi-écriture* ["archiwriting"]. In just the same way, the more Rousseau tries to distance masturbation from "true" or "natural" sexuality, the more the aberration proves central to the norm. Masturbation begins as a specialized and aberrant form of sex, but in the end both sex and masturbation are shown to be specialized cases of a more generalized masturbation, an *archi-masturbation*.[3]

Few would characterize Derrida's reading of Rousseau in *Of Grammatology* as either a treatise on masturbation or Rousseau; the subject, if we had to choose one, would more likely be something along the lines of "writing as supplementarity." Masturbation, then, like Rousseau, is merely an *example*[4]—and, as such, subsidiary to the theoretical problem it is meant to illustrate. Examples, to state the obvious, are (examples of) supplements: they support and/or supplant the theories they are supposed to exemplify. For *writing* is only one of a set of privileged terms in *Of Grammatology,* all of which describe *supplementarity* in different ways (245).[5] Viewed as standing outside and after speech (*phoné*), for which it is merely a visible or durable notation, writing is called upon, nonetheless, to replace it. By *writing,* then, Derrida refers to the *supplement as exterior* (144-45), that which culture presumes to come after, or be left behind. And Rousseau's characterization of masturbation is, for Derrida, an *example of* the supplementarity of writing, a way of demonstrating that supplementarity is pervasive, inescapable, the very condition of signification (that it is the same as writing, in other words).

Nor is Derrida the point of this essay. Derrida, here, is an example, nothing more, summoned, *anecdotally,* as it were, to illustrate a point: namely, that illustrations have a way of becoming the point. A word on the *anecdote* here, for the anecdote is at once the least exemplary and the most exemplary of examples. Now examples are always contradictory, in the sense that they must fulfill two antithetical conditions: to be ordinary (an instance of the norm), and extraordinary (a particular instance, one in which the norm is rendered translucent). So with the anecdote. On the one hand, the anecdote is the most eccentric of examples, the example as superfluous and extraneous interpolation. In the anecdote, for example, theory falls, embarrassingly, back into the status of text (the narrative, the material) from which it (theory) tries to keep aloof. On the other hand, if it is the defining feature of the example to be supplementary, and if the anecdote is the most supplementary of examples, then it would also appear to be the example in its quintessential form, the example *par excellence.* This contradiction has a special bearing on Ronsard's **Les Amours Diverse 45,** which has long been regarded as an embarrassing anecdote to the poet's oeuvre. If illustrations are a way of articulating rules, then the more graphic the illustration, we might say, the more it appears both to coincide with the rule at hand, and to be its exception.

To return to Derrida as anecdote: one might approach the supplement as but the latest—and most graphic— illustration of a far more pervasive phenomenon, the *exemplum* or *paradeigma,* which was a central feature of discourse in the West from the late classical to the early modern period. Curtius defines the *exemplum* as an "interpolated anecdote serving as an example" (1953: 59). In the end, the definition is not a very satisfying one; above all, because what constitutes an *interpolation* is far from clear. All writing, Derrida argues, is a

form of citation; all writing, too, may be considered an act of interpolation. François Rigolot, in "The Renaissance Crisis of Exemplarity," notes how, in the early modern period, the concept of the *exemplum,* by way of the many vernacular derivatives from the Latin (from *ejemplo* to *exemple*) becomes increasingly elastic. J. T. Welter offers us a catalogue of medieval *exempla* in *L'Exemplum dans la littérature du moyen âge;* but the more precise he tries to be—in other words, the more examples he gives—the less precise the point (1927: 20). In the end, it would appear, almost everything can be an *exemplum.*

Examples, we may conclude, are powerful ways of authorizing discourse, of controlling what is being said or heard. Calling something (A) an example of something else (B) is a way of turning the former (A) into the supplement of the latter (B). But it is always possible, according to the logic of the supplement, that that something else (B) itself becomes the example of that (A) which was formerly its (B's) example. In Derrida's reading of Rousseau (for example), a theory of the supplement (with masturbation as an example) becomes a theory of masturbation (with the supplement as an example). If masturbation is understood as a privileging of distance over proximity, memory over immediacy, absence over presence, the rehearsed over the real, then it would appear to be a name for the very condition of all supplementarity. By the very logic of supplementarity, in other words, we are led to the following proposition: that *the supplement is always masturbatory,* and that *all writing,* which is supplementary, *is a form of masturbation.*[6] That may sound almost commonplace to the ear today; but Ronsard will help to remind us what it means, and rather rudely.[7]

Derrida's descriptions of the supplement resort then, perhaps inevitably, to masturbatory metaphor. This is hardly surprising, given that Derrida's own writing, on the level of the signifier as much as the signified, everywhere stages the return of the repressed. Focusing on what appears to be incidental material (footnotes, parentheses, anecdotes, examples) or stylistic nuances (verbal tics, figures, puns) as symptoms of contradiction or control is itself one of Derrida's own favorite strategies for reading. For Derrida just as much as for Freud, language (not just what is said, but how it is said) is overdetermined: a symptom.[8] Which is why the very language Derrida uses to refer to the supplement is predictably phallic: "It adds only to replace. It intervenes or insinuates itself *in-the-place-of;* if it fills, it is as if one fills a void." It appears difficult to talk about supplementarity except in fetishistic terms. A more explicit example of this kind of overdetermination is in the following passage from "La Pharmacie de Platon":

> Ce que Platon vise donc dans la sophistique, ce n'est pas le recours à la mémoire, mais dans un tel recours,

la substitution de l'aide-mémoire à la mémoire vive, de
la prothèse à l'organe, la perversion qui consiste à rem-
placer un membre par une chose.[9]

(1972: 123-24)

This is precisely the scenario dramatized in Ronsard's
Les Amours Diverses **45**: the *perversion that consists of
replacing a limb by a thing.*

LES AMOURS DIVERSES 45: THE CRITICAL TRADITION

Amour, je ne me plains de l'orgueil endurcy,
Ny de la cruauté de ma jeune Lucresse,
Ny comme sans secours languir elle me laisse:
Je me plains de sa main & de son godmicy.
　　　　C'est un gros instrument qui se fait pres
　　　　　　　d'icy,
Dont chaste elle corrompt toute nuict sa jeunesse:
Voila contre l'Amour sa prudente finesse,
Voila comme elle trompe un amoureux soucy.
Aussi pour recompense une haleine puante,
Une glaire espessie entre les draps gluante,
Un oeil have & battu, un teint palle & desfait,
　　　　Monstrent qu'un faux plaisir toute nuict la
　　　　　　　possede.
Il vaut mieux estre Phryne & Laïs tout à fait,
Que se feindre Portie avec un tel remede.[10]

Originally published in the first edition of the *Amours
Diverses* (1578), **Sonnet 45** was removed from the
second edition (1584), reappearing only with the *Recueil des Pièces retranchées* (1609). A slightly altered
version of the poem is found in a second manuscript
belonging to Rasse des Noeux. It is likely that the sonnet was originally intended for the *Sonnets pour
Hélène,* since most of the poems in *Les Amours Diverses* found their place in later editions of this, Ronsard's last sonnet cycle. The poem has more often than
not been excluded from collections of Ronsard's work.
Ronsard himself seems to have made efforts to suppress
it (Laumonier 331, de Rocher 149), as have Ronsard's
readers.[11]

One might say that *Les Amours Diverses* **45,** which
tells the story of a particularly embarrassing brand of
supplement, bears a supplementary relation to the main
body of Ronsard's work. But the supplement, we have
already seen, has a way of taking its revenge. Despite
Ronsard's own attempts to detach the sonnet from his
corpus, as it were,[12] it looms rather large in Huguet's
Dictionnaire de la langue française du seizième siècle,
where it is cited as the earliest instance of *godemichi,*
and in the *Trésor de la langue française,* as the earliest
appearance of one of a handful of variant forms grouped
under *godemichet* (defined, in the latter work, as a
"Phallus artificiel, destiné au plaisir sexuel."[13] Ronsard
becomes, in effect, one of several authorities on the
dildo; **Sonnet 45** in Huguet's dictionary is not execrable,
but exemplary. The supplement is the exception that

proves the rule. And the rule proved by the suppression,
excision, and rejection of this sonnet is that, it would
appear, of supplementarity itself.

When Ronsard's commentators have responded to *Les
Amours Diverses* **45,** it has more often than not been to
ascertain the identity of its addressee and the authenticity of its charges against her. This is as we might expect:
Ronsard's sonnet cycles have traditionally been read as
pseudo-biographical narratives. Petrarchan sonnets and
sonnet cycles in general, of course, encourage us to
read them this way.[14] And like Ronsard's earlier *Amours,*
cycles dedicated, variously, to Cassandre, Marie, and
Sinope, the *Sonnets pour Hélène* adheres closely to the
standard Petrarchan scenario of frustrated love, staged
as a serial confession. There was, it is generally agreed,
a "real" Helen—one Hélène de Surgères, *fille d'honneur*
of Catherine de Medicis—just as there was almost
certainly a "real" Laura behind Petrarch's *Canzoniere.*[15]
Both, however, are really beside the point when it comes
to the poetry ostensibly written to and about them. The
real object of desire, here as in any early modern sonnet
cycle, is not so much the beloved herself as various
metonymic or metaphorical substitutes for her (fantasies,
phantoms, dreams, memories, mythic avatars, portraits,
letters, articles of clothing, etc.).[16]

Whether the sonnet's protagonist is or isn't Helen does
have certain ramifications, of course, for the shape of
Ronsard's oeuvre, suggesting either the inclusion or
exclusion of **Sonnet 45** from the *Sonnets pour Hélène.*
Regardless of their position on this question, critics
tend to base it almost entirely on biographical readings.
Lebègue, for example, along with Laumonier, rejects
Helen as a possible candidate based on the historical
record: "Si cette pièce grossière avait concerné Hélène,
Ronsard n'eût pu conserver avec elle les relations cor-
diales qu'atteste une lettre qu'il écrivit à son ami Gal-
land. L'héroïne de ce sonnet satirique reste inconnue"
(qtd. in Ronsard 1959: 17.3: 332-33.n3).

Longnon, on the other hand, along with de Rocher,
argues that the woman referred to is without a doubt
Ronsard's beloved (72-74). Longnon's case rests on
hearsay, a piece of court gossip recorded by Ronsard's
contemporary Pierre de Bourdeille, Seigneur de
Brantôme. Brantôme's *Dames galantes* is an encyclopedia of scandal and a sixteenth-century *dictionnaire
d'idées reçues.* In the "Premier Discours" of Part 2, one
finds the following anecdote, embedded in a series of
stories about women notorious for their unconventional
erotic proclivities. Following the execution of an order
given by *la reine mère* to search the apartments of the
Louvre for hidden weapons, "il y en eut une qui fut
trouvée saisie dans un coffre par le capitaine des gardes
. . . de quatre gros godmicy gentiment façonnez qui
donnèrent bien de la risée au monde" (Bourdeille 125).
Despite its uncertain provenance, Brantôme's anecdote

is cited by Longnon as historical fact, a referential foundation for Ronsard's sonnet.[17]

Sonnet 45 may or may not be a response to the scandal of the *godmicy*. It may or may not be about Hélène de Surgères. It may or may not be something Ronsard regretted writing. A second version of the poem may or may not be Ronsard's (I return to this issue in a moment). All of these uncertainties, in any case, have something to do with the question of *authenticity* and *imitation,* with the extent to which the poem faithfully reproduces an historical or biographical or psychological or sentimental *reality*.

But even a cursory glance at the sonnet itself suggests that this is a poem precisely about the difficulty distinguishing the genuine from the fraudulent. The problem is not that Helen has refused the speaker's advances, but that she has misinformed him as to the reasons why. Her conduct has been a charade: playing Portia upon the public stage, she is, in fact, another Phryne. Helen's sin, then, is deception more than masturbation *per se* (although it is not clear we can separate the two), as the poet's concluding tercet clearly announces; her pleasure, too, is false (*un faux plaisir*), and betrayed through a host of visible signs or diagnosable symptoms. The sonnet is simply the catalogue of those signs/symptoms, which makes it a kind of *blason* (or *contreblason*) of masturbation: Helen's pride (line 1), her cruelty (2), her desertion (3), her over-refined display of modesty (7), her deceit (8), the visible symptoms marking her body (9 and 11)[18] and her bed (10) and, of course, her dildo (4).

If all this sounds a trifle clinical, there is a sense in which all of Ronsard's Petrarchan sonnets are medical reports. Like Petrarchan sonnets in general, Ronsard's always function as *visible signs* and *diagnosable symptoms*; they are designed to be read as the record of or replacement for something that really happened, or failed to happen. To say that **Sonnet 45,** for example, is a *complaint* ("je me plains," lines 1 and 4), means that it is a *translation* of pain: what a lover might say to a beloved, or a patient to a doctor. That makes the complaint a compensatory act: a way of expressing and explaining pain, a mechanism for reliving and relieving it. Which should help to remind us that the love sonnet (like the *complaint*) is a poetic form: not pain itself, but a prescribed way of speaking for it. Thus the very presence of the dildo should alert us from the beginning to the extent to which the love sonnet is itself a supplement: a *remede* (line 14), a remedy and replacement for something "real."[19]

A Few Comments on Early Modern Writings on Masturbation

Ronsard's imprecations in *Les Amours Diverses* **45** would seem to be consistent with a larger order of cultural fears about imitation and fraudulence. Let us return to Brantôme for a moment. Longnon fails to point out that Brantôme's story of the dildo is the concluding entry in a chapter of *Dames galantes* devoted to female homoeroticism. Now female same-sex sexual activity,[20] or what he terms *la fricarelle*,[21] is for Brantôme a strictly supplementary activity: at best preparatory to opposite-sex sexual activity, always a substitute for it. Regarding a particularly notorious couple, Brantôme writes, as if to reassure, "ces fricarelles ne leur servent qu'à faute des hommes" (123).[22] What today we might call a *lesbian*—for example, a woman who actually preferred sex with other women, whether occasionally or absolutely[23]—is a species Brantôme cannot conceive.[24] The proof is the dildo itself. Brantôme reports the case of two women discovered making use of the device: "L'une se trouva saisie et accommodée d'un gros entre les jambes, gentiment attaché avec de petites bandelettes à l'entour du corps, qu'il sembloit un membre naturel" (124-25). The dildo here is a perversion because it so clearly mimics the "real thing."[25] (At the same time, the fact that it functions only as a substitute can serve to reassure.) The dildo, therefore, is dangerous, a threat even to health:[26]

> Et mesmes pour la guerison de tel mal, comme j'ay ouy conter à aucuns chirurgiens, qu'il n'y a rien plus propre que de les faire bien nettoyer là-dedans par ces membres naturels des hommes, qui sont meilleurs que des pesseres qu'usent les medecins et chirurgiens . . . et toutefois il y a plusieurs femmes, nonobstant les inconveniens qu'elles en voyent arriver souvent, si faut-il qu'elles en ayent de ces engins contrefaits.
>
> (125)

Brantôme's defensiveness backfires here. In his effort to defend the true organ over the imposture of the dildo, he turns the real phallus into the supplement: a replacement, infinitely superior, it is true, but a replacement all the same, for the instruments "normally" preferred by doctors. The penis becomes a remedy, just as surely as the dildo seems to be for Helen.

One cannot help but note Brantôme's and Ronsard's reliance on a distinctly pathological discourse. Publication of the anonymous diatribe *Onania* circa 1710 is often cited as a crucial event in the medicalization of masturbation. Prior to that date, masturbation is condemned as a mortal sin, a "sin against nature"; only after, most critics argue, is it understood as a medical disorder, and something to be ruthlessly extirpated. Stengers and Neck review the literature and conclude that, up to the eighteenth-century, the injunction against masturbation is mostly an ecclesiastical affair, and never based on medical grounds (34-35).[27]

Foucault is no doubt right that in the eighteenth-century new centers of power produce new discourses on the body (medicine, psychiatry, onanism), constituting a veritable science of sex; and, along with them, new forms of perversion.[28] But these categories, while undoubtedly codified in the modern period, are discernable long before. In *The History of Sexuality* Foucault presents four figures who emerge in the modern period as "privileged objects of knowledge": the "hysterical woman," the "masturbating child," the "Malthusian [in other words, sterile] couple," and the "perverse adult" (105). Now these figures, less distinctly drawn and variously conflated, are already present in early modern pseudo-scientific writings long before the eighteenth-century, objects not so much of knowledge as of fear. The figure equipped with a dildo in Ronsard's sonnet, after all, is a woman at once hysterical, masturbating, non-reproductive, and perverse. It is not enough to say, therefore, that in the sixteenth-century and before, masturbation is proscribed above all as a "sin against nature," what Aquinas calls "vitium contra naturam" (qtd. in Stengers 30).[29] The question is, why? In other words, what kind of science is already implicit in that proscription?

It is, I propose, a science of (anti)supplementarity. The injunctions of the church against masturbation, like its exhortations against homosexuality, represent less a *moral* position in regard to what constitutes the *natural,* as an abhorrence of imitation as that which poses as and threatens to take the place of the *natural.*[30] Consider the following excerpt from Thomas de Cantimpré's *Bonum universale de apibus*:

> La colère de Dieu face à ce péché abject, selon Thomas, se manifeste non seulement par le châtiment suprême, mais aussi à l'occasion par des miracles, qui sont autant d'avertissements. C'est ainsi, nous raconte-t-il, qu'un masturbateur ayant voulu, dans une intention coupable, saisir sa verge, sentit soudain dans sa main une couleuvre.

> (Stengers 30)

How is this archetypal masturbator punished? By becoming a victim of supplementarity itself. Divine intervention terrifies in this case not so much through the disappearance of the penis but its replacement by something that resembles it. The snake is both a warning and a clarification, and shows us that this, in fact, is what the penis is: bestial and monstrous, unnatural and perverse.

Thus, to masturbate is not only to circumvent copulation but, more importantly, to *mimic* it.[31] Sodomy, in other words, is an *aesthetic,* not an *ethical* category.[32] Crompton recalls the case of a woman executed in 1535 in Fontaine for "wickedness which she used to counterfeit the office of a husband" (17). It is not clear, however, if the crime for which this woman is executed is really sodomy, or counterfeiting.[33] In the end, both may be variations of the same transgression.

No surprise, then, if the dildo is a scandalous object, just as much in the sixteenth- as in the eighteenth-century.[34] Which is why in early modern medical writings (such as they can be labeled) the dildo unleashes a whole set of cultural anxieties over the categories of the *natural* and the *authentic.* In Chapter 4 of Laurent Joubert's *Erreurs populaires* (1578), "Whether there is certain knowledge of the virginity of a maiden," the author spends a good deal of time carefully distinguishing deceptive appearances from verifiable realities. A woman may appear to have lost her virginity, but "how would you be able to tell," asks Joubert, "that the opening was attributable to the virile member rather than to a candle, or a pessary, or the finger of the maiden herself . . . ?" (216). Joubert's speculations suggest that virginity is a matter of causality, not effect (that is, physiology). Note that even rehearsing causality is condemned. There is only supposed to be one cause, and one premiere performance. Anything else is a sham:[35] both the pleasure, and the object causing it. Thus the problem of telling true from false is replayed in the distinction between the "virile member" on the one hand, and the candle, the pessary, and the finger on the other, all supplements. Finally, if Joubert's task is to dispel the ambiguities blurring the true and the false (this is, after all, a medical treatise), his writing would appear to end up reinstating them. Joubert continues his analysis:

> For the membranes . . . mentioned above can be opened and pushed back by the maiden herself upon inserting her finger often. This is the case with a few who are unchaste of heart, and who would willingly receive into their hell the good hermit's devil.

> (220)[36]

Note how Joubert's writing, which would unmask the mechanism of phallic simulation, in fact cooperates with it, repeating it coyly through the artifice of circumlocution, a form of linguistic camouflage. This medical treatise is itself a textual striptease for the "unchaste of heart."

PERFORMANCE ANXIETY AND THE SONNET

This is precisely what Ronsard's sonnet is, with its pseudo-medical diagnosis and its tone of righteous indignation over sins it voyeuristically repeats. Of these the most shocking is not, I have suggested, masturbation but simulation (something which the poet, in effect, cheerfully practices in every sonnet). But critics who have turned their attention to **Sonnet 45,** and more often than not, by approaching the sonnet as testimony, taking imitation for the real thing, end up confirming the very cultural fears they set out, in part, to dispel.

Consider de Rocher's analysis in "Ronsard's Dildo Sonnet: The Scandal of Poissy and Rasse des Noeux," one of the rare examples of recent criticism to even touch the subject.[37] De Rocher links the story of the dildo to a local Catholic gathering at which Ronsard may have played a role, and to the apparent rewriting of the sonnet by a Protestant irritated at his presence. "Cest un gros instrument qui se fait pres d'icy." *Here,* in a "corrected" version of the poem by François Rasse des Noeux, *chirurgien ordinaire* of Charles IX (1500-73) and a Protestant, is Poissy ("C'est un gros instrument qu'on pratique à Poissy," l.5), a Dominican convent where a group of prominent Catholics connected to Ronsard had recently convened. Rasse des Noeux, de Rocher argues, rewrites Ronsard's sonnet and publishes it as a means of disparaging the Catholics and the Colloquy of Poissy. According to de Rocher, the Colloquy marks a definitive rupture between Catholics and Protestants, the Sorbonne demanding "[s]igns," as de Rocher puts it, "of the validity of the New Religion" (159). And so events at Poissy appear to prefigure the sonnet's concern with telling true from false. Thus the dildo in Ronsard's sonnet, as rewritten by Rasse des Noeux, would be a way of pointing to the spuriousness of the Colloquy's faith.[38]

In effect de Rocher argues that Ronsard deploys the dildo as a rhetorical, rather than an actual, instrument, one that serves as an emblem for the category of the *unnatural* or the *artificial.* His subsequent efforts to make sense out of **Sonnet 45** by reinserting it into an historical-biographical context, however, suggest that his real interest is not rhetoricity at all. Perhaps this return to the biographical is inevitable from the moment de Rocher subsumes rhetoric in historical context. The trope of the *unnatural* in the sonnet is linked to Ronsard's Catholic activism: the poet makes allusion, de Rocher notes, in an anti-Protestant pamphlet written while at Poissy, to the "unnatural" acts of a renegade theologian (162). The unusual vehemence of the rhetoric in **Sonnet 45** allows de Rocher to forget that it is still just that, rhetoric. Only a truly, deeply wounded lover, de Rocher argues, in effect, could write a sonnet this crude and this lewd.[39] Meanwhile, de Rocher's lengthy discussion of whether or not the original sonnet is really addressed to Helen (149-150), or really authored by Ronsard at all,[40] suggests an ironic repetition of the anxiety over falsehood that is, I am suggesting, the sonnet's central concern.[41]

What makes this poem worth reading, I would argue, beyond its interest as a psychological document, or a casualty of religious conflict, or a piece of cultural evidence reflecting early modern apprehensions over an autonomous female eroticism, is that it appears to exploit all of these readings in the service of *rhetoricity* itself. Authenticity is important in this poem, but to the extent that it is something to be performed. And if there is performance anxiety here, it is probably ours, not Ronsard's: for it is performance itself—by which I mean that which strives for effect, not truth—that continues to

make us anxious. I have suggested that the dildo sonnet stages a search for the real and the genuine. But it is probably safe to say that the poem would not be particularly interesting if it did not at the same time challenge the coherence of those terms, or exposed them as rhetorical positions.

To a large degree these are positions dictated, again, by the conventions of Petrarchism. Like all of the sonnets in the *Sonnets pour Hélène,* this one only poses as an earnest battle with deception. If Helen's conduct is a performance, then so is Ronsard's. It is, one could argue, the central convention of the Petrarchan sonnet that it pose as confession, that it claim to be absolutely unconventional.[42] In this respect **Sonnet 45** is no different than its Petrarchan counterparts. Readers, however, have generally been so repelled by the subject of the performance in *Les Amours Diverses* 45 that they have been unable or unwilling to appreciate its technique, or what it shares with other performances. And yet nothing that this sonnet *does* departs from the standard Petrarchan paradigm.

In some sense the Petrarchan sonnet is the speaker's way of taking revenge on the object of his pursuit, transferring that object to the realm of fantasy, a realm over which the poet has complete mastery. (Hence the familiar references to Greco-Roman figures—Portia, Lais, Lucretia and, above all, Helen herself—which give the poem the required classical veneer, and help to turn mere scandal-mongering into "literature." The same logic, of course, helps to explain why Ronsard's first sonnet cycle is addressed to a "Cassandre," and his last to a "Helene.") Once the beloved is turned into text, the poet can have his way with her.

This is precisely what the form of the *blason* accomplishes: nature turned into artifice, the female body divided into fragments or percepts, the beloved broken down and put back together again at will. Will is an important notion here.[43] The *blason,* Kritzman argues, is the expression of poetic will or domination on the level of form:

> If such an anatomical discourse represents a fragmented body behind which the feminine subject effectively disappears, it is because the *blasonneur* depicts both the violence of the subject's relation to a fetishized body and the sadism linked to the manipulation of textual material. The poet attempts to evoke the woman's presence by means of a text that manipulates the architecture of the body into a synecdochical collage of the desired object; idealization entails a fetishism of the object in the form of a succession of disjunctive images.
>
> (98)

Perhaps Helen is not the only one masturbating here; this sonnet, after all, is Ronsard's fantasy, not Helen's.[44]

The description of Helen's "symptoms" in **Sonnet 45** allows the speaker, like any *blasonneur,* to enumerate and catalogue the beloved, to turn her into a selection of percepts or synecdoches.[45] The dildo in Ronsard's *blason* (more properly, a *contreblason*—although Kritzman's argument implies that every *blason is* a *contreblason*) is just such a synecdoche. It is, however, a very unusual synecdoche. Phallic instrument par excellence, standing in for the male's body, it is now, effectively, part of the female's. Note the distinction/conflation between the two objects of the speaker's scorn: "Je me plains de sa main & de son godmicy." Kritzman also comments on the metaphorical tendencies of the *blason,* in which the natural female anatomy is translated into a new organic architecture, built out of "precious metals" and "more prosaic objects" (97). The dildo is one of these prosaic objects, but now transferred, in its practical use, to the realm of flesh-and-blood.[46]

Sonnet 45 adheres faithfully to Petrarchan content and form, while, simultaneously, turning both upside down. That, too, is part of the game: turning Petrarchism upside down, I have suggested, is itself a standard move in Petrarchism. In **Sonnet 45** it is the beloved, instead of the poet, who takes refuge—and, even worse, pleasure—in simulacra and substitutes. This is, according to the speaker, "un faux plaisir." That, too, we know is a lie. Here the speaker's rage is both prompted, and rendered comical, by the knowledge, shared by speaker and reader alike, that this pleasure is all too real (at least within the fictive frame of the sonnet and the cycle), and enjoyed without the presence of either one of us being required. This is the revenge, again, of supplementarity. Helen does not simply resort to the dildo: she *prefers* it. Meanwhile, the speaker appears to measure himself in "dildo-ic" terms when he complains of Helen's "orgueil endurcy", and that "languir elle me laisse." Ronsard's sonnet thereby appears to point to the natural inconstancy of the real phallus, as opposed to the unnatural reliability of its surrogate.[47] The failure of the phallus is one of the themes of this poem. The idea of inadequacy is reinforced by Helen's own stamina, the fact that her corruption lasts "toute nuict," a phrase which appears twice in the poem. One might also speak of the unnatural reliability and stamina of poetry. Ronsard's love sonnets, like many early modern love sonnets, claim to be *natural*: earnest, authentic, spontaneous, and ephemeral. That is the game the poet plays; and we, the reader, are happy to play along.[48]

For it is a role we, too, are playing when we read: that of the innocent bystander who just happens to be near the scene of a crime (something, in other words, that happens to someone else). But readers are not innocent bystanders (or bystanders are not as innocent, perhaps, as they profess): we *enjoy* the scene of a crime. Even professional readers, or critics, those distanced and dispassionate analysts of the text, *take pleasure in* what

they read. Readers are always eavesdroppers and voyeurs.[49] Which is fine, as long as the sonnet is a polite affair. The problem with a sonnet about masturbation is that it reminds us, irritatingly, just how strange all sonnets are, and how strange that we enjoy reading them.

If *Les Amours Diverses* **45** only does what a Petrarchan sonnet is supposed to, then what makes this particular sonnet so troubling, we can see, is that it does it so transparently. Ronsard's dildo sonnet brazenly flaunts what ordinarily remains implicit: namely, that poetry is always, by its very nature, a perverse act of substitution (and reading poetry, therefore, a perverse act of voyeurism). None of that is news to us now; but it still is not something we like to see broadcast. The dildo is obscene because it refers so obviously to something else; indeed, so obviously that it becomes, in effect, a signifier for all signifiers.[50] It is signification itself—as substitution, imitation, and supplementarity—that is obscene. Standing in place of the "real thing," the dildo becomes the very icon of substitution. In other words: the dildo stands for the power to stand for. Recalling Derrida's description of the supplement: "It intervenes or insinuates itself *in-the-place-of*; if it fills, it is as if one fills a void. . . ." The problem is, the dildo does it *too literally.* This makes the dildo the naked supplement, the supplement *par excellence.* As such, the dildo is not a perversion within the erotic and poetic economy of the early modern sonnet cycle, but its perfect emblem. In other words: every sonnet is a dildo.

Notes

1. See n50 below. All translations, unless otherwise stated, are by the author.

2. Culler, as always, provides cogent paraphrases of Derrida's argument: "the superior term belongs to the logos and is a higher presence; the inferior term marks a fall. Logocentrism thus assumes the priority of the first term and conceives the second in relation to it, as a complication, a negation, a manifestation, or a disruption of the first" (93).

3. Culler considers the opposition *presence/absence*:

   A deconstruction would involve the demonstration that for presence to function as it is said to, it must have the qualities that supposedly belong to its opposite, absence. Thus, instead of defining absence in terms of presence, as *its* negation, we can treat "presence" as the effect of a generalized absence

   (95).

4. One situated, conveniently for Derrida's purposes in *Of Grammatology,* on the cusp of modernity. But what makes Rousseau, *specifically,* a good example is that he is, to a large extent, *generalizable*: a synecdoche for tradition. In the earliest references to it in Western literature, masturbation is described as a supplement—as in Aristophanes's *Lysistrata* (l. 108-110, 158-59, etc.). See the epigraph to this essay, and n34 and n50 below.

5. As Spivak puts it, "Derrida would not privilege a signifier into transcendence . . . Derrida's vocabulary is always on the move" (lxx-lxxi).

6. The two are closely linked in *Du côté de chez Swann,* where Marcel recalls "une petite pièce sentant l'iris" ["a little room fragrant with iris"] from his childhood. This room is, in fact, a kind of private annex—a supplement—to the public domain of the family house:

> Destinée à un usage plus spécial et plus vulgaire, cette pièce . . . servit longtemps de refuge pour moi, sans doute parce qu'elle était la seule qu'il me fût permis de fermer à clef, à toutes celles de mes occupations qui réclamaient une inviolable solitude: la lecture, la rêverie, les larmes et la volupté.
>
> (12)

Moreover, if both literature (*la lecture*) and masturbation (*la volupté*) depend on the supplementary logic of the vicarious, so, Proust insists, does our experience of reality itself. It may be true, as Françoise insists, that characters in books are not "réels" ["real"]; "Mais tous les sentiments que nous font éprouver la joie ou l'infortune d'un personnage réel ne se produisent en nous que par l'intermédiaire d'une image de cette joie ou de cette infortune" (83-84).

7. In fact this very proposition is intimated by Cixous in her description of an autonomous female eroticism in "The Laugh of the Medusa":

> A world of searching, the elaboration of a knowledge, on the basis of a systematic experimentation with the bodily functions, a passionate and precise interrogation of . . . erotogeneity. This practice . . . in particular as concerns masturbation, is *prolonged* or *accompanied by* a production of forms, a veritable aesthetic activity, each stage of rapture inscribing a resonant vision, a composition, something beautiful.
>
> (876; my italics)

For Cixous, masturbation and writing do not simply coincide in the female body; writing, rather, is there as supplement to masturbation.

8. Culler's reading of Derrida's reading of Rousseau suggests this kind of overdetermination at work: it is only after citing first writing, and then education, as examples of the supplement in Rousseau, that Culler brings up the subject, unnecessarily, it would appear, of masturbation: "Rousseau also speaks of masturbation as a 'dangerous supplement.' Like writing, it is a perverse addition, a practice or technique added to normal sexuality as writing is added to speech" (104). The deployment here of "also" and "like" suggest precisely the kind of "perverse addition" Culler is attempting to elucidate. Culler's example of masturbation as supplement, which would seem to add little to his argument, is itself a perverse supplement to that argument.

9. This kind of phallic imagery continues in "Plato's Pharmacy" and grows increasingly violent when Derrida equates the supplement with the *pharmakon*: "Plato maintains both the exteriority of writing *and* its power of maleficent penetration, its ability to affect or infect what lies deepest inside. The *pharmakon* is that dangerous supplement that breaks into the very thing that would have liked to do without it yet lets itself *at once* be breached, roughed up, fulfilled . . . replaced, completed" (1981: 125-26).

10. Ronsard 1963: 477-78, 786.

11. It is not mentioned, for example, in Desonay's *Ronsard poète de l'amour,* nor Stone's *Ronsard's Sonnet Cycles,* nor Fallon's *Voice and Vision in Ronsard* 's Les Sonnets pour Helene, nor Cave's *Ronsard the Poet* (which nonetheless has detailed references to both *Les Amours Diverses* and *Recueil des Pièces retranchées*).

12. De Rocher refers to "the momentary insertion of the dildo poem into," and later its "excision from," the "Ronsardian corpus" (150). In critical discussions of sonnet 45, my own included, phallic punning appears to recur like a neurotic symptom. See n8 above.

13. These variant forms include: *godemiché, godemichi, godemiche,* and Ronsard's own *godmicy.* The origin of this term is unclear. While the *Trésor* suggests the Spanish *gaudamecí,* that is, "cuir de Gaudames," most sources point to the Latin *gaude mihi,* "réjouis-moi." The origin of the English *dildo* is also uncertain; the word appears as early as 1593, and may be a corruption of the Italian *deletto,* "delight." Pleasure would seem to be the essential feature.

14. "It is this self-dramatization . . . that accounts for Petrarch's critical identification ever since the Renaissance with a highly subjective, even 'confessional' poetry" (Bermann 13).

15. For a biographical approach to Ronsard's *Sonnets pour Hélène,* see Desonay *passim.*

16. On the *Sonnets pour Hélène* as a supplementary system, see Quainton 1995 and Dubois 1989.

17. Thus Weber and Weber: "Ce sonnet est évidemment en rapport avec un incident rapporté par Brantôme" (Ronsard 1963: 786).

18. All of the symptoms here are probably commonplace. Exactly why Helen's *breath* should be affected is unclear (would it be too far-fetched to detect an allusion to fellatio?). But the play on *Hélène/haleine* is common in the *Sonnets pour Hélène,* and the explicit subject of at least one of its sonnets (3).

19. Vance captures the perversity of this routine Petrarchan scenario of substitution and deferral in a rather clinical analysis of its literary ancestor, the troubadour performance: "it is clear that if I were to really enjoy that lady (or any lady), the *je* of the singing poet and his audience would instantly die: semen and ink cannot flow in the same vein, if I may abuse a profoundly medieval analogy" (101). Note that words with the *re-* prefix denoting repetition, like *remede* and *recompense,* which otherwise might seem out of place in sonnet 45, serve to reinforce the theme of substitution or replacement.

20. An unwieldy formulation, I admit; but see n21.

21. See Bonnet's review of the changing lexicon of women's same-sex behavior in France, *Un choix sans équivoque.* Three terms are cited from the seventeenth-century *Dictionnaire érotique latin-francais: tribade* (from the Greek *tribein,* "to rub"), *lesbian,* and *fricatrix* (43).

22. The same structure of supplementarity is found in a sixteenth-century instance of *godemichi* listed in Huguet: "O legere fortune! Qui donne à l'un un oeuf, et à l'autre une prune; Qui fait que d'un vieil gant les dames de Paris font des gaudemichés, a faute de maris" (330). For the classical formulation of this structure, see n4 above, and n34, n50 below.

23. For example Vicinus, in "'They Wonder to Which Sex I Belong': The Historical Roots of the Modern Lesbian Identity," argues that "Conceptual confusion is perhaps inevitable in regard to lesbians, given the historical suppression of female identity in general" (434); in fact, "we lack any general agreement as to what constitutes a lesbian" (433).

24. It may indeed be the case that an autonomous female sexuality has never been something possible to acknowledge, given that, historically, as Irigaray puts it in *This Sex Which Is Not One,* "the feminine occurs only within models and laws devised by male subjects" (1985a: 86). Within what de Lauretis, in "Sexual Indifference and Lesbian Representation," calls this "phallic regime" (142), "[t]hat a woman might desire a woman 'like' herself, someone of the 'same' sex, that she might also have auto- and homosexual appetites, is simply incomprehensible" (Irigaray 86). Irigaray, in *Speculum of the Other Woman,* calls this phallic regime the regime of "sexual indifference" (1985b: 28) or *hommo-sexualité* as opposed to *homo-sexualité* (101-103).

25. Brantôme thus adheres to what Maines, in *The Technology of Orgasm,* calls the "androcentric definition of sex," namely penetration and male orgasm (7). Sex without those two steps "has not been popularly or medically (or for that matter legally) regarded as 'the real thing.'" On the persistence of what Rich most famously called "compulsory heterosexuality" and the phallocentric or androcentric model, see Juffer 1998. Does this model apply to the early modern period? Weigert's study of the homoerotic representation of witches in sixteenth-century Germany would seem to suggest it does. In all of the images Weigert examines, the phallus is always present in absentia, signaled by way of various substitutes (fingers, broomsticks, sausages, etc.). Indeed, according to Weigert, trial records in sixteenth-century Europe of women accused of sodomy suggest that "sexual relations between women could not be conceived of without the use of some kind of penis substitute" (36).

26. And to social order, potentially. The woman equipped with a substitute phallus may be understood as effectively performing or miming the role of the male. A more thorough study of the dildo in early modern culture would link it to other practices of sexual inversion or transvestism. See Davis' study of gender role reversal as social resistance, "Women on Top" in her *Society and Culture in Early Modern France* (1975: 124-51). On gender and French Renaissance culture more generally, see Gray 2000.

27. This would seem to be contradicted by the medical and alchemical terminology that, according to Halpern's *Shakespeare's Perfume: Sodomy and Sublimity in the Sonnets, Wilde, Freud, and Lacan,* underlies Shakespeare's paradoxical proscriptions of sodomy in the *Sonnets*—paradoxical because this rejection of sodomy (understood here as any use of semen for purposes other than procreation, from masturbation to homosexuality) thereby links it both to the *sublimate* (the unusable, in alchemical terms) and to the *sublime* (the unspeakable, in aesthetic terms).

28. See *The History of Sexuality* (1: 28-30, 103-105). New forms, too, of social resistance. Davis 1975 is helpful on the role of ritually prescribed sexual inversion and transvestism in sixteenth- and seventeenth-century century Europe as a way of simultaneously confirming and challenging patriarchy.

29. Not enough attention has been paid, likewise, to the distinction made, theologically, between male and female masturbation—something that could have important consequences for how we read Ronsard's *Les Amours Diverses* 45. It is not even clear to what extent female masturbation can be conceptualized at all in medieval and early modern theology, far more interested in the fate of the

male seed than the female ovum. So Jordan argues, in *The Invention of Sodomy in Christian Theology*: "Albertus Magnus even goes so far as to state that female masturbation is not necessarily sinful since it does not entail a waste of male seed" (158). See n36 below. The fact that, as Vicinus puts it, "Women's same-sex behavior [has] remained marginal to male sexual and societal discourses" (438) explains in part how little we know about the history of lesbianism, as well as its relative neglect by the church. See Vicinus 449n35.

30. In the social realm the "natural" may include the normative hierarchy of gender; a hierarchy which may be threatened, or confirmed, by the assuming of transgressive sexual roles. See Davis 1975.

31. Similarly, the debate amongst feminist writers in the 1970s on the use of women's sex toys as masturbatory aids is to a large extent a confrontation with the mimetic implications of supplementarity. The vibrator, for example, is both a way of insisting on the "naturalness" of an autonomous female sexuality, and a threat to it. So Juffer: "if the vibrator is intended to free women from reliance on men for their pleasures, then isn't there something ironic about using an artificial penis to get off?" (84).

32. Compare this formulation to Halpern's. Halpern's point is that sodomy in Shakespeare's *Sonnets* is essentially an aesthetic category. As such, however, it is precisely the antithesis of that found in Ronsard's *Sonnets pour Hélène*. For Shakespeare, Halpern contends, sodomy is the *unrepresentable*; for Ronsard, I am arguing, sodomy is the *representable*. For Butler, in "Imitation and Gender," if "compulsory heterosexuality" "sets itself up as the original, the true, the authentic," then "'being' lesbian is always a kind of miming, a vain effort to participate in the phantasmatic plenitude of naturalized heterosexuality" (1993: 312). But without the proposition "the homosexual is a copy" the axiomatic identification of "heterosexuality as origin" is impossible, Butler argues: "Heterosexuality . . . presupposes homosexuality." The implication here is that, as Butler claims in *Gender Trouble,* gender has always been a matter of representation, political or mimetic; the performative mirroring of an elusive—and, ultimately, illusory—core identity (1990: 6-7).

33. Compare this case with that of Catharine Margaretha Linck, executed, in Germany in 1721, for the crime of sodomy. Whatever weight the legal charge may have carried, Linck's real transgression seems to have been, as was the case in Fontaine in 1535, the all-too comfortable mimicry of a male social and sexual identity. "Dressed as a man," Vicinus writes, describing the case, "she served in a Prussian volunteer corps, worked as a weaver, and married a woman, with whom she had sex, using a homemade dildo" (439). In this narrative of deception and disguise, Linck's mother-in-law plays the role of the detective who reveals (quite literally, tearing Linck's clothing off her body) the true identity of the impostor. Vicinus' findings must be read against Davis' suggestion that local or ephemeral opportunities for tactical social resistance through sexual inversion were common in the early modern period. See Vicinus 447n7.

34. Indeed, long before. In classical Greek settings the dildo (*olisbos*; more rarely, *baubon*) is always represented as a scandalous supplement, a sign of female perversity. See Henderson (15, 221, 222), Mention of female masturbation is rare in the classical world, appearing almost exclusively in a satirical or comic vein. See n4 above, n50 below. Richlin notes that while "jokes about female masturbation are not uncommon" in ancient Greek literature, "there is not even a word for 'dildo' in Latin" (231). For references to autoeroticism in general in classical antiquity, see Henderson (*passim*), Richlin (135-36, 159-60, 231n27), and Halpern (11, 57, 61, 70, 71, 472-76).

35. Not to mention a waste. The intersection of medical and economic rhetorical models in medieval and early modern proscriptions of masturbation (Brantôme, we recall, referred to dildos as "ces engins contrefaits") should not go unmentioned. Masturbation is also *unnatural* because it is *wasteful*. This charge is already present in Ronsard's sonnet, where Helen's maladies are her "recompense" (9). Shakespeare's references to masturbation in the *Sonnets* (4, 6, 9) exploit various economic double-entendres in reproductive terminology. Booth notes the Elizabethan "pseudo-medical belief" that "each sexual emission diminished a man's lifespan" (142), a belief which appears to inform sonnets 6, 11, and 129. See n28 above. Vendler's reading of the same sonnets more clearly underscores their mimetic concerns. In sonnet 4 (61-64) masturbation represents a kind of monstrous and mechanical repetition of the self: note the repetition of "self" and the second-person pronouns: "For having traffic with thyself alone, / Thou of thyself thy sweet self dost deceive" (l.9-10); in sonnet 9 (83-86) the young man's refusal to reproduce leads, on the other hand, to a failure of representation: "The world will be thy widow and still weep, / That thou no form of thee has left behind" (l.5-6). This mimetic imperative is encoded on the level of the signifier; Vendler calls sonnet 9 a "Fantasy on the Letter W," noting, with regard to the lines just cited, that "The initial and

final *w*'s of *widdow* [the Quarto spelling] are mirror images of each other, and its middle letter is repeated—*dd*—in self-identity" (84).

36. The last phrase would appear to be a reference to Boccaccio's story of Alibech and Rustico in the *Decameron* (274); a fable, itself, about the hazards of circumlocution. For the narrator (Dioneo) spends less time exposing Rustico's double-entendres—shocking because they conflate religious and erotic rhetoric—than conspiring with them ("During the next few days, however, the devil's pride frequently reared its head again" [277], etc.).

37. *Les Amours Diverses* 45 is often referred to as the "dildo sonnet"; a title I have specifically avoided, given that, in taking a part for the whole, it reproduces the very synecdochic and supplementary logic which the poem itself, I am arguing, exposes and exploits.

38. In *The Return of Martin Guerre* Davis observes that Jean de Coras' report on the impersonation of Martin Guerre was published against the backdrop of an increasingly violent debate between Protestants and Catholics over what constituted authentic faith. Coras' story of an "impostor husband" is written at the very moment when partisans are "fighting about the true and false church" (115). Montaigne brings up the case in "Des boyteux" in order to suggest how difficult it is to tell the real from the illusory: "Truth and falsehood have both alike countenances. . . . Wee behold them with one same eye" (Montaigne 3.11: 612-17, qtd. in Davis 1983: 119). See also Montaigne 3.5 on the simulacrum.

39. Of Ronsard's pursuit of Helen, de Rocher asserts: "what had started out as a game soon became love in earnest" (152); and on the dildo sonnet: "It is as though . . . Ronsard distilled all the yellow bile provoked by distant, hesitant, or otherwise unyielding Egerias and spilled it in one violent access of poetic fury" (151).

40. Laumonier remains unsure as to whether Ronsard or Rasse des Noeux is the author of the sonnet in its variant form (477).

41. This "anxiety of falsehood" is particularly blatant in the Rasse des Noeux manuscript version: for "ma jeune Lucresse," "ma feinte maistresse" (line 2); for "Monstrent qu'un faux plaisir toute nuict la possede," "Monstrent qu'au lieu du vray tousjours le faux y entre" (line 12). On early modern conceptions of *falsehood*, see Grafton 1990.

42. For a poem that performs as it exposes all the requisite moves of this Petrarchan choreography, see Du Bellay's "Contre les Petrarquistes," from *Divers Jeux Rustiques*. Note also Du Bellay's

reference to female auto-eroticism in "La Contre-Repentie," also from *Divers Jeux Rustiques* (Saulnier 147).

43. See Ronsard's "Elegie a Janet Peintre du Roi," from the *Meslanges* (1555), an extended blazon in which Ronsard's commission of a portrait of the beloved turns into a Pygmalionesque fantasy.

44. The phallus here, then, continues to play its favorite role, that of the exception which proves the rule: the rule of sexual indifference. For the *blason,* one might argue, is the extension of that rule or regime as poetic form, a form which effaces any autonomous feminine sexual identity, segmenting it into a concatenation of (masculine) percepts, parts for a missing whole. The dildo is the synecdoche that makes a difference—ironically, by erasing difference. And sonnet 45 as *blason* would appear to be a convincing demonstration of Irigaray's pronouncement: "So there will be no female homosexuality, just a hommosexuality in which women will be involved in the process of specularizing the phallus, begged to maintain the desire for the same that man has" (1985: 101-103). See also *Amours* 90, a blazon in which it is not clear whether the sum of Cassandre's parts add up to a male or female whole. The speaker's critical assessment, there, of what he sees, takes the form of a masturbatory response, one reflected on the very level of the signifier itself: "Je me contente en mon contentement." On gender and the blazon more generally, see the work of Freccero, and Persels.

45. See n18 above, on the play on or confusion between "haleine," the symptom, and "Hélène," the subject.

46. A similar confusion between the organic/somatic and the inorganic/prosthetic is found in chapter 8 of Rabelais' *Gargantua,* "Comment on vestit Gargantua" ["How Gargantua was dressed" (trans. Cohen)]. This chapter is, in fact, a *blason* of the male body; one in which the body itself is repeatedly obscured by or conflated with the fabrics and accouterments that conceal it. Of the four or five paragraphs in this chapter, by far the longest is devoted to Gargantua's *braguette,* or "codpiece." The "natural member" itself is incomplete without it: the clasp of the codpiece is ornamented with emeralds, a stone which "has an erective virtue and is encouraging to the natural member" (Cohen 55). The codpiece is a supplement, then; one which, however, is here so expansively described, in such detail, that we soon forget what it contains, or forget there is a difference between container and contained. Gargantua's codpiece becomes a living organism, the very symbol of fertility: "you would have compared it to one of those grand

Horns of Plenty" (Cohen 55). The image of the *cornucopia* suggests the early modern obsession with *copia* or verbal *plenitude*: the triumph of verbal artifice, of the rhetoric as the real: for it is

> always brave, sappy, and moist, always green, always flourishing, always fructifying, full of humours, full of flowers, full of fruit, full of every delight. . . . But I will tell you a good deal more about it in the book that I have written, *On the Dignity of Codpieces* . . . not only was it long and capacious, but well furnished within and victualled, having no resemblance to the fraudulent codpieces of so many young gentlemen which contain nothing but wind.

(On the theme of *copia* in early modern writing, see Cave *passim.*) Consider the "fraudulent codpiece": for are not all codpieces by definition fraudulent, an empty sign? But here the signifier is *full,* and takes on an epic life of its own. Note, finally, the reference to a *supplementary work, On the Dignity of Codpieces,* pointing to the potential incompleteness of the very text we are reading (and, by extension, all texts).

47. Lamenting the unreliability of the male organ is a standard trope in poetry, already to be found in Ovid's *Amores* 3.7 (Showerman 475-79) and Petronius's *Satyricon* (Arrowsmith 150-52). Openly praising the superior virtues of that organ's simulacrum is more unusual. But see Thomas Nash's *The Choice of Valentines: Or, The Merie Ballad* (1593). In this frank account of an adventure in a brothel, the speaker strives heroically, but unsuccessfully, to keep pace with his female partner: "Thus gazing and thus striuing, we perseuer: / But what so firme that maie continue euer?" (Farmer 177-78). Now it is the turn of the woman to speak, who presents the dildo, explicitly, as his replacement:

> Adieu! Faint-hearted instrument of lust;
> That falselie hath betrayed our equale trust.
> Henceforth no more will I implore thine ayde,
> Or thee, or man of cowardize upbrayde.

> My little dilldo shall suply their kinde:
> A knave, that moues as light as leaues by winde;
> That bendeth not, nor fouldeth anie deale,
> But stands as stiff as he were made of steele. . . .
> Poore Priapus! Whose triumph now must falle,
> Except thou thrust this weakeling to the walle.
> Behould! How he usurps, in bed and bowre
> And undermines thy kingdom euerie howre.

(233-48)

Note that the true penis is now labeled false, while the false one proves true. One would be hard pressed to find a starker example of the logic of the supplement at work.

48. This is true, of course, of love poetry long before the sonnet. In both Ovid and Petronius, phallic failure becomes the occasion (convincing, because confessional, masochistic, therefore *authentic*) for poetic virtuosity (that is, *artifice*): one performance compensating for the other. But in order to fully understand this game of substitution in Ronsard's sonnet 45, it needs to be read within the specific context of the Renaissance debate on *art* versus *nature.* This is a subject, clearly, too vast to treat here; but see Rigolot's *L'Erreur de la Renaissance* (2002a: 25ff). Throughout his poetry, in any case, Ronsard negotiates between the poles of the *natural* and the *unnatural.* In *Les Continuations des Amours,* as elsewhere, the speaker continually makes a grand show of rejecting Petrarchism because of its artificiality. This is also the game, of course, of *intertextuality.* On mimesis and intertextuality in Renaissance poetry, see above all Greene 1982, Quint 1983, and Rigolot 2002b.

49. "The artist, as John Stuart Mill saw in a wonderful flash of critical insight, is not heard but overheard" (qtd. in Frye 5); Frye later inflects that insight: "The lyric is, to go back to Mill's aphorism . . . preeminently the utterance that is overheard" (249). Overhearing and eavesdropping, when it comes to literature, can, of course, be perverse and perverting acts: as Dante's Paolo and Francesca discover reading "the rhyme / of Lancelot" (Ciardi l.124-25). Their first adulterous kiss, Francesca's tells us in *Inferno* 5.88-135, is an imitation of Lancelot and Guinevere's.

50. See *Lysistrata* l.157-159, where Lysistrata proposes the dildo as a substitute for sex. She does so, however, by way of circumlocution, a rather obscure figure of speech: *to tou Pherekratous, kuna derein dedarmenen,* "as Pherecrates said, you'll have to skin the skinned dog" (l.158). Calonice's response (l.159), which is the epigraph to this essay, *phluaria taut'esti ta memimemena,* "these things are mere nonsense," rejects Lysistrata's suggestion, classifying the dildo within the larger category of *memimemena,* "imitations" or "mimeses," a category regarded as deficient, mere *phluaria.* This last term, I want to point out, designates a specifically verbal or semiotic form of deficiency: "nonsense," or "silly talk," according to Liddell and Scott, from *phluo,* to "boil" or "bubble over," a metaphor for "to overflow with words," "talk idly." The dildo, in other words, is just one particular instance of *writing,* in the Derridean sense. This *semioticization* of the dildo is something erased or elided in most translations of the passage, which substitute various circumlocutions for the original Greek—thereby reenacting the very supplementary necessity that prompted Lysistrata's mention (by way, in turn, of circumlocutory language) of the dildo in the first place. Henderson: "[Lysistrata:] As the saying goes,

you've got to use your head. [Calonice:] But that's no good, I wouldn't stoop to that"; McLeish: "[L:] Then it's back to carrots, as the proverb says. [Myrrhine, for Calonice:] I never could stand proverbs. Or carrots" (203); but see Sommerstein, who renders the line more literally. Rogers, finally, renders 1.158 as "O faddle! then we'll find some substitute," omitting Calonice's response entirely—while offering an explicit translation of the whole exchange in the critical apparatus (19). See n4 and n35 above.

Works Cited

Arrowsmith, W., trans. *Petronius. The Satyricon.* New York: Penguin, 1977.

Barthes, Roland. *Le Plaisir du texte.* Paris: Editions du Seuil, 1973.

Bennet, Paula and Vernon A. Rosario II, eds. *Solitary Pleasures: The Historical, Literary, and Artistic Discourses of Autoeroticism.* New York: Routledge, 1995.

Bermann, Sandra L. *The Sonnet Over Time.* Chapel Hill: University of North Carolina Press, 1988.

Boccaccio, Giovanni. *The Decameron.* Trans. G. H. McWilliam. London: Penguin, 1995.

Bonnet, Marie-Jo. *Un choix sans équivoque.* Paris: Denöel, 1981.

Booth, Stephen, ed. *Shakespeare's Sonnets.* New Haven: Yale University Press, 1977.

Brantôme, P. Bourdeille, Seigneur de. *Les Dames galantes.* Ed. Maurice Rat. Paris: Editions Garnier Frères, 1967.

Butler, Judith. *Gender Trouble: Feminism and the Subversion of Identity.* New York: Routledge, 1990.

———. "Imitation and Gender Insubordination." *The Lesbian and Gay Studies Reader.* Ed. Henry Abelove, Michèle Aina Barale, and David M. Halperin. New York: Routledge, 1993. 307-20.

Cave, Terence, ed. *Ronsard the Poet.* London: Methuen, 1973.

———. *The Cornucopian Text: Problems in Writing in the French Renaissance.* London: Clarendon, 1985.

Cixous, Hélène. "The Laugh of the Medusa." Trans. Keith Cohen and Paula Cohen. *Signs: Journal of Women in Culture and Society* 1 (1976): 875-91.

Crompton, Louis. "The Myth of Lesbian Impunity: Capital Laws from 1270 to 1791." *Journal of Homosexuality* 6 (1981): 11-25.

Culler, Jonathan. *On Deconstruction: Theory and Criticism After Structuralism.* Ithaca: Cornell University Press, 1982.

Curtius, E. R. *European Literature and the Latin Middle Ages.* Trans. W. R. Trask. Princeton: Princeton University Press, 1953.

Dante. *Inferno.* Trans. John Ciardi. New York: Signet Classic, 2001.

Davis, Natalie Zemon. *Society and Culture in Early Modern France.* Stanford: Stanford University Press, 1975.

———. *The Return of Martin Guerre.* Cambridge MA: Harvard University Press, 1983.

De Lauretis, Teresa. "Sexual Indifference and Lesbian Representation." *The Lesbian and Gay Studies Reader.* Ed. Henry Abelove, Michèle Aina Barale, and David M. Halperin. New York: Routledge, 1993. 141-58.

De Man, Paul. "Lyric Voice in Contemporary Theory: Riffaterre and Jauss." *Lyric Poetry: Beyond New Criticism.* Ed. Chaviva Hosek and Patricia Parker. New York: Cornell University Press, 1985. 55-72.

De Rocher, Gregory. "Ronsard's Dildo Sonnet: The Scandal of Poissy and Rasse des Noeux." *Writing the Renaissance: Essays on Sixteenth Century French Literature in Honor of Floyd Gray.* Ed. Raymond C. La Charité. Lexington, Kentucky: *French Forum* (1992): 149-164.

Derrida, Jacques. *La dissémination.* Paris: Editions du Seuil, 1972.

———. *Of Grammatology.* Trans. Gayatri C. Spivak. Baltimore: Johns Hopkins University Press, 1976.

———. *The Truth in Painting.* Trans. Geoff Bennington and Ian McLeod. Chicago: University of Chicago Press, 1981.

Desonay, Fernand. *Ronsard, poète de l'amour.* Bruxelles: Palais des académies, 1952-59.

Du Bellay, Joachim. *Œuvres poétiques de Joachim du Bellay.* Ed. Henri Chamard. Paris: Société des textes français modernes, 1948.

Dubois, C.-G. "Autour du nom d'Hélène: Doubles et couples, similitudes et simulacres." *Etudes Ronsardiennes II: Ronsard et son 4ᵉ centenaire.* Eds. J. Cedard, D. Menanger, M. Simonin. Geneva, 1989. 173-81.

Durling, R. M., ed. *Petrarch's Lyric Poems: The Rime Sparse and Other Lyrics.* With translation and introduction. Cambridge MA: Harvard University Press, 1976.

Fallon, Jean M. *Voice and Vision in Ronsard's Les Sonnets pour Helene.* New York: Peter Lang, 1993.

Farmer, John S., ed. *Thomas Nash. The Choice of Valentines: Or, The Merie Ballad of Nash his Dildo.* London, 1899.

Foucault, Michel. *The History of Sexuality.* Trans. Robert Hurley. Vol. 1. New York: Penguin, 1978.

Frye, Northrop. *Anatomy of Criticism: Four Essays.* London: Penguin, 1957.

Grafton, Anthony. *Forgers and Critics: Creativity and Duplicity in Western Scholarship.* Princeton: Princeton University Press, 1990.

Gray, Floyd. *Gender, Rhetoric and Print Culture in French Renaissance Writing.* New York: Cambridge University Press, 2000.

Gray, Floyd and Marcel Tetel, eds. *Textes et intertextes: études sur le XVIe siècle pour Alfred Glauser.* Paris: Nizet 1979.

Greene, Thomas. *The Light in Troy: Imitation and Discovery in Renaissance Poetry.* New Haven: Yale University Press, 1982.

Halperin, David M., John J. Winkler, and Froma I. Zeitlin, eds. *Before Sexuality: The Construction of Erotic Experience in the Ancient Greek World.* Princeton: Princeton University Press, 1990.

Halpern, Richard. *Shakespeare's Perfume: Sodomy and Sublimity in the Sonnets, Wilde, Freud, and Lacan.* Philadelphia: University of Pennsylvania Press, 2002.

Henderson, Jeffrey. *The Maculate Muse: Obscene Language in Attic Comedy.* New Haven: Yale University Press, 1975.

Henderson, Jeffrey, trans. *Staging Women: Three Plays by Aristophanes.* New York: Routledge, 1996.

Huguet, Edmond. *Dictionnaire de la langue française du seizième siècle.* Paris: E. Champion, 1950. 7 vols. 1925-73.

Irigaray, Luce. *This Sex Which Is Not One.* Trans. Catherine Porter. Ithaca: Cornell University Press, 1985.

———. *Speculum of the Other Woman.* Trans. Gillian C. Gill. Ithaca: Cornell University Press, 1985.

Jordan, Mark D. *The Invention of Sodomy in Christian Theology.* Chicago: University of Chicago Press, 1997.

Joubert, Laurent. *Popular Errors.* Trans. Gregory de Rocher. Tuscaloosa: University of Alabama Press, 1989.

Juffer, Jane. *At Home With Pornography: Women, Sex, and Everyday Life.* New York: NYU Press, 1998.

Kritzman, Lawrence D. *The Rhetoric of Sexuality and the Literature of the French Renaissance.* Cambridge: Cambridge University Press, 1991.

La Charité, Raymond C., ed. *Writing the Renaissance: Essays on Sixteenth-Century French Literature in Honor of Floyd Gray.* Lexington, KY: French Forum, 1992.

Leitch, Vincent B. *Deconstructive Criticism: An Advanced Introduction.* New York: Columbia University Press, 1983.

Liddell, H. G. and Scott, eds. *An Intermediate Greek-English Lexicon.* Oxford: Oxford University Press, 1985.

Longnon, H. "Les Déboires de Ronsard à la Cour." *Bibliothèque d'humanisme et Renaissance* 12 (1950): 60-80.

Maines, Rachel P. *The Technology of Orgasm: "Hysteria," the Vibrator, and Women's Sexual Satisfaction.* Baltimore: Johns Hopkins University Press, 1999.

McLeish, Kenneth, trans. *Plays. Aristophanes.* London: Methuen Drama, 1993.

Montaigne, Michel de. *Michel de Montaigne. Œuvres complètes.* Trans. John Florio. London, 1610.

Onania, or, The heinous sin of self-pollution: and all its frightful consequences, in both sexes, consider'd: with spiritual and physical advice to those who have already injur'd themselves by this abominable practice. 1710-1722. London: E. R., 1610.

Proust, Marcel. *Du Côté de chez Swann.* Paris: Gallimard, 1987. Vol. 1 of *A la Recherche du temps perdu.*

Quainton, M. 1995. "Ronsard's *Sonnets pour Hélène* and the Alternative Helen Myth." *Michigan Romance Studies* 15: 77-112.

Quint, David. *Origin and Originality in Renaissance Literature: Versions of the Source.* New Haven: Yale University Press, 1983.

Rabelais, François de. *Histories of Gargantua and Pantagruel.* Trans. J. M. Cohen. New York: Viking Press, 1955.

Rey, Alain and Josette Rey-Debove. *Le Petit Robert.* Volume 1. *Dictionnaire alphabétique et analogique de la langue française.* Paris: Les Dictionnaires Robert, 1984.

Rich, Adrienne. "Compulsory Heterosexuality and Lesbian Existence." *The Lesbian and Gay Studies Reader.* Ed. Henry Abelove, Michèle Aina Barale, and David M. Halperin. NY: Routledge, 1993. 227-54.

Richlin, Amy. *The Garden of Priapus: Sexuality and Aggression in Roman Humor.* Oxford: Oxford University Press, 1992.

Rigolot, François. "The Renaissance Crisis of Exemplarity." *Journal of the History of Ideas* 59 (1998): 557.

———. *L'Erreur de la Renaissance.* Paris: Champion, 2002.

———. *Poésie et Renaissance.* Paris: Seuil, 2002.

Rogers, Benjamin B., ed. *Aristophanes.* Volume 3. With translation. Cambridge, MA: Harvard University Press, 1996.

Ronsard, Pierre de. *Œuvres Complètes*. Ed. Paul Laumonier. Vol. 17.2. Paris: Société des textes français
modernes, 1959. 20 vols. 1914-75.

――――. *Les Amours*. Ed. Henri and Catherine Weber.
With introduction and notes. Paris: Editions Garnier
Frères, 1963.

――――. *Œuvres Complètes. Edition établie, présentée
et annotée par Jean Céard, Daniel Ménager et Michel
Simonin.* Paris: Gallimard, 1993.

Saulnier, V.-L. *Du Bellay. Divers Jeux Rustiques*.
Geneva: Droz, 1965.

Seifert, Lewis C. "Eroticizing the Fronde: Sexual Deviance and Political Disorder in the *Mazarinades*."
L'Esprit Créateur 35.2 (1999): 22-36.

Showerman, Grant, trans. *Ovid. Heroides and Amores*.
Cambridge, MA: Harvard University Press, 1977.

Simonin, Michel. "Hélène avant Surgères. Pour une
lecture humaniste des *Sonnets pour Hélène*." *Sur des
vers de Ronsard*. Paris: Aux Amateurs de Lunès, 1989.

Sommerstein, Alan H., trans. *Aristophanes*. London:
Penguin, 1973.

Spivak, Gayatri Chakravorty. "Translator's Preface." *Of
Grammatology*. By Jacques Derrida. Baltimore: Johns
Hopkins University Press, 1976. ix-lxxxvii.

Stengers, Jean and Anne Van Neck. *Histoire d'une
grande peur, la masturbation*. Paris: Institut Synthélabo,
1998.

Stone, Donald Jr. *Ronsard's Sonnet Cycles: A Study in
Tone and Vision*. New Haven: Yale University Press,
1966.

*Trésor de la langue française; dictionnaire de la langue
du XIXe et XXe siècle (1789-1960)*. Paris: CNRS. 16
vols. 1971-94.

Vance, Eugene. "Greimas, Freud, and the Story of Trou-
vère Lyric." *Lyric Poetry: Beyond New Criticism*. Ed.
Chaviva Hosek and Patricia Parker. New York: Cornell
University Press, 1985. 93-105.

Vendler, Helen. *The Art of Shakespeare's Sonnets*.
Cambridge MA: Harvard University Press, 1997.

Vicinus, Martha. "'They Wonder to Which Sex I
Belong': The Historical Roots of the Modern Lesbian
Identity." *The Lesbian and Gay Studies Reader*. Ed.
Henry Abelove, Michèle Aina Barale, and David M.
Halperin. New York: Routledge, 1993. 432-52.

Weigert, Laura. "Autonomy as Deviance: Sixteenth-
Century Images of Witches and Prostitutes." *Solitary
Pleasures: The Historical, Literary, and Artistic
Discourses of Autoeroticism*. Ed. Paula Bennet and Ver-
non A. Rosario II. New York: Routledge, 1995. 19-47.

Welter, J. T. *L'exemplum dans la littérature du moyen
âge*. Paris: Occitania, 1927.

Anna Klosowska (essay date winter 2007)

SOURCE: Klosowska, Anna. "Madeleine de
l'Aubespine: Life, Works, and Auto-Mythography: An
Exchange with Ronsard, ca. 1570-80.[1]" *French Forum*
32, nos. 1/2 (winter 2007): 19-38.

[*In the following essay, Klosowska discusses the
relationship between Ronsard and Madeleine de
l'Aubespine, one of the few female poets Ronsard
praised for her work.*]

In 1587, the posthumous printing of Ronsard's ***Amours
diverses*** included for the first time among the *Gayetez* a
sonnet praising a woman poet quite forgotten today,
Madeleine de l'Aubespine (1546-96).[2] That poem is one
of the very few in Ronsard's *œuvre* where he praised a
woman for her writing.[3] L'Aubespine answered by a
sonnet where she compared herself to Phaeton, and
called Ronsard "her Apollo" (7).[4] Ronsard's reply
continued the theme of Phaeton. Only the last tercet of
this unpublished sonnet remains:[5]

> Si vollant vous tombez pour me vouloir trop croire
> Au moings vous acquerez pour tombe ceste gloire
> Qu'une femme a vaincu les plus doctes françois.

> If, flying, you fall, too willing to believe me,
> At least you will have earned this glory for your tomb
> That a woman surpassed the most learned French men.

The source of the Ronsard fragment is a nine-page
handwritten description (including incipits and quotes)
of the lost posthumous manuscript of l'Aubespine's
poetry.[6] That volume, containing over 4500 lines, disappeared in the fire of the Turin library in 1904.[7] However,
the description of l'Aubespine's lost volume, especially
the incipits, led to the rediscovery of her works
contained in other manuscripts, until now considered
anonymous or attributed to other (male) poets. I will
briefly describe l'Aubespine's life and major works,
and then focus on her exchange with Ronsard. Rather
than use the topos of feminine modesty, l'Aubespine
and Ronsard fashion a national, heroic, masculine figure
of the author: l'Aubespine is Ronsard's successor, the
French Phaeton to his French Apollo.

LIFE AND WORKS

Louise Labé, a hoax?[8] If Labé has a "problem"—as Huchon's recent study claims, she may have not existed,
and instead was a fictional character invented and
maintained by a group of poets and an eager public that
took the bait and responded to the fiction as if it was
reality, at the time, and over the centuries—

l'Aubespine's "problem" is the opposite: she did exist and write, but had no public that sustained the tradition of reading her works with her name attached to them, into the present time. In view of this opposition, we may ask ourselves what is a canonical author but *une créature de papier,* a nexus of discourses that actual presence and poetry written in an originary moment in history only anchor but do not determine? I believe we have always answered this question by editing and discussing anew certain forgotten writers, including women. The canon is not a matter of universally recognized beauty, but a matter of maintaining the old or creating new discursive fields that are trendy enough to attract attention. Once a certain critical mass of responses is reached, the field takes on a life of its own. By contrast with Labé, l'Aubespine's life in letters was limited by the nearly intangible practice of writing poetry shared in the ephemeral context of a literary circle. Manuscripts vanish, memories fade, unpublished authors disappear. It took the current confluence of scholars, access, and accidents of preservation, to bring out l'Aubespine's legacy. What will be its assessment? That will be determined in the conversational space formed around her writing: her auctorial and erotic self-fashioning, nothing short of exciting because it emphasizes two trends that go against the stereotype of "feminine modesty": one, the fact that women authors had literary ambitions expressed by myths of creation and author personas that we would consider "masculine," and two, that women in the period read, wrote, and publicly shared erotic poetry, sometimes with lesbian themes; the emergence of her works, of which only a third has been recovered; Colette Winn's uncertain attribution to l'Aubespine of the *Cabinet des saines affections*;[9] Isabelle de Conihout and Pascal Ract-Madoux's discovery of the magnificent *bibliothèque évanouie,* inventoried at l'Aubespine's death: some three thousand volumes including, for instance, an Aldus Manutius Ovid decorated with silver roses (for *l'aubespine,* hawthorn, whose flowers resemble white wild roses), and the *oraison funèbre* from Ronsard's burial that she attended in 1585.

Fortunately, unlike most early modern women poets, l'Aubespine is quite well documented. De Conihout and Ract-Madoux have accomplished an impressive recovery of historical details concerning her (their book is much awaited). She belonged by birth to an elite family of servants to the State and was married to the most notable royal secretary of the sixteenth century, Nicolas de Neufville sieur de Villeroy (1543-1617). He served four kings (Charles IX, Henry III, Henry IV and Louis XIII), having begun his career early, at sixteen (1559), the year he signed his marriage contract with l'Aubespine, who was then thirteen.[10] Already during that year, he was sent on two diplomatic missions, to Spain and Rome.[11] The couple owned l'hôtel de la Chasse, one of the most notable Renaissance *hôtels*

particuliers, in rue Bourdonnais, near the Halles—a fashionable address—as well as palaces outside the city, including Conflans, described in Ronsard's poems, and Villeroy, l'Aubespine's favorite retreat.[12] Villeroy and l'Aubespine's only surviving son, Charles (1566-1642), became the governor of Lyon and the Lyonnais, and was made marquis by Louis XIII in 1619. He was baptized in 1567 in the royal parish church of St Germain l'Auxerrois, across the street from the Louvre, "in the presence of their majesties and so many ladies and gentlemen of the court; whereupon M. de Ronsard made beautiful verse, and the King gave him his name, Charles."[13] In addition to such documents as the marriage contract with l'Aubespine's signature, we have at least two portraits of her, an oil on canvas in the Musée Carnavalet and a drawing in the Cabinet des Estampes (Bibliothèque nationale de France).[14]

Ronsard was the most prominent of a dozen writers whom Villeroy and l'Aubespine patronized. He dedicated to Villeroy five poems that open the ***Amours Diverses*** cycle (1584); the first of these poems was written as early as 1570.[15] At Villeroy's initiative, Ronsard and other leading poets (Dorat, Jodelle, Baïf, Desportes) created a poetic *tumulus* commemorating l'Aubespine's brilliant brother, Claude III, who died unexpectedly at the age of 25 (d. 1570), her father (d. 1567), and her uncle, Jean de Morvilliers (d. 1577); all three were important statesmen.[16] L'Aubespine also received literary homages independently of her husband. She was mentioned by bibliographers and memorialists: La Croix du Maine, Père Louis Jacob, Père Hilarion de Coste, François le Poulchre de La Roche Messemé, Pierre de Dampmartin, Pierre de L'Estoile, Brantôme.[17] She was celebrated by poets: Agrippa d'Aubigné, Rémy Belleau, Amadis Jamyn, Biard, Françoys Chouayne, Jean Bertaut, Abel de Sainte-Marthe and, most importantly, Philippe Desportes, who was her "poet-lover."[18] She authored one of the liminary poems in Desportes' *Premières œuvres* (first edition, 1573; reprinted in subsequent editions). The encomiasts of Desportes in *Premières œuvres* also included Jean Dorat, and the popular poet Jean-Antoine de Baïf; both were part of Villeroy's and l'Aubespine's circle.[19] These facts underscore the importance of l'Aubespine at the beginning of Desportes' career. Desportes later eclipsed Ronsard in the eyes of his contemporaries and, unlike Ronsard, became wealthy thanks to royal patronage.

In addition to her own *salon,* l'Aubespine was also an important participant in three leading literary circles: the court of Marguerite de Valois, the *salon vert* of Catherine de Clairemont, the maréchale de Retz, and the *Académie du Palais* of Henry III, who favored l'Aubespine so much that he gave her an abbey (1582), to the consternation of Rome (L'Aubespine, 20).[20] The accounts of memorialists as well as the works produced in these circles document their literary collaboration.

L'Aubespine's principal translation of Ariosto's *Orlando Furioso* (first two cantos) is dedicated to Marguerite de Valois.[21] An Ovid translation by l'Aubespine (*Heroides* 2) is part of a manuscript that belonged to the princess. A short Ariosto translation (fragment of canto 32) is conserved in the principal poetic album of the maréchale de Retz. L'Aubespine is also mentioned among the maréchale's companions in other poems in that album.

L'Aubespine's best-known poetic collaborations involve Desportes. The sonnet that she contributed to his *Premières œuvres* was one of the few of her poems in print during her lifetime. Another was part of a famous exchange: one of three *villanelles* sharing the same refrain, written respectively by Desportes, l'Aubespine and Agrippa d'Aubigné, probably soon after Desportes' return from Poland in 1574, where he accompanied the duke of Anjou (future Henry III), elected king of Poland. The narrator of Desportes' *villanelle* reproaches "Rozette" for her inconstancy in love, l'Aubespine's Rozette blames him in turn, and d'Aubigné chastises them both. This popular group of poems appeared in print several times, beginning as early as 1576, in small format "song books" (in-16°), including both Deportes and l'Aubespine's texts.[22] Desportes' "Rozette" was one of his most popular pieces, appearing in anthologies from the seventeenth through the twentieth century.[23]

Desportes was the first lover attributed to l'Aubespine by contemporary sources (from 1573-77), followed by Livarot (killed in a duel in 1581) and François de Fourquevaux (born ca. 1561-died 1611). Fourquevaux was the son of Raymond de Beccarie de Pavie de Fourquevaux, the ambassador to Spain and close advisor to Catherine de' Medici. He edited his father's military science compendium, a popular work translated into Italian, English and Castillan (to the chagrin of Fourquevaux *fils*, this work was frequently misattributed to Guillaume du Bellay, sieur de Langé). He was also a noted author of literary works, according to contemporary sources. While his published works are usually believed to have been lost—only a lively manuscript account of his travels to Egypt, Syria and Romania in 1585 is generally known—one volume does exist: a posthumous edition of his *Vies des grands capitaines* (1643), where he describes his father among fourteen great captains (I thank George Satterfield for this reference). Fourquevaux later courted Marguerite de Valois, and he and his wife became close friends of the queen after her divorce from Henry IV, when she reestablished her literary salon in Paris.[24]

L'Aubespine's poetic works, listed in the description of the lost posthumous volume, consisted of 59 sonnets, *chansons,* poetic dialogues and epigrams, but the lengthiest portions are her translations of narrative poems from Italian and Latin: the first two cantos of Ariosto's *Orlando furioso* and four epistles from Ovid's

Heroides (2, 5, 16 and 17). The contents of the lost posthumous volume were described in detail by the cataloguer, the head of the Turin library:[25]

> liminary poem fo. 1-2 (by the anonymous owner of the volume, who claims to be l'Aubespine's lover, and speaks of her recent death)
>
> sonnets fo. 3-20 (including two sonnets by Ronsard and "other poets")
>
> *chansons* fo. 21-23
>
> dialogues fo. 24-25
>
> epigrams fo. 26-30
>
> Ariosto 1 fo. 31-43
>
> Ariosto 2 fo. 44-57
>
> Ovid 2 fo. 58-63 (Phillis to Demophon)
>
> Ovid 5 fo. 63-67 (Oenona to Paris)
>
> Ovid 16 fo. 68-78 (Paris to Helena)
>
> Ovid 17 fo. 79-89 (Helena to Paris)
>
> *Espitre* [sic] fo. 90
>
> Two prose letters (ending on fo. 94?)

I hope that the incipits included below may lead someone to the discovery of the full text of these translations: *Heroides* 5, Oenona to Paris ("Lis tu ces tristes vers messagers de ma flame," f. 63), *Heroides* 16, Paris to Helena ("Helene, je ne puis plus receller la flame", f. 68), *Heroides* 17, Helena to Paris ("As tu donc bien ozé temeraire effronté," f. 79). The volume closed by two letters in prose, "dell'amica all'amico." According to the cataloguer, "they are without doubt by Madeleine and concern private quarrels (dissidi [?] privati) and petty affairs of the court." The remaining unidentified incipits are: the opening poem of the cycle of *chansons* ("Quand vostre cueur d'amour attaint"), and the closing *espitre* ("Ores que je suis loing de vous mon serviteur").

Only a portion of the lost volume, about one third, has been recovered from other manuscripts, including all of l'Aubespine's Ariosto translations.[26] These translations were mentioned by Alexandre Cioranescu in his thesis on Ariosto in France, although, not aware of l'Aubespine's authorship, Cioranescu tentatively attributed them to other poets.[27] It was also Cioranescu who connected the manuscript of the two first cantos of Ariosto dedicated to Marguerite de Valois, to a short fragment of canto 32, contained in maréchale de Retz's album, on the basis of script, form and style.[28] The newly discovered texts represent a major increase over the existing edition of l'Aubespine by Roger Sorg, a Ronsard specialist (in 1926), which only contains fourteen sonnets, seven other lyric poems, one Ovidian epistle (Phillis, 243 lines), and which does not mention Ariosto.

Although Cioranescu did not know who was the author of the Ariosto fragments, he praised their clarity, concision, and the fluidity of their *alexandrin*, qualities that also characterize l'Aubespine's translation of Ovid's epistles. Her choice of epistles to translate is interesting in itself. Against the stereotype that defines early modern women's translations and imitations of the *Heroides* as a masochistic preoccupation with abandoned women lovers, precursors of "love martyr" protagonists of the sentimental and epistolary novels of the seventeenth and eighteenth centuries, l'Aubespine devotes as much attention to abandoned females (Phyllis, Oenona) as she does to unleashed adulterous passions and unabashed narcissism (Paris, Helena).

While many of l'Aubespine's Petrarchist and pious sonnets are typical for her time, in some love poems she goes blatantly against the stereotype of female modesty. Three of her poems appear (anonymously) in the *Cabinet Satyrique,* a volume that Rousseau would have included among those he read "with one hand" (the *Cabinet,* alongside the *Parnasse Satyrique,* is one of the two most popular French anthologies of this kind, with twenty editions between 1618 and 1800). L'Aubespine is also, to my knowledge, the only early modern French woman author of a lesbian poem, where the woman narrator disputes the favors of her beloved with a man whom she calls her "co-rival."[29] She taunts him with a compromise:

> Je serviray les jours, vous servirez les nuictz
> Ha vous ne voulez pas, et bien, j'en suis contente[30]

> I will serve her in the daytime, you will serve her at
>   night.
> Ha, you don't want to? Well, then, I'm glad.

(13-14)

The interpretations of this poem cover a wide spectrum, from reading its lesbian content as a *roman à clef,* in the context of the sexual latitude attributed to the late Valois court (Lachèvre 1937, 8), to treating the avowed same-sex love as a joke, a frivolous hyperbole of the relationship between a lady-in-waiting and her mistress (Lavaud, 1936b, 510-11). But, if this poem is a joke, it still presupposes a late sixteenth century Paris audience amused by a lesbian joke. It is certainly not the kind of joke that passes undetected because erotic relationships between women cannot be imagined at the time. On the contrary, same-sex acts between women are a predictable if minor component of erotica (ex. the *Cabinet,* 1618, or a decade earlier, 1608, *Premier acte . . .* , 22).

The "Riddle,"[31] possibly l'Aubespine's best-known poem, included in the *Cabinet Satyrique,* describes playing a lute, but suggests a very different exercise.[32] The instrument was a frequent metaphor for both the male and the female body, and other poems on the lute were written in the maréchale de Retz's circle (Jamyn, Tyard).[33] What makes l'Aubespine's "Riddle" particularly interesting is the objectification of the male lover by the woman narrator of the poem. The beloved is literally an instrument, but it/he also functions as an instrument in the conceptual sense. He is metonymically reduced to a penis, animated by the hands of the woman narrator:

> Je prens le manche en main je le touche et manye
> Tant qu'il soit en estat de me donner plaisir
> Sur mon lict je me Jecte et sans m'en dessaisir
> Je l'estreins de mes bras sur mon sain je l'appuye
> Et remuant bien fort d'aise toute ravie
> Entre mille douceurs j'accompliz mon desir.[34]

> I take the neck[35] in hand, I touch it and I handle it,
> Until he is fit to give me pleasure.
> I throw myself on my bed and, without letting go of
>   him,
> I grasp him in my arms, I press him to my bosom,
> And moving hard, ravished by pleasure,
> Through a thousand delights I fulfill my desire

(3-8)

The text is at the same time conventional because it structures the erotic encounter as a one-way transaction where the subject's lust is serviced by the object, and revolutionary because it reverses stereotypical Renaissance gender and sexual roles, making the woman the subject, the man, the object from which she derives sexual pleasure—a reversal that has serious consequences for our understanding of early modern constructions of subjectivity, sexuality, and femininity. In the last line, the lyric narrator borrows word for word from Juvenal's portrait of Messalina, an archetypal female monster filled with insatiable lust (Satire 6): *Lasse et non assouvye* (14), "tired but not sated."[36] By conspicuously placing her female narrator in the context of Messalina, l'Aubespine repossesses, rewrites, and legitimizes the image of woman as a sexual subject. L'Aubespine's erotica and their circulation recall a trend described by Ian Frederic Moulton, who analyzes manuscripts containing erotica written or circulated by women in England in the first half of the seventeenth century, concluding that "women were seen as a potential audience for bawdy verse," and noting that they were sometimes credited with the authorship or the command to copy and distribute erotica (56).

The Exchange with Ronsard

Although we must read Ronsard's hyperbolic praise in the context of the address of a poet to his patroness, the fact remains: l'Aubespine is one of the rare women whom he distinguishes in that way. His first sonnet, "Madelene, ostez moy ce nom de l'Aubespine," multiplies allusions to classical myths of poetic creation. Ronsard opens by urging her to exchange her name (hawthorn), for the "palms and laurels . . . [of] Parnassus," "worthy to take root in her" (1-4). Her head is "crowned with honor," in her "chaste and rare bosom," "virtues and arts" are "borne by the thousands" (5-8). Ronsard encourages her ("O holy new seed / Of Pallas, take heart," 12-13), and says that even as her poetic star rises, his own is setting:

> Je suis en vous voyant heureux et malheureux:
> Heureux de voir vos vers, ouvrage genereux:
> Et malheureux de voir ma muse qui se couche
> Dessous vostre Orient. . . .
>
> When I see you, I am both happy and unhappy:
> Happy to see your verse, generous work,
> And unhappy to see my Muse who's setting down
> Beneath your Orient. . . .
>
> (9-12)

Ronsard recasts this image of a new poet that supersedes the old, in the last line of his second sonnet for l'Aubespine, "If you fall," where he predicts that "a woman" will have "defeated the most learned Frenchmen" (14)—giving the image a distinctly gendered aspect (woman defeating men).

Ronsard's hallmark combination of erudition and intimacy marks the closing lines of his first sonnet, where he creates an unexpectedly visceral image of the Muses filling l'Aubespine's mouth with the water from the source of poetic inspiration:[37]

> . . . O saint germe nouveau
> De Pallas, prenez cueur: les Soeurs n'ont assez d'eau
> Sur le mont d'Helicon pour laver vostre bouche.
>
> . . . O holy new seed
> Of Pallas, take heart: the Sisters don't have enough
>   water
> On Mount Helicon to moisten your mouth.
>
> (12-14)

If Ronsard links l'Aubespine to Parnassus, Pallas and the Muses, he also associates her with Apollo: "and the gifts of Apollo that are familiar to you, / So that nothing is worthy of you but yourself" (5-8). The motif of "familiar gifts of Apollo" from the second quatrain continues in the first tercet, in the "change of guard" image ("my Muse who's setting down / Beneath your Orient," 11-12). That image in lines 11-12 expands the reference to Apollo in line 5, evoking the sun god who departs at dawn from his palace in the Orient.

Among the many motifs proffered in Ronsard's first sonnet, l'Aubespine chose Apollo and Phaeton as the theme of her response. Since the myth of Phaeton occupies a prominent position as the opening of the second book of Ovid's *Metamorphoses,* there is a picture of Phaeton in every illustrated Renaissance edition of that work. The "Fall of Phaeton" was also a frequent choice for mannerist and baroque ceiling decorations. The

myth, as narrated by Ovid, describes the adventures of a son of Apollo. Growing up fatherless, derided by his companions, he travels from Egypt to the Orient to meet his father. When Phaeton arrives, his father acknowledges him as his son and, as a pledge of paternal love, grants him a wish. Phaeton asks to drive Apollo's chariot on the path through the stars. Apollo begs him to change his request, but Phaeton refuses, and tragedy unfolds. He is inexperienced and flies either too high or too low, causing darkness and cold, or scorching heat. Finally, frightened by the constellation of Scorpio, Phaeton drops the reins. The falling chariot is about to set the Earth ablaze. To prevent the cosmic catastrophe, Zeus throws a thunderbolt at the chariot, killing Phaeton. Vulcan fashions a new sun chariot, but Apollo, mourning his son, refuses to drive. The earth is plunged into darkness until he relents.

Like Icarus and Bellerophon, Phaeton illustrates the dangers of *hubris.* Alain Moreau elegantly designates these myths as "presumptuous anabasis," ascension doomed to failure. Ronsard uses the myth of Phaeton to condemn arrogance in his political texts, as does Montaigne.[38] However, as Moreau observes, when Ronsard uses presumptuous anabasis in love lyrics, "the sign is inversed: condemnation becomes praise." To aim too high in love warrants a glorious fall. "Ambivalence? Contradiction? No doubt, but after all a contradiction shared by Pindar, one of Ronsard's masters," notes Moreau (72-3).[39]

In l'Aubespine's response, the explicit reference to Phaeton only appears in the second part of her poem, foreshadowed by allusions in the first part. She acknowledges that Ronsard's praise is important to her because he is the "French Apollo" (7). The first image of l'Aubespine's poem consists of "flame and love" with which Ronsard "lights the night of [her] writings" (1-2): the flame (of the sun) and paternal love are also Apollo's gifts to Phaeton. L'Aubespine continues by saying that her *"esprit"* (mind, wit, intellect, talents) "dragged low," but Ronsard's praise makes her "treasure myself, please and value myself" (3). Her *esprit* "presumes to fly to the skies, if [Ronsard] favors it" (6). This trajectory also recalls Phaeton's adventure. Then, l'Aubespine implores: "o divine Ronsard, help in my undertaking" (7), "without you, in vain would I dare" (8). She reveals the meaning of her allusions (Apollo, flames, and flight into the sky) in the opening of the first tercet. She speaks of her newfound audacity that makes her "like Phaeton" (9). "O my Apollo," she says, "I call myself your daughter" (10), her only reference to her sex. Like Phaeton, l'Aubespine asks Ronsard/Apollo for "a gift, the proof of your love" (11). Ronsard, whose "glory [is] brighter than day," is now supposed to "show [her] the way," again recalling Apollo, who gave the reins of the sun chariot to Phaeton:

Monstre moy le chemin et la sente incongnue
Par qui tant de lumière en la France est venue
Et qui rend ton renom plus luysant que le Jour.

Show me the way and the unknown path
Through which so much light came into France
And that makes your renown more brilliant than day

(12-14).

Although we only have the last three lines of Ronsard's response ("If you fall"), it is clear from the fragment that Ronsard continues the theme of Phaeton chosen by l'Aubespine. Like Phaeton, by taking on an impossible task, she will achieve immortal glory:

Si vollant vous tombez pour me vouloir trop croire
Au moings vous acquerez pour tombe ceste gloire
Q'une femme a vaincu les plus doctes françois

If, flying, you fall, too willing to believe me,
At least you will have earned this glory for your tomb
That a woman surpassed the most learned French men

(12-14).

The myth of the author co-written for l'Aubespine by herself and Ronsard is twice removed from the "modesty of her sex" *topos*. L'Aubespine and Ronsard do not attempt to prove that she is not an excessively daring female. Instead, they draw on the extreme heroic tradition, not in the tragic sense that characterizes the political uses of presumptuous anabasis, but in the heroic version present in Pindar and exploited by Ronsard in his love lyrics.

When l'Aubespine calls herself Ronsard's "daughter" (10), her emphasis is not on her femaleness, but on her being the Phaeton to Ronsard's Apollo. In turn, for Ronsard, l'Aubespine promises to become a fellow master poet in her own right, whose tomb will proclaim that she "surpassed the most learned French men." No less important is Ronsard's emphasis on *French* men (14), in response to l'Aubespine's acknowledgement that Ronsard, through whom "so much light came into *France*" (13), was the star poet of the Pléiade, the project in national poetics set forth in the *Défense et illustration de la langue française*. The reference to France, initiated by l'Aubespine and emphatically taken up by Ronsard—the word *françois* closes his second sonnet—shows that l'Aubespine constructed herself as the heroic masculine *national* poet, like the members of the Pléiade, and not as an exceptional denizen of the "royaume de Fémynie." As Myriam Maître and Chloé Hogg have most recently shown, women authors including Montaigne's *fille d'alliance* and editor Marie de Gournay, and later Mme de Scudéry in *Clélie*, attempted to define a space for women's writings within the mainstream tradition. L'Aubespine's auto-mythography can be counted among the precursors of that trend.

Ronsard to l'Aubespine. Ronsard, *Œuvres complètes,* vol. 1, 553. Peyron, 4-5. *Chansons,* 25-6.

Madelene, ostez moy ce nom de l'Aubespine,
Et prenez a sa place et Palmes et Lauriers,
Qui croissent sur Parnasse en verdeur les premiers,
Dignes de prendre en vous et tiges et racine.

Chef couronné d'honneur, rare et chaste poitrine,
Où naissent les vertus et les arts à miliers,
Et les dons d'Apollon qui vous sont familiers,
Si bien que rien de vous, que vous-mesme n'est digne,

Je suis en vous voyant heureux et malheureux:
Heureux de voir vos vers, ouvrage genereux:
Et malheureux de voir ma muse qui se couche

Dessous vostre Orient. O saint germe nouveau
De Pallas, prenez cueur: les Soeurs n'ont assez d'eau
Sur le mont d'Helicon pour laver vostre bouche.

L'Aubespine. Sonnet pour Monsieur de Ronsard. BnF ms fr 1718, fo 80r. Peyron, 5. *Chansons,* 27.

Tant de flame et d'amour, dont tu vas allumant
La nuict de mes escriptz que ta muse eternise
Font que je me tiens chere et me plais et me prise
Car je ne puis faillir, suyvant ton Jugement.

Mon Esprit[40] qui devant se trainoit bassement
Pretend voller au ciel si tu le favorise
Donc ô divin Ronsard, ayde a mon entreprise
Je scay bien que sans toy j'ozerois vainement

Ainsy que Phaeton d'une audace nouvelle
Puisque o mon Apollon ta fille je m'apelle
Je te demande un don gaige de ton amour

Monstre moy le chemin et la sente incongnue
Par qui tant de lumière en la France est venue
Et qui rend ton renom plus luysant que le Jour.

Bibliothèque municipale de Lyon ms 745 (Ariosto, *Roland furieux,* cantos 1 and 2)

Paris, BnF ms fr 1662 (epigram on her name)

Paris, BnF ms fr 1663 (Gassot's album, "le tombeau des l'Aubespine")

Paris, BnF ms fr 1718 (lyric poems)

Paris, BnF ms fr 6604 (l'Aubespine's marriage contract)

Paris, BnF ms fr 24320 (Anne Olivier's album; two epigrams by l'Aubespine)

Paris, BnF ms fr 25455 (maréchale de Retz' album; Ariosto, *Roland furieux,* fragment of canto 32)

Paris, Bibliothèque du protestantisme français ms 816-12 (Ovid, *Phyllis to Demophon*)

Turin, Biblioteca Nazionale Universitaria, ms M.IV.12 (lost posthumous volume)

Turin, Biblioteca Nazionale Universitaria, Cons[ultazione] Mss 8 Peyron Franc. (Peyron, Bernardino. *Catalogo dei manoscritti francesi della Biblioteca nazionale di Torino*. Photocopy of a handwritten copy of Peyron's manuscript, made in the 20th c. by par Gino Tamburini. [n.d.]).

Notes

I wish to thank the anonymous Reader at *French Forum,* and the friends and colleagues who had the generosity to pore over my manuscripts concerning l'Aubespine in the last few years: Jim Creech, Elisabeth Hodges, Chloé Hogg. I also want to thank those who discussed l'Aubespine with me and gave brilliant answers to my arcane questions: Jean Céard, Isabelle de Conihout, Wendy Fisher, Philip Ford, Bonnie Krueger, Ann Moss, Pascal Ract-Madoux, Charles Ross, George Satterfield, Janet Smarr, Eliane Viennot, Colette Winn. I also would like to announce a bilingual edition of l'Aubespine's poetic works, forthcoming in 2007 in the Other Voice in Early Modern Europe series from University of Chicago Press, and a critical edition, under review at Honoré Champion Editeur, Paris (both edited by me).

1. I borrow the term "auto-mythography" from Jane Chance's work on Christine de Pisan.

2. Ronsard, *Œuvres complètes,* vol. 1, 553. The sonnet for l'Aubespine was added to *Gayetez* between the epigrams [IX] and [X].

3. Ronsard wrote a poem, now lost, in praise of Catherine Des Roches' *Sincero,* "during his stay with the Villeroys, in Conflans," in September 1575 (Anne R. Larsen in Des Roches, *Les Œuvres,* 30, citing Michel Simonin, *Pierre de Ronsard,* 30); I thank the anonymous Reader at University of Chicago Press for this reference. Ronsard also wrote a poem praising the piety of Anne de Marquets.

4. L'Aubespine, *Chansons de Callianthe,* p. X. Please see the Appendix, below, for the full text of l'Aubespine's and Ronsard's poems.

5. I thank Jean Céard for confirming that, to his knowledge, this fragment is unpublished.

6. Bernardino Peyron, Turin, Biblioteca Nazionale Universitaria Cons[ultazione] Mss 8 Peyron Franc. The discovery of this description confirms Roger Sorg's attribution to l'Aubespine of the poems edited in his 1926 volume (see L'Aubespine), an attribution supported by the great Desportes

scholar Jacques Lavaud, but energetically disputed by Frédéric Lachèvre, who believed the author was Héliette de Vivonne.

7. Turin, Biblioteca Nazionale M.IV.12.

8. Huchon, *Louise Labé.*

9. The *Cabinet,* first published in 1584, is a small prose volume inspired by Stoicism, reprinted five times before l'Aubespine's death, translated into German and Italian (1623), and imitated in English (1612). Winn calls l'Aubespine the "uncertain author" of the *Cabinet.*

10. For genealogies of l'Aubespine and Villeroy, see Père Anselme. For Villeroy's career, see Dickerman and Sutherland.

11. Dickerman, 5; De Conihout and Ract-Madoux, 75.

12. De Conihout and Ract-Madoux, 74-77.

13. De Conihout and Ract-Madoux, 74, citing the description by Villeroy's secretary Jules Gassot, 70.

14. The painting, Musée Carnavalet, Ancien Fonds inv. P. 56 (ca. 1560), and the drawing, Paris, BnF, Cabinet des Estampes, Na22 Réserve boîte 25.

15. Pierre de Ronsard, *Œuvres complètes: Amours diverses,* vol. 1, 439-445. "Le sonnet à Madame de Villeroy," vol. 1, 553. "L'épitaphe de Claude de l'Aubespine," vol. 2, 949. "Le sizain pour les coeurs de Messieurs de l'Aubespine," 2, 949. "A Monsieur de Villeroy" (pièces attribuées, 2, 1277-8; written "at Confians, the 8th of September 1570"). "L'épitaphe de feu Monsr de l'Aubespine" (pièces attribuées, 2, 1277-8). "L'épitaphe de la Barbiche de Mme de Villeroy" (published in *Œuvres,* 1584), 2, 971-2.

16. The elegies form the core of the manuscript album BnF ms fr 1663, calligraphied by Villeroy's secretary Gassot. See Champion and Flèges. Claude III was an important figure at court: "in the summer of 1569, according to the Spanish ambassador, Charles IX 'had no other confidants but the count de Retz and M. de Laubespine'" (De Conihout and Ract-Madoux, 73-4). De Conihout also cites Brantôme (156) who claims a friendship with Claude III and mentions his "love of nobility" and "great beauty" (73).

17. La Croix du Maine mentioned that l'Aubespine composed in prose and verse and singles out her translations of Ovid (La Croix du Maine, 2, 70). Père Jacob mentioned her in his *Bibliothèque des femmes illustres par leurs écrits,* a lost work (Lavaud 1936b, 504). De Coste included her biography in the *Eloges et les vies des Reynes*

. . . (2, p. 219), later published in a shorter version by La Croix in his biographical *Dictionnaire portatif des femmes célèbres* (1769). I want to thank Chloé Hogg for the reference to La Croix. Le Poulchre attributed to l'Aubespine the *Cabinet des saines affections* (Attributed to l'Aubespine, 13-16; La Croix du Maine, 2, p. 70; Le Poulchre, 1597, fo 33). Dampmartin evoked "the meetings and vivacities of Madame de Villeroy" (Dampmartin, fo 27; cited by Lavaud, 1936b, p. 504). L'Estoile and Brantôme provided information on l'Aubespine's liaisons (L'Estoile, 3, 173; 5, 122-23 and 350; Brantôme, 6, 178-179, 183; cited by Lavaud, 1936b, 310-11). L'Estoile also noted her death (May 17, 1596).

18. D'Aubigné included two anecdotes concerning l'Aubespine in the *Avantures du baron de Faeneste* (Lavaud 1936b, 514; d'Aubigné 2, 248 and l'Aubespine 19). Belleau devoted to her "The Eagle Stone Called Aetités" in his cycle *Pierres précieuses* (Lavaud, 1936b, 504; Attributed to l'Aubespine, p. 16-17). Jamyn wrote three quatrains for l'Aubespine, included in the maréchale de Retz' album ("Pour une Magdaleine," cited by Lavaud, 1936b, 503). Bertaut, bishop of Séez (Savoy; 1552-1611), wrote stanzas for l'Aubespine's epitaph (cited in La Croix, 1, 255-56). Abel de Sainte-Marthe (1566-1652), *conseiller d'état,* the eldest son of Scévole, praised her in the "Eloge de la très-illustre Maison de l'Aubespine" (La Coste, 2, 219; La Croix, 1, 255).

19. The liminary poems of *Premières Œuvres* (1573) also included contributions by Germain Vaillant de la Guesle, Grojanus, Nicolas Vauquelin des Yvetaux, François Chouayne and Biard. Chouayne (ca. 1551-1616) was the author of *L'Adieu d'Amynte et de Clorice.* He also contributed liminary poems to collections by Jamyn and Antoine Mathieu de Laval (Lavaud, 1936b, 328-29, n2; on Laval, author of a prose translation of the psalms, see Lavaud, 1936b, 97-98 n4). Biard was an otherwise unknown author (Lavaud 1936b, 97-98). Chouayne and Biard were also among the authors of l'Aubespine's other poetic album, lost since the nineteenth century, last seen by Feuillet de Conches (Conches, 2, 392; Lavaud 1936b, 516).

20. In an introductory chapter to *L'accès de femmes à la culture,* Timmermans summarizes the history of literary salons at the turn of the sixteenth century, highlighting Mathieu-Castellani's revision of the *salon* history (Mathieu-Castellani 214-219). Previous critics placed that originary moment much later, in the 1620s (Mongrédien). Concerning l'Aubespine's place in the *salon* culture in Paris in the 1570s, see Keating, 81-102, and the essays destined for the general public by Ratel and recently by Lazard, 295-97.

21. L'Aubespine had other, less definite connections to Marguerite de Valois. They shared a monogram that the queen used, among others, in her correspondence with a former lover of l'Aubespine, François de Fourquevaux. For the biography of Fourquevaux, see Marguerite de Valois, 183 n2, 271, 424-25, 424 n1, 429-33 and 629-30. I would like to thank Eliane Viennot for her kind response to my questions concerning Fourquevaux. For Marguerite de Valois' use of the monogram MW between two "fermesses" (crossed S), as well as her use of the monogram W, see Marguerite de Valois, pages cited above in reference to Fourquevaux, as well as 39-40, 123, 125, 271, 610, and Hobson and Hobson, 80-81, 109, 115. For the use of the two monograms associated with l'Aubespine, see Lavaud 1936b, 510-11, L'Aubespine, 7-21, and Lachèvre, 1932, 7-27.

22. The two poems appeared in the *Sommaire de tous les recueils des chansons, tant amoureuses, rustiques, que musicales . . .* (Lavaud, 1936b, 509 n2). The 1585 edition of the *Sommaire* printed by Bonfons in Paris also contains the two poems by Desportes and l'Aubespine. It seems to me that these small-format editions imply that Desportes' and l'Aubespine's poems were one of the most popular pieces circulating at the time.

23. Lavaud, 1936b, 509; L'Aubespine, 15.

24. On Fourquevaux, see Marguerite de Valois, 39-40, 424-25, 429-33.

25. The handwritten original of Peyron's *Catalogo dei manoscritti francesi,* of which the 9-page description of the lost l'Aubespine volume is a part, was lost in the fire of 1904, but the library has a handwritten copy of Peyron's notes, by Gino Tamburini, Peyron's successor as the head of the library. Peyron belonged to a distinguished family of *savants* and librarians. Head of the library between 1842-70, Peyron initiated in 1855 a new classification order where French manuscripts were collected in the sections L and M (with some *varia* in P and Q). The section M, where l'Aubespine's manuscript was placed, contained mostly new acquisitions (chiefly gifts from the collection of Cesare Saluzzo focused on military works in French, from the collection of Perrone de St Martino, and a small group of 15th and 16th c. manuscripts whose provenance was not indicated by Peyron). Section M was almost completely destroyed in the 1904 fire (only eleven of 136 volumes in this section, and some pages, including from volumes neighboring l'Aubespine's volume on the shelf, survived). The scholars who

compiled lists of extant and lost French manuscripts after the 1904 fire (most notably,
Wahlgren), had no access to Peyron's *Catalogo
dei manoscritti francesi,* which explains why Sorg
didn't know about l'Aubespine's lost volume
when he published his 1926 edition of her poems.

26. Since we know that Ovid's second epistle, 243
    lines, occupied ff. 58-62 of the lost volume, we
    can estimate that the epistle portion may have
    contained some 1800 lines. If this density was
    similar in the first portion of the manuscript, the
    volume may have contained more than 4500 lines,
    almost ten times more than the volume edited by
    Sorg in 1926.

27. Cioranescu, *L'Arioste en France,* 102.

28. Respectively, Bibliothèque municipale de Lyon
    ms 745 and Paris BnF ms fr 25455 fo 14.

29. I discuss this poem at length in another article,
    currently under review.

30. BnF ms français 1718, fo 38r; L'Aubespine, 34.

31. I thank the anonymous Reader at University of
    Chicago Press for suggesting this translation for
    the poem's title.

32. I discuss this poem at length in another article,
    currently under review.

33. Pontus de Tyard and Amadis Jamyn both authored
    poems on the lute. On the connection between
    Tyard and l'Aubespine, see Eva Kushner, *Pontus
    de Tyard.* I thank the anonymous Reader at the
    PMLA for the reference to Kushner's work. On
    the lute as metaphor for the body, see Karla
    Zecher, "The Gendering of the Lute." I thank
    Charles Ross for this reference.

34. BnF ms français 1718, fo 57r; L'Aubespine, 70.

35. I thank the anonymous Reader at the University
    of Chicago Press for suggesting this translation of
    manche.

36. Juvenal, Sat. 6, l. 125: *et lassata uiris necdum sa-
    tiata recessit.*

37. I thank Chloé Hogg for emphasizing the interest
    and noting the visceral nature of this image.

38. Ronsard, *Remonstrance au peuple françoys*; Mon-
    taigne, "Apologie de Raymond Sebond," in the
    Essays.

39. Moreau cites three love poems by Ronsard that
    use the image of Phaeton and Icarus: *Sonnets pour
    Hélène* II, I (1578), *Sonnets et madrigals pour As-
    trée* I and II (1578) (Moreau, 59 n. 12).

40. In the manuscript, "Jamais mon Esprit," which
    Sorg silently corrects to "Mon esprit."

Works Cited

Adhémar, Jean, and Christine Moulin. "Les portraits
dessinés du XVIe siècle au cabinet des estampes,"
Gazette des Beaux-Arts (September-December 1973).

Anselme, Père. *Histoire généalogique . . . ,* 9 vols.
Paris: [n.p.], 1726-1732, vol. 6.

L'Aubespine, Madeleine de. *Les chansons de Callianthe, fille de Ronsard.* Ed. Roger Sorg. Paris: Léon Pi-
chon, 1926.

Attributed to de l'Aubespine, Madeleine. *Cabinet de
saines affections.* Ed. Colette Winn. Paris, Champion:
2001.

Aubigné, Agrippa de. *Œuvres complètes.* Eds. Eugène
Réaume and F. de Caussade. 6 vols. Paris: A. Lemestre,
1873-1892.

Belleau, Remy. *Œuvres poétiques.* Ed. Guy Demerson.
Paris: Champion, 1995-2003.

Boucher, Jacqueline. *Société et mentalités autour de
Henri III.* 4 vols. Paris: Honoré Champion, 1981; thesis,
Université de Lyon, 1971.

Boucher, Jacqueline. *La cour de Henri III.* (n.p.): Ouest
France Université, 1986.

Brantôme, Pierre de Bourdeille seigneur de. *Œuvres
complètes.* Ed. Ludovic Lalanne. 11 vols. Paris: Veuve
Jules Renouard, 1864-82. Vol. 6, *Grands capitaines,*
1866.

Brooks, Jeanice and Philip Ford, eds. *Poetry and Music
in the French Renaissance: Proceedings of the Sixth
Cambridge Renaissance Colloquium, 5-7 July 1999.*
Cambridge: Cambridge French Colloquia, 2001.

*Le Cabinet satyrique. Première édition complète et
critique, d'après l'édition originale de 1618, augmentée
des éditions suivantes, avec une notice, une bibliogra-
phie, un glossaire, des variantes et des notes.* Ed.
Fernand Fleuret and Louis Perceau. Paris: Librairie du
bon vieux temps, 1924.

Champion, Pierre. *Ronsard et Villeroy: Les sécretaires
du roy et les poètes, d'après le manuscrit français 1663
de la Bibliothèque nationale.* Paris: Champion, 1925.

Chouaine, François. *L'Adieu d'Amynte et de Clorice,
par François Chouayne, sieur de Chambellay, conseiller
du Roy, président au baillage et siège présidial de Chartres.* Chartres: Claude Cottereau, 1610).

Cioranescu, Alexandre. *L'Arioste en France, des origines à la fin du XVIIIe siècle.* 2 vols. Paris: Les Presses
Modernes, 1938.

Conihout, Isabelle de, and Pascal Ract-Madoux. "Ni
Grolier, ni Mahieu: Laubespine." *Bulletin du Bibliophile*
(June 2004): 63-88.

Coste, Hilarion de. *Les Eloges et les vies des Reynes, des princesses, et des dames illustres.* 2 vols. Paris: Cramoisy, 1647.

Dampmartin, Pierre. *Du bon-heur de la Cour, et vraye félicité de l'homme.* Antwerp: François de Nue, 1592.

Desportes, Philippe. *Œuvres de Philippe Desportes.* Ed. Alfred Michiels. Paris: Adolphe Delahays, 1858.

Desportes, Philippe. *Diverses amours et autres œuvres meslées.* Ed. Victor E. Graham. Geneva: Droz, 1963.

Dickerman, Edmund H. *Bellièvre and Villeroy: Power in France under Henry III and Henry IV.* Providence: Brown UP, 1971.

Feuillet de Conches, *Causeries d'un curieux.* 2 vols. Paris: (n.p., n.d.).

Flèges, Amaury. "Le tombeau des l'Aubespine: Autour du manuscrit 1663 de la Bibliothèque Nationale." *La Licorne* 29 (1994): 17-68.

Gassot, Jules. *Sommaire mémorial (souvenirs) de Jules Gassot, secrétaire du roi, 1555-1623, publié . . . par Pierre Champion.* Paris: Champion, 1934.

Hobson, Geoffrey D. and Anthony R. A. Hobson. *Les reliures à la fanfare. Le problème de l'S fermé (SI). Une étude historique et critique de l'art de la reliure en France au XVIe siècle, fixée sur le style à la fanfare et l'usage de l'S fermé. Deuxième édition, augmentée d'un supplément contenant des additions et corrections par Anthony R. A. Hobson.* Amsterdam: Gérard Th. Van Huesden, 1970.

Hogg, Chloé. *Novel Histories and Historical Novels in France, 1654-1700.* Diss. U of Pennsylvania, 2002.

Huchon, Mireille. *Louise Labé, créature de papier.* Geneva: Droz, 2006.

Jamyn, Amadis. *Les œuvres poétiques. Premières poésies et Livre premier.* Ed. Samuel M. Carrington. Geneva: Droz, 1973.

Jamyn, Amadis. *Les œuvres poétiques. Livre II, III et IV (1575).* Ed. Samuel M. Carrington. Geneva: Droz, 1978.

Juvenal (Juvenalis Decimus Junius). *Juvenal and Persius, with an English Translation.* Trnas. George G. Ramsay. Cambridge: Harvard UP, 1940.

Keating, Louis Clark. *Studies on the Literary Salon in France, 1550-1615.* Cambridge: Harvard University Press, 1941.

Kushner, Eva. *Pontus de Tyard et son œuvre poétique.* Paris: Champion, 2001.

Lachèvre, Frédéric. *Poésies de Héliette de Vivonne attribuées à tort à Madeleine de Laubespine sous le titre "Chansons de Callianthe," précédées d'une introduction.* Paris: Librairie Historique Alph. Margraff, 1932.

Lachèvre, Frédéric. *Les Chansons de Calianthe, éditées par M. Sorg, ne sont pas de Madeleine de Laubespine.* (n.p.), 1937.

La Croix, Jean-François de. *Dictionnaire historique portatif des femmes célèbres.* 2 vols. Paris: L. Cellot, 1769.

La Croix du Maine, François Grudé, sieur de. *Les bibliothèques françoises.* Ed. Jean Antoine Rigoley de Juvigny. 6 vols. Paris: Saillant et Nyon, 1772-3.

Lalanne, Ludovic. *Dictionnaire historique de la France.* New York: Burt Franklin, 1877, 1968.

Laval, Antoine Mathieu de. *Paraphrase des pseaumes de David, tant literalle que mystique . . . par Anthoine de Laval, . . .* Paris: Abel Langellier, 1610.

Lavaud, Jacques. *Les imitations de l'Arioste par Philippe Desportes, suivies de poésies inédites ou non recueilles du même auteur.* Paris: Droz, 1936a.

Lavaud, Jacques. *Un poète de cour au temps des derniers Valois: Philippe Desportes (1546-1606).* Paris: Droz, 1936b.

Lavaud, Jacques. "Les dépenses extraordinaires d'un ambassadeur en 1574." *Mélanges offerts à Abel Lefranc . . . 1972.* Genève: Slatkine Reprints, 1936. 418-424.

Lazard, Madeleine. *Les avenues de Fémynie: Les femmes et la Renaissance.* Paris: Fayard, 2001.

Le Poulchre de la Motte Messemé, François. *Le passetemps.* 2nd edition. Paris: Jean le Blanc, 1597.

L'Estoile, Pierre de. *Registre-journal du règne de Henri III.* Eds. Madeleine Lazard and Gilbert Schrenck. 6 vols. Geneva: Droz, 1992-2003.

Maître, Myriam. "Editer, imprimer, publier: quelques stratégies féminines au XVIIe siècle." *Travaux de littérature* 14 (2001):257-76.

Maître, Myriam. "Les 'Belles' et les Belles Lettres: femmes, instances du féminin et nouvelles configurations du savoir." *Le savoir au XVIIe siècle.* Eds. John D. Lyons and Cara Welch. Tübingen, Germany: Narr, 2003. 35-64.

de Valois, Marguerite. *Correspondance, 1569-1614.* Ed. Eliane Viennot. Paris: Champion, 1998.

Mathieu-Castellani, Gisèle. *Les thèmes amoureux dans la poésie française (1570-1600).* Paris: Klincksieck, 1975.

Moreau, Alain. "Ronsard: Variations sur les mythes de l'anabase présomptueuse." *Ronsard et la Grèce: Actes du colloque d'Athènes et de Delphes, 4-7 octobre 1985.* Ed. Kyriaki Christodoulou. Paris: Nizet, 1988. 55-73.

Moulton, Ian Frederick. *Before Pornography: Erotic Writing in Early Modern England.* Oxford: Oxford UP, 2000.

Premier acte du synode nocturne des Tribades, Lemanes, Unelmanes, Propetides à la ruine des biens, vie, et honneur de Calianthe. Guillaume Reboul, 1608.

Ratel, S. "La cour de la reine Marguerite." *Revue du XVIe* s., 11 (1924) 1-29, 193-207, and 12 (1924), 1-43.

Ronsard, Pierre de. *Œuvres complètes.* Eds. Jean Céard, Daniel Ménager and Michel Simonin. 2 vols. Paris: Gallimard, 1993-4.

Sommaire de tous les recueils des chansons, tant amoureuses, rustiques, que musicales. . . . Paris: Nicolas Bonfons, 1576.

Sorg, Roger. "Une fille de Ronsard, la bergère Rozette." *Revue des deux mondes.* (January 1, 1923).

Simonin, Michel. *Pierre de Ronsard.* Paris: Fayard, 1990.

Sutherland, Nicola Mary. *The French Secretaries of State in the Age of Catherine de Medici.* London: U of London, Athlone Press, 1962.

Timmermans, Linda. *L'accès de femmes à la culture (1598-1715): Un débat d'idées de Saint François de Salles à la Marquise de Lambert.* Paris: Champion, 1993.

Tombeau de feu monsieur m. François Chouayne, escuyer, sieur de Chamblay, conseiller du Roy, Maistre des requestes ordinaire de la Reyne Mère, president et lieutenant general au baillage et siege presidial de Chartres, et auparavant conseiller de Sa Majesté en son grand Conseil et en son Eschiquier d'Alençon (Chartres: Claude Cottereau, 1616).

Zecher, Karla. "The Gendering of the Lute in Sixteenth-century French Love Poetry," *Renaissance Quarterly* 53 (2000): 769-791.

Lance K. Donaldson-Evans (essay date 2007)

SOURCE: Donaldson-Evans, Lance K. "Ronsard's *Folies Bergéres*: The *Livret des Folastries* and Petrarch." *Neophilologus* 91 (2007): 1-17.

[*In the following essay, Donaldson-Evans examines Ronsard's* Folastries, *a volume of poetry the critic describes as "Ronsard's most anti-Petrarchan text."*]

Whether or not Ronsard played any role in the elaboration or composition of Du Bellay's *Deffence et illustration de la langue françoyse,* as has sometimes been suggested, he certainly subscribed to its basic theses. One of the great paradoxes of the *Deffence* is that, although it recommends the renewal of French verse by an "imitation" of the poetry of Greek and Latin antiquity, Du Bellay in fact opts for an "imitation" of Petrarch in his very first poetic work, the *Olive,* the first version of which appeared soon after the publication of the *Deffence* in 1549. For all his apparent revolutionary ardor, Du Bellay chose a safe and well-trodden path to inaugurate his career as a poet, the *Olive*'s principal innovation being the choice of the sonnet as its poetic unit.[1]

In many ways, Ronsard was much more radical than Du Bellay in his adoption of the new poetics which the *Deffence* announced. Promising in the preface to his *Odes* nothing less than a "stile apart, sens apart, euvre apart,"[2] he delivers on this vow by going back to the poets of antiquity and providing a credible and original French rewriting of a poetic form perfected by Greek and Latin poets. Indeed one of the many striking features of the *Odes* is not merely their poetic quality, but the sheer variety of tone and subject, ranging from the serious and erudite Pindaric-style odes to the light and frothy versions of the Anacreontic and Horatian corpus. This poetic stance of Ronsard was no doubt a way of marking his distance from his cousin Du Bellay,[3] but at the same time it enabled him to show his independence from the Petrarchan, or neo-Petrarchan tradition which had already gripped France.

Two years later however, Ronsard was forced to capitulate to the prevailing mode in his *Amours,* since his *Odes* had not brought him the fame and glory he hoped, Ronsard knew Petrarch's verse well and he has used many of the images and tropes which derive from Petrarch in the *Amours* of 1552, as generations of Ronsard critics have shown. It is interesting to note, however, that whereas Du Bellay took not only Petrarch but above all Petrarch's Italian imitators as his inspiration, Ronsard more often went directly to Petrarch himself. Sara Sturm-Maddox, who in her excellent study *Ronsard, Petrarch and the «Amours»,*[4] reminds us that Olivier de Magny bestowed the title of "Pétrarque Vandomois" on Ronsard, illuminates Ronsard's many borrowings from his Tuscan predecessor. Yet Ronsard, while conforming to the letter of Petrarch's text in many cases, in fact subverted the whole Petrarchan enterprise by resolutely removing any Christian or indeed any spiritual content from his sonnets, by insisting on the physical aspects of love (although there are some neoplatonic elements in the *Amours*), and by adding a plethora of references to classical antiquity and to Greek and Roman mythology.[5] This last practice we certainly find in Scève, but in the *Rime* of Petrarch himself, mythological references are much more sparse than in Ronsard's love poetry. It is also significant that whereas Scève and Du Bellay chose the Beloved's name as title of their respective works, Ronsard chose a title which evokes Ovid rather than Petrarch,[6] and indeed the name of the woman who is the object of his love, Cassandra, recalls Homer, Greek antiquity and the epic rather than a lyric form like the sonnet.

This subversion of the Petrarchan model is already in evidence graphically in the two engraved portraits which form the frontispiece of the 1552 edition. One represents Ronsard, crowned with a laurel wreath, the usual attribute of the poet, but quite possibly a sly reference to Petrarch for whom the laurel was the emblematic plant for Laura. The other portrait depicts Cassandra, whose *décolletage* is particularly revealing. Indeed her bare bosom suggests pictorially at the outset of the work the sensuality and sexuality which set Ronsard's poetry apart from that of Petrarch and from most of the latter's French imitators.

However, Ronsard's most anti-Petrarchan text, even though it does not overtly present itself as such, is one of his least studied works, the curious *Livret de folastries* which appeared anonymously in 1553, 1 month before the 1553 edition of the *Amours,* and printed by the same publisher, La Veuve Maurice de la Porte. This collection has recently been analyzed provocatively by Catharine Randall,[7] David Dorais[8] and Cathy Yandell[9] who see in it respectively an early form of pornography, an example of neo-pagan eroticism (following Laumonier's description of Ronsard and his fellow poets as "pagan"), and an investigation of the ambiguity which underlies the notion of virility in Ronsard's verse.

All of these interpretations have merit. Certainly, as Catharine Randall has noted, the work was "not adequately 'politically correct'" in Ronsard's time. Indeed its detractors (and they were many) wanted the book to be burned publicly, and it was officially censured (and censored) by the Parlement of Paris. However, curiously, critics have failed to address the question of why Ronsard chose to write such a work. André Gendre, editor of one of the few modern versions of this poetic collection,[10] sees it as a return to the Marotic tradition ("Voici Ronsard bien près de renouer [. . .] avec l'école marotique qu'il avait dédaignée," p. 13) and there are certainly echoes of the "veine gauloise" of earlier poetry, both that of Marot and the Middle Ages. However, what is striking is the strange juxtaposition of popular erotic poetry, as much in the "fabliaux" as in the Marotic tradition, with imitations of the Greek dithyramb and translations of Greek epigrammes.

I would like to suggest that the composition and publication of the *Folastries* is a bold affirmation of the more subtle, covert anti-Petrarchism one encounters in the *Amours.* The fact that the work was published anonymously does not weaken this hypothesis, since everyone knew who the author was (just as nobody was deceived by the nom de plume adopted by Rabelais when he published his *Pantagruel*) and since in any case Ronsard incorporated most of the original pieces of the *Livret* into subsequent editions of his work.[11] While the *anonymat* afforded the poet some protection against direct attack by the Royal authorities (although not from the Parlement), it did not spare him the criticism of some of his friends and colleagues who felt that the work was unworthy of him.[12] However, the fact that Ronsard discarded definitively only one of the original pieces shows that he was not willing to renounce paternity of this unruly offspring.

The title of the work is important. Firstly, "Livret" evokes the lightness of tone that obtains whenever Ronsard uses diminutives. However, "lightness" does not necessarily mean that the poems in question are of little importance, since Ronsard can also use this stylistic element for serious matters, as we see in the epitaph, he wrote for himself:

> Amelette Ronsardelette,
> Mignonnelette doucelette,
> Treschere hostesse de mon corps,
> Tu descens là bas foiblette,
> Pasle, maigrelette, seulette
> Dans le froid Royaume des mors.[13]

Secondly, while the use of the word "folastries" suggests playfulness, it is also often associated with sexual and erotic activities and brings to mind the "fol amour" which, in the works of Marot and Scève, is usually contrasted with the much more desirable "ferme amour," a concept which, interestingly enough, is quite foreign to Ronsard's poetry.

The *Livret* is dedicated to "Janot Parisien," in all likelihood Jean-Antoine de Baïf whose second book of *Amours* had appeared in 1552 and whom Ronsard praises for having appreciated the "vers raillars" of his own "amours."[14] What is surprising in Ronsard's dedicatory poem is the shift in tone that follows line 16. Written in the low style one would expect from the title, the introductory section finishes as follows:

> Pource, mon Janot, je te livre
> Ce qui est de gay dans ce livre,
> Ce qui est de mignardelet
> Dedans ce livre nouvelet

> (ll. 13-16)

However, when he arrives at the second part of this poem, Ronsard adopts an elevated style as a sign that the work to follow may be *gay* but it is not frivolous. He thus introduces the reader to the dual nature of the *Folastries* which contain poetry inspired both by the French tradition (in particular the *gaulois* tradition), and also by Ancient Greek verse:

> Livre que les sœurs Thespiennes,
> Dessus les rives Pympléennes,
> Ravi, me firent concevoir,
> Quand jeune garson j'allay voir
> Le brisement de leur cadance
> Et Apollon le guidedance.

> (ll. 17-22).

In much the same way as the works of Rabelais, the *Folastries* are therefore destined for the serious and learned reader, their apparently popular component notwithstanding.

The first *Folastrie* shows its anti-Petrarchan stance not only by its low style—it is heptasyllabic like some of Ronsard's lighter odes and is in rhymed couplets—but by its direct and sensual approach. This is in sharp contrast to the last lines of the opening sonnet of Petrarch's *Rime,* where everything that pleases in this world is described as simply a passing dream ("e 'l pentersi, e 'l conoscer chiaramente / che quanto piace al mondo è breve sogno"[15]). Ronsard immediately shows himself to be much more interested in the material world, which for him is no mere dream. Indeed he is entranced with his lady's "grasset enbonpoint" rather than with her spiritual qualities. Could it be coincidence that he claims to love this "pucelette grasselette" more than he loves his heart or his eyes (a traditional hyperbole, it is true), when both these parts of the body are mentioned in Petrarch's second sonnet ("era la mia virtute al *cor* ristretta / per far ivi e negli *occhi* sue difese . . ."; "My virtue had withdrawn to my heart to set up there and in my eyes its defenses [against Love]"). Ronsard seems to provide an ironic echo to these typically Petrarchan lines when he writes

> Qu'éperdument j'ayme mieux
> Que mon cœur, ny que mes yeux

words which become become, with slight variations, a refrain for this song-like poem.

The fact that, in this first *Folastrie,* Ronsard's persona is torn between two women can also be seen as a repudiation of Petrarch's unwavering love for Laura, one of the dominant themes of Petrarchan poetry, which is echoed by Marot and Scève in the notion "ferme Amour."[16] The poem assumes the form of a *débat* as to the relative merits of the "pucelette maigrelette" and the "pucelette grasselette," merits which are spelled out in graphic physical detail. The protagonist of the poem permits himself to engage in all sorts of liberties, as he caresses

> Or le bel yvoire blanc
> De sa cuisse rondelette,
> Or sa grosse motelette
> Où les doux troupeaux ailez
> Des freres enquarquelez
> Dix mille fleches decochent . . .

> (ll. 78-83).

What is incongruous here is the ironic coupling of very explicit physical description with the delicate mythological reference to hosts of little Cupids who hover over the lady's body like the *putti* of an Italian Renaissance painting.

That Ronsard is concerned only with sensual love becomes even more obvious when he turns to the "maigre pucelette" whose bony frame diminishes the pleasure of sexual intimacy in an age when a certain corpulence was sometimes considered to be sexually desirable (although this is certainly not apparent in the female bodies depicted by painters of the Fontainebleau school):

> Si bien, que quand je la perse
> Je sen les dentz d'une herse,
> J'enten mill' ossetz cornus
> Qui me blessent les flancs nus.

> (ll. 111-114).

Once again, the language is crude and indeed this representation of the woman evokes the specter of the *vagina dentata,* that terrifying representation of the *femme castratrice.* Ronsard's emaciated Beloved is, fortunately, possessed of musical talents which compensate for her lack of corpulence and which, appropriately enough, charm the poet's heart:

> Mais en lieu de beautez telles
> Elle en ha bien de plus belles,
> Un chant qui ravit mon cœur,
> Et qui dedans moy vainqueur,
> Toutes mes veines attise:

> (ll. 115-119)

After this curious declaration of love to two different women, the poem's persona adopts a tone of reproach, since in the past 2 or 3 months he has only once had the opportunity to dally with the "estomac grasselet" and the "sein maigrelet" of his mistresses. Nonetheless, in a final flourish, Ronsard, in a parody of the oaths of constancy sworn by Petrarchan lovers, finishes his poem by listing all the obstacles he is willing to overcome in order to remain constant to *both* his Beloveds. The vehement tone created by the anaphora *Ny*[17]—used in 12 of the 14 lines to specify the obstacles to his passion—is subverted by the disparate nature of the obstacles themselves, in a list where "violence de Mort" is juxtaposed with "maris menaçans," the "préchemens des meres" with "dangers perilleux." The tone is mock heroic and represents an ironic subversion of this common Petrarchan theme.

The second *Folastrie* is of quite a different order, since it has a political dimension, lauding Henri II's victory over the Emperor Charles V at Metz, Toul and Verdun in 1552. However, it is also a parody of the type of war song associated with the Greek schoolmaster, Tyrtaeus, who was sent to Sparta and rallied the Spartans in the war of Messenia.[18] The poem, purportedly written during the truce that followed Henri's victory, qualifies as a "folastrie" since it focusses, not on the war and its political aftermath, but on *la chasse à la femme.* Here, the "pucelette grasselette" and the "maigrelette" to whom he had sworn fidelity in the preceding poem are forgotten, to be replaced by yet another young woman, a further renunciation of Petrarchan constancy. The temporary cessation of war has had a deleterious effect on the protagonist's amorous designs, since the truce has meant the return of the Beloved's brothers, who were fighting as soldiers in the royal army. This has, ironically, caused an involuntary truce in his own attempted conquest. While her brothers were at war, he was

> Mieux fortuné que les Roys
> De la plus fertile Asie
>
> (ll. 2-3).

Since their return, he is

> . . . plus malheureux
> Qu'un Empereur de l'Asie,
> De qui la terre est saisie
>
> (ll 14-16)

The mock-heroic comparisons, Petrarchan-like in their hyperbole, if not their intent, suggest the parallels between the war in which the soldiers are engaged and the protagonist's own battle for his lady's favors. The poem even goes so far as to engage in a mock patriotic entreaty, encouraging the two soldiers who are spoiling his chances in love to do their duty to King and country and return to war:

> Donc, si quelque honneur vous point,
> Soldars, ne cagnardez point,
> Suivez le train de voz Peres
> Et raportez à voz Meres
> Double honneur et double bien.
> Sans vous je garderay bien . . .
> Secourez la fleur de lis . . .
>
> (ll. 77-81; 85)

This highly egotistical call to arms is placed under the ægis of Bacchus, invoked as the soldiers' protector several times in the poem. Such an invocation transforms the poem from war-song into drinking song, since Bacchus replaces Mars, the usual patron of soldiers. In this parodic transformation, Ronsard depicts the traditional thyrsus of Bacchus as a lance, and Bacchus as a carousing warrior, using this transposition to suggest the propensity of soldiers for excessive drinking:

> Ainsi le vineux Denys
> Le bon Bacchus portelance
> Soit tousjours votre defence.
>
> (ll. 86-88).

However successful this poem may be as a parody of the war song, it would be reductive to assume that it is *merely* tongue-in-cheek. In fact, it has two important functions, one practical, the other structural. In the first place, it serves to ingratiate the poet with the King whose support will be needed if the *Folastries* antagonize the public; in the second, it introduces the theme of Bacchus and his revelries, a theme which will be taken up later in the text, and which stands in stark contrast to the languid sufferings endured by the typical Petrarchan lover.

Folastrie **III,** subsequently moved to the *Gayetz,* is a misogynistic poem somewhat reminiscent of the *Blason du laid tetin* of Clément Marot. Here it is quite obvious that the woman's body is, as Catharine Randall has stated, "a commodity, an object appropriated to fulfil Ronsard's own purposes."[19] This poem criticizes the behavior of a woman named Catin, and notwithstanding the fact that modern editions of the *Folastries* note simply that "Catin" is a diminutive of "Catherine," the name was already being used in its later sense of "prostitute" or "loose woman" by Marot as early as 1547. Given the nature of the poem, this word most probably has a pejorative sense, particularly since this "Catin" is the caricature of the promiscuous woman we find in many Renaissance texts, her activities being described in appropriately lewd language. Perhaps more akin to the loose woman than to the prostitute, since she accepts no remuneration for her sexual favors, she appears to be ruled by her inordinate sexual desire and exemplifies the type of female behavior Dr. Rondibilis describes in his diatribe against women in Chapter 32 of the *Tiers Livre.*[20]

Ronsard's description is very explicit:

> Ceste Catin en sa jeunesse
> Fut si nayve de simplesse,
> Qu'autant le pauvre luy plaisoit
> Comme le riche, et ne faisoit
> Le soubresaut pour l'avarice,
> Mais ell' disoit que c'estoit vice
> De prendre, ou cheine, ou diamant,
> De pauvre, ny de riche amant,
> Pourveu qu'il servist bien en chambre,
> Et qu'il eust plus d'un pié de membre.
>
> (ll. 17-26).

Whereas in most of the other *folastries* we are confronted with simple obscenity, here we approach pornography, with its exaggerated representations of sexual activity and the genital organs. Yet Catin, despite her willingness to have intercourse with any available male (provided he meets her physical criteria!) is presented as someone who evokes revulsion rather than desire:

> Tel bouc sortoit de ses esselles,
> Et tel parfum de ses mammelles,
> Qu'un mont Liban ensafrané
> En est esté bien embrené.
>
> (ll. 13-16)

Here the female body is not the idealized object of worship we find in he Petrarchan tradition, but rather the grotesque and repugnant body depicted by Marot in his anti-blason *Du laid Tetin,* a body from which foul odors emanate and which is associated with excrement ("bien embrené").

Given the usually highly sexual nature of Ronsard's portrayal of women, we are at first puzzled by his supremely unflattering representation of Catin. However, when he describes her present state as that of an older woman, who, because she has lost all appeal for the opposite sex, has become "une bigote," we begin to understand, and the links to Marot's poem become even more apparent. Ronsard is in fact penning a revenge poem, because Catin has managed to persuade the young woman, on whom the poem's protagonist dotes, to embrace religion instead of carnal love. This results in extreme sexual frustration for the male protagonist, frustration that Ronsard does not hesitate to express in the crudest possible terms:

> Ainsi depuis une semeine,
> La longue roydeur de ma veine
> Pourneant rouge et bien enpoint
> Bat ma chemise et mon proupoint,
> Qu'à cent diables soit la prestresse
> Qui a bigotté ma maistresse

> (ll. 151-156)

Thus, in the final analysis, the poem is not strictly pornographic, since pornography is about performance, whereas this piece describes frustration and non-performance. The only performance involved is that of the poet, who uses poetry for vengeance and presumably personal satisfaction.

The fourth *Folastrie* is much more rustic in tone and setting and thus recalls the *pastourelle* and the *fabliau.* Once again, the style is unadorned and the narrative simple: Jaquet and Robine are two peasants who find themselves together in the countryside in winter, and build a fire to keep warm. The cold also whets their appetite, another transparent symbol, and they sit before the fire to partake of the food they have brought with them. The peasant smocks they wear are apparently hitched up, for, as they eat before the fire, each one notices and admires the sexual organs of the other. The description of Robine's attributes is a curious mixture of crudity and refinement, with the traditional rose imagery linking the rather raw sexuality of the lines to a more courtly tradition, although this tradition is subverted by the lewd language used by the poet:

> Comme il [Jaquet] repaissoit, il a veu,
> Guignant par le travers du feu,
> De sa Robine recourssée
> La grosse motte retroussée
> Et son petit cas barbelu

> D'un or jaunement crespelu,
> Dont le fond sembloit une rose
> Non encor' à demy déclose

> (ll. 59-66).

Robine in turn notices Jaquart's attributes[21] and, inflamed with desire, she invites him to make love to her in the most direct of language:

> Je te pry, Jaquet, jauche moy
> Et metz le grand pau que je voy
> Dedans le rond de ma fossette

> (ll. 81-83).

We are far removed from the delicate discourse of the Petrarchan lover here, both with respect to the prelude and the aftermath, for, having yielded spontaneously to their passion, the lovers are now both sated, happy and unremorseful. Love here is purely physical and natural, untainted by guilt, and the poem expresses the direct sensuality of the *gauloise* tradition, in contradistinction to the refinement and sublimated desire of Petrarch.

Folastrie **V** recalls **III** in that it too is a malediction called down upon another obstacle to the love of the poem's persona, a malediction upon another traitor like Catin. However, here the culprit is a hapless dog, who, like Catin, is described in the most unflattering of terms. More sophisticated than the previous pastoral poem, this *folastrie* contains a number of mythological and learned references. In the style of the Pindaric odes, Ronsard recalls the Golden Age when dogs were faithful and Zeus ("l'enfant de Rhée" in the poem) had not yet overthrown Chronos. The traditional canine virtue evoked here does not however belong to the dog to which this poem is addressed. This particular animal is cursed as a "chien de mechante race," which, instead of guarding the door of the bedroom in which the poet's persona and his beloved are cavorting, barks incessantly and arouses the suspicions of friends, family and neighbors, thus bringing shame and criticism upon the lovers.

In order to punish this disloyal action, Ronsard invokes, *a contrario,* the poet's traditional power to immortalize the people and objects described in his poetry. Usually, this strategy is used by Ronsard to overcome the resistance of a lady to his advances and is offered as a reward for compliance. Here, it becomes a means of punishment, for not only will this particular dog not be placed among the stars (that is, immortalized in poetry for his fidelity) like Orion's faithful companion, but he will become instead an eternal object of shame and derision despite a physical beauty worthy of being immortalized:

> Mais en lieu d'une gloire telle
> Une demangeante gratelle,
> Une fourmilliere de poux,

Un camp de puces et de loups,
La rage, le farcin, la taigne,
Un dogue afamé de Bretaigne,
Jusque aux oz te puissent manger

(ll. 49-55).

Of course, given the similarities between the vilification of the dog (which recalls by its actions the spies of courtly love poetry), and that of Catin in the previous poem, it becomes quite obvious that this *folastrie* is also a warning to any woman who might spurn the poet, for she risks the same fate as the dog in this *folastrie,* that of being the object of eternal scorn and ridicule instead of enjoying the favorable immortalization that the poet is able to confer on those about whom he writes.

The next **Folastrie (VI)** addresses, not a faithless dog, but a 3-year-old child, envied because he (or she) has a desirable wet nurse. Once again, the poem shows a decidedly anti-Petrarchan character in its earthy sensuality. The child, still at the breast, inspires in the protagonist dreams of an equivalent intimacy, all the more so since the nurse has apparently resisted his advances.

Although this poem shares with **Folastrie IV** a down-to-earth, peasant-like sensuality, it differs from the earlier poem in its references to classical antiquity. The allusion to *les ars Medeans* in this excerpt presupposes a learned reader, as does the mythological reference to Venus' pursuit of Adonis which closes the poem. This juxtaposition of erudite allusions with low style is yet another example of Ronsard's anti-Petrarchan agenda.

The pains of love are again the subject in the **Folastrie VII,** but this eminently Petrarchan subject is treated in a thoroughly non-Petrarchan manner. Here, the non-Petrarchan elements do not come from the poem's sensuality but from its espousal of Classical rather than Italian models. In the opening lines of the poem, Ronsard salutes Homer, and presents him in accordance with typical Renaissance imagery as an old man inspired by the fruit of the vine and living a joyously Sybaritic life.

Tu voulois dire, bon Homere,
Que l'on doit faire bonne chere
Tandis que l'âge, et la saison
Et la peu maistrese raison,
Permetent à nostre jeunesse,
Les libertez de la liesse,
Sans avoir soin du lendemain:

(ll. 21-27)

The theme of *carpe diem* that inspires these lines soon disappears as the poem takes an elegiac turn when the onset of winter is evoked, symbolizing the unrequited love that Ronsard's protagonist is enduring. However, in conformity with the opening lines of the poem, wine again becomes an antidote to melancholy:

Verse, page, et reverse encor,
Il me plaist de noyer ma peine
Au fond de ceste tasse pleine

(ll. 60-62).

Ronsard proceeds to suggest yet another remedy for the pangs of love: poetry itself. Significantly, the inspiration for this poetry will come, not from Petrarch, who does not even merit a mention, but from Catullus, Tibullus and Marullus. This allusion to the *fureur poétique* inspired by writers of Antiquity is followed immediately in the poem by a reference to another sort of *fureur,* as Ronsard returns again to the theme of wine. This time, he treats the subject in a more elevated manner, invoking Bacchic *furor,* one of the four Platonic furors leading to enlightenment. However, he can conjure up the carefree joy of poetic inspiration and become a worshiper of Bacchus only if this furor is strong enough to overcome the pangs of love. Only then will the protagonist become a true disciple and be able to perform adequately in Bacchic revelry, as the prayer contained in the poem's closing lines makes clear:

Ce n'est pas moy, las! ce n'est pas,
Qui dedaigne suivre tes pas
Et couvert de lierre brére
Par la Thrace Evan, pourveu pere,
Las! pourveu pere, las! pourveu
Que ta flamme esteigne le feu
Qu'amour, de ses rouges tenailles
Me tournasse dans les antrailles.

(ll. 83-90).

The last **Folastrie (VIII)** takes up the Bacchanalian theme evoked at the end of the previous poem. However, here, the protagonist is not a *je parlant* but a third-person character named Thenot. According to Laumonier's note reprised by Gendre (p. 277, note 2), this was the stock name given to the typical drunken soldier, who here becomes inebriated in the course of celebrating the Feast of Saint Martin. Attempting to sleep off his drunkenness, Thenot looks up at the sky and in his stupor sees in the clouds a parade of monsters, human, semi-human and animal, worthy of some of the bizarre creations of the painter Bosch:

Voicy deux nuages tous plains
De Mores, qui n'ont point de mains
Ny de corps, et ont les visages
Semblables à des chatz sauvages:
Les uns portent des piedz de chevre,
Et les autres n'ont qu'une levre . . .

(ll. 53-58)

This series of bizarre hallucinations in which Bacchus plays an active role culminates in two final visions, first of a forest where Thenot sees "cent mille Satyreaux" chasing "mille Naiades," and then of the dance of the "Dryades" who bathe in the stream. As he watches the changing cloud formations, the intoxicated soldier is frightened by a crack of thunder which he interprets as punishment from heaven. In his drunken stupor, he believes he has been struck by lightning, a belief underlined by the onomatopoeia of lines 117, 118 and 120:

> Bré bré bré bré, voici le foudre
> Craq craq craq, n'oyez-vous decoudre
> Le ventre d'un nuau? J'ay veu
> J'ay veu, craq, craq j'ay veu le feu,
> J'ay veu l'orage, et le Tonnerre
> Tout mort me brise contre terre.

> (ll. 117-122).

This series of eight poems ends with the derisive portrait of a fool who had imbibed Bacchus's potion. Significantly, the poem's only erotic content is the brief description of the woodland activities of Satyrs, Naiades and Dryades. Its ironic conclusion notwithstanding, perhaps the message of this poem is that Bacchus's *furor* can be a catalyst for the generation of fantastic images and a source of poetic inspiration, even in the befuddled brain of a drunken soldier.[22]

A reading of these eight *folastries* leads us to a broader understanding of the significance of their title. "Fol-" suggests not simply the notion of frivolity and of *fol amour,* both abundantly illustrated in many of the poems, but also the wine-induced *folie* of Thenot, which although ultimately treated ironically and comically, reminds us of the divine folly of the poet. Creating fantastic images out of insubstantial words for the pleasure and edification of his readers, he, like the hapless Thenot, may remain thunderstruck after expending his creative efforts. The title can also be read as an ironic and somewhat self-deprecating commentary on the travail and artistic suffering the poet must endure in order to create his poems, poems which some dismiss as insubstantial and fantastical.

The second part of the **Livret** contains more surprises, because, in addition to a change of tone, the reader discovers that the focus of the work has changed from the *folie* engendered by love to the productive madness associated with the divine mysteries of Bacchus, and the art of poetic creation. The link between the two parts comes from the last of the *folastries* and its evocation of Bacchus and drunkenness. The first poem of the second part, entitled **Dithyrambes,** presents Bacchus in his more serious role of God of religious mysteries and initiations. Here, the *furor* of Bacchus is given particular prominence because it is represented in high style. Moreover, the description evokes the neo-pagan revelries in which Ronsard and his fellow poets of the Brigade were said to indulge in order to celebrate the performance of Jodelle's Greek style tragedy, *Cléopâtre captive.*

In this poem, the *je parlant* appears to be under the influence of something much more powerful than simple drunkenness. He is "Tout ravy d'esprit," to the point that "[Il] forcene", (he acts like a crazed man), as he describes his Bacchanalian revels and participates in the secret mysteries and rituals associated with Dionysos. It is significant that this praise of the Greek God adopts the style of many of Ronsard's odes and that its subject is both a description of the rites and an extended eulogy of the god himself. The numerous mythological references and the many words formed in imitation of the Greek ("un Thyrse *portelierre*" for example) solidify the link with antiquity. Even the chorus which evokes the refrain of the Bacchantes: "Iach ïach Evoé / Evoé ïach ïach," and the irregular versification and choppy rhythm of the poem suggest the wild cavortings of the bacchanalian worshippers. What is particularly interesting about this long piece[23] is that the *je parlant* of the poem is identified towards the end of the poem as Jodelle, and not as Ronsard, and that Ronsard is mentioned in the third person in line 138, causing some critics to doubt his authorship of the poem. However, the notion of lending one's poetic voice to someone else was a common practice at the time, and this could well have been Ronsard's way of participating in the glory Jodelle received for his tragedy, by showing his remarkably detailed knowledge of Greek mythology, and by attributing his poetry to the playwright himself. The fact that this was by far the longest piece in the **Livret** (396 lines) and that it contains no references to erotic love and no *gauloiseries,* underlines its importance, while stressing the Greek vein of inspiration which runs through the **Livret** as a whole. While not overtly anti-Petrarchan, this poem affirms the primacy of the Grecian muse in Ronsard's poetry and is a covert repudiation of the Italianate tradition.

The next section of the **Livret** confirms the central role of classical Greek poetry in this text. It consists of a series of translations from various Greek epigrammes, some in a moralistic vein offering advice or consolation in the face of life's vicissitudes, others in a satirical mode. However, lest the reader forget that we are dealing with a collection of poems entitled **Folastries,** the two final poems, both *sonnets-blasons,* return to the erotic and obscene dimension of the text.

The first one, reminiscent of the Bacchanalian poems encountered earlier, sings the praises of the male member in suitably pornographic terms:

> Lance au bout d'or, qui sais et poindre et oindre
> De qui jamais la roideur ne defaut . . .

> (ll. 1-2)

The companion piece is, appropriately, a blason on the female pudenda, also presented as a Goddess to be worshiped by her admirers and praised in a way which is somewhat blasphemous since the locution "Je te salue . . ." echoes the *incipit* of the *Ave Maria*:

> Je te salue, ô vermeillette fante,
> Qui vivement entre ces flancs reluis:
> Je te salue, o bienheuré pertuis,
> Qui rens ma vie heureusement contante
>
> (ll. 1-4).

Since the sonnet is discretely entitled L.M.F (for "la motte féminine"), we are in fact returned to the ambiance of the first *folastrie* where, among other attributes "la grosse motelette" of the "Pucelette grasselette" had been singled out for special praise in line 80. The wheel has come full circle and the **Folastries** have run the gamut from crude, sexually explicit, often misogynistic pieces to imitations of both low and high style Greek and Roman poetry only to return to the *gauloiserie* of the earlier poems. However, whether the style of the individual poems in this collection be high or low, each marks its distance from the Petrarchan tradition. By their suppression of the Petrarchan intertext, the **Folastries** express Ronsard's fundamental rebellion both against the title "French Petrarch" which was bestowed upon him, and against the tyranny of the Petrarchan mode in general. Boldly proclaiming the pre-eminence of Greek and Latin poetry as the appropriate models for the rejuvenation of French poetry, the **Folastries** may well be Ronsard's most subversive collection, calling into question the prevailing poetic practice of his contemporaries.

Notes

1. Scève had used the *dizain* in his *Délie* and indeed the sonnet was little used in France before the publication of Du Bellay's sonnet cycle.

2. "Au lecteur" in Ronsard's *Œuvres complètes* (Bibliothèque de la Pléiade, Paris: Gallimard, 1993, vol I, p. 995). Unless otherwise indicated, all quotations from Ronsard come from this edition, which will be referred to simply as *OC* henceforward.

3. In a recent article, the late Gérard Defaux has reminded us that a rivalry (perhaps more strongly felt by Ronsard) existed between the two poets despite the laudatory poems each wrote about the other's works (see "«Moy ton Poëte, ayant premier osé . . . »: Du Bellay, Ronsard et l'Envie" in *Cité des hommes, Cité de Dieu: travaux sur la littérature de la Renaissance en l'honneur de Daniel Ménager* Geneva: Droz, 2003, pp. 197-205. See also the article of Henri Weber "Quand Ronsard

veut rivaliser avec Du Bellay" in *Les Amours (1552-1553) de Ronsard,* ed. Gisèle Mathieu-Castellani, Paris, Cahiers Textuels, 1998, pp. 11-24.

4. Sara Sturm-Maddox. *Ronsard, Petrarch, and the «Amours»* Gainesville: UP of Florida, 1999.

5. It is interesting to note that the 1552 edition of the *Amours* contains the first version of the Fifth Book of the *Odes,* a clear sign that Ronsard still considered Greek and Latin poetry to be pre-eminent.

6. While Petrarch gave the generic name *Rime* to his work, in the minds of his readers it was always associated with the single female name, Laura.

7. "Poetic License, Censorship and the Unrestrained Self: Ronsard's *Livret de folastries* in *Papers in French Seventeenth Century Literature,* XXIII, 45, 1966, pp. 449-462.

8. "«Les Païens de la Pléiade»: l'érotisme dans les *Folastries* de Ronsard et dans les *Gayetez* d'Olivier de Magny" in *Renaissance and Reformation,* XXIII, 3 (1999), pp. 65-79.

9. "Rhetoric and virility in Ronsard's *Folastries,*" to appear in *Masculinities in the French Renaissance,* ed. Philip Ford. Cambridge: Cambridge French Colloquia, forthcoming.

10. *Ronsard: «Les Amours»,* ed. André Gendre, Paris: Livre de poche classique, 1993. The otherwise excellent *OC* do not reproduce the *Folastries* as a complete work. All quotations of the *Folastries* are therefore taken from Gendre's edition.

11. The only pieces which were not transferred, in some form or another, to subsequent *recueils* were the last of the actual *folastries* (VIII), the *Dithyrambes à la pompe du Bouc d'E. Jodelle poëte Tragicq,* two translations of Greek epigrammes (10 and 13 both entitled "De Nicarche") and the two final pornographic sonnets-blasons in praise of the male and female sexual organs, respectively. One can speculate that *Folastrie VIII* was abandoned because its principal purpose was to serve as a transition between the two parts of the collection (see *OC,* vol II, p. 1461). The *Dithyrambes* was most likely suppressed because of the charges of paganism which the celebration of the performance of Jodelle's tragedy elicited, while the two epigramme translations were of minor importance. As for the two sonnets, Ronsard apparently decided they were too dangerously lascivious to be recycled in a later collection.

12. See Gendre, p. 14.

13. Ronsard, *OC,* II, 1105, ll. 1-6.

14. Gendre, p. 245, l. 4 and 6.

15. Franceso Petrarca. *Rime,* ed Guido Bezzola, Milano: Rizzoli, 1998, p. 89.

16. On this score, Ronsard later castigates Petrarch, suggesting that he was either a fool to have courted Laura for 30 years without receiving any physical satisfaction, or he was simply a lair. See "Elégie à son livre", ll 33-51 in *OC,* t. I, pp. 168-169. I cannot agree with André Gendre's contention that "La réaction antipétrarquiste de Ronsard n'est qu'un épisode." "Pierre de Ronsard" in *Les Poètes français de la Renaissance et Pétrarque,* ed. Jean Balsamo, Geneva: Droz, 2004, p. 244.

17. *Ny* suggests, ironically, denial and also parodies the opening line of Petrarch's sonnet 312: "Né per sereno ciel ir vaghe stelle . . .".

18. Ronsard, Pléiade edition, II. 1538.

19. Catharine Randall, "Poetic License, Censorship and unrestrained Self: Ronsard's *Livret de folastries,*" p. 450.

20. "Quand je diz femme, je diz un sexe tant fragil, tant variable, tant muable, tant inconstant et tant imperfaict, que Nature me semble . . . s'estre esguarée de [son] bon sens . . .". Rabelais, *Œuvres complètes,* ed. Guy Demerson, Paris: Seuil, 1973, p. 490.

21. It should be noted that women wore no underclothes, apart from the *chemise,* until the 19th century, since underpants were considered to be male clothing. Moreover, paintings from the period indicate that male peasants did not always wear underpants beneath their smocks. Hence what may appear to be gratuitous obscenity to the modern reader is referentially accurate. See Ann Hollander, *Seeing Through Clothes,* Berkeley: U. of California, 1993, p. 159 ff.

22. See the introduction of André Gendre's edition (pp. 40-49) for a valuable analysis of the role of Bacchus in the *Folastries.*

23. Ronsard reworked parts of this poem for his later "Hymne de Bacchus," in which he portrayed the Roman God, not merely as a fun-loving, drunken reveler, but as a serious deity whose inspiration was one of the paths leading to superior knowledge and wisdom.

Tom Conley (essay date 2007)

SOURCE: Conley, Tom. "Ronsard on Speed: 'Ciel, air, & vens . . . .'" In *In Memory of Elaine Marks: Life Writing, Writing Death,* edited by Richard E. Goodkin, pp. 147-62. Madison, Wis.: University of Wisconsin Press, 2007.

[*In the following essay, Conley examines Ronsard's treatment of geographical space in* Amours.]

PLACES WRITING LIVES

For Elaine Marks literature was, as went the last line of Baudelaire's translation of the artist's last words in Poe's "Oval Portrait," *la vie elle-même.* Literature was life itself: Elaine Marks invented the vital spaces of her days and years by living her reading. To live was to write, and to write was to feel and touch the fragile beauty of the world in which we live. When she stared at the gelid surface of Lake Mendota in the middle of winter, its expanse of ice and snow extending from the south toward Picnic Point and the distant northern shores beyond, she saw the landscape through the words of Mallarmé's sonnet, "Le vierge, le vivace, et le bel aujourd'hui" [The virginal, the lively, and the beautiful today]. When, years later it seemed, spring came to Madison in the month of May, only days after the melting of Mendota's waters, she would gleefully quote Victor Hugo's "Le Satyre" to tell us that the sudden change was indeed "La palpitation sauvage du printemps" [The wild throbbing of spring]. When, time and again in Paris, she turned from the Boulevard Saint-Germain, the wide avenue on which she had been strutting with the ghosts of Jean-Paul Sartre and Marguerite Duras, and then meandered down the rue des Saints-Pères, she often passed by the Bibliothèque de l'Histoire du Protestantisme. There she was suddenly transported back to the Wars of Religion and trembled in her memory of Ronsard's *Discours,* the polemical rhapsodies that turned a poet-lover into an indomitable warrior, and that made her think twice about the meaning of *engagement* for the existential writer. And as she continued along the street, going by the Bibliothèque de l'Ecole des Ponts et Chaussées, she imagined herself rolling on the roads that engineers built for the carriages that took Voltaire and Rousseau to and from Paris and the Jura mountains along the northwestern border of Switzerland.

Elaine was a pilgrim for whom literature was a breviary, a love, and a geography. Life-writing, one of the themes of this volume, can be understood to include the spaces and places people invent in their sentient lives through their animated and vibrant commitment to literature. Requiring extensive training and years of labor spent in libraries, the commitment is rewarded by unforeseen epiphanies that take place when the poetry one loves, that one carries neither in books heaped in a satchel or backpack nor in the memory seen on the screen of a laptop, ripples through our bodies. The poem and the body meld into the impressions of the place one happens to be passing. These moments and sites in which we find ourselves lost, possessed by poetry, cannot be monitored or controlled. They are not the privilege of the literary tourist or the historian of poetic conventions. They bring the life-writer to an enthralling edge where what matters is a sudden and intense, immediate and compelling capture and release of the body in space and words. The life-writer often feels the moments and sites over and over again, in an invigorating continuum of repetition and difference, in which variation meshes with memory, reiteration, and reinvention.

In her address that celebrated the end of her tenure as president of the Modern Language Association, Elaine Marks dared to avow that a certain number of poems had determined her life. The students in her courses on poetry—the author of this essay among them—knew well that Poe and Valéry were pole stars in her travels and navigations. Readers of *French Poetry from Baudelaire to the Present,* an anthology that Elaine edited and that formed generations of students of literature, knew that Apollinaire, Saint-John Perse, Desnos, Ponge, Jacottet, Bonnefoy, and Char figured in her pantheon of modern masters. Until that speech few were aware that her life had been written, too, by poets of earlier and more obscure ages, which reached back to the Troubadours but were especially marked by the bards who fashioned new lyrics during the growth of print culture. Included were the Villon of the poem that Clément Marot called "La Ballade des femmes du temps jadis" [Ballad of the women of former times] and the Ronsard of the *Amours,* especially the sonnets attesting to the speed of life passing so rapidly that the names applied to the topoi associated with life's ephemeral nature, *carpe diem* and *ubi sunt,* seemed to be (as they still and always are) light years away from the body that feels the impact of passage and of loss. Elaine admired the seductive poet who forever begged his coy mistress to come with him to see a rose unfolding its delicate petals in the warm light of dawn. She loved no less the flower— "Comme sur la branche au moys de mai la rose" [As on the branch in the month of May the rose]—battered in rain and cold and withering on the very branch of its line. At the end of her life she gaily, even laughingly anticipated how she would be "sous la terre et fantôme sans os" [under the earth and a ghost without bones], becoming for those who knew her a fleeting incarnation of poems with which she brought to us, her children, the writings of our lives.

In what follows, in homage to the memory of Elaine Marks, I should like to see how Ronsard might have been an embodiment of the life-writer whose poems invent spaces and become lives in and unto themselves, in other words, objects that, as we read and carry them in our lives, become events we relive and sustain when we think about them wherever we are; when, over and again, with fabulous variation, we read and teach them to ourselves and to our kin. The stakes are to see how the poem turns what is given in a neutral and geographical way as a place, a place-name, a toponym—*lieu-dit,* a common place, or a topos—into a site in which we get lost within the writing of the poem. Life-writing begins when the geography represented in the poem becomes a lyrical space in which the very character of

the writing co-extends with its field of reference. When the geography of the poem overtakes its own toponyms, and when the latter—which we continue to know insofar as they are referring to real places—turn into these enthralling edges of new registers of experience, we are, all of a sudden, captives of life-writing.

OF EARTH AND BEINGS

Such is what Ronsard offers in what seems to be a textbook sample of a simple *sonnet rapporté,* a poem designed to put forward in its first two quatrains the elements of what will be brought back in an accelerated enumeration in the final tercet.[1] Ronsard's variant on the model treats of places dear to the author, of his own origin. The sonnet appeared in the first (1552) and second (1553) edition of the ***Amours***:

> Ciel, air, & vens, plains, & mons decouvers,
> Tertres fourchus, & forets verdoiantes,
> Rivages tors, & sources ondoiantes,
> Taillis rasés, & vous bocages vers,
>   Antres moussus à demifront ouvers,
> Prés, boutons, fleurs, & herbes rousoiantes,
> Coutaus vineus, & plages blondoiantes,
> Gâtine, Loir, & vous mes tristes vers:
>   Puis qu'au partir, rongé de soin & d'ire,
> A ce bel œil, l'Adieu je n'ai seu dire,
> Qui pres & loin me detient en émoi:
>   Je vous suppli, Ciel, air, vens, mons, & plaines,
> Taillis, forest, rivages & fontaines,
> Antres, prés, fleurs, dites le lui pour moi.[2]

> [Sky, air, and winds, plains and uncovered mountains,
> Forked hillocks, and flourishing forests,
> Twined shorelines and wavy springs,
> Pruned thickets and you green groves,
>   Mossy lairs half-open to the air,
> Meadows, buds, flowers, and bedewed grasses,
> Winey slopes, and flaxen flatlands,
> Gâtine, Loir, and you my sad verses:
>   Upon my departure, gnawed by worry and ire,
> To this lovely eye, I knew not how to say farewell,
> Which near and far holds me in thrall:
>   I beg you, Sky, air, winds, mountains and plains,
> Thickets, forests, shores and fountains,
> Lairs, meadows, flowers, say it to her for me.]

The poem stages a scene of separation, known well in modern literature running from Montaigne to Proust or in a critical canon from Lacan to Barthes, in which the voice of the text writes of the almost originary pain and trauma of breakage by which the speaker tells how he or she is awakened into subjectivity. For the author of the *Essais,* the separation from Rome, Paris, and his friend Etienne de la Boétie, three nourishing beings, leads the writer to make antiquity no different from the recent memories of his frightful separation from his father.[3] For Marcel of *A la recherche du temps perdu* the event of being torn from the landscape is devastating but vital to a reparative and generous act of writing.[4] Following the lead of Montaigne, Lacan tells us that the handsome fragility of our lives is affirmed when we realize that *séparer* is the same as *se parer,* that to be separated is tantamount to being decorated.[5] Roland Barthes reminds us that we rehearse the event of birth into life when we wave goodbye to our friends who waft kisses to us from the windows of the trains that leave the platforms of the railway stations on which we stand immobile.

Ronsard is no different. "Puis qu'au partir, rongé de soin et d'ire," he says, expressing angry confusion over his lover's departure, avowing that he is unable to look straight in the eye of the object of his affections when he bids her adieu. He cannot find the words to say good-bye to an unnamed lover (who goes by Cassandre elsewhere in the collection) but replaces them with an unparalleled motion of writing that seems to accelerate as it goes. Ronsard is on speed. It comes with the words that follow in the final tercet after an arrest, suspension, and mystic rapture by an image, a moment of self-mir-roring—the writing of the poem itself—*qui pres & loin me detient en émoi.*

In what might be one of the first critical editions of French literature, in his gloss of the sonnets, songs, and odes of the **Amours,** Marc-Antoine Muret sums up the poem in few words, unlike what he does elsewhere in copious commentary on the sources, vocabulary, and mythic personages inspiring many of the other poems. He merely states that the poet is "contraint quelque fois de prendre congé de sa dame, & n'aiant pas le pouvoir de lui dire Adieu, il prie, toutes les choses qu'il voit, de le lui dire en son nom" [sometimes constrained to take leave of his lady, and not having the power to bid her farewell, he begs all the things he sees to bid her farewell in his name].[6] For Muret the implied psycho-drama of separation prompts an appeal on the part of the poet to have the things the poet *sees* in his midst *speak* in his place. Ronsard, he implies, can animate the world about him by naming it but cannot find the words fitting for separation. Muret indirectly avows that the elements the poet sees in the field of his gaze, except for the *bel oeil* of the beloved that leaves him speech-less, will, if they respond to his entreaty, release speech, yield emotive meaning, and, ultimately, speak for him on his behalf.

The poet finds *other* words, the names that describe his *terroir,* to inspire the world to say what he cannot. He hopes that the fragments he discerns in a landscape will speak silently and graphically, like hieroglyphs, in the absence of his voice. The self, the *moi,* is evacuated when it begins to move and multiply, growing out of emotion, *émoi.* The self dissolves into the words depict-ing the landscape that he takes to be both his own—it is marked by toponyms he has known from his earliest childhood—and belonging to an overriding Nature that

in other poems he fills with mythic creatures reaching back to antiquity.[7] What is at stake for the poet is hav-ing the words that could be marshaled to describe any landscape apply to himself and his own milieu. The substantives become the raw matter of a topography, that of Ronsard's Gâtine and Loir (1. 8), the place-names that figure near the visual axis of the poem.

On first glace "mons decouvers," "tertres fourchus," "forets verdoiantes," "rivages tors," "sources on-doiantes," "taillis rasés," "bocages vers," "antres mous-sus," "herbes rousoiantes," "coutaux vineux," and "plages blondoiantes"—all formulas coined to motivate the elements of a landscape by attaching an ostensively natural and appropriate adjective to the substantive—figure in an idiolect that here and elsewhere in the **Amours** reattaches the signature of the poet to the world from which he shows that he is separated. But, prior to being identified on a map of the Touraine, are mountains always "uncovered"? Are hillocks forever "forked"? It is a fact that forests are "flourishing"? Do shorelines find themselves "twined"? Are thickets "pruned"? Groves "green"? Lairs "mossy"? Grasses "bedewed"? Slopes "winey"? Flatlands "flaxen"?[8] If they are not, or if the descriptives attached to the nouns are of a signature of his own, the landscape will have spoken for the poet *before* he asks them to do so in the name of his beloved. Thus the poem will have responded to the question before it is posed.

It can be said that the formulas are Ronsard's insofar as the sonnet betrays the dilemma of being separated from itself and its author, located anywhere and everywhere in the world at large, and belonging to a topography that might and might not be rooted in the place where the poet situates it. In current manuals of cosmography the first sentences of Ptolemy's *Geographia* were il-lustrated by a similitude that compared the construction of a world map to the portrait of a human being and a landscape or city-view to any of its isolated details. A French translation of Pieter Apian's *Cosmographie,* published two years before the first edition of Ron-sard's **Amours,** asserts,

> La consummation & fin de la Geographie est constituée au regard de toute la rondeur de la terre, a l'exemple de ceulx qui veulent entierement paindre la teste d'une personne avec ses proportions. Chorographie . . . est aussi appellée Topographie, elle considere seulement aucuns lieux ou places particulieres en soy-mesmes, sans avoir entre eulx quelque comparaison ou sem-blance a l'environnement de la terre. Car elle demon-stre toutes les choses, & a peu pres les moindres en iceulx lieux contenues, comme sont villes, portz de mer, peuples, pays, cours des rivieres, & plusieurs au-tres choses, comme edifices, maisons, tours, & autres choses semblables. Et la fin d'icelle s'accomplit en fai-sant la similitude d'aucuns lieux particuliers, comme si un painctre vouloit contrefaire, un seul œil, ou une or-eille.[9]

[The achievement and end of Geography is constituted in regard to the earth's entire fullness, following the example of those who wish to paint in its entirety the head of a person with its proportions. Chorography . . . is also called Topography, it only considers various places with their own peculiarities, without establishing among them any comparison or similarity to the earth as a whole. For it demonstrates all things, even, nearly, the smallest contained in these places, as are cities, seaports, populations, countries, courses of rivers, and several other things, like buildings, houses, towers, and other like things. And it accomplishes its goal by creating a likeness of various particular places, as if a painter wished to picture a single eye, or an ear.]

Between the sentence defining the ends of geography and those of topography, Apian inserts a rectangular woodcut, containing two spheres of equal radius. Within the circle on the left, below a printed title outside of the frame stating that the projection is "La Geographie," is an image of the world seen from north (bottom) to south (top). On a *mer oceane* float Europe, Asia, and Africa (dominated by the image of the Nile and three tributaries), Taprobana, and even Antarctica. Within the circle on the right, below the printed title "La similitude d'icelle" [The similitude of Geography] is a portrait of a man in profile, who strangely resembles contemporary images of Christ, who looks to the left and seems to be contemplating the world map on the other side of the frame. Below the paragraph describing the ends of topography is another, slightly longer rectangle, in which almost three-quarters of the space encloses a view of a city built upon an island floating on water. It is identified as "La Chorographie." To the right, on the other side of a vertical line that marks the left-hand edge of the remaining space of the image, is an ear (above) and an eye (below), the latter apparently looking at the city-view to its left.[10]

Located in the construction is not so much the relation of cosmography to the art of the portrait—or of topography to details contained in either of the encompassing parts of the images—as the reign of confusion implied by the drawing, one in which it would be impossible to attach parts to a whole, if indeed a whole there be. The world map is seen as a cut or a fragment taken from what is greater than what is framed, while the portrait to the right is autonomous if, say, it were taken to resemble a figure struck on a medallion. The city seen in the view occupies the sum of the island that is shown and thus floats without any mooring. The same can be said of the eye and ear that become islands or even, if they are studied for their erotic ridges and folds, "mossy lairs" that have no analogues in the portrait of the man next to the world map. In both the text and the image of Apian's similitude it is averred that no "comparison or similarity to the earth as a whole" can be seen in "various places with their own peculiarities." The construction of the text and image beguiles the reader and spectator to construct analogy where it is shown to be tenuous and even unlikely, even if, at the same time, its effectiveness as a memory-image is indelible. Like a poem, the similitude does things other than what it states it is doing.

It bears directly on the life-writing of Ronsard's sonnet. The incipit, graced by a majuscule C (shown again, in the twelfth line, when *Ciel* returns in the second enumeration) forms an open totality, an open O, that implies a sum of things infinite, a centurial ideal. The sky of the incipit stands over what the rest of the line distinguishes as pieces and parts—air, wind, plains, mountains—of the world below or adjacent to it. The enumeration leads to the presence of concealed worlds and of revealed landscapes, that is, of details of a picture that may or may not bear on a totality in the self-contained world or topographic picture given by the greater form of the sonnet: *mons decouvers* [uncovered mountains] reads in the graphic matter as might an accidental line of mountains visible on a horizon, but its homonym in the vocal register, *mondes couvers* [covered worlds], signals that entire geographies, greater wholes, might be hidden in the words that follow. Mountains shown to be uncovered reveal greater worlds covered. The spacing of the letters and words mobilizes the image they make of a landscape as it might be drawn or engraved in a woodcut.

In turn, the mimetic register of the sonnet is transformed into the vital drive of writing. The "forked" hillock is split when the referent is seen through the word both as a knoll cut in half by a depressed line and as divided into two equal parts that mirror each other (*ter-tres*) and anticipate the image of the "fo*r*ets ve*r*doian*tes*," while the echo of "worlds" in the opening line can only make the earth, or *terre,* emerge from the incipit of the second line. The *forets* splitting out of *four*chus would be branches ramifying from what, in Ronsard's typical idiolect, would be an apical origin, a site of division and growth that thrusts forward. The bending shorelines seem vagabond, and the springs at the origins of the waters (*ondoiantes*) of the rivers shimmer and flow before they reach their name. Pruning the trees in the thickets seems to generate groves that are poems in themselves, *bocages vers* [green groves / verse groves], that give rise to fabulously erotic sites, frothy and mossy lairs whose openings dilate and pulsate in the midst of flora, moistened with fluids of desire, and that redden and blush.

The origin and effect of the landscape are found in the strange combination of *coutaus vineus,* hillsides cut by the veined lines of rivulets in the flesh of the countryside or else, too, slopes cultivated with grapevines that ramify no less than the branches and rivers figured just above. *Coutaus* would also be the pruning shears or the knives the laborers use to cut and manage the stocks, branches, and tendrils of the vines. Or, too, they might be the burins and blades that incise woodblocks on which the scenes are printed and reproduced. If so, they qualify as an image, common to woodcut illustrations of landscapes in the 1550s, of a stylized sign, based on the transformation of a drawing of a stock into a graphic figure, a process by which a mimetic form turns into a stenographic mark, a *festina lente,* a sort of ampersand of the kind that marks the sonnet twelve times. The description contains the image of a miniature flourish of straight and curved lines approximating the vine and its support.[11] The fields that seem to whiten in the sunshine, *plages blondoiantes,* require Muret to note that the adjective Ronsard has coined to describe the undulating landscape merely means "covered with already ripened wheat," in other words, stalks bearing tips and seeds that promise procreation and production.

The elements of the description, ten couples of substantives and adjectives, converge toward the toponyms *Gâtine* and *Loir* on the left side of the eighth line—a border, an edge, even a boundary in the scheme of quatrains and tercets marked by the indentations of their incipits—and on the right, before the narration of the sonnet begins, the poet appeals to (or even interpellates) his own poetry: *vous mes tristes vers.* These verbal couples, each a detail that comprises the general and a local character of the landscape, move in rapid enumeration toward the place-names located near the center of the virtual map of the poem. They are no sooner assimilated into "you my sad verses" than the region is metamorphosed into the poet's own tropes. The formula inverts an order that had become routine in the first seven lines of the exposition. For the first time the poem puts, like a cart before a horse, a modifier in front of what it modifies. The reversal in the pattern of the enumeration is all the more striking, in view of the dazzling combinations and the speed of their exposition, than it would be if *mes tristes vers* were taken at face value, which would suggest the idea of poetry malformed, maladroit, or of melancholic bent. Nor does the expression yield signs of affected modesty unless, of course, antithesis or irony might be implied as a ruse, a way of beguiling the reader through the radiance and glory of the enumeration that leads to a falsely disparaging description of the verse.

The landscape becomes the poet's property at the turning point of the poem. The region is transformed into the verse itself, and the implied reader who is captured by the poet (*vous mes . . .* , or "you my . . .") also falls under the spell of his lines *(vers).*[12] At the juncture of the second quatrain and the first tercet it is not clear if the story he tells about his inability to bid adieu to his beloved is addressed to a reader, to himself and his own verse, to the landscape, or to everything and everyone at large. In the second tercet he now begs twelve elements—not listed in the order they had been enumerated in the quatrains above—to listen to the poem which has confined them. The first four (*ciel, air, vens, mons*) reiterate the gist of the incipit. *Tertres* gives way to *plaines; taillis* jumps ahead in the list, in place of *rivages* (that now soon follows) and *sources* becomes *fontaines.*

Bocages is left aside, possibly because the image is already suggested by *taillis* and *forets,* or perhaps because "bocages vers" had already signaled the totality of the sonnets themselves in the forest of **Les Amours.** Implied is the suggestive allusion to a grove of trees as a poem, indeed as a sonnet, marked off and drawn according to the way its squarish shape as a block of words on a page might resemble the sight on a map of a grove of trees in a greater pasture of rolling hills or flatlands.[13] Surely the formula at the end of the first quatrain anticipates the "vers" or the poem itself as it is announced at the end of the second. But the *bocage* can also be a unit of cultivated land and language somewhere between "poetry" and a "poem," analogous to "geography" and "topography" in Ptolemy and in Apian's emblematic memory-image.

This is all the more true if the reader keeps in mind one of Ronsard's comparisons of verse to field and forest, taken from the preface to his posthumous complete works of 1587:

> Poëme et Poësie ont grande difference.
> Poësie est un pré de diverse apparence,
> Orgueilleux de ses biens, et riche de ses fleurs,
> Diapré, peinturé de cent mille couleurs,
> Qui fournist de bouquets les amantes Pucelles,
> Et de vivres les camps des Abeilles nouvelles.
> Poëme est une fleur, ou comme en des Forés
> Un seul Chesne, un seul Orme, un Sapin, un Cyprès,
> Qu'un nerveux Charpentier tourne en courbes charrues,
> Ou en carreaux voutez des navires ventrues,
> Pour aller voir auprès de Thetis les dangers
> Et les bords enrichis des biens des estrangers.[14]

> [Poem and Poetry have a great difference.
> Poetry is a meadow of varied mien,
> Proud of its possessions, and rich with its flowers,
> Mottled, painted with a hundred thousand colors,
> It provides bouquets to virginal lovers,
> And feeds the swarms of new Bees.
> Poem is a flower, or, as in Forests
> A single Oak, a single Elm, a Fir, a Cypress,
> That a wiry Carpenter turns into curved plows,
> Or the arched planks of stout ships,
> To go visit the dangers in Thetis's realm
> And the shores enriched by foreigners' goods.]

Here, akin to the Saussurian linguist's distinction between speech *(parole)* and language *(langue),* a poem is an instantiation, a not-so-arbitrary tree that can be cut and fashioned for strategic ends, while poetry is inferred to be a commanding forest of many species from which a given type can be cut, drawn, and fashioned according to the will of the poet. The grove would be a collection or a single volume of poems that the author cultivates by cutting, planting, pruning, and shearing.[15] In respect to Ronsard's figure of the forest that serves to theorize his poetry, the sonnet certifies that "vous bocages vers" becomes "vous mes tristes vers" and that the one formula and the other indeed do dissolve into the movement of the accelerating enumeration of the last tercet.

The cornerstone or defining edge of the poem is *moi,* the last word, the keystone that responds first to *émoi* just above, stabilizing the expression of distress in line eleven and also arching back to *Ciel* at the opposite side of the poem. In the same fashion *decouvers,* the end of the first line, corresponds to *antres,* the substantive that marks the beginning of the last line. If these words are considered plot points in the cartography of the poem, they can also, given the gusts of air that seem to blow across the text, be compared to wind roses or even wind heads that allow the reader to look upon the text from each of its four cardinal angles.[16] The sky is at the top before the text gives way to worlds and mountains, then to the landscape, before ending with the immanence and transcendence of the *moi.* And *antres* would be a tiny entry, a lair into which the eye can peer to see the poem whose greater sum is anticipated in *mons decou*vers.[17]

The reader is invited to see the landscape-sonnet from different angles but also, at the same time, to feel the wind of its inspiration. A dilemma for the poet and painter of the Renaissance has always centered on how to represent wind. A painting could simulate movement only through effects of shading and slight distortions brought to vegetation. Leonardo da Vinci noted that boughs of trees and leaves needed to be bent in an atmosphere where "clouds of fine dust [are] mingled with the troubled air."[18] For the poet, the task was less evident. How could writing embody movement where words would otherwise only refer to atmospheric turmoil? Ronsard responds to the challenge by deploying at least two graphic strategies. In the italic font of the first two editions of the **Amours,** the letters seem to be pushed over and to bend back under the thrust of a force that pushes them down.[19] "Ciel, air & vens" is especially effective because the poem begins with convection and winds that blow over the landscape. The aeolian thrust of the words pushes the reader ahead.

And so also do the ampersands that stud the poem as they do no other piece in all of the **Amours** of 1553. The ampersand is in a cascade. The reader sees "air, & vens," "plains, & mons," "fourchus, & forets," "tors, & sources," "rasés, & vous," "fleurs, & herbes," "vineus, & plages," "Loir, & vous," "soin & d'ire," "pres & loin," "mons, & plaines," and "rivages & fontaines."

Each is part of a construction implementing graphic signs that seem to belong to a speed-writing, an elegant stenography in which a typographic letter takes the shape of a *festina lente,* a form in which a single letter ties the serpentine flow of a curved line to the straight and anchored aspect of an orthogonal trait. Everywhere the sonnet "makes haste slowly." The ampersand signals how the poem changes speed, driving forward under the propulsion of wind from the left, but also slowing down or being tempered by the comma stops set in front of each of the first eight inscriptions. The ampersand appears to cut the poem in half in the middle area (11. 2-4 and 7-8, after the fourth syllable, and 1. 1, after the third and sixth syllable), to give the appearance of a separation and division that exists within the poem, before the same letter scatters in the tercets.

Throughout the poem the ampersand suggests that its printed writing belongs to the arts of furrowing, grafting, cutting, incising, and drawing that are coordinated with both respiration of the poet and the rhythms of his body with the world at large. The rhythm is nonetheless predominantly visual, graphed according to spacings and intersections of letters and words. If indeed the sonnet is composed as a picture according to perspectival composition and thus, as might an emblematic image, marks a vanishing point within and among its signs, it would emerge among the ampersands between either—or both—*cousteaus vineus* and *plages blondoiantes* (1. 7) and *Gâtine, Loir* and *vous mes tristes vers* (1. 8).[20] In this way the sign figures in a visual rhetoric that centers the interest of the poem on its own geography. The poetic space of the sonnet is made visible where the verbal and visual tensions originate from each of the four angles at the corners of the poem. The point of intersection of the imaginary diagonals that begin and end at the corners would be the site of an enigma set at once in a central area at or about their crossing. The ampersand is seen in this zone and, furthermore, it seems to be inscribed elsewhere over the greater landscape of vocables.

Where the ampersand suggests that the poem is based on an additive composition, of endless movement, *et + et + et . . . ,* arrested only by the confines of the rectangular form, *Gâtine* and *Loir* anchor the text in a topography given by their reiteration in other poems and, perhaps, the memory of the way the place-names are attached both to cartographic representations and to the milieu itself. A sense of locale is underscored by similar formulas in ambient poems ("o coutaux plantureus" [sonnet 55], "antres & prés, & vous foréts" [sonnet 63], etc.), such that "Ciel, air & vens" merely links together, for an instant, a number of the elements that comprise an open totality.

The poem can be read as a piece of life-writing to the degree that it plots a poetic geography both in the stakes of the writer's life and times and, no less, in its construction of a lived space that is at once the poem and its vital biological relation to the poet, that is, to Ronsard as we imagine him through our own rapport with his strange language and deceptively familiar geography. It is known that Ronsard and his cohorts of the Pléiade "sought to bring classical culture to France as a way of increasing their own cultural capital."[21] They could advance themselves, historians write, by attaching themselves to a *terroir* that would become part of their own merit and signature. In the same line of reasoning, Ronsard affirms a national cause with universal claims through the welter of figures that tie the topography of local character and landscape to a geographic whole, to a world that will soon be seen both in atlases and in the poet's future tomb, a folio edition of his *œuvres complètes*.

Yet, despite what would seem to be the geographic investment in Ronsard's aims to curry favor at the French court and to plant himself in a pantheon of poets born in France and descending from the likes of Pindar and Virgil, in the **Amours** we cannot fail to imagine the topography of the author's Gâtine and Loir through the kind of life-writing that Elaine Marks embodied and personified for her readers and students. Ronsard represents and invents space in his lyric as no poet had ever done. He speeds over and about it in ways that tell us how we, too, produce and foster the illusions we need in order to feel we belong to the world about us. In her teachings and writing about poetry, Elaine Marks did for our generation what Ronsard had done for his legions of readers, which include our teacher, a fervent admirer of the **Amours,** whose words and memory are graven in the landscapes of our lives.

Notes

1. Ronsard here displays a model for other users. The most remarkable *sonnet rapporté* in the production of the Pléiade may indeed be Etienne Jodelle's "Myrrhe brusloit jadis d'une flamme enragée," in his *Contr-amours,* as François Rigolot notes well in *Poésie et Renaissance,* 220-21. Christofle de Beaujeu engineers an extraordinary inversion of the form in "Ganymède, Uranie, Io, Laède, Léandre," in Gisèle Mathieu-Castellani's edited collection, *Anthologie de la poésie amoureuse de l'âge baroque,* 73-74.

   The heading for this section is taken from the observation of Proust's older narrator in *Combray,* who, in casting a backward look at his childhood, notes: "la terre et les êtres, je ne les séparais pas" [earth and beings, I did not separate them] (*A la recherche du temps perdu* 1:155).

2. Buzon and Martin, eds., *Ronsard & Muret, Les Amours, leurs Commentaires,* 99 (translation mine). Based on the *Amours* of 1553, this edition

includes both the poems and the commentary supplied by the humanist Marc-Antoine de Muret. The poem can be downloaded in the original typography of the 1553 edition from the "Gallica" website of the Bibliothèque Nationale de France, http://gallica.bnf.fr/ (last consulted June 12, 2006). See also Henri Weber and Catherine Weber's critical edition of Ronsard, *Les Amours,* 43, 534. They speculate that the poem is inspired by the movement of Astemio Bevilacqua's sonnet "Herbe felici et prato aventuroso."

3. "Nous remplissions mieux et estandions la possession de la vie en nous separant," writes Montaigne in the *Essais,* 977 (while the presence of the father is noted on 996).

4. The older narrator of *Combray* fathoms his past, castigating himself by noting, "Et la terre et les êtres, je ne les séparais pas." Again, for Proust's elderly narrator reminiscing about Combray, life itself was the illusion of the land and not the separation from it. In his past life the narrator would have wished to meld with the *terroir* of his youth in loving any of its representative peasants, thus being charged with "cet émoi nouveau" [this new excitement] that made the landscape and beings look all the more desirable to him (*A la recherche du temps perdu* 1:154).

5. Montaigne's words on self-styling are in "De l'exercitation" (*Essais,* 378-79).

6. In Buzon and Martin, *Ronsard & Muret,* 99.

7. Rigolot, in *Poésie et Renaissance,* notes that "le paysage du Vendômois natal offre aussi ses prés, ses vignobles et ses antres sauvages. Les chênes et les lauriers n'y sont plus de froids emblèmes mais retrouvent la verdeur 'naïve' de la Nature. La géographie lointaine d'Homère et de Virgile redevient familière" (193) [the landscape of the native Vendôme region also offers its meadows, its vineyards and its wild lairs. Oaks and laurel trees are no longer cold emblems there, but rather reassume the "naive" greenness of Nature. Homer's and Virgil's distant geography becomes familiar once again].

8. Translation is made from Randle Cotgrave, *A Dictionarie of the French and English Tongues* (1611), a dictionary in which all of the descriptives of the poem are found.

9. Apian, *Cosmographie,* 4 (translation mine).

10. The woodcut was a celebrated memory-image of what might be called "ut pictura geographia." A fairly close reading of this passage is offered by Lucia Nuti, "Le langage de la peinture dans la cartographie topographique," 54-55.

11. Père François de Dainville shows how, in his *Cosmographia* of 1550, Sébastian Münster used his own figurative representation of vines to produce a sign "that reduced it to the stock attached to its stake," in *Le Langage des géographes,* 327 (fig. 47). Elsewhere Dainville describes it as might an emblematist a *festina lente*: "a kind of snake or zigzag around each pole, or little Saint André's crosses below which a line of shade is drawn" (209).

12. Every student of poetry knows Emile Benveniste's remarks about how shifters betray relations of power, presence, and absence. Suffice it here to recall how, during their seasonal campaigns to raise money, announcers on National Public Radio assert, "we are funded by you our listeners."

13. Dainville notes that in French *bois* generates diminutives similar to *silvula* in Latin. *Bocage,* he adds, is "a diminutive of forest" and has always connoted a charming and agreeable place (195).

14. In Ronsard, *Œuvres complètes,* 2:849 (translation mine).

15. The metaphor applies well to the shape of each of Ronsard's volumes in the perspective of their evolution in the composition of the oeuvre. Some pieces are cut away, others added; almost every poem is manicured and retouched over the course of the author's career.

16. Christian Jacob notes that, in the case of mnemographic maps that bear wind heads along their borders or in the spandrels, viewers are enabled to look at the projection as they might from the wind head's point of view but also discern their own capacity to see the work from all sides and altitudes in the same blow. Wind heads give the viewer a sense of the multiplicity of ways that a spatial representation can be beheld (*L'Empire des cartes,* 153-54). A similar observation can be made about how we can draw words at the edges of the poem across its surface in order to survey it, if only as an essay, as a way of seeing the poem from different perspectives.

17. The *antre* could resemble an eye socket. Such is the image given in Gilles Corrozet, *Hécatomgraphie,* in the emblem entitled "Secret est à louer." In "Une histoire taillée en images," 90-92, I have juxtaposed the isolated eye in Pieter Apian's illustration of the similitude of "cosmography/portraiture: topography/detail" with the outline of the *antre,* or lair, from which emerges a giant snail (or pupil of an eye) in Corrozet's emblem.

18. Leonardo, *The Notebooks of Leonardo da Vinci,* vol. 1, entry 470 (236). The observer of popular culture witnessed, at the time of the Apollo mission, the difficulty that American emissaries to the moon had in displaying the flag to the faraway public. The voyagers needed to find a strut to prop up the limp and useless cloth. The fantasy for many viewers of the Apollo mission was that the resourceful astronauts used a wire coat hanger to make the emblem of America stand aloft and proud on a breezeless and barren terrain.

19. See Henri Meschonnic on Claudel's *Locomotive*: "Claudel et l'hiéroglyphe ou la Ahité des Choses," 102-3.

20. In my *L'Inconscient graphique,* chapter 4, I read two poems (*Amours* 60 and 90 of the 1553 edition) according to this mode of composition.

21. Hampton, *Literature and Nation in the Sixteenth Century,* 161. Hampton argues compellingly that for the poets, especially Du Bellay, a crisis of social identity leads to the creation of a "*national character*" (190).

Works Cited

Apian, Pieter. *Cosmographie.* Paris: Gualtherot, 1551.

Buzon, Christine de, and Pierre Martin, eds. *Ronsard & Muret, Les Amours, leurs Commentaires.* Paris: Classiques Didier Erudition, 1999.

Conley, Tom. *The Graphic Unconscious in Early Modern French Writing.* New York: Cambridge University Press, 1992. Published in French as *L'Inconscient graphique: Essai sur l'écriture de la Renaissance (Marot, Ronsard, Rabelais, Montaigne)* (Paris: Presses Universitaires de Vincennes, 2000).

Corrozet, Gilles. *Hécatomgraphie.* Paris: D. Janot, 1541.

Cotgrave, Randle. *A Dictionarie of the French and English Tongues.* London: Islip, 1611.

Dainville, Père François de. *Le Langage des géographes.* Paris: Picard, 1964.

Hampton, Timothy. *Literature and Nation in the Sixteenth Century: Inventing Renaissance France.* Ithaca, N.Y.: Cornell University Press, 2001.

Jacob, Christian. *L'Empire des cartes: Approche théorique à travers l'histoire de la cartographie.* Paris: Albin Michel, 1992.

Leonardo da Vinci. *The Notebooks of Leonardo da Vinci.* Edited by Jean-Paul Richter. 2 vols. New York: Dover Reprints, 1970.

Mathieu-Castellani, Gisèle, ed. *Anthologie de la poésie amoureuse de l'âge baroque, 1570-1640.* Paris: Livre de Poche, 1990.

Meschonnic, Henri. "Claudel et l'hiéroglyphe ou la Ahité des Choses." In *La Pensée de l'image: Significa-*

tion et figuration dans le text et la peinture, edited by Gisèle Mathieu-Castellani. Paris: Presses Universitaires de Vincennes, 1994.

Montaigne, Michel de. *Essais.* Edited by Pierre Villey. Quadrige. Paris: PUF, 1988.

Nuti, Lucia. "Le langage de la peinture dans la cartographie topographique." In *L'Œil du cartographe et la representation géographique du Moyen Âge à nos jours,* edited by Catherine Bousquet-Bressolier, 53-70. Mémoires de la section de géographie physique et humaine 18. Paris: CTHS, 1995.

Proust, Marcel. *A la recherche du temps perdu.* Edited by Jean-Yves Tadié. 4 vols. Bibliothèque de la Pléiade. Paris: Gallimard, 1987-1989. Translated by C. K. Scott Moncrieff and Terence Kilmartin as *Remembrance of Things Past* (New York: Vintage, 1982).

Rigolot, François. *Poésie et Renaissance.* Paris: Seuil, 2001.

Ronsard, Pierre de. *Discours.* In *Œuvres complètes.* Vol. 2, edited by Jean Céard, Daniel Ménager, and Michel Simonin. Bibliothèque de la Pléiade. Paris: Gallimard, 1994.

———. *Les Amours.* Edited by Henri Weber and Catherine Weber. Paris: Garnier, 1964.

JoAnn DellaNeva (essay date September 2008)

SOURCE: DellaNeva, JoAnn. "Ronsard and the 'sein verdelet' of Cassandre: Uncovering an Unexplored Italian Source." *Renaissance Studies* 22, no. 4 (September 2008): 542-56.

[*In the following essay, DellaNeva explores sources for Ronsard's descriptions of female beauty in the* Amours, *noting that Ronsard followed the convention of the day in that he derived his descriptions from other texts—the poems of Petrarch, Ariosto, and Pietro Bembo—rather than from his personal observations of real women.*]

The love poetry of the Renaissance Petrarchist tradition is teeming with descriptions of the female body. While some poems seemingly fetishize a particular body part in the manner of the celebratory *blason,* others fragment and catalogue the female anatomy, often by using the rhetorical device of *effictio,* which scans the body from head to toe.[1] In both types of poems, descriptions of feminine beauty are clearly based less on the poets' observation of actual women and more on their reading of previous literary texts. Hair, for example, does not really share all of the attributes of genuine gold, nor are cheeks literally comprised of roses, yet such metaphors and similes—which generally suggest a point of comparison based on a single trait (for example, colour

or texture)—are ubiquitous in this type of poetry. Indeed, during the Renaissance, certain stock images (often pairing a vegetative or mineral image with a given body part) drawn from the poems of the famed fourteenth-century lyricist Francesco Petrarca, as well as Petrarch's many followers, came to be viewed as *de rigueur.*[2] Aspiring poets could avail themselves of such tools as Francesco Alunno's *Osservazioni sopra il Petrarca* (originally published in 1539), a concordance of Petrarch's vocabulary that allowed writers, with a bit of effort, to match the poet's nouns with authentically Petrarchan adjectives.[3] These 'canonical' and authorized epithets were also compiled and discussed in Renaissance handbooks and treatises—including the 'Dialogo delle bellezze delle donne' of Agnolo Firenzuola (written in 1541 and first published in 1548) and 'Il libro della bella donna' by Federico Luigini da Udine (1554)—which facilitated the imitation of poetic best practices. Thus, instead of gazing at flesh-and-blood models for inspiration, Renaissance poets could turn primarily to other texts—to manuals, concordances of epithets, and collections of poems by various other authors—when writing descriptions of the female body.[4]

Among French Renaissance poets, Pierre de Ronsard was certainly an admirable inheritor of and frequent participant in the blazon tradition. While his love poems are sufficiently diverse to satisfy the Renaissance penchant for *varietas,* they do, nevertheless, tend to demonstrate Ronsard's particular predilection for describing the female breast, often with great sensual detail. Numerous critics have commented on the Frenchman's characterizations that emphasize the breast's roundness or undulating movement, through such designations as 'Tertres d'Agathe blanc' and 'flotz jumeaulx de laict'.[5] Additionally, both of these expressions suggest the white colour of the breasts, a characteristic that is perfectly in conformity with the Petrarchan tradition. The conventionality—indeed the exigency—of describing the breast as white can be verified in Firenzuola's dialogue, where the author categorically states that 'the bosom needs only to be white, and since the creation of complete beauty requires the perfect beauty of each part, it will be necessary that each has the right colour, that is, the colour that is necessary to its own particular beauty or essence'.[6]

Yet, on two different occasions, Ronsard also describes the young Cassandre, the mistress lauded in his earliest love poetry, as having a 'sein verdelet'.[7] This is a rather puzzling expression, which, following Cotgrave's primary definition of the adjective ('Prettie and green'), one might translate as 'greenish bosom', or 'pretty green bosom'.[8] The image is no doubt jarring, especially in light of the Renaissance reader's expectations that the female breast be praised for its whiteness. Even if one assumes that the word 'verdelet' must be understood in its more figurative senses, the colour green still intrudes to a certain extent. This is confirmed by considering its more complete context in the sonnet 'Ha, seigneur dieu' (vv. 1-8), first printed in 1553 and addressed to Cassandre:

> Ha, Seigneur dieu, que de graces écloses
> Dans le jardin de ce sein verdelet,
> Enflent le rond de deus gazons de lait,
> Où des Amours les fléches sont encloses!
> Je me transforme en cent metamorfoses,
> Quant je te voi, petit mont jumelet,
> Ains du printans un rosier nouvelet,
> Qui le matin bienveigne de ses roses.

It is no doubt the colour green that dominates here, especially in the first quatrain through the pairing of 'le jardin de ce sein verdelet' with its equally startling rhyme 'deux gazons de lait', another expression suggesting 'greenness' through an image of vegetation. Clearly, the markers 'jardin', 'gazons', and 'rosier' (which would, of course, have leaves), serve to transform the lady's body into a green landscape, making it impossible for the reader to forget the literal meaning of 'verdelet'.[9]

The 'blatant oddness' of this insistence on the colour green begs for an explanation, and a rather intriguing one has been provided by Michael Riffaterre.[10] As Riffaterre acknowledges, this colour, though certainly capable of carrying positive connotations related to springtime and fertility, is nevertheless not normally associated with female beauty. Rather, when applied to the human body, the colour green invariably signals 'pathology or monstrousness: sickliness, morbid decay, envy, outer-space complexion, etc'.[11] Nevertheless, according to Riffaterre, its presence in this poem extolling the female breast can be redeemed in part by reference to another literary text—and not the natural world— thus attesting to the importance of intertextuality in the Renaissance. The passage in question is the celebrated portrait of Alcina found in Ludovico Ariosto's *Orlando furioso* 7: 14, one of the texts that constitute a virtual canon of female beauty for subsequent Renaissance poets.[12] There, Ariosto describes the colour, shape, and movement of Alcina's bosom using the images of snow, milk, apples, ivory, and waves:

> Bianca nieve è il bel collo, e 'l petto latte;
> il collo è tondo, il petto colmo e largo:
> due pome acerbe, e pur d'avorio fatte,
> vengono e van come onda al primo margo,
> quando piacevole aura il mar combatte.[13]

The mention of fruit—specifically apples—is intended to suggest the roundness of the lady's breasts, while references to snow, milk, and ivory emphasize their whiteness. By adding the adjective 'acerbe'—literally meaning 'unripe' or 'bitter'—to the apple image, Ariosto is, above all, introducing the notion of Alcina's apparent youth (though it is later revealed that she is, in

actuality, an old hag who merely projects the image of youthful beauty for the benefit of her hapless victims whom she instantly seduces through her physical charms).[14] Furthermore, as Riffaterre reminds us, the apple image is related to the traditional vision of the body-as-garden, a topos that can be traced back through medieval poetry (and, one might add, beyond, to the Song of Songs).

Although this image apparently works well enough in the original Italian, Riffaterre shows that a problem arises when later French poets, such as Ronsard, attempt to translate this into their native language: for, the critic asserts (84), 'pome *acerbe*' would normally yield, in French, 'pommes *vertes*', thereby unequivocally introducing the colour green into the bodily description. Although Ronsard does not actualize this translation in his poem—it does not mention 'apples', only 'bosom'—the expression 'pommes vertes' can be seen as an intermediary sign between 'pome acerbe' and 'sein verdelet'. Once 'pomme vertes' is present in the poet's mind as a preliminary literal translation of 'pome acerbe', it could then give rise to the diminutive 'verdelet', a poetic form of 'vert' that had previously been used in descriptions of female beauty only in reference to the colour of the lady's eyes.[15] Although Riffaterre does not mention this, the movement from 'pome acerbe' to 'sein verdelet' through 'pommes vertes' might possibly have been facilitated by another meaning of 'verdelet': for as a substantive, the word is defined by Cotgrave as 'the tender, and delicate peare, called a Greening', thereby evoking another (somewhat similar) kind of fruit.[16]

In turn, the word 'verdelet' placed at the rhyme, Riffaterre asserts, 'lends itself to punning: it sounds exactly like a fantasy *vert de lait,* "milk green,"' and this ultimately engenders the phrase *gazons de lait* 'since *gazon . . .* is *the* word for 'viridity' in a garden description' (85). Riffaterre, however, wrongly interprets 'deux gazons de lait' to mean 'two green lawns' (an image that brings to mind a flat plain) whereas the word 'gazons', in sixteenth-century French, actually meant 'mounds' or 'little hills' (Cotgrave defines it as 'a hill covered with greene sodds'), thus conveying a sense of roundness that corresponds to the apple image already present in Ariosto's text.[17] While this misinterpretation might detract from the correct nuance of firm, youthful, round breasts inherent in Ronsard's image, the point that Riffaterre makes, regarding the association of 'gazons' with 'viridity' or greenness, nevertheless obtains. As the French critic claims, once the Ariostean intertext is recognized, the peculiarity of the expressions 'verdelet' and 'gazon de lait' is diminished and their proper metonymical association with 'greenness' merely to mark *youth* (and not actual *colour* or *taste*) comes to the fore.[18]

Riffaterre's explanation of this intertextual punning is, as has been noted, based on its use in the sonnet 'Ha, seigneur dieu', which Ronsard added to his first *canzoniere*, the *Amours*, when it was republished in augmented form in 1553.[19] Before that, however, Ronsard had already referred to the '*boutons* verdeletz' of Cassandre's bosom in the sixth sonnet of the 1552 version of the *Amours*, beginning 'Ces liens d'or':

> Ces mains, ce col, ce front, & cette oreille,
> Et de ce sein les boutons verdelets

(vv. 5-6)

Riffaterre suggests that *this* use of 'verdelet' (paired with 'bouton' rather than 'sein') is a more transparent allusion to nubile beauty using the body-as-garden image; indeed, here, he states, 'the image is quite acceptable, because the same word *bouton* means, according to the text, either "nipples" or "flower buds"—a happy coincidence for one striving to suggest nubility as a promise of beauty to come' (85). But what Riffaterre does not address is the fact that the more puzzling expression 'sein verdelet' also appeared for the first time in the *Amours* of 1552, in **Sonnet 18** ('Un chaste feu'), several months before the publication of 'Ha, seigneur dieu'.[20] While the exact dating of Ronsard's numerous sonnets is not known, it is presumed that the poems forming the original 1552 edition predate those that appear only in 1553. If this is true, then the presence of the expression 'sein verdelet' in *Amours* 1552, **Sonnet 18,** might render Riffaterre's analysis somewhat problematic: for one would expect the rationale behind Ronsard's choice to be in operation from the first instance of its use, and not merely in subsequent appearances of this expression. In order for Riffaterre's elaborate explanation to be fully satisfactory, then, the question must be raised as to whether the Ariosto subtext is, in fact, also pertinent to the 1552 *Amours* S. 18, or whether there might be an alternative intertext that helps to explain the pairing of 'sein' and 'verdelet' in this earlier sonnet. It would also be legitimate to investigate if there are other possible intertexts that could shed light on Ronsard's use of the adjective 'verdelet' (coupled with 'boutons') in **Sonnet 6,** which might also have inspired the subsequent reappearance of this poetic epithet in conjunction with breast imagery.

Ronsard's first formal commentator, Marc-Antoine de Muret, writing in 1553, glossed **S. 18** with a reference to a Petrarchan sonnet, saying that 'Un chaste feu' was 'presque tout traduit' from *Rime sparse* 213, 'Gratie ch'a pochi', which he then transcribed in its entirety; notably, Muret does not mention Ariosto here, nor does he see the need to gloss the expression 'sein verdelet' at all.[21] More recent commentators, including Laumonier and Weber, likewise point to this same Petrarchan sonnet as an important source for Ronsard's themes, imagery, and structure.[22] Clearly, *RS* 213 does provide many parallels to the Ronsardian sonnet, as a side-by-side comparison of the texts reveals:

> Un chaste feu qui les coeurs illumine,
> Un or frisé de meint crespe anelet,
> Un front de rose, un teint damoiselet,
> Un ris qui l'ame aus astres achemine:
>   Une vertu de telles graces digne,
> Un col de neige, une gorge de laict,
> Un coeur ja meur dans un sein verdelet,
> En dame humaine une beaulté divine:
>   Un oeil puissant de faire jours les nuits,
> Une main forte à piller les ennuis,
> Qui tient ma vie en ses dois enfermée:
>   Avec un chant offensé doucement
> Ores d'un ris, or d'un gemissement:
> De tels sorciers ma raison fut charmée.

> Gratie ch'a pochi il ciel largo destina:
> rara vertù, non già d'umana gente,
> sotto biondi capei canuta mente,
> e 'n humil donna alta beltà divina;
>   leggiadria singular et pellegrina,
> e 'l cantar che ne l'anima si sente,
> l'andar celeste, e 'l vago spirto ardente,
> ch'ogni dur rompe et ogni altezza inchina;
>   et que' belli occhi che i cor' fanno smalti,
> possenti a rischiarar abisso et notti,
> et torre l'alme a' corpi, et darle altrui;
>   col dir pien d'intellecti dolci et alti,
> coi sospiri soave-mente rotti:
> da questi magi transformato fui.[23]

Petrarch's poem is remarkable because it uses no determinant in its early evocations of the lady but gradually introduces the use of the definite article and finally the demonstrative adjective, thereby succeeding in making Laura's person more and more truly present before the eyes of the reader.[24] Ronsard's sonnet differs from its Italian predecessor thanks particularly to its consistent use of the determinant 'un'/'une' that comprises the anaphora—a rhetorical device of which the Frenchman was evidently quite fond—seen throughout the text.

Despite this basic difference, however, the two poems share several significant elements. Among the more obvious similarities are their respective rhyme schemes, in which Ronsard echoes Petrarch's 'A' rhymes ending in '-ina', through his own use of rhymes ending in their French equivalent, '-ine'. As for specific imagery, one quickly notes that the coupling of 'gratie' and 'vertù' (which is found in the first two verses of Petrarch's poem) is relocated to verse five of Ronsard's sonnet, 'une *vertu* de telles *graces* digne'.[25] At the end of that same stanza, Ronsard virtually translates Petrarch's v. 4 ('e'n humil donna alta beltà divina'). This is lightly recast as 'En dame humaine une beauté divine', retaining the same rhyme, but changing 'humil' to 'humaine', a word whose Italian equivalent is found in verse two. Both 'humil' and 'umana' or 'humaine' are, of course, related etymologically to each other, stemming from the

Latin 'humus', meaning 'earth' or 'soil', so that the movement from 'humil' to 'humaine' is still almost a translation on Ronsard's part.

Ronsard's first tercet also draws from Petrarch's, as both poems focus on the lady's eye, or eyes, which have the power to brighten the night. Again, Ronsard translates the rhyme word 'notti' into his French sonnet, likewise placing 'les nuits' at the end of his verse. In his last tercet, Ronsard turns once more to Petrarch by evoking the image of the lady's voice (in this case, her song) which is sweetly interrupted by laughter or sighing, a detail which is expressed by the Italian's verse thirteen, 'coi sospiri soave-mente rotti'. Finally, Ronsard sums up the effects of his lady's charms by referring to them as 'De tels sorciers', a close equivalent of the Italian's expression 'da questi magi', and it is the similarity of their *pointes* that makes this intertextuality most evident.

What is *not* present in the Petrarchan sonnet is an allusion to the lady's lovely bosom, and this is no surprise as the Trecento poet rarely described this part of Laura's body.[26] For that detail, Weber refers the reader of his edition to Ariosto's portrait of Alcina, a text that he had already mentioned in connection with Ronsard's sixth sonnet. Specifically, Weber finds Ronsard's verse seven, 'Un coeur ja meur dans un sein verdelet', to be an amalgam of Petrarch's verse three ('sotto biondi capei canuta mente') and Ariosto's description of Alcina's bosom as 'pome acerbe'. While he does not offer the elaborate explanation proffered by Riffaterre, it should be noted that Weber's notes to Sonnets six and eighteen show that he too saw a connection between the unusual term 'verdelet' and the 'pome acerbe' of Ariosto's Alcina figure.

To fill out what Weber merely suggests, we can say that Ronsard, wishing to evoke the paradox of youthful wisdom found in Petrarch's verse three, moved the locus of this quality from the lady's mind to her heart, thus allowing him to focus on her bosom in a seemingly innocent—or at least natural—fashion.[27] In so doing, Ronsard also naturally changes the colouration of the lady's portrait found in the model text. Petrarch's evocation of wisdom was rendered by the phrase 'canuta mente', literally, a white-haired or hoary mind; this implies that wisdom is something one acquires with age (along with, alas, grey hair). Laura is remarkable, however, because she already possesses this mature wisdom while still enjoying the beauties of her blond locks. Clearly, this same idea is depicted by Ronsard's pairing of a mature heart in a 'sein verdelet', whereby 'verdelet' connotes youthfulness (or more literally and somewhat less flatteringly 'greenishness').

Though Weber's notes do not mention this, it is actually Ronsard's verse six, 'Un col de neige, une gorge de lait', that most closely matches Ariosto's depiction of

Alcina's breast, as it is a virtual translation of the line 'Bianca nieve è il bel collo, e'l petto latte', a verse that, like Ronsard's, combines images of snow and milk to describe the female breast.[28] This insistence on whiteness (which was present in the Petrarchan sonnet in reference to hair colour) permits Ronsard to downplay the physicality of the greenness implied in the word 'verdelet', for Cassandre's bosom has already been shown to be the colour of snow and milk. This then allows 'verdelet' to be interpreted purely metonymically in its association with youth.[29] Ronsard's verse seven thus does indeed seem to be a unique amalgam of Ariosto's sensual description of nubile female beauty and Petrarch's ethereal evocation of youthful wisdom, just as Weber has suggested. The influence of Ariosto's portrait of Alcina in this poem thus seems to render Riffaterre's explanation of the 'sein verdelet' equally pertinent here as well, thus further strengthening its validity.

But further research into the realm of Italian Renaissance poetry reveals that there may well be yet a third important, but heretofore undiscovered, subtext present in Ronsard's sonnet. For, as Ronsard was bound to know, Petrarch's Sonnet 213 was the source of a very well-known poem by Pietro Bembo, 'Crin d'oro crespo', that became, in its own right, another canonical description of female beauty:[30]

> Crin d'oro crespo e d'ambra tersa e pura,
> ch'a l'aura su la neve ondeggi e vole,
> occhi soavi e più chiari che 'l sole,
> da far giorno seren la notte oscura,
>   riso, qu'acqueta ogni aspra pena e dura,
> rubini e perle, ond'escono parole
> sì dolci, ch'altro ben l'alma non vòle,
> man d'avorio, che i cor distringe e fura,
>   cantar, che sembra d'armonia divina,
> senno maturo a la più verde etate,
> leggiadria non veduta unqua fra noi,
>   giunta a somma beltà somma onestade,
> fur l'esca del mio foco, e sono in voi
> grazie, ch'a poche il ciel largo destina.[31]

The relationship between Bembo's sonnet and its Petrarchan predecessor is obvious, thanks to Bembo's complete citation of S. 213's *incipit*, 'Grazie ch'a pochi il ciel largo destina', the unofficial title by which it would have been known in Renaissance circles.[32] However, this first verse is moved by Bembo into the *pointe* or final verse of his imitation, where he also changes Petrarch's word 'pochi' to the feminine 'poche', specifying that these graces are destined to few *women*.

Otherwise, 'Crin d'oro crespo' follows the general movement of its model and retains much of the original's lexicon, including the rhyme word 'divina', allusions to the lady's 'alta beltà' (in Bembo's 'somma beltà' of verse 12), and other individual words, including 'occhi', 'notte', 'l'alma', 'i cor' (that is, 'cuori'), 'l'alma' and 'dolci'. In turn, Bembo's poem became so well known as a canon for the description of female beauty that it quickly became the fodder for parody: namely, in Francesco Berni's merciless 'Chiome d'argento fino', which cleverly mismatches epithets that were part of traditional Petrarchan descriptions with the wrong, but equally traditional, body parts blazoned by countless poets.[33] Thus Berni's lady love boasts, for example, 'un bel viso d'oro' (or a beautiful golden face) and a 'fronte crespa' (or wrinkled forehead), thereby exhibiting the attributes of waviness and gold colour present in the 'crin d'oro crespo' or 'wavy golden hair' of Bembo's lady. She is further endowed with 'ciglia di neve' (or snowy eyebrows) and 'occhi di perle' (or pearly eyes) instead of snowy breasts and a pearly smile.[34]

It is in part thanks to this evidence regarding its popularity that Bembo's poem can be claimed as an important, though hitherto undiscovered, subtext for *Amours* 18.[35] In addition to using vocabulary that is found in both Bembo and Petrarch (such as 'coeurs', 'ame', 'graces', 'oeil', 'nuits' and 'chant'), Ronsard uses certain images that come solely from Bembo and not from Petrarch. He begins, for example, by referring to the element of fire, found in Bembo's verse thirteen, and goes on to evoke the curly *golden* hair (or 'un *or* frisé de meint crespe anelet') found in Bembo's first verse, thus translating the *incipit* 'crin d'*oro* crespo' (and significantly, not depicting merely *blonde* hair or the '*biondi* capei' of Petrarch's verse three). Another attribute which was denied Laura but that was lauded by Bembo is the lady's hand, mentioned in Ronsard's verse ten and the Italian's verse eight. In both cases, this feature is described quite graphically as grasping and imprisoning the lover's heart or life in a somewhat violent manner that belies its delicate beauty.[36]

Ronsard also ends his first stanza with a reference to his lady's smile or laughter, a quality not described by Petrarch but to which Bembo alludes in his second stanza. The effects of this smile, which guides one's soul to the heavens, is reminiscent, however, of one of the powers Petrarch assigns in verse eleven to Laura's eyes, which likewise affect the souls of those who come under her spell. While Bembo *does* mention (in verse seven) the beholder's soul as being so smitten by the lady's sweet words that it desires no other good, he does not ascribe movement to the soul in the way that Petrarch did and that Ronsard emulates. This coupling of characteristics taken from both Bembo and Petrarch is also seen in the intriguing way in which Ronsard depicts Cassandre's eye. All three poets claim that this feature brightens the dark night, but Ronsard clearly takes the adjective 'puissant' from Petrarch's 'possenti', pairing it, however, with a close French translation of Bembo's verbal construction 'da far giorno . . . la

notte', that is 'de faire jours les nuits', thus eschewing Petrarch's more unique verb 'rischiarar' and avoiding the noun 'abisso' while echoing Bembo's antithesis of night and day.

So far, however, Bembo's poem does not appear to provide any sustained image of the lady's bosom that might account for Ronsard's insistence on Cassandre's breasts. Still, there is some hint of this erotically charged body part in Bembo's second verse, for soon after describing his lady's curly gold hair, he evokes the image of its movement in the breeze, as it ripples and flies across the snow. It is only this single metonym, 'la neve', that allows a glimpse at his lady's bosom or neckline, for what other body part could it describe if not the 'bel collo' of white snow evoked by Ariosto? Indeed, one could argue that Bembo's combination of the words 'l'aura', 'ondeggi' and 'neve' economically conjures the salient features of Ariosto's more elaborate portrait of Alcina's bosom.

It is difficult to determine if there is any direct influence of Ariosto on Bembo's sonnet, in part because Bembo's poems are undated. According to Carlo Dionisotti, Bembo's modern editor, this particular poem might have been written in the first decade of the sixteenth century, long before the publication of Bembo's *Rime* in 1530. If this is so, Sonnet five was thus completed in advance of Ariosto's first edition of the *Orlando furioso,* in 1516. But this question of influence is a moot point and totally irrelevant, insofar as it would not have mattered much to Ronsard, who had equal access to both Ariosto and Bembo when writing his own sonnet. It is easy enough to imagine, then, that Ronsard might have been reminded, when reading Bembo's evocative verse two, of Ariosto's far more explicit and sustained rendering of the female bosom and that it was this connection that encouraged him to describe Cassandre's 'col de neige' and 'gorge de lait' in terms more clearly reminiscent of Ariosto than Bembo here. In this way, Ronsard's poem constitutes a conflation of several sources—verses by Petrarch, Ariosto, and Bembo—in a manner that exemplifies the French poet's adherence to the principles of eclectic imitation.[37]

Still, even if we accept the intrusion of Ariosto's portrait of Alcina on Ronsard's rewriting of two Italian sonnets, this does not necessarily mean that the Frenchman found the model for Cassandre's 'sein verdelet' in Ariosto's 'due pome acerbe'. For there is indeed another expression in Bembo's sonnet that might account for the pairing of 'sein' and 'verdelet'. This is found precisely in Bembo's own rendition of Petrarch's verse three (*RS* 213: 'sotto biondi capei canuta mente'), in which the beloved's unique youthful wisdom is evoked: 'senno maturo a la più verde etate', a paradox that Ronsard expressed by the verse 'un coeur ja meur dans un sein verdelet'. Bembo certainly does not merely repeat Petrarch's depiction of a hoary mind located under blond hair. Instead, like Ronsard, Bembo changes the colouration of Petrarch's description from yellow to green, using the expression 'la più verde etade', or 'greenest years', a phrase that signifies 'youth'. This is because Bembo gives no location as the seat of his lady's maturity, referring not to her mind but only to her 'senno maturo' or mature wisdom, judgment or sense, thereby making the quality of yellowness or blondness (that is, youthful hair colour) superfluous. Bembo's choice of the word 'senno' instead of 'mente' also has the advantage of evoking, by means of paronomasia, the Latin word 'senex': the word used to designate a man who is essentially a community 'elder', suggesting not only mature years but also the accumulated wisdom associated with maturity. Though the words are not related etymologically, the learned Renaissance reader might still find in their similar sounds sufficient proof that wisdom or good judgment is a product of experience rather than youth;[38] Bembo's adjective 'maturo' merely emphasizes this claim even further.

Clearly Ronsard's rendering of this aspect of Cassandre's attributes is much closer to Bembo's than it is to Petrarch's, for he uses the word 'meur' (the French equivalent of 'maturo' rather than 'canuta') in addition to the word 'verdelet', which is an obvious echo of 'verde' rather than 'biondi'. But what is most of interest here is that Ronsard's innovative image of the 'sein verdelet' may well have been inspired by the pairing of the words 'senno' and 'verde' in Bembo's verse. It is certainly possible that, in first reading the word 'senno', Ronsard mistook it for the Italian word 'seno' or breast, which he might have understood to be used by Bembo metonymically to evoke a mature heart, which he then rendered in his own poem as 'coeur meur'. He might then have thought himself rather clever to place this 'coeur meur' within the confines of a 'sein verdelet', thus reverting to what he might have thought was the more literal meaning of the word used by Bembo. On the other hand, it is at least equally likely that Ronsard realized that 'seno' and 'senno' were two different words, but that he too was engaging in the widespread practice among humanists (such as his colleagues Du Bellay and Dorat) of *allusio,* that is, relating similarly sounding but differently meaning words in an effort to see some profound connection between the two.[39]

Whether or not Ronsard understood or misunderstood the word 'senno', there is no doubt, however, that this word is both graphically and acoustically (though not semantically) suggestive of the French word 'sein'. It is quite possible, then, that the text that most directly suggested the specific coupling of the word 'sein' with 'verdelet' may well have been Bembo's Sonnet five and not Ariosto's portrait of Alcina. For there, it must be recognized, one does not find any close equivalent to the French words 'sein' or 'verdelet'. Ariosto speaks

only of Alcina's 'collo' and 'petto', not her 'seno', and the quality of greenness is not evoked by the phoneme 'verde' but only distantly and metonymically through the image of 'bitter' or 'unripe apples'. Bembo, on the other hand, evokes in a single line both the sound and the form of the word 'sein' through the unrelated noun 'senno' and that of 'verdelet' in the adjective 'verde'. While metonymical thinking is certainly common among poets, the impact of letters on a page and the sounds they represent should not be minimized, especially with regard to a poet who was as sensitive to sonority as Ronsard.

Nor would this be the only case in which Ronsard ignores the meaning of Italian words found in his sources in favor of emphasizing their graphic and acoustic affinity to an unrelated word in French, thus engaging in a kind of intertextual and bilingual paronomasia. In **Sonnet 56 [S. 55]** of the *Amours* ('Verrai-je point le dous jour'), for example, Ronsard provides a close rendition of the *incipit* of a sonnet by the minor poet Giovanni Andrea Gesualdo, 'Verrà mai il di', published in the collection of Italian lyrics commonly known as the Giolito anthologies.[40] While Ronsard pays close attention to the meaning of Gesualdo's verses and repeats much of the Italian's vocabulary, he definitely does *not* translate the meaning of Gesualdo's opening verb 'Verrà', which stems from the irregular verb 'venire', meaning 'to come'. Instead, Ronsard commences his poem with the graphically and acoustically similar verb 'Verrai', which derives from the irregular verb 'voir', 'to see'.[41] Clearly, Ronsard has no qualms here about changing the meaning of the Italian's expression, for what mattered to him most was echoing the sounds of his model and its written appearance in his own poem.

Indeed, there may be further evidence of this *modus operandi* in Ronsard's **Sonnet 6** ('Ces liens d'or', vv. 1-8), which is the other poem of the *Amours* of 1552 to use the adjective 'verdelet' in conjunction with the noun 'sein'. This poem owes much of its imagery to another Petrarchan model, *RS* 200 ('Non pur quell' una', vv. 9-14), as a side-by-side comparison of the poems demonstrates:

> Ces liens d'or, cette bouche vermeille,
> Pleine de lis, de roses, & d'oeuillets,
> Et ces couraus chastement vermeillets
> Et cette joüe à l'Aurore pareille.
> Ces mains, ce col, ce front, & cette oreille,
> Et de ce sein les boutons verdelets,
> Et de ces yeus les astres jumelets,
> Qui font trembler les ames de merveille.
>
> li occhi sereni et le stellanti ciglia,
> la bella bocca angelica, di perle
> piena et di rose et di dolci parole,
> che fanno altrui tremar di meraviglia

et la fronte, et le chiome, ch'a vederle
di state, a mezzo dì, vincono il sole.

Here, Ronsard transposes the imagery of Petrarch's tercets to his own quatrains, including allusions to his lady's forehead and eyes. In particular, the expression 'bouche . . . pleine de roses' appears to have been inspired by Petrarch's 'bocca . . . piena di rose'; furthermore, Ronsard's verse eight, 'qui font trembler les ames de merveille', is a close rendition of Petrarch's verse twelve, 'che fanno altrui tremar di meraviglia'. It will be noted that Ronsard retains the equivalent of Petrarch's rhyme word 'meraviglia', and this attention to rhyme is indeed quite common for Ronsard, thus providing further testimony to the importance of graphic and phonemic mimicry in Ronsard's imitations. But what is even more intriguing is the rhyme word of the verse that immediately follows this one, verse thirteen of the Italian sonnet, which ends with the seemingly uninspired verb 'vederle', meaning 'to see them'. Is it just coincidence that Ronsard places his poetic diminutive 'verdelets' at the rhyme, in the same stanza as 'merveille', just as Petrarch had followed 'meraviglia' with 'vederle'? Or did this simple Italian verb/pronoun composite suggest to him, through its sounds and letters, but certainly not its meaning, this evocative diminutive that seemed perfect to pair with the noun 'boutons', to suggest the notion of nubile feminine beauty? Of course, once the term 'verdelet' became part of his poetic repertoire in 1552—thanks to his reading of Petrarch and Bembo—one would fully expect Ronsard subsequently to reuse the expression at will, as he apparently did in the sonnet 'Ha, seigneur dieu' of 1553. If this is so, then the wording of the striking image 'sein verdelet' in the **Amours de Cassandre** may indeed have been inspired by an Italian source—though not uniquely (nor, perhaps, even primarily) the one that many of Ronsard's readers, from Weber to Riffaterre, may have supposed.

Notes

A preliminary version of this paper was read at the 2006 Renaissance Society of America Conference in San Francisco. I am grateful for the many useful comments offered by participants at that session as well as by the two anonymous referees of this article.

1. For an overview of these types of poetic portraits, consult François Lecercle, *La Chimère de Zeuxis: Portrait poétique et portrait peint en France et en Italie à la Renaissance* (Tubingen: Gunter Narr, 1987). For more on the *blason* genre, which has received considerable critical attention in recent years, consult Alison Saunders, *The Sixteenth-Century Blason Poétique* (Bern: Peter Lang, 1981). Also see the selection of 'Blasons du corps féminin' (written for a competition among poets in the 1530s that was said to have been won by Maurice Scève for his contribution on 'Le Sourcil' or 'eyebrow') in *Poètes du XVIe siècle,* ed. Albert-Marie Schmidt (Paris: Gallimard, 1953), 291-364. This selection also contains a number of 'contre-blasons', that is, parodies of proper *blasons.* Such poems include the 'Blason du Laid Tétin' by Clément Marot.

2. For a detailed analysis of the conventions of describing female beauty, consult Giovanni Pozzi, 'Temi, tópoi, stereotipi', *Letteratura italiana 3: Le forme del testo. 1. Teoria e poesia,* ed. Alberto Asor Rosa (Turin: Einaudi, 1984), 391-436.

3. In his preface to the *Osservazioni,* Alunno instructs prospective writers to employ expressions sanctioned by Petrarch by first consulting his concordance for a noun (the author gives the example of 'cielo' or 'sky'), then searching for appropriate adjectives (e.g., 'stellato' or 'starry'), then finally comparing the two entries to check for coincidences of references. The result of this tedious search would be an authentically Petrarchan formula that, with respect to the new poet, might have little to do with reality and even less to do with originality. Alunno's revised edition, published in 1550, facilitates the search by citing the entire verse in which any word appears, thereby more easily supplying the 'correct' Petrarchan epithet.

4. For an excellent overview of Renaissance *imitatio,* that is, the practice of imitating prior texts (as opposed, in this instance, to describing simply the natural world that one sees), consult Thomas M. Greene, *The Light in Troy: Imitation and Discovery in Renaissance Poetry* (New Haven: Yale University Press, 1982).

5. Ronsard's poems were frequently revised in later years, often changing places within a single collection and sometimes even migrating between different collections. Because this study is concerned with the early uses of these images (which date from 1552-53), the most pertinent editions, for our purpose, will be *Les Amours,* eds. Henri Weber and Catherine Weber (Paris: Garnier, 1963) and *Ronsard & Muret: Les Amours, leurs Commentaires,* eds. Christine de Buzon and Pierre Martin (Paris: Didier, 1999); sonnet numbers given thus refer to the numbering of these editions and quotations will be drawn from Buzon/Martin. For an authoritative, recent edition based on the 1584 text, consult Ronsard's *Oeuvres complètes,* eds. Jean Céard, Daniel Ménager and Michel Simonin (Paris: Gallimard, 1993); the sonnet number provided in brackets refers to this edition (but only if the sonnet is indeed differently numbered from the 1552-53 editions). For the expression 'Tertres d'Agathe blanc', see the sonnet 'Belle

gorge d'albastre', *Le Second Livre des Sonnets pour Hélène*, [S. 53, v. 3]); for the expression 'Ces flotz jumeaulx de laict', see *Amours* 1552-53, s. 187 [S. 193], v. 1.

6. '. . . conviene . . . al petto la bianchezza solamente; e bisognando che per la eccitazione della bellezza universale, tutte le membra nella separazione sieno perfette; sarà mestieri che ell'abbiano il dovuto colore, cioè quello ch'era necessario alla loro propria e particolare bellezza, ovvero essenza . . .' Quoted from Agnolo Firenzuola, 'Celso: Dialogo delle bellezze delle donne', in *Opere,* ed. Adriano Seroni (1958; Florence: Sansoni, 1993), 521-596 (540). For the English translation, see *On the Beauty of Women,* trans. Konrad Eisenbichler and Jacqueline Murray (Philadelphia: University of Pennsylvania Press, 1992) 15. Earlier in this passage, Firenzuola distinguishes between the metaphors of ivory and snow, which both designate whiteness, stating that ivory (rendered by the Italian adjective 'candido' or 'fair') entails lustre while snow does not glow.

7. This expression is found in the sonnets 'Un chaste feu' (S. 18, v. 7) and 'Ha, seigneur dieu' (S. 41 [S. 40], v. 2) of the *Amours* 1552-53. In later editions, the *incipit* of 'Un chaste feu' was emended to 'Une beauté de quinze ans enfantine', while 'Ha, seigneur dieu' was changed to 'Que de Beautez'.

8. See Randall Cotgrave, *A Dictionarie of the French and English Tongues* (1611; repr. 1950, Columbia, S.C.: University of South Carolina Press, 1968).

9. For a more general study of Ronsard's use of vegetative and landscape imagery, consult Danièle Duport, *Les Jardins qui sentent le sauvage. Ronsard et la poétique du paysage* (Geneva: Droz, 2000). For another analysis of conventional metaphors evoking the beloved lady, see Yvonne Bellenger, *Lisez la Cassandre de Ronsard: Etude sur 'Les Amours' (1553)* (Paris: Champion, 1997).

10. Michael Riffaterre, *Semiotics of Poetry* (Bloomington: Indiana University Press, 1978), 81-6. It is Riffaterre who suggests the translation 'pretty green bosom' (82).

11. Riffaterre, *Semiotics of Poetry,* 85. Riffaterre's assertion is certainly confirmed by Hollywood's portrayal of Frankenstein's monster, the Wicked Witch of the West, and little green men from Mars.

12. For more on Ariosto's influential description, see Henri Weber, *La Création poétique au XVIe siècle en France de Maurice Scève à Agrippa d'Aubigné* (Paris: Nizet 1955), 265-8. Ariosto's passage is also cited numerous times as a model for female bodily description by Federico Luigini da Udine, 'Il libro della bella donna' in *Trattati del Cinque-*

cento sulla donna, ed. Giuseppe Zonta (Bari: Laterza, 1913), 221-305.

13. The Italian text is taken from Ariosto, *Opere,* ed. Adriano Seroni (1961; Milan: Mursia, 1966); for an English translation, see *Orlando furioso (The Frenzy of Orlando),* trans. Barbara Reynolds (1975; New York: Penguin, 1977), 2 vols.

14. The word 'acerbe' or 'bitter' can, of course, also carry negative connotations and was used by Petrarch to convey a sense of moral dissatisfaction with his forbidden love for Laura. For an example, see especially *Rime sparse* 6. One also thinks, in this regard, of the tasting of forbidden fruit, traditionally identified as an apple, in the book of Genesis. Perhaps Ariosto's 'pome acerbe' image was also meant to convey a certain ambiguity that anticipates Alcina's negative role later in the poem.

15. See, for example, Pierre Danché, 'Blason de la belle fille', which is found in the *Jardin de Plaisance* (1501), where the poet speaks of the lady's 'Oeil verdelet'. Quoted in Saunders, *Blason Poétique,* 62. I am grateful to the author for pointing out this reference.

16. This connection was suggested by an anonymous reader of this article. It should be noted, however, that this meaning is not attested by Huguet or Greimas, and Cotgrave gives no specific citation of its contemporary use. Therefore, it might be somewhat imprudent—though certainly intriguing—to suggest that, when Ronsard read of Ariosto's green apples, he thought of the pear he might have known as a 'verdelet', transforming that noun into an adjective to describe the same body part evoked by the Italian.

17. Weber also treats this image, saying 'L'image du sein verdelet peut paraître étrange, elle évoque la jeunesse et a pour origine l'Arioste: "due pome acerbe". Ronsard, n'oublie pas le sens premier de l'adjectif, il en poursuit l'image avec les deux gazons de lait: gazon ayant son sens premier de motte couverte d'herbe. L'image traditionnelle des deux monts de lait s'unit à celle d'une végétation qui va s'épanouir en jardin dans le second quatrain'. See 'La Célébration du corps féminin dans *Les Amours* de Ronsard: variation sur un répertoire connu', *RHR: Réforme, Humanisme, Renaissance* 45 (1997) 7-23, especially 18. The full verse, beginning 'Enfler son rond', also indicates that these 'gazons' are round, not flat; the idea is reinforced in verse six, which refers to the beloved's 'petit mont jumelet'.

18. Given Ronsard's penchant for sensual description, the sense of taste might still be subtly present, particularly in light of this sonnet's last tercet,

which describes the lover's desire to transform himself into a flea, so that 'La baisotant, tous les jours je mordroi / Ses beaus tetins'. In *Le Petit Robert: Dictionnaire alphabétique de la langue française,* ed. Paul Robert, et al. Nouvelle édition (Paris: Société du Nouveau Littré, 1977), 2077, it indeed states that the term 'verdelet' is used in non-poetic situations to refer to wine that is a little 'green' or acidic in taste ('vin verdelet, un peu vert, légèrement acide'), very much like the Italian 'acerbo'. Cotgrave also suggests this definition: 'onely beginning to be greene, but young, not yet ripe; also a little raw, tart, sharpe', fol. L111 ii r. While the notion of bitter taste might bring additional resonances to Ronsard's poem, there is no doubt that it does not carry the same sense of moral dissatisfaction that was present in Petrarch's use of 'acerbo'.

19. The title page of this edition reads: *'Les Amours de P. de Ronsard Vandomois, nouvellement augmentées par lui . . .'*. See the edition of Buzon and Martin, *Ronsard et Muret,* for a facsimile reproduction of this page.

20. For the complete original 1552 version of the *Amours,* consult Ronsard, *Oeuvres Complètes* IV, eds. Paul Laumonier and Rayomond Lebègue (1925; Paris: Nizet, 1982).

21. For the Muret commentary on this poem, see Buzon and Martin, *Ronsard & Muret,* 36-38. For another modern edition that reproduces in facsimile form Muret's commentary as it appeared in the 1623 edition (along with other variants in the commentary introduced after 1553), consult *Commentaires au Premier Livre des Amours de Ronsard,* ed. Gisèle Mathieu-Castellani (Geneva: Droz, 1985).

22. See their notes to Sonnet 18 in their respective editions; also consult Weber, *La Création poétique,* 270-73 and Dario Cecchetti, *Il Petrarchismo in Francia* (Turin: Giappichelli, 1970), 40-41.

23. Quoted from Petrarca, *Canzoniere,* ed. Marco Santagata (Milan: Mondadori, 1996). For an English translation, see *Petrarch's Lyric Poems: The Rime sparse and Other Lyrics,* trans. Robert M. Durling (Cambridge, Mass.: Harvard University Press, 1976). All subsequent quotations of Petrarch are from the Santagata edition.

24. This difference is the focus of the analysis made by Lecercle, who emphasizes that this 'détermination de plus en plus précise' of *RS* 213 is generally not imitated by Petrarch's French and Italian followers, who prefer to structure the presentation of their lady's charms through the anaphoric repetition of the article or demonstrative adjective. See *La Chimère de Zeuxis* 91-3.

25. The coupling of 'graces' and 'vertu' holds only for the 1553 version of this sonnet. In 1552, verse five was rendered: 'Une vertu de telles beaultez digne'. See the Laumonier edition for that version.

26. For some notable exceptions, see *RS* 37, where Petrarch describes Laura's 'bel giovenil petto' ('lovely youthful breast', v. 102), *RS* 126, where he refers to her 'angelico seno' ('angelic breast', v. 9), and. *RS* 160, where he mentions 'suo candido seno' ('her white breast', v. 11).

27. In *La Création poétique,* Weber also suggests that Ronsard's image might also owe something to these verses from the next sonnet in Petrarch's sequence, *RS* 215: 'In nobil sangue vita humile et queta / et in alto intellecto un puro core, / frutto senile in sul giovenil fiore . . .'. (vv. 1-3).

28. See, however, Weber, *La Création poétique,* 272 for a similar suggestion.

29. Ronsard's later variant of the *incipit* of this sonnet, 'Une beauté de quinze ans enfantine', likewise stresses Cassandre's youthfulness.

30. This sonnet is cited five times by Luigini as an authoritative source for describing the beloved's hair (which is golden and curly), hand (which is ivory-like), and teeth (like pearls). See 'Il libro della bella donna', 230-231, 243, 248, and 250.

31. Quoted from Pietro Bembo, *Prose della volgar lingua, Gli Asolani, Rime,* ed. Carlo Dionisotti (Turin: UTET, 1966), S. 5 (pp. 510-511). For an English translation, see *Italian Poets of the Renaissance,* trans. and intro. Joseph Tusiani (Long Island City, N.Y.: Baroque Press, 1971) 118.

32. This technique of excerpting whole lines from a famous model poem, such as Petrarch's sonnets, was not uncommon in the sixteenth century. Known as the *cento* or patchwork, this genre was facilitated by the publication of *rimari* or rhyme dictionaries that listed Petrarch's rhyme words in alphabetical order, often including the entire verse where the rhyme is found. For an example of such a *rimario,* see the *Tavola di tutte le rime de i sonetti e canzoni del Petrarca ridotte co i versi interi sotto le lettere vocali* by Luc'Antonio Ridolfi which was appended to several Lyonnais editions of Petrarch (published in 1550, 1551, 1558, 1564, and 1574 by Guillaume Roville). For more on the *cento* form and its relationship to Petrarchism, consult Frank Erspamer, 'Centoni e petrarchismo nel Cinquecento' in *Scritture di Scritture: Testi, Generi, Modelli nel Rinascimento* (Rome: Bulzoni, 1987), 463-95; see especially p. 485 for its connection to *rimari*. The popularity of *cento* writing (which was not limited to Petrarch but was sometimes done with classical texts, most espe-

cially Virgil's) is attested to by the manner in which it is dismissed by Du Bellay in his *Deffence et illustration de la langue françoyse* (Bk.1.11).

33. This sonnet was printed in the anthology *Il Primo Libro dell'opere burlesche, di M. Francesco Berni,* et al., published in 1548. For a modern version, see Francesco Berni, *Rime,* ed. Danilo Romei (Milan: Mursia, 1985) from which these quotations are taken.

34. Berni's parody made its way into France thanks to its imitation by Saint-Gelais in the sonnet 'Cheveux d'argent'. Later, Du Bellay himself also imitates this poem in his *Regrets* 91, 'O beaux cheveux d'argent'. For more on the relationship between the sonnets of Berni and Bembo (as well as the role played here by Firenzuola's prescriptive formulas in his dialogue 'On the Beauty of Women'), consult Patrizia Bettella, 'Discourse of Resistance: The Parody of Feminine Beauty in Berni, Doni and Firenzuola', *MLN* 113.1 (1998) 192-203.

35. For another study of Bembo's influence on Ronsard (that does not treat this particular case), see Charles Dédéyan, 'Ronsard et Bembo', in *Ronsard e l'Italia, Ronsard in Italia: Atti del primo covegno del gruppo di studio sul Cinquecento francese* (Fasano: Schena, 1988), 27-51.

36. For a Petrarchan analogue of this image, see *RS* 199: 1 'O bella man, che mi distringi 'l core'.

37. For more on this aspect of Ronsard's imitative practice, see Greene, *The Light in Troy,* 199-201.

38. Renaissance humanists often engaged in this learned game of *allusio* whereby meaning is sought through the *rapprochement* of two similarly sounding words or names, whether or not these are in fact derived from the same root. For an example of such wordplay, see Du Bellay's *Xenia,* which explicates the meaning of names in this fashion (e.g. the poet Olivier de Magny's name is related to the words 'magnus' or 'great' and 'magnes' or 'magnetism'). For this, see Du Bellay, *Oeuvres poétiques* VIII (*Autres oeuvres latines*), ed. Geneviève Demerson (Paris: Nizet, 1985), 94-5 (*Xenia* 50). I am indebted to Philip Ford for this reference.

39. For more on this topic with respect to the Pléiade poets' learned master, Jean Dorat, consult Geneviève Demerson, *Dorat en son temps: Culture classique et présence au monde* (Clermont-Ferrand: ADOSA, 1983) 210-212. See also the 'Introduction' to Dorat, *Mythologicum,* ed. Philip Ford (Geneva: Droz, 2000), xxi-xxix. For Du Bellay's use of *allusio,* see note 38 above. For a discussion of a similar (but perhaps less

intentional) slippage in meaning regarding the adjective 'vair' (from 'soft' or 'bright' to 'green') to describe a lady's eyes in medieval French texts, consult Saunders, *Blason Poétique,* 65-66, who shows how this word was sometimes replaced by the unequivocal 'doux' or 'verdelet', depending on how the author understood the term.

40. *Rime diverse di molti eccellentissimi auttori nuovamente raccolte* (Venice: Giolito, 1546). This anthology was first published in 1545, but Ronsard's personal copy is the second edition, printed in 1546. For a modern edition of the first Giolito volume, see *Rime diverse di molti eccellentissimi autori,* eds. Franco Tomasi and Paolo Zaja (Turin: Edizione RES, 2001).

41. For a more extensive analysis of Ronsard's reuse of the Gesualdo poems, which he underscored in his personal copy of the first volume of the Giolito anthologies, see my 'Marginal Notes on Marginal Poets: Ronsard Reading the Giolito Anthologies', forthcoming in *Esprit généreux, esprit pantagruélique: Essays in Honor of François Rigolot* (Geneva: Droz).

FURTHER READING

Criticism

Campo, Roberto E. "Ronsard's Eutrapelian *Gaillardise.*" *Neophilologus* 87 (2003): 529-51.

Discusses Ronsard's use of the term "gaillard," contending that it is one of "the most semantically loaded and etymologically enigmatic words of the early modern French language."

Ford, Philip. "The Theoretical Background." In *Ronsard's* Hymnes: *A Literary and Iconographical Study,* pp. 19-57. Tempe, Ariz.: Medieval and Renaissance Texts and Studies, 1997.

Examination of Ronsard's ideas on the nature of poetry as envisioned by the Neo-Platonists, as well as the development of his own poetic theory that informed his own poems, particularly those in the *Hymnes.*

MacPhail, Eric. "Rich Rhyme: Acoustic Allusions in Ronsard's *Amours.*" *French Forum* 27, no. 2 (spring 2002): 1-12.

Discussion of verbal echoes such as rhyme, alliteration, and assonance in Ronsard's *Amours.*

Murphy, Stephen. "Ronsard, Polemic, and Palinode." *Mediaevalia* 22, no. Special Issue (1999): 75-101.

Examines Ronsard's *Discours des misères de ce temps* and the responses to it in the literary discourse surrounding the French civil wars of the sixteenth century.

Additional coverage of Ronsard's life and work is contained in the following sources published by Gale: *Dictionary of Literary Biography,* **Vol. 327;** *European Writers,* **Vol. 2;** *Guide to French Literature: Beginnings to 1789*; *Literature Criticism from 1400 to 1800,* **Vols. 6, 54;** *Literature Resource Center*; *Poetry Criticism,* **Vol. 11;** *Reference Guide to World Literature,* **Eds. 2, 3; and** *Twayne's World Authors.*

How to Use This Index

The main references

Calvino, Italo
1923-1985 .... **CLC 5, 8, 11, 22, 33, 39,
73; SSC 3, 48**

list all author entries in the following Gale Literary Criticism series:

AAL = *Asian American Literature*
BG = *The Beat Generation: A Gale Critical Companion*
BLC = *Black Literature Criticism*
BLCS = *Black Literature Criticism Supplement*
CLC = *Contemporary Literary Criticism*
CLR = *Children's Literature Review*
CMLC = *Classical and Medieval Literature Criticism*
DC = *Drama Criticism*
FL = *Feminism in Literature: A Gale Critical Companion*
GL = *Gothic Literature: A Gale Critical Companion*
HLC = *Hispanic Literature Criticism*
HLCS = *Hispanic Literature Criticism Supplement*
HR = *Harlem Renaissance: A Gale Critical Companion*
LC = *Literature Criticism from 1400 to 1800*
NCLC = *Nineteenth-Century Literature Criticism*
NNAL = *Native North American Literature*
PC = *Poetry Criticism*
SSC = *Short Story Criticism*
TCLC = *Twentieth-Century Literary Criticism*
WLC = *World Literature Criticism, 1500 to the Present*
WLCS = *World Literature Criticism Supplement*

The cross-references

See also CA 85-88, 116; CANR 23, 61;
DAM NOV; DLB 196; EW 13; MTCW 1, 2;
RGSF 2; RGWL 2; SFW 4; SSFS 12

list all author entries in the following Gale biographical and literary sources:

AAYA = *Authors & Artists for Young Adults*
AFAW = *African American Writers*
AFW = *African Writers*
AITN = *Authors in the News*
AMW = *American Writers*
AMWR = *American Writers Retrospective Supplement*
AMWS = *American Writers Supplement*
ANW = *American Nature Writers*
AW = *Ancient Writers*
BEST = *Bestsellers*
BPFB = *Beacham's Encyclopedia of Popular Fiction: Biography and Resources*
BRW = *British Writers*
BRWS = *British Writers Supplement*
BW = *Black Writers*
BYA = *Beacham's Guide to Literature for Young Adults*
CA = *Contemporary Authors*
CAAS = *Contemporary Authors Autobiography Series*
CABS = *Contemporary Authors Bibliographical Series*
CAD = *Contemporary American Dramatists*
CANR = *Contemporary Authors New Revision Series*
CAP = *Contemporary Authors Permanent Series*
CBD = *Contemporary British Dramatists*
CCA = *Contemporary Canadian Authors*
CD = *Contemporary Dramatists*
CDALB = *Concise Dictionary of American Literary Biography*

CDALBS = Concise Dictionary of American Literary Biography Supplement
CDBLB = Concise Dictionary of British Literary Biography
CMW = St. James Guide to Crime & Mystery Writers
CN = Contemporary Novelists
CP = Contemporary Poets
CPW = Contemporary Popular Writers
CSW = Contemporary Southern Writers
CWD = Contemporary Women Dramatists
CWP = Contemporary Women Poets
CWRI = St. James Guide to Children's Writers
CWW = Contemporary World Writers
DA = DISCovering Authors
DA3 = DISCovering Authors 3.0
DAB = DISCovering Authors: British Edition
DAC = DISCovering Authors: Canadian Edition
DAM = DISCovering Authors: Modules
   DRAM: Dramatists Module; **MST:** Most-studied Authors Module;
   MULT: Multicultural Authors Module; **NOV:** Novelists Module;
   POET: Poets Module; **POP:** Popular Fiction and Genre Authors Module
DFS = Drama for Students
DLB = Dictionary of Literary Biography
DLBD = Dictionary of Literary Biography Documentary Series
DLBY = Dictionary of Literary Biography Yearbook
DNFS = Literature of Developing Nations for Students
EFS = Epics for Students
EW = European Writers
EWL = Encyclopedia of World Literature in the 20th Century
EXPN = Exploring Novels
EXPP = Exploring Poetry
EXPS = Exploring Short Stories
FANT = St. James Guide to Fantasy Writers
FW = Feminist Writers
GFL = Guide to French Literature, Beginnings to 1789, 1798 to the Present
GLL = Gay and Lesbian Literature
HGG = St. James Guide to Horror, Ghost & Gothic Writers
HW = Hispanic Writers
IDFW = International Dictionary of Films and Filmmakers: Writers and Production Artists
IDTP = International Dictionary of Theatre: Playwrights
LAIT = Literature and Its Times
LAW = Latin American Writers
JRDA = Junior DISCovering Authors
MAICYA = Major Authors and Illustrators for Children and Young Adults
MAICYAS = Major Authors and Illustrators for Children and Young Adults Supplement
MAWW = Modern American Women Writers
MJW = Modern Japanese Writers
MTCW = Major 20th-Century Writers
NCFS = Nonfiction Classics for Students
NFS = Novels for Students
PAB = Poets: American and British
PFS = Poetry for Students
RGAL = Reference Guide to American Literature
RGEL = Reference Guide to English Literature
RGSF = Reference Guide to Short Fiction
RGWL = Reference Guide to World Literature
RHW = Twentieth-Century Romance and Historical Writers
SAAS = Something about the Author Autobiography Series
SATA = Something about the Author
SFW = St. James Guide to Science Fiction Writers
SSFS = Short Stories for Students
TCWW = Twentieth-Century Western Writers
WLIT = World Literature and Its Times
WP = World Poets
YABC = Yesterday's Authors of Books for Children
YAW = St. James Guide to Young Adult Writers

Literary Criticism Series
Cumulative Author Index

Antschel, Paul
See Celan, Paul

Anwar, Chairil 1922-1949 .... **TCLC 22**
See also CA 121; 219; EWL 3; RGWL 3

Anyidoho, Kofi 1947- .... **BLC 2:1**
See also BW 3; CA 178; CP 5, 6, 7; DLB
157; EWL 3

Anzaldua, Gloria (Evanjelina)
1942-2004 .... **CLC 200; HLCS 1**
See also CA 175; 227; CSW; CWP; DLB
122; FW; LLW; RGAL 4; SATA-Obit 154

Apess, William 1798-1839(?) .... **NCLC 73;
NNAL**
See also DAM MULT; DLB 175, 243

Apollinaire, Guillaume 1880-1918 .... **PC 7;
TCLC 3, 8, 51**
See also CA 104; 152; DAM POET; DLB
258, 321; EW 9; EWL 3; GFL 1789 to
the Present; MTCW 2; PFS 24; RGWL 2,
3; TWA; WP

Apollonius of Rhodes
See Apollonius Rhodius

Apollonius Rhodius c. 300B.C.-c.
220B.C. .... **CMLC 28**
See also AW 1; DLB 176; RGWL 2, 3

Appelfeld, Aharon 1932- ... **CLC 23, 47; SSC
42**
See also CA 112; 133; CANR 86, 160;
CWW 2; DLB 299; EWL 3; RGHL;
RGSF 2; WLIT 6

Appelfeld, Aron
See Appelfeld, Aharon

Apple, Max (Isaac) 1941- .... **CLC 9, 33; SSC
50**
See also AMWS 17; CA 81-84; CANR 19,
54; DLB 130

Appleman, Philip (Dean) 1926- .... **CLC 51**
See also CA 13-16R; CAAS 18; CANR 6,
29, 56

Appleton, Lawrence
See Lovecraft, H. P.

Apteryx
See Eliot, T. S.

Apuleius, (Lucius Madaurensis) c. 125-c.
164 .... **CMLC 1, 84**
See also AW 2; CDWLB 1; DLB 211;
RGWL 2, 3; SUFW; WLIT 8

Aquin, Hubert 1929-1977 .... **CLC 15**
See also CA 105; DLB 53; EWL 3

Aquinas, Thomas 1224(?)-1274 ..... **CMLC 33**
See also DLB 115; EW 1; TWA

Aragon, Louis 1897-1982 .... **CLC 3, 22;
TCLC 123**
See also CA 69-72; 108; CANR 28, 71;
DAM NOV, POET; DLB 72, 258; EW 11;
EWL 3; GFL 1789 to the Present; GLL 2;
LMFS 2; MTCW 1, 2; RGWL 2, 3

Arany, Janos 1817-1882 .... **NCLC 34**

Aranyos, Kakay 1847-1910
See Mikszath, Kalman

Aratus of Soli c. 315B.C.-c.
240B.C. .... **CMLC 64, 114**
See also DLB 176

Arbuthnot, John 1667-1735 .... **LC 1**
See also DLB 101

Archer, Herbert Winslow
See Mencken, H. L.

Archer, Jeffrey 1940- .... **CLC 28**
See also AAYA 16; BEST 89:3; BPFB 1;
CA 77-80; CANR 22, 52, 95, 136; CPW;
DA3; DAM POP; INT CANR-22; MTFW
2005

Archer, Jeffrey Howard
See Archer, Jeffrey

Archer, Jules 1915- .... **CLC 12**
See also CA 9-12R; CANR 6, 69; SAAS 5;
SATA 4, 85

Archer, Lee
See Ellison, Harlan

Archilochus c. 7th cent. B.C.- .... **CMLC 44**
See also DLB 176

Ard, William
See Jakes, John

Arden, John 1930- .... **CLC 6, 13, 15**
See also BRWS 2; CA 13-16R; CAAS 4;
CANR 31, 65, 67, 124; CBD; CD 5, 6;
DAM DRAM; DFS 9; DLB 13, 245;
EWL 3; MTCW 1

Arenas, Reinaldo 1943-1990 .. **CLC 41; HLC
1; TCLC 191**
See also CA 124; 128; 133; CANR 73, 106;
DAM MULT; DLB 145; EWL 3; GLL 2;
HW 1; LAW; LAWS 1; MTCW 2; MTFW
2005; RGSF 2; RGWL 3; WLIT 1

Arendt, Hannah 1906-1975 .... **CLC 66, 98;
TCLC 193**
See also CA 17-20R; 61-64; CANR 26, 60,
172; DLB 242; MTCW 1, 2

Aretino, Pietro 1492-1556 .... **LC 12, 165**
See also RGWL 2, 3.

Arghezi, Tudor
See Theodorescu, Ion N.

Arguedas, Jose Maria 1911-1969 .... **CLC 10,
18; HLCS 1; TCLC 147**
See also CA 89-92; CANR 73; DLB 113;
EWL 3; HW 1; LAW; RGWL 2, 3; WLIT
1

Argueta, Manlio 1936- .... **CLC 31**
See also CA 131; CANR 73; CWW 2; DLB
145; EWL 3; HW 1; RGWL 3

Arias, Ron 1941- .... **HLC 1**
See also CA 131; CANR 81, 136; DAM
MULT; DLB 82; HW 1, 2; MTCW 2;
MTFW 2005

Ariosto, Lodovico
See Ariosto, Ludovico

Ariosto, Ludovico 1474-1533 ... **LC 6, 87; PC
42**
See also EW 2; RGWL 2, 3; WLIT 7

Aristides
See Epstein, Joseph

Aristophanes 450B.C.-385B.C. .... **CMLC 4,
51; DC 2; WLCS**
See also AW 1; CDWLB 1; DA; DA3;
DAB; DAC; DAM DRAM, MST; DFS
10; DLB 176; LMFS 1; RGWL 2, 3;
TWA; WLIT 8

Aristotle 384B.C.-322B.C. .... **CMLC 31;
WLCS**
See also AW 1; CDWLB 1; DA; DA3;
DAB; DAC; DAM MST; DLB 176;
RGWL 2, 3; TWA; WLIT 8

Arlt, Roberto 1900-1942 .. **HLC 1; TCLC 29**
See also CA 123; 131; CANR 67; DAM
MULT; DLB 305; EWL 3; HW 1, 2;
IDTP; LAW

Arlt, Roberto Godofredo Christophersen
See Arlt, Roberto

Armah, Ayi Kwei 1939- . **BLC 1:1, 2:1; CLC
5, 33, 136**
See also AFW; BRWS 10; BW 1; CA 61-
64; CANR 21, 64; CDWLB 3; CN 1, 2,
3, 4, 5, 6, 7; DAM MULT, POET; DLB
117; EWL 3; MTCW 1; WLIT 2

Armatrading, Joan 1950- .... **CLC 17**
See also CA 114; 186

Armin, Robert 1568(?)-1615(?) .... **LC 120**

Armitage, Frank
See Carpenter, John

Armstrong, Jeannette (C.) 1948- .... **NNAL**
See also CA 149; CCA 1; CN 6, 7; DAC;
DLB 334; SATA 102

Arnauld, Antoine 1612-1694 .... **LC 169**
See also DLB 268

Arnette, Robert
See Silverberg, Robert

**Arnim, Achim von (Ludwig Joachim von
Arnim)** 1781-1831 .. **NCLC 5, 159; SSC
29**
See also DLB 90

Arnim, Bettina von 1785-1859 ...... **NCLC 38,
123**
See also DLB 90; RGWL 2, 3

Arnold, Matthew 1822-1888 ..... **NCLC 6, 29,
89, 126, 218; PC 5, 94; WLC 1**
See also BRW 5; CDBLB 1832-1890; DA;
DAB; DAC; DAM MST, POET; DLB 32,
57; EXPP; PAB; PFS 2; TEA; WP

Arnold, Thomas 1795-1842 .... **NCLC 18**
See also DLB 55

Arnow, Harriette (Louisa) Simpson
1908-1986 ...... **CLC 2, 7, 18; TCLC 196**
See also BPFB 1; CA 9-12R; 118; CANR
14; CN 2, 3, 4; DLB 6; FW; MTCW 1, 2;
RHW; SATA 42; SATA-Obit 47

Arouet, Francois-Marie
See Voltaire

Arp, Hans
See Arp, Jean

Arp, Jean 1887-1966 .... **CLC 5; TCLC 115**
See also CA 81-84; 25-28R; CANR 42, 77;
EW 10

Arrabal
See Arrabal, Fernando

Arrabal, Fernando 1932- .. **CLC 2, 9, 18, 58;
DC 35**
See also CA 9-12R; CANR 15; CWW 2;
DLB 321; EWL 3; LMFS 2

Arrabal Teran, Fernando
See Arrabal, Fernando

Arreola, Juan Jose 1918-2001 .... **CLC 147;
HLC 1; SSC 38**
See also CA 113; 131; 200; CANR 81;
CWW 2; DAM MULT; DLB 113; DNFS
2; EWL 3; HW 1, 2; LAW; RGSF 2

Arrian c. 89(?)-c. 155(?) .... **CMLC 43**
See also DLB 176

Arrick, Fran
See Angell, Judie

Arrley, Richmond
See Delany, Samuel R., Jr.

Artaud, Antonin 1896-1948 ... **DC 14; TCLC
3, 36**
See also CA 104; 149; DA3; DAM DRAM;
DFS 22; DLB 258, 321; EW 11; EWL 3;
GFL 1789 to the Present; MTCW 2;
MTFW 2005; RGWL 2, 3

Artaud, Antonin Marie Joseph
See Artaud, Antonin

Arthur, Ruth M(abel) 1905-1979 ..... **CLC 12**
See also CA 9-12R; 85-88; CANR 4; CWRI
5; SATA 7, 26

Artsybashev, Mikhail (Petrovich)
1878-1927 .... **TCLC 31**
See also CA 170; DLB 295

Arundel, Honor (Morfydd)
1919-1973 .... **CLC 17**
See also CA 21-22; 41-44R; CAP 2; CLR
35; CWRI 5; SATA 4; SATA-Obit 24

Arzner, Dorothy 1900-1979 .... **CLC 98**

Asch, Sholem 1880-1957 .... **TCLC 3**
See also CA 105; DLB 333; EWL 3; GLL
2; RGHL

Ascham, Roger 1516(?)-1568 .... **LC 101**
See also DLB 236

Ash, Shalom
See Asch, Sholem

Ashbery, John 1927- ... **CLC 2, 3, 4, 6, 9, 13,
15, 25, 41, 77, 125, 221; PC 26**
See also AMWS 3; CA 5-8R; CANR 9, 37,
66, 102, 132, 170; CP 1, 2, 3, 4, 5, 6, 7;
DA3; DAM POET; DLB 5, 165; DLBY
1981; EWL 3; GLL 1; INT CANR-9;
MAL 5; MTCW 1, 2; MTFW 2005; PAB;
PFS 11, 28; RGAL 4; TCLE 1:1; WP

Baudouin, Marcel
 See Peguy, Charles (Pierre)
Baudouin, Pierre
 See Peguy, Charles (Pierre)
Baudrillard, Jean 1929-2007 .... **CLC 60**
 See also CA 252; 258; DLB 296
Baum, L. Frank 1856-1919 ...... **TCLC 7, 132**
 See also AAYA 46; BYA 16; CA 108; 133;
 CLR 15, 107; CWRI 5; DLB 22; FANT;
 JRDA; MAICYA 1, 2; MTCW 1, 2; NFS
 13; RGAL 4; SATA 18, 100; WCH
Baum, Louis F.
 See Baum, L. Frank
Baum, Lyman Frank
 See Baum, L. Frank
Baumbach, Jonathan 1933- .... **CLC 6, 23**
 See also CA 13-16R, 284; CAAE 284;
 CAAS 5; CANR 12, 66, 140; CN 3, 4, 5,
 6, 7; DLBY 1980; INT CANR-12; MTCW
 1
Bausch, Richard 1945- .... **CLC 51**
 See also AMWS 7; CA 101; CAAS 14;
 CANR 43, 61, 87, 164, 200; CN 7; CSW;
 DLB 130; MAL 5
Bausch, Richard Carl
 See Bausch, Richard
Baxter, Charles 1947- .... **CLC 45, 78**
 See also AMWS 17; CA 57-60; CANR 40,
 64, 104, 133, 188; CPW; DAM POP; DLB
 130; MAL 5; MTCW 2; MTFW 2005;
 TCLE 1:1
Baxter, Charles Morley
 See Baxter, Charles
Baxter, George Owen
 See Faust, Frederick
Baxter, James K(eir) 1926-1972 .... **CLC 14**
 See also CA 77-80; CP 1; EWL 3
Baxter, John
 See Hunt, E. Howard
Bayer, Sylvia
 See Glassco, John
Bayle, Pierre 1647-1706 .... **LC 126**
 See also DLB 268, 313; GFL Beginnings to
 1789
Baynton, Barbara 1857-1929 . **TCLC 57, 211**
 See also DLB 230; RGSF 2
Beagle, Peter S. 1939- .... **CLC 7, 104**
 See also AAYA 47; BPFB 1; BYA 9, 10,
 16; CA 9-12R; CANR 4, 51, 73, 110;
 DA3; DLBY 1980; FANT; INT CANR-4;
 MTCW 2; MTFW 2005; SATA 60, 130;
 SUFW 1, 2; YAW
Beagle, Peter Soyer
 See Beagle, Peter S.
Bean, Normal
 See Burroughs, Edgar Rice
Beard, Charles A(ustin)
 1874-1948 .... **TCLC 15**
 See also CA 115; 189; DLB 17; SATA 18
Beardsley, Aubrey 1872-1898 .... **NCLC 6**
Beatrice of Nazareth 1200-1268 .. **CMLC 114**
Beattie, Ann 1947- ..... **CLC 8, 13, 18, 40, 63,
 146; SSC 11, 130**
 See also AMWS 5; BEST 90:2; BPFB 1;
 CA 81-84; CANR 53, 73, 128; CN 4, 5,
 6, 7; CPW; DA3; DAM NOV, POP; DLB
 218, 278; DLBY 1982; EWL 3; MAL 5;
 MTCW 1, 2; MTFW 2005; RGAL 4;
 RGSF 2; SSFS 9; TUS
Beattie, James 1735-1803 .... **NCLC 25**
 See also DLB 109
Beauchamp, Katherine Mansfield
 See Mansfield, Kathleen
Beaumarchais, Pierre-Augustin Caron de
 1732-1799 .... **DC 4; LC 61**
 See also DAM DRAM; DFS 14, 16; DLB
 313; EW 4; GFL Beginnings to 1789;
 RGWL 2, 3

Beaumont, Francis 1584(?)-1616 .. **DC 6; LC
 33**
 See also BRW 2; CDBLB Before 1660;
 DLB 58; TEA
Beauvoir, Simone de 1908-1986 .... **CLC 1, 2,
 4, 8, 14, 31, 44, 50, 71, 124; SSC 35;
 TCLC 221; WLC 1**
 See also BPFB 1; CA 9-12R; 118; CANR
 28, 61; DA; DA3; DAB; DAC; DAM
 MST, NOV; DLB 72; DLBY 1986; EW
 12; EWL 3; FL 1:5; FW; GFL 1789 to the
 Present; LMFS 2; MTCW 1, 2; MTFW
 2005; RGSF 2; RGWL 2, 3; TWA
**Beauvoir, Simone Lucie Ernestine Marie
 Bertrand de**
 See Beauvoir, Simone de
Becker, Carl (Lotus) 1873-1945 ..... **TCLC 63**
 See also CA 157; DLB 17
Becker, Jurek 1937-1997 .... **CLC 7, 19**
 See also CA 85-88; 157; CANR 60, 117;
 CWW 2; DLB 75, 299; EWL 3; RGHL
Becker, Walter 1950- .... **CLC 26**
Becket, Thomas a 1118(?)-1170 .... **CMLC 83**
Beckett, Samuel 1906-1989 ... **CLC 1, 2, 3, 4,
 6, 9, 10, 11, 14, 18, 29, 57, 59, 83; DC
 22; SSC 16, 74; TCLC 145; WLC 1**
 See also BRWC 2; BRWR 1; BRWS 1; CA
 5-8R; 130; CANR 33, 61; CBD; CDBLB
 1945-1960; CN 1, 2, 3, 4; CP 1, 2, 3, 4;
 DA; DA3; DAB; DAC; DAM DRAM,
 MST, NOV; DFS 2, 7, 18; DLB 13, 15,
 233, 319, 321, 329; DLBY 1990; EWL 3;
 GFL 1789 to the Present; LATS 1:2;
 LMFS 2; MTCW 1, 2; MTFW 2005;
 RGSF 2; RGWL 2, 3; SSFS 15; TEA;
 WLIT 4
Beckett, Samuel Barclay
 See Beckett, Samuel
Beckford, William 1760-1844 .... **NCLC 16,
 214**
 See also BRW 3; DLB 39, 213; GL 2; HGG;
 LMFS 1; SUFW
Beckham, Barry (Earl) 1944- .... **BLC 1:1**
 See also BW 1; CA 29-32R; CANR 26, 62;
 CN 1, 2, 3, 4, 5, 6; DAM MULT; DLB 33
Beckman, Gunnel 1910- .... **CLC 26**
 See also CA 33-36R; CANR 15, 114; CLR
 25; MAICYA 1, 2; SAAS 9; SATA 6
Becque, Henri 1837-1899 .... **DC 21; NCLC 3**
 See also DLB 192; GFL 1789 to the Present
Becquer, Gustavo Adolfo
 1836-1870 .... **HLCS 1; NCLC 106**
 See also DAM MULT
Beddoes, Thomas Lovell 1803-1849 .. **DC 15;
 NCLC 3, 154**
 See also BRWS 11; DLB 96
Bede c. 673-735 .... **CMLC 20**
 See also DLB 146; TEA
Bedford, Denton R. 1907-(?) .... **NNAL**
Bedford, Donald F.
 See Fearing, Kenneth
Beecher, Catharine Esther
 1800-1878 .... **NCLC 30**
 See also DLB 1, 243
Beecher, John 1904-1980 .... **CLC 6**
 See also AITN 1; CA 5-8R; 105; CANR 8;
 CP 1, 2, 3
Beer, Johann 1655-1700 .... **LC 5**
 See also DLB 168
Beer, Patricia 1924- .... **CLC 58**
 See also BRWS 14; CA 61-64; 183; CANR
 13, 46; CP 1, 2, 3, 4, 5, 6; CWP; DLB
 40; FW
Beerbohm, Max
 See Beerbohm, (Henry) Max(imilian)
Beerbohm, (Henry) Max(imilian)
 1872-1956 .... **TCLC 1, 24**
 See also BRWS 2; CA 104; 154; CANR 79;
 DLB 34, 100; FANT; MTCW 2

Beer-Hofmann, Richard
 1866-1945 .... **TCLC 60**
 See also CA 160; DLB 81
Beg, Shemus
 See Stephens, James
Begiebing, Robert J(ohn) 1946- .... **CLC 70**
 See also CA 122; CANR 40, 88
Begley, Louis 1933- .... **CLC 197**
 See also CA 140; CANR 98, 176; DLB 299;
 RGHL; TCLE 1:1
Behan, Brendan 1923-1964 ...... **CLC 1, 8, 11,
 15, 79**
 See also BRWS 2; CA 73-76; CANR 33,
 121; CBD; CDBLB 1945-1960; DAM
 DRAM; DFS 7; DLB 13, 233; EWL 3;
 MTCW 1, 2
Behan, Brendan Francis
 See Behan, Brendan
Behn, Aphra 1640(?)-1689 .. **DC 4; LC 1, 30,
 42, 135; PC 13, 88; WLC 1**
 See also BRWR 3; BRWS 3; DA; DA3;
 DAB; DAC; DAM DRAM, MST, NOV,
 POET; DFS 16, 24; DLB 39, 80, 131; FW;
 TEA; WLIT 3
Behrman, S(amuel) N(athaniel)
 1893-1973 .... **CLC 40**
 See also CA 13-16; 45-48; CAD; CAP 1;
 DLB 7, 44; IDFW 3; MAL 5; RGAL 4
Bekederemo, J. P. Clark
 See Clark-Bekederemo, J. P.
Belasco, David 1853-1931 .... **TCLC 3**
 See also CA 104; 168; DLB 7; MAL 5;
 RGAL 4
Belben, Rosalind 1941- .... **CLC 280**
 See also CA 291
Belben, Rosalind Loveday
 See Belben, Rosalind
Belcheva, Elisaveta Lyubomirova
 1893-1991 .... **CLC 10**
 See also CA 178; CDWLB 4; DLB 147;
 EWL 3
Beldone, Phil "Cheech"
 See Ellison, Harlan
Beleno
 See Azuela, Mariano
Belinski, Vissarion Grigoryevich
 1811-1848 .... **NCLC 5**
 See also DLB 198
Belitt, Ben 1911- .... **CLC 22**
 See also CA 13-16R; CAAS 4; CANR 7,
 77; CP 1, 2, 3, 4, 5, 6; DLB 5
Belknap, Jeremy 1744-1798 .... **LC 115**
 See also DLB 30, 37
Bell, Gertrude (Margaret Lowthian)
 1868-1926 .... **TCLC 67**
 See also CA 167; CANR 110; DLB 174
Bell, J. Freeman
 See Zangwill, Israel
Bell, James Madison 1826-1902 ..... **BLC 1:1;
 TCLC 43**
 See also BW 1; CA 122; 124; DAM MULT;
 DLB 50
Bell, Madison Smartt 1957- ..... **CLC 41, 102,
 223**
 See also AMWS 10; BPFB 1; CA 111, 183;
 CAAE 183; CANR 28, 54, 73, 134, 176;
 CN 5, 6, 7; CSW; DLB 218, 278; MTCW
 2; MTFW 2005
Bell, Marvin (Hartley) 1937- ...... **CLC 8, 31;
 PC 79**
 See also CA 21-24R; CAAS 14; CANR 59,
 102; CP 1, 2, 3, 4, 5, 6, 7; DAM POET;
 DLB 5; MAL 5; MTCW 1; PFS 25
Bell, W. L. D.
 See Mencken, H. L.
Bellamy, Atwood C.
 See Mencken, H. L.

Bissoondath, Neil Devindra
See Bissoondath, Neil
Bitov, Andrei (Georgievich) 1937- ... **CLC 57**
See also CA 142; DLB 302
Biyidi, Alexandre
See Beti, Mongo
Bjarme, Brynjolf
See Ibsen, Henrik
Bjoernson, Bjoernstjerne (Martinius)
1832-1910 .... **TCLC 7, 37**
See also CA 104
Black, Benjamin
See Banville, John
Black, Robert
See Holdstock, Robert
Blackburn, Paul 1926-1971 .... **CLC 9, 43**
See also BG 1:2; CA 81-84; 33-36R; CANR
34; CP 1; DLB 16; DLBY 1981
Black Elk 1863-1950 .... **NNAL; TCLC 33**
See also CA 144; DAM MULT; MTCW 2;
MTFW 2005; WP
Black Hawk 1767-1838 .... **NNAL**
Black Hobart
See Sanders, Ed
Blacklin, Malcolm
See Chambers, Aidan
Blackmore, R(ichard) D(oddridge)
1825-1900 .... **TCLC 27**
See also CA 120; DLB 18; RGEL 2
Blackmur, R(ichard) P(almer)
1904-1965 .... **CLC 2, 24**
See also AMWS 2; CA 11-12; 25-28R;
CANR 71; CAP 1; DLB 63; EWL 3;
MAL 5
Black Tarantula
See Acker, Kathy
Blackwood, Algernon 1869-1951 .... **SSC 107;**
TCLC 5
See also AAYA 78; CA 105; 150; CANR
169; DLB 153, 156, 178; HGG; SUFW 1
Blackwood, Algernon Henry
See Blackwood, Algernon
Blackwood, Caroline (Maureen)
1931-1996 .... **CLC 6, 9, 100**
See also BRWS 9; CA 85-88; 151; CANR
32, 61, 65; CN 3, 4, 5, 6; DLB 14, 207;
HGG; MTCW 1
Blade, Alexander
See Hamilton, Edmond; Silverberg, Robert
Blaga, Lucian 1895-1961 .... **CLC 75**
See also CA 157; DLB 220; EWL 3
Blair, Eric
See Orwell, George
Blair, Eric Arthur
See Orwell, George
Blair, Hugh 1718-1800 .... **NCLC 75**
Blais, Marie-Claire 1939- .... **CLC 2, 4, 6, 13,**
22
See also CA 21-24R; CAAS 4; CANR 38,
75, 93; CWW 2; DAC; DAM MST; DLB
53; EWL 3; FW; MTCW 1, 2; MTFW
2005; TWA
Blaise, Clark 1940- .... **CLC 29, 261**
See also AITN 2; CA 53-56, 231; CAAE
231; CAAS 3; CANR 5, 66, 106; CN 4,
5, 6, 7; DLB 53; RGSF 2
Blake, Fairley
See De Voto, Bernard (Augustine)
Blake, Nicholas
See Day Lewis, C.
Blake, Sterling
See Benford, Gregory
Blake, William 1757-1827 . **NCLC 13, 37, 57,**
127, 173, 190, 201; PC 12, 63; WLC 1
See also AAYA 47; BRW 3; BRWR 1; CD-
BLB 1789-1832; CLR 52; DA; DA3;
DAB; DAC; DAM MST, POET; DLB 93,

163; EXPP; LATS 1:1; LMFS 1; MAI-
CYA 1, 2; PAB; PFS 2, 12, 24; SATA 30;
TEA; WCH; WLIT 3; WP
Blanchot, Maurice 1907-2003 .... **CLC 135**
See also CA 117; 144; 213; CANR 138;
DLB 72, 296; EWL 3
Blasco Ibanez, Vicente 1867-1928 . **TCLC 12**
See also BPFB 1; CA 110; 131; CANR 81;
DA3; DAM NOV; DLB 322; EW 8; EWL
3; HW 1, 2; MTCW 1
Blatty, William Peter 1928- .... **CLC 2**
See also CA 5-8R; CANR 9, 124; DAM
POP; HGG
Bleeck, Oliver
See Thomas, Ross (Elmore)
Bleecker, Ann Eliza 1752-1783 .... **LC 161**
See also DLB 200
Blessing, Lee 1949- .... **CLC 54**
See also CA 236; CAD; CD 5, 6; DFS 23,
26
Blessing, Lee Knowlton
See Blessing, Lee
Blight, Rose
See Greer, Germaine
Blind, Mathilde 1841-1896 .... **NCLC 202**
See also DLB 199
Blish, James 1921-1975 .... **CLC 14**
See also BPFB 1; CA 1-4R; 57-60; CANR
3; CN 2; DLB 8; MTCW 1; SATA 66;
SCFW 1, 2; SFW 4
Blish, James Benjamin
See Blish, James
Bliss, Frederick
See Card, Orson Scott
Bliss, Gillian
See Paton Walsh, Jill
Bliss, Reginald
See Wells, H. G.
Blixen, Karen 1885-1962 ..... **CLC 10, 29, 95;**
SSC 7, 75
See also CA 25-28; CANR 22, 50; CAP 2;
DA3; DLB 214; EW 10; EWL 3; EXPS;
FW; GL 2; HGG; LAIT 3; LMFS 1;
MTCW 1; NCFS 2; NFS 9; RGSF 2;
RGWL 2, 3; SATA 44; SSFS 3, 6, 13;
WLIT 2
Blixen, Karen Christentze Dinesen
See Blixen, Karen
Bloch, Robert (Albert) 1917-1994 .... **CLC 33**
See also AAYA 29; CA 5-8R; 179; 146;
CAAE 179; CAAS 20; CANR 5, 78;
DA3; DLB 44; HGG; INT CANR-5;
MTCW 2; SATA 12; SATA-Obit 82; SFW
4; SUFW 1, 2
Blok, Alexander (Alexandrovich)
1880-1921 .... **PC 21; TCLC 5**
See also CA 104; 183; DLB 295; EW 9;
EWL 3; LMFS 2; RGWL 2, 3
Blom, Jan
See Breytenbach, Breyten
Bloom, Harold 1930- .... **CLC 24, 103, 221**
See also CA 13-16R; CANR 39, 75, 92,
133, 181; DLB 67; EWL 3; MTCW 2;
MTFW 2005; RGAL 4
Bloomfield, Aurelius
See Bourne, Randolph S(illiman)
Bloomfield, Robert 1766-1823 ..... **NCLC 145**
See also DLB 93
Blount, Roy, Jr. 1941- .... **CLC 38**
See also CA 53-56; CANR 10, 28, 61, 125,
176; CSW; INT CANR-28; MTCW 1, 2;
MTFW 2005
Blount, Roy Alton
See Blount, Roy, Jr.
Blowsnake, Sam 1875-(?) .... **NNAL**
Bloy, Leon 1846-1917 .... **TCLC 22**
See also CA 121; 183; DLB 123; GFL 1789
to the Present

Blue Cloud, Peter (Aroniawenrate)
1933- .... **NNAL**
See also CA 117; CANR 40; DAM MULT;
DLB 342
Bluggage, Oranthy
See Alcott, Louisa May
Blume, Judy 1938- .... **CLC 12, 30**
See also AAYA 3, 26; BYA 1, 8, 12; CA 29-
32R; CANR 13, 37, 66, 124, 186; CLR 2,
15, 69; CPW; DA3; DAM NOV, POP;
DLB 52; JRDA; MAICYA 1, 2; MAIC-
YAS 1; MTCW 1, 2; MTFW 2005; NFS
24; SATA 2, 31, 79, 142, 195; WYA; YAW
Blume, Judy Sussman
See Blume, Judy
Blunden, Edmund (Charles)
1896-1974 .... **CLC 2, 56; PC 66**
See also BRW 6; BRWS 11; CA 17-18; 45-
48; CANR 54; CAP 2; CP 1, 2; DLB 20,
100, 155; MTCW 1; PAB
Bly, Robert 1926- ..... **CLC 1, 2, 5, 10, 15, 38,**
128; PC 39
See also AMWS 4; CA 5-8R; CANR 41,
73, 125; CP 1, 2, 3, 4, 5, 6, 7; DA3; DAM
POET; DLB 5, 342; EWL 3; MAL 5;
MTCW 1, 2; MTFW 2005; PFS 6, 17;
RGAL 4
Bly, Robert Elwood
See Bly, Robert
Boas, Franz 1858-1942 .... **TCLC 56**
See also CA 115; 181
Bobette
See Simenon, Georges
Boccaccio, Giovanni 1313-1375 ... **CMLC 13,**
57; SSC 10, 87
See also EW 2; RGSF 2; RGWL 2, 3; TWA;
WLIT 7
Bochco, Steven 1943- .... **CLC 35**
See also AAYA 11, 71; CA 124; 138
Bode, Sigmund
See O'Doherty, Brian
Bodel, Jean 1167(?)-1210 .... **CMLC 28**
Bodenheim, Maxwell 1892-1954 .... **TCLC 44**
See also CA 110; 187; DLB 9, 45; MAL 5;
RGAL 4
Bodenheimer, Maxwell
See Bodenheim, Maxwell
Bodker, Cecil
See Bodker, Cecil
Bodker, Cecil 1927- .... **CLC 21**
See also CA 73-76; CANR 13, 44, 111;
CLR 23; MAICYA 1, 2; SATA 14, 133
Boell, Heinrich 1917-1985 ..... **CLC 2, 3, 6, 9,**
11, 15, 27, 32, 72; SSC 23; TCLC 185;
WLC 1
See also BPFB 1; CA 21-24R; 116; CANR
24; CDWLB 2; DA; DA3; DAB; DAC;
DAM MST, NOV; DLB 69, 329; DLBY
1985; EW 13; EWL 3; MTCW 1, 2;
MTFW 2005; RGHL; RGSF 2; RGWL 2,
3; SSFS 20; TWA
Boell, Heinrich Theodor
See Boell, Heinrich
Boerne, Alfred
See Doeblin, Alfred
Boethius c. 480-c. 524 .... **CMLC 15**
See also DLB 115; RGWL 2, 3; WLIT 8
Boff, Leonardo (Genezio Darci)
1938- .... **CLC 70; HLC 1**
See also CA 150; DAM MULT; HW 2
Bogan, Louise 1897-1970 .... **CLC 4, 39, 46,**
93; PC 12
See also AMWS 3; CA 73-76; 25-28R;
CANR 33, 82; CP 1; DAM POET; DLB
45, 169; EWL 3; MAL 5; MBL; MTCW
1, 2; PFS 21; RGAL 4
Bogarde, Dirk
See Van Den Bogarde, Derek Jules Gaspard
Ulric Niven

DAC; DAM NOV; DLB 14, 194, 261; DLBY 1998; EWL 3; MTCW 1, 2; MTFW 2005; NFS 15; RGEL 2; RHW; SFW 4; TEA; YAW

Buridan, John c. 1295-c. 1358 ...... **CMLC 97**

Burke, Edmund 1729(?)-1797 .... **LC 7, 36, 146; WLC 1**
See also BRW 3; DA; DA3; DAB; DAC; DAM MST; DLB 104, 252, 336; RGEL 2; TEA

Burke, Kenneth (Duva) 1897-1993 ... **CLC 2, 24**
See also AMW; CA 5-8R; 143; CANR 39, 74, 136; CN 1, 2; CP 1, 2, 3, 4, 5; DLB 45, 63; EWL 3; MAL 5; MTCW 1, 2; MTFW 2005; RGAL 4

Burke, Leda
See Garnett, David

Burke, Ralph
See Silverberg, Robert

Burke, Thomas 1886-1945 .... **TCLC 63**
See also CA 113; 155; CMW 4; DLB 197

Burney, Fanny 1752-1840 .... **NCLC 12, 54, 107**
See also BRWS 3; DLB 39; FL 1:2; NFS 16; RGEL 2; TEA

Burney, Frances
See Burney, Fanny

Burns, Robert 1759-1796 ... **LC 3, 29, 40; PC 6; WLC 1**
See also AAYA 51; BRW 3; CDBLB 1789-1832; DA; DA3; DAB; DAC; DAM MST, POET; DLB 109; EXPP; PAB; RGEL 2; TEA; WP

Burns, Tex
See L'Amour, Louis

Burnshaw, Stanley 1906-2005 ..... **CLC 3, 13, 44**
See also CA 9-12R; 243; CP 1, 2, 3, 4, 5, 6, 7; DLB 48; DLBY 1997

Burr, Anne 1937- .... **CLC 6**
See also CA 25-28R

Burroughs, Augusten 1965- .... **CLC 277**
See also AAYA 73; CA 214; CANR 168

Burroughs, Edgar Rice 1875-1950 . **TCLC 2, 32**
See also AAYA 11; BPFB 1; BYA 4, 9; CA 104; 132; CANR 131; DA3; DAM NOV; DLB 8; FANT; MTCW 1, 2; MTFW 2005; RGAL 4; SATA 41; SCFW 1, 2; SFW 4; TCWW 1, 2; TUS; YAW

Burroughs, William S. 1914-1997 . **CLC 1, 2, 5, 15, 22, 42, 75, 109; TCLC 121; WLC 1**
See also AAYA 60; AITN 2; AMWS 3; BG 1:2; BPFB 1; CA 9-12R; 160; CANR 20, 52, 104; CN 1, 2, 3, 4, 5, 6; CPW; DA; DA3; DAB; DAC; DAM MST, NOV, POP; DLB 2, 8, 16, 152, 237; DLBY 1981, 1997; EWL 3; GLL 1; HGG; LMFS 2; MAL 5; MTCW 1, 2; MTFW 2005; RGAL 4; SFW 4

Burroughs, William Seward
See Burroughs, William S.

Burton, Sir Richard F(rancis) 1821-1890 .... **NCLC 42**
See also DLB 55, 166, 184; SSFS 21

Burton, Robert 1577-1640 .... **LC 74**
See also DLB 151; RGEL 2

Buruma, Ian 1951- .... **CLC 163**
See also CA 128; CANR 65, 141, 195

Bury, Stephen
See Stephenson, Neal

Busch, Frederick 1941-2006 .. **CLC 7, 10, 18, 47, 166**
See also CA 33-36R; 248; CAAS 1; CANR 45, 73, 92, 157; CN 1, 2, 3, 4, 5, 6, 7; DLB 6, 218

Busch, Frederick Matthew
See Busch, Frederick

Bush, Barney (Furman) 1946- .... **NNAL**
See also CA 145

Bush, Ronald 1946- .... **CLC 34**
See also CA 136

Busia, Abena, P. A. 1953- .... **BLC 2:1**

Bustos, Francisco
See Borges, Jorge Luis

Bustos Domecq, Honorio
See Bioy Casares, Adolfo; Borges, Jorge Luis

Butler, Octavia 1947-2006 . **BLC 2:1; BLCS; CLC 38, 121, 230, 240**
See also AAYA 18, 48; AFAW 2; AMWS 13; BPFB 1; BW 2, 3; CA 73-76; 248; CANR 12, 24, 38, 73, 145, 240; CLR 65; CN 7; CPW; DA3; DAM MULT, POP; DLB 33; LATS 1:2; MTCW 1, 2; MTFW 2005; NFS 8, 21; SATA 84; SCFW 2; SFW 4; SSFS 6; TCLE 1:1; YAW

Butler, Octavia E.
See Butler, Octavia

Butler, Octavia Estelle
See Butler, Octavia

Butler, Robert Olen, Jr.
See Butler, Robert Olen

Butler, Robert Olen 1945- .... **CLC 81, 162; SSC 117**
See also AMWS 12; BPFB 1; CA 112; CANR 66, 138, 194; CN 7; CSW; DAM POP; DLB 173, 335; INT CA-112; MAL 5; MTCW 2; MTFW 2005; SSFS 11, 22

Butler, Samuel 1612-1680 .... **LC 16, 43, 173; PC 94**
See also DLB 101, 126; RGEL 2

Butler, Samuel 1835-1902 .... **TCLC 1, 33; WLC 1**
See also BRWS 2; CA 143; CDBLB 1890-1914; DA; DA3; DAB; DAC; DAM MST, NOV; DLB 18, 57, 174; RGEL 2; SFW 4; TEA

Butler, Walter C.
See Faust, Frederick

Butor, Michel (Marie Francois) 1926- ...... **CLC 1, 3, 8, 11, 15, 161**
See also CA 9-12R; CANR 33, 66; CWW 2; DLB 83; EW 13; EWL 3; GFL 1789 to the Present; MTCW 1, 2; MTFW 2005

Butts, Mary 1890(?)-1937 ... **SSC 124; TCLC 77**
See also CA 148; DLB 240

Buxton, Ralph
See Silverstein, Alvin; Silverstein, Virginia B.

Buzo, Alex
See Buzo, Alexander (John)

Buzo, Alexander (John) 1944- .... **CLC 61**
See also CA 97-100; CANR 17, 39, 69; CD 5, 6; DLB 289

Buzzati, Dino 1906-1972 .... **CLC 36**
See also CA 160; 33-36R; DLB 177; RGWL 2, 3; SFW 4

Byars, Betsy 1928- .... **CLC 35**
See also AAYA 19; BYA 3; CA 33-36R; 183; CAAE 183; CANR 18, 36, 57, 102, 148; CLR 1, 16, 72; DLB 52; INT CANR-18; JRDA; MAICYA 1, 2; MAICYAS 1; MTCW 1; SAAS 1; SATA 4, 46, 80, 163; SATA-Essay 108; WYA; YAW

Byars, Betsy Cromer
See Byars, Betsy

Byatt, A. S. 1936- .... **CLC 19, 65, 136, 223; SSC 91**
See also BPFB 1; BRWC 2; BRWS 4; CA 13-16R; CANR 13, 33, 50, 75, 96, 133; CN 1, 2, 3, 4, 5, 6; DA3; DAM NOV, POP; DLB 14, 194, 319, 326; EWL 3; MTCW 1, 2; MTFW 2005; RGSF 2; RHW; SSFS 26; TEA

Byatt, Antonia Susan Drabble
See Byatt, A. S.

Byrd, William II 1674-1744 .... **LC 112**
See also DLB 24, 140; RGAL 4

Byrne, David 1952- .... **CLC 26**
See also CA 127

Byrne, John Joseph
See Leonard, Hugh

Byrne, John Keyes
See Leonard, Hugh

Byron, George Gordon
See Lord Byron

Byron, George Gordon Noel
See Lord Byron

Byron, Robert 1905-1941 .... **TCLC 67**
See also CA 160; DLB 195

C. 3. 3.
See Wilde, Oscar

Caballero, Fernan 1796-1877 .... **NCLC 10**

Cabell, Branch
See Cabell, James Branch

Cabell, James Branch 1879-1958 .... **TCLC 6**
See also CA 105; 152; DLB 9, 78; FANT; MAL 5; MTCW 2; RGAL 4; SUFW 1

Cabeza de Vaca, Alvar Nunez 1490-1557(?) .... **LC 61**

Cable, George Washington 1844-1925 .... **SSC 4; TCLC 4**
See also CA 104; 155; DLB 12, 74; DLBD 13; RGAL 4; TUS

Cabral de Melo Neto, Joao 1920-1999 .... **CLC 76**
See also CA 151; CWW 2; DAM MULT; DLB 307; EWL 3; LAW; LAWS 1

Cabrera, Lydia 1900-1991 .... **TCLC 223**
See also CA 178; DLB 145; EWL 3; HW 1; LAWS 1

Cabrera Infante, G. 1929-2005 ... **CLC 5, 25, 45, 120; HLC 1; SSC 39**
See also CA 85-88; 236; CANR 29, 65, 110; CDWLB 3; CWW 2; DA3; DAM MULT; DLB 113; EWL 3; HW 1, 2; LAW; LAWS 1; MTCW 1, 2; MTFW 2005; RGSF 2; WLIT 1

Cabrera Infante, Guillermo
See Cabrera Infante, G.

Cade, Toni
See Bambara, Toni Cade

Cadmus and Harmonia
See Buchan, John

Caedmon fl. 658-680 .... **CMLC 7**
See also DLB 146

Caeiro, Alberto
See Pessoa, Fernando

Caesar, Julius
See Julius Caesar

Cage, John (Milton), (Jr.) 1912-1992 .... **CLC 41; PC 58**
See also CA 13-16R; 169; CANR 9, 78; DLB 193; INT CANR-9; TCLE 1:1

Cahan, Abraham 1860-1951 .... **TCLC 71**
See also CA 108; 154; DLB 9, 25, 28; MAL 5; RGAL 4

Cain, Christopher
See Fleming, Thomas

Cain, G.
See Cabrera Infante, G.

Cain, Guillermo
See Cabrera Infante, G.

Cain, James M(allahan) 1892-1977 .. **CLC 3, 11, 28**
See also AITN 1; BPFB 1; CA 17-20R; 73-76; CANR 8, 34, 61; CMW 4; CN 1, 2; DLB 226; EWL 3; MAL 5; MSW; MTCW 1; RGAL 4

Clifford, Lady Anne 1590-1676 .... **LC 76**
 See also DLB 151
Clifton, Lucille 1936- ..... **BLC 1:1, 2:1; CLC**
 19, 66, 162, 283; PC 17
 See also AFAW 2; BW 2, 3; CA 49-52;
 CANR 2, 24, 42, 76, 97, 138; CLR 5; CP
 2, 3, 4, 5, 6, 7; CSW; CWP; CWRI 5;
 DA3; DAM MULT, POET; DLB 5, 41;
 EXPP; MAICYA 1, 2; MTCW 1, 2;
 MTFW 2005; PFS 1, 14, 29; SATA 20,
 69, 128; WP
Clifton, Thelma Lucille
 See Clifton, Lucille
Clinton, Dirk
 See Silverberg, Robert
Clough, Arthur Hugh 1819-1861 .. **NCLC 27,**
 163; PC 103
 See also BRW 5; DLB 32; RGEL 2
Clutha, Janet Paterson Frame
 See Frame, Janet
Clyne, Terence
 See Blatty, William Peter
Cobalt, Martin
 See Mayne, William (James Carter)
Cobb, Irvin S(hrewsbury)
 1876-1944 .... **TCLC 77**
 See also CA 175; DLB 11, 25, 86
Cobbett, William 1763-1835 .... **NCLC 49**
 See also DLB 43, 107, 158; RGEL 2
Coben, Harlan 1962- .... **CLC 269**
 See also CA 164; CANR 162, 199
Coburn, D(onald) L(ee) 1938- .... **CLC 10**
 See also CA 89-92; DFS 23
Cocteau, Jean 1889-1963 ... **CLC 1, 8, 15, 16,**
 43; DC 17; TCLC 119; WLC 2
 See also AAYA 74; CA 25-28; CANR 40;
 CAP 2; DA; DA3; DAB; DAC; DAM
 DRAM, MST, NOV; DFS 24; DLB 65,
 258, 321; EW 10; EWL 3; GFL 1789 to
 the Present; MTCW 1, 2; RGWL 2, 3;
 TWA
Cocteau, Jean Maurice Eugene Clement
 See Cocteau, Jean
Codrescu, Andrei 1946- .... **CLC 46, 121**
 See also CA 33-36R; CAAS 19; CANR 13,
 34, 53, 76, 125; CN 7; DA3; DAM POET;
 MAL 5; MTCW 2; MTFW 2005
Coe, Max
 See Bourne, Randolph S(illiman)
Coe, Tucker
 See Westlake, Donald E.
Coelho, Paulo 1947- .... **CLC 258**
 See also CA 152; CANR 80, 93, 155, 194;
 NFS 29
Coen, Ethan 1957- .... **CLC 108, 267**
 See also AAYA 54; CA 126; CANR 85
Coen, Joel 1954- .... **CLC 108, 267**
 See also AAYA 54; CA 126; CANR 119
The Coen Brothers
 See Coen, Ethan; Coen, Joel
Coetzee, J. M. 1940- ..... **CLC 23, 33, 66, 117,**
 161, 162
 See also AAYA 37; AFW; BRWS 6; CA 77-
 80; CANR 41, 54, 74, 114, 133, 180; CN
 4, 5, 6, 7; DA3; DAM NOV; DLB 225,
 326, 329; EWL 3; LMFS 2; MTCW 1, 2;
 MTFW 2005; NFS 21; WLIT 2; WWE 1
Coetzee, John Maxwell
 See Coetzee, J. M.
Coffey, Brian
 See Koontz, Dean
Coffin, Robert P. Tristram
 1892-1955 .... **TCLC 95**
 See also CA 123; 169; DLB 45
Coffin, Robert Peter Tristram
 See Coffin, Robert P. Tristram
Cohan, George M. 1878-1942 .... **TCLC 60**
 See also CA 157; DLB 249; RGAL 4

Cohan, George Michael
 See Cohan, George M.
Cohen, Arthur A(llen) 1928-1986 ...... **CLC 7,**
 31
 See also CA 1-4R; 120; CANR 1, 17, 42;
 DLB 28; RGHL
Cohen, Leonard 1934- .... **CLC 3, 38, 260**
 See also CA 21-24R; CANR 14, 69; CN 1,
 2, 3, 4, 5, 6; CP 1, 2, 3, 4, 5, 6, 7; DAC;
 DAM MST; DLB 53; EWL 3; MTCW 1
Cohen, Leonard Norman
 See Cohen, Leonard
Cohen, Matt(hew) 1942-1999 .... **CLC 19**
 See also CA 61-64; 187; CAAS 18; CANR
 40; CN 1, 2, 3, 4, 5, 6; DAC; DLB 53
Cohen-Solal, Annie 1948- .... **CLC 50**
 See also CA 239
Colegate, Isabel 1931- .... **CLC 36**
 See also CA 17-20R; CANR 8, 22, 74; CN
 4, 5, 6, 7; DLB 14, 231; INT CANR-22;
 MTCW 1
Coleman, Emmett
 See Reed, Ishmael
Coleridge, Hartley 1796-1849 .... **NCLC 90**
 See also DLB 96
Coleridge, M. E.
 See Coleridge, Mary E(lizabeth)
Coleridge, Mary E(lizabeth)
 1861-1907 .... **TCLC 73**
 See also CA 116; 166; DLB 19, 98
Coleridge, Samuel Taylor
 1772-1834 ..... **NCLC 9, 54, 99, 111, 177,**
 197; PC 11, 39, 67, 100; WLC 2
 See also AAYA 66; BRW 4; BRWR 2; BYA
 4; CDBLB 1789-1832; DA; DA3; DAB;
 DAC; DAM MST, POET; DLB 93, 107;
 EXPP; LATS 1:1; LMFS 1; PAB; PFS 4,
 5; RGEL 2; TEA; WLIT 3; WP
Coleridge, Sara 1802-1852 .... **NCLC 31**
 See also DLB 199
Coles, Don 1928- .... **CLC 46**
 See also CA 115; CANR 38; CP 5, 6, 7
Coles, Robert (Martin) 1929- .... **CLC 108**
 See also CA 45-48; CANR 3, 32, 66, 70,
 135; INT CANR-32; SATA 23
Colette 1873-1954 ... **SSC 10, 93; TCLC 1, 5,**
 16
 See also CA 104; 131; DA3; DAM NOV;
 DLB 65; EW 9; EWL 3; GFL 1789 to the
 Present; GLL 1; MTCW 1, 2; MTFW
 2005; RGWL 2, 3; TWA
Colette, Sidonie-Gabrielle
 See Colette
Collett, (Jacobine) Camilla (Wergeland)
 1813-1895 .... **NCLC 22**
 See also DLB 354
Collier, Christopher 1930- .... **CLC 30**
 See also AAYA 13; BYA 2; CA 33-36R;
 CANR 13, 33, 102; CLR 126; JRDA;
 MAICYA 1, 2; SATA 16, 70; WYA; YAW
 1
Collier, James Lincoln 1928- .... **CLC 30**
 See also AAYA 13; BYA 2; CA 9-12R;
 CANR 4, 33, 60, 102; CLR 3, 126; DAM
 POP; JRDA; MAICYA 1, 2; SAAS 21;
 SATA 8, 70, 166; WYA; YAW 1
Collier, Jeremy 1650-1726 .... **LC 6, 157**
 See also DLB 336
Collier, John 1901-1980 . **SSC 19; TCLC 127**
 See also CA 65-68; 97-100; CANR 10; CN
 1, 2; DLB 77, 255; FANT; SUFW 1
Collier, Mary 1690-1762 .... **LC 86**
 See also DLB 95
Collingwood, R(obin) G(eorge)
 1889(?)-1943 .... **TCLC 67**
 See also CA 117; 155; DLB 262
Collins, Billy 1941- .... **PC 68**
 See also AAYA 64; CA 151; CANR 92; CP
 7; MTFW 2005; PFS 18

Collins, Hunt
 See Hunter, Evan
Collins, Linda 1931- .... **CLC 44**
 See also CA 125
Collins, Merle 1950- .... **BLC 2:1**
 See also BW 3; CA 175; DLB 157
Collins, Tom
 See Furphy, Joseph
Collins, Wilkie 1824-1889 ... **NCLC 1, 18, 93;**
 SSC 93
 See also BRWS 6; CDBLB 1832-1890;
 CMW 4; DLB 18, 70, 159; GL 2; MSW;
 RGEL 2; RGSF 2; SUFW 1; WLIT 4
Collins, William 1721-1759 ...... **LC 4, 40; PC**
 72
 See also BRW 3; DAM POET; DLB 109;
 RGEL 2
Collins, William Wilkie
 See Collins, Wilkie
Collodi, Carlo
 See Lorenzini, Carlo
Colman, George
 See Glassco, John
Colman, George, the Elder
 1732-1794 .... **LC 98**
 See also RGEL 2
Colonna, Vittoria 1492-1547 .... **LC 71**
 See also RGWL 2, 3
Colt, Winchester Remington
 See Hubbard, L. Ron
Colter, Cyrus J. 1910-2002 .... **CLC 58**
 See also BW 1; CA 65-68; 205; CANR 10,
 66; CN 2, 3, 4, 5, 6; DLB 33
Colton, James
 See Hansen, Joseph
Colum, Padraic 1881-1972 .... **CLC 28**
 See also BYA 4; CA 73-76; 33-36R; CANR
 35; CLR 36; CP 1; CWRI 5; DLB 19;
 MAICYA 1, 2; MTCW 1; RGEL 2; SATA
 15; WCH
Colvin, James
 See Moorcock, Michael
Colwin, Laurie (E.) 1944-1992 .... **CLC 5, 13,**
 23, 84
 See also CA 89-92; 139; CANR 20, 46;
 DLB 218; DLBY 1980; MTCW 1
Comfort, Alex(ander) 1920-2000 .... **CLC 7**
 See also CA 1-4R; 190; CANR 1, 45; CN
 1, 2, 3, 4; CP 1, 2, 3, 4, 5, 6, 7; DAM
 POP; MTCW 2
Comfort, Montgomery
 See Campbell, Ramsey
Compton-Burnett, I. 1892(?)-1969 .... **CLC 1,**
 3, 10, 15, 34; TCLC 180
 See also BRW 7; CA 1-4R; 25-28R; CANR
 4; DAM NOV; DLB 36; EWL 3; MTCW
 1, 2; RGEL 2
Compton-Burnett, Ivy
 See Compton-Burnett, I.
Comstock, Anthony 1844-1915 ...... **TCLC 13**
 See also CA 110; 169
Comte, Auguste 1798-1857 .... **NCLC 54**
Conan Doyle, Arthur
 See Doyle, Sir Arthur Conan
Conde (Abellan), Carmen
 1901-1996 .... **HLCS 1**
 See also CA 177; CWW 2; DLB 108; EWL
 3; HW 2
Conde, Maryse 1937- .... **BLC 2:1; BLCS;**
 CLC 52, 92, 247
 See also BW 2, 3; CA 110, 190; CAAE 190;
 CANR 30, 53, 76, 171; CWW 2; DAM
 MULT; EWL 3; MTCW 2; MTFW 2005
Condillac, Etienne Bonnot de
 1714-1780 .... **LC 26**
 See also DLB 313

Crowley, Edward Alexander
1875-1947 .... **TCLC 7**
See also CA 104; GLL 1; HGG
Crowley, John 1942- .... **CLC 57**
See also AAYA 57; BPFB 1; CA 61-64;
CANR 43, 98, 138, 177; DLBY 1982;
FANT; MTFW 2005; SATA 65, 140; SFW
4; SUFW 2
Crowne, John 1641-1712 .... **LC 104**
See also DLB 80; RGEL 2
Crud
See Crumb, R.
Crumarums
See Crumb, R.
Crumb, R. 1943- .... **CLC 17**
See also CA 106; CANR 107, 150
Crumb, Robert
See Crumb, R.
Crumbum
See Crumb, R.
Crumski
See Crumb, R.
Crum the Bum
See Crumb, R.
Crunk
See Crumb, R.
Crustt
See Crumb, R.
Crutchfield, Les
See Trumbo, Dalton
Cruz, Victor Hernandez 1949- ... **HLC 1; PC 37**
See also BW 2; CA 65-68, 271; CAAE 271;
CAAS 17; CANR 14, 32, 74, 132; CP 1,
2, 3, 4, 5, 6, 7; DAM MULT, POET; DLB
41; DNFS 1; EXPP; HW 1, 2; LLW;
MTCW 2; MTFW 2005; PFS 16; WP
Cryer, Gretchen (Kiger) 1935- .... **CLC 21**
See also CA 114; 123
Csath, Geza
See Brenner, Jozef
Cudlip, David R(ockwell) 1933- .... **CLC 34**
See also CA 177
Cullen, Countee 1903-1946 ..... **BLC 1:1; HR 1:2; PC 20; TCLC 4, 37, 220; WLCS**
See also AAYA 78; AFAW 2; AMWS 4; BW
1; CA 108; 124; CDALB 1917-1929; DA;
DA3; DAC; DAM MST, MULT, POET;
DLB 4, 48, 51; EWL 3; EXPP; LMFS 2;
MAL 5; MTCW 1, 2; MTFW 2005; PFS
3; RGAL 4; SATA 18; WP
Culleton, Beatrice 1949- .... **NNAL**
See also CA 120; CANR 83; DAC
Culver, Timothy J.
See Westlake, Donald E.
Culver, Timothy J.
See Westlake, Donald E.
Cum, R.
See Crumb, R.
Cumberland, Richard
1732-1811 .... **NCLC 167**
See also DLB 89; RGEL 2
Cummings, Bruce F. 1889-1919 ..... **TCLC 24**
See also CA 123
Cummings, Bruce Frederick
See Cummings, Bruce F.
Cummings, E. E. 1894-1962 ...... **CLC 1, 3, 8, 12, 15, 68; PC 5; TCLC 137; WLC 2**
See also AAYA 41; AMW; CA 73-76;
CANR 31; CDALB 1929-1941; DA;
DA3; DAB; DAC; DAM MST, POET;
DLB 4, 48; EWL 3; EXPP; MAL 5;
MTCW 1, 2; MTFW 2005; PAB; PFS 1,
3, 12, 13, 19, 30; RGAL 4; TUS; WP
Cummings, Edward Estlin
See Cummings, E. E.
Cummins, Maria Susanna
1827-1866 .... **NCLC 139**
See also DLB 42; YABC 1

Cunha, Euclides (Rodrigues Pimenta) da
1866-1909 .... **TCLC 24**
See also CA 123; 219; DLB 307; LAW;
WLIT 1
Cunningham, E. V.
See Fast, Howard
Cunningham, J. Morgan
See Westlake, Donald E.
Cunningham, J(ames) V(incent)
1911-1985 .... **CLC 3, 31; PC 92**
See also CA 1-4R; 115; CANR 1, 72; CP 1,
2, 3, 4; DLB 5
Cunningham, Julia (Woolfolk)
1916- .... **CLC 12**
See also CA 9-12R; CANR 4, 19, 36; CWRI
5; JRDA; MAICYA 1, 2; SAAS 2; SATA
1, 26, 132
Cunningham, Michael 1952- .... **CLC 34, 243**
See also AMWS 15; CA 136; CANR 96,
160; CN 7; DLB 292; GLL 2; MTFW
2005; NFS 23
Cunninghame Graham, R. B.
See Cunninghame Graham, Robert Bontine
Cunninghame Graham, Robert Bontine
1852-1936 .... **TCLC 19**
See also CA 119; 184; DLB 98, 135, 174;
RGEL 2; RGSF 2
Cunninghame Graham, Robert Gallnigad Bontine
See Cunninghame Graham, Robert Bontine
Curnow, (Thomas) Allen (Monro)
1911-2001 .... **PC 48**
See also CA 69-72; 202; CANR 48, 99; CP
1, 2, 3, 4, 5, 6, 7; EWL 3; RGEL 2
Currie, Ellen 19(?)- .... **CLC 44**
Curtin, Philip
See Lowndes, Marie Adelaide (Belloc)
Curtin, Phillip
See Lowndes, Marie Adelaide (Belloc)
Curtis, Price
See Ellison, Harlan
Cusanus, Nicolaus 1401-1464
See Nicholas of Cusa
Cutrate, Joe
See Spiegelman, Art
Cynewulf fl. 9th cent. - .... **CMLC 23, 117**
See also DLB 146; RGEL 2
Cyrano de Bergerac, Savinien de
1619-1655 .... **LC 65**
See also DLB 268; GFL Beginnings to
1789; RGWL 2, 3
Cyril of Alexandria c. 375-c. 430 . **CMLC 59**
Czaczkes, Shmuel Yosef Halevi
See Agnon, S.Y.
Dabrowska, Maria (Szumska)
1889-1965 .... **CLC 15**
See also CA 106; CDWLB 4; DLB 215;
EWL 3
Dabydeen, David 1955- .... **CLC 34**
See also BW 1; CA 125; CANR 56, 92; CN
6, 7; CP 5, 6, 7; DLB 347
Dacey, Philip 1939- .... **CLC 51**
See also CA 37-40R, 231; CAAE 231;
CAAS 17; CANR 14, 32, 64; CP 4, 5, 6,
7; DLB 105
Dacre, Charlotte c. 1772-1825(?) . **NCLC 151**
Dafydd ap Gwilym c. 1320-c. 1380 ..... **PC 56**
Dagerman, Stig (Halvard)
1923-1954 .... **TCLC 17**
See also CA 117; 155; DLB 259; EWL 3
D'Aguiar, Fred 1960- ..... **BLC 2:1; CLC 145**
See also CA 148; CANR 83, 101; CN 7;
CP 5, 6, 7; DLB 157; EWL 3
Dahl, Roald 1916-1990 ...... **CLC 1, 6, 18, 79; TCLC 173**
See also AAYA 15; BPFB 1; BRWS 4; BYA
5; CA 1-4R; 133; CANR 6, 32, 37, 62;
CLR 1, 7, 41, 111; CN 1, 2, 3, 4; CPW;
DA3; DAB; DAC; DAM MST, NOV,

POP; DLB 139, 255; HGG; JRDA; MAI-
CYA 1, 2; MTCW 1, 2; MTFW 2005;
RGSF 2; SATA 1, 26, 73; SATA-Obit 65;
SSFS 4; TEA; YAW
Dahlberg, Edward 1900-1977 . **CLC 1, 7, 14; TCLC 208**
See also CA 9-12R; 69-72; CANR 31, 62;
CN 1, 2; DLB 48; MAL 5; MTCW 1;
RGAL 4
Daitch, Susan 1954- .... **CLC 103**
See also CA 161
Dale, Colin
See Lawrence, T. E.
Dale, George E.
See Asimov, Isaac
d'Alembert, Jean Le Rond
1717-1783 .... **LC 126**
Dalton, Roque 1935-1975(?) ..... **HLCS 1; PC 36**
See also CA 176; DLB 283; HW 2
Daly, Elizabeth 1878-1967 .... **CLC 52**
See also CA 23-24; 25-28R; CANR 60;
CAP 2; CMW 4
Daly, Mary 1928-2010 .... **CLC 173**
See also CA 25-28R; CANR 30, 62, 166;
FW; GLL 1; MTCW 1
Daly, Maureen 1921-2006 .... **CLC 17**
See also AAYA 5, 58; BYA 6; CA 253;
CANR 37, 83, 108; CLR 96; JRDA; MAI-
CYA 1, 2; SAAS 1; SATA 2, 129; SATA-
Obit 176; WYA; YAW
Damas, Leon-Gontran 1912-1978 ... **CLC 84; TCLC 204**
See also BW 1; CA 125; 73-76; EWL 3
Damocles
See Benedetti, Mario
Dana, Richard Henry Sr.
1787-1879 .... **NCLC 53**
Dangarembga, Tsitsi 1959- .... **BLC 2:1**
See also BW 3; CA 163; NFS 28; WLIT 2
Daniel, Samuel 1562(?)-1619 .... **LC 24, 171**
See also DLB 62; RGEL 2
Daniels, Brett
See Adler, Renata
Dannay, Frederic 1905-1982 .... **CLC 3, 11**
See also BPFB 3; CA 1-4R; 107; CANR 1,
39; CMW 4; DAM POP; DLB 137; MSW;
MTCW 1; RGAL 4
D'Annunzio, Gabriele 1863-1938 ... **TCLC 6, 40, 215**
See also CA 104; 155; EW 8; EWL 3;
RGWL 2, 3; TWA; WLIT 7
Danois, N. le
See Gourmont, Remy(-Marie-Charles) de
Dante 1265-1321 .... **CMLC 3, 18, 39, 70; PC 21; WLCS**
See also DA; DA3; DAB; DAC; DAM
MST, POET; EFS 1; EW 1; LAIT 1;
RGWL 2, 3; TWA; WLIT 7; WP
d'Antibes, Germain
See Simenon, Georges
Danticat, Edwidge 1969- . **BLC 2:1; CLC 94, 139, 228; SSC 100**
See also AAYA 29; CA 152, 192; CAAE
192; CANR 73, 129, 179; CN 7; DLB
350; DNFS 1; EXPS; LATS 1:2; LNFS 3;
MTCW 2; MTFW 2005; NFS 28; SSFS
1, 25; YAW
Danvers, Dennis 1947- .... **CLC 70**
Danziger, Paula 1944-2004 .... **CLC 21**
See also AAYA 4, 36; BYA 6, 7, 14; CA
112; 115; 229; CANR 37, 132; CLR 20;
JRDA; MAICYA 1, 2; MTFW 2005;
SATA 36, 63, 102, 149; SATA-Brief 30;
SATA-Obit 155; WYA; YAW

Desbordes-Valmore, Marceline
1786-1859 .... **NCLC 97**
See also DLB 217

Descartes, Rene 1596-1650 .... **LC 20, 35, 150**
See also DLB 268; EW 3; GFL Beginnings
to 1789

Deschamps, Eustache 1340(?)-1404 .. **LC 103**
See also DLB 208

De Sica, Vittorio 1901(?)-1974 .... **CLC 20**
See also CA 117

Desnos, Robert 1900-1945 .... **TCLC 22**
See also CA 121; 151; CANR 107; DLB
258; EWL 3; LMFS 2

Destouches, Louis-Ferdinand
See Celine, Louis-Ferdinand

de Teran, Lisa St. Aubin
See St. Aubin de Teran, Lisa

de Tolignac, Gaston
See Griffith, D.W.

Deutsch, Babette 1895-1982 .... **CLC 18**
See also BYA 3; CA 1-4R; 108; CANR 4,
79; CP 1, 2, 3; DLB 45; SATA 1; SATA-
Obit 33

Devenant, William 1606-1649 .... **LC 13**

Deville, Rene
See Kacew, Romain

Devkota, Laxmiprasad 1909-1959 . **TCLC 23**
See also CA 123

De Voto, Bernard (Augustine)
1897-1955 .... **TCLC 29**
See also CA 113; 160; DLB 9, 256; MAL
5; TCWW 1, 2

De Vries, Peter 1910-1993 ..... **CLC 1, 2, 3, 7,
10, 28, 46**
See also CA 17-20R; 142; CANR 41; CN
1, 2, 3, 4, 5; DAM NOV; DLB 6; DLBY
1982; MAL 5; MTCW 1, 2; MTFW 2005

Dewey, John 1859-1952 .... **TCLC 95**
See also CA 114; 170; CANR 144; DLB
246, 270; RGAL 4

Dexter, John
See Bradley, Marion Zimmer

Dexter, Martin
See Faust, Frederick

Dexter, Pete 1943- .... **CLC 34, 55**
See also BEST 89:2; CA 127; 131; CANR
129; CPW; DAM POP; INT CA-131;
MAL 5; MTCW 1; MTFW 2005

Diamano, Silmang
See Senghor, Leopold Sedar

Diamant, Anita 1951- .... **CLC 239**
See also CA 145; CANR 126

Diamond, Neil 1941- .... **CLC 30**
See also CA 108

Diaz, Junot 1968- .... **CLC 258**
See also BYA 12; CA 161; CANR 119, 183;
LLW; SSFS 20

Diaz del Castillo, Bernal c.
1496-1584 .... **HLCS 1; LC 31**
See also DLB 318; LAW

di Bassetto, Corno
See Shaw, George Bernard

Dick, Philip K. 1928-1982 ... **CLC 10, 30, 72;
SSC 57**
See also AAYA 24; BPFB 1; BYA 11; CA
49-52; 106; CANR 2, 16, 132; CN 2, 3;
CPW; DA3; DAM NOV, POP; DLB 8;
MTCW 1, 2; MTFW 2005; NFS 5, 26;
SCFW 1, 2; SFW 4

Dick, Philip Kindred
See Dick, Philip K.

Dickens, Charles 1812-1870 . **NCLC 3, 8, 18,
26, 37, 50, 86, 105, 113, 161, 187, 203,
206, 211, 217, 219; SSC 17, 49, 88;
WLC 2**
See also AAYA 23; BRW 5; BRWC 1, 2;
BYA 1, 2, 3, 13, 14; CDBLB 1832-1890;
CLR 95; CMW 4; DA; DA3; DAB; DAC;
DAM MST, NOV; DLB 21, 55, 70, 159,

166; EXPN; GL 2; HGG; JRDA; LAIT 1,
2; LATS 1:1; LMFS 1; MAICYA 1, 2;
NFS 4, 5, 10, 14, 20, 25, 30; RGEL 2;
RGSF 2; SATA 15; SUFW 1; TEA; WCH;
WLIT 4; WYA

Dickens, Charles John Huffam
See Dickens, Charles

Dickey, James 1923-1997 .... **CLC 1, 2, 4, 7,
10, 15, 47, 109; PC 40; TCLC 151**
See also AAYA 50; AITN 1, 2; AMWS 4;
BPFB 1; CA 9-12R; 156; CABS 2; CANR
10, 48, 61, 105; CDALB 1968-1988; CP
1, 2, 3, 4, 5, 6; CPW; CSW; DA3; DAM
NOV, POET, POP; DLB 5, 193, 342;
DLBD 7; DLBY 1982, 1993, 1996, 1997,
1998; EWL 3; INT CANR-10; MAL 5;
MTCW 1, 2; NFS 9; PFS 6, 11; RGAL 4;
TUS

Dickey, James Lafayette
See Dickey, James

Dickey, William 1928-1994 .... **CLC 3, 28**
See also CA 9-12R; 145; CANR 24, 79; CP
1, 2, 3, 4; DLB 5

Dickinson, Charles 1951- .... **CLC 49**
See also CA 128; CANR 141

Dickinson, Emily 1830-1886 ... **NCLC 21, 77,
171; PC 1; WLC 2**
See also AAYA 22; AMW; AMWR 1;
CDALB 1865-1917; DA; DA3; DAB;
DAC; DAM MST, POET; DLB 1, 243;
EXPP; FL 1:3; MBL; PAB; PFS 1, 2, 3,
4, 5, 6, 8, 10, 11, 13, 16, 28; RGAL 4;
SATA 29; TUS; WP; WYA

Dickinson, Emily Elizabeth
See Dickinson, Emily

Dickinson, Mrs. Herbert Ward
See Phelps, Elizabeth Stuart

Dickinson, Peter 1927- .... **CLC 12, 35**
See also AAYA 9, 49; BYA 5; CA 41-44R;
CANR 31, 58, 88, 134, 195; CLR 29, 125;
CMW 4; DLB 87, 161, 276; JRDA; MAI-
CYA 1, 2; SATA 5, 62, 95, 150; SFW 4;
WYA; YAW

Dickinson, Peter Malcolm de Brissac
See Dickinson, Peter

Dickson, Carr
See Carr, John Dickson

Dickson, Carter
See Carr, John Dickson

Diderot, Denis 1713-1784 .... **LC 26, 126**
See also DLB 313; EW 4; GFL Beginnings
to 1789; LMFS 1; RGWL 2, 3

Didion, Joan 1934- . **CLC 1, 3, 8, 14, 32, 129**
See also AITN 1; AMWS 4; CA 5-8R;
CANR 14, 52, 76, 125, 174; CDALB
1968-1988; CN 2, 3, 4, 5, 6, 7; DA3;
DAM NOV; DLB 2, 173, 185; DLBY
1981, 1986; EWL 3; MAL 5; MBL;
MTCW 1, 2; MTFW 2005; NFS 3; RGAL
4; TCLE 1:1; TCWW 2; TUS

di Donato, Pietro 1911-1992 .... **TCLC 159**
See also CA 101; 136; DLB 9

Dietrich, Robert
See Hunt, E. Howard

Difusa, Pati
See Almodovar, Pedro

di Lampedusa, Giuseppe Tomasi
See Tomasi di Lampedusa, Giuseppe

Dillard, Annie 1945- ...... **CLC 9, 60, 115, 216**
See also AAYA 6, 43; AMWS 6; ANW; CA
49-52; CANR 3, 43, 62, 90, 125; DA3;
DAM NOV; DLB 275, 278; DLBY 1980;
LAIT 4, 5; MAL 5; MTCW 1, 2; MTFW
2005; NCFS 1; RGAL 4; SATA 10, 140;
TCLE 1:1; TUS

Dillard, R(ichard) H(enry) W(ilde)
1937- .... **CLC 5**
See also CA 21-24R; CAAS 7; CANR 10;
CP 2, 3, 4, 5, 6, 7; CSW; DLB 5, 244

Dillon, Eilis 1920-1994 .... **CLC 17**
See also CA 9-12R, 182; 147; CAAE 182;
CAAS 3; CANR 4, 38, 78; CLR 26; MAI-
CYA 1, 2; MAICYAS 1; SATA 2, 74;
SATA-Essay 105; SATA-Obit 83; YAW

Dimont, Penelope
See Mortimer, Penelope (Ruth)

Dinesen, Isak
See Blixen, Karen

Ding Ling
See Chiang, Pin-chin

Diodorus Siculus c. 90B.C.-c.
31B.C. .... **CMLC 88**

Diphusa, Patty
See Almodovar, Pedro

Disch, Thomas M. 1940-2008 .... **CLC 7, 36**
See also AAYA 17; BPFB 1; CA 21-24R;
274; CAAS 4; CANR 17, 36, 54, 89; CLR
18; CP 5, 6, 7; DA3; DLB 8, 282; HGG;
MAICYA 1, 2; MTCW 1, 2; MTFW 2005;
SAAS 15; SATA 92; SATA-Obit 195;
SCFW 1, 2; SFW 4; SUFW 2

Disch, Thomas Michael
See Disch, Thomas M.

Disch, Tom
See Disch, Thomas M.

d'Isly, Georges
See Simenon, Georges

Disraeli, Benjamin 1804-1881 ... **NCLC 2, 39,
79**
See also BRW 4; DLB 21, 55; RGEL 2

D'Israeli, Isaac 1766-1848 .... **NCLC 217**
See also DLB 107

Ditcum, Steve
See Crumb, R.

Dixon, Paige
See Corcoran, Barbara (Asenath)

Dixon, Stephen 1936- .... **CLC 52; SSC 16**
See also AMWS 12; CA 89-92; CANR 17,
40, 54, 91, 175; CN 4, 5, 6, 7; DLB 130;
MAL 5

Dixon, Thomas, Jr. 1864-1946 ..... **TCLC 163**
See also RHW

Djebar, Assia 1936- .... **BLC 2:1; CLC 182;
SSC 114**
See also CA 188; CANR 169; DLB 346;
EWL 3; RGWL 3; WLIT 2

Doak, Annie
See Dillard, Annie

Dobell, Sydney Thompson
1824-1874 .... **NCLC 43; PC 100**
See also DLB 32; RGEL 2

Doblin, Alfred
See Doeblin, Alfred

Dobroliubov, Nikolai Aleksandrovich
See Dobrolyubov, Nikolai Alexandrovich

Dobrolyubov, Nikolai Alexandrovich
1836-1861 .... **NCLC 5**
See also DLB 277

Dobson, Austin 1840-1921 .... **TCLC 79**
See also DLB 35, 144

Dobyns, Stephen 1941- .... **CLC 37, 233**
See also AMWS 13; CA 45-48; CANR 2,
18, 99; CMW 4; CP 4, 5, 6, 7; PFS 23

Doctorow, Cory 1971- .... **CLC 273**
See also CA 221

Doctorow, E. L. 1931- ...... **CLC 6, 11, 15, 18,
37, 44, 65, 113, 214**
See also AAYA 22; AITN 2; AMWS 4;
BEST 89:3; BPFB 1; CA 45-48; CANR
2, 33, 51, 76, 97, 133, 170; CDALB 1968-
1988; CN 3, 4, 5, 6, 7; CPW; DA3; DAM
NOV, POP; DLB 2, 28, 173; DLBY 1980;
EWL 3; LAIT 3; MAL 5; MTCW 1, 2;
MTFW 2005; NFS 6; RGAL 4; RGHL;
RHW; SSFS 27; TCLE 1:1; TCWW 1, 2;
TUS

Doctorow, Edgar Laurence
See Doctorow, E. L.

Ehrenburg, Ilya (Grigoryevich)
1891-1967 .... **CLC 18, 34, 62**
See Erenburg, Ilya (Grigoryevich)
See also CA 102; 25-28R; EWL 3

Ehrenburg, Ilyo (Grigoryevich)
See Ehrenburg, Ilya (Grigoryevich)

Ehrenreich, Barbara 1941- ..... **CLC 110, 267**
See also BEST 90:4; CA 73-76; CANR 16,
37, 62, 117, 167; DLB 246; FW; LNFS 1;
MTCW 1, 2; MTFW 2005

Ehrlich, Gretel 1946- .... **CLC 249**
See also ANW; CA 140; CANR 74, 146;
DLB 212, 275; TCWW 2

Eich, Gunter
See Eich, Gunter

Eich, Gunter 1907-1972 .... **CLC 15**
See also CA 111; 93-96; DLB 69, 124;
EWL 3; RGWL 2, 3

Eichendorff, Joseph 1788-1857 .... **NCLC 8,
225**
See also DLB 90; RGWL 2, 3

Eigner, Larry
See Eigner, Laurence (Joel)

Eigner, Laurence (Joel) 1927-1996 ..... **CLC 9**
See also CA 9-12R; 151; CAAS 23; CANR
6, 84; CP 1, 2, 3, 4, 5, 6, 7; DLB 5; WP

Eilhart von Oberge c. 1140-c.
1195 .... **CMLC 67**
See also DLB 148

Einhard c. 770-840 .... **CMLC 50**
See also DLB 148

Einstein, Albert 1879-1955 .... **TCLC 65**
See also CA 121; 133; MTCW 1, 2

Eiseley, Loren
See Eiseley, Loren Corey

Eiseley, Loren Corey 1907-1977 .... **CLC 7**
See also AAYA 5; ANW; CA 1-4R; 73-76;
CANR 6; DLB 275; DLBD 17

Eisenstadt, Jill 1963- .... **CLC 50**
See also CA 140

Eisenstein, Sergei (Mikhailovich)
1898-1948 .... **TCLC 57**
See also CA 114; 149

Eisner, Simon
See Kornbluth, C(yril) M.

Eisner, Will 1917-2005 .... **CLC 237**
See also AAYA 52; CA 108; 235; CANR
114, 140, 179; MTFW 2005; SATA 31,
165

Eisner, William Erwin
See Eisner, Will

Ekeloef, Bengt Gunnar
See Ekelof, Gunnar

Ekeloef, Gunnar
See Ekelof, Gunnar

Ekelof, Gunnar 1907-1968 ... **CLC 27; PC 23**
See also CA 123; 25-28R; DAM POET;
DLB 259; EW 12; EWL 3

Ekelund, Vilhelm 1880-1949 .... **TCLC 75**
See also CA 189; EWL 3

Ekman, Kerstin (Lillemor) 1933- ... **CLC 279**
See also CA 154; CANR 124; DLB 257;
EWL 3

Ekwensi, C. O. D.
See Ekwensi, Cyprian

Ekwensi, Cyprian 1921-2007 .... **BLC 1:1;
CLC 4**
See also AFW; BW 2, 3; CA 29-32R;
CANR 18, 42, 74, 125; CDWLB 3; CN 1,
2, 3, 4, 5, 6; CWRI 5; DAM MULT; DLB
117; EWL 3; MTCW 1, 2; RGEL 2; SATA
66; WLIT 2

Ekwensi, Cyprian Odiatu Duaka
See Ekwensi, Cyprian

Elaine
See Leverson, Ada Esther

El Conde de Pepe
See Mihura, Miguel

El Crummo
See Crumb, R.

Elder, Lonne III 1931-1996 .. **BLC 1:1; DC 8**
See also BW 1, 3; CA 81-84; 152; CAD;
CANR 25; DAM MULT; DLB 7, 38, 44;
MAL 5

Eleanor of Aquitaine 1122-1204 ... **CMLC 39**

Elia
See Lamb, Charles

Eliade, Mircea 1907-1986 .... **CLC 19**
See also CA 65-68; 119; CANR 30, 62; CD-
WLB 4; DLB 220; EWL 3; MTCW 1;
RGWL 3; SFW 4

Eliot, A. D.
See Jewett, Sarah Orne

Eliot, Alice
See Jewett, Sarah Orne

Eliot, Dan
See Silverberg, Robert

Eliot, George 1819-1880 ...... **NCLC 4, 13, 23,
41, 49, 89, 118, 183, 199, 209; PC 20;
SSC 72; WLC 2**
See also BRW 5; BRWC 1, 2; BRWR 2;
CDBLB 1832-1890; CN 7; CPW; DA;
DA3; DAB; DAC; DAM MST, NOV;
DLB 21, 35, 55; FL 1:3; LATS 1:1; LMFS
1; NFS 17, 20; RGEL 2; RGSF 2; SSFS
8; TEA; WLIT 3

Eliot, John 1604-1690 .... **LC 5**
See also DLB 24

Eliot, T. S. 1888-1965 .. **CLC 1, 2, 3, 6, 9, 10,
13, 15, 24, 34, 41, 55, 57, 113; DC 28;
PC 5, 31, 90; WLC 2**
See also AAYA 28; AMW; AMWC 1;
AMWR 1; BRW 7; BRWR 2; CA 5-8R;
25-28R; CANR 41; CBD; CDALB 1929-
1941; DA; DA3; DAB; DAC; DAM
DRAM, MST, POET; DFS 4, 13; DLB 7,
10, 45, 63, 245, 329; DLBY 1988; EWL
3; EXPP; LAIT 3; LATS 1:1; LMFS 2;
MAL 5; MTCW 1, 2; MTFW 2005; NCFS
5; PAB; PFS 1, 7, 20; RGAL 4; RGEL 2;
TUS; WLIT 4; WP

Eliot, Thomas Stearns
See Eliot, T. S.

Elisabeth of Schonau c.
1129-1165 .... **CMLC 82**

Elizabeth 1866-1941 .... **TCLC 41**

Elizabeth I 1533-1603 .... **LC 118**
See also DLB 136

Elkin, Stanley L. 1930-1995 ...... **CLC 4, 6, 9,
14, 27, 51, 91; SSC 12**
See also AMWS 6; BPFB 1; CA 9-12R;
148; CANR 8, 46; CN 1, 2, 3, 4, 5, 6;
CPW; DAM NOV, POP; DLB 2, 28, 218,
278; DLBY 1980; EWL 3; INT CANR-8;
MAL 5; MTCW 1, 2; MTFW 2005;
RGAL 4; TCLE 1:1

Elledge, Scott .... **CLC 34**

Eller, Scott
See Shepard, Jim

Elliott, Don
See Silverberg, Robert

Elliott, Ebenezer 1781-1849 .... **PC 96**
See also DLB 96, 190; RGEL 2

Elliott, George P(aul) 1918-1980 .... **CLC 2**
See also CA 1-4R; 97-100; CANR 2; CN 1,
2; CP 3; DLB 244; MAL 5

Elliott, Janice 1931-1995 .... **CLC 47**
See also CA 13-16R; CANR 8, 29, 84; CN
5, 6, 7; DLB 14; SATA 119

Elliott, Sumner Locke 1917-1991 ..... **CLC 38**
See also CA 5-8R; 134; CANR 2, 21; DLB
289

Elliott, William
See Bradbury, Ray

Ellis, A. E. .... **CLC 7**

Ellis, Alice Thomas
See Haycraft, Anna

Ellis, Bret Easton 1964- ..... **CLC 39, 71, 117,
229**
See also AAYA 2, 43; CA 118; 123; CANR
51, 74, 126; CN 6, 7; CPW; DA3; DAM
POP; DLB 292; HGG; INT CA-123;
MTCW 2; MTFW 2005; NFS 11

Ellis, (Henry) Havelock
1859-1939 .... **TCLC 14**
See also CA 109; 169; DLB 190

Ellis, Landon
See Ellison, Harlan

Ellis, Trey 1962- .... **CLC 55**
See also CA 146; CANR 92; CN 7

Ellison, Harlan 1934- .... **CLC 1, 13, 42, 139;
SSC 14**
See also AAYA 29; BPFB 1; BYA 14; CA
5-8R; CANR 5, 46, 115; CPW; DAM
POP; DLB 8, 335; HGG; INT CANR-5;
MTCW 1, 2; MTFW 2005; SCFW 2;
SFW 4; SSFS 13, 14, 15, 21; SUFW 1, 2

Ellison, Ralph 1914-1994 .... **BLC 1:1, 2:2;
CLC 1, 3, 11, 54, 86, 114; SSC 26, 79;
WLC 2**
See also AAYA 19; AFAW 1, 2; AMWC 2;
AMWR 2; AMWS 2; BPFB 1; BW 1, 3;
BYA 2; CA 9-12R; 145; CANR 24, 53;
CDALB 1941-1968; CN 1, 2, 3, 4, 5;
CSW; DA; DA3; DAB; DAC; DAM MST,
MULT, NOV; DLB 2, 76, 227; DLBY
1994; EWL 3; EXPN; EXPS; LAIT 4;
MAL 5; MTCW 1, 2; MTFW 2005; NCFS
3; NFS 2, 21; RGAL 4; RGSF 2; SSFS 1,
11; YAW

Ellison, Ralph Waldo
See Ellison, Ralph

Ellmann, Lucy 1956- .... **CLC 61**
See also CA 128; CANR 154

Ellmann, Lucy Elizabeth
See Ellmann, Lucy

Ellmann, Richard (David)
1918-1987 .... **CLC 50**
See also BEST 89:2; CA 1-4R; 122; CANR
2, 28, 61; DLB 103; DLBY 1987; MTCW
1, 2; MTFW 2005

Ellroy, James 1948- .... **CLC 215**
See also CA 138; CANR 74,
133; CMW 4; CN 6, 7; DA3; DLB 226;
MTCW 2; MTFW 2005

Elman, Richard (Martin)
1934-1997 .... **CLC 19**
See also CA 17-20R; 163; CAAS 3; CANR
47; TCLE 1:1

Elron
See Hubbard, L. Ron

El Saadawi, Nawal 1931- ...... **BLC 2:2; CLC
196, 284**
See also AFW; CA 118; CAAS 11; CANR
44, 92; CWW 2; DLB 346; EWL 3; FW;
WLIT 2

El-Shabazz, El-Hajj Malik
See Malcolm X

Eluard, Paul
See Grindel, Eugene

Eluard, Paul
See Grindel, Eugene

Elyot, Thomas 1490(?)-1546 .... **LC 11, 139**
See also DLB 136; RGEL 2

Elytis, Odysseus 1911-1996 .... **CLC 15, 49,
100; PC 21**
See also CA 102; 151; CANR 94; CWW 2;
DAM POET; DLB 329; EW 13; EWL 3;
MTCW 1, 2; RGWL 2, 3

Emecheta, Buchi 1944- ... **BLC 1:2; CLC 14,
48, 128, 214**
See also AAYA 67; AFW; BW 2, 3; CA 81-
84; CANR 27, 81, 126; CDWLB 3; CN
4, 5, 6, 7; CWRI 5; DA3; DAM MULT;
DLB 117; EWL 3; FL 1:5; FW; MTCW
1, 2; MTFW 2005; NFS 12, 14; SATA 66;
WLIT 2

Exley, Frederick (Earl) 1929-1992 .... **CLC 6, 11**
See also AITN 2; BPFB 1; CA 81-84; 138; CANR 117; DLB 143; DLBY 1981

Eynhardt, Guillermo
See Quiroga, Horacio (Sylvestre)

Ezekiel, Nissim (Moses) 1924-2004 .. **CLC 61**
See also CA 61-64; 223; CP 1, 2, 3, 4, 5, 6, 7; DLB 323; EWL 3

Ezekiel, Tish O'Dowd 1943- .... **CLC 34**
See also CA 129

Fadeev, Aleksandr Aleksandrovich
See Bulgya, Alexander Alexandrovich

Fadeev, Alexandr Alexandrovich
See Bulgya, Alexander Alexandrovich

Fadeyev, A.
See Bulgya, Alexander Alexandrovich

Fadeyev, Alexander
See Bulgya, Alexander Alexandrovich

Fagen, Donald 1948- .... **CLC 26**

Fainzil'berg, Il'ia Arnol'dovich
See Fainzilberg, Ilya Arnoldovich

Fainzilberg, Ilya Arnoldovich
1897-1937 .... **TCLC 21**
See also CA 120; 165; DLB 272; EWL 3

Fair, Ronald L. 1932- .... **CLC 18**
See also BW 1; CA 69-72; CANR 25; DLB 33

Fairbairn, Roger
See Carr, John Dickson

Fairbairns, Zoe (Ann) 1948- .... **CLC 32**
See also CA 103; CANR 21, 85; CN 4, 5, 6, 7

Fairfield, Flora
See Alcott, Louisa May

Falco, Gian
See Papini, Giovanni

Falconer, James
See Kirkup, James

Falconer, Kenneth
See Kornbluth, C(yril) M.

Falkland, Samuel
See Heijermans, Herman

Fallaci, Oriana 1930-2006 .... **CLC 11, 110**
See also CA 77-80; 253; CANR 15, 58, 134; FW; MTCW 1

Faludi, Susan 1959- .... **CLC 140**
See also CA 138; CANR 126, 194; FW; MTCW 2; MTFW 2005; NCFS 3

Faludy, George 1913- .... **CLC 42**
See also CA 21-24R

Faludy, Gyoergy
See Faludy, George

Fanon, Frantz 1925-1961 ...... **BLC 1:2; CLC 74; TCLC 188**
See also BW 1; CA 116; 89-92; DAM MULT; DLB 296; LMFS 2; WLIT 2

Fanshawe, Ann 1625-1680 .... **LC 11**

Fante, John (Thomas) 1911-1983 .... **CLC 60; SSC 65**
See also AMWS 11; CA 69-72; 109; CANR 23, 104; DLB 130; DLBY 1983

Far, Sui Sin
See Eaton, Edith Maude

Farah, Nuruddin 1945- .. **BLC 1:2, 2:2; CLC 53, 137**
See also AFW; BW 2, 3; CA 106; CANR 81, 148; CDWLB 3; CN 4, 5, 6, 7; DAM MULT; DLB 125; EWL 3; WLIT 2

Fardusi
See Ferdowsi, Abu'l Qasem

Fargue, Leon-Paul 1876(?)-1947 .... **TCLC 11**
See also CA 109; CANR 107; DLB 258; EWL 3

Farigoule, Louis
See Romains, Jules

Farina, Richard 1936(?)-1966 .... **CLC 9**
See also CA 81-84; 25-28R

Farley, Walter (Lorimer)
1915-1989 .... **CLC 17**
See also AAYA 58; BYA 14; CA 17-20R; CANR 8, 29, 84; DLB 22; JRDA; MAICYA 1, 2; SATA 2, 43, 132; YAW

Farmer, Philip Jose
See Farmer, Philip Jose

Farmer, Philip Jose 1918-2009 ..... **CLC 1, 19**
See also AAYA 28; BPFB 1; CA 1-4R; 283; CANR 4, 35, 111; DLB 8; MTCW 1; SATA 93; SATA-Obit 201; SCFW 1, 2; SFW 4

Farmer, Philipe Jos
See Farmer, Philip Jose

Farquhar, George 1677-1707 . **DC 38; LC 21**
See also BRW 2; DAM DRAM; DLB 84; RGEL 2

Farrell, J(ames) G(ordon)
1935-1979 .... **CLC 6**
See also CA 73-76; 89-92; CANR 36; CN 1, 2; DLB 14, 271, 326; MTCW 1; RGEL 2; RHW; WLIT 4

Farrell, James T(homas) 1904-1979 . **CLC 1, 4, 8, 11, 66; SSC 28**
See also AMW; BPFB 1; CA 5-8R; 89-92; CANR 9, 61; CN 1, 2; DLB 4, 9, 86; DLBD 2; EWL 3; MAL 5; MTCW 1, 2; MTFW 2005; RGAL 4

Farrell, M. J.
See Keane, Mary Nesta

Farrell, Warren (Thomas) 1943- ...... **CLC 70**
See also CA 146; CANR 120

Farren, Richard J.
See Betjeman, John

Farren, Richard M.
See Betjeman, John

Farrugia, Mario Benedetti
See Bentley, Eric

Farrugia, Mario Orlando Hardy Hamlet Brenno Benedetti
See Benedetti, Mario

Fassbinder, Rainer Werner
1946-1982 .... **CLC 20**
See also CA 93-96; 106; CANR 31

Fast, Howard 1914-2003 .... **CLC 23, 131**
See also AAYA 16; BPFB 1; CA 1-4R; 181; 214; CAAE 181; CAAS 18; CANR 1, 33, 54, 75, 98, 140; CMW 4; CN 1, 2, 3, 4, 5, 6, 7; CPW; DAM NOV; DLB 9; INT CANR-33; LATS 1:1; MAL 5; MTCW 2; MTFW 2005; RHW; SATA 7; SATA-Essay 107; TCWW 1, 2; YAW

Faulcon, Robert
See Holdstock, Robert

Faulkner, William 1897-1962 .... **CLC 1, 3, 6, 8, 9, 11, 14, 18, 28, 52, 68; SSC 1, 35, 42, 92, 97; TCLC 141; WLC 2**
See also AAYA 7; AMW; AMWR 1; BPFB 1; BYA 5, 15; CA 81-84; CANR 33; CDALB 1929-1941; DA; DA3; DAB; DAC; DAM MST, NOV; DLB 9, 11, 44, 102, 316, 330; DLBD 2; DLBY 1986, 1997; EWL 3; EXPN; EXPS; GL 2; LAIT 2; LATS 1:1; LMFS 2; MAL 5; MTCW 1, 2; MTFW 2005; NFS 4, 8, 13, 24; RGAL 4; RGSF 2; SSFS 2, 5, 6, 12, 27; TUS

Faulkner, William Cuthbert
See Faulkner, William

Fauset, Jessie Redmon
1882(?)-1961 ...... **BLC 1:2; CLC 19, 54; HR 1:2**
See also AFAW 2; BW 1; CA 109; CANR 83; DAM MULT; DLB 51; FW; LMFS 2; MAL 5; MBL

Faust, Frederick 1892-1944 .... **TCLC 49**
See also BPFB 1; CA 108; 152; CANR 143; DAM POP; DLB 256; TCWW 1, 2; TUS

Faust, Frederick Schiller
See Faust, Frederick

Faust, Irvin 1924- .... **CLC 8**
See also CA 33-36R; CANR 28, 67; CN 1, 2, 3, 4, 5, 6, 7; DLB 2, 28, 218, 278; DLBY 1980

Fawkes, Guy
See Benchley, Robert (Charles)

Fearing, Kenneth 1902-1961 .... **CLC 51**
See also CA 93-96; CANR 59; CMW 4; DLB 9; MAL 5; RGAL 4

Fearing, Kenneth Flexner
See Fearing, Kenneth

Fecamps, Elise
See Creasey, John

Federman, Raymond 1928-2009 .. **CLC 6, 47**
See also CA 17-20R; 208; 292; CAAE 208; CAAS 8; CANR 10, 43, 83, 108; CN 3, 4, 5, 6; DLBY 1980

Federspiel, J.F. 1931-2007 .... **CLC 42**
See also CA 146; 257

Federspiel, Juerg F.
See Federspiel, J.F.

Federspiel, Jurg F.
See Federspiel, J.F.

Feiffer, Jules 1929- .... **CLC 2, 8, 64**
See also AAYA 3, 62; CA 17-20R; CAD; CANR 30, 59, 129, 161, 192; CD 5, 6; DAM DRAM; DLB 7, 44; INT CANR-30; MTCW 1; SATA 8, 61, 111, 157, 201

Feiffer, Jules Ralph
See Feiffer, Jules

Feige, Hermann Albert Otto Maximilian
See Traven, B.

Fei-Kan, Li
See Jin, Ba

Feinberg, David B. 1956-1994 .... **CLC 59**
See also CA 135; 147

Feinstein, Elaine 1930- .... **CLC 36**
See also CA 69-72; CAAS 1; CANR 31, 68, 121, 162; CN 3, 4, 5, 6, 7; CP 2, 3, 4, 5, 6, 7; CWP; DLB 14, 40; MTCW 1

Feke, Gilbert David CLC 65

Feldman, Irving (Mordecai) 1928- ..... **CLC 7**
See also CA 1-4R; CANR 1; CP 1, 2, 3, 4, 5, 6, 7; DLB 169; TCLE 1:1

Felix-Tchicaya, Gerald
See Tchicaya, Gerald Felix

Fellini, Federico 1920-1993 .... **CLC 16, 85**
See also CA 65-68; 143; CANR 33

Felltham, Owen 1602(?)-1668 .... **LC 92**
See also DLB 126, 151

Felsen, Henry Gregor 1916-1995 ..... **CLC 17**
See also CA 1-4R; 180; CANR 1; SAAS 2; SATA 1

Felski, Rita CLC 65

Fenelon, Francois de Pons de Salignac de la Mothe- 1651-1715 .... **LC 134**
See also DLB 268; EW 3; GFL Beginnings to 1789

Fenno, Jack
See Calisher, Hortense

Fenollosa, Ernest (Francisco)
1853-1908 .... **TCLC 91**

Fenton, James 1949- .... **CLC 32, 209**
See also CA 102; CANR 108, 160; CP 2, 3, 4, 5, 6, 7; DLB 40; PFS 11

Fenton, James Martin
See Fenton, James

Ferber, Edna 1887-1968 .... **CLC 18, 93**
See also AITN 1; CA 5-8R; 25-28R; CANR 68, 105; DLB 9, 28, 86, 266; MAL 5; MTCW 1, 2; MTFW 2005; RGAL 4; RHW; SATA 7; TCWW 1, 2

Ferdousi
See Ferdowsi, Abu'l Qasem

Ferdovsi
See Ferdowsi, Abu'l Qasem

Ferdowsi
See Ferdowsi, Abu'l Qasem

Fowles, John Robert
See Fowles, John

Fox, Norma Diane
See Mazer, Norma Fox

Fox, Paula 1923- .... **CLC 2, 8, 121**
See also AAYA 3, 37; BYA 3, 8; CA 73-76;
CANR 20, 36, 62, 105, 200; CLR 1, 44,
96; DLB 52; JRDA; MAICYA 1, 2;
MTCW 1; NFS 12; SATA 17, 60, 120,
167; WYA; YAW

Fox, William Price, Jr.
See Fox, William Price

Fox, William Price 1926- .... **CLC 22**
See also CA 17-20R; CAAS 19; CANR 11,
142, 189; CSW; DLB 2; DLBY 1981

Foxe, John 1517(?)-1587 .... **LC 14, 166**
See also DLB 132

Frame, Janet 1924-2004 ...... **CLC 2, 3, 6, 22,**
66, 96, 237; SSC 29, 127
See also CA 1-4R; 224; CANR 2, 36, 76,
135; CN 1, 2, 3, 4, 5, 6, 7; CP 2, 3, 4;
CWP; EWL 3; MTCW 1,2; RGEL 2;
RGSF 2; SATA 119; TWA

France, Anatole 1844-1924 .... **TCLC 9**
See also CA 106; 127; DA3; DAM NOV;
DLB 123, 330; EWL 3; GFL 1789 to the
Present; MTCW 1, 2; RGWL 2, 3; SUFW
1; TWA

Francis, Claude CLC 50
See also CA 192

Francis, Dick 1920- .... **CLC 2, 22, 42, 102**
See also AAYA 5, 21; BEST 89:3; BPFB 1;
CA 5-8R; CANR 9, 42, 68, 100, 141, 179;
CDBLB 1960 to Present; CMW 4; CN 2,
3, 4, 5, 6; DA3; DAM POP; DLB 87; INT
CANR-9; MSW; MTCW 1, 2; MTFW
2005

Francis, Paula Marie
See Allen, Paula Gunn

Francis, Richard Stanley
See Francis, Dick

Francis, Robert (Churchill)
1901-1987 .... **CLC 15; PC 34**
See also AMWS 9; CA 1-4R; 123; CANR
1; CP 1, 2, 3, 4; EXPP; PFS 12; TCLE
1:1

Francis, Lord Jeffrey
See Jeffrey, Francis

Franco, Veronica 1546-1591 .... **LC 171**
See also WLIT 7

Frank, Anne 1929-1945 ... **TCLC 17; WLC 2**
See also AAYA 12; BYA 1; CA 113; 133;
CANR 68; CLR 101; DA; DA3; DAB;
DAC; DAM MST; LAIT 4; MAICYA 2;
MAICYAS 1; MTCW 1, 2; MTFW 2005;
NCFS 2; RGHL; SATA 87; SATA-Brief
42; WYA; YAW

Frank, Annelies Marie
See Frank, Anne

Frank, Bruno 1887-1945 .... **TCLC 81**
See also CA 189; DLB 118; EWL 3

Frank, Elizabeth 1945- .... **CLC 39**
See also CA 121; 126; CANR 78, 150; INT
CA-126

Frankl, Viktor E(mil) 1905-1997 ...... **CLC 93**
See also CA 65-68; 161; RGHL

Franklin, Benjamin
See Hasek, Jaroslav

Franklin, Benjamin 1706-1790 .. **LC 25, 134;**
WLCS
See also AMW; CDALB 1640-1865; DA;
DA3; DAB; DAC; DAM MST; DLB 24,
43, 73, 183; LAIT 1; RGAL 4; TUS

Franklin, Madeleine
See L'Engle, Madeleine

Franklin, Madeleine L'Engle
See L'Engle, Madeleine

Franklin, Madeleine L'Engle Camp
See L'Engle, Madeleine

Franklin, (Stella Maria Sarah) Miles
(Lampe) 1879-1954 .... **TCLC 7**
See also CA 104; 164; DLB 230; FW;
MTCW 2; RGEL 2; TWA

Franzen, Jonathan 1959- .... **CLC 202**
See also AAYA 65; CA 129; CANR 105,
166

Fraser, Antonia 1932- .... **CLC 32, 107**
See also AAYA 57; CA 85-88; CANR 44,
65, 119, 164; CMW; DLB 276; MTCW 1,
2; MTFW 2005; SATA-Brief 32

Fraser, George MacDonald
1925-2008 .... **CLC 7**
See also AAYA 48; CA 45-48, 180; 268;
CAAE 180; CANR 2, 48, 74, 192; DLB
352; MTCW 2; RHW

Fraser, Sylvia 1935- .... **CLC 64**
See also CA 45-48; CANR 1, 16, 60; CCA
1

Frater Perdurabo
See Crowley, Edward Alexander

Frayn, Michael 1933- .... **CLC 3, 7, 31, 47,**
176; DC 27
See also AAYA 69; BRWC 2; BRWS 7; CA
5-8R; CANR 30, 69, 114, 133, 166; CBD;
CD 5, 6; CN 1, 2, 3, 4, 5, 6, 7; DAM
DRAM, NOV; DFS 22; DLB 13, 14, 194,
245; FANT; MTCW 1, 2; MTFW 2005;
SFW 4

Fraze, Candida (Merrill) 1945- .... **CLC 50**
See also CA 126

Frazer, Andrew
See Marlowe, Stephen

Frazer, J(ames) G(eorge)
1854-1941 .... **TCLC 32**
See also BRWS 3; CA 118; NCFS 5

Frazer, Robert Caine
See Creasey, John

Frazer, Sir James George
See Frazer, J(ames) G(eorge)

Frazier, Charles 1950- .... **CLC 109, 224**
See also AAYA 34; CA 161; CANR 126,
170; CSW; DLB 292; MTFW 2005; NFS
25

Frazier, Charles R.
See Frazier, Charles

Frazier, Charles Robinson
See Frazier, Charles

Frazier, Ian 1951- .... **CLC 46**
See also CA 130; CANR 54, 93, 193

Frederic, Harold 1856-1898 ... **NCLC 10, 175**
See also AMW; DLB 12, 23; DLBD 13;
MAL 5; NFS 22; RGAL 4

Frederick, John
See Faust, Frederick

Frederick the Great 1712-1786 .... **LC 14**

Fredro, Aleksander 1793-1876 .... **NCLC 8**

Freeling, Nicolas 1927-2003 .... **CLC 38**
See also CA 49-52; 218; CAAS 12; CANR
1, 17, 50, 84; CMW 4; CN 1, 2, 3, 4, 5,
6; DLB 87

Freeman, Douglas Southall
1886-1953 .... **TCLC 11**
See also CA 109; 195; DLB 17; DLBD 17

Freeman, Judith 1946- .... **CLC 55**
See also CA 148; CANR 120, 179; DLB
256

Freeman, Mary E(leanor) Wilkins
1852-1930 .... **SSC 1, 47, 113; TCLC 9**
See also CA 106; 177; DLB 12, 78, 221;
EXPS; FW; HGG; MBL; RGAL 4; RGSF
2; SSFS 4, 8, 26; SUFW 1; TUS

Freeman, R(ichard) Austin
1862-1943 .... **TCLC 21**
See also CA 113; CANR 84; CMW 4; DLB
70

French, Albert 1943- .... **CLC 86**
See also BW 3; CA 167

French, Antonia
See Kureishi, Hanif

French, Marilyn 1929-2009 . **CLC 10, 18, 60,**
177
See also BPFB 1; CA 69-72; 286; CANR 3,
31, 134, 163; CN 5, 6, 7; CPW; DAM
DRAM, NOV, POP; FL 1:5; FW; INT
CANR-31; MTCW 1, 2; MTFW 2005

French, Paul
See Asimov, Isaac

Freneau, Philip Morin 1752-1832 .. **NCLC 1,**
111
See also AMWS 2; DLB 37, 43; RGAL 4

Freud, Sigmund 1856-1939 .... **TCLC 52**
See also CA 115; 133; CANR 69; DLB 296;
EW 8; EWL 3; LATS 1:1; MTCW 1, 2;
MTFW 2005; NCFS 3; TWA

Freytag, Gustav 1816-1895 .... **NCLC 109**
See also DLB 129

Friedan, Betty 1921-2006 .... **CLC 74**
See also CA 65-68; 248; CANR 18, 45, 74;
DLB 246; FW; MTCW 1, 2; MTFW
2005; NCFS 5

Friedan, Betty Naomi
See Friedan, Betty

Friedlander, Saul 1932- .... **CLC 90**
See also CA 117; 130; CANR 72; RGHL

Friedman, B(ernard) H(arper)
1926- .... **CLC 7**
See also CA 1-4R; CANR 25, 52,

Friedman, Bruce Jay 1930- ...... **CLC 3, 5, 56**
See also CA 9-12R; CAD; CANR 25, 52,
101; CD 5, 6; CN 1, 2, 3, 4, 5, 6, 7; DLB
2, 28, 244; INT CANR-25; MAL 5; SSFS
18

Friel, Brian 1929- .. **CLC 5, 42, 59, 115, 253;**
DC 8; SSC 76
See also BRWS 5; CA 21-24R; CANR 33,
69, 131; CBD; CD 5, 6; DFS 11; DLB
13, 319; EWL 3; MTCW 1; RGEL 2; TEA

Friis-Baastad, Babbis Ellinor
1921-1970 .... **CLC 12**
See also CA 17-20R; 134; SATA 7

Frisch, Max 1911-1991 ...... **CLC 3, 9, 14, 18,**
32, 44; TCLC 121
See also CA 85-88; 134; CANR 32, 74; CD-
WLB 2; DAM DRAM, NOV; DFS 25;
DLB 69, 124; EW 13; EWL 3; MTCW 1,
2; MTFW 2005; RGHL; RGWL 2, 3

Froehlich, Peter
See Gay, Peter

Fromentin, Eugene (Samuel Auguste)
1820-1876 .... **NCLC 10, 125**
See also DLB 123; GFL 1789 to the Present

Frost, Frederick
See Faust, Frederick

Frost, Robert 1874-1963 . **CLC 1, 3, 4, 9, 10,**
13, 15, 26, 34, 44; PC 1, 39, 71; WLC 2
See also AAYA 21; AMW; AMWR 1; CA
89-92; CANR 33; CDALB 1917-1929;
CLR 67; DA; DA3; DAB; DAC; DAM
MST, POET; DLB 54, 284, 342; DLBD
7; EWL 3; EXPP; MAL 5; MTCW 1, 2;
MTFW 2005; PAB; PFS 1, 2, 3, 4, 5, 6,
7, 10, 13; RGAL 4; SATA 14; TUS; WP;
WYA

Frost, Robert Lee
See Frost, Robert

Froude, James Anthony
1818-1894 .... **NCLC 43**
See also DLB 18, 57, 144

Froy, Herald
See Waterhouse, Keith

Fry, Christopher 1907-2005 .. **CLC 2, 10, 14;**
DC 36
See also BRWS 3; CA 17-20R; 240; CAAS
23; CANR 9, 30, 74, 132; CBD; CD 5, 6;
CP 1, 2, 3, 4, 5, 6, 7; DAM DRAM; DLB
13; EWL 3; MTCW 1, 2; MTFW 2005;
RGEL 2; SATA 66; TEA

Gordon, Adam Lindsay
1833-1870 .... **NCLC 21**
See also DLB 230
Gordon, Caroline 1895-1981 . **CLC 6, 13, 29, 83; SSC 15**
See also AMW; CA 11-12; 103; CANR 36; CAP 1; CN 1, 2; DLB 4, 9, 102; DLBD 17; DLBY 1981; EWL 3; MAL 5; MTCW 1, 2; MTFW 2005; RGAL 4; RGSF 2
Gordon, Charles William
1860-1937 .... **TCLC 31**
See also CA 109; DLB 92; TCWW 1, 2
Gordon, Mary 1949- .. **CLC 13, 22, 128, 216; SSC 59**
See also AMWS 4; BPFB 2; CA 102; CANR 44, 92, 154, 179; CN 4, 5, 6, 7; DLB 6; DLBY 1981; FW; INT CA-102; MAL 5; MTCW 1
Gordon, Mary Catherine
See Gordon, Mary
Gordon, N. J.
See Bosman, Herman Charles
Gordon, Sol 1923- .... **CLC 26**
See also CA 53-56; CANR 4; SATA 11
Gordone, Charles 1925-1995 .... **BLC 2:2; CLC 1, 4; DC 8**
See also BW 1, 3; CA 93-96; 180; 150; CAAE 180; CAD; CANR 55; DAM DRAM; DLB 7; INT CA-93-96; MTCW 1
Gore, Catherine 1800-1861 .... **NCLC 65**
See also DLB 116, 344; RGEL 2
Gorenko, Anna Andreevna
See Akhmatova, Anna
Gor'kii, Maksim
See Gorky, Maxim
Gorky, Maxim 1868-1936 ..... **SSC 28; TCLC 8; WLC 3**
See also CA 105; 141; CANR 83; DA; DAB; DAC; DAM DRAM, MST, NOV; DFS 9; DLB 295; EW 8; EWL 3; MTCW 2; MTFW 2005; RGSF 2; RGWL 2, 3; TWA
Goryan, Sirak
See Saroyan, William
Gosse, Edmund (William)
1849-1928 .... **TCLC 28**
See also CA 117; DLB 57, 144, 184; RGEL 2
Gotlieb, Phyllis 1926-2009 .... **CLC 18**
See also CA 13-16R; CANR 7, 135; CN 7; CP 1, 2, 3, 4; DLB 88, 251; SFW 4
Gotlieb, Phyllis Fay Bloom
See Gotlieb, Phyllis
Gottesman, S. D.
See Kornbluth, C(yril) M.; Pohl, Frederik
Gottfried von Strassburg fl. c.
1170-1215 .... **CMLC 10, 96**
See also CDWLB 2; DLB 138; EW 1; RGWL 2, 3
Gotthelf, Jeremias 1797-1854 .... **NCLC 117**
See also DLB 133; RGWL 2, 3
Gottschalk, Laura Riding
See Jackson, Laura
Gould, Lois 1932(?)-2002 .... **CLC 4, 10**
See also CA 77-80; 208; CANR 29; MTCW 1
Gould, Stephen Jay 1941-2002 .... **CLC 163**
See also AAYA 26; BEST 90:2; CA 77-80; 205; CANR 10, 27, 56, 75, 125; CPW; INT CANR-27; MTCW 1, 2; MTFW 2005
Gourmont, Remy(-Marie-Charles) de
1858-1915 .... **TCLC 17**
See also CA 109; 150; GFL 1789 to the Present; MTCW 2
Gournay, Marie le Jars de
See de Gournay, Marie le Jars

Govier, Katherine 1948- .... **CLC 51**
See also CA 101; CANR 18, 40, 128; CCA 1
Gower, John c. 1330-1408 .... **LC 76; PC 59**
See also BRW 1; DLB 146; RGEL 2
Goyen, (Charles) William
1915-1983 .... **CLC 5, 8, 14, 40**
See also AITN 2; CA 5-8R; 110; CANR 6, 71; CN 1, 2, 3; DLB 2, 218; DLBY 1983; EWL 3; INT CANR-6; MAL 5
Goytisolo, Juan 1931- .... **CLC 5, 10, 23, 133; HLC 1**
See also CA 85-88; CANR 32, 61, 131, 182; CWW 2; DAM MULT; DLB 322; EWL 3; GLL 2; HW 1, 2; MTCW 1, 2; MTFW 2005
Gozzano, Guido 1883-1916 .... **PC 10**
See also CA 154; DLB 114; EWL 3
Gozzi, (Conte) Carlo 1720-1806 .... **NCLC 23**
Grabbe, Christian Dietrich
1801-1836 .... **NCLC 2**
See also DLB 133; RGWL 2, 3
Grace, Patricia 1937- .... **CLC 56**
See also CA 176; CANR 118; CN 4, 5, 6, 7; EWL 3; RGSF 2
Grace, Patricia Frances
See Grace, Patricia
Gracian, Baltasar 1601-1658 .... **LC 15, 160**
Gracian y Morales, Baltasar
See Gracian, Baltasar
Gracq, Julien 1910-2007 ..... **CLC 11, 48, 259**
See also CA 122; 126; 267; CANR 141; CWW 2; DLB 83; GFL 1789 to the present
Grade, Chaim 1910-1982 .... **CLC 10**
See also CA 93-96; 107; DLB 333; EWL 3; RGHL
Grade, Khayim
See Grade, Chaim
Graduate of Oxford, A
See Ruskin, John
Grafton, Garth
See Duncan, Sara Jeannette
Grafton, Sue 1940- .... **CLC 163**
See also AAYA 11, 49; BEST 90:3; CA 108; CANR 31, 55, 111, 134, 195; CMW 4; CPW; CSW; DA3; DAM POP; DLB 226; FW; MSW; MTFW 2005
Graham, John
See Phillips, David Graham
Graham, Jorie 1950- .... **CLC 48, 118; PC 59**
See also AAYA 67; CA 111; CANR 63, 118; CP 4, 5, 6, 7; CWP; DLB 120; EWL 3; MTFW 2005; PFS 10, 17; TCLE 1:1
Graham, R. B. Cunninghame
See Cunninghame Graham, Robert Bontine
Graham, Robert
See Haldeman, Joe
Graham, Robert Bontine Cunninghame
See Cunninghame Graham, Robert Bontine
Graham, Tom
See Lewis, Sinclair
Graham, W(illiam) S(ydney)
1918-1986 .... **CLC 29**
See also BRWS 7; CA 73-76; 118; CP 1, 2, 3, 4; DLB 20; RGEL 2
Graham, Winston (Mawdsley)
1910-2003 .... **CLC 23**
See also CA 49-52; 218; CANR 2, 22, 45, 66; CMW 4; CN 1, 2, 3, 4, 5, 6, 7; DLB 77; RHW
Grahame, Kenneth 1859-1932 ...... **TCLC 64, 136**
See also BYA 5; CA 108; 136; CANR 80; CLR 5, 135; CWRI 5; DA3; DAB; DLB 34, 141, 178; FANT; MAICYA 1, 2; MTCW 2; NFS 20; RGEL 2; SATA 100; TEA; WCH; YABC 1

Granger, Darius John
See Marlowe, Stephen
Granin, Daniil 1918- .... **CLC 59**
See also DLB 302
Granovsky, Timofei Nikolaevich
1813-1855 .... **NCLC 75**
See also DLB 198
Grant, Skeeter
See Spiegelman, Art
Granville-Barker, Harley
1877-1946 .... **TCLC 2**
See also CA 104; 204; DAM DRAM; DLB 10; RGEL 2
Granzotto, Gianni
See Granzotto, Giovanni Battista
Granzotto, Giovanni Battista
1914-1985 .... **CLC 70**
See also CA 166
Grasemann, Ruth Barbara
See Rendell, Ruth
Grass, Guenter
See Grass, Gunter
Grass, Gunter 1927- .. **CLC 1, 2, 4, 6, 11, 15, 22, 32, 49, 88, 207; WLC 3**
See also BPFB 2; CA 13-16R; CANR 20, 75, 93, 133, 174; CDWLB 2; CWW 2; DA; DA3; DAB; DAC; DAM MST, NOV; DLB 330; EW 13; EWL 3; MTCW 1, 2; MTFW 2005; RGHL; RGWL 2, 3; TWA
Grass, Gunter Wilhelm
See Grass, Gunter
Gratton, Thomas
See Hulme, T(homas) E(rnest)
Grau, Shirley Ann 1929- .... **CLC 4, 9, 146; SSC 15**
See also CA 89-92; CANR 22, 69; CN 1, 2, 3, 4, 5, 6, 7; CSW; DLB 2, 218; INT CA-89-92; CANR-22; MTCW 1
Gravel, Fern
See Hall, James Norman
Graver, Elizabeth 1964- .... **CLC 70**
See also CA 135; CANR 71, 129
Graves, Richard Perceval
1895-1985 .... **CLC 44**
See also CA 65-68; CANR 9, 26, 51
Graves, Robert 1895-1985 ... **CLC 1, 2, 6, 11, 39, 44, 45; PC 6**
See also BPFB 2; BRW 7; BYA 4; CA 5-8R; 117; CANR 5, 36; CDBLB 1914-1945; CN 1, 2, 3; CP 1, 2, 3, 4; DA3; DAB; DAC; DAM MST, POET; DLB 20, 100, 191; DLBD 18; DLBY 1985; EWL 3; LATS 1:1; MTCW 1, 2; MTFW 2005; NCFS 2; NFS 21; RGEL 2; RHW; SATA 45; TEA
Graves, Robert von Ranke
See Graves, Robert
Graves, Valerie
See Bradley, Marion Zimmer
Gray, Alasdair 1934- .... **CLC 41, 275**
See also BRWS 9; CA 126; CANR 47, 69, 106, 140; CN 4, 5, 6, 7; DLB 194, 261, 319; HGG; INT CA-126; MTCW 1, 2; MTFW 2005; RGSF 2; SUFW 2
Gray, Amlin 1946- .... **CLC 29**
See also CA 138
Gray, Francine du Plessix 1930- ..... **CLC 22, 153**
See also BEST 90:3; CA 61-64; CAAS 2; CANR 11, 33, 75, 81, 197; DAM NOV; INT CANR-11; MTCW 1, 2; MTFW 2005
Gray, John (Henry) 1866-1934 ...... **TCLC 19**
See also CA 119; 162; RGEL 2
Gray, John Lee
See Jakes, John
Gray, Simon 1936-2008 .... **CLC 9, 14, 36**
See also AITN 1; CA 21-24R; 275; CAAS 3; CANR 32, 69; CBD; CD 5, 6; CN 1, 2, 3; DLB 13; EWL 3; MTCW 1; RGEL 2

Grumbach, Doris 1918- .... **CLC 13, 22, 64**
See also CA 5-8R; CAAS 2; CANR 9, 42, 70, 127; CN 6, 7; INT CANR-9; MTCW 2; MTFW 2005

Grundtvig, Nikolai Frederik Severin
1783-1872 .... **NCLC 1, 158**
See also DLB 300

Grunge
See Crumb, R.

Grunwald, Lisa 1959- .... **CLC 44**
See also CA 120; CANR 148

Gryphius, Andreas 1616-1664 .... **LC 89**
See also CDWLB 2; DLB 164; RGWL 2, 3

Guare, John 1938- .... **CLC 8, 14, 29, 67; DC 20**
See also CA 73-76; CAD; CANR 21, 69, 118; CD 5, 6; DAM DRAM; DFS 8, 13; DLB 7, 249; EWL 3; MAL 5; MTCW 1, 2; RGAL 4

Guarini, Battista 1538-1612 .... **LC 102**
See also DLB 339

Gubar, Susan 1944- .... **CLC 145**
See also CA 108; CANR 45, 70, 139, 179; FW; MTCW 1; RGAL 4

Gubar, Susan David
See Gubar, Susan

Gudjonsson, Halldor Kiljan
1902-1998 .... **CLC 25**
See also CA 103; 164; CWW 2; DLB 293, 331; EW 12; EWL 3; RGWL 2, 3

Guedes, Vincente
See Pessoa, Fernando

Guenter, Erich
See Eich, Gunter

Guest, Barbara 1920-2006 ... **CLC 34; PC 55**
See also BG 1:2; CA 25-28R; 248; CANR 11, 44, 84; CP 1, 2, 3, 4, 5, 6, 7; CWP; DLB 5, 193

Guest, Edgar A(lbert) 1881-1959 ... **TCLC 95**
See also CA 112; 168

Guest, Judith 1936- .... **CLC 8, 30**
See also AAYA 7, 66; CA 77-80; CANR 15, 75, 138; DA3; DAM NOV, POP; EXPN; INT CANR-15; LAIT 5; MTCW 1, 2; MTFW 2005; NFS 1

Guest, Judith Ann
See Guest, Judith

Guevara, Che
See Guevara (Serna), Ernesto

Guevara (Serna), Ernesto
1928-1967 .... **CLC 87; HLC 1**
See also CA 127; 111; CANR 56; DAM MULT; HW 1

Guicciardini, Francesco 1483-1540 ..... **LC 49**

Guido delle Colonne c. 1215-c.
1290 .... **CMLC 90**

Guild, Nicholas M. 1944- .... **CLC 33**
See also CA 93-96

Guillemin, Jacques
See Sartre, Jean-Paul

Guillen, Jorge 1893-1984 . **CLC 11; HLCS 1; PC 35; TCLC 233**
See also CA 89-92; 112; DAM MULT, POET; DLB 108; EWL 3; HW 1; RGWL 2, 3

Guillen, Nicolas 1902-1989 ... **BLC 1:2; CLC 48, 79; HLC 1; PC 23**
See also BW 2; CA 116; 125; 129; CANR 84; DAM MST, MULT, POET; DLB 283; EWL 3; HW 1; LAW; RGWL 2, 3; WP

Guillen, Nicolas Cristobal
See Guillen, Nicolas

Guillen y Alvarez, Jorge
See Guillen, Jorge

Guillevic, (Eugene) 1907-1997 .... **CLC 33**
See also CA 93-96; CWW 2

Guillois
See Desnos, Robert

Guillois, Valentin
See Desnos, Robert

Guimaraes Rosa, Joao 1908-1967 ... **CLC 23; HLCS 1**
See also CA 175; 89-92; DLB 113, 307; EWL 3; LAW; RGSF 2; RGWL 2, 3; WLIT 1

Guiney, Louise Imogen
1861-1920 .... **TCLC 41**
See also CA 160; DLB 54; RGAL 4

Guinizelli, Guido c. 1230-1276 ...... **CMLC 49**
See also WLIT 7

Guinizzelli, Guido
See Guinizelli, Guido

Guiraldes, Ricardo (Guillermo)
1886-1927 .... **TCLC 39**
See also CA 131; EWL 3; HW 1; LAW; MTCW 1

Guma, Alex La
See La Guma, Alex

Gumilev, Nikolai (Stepanovich)
1886-1921 .... **TCLC 60**
See also CA 165; DLB 295; EWL 3

Gumilyov, Nikolay Stepanovich
See Gumilev, Nikolai (Stepanovich)

Gump, P. Q.
See Card, Orson Scott

Gump, P.Q.
See Card, Orson Scott

Gunesekera, Romesh 1954- .... **CLC 91**
See also BRWS 10; CA 159; CANR 140, 172; CN 6, 7; DLB 267, 323

Gunn, Bill
See Gunn, William Harrison

Gunn, Thom 1929-2004 ..... **CLC 3, 6, 18, 32, 81; PC 26**
See also BRWR 3; BRWS 4; CA 17-20R; 227; CANR 9, 33, 116; CDBLB 1960 to Present; CP 1, 2, 3, 4, 5, 6, 7; DAM POET; DLB 27; INT CANR-33; MTCW 1; PFS 9; RGEL 2

Gunn, William Harrison
1934(?)-1989 .... **CLC 5**
See also AITN 1; BW 1, 3; CA 13-16R; 128; CANR 12, 25, 76; DLB 38

Gunn Allen, Paula
See Allen, Paula Gunn

Gunnars, Kristjana 1948- .... **CLC 69**
See also CA 113; CCA 1; CP 6, 7; CWP; DLB 60

Gunter, Erich
See Eich, Gunter

Gurdjieff, G(eorgei) I(vanovich)
1877(?)-1949 .... **TCLC 71**
See also CA 157

Gurganus, Allan 1947- .... **CLC 70**
See also BEST 90:1; CA 135; CANR 114; CN 6, 7; CPW; CSW; DAM POP; DLB 350; GLL 1

Gurney, A. R.
See Gurney, A(lbert) R(amsdell), Jr.

Gurney, A(lbert) R(amsdell), Jr.
1930- .... **CLC 32, 50, 54**
See also AMWS 5; CA 77-80; CAD; CANR 32, 64, 121; CD 5, 6; DAM DRAM; DLB 266; EWL 3

Gurney, Ivor (Bertie) 1890-1937 ... **TCLC 33**
See also BRW 6; CA 167; DLBY 2002; PAB; RGEL 2

Gurney, Peter
See Gurney, A(lbert) R(amsdell), Jr.

Guro, Elena (Genrikhovna)
1877-1913 .... **TCLC 56**
See also DLB 295

Gustafson, James M(oody) 1925- ... **CLC 100**
See also CA 25-28R; CANR 37

Gustafson, Ralph (Barker)
1909-1995 .... **CLC 36**
See also CA 21-24R; CANR 8, 45, 84; CP 1, 2, 3, 4, 5, 6; DLB 88; RGEL 2

Gut, Gom
See Simenon, Georges

Guterson, David 1956- .... **CLC 91**
See also CA 132; CANR 73, 126, 194; CN 7; DLB 292; MTCW 2; MTFW 2005; NFS 13

Guthrie, A(lfred) B(ertram), Jr.
1901-1991 .... **CLC 23**
See also CA 57-60; 134; CANR 24; CN 1, 2, 3; DLB 6, 212; MAL 5; SATA 62; SATA-Obit 67; TCWW 1, 2

Guthrie, Isobel
See Grieve, C. M.

Gutierrez Najera, Manuel
1859-1895 .... **HLCS 2; NCLC 133**
See also DLB 290; LAW

Guy, Rosa (Cuthbert) 1925- .... **CLC 26**
See also AAYA 4, 37; BW 2; CA 17-20R; CANR 14, 34, 83; CLR 13, 137; DLB 33; DNFS 1; JRDA; MAICYA 1, 2; SATA 14, 62, 122; YAW

Gwendolyn
See Bennett, (Enoch) Arnold

H. D.
See Doolittle, Hilda

H. de V.
See Buchan, John

Haavikko, Paavo Juhani 1931- .. **CLC 18, 34**
See also CA 106; CWW 2; EWL 3

Habbema, Koos
See Heijermans, Herman

Habermas, Juergen 1929- .... **CLC 104**
See also CA 109; CANR 85, 162; DLB 242

Habermas, Jurgen
See Habermas, Juergen

Hacker, Marilyn 1942- ...... **CLC 5, 9, 23, 72, 91; PC 47**
See also CA 77-80; CANR 68, 129; CP 3, 4, 5, 6, 7; CWP; DAM POET; DLB 120, 282; FW; GLL 2; MAL 5; PFS 19

Hadewijch of Antwerp fl. 1250- ... **CMLC 61**
See also RGWL 3

Hadrian 76-138 .... **CMLC 52**

Haeckel, Ernst Heinrich (Philipp August)
1834-1919 .... **TCLC 83**
See also CA 157

Hafiz c. 1326-1389(?) .... **CMLC 34**
See also RGWL 2, 3; WLIT 6

Hagedorn, Jessica T(arahata)
1949- .... **CLC 185**
See also CA 139; CANR 69; CWP; DLB 312; RGAL 4

Haggard, H(enry) Rider
1856-1925 .... **TCLC 11**
See also AAYA 81; BRWS 3; BYA 4, 5; CA 108; 148; CANR 112; DLB 70, 156, 174, 178; FANT; LMFS 1; MTCW 2; RGEL 2; RHW; SATA 16; SCFW 1, 2; SFW 4; SUFW 1; WLIT 4

Hagiosy, L.
See Larbaud, Valery (Nicolas)

Hagiwara, Sakutaro 1886-1942 .... **PC 18; TCLC 60**
See also CA 154; EWL 3; RGWL 3

Hagiwara Sakutaro
See Hagiwara, Sakutaro

Haig, Fenil
See Ford, Ford Madox

Haig-Brown, Roderick (Langmere)
1908-1976 .... **CLC 21**
See also CA 5-8R; 69-72; CANR 4, 38, 83; CLR 31; CWRI 5; DLB 88; MAICYA 1, 2; SATA 12; TCWW 2

Haight, Rip
See Carpenter, John

Hargrave, Leonie
 See Disch, Thomas M.
**Hariri, Al- al-Qasim ibn 'Ali Abu
  Muhammad al-Basri**
 See al-Hariri, al-Qasim ibn 'Ali Abu Mu-
  hammad al-Basri
Harjo, Joy 1951- .... **CLC 83; NNAL; PC 27**
 See also AMWS 12; CA 114; CANR 35,
  67, 91, 129; CP 6, 7; CWP; DAM MULT;
  DLB 120, 175, 342; EWL 3; MTCW 2;
  MTFW 2005; PFS 15; RGAL 4
Harlan, Louis R. 1922-2010 .... **CLC 34**
 See also CA 21-24R; CANR 25, 55, 80
Harlan, Louis Rudolph
 See Harlan, Louis R.
Harling, Robert 1951(?)- .... **CLC 53**
 See also CA 147
Harmon, William (Ruth) 1938- .... **CLC 38**
 See also CA 33-36R; CANR 14, 32, 35;
  SATA 65
Harper, F. E. W.
 See Harper, Frances Ellen Watkins
Harper, Frances E. W.
 See Harper, Frances Ellen Watkins
Harper, Frances E. Watkins
 See Harper, Frances Ellen Watkins
Harper, Frances Ellen
 See Harper, Frances Ellen Watkins
Harper, Frances Ellen Watkins
  1825-1911 . **BLC 1:2; PC 21; TCLC 14,
  217**
 See also AFAW 1, 2; BW 1, 3; CA 111; 125;
  CANR 79; DAM MULT, POET; DLB 50,
  221; MBL; RGAL 4
Harper, Michael S(teven) 1938- ..... **BLC 2:2;
  CLC 7, 22**
 See also AFAW 2; BW 1; CA 33-36R; 224;
  CAAE 224; CANR 24, 108; CP 2, 3, 4, 5,
  6, 7; DLB 41; RGAL 4; TCLE 1:1
Harper, Mrs. F. E. W.
 See Harper, Frances Ellen Watkins
Harpur, Charles 1813-1868 .... **NCLC 114**
 See also DLB 230; RGEL 2
Harris, Christie
 See Harris, Christie (Lucy) Irwin
Harris, Christie (Lucy) Irwin
  1907-2002 .... **CLC 12**
 See also CA 5-8R; CANR 6, 83; CLR 47;
  DLB 88; JRDA; MAICYA 1, 2; SAAS 10;
  SATA 6, 74; SATA-Essay 116
Harris, Frank 1856-1931 .... **TCLC 24**
 See also CA 109; 150; CANR 80; DLB 156,
  197; RGEL 2
Harris, George Washington
  1814-1869 .... **NCLC 23, 165**
 See also DLB 3, 11, 248; RGAL 4
Harris, Joel Chandler 1848-1908 ..... **SSC 19,
  103; TCLC 2**
 See also CA 104; 137; CANR 80; CLR 49,
  128; DLB 11, 23, 42, 78, 91; LAIT 2;
  MAICYA 1, 2; RGSF 2; SATA 100; WCH;
  YABC 1
**Harris, John (Wyndham Parkes Lucas)
  Beynon** 1903-1969 .... **CLC 19**
 See also BRWS 13; CA 102; 89-92; CANR
  84; DLB 255; SATA 118; SCFW 1, 2;
  SFW 4
Harris, MacDonald
 See Heiney, Donald (William)
Harris, Mark 1922-2007 .... **CLC 19**
 See also CA 5-8R; 260; CAAS 3; CANR 2,
  55, 83; CN 1, 2, 3, 4, 5, 6, 7; DLB 2;
  DLBY 1980
Harris, Norman CLC 65
Harris, (Theodore) Wilson 1921- ... **BLC 2:2;
  CLC 25, 159**
 See also BRWS 5; BW 2, 3; CA 65-68;
  CAAS 16; CANR 11, 27, 69, 114; CD-
  WLB 3; CN 1, 2, 3, 4, 5, 6, 7; CP 1, 2, 3,
  4, 5, 6, 7; DLB 117; EWL 3; MTCW 1;
  RGEL 2

Harrison, Barbara Grizzuti
  1934-2002 .... **CLC 144**
 See also CA 77-80; 205; CANR 15, 48; INT
  CANR-15
Harrison, Elizabeth (Allen) Cavanna
  1909-2001 .... **CLC 12**
 See also CA 9-12R; 200; CANR 6, 27, 85,
  104, 121; JRDA; MAICYA 1; SAAS 4;
  SATA 1, 30; YAW
Harrison, Harry 1925- .... **CLC 42**
 See also CA 1-4R; CANR 5, 21, 84; DLB
  8; SATA 4; SCFW 2; SFW 4
Harrison, Harry Max
 See Harrison, Harry
Harrison, James
 See Harrison, Jim
Harrison, James Thomas
 See Harrison, Jim
Harrison, Jim 1937- .... **CLC 6, 14, 33, 66,
  143; SSC 19**
 See also AMWS 8; CA 13-16R; CANR 8,
  51, 79, 142, 198; CN 5, 6; CP 1, 2, 3, 4,
  5, 6; DLBY 1982; INT CANR-8; RGAL
  4; TCWW 2; TUS
Harrison, Kathryn 1961- .... **CLC 70, 151**
 See also CA 144; CANR 68, 122, 194
Harrison, Tony 1937- .... **CLC 43, 129**
 See also BRWS 5; CA 65-68; CANR 44,
  98; CBD; CD 5, 6; CP 2, 3, 4, 5, 6, 7;
  DLB 40, 245; MTCW 1; RGEL 2
Harriss, Will(ard Irvin) 1922- .... **CLC 34**
 See also CA 111
Hart, Ellis
 See Ellison, Harlan
Hart, Josephine 1942(?)- .... **CLC 70**
 See also CA 138; CANR 70, 149; CPW;
  DAM POP
Hart, Moss 1904-1961 .... **CLC 66**
 See also CA 109; 89-92; CANR 84; DAM
  DRAM; DFS 1; DLB 7, 266; RGAL 4
Harte, Bret 1836(?)-1902 ... **SSC 8, 59; TCLC
  1, 25; WLC 3**
 See also AMWS 2; CA 104; 140; CANR
  80; CDALB 1865-1917; DA; DA3; DAC;
  DAM MST; DLB 12, 64, 74, 79, 186;
  EXPS; LAIT 2; RGAL 4; RGSF 2; SATA
  26; SSFS 3; TUS
Harte, Francis Brett
 See Harte, Bret
Hartley, L(eslie) P(oles) 1895-1972 ... **CLC 2,
  22; SSC 125**
 See also BRWS 7; CA 45-48; 37-40R;
  CANR 33; CN 1; DLB 15, 139; EWL 3;
  HGG; MTCW 1, 2; MTFW 2005; RGEL
  2; RGSF 2; SUFW 1
Hartman, Geoffrey H. 1929- .... **CLC 27**
 See also CA 117; 125; CANR 79; DLB 67
Hartmann, Sadakichi 1869-1944 ... **TCLC 73**
 See also CA 157; DLB 54
Hartmann von Aue c. 1170-c.
  1210 .... **CMLC 15**
 See also CDWLB 2; DLB 138; RGWL 2, 3
Hartog, Jan de
 See de Hartog, Jan
Haruf, Kent 1943- .... **CLC 34**
 See also AAYA 44; CA 149; CANR 91, 131
Harvey, Caroline
 See Trollope, Joanna
Harvey, Gabriel 1550(?)-1631 .... **LC 88**
 See also DLB 167, 213, 281
Harvey, Jack
 See Rankin, Ian
Harwood, Ronald 1934- .... **CLC 32**
 See also CA 1-4R; CANR 4, 55, 150; CBD;
  CD 5, 6; DAM DRAM, MST; DLB 13
Hasegawa Tatsunosuke
 See Futabatei, Shimei

Hasek, Jaroslav 1883-1923 ... **SSC 69; TCLC
  4**
 See also CA 104; 129; CDWLB 4; DLB
  215; EW 9; EWL 3; MTCW 1, 2; RGSF
  2; RGWL 2, 3
Hasek, Jaroslav Matej Frantisek
 See Hasek, Jaroslav
Hass, Robert 1941- ...... **CLC 18, 39, 99, 287;
  PC 16**
 See also AMWS 6; CA 111; CANR 30, 50,
  71, 187; CP 3, 4, 5, 6, 7; DLB 105, 206;
  EWL 3; MAL 5; MTFW 2005; RGAL 4;
  SATA 94; TCLE 1:1
Hassler, Jon 1933-2008 .... **CLC 263**
 See also CA 73-76; 270; CANR 21, 80, 161;
  CN 6, 7; INT CANR-21; SATA 19; SATA-
  Obit 191
Hassler, Jon Francis
 See Hassler, Jon
Hastings, Hudson
 See Kuttner, Henry
Hastings, Selina CLC 44
 See also CA 257
Hastings, Selina Shirley
 See Hastings, Selina
Hastings, Victor
 See Disch, Thomas M.
Hathorne, John 1641-1717 .... **LC 38**
Hatteras, Amelia
 See Mencken, H. L.
Hatteras, Owen
 See Mencken, H. L.; Nathan, George Jean
Hauff, Wilhelm 1802-1827 .... **NCLC 185**
 See also DLB 90; SUFW 1
Hauptmann, Gerhart 1862-1946 .... **DC 34;
  SSC 37; TCLC 4**
 See also CA 104; 153; CDWLB 2; DAM
  DRAM; DLB 66, 118, 330; EW 8; EWL
  3; RGSF 2; RGWL 2, 3; TWA
Hauptmann, Gerhart Johann Robert
 See Hauptmann, Gerhart
Havel, Vaclav 1936- ..... **CLC 25, 58, 65, 123;
  DC 6**
 See also CA 104; CANR 36, 63, 124, 175;
  CDWLB 4; CWW 2; DA3; DAM DRAM;
  DFS 10; DLB 232; EWL 3; LMFS 2;
  MTCW 1, 2; RGWL 3
Haviaras, Stratis
 See Chaviaras, Strates
Hawes, Stephen 1475(?)-1529(?) .... **LC 17**
 See also DLB 132; RGEL 2
Hawkes, John 1925-1998 .. **CLC 1, 2, 3, 4, 7,
  9, 14, 15, 27, 49**
 See also BPFB 2; CA 1-4R; 167; CANR 2,
  47, 64; CN 1, 2, 3, 4, 5, 6; DLB 2, 7, 227;
  DLBY 1980, 1998; EWL 3; MAL 5;
  MTCW 1, 2; MTFW 2005; RGAL 4
Hawking, S. W.
 See Hawking, Stephen W.
Hawking, Stephen W. 1942- ..... **CLC 63, 105**
 See also AAYA 13; BEST 89:1; CA 126;
  129; CANR 48, 115; CPW; DA3; MTCW
  2; MTFW 2005
Hawking, Stephen William
 See Hawking, Stephen W.
Hawkins, Anthony Hope
 See Hope, Anthony
Hawthorne, Julian 1846-1934 .... **TCLC 25**
 See also CA 165; HGG
Hawthorne, Nathaniel 1804-1864 ... **NCLC 2,
  10, 17, 23, 39, 79, 95, 158, 171, 191,
  226; SSC 3, 29, 39, 89, 130; WLC 3**
 See also AAYA 18; AMW; AMWC 1;
  AMWR 1; BPFB 2; BYA 3; CDALB
  1640-1865; CLR 103; DA; DA3; DAB;
  DAC; DAM MST, NOV; DLB 1, 74, 183,

223, 269; EXPN; EXPS; GL 2; HGG; LAIT 1; NFS 1, 20; RGAL 4; RGSF 2; SSFS 1, 7, 11, 15; SUFW 1; TUS; WCH; YABC 2

Hawthorne, Sophia Peabody
1809-1871 .... **NCLC 150**
See also DLB 183, 239

Haxton, Josephine Ayres
See Douglas, Ellen

Hayaseca y Eizaguirre, Jorge
See Echegaray (y Eizaguirre), Jose (Maria Waldo)

Hayashi, Fumiko 1904-1951 .... **TCLC 27**
See also CA 161; DLB 180; EWL 3

Hayashi Fumiko
See Hayashi, Fumiko

Haycraft, Anna 1932-2005 .... **CLC 40**
See also CA 122; 237; CANR 90, 141; CN 4, 5, 6; DLB 194; MTCW 2; MTFW 2005

Haycraft, Anna Margaret
See Haycraft, Anna

Hayden, Robert
See Hayden, Robert Earl

Hayden, Robert E.
See Hayden, Robert Earl

Hayden, Robert Earl 1913-1980 .... **BLC 1:2; CLC 5, 9, 14, 37; PC 6**
See also AFAW 1, 2; AMWS 2; BW 1, 3; CA 69-72; 97-100; CABS 1; CANR 24, 75, 82; CDALB 1941-1968; CP 1, 2, 3; DA; DAC; DAM MST, MULT, POET; DLB 5, 76; EWL 3; EXPP; MAL 5; MTCW 1, 2; PFS 1, 31; RGAL 4; SATA 19; SATA-Obit 26; WP

Haydon, Benjamin Robert
1786-1846 .... **NCLC 146**
See also DLB 110

Hayek, F(riedrich) A(ugust von)
1899-1992 .... **TCLC 109**
See also CA 93-96; 137; CANR 20; MTCW 1, 2

Hayford, J(oseph) E(phraim) Casely
See Casely-Hayford, J(oseph) E(phraim)

Hayman, Ronald 1932- .... **CLC 44**
See also CA 25-28R; CANR 18, 50, 88; CD 5, 6; DLB 155

Hayne, Paul Hamilton 1830-1886 . **NCLC 94**
See also DLB 3, 64, 79, 248; RGAL 4

Hays, Mary 1760-1843 .... **NCLC 114**
See also DLB 142, 158; RGEL 2

Haywood, Eliza (Fowler)
1693(?)-1756 .... **LC 1, 44, 177**
See also BRWS 12; DLB 39; RGEL 2

Hazlitt, William 1778-1830 ...... **NCLC 29, 82**
See also BRW 4; DLB 110, 158; RGEL 2; TEA

Hazzard, Shirley 1931- .... **CLC 18, 218**
See also CA 9-12R; CANR 4, 70, 127; CN 1, 2, 3, 4, 5, 6, 7; DLB 289; DLBY 1982; MTCW 1

Head, Bessie 1937-1986 . **BLC 1:2, 2:2; CLC 25, 67; SSC 52**
See also AFW; BW 2, 3; CA 29-32R; 119; CANR 25, 82; CDWLB 3; CN 1, 2, 3, 4; DA3; DAM MULT; DLB 117, 225; EWL 3; EXPS; FL 1:6; FW; MTCW 1, 2; MTFW 2005; RGSF 2; SSFS 5, 13; WLIT 2; WWE 1

Headley, Elizabeth
See Harrison, Elizabeth (Allen) Cavanna

Headon, (Nicky) Topper 1956(?)- ..... **CLC 30**

Heaney, Seamus 1939- . **CLC 5, 7, 14, 25, 37, 74, 91, 171, 225; PC 18, 100; WLCS**
See also AAYA 61; BRWR 1; BRWS 2; CA 85-88; CANR 25, 48, 75, 91, 128, 184; CDBLB 1960 to Present; CP 1, 2, 3, 4, 5, 6, 7; DA3; DAB; DAM POET; DLB 40,

330; DLBY 1995; EWL 3; EXPP; MTCW 1, 2; MTFW 2005; PAB; PFS 2, 5, 8, 17, 30; RGEL 2; TEA; WLIT 4

Heaney, Seamus Justin
See Heaney, Seamus

Hearn, Lafcadio 1850-1904 .... **TCLC 9**
See also AAYA 79; CA 105; 166; DLB 12, 78, 189; HGG; MAL 5; RGAL 4

Hearn, Patricio Lafcadio Tessima Carlos
See Hearn, Lafcadio

Hearne, Samuel 1745-1792 .... **LC 95**
See also DLB 99

Hearne, Vicki 1946-2001 .... **CLC 56**
See also CA 139; 201

Hearon, Shelby 1931- .... **CLC 63**
See also AITN 2; AMWS 8; CA 25-28R; CAAS 11; CANR 18, 48, 103, 146; CSW

Heat-Moon, William Least 1939- ..... **CLC 29**
See also AAYA 9, 66; ANW; CA 115; 119; CANR 47, 89; CPW; INT CA-119

Hebbel, Friedrich 1813-1863 . **DC 21; NCLC 43**
See also CDWLB 2; DAM DRAM; DLB 129; EW 6; RGWL 2, 3

Hebert, Anne 1916-2000 . **CLC 4, 13, 29, 246**
See also CA 85-88; 187; CANR 69, 126; CCA 1; CWP; CWW 2; DA3; DAC; DAM MST, POET; DLB 68; EWL 3; GFL 1789 to the Present; MTCW 1, 2; MTFW 2005; PFS 20

Hecht, Anthony (Evan) 1923-2004 .... **CLC 8, 13, 19; PC 70**
See also AMWS 10; CA 9-12R; 232; CANR 6, 108; CP 1, 2, 3, 4, 5, 6, 7; DAM POET; DLB 5, 169; EWL 3; PFS 6; WP

Hecht, Ben 1894-1964 ..... **CLC 8; TCLC 101**
See also CA 85-88; DFS 9; DLB 7, 9, 25, 26, 28, 86; FANT; IDFW 3, 4; RGAL 4

Hedayat, Sadeq 1903-1951 . **SSC 131; TCLC 21**
See also CA 120; EWL 3; RGSF 2

Hegel, Georg Wilhelm Friedrich
1770-1831 .... **NCLC 46, 151**
See also DLB 90; TWA

Heidegger, Martin 1889-1976 .... **CLC 24**
See also CA 81-84; 65-68; CANR 34; DLB 296; MTCW 1, 2; MTFW 2005

Heidenstam, (Carl Gustaf) Verner von
1859-1940 .... **TCLC 5**
See also CA 104; DLB 330

Heidi Louise
See Erdrich, Louise

Heifner, Jack 1946- .... **CLC 11**
See also CA 105; CANR 47

Heijermans, Herman 1864-1924 .... **TCLC 24**
See also CA 123; EWL 3

Heilbrun, Carolyn G. 1926-2003 ..... **CLC 25, 173**
See also BPFB 1; CA 45-48; 220; CANR 1, 28, 58, 94; CMW; CPW; DLB 306; FW; MSW

Heilbrun, Carolyn Gold
See Heilbrun, Carolyn G.

Hein, Christoph 1944- .... **CLC 154**
See also CA 158; CANR 108; CDWLB 2; CWW 2; DLB 124

Heine, Heinrich 1797-1856 .... **NCLC 4, 54, 147; PC 25**
See also CDWLB 2; DLB 90; EW 5; RGWL 2, 3; TWA

Heinemann, Larry 1944- .... **CLC 50**
See also CA 110; CAAS 21; CANR 31, 81, 156; DLBD 9; INT CANR-31

Heinemann, Larry Curtiss
See Heinemann, Larry

Heiney, Donald (William) 1921-1993 . **CLC 9**
See also CA 1-4R; 142; CANR 3, 58; FANT

Heinlein, Robert A. 1907-1988 .. **CLC 1, 3, 8, 14, 26, 55; SSC 55**
See also AAYA 17; BPFB 2; BYA 4, 13; CA 1-4R; 125; CANR 1, 20, 53; CLR 75; CN 1, 2, 3, 4; CPW; DA3; DAM POP; DLB 8; EXPS; JRDA; LAIT 5; LMFS 2; MAICYA 1, 2; MTCW 1, 2; MTFW 2005; RGAL 4; SATA 9, 69; SATA-Obit 56; SCFW 1, 2; SFW 4; SSFS 7; YAW

Held, Peter
See Vance, Jack

Heldris of Cornwall fl. 13th cent.
- .... **CMLC 97**

Helforth, John
See Doolittle, Hilda

Heliodorus fl. 3rd cent. - .... **CMLC 52**
See also WLIT 8

Hellenhofferu, Vojtech Kapristian z
See Hasek, Jaroslav

Heller, Joseph 1923-1999 . **CLC 1, 3, 5, 8, 11, 36, 63; TCLC 131, 151; WLC 3**
See also AAYA 24; AITN 1; AMWS 4; BPFB 2; BYA 1; CA 5-8R; 187; CABS 1; CANR 8, 42, 66, 126; CN 1, 2, 3, 4, 5, 6; CPW; DA; DA3; DAB; DAC; DAM MST, NOV, POP; DLB 2, 28, 227; DLBY 1980, 2002; EWL 3; EXPN; INT CANR-8; LAIT 4; MAL 5; MTCW 1, 2; MTFW 2005; NFS 1; RGAL 4; TUS; YAW

Hellman, Lillian 1905-1984 . **CLC 2, 4, 8, 14, 18, 34, 44, 52; DC 1; TCLC 119**
See also AAYA 47; AITN 1, 2; AMWS 1; CA 13-16R; 112; CAD; CANR 33; CWD; DA3; DAM DRAM; DFS 1, 3, 14; DLB 7, 228; DLBY 1984; EWL 3; FL 1:6; FW; LAIT 3; MAL 5; MBL; MTCW 1, 2; MTFW 2005; RGAL 4; TUS

Hellman, Lillian Florence
See Hellman, Lillian

Helprin, Mark 1947- .... **CLC 7, 10, 22, 32**
See also CA 81-84; CANR 47, 64, 124; CDALBS; CN 7; CPW; DA3; DAM NOV, POP; DLB 335; DLBY 1985; FANT; MAL 5; MTCW 1, 2; MTFW 2005; SSFS 25; SUFW 2

Helvetius, Claude-Adrien 1715-1771 .. **LC 26**
See also DLB 313

Helyar, Jane Penelope Josephine
1933- .... **CLC 17**
See also CA 21-24R; CANR 10, 26; CWRI 5; SAAS 2; SATA 5; SATA-Essay 138

Hemans, Felicia 1793-1835 ...... **NCLC 29, 71**
See also DLB 96; RGEL 2

Hemingway, Ernest 1899-1961 .. **CLC 1, 3, 6, 8, 10, 13, 19, 30, 34, 39, 41, 44, 50, 61, 80; SSC 1, 25, 36, 40, 63, 117, 137; TCLC 115, 203; WLC 3**
See also AAYA 19; AMW; AMWC 1; AMWR 1; BPFB 2; BYA 2, 3, 13, 15; CA 77-80; CANR 34; CDALB 1917-1929; DA; DA3; DAB; DAC; DAM MST, NOV; DLB 4, 9, 102, 210, 308, 316, 330; DLBD 1, 15, 16; DLBY 1981, 1987, 1996, 1998; EWL 3; EXPN; EXPS; LAIT 3, 4; LATS 1:1; MAL 5; MTCW 1, 2; MTFW 2005; NFS 1, 5, 6, 14; RGAL 4; RGSF 2; SSFS 17; TUS; WYA

Hemingway, Ernest Miller
See Hemingway, Ernest

Hempel, Amy 1951- .... **CLC 39**
See also CA 118; 137; CANR 70, 166; DA3; DLB 218; EXPS; MTCW 2; MTFW 2005; SSFS 2

Henderson, F. C.
See Mencken, H. L.

Henderson, Mary
See Mavor, Osborne Henry

Henderson, Sylvia
See Ashton-Warner, Sylvia (Constance)

Hikmet, Nazim 1902-1963 .... **CLC 40**
 See also CA 141; 93-96; EWL 3; WLIT 6
Hildegard von Bingen
 1098-1179 .... **CMLC 20, 118**
 See also DLB 148
Hildesheimer, Wolfgang 1916-1991 .. **CLC 49**
 See also CA 101; 135; DLB 69, 124; EWL
 3; RGHL
Hill, Aaron 1685-1750 .... **LC 148**
 See also DLB 84; RGEL 2
Hill, Geoffrey 1932- .... **CLC 5, 8, 18, 45, 251**
 See also BRWR 3; BRWS 5; CA 81-84;
 CANR 21, 89; CDBLB 1960 to Present;
 CP 1, 2, 3, 4, 5, 6, 7; DAM POET; DLB
 40; EWL 3; MTCW 1; RGEL 2; RGHL
Hill, George Roy 1921-2002 .... **CLC 26**
 See also CA 110; 122; 213
Hill, John
 See Koontz, Dean
Hill, Susan 1942- .... **CLC 4, 113**
 See also BRWS 14; CA 33-36R; CANR 29,
 69, 129, 172, 201; CN 2, 3, 4, 5, 6, 7;
 DAB; DAM MST, NOV; DLB 14, 139;
 HGG; MTCW 1; RHW; SATA 183
Hill, Susan Elizabeth
 See Hill, Susan
Hillard, Asa G. III CLC 70
Hillerman, Anthony Grove
 See Hillerman, Tony
Hillerman, Tony 1925-2008 ...... **CLC 62, 170**
 See also AAYA 40; BEST 89:1; BPFB 2;
 CA 29-32R; 278; CANR 21, 42, 65, 97,
 134; CMW 4; CPW; DA3; DAM POP;
 DLB 206, 306; MAL 5; MSW; MTCW 2;
 MTFW 2005; RGAL 4; SATA 6; SATA-
 Obit 198; TCWW 2; YAW
Hillesum, Etty 1914-1943 .... **TCLC 49**
 See also CA 137; RGHL
Hilliard, Noel (Harvey) 1929-1996 ... **CLC 15**
 See also CA 9-12R; CANR 7, 69; CN 1, 2,
 3, 4, 5, 6
Hillis, Rick 1956- .... **CLC 66**
 See also CA 134
Hilton, James 1900-1954 .... **TCLC 21**
 See also AAYA 76; CA 108; 169; DLB 34,
 77; FANT; SATA 34
Hilton, Walter (?)-1396 .... **CMLC 58**
 See also DLB 146; RGEL 2
Himes, Chester (Bomar)
 1909-1984 .... **BLC 1:2; CLC 2, 4, 7, 18,
 58, 108; TCLC 139**
 See also AFAW 2; AMWS 16; BPFB 2; BW
 2; CA 25-28R; 114; CANR 22, 89; CMW
 4; CN 1, 2, 3; DAM MULT; DLB 2, 76,
 143, 226; EWL 3; MAL 5; MSW; MTCW
 1, 2; MTFW 2005; RGAL 4
Himmelfarb, Gertrude 1922- .... **CLC 202**
 See also CA 49-52; CANR 28, 66, 102, 166
Hinde, Thomas
 See Chitty, Thomas Willes
Hine, (William) Daryl 1936- .... **CLC 15**
 See also CA 1-4R; CAAS 15; CANR 1, 20;
 CP 1, 2, 3, 4, 5, 6, 7; DLB 60
Hinkson, Katharine Tynan
 See Tynan, Katharine
Hinojosa, Rolando 1929- .... **HLC 1**
 See also CA 131; CAAS 16; CANR 62;
 DAM MULT; DLB 82; EWL 3; HW 1, 2;
 LLW; MTCW 2; MTFW 2005; RGAL 4
Hinton, S. E. 1950- .... **CLC 30, 111**
 See also AAYA 2, 33; BPFB 2; BYA 2, 3;
 CA 81-84; CANR 32, 62, 92, 133;
 CDALBS; CLR 3, 23; CPW; DA; DA3;
 DAB; DAC; DAM MST, NOV; JRDA;
 LAIT 5; MAICYA 1, 2; MTCW 1, 2;
 MTFW 2005; NFS 5, 9, 15, 16; SATA 19,
 58, 115, 160; WYA; YAW
Hinton, Susan Eloise
 See Hinton, S. E.

Hippius, Zinaida
 See Gippius, Zinaida
Hiraoka, Kimitake 1925-1970 ... **CLC 2, 4, 6,
 9, 27; DC 1; SSC 4; TCLC 161; WLC
 4**
 See also AAYA 50; BPFB 2; CA 97-100;
 29-32R; DA3; DAM DRAM; DLB 182;
 EWL 3; GLL 1; MJW; MTCW 1, 2;
 RGSF 2; RGWL 2, 3; SSFS 5, 12
Hirsch, E.D., Jr. 1928- .... **CLC 79**
 See also CA 25-28R; CANR 27, 51, 146,
 181; DLB 67; INT CANR-27; MTCW 1
Hirsch, Edward 1950- .... **CLC 31, 50**
 See also CA 104; CANR 20, 42, 102, 167;
 CP 6, 7; DLB 120; PFS 22
Hirsch, Eric Donald, Jr.
 See Hirsch, E.D., Jr.
Hitchcock, Alfred (Joseph)
 1899-1980 .... **CLC 16**
 See also AAYA 22; CA 159; 97-100; SATA
 27; SATA-Obit 24
Hitchens, Christopher 1949- .... **CLC 157**
 See also CA 152; CANR 89, 155, 191
Hitchens, Christopher Eric
 See Hitchens, Christopher
Hitler, Adolf 1889-1945 .... **TCLC 53**
 See also CA 117; 147
Hoagland, Edward (Morley) 1932- .. **CLC 28**
 See also ANW; CA 1-4R; CANR 2, 31, 57,
 107; CN 1, 2, 3, 4, 5, 6, 7; DLB 6; SATA
 51; TCWW 2
Hoban, Russell 1925- .... **CLC 7, 25**
 See also BPFB 2; CA 5-8R; CANR 23, 37,
 66, 114, 138; CLR 3, 69, 139; CN 4, 5, 6,
 7; CWRI 5; DAM NOV; DLB 52; FANT;
 MAICYA 1, 2; MTCW 1, 2; MTFW 2005;
 SATA 1, 40, 78, 136; SFW 4; SUFW 2;
 TCLE 1:1
Hobbes, Thomas 1588-1679 .... **LC 36, 142**
 See also DLB 151, 252, 281; RGEL 2
Hobbs, Perry
 See Blackmur, R(ichard) P(almer)
Hobson, Laura Z(ametkin)
 1900-1986 .... **CLC 7, 25**
 See also BPFB 2; CA 17-20R; 118; CANR
 55; CN 1, 2, 3, 4; DLB 28; SATA 52
Hoccleve, Thomas c. 1368-c. 1437 ...... **LC 75**
 See also DLB 146; RGEL 2
Hoch, Edward D. 1930-2008 .... **SSC 119**
 See also CA 29-32R; CANR 11, 27, 51, 97;
 CMW 4; DLB 306; SFW 4
Hoch, Edward Dentinger
 See Hoch, Edward D.
Hochhuth, Rolf 1931- .... **CLC 4, 11, 18**
 See also CA 5-8R; CANR 33, 75, 136;
 CWW 2; DAM DRAM; DLB 124; EWL
 3; MTCW 1, 2; MTFW 2005; RGHL
Hochman, Sandra 1936- .... **CLC 3, 8**
 See also CA 5-8R; CP 1, 2, 3, 4, 5; DLB 5
Hochwaelder, Fritz 1911-1986 .... **CLC 36**
 See also CA 29-32R; 120; CANR 42; DAM
 DRAM; EWL 3; MTCW 1; RGWL 2, 3
Hochwalder, Fritz
 See Hochwaelder, Fritz
Hocking, Mary (Eunice) 1921- .... **CLC 13**
 See also CA 101; CANR 18, 40
Hodge, Merle 1944- .... **BLC 2:2**
 See also EWL 3
Hodgins, Jack 1938- .... **CLC 23; SSC 132**
 See also CA 93-96; CN 4, 5, 6, 7; DLB 60
Hodgson, William Hope
 1877(?)-1918 .... **TCLC 13**
 See also CA 111; 164; CMW 4; DLB 70,
 153, 156, 178; HGG; MTCW 2; SFW 4;
 SUFW 1
Hoeg, Peter 1957- .... **CLC 95, 156**
 See also CA 151; CANR 75; CMW 4; DA3;
 DLB 214; EWL 3; MTCW 2; MTFW
 2005; NFS 17; RGWL 3; SSFS 18

Hoffman, Alice 1952- .... **CLC 51**
 See also AAYA 37; AMWS 10; CA 77-80;
 CANR 34, 66, 100, 138, 170; CN 4, 5, 6,
 7; CPW; DAM NOV; DLB 292; MAL 5;
 MTCW 1, 2; MTFW 2005; TCLE 1:1
Hoffman, Daniel (Gerard) 1923- . **CLC 6, 13,
 23**
 See also CA 1-4R; CANR 4, 142; CP 1, 2,
 3, 4, 5, 6, 7; DLB 5; TCLE 1:1
Hoffman, Eva 1945- .... **CLC 182**
 See also AMWS 16; CA 132; CANR 146
Hoffman, Stanley 1944- .... **CLC 5**
 See also CA 77-80
Hoffman, William 1925- .... **CLC 141**
 See also AMWS 18; CA 21-24R; CANR 9,
 103; CSW; DLB 234; TCLE 1:1
Hoffman, William M.
 See Hoffman, William M(oses)
Hoffman, William M(oses) 1939- ..... **CLC 40**
 See also CA 57-60; CAD; CANR 11, 71;
 CD 5, 6
Hoffmann, E(rnst) T(heodor) A(madeus)
 1776-1822 ..... **NCLC 2, 183; SSC 13, 92**
 See also CDWLB 2; CLR 133; DLB 90;
 EW 5; GL 2; RGSF 2; RGWL 2, 3; SATA
 27; SUFW 1; WCH
Hofmann, Gert 1931-1993 .... **CLC 54**
 See also CA 128; CANR 145; EWL 3;
 RGHL
Hofmannsthal, Hugo von 1874-1929 ... **DC 4;
 TCLC 11**
 See also CA 106; 153; CDWLB 2; DAM
 DRAM; DFS 17; DLB 81, 118; EW 9;
 EWL 3; RGWL 2, 3
Hogan, Linda 1947- ..... **CLC 73; NNAL; PC
 35**
 See also AMWS 4; ANW; BYA 12; CA 120,
 226; CAAE 226; CANR 45, 73, 129, 196;
 CWP; DAM MULT; DLB 175; SATA
 132; TCWW 2
Hogarth, Charles
 See Creasey, John
Hogarth, Emmett
 See Polonsky, Abraham (Lincoln)
Hogarth, William 1697-1764 .... **LC 112**
 See also AAYA 56
Hogg, James 1770-1835 .. **NCLC 4, 109; SSC
 130**
 See also BRWS 10; DLB 93, 116, 159; GL
 2; HGG; RGEL 2; SUFW 1
Holbach, Paul-Henri Thiry
 1723-1789 .... **LC 14**
 See also DLB 313
Holberg, Ludvig 1684-1754 .... **LC 6**
 See also DLB 300; RGWL 2, 3
Holbrook, John
 See Vance, Jack
Holcroft, Thomas 1745-1809 .... **NCLC 85**
 See also DLB 39, 89, 158; RGEL 2
Holden, Ursula 1921- .... **CLC 18**
 See also CA 101; CAAS 8; CANR 22
Holderlin, (Johann Christian) Friedrich
 1770-1843 .... **NCLC 16, 187; PC 4**
 See also CDWLB 2; DLB 90; EW 5; RGWL
 2, 3
Holdstock, Robert 1948-2009 .... **CLC 39**
 See also CA 131; CANR 81; DLB 261;
 FANT; HGG; SFW 4; SUFW 2
Holdstock, Robert P.
 See Holdstock, Robert
Holinshed, Raphael fl. 1580- .... **LC 69**
 See also DLB 167; RGEL 2
Holland, Isabelle (Christian)
 1920-2002 .... **CLC 21**
 See also AAYA 11, 64; CA 21-24R; 205;
 CAAE 181; CANR 10, 25, 47; CLR 57;
 CWRI 5; JRDA; LAIT 4; MAICYA 1, 2;
 SATA 8, 70; SATA-Essay 103; SATA-Obit
 132; WYA

Huxley, Aldous 1894-1963 . **CLC 1, 3, 4, 5, 8, 11, 18, 35, 79; SSC 39; WLC 3**
See also AAYA 11; BPFB 2; BRW 7; CA 85-88; CANR 44, 99; CDBLB 1914-1945; DA; DA3; DAB; DAC; DAM MST, NOV; DLB 36, 100, 162, 195, 255; EWL 3; EXPN; LAIT 5; LMFS 2; MTCW 1, 2; MTFW 2005; NFS 6; RGEL 2; SATA 63; SCFW 1, 2; SFW 4; TEA; YAW

Huxley, Aldous Leonard
See Huxley, Aldous

Huxley, T(homas) H(enry)
1825-1895 .... **NCLC 67**
See also DLB 57; TEA

Huygens, Constantijn 1596-1687 .... **LC 114**
See also RGWL 2, 3

Huysmans, Joris-Karl 1848-1907 ... **TCLC 7, 69, 212**
See also CA 104; 165; DLB 123; EW 7; GFL 1789 to the Present; LMFS 2; RGWL 2, 3

Hwang, David Henry 1957- .... **CLC 55, 196; DC 4, 23**
See also CA 127; 132; CAD; CANR 76, 124; CD 5, 6; DA3; DAM DRAM; DFS 11, 18; DLB 212, 228, 312; INT CA-132; MAL 5; MTCW 2; MTFW 2005; RGAL 4

Hyatt, Daniel
See James, Daniel (Lewis)

Hyde, Anthony 1946- .... **CLC 42**
See also CA 136; CCA 1

Hyde, Margaret O. 1917- .... **CLC 21**
See also CA 1-4R; CANR 1, 36, 137, 181; CLR 23; JRDA; MAICYA 1, 2; SAAS 8; SATA 1, 42, 76, 139

Hyde, Margaret Oldroyd
See Hyde, Margaret O.

Hynes, James 1956(?)- .... **CLC 65**
See also CA 164; CANR 105

Hypatia c. 370-415 .... **CMLC 35**

Ian, Janis 1951- .... **CLC 21**
See also CA 105; 187

Ibanez, Vicente Blasco
See Blasco Ibanez, Vicente

Ibarbourou, Juana de
1895(?)-1979 .... **HLCS 2**
See also DLB 290; HW 1; LAW

Ibarguengoitia, Jorge 1928-1983 ..... **CLC 37; TCLC 148**
See also CA 124; 113; EWL 3; HW 1

Ibn Arabi 1165-1240 .... **CMLC 105**

Ibn Battuta, Abu Abdalla
1304-1368(?) .... **CMLC 57**
See also WLIT 2

Ibn Hazm 994-1064 .... **CMLC 64**

Ibn Zaydun 1003-1070 .... **CMLC 89**

Ibsen, Henrik 1828-1906 .... **DC 2, 30; TCLC 2, 8, 16, 37, 52; WLC 3**
See also AAYA 46; CA 104; 141; DA; DA3; DAB; DAC; DAM DRAM, MST; DFS 1, 6, 8, 10, 11, 15, 16, 25; DLB 354; EW 7; LAIT 2; LATS 1:1; MTFW 2005; RGWL 2, 3

Ibsen, Henrik Johan
See Ibsen, Henrik

Ibuse, Masuji 1898-1993 .... **CLC 22**
See also CA 127; 141; CWW 2; DLB 180; EWL 3; MJW; RGWL 3

Ibuse Masuji
See Ibuse, Masuji

Ichikawa, Kon 1915-2008 .... **CLC 20**
See also CA 121; 269

Ichiyo, Higuchi 1872-1896 .... **NCLC 49**
See also MJW

Idle, Eric 1943- .... **CLC 21**
See also CA 116; CANR 35, 91, 148; DLB 352

Idris, Yusuf 1927-1991 ... **SSC 74; TCLC 232**
See also AFW; DLB 346; EWL 3; RGSF 2, 3; RGWL 3; WLIT 2

Ignatieff, Michael 1947- .... **CLC 236**
See also CA 144; CANR 88, 156; CN 6, 7; DLB 267

Ignatieff, Michael Grant
See Ignatieff, Michael

Ignatow, David 1914-1997 .... **CLC 4, 7, 14, 40; PC 34**
See also CA 9-12R; 162; CAAS 3; CANR 31, 57, 96; CP 1, 2, 3, 4, 5, 6; DLB 5; EWL 3; MAL 5

Ignotus
See Strachey, (Giles) Lytton

Ihimaera, Witi (Tame) 1944- .... **CLC 46**
See also CA 77-80; CANR 130; CN 2, 3, 4, 5, 6, 7; RGSF 2; SATA 148

Il'f, Il'ia
See Fainzilberg, Ilya Arnoldovich

Ilf, Ilya
See Fainzilberg, Ilya Arnoldovich

Illyes, Gyula 1902-1983 .... **PC 16**
See also CA 114; 109; CDWLB 4; DLB 215; EWL 3; RGWL 2, 3

Imalayen, Fatima-Zohra
See Djebar, Assia

Immermann, Karl (Lebrecht)
1796-1840 .... **NCLC 4, 49**
See also DLB 133

Ince, Thomas H. 1882-1924 .... **TCLC 89**
See also IDFW 3, 4

Inchbald, Elizabeth 1753-1821 ...... **NCLC 62**
See also BRWS 15; DLB 39, 89; RGEL 2

Inclan, Ramon del Valle
See Valle-Inclan, Ramon del

Incogniteau, Jean-Louis
See Kerouac, Jack

Infante, Guillermo Cabrera
See Cabrera Infante, G.

Ingalls, Rachel 1940- .... **CLC 42**
See also CA 123; 127; CANR 154

Ingalls, Rachel Holmes
See Ingalls, Rachel

Ingamells, Reginald Charles
See Ingamells, Rex

Ingamells, Rex 1913-1955 .... **TCLC 35**
See also CA 167; DLB 260

Inge, William (Motter) 1913-1973 ..... **CLC 1, 8, 19; DC 37**
See also CA 9-12R; CAD; CDALB 1941-1968; DA3; DAM DRAM; DFS 1, 3, 5, 8; DLB 7, 249; EWL 3; MAL 5; MTCW 1, 2; MTFW 2005; RGAL 4; TUS

Ingelow, Jean 1820-1897 .... **NCLC 39, 107**
See also DLB 35, 163; FANT; SATA 33

Ingram, Willis J.
See Harris, Mark

Innaurato, Albert (F.) 1948(?)- ... **CLC 21, 60**
See also CA 115; 122; CAD; CANR 78; CD 5, 6; INT CA-122

Innes, Michael
See Stewart, J(ohn) I(nnes) M(ackintosh)

Innis, Harold Adams 1894-1952 .... **TCLC 77**
See also CA 181; DLB 88

Insluis, Alanus de
See Alain de Lille

Iola
See Wells-Barnett, Ida B(ell)

Ionesco, Eugene 1909-1994 ... **CLC 1, 4, 6, 9, 11, 15, 41, 86; DC 12; TCLC 232; WLC 3**
See also CA 9-12R; 144; CANR 55, 132; CWW 2; DA; DA3; DAB; DAC; DAM DRAM, MST; DFS 4, 9, 25; DLB 321; EW 13; EWL 3; GFL 1789 to the Present; LMFS 2; MTCW 1, 2; MTFW 2005; RGWL 2, 3; SATA 7; SATA-Obit 79; TWA

Iqbal, Muhammad 1877-1938 .... **TCLC 28**
See also CA 215; EWL 3

Ireland, Patrick
See O'Doherty, Brian

Irenaeus St. 130- .... **CMLC 42**

Irigaray, Luce 1930- .... **CLC 164**
See also CA 154; CANR 121; FW

Irish, William
See Hopley-Woolrich, Cornell George

Irland, David
See Green, Julien

Iron, Ralph
See Schreiner, Olive

Irving, John 1942- . **CLC 13, 23, 38, 112, 175**
See also AAYA 8, 62; AMWS 6; BEST 89:3; BPFB 2; CA 25-28R; CANR 28, 73, 112, 133; CN 3, 4, 5, 6, 7; CPW; DA3; DAM NOV, POP; DLB 6, 278; DLBY 1982; EWL 3; MAL 5; MTCW 1, 2; MTFW 2005; NFS 12, 14; RGAL 4; TUS

Irving, John Winslow
See Irving, John

Irving, Washington 1783-1859 . **NCLC 2, 19, 95; SSC 2, 37, 104; WLC 3**
See also AAYA 56; AMW; CDALB 1640-1865; CLR 97; DA; DA3; DAB; DAC; DAM MST; DLB 3, 11, 30, 59, 73, 74, 183, 186, 250, 254; EXPS; GL 2; LAIT 1; RGAL 4; RGSF 2; SSFS 1, 8, 16; SUFW 1; TUS; WCH; YABC 2

Irwin, P. K.
See Page, P.K.

Isaacs, Jorge Ricardo 1837-1895 ... **NCLC 70**
See also LAW

Isaacs, Susan 1943- .... **CLC 32**
See also BEST 89:1; BPFB 2; CA 89-92; CANR 20, 41, 65, 112, 134, 165; CPW; DA3; DAM POP; INT CANR-20; MTCW 1, 2; MTFW 2005

Isherwood, Christopher 1904-1986 ... **CLC 1, 9, 11, 14, 44; SSC 56; TCLC 227**
See also AMWS 14; BRW 7; CA 13-16R; 117; CANR 35, 97, 133; CN 1, 2, 3; DA3; DAM DRAM, NOV; DLB 15, 195; DLBY 1986; EWL 3; IDTP; MTCW 1, 2; MTFW 2005; RGAL 4; RGEL 2; TUS; WLIT 4

Isherwood, Christopher William Bradshaw
See Isherwood, Christopher

Ishiguro, Kazuo 1954- . **CLC 27, 56, 59, 110, 219**
See also AAYA 58; BEST 90:2; BPFB 2; BRWR 3; BRWS 4; CA 120; CANR 49, 95, 133; CN 5, 6, 7; DA3; DAM NOV; DLB 194, 326; EWL 3; MTCW 1, 2; MTFW 2005; NFS 13; WLIT 4; WWE 1

Ishikawa, Hakuhin
See Ishikawa, Takuboku

Ishikawa, Takuboku 1886(?)-1912 ..... **PC 10; TCLC 15**
See also CA 113; 153; DAM POET

Isidore of Seville c. 560-636 .... **CMLC 101**

Iskander, Fazil (Abdulovich) 1929- .. **CLC 47**
See also CA 102; DLB 302; EWL 3

Iskander, Fazil' Abdulevich
See Iskander, Fazil (Abdulovich)

Isler, Alan (David) 1934- .... **CLC 91**
See also CA 156; CANR 105

Ivan IV 1530-1584 .... **LC 17**

Ivanov, V.I.
See Ivanov, Vyacheslav

Ivanov, Vyacheslav 1866-1949 .... **TCLC 33**
See also CA 122; EWL 3

Ivanov, Vyacheslav Ivanovich
See Ivanov, Vyacheslav

Ivask, Ivar Vidrik 1927-1992 .... **CLC 14**
See also CA 37-40R; 139; CANR 24

Ives, Morgan
See Bradley, Marion Zimmer

Izumi Shikibu c. 973-c. 1034 .... **CMLC 33**

J. R. S.
  See Gogarty, Oliver St. John

Jabran, Kahlil
  See Gibran, Kahlil

Jabran, Khalil
  See Gibran, Kahlil

Jaccottet, Philippe 1925- .... **PC 98**
  See also CA 116; 129; CWW 2; GFL 1789
  to the Present

Jackson, Daniel
  See Wingrove, David

Jackson, Helen Hunt 1830-1885 .... **NCLC 90**
  See also DLB 42, 47, 186, 189; RGAL 4

Jackson, Jesse 1908-1983 .... **CLC 12**
  See also BW 1; CA 25-28R; 109; CANR
  27; CLR 28; CWRI 5; MAICYA 1, 2;
  SATA 2, 29; SATA-Obit 48

Jackson, Laura 1901-1991 . **CLC 3, 7; PC 44**
  See also CA 65-68; 135; CANR 28, 89; CP
  1, 2, 3, 4, 5; DLB 48; RGAL 4

Jackson, Laura Riding
  See Jackson, Laura

Jackson, Sam
  See Trumbo, Dalton

Jackson, Sara
  See Wingrove, David

Jackson, Shirley 1919-1965 . **CLC 11, 60, 87;
  SSC 9, 39; TCLC 187; WLC 3**
  See also AAYA 9; AMWS 9; BPFB 2; CA
  1-4R; 25-28R; CANR 4, 52; CDALB
  1941-1968; DA; DA3; DAC; DAM MST;
  DLB 6, 234; EXPS; HGG; LAIT 4; MAL
  5; MTCW 2; MTFW 2005; RGAL 4;
  RGSF 2; SATA 2; SSFS 1, 27; SUFW 1,
  2

Jacob, (Cyprien-)Max 1876-1944 .... **TCLC 6**
  See also CA 104; 193; DLB 258; EWL 3;
  GFL 1789 to the Present; GLL 2; RGWL
  2, 3

Jacobs, Harriet A. 1813(?)-1897 ... **NCLC 67,
  162**
  See also AFAW 1, 2; DLB 239; FL 1:3; FW;
  LAIT 2; RGAL 4

Jacobs, Harriet Ann
  See Jacobs, Harriet A.

Jacobs, Jim 1942- .... **CLC 12**
  See also CA 97-100; INT CA-97-100

Jacobs, W(illiam) W(ymark)
  1863-1943 .... **SSC 73; TCLC 22**
  See also CA 121; 167; DLB 135; EXPS;
  HGG; RGEL 2; RGSF 2; SSFS 2; SUFW
  1

Jacobsen, Jens Peter 1847-1885 .... **NCLC 34**

Jacobsen, Josephine (Winder)
  1908-2003 .... **CLC 48, 102; PC 62**
  See also CA 33-36R; 218; CAAS 18; CANR
  23, 48; CCA 1; CP 2, 3, 4, 5, 6, 7; DLB
  244; PFS 23; TCLE 1:1

Jacobson, Dan 1929- ...... **CLC 4, 14; SSC 91**
  See also AFW; CA 1-4R; CANR 2, 25, 66,
  170; CN 1, 2, 3, 4, 5, 6, 7; DLB 14, 207,
  225, 319; EWL 3; MTCW 1; RGSF 2

Jacopone da Todi 1236-1306 .... **CMLC 95**

Jacqueline
  See Carpentier, Alejo

Jacques de Vitry c. 1160-1240 ...... **CMLC 63**
  See also DLB 208

Jagger, Michael Philip
  See Jagger, Mick

Jagger, Mick 1943- .... **CLC 17**
  See also CA 239

Jahiz, al- c. 780-c. 869 .... **CMLC 25**
  See also DLB 311

Jakes, John 1932- .... **CLC 29**
  See also AAYA 32; BEST 89:4; BPFB 2;
  CA 57-60, 214; CAAE 214; CANR 10,
  43, 66, 111, 142, 171; CPW; CSW; DA3;

DAM NOV, POP; DLB 278; DLBY 1983;
FANT; INT CANR-10; MTCW 1, 2;
MTFW 2005; RHW; SATA 62; SFW 4;
TCWW 1, 2

Jakes, John William
  See Jakes, John

James I 1394-1437 .... **LC 20**
  See also RGEL 2

James, Alice 1848-1892 .... **NCLC 206**
  See also DLB 221

James, Andrew
  See Kirkup, James

James, C(yril) L(ionel) R(obert)
  1901-1989 .... **BLCS; CLC 33**
  See also BW 2; CA 117; 125; 128; CANR
  62; CN 1, 2, 3, 4; DLB 125; MTCW 1

James, Daniel (Lewis) 1911-1988 ..... **CLC 33**
  See also CA 174; 125; DLB 122

James, Dynely
  See Mayne, William (James Carter)

James, Henry Sr. 1811-1882 .... **NCLC 53**

James, Henry 1843-1916 .... **SSC 8, 32, 47,
  108; TCLC 2, 11, 24, 40, 47, 64, 171;
  WLC 3**
  See also AMW; AMWC 1; AMWR 1; BPFB
  2; BRW 6; CA 104; 132; CDALB 1865-
  1917; DA; DA3; DAB; DAC; DAM MST,
  NOV; DLB 12, 71, 74, 189; DLBD 13;
  EWL 3; EXPS; GL 2; HGG; LAIT 2;
  MAL 5; MTCW 1, 2; MTFW 2005; NFS
  12, 16, 19; RGAL 4; RGEL 2; RGSF 2;
  SSFS 9; SUFW 1; TUS

James, M. R.
  See James, Montague

James, Mary
  See Meaker, Marijane

James, Montague 1862-1936 ...... **SSC 16, 93;
  TCLC 6**
  See also CA 104; 203; DLB 156, 201;
  HGG; RGEL 2; RGSF 2; SUFW 1

James, Montague Rhodes
  See James, Montague

James, P.D. 1920- .... **CLC 18, 46, 122, 226**
  See also BEST 90:2; BPFB 2; BRWS 4;
  CA 21-24R; CANR 17, 43, 65, 112, 201;
  CDBLB 1960 to Present; CMW 4; CN 4,
  5, 6, 7; CPW; DA3; DAM POP; DLB 87,
  276; DLBD 17; MSW; MTCW 1, 2;
  MTFW 2005; TEA

James, Philip
  See Moorcock, Michael

James, Samuel
  See Stephens, James

James, Seumas
  See Stephens, James

James, Stephen
  See Stephens, James

James, T. F.
  See Fleming, Thomas

James, William 1842-1910 .... **TCLC 15, 32**
  See also AMW; CA 109; 193; DLB 270,
  284; MAL 5; NCFS 5; RGAL 4

Jameson, Anna 1794-1860 .... **NCLC 43**
  See also DLB 99, 166

Jameson, Fredric 1934- .... **CLC 142**
  See also CA 196; CANR 169; DLB 67;
  LMFS 2

Jameson, Fredric R.
  See Jameson, Fredric

James VI of Scotland 1566-1625 .... **LC 109**
  See also DLB 151, 172

Jami, Nur al-Din 'Abd al-Rahman
  1414-1492 .... **LC 9**

Jammes, Francis 1868-1938 .... **TCLC 75**
  See also CA 198; EWL 3; GFL 1789 to the
  Present

Jandl, Ernst 1925-2000 .... **CLC 34**
  See also CA 200; EWL 3

Janowitz, Tama 1957- .... **CLC 43, 145**
  See also CA 106; CANR 52, 89, 129; CN
  5, 6, 7; CPW; DAM POP; DLB 292;
  MTFW 2005

Jansson, Tove (Marika) 1914-2001 ... **SSC 96**
  See also CA 17-20R; 196; CANR 38, 118;
  CLR 2, 125; CWW 2; DLB 257; EWL 3;
  MAICYA 1, 2; RGSF 2; SATA 3, 41

Japrisot, Sebastien 1931-
  See Rossi, Jean-Baptiste

Jarrell, Randall 1914-1965 .... **CLC 1, 2, 6, 9,
  13, 49; PC 41; TCLC 177**
  See also AMW; BYA 5; CA 5-8R; 25-28R;
  CABS 2; CANR 6, 34; CDALB 1941-
  1968; CLR 6, 111; CWRI 5; DAM POET;
  DLB 48, 52; EWL 3; EXPP; MAICYA 1,
  2; MAL 5; MTCW 1, 2; PAB; PFS 2, 31;
  RGAL 4; SATA 7

Jarry, Alfred 1873-1907 .... **SSC 20; TCLC 2,
  14, 147**
  See also CA 104; 153; DA3; DAM DRAM;
  DFS 8; DLB 192, 258; EW 9; EWL 3;
  GFL 1789 to the Present; RGWL 2, 3;
  TWA

Jarvis, E.K.
  See Ellison, Harlan; Silverberg, Robert

Jawien, Andrzej
  See John Paul II, Pope

Jaynes, Roderick
  See Coen, Ethan

Jeake, Samuel, Jr.
  See Aiken, Conrad

Jean-Louis
  See Kerouac, Jack

Jean Paul 1763-1825 .... **NCLC 7**

Jefferies, (John) Richard
  1848-1887 .... **NCLC 47**
  See also BRWS 15; DLB 98, 141; RGEL 2;
  SATA 16; SFW 4

Jeffers, John Robinson
  See Jeffers, Robinson

Jeffers, Robinson 1887-1962 .... **CLC 2, 3, 11,
  15, 54; PC 17; WLC 3**
  See also AMWS 2; CA 85-88; CANR 35;
  CDALB 1917-1929; DA; DAC; DAM
  MST, POET; DLB 45, 212, 342; EWL 3;
  MAL 5; MTCW 1, 2; MTFW 2005; PAB;
  PFS 3, 4; RGAL 4

Jefferson, Janet
  See Mencken, H. L.

Jefferson, Thomas 1743-1826 . **NCLC 11, 103**
  See also AAYA 54; ANW; CDALB 1640-
  1865; DA3; DLB 31, 183; LAIT 1; RGAL
  4

Jeffrey, Francis 1773-1850 .... **NCLC 33**
  See also DLB 107

Jelakowitch, Ivan
  See Heijermans, Herman

Jelinek, Elfriede 1946- .... **CLC 169**
  See also AAYA 68; CA 154; CANR 169;
  DLB 85, 330; FW

Jellicoe, (Patricia) Ann 1927- .... **CLC 27**
  See also CA 85-88; CBD; CD 5, 6; CWD;
  CWRI 5; DLB 13, 233; FW

Jelloun, Tahar ben
  See Ben Jelloun, Tahar

Jemyma
  See Holley, Marietta

Jen, Gish 1955- .... **AAL; CLC 70, 198, 260**
  See also AMWC 2; CA 135; CANR 89,
  130; CN 7; DLB 312; NFS 30

Jen, Lillian
  See Jen, Gish

Jenkins, (John) Robin 1912- .... **CLC 52**
  See also CA 1-4R; CANR 1, 135; CN 1, 2,
  3, 4, 5, 6, 7; DLB 14, 271

Jennings, Elizabeth (Joan)
1926-2001 .... **CLC 5, 14, 131**
See also BRWS 5; CA 61-64; 200; CAAS 5; CANR 8, 39, 66, 127; CP 1, 2, 3, 4, 5, 6, 7; CWP; DLB 27; EWL 3; MTCW 1; SATA 66

Jennings, Waylon 1937-2002 .... **CLC 21**

Jensen, Johannes V(ilhelm)
1873-1950 .... **TCLC 41**
See also CA 170; DLB 214, 330; EWL 3; RGWL 3

Jensen, Laura (Linnea) 1948- .... **CLC 37**
See also CA 103

Jerome, Saint 345-420 .... **CMLC 30**
See also RGWL 3

Jerome, Jerome K(lapka)
1859-1927 .... **TCLC 23**
See also CA 119; 177; DLB 10, 34, 135; RGEL 2

Jerrold, Douglas William
1803-1857 .... **NCLC 2**
See also DLB 158, 159, 344; RGEL 2

Jewett, Sarah Orne 1849-1909 ..... **SSC 6, 44, 110; TCLC 1, 22**
See also AAYA 76; AMW; AMWC 2; AMWR 2; CA 108; 127; CANR 71; DLB 12, 74, 221; EXPS; FL 1:3; FW; MAL 5; MBL; NFS 15; RGAL 4; RGSF 2; SATA 15; SSFS 4

Jewett, Theodora Sarah Orne
See Jewett, Sarah Orne

Jewsbury, Geraldine (Endsor)
1812-1880 .... **NCLC 22**
See also DLB 21

Jhabvala, Ruth Prawer 1927- . **CLC 4, 8, 29, 94, 138, 284; SSC 91**
See also BRWS 5; CA 1-4R; CANR 2, 29, 51, 74, 91, 128; CN 1, 2, 3, 4, 5, 6, 7; DAB; DAM NOV; DLB 139, 194, 323, 326; EWL 3; IDFW 3, 4; INT CANR-29; MTCW 1, 2; MTFW 2005; RGSF 2; RGWL 2; RHW; TEA

Jibran, Kahlil
See Gibran, Kahlil

Jibran, Khalil
See Gibran, Kahlil

Jiles, Paulette 1943- .... **CLC 13, 58**
See also CA 101; CANR 70, 124, 170; CP 5; CWP

Jimenez, Juan Ramon 1881-1958 ..... **HLC 1; PC 7; TCLC 4, 183**
See also CA 104; 131; CANR 74; DAM MULT, POET; DLB 134, 330; EW 9; EWL 3; HW 1; MTCW 1, 2; MTFW 2005; RGWL 2, 3

Jimenez, Ramon
See Jimenez, Juan Ramon

Jimenez Mantecon, Juan
See Jimenez, Juan Ramon

Jimenez Mantecon, Juan Ramon
See Jimenez, Juan Ramon

Jin, Ba 1904-2005 .... **CLC 18**
See Cantu, Robert Clark
See also CA 105; 244; CWW 2; DLB 328; EWL 3

Jin, Xuefei 1956- .... **CLC 109, 262**
See also CA 152; CANR 91, 130, 184; DLB 244, 292; MTFW 2005; NFS 25; SSFS 17

Jin Ha
See Jin, Xuefei

Jodelle, Etienne 1532-1573 .... **LC 119**
See also DLB 327; GFL Beginnings to 1789

Joel, Billy
See Joel, William Martin

Joel, William Martin 1949- .... **CLC 26**
See also CA 108

John, St.
See John of Damascus, St.

John of Damascus, St. c.
675-749 .... **CMLC 27, 95**

John of Salisbury c. 1115-1180 ..... **CMLC 63**

John of the Cross, St. 1542-1591 .... **LC 18, 146**
See also RGWL 2, 3

John Paul II, Pope 1920-2005 .... **CLC 128**
See also CA 106; 133; 238

Johnson, B(ryan) S(tanley William)
1933-1973 .... **CLC 6, 9**
See also CA 9-12R; 53-56; CANR 9; CN 1; CP 1, 2; DLB 14, 40; EWL 3; RGEL 2

Johnson, Benjamin F., of Boone
See Riley, James Whitcomb

Johnson, Charles (Richard) 1948- . **BLC 1:2, 2:2; CLC 7, 51, 65, 163**
See also AFAW 2; AMWS 6; BW 2, 3; CA 116; CAAS 18; CANR 42, 66, 82, 129; CN 5, 6, 7; DAM MULT; DLB 33, 278; MAL 5; MTCW 2; MTFW 2005; RGAL 4; SSFS 16

Johnson, Charles S(purgeon)
1893-1956 .... **HR 1:3**
See also BW 1, 3; CA 125; CANR 82; DLB 51, 91

Johnson, Denis 1949- . **CLC 52, 160; SSC 56**
See also CA 117; 121; CANR 71, 99, 178; CN 4, 5, 6, 7; DLB 120

Johnson, Diane 1934- ...... **CLC 5, 13, 48, 244**
See also BPFB 2; CA 41-44R; CANR 17, 40, 62, 95, 155, 198; CN 4, 5, 6, 7; DLB 350; DLBY 1980; INT CANR-17; MTCW 1

Johnson, E(mily) Pauline 1861-1913 . **NNAL**
See also CA 150; CCA 1; DAC; DAM MULT; DLB 92, 175; TCWW 2

Johnson, Eyvind (Olof Verner)
1900-1976 .... **CLC 14**
See also CA 73-76; 69-72; CANR 34, 101; DLB 259, 330; EW 12; EWL 3

Johnson, Fenton 1888-1958 .... **BLC 1:2**
See also BW 1; CA 118; 124; DAM MULT; DLB 45, 50

Johnson, Georgia Douglas (Camp)
1880-1966 .... **HR 1:3**
See also BW 1; CA 125; DLB 51, 249; WP

Johnson, Helene 1907-1995 .... **HR 1:3**
See also CA 181; DLB 51; WP

Johnson, J. R.
See James, C(yril) L(ionel) R(obert)

Johnson, James Weldon
1871-1938 .... **BLC 1:2; HR 1:3; PC 24; TCLC 3, 19, 175**
See also AAYA 73; AFAW 1, 2; BW 1, 3; CA 104; 125; CANR 82; CDALB 1917-1929; CLR 32; DA3; DAM MULT, POET; DLB 51; EWL 3; EXPP; LMFS 2; MAL 5; MTCW 1, 2; MTFW 2005; NFS 22; PFS 1; RGAL 4; SATA 31; TUS

Johnson, Joyce 1935- .... **CLC 58**
See also BG 1:3; CA 125; 129; CANR 102

Johnson, Judith 1936- .... **CLC 7, 15**
See also CA 25-28R; 153; CANR 34, 85; CP 2, 3, 4, 5, 6, 7; CWP

Johnson, Judith Emlyn
See Johnson, Judith

Johnson, Lionel (Pigot)
1867-1902 .... **TCLC 19**
See also CA 117; 209; DLB 19; RGEL 2

Johnson, Marguerite Annie
See Angelou, Maya

Johnson, Mel
See Malzberg, Barry N(athaniel)

Johnson, Pamela Hansford
1912-1981 .... **CLC 1, 7, 27**
See also CA 1-4R; 104; CANR 2, 28; CN 1, 2, 3; DLB 15; MTCW 1, 2; MTFW 2005; RGEL 2

Johnson, Paul 1928- .... **CLC 147**
See also BEST 89:4; CA 17-20R; CANR 34, 62, 100, 155, 197

Johnson, Paul Bede
See Johnson, Paul

Johnson, Robert CLC 70

Johnson, Robert 1911(?)-1938 .... **TCLC 69**
See also BW 3; CA 174

Johnson, Samuel 1709-1784 . **LC 15, 52, 128; PC 81; WLC 3**
See also BRW 3; BRWR 1; CDBLB 1660-1789; DA; DAB; DAC; DAM MST; DLB 39, 95, 104, 142, 213; LMFS 1; RGEL 2; TEA

Johnson, Stacie
See Myers, Walter Dean

Johnson, Uwe 1934-1984 .. **CLC 5, 10, 15, 40**
See also CA 1-4R; 112; CANR 1, 39; CD-WLB 2; DLB 75; EWL 3; MTCW 1; RGWL 2, 3

Johnston, Basil H. 1929- .... **NNAL**
See also CA 69-72; CANR 11, 28, 66; DAC; DAM MULT; DLB 60

Johnston, George (Benson) 1913- .... **CLC 51**
See also CA 1-4R; CANR 5, 20; CP 1, 2, 3, 4, 5, 6, 7; DLB 88

Johnston, Jennifer (Prudence)
1930- .... **CLC 7, 150, 228**
See also CA 85-88; CANR 92; CN 4, 5, 6, 7; DLB 14

Joinville, Jean de 1224(?)-1317 ..... **CMLC 38**

Jolley, Elizabeth 1923-2007 ..... **CLC 46, 256, 260; SSC 19**
See also CA 127; 257; CAAS 13; CANR 59; CN 4, 5, 6, 7; DLB 325; EWL 3; RGSF 2

Jolley, Monica Elizabeth
See Jolley, Elizabeth

Jones, Arthur Llewellyn 1863-1947 . **SSC 20; TCLC 4**
See Machen, Arthur
See also CA 104; 179; DLB 36; HGG; RGEL 2; SUFW 1

Jones, D(ouglas) G(ordon) 1929- ..... **CLC 10**
See also CA 29-32R; CANR 13, 90; CP 1, 2, 3, 4, 5, 6, 7; DLB 53

Jones, David (Michael) 1895-1974 .... **CLC 2, 4, 7, 13, 42**
See also BRW 6; BRWS 7; CA 9-12R; 53-56; CANR 28; CDBLB 1945-1960; CP 1, 2; DLB 20, 100; EWL 3; MTCW 1; PAB; RGEL 2

Jones, David Robert 1947- .... **CLC 17**
See also CA 103; CANR 104

Jones, Diana Wynne 1934- .... **CLC 26**
See also AAYA 12; BYA 6, 7, 9, 11, 13, 16; CA 49-52; CANR 4, 26, 56, 120, 167; CLR 23, 120; DLB 161; FANT; JRDA; MAICYA 1, 2; MTFW 2005; SAAS 7; SATA 9, 70, 108, 160; SFW 4; SUFW 2; YAW

Jones, Edward P. 1950- .. **BLC 2:2; CLC 76, 223**
See also AAYA 71; BW 2, 3; CA 142; CANR 79, 134, 190; CSW; LNFS 2; MTFW 2005; NFS 26

Jones, Edward Paul
See Jones, Edward P.

Jones, Ernest Charles
1819-1869 .... **NCLC 222**
See also DLB 32

Jones, Everett LeRoi
See Baraka, Amiri

Jones, Gayl 1949- .. **BLC 1:2; CLC 6, 9, 131, 270**
See also AFAW 1, 2; BW 2, 3; CA 77-80; CANR 27, 66, 122; CN 4, 5, 6, 7; CSW; DA3; DAM MULT; DLB 33, 278; MAL 5; MTCW 1, 2; MTFW 2005; RGAL 4

Kandinsky, Wassily 1866-1944 .... **TCLC 92**
    See also AAYA 64; CA 118; 155
Kane, Francis
    See Robbins, Harold
Kane, Paul
    See Simon, Paul
Kane, Sarah 1971-1999 .... **DC 31**
    See also BRWS 8; CA 190; CD 5, 6; DLB
    310
Kanin, Garson 1912-1999 .... **CLC 22**
    See also AITN 1; CA 5-8R; 177; CAD;
    CANR 7, 78; DLB 7; IDFW 3, 4
Kaniuk, Yoram 1930- .... **CLC 19**
    See also CA 134; DLB 299; RGHL
Kant, Immanuel 1724-1804 ..... **NCLC 27, 67**
    See also DLB 94
Kantor, MacKinlay 1904-1977 .... **CLC 7**
    See also CA 61-64; 73-76; CANR 60, 63;
    CN 1, 2; DLB 9, 102; MAL 5; MTCW 2;
    RHW; TCWW 1, 2
Kanze Motokiyo
    See Zeami
Kaplan, David Michael 1946- .... **CLC 50**
    See also CA 187
Kaplan, James 1951- .... **CLC 59**
    See also CA 135; CANR 121
Karadzic, Vuk Stefanovic
    1787-1864 .... **NCLC 115**
    See also CDWLB 4; DLB 147
Karageorge, Michael
    See Anderson, Poul
Karamzin, Nikolai Mikhailovich
    1766-1826 .... **NCLC 3, 173**
    See also DLB 150; RGSF 2
Karapanou, Margarita 1946- .... **CLC 13**
    See also CA 101
Karinthy, Frigyes 1887-1938 .... **TCLC 47**
    See also CA 170; DLB 215; EWL 3
Karl, Frederick R(obert)
    1927-2004 .... **CLC 34**
    See also CA 5-8R; 226; CANR 3, 44, 143
Karr, Mary 1955- .... **CLC 188**
    See also AMWS 11; CA 151; CANR 100,
    191; MTFW 2005; NCFS 5
Kastel, Warren
    See Silverberg, Robert
Kataev, Evgeny Petrovich
    1903-1942 .... **TCLC 21**
    See also CA 120; DLB 272
Kataphusin
    See Ruskin, John
Katz, Steve 1935- .... **CLC 47**
    See also CA 25-28R; CAAS 14, 64; CANR
    12; CN 4, 5, 6, 7; DLBY 1983
Kauffman, Janet 1945- .... **CLC 42**
    See also CA 117; CANR 43, 84; DLB 218;
    DLBY 1986
Kaufman, Bob (Garnell)
    1925-1986 .... **CLC 49; PC 74**
    See also BG 1:3; BW 1; CA 41-44R; 118;
    CANR 22; CP 1; DLB 16, 41
Kaufman, George S. 1889-1961 ...... **CLC 38;
    DC 17**
    See also CA 108; 93-96; DAM DRAM;
    DFS 1, 10; DLB 7; INT CA-108; MTCW
    2; MTFW 2005; RGAL 4; TUS
Kaufman, Moises 1963- .... **DC 26**
    See also CA 211; DFS 22; MTFW 2005
Kaufman, Sue
    See Barondess, Sue K.
Kavafis, Konstantinos Petrov
    See Cavafy, Constantine
Kavan, Anna 1901-1968 .... **CLC 5, 13, 82**
    See also BRWS 7; CA 5-8R; CANR 6, 57;
    DLB 255; MTCW 1; RGEL 2; SFW 4
Kavanagh, Dan
    See Barnes, Julian

Kavanagh, Julie 1952- .... **CLC 119**
    See also CA 163; CANR 186
Kavanagh, Patrick (Joseph)
    1904-1967 .... **CLC 22; PC 33, 105**
    See also BRWS 7; CA 123; 25-28R; DLB
    15, 20; EWL 3; MTCW 1; RGEL 2
Kawabata, Yasunari 1899-1972 ..... **CLC 2, 5,
    9, 18, 107; SSC 17**
    See also CA 93-96; 33-36R; CANR 88;
    DAM MULT; DLB 180, 330; EWL 3;
    MJW; MTCW 2; MTFW 2005; RGSF 2;
    RGWL 2, 3
Kawabata Yasunari
    See Kawabata, Yasunari
Kaye, Mary Margaret
    See Kaye, M.M.
Kaye, M.M. 1908-2004 .... **CLC 28**
    See also CA 89-92; 223; CANR 24, 60, 102,
    142; MTCW 1, 2; MTFW 2005; RHW;
    SATA 62; SATA-Obit 152
Kaye, Mollie
    See Kaye, M.M.
Kaye-Smith, Sheila 1887-1956 .... **TCLC 20**
    See also CA 118; 203; DLB 36
Kaymor, Patrice Maguilene
    See Senghor, Leopold Sedar
Kazakov, Iurii Pavlovich
    See Kazakov, Yuri Pavlovich
Kazakov, Yuri Pavlovich 1927-1982 . **SSC 43**
    See also CA 5-8R; CANR 36; DLB 302;
    EWL 3; MTCW 1; RGSF 2
Kazakov, Yury
    See Kazakov, Yuri Pavlovich
Kazan, Elia 1909-2003 .... **CLC 6, 16, 63**
    See also CA 21-24R; 220; CANR 32, 78
Kazantzakis, Nikos 1883(?)-1957 .... **TCLC 2,
    5, 33, 181**
    See also BPFB 2; CA 105; 132; DA3; EW
    9; EWL 3; MTCW 1, 2; MTFW 2005;
    RGWL 2, 3
Kazin, Alfred 1915-1998 ..... **CLC 34, 38, 119**
    See also AMWS 8; CA 1-4R; CAAS 7;
    CANR 1, 45, 79; DLB 67; EWL 3
Keane, Mary Nesta 1904-1996 .... **CLC 31**
    See also CA 108; 114; 151; CN 5, 6; INT
    CA-114; RHW; TCLE 1:1
Keane, Mary Nesta Skrine
    See Keane, Mary Nesta
Keane, Molly
    See Keane, Mary Nesta
Keates, Jonathan 1946(?)- .... **CLC 34**
    See also CA 163; CANR 126
Keaton, Buster 1895-1966 .... **CLC 20**
    See also AAYA 79; CA 194
Keats, John 1795-1821 ...... **NCLC 8, 73, 121,
    225; PC 1, 96; WLC 3**
    See also AAYA 58; BRW 4; BRWR 1; CD-
    BLB 1789-1832; DA; DA3; DAB; DAC;
    DAM MST, POET; DLB 96, 110; EXPP;
    LMFS 1; PAB; PFS 1, 2, 3, 9, 17; RGEL
    2; TEA; WLIT 3; WP
Keble, John 1792-1866 .... **NCLC 87**
    See also DLB 32, 55; RGEL 2
Keene, Donald 1922- .... **CLC 34**
    See also CA 1-4R; CANR 5, 119, 190
Keillor, Garrison 1942- ..... **CLC 40, 115, 222**
    See also AAYA 2, 62; AMWS 16; BEST
    89:3; BPFB 2; CA 111; 117; CANR 36,
    59, 124, 180; CPW; DA3; DAM POP;
    DLBY 1987; EWL 3; MTCW 1, 2; MTFW
    2005; SATA 58; TUS
Keillor, Gary Edward
    See Keillor, Garrison
Keith, Carlos
    See Lewton, Val
Keith, Michael
    See Hubbard, L. Ron
Kell, Joseph
    See Burgess, Anthony

Keller, Gottfried 1819-1890 .... **NCLC 2; SSC
    26, 107**
    See also CDWLB 2; DLB 129; EW; RGSF
    2; RGWL 2, 3
Keller, Nora Okja 1965- .... **CLC 109, 281**
    See also CA 187
Kellerman, Jonathan 1949- .... **CLC 44**
    See also AAYA 35; BEST 90:1; CA 106;
    CANR 29, 51, 150, 183; CMW 4; CPW;
    DA3; DAM POP; INT CANR-29
Kelley, William Melvin 1937- .... **BLC 2:2;
    CLC 22**
    See also BW 1; CA 77-80; CANR 27, 83;
    CN 1, 2, 3, 4, 5, 6, 7; DLB 33; EWL 3
Kellock, Archibald P.
    See Mavor, Osborne Henry
Kellogg, Marjorie 1922-2005 .... **CLC 2**
    See also CA 81-84; 246
Kellow, Kathleen
    See Hibbert, Eleanor Alice Burford
Kelly, Lauren
    See Oates, Joyce Carol
Kelly, M(ilton) T(errence) 1947- ...... **CLC 55**
    See also CA 97-100; CAAS 22; CANR 19,
    43, 84; CN 6
Kelly, Robert 1935- .... **SSC 50**
    See also CA 17-20R; CAAS 19; CANR 47;
    CP 1, 2, 3, 4, 5, 6, 7; DLB 5, 130, 165
Kelman, James 1946- .... **CLC 58, 86**
    See also BRWS 5; CA 148; CANR 85, 130,
    199; CN 5, 6, 7; DLB 194, 319, 326;
    RGSF 2; WLIT 4
Kemal, Yasar
    See Kemal, Yashar
Kemal, Yashar 1923(?)- .... **CLC 14, 29**
    See also CA 89-92; CANR 44; CWW 2;
    EWL 3; WLIT 6
Kemble, Fanny 1809-1893 .... **NCLC 18**
    See also DLB 32
Kemelman, Harry 1908-1996 .... **CLC 2**
    See also AITN 1; BPFB 2; CA 9-12R; 155;
    CANR 6, 71; CMW 4; DLB 28
Kempe, Margery 1373(?)-1440(?) ... **LC 6, 56**
    See also BRWS 12; DLB 146; FL 1:1;
    RGEL 2
Kempis, Thomas a 1380-1471 .... **LC 11**
Kenan, Randall (G.) 1963- .... **BLC 2:2**
    See also BW 2, 3; CA 142; CANR 86; CN
    7; CSW; DLB 292; GLL 1
Kendall, Henry 1839-1882 .... **NCLC 12**
    See also DLB 230
Keneally, Thomas 1935- .... **CLC 5, 8, 10, 14,
    19, 27, 43, 117, 279**
    See also BRWS 4; CA 85-88; CANR 10,
    50, 74, 130, 165, 198; CN 1, 2, 3, 4, 5, 6,
    7; CPW; DA3; DAM NOV; DLB 289,
    299, 326; EWL 3; MTCW 1, 2; MTFW
    2005; NFS 17; RGEL 2; RGHL; RHW
Keneally, Thomas Michael
    See Keneally, Thomas
Keneally, Tom
    See Keneally, Thomas
Kennedy, A. L. 1965- .... **CLC 188**
    See also CA 168, 213; CAAE 213; CANR
    108, 193; CD 5, 6; CN 6, 7; DLB 271;
    RGSF 2
Kennedy, Adrienne (Lita) 1931- .... **BLC 1:2;
    CLC 66; DC 5**
    See also AFAW 2; BW 2, 3; CA 103; CAAS
    20; CABS 3; CAD; CANR 26, 53, 82;
    CD 5, 6; DAM MULT; DFS 9; DLB 38,
    341; FW; MAL 5
Kennedy, Alison Louise
    See Kennedy, A. L.
Kennedy, John Pendleton
    1795-1870 .... **NCLC 2**
    See also DLB 3, 248, 254; RGAL 4

Kennedy, Joseph Charles 1929- .. **CLC 8, 42; PC 93**
See Kennedy, X. J.
See also AMWS 15; CA 1-4R, 201; CAAE 201; CAAS 9; CANR 4, 30, 40; CLR 27; CP 1, 2, 3, 4, 5, 6, 7; CWRI 5; DLB 5; MAICYA 2; MAICYAS 1; SAAS 22; SATA 14, 86, 130; SATA-Essay 130

Kennedy, William 1928- .. **CLC 6, 28, 34, 53, 239**
See also AAYA 1, 73; AMWS 7; BPFB 2; CA 85-88; CANR 14, 31, 76, 134; CN 4, 5, 6, 7; DA3; DAM NOV; DLB 143; DLBY 1985; EWL 3; INT CANR-31; MAL 5; MTCW 1, 2; MTFW 2005; SATA 57

Kennedy, William Joseph
See Kennedy, William

Kennedy, X. J. CLC 8, 42
See Kennedy, Joseph Charles
See also CAAS 9; CLR 27; DLB 5; SAAS 22

Kenny, Maurice (Francis) 1929- ..... **CLC 87; NNAL**
See also CA 144; CAAS 22; CANR 143; DAM MULT; DLB 175

Kent, Kathleen CLC 280
See also CA 288

Kent, Kelvin
See Kuttner, Henry

Kenton, Maxwell
See Southern, Terry

Kenyon, Jane 1947-1995 .... **PC 57**
See also AAYA 63; AMWS 7; CA 118; 148; CANR 44, 69, 172; CP 6, 7; CWP; DLB 120; PFS 9, 17; RGAL 4

Kenyon, Robert O.
See Kuttner, Henry

Kepler, Johannes 1571-1630 .... **LC 45**

Ker, Jill
See Conway, Jill K.

Kerkow, H. C.
See Lewton, Val

Kerouac, Jack 1922-1969 ...... **CLC 1, 2, 3, 5, 14, 61; TCLC 117; WLC**
See also AAYA 25; AITN 1; AMWC 1; AMWS 3; BG 3; BPFB 2; CA 5-8R; 25-28R; CANR 26, 54, 95, 184; CDALB 1941-1968; CP 1; CPW; DA; DA3; DAB; DAC; DAM MST, NOV, POET, POP; DLB 2, 16, 237; DLBY 1995; EWL 3; GLL 1; LATS 1:2; LMFS 2; MAL 5; MTCW 1, 2; MTFW 2005; NFS 8; RGAL 4; TUS; WP

Kerouac, Jean-Louis le Brisde
See Kerouac, Jack

Kerouac, John
See Kerouac, Jack

Kerr, (Bridget) Jean (Collins)
1923(?)-2003 .... **CLC 22**
See also CA 5-8R; 212; CANR 7; INT CANR-7

Kerr, M. E.
See Meaker, Marijane

Kerr, Robert CLC 55

Kerrigan, (Thomas) Anthony 1918- .. **CLC 4, 6**
See also CA 49-52; CAAS 11; CANR 4

Kerry, Lois
See Duncan, Lois

Kesey, Ken 1935-2001 .... **CLC 1, 3, 6, 11, 46, 64, 184; WLC 3**
See also AAYA 25; BG 1:3; BPFB 2; CA 1-4R; 204; CANR 22, 38, 66, 124; CDALB 1968-1988; CN 1, 2, 3, 4, 5, 6, 7; CPW; DA; DA3; DAB; DAC; DAM MST, NOV, POP; DLB 2, 16, 206; EWL

3; EXPN; LAIT 4; MAL 5; MTCW 1, 2; MTFW 2005; NFS 2; RGAL 4; SATA 66; SATA-Obit 131; TUS; YAW

Kesselring, Joseph (Otto)
1902-1967 .... **CLC 45**
See also CA 150; DAM DRAM, MST; DFS 20

Kessler, Jascha (Frederick) 1929- ...... **CLC 4**
See also CA 17-20R; CANR 8, 48, 111; CP 1

Kettelkamp, Larry (Dale) 1933- .... **CLC 12**
See also CA 29-32R; CANR 16; SAAS 3; SATA 2

Key, Ellen (Karolina Sofia)
1849-1926 .... **TCLC 65**
See also DLB 259

Keyber, Conny
See Fielding, Henry

Keyes, Daniel 1927- .... **CLC 80**
See also AAYA 23; BYA 11; CA 17-20R, 181; CAAE 181; CANR 10, 26, 54, 74; DA; DA3; DAC; DAM MST, NOV; EXPN; LAIT 4; MTCW 2; MTFW 2005; NFS 2; SATA 37; SFW 4

Keynes, John Maynard
1883-1946 .... **TCLC 64**
See also CA 114; 162, 163; DLBD 10; MTCW 2; MTFW 2005

Khanshendel, Chiron
See Rose, Wendy

Khayyam, Omar 1048-1131 ... **CMLC 11; PC 8**
See also DA3; DAM POET; RGWL 2, 3; WLIT 6

Kherdian, David 1931- .... **CLC 6, 9**
See also AAYA 42; CA 21-24R, 192; CAAE 192; CAAS 2; CANR 39, 78; CLR 24; JRDA; LAIT 3; MAICYA 1, 2; SATA 16, 74; SATA-Essay 125

Khlebnikov, Velimir TCLC 20
See Khlebnikov, Viktor Vladimirovich
See also DLB 295; EW 10; EWL 3; RGWL 2, 3

Khlebnikov, Viktor Vladimirovich 1885-1922
See Khlebnikov, Velimir
See also CA 117; 217

Khodasevich, V.F.
See Khodasevich, Vladislav

Khodasevich, Vladislav
1886-1939 .... **TCLC 15**
See also CA 115; DLB 317; EWL 3

Khodasevich, Vladislav Felitsianovich
See Khodasevich, Vladislav

Kidd, Sue Monk 1948- .... **CLC 267**
See also AAYA 72; CA 202; LNFS 1; MTFW 2005; NFS 27

Kielland, Alexander Lange
1849-1906 .... **TCLC 5**
See also CA 104; DLB 354

Kiely, Benedict 1919-2007 . **CLC 23, 43; SSC 58**
See also CA 1-4R; 257; CANR 2, 84; CN 1, 2, 3, 4, 5, 6, 7; DLB 15, 319; TCLE 1:1

Kienzle, William X. 1928-2001 .... **CLC 25**
See also CA 93-96; 203; CAAS 1; CANR 9, 31, 59, 111; CMW 4; DA3; DAM POP; INT CANR-31; MSW; MTCW 1, 2; MTFW 2005

Kierkegaard, Soren 1813-1855 ..... **NCLC 34, 78, 125**
See also DLB 300; EW 6; LMFS 2; RGWL 3; TWA

Kieslowski, Krzysztof 1941-1996 .... **CLC 120**
See also CA 147; 151

Killens, John Oliver 1916-1987 ...... **BLC 2:2; CLC 10**
See also BW 2; CA 77-80; 123; CAAS 2; CANR 26; CN 1, 2, 3, 4; DLB 33; EWL 3

Killigrew, Anne 1660-1685 .... **LC 4, 73**
See also DLB 131

Killigrew, Thomas 1612-1683 .... **LC 57**
See also DLB 58; RGEL 2

Kim
See Simenon, Georges

Kincaid, Jamaica 1949- . **BLC 1:2, 2:2; CLC 43, 68, 137, 234; SSC 72**
See also AAYA 13, 56; AFAW 2; AMWS 7; BRWS 7; BW 2, 3; CA 125; CANR 47, 59, 95, 133; CDALBS; CDWLB 3; CLR 63; CN 4, 5, 6, 7; DA3; DAM MULT, NOV; DLB 157, 227; DNFS 1; EWL 3; EXPS; FW; LATS 1:2; LMFS 2; MAL 5; MTCW 2; MTFW 2005; NCFS 1; NFS 3; SSFS 5, 7; TUS; WWE 1; YAW

King, Francis (Henry) 1923- .... **CLC 8, 53, 145**
See also CA 1-4R; CANR 1, 33, 86; CN 1, 2, 3, 4, 5, 6, 7; DAM NOV; DLB 15, 139; MTCW 1

King, Kennedy
See Brown, George Douglas

King, Martin Luther, Jr.
1929-1968 ... **BLC 1:2; CLC 83; WLCS**
See also BW 2, 3; CA 25-28; CANR 27, 44; CAP 2; DA; DA3; DAB; DAM MST, MULT; LAIT 5; LATS 1:2; MTCW 1, 2; MTFW 2005; SATA 14

King, Stephen 1947- .... **CLC 12, 26, 37, 61, 113, 228, 244; SSC 17, 55**
See also AAYA 1, 17, 82; AMWS 5; BEST 90:1; BPFB 2; CA 61-64; CANR 1, 30, 52, 76, 119, 134, 168; CLR 124; CN 7; CPW; DA3; DAM NOV, POP; DLB 143, 350; DLBY 1980; HGG; JRDA; LAIT 5; LNFS 1; MTCW 1, 2; MTFW 2005; RGAL 4; SATA 9, 55, 161; SUFW 1, 2; WYAS 1; YAW

King, Stephen Edwin
See King, Stephen

King, Steve
See King, Stephen

King, Thomas 1943- .... **CLC 89, 171, 276; NNAL**
See also CA 144; CANR 95, 175; CCA 1; CN 6, 7; DAC; DAM MULT; DLB 175, 334; SATA 96

King, Thomas Hunt
See King, Thomas

Kingman, Lee
See Natti, Lee

Kingsley, Charles 1819-1875 .... **NCLC 35**
See also CLR 77; DLB 21, 32, 163, 178, 190; FANT; MAICYA 2; MAICYAS 1; RGEL 2; WCH; YABC 2

Kingsley, Henry 1830-1876 .... **NCLC 107**
See also DLB 21, 230; RGEL 2

Kingsley, Sidney 1906-1995 .... **CLC 44**
See also CA 85-88; 147; CAD; DFS 14, 19; DLB 7; MAL 5; RGAL 4

Kingsolver, Barbara 1955- .... **CLC 55, 81, 130, 216, 269**
See also AAYA 15; AMWS 7; CA 129; 134; CANR 60, 96, 133, 179; CDALBS; CN 7; CPW; CSW; DA3; DAM POP; DLB 206; INT CA-134; LAIT 5; MTCW 2; MTFW 2005; NFS 5, 10, 12, 24; RGAL 4; TCLE 1:1

Kingston, Maxine Hong 1940- .... **AAL; CLC 12, 19, 58, 121, 271; SSC 136; WLCS**
See also AAYA 8, 55; AMWS 5; BPFB 2; CA 69-72; CANR 13, 38, 74, 87, 128; CDALBS; CN 6, 7; DA3; DAM MULT, NOV; DLB 173, 212, 312; DLBY 1980;

Lacolere, Francois
See Aragon, Louis

Lactantius c. 250-c. 325 .... **CMLC 118**

La Deshabilleuse
See Simenon, Georges

Lady Gregory
See Gregory, Lady Isabella Augusta (Persse)

Lady of Quality, A
See Bagnold, Enid

**La Fayette, Marie-(Madelaine Pioche de la
Vergne)** 1634-1693 .... **LC 2, 144**
See also DLB 268; GFL Beginnings to
1789; RGWL 2, 3

Lafayette, Marie-Madeleine
See La Fayette, Marie-(Madelaine Pioche
de la Vergne)

Lafayette, Rene
See Hubbard, L. Ron

La Flesche, Francis 1857(?)-1932 ...... **NNAL**
See also CA 144; CANR 83; DLB 175

La Fontaine, Jean de 1621-1695 .... **LC 50**
See also DLB 268; EW 3; GFL Beginnings
to 1789; MAICYA 1, 2; RGWL 2, 3;
SATA 18

LaForet, Carmen 1921-2004 .... **CLC 219**
See also CA 246; CWW 2; DLB 322; EWL
3

LaForet Diaz, Carmen
See LaForet, Carmen

Laforgue, Jules 1860-1887 .... **NCLC 5, 53,
221; PC 14; SSC 20**
See also DLB 217; EW 7; GFL 1789 to the
Present; RGWL 2, 3

Lagerkvist, Paer 1891-1974 ... **CLC 7, 10, 13,
54; SSC 12; TCLC 144**
See also CA 85-88; 49-52; DA3; DAM
DRAM, NOV; DLB 259, 331; EW 10;
EWL 3; MTCW 1, 2; MTFW 2005; RGSF
2; RGWL 2, 3; TWA

Lagerkvist, Paer Fabian
See Lagerkvist, Paer

Lagerkvist, Par
See Lagerkvist, Paer

Lagerloef, Selma
See Lagerlof, Selma

Lagerloef, Selma Ottiliana Lovisa
See Lagerlof, Selma

Lagerlof, Selma 1858-1940 .... **TCLC 4, 36**
See also CA 108; 188; CLR 7; DLB 259,
331; MTCW 2; RGWL 2, 3; SATA 15;
SSFS 18

Lagerlof, Selma Ottiliana Lovisa
See Lagerlof, Selma

La Guma, Alex 1925-1985 .. **BLCS; CLC 19;
TCLC 140**
See also AFW; BW 1, 3; CA 49-52; 118;
CANR 25, 81; CDWLB 3; CN 1, 2, 3;
CP 1; DAM NOV; DLB 117, 225; EWL
3; MTCW 1, 2; MTFW 2005; WLIT 2;
WWE 1

La Guma, Justin Alexander
See La Guma, Alex

Lahiri, Jhumpa 1967- .... **CLC 282; SSC 96**
See also AAYA 56; CA 193; CANR 134,
184; DLB 323; MTFW 2005; SSFS 19,
27

Laidlaw, A. K.
See Grieve, C. M.

Lainez, Manuel Mujica
See Mujica Lainez, Manuel

Laing, R(onald) D(avid) 1927-1989 . **CLC 95**
See also CA 107; 129; CANR 34; MTCW 1

Laishley, Alex
See Booth, Martin

Lamartine, Alphonse de
1790-1869 .... **NCLC 11, 190; PC 16**
See also DAM POET; DLB 217; GFL 1789
to the Present; RGWL 2, 3

Lamartine, Alphonse Marie Louis Prat de
See Lamartine, Alphonse de

Lamb, Charles 1775-1834 ..... **NCLC 10, 113;
SSC 112; WLC 3**
See also BRW 4; CDBLB 1789-1832; DA;
DAB; DAC; DAM MST; DLB 93, 107,
163; RGEL 2; SATA 17; TEA

Lamb, Lady Caroline 1785-1828 ... **NCLC 38**
See also DLB 116

Lamb, Mary Ann 1764-1847 ...... **NCLC 125;
SSC 112**
See also DLB 163; SATA 17

Lame Deer 1903(?)-1976 .... **NNAL**
See also CA 69-72

Lamming, George (William)
1927- . **BLC 1:2, 2:2; CLC 2, 4, 66, 144**
See also BW 2, 3; CA 85-88; CANR 26,
76; CDWLB 3; CN 1, 2, 3, 4, 5, 6, 7; CP
1; DAM MULT; DLB 125; EWL 3;
MTCW 1, 2; MTFW 2005; NFS 15;
RGEL 2

L'Amour, Louis 1908-1988 .... **CLC 25, 55**
See also AAYA 16; AITN 2; BEST 89:2;
BPFB 2; CA 1-4R; 125; CANR 3, 25, 40;
CPW; DA3; DAM NOV, POP; DLB 206;
DLBY 1980; MTCW 1, 2; MTFW 2005;
RGAL 4; TCWW 1, 2

Lampedusa, Giuseppe di
See Tomasi di Lampedusa, Giuseppe

Lampedusa, Giuseppe Tomasi di
See Tomasi di Lampedusa, Giuseppe

Lampman, Archibald 1861-1899 .. **NCLC 25,
194**
See also DLB 92; RGEL 2; TWA

Lancaster, Bruce 1896-1963 .... **CLC 36**
See also CA 9-10; CANR 70; CAP 1; SATA
9

Lanchester, John 1962- .... **CLC 99, 280**
See also CA 194; DLB 267

Landau, Mark Alexandrovich
See Aldanov, Mark (Alexandrovich)

Landau-Aldanov, Mark Alexandrovich
See Aldanov, Mark (Alexandrovich)

Landis, Jerry
See Simon, Paul

Landis, John 1950- .... **CLC 26**
See also CA 112; 122; CANR 128

Landolfi, Tommaso 1908-1979 .... **CLC 11, 49**
See also CA 127; 117; DLB 177; EWL 3

Landon, Letitia Elizabeth
1802-1838 .... **NCLC 15**
See also DLB 96

Landor, Walter Savage
1775-1864 .... **NCLC 14**
See also BRW 4; DLB 93, 107; RGEL 2

Landwirth, Heinz
See Lind, Jakov

Lane, Patrick 1939- .... **CLC 25**
See also CA 97-100; CANR 54; CP 3, 4, 5,
6, 7; DAM POET; DLB 53; INT CA-97-
100

Lane, Rose Wilder 1887-1968 ...... **TCLC 177**
See also CA 102; CANR 63; SATA 29;
SATA-Brief 28; TCWW 2

Lang, Andrew 1844-1912 .... **TCLC 16**
See also CA 114; 137; CANR 85; CLR 101;
DLB 98, 141, 184; FANT; MAICYA 1, 2;
RGEL 2; SATA 16; WCH

Lang, Fritz 1890-1976 .... **CLC 20, 103**
See also AAYA 65; CA 77-80; 69-72;
CANR 30

Lange, John
See Crichton, Michael

Langer, Elinor 1939- .... **CLC 34**
See also CA 121

Langland, William 1332(?)-1400(?) .... **LC 19,
120**
See also BRW 1; DA; DAB; DAC; DAM
MST, POET; DLB 146; RGEL 2; TEA;
WLIT 3

Langstaff, Launcelot
See Irving, Washington

Lanier, Sidney 1842-1881 . **NCLC 6, 118; PC
50**
See also AMWS 1; DAM POET; DLB 64;
DLBD 13; EXPP; MAICYA 1; PFS 14;
RGAL 4; SATA 18

Lanyer, Aemilia 1569-1645 .... **LC 10, 30, 83;
PC 60**
See also DLB 121

Lao Tzu c. 6th cent. B.C.-3rd cent.
B.C. .... **CMLC 7**

Lao-Tzu
See Lao Tzu

Lapine, James (Elliot) 1949- .... **CLC 39**
See also CA 123; 130; CANR 54, 128; DFS
25; DLB 341; INT CA-130

La Ramee, Pierre de 1515(?)-1572 .... **LC 174**
See also DLB 327

Larbaud, Valery (Nicolas)
1881-1957 .... **TCLC 9**
See also CA 106; 152; EWL 3; GFL 1789
to the Present

Larcom, Lucy 1824-1893 .... **NCLC 179**
See also AMWS 13; DLB 221, 243

Lardner, Ring 1885-1933 .... **SSC 32, 118;
TCLC 2, 14**
See also AMW; BPFB 2; CA 104; 131;
CDALB 1917-1929; DLB 11, 25, 86, 171;
DLBD 16; MAL 5; MTCW 1, 2; MTFW
2005; RGAL 4; RGSF 2; TUS

Lardner, Ring W., Jr.
See Lardner, Ring

Lardner, Ringold Wilmer
See Lardner, Ring

Laredo, Betty
See Codrescu, Andrei

Larkin, Maia
See Wojciechowska, Maia (Teresa)

Larkin, Philip 1922-1985 .... **CLC 3, 5, 8, 9,
13, 18, 33, 39, 64; PC 21**
See also BRWR 3; BRWS 1; CA 5-8R; 117;
CANR 24, 62; CDBLB 1960 to Present;
CP 1, 2, 3, 4; DA3; DAB; DAM MST,
POET; DLB 27; EWL 3; MTCW 1, 2;
MTFW 2005; PFS 3, 4, 12; RGEL 2

Larkin, Philip Arthur
See Larkin, Philip

La Roche, Sophie von
1730-1807 .... **NCLC 121**
See also DLB 94

La Rochefoucauld, Francois
1613-1680 .... **LC 108, 172**
See also DLB 268; EW 3; GFL Beginnings
to 1789; RGWL 2, 3

**Larra (y Sanchez de Castro), Mariano Jose
de** 1809-1837 .... **NCLC 17, 130**

Larsen, Eric 1941- .... **CLC 55**
See also CA 132

Larsen, Nella 1893(?)-1963 ... **BLC 1:2; CLC
37; HR 1:3; TCLC 200**
See also AFAW 1, 2; AMWS 18; BW 1;
CA 125; CANR 83; DAM MULT; DLB
51; FW; LATS 1:1; LMFS 2

Larson, Charles R(aymond) 1938- ... **CLC 31**
See also CA 53-56; CANR 4, 121

Larson, Jonathan 1960-1996 .... **CLC 99**
See also AAYA 28; CA 156; DFS 23;
MTFW 2005

La Sale, Antoine de c. 1386-1460(?) . **LC 104**
See also DLB 208

Las Casas, Bartolome de
1474-1566 .... **HLCS; LC 31**
See also DLB 318; LAW; WLIT 1

Macaulay, (Emilie) Rose
1881(?)-1958 .... **TCLC 7, 44**
See also CA 104; DLB 36; EWL 3; RGEL
2; RHW

Macaulay, Thomas Babington
1800-1859 .... **NCLC 42**
See also BRW 4; CDBLB 1832-1890; DLB
32, 55; RGEL 2

MacBeth, George (Mann)
1932-1992 .... **CLC 2, 5, 9**
See also CA 25-28R; 136; CANR 61, 66;
CP 1, 2, 3, 4, 5; DLB 40; MTCW 1; PFS
8; SATA 4; SATA-Obit 70

MacCaig, Norman (Alexander)
1910-1996 .... **CLC 36**
See also BRWS 6; CA 9-12R; CANR 3, 34;
CP 1, 2, 3, 4, 5, 6; DAB; DAM POET;
DLB 27; EWL 3; RGEL 2

MacCarthy, Sir (Charles Otto) Desmond
1877-1952 .... **TCLC 36**
See also CA 167

MacDiarmid, Hugh
See Grieve, C. M.

MacDonald, Anson
See Heinlein, Robert A.

Macdonald, Cynthia 1928- .... **CLC 13, 19**
See also CA 49-52; CANR 4, 44, 146; DLB
105

MacDonald, George 1824-1905 .... **TCLC 9,
113, 207**
See also AAYA 57; BYA 5; CA 106; 137;
CANR 80; CLR 67; DLB 18, 163, 178;
FANT; MAICYA 1, 2; RGEL 2; SATA 33,
100; SFW 4; SUFW; WCH

Macdonald, John
See Millar, Kenneth

MacDonald, John D. 1916-1986 .. **CLC 3, 27,
44**
See also BPFB 2; CA 1-4R; 121; CANR 1,
19, 60; CMW 4; CPW; DAM NOV, POP;
DLB 8, 306; DLBY 1986; MSW; MTCW
1, 2; MTFW 2005; SFW 4

Macdonald, John Ross
See Millar, Kenneth

Macdonald, Ross
See Millar, Kenneth

MacDonald Fraser, George
See Fraser, George MacDonald

MacDougal, John
See Blish, James

MacDowell, John
See Parks, Tim(othy Harold)

MacEwen, Gwendolyn (Margaret)
1941-1987 .... **CLC 13, 55**
See also CA 9-12R; 124; CANR 7, 22; CP
1, 2, 3, 4; DLB 53, 251; SATA 50; SATA-
Obit 55

MacGreevy, Thomas 1893-1967 .... **PC 82**
See also CA 262

Macha, Karel Hynek 1810-1846 .... **NCLC 46**

Machado (y Ruiz), Antonio
1875-1939 .... **TCLC 3**
See also CA 104; 174; DLB 108; EW 9;
EWL 3; HW 2; PFS 23; RGWL 2, 3

Machado de Assis, Joaquim Maria
1839-1908 . **BLC 1:2; HLCS 2; SSC 24,
118; TCLC 10**
See also CA 107; 153; CANR 91; DLB 307;
LAW; RGSF 2; RGWL 2, 3; TWA; WLIT
1

Machaut, Guillaume de c.
1300-1377 .... **CMLC 64**
See also DLB 208

Machen, Arthur .... **SSC 20; TCLC 4**
See Jones, Arthur Llewellyn
See also CA 179; DLB 156, 178; RGEL 2

Machen, Arthur Llewelyn Jones
See Jones, Arthur Llewellyn

Machiavelli, Niccolo 1469-1527 ... **DC 16; LC
8, 36, 140; WLCS**
See also AAYA 58; DA; DAB; DAC; DAM
MST; EW 2; LAIT 1; LMFS 1; NFS 9;
RGWL 2, 3; TWA; WLIT 7

MacInnes, Colin 1914-1976 .... **CLC 4, 23**
See also CA 69-72; 65-68; CANR 21; CN
1, 2; DLB 14; MTCW 1, 2; RGEL 2;
RHW

MacInnes, Helen (Clark)
1907-1985 .... **CLC 27, 39**
See also BPFB 2; CA 1-4R; 117; CANR 1,
28, 58; CMW 4; CN 1, 2; CPW; DAM
POP; DLB 87; MSW; MTCW 1, 2;
MTFW 2005; SATA 22; SATA-Obit 44

Mackay, Mary 1855-1924 .... **TCLC 51**
See also CA 118; 177; DLB 34, 156; FANT;
RGEL 2; RHW; SUFW 1

Mackay, Shena 1944- .... **CLC 195**
See also CA 104; CANR 88, 139; DLB 231,
319; MTFW 2005

Mackenzie, Compton (Edward Montague)
1883-1972 .... **CLC 18; TCLC 116**
See also CA 21-22; 37-40R; CAP 2; CN 1;
DLB 34, 100; RGEL 2

Mackenzie, Henry 1745-1831 .... **NCLC 41**
See also DLB 39; RGEL 2

Mackey, Nathaniel 1947- .... **BLC 2:3; PC 49**
See also CA 153; CANR 114; CP 6, 7; DLB
169

Mackey, Nathaniel Ernest
See Mackey, Nathaniel

MacKinnon, Catharine
See MacKinnon, Catharine A.

MacKinnon, Catharine A. 1946- .... **CLC 181**
See also CA 128; 132; CANR 73, 140, 189;
FW; MTCW 2; MTFW 2005

Mackintosh, Elizabeth
1896(?)-1952 .... **TCLC 14**
See also CA 110; CMW 4; DLB 10, 77;
MSW

Macklin, Charles 1699-1797 .... **LC 132**
See also DLB 89; RGEL 2

MacLaren, James
See Grieve, C. M.

MacLaverty, Bernard 1942- ..... **CLC 31, 243**
See also CA 116; 118; CANR 43, 88, 168;
CN 5, 6, 7; DLB 267; INT CA-118; RGSF
2

MacLean, Alistair 1922(?)-1987 .. **CLC 3, 13,
50, 63**
See also CA 57-60; 121; CANR 28, 61;
CMW 4; CP 2, 3, 4, 5, 6, 7; CPW; DAM
POP; DLB 276; MTCW 1; SATA 23;
SATA-Obit 50; TCWW 2

MacLean, Alistair Stuart
See MacLean, Alistair

Maclean, Norman (Fitzroy)
1902-1990 .... **CLC 78; SSC 13, 136**
See also AMWS 14; CA 102; 132; CANR
49; CPW; DAM POP; DLB 206; TCWW
2

MacLeish, Archibald 1892-1982 ... **CLC 3, 8,
14, 68; PC 47**
See also AMW; CA 9-12R; 106; CAD;
CANR 33, 63; CDALBS; CP 1, 2; DAM
POET; DFS 15; DLB 4, 7, 45; DLBY
1982; EWL 3; EXPP; MAL 5; MTCW 1,
2; MTFW 2005; PAB; PFS 5; RGAL 4;
TUS

MacLennan, (John) Hugh
1907-1990 .... **CLC 2, 14, 92**
See also CA 5-8R; 142; CANR 33; CN 1,
2, 3, 4; DAC; DAM MST; DLB 68; EWL
3; MTCW 1, 2; MTFW 2005; RGEL 2;
TWA

MacLeod, Alistair 1936- .. **CLC 56, 165; SSC
90**
See also CA 123; CCA 1; DAC; DAM
MST; DLB 60; MTCW 2; MTFW 2005;
RGSF 2; TCLE 1:2

Macleod, Fiona
See Sharp, William

MacNeice, (Frederick) Louis
1907-1963 .... **CLC 1, 4, 10, 53; PC 61**
See also BRW 7; CA 85-88; CANR 61;
DAB; DAM POET; DLB 10, 20; EWL 3;
MTCW 1, 2; MTFW 2005; RGEL 2

MacNeill, Dand
See Fraser, George MacDonald

Macpherson, James 1736-1796 .... **CMLC 28;
LC 29; PC 97**
See also BRWS 8; DLB 109, 336; RGEL 2

Macpherson, (Jean) Jay 1931- .... **CLC 14**
See also CA 5-8R; CANR 90; CP 1, 2, 3, 4,
6, 7; CWP; DLB 53

Macrobius fl. 430- .... **CMLC 48**

MacShane, Frank 1927-1999 .... **CLC 39**
See also CA 9-12R; 186; CANR 3, 33; DLB
111

Macumber, Mari
See Sandoz, Mari(e Susette)

Madach, Imre 1823-1864 .... **NCLC 19**

Madden, (Jerry) David 1933- .... **CLC 5, 15**
See also CA 1-4R; CAAS 3; CANR 4, 45;
CN 3, 4, 5, 6, 7; CSW; DLB 6; MTCW 1

Maddern, Al(an)
See Ellison, Harlan

Madhubuti, Haki R. 1942- .... **BLC 1:2; CLC
2; PC 5**
See also BW 2, 3; CA 73-76; CANR 24,
51, 73, 139; CP 2, 3, 4, 5, 6, 7; CSW;
DAM MULT, POET; DLB 5, 41; DLBD
8; EWL 3; MAL 5; MTCW 2; MTFW
2005; RGAL 4

Madison, James 1751-1836 .... **NCLC 126**
See also DLB 37

Maepenn, Hugh
See Kuttner, Henry

Maepenn, K. H.
See Kuttner, Henry

Maeterlinck, Maurice 1862-1949 .... **DC 32;
TCLC 3**
See also CA 104; 136; CANR 80; DAM
DRAM; DLB 192, 331; EW 8; EWL 3;
GFL 1789 to the Present; LMFS 2; RGWL
2, 3; SATA 66; TWA

Maginn, William 1794-1842 .... **NCLC 8**
See also DLB 110, 159

Mahapatra, Jayanta 1928- .... **CLC 33**
See also CA 73-76; CAAS 9; CANR 15,
33, 66, 87; CP 4, 5, 6, 7; DAM MULT;
DLB 323

Mahfouz, Nagib
See Mahfouz, Naguib

Mahfouz, Naguib 1911(?)-2006 . **CLC 52, 55,
153; SSC 66**
See also AAYA 49; AFW; BEST 89:2; CA
128; 253; CANR 55, 101; DA3; DAM
NOV; DLB 346; DLBY 1988; MTCW 1,
2; MTFW 2005; RGSF 2; RGWL 2, 3;
SSFS 9; WLIT 2

Mahfouz, Naguib Abdel Aziz Al-Sabilgi
See Mahfouz, Naguib

Mahfouz, Najib
See Mahfouz, Naguib

Mahfuz, Najib
See Mahfouz, Naguib

Mahon, Derek 1941- .... **CLC 27; PC 60**
See also BRWS 6; CA 113; 128; CANR 88;
CP 1, 2, 3, 4, 5, 6, 7; DLB 40; EWL 3

Maiakovskii, Vladimir
See Mayakovski, Vladimir

Map, Walter 1140-1209 .... **CMLC 32**
Mapu, Abraham (ben Jekutiel)
     1808-1867 .... **NCLC 18**
Mara, Sally
     See Queneau, Raymond
Maracle, Lee 1950- .... **NNAL**
     See also CA 149
Marat, Jean Paul 1743-1793 .... **LC 10**
Marcel, Gabriel Honore 1889-1973 . **CLC 15**
     See also CA 102; 45-48; EWL 3; MTCW 1,
     2
March, William
     See Campbell, William Edward March
Marchbanks, Samuel
     See Davies, Robertson
Marchi, Giacomo
     See Bassani, Giorgio
Marcus Aurelius
     See Aurelius, Marcus
Marcuse, Herbert 1898-1979 .... **TCLC 207**
     See also CA 188; 89-92; DLB 242
Marguerite
     See de Navarre, Marguerite
Marguerite d'Angouleme
     See de Navarre, Marguerite
Marguerite de Navarre
     See de Navarre, Marguerite
Margulies, Donald 1954- .... **CLC 76**
     See also AAYA 57; CA 200; CD 6; DFS 13;
     DLB 228
Marias, Javier 1951- .... **CLC 239**
     See also CA 167; CANR 109, 139; DLB
     322; HW 2; MTFW 2005
Marie de France c. 12th cent. - ...... **CMLC 8,
     111; PC 22**
     See also DLB 208; FW; RGWL 2, 3
Marie de l'Incarnation 1599-1672 ..... **LC 10,
     168**
Marier, Captain Victor
     See Griffith, D.W.
Mariner, Scott
     See Pohl, Frederik
Marinetti, Filippo Tommaso
     1876-1944 .... **TCLC 10**
     See also CA 107; DLB 114, 264; EW 9;
     EWL 3; WLIT 7
Marivaux, Pierre Carlet de Chamblain de
     1688-1763 .... **DC 7; LC 4, 123**
     See also DLB 314; GFL Beginnings to
     1789; RGWL 2, 3; TWA
Markandaya, Kamala 1924-2004 . **CLC 8, 38**
     See also BYA 13; CA 77-80; 227; CN 1, 2,
     3, 4, 5, 6, 7; DLB 323; EWL 3; MTFW
     2005; NFS 13
Markfield, Wallace (Arthur)
     1926-2002 .... **CLC 8**
     See also CA 69-72; 208; CAAS 3; CN 1, 2,
     3, 4, 5, 6, 7; DLB 2, 28; DLBY 2002
Markham, Edwin 1852-1940 .... **TCLC 47**
     See also CA 160; DLB 54, 186; MAL 5;
     RGAL 4
Markham, Robert
     See Amis, Kingsley
Marks, J.
     See Highwater, Jamake (Mamake)
Marks-Highwater, J.
     See Highwater, Jamake (Mamake)
Markson, David M. 1927- .... **CLC 67**
     See also AMWS 17; CA 49-52; CANR 1,
     91, 158; CN 5, 6
Markson, David Merrill
     See Markson, David M.
Marlatt, Daphne (Buckle) 1942- .... **CLC 168**
     See also CA 25-28R; CANR 17, 39; CN 6,
     7; CP 4, 5, 6, 7; CWP; DLB 60; FW
Marley, Bob
     See Marley, Robert Nesta

Marley, Robert Nesta 1945-1981 ...... **CLC 17**
     See also CA 107; 103
Marlowe, Christopher 1564-1593 . **DC 1; LC
     22, 47, 117; PC 57; WLC 4**
     See also BRW 1; BRWR 1; CDBLB Before
     1660; DA; DA3; DAB; DAC; DAM
     DRAM, MST; DFS 1, 5, 13, 21; DLB 62;
     EXPP; LMFS 1; PFS 22; RGEL 2; TEA;
     WLIT 3
Marlowe, Stephen 1928-2008 .... **CLC 70**
     See also CA 13-16R; 269; CANR 6, 55;
     CMW 4; SFW 4
Marmion, Shakerley 1603-1639 .... **LC 89**
     See also DLB 58; RGEL 2
Marmontel, Jean-Francois 1723-1799 .. **LC 2**
     See also DLB 314
Maron, Monika 1941- .... **CLC 165**
     See also CA 201
Marot, Clement c. 1496-1544 .... **LC 133**
     See also DLB 327; GFL Beginnings to 1789
Marquand, John P(hillips)
     1893-1960 .... **CLC 2, 10**
     See also AMW; BPFB 2; CA 85-88; CANR
     73; CMW 4; DLB 9, 102; EWL 3; MAL
     5; MTCW 2; RGAL 4
Marques, Rene 1919-1979 .. **CLC 96; HLC 2**
     See also CA 97-100; 85-88; CANR 78;
     DAM MULT; DLB 305; EWL 3; HW 1,
     2; LAW; RGSF 2
Marquez, Gabriel Garcia
     See Garcia Marquez, Gabriel
Marquis, Don(ald Robert Perry)
     1878-1937 .... **TCLC 7**
     See also CA 104; 166; DLB 11, 25; MAL
     5; RGAL 4
Marquis de Sade
     See Sade, Donatien Alphonse Francois
Marric, J. J.
     See Creasey, John
Marryat, Frederick 1792-1848 .... **NCLC 3**
     See also DLB 21, 163; RGEL 2; WCH
Marsden, James
     See Creasey, John
Marsh, Edith Ngaio
     See Marsh, Ngaio
Marsh, Edward 1872-1953 .... **TCLC 99**
Marsh, Ngaio 1895-1982 .... **CLC 7, 53**
     See also CA 9-12R; CANR 6, 58; CMW 4;
     CN 1, 2, 3; CPW; DAM POP; DLB 77;
     MSW; MTCW 1, 2; RGEL 2; TEA
Marshall, Alan
     See Westlake, Donald E.
Marshall, Allen
     See Westlake, Donald E.
Marshall, Garry 1934- .... **CLC 17**
     See also AAYA 3; CA 111; SATA 60
Marshall, Paule 1929- .... **BLC 1:3, 2:3; CLC
     27, 72, 253; SSC 3**
     See also AFAW 1, 2; AMWS 11; BPFB 2;
     BW 2, 3; CA 77-80; CANR 25, 73, 129;
     CN 1, 2, 3, 4, 5, 6, 7; DA3; DAM MULT;
     DLB 33, 157, 227; EWL 3; LATS 1:2;
     MAL 5; MTCW 1, 2; MTFW 2005;
     RGAL 4; SSFS 15
Marshallik
     See Zangwill, Israel
Marsilius of Inghen c.
     1340-1396 .... **CMLC 106**
Marsten, Richard
     See Hunter, Evan
Marston, John 1576-1634 ...... **DC 37; LC 33,
     172**
     See also BRW 2; DAM DRAM; DLB 58,
     172; RGEL 2
Martel, Yann 1963- .... **CLC 192**
     See also AAYA 67; CA 146; CANR 114;
     DLB 326, 334; LNFS 2; MTFW 2005;
     NFS 27

Martens, Adolphe-Adhemar
     See Ghelderode, Michel de
Martha, Henry
     See Harris, Mark
Marti, Jose 1853-1895 ..... **HLC 2; NCLC 63;
     PC 76**
     See also DAM MULT; DLB 290; HW 2;
     LAW; RGWL 2, 3; WLIT 1
Martial c. 40-c. 104 .... **CMLC 35; PC 10**
     See also AW 2; CDWLB 1; DLB 211;
     RGWL 2, 3
Martin, Ken
     See Hubbard, L. Ron
Martin, Richard
     See Creasey, John
Martin, Steve 1945- .... **CLC 30, 217**
     See also AAYA 53; CA 97-100; CANR 30,
     100, 140, 195; DFS 19; MTCW 1; MTFW
     2005
Martin, Valerie 1948- .... **CLC 89**
     See also BEST 90:2; CA 85-88; CANR 49,
     89, 165, 200
Martin, Violet Florence 1862-1915 .. **SSC 56;
     TCLC 51**
Martin, Webber
     See Silverberg, Robert
Martindale, Patrick Victor
     See White, Patrick
Martin du Gard, Roger
     1881-1958 .... **TCLC 24**
     See also CA 118; CANR 94; DLB 65, 331;
     EWL 3; GFL 1789 to the Present; RGWL
     2, 3
Martineau, Harriet 1802-1876 ...... **NCLC 26,
     137**
     See also BRWS 15; DLB 21, 55, 159, 163,
     166, 190; FW; RGEL 2; YABC 2
Martines, Julia
     See O'Faolain, Julia
Martinez, Enrique Gonzalez
     See Gonzalez Martinez, Enrique
Martinez, Jacinto Benavente y
     See Benavente, Jacinto
Martinez de la Rosa, Francisco de Paula
     1787-1862 .... **NCLC 102**
     See also TWA
Martinez Ruiz, Jose 1873-1967 .... **CLC 11**
     See also CA 93-96; DLB 322; EW 3; EWL
     3; HW 1
Martinez Sierra, Gregorio
     See Martinez Sierra, Maria
Martinez Sierra, Gregorio
     1881-1947 .... **TCLC 6**
     See also CA 115; EWL 3
Martinez Sierra, Maria 1874-1974 .. **TCLC 6**
     See also CA 250; 115; EWL 3
Martinsen, Martin
     See Follett, Ken
Martinson, Harry (Edmund)
     1904-1978 .... **CLC 14**
     See also CA 77-80; CANR 34, 130; DLB
     259, 331; EWL 3
Marti y Perez, Jose Julian
     See Marti, Jose
Martyn, Edward 1859-1923 .... **TCLC 131**
     See also CA 179; DLB 10; RGEL 2
Marut, Ret
     See Traven, B.
Marut, Robert
     See Traven, B.
Marvell, Andrew 1621-1678 .... **LC 4, 43; PC
     10, 86; WLC 4**
     See also BRW 2; BRWR 2; CDBLB 1660-
     1789; DA; DAB; DAC; DAM MST,
     POET; DLB 131; EXPP; PFS 5; RGEL 2;
     TEA; WP
Marx, Karl 1818-1883 .... **NCLC 17, 114**
     See also DLB 129; LATS 1:1; TWA

McCabe, Patrick 1955- .... **CLC 133**
See also BRWS 9; CA 130; CANR 50, 90, 168, 202; CN 6, 7; DLB 194
McCaffrey, Anne 1926- .... **CLC 17**
See also AAYA 6, 34; AITN 2; BEST 89:2; BPFB 2; BYA 5; CA 25-28R, 227; CAAE 227; CANR 15, 35, 55, 96, 169; CLR 49, 130; CPW; DA3; DAM NOV, POP; DLB 8; JRDA; MAICYA 1, 2; MTCW 1, 2; MTFW 2005; SAAS 11; SATA 8, 70, 116, 152; SATA-Essay 152; SFW 4; SUFW 2; WYA; YAW
McCaffrey, Anne Inez
See McCaffrey, Anne
McCall, Nathan 1955(?)- .... **CLC 86**
See also AAYA 59; BW 3; CA 146; CANR 88, 186
McCall Smith, Alexander
See Smith, Alexander McCall
McCann, Arthur
See Campbell, John W(ood, Jr.)
McCann, Edson
See Pohl, Frederik
McCarthy, Charles
See McCarthy, Cormac
McCarthy, Charles, Jr.
See McCarthy, Cormac
McCarthy, Cormac 1933- .... **CLC 4, 57, 101, 204**
See also AAYA 41; AMWS 8; BPFB 2; CA 13-16R; CANR 10, 42, 69, 101, 161, 171; CN 6, 7; CPW; CSW; DA3; DAM POP; DLB 6, 143, 256; EWL 3; LATS 1:2; LNFS 3; MAL 5; MTCW 2; MTFW 2005; TCLE 1:2; TCWW 2
McCarthy, Mary 1912-1989 ...... **CLC 1, 3, 5, 14, 24, 39, 59; SSC 24**
See also AMW; BPFB 2; CA 5-8R; 129; CANR 16, 50, 64; CN 1, 2, 3, 4; DA3; DLB 2; DLBY 1981; EWL 3; FW; INT CANR-16; MAL 5; MBL; MTCW 1, 2; MTFW 2005; RGAL 4; TUS
McCarthy, Mary Therese
See McCarthy, Mary
McCartney, James Paul
See McCartney, Paul
McCartney, Paul 1942- .... **CLC 12, 35**
See also CA 146; CANR 111
McCauley, Stephen (D.) 1955- .... **CLC 50**
See also CA 141
McClaren, Peter CLC 70
McClure, Michael (Thomas) 1932- ... **CLC 6, 10**
See also BG 1:3; CA 21-24R; CAD; CANR 17, 46, 77, 131; CD 5, 6; CP 1, 2, 3, 4, 5, 6, 7; DLB 16; WP
McCorkle, Jill (Collins) 1958- .... **CLC 51**
See also CA 121; CANR 113; CSW; DLB 234; DLBY 1987; SSFS 24
McCourt, Francis
See McCourt, Frank
McCourt, Frank 1930-2009 .... **CLC 109**
See also AAYA 61; AMWS 12; CA 157; 288; CANR 97, 138; MTFW 2005; NCFS 1
McCourt, James 1941- .... **CLC 5**
See also CA 57-60; CANR 98, 152, 186
McCourt, Malachy 1931- .... **CLC 119**
See also SATA 126
McCoy, Edmund
See Gardner, John
McCoy, Horace (Stanley) 1897-1955 .... **TCLC 28**
See also AMWS 13; CA 108; 155; CMW 4; DLB 9
McCrae, John 1872-1918 .... **TCLC 12**
See also CA 109; DLB 92; PFS 5
McCreigh, James
See Pohl, Frederik

McCullers, Carson 1917-1967 . **CLC 1, 4, 10, 12, 48, 100; DC 35; SSC 9, 24, 99; TCLC 155; WLC 4**
See also AAYA 21; AMW; AMWC 2; BPFB 2; CA 5-8R; 25-28R; CABS 1, 3; CANR 18, 132; CDALB 1941-1968; DA; DA3; DAB; DAC; DAM MST, NOV; DFS 5, 18; DLB 2, 7, 173, 228; EWL 3; EXPS; FW; GLL 1; LAIT 3, 4; MAL 5; MBL; MTCW 1, 2; MTFW 2005; NFS 6, 13; RGAL 4; RGSF 2; SATA 27; SSFS 5; TUS; YAW
McCullers, Lula Carson Smith
See McCullers, Carson
McCulloch, John Tyler
See Burroughs, Edgar Rice
McCullough, Colleen 1937- ...... **CLC 27, 107**
See also AAYA 36; BPFB 2; CA 81-84; CANR 17, 46, 67, 98, 139; CPW; DA3; DAM NOV, POP; MTCW 1, 2; MTFW 2005; RHW
McCunn, Ruthanne Lum 1946- .... **AAL**
See also CA 119; CANR 43, 96; DLB 312; LAIT 2; SATA 63
McDermott, Alice 1953- .... **CLC 90**
See also AMWS 18; CA 109; CANR 40, 90, 126, 181; CN 7; DLB 292; MTFW 2005; NFS 23
McElroy, Joseph 1930- .... **CLC 5, 47**
See also CA 17-20R; CANR 149; CN 3, 4, 5, 6, 7
McElroy, Joseph Prince
See McElroy, Joseph
McEwan, Ian 1948- ... **CLC 13, 66, 169, 269; SSC 106**
See also BEST 90:4; BRWS 4; CA 61-64; CANR 14, 41, 69, 87, 132, 179; CN 3, 4, 5, 6, 7; DAM NOV; DLB 14, 194, 319, 326; HGG; MTCW 1, 2; MTFW 2005; RGSF 2; SUFW 2; TEA
McEwan, Ian Russell
See McEwan, Ian
McFadden, David 1940- .... **CLC 48**
See also CA 104; CP 1, 2, 3, 4, 5, 6, 7; DLB 60; INT CA-104
McFarland, Dennis 1950- .... **CLC 65**
See also CA 165; CANR 110, 179
McGahern, John 1934-2006 .... **CLC 5, 9, 48, 156; SSC 17**
See also CA 17-20R; 249; CANR 29, 68, 113; CN 1, 2, 3, 4, 5, 6, 7; DLB 14, 231, 319; MTCW 1
McGinley, Patrick (Anthony) 1937- . **CLC 41**
See also CA 120; 127; CANR 56; INT CA-127
McGinley, Phyllis 1905-1978 .... **CLC 14**
See also CA 9-12R; 77-80; CANR 19; CP 1, 2; CWRI 5; DLB 11, 48; MAL 5; PFS 9, 13; SATA 2, 44; SATA-Obit 24
McGinniss, Joe 1942- .... **CLC 32**
See also AITN 2; BEST 89:2; CA 25-28R; CANR 26, 70, 152; CPW; DLB 185; INT CANR-26
McGivern, Maureen Daly
See Daly, Maureen
McGivern, Maureen Patricia Daly
See Daly, Maureen
McGrath, Patrick 1950- .... **CLC 55**
See also CA 136; CANR 65, 148, 190; CN 5, 6, 7; DLB 231; HGG; SUFW 2
McGrath, Thomas (Matthew) 1916-1990 .... **CLC 28, 59**
See also AMWS 10; CA 9-12R; 132; CANR 6, 33, 95; CP 1, 2, 3, 4, 5; DAM POET; MAL 5; MTCW 1; SATA 41; SATA-Obit 66

McGuane, Thomas 1939- .. **CLC 3, 7, 18, 45, 127**
See also AITN 2; BPFB 2; CA 49-52; CANR 5, 24, 49, 94, 164; CN 2, 3, 4, 5, 6, 7; DLB 2, 212; DLBY 1980; EWL 3; INT CANR-24; MAL 5; MTCW 1; MTFW 2005; TCWW 1, 2
McGuane, Thomas Francis III
See McGuane, Thomas
McGuckian, Medbh 1950- .... **CLC 48, 174; PC 27**
See also BRWS 5; CA 143; CP 4, 5, 6, 7; CWP; DAM POET; DLB 40
McHale, Tom 1942(?)-1982 .... **CLC 3, 5**
See also AITN 1; CA 77-80; 106; CN 1, 2, 3
McHugh, Heather 1948- .... **PC 61**
See also CA 69-72; CANR 11, 28, 55, 92; CP 4, 5, 6, 7; CWP; PFS 24
McIlvanney, William 1936- .... **CLC 42**
See also CA 25-28R; CANR 61; CMW 4; DLB 14, 207
McIlwraith, Maureen Mollie Hunter
See Hunter, Mollie
McInerney, Jay 1955- .... **CLC 34, 112**
See also AAYA 18; BPFB 2; CA 116; 123; CANR 45, 68, 116, 176; CN 5, 6, 7; CPW; DA3; DAM POP; DLB 292; INT CANR-123; MAL 5; MTCW 2; MTFW 2005
McIntyre, Vonda N. 1948- .... **CLC 18**
See also CA 81-84; CANR 17, 34, 69; MTCW 1; SFW 4; YAW
McIntyre, Vonda Neel
See McIntyre, Vonda N.
McKay, Claude 1889-1948 ...... **BLC 1:3; HR 1:3; PC 2; TCLC 7, 41; WLC 4**
See also AFAW 1, 2; AMWS 10; BW 1, 3; CA 104; 124; CANR 73; DA; DAB; DAC; DAM MST, MULT, NOV, POET; DLB 4, 45, 51, 117; EWL 3; EXPP; GLL 2; LAIT 3; LMFS 2; MAL 5; MTCW 1, 2; MTFW 2005; PAB; PFS 4; RGAL 4; TUS; WP
McKay, Festus Claudius
See McKay, Claude
McKuen, Rod 1933- .... **CLC 1, 3**
See also AITN 1; CA 41-44R; CANR 40; CP 1
McLoughlin, R. B.
See Mencken, H. L.
McLuhan, (Herbert) Marshall 1911-1980 .... **CLC 37, 83**
See also CA 9-12R; 102; CANR 12, 34, 61; DLB 88; INT CANR-12; MTCW 1, 2; MTFW 2005
McMahon, Pat
See Hoch, Edward D.
McManus, Declan Patrick Aloysius
See Costello, Elvis
McMillan, Terry 1951- .. **BLCS; CLC 50, 61, 112**
See also AAYA 21; AMWS 13; BPFB 2; BW 2, 3; CA 140; CANR 60, 104, 131; CN 7; CPW; DA3; DAM MULT, NOV, POP; MAL 5; MTCW 2; MTFW 2005; RGAL 4; YAW
McMillan, Terry L.
See McMillan, Terry
McMurtry, Larry 1936- .... **CLC 2, 3, 7, 11, 27, 44, 127, 250**
See also AAYA 15; AITN 2; AMWS 5; BEST 89:2; BPFB 2; CA 5-8R; CANR 19, 43, 64, 103, 170; CDALB 1968-1988; CN 2, 3, 4, 5, 6, 7; CPW; CSW; DA3; DAM NOV, POP; DLB 2, 143, 256; DLBY 1980, 1987; EWL 3; MAL 5; MTCW 1, 2; MTFW 2005; RGAL 4; TCWW 1, 2
McMurtry, Larry Jeff
See McMurtry, Larry

McNally, Terrence 1939- ... **CLC 4, 7, 41, 91, 252; DC 27**
See also AAYA 62; AMWS 13; CA 45-48; CAD; CANR 2, 56, 116; CD 5, 6; DA3; DAM DRAM; DFS 16, 19; DLB 7, 249; EWL 3; GLL 1; MTCW 2; MTFW 2005

McNally, Thomas Michael
See McNally, T.M.

McNally, T.M. 1961- .... **CLC 82**
See also CA 246

McNamer, Deirdre 1950- .... **CLC 70**
See also CA 188; CANR 163, 200

McNeal, Tom CLC 119
See also CA 252; CANR 185; SATA 194

McNeile, Herman Cyril
1888-1937 .... **TCLC 44**
See also CA 184; CMW 4; DLB 77

McNickle, D'Arcy 1904-1977 .... **CLC 89; NNAL**
See also CA 9-12R; 85-88; CANR 5, 45; DAM MULT; DLB 175, 212; RGAL 4; SATA-Obit 22; TCWW 1, 2

McNickle, William D'Arcy
See McNickle, D'Arcy

McPhee, John 1931- .... **CLC 36**
See also AAYA 61; AMWS 3; ANW; BEST 90:1; CA 65-68; CANR 20, 46, 64, 69, 121, 165; CPW; DLB 185, 275; MTCW 1, 2; MTFW 2005; TUS

McPhee, John Angus
See McPhee, John

McPherson, James Alan, Jr.
See McPherson, James Alan

McPherson, James Alan 1943- . **BLCS; CLC 19, 77; SSC 95**
See also BW 1, 3; CA 25-28R, 273; CAAE 273; CAAS 17; CANR 24, 74, 140; CN 3, 4, 5, 6; CSW; DLB 38, 244; EWL 3; MTCW 1, 2; MTFW 2005; RGAL 4; RGSF 2; SSFS 23

McPherson, William (Alexander)
1933- .... **CLC 34**
See also CA 69-72; CANR 28; INT CANR-28

McTaggart, J. McT. Ellis
See McTaggart, John McTaggart Ellis

McTaggart, John McTaggart Ellis
1866-1925 .... **TCLC 105**
See also CA 120; DLB 262

Mda, Zakes 1948- .... **BLC 2:3; CLC 262**
See also BRWS 15; CA 205; CANR 151, 185; CD 5, 6; DLB 225

Mda, Zanemvula
See Mda, Zakes

Mda, Zanemvula Kizito Gatyeni
See Mda, Zakes

Mead, George Herbert 1863-1931 . **TCLC 89**
See also CA 212; DLB 270

Mead, Margaret 1901-1978 .... **CLC 37**
See also AITN 1; CA 1-4R; 81-84; CANR 4; DA3; FW; MTCW 1, 2; SATA-Obit 20

Meaker, M. J.
See Meaker, Marijane

Meaker, Marijane 1927- .... **CLC 12, 35**
See also AAYA 2, 23, 82; BYA 1, 7, 8; CA 107; CANR 37, 63, 145, 180; CLR 29; GLL 2; INT CA-107; JRDA; MAICYA 1, 2; MAICYAS 1; MTCW 1; SAAS 1; SATA 20, 61, 99, 160; SATA-Essay 111; WYA; YAW

Meaker, Marijane Agnes
See Meaker, Marijane

Mechthild von Magdeburg c. 1207-c. 1282 .... **CMLC 91**
See also DLB 138

Medoff, Mark (Howard) 1940- .... **CLC 6, 23**
See also AITN 1; CA 53-56; CAD; CANR 5; CD 5, 6; DAM DRAM; DFS 4; DLB 7; INT CANR-5

Medvedev, P. N.
See Bakhtin, Mikhail Mikhailovich

Meged, Aharon
See Megged, Aharon

Meged, Aron
See Megged, Aharon

Megged, Aharon 1920- .... **CLC 9**
See also CA 49-52; CAAS 13; CANR 1, 140; EWL 3; RGHL

Mehta, Deepa 1950- .... **CLC 208**

Mehta, Gita 1943- .... **CLC 179**
See also CA 225; CN 7; DNFS 2

Mehta, Ved 1934- .... **CLC 37**
See also CA 1-4R, 212; CAAE 212; CANR 2, 23, 69; DLB 323; MTCW 1; MTFW 2005

Melanchthon, Philipp 1497-1560 .... **LC 90**
See also DLB 179

Melanter
See Blackmore, R(ichard) D(oddridge)

Meleager c. 140B.C.-c. 70B.C. ...... **CMLC 53**

Melies, Georges 1861-1938 .... **TCLC 81**

Melikow, Loris
See Hofmannsthal, Hugo von

Melmoth, Sebastian
See Wilde, Oscar

Melo Neto, Joao Cabral de
See Cabral de Melo Neto, Joao

Meltzer, Milton 1915-2009 .... **CLC 26**
See also AAYA 8, 45; BYA 2, 6; CA 13-16R; 290; CANR 38, 92, 107, 192; CLR 13; DLB 61; JRDA; MAICYA 1, 2; SAAS 1; SATA 1, 50, 80, 128, 201; SATA-Essay 124; WYA; YAW

Melville, Herman 1819-1891 ..... **NCLC 3, 12, 29, 45, 49, 91, 93, 123, 157, 181, 193, 221; PC 82; SSC 1, 17, 46, 95; WLC 4**
See also AAYA 25; AMW; AMWR 1; CDALB 1640-1865; DA; DA3; DAB; DAC; DAM MST, NOV; DLB 3, 74, 250, 254, 349; EXPN; EXPS; GL 3; LAIT 1, 2; NFS 7, 9; RGAL 4; RGSF 2; SATA 59; SSFS 3; TUS

Members, Mark
See Powell, Anthony

Membreno, Alejandro CLC 59

Menand, Louis 1952- .... **CLC 208**
See also CA 200

Menander c. 342B.C.-c. 293B.C. .... **CMLC 9, 51, 101; DC 3**
See also AW 1; CDWLB 1; DAM DRAM; DLB 176; LMFS 1; RGWL 2, 3

Menchu, Rigoberta 1959- .. **CLC 160; HLCS 2**
See also CA 175; CANR 135; DNFS 1; WLIT 1

Mencken, H. L. 1880-1956 .... **TCLC 13, 18**
See also AMW; CA 105; 125; CDALB 1917-1929; DLB 11, 29, 63, 137, 222; EWL 3; MAL 5; MTCW 1, 2; MTFW 2005; NCFS 4; RGAL 4; TUS

Mencken, Henry Louis
See Mencken, H. L.

Mendelsohn, Jane 1965- .... **CLC 99**
See also CA 154; CANR 94

Mendelssohn, Moses 1729-1786 .... **LC 142**
See also DLB 97

Mendoza, Inigo Lopez de
See Santillana, Inigo Lopez de Mendoza, Marques de

Menton, Francisco de
See Chin, Frank

Mercer, David 1928-1980 .... **CLC 5**
See also CA 9-12R; 102; CANR 23; CBD; DAM DRAM; DLB 13, 310; MTCW 1; RGEL 2

Merchant, Paul
See Ellison, Harlan

Meredith, George 1828-1909 .. **PC 60; TCLC 17, 43**
See also CA 117; 153; CANR 80; CDBLB 1832-1890; DAM POET; DLB 18, 35, 57, 159; RGEL 2; TEA

Meredith, William 1919-2007 ...... **CLC 4, 13, 22, 55; PC 28**
See also CA 9-12R; 260; CAAS 14; CANR 6, 40, 129; CP 1, 2, 3, 4, 5, 6, 7; DAM POET; DLB 5; MAL 5

Meredith, William Morris
See Meredith, William

Merezhkovsky, Dmitrii Sergeevich
See Merezhkovsky, Dmitry Sergeyevich

Merezhkovsky, Dmitry Sergeevich
See Merezhkovsky, Dmitry Sergeyevich

Merezhkovsky, Dmitry Sergeyevich
1865-1941 .... **TCLC 29**
See also CA 169; DLB 295; EWL 3

Merezhkovsky, Zinaida
See Gippius, Zinaida

Merimee, Prosper 1803-1870 . **DC 33; NCLC 6, 65; SSC 7, 77**
See also DLB 119, 192; EW 6; EXPS; GFL 1789 to the Present; RGSF 2; RGWL 2, 3; SSFS 8; SUFW

Merkin, Daphne 1954- .... **CLC 44**
See also CA 123

Merleau-Ponty, Maurice
1908-1961 .... **TCLC 156**
See also CA 114; 89-92; DLB 296; GFL 1789 to the Present

Merlin, Arthur
See Blish, James

Mernissi, Fatima 1940- .... **CLC 171**
See also CA 152; DLB 346; FW

Merrill, James 1926-1995 ...... **CLC 2, 3, 6, 8, 13, 18, 34, 91; PC 28; TCLC 173**
See also AMWS 3; CA 13-16R; 147; CANR 10, 49, 63, 108; CP 1, 2, 3, 4; DA3; DAM POET; DLB 5, 165; DLBY 1985; EWL 3; INT CANR-10; MAL 5; MTCW 1, 2; MTFW 2005; PAB; PFS 23; RGAL 4

Merrill, James Ingram
See Merrill, James

Merriman, Alex
See Silverberg, Robert

Merriman, Brian 1747-1805 .... **NCLC 70**

Merritt, E. B.
See Waddington, Miriam

Merton, Thomas 1915-1968 ..... **CLC 1, 3, 11, 34, 83; PC 10**
See also AAYA 61; AMWS 8; CA 5-8R; 25-28R; CANR 22, 53, 111, 131; DA3; DLB 48; DLBY 1981; MAL 5; MTCW 1, 2; MTFW 2005

Merton, Thomas James
See Merton, Thomas

Merwin, William Stanley
See Merwin, W.S.

Merwin, W.S. 1927- ..... **CLC 1, 2, 3, 5, 8, 13, 18, 45, 88; PC 45**
See also AMWS 3; CA 13-16R; CANR 15, 51, 112, 140; CP 1, 2, 3, 4, 5, 6, 7; DA3; DAM POET; DLB 5, 169, 342; EWL 3; INT CANR-15; MAL 5; MTCW 1, 2; MTFW 2005; PAB; PFS 5, 15; RGAL 4

Metastasio, Pietro 1698-1782 .... **LC 115**
See also RGWL 2, 3

Metcalf, John 1938- .... **CLC 37; SSC 43**
See also CA 113; CN 4, 5, 6, 7; DLB 60; RGSF 2; TWA

Metcalf, Suzanne
See Baum, L. Frank

Mew, Charlotte (Mary) 1870-1928 .. **TCLC 8**
See also CA 105; 189; DLB 19, 135; RGEL 2

Mister X
See Hoch, Edward D.

Mistral, Frederic 1830-1914 .... **TCLC 51**
See also CA 122; 213; DLB 331; GFL 1789
to the Present

Mistral, Gabriela 1899-1957 .... **HLC 2; PC
32; TCLC 2**
See also BW 2; CA 104; 131; CANR 81;
DAM MULT; DLB 283, 331; DNFS;
EWL 3; HW 1, 2; LAW; MTCW 1, 2;
MTFW 2005; RGWL 2, 3; WP

Mistry, Rohinton 1952- ... **CLC 71, 196, 281;
SSC 73**
See also BRWS 10; CA 141; CANR 86,
114; CCA 1; CN 6, 7; DAC; DLB 334;
SSFS 6

Mitchell, Clyde
See Ellison, Harlan; Silverberg, Robert

Mitchell, Emerson Blackhorse Barney
1945- .... **NNAL**
See also CA 45-48

Mitchell, James Leslie 1901-1935 .... **TCLC 4**
See also BRWS 14; CA 104; 188; DLB 15;
RGEL 2

Mitchell, Joni 1943- .... **CLC 12**
See also CA 112; CCA 1

Mitchell, Joseph (Quincy)
1908-1996 .... **CLC 98**
See also CA 77-80; 152; CANR 69; CN 1,
2, 3, 4, 5, 6; CSW; DLB 185; DLBY 1996

Mitchell, Margaret 1900-1949 .... **TCLC 11,
170**
See also AAYA 23; BPFB 2; BYA 1; CA
109; 125; CANR 55, 94; CDALBS; DA3;
DAM NOV, POP; DLB 9; LAIT 2; MAL
5; MTCW 1, 2; MTFW 2005; NFS 9;
RGAL 4; RHW; TUS; WYAS 1; YAW

Mitchell, Margaret Munnerlyn
See Mitchell, Margaret

Mitchell, Peggy
See Mitchell, Margaret

Mitchell, S(ilas) Weir 1829-1914 .... **TCLC 36**
See also CA 165; DLB 202; RGAL 4

Mitchell, W(illiam) O(rmond)
1914-1998 .... **CLC 25**
See also CA 77-80; 165; CANR 15, 43; CN
1, 2, 3, 4, 5, 6; DAC; DAM MST; DLB
88; TCLE 1:2

Mitchell, William (Lendrum)
1879-1936 .... **TCLC 81**
See also CA 213

Mitford, Mary Russell 1787-1855 ... **NCLC 4**
See also DLB 110, 116; RGEL 2

Mitford, Nancy 1904-1973 .... **CLC 44**
See also BRWS 10; CA 9-12R; CN 1; DLB
191; RGEL 2

Miyamoto, (Chujo) Yuriko
1899-1951 .... **TCLC 37**
See also CA 170, 174; DLB 180

Miyamoto Yuriko
See Miyamoto, (Chujo) Yuriko

Miyazaki, Kenji 1896-1933 .... **TCLC 76**
See also CA 157; EWL 3; RGWL 3

Miyazawa Kenji
See Miyazawa, Kenji

Mizoguchi, Kenji 1898-1956 .... **TCLC 72**
See also CA 167

Mo, Timothy (Peter) 1950- .... **CLC 46, 134**
See also CA 117; CANR 128; CN 5, 6, 7;
DLB 194; MTCW 1; WLIT 4; WWE 1

Mo, Yan
See Yan, Mo

Moberg, Carl Arthur
See Moberg, Vilhelm

Moberg, Vilhelm 1898-1973 .... **TCLC 224**
See also CA 97-100; 45-48; CANR 135;
DLB 259; EW 11; EWL 3

Modarressi, Taghi (M.) 1931-1997 ... **CLC 44**
See also CA 121; 134; INT CA-134

Modiano, Patrick (Jean) 1945- .... **CLC 18,
218**
See also CA 85-88; CANR 17, 40, 115;
CWW 2; DLB 83, 299; EWL 3; RGHL

Mofolo, Thomas 1875(?)-1948 .... **BLC 1:3;
TCLC 22**
See also AFW; CA 121; 153; CANR 83;
DAM MULT; DLB 225; EWL 3; MTCW
2; MTFW 2005; WLIT 2

Mofolo, Thomas Mokopu
See Mofolo, Thomas

Mohr, Nicholasa 1938- .... **CLC 12; HLC 2**
See also AAYA 8, 46; CA 49-52; CANR 1,
32, 64; CLR 22; DAM MULT; DLB 145;
HW 1, 2; JRDA; LAIT 5; LLW; MAICYA
2; MAICYAS 1; RGAL 4; SAAS 8; SATA
8, 97; SATA-Essay 113; WYA; YAW

Moi, Toril 1953- .... **CLC 172**
See also CA 154; CANR 102; FW

Mojtabai, A(nn) G(race) 1938- ..... **CLC 5, 9,
15, 29**
See also CA 85-88; CANR 88

Moliere 1622-1673 ..... **DC 13; LC 10, 28, 64,
125, 127; WLC 4**
See also DA; DA3; DAB; DAC; DAM
DRAM, MST; DFS 13, 18, 20; DLB 268;
EW 3; GFL Beginnings to 1789; LATS
1:1; RGWL 2, 3; TWA

Molin, Charles
See Mayne, William (James Carter)

Molnar, Ferenc 1878-1952 .... **TCLC 20**
See also CA 109; 153; CANR 83; CDWLB
4; DAM DRAM; DLB 215; EWL 3;
RGWL 2, 3

Momaday, N. Scott 1934- ...... **CLC 2, 19, 85,
95, 160; NNAL; PC 25; WLCS**
See also AAYA 11, 64; AMWS 4; ANW;
BPFB 2; BYA 12; CA 25-28R; CANR 14,
34, 68, 134; CDALBS; CN 2, 3, 4, 5, 6,
7; CPW; DA; DA3; DAB; DAC; DAM
MST, MULT, NOV, POP; DLB 143, 175,
256; EWL 3; EXPP; INT CANR-14;
LAIT 4; LATS 1:2; MAL 5; MTCW 1, 2;
MTFW 2005; NFS 10; PFS 2, 11; RGAL
4; SATA 48; SATA-Brief 30; TCWW 1,
2; WP; YAW

Momaday, Navarre Scott
See Momaday, N. Scott

Momala, Ville i
See Moberg, Vilhelm

Monette, Paul 1945-1995 .... **CLC 82**
See also AMWS 10; CA 139; 147; CN 6;
DLB 350; GLL 1

Monroe, Harriet 1860-1936 .... **TCLC 12**
See also CA 109; 204; DLB 54, 91

Monroe, Lyle
See Heinlein, Robert A.

Montagu, Elizabeth 1720-1800 .... **NCLC 7,
117**
See also FW

Montagu, Mary (Pierrepont) Wortley
1689-1762 .... **LC 9, 57; PC 16**
See also DLB 95, 101; FL 1:1; RGEL 2

Montagu, W. H.
See Coleridge, Samuel Taylor

Montague, John (Patrick) 1929- ..... **CLC 13,
46**
See also BRWS 15; CA 9-12R; CANR 9,
69, 121; CP 1, 2, 3, 4, 5, 6, 7; DLB 40;
EWL 3; MTCW 1; PFS 12; RGEL 2;
TCLE 1:2

Montaigne, Michel de 1533-1592 .... **LC 8,
105; WLC 4**
See also DA; DAB; DAC; DAM MST;
DLB 327; EW 2; GFL Beginnings to
1789; LMFS 1; RGWL 2, 3; TWA

Montaigne, Michel Eyquem de
See Montaigne, Michel de

Montale, Eugenio 1896-1981 ... **CLC 7, 9, 18;
PC 13**
See also CA 17-20R; 104; CANR 30; DLB
114, 331; EW 11; EWL 3; MTCW 1; PFS
22; RGWL 2, 3; TWA; WLIT 7

Montesquieu, Charles-Louis de Secondat
1689-1755 .... **LC 7, 69**
See also DLB 314; EW 3; GFL Beginnings
to 1789; TWA

Montessori, Maria 1870-1952 ...... **TCLC 103**
See also CA 115; 147

Montgomery, Bruce 1921(?)-1978 .... **CLC 22**
See also CA 179; 104; CMW 4; DLB 87;
MSW

Montgomery, L. M. 1874-1942 ..... **TCLC 51,
140**
See also AAYA 12; BYA 1; CA 108; 137;
CLR 8, 91, 145; DA3; DAC; DAM MST;
DLB 92; DLBD 14; JRDA; MAICYA 1,
2; MTCW 2; MTFW 2005; RGEL 2;
SATA 100; TWA; WCH; WYA; YABC 1

Montgomery, Lucy Maud
See Montgomery, L. M.

Montgomery, Marion, Jr. 1925- .... **CLC 7**
See also AITN 1; CA 1-4R; CANR 3, 48,
162; CSW; DLB 6

Montgomery, Marion H. 1925-
See Montgomery, Marion, Jr.

Montgomery, Max
See Davenport, Guy (Mattison, Jr.)

Montgomery, Robert Bruce
See Montgomery, Bruce

Montherlant, Henry de 1896-1972 .... **CLC 8,
19**
See also CA 85-88; 37-40R; DAM DRAM;
DLB 72, 321; EW 11; EWL 3; GFL 1789
to the Present; MTCW 1

Montherlant, Henry Milon de
See Montherlant, Henry de

Monty Python
See Chapman, Graham; Cleese, John
(Marwood); Gilliam, Terry; Idle, Eric;
Jones, Terence Graham Parry; Palin,
Michael

Moodie, Susanna (Strickland)
1803-1885 .... **NCLC 14, 113**
See also DLB 99

Moody, Hiram
See Moody, Rick

Moody, Hiram F. III
See Moody, Rick

Moody, Minerva
See Alcott, Louisa May

Moody, Rick 1961- .... **CLC 147**
See also CA 138; CANR 64, 112, 179;
MTFW 2005

Moody, William Vaughan
1869-1910 .... **TCLC 105**
See also CA 110; 178; DLB 7, 54; MAL 5;
RGAL 4

Mooney, Edward 1951- .... **CLC 25**
See also CA 130

Mooney, Ted
See Mooney, Edward

Moorcock, Michael 1939- ...... **CLC 5, 27, 58,
236**
See also AAYA 26; CA 45-48; CAAS 5;
CANR 2, 17, 38, 64, 122; CN 5, 6, 7;
DLB 14, 231, 261, 319; FANT; MTCW 1,
2; MTFW 2005; SATA 93, 166; SCFW 1,
2; SFW 4; SUFW 1, 2

Moorcock, Michael John
See Moorcock, Michael

Moorcock, Michael John
See Moorcock, Michael

Moore, Al
See Moore, Alan

Porter, Gene Stratton
See Stratton-Porter, Gene

Porter, Geneva Grace
See Stratton-Porter, Gene

Porter, Katherine Anne 1890-1980 ... **CLC 1, 3, 7, 10, 13, 15, 27, 101; SSC 4, 31, 43, 108; TCLC 233**
See also AAYA 42; AITN 2; AMW; BPFB 3; CA 1-4R; 101; CANR 1, 65; CDALBS; CN 1, 2; DA; DA3; DAB; DAC; DAM MST, NOV; DLB 4, 9, 102; DLBD 12; DLBY 1980; EWL 3; EXPS; LAIT 3; MAL 5; MBL; MTCW 1, 2; MTFW 2005; NFS 14; RGAL 4; RGSF 2; SATA 39; SATA-Obit 23; SSFS 1, 8, 11, 16, 23; TCWW 2; TUS

Porter, Peter (Neville Frederick)
1929- .... **CLC 5, 13, 33**
See also CA 85-88; CP 1, 2, 3, 4, 5, 6, 7; DLB 40, 289; WWE 1

Porter, R. E.
See Hoch, Edward D.

Porter, William Sydney
See Henry, O.

Portillo (y Pacheco), Jose Lopez
See Lopez Portillo (y Pacheco), Jose

Portillo Trambley, Estela
1927-1998 .... **HLC 2; TCLC 163**
See also CA 77-80; CANR 32; DAM MULT; DLB 209; HW 1; RGAL 4

Posey, Alexander (Lawrence)
1873-1908 .... **NNAL**
See also CA 144; CANR 80; DAM MULT; DLB 175

Posse, Abel CLC 70, 273
See also CA 252

Post, Melville Davisson
1869-1930 .... **TCLC 39**
See also CA 110; 202; CMW 4

Postman, Neil 1931(?)-2003 .... **CLC 244**
See also CA 102; 221

Potok, Chaim 1929-2002 ... **CLC 2, 7, 14, 26, 112**
See also AAYA 15, 50; AITN 1, 2; BPFB 3; BYA 1; CA 17-20R; 208; CANR 19, 35, 64, 98; CLR 92; CN 4, 5, 6; DA3; DAM NOV; DLB 28, 152; EXPN; INT CANR-19; LAIT 4; MTCW 1, 2; MTFW 2005; NFS 4; RGHL; SATA 33, 106; SATA-Obit 134; TUS; YAW

Potok, Herbert Harold
See Potok, Chaim

Potok, Herman Harold
See Potok, Chaim

Potter, Dennis (Christopher George)
1935-1994 .... **CLC 58, 86, 123**
See also BRWS 10; CA 107; 145; CANR 33, 61; CBD; DLB 233; MTCW 1

Pound, Ezra 1885-1972 . **CLC 1, 2, 3, 4, 5, 7, 10, 13, 18, 34, 48, 50, 112; PC 4, 95; WLC 5**
See also AAYA 47; AMW; AMWR 1; CA 5-8R; 37-40R; CANR 40; CDALB 1917-1929; CP 1; DA; DA3; DAB; DAC; DAM MST, POET; DLB 4, 45, 63; DLBD 15; EFS 2; EWL 3; EXPP; LMFS 2; MAL 5; MTCW 1, 2; MTFW 2005; PAB; PFS 2, 8, 16; RGAL 4; TUS; WP

Pound, Ezra Weston Loomis
See Pound, Ezra

Povod, Reinaldo 1959-1994 .... **CLC 44**
See also CA 136; 146; CANR 83

Powell, Adam Clayton, Jr.
1908-1972 .... **BLC 1:3; CLC 89**
See also BW 1, 3; CA 102; 33-36R; CANR 86; DAM MULT; DLB 345

Powell, Anthony 1905-2000 ... **CLC 1, 3, 7, 9, 10, 31**
See also BRW 7; CA 1-4R; 189; CANR 1, 32, 62, 107; CDBLB 1945-1960; CN 1, 2, 3, 4, 5, 6; DLB 15; EWL 3; MTCW 1, 2; MTFW 2005; RGEL 2; TEA

Powell, Dawn 1896(?)-1965 .... **CLC 66**
See also CA 5-8R; CANR 121; DLBY 1997

Powell, Padgett 1952- .... **CLC 34**
See also CA 126; CANR 63, 101; CSW; DLB 234; DLBY 01; SSFS 25

Power, Susan 1961- .... **CLC 91**
See also BYA 14; CA 160; CANR 135; NFS 11

Powers, J(ames) F(arl) 1917-1999 ..... **CLC 1, 4, 8, 57; SSC 4**
See also CA 1-4R; 181; CANR 2, 61; CN 1, 2, 3, 4, 5, 6; DLB 130; MTCW 1; RGAL 4; RGSF 2

Powers, John
See Powers, John R.

Powers, John R. 1945- .... **CLC 66**
See also CA 69-72

Powers, Richard 1957- .... **CLC 93**
See also AMWS 9; BPFB 3; CA 148; CANR 80, 180; CN 6, 7; DLB 350; MTFW 2005; TCLE 1:2

Powers, Richard S.
See Powers, Richard

Pownall, David 1938- .... **CLC 10**
See also CA 89-92, 180; CAAS 18; CANR 49, 101; CBD; CD 5, 6; CN 4, 5, 6, 7; DLB 14

Powys, John Cowper 1872-1963 ... **CLC 7, 9, 15, 46, 125**
See also CA 85-88; CANR 106; DLB 15, 255; EWL 3; FANT; MTCW 1, 2; MTFW 2005; RGEL 2; SUFW

Powys, T(heodore) F(rancis)
1875-1953 .... **TCLC 9**
See also BRWS 8; CA 106; 189; DLB 36, 162; EWL 3; FANT; RGEL 2; SUFW

Pozzo, Modesta
See Fonte, Moderata

Prado (Calvo), Pedro 1886-1952 ... **TCLC 75**
See also CA 131; DLB 283; HW 1; LAW

Prager, Emily 1952- .... **CLC 56**
See also CA 204

Pratchett, Terence David John
See Pratchett, Terry

Pratchett, Terry 1948- .... **CLC 197**
See also AAYA 19, 54; BPFB 3; CA 143; CANR 87, 126, 170; CLR 64; CN 6, 7; CPW; CWRI 5; FANT; MTFW 2005; SATA 82, 139, 185; SFW 4; SUFW 2

Pratolini, Vasco 1913-1991 .... **TCLC 124**
See also CA 211; DLB 177; EWL 3; RGWL 2, 3

Pratt, E(dwin) J(ohn) 1883(?)-1964 . **CLC 19**
See also CA 141; 93-96; CANR 77; DAC; DAM POET; DLB 92; EWL 3; RGEL 2; TWA

Premacanda
See Srivastava, Dhanpat Rai

Premchand
See Srivastava, Dhanpat Rai

Prem Chand, Munshi
See Srivastava, Dhanpat Rai

Premchand, Munshi
See Srivastava, Dhanpat Rai

Prescott, William Hickling
1796-1859 .... **NCLC 163**
See also DLB 1, 30, 59, 235

Preseren, France 1800-1849 .... **NCLC 127**
See also CDWLB 4; DLB 147

Preussler, Otfried 1923- .... **CLC 17**
See also CA 77-80; SATA 24

Prevert, Jacques (Henri Marie)
1900-1977 .... **CLC 15**
See also CA 77-80; 69-72; CANR 29, 61; DLB 258; EWL 3; GFL 1789 to the Present; IDFW 3, 4; MTCW 1; RGWL 2, 3; SATA-Obit 30

Prevost, (Antoine Francois)
1697-1763 .... **LC 1, 174**
See also DLB 314; EW 4; GFL Beginnings to 1789; RGWL 2, 3

Price, Edward Reynolds
See Price, Reynolds

Price, Reynolds 1933- .. **CLC 3, 6, 13, 43, 50, 63, 212; SSC 22**
See also AMWS 6; CA 1-4R; CANR 1, 37, 57, 87, 128, 177; CN 1, 2, 3, 4, 5, 6, 7; CSW; DAM NOV; DLB 2, 218, 278; EWL 3; INT CANR-37; MAL 5; MTCW 2005; NFS 18

Price, Richard 1949- .... **CLC 6, 12**
See also CA 49-52; CANR 3, 147, 190; CN 7; DLBY 1981

Prichard, Katharine Susannah
1883-1969 .... **CLC 46**
See also CA 11-12; CANR 33; CAP 1; DLB 260; MTCW 1; RGEL 2; RGSF 2; SATA 66

Priestley, J(ohn) B(oynton)
1894-1984 .... **CLC 2, 5, 9, 34**
See also BRW 7; CA 9-12R; 113; CANR 33; CDBLB 1914-1945; CN 1, 2, 3; DA3; DAM DRAM, NOV; DLB 10, 34, 77, 100, 139; DLBY 1984; EWL 3; MTCW 1, 2; MTFW 2005; RGEL 2; SFW 4

Prince 1958- .... **CLC 35**
See also CA 213

Prince, F(rank) T(empleton)
1912-2003 .... **CLC 22**
See also CA 101; 219; CANR 43, 79; CP 1, 2, 3, 4, 5, 6, 7; DLB 20

Prince Kropotkin
See Kropotkin, Peter

Prior, Matthew 1664-1721 ...... **LC 4; PC 102**
See also DLB 95; RGEL 2

Prishvin, Mikhail 1873-1954 .... **TCLC 75**
See also DLB 272; EWL 3 !**

Prishvin, Mikhail Mikhailovich
See Prishvin, Mikhail

Pritchard, William H(arrison)
1932- .... **CLC 34**
See also CA 65-68; CANR 23, 95; DLB 111

Pritchett, V(ictor) S(awdon)
1900-1997 .. **CLC 5, 13, 15, 41; SSC 14, 126**
See also BPFB 3; BRWS 3; CA 61-64; 157; CANR 31, 63; CN 1, 2, 3, 4, 5, 6; DA3; DAM NOV; DLB 15, 139; EWL 3; MTCW 1, 2; MTFW 2005; RGEL 2; RGSF 2; TEA

Private 19022
See Manning, Frederic

Probst, Mark 1925- .... **CLC 59**
See also CA 130

Procaccino, Michael
See Cristofer, Michael

Proclus c. 412-c. 485 .... **CMLC 81**

Prokosch, Frederic 1908-1989 ...... **CLC 4, 48**
See also CA 73-76; 128; CANR 82; CN 1, 2, 3, 4; CP 1, 2, 3, 4; DLB 48; MTCW 2

Propertius, Sextus c. 50B.C.-c. 16B.C. .... **CMLC 32**
See also AW 2; CDWLB 1; DLB 211; RGWL 2, 3; WLIT 8

Prophet, The
See Dreiser, Theodore

Richler, Mordecai 1931-2001 .... **CLC 3, 5, 9, 13, 18, 46, 70, 185, 271**
See also AITN 1; CA 65-68; 201; CANR 31, 62, 111; CCA 1; CLR 17; CN 1, 2, 3, 4, 5, 7; CWRI 5; DAC; DAM MST, NOV; DLB 53; EWL 3; MAICYA 1, 2; MTCW 1, 2; MTFW 2005; RGEL 2; RGHL; SATA 44, 98; SATA-Brief 27; TWA

Richter, Conrad (Michael)
1890-1968 .... **CLC 30**
See also AAYA 21; AMWS 18; BYA 2; CA 5-8R; 25-28R; CANR 23; DLB 9, 212; LAIT 1; MAL 5; MTCW 1, 2; MTFW 2005; RGAL 4; SATA 3; TCWW 1, 2; TUS; YAW

Ricostranza, Tom
See Ellis, Trey

Riddell, Charlotte 1832-1906 .... **TCLC 40**
See also CA 165; DLB 156; HGG; SUFW

Riddell, Mrs. J. H.
See Riddell, Charlotte

Ridge, John Rollin 1827-1867 ...... **NCLC 82; NNAL**
See also CA 144; DAM MULT; DLB 175

Ridgeway, Jason
See Marlowe, Stephen

Ridgway, Keith 1965- .... **CLC 119**
See also CA 172; CANR 144

Riding, Laura
See Jackson, Laura

Riefenstahl, Berta Helene Amalia
1902-2003 .... **CLC 16, 190**
See also CA 108; 220

Riefenstahl, Leni
See Riefenstahl, Berta Helene Amalia

Riffe, Ernest
See Bergman, Ingmar

Riffe, Ernest Ingmar
See Bergman, Ingmar

Riggs, (Rolla) Lynn
1899-1954 .... **NNAL; TCLC 56**
See also CA 144; DAM MULT; DLB 175

Riis, Jacob A(ugust) 1849-1914 ..... **TCLC 80**
See also CA 113; 168; DLB 23

Rikki
See Ducornet, Erica

Riley, James Whitcomb 1849-1916 .... **PC 48; TCLC 51**
See also CA 118; 137; DAM POET; MAICYA 1, 2; RGAL 4; SATA 17

Riley, Tex
See Creasey, John

Rilke, Rainer Maria 1875-1926 .... **PC 2; TCLC 1, 6, 19, 195**
See also CA 104; 132; CANR 62, 99; CD-WLB 2; DA3; DAM POET; DLB 81; EW 9; EWL 3; MTCW 1, 2; MTFW 2005; PFS 19, 27; RGWL 2, 3; TWA; WP

Rimbaud, Arthur 1854-1891 ..... **NCLC 4, 35, 82; PC 3, 57; WLC 5**
See also DA; DA3; DAB; DAC; DAM MST, POET; DLB 217; EW 7; GFL 1789 to the Present; LMFS 2; PFS 28; RGWL 2, 3; TWA; WP

Rimbaud, Jean Nicholas Arthur
See Rimbaud, Arthur

Rinehart, Mary Roberts
1876-1958 .... **TCLC 52**
See also BPFB 3; CA 108; 166; RGAL 4; RHW

Ringmaster, The
See Mencken, H. L.

Ringwood, Gwen(dolyn Margaret) Pharis
1910-1984 .... **CLC 48**
See also CA 148; 112; DLB 88

Rio, Michel 1945(?)- .... **CLC 43**
See also CA 201

Rios, Alberto 1952- .... **PC 57**
See also AAYA 66; AMWS 4; CA 113; CANR 34, 79, 137; CP 6, 7; DLB 122; HW 2; MTFW 2005; PFS 11

Rios, Alberto Alvaro
See Rios, Alberto

Ritsos, Giannes
See Ritsos, Yannis

Ritsos, Yannis 1909-1990 .... **CLC 6, 13, 31**
See also CA 77-80; 133; CANR 39, 61; EW 12; EWL 3; MTCW 1; RGWL 2, 3

Ritter, Erika 1948(?)- .... **CLC 52**
See also CD 5, 6; CWD

Rivera, Jose Eustasio 1889-1928 ... **TCLC 35**
See also CA 162; EWL 3; HW 1, 2; LAW

Rivera, Tomas 1935-1984 .... **HLCS 2**
See also CA 49-52; CANR 32; DLB 82; HW 1; LLW; RGAL 4; SSFS 15; TCWW 2; WLIT 1

Rivers, Conrad Kent 1933-1968 .... **CLC 1**
See also BW 1; CA 85-88; DLB 41

Rivers, Elfrida
See Bradley, Marion Zimmer

Riverside, John
See Heinlein, Robert A.

Rizal, Jose 1861-1896 .... **NCLC 27**
See also DLB 348

Roa Bastos, Augusto 1917-2005 ...... **CLC 45; HLC 2**
See also CA 131; 238; CWW 2; DAM MULT; DLB 113; EWL 3; HW 1; LAW; RGSF 2; WLIT 1

Roa Bastos, Augusto Jose Antonio
See Roa Bastos, Augusto

Robbe-Grillet, Alain 1922-2008 ..... **CLC 1, 2, 4, 6, 8, 10, 14, 43, 128, 287**
See also BPFB 3; CA 9-12R; 269; CANR 33, 65, 115; CWW 2; DLB 83; EW 13; EWL 3; GFL 1789 to the Present; IDFW 3, 4; MTCW 1, 2; MTFW 2005; RGWL 2, 3; SSFS 15

Robbins, Harold 1916-1997 .... **CLC 5**
See also BPFB 3; CA 73-76; 162; CANR 26, 54, 112, 156; DA3; DAM NOV; MTCW 1, 2

Robbins, Thomas Eugene 1936- . **CLC 9, 32, 64**
See also AAYA 32; AMWS 10; BEST 90:3; BPFB 3; CA 81-84; CANR 29, 59, 95, 139; CN 3, 4, 5, 6, 7; CPW; CSW; DA3; DAM NOV, POP; DLBY 1980; MTCW 1, 2; MTFW 2005

Robbins, Tom
See Robbins, Thomas Eugene

Robbins, Trina 1938- .... **CLC 21**
See also AAYA 61; CA 128; CANR 152

Robert de Boron fl. 12th cent. - .... **CMLC 94**

Roberts, Charles G(eorge) D(ouglas)
1860-1943 .... **SSC 91; TCLC 8**
See also CA 105; 188; CLR 33; CWRI 5; DLB 92; RGEL 2; RGSF 2; SATA 88; SATA-Brief 29

Roberts, Elizabeth Madox
1886-1941 .... **TCLC 68**
See also CA 111; 166; CLR 100; CWRI 5; DLB 9, 54, 102; RGAL 4; RHW; SATA 33; SATA-Brief 27; TCWW 2; WCH

Roberts, Kate 1891-1985 .... **CLC 15**
See also CA 107; 116; DLB 319

Roberts, Keith (John Kingston)
1935-2000 .... **CLC 14**
See also BRWS 10; CA 25-28R; CANR 46; DLB 261; SFW 4

Roberts, Kenneth (Lewis)
1885-1957 .... **TCLC 23**
See also CA 109; 199; DLB 9; MAL 5; RGAL 4; RHW

Roberts, Michele 1949- .... **CLC 48, 178**
See also BRWS 15; CA 115; CANR 58, 120, 164, 200; CN 6, 7; DLB 231; FW

Roberts, Michele Brigitte
See Roberts, Michele

Robertson, Ellis
See Ellison, Harlan; Silverberg, Robert

Robertson, Thomas William
1829-1871 .... **NCLC 35**
See also DAM DRAM; DLB 344; RGEL 2

Robertson, Tom
See Robertson, Thomas William

Robeson, Kenneth
See Dent, Lester

Robinson, Edwin Arlington
1869-1935 .... **PC 1, 35; TCLC 5, 101**
See also AAYA 72; AMW; CA 104; 133; CDALB 1865-1917; DA; DAC; DAM MST, POET; DLB 54; EWL 3; EXPP; MAL 5; MTCW 1, 2; MTFW 2005; PAB; PFS 4; RGAL 4; WP

Robinson, Henry Crabb
1775-1867 .... **NCLC 15**
See also DLB 107

Robinson, Jill 1936- .... **CLC 10**
See also CA 102; CANR 120; INT CA-102

Robinson, Kim Stanley 1952- ... **CLC 34, 248**
See also AAYA 26; CA 126; CANR 113, 139, 173; CN 6, 7; MTFW 2005; SATA 109; SCFW 2; SFW 4

Robinson, Lloyd
See Silverberg, Robert

Robinson, Marilynne 1943- ..... **CLC 25, 180, 276**
See also AAYA 69; CA 116; CANR 80, 140, 192; CN 4, 5, 6, 7; DLB 206, 350; MTFW 2005; NFS 24

Robinson, Mary 1758-1800 .... **NCLC 142**
See also BRWS 13; DLB 158; FW

Robinson, Smokey
See Robinson, William, Jr.

Robinson, William, Jr. 1940- .... **CLC 21**
See also CA 116

Robison, Mary 1949- .... **CLC 42, 98**
See also CA 113; 116; CANR 87; CN 4, 5, 6, 7; DLB 130; INT CA-116; RGSF 2

Roches, Catherine des 1542-1587 ...... **LC 117**
See also DLB 327

Rochester
See Wilmot, John

Rod, Edouard 1857-1910 .... **TCLC 52**

Roddenberry, Eugene Wesley
1921-1991 .... **CLC 17**
See also AAYA 5; CA 110; 135; CANR 37; SATA 45; SATA-Obit 69

Roddenberry, Gene
See Roddenberry, Eugene Wesley

Rodgers, Mary 1931- .... **CLC 12**
See also BYA 5; CA 49-52; CANR 8, 55, 90; CLR 20; CWRI 5; INT CANR-8; JRDA; MAICYA 1, 2; SATA 8, 130

Rodgers, W(illiam) R(obert)
1909-1969 .... **CLC 7**
See also CA 85-88; DLB 20; RGEL 2

Rodman, Eric
See Silverberg, Robert

Rodman, Howard 1920(?)-1985 .... **CLC 65**
See also CA 118

Rodman, Maia
See Wojciechowska, Maia (Teresa)

Rodo, Jose Enrique 1871(?)-1917 .... **HLCS 2**
See also CA 178; EWL 3; HW 2; LAW

Rodolph, Utto
See Ouologuem, Yambo

Rodriguez, Claudio 1934-1999 .... **CLC 10**
See also CA 188; DLB 134

Sargeson, Frank 1903-1982 ..... **CLC 31; SSC 99**
See also CA 25-28R; 106; CANR 38, 79; CN 1, 2, 3; EWL 3; GLL 2; RGEL 2; RGSF 2; SSFS 20

Sarmiento, Domingo Faustino 1811-1888 .... **HLCS 2; NCLC 123**
See also LAW; WLIT 1

Sarmiento, Felix Ruben Garcia
See Dario, Ruben

Saro-Wiwa, Ken(ule Beeson) 1941-1995 .... **CLC 114; TCLC 200**
See also BW 2; CA 142; 150; CANR 60; DLB 157

Saroyan, William 1908-1981 ... **CLC 1, 8, 10, 29, 34, 56; DC 28; SSC 21; TCLC 137; WLC 5**
See also AAYA 66; CA 5-8R; 103; CAD; CANR 30; CDALBS; CN 1, 2; DA; DA3; DAB; DAC; DAM DRAM, MST, NOV; DFS 17; DLB 7, 9, 86; DLBY 1981; EWL 3; LAIT 4; MAL 5; MTCW 1, 2; MTFW 2005; RGAL 4; RGSF 2; SATA 23; SATA-Obit 24; SSFS 14; TUS

Sarraute, Nathalie 1900-1999 .... **CLC 1, 2, 4, 8, 10, 31, 80; TCLC 145**
See also BPFB 3; CA 9-12R; 187; CANR 23, 66, 134; CWW 2; DLB 83, 321; EW 12; EWL 3; GFL 1789 to the Present; MTCW 1, 2; MTFW 2005; RGWL 2, 3

Sarton, May 1912-1995 ... **CLC 4, 14, 49, 91; PC 39; TCLC 120**
See also AMWS 8; CA 1-4R; 149; CANR 1, 34, 55, 116; CN 1, 2, 3, 4, 5, 6; CP 1, 2, 3, 4, 5, 6; DAM POET; DLB 48; DLBY 1981; EWL 3; FW; INT CANR-34; MAL 5; MTCW 1, 2; MTFW 2005; RGAL 4; SATA 36; SATA-Obit 86; TUS

Sartre, Jean-Paul 1905-1980 . **CLC 1, 4, 7, 9, 13, 18, 24, 44, 50, 52; DC 3; SSC 32; WLC 5**
See also AAYA 62; CA 9-12R; 97-100; CANR 21; DA; DA3; DAB; DAC; DAM DRAM, MST, NOV; DFS 5, 26; DLB 72, 296, 321, 332; EW 12; EWL 3; GFL 1789 to the Present; LMFS 2; MTCW 1, 2; MTFW 2005; NFS 21; RGHL; RGSF 2; RGWL 2, 3; SSFS 9; TWA

Sassoon, Siegfried 1886-1967 .. **CLC 36, 130; PC 12**
See also BRW 6; CA 104; 25-28R; CANR 36; DAB; DAM MST, NOV, POET; DLB 20, 191; DLBD 18; EWL 3; MTCW 1, 2; MTFW 2005; PAB; PFS 28; RGEL 2; TEA

Sassoon, Siegfried Lorraine
See Sassoon, Siegfried

Satterfield, Charles
See Pohl, Frederik

Satyremont
See Peret, Benjamin

Saul, John III
See Saul, John

Saul, John 1942- .... **CLC 46**
See also AAYA 10, 62; BEST 90:4; CA 81-84; CANR 16, 40, 81, 176; CPW; DAM NOV, POP; HGG; SATA 98

Saul, John W.
See Saul, John

Saul, John W. III
See Saul, John

Saul, John Woodruff III
See Saul, John

Saunders, Caleb
See Heinlein, Robert A.

Saura (Atares), Carlos 1932-1998 .... **CLC 20**
See also CA 114; 131; CANR 79; HW 1

Sauser, Frederic Louis
See Sauser-Hall, Frederic

Sauser-Hall, Frederic 1887-1961 ..... **CLC 18, 106**
See also CA 102; 93-96; CANR 36, 62; DLB 258; EWL 3; GFL 1789 to the Present; MTCW 1; WP

Saussure, Ferdinand de 1857-1913 .... **TCLC 49**
See also DLB 242

Savage, Catharine
See Brosman, Catharine Savage

Savage, Richard 1697(?)-1743 .... **LC 96**
See also DLB 95; RGEL 2

Savage, Thomas 1915-2003 .... **CLC 40**
See also CA 126; 132; 218; CAAS 15; CN 6, 7; INT CA-132; SATA-Obit 147; TCWW 2

Savan, Glenn 1953-2003 .... **CLC 50**
See also CA 225

Savonarola, Girolamo 1452-1498 ...... **LC 152**
See also LMFS 1

Sax, Robert
See Johnson, Robert

Saxo Grammaticus c. 1150-c. 1222 .... **CMLC 58**

Saxton, Robert
See Johnson, Robert

Sayers, Dorothy L(eigh) 1893-1957 . **SSC 71; TCLC 2, 15**
See also BPFB 3; BRWS 3; CA 104; 119; CANR 60; CDBLB 1914-1945; CMW 4; DAM POP; DLB 10, 36, 77, 100; MSW; MTCW 1, 2; MTFW 2005; RGEL 2; SSFS 12; TEA

Sayers, Valerie 1952- .... **CLC 50, 122**
See also CA 134; CANR 61; CSW

Sayles, John (Thomas) 1950- .... **CLC 7, 10, 14, 198**
See also CA 57-60; CANR 41, 84; DLB 44

Scamander, Newt
See Rowling, J. K.

Scammell, Michael 1935- .... **CLC 34**
See also CA 156

Scannel, John Vernon
See Scannell, Vernon

Scannell, Vernon 1922-2007 .... **CLC 49**
See also CA 5-8R; 266; CANR 8, 24, 57, 143; CN 1, 2; CP 1, 2, 3, 4, 5, 6, 7; CWRI 5; DLB 27; SATA 59; SATA-Obit 188

Scarlett, Susan
See Streatfeild, Noel

Scarron 1847-1910
See Mikszath, Kalman

Scarron, Paul 1610-1660 .... **LC 116**
See also GFL Beginnings to 1789; RGWL 2, 3

Schaeffer, Susan Fromberg 1941- ..... **CLC 6, 11, 22**
See also CA 49-52; CANR 18, 65, 160; CN 4, 5, 6, 7; DLB 28, 299; MTCW 1, 2; MTFW 2005; SATA 22

Schama, Simon 1945- .... **CLC 150**
See also BEST 89:4; CA 105; CANR 39, 91, 168

Schama, Simon Michael
See Schama, Simon

Schary, Jill
See Robinson, Jill

Schell, Jonathan 1943- .... **CLC 35**
See also CA 73-76; CANR 12, 117, 187

Schelling, Friedrich Wilhelm Joseph von 1775-1854 .... **NCLC 30**
See also DLB 90

Scherer, Jean-Marie Maurice
See Rohmer, Eric

Schevill, James (Erwin) 1920- .... **CLC 7**
See also CA 5-8R; CAAS 12; CAD; CD 5, 6; CP 1, 2, 3, 4, 5

Schiller, Friedrich von 1759-1805 ...... **DC 12; NCLC 39, 69, 166**
See also CDWLB 2; DAM DRAM; DLB 94; EW 5; RGWL 2, 3; TWA

Schisgal, Murray (Joseph) 1926- .... **CLC 6**
See also CA 21-24R; CAD; CANR 48, 86; CD 5, 6; MAL 5

Schlee, Ann 1934- .... **CLC 35**
See also CA 101; CANR 29, 88; SATA 44; SATA-Brief 36

Schlegel, August Wilhelm von 1767-1845 .... **NCLC 15, 142**
See also DLB 94; RGWL 2, 3

Schlegel, Friedrich 1772-1829 .... **NCLC 45, 226**
See also DLB 90; EW 5; RGWL 2, 3; TWA

Schlegel, Johann Elias (von) 1719(?)-1749 .... **LC 5**

Schleiermacher, Friedrich 1768-1834 .... **NCLC 107**
See also DLB 90

Schlesinger, Arthur M., Jr. 1917-2007 .... **CLC 84**
See Schlesinger, Arthur Meier
See also AITN 1; CA 1-4R; 257; CANR 1, 28, 58, 105, 187; DLB 17; INT CANR-28; MTCW 1, 2; SATA 61; SATA-Obit 181

Schlink, Bernhard 1944- .... **CLC 174**
See also CA 163; CANR 116, 175; RGHL

Schmidt, Arno (Otto) 1914-1979 ...... **CLC 56**
See also CA 128; 109; DLB 69; EWL 3

Schmitz, Aron Hector 1861-1928 ..... **SSC 25; TCLC 2, 35**
See also CA 104; 122; DLB 264; EW 8; EWL 3; MTCW 1; RGWL 2, 3; WLIT 7

Schnackenberg, Gjertrud 1953- ...... **CLC 40; PC 45**
See also AMWS 15; CA 116; CANR 100; CP 5, 6, 7; CWP; DLB 120, 282; PFS 13, 25

Schnackenberg, Gjertrud Cecelia
See Schnackenberg, Gjertrud

Schneider, Leonard Alfred 1925-1966 .... **CLC 21**
See also CA 89-92

Schnitzler, Arthur 1862-1931 ..... **DC 17; SSC 15, 61; TCLC 4**
See also CA 104; CDWLB 2; DLB 81, 118; EW 8; EWL 3; RGSF 2; RGWL 2, 3

Schoenberg, Arnold Franz Walter 1874-1951 .... **TCLC 75**
See also CA 109; 188

Schonberg, Arnold
See Schoenberg, Arnold Franz Walter

Schopenhauer, Arthur 1788-1860 . **NCLC 51, 157**
See also DLB 90; EW 5

Schor, Sandra (M.) 1932(?)-1990 ..... **CLC 65**
See also CA 132

Schorer, Mark 1908-1977 .... **CLC 9**
See also CA 5-8R; 73-76; CANR 7; CN 1, 2; DLB 103

Schrader, Paul (Joseph) 1946- . **CLC 26, 212**
See also CA 37-40R; CANR 41; DLB 44

Schreber, Daniel 1842-1911 .... **TCLC 123**

Schreiner, Olive 1855-1920 ...... **TCLC 9, 235**
See also AFW; BRWS 2; CA 105; 154; DLB 18, 156, 190, 225; EWL 3; FW; RGEL 2; TWA; WLIT 2; WWE 1

Schreiner, Olive Emilie Albertina
See Schreiner, Olive

Schulberg, Budd 1914-2009 .... **CLC 7, 48**
See also AMWS 18; BPFB 3; CA 25-28R; 289; CANR 19, 87, 178; CN 1, 2, 3, 4, 5, 6, 7; DLB 6, 26, 28; DLBY 1981, 2001; MAL 5

Schulberg, Budd Wilson
See Schulberg, Budd

Schulberg, Seymour Wilson
See Schulberg, Budd

Schulman, Arnold
See Trumbo, Dalton

Schulz, Bruno 1892-1942 .. **SSC 13; TCLC 5, 51**
See also CA 115; 123; CANR 86; CDWLB 4; DLB 215; EWL 3; MTCW 2; MTFW 2005; RGSF 2; RGWL 2, 3

Schulz, Charles M. 1922-2000 .... **CLC 12**
See also AAYA 39; CA 9-12R; 187; CANR 6, 132; INT CANR-6; MTFW 2005; SATA 10; SATA-Obit 118

Schulz, Charles Monroe
See Schulz, Charles M.

Schumacher, E(rnst) F(riedrich)
1911-1977 .... **CLC 80**
See also CA 81-84; 73-76; CANR 34, 85

Schumann, Robert 1810-1856 ...... **NCLC 143**

Schuyler, George Samuel 1895-1977 . **HR 1:3**
See also BW 2; CA 81-84; 73-76; CANR 42; DLB 29, 51

Schuyler, James Marcus 1923-1991 .. **CLC 5, 23; PC 88**
See also CA 101; 134; CP 1, 2, 3, 4, 5; DAM POET; DLB 5, 169; EWL 3; INT CA-101; MAL 5; WP

Schwartz, Delmore (David)
1913-1966 . **CLC 2, 4, 10, 45, 87; PC 8; SSC 105**
See also AMWS 2; CA 17-18; 25-28R; CANR 35; CAP 2; DLB 28, 48; EWL 3; MAL 5; MTCW 1, 2; MTFW 2005; PAB; RGAL 4; TUS

Schwartz, Ernst
See Ozu, Yasujiro

Schwartz, John Burnham 1965- .... **CLC 59**
See also CA 132; CANR 116, 188

Schwartz, Lynne Sharon 1939- .... **CLC 31**
See also CA 103; CANR 44, 89, 160; DLB 218; MTCW 2; MTFW 2005

Schwartz, Muriel A.
See Eliot, T. S.

Schwarz-Bart, Andre 1928-2006 .... **CLC 2, 4**
See also CA 89-92; 253; CANR 109; DLB 299; RGHL

Schwarz-Bart, Simone 1938- . **BLCS; CLC 7**
See also BW 2; CA 97-100; CANR 117; EWL 3

Schwerner, Armand 1927-1999 .... **PC 42**
See also CA 9-12R; 179; CANR 50, 85; CP 2, 3, 4, 5, 6; DLB 165

Schwitters, Kurt (Hermann Edward Karl Julius) 1887-1948 .... **TCLC 95**
See also CA 158

Schwob, Marcel (Mayer Andre)
1867-1905 .... **TCLC 20**
See also CA 117; 168; DLB 123; GFL 1789 to the Present

Sciascia, Leonardo 1921-1989 .. **CLC 8, 9, 41**
See also CA 85-88; 130; CANR 35; DLB 177; EWL 3; MTCW 1; RGWL 2, 3

Scoppettone, Sandra 1936- .... **CLC 26**
See also AAYA 11, 65; BYA 8; CA 5-8R; CANR 41, 73, 157; GLL 1; MAICYA 2; MAICYAS 1; SATA 9, 92; WYA; YAW

Scorsese, Martin 1942- .... **CLC 20, 89, 207**
See also AAYA 38; CA 110; 114; CANR 46, 85

Scotland, Jay
See Jakes, John

Scott, Duncan Campbell
1862-1947 .... **TCLC 6**
See also CA 104; 153; DAC; DLB 92; RGEL 2

Scott, Evelyn 1893-1963 .... **CLC 43**
See also CA 104; 112; CANR 64; DLB 9, 48; RHW

Scott, F(rancis) R(eginald)
1899-1985 .... **CLC 22**
See also CA 101; 114; CANR 87; CP 1, 2, 3, 4; DLB 88; INT CA-101; RGEL 2

Scott, Frank
See Scott, F(rancis) R(eginald)

Scott, Joan CLC 65

Scott, Joanna 1960- .... **CLC 50**
See also AMWS 17; CA 126; CANR 53, 92, 168

Scott, Joanna Jeanne
See Scott, Joanna

Scott, Paul (Mark) 1920-1978 ...... **CLC 9, 60**
See also BRWS 1; CA 81-84; 77-80; CANR 33; CN 1, 2; DLB 14, 207, 326; EWL 3; MTCW 1; RGEL 2; RHW; WWE 1

Scott, Ridley 1937- .... **CLC 183**
See also AAYA 13, 43

Scott, Sarah 1723-1795 .... **LC 44**
See also DLB 39

Scott, Sir Walter 1771-1832 .... **NCLC 15, 69, 110, 209; PC 13; SSC 32; WLC 5**
See also AAYA 22; BRW 4; BYA 2; CD-BLB 1789-1832; DA; DAB; DAC; DAM MST, NOV, POET; DLB 93, 107, 116, 144, 159; GL 3; HGG; LAIT 1; RGEL 2; RGSF 2; SSFS 10; SUFW 1; TEA; WLIT 3; YABC 2

Scribe, Augustin Eugene
See Scribe, (Augustin) Eugene

Scribe, (Augustin) Eugene 1791-1861 . **DC 5; NCLC 16**
See also DAM DRAM; DLB 192; GFL 1789 to the Present; RGWL 2, 3

Scrum, R.
See Crumb, R.

Scudery, Georges de 1601-1667 .... **LC 75**
See also GFL Beginnings to 1789

Scudery, Madeleine de 1607-1701 .. **LC 2, 58**
See also DLB 268; GFL Beginnings to 1789

Scum
See Crumb, R.

Scumbag, Little Bobby
See Crumb, R.

Seabrook, John
See Hubbard, L. Ron

Seacole, Mary Jane Grant
1805-1881 .... **NCLC 147**
See also DLB 166

Sealy, I(rwin) Allan 1951- .... **CLC 55**
See also CA 136; CN 6, 7

Search, Alexander
See Pessoa, Fernando

Seare, Nicholas
See Whitaker, Rod

Sebald, W(infried) G(eorg)
1944-2001 .... **CLC 194**
See also BRWS 8; CA 159; 202; CANR 98; MTFW 2005; RGHL

Sebastian, Lee
See Silverberg, Robert

Sebastian Owl
See Thompson, Hunter S.

Sebestyen, Igen
See Sebestyen, Ouida

Sebestyen, Ouida 1924- .... **CLC 30**
See also AAYA 8; BYA 7; CA 107; CANR 40, 114; CLR 17; JRDA; MAICYA 1, 2; SAAS 10; SATA 39, 140; WYA; YAW

Sebold, Alice 1963- .... **CLC 193**
See also AAYA 56; CA 203; CANR 181; LNFS 1; MTFW 2005

Second Duke of Buckingham
See Villiers, George

Secundus, H. Scriblerus
See Fielding, Henry

Sedges, John
See Buck, Pearl S.

Sedgwick, Catharine Maria
1789-1867 .... **NCLC 19, 98**
See also DLB 1, 74, 183, 239, 243, 254; FL 1:3; RGAL 4

Sedley, Sir Charles 1639-1701 .... **LC 168**
See also BRW 2; DLB 131; RGEL 2

Sedulius Scottus 9th cent. -c. 874 .. **CMLC 86**

Seebohm, Victoria
See Glendinning, Victoria

Seelye, John (Douglas) 1931- .... **CLC 7**
See also CA 97-100; CANR 70; INT CA-97-100; TCWW 1, 2

Seferiades, Giorgos Stylianou
See Seferis, George

Seferis, George 1900-1971 .... **CLC 5, 11; TCLC 213**
See also CA 5-8R; 33-36R; CANR 5, 36; DLB 332; EW 12; EWL 3; MTCW 1; RGWL 2, 3

Segal, Erich 1937-2010 .... **CLC 3, 10**
See also BEST 89:1; BPFB 3; CA 25-28R; CANR 20, 36, 65, 113; CPW; DAM POP; DLBY 1986; INT CANR-20; MTCW 1

Segal, Erich Wolf
See Segal, Erich

Seger, Bob 1945- .... **CLC 35**

Seghers
See Radvanyi, Netty

Seghers, Anna
See Radvanyi, Netty

Seidel, Frederick 1936- .... **CLC 18**
See also CA 13-16R; CANR 8, 99, 180; CP 1, 2, 3, 4, 5, 6, 7; DLBY 1984

Seidel, Frederick Lewis
See Seidel, Frederick

Seifert, Jaroslav 1901-1986 . **CLC 34, 44, 93; PC 47**
See also CA 127; CDWLB 4; DLB 215, 332; EWL 3; MTCW 1, 2

Sei Shonagon c. 966-1017(?) ..... **CMLC 6, 89**

Sejour, Victor 1817-1874 .... **DC 10**
See also DLB 50

Sejour Marcou et Ferrand, Juan Victor
See Sejour, Victor

Selby, Hubert, Jr. 1928-2004 ..... **CLC 1, 2, 4, 8; SSC 20**
See also CA 13-16R; 226; CANR 33, 85; CN 1, 2, 3, 4, 5, 6, 7; DLB 2, 227; MAL 5

Self, Will 1961- .... **CLC 282**
See also BRWS 5; CA 143; CANR 83, 126, 171, 201; CN 6, 7; DLB 207

Self, William
See Self, Will

Self, William Woodward
See Self, Will

Selzer, Richard 1928- .... **CLC 74**
See also CA 65-68; CANR 14, 106

Sembene, Ousmane
See Ousmane, Sembene

Senancour, Etienne Pivert de
1770-1846 .... **NCLC 16**
See also DLB 119; GFL 1789 to the Present

Sender, Ramon (Jose) 1902-1982 ...... **CLC 8; HLC 2; TCLC 136**
See also CA 5-8R; 105; CANR 8; DAM MULT; DLB 322; EWL 3; HW 1; MTCW 1; RGWL 2, 3

Seneca, Lucius Annaeus c. 4B.C.-c.
65 .... **CMLC 6, 107; DC 5**
See also AW 2; CDWLB 1; DAM DRAM; DLB 211; RGWL 2, 3; TWA; WLIT 8

Seneca the Younger
See Seneca, Lucius Annaeus

Shepard, Jim 1956- .... **CLC 36**
See also AAYA 73; CA 137; CANR 59, 104, 160, 199; SATA 90, 164

Shepard, Lucius 1947- .... **CLC 34**
See also CA 128; 141; CANR 81, 124, 178; HGG; SCFW 2; SFW 4; SUFW 2

Shepard, Sam 1943- .... **CLC 4, 6, 17, 34, 41, 44, 169; DC 5**
See also AAYA 1, 58; AMWS 3; CA 69-72; CABS 3; CAD; CANR 22, 120, 140; CD 5, 6; DA3; DAM DRAM; DFS 3, 6, 7, 14; DLB 7, 212, 341; EWL 3; IDFW 3, 4; MAL 5; MTCW 1, 2; MTFW 2005; RGAL 4

Shepherd, Jean (Parker) 1921-1999 .... **TCLC 177**
See also AAYA 69; AITN 2; CA 77-80; 187

Shepherd, Michael
See Ludlum, Robert

Sherburne, Zoa (Lillian Morin) 1912-1995 .... **CLC 30**
See also AAYA 13; CA 1-4R; 176; CANR 3, 37; MAICYA 1, 2; SAAS 18; SATA 3; YAW

Sheridan, Frances 1724-1766 .... **LC 7**
See also DLB 39, 84

Sheridan, Richard Brinsley 1751-1816 . **DC 1; NCLC 5, 91; WLC 5**
See also BRW 3; CDBLB 1660-1789; DA; DAB; DAC; DAM DRAM, MST; DFS 15; DLB 89; WLIT 3

Sherman, Jonathan Marc 1968- .... **CLC 55**
See also CA 230

Sherman, Martin 1941(?)- .... **CLC 19**
See also CA 116; 123; CAD; CANR 86; CD 5, 6; DFS 20; DLB 228; GLL 1; IDTP; RGHL

Sherwin, Judith Johnson
See Johnson, Judith

Sherwood, Frances 1940- .... **CLC 81**
See also CA 146, 220; CAAE 220; CANR 158

Sherwood, Robert E(mmet) 1896-1955 .... **DC 36; TCLC 3**
See also CA 104; 153; CANR 86; DAM DRAM; DFS 11, 15, 17; DLB 7, 26, 249; IDFW 3, 4; MAL 5; RGAL 4

Shestov, Lev 1866-1938 .... **TCLC 56**

Shevchenko, Taras 1814-1861 .... **NCLC 54**

Shiel, M. P. 1865-1947 .... **TCLC 8**
See also CA 106; 160; DLB 153; HGG; MTCW 2; MTFW 2005; SCFW 1, 2; SFW 4; SUFW

Shiel, Matthew Phipps
See Shiel, M. P.

Shields, Carol 1935-2003 . **CLC 91, 113, 193; SSC 126**
See also AMWS 7; CA 81-84; 218; CANR 51, 74, 98, 133; CCA 1; CN 6, 7; CPW; DA3; DAC; DLB 334, 350; MTCW 2; MTFW 2005; NFS 23

Shields, David 1956- .... **CLC 97**
See also CA 124; CANR 48, 99, 112, 157

Shields, David Jonathan
See Shields, David

Shiga, Naoya 1883-1971 .... **CLC 33; SSC 23; TCLC 172**
See also CA 101; 33-36R; DLB 180; EWL 3; MJW; RGWL 3

Shiga Naoya
See Shiga, Naoya

Shilts, Randy 1951-1994 .... **CLC 85**
See also AAYA 19; CA 115; 127; 144; CANR 45; DA3; GLL 1; INT CA-127; MTCW 2; MTFW 2005

Shimazaki, Haruki 1872-1943 .... **TCLC 5**
See also CA 105; 134; CANR 84; DLB 180; EWL 3; MJW; RGWL 3

Shimazaki Toson
See Shimazaki, Haruki

Shirley, James 1596-1666 .... **DC 25; LC 96**
See also DLB 58; RGEL 2

Shirley Hastings, Selina
See Hastings, Selina

Sholem Aleykhem
See Rabinovitch, Sholem

Sholokhov, Mikhail 1905-1984 ..... **CLC 7, 15**
See also CA 101; 112; DLB 272, 332; EWL 3; MTCW 1, 2; MTFW 2005; RGWL 2, 3; SATA-Obit 36

Sholokhov, Mikhail Aleksandrovich
See Sholokhov, Mikhail

Sholom Aleichem 1859-1916
See Rabinovitch, Sholem

Shone, Patric
See Hanley, James

Showalter, Elaine 1941- .... **CLC 169**
See also CA 57-60; CANR 58, 106; DLB 67; FW; GLL 2

Shreve, Susan
See Shreve, Susan Richards

Shreve, Susan Richards 1939- .... **CLC 23**
See also CA 49-52; CAAS 5; CANR 5, 38, 69, 100, 159, 199; MAICYA 1, 2; SATA 46, 95, 152; SATA-Brief 41

Shue, Larry 1946-1985 .... **CLC 52**
See also CA 145; 117; DAM DRAM; DFS 7

Shu-Jen, Chou 1881-1936 . **SSC 20; TCLC 3**
See also CA 104; EWL 3

Shulman, Alix Kates 1932- .... **CLC 2, 10**
See also CA 29-32R; CANR 43, 199; FW; SATA 7

Shuster, Joe 1914-1992 .... **CLC 21**
See also AAYA 50

Shute, Nevil 1899-1960 .... **CLC 30**
See also BPFB 3; CA 102; 93-96; CANR 85; DLB 255; MTCW 2; NFS 9; RHW 4; SFW 4

Shuttle, Penelope (Diane) 1947- .... **CLC 7**
See also CA 93-96; CANR 39, 84, 92, 108; CP 3, 4, 5, 6, 7; CWP; DLB 14, 40

Shvarts, Elena 1948- .... **PC 50**
See also CA 147

Sidhwa, Bapsi 1939-
See Sidhwa, Bapsy (N.)

Sidhwa, Bapsy (N.) 1938- .... **CLC 168**
See also CA 108; CANR 25, 57; CN 6, 7; DLB 323; FW

Sidney, Mary 1561-1621 .... **LC 19, 39**
See also DLB 167

Sidney, Sir Philip 1554-1586 .... **LC 19, 39, 131; PC 32**
See also BRW 1; BRWR 2; CDBLB Before 1660; DA; DA3; DAB; DAC; DAM MST, POET; DLB 167; EXPP; PAB; PFS 30; RGEL 2; TEA; WP

Sidney Herbert, Mary
See Sidney, Mary

Siegel, Jerome 1914-1996 .... **CLC 21**
See also AAYA 50; CA 116; 169; 151

Siegel, Jerry
See Siegel, Jerome

Sienkiewicz, Henryk (Adam Alexander Pius) 1846-1916 .... **TCLC 3**
See also CA 104; 134; CANR 84; DLB 332; EWL 3; RGSF 2; RGWL 2, 3

Sierra, Gregorio Martinez
See Martinez Sierra, Gregorio

Sierra, Maria de la O'LeJarraga Martinez
See Martinez Sierra, Maria

Sigal, Clancy 1926- .... **CLC 7**
See also CA 1-4R; CANR 85, 184; CN 1, 2, 3, 4, 5, 6, 7

Siger of Brabant 1240(?)-1284(?) . **CMLC 69**
See also DLB 115

Sigourney, Lydia H.
See Sigourney, Lydia Howard
See also DLB 73, 183

Sigourney, Lydia Howard 1791-1865 .... **NCLC 21, 87**
See Sigourney, Lydia H.
See also DLB 1, 42, 239, 243

Sigourney, Lydia Howard Huntley
See Sigourney, Lydia Howard

Sigourney, Lydia Huntley
See Sigourney, Lydia Howard

Siguenza y Gongora, Carlos de 1645-1700 .... **HLCS 2; LC 8**
See also LAW

Sigurjonsson, Johann
See Sigurjonsson, Johann

Sigurjonsson, Johann 1880-1919 ... **TCLC 27**
See also CA 170; DLB 293; EWL 3

Sikelianos, Angelos 1884-1951 .... **PC 29; TCLC 39**
See also EWL 3; RGWL 2, 3

Silkin, Jon 1930-1997 .... **CLC 2, 6, 43**
See also CA 5-8R; CAAS 5; CANR 89; CP 1, 2, 3, 4, 5, 6; DLB 27

Silko, Leslie 1948- ...... **CLC 23, 74, 114, 211; NNAL; SSC 37, 66; WLCS**
See also AAYA 14; AMWS 4; ANW; BYA 12; CA 115; 122; CANR 45, 65, 118; CN 4, 5, 6, 7; CP 4, 5, 6, 7; CPW 1; CWP; DA; DA3; DAC; DAM MST, MULT, POP; DLB 143, 175, 256, 275; EWL 3; EXPP; EXPS; LAIT 4; MAL 5; MTCW 2; MTFW 2005; NFS 4; PFS 9, 16; RGAL 4; RGSF 2; SSFS 4, 8, 10, 11; TCWW 1, 2

Silko, Leslie Marmon
See Silko, Leslie

Sillanpaa, Frans Eemil 1888-1964 ... **CLC 19**
See also CA 129; 93-96; DLB 332; EWL 3; MTCW 1

Sillitoe, Alan 1928- .. **CLC 1, 3, 6, 10, 19, 57, 148**
See also AITN 1; BRWS 5; CA 9-12R, 191; CAAE 191; CAAS 2; CANR 8, 26, 55, 139; CDBLB 1960 to Present; CN 1, 2, 3, 4, 5, 6; CP 1, 2, 3, 4, 5; DLB 14, 139; EWL 3; MTCW 1, 2; MTFW 2005; RGEL 2; RGSF 2; SATA 61

Silone, Ignazio 1900-1978 .... **CLC 4**
See also CA 25-28; 81-84; CANR 34; CAP 2; DLB 264; EW 12; EWL 3; MTCW 1; RGSF 2; RGWL 2, 3

Silone, Ignazione
See Silone, Ignazio

Siluriensis, Leolinus
See Jones, Arthur Llewellyn

Silver, Joan Micklin 1935- .... **CLC 20**
See also CA 114; 121; INT CA-121

Silver, Nicholas
See Faust, Frederick

Silverberg, Robert 1935- .... **CLC 7, 140**
See also AAYA 24; BPFB 3; BYA 7, 9; CA 1-4R; 186; CAAE 186; CAAS 3; CANR 1, 20, 36, 85, 140, 175; CLR 59; CN 6, 7; CPW; DAM POP; DLB 8; INT CANR-20; MAICYA 1, 2; MTCW 1, 2; MTFW 2005; SATA 13, 91; SATA-Essay 104; SCFW 1, 2; SFW 4; SUFW 2

Silverstein, Alvin 1933- .... **CLC 17**
See also CA 49-52; CANR 2; CLR 25; JRDA; MAICYA 1, 2; SATA 8, 69, 124

Silverstein, Shel 1932-1999 .... **PC 49**
See also AAYA 40; BW 3; CA 107; 179; CANR 47, 74, 81; CLR 5, 96; CWRI 5; JRDA; MAICYA 1, 2; MTCW 2; MTFW 2005; SATA 33, 92; SATA-Brief 27; SATA-Obit 116

Silverstein, Sheldon Allan
See Silverstein, Shel

Silverstein, Virginia B. 1937- .... **CLC 17**
See also CA 49-52; CANR 2; CLR 25; JRDA; MAICYA 1, 2; SATA 8, 69, 124

Silverstein, Virginia Barbara Opshelor
See Silverstein, Virginia B.

Sim, Georges
See Simenon, Georges

Simak, Clifford D(onald) 1904-1988 . **CLC 1, 55**
See also CA 1-4R; 125; CANR 1, 35; DLB 8; MTCW 1; SATA-Obit 56; SCFW 1, 2; SFW 4

Simenon, Georges 1903-1989 .... **CLC 1, 2, 3, 8, 18, 47**
See also BPFB 3; CA 85-88; 129; CANR 35; CMW 4; DA3; DAM POP; DLB 72; DLBY 1989; EW 12; EWL 3; GFL 1789 to the Present; MSW; MTCW 1, 2; MTFW 2005; RGWL 2, 3

Simenon, Georges Jacques Christian
See Simenon, Georges

Simic, Charles 1938- .... **CLC 6, 9, 22, 49, 68, 130, 256; PC 69**
See also AAYA 78; AMWS 8; CA 29-32R; CAAS 4; CANR 12, 33, 52, 61, 96, 140; CP 2, 3, 4, 5, 6, 7; DA3; DAM POET; DLB 105; MAL 5; MTCW 2; MTFW 2005; PFS 7; RGAL 4; WP

Simmel, Georg 1858-1918 .... **TCLC 64**
See also CA 157; DLB 296

Simmons, Charles (Paul) 1924- .... **CLC 57**
See also CA 89-92; INT CA-89-92

Simmons, Dan 1948- .... **CLC 44**
See also AAYA 16, 54; CA 138; CANR 53, 81, 126, 174; CPW; DAM POP; HGG; SUFW 2

Simmons, James (Stewart Alexander) 1933- .... **CLC 43**
See also CA 105; CAAS 21; CP 1, 2, 3, 4, 5, 6, 7; DLB 40

Simmons, Richard
See Simmons, Dan

Simms, William Gilmore 1806-1870 .... **NCLC 3**
See also DLB 3, 30, 59, 73, 248, 254; RGAL 4

Simon, Carly 1945- .... **CLC 26**
See also CA 105

Simon, Claude 1913-2005 ... **CLC 4, 9, 15, 39**
See also CA 89-92; 241; CANR 33, 117; CWW 2; DAM NOV; DLB 83, 332; EW 13; EWL 3; GFL 1789 to the Present; MTCW 1

Simon, Claude Eugene Henri
See Simon, Claude

Simon, Claude Henri Eugene
See Simon, Claude

Simon, Marvin Neil
See Simon, Neil

Simon, Myles
See Follett, Ken

Simon, Neil 1927- .... **CLC 6, 11, 31, 39, 70, 233; DC 14**
See also AAYA 32; AITN 1; AMWS 4; CA 21-24R; CAD; CANR 26, 54, 87, 126; CD 5, 6; DA3; DAM DRAM; DFS 2, 6, 12, 18,, 24; DLB 7, 266; LAIT 4; MAL 5; MTCW 1, 2; MTFW 2005; RGAL 4; TUS

Simon, Paul 1941(?)- .... **CLC 17**
See also CA 116; 153; CANR 152

Simon, Paul Frederick
See Simon, Paul

Simonon, Paul 1956(?)- .... **CLC 30**

Simonson, Rick CLC 70

Simpson, Harriette
See Arnow, Harriette (Louisa) Simpson

Simpson, Louis 1923- ... **CLC 4, 7, 9, 32, 149**
See also AMWS 9; CA 1-4R; CAAS 4; CANR 1, 61, 140; CP 1, 2, 3, 4, 5, 6, 7; DAM POET; DLB 5; MAL 5; MTCW 1, 2; MTFW 2005; PFS 7, 11, 14; RGAL 4

Simpson, Mona 1957- .... **CLC 44, 146**
See also CA 122; 135; CANR 68, 103; CN 6, 7; EWL 3

Simpson, Mona Elizabeth
See Simpson, Mona

Simpson, N(orman) F(rederick) 1919- .... **CLC 29**
See also CA 13-16R; CBD; DLB 13; RGEL 2

Sinclair, Andrew (Annandale) 1935- . **CLC 2, 14**
See also CA 9-12R; CAAS 5; CANR 14, 38, 91; CN 1, 2, 3, 4, 5, 6, 7; DLB 14; FANT; MTCW 1

Sinclair, Emil
See Hesse, Hermann

Sinclair, Iain 1943- .... **CLC 76**
See also BRWS 14; CA 132; CANR 81, 157; CP 5, 6, 7; HGG

Sinclair, Iain MacGregor
See Sinclair, Iain

Sinclair, Irene
See Griffith, D.W.

Sinclair, Julian
See Sinclair, May

Sinclair, Mary Amelia St. Clair (?)-
See Sinclair, May

Sinclair, May 1865-1946 .... **TCLC 3, 11**
See also CA 104; 166; DLB 36, 135; EWL 3; HGG; RGEL 2; RHW; SUFW

Sinclair, Roy
See Griffith, D.W.

Sinclair, Upton 1878-1968 ...... **CLC 1, 11, 15, 63; TCLC 160; WLC 5**
See also AAYA 63; AMWS 5; BPFB 3; BYA 2; CA 5-8R; 25-28R; CANR 7; CDALB 1929-1941; DA; DA3; DAB; DAC; DAM MST, NOV; DLB 9; EWL 3; INT CANR-7; LAIT 3; MAL 5; MTCW 1, 2; MTFW 2005; NFS 6; RGAL 4; SATA 9; TUS; YAW

Sinclair, Upton Beall
See Sinclair, Upton

Singe, (Edmund) J(ohn) M(illington) 1871-1909 .... **WLC**

Singer, Isaac
See Singer, Isaac Bashevis

Singer, Isaac Bashevis 1904-1991 .. **CLC 1, 3, 6, 9, 11, 15, 23, 38, 69, 111; SSC 3, 53, 80; WLC 5**
See also AAYA 32; AITN 1, 2; AMW; AMWR 2; BPFB 3; BYA 1, 4; CA 1-4R; 134; CANR 1, 39, 106; CDALB 1941-1968; CLR 1; CN 1, 2, 3, 4; CWRI 5; DA; DA3; DAB; DAC; DAM MST, NOV; DLB 6, 28, 52, 278, 332, 333; DLBY 1991; EWL 3; EXPS; HGG; JRDA; LAIT 3; MAICYA 1, 2; MAL 5; MTCW 1, 2; MTFW 2005; RGAL 4; RGHL; RGSF 2; SATA 3, 27; SATA-Obit 68; SSFS 2, 12, 16, 27; TUS; TWA

Singer, Israel Joshua 1893-1944 .... **TCLC 33**
See also CA 169; DLB 333; EWL 3

Singh, Khushwant 1915- .... **CLC 11**
See also CA 9-12R; CAAS 9; CANR 6, 84; CN 1, 2, 3, 4, 5, 6, 7; DLB 323; EWL 3; RGEL 2

Singleton, Ann
See Benedict, Ruth

Singleton, John 1968(?)- .... **CLC 156**
See also AAYA 50; BW 2, 3; CA 138; CANR 67, 82; DAM MULT

Siniavskii, Andrei
See Sinyavsky, Andrei (Donatevich)

Sinibaldi, Fosco
See Kacew, Romain

Sinjohn, John
See Galsworthy, John

Sinyavsky, Andrei (Donatevich) 1925-1997 .... **CLC 8**
See also CA 85-88; 159; CWW 2; EWL 3; RGSF 2

Sinyavsky, Andrey Donatovich
See Sinyavsky, Andrei (Donatevich)

Sirin, V.
See Nabokov, Vladimir

Sissman, L(ouis) E(dward) 1928-1976 .... **CLC 9, 18**
See also CA 21-24R; 65-68; CANR 13; CP 2; DLB 5

Sisson, C(harles) H(ubert) 1914-2003 .... **CLC 8**
See also BRWS 11; CA 1-4R; 220; CAAS 3; CANR 3, 48, 84; CP 1, 2, 3, 4, 5, 6, 7; DLB 27

Sitting Bull 1831(?)-1890 .... **NNAL**
See also DA3; DAM MULT

Sitwell, Dame Edith 1887-1964 ..... **CLC 2, 9, 67; PC 3**
See also BRW 7; CA 9-12R; CANR 35; CDBLB 1945-1960; DAM POET; DLB 20; EWL 3; MTCW 1, 2; MTFW 2005; RGEL 2; TEA

Siwaarmill, H. P.
See Sharp, William

Sjoewall, Maj 1935- .... **CLC 7**
See also BPFB 3; CA 65-68; CANR 73; CMW 4; MSW

Sjowall, Maj
See Sjoewall, Maj

Skelton, John 1460(?)-1529 ..... **LC 71; PC 25**
See also BRW 1; DLB 136; RGEL 2

Skelton, Robin 1925-1997 .... **CLC 13**
See also AITN 2; CA 5-8R; 160; CAAS 5; CANR 28, 89; CCA 1; CP 1, 2, 3, 4, 5, 6; DLB 27, 53

Skolimowski, Jerzy 1938- .... **CLC 20**
See also CA 128

Skram, Amalie (Bertha) 1846-1905 .... **TCLC 25**
See also CA 165; DLB 354

Skvorecky, Josef 1924- . **CLC 15, 39, 69, 152**
See also CA 61-64; CAAS 1; CANR 10, 34, 63, 108; CDWLB 4; CWW 2; DA3; DAC; DAM NOV; DLB 232; EWL 3; MTCW 1, 2; MTFW 2005

Skvorecky, Josef Vaclav
See Skvorecky, Josef

Slade, Bernard 1930-
See Newbound, Bernard Slade

Slaughter, Carolyn 1946- .... **CLC 56**
See also CA 85-88; CANR 85, 169; CN 5, 6, 7

Slaughter, Frank G(ill) 1908-2001 ... **CLC 29**
See also AITN 2; CA 5-8R; 197; CANR 5, 85; INT CANR-5; RHW

Slavitt, David R. 1935- .... **CLC 5, 14**
See also CA 21-24R; CAAS 3; CANR 41, 83; CN 1, 2; CP 1, 2, 3, 4, 5, 6, 7; DLB 5, 6

Slavitt, David Rytman
See Slavitt, David R.

Slesinger, Tess 1905-1945 .... **TCLC 10**
See also CA 107; 199; DLB 102

Slessor, Kenneth 1901-1971 .... **CLC 14**
See also CA 102; 89-92; DLB 260; RGEL 2

Slowacki, Juliusz 1809-1849 .... **NCLC 15**
See also RGWL 3

Smart, Christopher 1722-1771 .... **LC 3, 134; PC 13**
See also DAM POET; DLB 109; RGEL 2

Song, Cathy 1955- .... **AAL; PC 21**
   See also CA 154; CANR 118; CWP; DLB
   169, 312; EXPP; FW; PFS 5

Sontag, Susan 1933-2004 ... **CLC 1, 2, 10, 13,**
   31, 105, 195, 277
   See also AMWS 3; CA 17-20R; 234; CANR
   25, 51, 74, 97, 184; CN 1, 2, 3, 4, 5, 6, 7;
   CPW; DA3; DAM POP; DLB 2, 67; EWL
   3; MAL 5; MBL; MTCW 1, 2; MTFW
   2005; RGAL 4; RHW; SSFS 10

Sophocles 496(?)B.C.-406(?)B.C. .... **CMLC 2,**
   47, 51, 86; DC 1; WLCS
   See also AW 1; CDWLB 1; DA; DA3;
   DAB; DAC; DAM DRAM, MST; DFS 1,
   4, 8, 24; DLB 176; LAIT 1; LATS 1:1;
   LMFS 1; RGWL 2, 3; TWA; WLIT 8

Sordello 1189-1269 .... **CMLC 15**

Sorel, Georges 1847-1922 .... **TCLC 91**
   See also CA 118; 188

Sorel, Julia
   See Drexler, Rosalyn

Sorokin, Vladimir CLC 59
   See also CA 258; DLB 285

Sorokin, Vladimir Georgievich
   See Sorokin, Vladimir

Sorrentino, Gilbert 1929-2006 .... **CLC 3, 7,**
   14, 22, 40, 247
   See also CA 77-80; 250; CANR 14, 33, 115,
   157; CN 3, 4, 5, 6, 7; CP 1, 2, 3, 4, 5, 6,
   7; DLB 5, 173; DLBY 1980; INT
   CANR-14

Soseki
   See Natsume, Soseki

Soto, Gary 1952- ... **CLC 32, 80; HLC 2; PC**
   28
   See also AAYA 10, 37; BYA 11; CA 119;
   125; CANR 50, 74, 107, 157; CLR 38;
   CP 4, 5, 6, 7; DAM MULT; DFS 26; DLB
   82; EWL 3; EXPP; HW 1, 2; INT CA-
   125; JRDA; LLW; MAICYA 2; MAIC-
   YAS 1; MAL 5; MTCW 2; MTFW 2005;
   PFS 7, 30; RGAL 4; SATA 80, 120, 174;
   WYA; YAW

Soupault, Philippe 1897-1990 .... **CLC 68**
   See also CA 116; 147; 131; EWL 3; GFL
   1789 to the Present; LMFS 2

Souster, (Holmes) Raymond 1921- .... **CLC 5,**
   14
   See also CA 13-16R; CAAS 14; CANR 13,
   29, 53; CP 1, 2, 3, 4, 5, 6, 7; DA3; DAC;
   DAM POET; DLB 88; RGEL 2; SATA 63

Southern, Terry 1924(?)-1995 .... **CLC 7**
   See also AMWS 11; BPFB 3; CA 1-4R;
   150; CANR 1, 55, 107; CN 1, 2, 3, 4, 5,
   6; DLB 2; IDFW 3, 4

Southerne, Thomas 1660-1746 .... **LC 99**
   See also DLB 80; RGEL 2

Southey, Robert 1774-1843 .... **NCLC 8, 97**
   See also BRW 4; DLB 93, 107, 142; RGEL
   2; SATA 54

Southwell, Robert 1561(?)-1595 .... **LC 108**
   See also DLB 167; RGEL 2; TEA

Southworth, Emma Dorothy Eliza Nevitte
   1819-1899 .... **NCLC 26**
   See also DLB 239

Souza, Ernest
   See Scott, Evelyn

Soyinka, Wole 1934- .. **BLC 1:3, 2:3; CLC 3,**
   5, 14, 36, 44, 179; DC 2; WLC 5
   See also AFW; BW 2, 3; CA 13-16R;
   CANR 27, 39, 82, 136; CD 5, 6; CDWLB
   3; CN 6, 7; CP 1, 2, 3, 4, 5, 6 ,7; DA;
   DA3; DAB; DAC; DAM DRAM, MST,
   MULT; DFS 10, 26; DLB 125, 332; EWL
   3; MTCW 1, 2; MTFW 2005; PFS 27;
   RGEL 2; TWA; WLIT 2; WWE 1

Spackman, W(illiam) M(ode)
   1905-1990 .... **CLC 46**
   See also CA 81-84; 132

Spacks, Barry (Bernard) 1931- .... **CLC 14**
   See also CA 154; CANR 33, 109; CP 3, 4,
   5, 6, 7; DLB 105

Spanidou, Irini 1946- .... **CLC 44**
   See also CA 185; CANR 179

Spark, Muriel 1918-2006 .... **CLC 2, 3, 5, 8,**
   13, 18, 40, 94, 242; PC 72; SSC 10, 115
   See also BRWS 1; CA 5-8R; 251; CANR
   12, 36, 76, 89, 131; CDBLB 1945-1960;
   CN 1, 2, 3, 4, 5, 6, 7; CP 1, 2, 3, 4, 5, 6,
   7; DA3; DAB; DAC; DAM MST, NOV;
   DLB 15, 139; EWL 3; FW; INT CANR-
   12; LAIT 4; MTCW 1, 2; MTFW 2005;
   NFS 22; RGEL 2; TEA; WLIT 4; YAW

Spark, Muriel Sarah
   See Spark, Muriel

Spaulding, Douglas
   See Bradbury, Ray

Spaulding, Leonard
   See Bradbury, Ray

Speght, Rachel 1597-c. 1630 .... **LC 97**
   See also DLB 126

Spence, J. A. D.
   See Eliot, T. S.

Spencer, Anne 1882-1975 ...... **HR 1:3; PC 77**
   See also BW 2; CA 161; DLB 51, 54

Spencer, Elizabeth 1921- .... **CLC 22; SSC 57**
   See also CA 13-16R; CANR 32, 65, 87; CN
   1, 2, 3, 4, 5, 6, 7; CSW; DLB 6, 218;
   EWL 3; MTCW 1; RGAL 4; SATA 14

Spencer, Leonard G.
   See Silverberg, Robert

Spencer, Scott 1945- .... **CLC 30**
   See also CA 113; CANR 51, 148, 190;
   DLBY 1986

Spender, Stephen 1909-1995 ..... **CLC 1, 2, 5,**
   10, 41, 91; PC 71
   See also BRWS 2; CA 9-12R; 149; CANR
   31, 54; CDBLB 1945-1960; CP 1, 2, 3, 4,
   5, 6; DA3; DAM POET; DLB 20; EWL
   3; MTCW 1, 2; MTFW 2005; PAB; PFS
   23; RGEL 2; TEA

Spender, Stephen Harold
   See Spender, Stephen

Spengler, Oswald (Arnold Gottfried)
   1880-1936 .... **TCLC 25**
   See also CA 118; 189

Spenser, Edmund 1552(?)-1599 ...... **LC 5, 39,**
   117; PC 8, 42; WLC 5
   See also AAYA 60; BRW 1; CDBLB Before
   1660; DA; DA3; DAB; DAC; DAM MST,
   POET; DLB 167; EFS 2; EXPP; PAB;
   RGEL 2; TEA; WLIT 3; WP

Spicer, Jack 1925-1965 .... **CLC 8, 18, 72**
   See also BG 1:3; CA 85-88; DAM POET;
   DLB 5, 16, 193; GLL 1; WP

Spiegelman, Art 1948- .... **CLC 76, 178**
   See also AAYA 10, 46; CA 125; CANR 41,
   55, 74, 124; DLB 299; MTCW 2; MTFW
   2005; RGHL; SATA 109, 158; YAW

Spielberg, Peter 1929- .... **CLC 6**
   See also CA 5-8R; CANR 4, 48; DLBY
   1981

Spielberg, Steven 1947- .... **CLC 20, 188**
   See also AAYA 8, 24; CA 77-80; CANR
   32; SATA 32

Spillane, Frank Morrison
   See Spillane, Mickey

Spillane, Mickey 1918-2006 .. **CLC 3, 13, 241**
   See also BPFB 3; CA 25-28R; 252; CANR
   28, 63, 125; CMW 4; DA3; DLB 226;
   MSW; MTCW 1, 2; MTFW 2005; SATA
   66; SATA-Obit 176

Spinoza, Benedictus de 1632-1677 . **LC 9, 58,**
   177

Spinrad, Norman (Richard) 1940- ... **CLC 46**
   See also BPFB 3; CA 37-40R, 233; CAAE
   233; CAAS 19; CANR 20, 91; DLB 8;
   INT CANR-20; SFW 4

Spitteler, Carl 1845-1924 .... **TCLC 12**
   See also CA 109; DLB 129, 332; EWL 3

Spitteler, Karl Friedrich Georg
   See Spitteler, Carl

Spivack, Kathleen (Romola Drucker)
   1938- .... **CLC 6**
   See also CA 49-52

Spivak, Gayatri Chakravorty
   1942- .... **CLC 233**
   See also CA 110; 154; CANR 91; FW;
   LMFS 2

Spofford, Harriet (Elizabeth) Prescott
   1835-1921 .... **SSC 87**
   See also CA 201; DLB 74, 221

Spoto, Donald 1941- .... **CLC 39**
   See also CA 65-68; CANR 11, 57, 93, 173

Springsteen, Bruce 1949- .... **CLC 17**
   See also CA 111

Springsteen, Bruce F.
   See Springsteen, Bruce

Spurling, Hilary 1940- .... **CLC 34**
   See also CA 104; CANR 25, 52, 94, 157

Spurling, Susan Hilary
   See Spurling, Hilary

Spyker, John Howland
   See Elman, Richard (Martin)

Squared, A.
   See Abbott, Edwin A.

Squires, (James) Radcliffe
   1917-1993 .... **CLC 51**
   See also CA 1-4R; 140; CANR 6, 21; CP 1,
   2, 3, 4, 5

Srivastav, Dhanpat Ray
   See Srivastava, Dhanpat Rai

Srivastav, Dheanpatrai
   See Srivastava, Dhanpat Rai

Srivastava, Dhanpat Rai
   1880(?)-1936 .... **TCLC 21**
   See also CA 118; 197; EWL 3

Ssu-ma Ch'ien c. 145B.C.-c.
   86B.C. .... **CMLC 96**

Ssu-ma T'an (?)-c. 110B.C. .... **CMLC 96**

Stacy, Donald
   See Pohl, Frederik

Stael
   See Stael-Holstein, Anne Louise Germaine
   Necker

Stael, Germaine de
   See Stael-Holstein, Anne Louise Germaine
   Necker

Stael-Holstein, Anne Louise Germaine
   Necker 1766-1817 .... **NCLC 3, 91**
   See also DLB 119, 192; EW 5; FL 1:3; FW;
   GFL 1789 to the Present; RGWL 2, 3;
   TWA

Stafford, Jean 1915-1979 .. **CLC 4, 7, 19, 68;**
   SSC 26, 86
   See also CA 1-4R; 85-88; CANR 3, 65; CN
   1, 2; DLB 2, 173; MAL 5; MTCW 1, 2;
   MTFW 2005; RGAL 4; RGSF 2; SATA-
   Obit 22; SSFS 21; TCWW 1, 2; TUS

Stafford, William 1914-1993 ... **CLC 4, 7, 29;**
   PC 71
   See also AMWS 11; CA 5-8R; 142; CAAS
   3; CANR 5, 22; CP 1, 2, 3, 4, 5; DAM
   POET; DLB 5, 206; EXPP; INT CANR-
   22; MAL 5; PFS 2, 8, 16; RGAL 4; WP

Stafford, William Edgar
   See Stafford, William

Stagnelius, Eric Johan 1793-1823 . **NCLC 61**

Staines, Trevor
   See Brunner, John (Kilian Houston)

Stairs, Gordon
   See Austin, Mary Hunter

Stalin, Joseph 1879-1953 .... **TCLC 92**

Stampa, Gaspara c. 1524-1554 .. **LC 114; PC**
   43
   See also RGWL 2, 3; WLIT 7

Stitt, Milan 1941-2009 .... **CLC 29**
See also CA 69-72; 284
Stitt, Milan William
See Stitt, Milan
Stockton, Francis Richard
1834-1902 .... **TCLC 47**
See also AAYA 68; BYA 4, 13; CA 108;
137; DLB 42, 74; DLBD 13; EXPS; MAI-
CYA 1, 2; SATA 44; SATA-Brief 32; SFW
4; SSFS 3; SUFW; WCH
Stockton, Frank R.
See Stockton, Francis Richard
Stoddard, Charles
See Kuttner, Henry
Stoker, Abraham
See Stoker, Bram
Stoker, Bram 1847-1912 ... **SSC 62; TCLC 8,**
144; WLC 6
See also AAYA 23; BPFB 3; BRWS 3; BYA
5; CA 105; 150; CDBLB 1890-1914; DA;
DA3; DAB; DAC; DAM MST, NOV;
DLB 304; GL 3; HGG; LATS 1:1; MTFW
2005; NFS 18; RGEL 2; SATA 29; SUFW;
TEA; WLIT 4
Stolz, Mary 1920-2006 .... **CLC 12**
See also AAYA 8, 73; AITN 1; CA 5-8R;
255; CANR 13, 41, 112; JRDA; MAICYA
1, 2; SAAS 3; SATA 10, 71, 133; SATA-
Obit 180; YAW
Stolz, Mary Slattery
See Stolz, Mary
Stone, Irving 1903-1989 .... **CLC 7**
See also AITN 1; BPFB 3; CA 1-4R; 129;
CAAS 3; CANR 1, 23; CN 1, 2, 3, 4;
CPW; DA3; DAM POP; INT CANR-23;
MTCW 1, 2; MTFW 2005; RHW; SATA
3; SATA-Obit 64
Stone, Oliver 1946- .... **CLC 73**
See also AAYA 15, 64; CA 110; CANR 55,
125
Stone, Oliver William
See Stone, Oliver
Stone, Robert 1937- .... **CLC 5, 23, 42, 175**
See also AMWS 5; BPFB 3; CA 85-88;
CANR 23, 66, 95, 173; CN 4, 5, 6, 7;
DLB 152; EWL 3; INT CANR-23; MAL
5; MTCW 1; MTFW 2005
Stone, Robert Anthony
See Stone, Robert
Stone, Ruth 1915- .... **PC 53**
See also CA 45-48; CANR 2, 91; CP 5, 6,
7; CSW; DLB 105; PFS 19
Stone, Zachary
See Follett, Ken
Stoppard, Tom 1937- ... **CLC 1, 3, 4, 5, 8, 15,**
29, 34, 63, 91; DC 6, 30; WLC 6
See also AAYA 63; BRWC 1; BRWR 2;
BRWS 1; CA 81-84; CANR 39, 67, 125;
CBD; CD 5, 6; CDBLB 1960 to Present;
DA; DA3; DAB; DAC; DAM DRAM,
MST; DFS 2, 5, 8, 11, 13, 16; DLB 13,
233; DLBY 1985; EWL 3; LATS 1:2;
LNFS 3; MTCW 1, 2; MTFW 2005;
RGEL 2; TEA; WLIT 4
Storey, David (Malcolm) 1933- . **CLC 2, 4, 5,**
8
See also BRWS 1; CA 81-84; CANR 36;
CBD; CD 5, 6; CN 1, 2, 3, 4, 5, 6; DAM
DRAM; DLB 13, 14, 207, 245, 326; EWL
3; MTCW 1; RGEL 2
Storm, Hyemeyohsts 1935- ... **CLC 3; NNAL**
See also CA 81-84; CANR 45; DAM MULT
Storm, (Hans) Theodor (Woldsen)
1817-1888 ... **NCLC 1, 195; SSC 27, 106**
See also CDWLB 2; DLB 129; EW; RGSF
2; RGWL 2, 3
Storni, Alfonsina 1892-1938 . **HLC 2; PC 33;**
TCLC 5
See also CA 104; 131; DAM MULT; DLB
283; HW 1; LAW

Stoughton, William 1631-1701 .... **LC 38**
See also DLB 24
Stout, Rex (Todhunter) 1886-1975 ..... **CLC 3**
See also AAYA 79; AITN 2; BPFB 3; CA
61-64; CANR 71; CMW 4; CN 2; DLB
306; MSW; RGAL 4
Stow, (Julian) Randolph 1935- ... **CLC 23, 48**
See also CA 13-16R; CANR 33; CN 1, 2,
3, 4, 5, 6, 7; CP 1, 2, 3, 4; DLB 260;
MTCW 1; RGEL 2
Stowe, Harriet Beecher 1811-1896 . **NCLC 3,**
50, 133, 195; WLC 6
See also AAYA 53; AMWS 1; CDALB
1865-1917; CLR 131; DA; DA3; DAB;
DAC; DAM MST, NOV; DLB 1, 12, 42,
74, 189, 239, 243; EXPN; FL 1:3; JRDA;
LAIT 2; MAICYA 1, 2; NFS 6; RGAL 4;
TUS; YABC 1
Stowe, Harriet Elizabeth Beecher
See Stowe, Harriet Beecher
Strabo c. 64B.C.-c. 25 .... **CMLC 37**
See also DLB 176
Strachey, (Giles) Lytton
1880-1932 .... **TCLC 12**
See also BRWS 2; CA 110; 178; DLB 149;
DLBD 10; EWL 3; MTCW 2; NCFS 4
Stramm, August 1874-1915 .... **PC 50**
See also CA 195; EWL 3
Strand, Mark 1934- .. **CLC 6, 18, 41, 71; PC**
63
See also AMWS 4; CA 21-24R; CANR 40,
65, 100; CP 1, 2, 3, 4, 5, 6, 7; DAM
POET; DLB 5, 342; EWL 3; MAL 5; PAB;
PFS 9, 18; RGAL 4; SATA 41; TCLE 1:2
Stratton-Porter, Gene 1863-1924 ... **TCLC 21**
See also ANW; BPFB 3; CA 112; 137; CLR
87; CWRI 5; DLB 221; DLBD 14; MAI-
CYA 1, 2; RHW; SATA 15
Stratton-Porter, Geneva Grace
See Stratton-Porter, Gene
Straub, Peter 1943- .... **CLC 28, 107**
See also AAYA 82; BEST 89:1; BPFB 3;
CA 85-88; CANR 28, 65, 109; CPW;
DAM POP; DLBY 1984; HGG; MTCW
1, 2; MTFW 2005; SUFW 2
Straub, Peter Francis
See Straub, Peter
Strauss, Botho 1944- .... **CLC 22**
See also CA 157; CWW 2; DLB 124
Strauss, Leo 1899-1973 .... **TCLC 141**
See also CA 101; 45-48; CANR 122
Streatfeild, Mary Noel
See Streatfeild, Noel
Streatfeild, Noel 1897(?)-1986 .... **CLC 21**
See also CA 81-84; 120; CANR 31; CLR
17, 83; CWRI 5; DLB 160; MAICYA 1,
2; SATA 20; SATA-Obit 48
Stribling, T(homas) S(igismund)
1881-1965 .... **CLC 23**
See also CA 189; 107; CMW 4; DLB 9;
RGAL 4
Strindberg, August 1849-1912 .... **DC 18;**
TCLC 1, 8, 21, 47, 231; WLC 6
See also CA 104; 135; DA; DA3; DAB;
DAC; DAM DRAM, MST; DFS 4, 9;
DLB 259; EW 7; EWL 3; IDTP; LMFS
2; MTCW 2; MTFW 2005; RGWL 2, 3;
TWA
Strindberg, Johan August
See Strindberg, August
Stringer, Arthur 1874-1950 .... **TCLC 37**
See also CA 161; DLB 92
Stringer, David
See Roberts, Keith (John Kingston)
Stroheim, Erich von 1885-1957 ..... **TCLC 71**
Strugatskii, Arkadii 1925-1991 .... **CLC 27**
See also CA 106; 135; DLB 302; SFW 4
Strugatskii, Arkadii Natanovich
See Strugatskii, Arkadii

Strugatskii, Boris 1933- .... **CLC 27**
See also CA 106; DLB 302; SFW 4
Strugatskii, Boris Natanovich
See Strugatskii, Boris
Strugatsky, Arkadii Natanovich
See Strugatskii, Arkadii
Strugatsky, Boris
See Strugatskii, Boris
Strugatsky, Boris Natanovich
See Strugatskii, Boris
Strummer, Joe 1952-2002 .... **CLC 30**
Strunk, William, Jr. 1869-1946 ...... **TCLC 92**
See also CA 118; 164; NCFS 5
Stryk, Lucien 1924- .... **PC 27**
See also CA 13-16R; CANR 10, 28, 55,
110; CP 1, 2, 3, 4, 5, 6, 7
Stuart, Don A.
See Campbell, John W(ood, Jr.)
Stuart, Ian
See MacLean, Alistair
Stuart, Jesse (Hilton) 1906-1984 ... **CLC 1, 8,**
11, 14, 34; SSC 31
See also CA 5-8R; 112; CANR 31; CN 1,
2, 3; DLB 9, 48, 102; DLBY 1984; SATA
2; SATA-Obit 36
Stubblefield, Sally
See Trumbo, Dalton
Sturgeon, Theodore (Hamilton)
1918-1985 .... **CLC 22, 39**
See also AAYA 51; BPFB 3; BYA 9, 10;
CA 81-84; 116; CANR 32, 103; DLB 8;
DLBY 1985; HGG; MTCW 1, 2; MTFW
2005; SCFW; SFW 4; SUFW
Sturges, Preston 1898-1959 .... **TCLC 48**
See also CA 114; 149; DLB 26
Styron, William 1925-2006 .. **CLC 1, 3, 5, 11,**
15, 60, 232, 244; SSC 25
See also AMW; AMWC 2; BEST 90:4;
BPFB 3; CA 5-8R; 255; CANR 6, 33, 74,
126, 191; CDALB 1968-1988; CN 1, 2,
3, 4, 5, 6, 7; CPW; CSW; DA3; DAM
NOV, POP; DLB 2, 143, 299; DLBY
1980; EWL 3; INT CANR-6; LAIT 2;
MAL 5; MTCW 1, 2; MTFW 2005; NCFS
1; NFS 22; RGAL 4; RGHL; RHW; TUS
Styron, William C.
See Styron, William
Styron, William Clark
See Styron, William
Su, Chien 1884-1918 .... **TCLC 24**
See also CA 123; EWL 3
Suarez Lynch, B.
See Bioy Casares, Adolfo; Borges, Jorge
Luis
Suassuna, Ariano Vilar 1927- .... **HLCS 1**
See also CA 178; DLB 307; HW 2; LAW
Suckert, Kurt Erich
See Malaparte, Curzio
Suckling, Sir John 1609-1642 . **LC 75; PC 30**
See also BRW 2; DAM POET; DLB 58,
126; EXPP; PAB; RGEL 2
Suckow, Ruth 1892-1960 .... **SSC 18**
See also CA 193; 113; DLB 9, 102; RGAL
4; TCWW 2
Sudermann, Hermann 1857-1928 .. **TCLC 15**
See also CA 107; 201; DLB 118
Sue, Eugene 1804-1857 .... **NCLC 1**
See also DLB 119
Sueskind, Patrick
See Suskind, Patrick
Suetonius c. 70-c. 130 .... **CMLC 60**
See also AW 2; DLB 211; RGWL 2, 3;
WLIT 8
Su Hsuan-ying
See Su, Chien
Su Hsuean-ying
See Su, Chien

Trollope, Anthony 1815-1882 .... **NCLC 6, 33, 101, 215; SSC 28, 133; WLC 6**
See also BRW 5; CDBLB 1832-1890; DA; DA3; DAB; DAC; DAM MST, NOV; DLB 21, 57, 159; RGEL 2; RGSF 2; SATA 22

Trollope, Frances 1779-1863 .... **NCLC 30**
See also DLB 21, 166

Trollope, Joanna 1943- .... **CLC 186**
See also CA 101; CANR 58, 95, 149, 191; CN 7; CPW; DLB 207; RHW

Trotsky, Leon 1879-1940 .... **TCLC 22**
See also CA 118; 167

Trotter (Cockburn), Catharine 1679-1749 .... **LC 8, 165**
See also DLB 84, 252

Trotter, Wilfred 1872-1939 .... **TCLC 97**

Troupe, Quincy 1943- .... **BLC 2:3**
See also BW 2; CA 113; 124; CANR 43, 90, 126; DLB 41

Trout, Kilgore
See Farmer, Philip Jose

Trow, George William Swift
See Trow, George W.S.

Trow, George W.S. 1943-2006 .... **CLC 52**
See also CA 126; 255; CANR 91

Troyat, Henri 1911-2007 .... **CLC 23**
See also CA 45-48; 258; CANR 2, 33, 67, 117; GFL 1789 to the Present; MTCW 1

Trudeau, Garretson Beekman
See Trudeau, G.B.

Trudeau, Garry
See Trudeau, G.B.

Trudeau, Garry B.
See Trudeau, G.B.

Trudeau, G.B. 1948- .... **CLC 12**
See also AAYA 10, 60; AITN 2; CA 81-84; CANR 31; SATA 35, 168

Truffaut, Francois 1932-1984 ... **CLC 20, 101**
See also CA 81-84; 113; CANR 34

Trumbo, Dalton 1905-1976 .... **CLC 19**
See also CA 21-24R; 69-72; CANR 10; CN 1, 2; DLB 26; IDFW 3, 4; YAW

Trumbull, John 1750-1831 .... **NCLC 30**
See also DLB 31; RGAL 4

Trundlett, Helen B.
See Eliot, T. S.

Truth, Sojourner 1797(?)-1883 ...... **NCLC 94**
See also DLB 239; FW; LAIT 2

Tryon, Thomas 1926-1991 .... **CLC 3, 11**
See also AITN 1; BPFB 3; CA 29-32R; 135; CANR 32, 77; CPW; DA3; DAM POP; HGG; MTCW 1

Tryon, Tom
See Tryon, Thomas

Ts'ao Hsueh-ch'in 1715(?)-1763 .... **LC 1**

Tsurayuki Ed. fl. 10th cent. - .... **PC 73**

Tsvetaeva, Marina 1892-1941 . **PC 14; TCLC 7, 35**
See also CA 104; 128; CANR 73; DLB 295; EW 11; MTCW 1, 2; PFS 29; RGWL 2, 3

Tsvetaeva Efron, Marina Ivanovna
See Tsvetaeva, Marina

Tuck, Lily 1938- .... **CLC 70**
See also AAYA 74; CA 139; CANR 90, 192

Tuckerman, Frederick Goddard 1821-1873 .... **PC 85**
See also DLB 243; RGAL 4

Tu Fu 712-770 .... **PC 9**
See also DAM MULT; RGWL 2, 3; TWA; WP

Tulsidas, Gosvami 1532(?)-1623 .... **LC 158**
See also RGWL 2, 3

Tunis, John R(oberts) 1889-1975 ..... **CLC 12**
See also BYA 1; CA 61-64; CANR 62; DLB 22, 171; JRDA; MAICYA 1, 2; SATA 37; SATA-Brief 30; YAW

Tuohy, Frank
See Tuohy, John Francis

Tuohy, John Francis 1925- .... **CLC 37**
See also CA 5-8R; 178; CANR 3, 47; CN 1, 2, 3, 4, 5, 6, 7; DLB 14, 139

Turco, Lewis 1934- .... **CLC 11, 63**
See also CA 13-16R; CAAS 22; CANR 24, 51, 185; CP 1, 2, 3, 4, 5, 6, 7; DLBY 1984; TCLE 1:2

Turco, Lewis Putnam
See Turco, Lewis

Turgenev, Ivan 1818-1883 . **DC 7; NCLC 21, 37, 122; SSC 7, 57; WLC 6**
See also AAYA 58; DA; DAB; DAC; DAM MST, NOV; DFS 6; DLB 238, 284; EW 6; LATS 1:1; NFS 16; RGSF 2; RGWL 2, 3; TWA

Turgenev, Ivan Sergeevich
See Turgenev, Ivan

Turgot, Anne-Robert-Jacques 1727-1781 .... **LC 26**
See also DLB 314

Turner, Frederick 1943- .... **CLC 48**
See also CA 73-76, 227; CAAE 227; CAAS 10; CANR 12, 30, 56; DLB 40, 282

Turton, James
See Crace, Jim

Tutu, Desmond M(pilo) 1931- .... **BLC 1:3; CLC 80**
See also BW 1, 3; CA 125; CANR 67, 81; DAM MULT

Tutuola, Amos 1920-1997 .... **BLC 1:3, 2:3; CLC 5, 14, 29; TCLC 188**
See also AAYA 76; AFW; BW 2, 3; CA 9-12R; 159; CANR 27, 66; CDWLB 3; CN 1, 2, 3, 4, 5, 6; DA3; DAM MULT; DLB 125; DNFS 2; EWL 3; MTCW 1, 2; MTFW 2005; RGEL 2; WLIT 2

Twain, Mark 1835-1910 ... **SSC 6, 26, 34, 87, 119; TCLC 6, 12, 19, 36, 48, 59, 161, 185; WLC 6**
See also AAYA 20; AMW; AMWC 1; BPFB 3; BYA 2, 3, 11, 14; CA 104; 135; CDALB 1865-1917; CLR 58, 60, 66; DA; DA3; DAB; DAC; DAM MST, NOV; DLB 12, 23, 64, 74, 186, 189, 11, 343; EXPN; EXPS; JRDA; LAIT 2; LMFS 1; MAI-CYA 1, 2; MAL 5; NCFS 4; NFS 1, 6; RGAL 4; RGSF 2; SATA 100; SFW 4; SSFS 1, 7, 16, 21, 27; SUFW; TUS; WCH; WYA; YABC 2; YAW

Twohill, Maggie
See Angell, Judie

Tyler, Anne 1941- . **CLC 7, 11, 18, 28, 44, 59, 103, 205, 265**
See also AAYA 18, 60; AMWS 4; BEST 89:1; BPFB 3; BYA 12; CA 9-12R; CANR 11, 33, 53, 109, 132, 168; CDALBS; CN 1, 2, 3, 4, 5, 6, 7; CPW; CSW; DAM NOV, POP; DLB 6, 143; DLBY 1982; EWL 3; EXPN; LATS 1:2; MAL 5; MBL; MTCW 1, 2; MTFW 2005; NFS 2, 7, 10; RGAL 4; SATA 7, 90, 173; SSFS 17; TCLE 1:2; TUS; YAW

Tyler, Royall 1757-1826 .... **NCLC 3**
See also DLB 37; RGAL 4

Tynan, Katharine 1861-1931 ... **TCLC 3, 217**
See also CA 104; 167; DLB 153, 240; FW

Tyndale, William c. 1484-1536 .... **LC 103**
See also DLB 132

Tyutchev, Fyodor 1803-1873 .... **NCLC 34**

Tzara, Tristan 1896-1963 .... **CLC 47; PC 27; TCLC 168**
See also CA 153; 89-92; DAM POET; EWL 3; MTCW 2

Uc de Saint Circ c. 1190B.C.-13th cent. B.C. .... **CMLC 102**

Uchida, Yoshiko 1921-1992 .... **AAL**
See also AAYA 16; BYA 2, 3; CA 13-16R; 139; CANR 6, 22, 47, 61; CDALBS; CLR 6, 56; CWRI 5; DLB 312; JRDA; MAI-CYA 1, 2; MTCW 1, 2; MTFW 2005; NFS 26; SAAS 1; SATA 1, 53; SATA-Obit 72

Udall, Nicholas 1504-1556 .... **LC 84**
See also DLB 62; RGEL 2

Ueda Akinari 1734-1809 .... **NCLC 131**

Uhry, Alfred 1936- .... **CLC 55; DC 28**
See also CA 127; 133; CAD; CANR 112; CD 5, 6; CSW; DA3; DAM DRAM, POP; DFS 11, 15; INT CA-133; MTFW 2005

Ulf, Haervéd
See Strindberg, August

Ulf, Harved
See Strindberg, August

Ulibarri, Sabine R(eyes) 1919-2003 .... **CLC 83; HLCS 2**
See also CA 131; 214; CANR 81; DAM MULT; DLB 82; HW 1, 2; RGSF 2

Ulyanov, V. I.
See Lenin

Ulyanov, Vladimir Ilyich
See Lenin

Ulyanov-Lenin
See Lenin

Unamuno, Miguel de 1864-1936 .... **HLC 2; SSC 11, 69; TCLC 2, 9, 148**
See also CA 104; 131; CANR 81; DAM MULT, NOV; DLB 108, 322; EW 8; EWL 3; HW 1, 2; MTCW 1, 2; MTFW 2005; RGSF 2; RGWL 2, 3; SSFS 20; TWA

Unamuno y Jugo, Miguel de
See Unamuno, Miguel de

Uncle Shelby
See Silverstein, Shel

Undercliffe, Errol
See Campbell, Ramsey

Underwood, Miles
See Glassco, John

Undset, Sigrid 1882-1949 .... **TCLC 3, 197; WLC 6**
See also AAYA 77; CA 104; 129; DA; DA3; DAB; DAC; DAM MST, NOV; DLB 293, 332; EW 9; EWL 3; FW; MTCW 1, 2; MTFW 2005; RGWL 2, 3

Ungaretti, Giuseppe 1888-1970 ... **CLC 7, 11, 15; PC 57; TCLC 200**
See also CA 19-20; 25-28R; CAP 2; DLB 114; EW 10; EWL 3; PFS 20; RGWL 2, 3; WLIT 7

Unger, Douglas 1952- .... **CLC 34**
See also CA 130; CANR 94, 155

Unsworth, Barry 1930- .... **CLC 76, 127**
See also BRWS 7; CA 25-28R; CANR 30, 54, 125, 171, 202; CN 6, 7; DLB 194, 326

Unsworth, Barry Forster
See Unsworth, Barry

Updike, John 1932-2009 .... **CLC 1, 2, 3, 5, 7, 9, 13, 15, 23, 34, 43, 70, 139, 214, 278; PC 90; SSC 13, 27, 103; WLC 6**
See also AAYA 36; AMW; AMWC 1; AMWR 1; BPFB 3; BYA 12; CA 1-4R; 282; CABS 1; CANR 4, 33, 51, 94, 133, 197; CDALB 1968-1988; CN 1, 2, 3, 4, 5, 6, 7; CP 1, 2, 3, 4, 5, 6, 7; CPW 1; DA; DA3; DAB; DAC; DAM MST, NOV, POET, POP; DLB 2, 5, 143, 218, 227; DLBD 3; DLBY 1980, 1982, 1997; EWL 3; EXPP; HGG; MAL 5; MTCW 1, 2; MTFW 2005; NFS 12, 24; RGAL 4; RGSF 2; SSFS 3, 19; TUS

Updike, John Hoyer
See Updike, John

Upshaw, Margaret Mitchell
See Mitchell, Margaret

Upton, Mark
See Sanders, Lawrence

Upward, Allen 1863-1926 .... **TCLC 85**
  See also CA 117; 187; DLB 36
Urdang, Constance (Henriette)
  1922-1996 .... **CLC 47**
  See also CA 21-24R; CANR 9, 24; CP 1, 2,
  3, 4, 5, 6; CWP
Urfe, Honore d' 1567(?)-1625 .... **LC 132**
  See also DLB 268; GFL Beginnings to
  1789; RGWL 2, 3
Uriel, Henry
  See Faust, Frederick
Uris, Leon 1924-2003 .... **CLC 7, 32**
  See also AITN 1, 2; BEST 89:2; BPFB 3;
  CA 1-4R; 217; CANR 1, 40, 65, 123; CN
  1, 2, 3, 4, 5, 6; CPW 1; DA3; DAM NOV,
  POP; MTCW 1, 2; MTFW 2005; RGHL;
  SATA 49; SATA-Obit 146
Urista, Alberto 1947- .... **HLCS 1; PC 34**
  See also CA 45-48R; CANR 2, 32; DLB
  82; HW 1; LLW
Urista Heredia, Alberto Baltazar
  See Urista, Alberto
Urmuz
  See Codrescu, Andrei
Urquhart, Guy
  See McAlmon, Robert (Menzies)
Urquhart, Jane 1949- .... **CLC 90, 242**
  See also CA 113; CANR 32, 68, 116, 157;
  CCA 1; DAC; DLB 334
Usigli, Rodolfo 1905-1979 .... **HLCS 1**
  See also CA 131; DLB 305; EWL 3; HW 1;
  LAW
Usk, Thomas (?)-1388 .... **CMLC 76**
  See also DLB 146
Ustinov, Peter (Alexander)
  1921-2004 .... **CLC 1**
  See also AITN 1; CA 13-16R; 225; CANR
  25, 51; CBD; CD 5, 6; DLB 13; MTCW
  2
U Tam'si, Gerald Felix Tchicaya
  See Tchicaya, Gerald Felix
U Tam'si, Tchicaya
  See Tchicaya, Gerald Felix
Vachss, Andrew 1942- .... **CLC 106**
  See also CA 118, 214; CAAE 214; CANR
  44, 95, 153, 197; CMW 4
Vachss, Andrew H.
  See Vachss, Andrew
Vachss, Andrew Henry
  See Vachss, Andrew
Vaculik, Ludvik 1926- .... **CLC 7**
  See also CA 53-56; CANR 72; CWW 2;
  DLB 232; EWL 3
Vaihinger, Hans 1852-1933 .... **TCLC 71**
  See also CA 116; 166
Valdez, Luis (Miguel) 1940- ..... **CLC 84; DC
  10; HLC 2**
  See also CA 101; CAD; CANR 32, 81; CD
  5, 6; DAM MULT; DFS 5; DLB 122;
  EWL 3; HW 1; LAIT 4; LLW
Valenzuela, Luisa 1938- .... **CLC 31, 104;
  HLCS 2; SSC 14, 82**
  See also CA 101; CANR 32, 65, 123; CD-
  WLB 3; CWW 2; DAM MULT; DLB 113;
  EWL 3; FW; HW 1, 2; LAW; RGSF 2;
  RGWL 3
Valera y Alcala-Galiano, Juan
  1824-1905 .... **TCLC 10**
  See also CA 106
Valerius Maximus CMLC 64
  See also DLB 211
Valery, Ambroise Paul Toussaint Jules
  See Valery, Paul
Valery, Paul 1871-1945 ... **PC 9; TCLC 4, 15,
  231**
  See also CA 104; 122; DA3; DAM POET;
  DLB 258; EW 8; EWL 3; GFL 1789 to
  the Present; MTCW 1, 2; MTFW 2005;
  RGWL 2, 3; TWA

Valle-Inclan, Ramon del 1866-1936 .. **HLC 2;
  TCLC 5, 228**
  See also CA 106; 153; CANR 80; DAM
  MULT; DLB 134, 322; EW 8; EWL 3;
  HW 2; RGSF 2; RGWL 2, 3
Valle-Inclan, Ramon Maria del
  See Valle-Inclan, Ramon del
Vallejo, Antonio Buero
  See Buero Vallejo, Antonio
Vallejo, Cesar 1892-1938 ... **HLC 2; TCLC 3,
  56**
  See also CA 105; 153; DAM MULT; DLB
  290; EWL 3; HW 1; LAW; PFS 26;
  RGWL 2, 3
Vallejo, Cesar Abraham
  See Vallejo, Cesar
Valles, Jules 1832-1885 .... **NCLC 71**
  See also DLB 123; GFL 1789 to the Present
Vallette, Marguerite Eymery
  1860-1953 .... **TCLC 67**
  See also CA 182; DLB 123, 192; EWL 3
Valle Y Pena, Ramon del
  See Valle-Inclan, Ramon del
Van Ash, Cay 1918-1994 .... **CLC 34**
  See also CA 220
Vanbrugh, Sir John 1664-1726 .... **LC 21**
  See also BRW 2; DAM DRAM; DLB 80;
  IDTP; RGEL 2
Van Campen, Karl
  See Campbell, John W(ood, Jr.)
Vance, Gerald
  See Silverberg, Robert
Vance, Jack 1916- .... **CLC 35**
  See also CA 29-32R; CANR 17, 65, 154;
  CMW 4; DLB 8; FANT; MTCW 1; SCFW
  1, 2; SFW 4; SUFW 1, 2
Vance, John Holbrook
  See Vance, Jack
**Van Den Bogarde, Derek Jules Gaspard
  Ulric Niven** 1921-1999 .... **CLC 14**
  See also CA 77-80; 179; DLB 14
Vandenburgh, Jane CLC 59
  See also CA 168
Vanderhaeghe, Guy 1951- .... **CLC 41**
  See also BPFB 3; CA 113; CANR 72, 145;
  CN 7; DLB 334
van der Post, Laurens (Jan)
  1906-1996 .... **CLC 5**
  See also AFW; CA 5-8R; 155; CANR 35;
  CN 1, 2, 3, 4, 5, 6; DLB 204; RGEL 2
van de Wetering, Janwillem
  1931-2008 .... **CLC 47**
  See also CA 49-52; 274; CANR 4, 62, 90;
  CMW 4
Van Dine, S. S.
  See Wright, Willard Huntington
Van Doren, Carl (Clinton)
  1885-1950 .... **TCLC 18**
  See also CA 111; 168
Van Doren, Mark 1894-1972 .... **CLC 6, 10**
  See also CA 1-4R; 37-40R; CANR 3; CN
  1; CP 1; DLB 45, 284, 335; MAL 5;
  MTCW 1, 2; RGAL 4
Van Druten, John (William)
  1901-1957 .... **TCLC 2**
  See also CA 104; 161; DLB 10; MAL 5;
  RGAL 4
Van Duyn, Mona 1921-2004 .... **CLC 3, 7, 63,
  116**
  See also CA 9-12R; 234; CANR 7, 38, 60,
  116; CP 1, 2, 3, 4, 5, 6, 7; CWP; DAM
  POET; DLB 5; MAL 5; MTFW 2005;
  PFS 20
Van Dyne, Edith
  See Baum, L. Frank
van Herk, Aritha 1954- .... **CLC 249**
  See also CA 101; CANR 94; DLB 334

van Itallie, Jean-Claude 1936- .... **CLC 3**
  See also CA 45-48; CAAS 2; CAD; CANR
  1, 48; CD 5, 6; DLB 7
Van Loot, Cornelius Obenchain
  See Roberts, Kenneth (Lewis)
van Ostaijen, Paul 1896-1928 .... **TCLC 33**
  See also CA 163
Van Peebles, Melvin 1932- .... **CLC 2, 20**
  See also BW 2, 3; CA 85-88; CANR 27,
  67, 82; DAM MULT
van Schendel, Arthur(-Francois-Emile)
  1874-1946 .... **TCLC 56**
  See also EWL 3
Van See, John
  See Vance, Jack
Vansittart, Peter 1920-2008 .... **CLC 42**
  See also CA 1-4R; 278; CANR 3, 49, 90;
  CN 4, 5, 6, 7; RHW
Van Vechten, Carl 1880-1964 ... **CLC 33; HR
  1:3**
  See also AMWS 2; CA 183; 89-92; DLB 4,
  9, 51; RGAL 4
van Vogt, A(lfred) E(lton) 1912-2000 . **CLC 1**
  See also BPFB 3; BYA 13, 14; CA 21-24R;
  190; CANR 28; DLB 8, 251; SATA 14;
  SATA-Obit 124; SCFW 1, 2; SFW 4
Vara, Madeleine
  See Jackson, Laura
Varda, Agnes 1928- .... **CLC 16**
  See also CA 116; 122
Vargas Llosa, Jorge Mario Pedro
  See Vargas Llosa, Mario
Vargas Llosa, Mario 1936- .. **CLC 3, 6, 9, 10,
  15, 31, 42, 85, 181; HLC 2**
  See also BPFB 3; CA 73-76; CANR 18, 32,
  42, 67, 116, 140, 173; CDWLB 3; CWW
  2; DA; DA3; DAB; DAC; DAM MST,
  MULT, NOV; DLB 145; DNFS 2; EWL
  3; HW 1, 2; LAIT 5; LATS 1:2; LAW;
  LAWS 1; MTCW 1, 2; MTFW 2005;
  RGWL 2, 3; SSFS 14; TWA; WLIT 1
Varnhagen von Ense, Rahel
  1771-1833 .... **NCLC 130**
  See also DLB 90
Vasari, Giorgio 1511-1574 .... **LC 114**
Vasilikos, Vasiles
  See Vassilikos, Vassilis
Vasiliu, Gheorghe
  See Bacovia, George
Vassa, Gustavus
  See Equiano, Olaudah
Vassilikos, Vassilis 1933- .... **CLC 4, 8**
  See also CA 81-84; CANR 75, 149; EWL 3
Vaughan, Henry 1621-1695 .... **LC 27; PC 81**
  See also BRW 2; DLB 131; PAB; RGEL 2
Vaughn, Stephanie CLC 62
Vazov, Ivan (Minchov) 1850-1921 . **TCLC 25**
  See also CA 121; 167; CDWLB 4; DLB
  147
Veblen, Thorstein B(unde)
  1857-1929 .... **TCLC 31**
  See also AMWS 1; CA 115; 165; DLB 246;
  MAL 5
Vega, Lope de 1562-1635 ... **HLCS 2; LC 23,
  119**
  See also EW 2; RGWL 2, 3
Veldeke, Heinrich von c. 1145-c.
  1190 .... **CMLC 85**
Vendler, Helen 1933- .... **CLC 138**
  See also CA 41-44R; CANR 25, 72, 136,
  190; MTCW 1, 2; MTFW 2005
Vendler, Helen Hennessy
  See Vendler, Helen
Venison, Alfred
  See Pound, Ezra
Ventsel, Elena Sergeevna
  1907-2002 .... **CLC 59**
  See also CA 154; CWW 2; DLB 302

Weldon, Fay 1931- . **CLC 6, 9, 11, 19, 36, 59, 122**
See also BRWS 4; CA 21-24R; CANR 16, 46, 63, 97, 137; CDBLB 1960 to Present; CN 3, 4, 5, 6, 7; CPW; DAM POP; DLB 14, 194, 319; EWL 3; FW; HGG; INT CANR-16; MTCW 1, 2; MTFW 2005; RGEL 2; RGSF 2

Wellek, Rene 1903-1995 .... **CLC 28**
See also CA 5-8R; 150; CAAS 7; CANR 8; DLB 63; EWL 3; INT CANR-8

Weller, Michael 1942- .... **CLC 10, 53**
See also CA 85-88; CAD; CD 5, 6

Weller, Paul 1958- .... **CLC 26**

Wellershoff, Dieter 1925- .... **CLC 46**
See also CA 89-92; CANR 16, 37

Welles, (George) Orson 1915-1985 .. **CLC 20, 80**
See also AAYA 40; CA 93-96; 117

Wellman, John McDowell 1945- ...... **CLC 65**
See also CA 166; CAD; CD 5, 6; RGAL 4

Wellman, Mac
See Wellman, John McDowell; Wellman, John McDowell

Wellman, Manly Wade 1903-1986 ... **CLC 49**
See also CA 1-4R; 118; CANR 6, 16, 44; FANT; SATA 6; SATA-Obit 47; SFW 4; SUFW

Wells, Carolyn 1869(?)-1942 .... **TCLC 35**
See also CA 113; 185; CMW 4; DLB 11

Wells, H. G. 1866-1946 . **SSC 6, 70; TCLC 6, 12, 19, 133; WLC 6**
See also AAYA 18; BPFB 3; BRW 6; CA 110; 121; CDBLB 1914-1945; CLR 64, 133; DA; DA3; DAB; DAC; DAM MST, NOV; DLB 34, 70, 156, 178; EWL 3; EXPS; HGG; LAIT 3; LMFS 2; MTCW 1, 2; MTFW 2005; NFS 17, 20; RGEL 2; RGSF 2; SATA 20; SCFW 1, 2; SFW 4; SSFS 3; SUFW; TEA; WCH; WLIT 4; YAW

Wells, Herbert George
See Wells, H. G.

Wells, Rosemary 1943- .... **CLC 12**
See also AAYA 13; BYA 7, 8; CA 85-88; CANR 48, 120, 179; CLR 16, 69; CWRI 5; MAICYA 1, 2; SAAS 1; SATA 18, 69, 114, 156, 207; YAW

Wells-Barnett, Ida B(ell) 1862-1931 .... **TCLC 125**
See also CA 182; DLB 23, 221

Welsh, Irvine 1958- .... **CLC 144, 276**
See also CA 173; CANR 146, 196; CN 7; DLB 271

Welty, Eudora 1909-2001 .... **CLC 1, 2, 5, 14, 22, 33, 105, 220; SSC 1, 27, 51, 111; WLC 6**
See also AAYA 48; AMW; AMWR 1; BPFB 3; CA 9-12R; 199; CABS 1; CANR 32, 65, 128; CDALB 1941-1968; CN 1, 2, 3, 4, 5, 6, 7; CSW; DA; DA3; DAB; DAC; DAM MST, NOV; DFS 26; DLB 2, 102, 143; DLBD 12; DLBY 1987, 2001; EWL 3; EXPS; HGG; LAIT 3; MAL 5; MBL; MTCW 1, 2; MTFW 2005; NFS 13, 15; RGAL 4; RGSF 2; RHW; SSFS 2, 10, 26; TUS

Welty, Eudora Alice
See Welty, Eudora

Wen I-to 1899-1946 .... **TCLC 28**
See also EWL 3

Wentworth, Robert
See Hamilton, Edmond

Werewere Liking 1950- .... **BLC 2:2**
See also EWL 3

Werfel, Franz (Viktor) 1890-1945 .... **PC 101; TCLC 8**
See also CA 104; 161; DLB 81, 124; EWL 3; RGWL 2, 3

Wergeland, Henrik Arnold 1808-1845 .... **NCLC 5**
See also DLB 354

Werner, Friedrich Ludwig Zacharias 1768-1823 .... **NCLC 189**
See also DLB 94

Werner, Zacharias
See Werner, Friedrich Ludwig Zacharias

Wersba, Barbara 1932- .... **CLC 30**
See also AAYA 2, 30; BYA 6, 12, 13; CA 29-32R, 182; CAAE 182; CANR 16, 38; CLR 3, 78; DLB 52; JRDA; MAICYA 1, 2; SAAS 2; SATA 1, 58; SATA-Essay 103; WYA; YAW

Wertmueller, Lina 1928- .... **CLC 16**
See also CA 97-100; CANR 39, 78

Wescott, Glenway 1901-1987 .. **CLC 13; SSC 35**
See also CA 13-16R; 121; CANR 23, 70; CN 1, 2, 3, 4; DLB 4, 9, 102; MAL 5; RGAL 4

Wesker, Arnold 1932- .... **CLC 3, 5, 42**
See also CA 1-4R; CAAS 7; CANR 1, 33; CBD; CD 5, 6; CDBLB 1960 to Present; DAB; DAM DRAM; DLB 13, 310, 319; EWL 3; MTCW 1; RGEL 2; TEA

Wesley, Charles 1707-1788 .... **LC 128**
See also DLB 95; RGEL 2

Wesley, John 1703-1791 .... **LC 88**
See also DLB 104

Wesley, Richard (Errol) 1945- .... **CLC 7**
See also BW 1; CA 57-60; CAD; CANR 27; CD 5, 6; DLB 38

Wessel, Johan Herman 1742-1785 .... **LC 7**
See also DLB 300

West, Anthony (Panther) 1914-1987 .... **CLC 50**
See also CA 45-48; 124; CANR 3, 19; CN 1, 2, 3, 4; DLB 15

West, C. P.
See Wodehouse, P. G.

West, Cornel 1953- .... **BLCS; CLC 134**
See also CA 144; CANR 91, 159; DLB 246

West, Cornel Ronald
See West, Cornel

West, Delno C(loyde), Jr. 1936- .... **CLC 70**
See also CA 57-60

West, Dorothy 1907-1998 ...... **HR 1:3; TCLC 108**
See also AMWS 18; BW 2; CA 143; 169; DLB 76

West, Edwin
See Westlake, Donald E.

West, (Mary) Jessamyn 1902-1984 ... **CLC 7, 17**
See also CA 9-12R; 112; CANR 27; CN 1, 2, 3; DLB 6; DLBY 1984; MTCW 1, 2; RGAL 4; RHW; SATA-Obit 37; TCWW 2; TUS; YAW

West, Morris L(anglo) 1916-1999 ..... **CLC 6, 33**
See also BPFB 3; CA 5-8R; 187; CANR 24, 49, 64; CN 1, 2, 3, 4, 5, 6; CPW; DLB 289; MTCW 1, 2; MTFW 2005

West, Nathanael 1903-1940 ...... **SSC 16, 116; TCLC 1, 14, 44, 235**
See also AAYA 77; AMW; AMWR 2; BPFB 3; CA 104; 125; CDALB 1929-1941; DA3; DLB 4, 9, 28; EWL 3; MAL 5; MTCW 1, 2; MTFW 2005; NFS 16; RGAL 4; TUS

West, Owen
See Koontz, Dean

West, Paul 1930- .... **CLC 7, 14, 96, 226**
See also CA 13-16R; CAAS 7; CANR 22, 53, 76, 89, 136; CN 1, 2, 3, 4, 5, 6, 7; DLB 14; INT CANR-22; MTCW 2; MTFW 2005

West, Rebecca 1892-1983 ... **CLC 7, 9, 31, 50**
See also BPFB 3; BRWS 3; CA 5-8R; 109; CANR 19; CN 1, 2, 3; DLB 36; DLBY 1983; EWL 3; FW; MTCW 1, 2; MTFW 2005; NCFS 4; RGEL 2; TEA

Westall, Robert (Atkinson) 1929-1993 .... **CLC 17**
See also AAYA 12; BYA 2, 6, 7, 8, 9, 15; CA 69-72; 141; CANR 18, 68; CLR 13; FANT; JRDA; MAICYA 1, 2; MAICYAS 1; SAAS 2; SATA 23, 69; SATA-Obit 75; WYA; YAW

Westermarck, Edward 1862-1939 . **TCLC 87**

Westlake, Donald E. 1933-2008 ... **CLC 7, 33**
See also BPFB 3; CA 17-20R; 280; CAAS 13; CANR 16, 44, 65, 94, 137, 192; CMW 4; CPW; DAM POP; INT CANR-16; MSW; MTCW 2; MTFW 2005

Westlake, Donald E. Edmund
See Westlake, Donald E.

Westlake, Donald Edwin
See Westlake, Donald E.

Westlake, Donald Edwin Edmund
See Westlake, Donald E.

Westmacott, Mary
See Christie, Agatha

Weston, Allen
See Norton, Andre

Wetcheek, J. L.
See Feuchtwanger, Lion

Wetering, Janwillem van de
See van de Wetering, Janwillem

Wetherald, Agnes Ethelwyn 1857-1940 .... **TCLC 81**
See also CA 202; DLB 99

Wetherell, Elizabeth
See Warner, Susan (Bogert)

Whale, James 1889-1957 .... **TCLC 63**
See also AAYA 75

Whalen, Philip (Glenn) 1923-2002 .... **CLC 6, 29**
See also BG 1:3; CA 9-12R; 209; CANR 5, 39; CP 1, 2, 3, 4, 5, 6, 7; DLB 16; WP

Wharton, Edith 1862-1937 ... **SSC 6, 84, 120; TCLC 3, 9, 27, 53, 129, 149; WLC 6**
See also AAYA 25; AMW; AMWC 2; AMWR 1; BPFB 3; CA 104; 132; CDALB 1865-1917; CLR 136; DA; DA3; DAB; DAC; DAM MST, NOV; DLB 4, 9, 12, 78, 189; DLBD 13; EWL 3; EXPS; FL 1:6; GL 3; HGG; LAIT 2, 3; LATS 1:1; MAL 5; MBL; MTCW 1, 2; MTFW 2005; NFS 5, 11, 15, 20; RGAL 4; RGSF 2; RHW; SSFS 6, 7; SUFW; TUS

Wharton, Edith Newbold Jones
See Wharton, Edith

Wharton, James
See Mencken, H. L.

Wharton, William 1925-2008 ..... **CLC 18, 37**
See also CA 93-96; 278; CN 4, 5, 6, 7; DLBY 1980; INT CA-93-96

Wheatley, Phillis 1753(?)-1784 .... **BLC 1:3; LC 3, 50; PC 3; WLC 6**
See also AFAW 1, 2; CDALB 1640-1865; DA; DA3; DAC; DAM MST, MULT, POET; DLB 31, 50; EXPP; FL 1:1; PFS 13, 29; RGAL 4

Wheatley Peters, Phillis
See Wheatley, Phillis

Wheelock, John Hall 1886-1978 .... **CLC 14**
See also CA 13-16R; 77-80; CANR 14; CP 1, 2; DLB 45; MAL 5

Whim-Wham
See Curnow, (Thomas) Allen (Monro)

Whisp, Kennilworthy
See Rowling, J. K.

Whitaker, Rod 1931-2005 .... **CLC 29**
See also CA 29-32R; 246; CANR 45, 153; CMW 4

PC Cumulative Nationality Index

AMERICAN

Ai **72**
Aiken, Conrad (Potter) **26**
Alexie, Sherman **53**
Ammons, A(rchie) R(andolph) **16**
Angelou, Maya **32**
Ashbery, John (Lawrence) **26**
Auden, W(ystan) H(ugh) **1, 92**
Baca, Jimmy Santiago **41**
Baraka, Amiri **4**
Benét, Stephen Vincent **64**
Berrigan, Ted **103**
Berry, Wendell (Erdman) **28**
Berryman, John **64**
Bishop, Elizabeth **3, 34**
Bly, Robert (Elwood) **39**
Bogan, Louise **12**
Bradstreet, Anne **10**
Braithwaite, William **52**
Brautigan, Richard **94**
Brodsky, Joseph **9**
Brooks, Gwendolyn (Elizabeth) **7**
Brown, Sterling Allen **55**
Bryant, William Cullen **20**
Bukowski, Charles **18**
Cage, John **58**
Carruth, Hayden **10**
Carver, Raymond **54**
Cervantes, Lorna Dee **35**
Chappell, Fred **105**
Chin, Marilyn (Mei Ling) **40**
Ciardi, John **69**
Cisneros, Sandra **52**
Clampitt, Amy **19**
Clifton, (Thelma) Lucille **17**
Collins, Billy **68**
Corso, (Nunzio) Gregory **33**
Crane, (Harold) Hart **3, 99**
Creeley, Robert **73**
Cullen, Countée **20**
Cummings, E(dward) E(stlin) **5**
Cunningham, J(ames) V(incent) **92**
Dickey, James (Lafayette) **40**
Dickinson, Emily (Elizabeth) **1**
Doolittle, Hilda **5**
Doty, Mark **53**
Dove, Rita (Frances) **6**
Dunbar, Paul Laurence **5**
Duncan, Robert (Edward) **2, 75**
Dylan, Bob **37**
Eberhart, Richard **76**
Eliot, T(homas) S(tearns) **5, 31**
Emerson, Ralph Waldo **18**
Erdrich, Louise **52**
Espada, Martín **74**
Ferlinghetti, Lawrence (Monsanto) **1**

Forché, Carolyn (Louise) **10**
Francis, Robert (Churchill) **34**
Frost, Robert (Lee) **1, 39, 71**
Gallagher, Tess **9**
Ginsberg, Allen **4, 47**
Giovanni, Nikki **19**
Glück, Louise (Elisabeth) **16**
Graham, Jorie **59**
Guest, Barbara **55**
Hacker, Marilyn **47**
Hall, Donald **70**
Hammon, Jupiter **16**
Harjo, Joy **27**
Harper, Frances Ellen Watkins **21**
Hass, Robert **16**
Hayden, Robert E(arl) **6**
Hecht, Anthony **70**
Hogan, Linda **35**
Holmes, Oliver Wendell **71**
Hongo, Garrett Kaoru **23**
Howe, Susan **54**
Hughes, (James) Langston **1, 53**
Hugo, Richard **68**
Ignatow, David **34**
Jackson, Laura (Riding) **44**
Jacobsen, Josephine **62**
Jarrell, Randall **41**
Jeffers, (John) Robinson **17**
Johnson, James Weldon **24**
Jordan, June **38**
Justice, Donald **64**
Kaufman, Bob **74**
Kennedy, X. J. **93**
Kenyon, Jane **57**
Kinnell, Galway **26**
Kizer, Carolyn **66**
Knight, Etheridge **14**
Komunyakaa, Yusef **51**
Kumin, Maxine (Winokur) **15**
Kunitz, Stanley (Jasspon) **19**
Lanier, Sidney **50**
Levertov, Denise **11**
Levine, Philip **22**
Lindsay, (Nicholas) Vachel **23**
Longfellow, Henry Wadsworth **30**
Lorde, Audre (Geraldine) **12**
Lowell, Amy **13**
Lowell, Robert (Traill Spence Jr.) **3**
Loy, Mina **16**
MacLeish, Archibald **47**
Mackey, Nathaniel **49**
Madhubuti, Haki R. **5**
Masters, Edgar Lee **1, 36**
McHugh, Heather **61**
Meredith, William (Morris) **28**

Merrill, James (Ingram) **28**
Merton, Thomas **10**
Merwin, W. S. **45**
Millay, Edna St. Vincent **6, 61**
Momaday, N(avarre) Scott **25**
Moore, Marianne (Craig) **4, 49**
Mueller, Lisel **33**
Nash, (Fredric) Ogden **21**
Nemerov, Howard (Stanley) **24**
Niedecker, Lorine **42**
O'Hara, Frank **45**
Olds, Sharon **22**
Oliver, Mary **75**
Olson, Charles (John) **19**
Oppen, George **35**
Ortiz, Simon J(oseph) **17**
Parker, Dorothy (Rothschild) **28**
Piercy, Marge **29**
Pinsky, Robert **27**
Plath, Sylvia **1, 37**
Poe, Edgar Allan **1, 54**
Pound, Ezra (Weston Loomis) **4, 95**
Quintana, Leroy V. **36**
Randall, Dudley **86**
Ransom, John Crowe **61**
Reed, Ishmael **68**
Reese, Lizette Woodworth **29**
Rexroth, Kenneth **20, 95**
Rich, Adrienne (Cecile) **5**
Riley, James Whitcomb **48**
Ríos, Alberto **57**
Robinson, Edwin Arlington **1, 35**
Roethke, Theodore (Huebner) **15**
Rose, Wendy **13**
Rukeyser, Muriel **12**
Sanchez, Sonia **9**
Sandburg, Carl (August) **2, 41**
Sarton, (Eleanor) May **39**
Schwartz, Delmore (David) **8**
Schnackenberg, Gjertrud **45**
Schuyler, James **88**
Schwerner, Armand **42**
Sexton, Anne (Harvey) **2**
Shapiro, Karl (Jay) **25**
Silverstein, Shel **49**
Simic, Charles **69**
Snodgrass, W. D. **74**
Snyder, Gary (Sherman) **21**
Song, Cathy **21**
Soto, Gary **28**
Spencer, Anne **77**
Spicer, Jack **78**
Stafford, William **71**
Stein, Gertrude **18**
Stevens, Wallace **6**
Stone, Ruth **53**

Nationality Index

PC-105 Title Index

Title Index

ISBN-13: 978-1-4144-4760-5
ISBN-10: 1-4144-4760-4

90000